Fodor's

FLORIDA

WELCOME TO FLORIDA

With its accessible and varied pleasures, Florida is a favorite of many. Drawn to the colonial charm of St. Augustine, Miami's pulsing nightlife, the glitz of Palm Beach, or the quiet expanse of the Everglades, almost all visitors find something to love here. From the powdery white beaches of the Panhandle to the vibrant coral reefs of the Florida Keys, the ocean is always calling—for sailing, fishing, diving, swimming, and other water sports. Stray off the path a few miles, and you might glimpse a bit of the Florida of old, including cigar makers and mermaids.

TOP REASONS TO GO

★ **Miami:** A vibrant, multicultural metropolis that buzzes both day and night.

★ **Beaches:** Surf-pounded on the Atlantic coast, powdery and pure white on the Gulf.

★ **Key West:** Quirky, fun, and tacky, it's both family-friendly and decidedly not.

★ **Golf:** Oceanfront and inland, some of the country's finest links are found here.

★ **Theme parks:** The state has some of the biggest and best, not all of them Disney.

★ **Family fun:** From shelling in Sanibel to meeting astronauts at Kennedy Space Center.

Fodor's FLORIDA

Editorial: Douglas Stallings, *Editorial Director*; Salwa Jabado and Margaret Kelly, *Senior Editors*; Alexis Kelly, Jacinta O'Halloran, and Amanda Sadlowski, *Editors*; Teddy Minford, *Associate Editor*; Rachael Roth, *Content Manager*

Design: Tina Malaney, *Associate Art Director*

Photography: Jennifer Arnow, *Senior Photo Editor*

Maps: Rebecca Baer, *Senior Map Editor*; David Lindroth, Mark Stroud (Moon Street Cartography), *Cartographers*

Production: Jennifer DePrima, *Editorial Production Manager*; Carrie Parker, *Senior Production Editor*; Elyse Rozelle, *Production Editor*

Business & Operations: Chuck Hoover, *Chief Marketing Officer*; Joy Lai, *Vice President and General Manager*; Stephen Horowitz, *Head of Business Development and Partnerships*

Public Relations: Joe Ewaskiw, *Manager*

Writers: Kate Bradshaw, Jennifer Greenhill-Taylor, Joseph Hayes, Lynne Helm, Jill Martin, Steve Master, Galena Mosovich, Jan Norris, Paul Rubio, Ashley Wright

Editor: Douglas Stallings

Production Editor: Elyse Rozelle

Production Design: Liliana Guia

33rd Edition

ISBN 978–1–101–88010–4

ISSN 0193–9556

All details in this book are based on information supplied to us at press time. Always confirm information when it matters, especially if you're making a detour to visit a specific place. Fodor's expressly disclaims any liability, loss, or risk, personal or otherwise, that is incurred as a consequence of the use of any of the contents of this book.

PRINTED IN THE UNITED STATES OF AMERICA

10 9 8 7 6 5 4 3 2 1

CONTENTS

MAPS

ABOUT THIS GUIDE

Fodor's Recommendations

Everything in this guide is worth doing—we don't cover what isn't—but exceptional sights, hotels, and restaurants are recognized with additional accolades. **Fodor's**Choice★ indicates our top recommendations. Care to nominate a new place? Visit Fodors.com/contact-us.

Trip Costs

We list prices wherever possible to help you budget well. Hotel and restaurant price categories from $ to $$$$ are noted alongside each recommendation. For hotels, we include the lowest cost of a standard double room in high season. For restaurants, we cite the average price of a main course at dinner or, if dinner isn't served, at lunch. For attractions, we always list adult admission fees; discounts are usually available for children, students, and senior citizens.

Hotels

Our local writers vet every hotel to recommend the best overnights in each price category, from budget to expensive. Unless otherwise specified, you can expect private bath, phone, and TV in your room. *For full hotel information, visit Fodors.com.*

Top Picks		Hotels &
★ **Fodor's**Choice		**Restaurants**
		⌂ Hotel
Listings		➷ Number of
✉ Address		rooms
✉ Branch address		ᵀᴼ�I Meal plans
☎ Telephone		✗ Restaurant
🖶 Fax		⚭ Reservations
⊕ Website		🏛 Dress code
✉ E-mail		▭ No credit cards
▨ Admission fee		$ Price
⊙ Open/closed		
times		**Other**
M Subway		⇨ See also
✛ Directions or		☞ Take note
Map coordinates		🏌 Golf facilities

Restaurants

Unless we state otherwise, restaurants are open for lunch and dinner daily. We mention dress code only when there's a specific requirement and reservations only when they're essential or not accepted. *For full restaurant information, visit Fodors.com.*

Credit Cards

The hotels and restaurants in this guide typically accept credit cards. If not, we'll say so.

EUGENE FODOR

Hungarian-born Eugene Fodor (1905–91) began his travel career as an interpreter on a French cruise ship. The experience inspired him to write *On the Continent* (1936), the first guidebook to receive annual updates and discuss a country's way of life as well as its sights. Fodor later joined the U.S. Army and worked for the OSS in World War II. After the war, he kept up his intelligence work while expanding his guidebook series. During the Cold War, many guides were written by fellow agents who understood the value of insider information. Today's guides continue Fodor's legacy by providing travelers with timely coverage, insider tips, and cultural context.

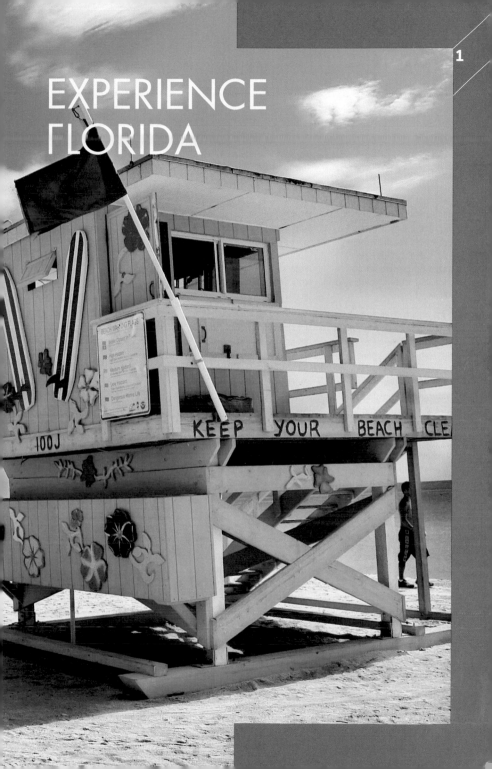

EXPERIENCE FLORIDA

WHAT'S WHERE

The following numbers refer to chapters.

2 Miami and Miami Beach. Greater Miami is hot—and we're not just talking about the weather. Art deco buildings and balmy beaches set the scene. Vacations here are as much about lifestyle as locale, so prepare for power shopping, club-hopping, and decadent dining.

3 The Everglades. Covering more than 1.5 million acres, the fabled "River of Grass" is the state's greatest natural treasure. Biscayne National Park (95% of which is underwater) runs a close second. It's the largest marine park in the United States.

4 The Florida Keys. This slender necklace of landfalls, strung together by a 113-mile highway, marks the southern edge of the continental United States. It's nirvana for anglers, divers, literature lovers, and Jimmy Buffett wannabes.

5 Fort Lauderdale with Broward County. The town *Where the Boys Are* has grown up. The beaches that first attracted college kids are now complemented by luxe lodgings and upscale entertainment options.

6 Palm Beach with the Treasure Coast. This area scores points for diversity. Palm Beach and environs are famous for their golden sand and glitzy residents, whereas the Treasure Coast has unspoiled natural delights.

7 The Tampa Bay Area. Tampa's Busch Gardens and Ybor City are only part of the area's appeal. Culture vultures flock to St. Petersburg and Sarasota for concerts and museums, and eco-adventurers veer north to the Nature Coast.

8 The Lower Gulf Coast. Blessed with beaches, this was the last bit of coast to be settled. But as Naples's manicured golf greens and Fort Myers's mansions-cum-museums prove, it is far from uncivilized.

9 Orlando and Environs. Theme parks are what draw most visitors to the area, yet downtown Orlando, Kissimmee, and Winter Park have enough sights, shops, and restaurants to make them destinations in their own right.

10 Walt Disney World. The granddaddy of attractions, Disney is four theme parks in one—Magic Kingdom, Animal Kingdom, Epcot, and Hollywood Studios. Plus, it has a pair of water parks and Disney Springs (an entertainment, dining, and shopping area).

11 Universal Orlando. The movies are brought to

life at Universal Studios, while Islands of Adventure delivers gravity-defying rides and special-effects surprises. Each has its own Wizarding World of Harry Potter (Diagon Alley and Hogsmeade, respectively). And there's Volcano Bay, a new water park.

12 SeaWorld Orlando. Marine mammals perform in SeaWorld's meticulously choreographed shows (which are being phased out by 2019), and thrill seekers find their adrenaline rush on coasters. Sister park Discovery Cove offers a daylong, swim-with-the-dolphins escape.

13 Northeast Florida. Though time rewinds in historic St. Augustine, it's on fast-forward in Daytona Beach and the Space Coast, where horse-drawn carriages are replaced by race cars and rocket ships.

14 The Panhandle. Southern gentility and redneck rambunctiousness make the Panhandle a colorful place—but it's the green Gulf waters and sugar-white sand that keep devotees coming back.

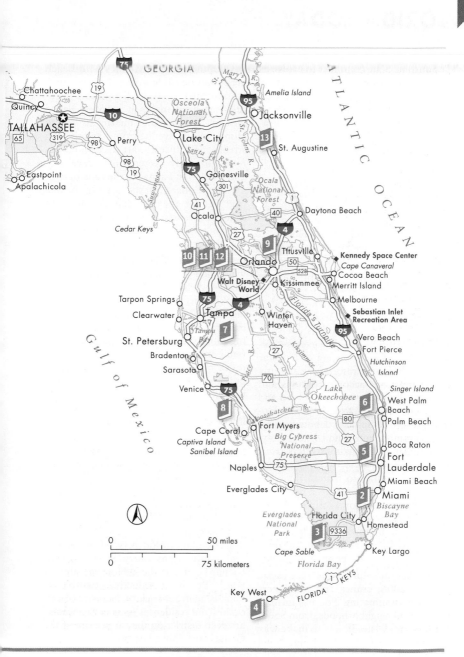

FLORIDA TODAY

The Sunshine State continues to evolve as a tourist destination to meet the growing demands of today's globalized traveler. From new high-end accommodations and experiences to improved access and infrastructure, Florida is keeping at the top of its game as one of America's superlative vacation spots.

More Luxury

From Orlando's timeless Walt Disney World to Miami's burgeoning Mid-Beach and expanding Sunny Isles Beach to Key West's charming Old Town, Florida is embracing a new luxury mantra and has plenty of new five-star residents to prove it.

Walt Disney World is proving that its secret recipe of fairy tales and imagination isn't just for tykes and tots. The arrival of the Four Seasons Resort Orlando at Walt Disney World Resort—and its over-the-top, near half-billion-dollar excess—has indeed ushered in a new era of five-star Disney. Eight Disney resorts have recently added Club Level accommodations and Club Level lounges with several food and wine presentations. Disney's Grand Floridian Resort & Spa has debuted pricey villa accommodations, and Disney's Polynesian Villas & Bungalows offers over-the-top, Tahitian-style overwater villas (with the price tag to match). In addition, Disney has opened up a new Tom Fazio–designed golf course and is offering new experiences like VIP escorts, where you jump the line for each ride and go across all parks in a single day (and travel between parks in some pretty hot wheels).

Just as they did during the real estate boom of 2006, cranes and bulldozers are again dominating South Florida's most coveted neighborhoods, from South Beach to Sunny Isles Beach, to make way for super-high-end residential and hotel developments. But Miami's Mid-Beach area may be undergoing the most dramatic transformation. Significant progress has been made in the new Faena District, a multi-block quarter stretching along Collins Avenue from 32nd to 35th streets, with historic art deco buildings reimagined by Argentinean developer and icon Alan Faena (to the tune of over a billion dollars). In the heart of the district lies the apex of Miami's onslaught of luxury resorts, the Faena Hotel Miami Beach, which is currently the talk of South Florida.

In November 2016, Downtown Miami welcomed its highly futuristic, Hong Kong–style $1.05-billion new resident: the Brickell City Centre complex, an 11-acre, high-tech, Arquitectonica-designed microcity in the heart of downtown encompassing more than 5.4 million square feet of retail and restaurant space, hotel rooms, office buildings, and two condominium buildings. The Design District continues to expand with ultra-high-design retail spaces for the big brands that are moving into the neighborhood monthly.

In the northern reaches of Miami Beach, Sunny Isles Beach has witnessed a new high-rise frenzy underscored by the 47-story Mansions at Acqualina and The Estates at Acqualina, neighbors of the Aqualina Resort & Spa. Never one to forgo the limelight, South Beach is also making waves with the half-billion-dollar collaboration between hotel and real estate titans Barry Sternlicht and Richard LeFrak: the 1 Hotel & Homes South Beach—a seductive, two-block-long, beachfront enclave, inclusive of 156 oceanfront residences—sits in the beach's art deco district on the former site of the Gansevoort South Beach.

Down in Key West, the opening of The Marker Key West heralded Old Town's first new-build since 1996. The arrival of the luxury 96-room resort has spawned a number of renovations and rebuilds, including the multimillion-dollar transformation of the Hyatt Key West to the Hyatt Centric Key West, a flagship for the Hyatt's new stylish lifestyle brand.

Improved Access

It's easier than ever to reach Florida by plane thanks to new flight routes and expanded airports. For example, Fort Lauderdale–Hollywood International Airport (FLL) is in the midst of a major expansion and renovation. So far, a new larger runway has been added, which permits jumbo-sized aircraft to utilize the airport, opening FLL to new destinations (e.g. Emirates now serves Fort Lauderdale directly from Dubai on a Boeing 777-200LR). In 2016, Orlando International Airport (MCO) also began a highly anticipated, $1.1-billion expansion.

To improve access between cities, Florida-based Brightline has opened the first phase of the first privately funded U.S. high-speed railway. Ultimately, state-of-the-art trains will travel from Miami to Orlando in three hours at speeds of up to 125 mph. Phase One, which opened in summer 2017, provides intercity express train service connecting Miami, Fort Lauderdale, and West Palm Beach in style and comfort. New stations have been constructed in the downtown areas of these three cities to provide service from one city center to the next (as opposed to using their often out-of-the-way Amtrak stations).

Response to Current Issues

Florida has been quick to respond to several of the negative issues that have overshadowed travel to the Sunshine State in the recent past. In response to increased threats of gun violence and terrorism, Walt Disney World has now added walk-through metal detectors at the entrance of its four theme parks, while Universal Orlando and SeaWorld Orlando are using wand-style metal detectors. Hearing the call of animal rights activists and protestors, SeaWorld Orlando will phase out its orca shows by 2019, while Ringling Bros. and Barnum & Bailey Circus in Sarasota shut down in May 2017. (The company's elephants, retired in 2016, are now living at the Ringling Bros. conservation center in rural Florida).

And while all of Miami-Dade County remains a Zika cautionary area, aggressive treatments have cut down on active transmissions. In September 2016, following three mosquito incubation periods, the CDC concluded that the Wynwood neighborhood is not a site of local mosquito-borne Zika virus transmission any longer. However, a 4½-square-mile area of Miami Beach (from 8th Street in South Beach to 63rd Street in Mid-Beach) and a 1-square-mile area of Little River (north of Little Haiti) have been declared Zika active transmission areas. Since the Zika issue changes frequently, we recommend expectant mothers and future mothers to review the CDC website and its special up-to-date Florida section.

FLORIDA'S TOP ATTRACTIONS

Walt Disney World

(A) Like one of Snow White's dwarfs, Orlando was sleepy until Uncle Walt turned this swampland into the world's most famous tourist attraction. Nowadays Walt Disney World is a 39-square-mile complex and growing, with four separate parks, scores of hotels, and satellite attractions. Thanks to innovative rides and dazzling animatronics, these parks feature prominently in every child's holiday fantasy. Walt Disney World also has grown-up amenities, including championship golf courses, sublime hotels and spas, and fine restaurants. If you have time for only one megapark, choose the original: Walt Disney World's Magic Kingdom. ⇨ *Chapter 10.*

South Beach

(B) You can't miss the distinctive forms, vibrant colors, and extravagant flourishes of SoBe's architectural gems. The world's largest concentration of art deco edifices

is right here. The neighborhood also has enough beautiful people to qualify for the Register of Hippest Places. The glitterati, along with assorted vacationing hedonists, are drawn by übertrendy shops and a surfeit of celeb-studded clubs. Divine eateries are the icing—umm, better make that the ganache—on South Beach's proverbial cake. ⇨ *Chapter 2.*

Key West

(C) These 800-plus islands in the Florida Keys are at once a unique landmass and a mass of contradictions. At the far end of this island chain, Key West is the main attraction. Its laid-back vibe is intoxicating. Eating, drinking, water sports, sunset cruises, kayaking, and more drinking are high on the agenda. Visitors never grow tired of the walking tours through the gingerbread-house-filled streets and channeling the spirit of Ernest Hemingway, who lived and worked here. Today, touring his former

digs and toasting his memory at Sloppy Joe's Bar on Duval Street is almost mandatory. ⇨ *Chapter 4.*

Shopping in Fort Lauderdale and Miami

(D) The Sunshine State is a shopaholic's dream. Visitors travel from overseas with the sole purpose of shopping weekends at Fort Lauderdale's 2 mile, alligator-shape Sawgrass Mills outlet mall. The alfresco addition to the mall, The Colonnade Outlets, features more upscale stores like David Yurman, Valentino, and Prada. For true high-end shoppers, Bal Harbour Shops in the swanky Miami suburb is a collection of 100 haute couture shops, boutiques, and department stores. Restaurants and cafés, in tropical garden settings, overflow with style-conscious diners. A formidable rival to Bal Harbour's haute couture empire is Miami's growing Design District. ⇨ *Chapters 2 and 5.*

Universal Orlando

(E) With rides and attractions more geared toward adults and teens, Universal's two theme parks—Universal Studios and Islands of Adventure—deliver gravity-defying rides and special-effects extravaganzas based on popular television shows and films. At the Wizarding World of Harry Potter: Hogsmeade (within Islands of Adventure), you'll get to see Hogwarts Castle and drink Butterbeer! ⇨ *Chapter 11.*

Kennedy Space Center

(F) Though there are enough wide-open expanses to justify the area's moniker, it was NASA that put the "space" in Space Coast—and this is its star attraction. Space memorabilia and aeronautic antiques, ranging from Redstone rockets to the *Apollo XIV* command module, turn an outing here into a trip back in time for anyone who lived through the space race. More down-to-earth types can also visit the Merrit Island National Wildlife

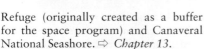

Refuge (originally created as a buffer for the space program) and Canaveral National Seashore. ⇨ *Chapter 13.*

Tampa Bay
(G) As a vibrant city with exceptional beaches, Tampa Bay is perfect for indecisive folks who want to enjoy surf and sand without sacrificing urban experiences. Families will love Busch Gardens, a major zoo and theme park. Football and hockey fans will relish the chance to see the Buccaneers and Lightning play. Baseball is big, too: the Rays are based here, and the Yankees descend annually for spring training. ⇨ *Chapter 7.*

The Dalí Museum
(H) St. Petersburg is home to a museum dedicated to the work of Salvador Dalí, showcasing the most comprehensive collection of the surrealist's artwork. This is the kind of first-class museum you'd expect to find in Paris or Madrid, but instead it's here on the Gulf Coast. The

state-of-the-art glass building housing the museum is quite a spectacle in and of itself. ⇨ *Chapter 7.*

Sportfishing
(I) Islamorada in the Florida Keys holds steadfast to its claim as Sportfishing Capital of the World. Up in the Panhandle, Destin proves it is the World's Luckiest Fishing Village each October by inviting anglers young and old to compete in the monthlong Destin Fishing Rodeo. However, if you'd prefer to throw fish rather than catch them, head to Pensacola in late April for the Interstate Mullet Toss. (Participants line up to throw dead fish across the Florida–Alabama state line.) ⇨ *Chapters 4 and 14.*

Stand-Up Paddleboarding
(J) Also called "YOLO Boarding," paddleboarding involves jumping on what looks like a wide surfboard and exploring calm waters with paddle in hand to push you forward. Requiring only a bit

of balance, almost anyone can do this (unlike surfing, which can be difficult to learn). Destin is paddleboard central, but you can enjoy the sport all over the Panhandle. ⇨ *Chapter 14.*

Palm Beach

(K) If money could talk, you'd hardly be able to hear above the din in Palm Beach. The upper crust started calling it home—during winter at least—in the early 1900s. And today it remains a ritzy, glitzy enclave for both old money and the nouveau riche (a coterie led by President Trump himself, who owns the landmark Mar-a-Lago Club). Simply put, Palm Beach is the sort of place where shopping is a full-time pursuit and residents don't just wear Polo—they play it. Ooh and aah to your heart's content; then, for more conspicuous consumption, continue south on the aptly named Gold Coast. ⇨ *Chapter 6.*

Broward's Inland Waterways

(L) Mariners should set their compass for Fort Lauderdale (aka the Venice of America), where vessels from around the world moor along some two dozen finger isles between the beach and the mainland. Tourists can cruise Broward County's 300 miles of inland waterways by water taxi and tour boat, or bob around the Atlantic in a chartered yacht. If you're in a buying mood, come in late October for the annual Fort Lauderdale International Boat Show. Billed as the world's largest, it has $3 billion worth of boats in every conceivable size, shape, and price range. ⇨ *Chapter 5.*

Little Havana

(M) On the streets of Miami's Little Havana, just west of downtown, salsa tunes blare and the smell of spicy chorizo fills the air. (You can get a good whiff of tobacco, too, thanks to the cigar makers who still hand-roll their products here.)

For nearly 50 years, the neighborhood's undisputed heart has been Calle Ocho, the commercial thoroughfare that hosts Carnaval Miami. The roaring 10-day block party each March culminates with the world's longest conga line. Ambience- and amenity-wise, it is as close as you'll get to Cuba without visiting the island itself. ⇨ *Chapter 2.*

The Everglades

(N) No trip to southern Florida is complete without seeing the Everglades. At its heart is a river—50 miles wide but merely 6 inches deep—flowing from Lake Okeechobee into Florida Bay. For an up-close look, speed demons can board an airboat that careens through the marshy waters. Purists, alternately, may placidly canoe or kayak within the boundaries of Everglades National Park. Just remember to keep your hands in the boat. The sharp saw grass and critters that call this unique ecosystem home (alligators, Florida panthers, cottonmouth snakes, and horseflies for starters) can add real cut, bite, or sting to your visit! ⇨ *Chapter 3.*

Sanibel Island

(O) Ready to do something slightly more vigorous than applying SPF 45 and rolling over? Trade beach-bumming for beachcombing in Sanibel, the Shell Capital of the World. Conchs, cockles, clams, coquinas—they're all here (the bounty is due to this barrier island's unusual east–west orientation). Of course, if you'd rather construct sand castles than do the Sanibel Stoop, you need only cross the 3-mile causeway to Fort Myers Beach. It has the finest building material and, every November, professional and amateur aficionados prove it during the American SandSculpting Championship. ⇨ *Chapter 8.*

Ringling Center for the Arts

(P) Sarasota, once winter headquarters for Ringling Bros. and Barnum & Bailey, is proud of its circus heritage. Ringling's former 32-room, 15-bathroom mansion is now the site of the Florida State University's Ringling Center for the Cultural Arts. Within this center, visitors can see an impressive collection of vintage costumes, props, and parade wagons at the stunning Ringling Circus Museum. In addition, the center's John and Mable Ringling Museum of Art showcases 500 years of art, including an impressive collection of tapestries and paintings by Rubens. The adjacent Tibbals Learning Center houses a mind-boggling ¾-inch-scale miniature circus with almost a million pieces. ⇨ *Chapter 7.*

St. Augustine

(Q) History comes to life in St. Augustine…and the same can perhaps be said of the undead. Ghosts are plentiful, thanks to all the pirates, plunderers, and other lost souls who formerly lived in this deceptively quiet city. To hear lurid lore about local haunts, sign on for one of the nightly outings organized by Ghost Tours of St. Augustine. These 90-minute lantern-lighted walks recount spirited stories full of goose-bump-inducing details. You can also opt for a trolley ride and enter the old jail if you dare, or take a cruise through the harbor shadows in the summer. Top off your tour with an overnight stay at St. Francis Inn or the Casablanca Inn on the Bay; both are reputedly haunted. ⇨ *Chapter 13.*

FLORIDA'S BEST BEACHES

Bahia Honda State Park

Though the Florida Keys aren't renowned for beautiful sandy beaches, this is an exception. The 524-acre park has three superb beaches over 2½ miles of sandy coastline at the crossroads of the Atlantic and the Gulf, idyllic for swimming, snorkeling, kayaking, and fishing. Atlantic-facing Sandspur beach flaunts long stretches of powdery sands. ⇨ *See Chapter 4.*

Bowman's Beach, Sanibel Island

On Sanibel's secluded northwest end, this beach doubles as a shell hunter's paradise and a beach wanderer's great escape. For the former, the likelihood of leaving with a bag full of gorgeous shells is high. For the latter, the chance of serene, inspiring vistas is guaranteed. ⇨ *See Chapter 8.*

Caladesi Island State Park

Accessible only by ferry from Honeymoon Island State Recreation Area, this park offers pure white beaches, beautiful sunsets, and excellent bird-watching ⇨ *See Chapter 7.*

Clearwater Beach

At what is arguably the state's best beach for families, kids and parents alike love the white stands and shallow, clear, warm waters by day, followed by sunset celebrations nightly, complete with musicians and artists. ⇨ *See Chapter 7.*

Fort de Soto Beach

Another winner of "America's Best Beach," the 1,136-acre park lies at the mouth of Tampa Bay, spread over five islands and housing 7 miles of beach, two fishing piers, and a 4-mile hiking/skating trail. The beaches are super packed on weekends but splendidly quiet on weekdays. ⇨ *See Chapter 7.*

Fort Lauderdale Beach

The former spring-break capital now plays host to a reinvented, more upscale beachfront; however, the downy sands and crystalline waters from the days of

Where the Boys Are haven't changed. The beach "scene" is found between Las Olas and Sunrise boulevards. ⇨ *See Chapter 5.*

John Pennekamp Coral Reef State Park

Florida's best bet for diving and snorkeling, this state park adjacent to the Florida Keys National Marine Sanctuary encompasses 78 square miles of ecological treasures, the majority of which are found underwater. Although the beaches here do attract families, the real draw is experiencing the underwater world of the 600 varieties of fish that call this park home. ⇨ *See Chapter 4.*

Panama City Beach

The former Spring Break Capital of the World is also a family-friendly 17-mile expanse of snowy-white sand and sparkling emerald-green water that's all about awesome fun in the sun. Pier Park offers great shopping and watering holes on the streets opposite the beachfront hotels. ⇨ *See Chapter 14.*

Siesta Key Beach

Crowned "America's Best Beach" in 2012, this one boasts the finest quartz sands in the world. The sand is so fine and powdery it appears like piles of flour and squeaks under your feet when you walk on it. The 40-acre beach park of this island is exceptionally wide and long, providing ample space for families, romantics, and Sunday's Drum Circle celebration. ⇨ *See Chapter 7.*

South Beach

The legend of beautiful people is very much a reality on the sands parallel to deco-drenched Ocean Drive from 5th to 15th Street, and upscale Collins Avenue from 15th to 23rd Street. Expect diesel bodies, plastic surgery, hunky gay guys, pretentious partygoers, and random families coming to see what the fuss is all about. ⇨ *See Chapter 2.*

GREAT ITINERARIES

NORTHERN FLORIDA IN ONE WEEK

As much as South Florida centers on the present and future, northern Florida is more about the past. From America's oldest city—the circa-1565 St. Augustine—to the lost-in-time seaside communities along the 250-mile coastline of the Florida Panhandle, northern Florida embraces the architecture, simplicity, and pace of yesteryear. Beyond dedicated party towns, don't expect much in terms of nightlife or glitz. Do expect stunning, wide expanses of white-sand beach, day-caught seafood served up in no-frills settings, regions rich in marine life, excellent fishing, a family-friendly atmosphere and plenty of fun-in-the-sun.

St. Augustine

1 or 2 days. Start your journey through northern Florida in the nation's oldest city, which was founded by the Spanish in 1565. To explore the state's Spanish past, visit Castillo de San Marcos (its colonial-era fortress), the Colonial Quarter (a 2-acre living history museum of Florida life in the 16th, 17th, and 18th centuries), or stroll the streets of the Old City that grew up around the colonial quarter, giving you a chance to experience life in the past lane. A whole city block of historic houses built between 1790 and 1910 has been turned into the Dow Museum. But St. Augustine's future isn't all in the past. Peruse the many boutiques and indulge at the prolific restaurants that line the town center, stay in one of the many charming bed-and-breakfasts, and discover why St. Augustine rivals Savannah and Charleston as one of America's most charming cities. To the east is Anastasia Island, a state park with a stunning beach. ⇨ *Chapter 13.*

Amelia Island and Vicinity

2 days. Head northeast beyond Jacksonville to reach prestigious Amelia Island, home to world-class beach resorts and wide swaths of family-friendly beaches. By day simply enjoy some fun-in-the-sun or beachcomb nearby undeveloped beaches for sand dollars and seashells. At night, search for nesting sea turtles. You can stay in one of Amelia Island's posh resorts, or for a similar experience that doesn't require such deep pockets, enjoy the beach action slightly south along one of the four quieter communities of Jacksonville Beaches, specifically Atlantic Beach or Ponte Vedra Beach. Jacksonville itself is a underrated vacation destination full of charm with a lively arts scene that often turns up on lists of the best places to live in the United States. Take a short detour into Jacksonville one day to visit the Museum of Contemporary Art Jacksonville or the Jacksonville Zoo and Gardens, two of the area's world-class attractions. ⇨ *Chapter 13.*

Tallahassee

1 day. Drive west toward the Panhandle to get a true taste of the Old South in Spanish moss–draped Tallahassee, visiting one or two of the region's 71 plantations, such as Goodwood Museum and Gardens. Then get a dose of Old Florida at Edward Ball Wakulla Springs State Park, protected since the 1930s and famous as the jungle setting of the original Tarzan films, which today houses the largest and deepest freshwater spring in the world and plenty of manatees, alligators, and turtles, plus more than 180 species of birds. ⇨ *Chapter 14.*

Atlantic Ocean

GEORGIA

Gulf of Mexico

Panama City Beach

1 or 2 days. Continue past the state capital to the 250-mile-plus belt known as Panhandle's Emerald Coast, heralded for its powdery white-sand beaches and sparkling water. If you take the coastal route, U.S. 98, along the way you may want to plan a stop in Apalachicola, a friendly and charming fishing town that's become a major regional tourist draw. Off the beach, this area feels more southern than South Florida. Sun-worship and indulge in Gulf-to-table seafood in Panama City Beach, enjoying enhanced nightlife options that go beyond the typical spring break options. Take a boat tour out to St. Andrews State Park to tour protected Shell Island, one of the few places in the world where you can swim with dolphins in the wild. ⇨ *Chapter 14.*

Pensacola Beach

1 or 2 days. From Panama City Beach to Pensacola, take a relaxing drive along scenic Route 30A, passing nostalgia-inducing communities like WaterColor and Seaside, with an optional stop in glorious Grayton Beach, where kayaking ranks high on the agenda—or have lunch in the Panhandle's poshest subcity, Sandestin. At Pensacola Beach—one of the longest barrier islands in the

TIPS

■ Begin this itinerary by flying into Jacksonville airport. You'll need to rent a car for the duration of the journey, dropping off the vehicle in Pensacola and returning home from Pensacola airport.

■ The Panhandle runs on Central Time, meaning it's one hour behind the rest of Florida, which is in the Eastern Time zone.

■ Unlike South and Central Florida, summer is high season for most of northern Florida.

■ Northern Florida can be cold in winter. In Pensacola, January temperatures on average fluctuate between 42 and 60 degrees.

world—enjoy such pursuits as fishing, boating, water sports, or simply relaxing and soaking in the laid-back beach vibe. Time and interest permitting, take a half-day trip up to Florida Caverns State Park, one of the state's lesser-known treasures, where rangers lead insightful cave tours. ⇨ *Chapter 14.*

GREAT ITINERARIES

CENTRAL FLORIDA IN ONE WEEK

Theme parks, nature, and beaches—oh my! Central Florida lures in the masses with the prospect of thrilling rides, handshakes with Mickey Mouse, overall Disney magic, and simply basking in the frivolity of childhood, though its appeal spans far beyond man-made attractions. In fact, Central Florida also stakes claim to the state's most exceptional natural riches, including some of the country's superlative beaches (with accolades to prove it) and unparalleled nature encounters, such as swimming with manatees in the wild and bird-watching at Merritt Island National Wildlife Refuge.

Orlando
2 or 3 days. You could easily spend a week at Walt Disney World alone. But unless you're a die-hard theme park devotee, a few days is sufficient. Spend a few days park-hopping at Walt Disney World between The Magic Kingdom, Epcot, Disney's Hollywood Studios, and Disney's Animal Kingdom. Smaller kids may enjoy a quieter time at nearby Legoland, some 50 miles from Orlando. For more intense thrills, allow a day or two for movie magic at Universal Studios or heart-pumping rides at Islands of Adventure, where Harry Potter now reigns and draws crowds by the millions. If you are theme parked–out after two days (or never really liked them to begin with), survey the collection of modern paintings at the Orlando Museum of Art, stroll through the 50-acre Harry P. Leu Gardens, or visit Orlando's serene sister city, Winter Park. Boaters can take advantage of the area's numerous lakes, and golfers can link up on courses designed by the sport's biggest stars. ⇨ *Chapter 9, 10, and 11.*

Cape Canaveral
1 day. Head east from Orlando to discover one of Florida's best central coast treasures. Spend the day bird-watching at Merritt Island National Wildlife Refuge, have an out-of-this-world- experience at the Kennedy Space Center (and enjoy the interactive Space Shuttle *Challenger* exhibit), catch a wave like local surfing legend Kelly Slater in Cocoa Beach, or blissfully hit the beach at Canaveral National Seashore—a 24-mile undeveloped preserve where you lounge in the shelter of dunes, not the shadow of high-rises. Adrenaline junkies may want to reset their GPS for Daytona Beach. Its International Speedway, which has hosted NASCAR's Daytona 500 every February since 1959, is a must-see for stock-car enthusiasts (and the plain ol' race-car curious). ⇨ *Chapter 13.*

Tampa
1 day. If you crave more theme park fun, scream through the hair-raising rides at Busch Gardens and admire the 2,000-animal zoo, intricately woven throughout the park. The more sports-minded may want to catch one of Tampa Bay's myriad sporting events (the city has professional baseball, football, and hockey teams). Beach-lovers who didn't get enough sand and surf in Cape Canaveral may want to head over to Clearwater Beach to find some of Central Florida's best sandy shores. At night, dine and imbibe in the Spanish-inflected Ybor City entertainment district. ⇨ *Chapter 7.*

St. Petersburg
2 days. Indulge in the culture and beaches of this sophisticated city, home to the riveting, world-class Salvador Dalí Museum, multiple art galleries, and a quaint, historic downtown. Hit the

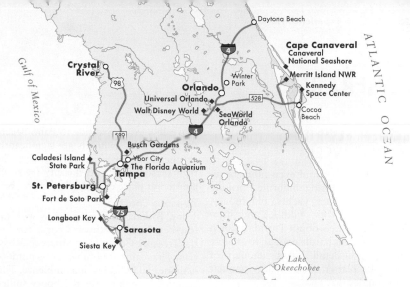

beach at Caladesi Island State Park to the west of the city or Fort De Soto Park at the mouth of Tampa Bay, both winners of the national "America's Best Beach" competition. Or explore the colorful waterfront community of Gulfport and its Art Village, which is full of locally owned boutiques, galleries, and eclectic eateries. Beer-lovers will want to set aside time to explore the city's burgeoning craft beer scene. ⇨ *Chapter 7.*

Sarasota

1 day. Drive south to Sarasota to appreciate Florida's thriving arts scene and stay overnight on one of the western barrier islands, namely Longboat Key or Siesta Key, the latter home to the finest quartz sand in the world and one of America's best beaches. In Sarasota, visit the John and Mable Ringling Museum of Art to learn all about the history of the Ringling circus and enjoy John Ringling's mind-blowingly expansive art collection. The museum encompasses the entire Ringling estate and offers something for guests of all ages and interests. ⇨ *Chapter 7.*

Crystal River

1/2 day. As a half-day trip, nature lovers should proceed north to Crystal River, less than two hours north of St. Petersburg, where you can snorkel with the

TIPS

■ Fly into and out of Orlando or Tampa, but you'll definitely need to rent a car.

■ In Orlando, a park-hopper pass will save you money and permit entry into multiple theme parks in a single day.

■ While within Disney World, leave your rental car in the hotel parking lot. Complimentary Disney buses transport you around this magical land.

■ The beaches around Tampa Bay and St. Petersburg are best on weekdays, when you are likely to have miles of sand all to yourself.

manatees that congregate in the warm waters from November through March. It's one of the few places on the planet where you can legally interact with them in natural waters. In off-season months, get your nature fix with a dolphin-watching cruise through the Florida Aquarium, back in Tampa. ⇨ *Chapter 7.*

GREAT ITINERARIES

SOUTH FLORIDA IN ONE WEEK

Beautiful beaches and even more beautiful people, pulsing nightlife, striking architecture, fancy yachts, old money, new money, exotic wildlife, and stunning marine life—South Florida's got it all. One week is hardly enough to explore the region in detail, but it's enough for a sampler platter of this wildly popular vacation destination.

Fort Lauderdale

1 day. Whether you fly into Miami or right into Fort Lauderdale, make the Yachting Capital of the World and the Venice of America your first stop; it's only an hour from the Miami airport. Known for its expansive beaches, show-stopping resort hotels, exploding food scene, and burgeoning cultural scene, Fort Lauderdale has a lot to like, so it may be hard to get your fill in a single day. Take to the waterways to appreciate this coastal beauty. Stroll picture-perfect Las Olas Boulevard, browsing the boutiques and enjoying the eclectic eateries lining Fort Lauderdale's principal thoroughfare. ⇨ *Chapter 5.*

Palm Beaches

1 day. Less than two hours north of Fort Lauderdale, the opulent mansions of Palm Beach's Ocean Boulevard give you a glimpse of how the richer half lives. For exclusive boutique shopping, art gallery browsing, and glittery sightseeing, sybarites should wander down "The Avenue" (that's Worth Avenue to non–Palm Beachers). The sporty set will find dozens of places to tee up in the Palm Beaches (hardly surprising given that the PGA is based here), along with tennis courts, polo clubs, even a croquet center. While there's

also a less expensive side to Palm Beach, the area's famous hotels are significantly cheaper after Easter weekend, when the high season ends and the city feels like a different place entirely. ⇨ *Chapter 6.*

Treasure Coast

1 day. To balance the highbrow with the low-key, head northward for a tour of the Treasure Coast, from Stuart to Sebastian. The region is notable for its outdoor activities and Old Florida ambience. This region was named for the booty spilled by a fleet of Spanish galleons shipwrecked here in 1715, though these days you're more likely to discover manatees and golden surfing opportunities than actual gold. You can also look for the sea turtles that lay their own little treasures in the sands March through October. As you drive north, you may want to stop in Jupiter, especially if you're a dog lover, to see one of the state's most dog-friendly beaches. ⇨ *Chapter 6.*

Miami

2 or 3 days. Greater Miami lays claim to the country's most celebrated strand—South Beach—and lingering there tops most tourist itineraries. Once you've checked out the candy-color art deco architecture, take time off to ogle the parade of stylish people along Lincoln Road Mall, Ocean Drive, or at the bars, restaurants, and sleek swimming pools within the ever-growing number of trendy hotels in both South Beach and Mid-Beach. Do some credit card damage up in the posh beach-front city of Bal Harbour or inland in the see-and-be-seen Design District. Later, *merengue* over to Calle Ocho, the center of Miami's Cuban community, and pay a visit to bohemian Coconut Grove or the Wynwood Arts District for some more culture. ⇨ *Chapter 2.*

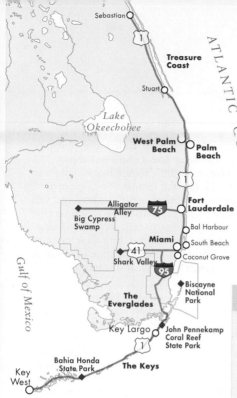

The Everglades

1/2 day. Miami is the only U.S. city with two national parks and a national preserve in its backyard, deeming it a convenient base for eco-excursions. Especially if you stay three days, keep your car long enough to take a day trip to the Everglades. The easiest access point is Shark Valley, where you can bike along a trail teeming with alligators and herons. Alternatively, get a spectacular view of Florida's coral reefs from a glass-bottom boat in Biscayne National Park; and then spot some rare wood storks in Big Cypress Swamp, which is best explored via Alligator Alley (Interstate 75). ⇨ *Chapter 3.*

The Keys

2 or 3 days. Head south from the Florida mainland to the überrelaxing island chain, planning a pit stop at John Pennekamp Coral Reef State Park in Key Largo (which offers unparalleled

TIPS

■ You can fly into either Miami International Airport or Fort Lauderdale–Hollywood International Airport; pick whichever is cheaper.

■ You'll definitely need a rental car to get between most destinations in South Florida, but expensive parking, pedestrian-friendly streets, and taxis make a car unnecessary in both South Beach and Key West.

■ If you have time, drive from Miami to Key West, but flights back can be quick and cheap; check the drop-off charge for a one-way rental.

snorkeling and scuba diving) or at Bahia Honda State Park farther south (it has ranger-led activities plus the Keys' best beach). Then plant yourself at the most famous key of all, Key West, where a come-as-you-are, do-as-you-please vibe rules. The Old Town has a funky, laid-back feel, with prolific nods to Ernest Hemingway. If you haven't imbibed too much at one of the renowned watering holes, rent a moped to tour the rest of the island. Clear waters and abundant marine life make underwater activities another must. ⇨ *Chapter 4.*

WHEN TO GO

Although Florida is a year-round vacation venue, it divides the calendar into regional tourism seasons. Holidays and school breaks are major factors. However, the clincher is weather, with the best months being designated as peak periods.

High season in southern Florida starts with the run-up to Christmas and continues through Easter. Snowbirds migrate down then to escape frosty weather back home, and festivalgoers flock in because major events are held this time of year to avoid summer's searing heat and high humidity. Winter is also *the* time to visit the Everglades, as temperatures, mosquito activity, and water levels are all lower (making wildlife easier to spot).

Northern Florida, conversely, receives the greatest influx of visitors from Memorial Day to Labor Day. Costs are highest then, but so are temperatures. (In winter, when the mercury dips into the 40s, you'd get a chilly reception on Panhandle beaches.) Specific areas, like Panama City Beach or Daytona Beach, attract throngs—and thongs—during spring break, too. In the latter location, expect revved-up revelers during Speedweeks (late January and February) and Bike Week (early March).

Thanks to its theme parks, Central Florida is a magnet for children, meaning the largest crowds gather, logically enough, whenever class lets out. Lineups at attractions do shrink after they return to school, though this area's hopping all year, with large numbers of international families and kid-free adults coming in the off-season. Spring and fall shoulder seasons are the optimal time to visit, both weather-wise and price-wise.

Climate

Florida is rightly called the Sunshine State—areas like Tampa Bay report 361 days of sunshine a year! But it could also be dubbed the Humid State. From June through September, 90% humidity levels aren't uncommon, nor are accompanying thunderstorms. In fact, more than half of the state's rain falls during these months. Florida's two-sided coastline also makes it a target for tropical storms.

Hurricanes

The hurricane season begins on June 1 and lasts through November 30 (roughly half the year). However, big storms are much more likely in August and September. Chances are, you'll be just fine if you travel to Florida in June or July, though it's always a good idea to buy travel insurance in case something does happen. In the summer, frequent afternoon thunderstorms are common, especially inland in places like Orlando. On the coast, the weather is almost universally hot and muggy, and rain is common, especially later in the summer.

MIAMI AND MIAMI BEACH

WELCOME TO MIAMI AND MIAMI BEACH

TOP REASONS TO GO

★ **The beach:** Miami Beach has been rated as one of the 10 best beaches in the world. White sand, warm water, and bronzed bodies everywhere provide just the right mix of relaxation and people-watching.

★ **Dining delights:** Miami's eclectic residents have transformed the city into a museum of epicurean wonders, ranging from Cuban and Argentine fare to fusion haute cuisine.

★ **Wee-hour parties:** A 24-hour liquor license means clubs stay open until 5 am, and after-parties go until noon the following day.

★ **Picture-perfect people:** Miami is a watering hole for the vain and beautiful of South America, Europe, and the Northeast. Watch them—or join them—as they strut their stuff and flaunt their tans on the white beds of renowned art deco hotels.

★ **Art Deco District:** Iconic pastels and neon lights accessorize the architecture that first put South Beach on the map in the 1930s.

1 **Downtown.** Weave through the glass-and-steel labyrinth of new condo construction to catch a game or a new exhibition.

2 **Coconut Grove.** Catch dinner and a movie, listen to live music, or cruise the bohemian shops.

3 **Coral Gables.** Dine and shop on family-friendly Miracle Mile, and take a driving tour of the surrounding neighborhoods.

4 **Key Biscayne.** Explore the pristine parks and stretches of award-winning beaches by boat, kayak, or foot.

5 **Wynwood.** Eat, shop, and gawk your way through this trendy, creative neighborhood north of Downtown.

6 **Midtown.** Experience yuppie life in this residential enclave chock-full of fabulous restaurants and lounges.

7 **Design District.** Browse the design showrooms and haute boutiques before dining at Miami's trendiest restaurants.

8 **Little Haiti.** Practice your Creole, sample Haitian food, and look for MiMo architecture around this interesting ethnic neighborhood.

9 **Little Havana.** Sip Cuban coffee, roll cigars, and play dominoes in the heart and soul of Cuba's exile community.

GETTING ORIENTED

Long considered the gateway to Latin America, Miami is as close to Cuba and the Caribbean as you can get within the United States. The 36-square-mile city is at the southern tip of the Florida peninsula, bordered on the east by Biscayne Bay. Over the bay lies a series of barrier islands, the largest being a thin 18-square-mile strip called Miami Beach. To the east of Miami Beach is the Atlantic Ocean. To the south are the Florida Keys.

10 South Beach. People-watch from sidewalk cafés, admire art deco, and party 'til dawn at the nation's hottest clubs.

11 Mid-Beach. Experience the booming restaurant scene and trendy hotels just beyond South Beach.

12 Fisher and Belle Isle. Be near the pulse of Miami Beach but a man-made island away.

13 North Beach. Shop and relax in the quieter northern end of Miami Beach, which also encompasses Aventura, Bal Harbour, and Sunny Isles.

CUBAN FOOD

If the tropical vibe has you hankering for Cuban food, you've come to the right place. Miami is the top spot in the country to enjoy authentic Cuban cooking.

The flavors and preparations of Cuban cuisine are influenced by the island nation's natural bounty (yuca, sugarcane, guava), as well as its rich immigrant history, from near (Caribbean countries) and far (Spanish and African traditions). Chefs in Miami tend to stick with the classic versions of beloved dishes, though you'll find some variation from restaurant to restaurant, as recipes have often been passed down through generations of home cooks. For a true Cuban experience, try either the popular **Versailles** (⊠ *3555 S.W. 8th St.* ☎ *305/444–0240* ⊕ *www.versaillesrestaurant.com*) or classic **La Carreta** (⊠ *3632 S.W. 8th St.* ☎ *305/444–7501*) in Little Havana, appealing to families seeking a home-cooked, Cuban-style meal. For a modern interpretation of Cuban eats, head to Coral Gable's **Havana Harry's** (⊠ *4612 S. Le Jeune Rd.* ☎ *305/661–2622*). South Beach eatery **Puerto Sagua Restaurant** (⊠ *700 Collins Ave.* ☎ *305/673–1115*) is the beach's favorite Cuban hole-in-the-wall, open daily from 7 am to 2 am.

THE CUBAN SANDWICH

A great *cubano* (Cuban sandwich) requires pillowy Cuban bread layered with ham, garlic-citrus-marinated slow-roasted pork, Swiss cheese, and pickles (plus salami in Tampa, lettuce and tomatoes in Key West), with butter and/or mustard. The sandwich is grilled in a sandwich press until the cheese melts and all the elements are fused together. Try one at **Enriqueta's Sandwich Shop** (⊠ *186 N.E. 29 St.* ☎ *305/573–4681* ⊗ Weekdays 6 am–4 pm, Sat. 6 am–2 pm) in Wynwood, or **Exquisito Restaurant** (⊠ *1510 S.W. 8th St.* ☎ *305/643–0227* ⊗ Daily 7 am–11 pm) in Little Havana.

KEY CUBAN DISHES

ARROZ CON POLLO

This chicken-and-rice dish is Cuban comfort food. Found throughout Latin America, the Cuban version is typically seasoned with garlic, paprika, and onions, then colored golden or reddish with saffron or achiote (a seed paste), and enlivened with a sizable splash of beer near the end of cooking. Green peas and sliced, roasted red peppers are standard toppings.

BISTEC DE PALOMILLA

This thinly sliced sirloin steak is marinated in lime juice and garlic and fried with onions. The steak is often served with *chimichurri* sauce, an olive oil, garlic, and cilantro sauce that sometimes comes with bread (slather bread with butter and dab on the chimichurri). Also try *ropa vieja,* a slow-cooked, shredded flank steak in a garlic-tomato sauce.

DESSERTS

Treat yourself to a slice of *tres leches* cake. The "three milks" come from the sweetened condensed milk, evaporated milk, and heavy cream that are poured over the cake until it's an utterly irresistible gooey mess. Also, don't miss the *pastelitos,* Cuban fruit-filled turnovers. Traditional flavors include plain guava, guava with cream cheese, and cream cheese with coconut.

DRINKS

Sip *guarapo* (gwa-RA-poh), a fresh sugarcane juice that isn't really as sweet as you might think, or grab a straw and enjoy a frothy *batido* (bah-TEE-doe), a Cuban-style milk shake made with tropical fruits like mango, *piña* (pineapple), or *mamey* (mah-MAY, a tropical fruit with a melon-cherry taste). For a real twist, try the *batido de trigo*—a wheat shake that will remind you of sugar-glazed breakfast cereal.

FRITAS

If you're in the mood for an inexpensive, casual Cuban meal, have a *frita*—a hamburger with distinctive Cuban flair. It's made with ground beef that's mixed with ground or finely chopped chorizo, spiced with pepper, paprika, and salt, topped with sautéed onions and shoestring potato fries, and then served on a bun slathered with a special tomato-based ketchup-like sauce.

LECHON ASADO

Fresh ham or an entire suckling pig marinated in *mojo criollo* (parsley, garlic, sour orange, and olive oil) is roasted until fork tender and served with white rice, black beans, and *tostones* (fried plantains) or yuca (pronounced YU-kah), a starchy tuber with a mild nut taste that's often sliced into fat sticks and deep-fried like fries.

Updated by
Paul Rubio

Three-quarters of a century after the art deco movement, Miami remains one of the world's trendiest and flashiest hot spots. Luckily for visitors, South Beach is no longer the only place to stand and pose in Miami. North of Downtown, the growing Wynwood and Design districts—along with nearby Midtown—are home to Miami's hipster and fashionista movements, and the South Beach "scene" continues to extend both north and west, with the addition of new venues north of 20th Street, south of 5th Street, and along the bay on West Avenue. The reopening of the mammoth Fontainebleau and its enclave of nightclubs and restaurants along Mid-Beach paved the way for a Mid-Beach renaissance, luring other globally renowned resorts, lounges, and restaurants into the neighborhood, such as the Soho Beach House and the Faena District Miami Beach, a multiblock project in Mid-Beach by Argentinean icon and developer Alan Faena.

Visit Miami today and it's hard to believe that 100 years ago it was a mosquito-infested swampland, with an Indian trading post on the Miami River. Then hotel builder Henry Flagler brought his railroad to the outpost known as Fort Dallas. Other visionaries—Carl Fisher, Julia Tuttle, William Brickell, and John Sewell, among others—set out to tame the unruly wilderness. Hotels were erected, bridges were built, the port was dredged, and electricity arrived. The narrow strip of mangrove coast was transformed into Miami Beach—and the tourists started to come. They haven't stopped since!

Greater Miami is many destinations in one. At its best it offers an unparalleled multicultural experience: melodic Latin and Caribbean tongues, international cuisines and cultural events, and an unmistakable joie de vivre—all against a beautiful beach backdrop. In Little Havana the air is tantalizing with the perfume of strong Cuban coffee. In Coconut Grove, Caribbean steel drums ring out during the Miami/Bahamas Goombay Festival. Anytime in colorful Miami Beach, restless crowds wait for entry to the hottest new clubs.

Many visitors don't know that Miami and Miami Beach are really separate cities. Miami, on the mainland, is South Florida's commercial hub. Miami Beach, on 17 islands in Biscayne Bay, is sometimes considered America's Riviera, luring refugees from winter with its warm sunshine; sandy beaches; graceful, shady palms; and tireless nightlife. The natives know well that there's more to Greater Miami than the bustle of South Beach and its Art Deco District. In addition to well-known places such as Ocean Drive and Lincoln Road, the less reported spots—like the burgeoning Design District in Miami, the historic buildings of Coral Gables, and the secluded beaches of Key Biscayne—are great insider destinations.

PLANNING

WHEN TO GO

Miami and Miami Beach are year-round destinations. Most people come from November through April, when the weather is close to perfect; hotels, restaurants, and attractions are busiest; and each weekend holds a festival or event. High season kicks off in December with Art Basel Miami Beach, and hotel rates don't come down until after the college kids have left after spring break in late March.

It's hot and steamy May through September, but nighttime temperatures are usually pleasant. Also, summer is a good time for the budget traveler. Many hotels lower their rates considerably, and many restaurants offer discounts—especially during Miami Spice in August and September, when a slew of top restaurants offer special tasting menus at a steep discount.

GETTING HERE AND AROUND

You'll need a car to visit many attractions and points of interest. If possible, avoid driving during the rush hours of 7–9 am and 5–7 pm—the hour just after and right before the peak times also can be slow going. During rainy weather, be especially cautious of flooding in South Beach and Key Biscayne.

AIR TRAVEL

Miami is serviced by Miami International Airport (MIA), 8 miles northwest of Downtown, and Fort Lauderdale–Hollywood International Airport (FLL), 26 miles northeast. Many discount carriers, like Spirit Airlines, Southwest Airlines, and JetBlue, fly into FLL, making it a smart bargain if you're renting a car. Otherwise, look for flights to MIA, which has undergone an extensive face-lift, improving facilities, common spaces, and the overall aesthetic of the airport.

CAR TRAVEL

Interstate 95 is the major expressway connecting South Florida with points north; State Road 836 is the major east–west expressway and connects to Florida's Turnpike, State Road 826, and Interstate 95. Seven causeways link Miami and Miami Beach, with Interstate 195 and Interstate 395 offering the most convenient routes; the Rickenbacker Causeway extends to Key Biscayne from Interstate 95 and U.S. 1. The high-speed lanes on the left-hand side of Interstate 95 require a prepaid toll pass called a Sunpass, available in most drug and grocery stores, or it can be ordered by mail before your trip. It is available with all rental cars (but you are billed for the tolls and associated fees later).

PUBLIC TRANSPORTATION

Some sights are accessible via the public transportation system, run by the **Metro-Dade Transit Agency,** which maintains 740 Metrobuses on 90 routes; the 23-mile Metrorail elevated rapid-transit system; and the Metromover, an elevated light-rail system. Those planning to use public transportation should get an EASY Card or EASY Ticket available at any Metrorail station and most supermarkets. Fares are discounted, and transfer fees are nominal. The bus stops for the **Metrobus** are marked with blue-and-green signs with a bus logo and route information. The fare is $2.25 (exact change only). Cash-paying customers must pay for another ride if transferring. Some express routes carry a surcharge of 40¢. Elevated **Metrorail** trains run from downtown Miami north to Hialeah and south along U.S. 1 to Dadeland. The system operates daily 5 am–midnight. The fare is $2.25; $0.60 transfers to Metrobus are available only for EASY Card and EASY Ticket holders. The free **Metromover** resembles an airport shuttle and runs on two loops around downtown Miami, linking major hotels, office buildings, and shopping areas. The system spans about 4½ miles, including the 1-mile Omni Loop and the 1-mile Brickell Loop. **Tri-Rail,** South Florida's commuter-train system, stops at 18 stations north of MIA along a 71-mile route. There's a Metrorail transfer station two stops north of MIA. Prices range from $2.50 to $6.90 for a one-way ticket.

Contacts Metro-Dade Transit Agency. ☎ *305/891–3131* ⊕ *www.miamidade. gov/transit/.* **Tri-Rail.** ☎ *800/874–7245* ⊕ *www.tri-rail.com.*

TAXI TRAVEL

Except in South Beach, it's difficult to hail a cab on the street; in most cases you'll need to call a cab company or have a hotel doorman hail one for you. Taxi drivers in Miami are notorious for bad customer service and not having credit card machines in their vehicles. These days, many people use Uber or Lyft to avoid this taxi drama, and for reasonable prices; however, in order to use Uber you must sign up with the company and have the Uber app installed on your smartphone. If using a regular taxi, note that fares run $2.50 for the first 1/6 of a mile and $0.40 for every additional 1/6 of a mile. Waiting time is $0.40 per minute. Flat-rate fares are also available from the airport to a variety of zones (including Miami Beach) for $35. Expect a $2 surcharge on rides leaving from Miami International Airport or the Port of Miami.

For those heading from MIA to Downtown, the 15-minute, 7-mile trip costs around $22. Some but not all cabs accept credit cards, so ask when you get in.

Taxi Companies Central Cab. ☎ *305/532-5555* ⊕ *www.centralcab.com.* **Uber.** ⊕ *www.uber.com.* **Yellow Cab.** ☎ *305/444-4444.*

TRAIN TRAVEL

New, privately operated high-speed Brightline service began in summer 2017, connecting downtown Miami, Fort Lauderdale, and West Palm Beach. The trip from downtown Miami to Fort Lauderdale takes about 30 minutes; it's another 30 minutes to West Palm Beach.

Amtrak provides service from 500 destinations to the Greater Miami area. The trains make several stops along the way; north–south service stops in the major Florida cities of Jacksonville, Orlando, Tampa, West Palm Beach, and Fort Lauderdale, but stations are not always conveniently located. The Auto Train (where you bring your car along) travels from Lorton, Virginia, just outside Washington, D.C., to Sanford, Florida, just outside Orlando. From there it's less than a four-hour drive to Miami. Fares vary, but expect to pay between around $275 and $350 for a basic sleeper seat and car passage each way. ■TIP→ You must be traveling with an automobile to purchase a ticket on the Auto Train.

Contacts Brightline. ⊕ *gobrightline.com.*

VISITOR INFORMATION

For additional information about Miami and Miami Beach, contact the city's visitor bureaus. You can also pick up a free Miami Beach INcard at the Miami Beach Visitors Center 10–4, seven days a week, entitling you to discounts and offers at restaurants, shops, galleries, and more.

Contacts City of Coral Gables. ⊠ *Coral Gables City Hall, 405 Biltmore Way, Coral Gables* ☎ *305/446-6800* ⊕ *www.coralgables.com.* **Coconut Grove Business Improvement District.** ⊠ *3390 Mary St., Suite 130, Coconut Grove* ☎ *305/461-5506* ⊕ *www.coconutgrove.com.* **Greater Miami Convention & Visitors Bureau.** ⊠ *701 Brickell Ave., Suite 2700* ☎ *305/539-3000, 800/933-8448 in U.S.* ⊕ *www.miamiandbeaches.com.* **Key Biscayne Chamber of Commerce and Visitors Center.** ⊠ *88 W. McIntyre St., Suite 100, Key Biscayne* ☎ *305/361-5207* ⊕ *www.keybiscaynechamber.org.* **Visit Miami Beach.** ⊠ *Visitor Center, 1901 Convention Center Dr., Hall C, Miami Beach* ☎ *786/276-2763, 305/673-7400 Miami Beach tourist hotline* ⊕ *www.miamibeachguest.com.*

EXPLORING

If you'd arrived here 50 years ago with a guidebook in hand, chances are you'd be thumbing through listings looking for alligator wrestlers and you-pick strawberry fields or citrus groves. Things have changed. While Disney sidetracked families in Orlando, Miami was developing a unique culture and attitude that's equal parts beach town/big business, Latino/Caribbean meets European/American—all of which fuels a great art and food scene, as well as exuberant nightlife and myriad festivals.

To find your way around Greater Miami, learn how the numbering system works (or better yet, use your phone's GPS). Miami is laid out on a grid with four quadrants—northeast, northwest, southeast, and southwest—that meet at Miami Avenue and Flagler Street. Miami Avenue separates east from west, and Flagler Street separates north from south. Avenues and courts run north–south; streets, terraces, and ways run east–west. Roads run diagonally, northwest–southeast. But other districts—Miami Beach, Coral Gables, and Hialeah—may or may not follow this system, and along the curve of Biscayne Bay the symmetrical grid shifts diagonally. If you do get lost, make sure you're in a safe neighborhood or public place when you seek guidance; cabdrivers and cops are good resources.

DOWNTOWN

Downtown Miami dazzles from a distance. America's third-largest skyline is fluid, thanks to the sheer number of sparkling glass high-rises between Biscayne Boulevard and the Miami River. Business is the key to downtown Miami's daytime bustle. However, the influx of massive, modern, and once-affordable condos has lured a young and trendy demographic to the areas in and around Downtown, giving Miami much more of a "city" feel come nightfall. In fact, Downtown has become a nighttime hot spot in recent years, inciting a cultural revolution that has fostered burgeoning areas north in Wynwood, Midtown, and the Design District, and south along Brickell Avenue. The pedestrian streets here tend to be very restaurant-centric, complemented by lounges and nightclubs.

The free, 4½-mile, elevated commuter system known as the Metromover runs inner and outer loops through Downtown and to nearby neighborhoods south and north. Many attractions are conveniently located within a few blocks of a station.

TOP ATTRACTIONS

Adrienne Arsht Center. Culture vultures and other artsy types are drawn to this stunning performing arts center, which includes the 2,400-seat Ziff Ballet Opera House, the 2,200-seat John S. and James L. Knight Concert Hall, the black-box Carnival Studio Theater, and an outdoor Plaza for the Arts. Throughout the year, you'll find top-notch performances by local and national touring groups, including Broadway hits like *Wicked* and *Jersey Boys,* intimate music concerts, and showstopping ballet. Think of it as a sliver of savoir faire to temper Miami's often-over-the-top vibe. The massive development was designed by architect César Pelli, and stands as the largest American performing arts center constructed since the 1980s. Complimentary one-hour tours of the Arsht Center, highlighting the architecture and its public art, are offered every Saturday and Monday at noon. Arrive early for your performance to dine at BRAVA By Brad Kilgore, located within the Arsht center and currently one of Miami's hottest restaurants. ⊠ *1300 Biscayne Blvd., at N.E. 13th St., Downtown* ☎ *305/949–6722 box office* ⊕ *www.arshtcenter.org.*

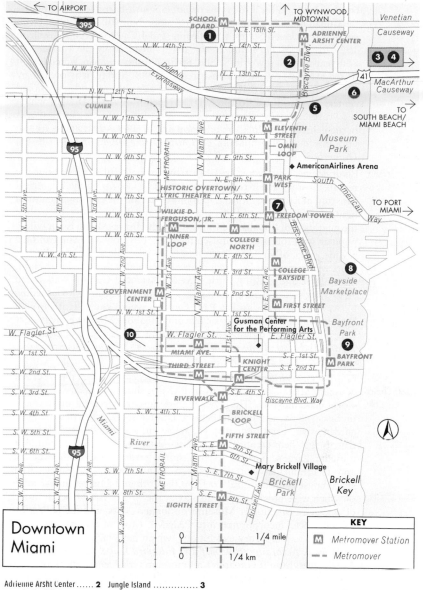

Downtown Miami

KEY

Ⓜ *Metromover Station*

- - - *Metromover*

Freedom Tower. In the 1960s this ornate Spanish-baroque structure was the Cuban Refugee Center, processing more than 500,000 Cubans who entered the United States after fleeing Fidel Castro's regime. Built in 1925 for the *Miami Daily News,* it was inspired by the Giralda, an 800-year-old bell tower in Seville, Spain. Preservationists were pleased to see the tower's exterior restored in 1988. Today, it is owned by Miami Dade College (MDC), functioning as a cultural and educational center; it's also home to the MDC Museum of Art + Design, which showcases a broad collection of contemporary Latin art as well works in the genres of minimalism and pop art. ■TIP➔ Admission is free to both the tower and museum. ⊠ *600 Biscayne Blvd., at N.E. 6th St., Downtown* ☎ *305/237-7700* ⊕ *www.mdcmoad.org.*

FAMILY **HistoryMiami.** Discover a treasure trove of colorful stories about the region's history at HistoryMiami, formerly known as the Historical Museum of Southern Florida. Exhibits celebrate the city's multicultural heritage, including an old Miami streetcar and unique items chronicling the migration of Cubans to Miami. Though HistoryMiami is not wildly popular with tourists, the museum's tours certainly are. You can take a wide range of walking, boat, coach, bike, gallery, and eco-history tours with varying prices, including culture walks through Little Haiti, informative and exciting Little Havana Arts and Culture Walks, and an evening of storytelling during the "Moon Over Miami" tour led by HistoryMiami historian Dr. Paul George, where you'll float through Downtown on the Miami River, learning all about Miami's early history circa the Tequesta Indians' days. ⊠ *101 W. Flagler St., between N.W. 1st and 2nd Aves., Downtown* ☎ *305/375-1492* ⊕ *www.historymiami. org* ⊠ *$10; tour costs vary.*

FAMILY **Pérez Art Museum Miami (PAMM).** Opened in December 2013, the Pérez Art
Fodor's Choice Museum Miami, known locally as PAMM, shines as the city's first true
★ world-class museum. This über-high-design architectural masterpiece on Biscayne Bay is a sight to behold. Double-story, cylindrical hanging gardens sway from high atop the museum, anchored to stylish wood trusses that help create this gotta-see-it-to-believe-it indoor-outdoor museum. Large sculptures, Asian-inspired gardens, sexy white benches, and steel frames envelop the property. Inside, the 120,000-square-foot space houses multicultural art from the 20th and 21st centuries, some of which were previously on display at the Miami Art Museum (note: downtown's Miami Art Museum no longer exists, and the collection has now been incorporated into PAMM). Most of the interior space is devoted to temporary exhibitions, which have included the likes of *Ai Weiwei: According to What?* and *Edouard Duval-Carrié: Imagined Landscapes.* Even if you aren't a "museum type," come check out this magnum opus over lunch at Verde at PAMM, the museum's sensational waterfront restaurant and bar. ■TIP➔ Admission is free every first Thursday of the month and every second Saturday of the month. ⊠ *1103 Biscayne Blvd., Downtown* ☎ *305/375-3000* ⊕ *www.pamm. org* ⊠ *$16* ⊗ *Closed Wed.*

WORTH NOTING

Bayfront Park. This pedestrian-friendly waterfront park sits on a 32-acre site smack in the heart of downtown Miami on Biscayne Bay, bordered by Bayside Marketplace to the north and the InterContinental Miami to the south. There's a small but lovely walking trail and two major event spaces—the Tina Hills Pavilion and Bayfront Park Amphitheater. American sculptor Isamu Noguchi helped redesign the park in the late 1980s, gracing the site with several works, including the white *Challenger* Memorial, commemorating the space shuttle that exploded in 1986. If you want to live like a local, join in the free yoga on the bay front Monday and Wednesday (6 pm) or Saturday (9 am). Seven blocks north of Bayfront Park is the 30-acre Museum Park (formerly Bicentennial Park), which houses the Patricia and Phillip Frost Museum of Science and the Pérez Art Museum Miami (PAMM), and is also managed by Bayfront Park Management Trust. ☒ *301 N. Biscayne Blvd., Downtown* ☎ *305/358–7550* ⊕ *www.bayfrontparkmiami.com.*

FAMILY **Bayside Marketplace.** The Bayside Marketplace, a waterfront complex of entertainment, dining, and retail stores, was en vogue circa 1992 and remains popular due to its location near PortMiami. You'll find the area awash in cruise-ship passenger chaos on most days (it's definitely *not* a draw for locals), so expect plenty of souvenir shops, a Hard Rock Cafe, and stores like Wet Seal and Sunglass Hut. Many boat tours leave from the marinas lining the festival marketplace. ☒ *401 Biscayne Blvd., Downtown* ☎ *305/577–3344* ⊕ *www.baysidemarketplace.com.*

Fredric Snitzer Gallery. The gallery of this longtime figure in the Miami arts scene highlights emerging and mid-career artists, providing them that tipping point needed for national and international exposure and recognition. The newly relocated space maintains its warehouse roots, letting the art speak for itself amid the raw walls and ample natural light. Though a commercial gallery, the selection is highly curated. Rotating monthly exhibitions are usually thematic, with works by one of its represented artists including Hernan Bas, Alice Aycock, Enrique Martinez Celaya, Rafael Domenech, and Jon Pylypchuk. For the art novice, the team, including Snitzer himself, are readily available and willing to share their knowledge. ☒ *1540 N.E. Miami Ct., Downtown* ☎ *305/448–8976* ⊕ *www.snitzer.com.*

FAMILY **Jungle Island.** Originally located deep in south Miami and known as Parrot Jungle, South Florida's original tourist attraction opened in 1936 and moved closer to Miami Beach in 2003. Now on Watson Island, a small stretch of land between downtown Miami and South Beach, Jungle Island is far more than a place where cockatoos ride tricycles; this interactive zoological park is home to just about every unusual and endangered species you would want to see (if you are into seeing them in zoo-like settings, that is), including a rare albino alligator, a liger (lion and tiger mix), and myriad exotic birds. With an emphasis on the experiential versus mere observation, the park now offers several new attractions and activities, including private beaches, treetop zip-lining, aquatic activities, adventure trails, cultural activities, and enhanced VIP packages where you mingle with an array of furry and feathered friends. Jungle Island offers complimentary shuttle service to most downtown

Miami and South Beach hotels. ⊠ *Watson Island, 1111 Parrot Jungle Trail, off MacArthur Causeway (I–395), Downtown* ☎ *305/400–7000* ⊕ *www.jungleisland.com* ⊠ *$39.95, plus $10 parking.*

FAMILY **Miami Children's Museum.** This Arquitectonica-designed museum, both imaginative and geometric in appearance, is directly across the MacArthur Causeway from Jungle Island. Twelve galleries house hundreds of interactive, bilingual exhibits. Children can scan plastic groceries in the supermarket, scramble through a giant sand castle, climb a rock wall, learn about the Everglades, and combine rhythms in the world-music studio. ⊠ *Watson Island, 980 MacArthur Causeway, off I–395, Downtown* ☎ *305/373–5437* ⊕ *www.miamichildrensmuseum.org* ⊠ *$20, parking $1/hr.*

FAMILY **Patricia and Phillip Frost Museum of Science.** In spring 2017, the Patricia and Phillip Frost Museum of Science relocated to its much larger (250,000-square-foot), hypermodern, $300 million-plus new home in Downtown's Museum Park. Marvel at the wealth of hands-on sound, gravity, and electricity displays for children and adults alike alongside a tri-level aquarium and a 250-seat state-of-the-art planetarium. There are also exhibits dedicated to space travel, the Everglades, and mind-blowing laser shows daily. Price of admission includes access to the museum as well as one Frost Planetarium show. ⊠ *1101 Biscayne Blvd., Downtown* ☎ *305/434–9600* ⊕ *www.frostscience.org* ⊠ *$27.*

COCONUT GROVE

A former haven for writers and artists, Coconut Grove has never quite outgrown its image as a small village. You can still feel the bohemian roots of this artsy neighborhood, but it has grown increasingly mainstream and residential over the past 20 years. Posh estates mingle with rustic cottages, modest frame homes, and stark modern dwellings, often on the same block. If you're into horticulture, you'll be impressed by the Garden of Eden–like foliage that seems to grow everywhere without care. In truth, residents are determined to keep up the Grove's village-in-a-jungle look, so they lavish attention on exotic plantings even as they battle to protect any remaining native vegetation.

The center of the Grove still attracts its fair share of locals and tourists who enjoy perusing the small boutiques, sidewalk cafés, and cute galleries that remind us of the old Grove. Activities here are family-friendly with easy access to bay-side parks, museums, and gardens.

TOP ATTRACTIONS

FAMILY

Fodor's Choice

★

Vizcaya Museum and Gardens. Of the 10,000 people living in Miami between 1912 and 1916, about 1,000 of them were gainfully employed by Chicago industrialist James Deering to build this European-inspired residence. Once comprising 180 acres, this National Historic Landmark now occupies a 30-acre tract that includes a rockland hammock (native forest) and more than 10 acres of formal gardens with fountains overlooking Biscayne Bay. The house, open to the public, contains 70 rooms, 34 of which are filled with paintings, sculpture, antique furniture, and other fine and decorative arts. The collection spans 2,000 years and represents the Renaissance, baroque, rococo, and neoclassical periods.

The 90-minute self-guided Discover Vizcaya Audio Tour is available in multiple languages for an additional $5. Moonlight tours, offered on evenings that are nearest the full moon, provide a magical look at the gardens; call for reservations. ✉ *3251 S. Miami Ave., Coconut Grove* ☎ *305/250–9133* ⊕ *www.vizcaya.org* 🎫 *$18* ⊗ *Closed Tues.*

CORAL GABLES

You can easily spot Coral Gables from the window of a Miami-bound jetliner—just look for the massive orange tower of the Biltmore Hotel rising from a lush green carpet of trees concealing the city's gracious homes. The canopy is as much a part of this planned city as its distinctive architecture, all attributed to the vision of George E. Merrick more than a century ago.

The story of this city began in 1911, when Merrick inherited 1,600 acres of citrus and avocado groves from his father. Through judicious investment he nearly doubled the tract to 3,000 acres by 1921. Merrick dreamed of building an American Venice here, complete with canals and homes. Working from this vision, he began designing a city based on centuries-old prototypes from Mediterranean countries. Unfortunately for Merrick, the devastating no-name hurricane of 1926, followed by the Great Depression, prevented him from fulfilling many of his plans. He died at 54, an employee of the post office. Today Coral Gables has a population of about 50,000. In its bustling Downtown more than 150 multinational companies maintain headquarters or regional offices, and the University of Miami campus in the southern part of the Gables brings a youthful vibrancy to the area. A southern branch of the city extends down the shore of Biscayne Bay through neighborhoods threaded with canals.

TOP ATTRACTIONS

Biltmore Hotel. Bouncing back stunningly from its dark days as an army hospital, this hotel has become the jewel of Coral Gables—a dazzling architectural gem with a colorful past. First opened in 1926, it was a hot spot for the rich and glamorous of the Jazz Age until it was converted to an army–air force regional hospital in 1942. Until 1968, the Veterans Administration continued to operate the hospital after World War II. The Biltmore then lay vacant for nearly 20 years before it underwent extensive renovations and reopened as a luxury hotel in 1987. Its 16-story tower, like the Freedom Tower in downtown Miami, is a replica of Seville's Giralda Tower. The magnificent pool is reportedly the largest hotel pool in the continental United States. ■ **TIP**➔ Because it functions as a full-service hotel, your ticket in—if you aren't staying here—is to patronize one of the hotel's several restaurants or bars. Try to get a courtyard table for the Sunday Champagne brunch, a local legend. ✉ *1200 Anastasia Ave., near De Soto Blvd., Coral Gables* ☎ *855/311–6903* ⊕ *www.biltmorehotel.com.*

FAMILY **Fairchild Tropical Botanic Garden.** With 83 acres of lakes, sunken gardens, a 560-foot vine pergola, orchids, bellflowers, coral trees, bougainvillea, rare palms, and flowering trees, Fairchild is the largest tropical botanical garden in the continental United States. The tram tour highlights the best of South

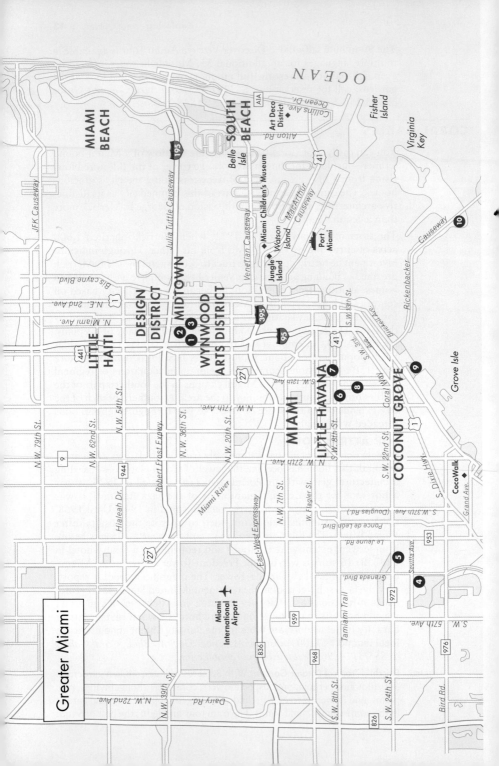

Greater Miami

OCEAN

MIAMI BEACH

SOUTH BEACH

Art Deco District

Fisher Island

Virginia Key

JFK Causeway

Julia Tuttle Causeway

195

Belle Isle

Collins Ave.

Ocean Dr.

A1A

Alton Rd.

Venetian Causeway

Miami Children's Museum

Watson Island

MacArthur Causeway

41

Port Miami

Jungle Island

Rickenbacker Causeway

10

Biscayne Blvd.

N.E. 2nd Ave.

N. Miami Ave.

1

DESIGN DISTRICT

MIDTOWN

WYNWOOD ARTS DISTRICT

2 3

1

395

95

Grove Isle

Brickell Ave.

S.W. 13th St.

441

LITTLE HAITI

N.W. 79th St.

N.W. 62nd St.

N.W. 54th St.

Hialeah Dr.

944

Robert Frost Expwy.

N.W. 36th St.

N.W. 17th Ave.

N.W. 20th Ave.

27

MIAMI

41

S.W. 3rd Ave.

S.W. 8th St.

LITTLE HAVANA

S.W. 12th Ave.

Coral Way

7

6 8

COCONUT GROVE

9

1

CocoWalk

Grand Ave.

9

Miami River

N.W. 27th Ave.

W. Flagler St.

N.W. 7th St.

East-West Expressway

Ponce de Leon Blvd. (Douglas Rd.)

Le Jeune Rd.

Granada Blvd.

Tamiami Trail

S.W. 22nd Ave.

S. Dixie HWY.

Sevilla Ave.

953

972

5

4

S.W. 37th Ave. (Douglas Rd.)

Miami International Airport

836

959

968

826

Dairy Rd.

N.W. 39th St.

N.W. 72nd Ave.

S.W. 8th St.

S.W. 24th St.

Bird Rd.

S.W. 57th Ave.

976

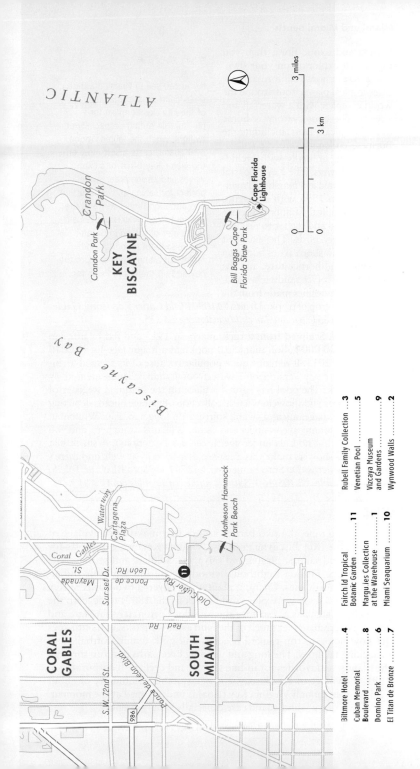

ATLANTIC

Crandon Park

Crandon
Park

Crandon Park

KEY
BISCAYNE

Bill Baggs Cape
Florida State Park

Cape Florida
Lighthouse

3 miles

3 km

0   0

Biscayne Bay

Coral Gables

Coral Gables

Maynada
St.

Sunset Dr.

León Rd.

Ponce de
León Rd.

Waterway

Cartagena
Plaza

Old Cutler Rd.

Red Rd.

Matheson Hammock
Park Beach

Ponce de León Blvd.

S.W. 72nd St.

986

CORAL
GABLES

SOUTH
MIAMI

Florida and exotic flora; then you can set off exploring on your own. The 2-acre Simons Rainforest showcases tropical plants from around the world complete with a waterfall and stream. The conservatory is home to rare tropical plants, including the Burmese endemic *Amherstia nobilis,* flowering annually with orchid-like pink flowers. The Keys Coastal Habitat, created in a marsh and mangrove area in 1995 with assistance from the Tropical Audubon Society, provides food and shelter to resident and migratory birds. The excellent bookstore–gift shop carries books on gardening and horticulture, and the Garden Café serves sandwiches and, seasonally, smoothies made from the garden's own crop of tropical fruits. ✉ *10901 Old Cutler Rd., Coral Gables* ☎ *305/667–1651* ⊕ *www.fairchildgarden.org* 🎟 *$25.*

FAMILY   **Venetian Pool.** Sculpted from a rock quarry in 1923 and fed by artesian wells, this 820,000-gallon municipal pool had a major face-lift in 2010 and again in 2015. It remains quite popular because of its themed architecture—a fantasy version of a waterfront Italian village—created by Denman Fink. The pool has earned a place on the National Register of Historic Places and showcases a nice collection of vintage photos depicting 1920s beauty pageants and swank soirees held long ago. Paul Whiteman played here, Johnny Weissmuller and Esther Williams swam here, and you should, too (but no kids under age three—no exceptions). A snack bar, lockers, and showers make this must-see user-friendly as well, and there's free parking across De Soto Boulevard. ✉ *2701 De Soto Blvd., at Toledo St., Coral Gables* ☎ *305/460–5306* ⊕ *www.coralgables.com* 🎟 *$13.*

SAIL AWAY

If you can sail in Miami, do. Blue skies, calm seas, and a view of the city skyline make for a pleasurable outing—especially at twilight, when the fabled "moon over Miami" casts a soft glow on the water. Key Biscayne's calm waves and strong breezes are perfect for sailing and windsurfing, and although Dinner Key and the Coconut Grove waterfront remain the center of sailing in Greater Miami, sailboat moorings and rentals sit along other parts of the bay and up the Miami River, too.

KEY BISCAYNE

Once upon a time, the two barrier islands that make up the village of Key Biscayne (Key Biscayne itself and Virginia Key) were outposts for fishermen and sailors, pirates and salvagers, soldiers and settlers. The 95-foot Cape Florida Lighthouse stood tall during Seminole Indian battles and hurricanes. Coconut plantations covered two-thirds of Key Biscayne, and there were plans as far back as the 1800s to develop the picturesque island as a resort for the wealthy. Fortunately, the state and county governments set much of the land aside for parks, and both keys are now home to top-ranked beaches and golf, tennis, softball, and picnicking facilities. The long and winding bike paths that run through the islands are favorites for in-line skaters and cyclists. Incorporated in 1991, the village of Key Biscayne is a hospitable community of about 12,500, even though Virginia Key remains undeveloped at the moment. These two playground islands are especially family-friendly.

TOP ATTRACTIONS

FAMILY **Miami Seaquarium.** This classic family attraction stages shows with sea lions, dolphins, and other marine animals. The Crocodile Flats exhibit has 26 Nile crocodiles. Discovery Bay, an endangered-mangrove habitat, is home to sea turtles, alligators, herons, egrets, and ibis. You can also visit a shark pool, a tropical reef aquarium, and West Indian and Florida manatees. A popular interactive attraction is the Stingray Touch Tank, where you can touch and feed cow-nose rays and southern stingrays. Another big draw is the Dolphin Interaction program, including the quite intensive Dolphin Odyssey ($210) experience and the lighter shallow-water Dolphin Encounter ($110). Make reservations for either experience. ✉ *4400 Rickenbacker Causeway, Virginia Key* ☎ *305/361–5705* ⊕ *www.miamiseaquarium.com* 🎫 *$44.99, parking $10 (cash only).*

WYNWOOD

North of Downtown, the formerly downtrodden Wynwood neighborhood has arrived, with an impressive mix of one-of-a-kind shops and art galleries, public art displays, see-and-be-seen bars, slick restaurants, and plenty of eye-popping graffiti. Wynwood's trendiness has proven infectious, also taking root in proximate neighborhoods. One thing is still missing from the emerging landscape: a decent hotel. On a positive note, it's kept the Wynwood vibe more local and less touristy. The downside: you'll need a vehicle to get here, and though in close proximity to one another, you'll also need a vehicle to get to nearby Midtown and the Design District.

Between Interstate 95 and Northeast 1st Avenue from 29th to 22nd streets lies the centerpiece of the edgy Wynwood neighborhood—the funky and edgy **Wynwood Art District** (⊕ *www.wynwoodmiami.com*), which is peppered with galleries, art studios, and private collections accessible to the public. Though the neighborhood hasn't completely shed its dodgy past, artist-painted graffiti walls and reinvented urban warehouses have transformed the area from plain old grimy to super-trendy. The Wynwood Walls on Northwest 2nd Avenue between Northeast 25th and 26th streets are a cutting-edge enclave of modern urban murals. However, these avant-garde graffiti displays by renowned artists are just the beginning; in fact, almost every street is colored with funky spray-paint art, making the neighborhood a photographer's dream. Wynwood's retail space is a hodgepodge of cheap garment stores, upscale boutiques, and contemporary galleries (some by appointment only). First-timers may want to visit during Wynwood's monthly gallery walk on the second Saturday evening of each month, when studios and galleries are all open at the same time.

TOP ATTRACTIONS

Margulies Collection at the Warehouse. Make sure a visit to Wynwood includes a stop at the Margulies Collection at the Warehouse. Martin Margulies's collection of vintage and contemporary photography, videos, and installation art in a 45,000-square-foot space makes for eye-popping viewing. Admission proceeds go to the Lotus House, a

Wynwood is famous for its walls covered by murals from famous contemporary artists, including these by Shepard Fairey.

local homeless shelter for women and children. ⊠ *591 N.W. 27th St., between N.W. 5th and 6th Aves., Wynwood* ☎ *305/576–1051* ⊕ *www. margulieswarehouse.com* ✉ *$10.*

Fodor's Choice
★ **Rubell Family Collection.** Fans of edgy art will appreciate the Rubell Family Collection. Mera and Don Rubell have accumulated work by artists from the 1970s to the present, including Jeff Koons, Cindy Sherman, Damien Hirst, and Keith Haring. New exhibitions for 2017 embodied a politically charged motif, including *High Anxiety: New Acquisitions,* a vast collection of art focused on today's social and political uncertainty. Admission always includes a complimentary audio tour; however, true art lovers should opt for a complimentary guided tour of the collection, offered Wednesday through Saturday at 3 pm. The collection plans to move to a new, larger home on the outskirts of Wynwood in 2018. ⊠ *95 N.W. 29th St., between N. Miami and N.W. 1st Aves., Wynwood* ☎ *305/573–6090* ⊕ *www.rfc.museum* ✉ *$10* ☉ *Closed Sept.–Nov. 2017.*

Fodor's Choice
★ **Wynwood Walls.** Between Northeast 25th and 26th streets on Northwest 2nd Avenue, the Wynwood Walls are a cutting-edge enclave of modern urban murals, reflecting diversity in graffiti and street art. More than 50 well-known and lesser-known artists have transformed 80,000 square feet of warehouse walls into an outdoor museum of sorts (bring your camera). The popularity of the walls spawned the neighboring Wynwood Doors, an industrial space rife with metal roll-down gates also used as blank canvases. The Outside the Walls project followed, which spreads the Walls love across the neighborhood, as artists are commissioned to transform Wynwood's surrounding warehouses and building spaces into singular pieces of painted art. ⊠ *2520 N.W. 2nd Ave., Wynwood* ⊕ *www.thewynwoodwalls.com.*

MIDTOWN

Northeast of Wynwood, Midtown (⊕ *www.midtownmiami.com*) lies between Northeast 29th and 36th streets, from North Miami Avenue to Northeast 2nd Avenue. This subcity is anchored by a multitower residential complex with prolific retail space, often housing the latest and greatest in dining and shopping trends.

DESIGN DISTRICT

North of Midtown, from about Northeast 38th to Northeast 42nd streets and across the other side of Interstate 195, the Design District (⊕ *www.miamidesigndistrict.net*) is yet another 18 blocks of clothiers, antiques shops, design stores, and bars and eateries. The real draws here are the interior design and furniture galleries as well as über-high-end shopping that's oh-so Rodeo Drive (and rivals Bal Harbour in North Beach).

Right outside Little Haiti's boundaries, running from 50th to 77th streets along Biscayne Boulevard, is the MiMo Biscayne Boulevard Historic District, known in short as the MiMo District. This strip is noted for its Miami modernist architecture and houses a number of boutiques and design galleries. It's sometimes seen as the latest extension of the growing Design District (with much cheaper rents). Within this district and in the neighborhoods to the east—collectively known as Miami's "Upper East Side"—several new restaurants are beginning to open.

LITTLE HAITI

Once a small farming community, Little Haiti is the heart and soul of Haitian society in the United States. In fact, Miami's Little Haiti is the largest Haitian community outside of Haiti itself. While people of different ethnic backgrounds have begun to move into the neighborhood, people here are still surprised to see tourists. However, owners of shops and restaurants tend to be welcoming. Creole is commonly spoken, although some people—especially younger folks—also speak English. Its northern and southern boundaries are 85th Street and 42nd Street, respectively, with Interstate 95 to the west and Biscayne Boulevard to the east in its southern reaches, then Northeast 4th Court to the east (two blocks west of Biscayne Boulevard). The best section to visit is along North Miami Avenue from 54th to 59th streets.

LITTLE HAVANA

First settled en masse by Cubans in the early 1960s, after Cuba's Communist revolution, Little Havana is a predominantly working-class area and the core of Miami's Hispanic community. Spanish is the principal language, but don't be surprised if the cadence is less Cuban and more Salvadoran or Nicaraguan: the neighborhood is now home to people from all Latin American countries.

If you come to Little Havana expecting the Latino version of New Orleans's French Quarter, you're apt to be disappointed—it's not about the architecture here. Rather, it's a place to soak in the atmosphere.

Little Havana is more about great, inexpensive food (not just Cuban; there's Vietnamese, Mexican, and Argentinean here as well), distinctive affordable Cuban-American art, cigars, and great coffee. It's not a prefab tourist destination—this is real life in Spanish-speaking Miami.

Little Havana's semiofficial boundaries are 27th Avenue to 4th Avenue on the west, Miami River to the north, and Southwest 13th Street to the south. Much of the neighborhood is residential; however, you'll quickly discover the area's flavor, both literally and figuratively, along Calle Ocho (Southwest 8th Street), between Southwest 11th and 17th avenues, which is lined with cigar factories, cafés selling guava pastries and rose-petal flan, *botanicas* brimming with candles, and Cuban clothes and crafts stores. Your "Welcome to Little Havana" photo op shines on 27th Avenue and 8th Street. Giant hand-painted roosters are found scattered throughout the entire neighborhood, an artistic nod to their real-life counterparts that roam the streets here. You'll need to drive into Little Havana, since public transportation here is limited; but once on Calle Ocho, it's best to experience the neighborhood on foot.

TOP ATTRACTIONS

Cuban Memorial Boulevard. Four blocks in the heart of Little Havana are filled with monuments to Cuba's freedom fighters. South of Calle Ocho (8th Street), Southwest 13th Avenue becomes a ceiba tree–lined parkway known as Cuban Memorial Boulevard, divided at the center by a narrow grassy mall with a walking path through the various memorials. Among them is the *Eternal Torch of the Brigade 2506*, blazing with an endless flame and commemorating those who were killed in the failed Bay of Pigs invasion of 1961. Another is a bas-relief map of Cuba depicting each of its *municipios*. There's also a bronze statue in honor of Nestory (Tony) Izquierdo, who participated in the Bay of Pigs invasion and served in Nicaragua's Somozan forces. ⊠ *S.W. 13th Ave., between S.W. 8th and S.W. 12th Sts., Little Havana.*

Domino Park. If you're not yet ready to take advantage of the relaxed restrictions on travel to Cuba, watch a slice of old Havana come to life in Miami's Little Havana. At Domino Park, officially known as Maximo Gomez Park, guayabera-clad seniors bask in the sun and play dominoes, while onlookers share neighborhood gossip and political opinions. ■ **TIP→ There is a little office at the park with a window where you can get information on Little Havana; the office also stores the dominoes for the older gents who play regularly, but it's BYOD (bring your own dominoes) for everyone else.** ⊠ *801 S.W. 15th Ave., Little Havana* ☎ *305/859–2717 park office.*

El Titan de Bronze. A peek at the intently focused cigar rollers through the windows doesn't prepare you for the rich, pungent scent that jolts your senses as you step inside the store. Millions of stogies are deftly hand-rolled at this family-owned cigar factory and retail store each year. Visitors are welcome to watch the rolling action (and of course buy some cigars). ⊠ *1071 S.W. 8th St., Little Havana* ☎ *305/860–1412* ⊕ *www.eltitancigars.com.*

SOUTH BEACH

Fodor's Choice
★

The hub of Miami Beach is South Beach (better known as SoBe), with its energetic Ocean Drive, Collins Avenue, and Washington Avenue. Here life unfolds 24 hours a day. Beautiful people pose in hotel lounges and sidewalk cafés, bronzed cyclists zoom past palm trees, and visitors flock to see the action. On Lincoln Road, café crowds spill onto the sidewalks, weekend markets draw all kinds of visitors and their dogs, and thanks to a few late-night lounges, the scene is just as alive at night. Farther north (in Mid-Beach and North Beach), the vibe is decidedly quieter.

TOP ATTRACTIONS

Española Way. There's a bohemian feel to this street lined with Mediterranean-revival buildings constructed in 1925. Al Capone's gambling syndicate ran its operations upstairs at what is now the Clay Hotel, a youth hostel. At a nightclub here in the 1930s, future bandleader Desi Arnaz strapped on a conga drum and started beating out a rumba rhythm. Visit this quaint avenue on a weekend afternoon, when merchants and craftspeople set up shop to sell everything from handcrafted bongo drums to fresh flowers. Between Washington and Drexel avenues the road has been narrowed to a single lane, and Miami Beach's trademark pink sidewalks have been widened to accommodate sidewalk cafés and shops selling imaginative clothing, jewelry, and art. ⊠ *Española Way, between 14th and 15th Sts. from Washington to Jefferson Aves., South Beach.*

Holocaust Memorial. A bronze sculpture depicts refugees clinging to a giant bronze arm that reaches out of the ground and 42 feet into the air. Enter the surrounding courtyard to see a memorial wall and hear the music that seems to give voice to the 6 million Jews who died at the hands of the Nazis. It's easy to understand why Kenneth Treister's dramatic memorial is in Miami Beach: the city's community of Holocaust survivors was once the second largest in the country. ⊠ *1933–1945 Meridian Ave., at Dade Blvd., South Beach* ☎ *305/538–1663* ⊕ *www. holocaustmemorialmiamibeach.org* ⊠ *Free.*

FAMILY
Fodor's Choice
★

Lincoln Road Mall. This open-air pedestrian mall flaunts some of Miami's best people-watching. The eclectic interiors of myriad fabulous restaurants, colorful boutiques, art galleries, lounges, and cafés are often upstaged by the bustling outdoor scene. It's here among the prolific alfresco dining enclaves that you can pass the hours easily beholding the beautiful people. Indeed, outdoor restaurant and café seating take center stage along this wide pedestrian road adorned with towering date palms, linear pools, and colorful broken-tile mosaics. A few of the shops on Lincoln Road are owner-operated boutiques carrying a smart variety of clothing, furnishings, jewelry, and decorative elements. But more often you'll find typical upscale chain stores—Apple Store, Nespresso, Gap, and so on. Lincoln Road is fun, lively, and friendly for people—old, young, gay, and straight—and their dogs. Lincoln Road is a great place to cool down with an icy treat while touring South Beach. If you visit on a Sunday, stop at one of the many juice vendors, who'll whip up made-to-order smoothies from mangoes, oranges, and other fresh local fruits.

Miami Beach and South Beach

MIAMI BEACH

SOUTH BEACH

Atlantic Ocean

ART DECO DISTRICT

SOFI DISTRICT

Lummus Park

Miami Beach

Ocean Front Park

Ocean Beach

Pier Park

Miami Beach Pier

MacArthur Causeway

Collins Park

South Pointe Park

SOUTH POINTE

0   400 yrds
0   400 meters

Two landmarks worth checking out at the eastern end of Lincoln Road are the massive 1940s keystone building at 420 Lincoln Road, which has a 1945 Leo Birchanky mural in the lobby, and the 1921 Mission-style Miami Beach Community Church, at Drexel Avenue. The Lincoln Theatre (541–545 Lincoln Rd.), at Pennsylvania Avenue, is a classical four-story art deco gem with friezes, which now houses H&M. At Euclid Avenue there's a monument to Morris Lapidus, the brains behind Lincoln Road Mall, who in his nineties watched the renaissance of his whimsical South Beach creation. At Lenox Avenue, a black-and-white art deco movie house with a Mediterranean barrel-tile roof is now the Colony Theater (1040 Lincoln Rd.), where live theater and experimental films are presented. ⊠ *Lincoln Rd., between Washington Ave. and Alton Rd., South Beach* ⊕ *www.lincolnroadmall.com.*

QUICK BITES

The Frieze Ice Cream Factory. A true South Beach original, this mom-and-pop ice-cream shop serves what could very well be the best ice cream in Florida (except Azucar in Little Havana). Delight in mouthwatering homemade ice cream and sorbets including Indian mango, key lime pie, cashew toffee crunch, and chocolate decadence. ⊠ *1626 Michigan Ave., just south of Lincoln Rd., South Beach* ☎ *305/538–0207.*

QUICK BITES

Gelateria 4D. Authentic Italian gelato is scooped up with plenty of authentic Miami attitude at this sleek glass-and-stainless-steel sweet spot. The gelato is delicious despite the not-so-sweet service and exorbitant price. ⊠ *670 Lincoln Rd., between Euclid and Pennsylvania Aves., South Beach* ☎ *786/276–9475* ⊕ *www.gelateria4d.com.*

WORTH NOTING

Art Deco Welcome Center and Museum. Run by the Miami Design Preservation League, the center provides information about the buildings in the district. An official art deco Museum opened within the center in October 2014, and an improved gift shop sells 1930s–50s art deco memorabilia, posters, and books on Miami's history. Several tours—covering Lincoln Road, Española Way, North Beach, and the entire Art Deco District, among others—start here. You can choose from a self-guided iPod audio tour or join one of the regular morning walking tours at 10:30 every day. On Thursday a second tour takes place at 6:30 pm. Prepurchase tickets online and arrive at the center 15 minutes beforehand; all tours leave from the gift shop. All of the options provide detailed histories of the art deco hotels as well as an introduction to the art deco, Mediterranean revival, and Miami Modern (MiMo) styles found within the Miami Beach Architectural Historic District. Don't miss the special boat tours during Art Deco Weekend, in early January. ⊠ *1001 Ocean Dr., South Beach* ☎ *305/672–2014, 305/531–3484 for tours* ⊕ *www.mdpl.org* ⧉ *Tours $25.*

World Erotic Art Museum (WEAM). Late millionaire Naomi Wilzig's collection of some 4,000 erotic items is on display at this unique museum. Expect sexy art of varying quality—fertility statues from around the globe and historic Chinese *shunga* books (erotic art offered as gifts to new brides on the wedding night) share the space with some kitschy

knickknacks. If this is your thing, an original phallic prop from Stanley Kubrick's *A Clockwork Orange* and an over-the-top Kama Sutra bed is worth the price of admission. Kids 17 and under are not admitted. ✉ *1205 Washington Ave., at 12th St., South Beach* ☎ *305/532–9336* ⊕ *www.weam.com* ▤ *$15.*

MID-BEACH

Where does South Beach end and Mid-Beach begin? With the massive amount of money being spent on former 1950s pleasure palaces like the Fontainebleau and Eden Roc, it could be that Mid-Beach will soon just be considered part of South Beach. North of 23rd Street, Collins Avenue curves its way to 44th Street, where it takes a sharp left turn after running into the Soho House Miami and then the Fontainebleau resort. The area between these two points—and up until 63rd Street—is officially Mid-Beach. The area has been experiencing a renaissance since the $1 billion re-debut of the Fontainebleau resort in 2008. Investors have followed suit with major other projects to revive the Mid-Beach area. Most recently, Argentinean developer Alan Faena has embarked on the neighborhood's latest $1 billion-plus mission: to restore the historic buildings along Collins Avenue from 32nd to 36th streets, creating new hotels, condos, and cultural institutions which will collectively become the Miami Beach Faena District. And the results have been nothing short of amazing.

FISHER AND BELLE ISLANDS

A private island community near the southern tip of South Beach, Fisher Island is accessible only by the island's ferry service. The island is predominantly residential with a few hotel rooms on offer at the Resort at Fisher Island Club. Belle Island is a small island connected to both the mainland and Miami Beach by road. It is a mile north of South Beach and just west over the Venetian Causeway.

NORTH BEACH

Though often referred to collectively as "North Beach," there are several neighborhoods above Mid-Beach before reaching the Dade-Broward border. In Miami Beach proper, nearing the 63rd Street mark on Collins Avenue, Mid-Beach gives way to North Beach (until 87th Street), followed by Surfside (up until 96th Street).

BAL HARBOUR

At 96th Street, the town of Bal Harbour takes over Collins Avenue from Miami Beach. Bal Harbour is famous for its outdoor high-end shops; and if you take your shopping seriously, you may want to spend some considerable time in this area. The town runs a mere 10 blocks to the north before the bridge to another barrier island. After crossing the bridge, you'll first come to Haulover Beach Park, which is still technically in the village of Bal Harbour.

SUNNY ISLES BEACH

Beyond Haulover Beach (and on the same barrier island) is the town of Sunny Isles Beach. Once over the bridge, Collins Avenue bypasses several dozen street numbers, picking up again in the 150s; that's when you know you've arrived in the town of Sunny Isles Beach—an appealing, calm, and predominantly upscale choice for families looking for a beautiful beach, and where Russian may be heard as often as English. There's no nightlife to speak of in Sunny Isles, and yet the half dozen mega-luxurious skyscraper hotels that have sprung up here in the past decade have created a niche-resort town from the demolished ashes of much older, affordable hotels.

NORTH MIAMI

This suburban city, north of Miami proper, is comprised predominantly of older homes in its western reaches—many derelict—but also some snazzy rebuilds in the sections around Biscayne Bay and U.S.1. Several strip malls and restaurants line U.S. 1.

NORTH MIAMI BEACH

Don't let the name fool you. North Miami Beach actually isn't on the beach, but its southeastern end does abut Biscayne Bay. Beyond the popular Oleta River State Park on the bay, the city offers little in terms of touristic appeal.

AVENTURA

West of Sunny Isles Beach and on the mainland are the high-rises of Aventura. This city is the heart and soul of South Florida's Jewish community as well as Miami's growing Russian community (along with Sunny Isles Beach). It is known for its high-end shopping opportunities, from the mega Aventura Mall to smaller boutiques in eclectic strip malls.

BEACHES

CORAL GABLES

FAMILY **Matheson Hammock Park and Beach.** Kids love the gentle waves and warm (albeit often murky) waters of this beach in Coral Gables's suburbia, near Fairchild Tropical Botanic Garden. But the beach is only part of the draw—the park includes a boardwalk trail, a playground, and a golf course. Plus, the park is a prime spot for kiteboarding. The man-made lagoon, or "atoll pool," is perfect for inexperienced swimmers, and it's one of the best places in mainland Miami for a picnic. Most tourists don't make the trek here; this park caters more to locals who don't want to travel all the way to Miami Beach. The park also offers a full-service marina. ■ TIP➜ With an emphasis on family fun, it's not the best place for singles. **Amenities:** parking (fee); toilets. **Best for:** swimming. ⊠ *9610 Old Cutler Rd., Coral Gables* ☎ *305/665–5475* ⊕ *www. miamidade.gov/parks/matheson-hammock.asp* ⊠ *$5 per vehicle weekdays, $7 weekends.*

KEY BISCAYNE

Fodor's Choice **Bill Baggs Cape Florida State Park.** Thanks to inviting beaches, sunsets, and
★ a tranquil lighthouse, this park at Key Biscayne's southern tip is worth
the drive. In fact, the 1-mile stretch of pure beachfront has been named
several times in Dr. Beach's revered America's Top 10 Beaches list. It has
18 picnic pavilions available as daily rentals, two cafés that serve light
lunches that include several Cuban specialties, and plenty of space to
enjoy the umbrella and chair rentals. A stroll or ride along walking and
bicycle paths provides wonderful views of Miami's dramatic skyline.
From the southern end of the park you can see a handful of houses
rising over the bay on wooden stilts, the remnants of Stiltsville, built
in the 1940s and now protected by the Stiltsville Trust. The nonprofit
group was established in 2003 to preserve the structures, because they
showcase the park's rich history. Bill Baggs has bicycle rentals, a playground, fishing piers, and guided tours of the **Cape Florida Lighthouse,**
South Florida's oldest structure. The lighthouse was erected in 1845 to
replace an earlier one damaged in an 1836 Seminole attack, in which the
keeper's helper was killed. Free tours are offered at the restored cottage
and lighthouse at 10 am and 1 pm Thursday to Monday. Be there a half
hour beforehand. **Amenities:** food and drink; lifeguards; parking (free);
showers; toilets. **Best for:** solitude; sunset; walking. ⊠ *1200 S. Crandon
Blvd., Key Biscayne* ☎ *305/361–5811* ⊕ *www.floridastateparks.org/
park/Cape-Florida* ⋈ *$8 per vehicle; $2 per pedestrian.*

FAMILY **Crandon Park Beach.** This relaxing oasis in northern Key Biscayne offers
renowned tennis facilities, a great golf course, a family amusement
center, and 2 miles of beach dotted with palm trees. The park is divided
by Key Biscayne's main road, with tennis and golf on the bay side, the
beaches on the ocean side. Families really enjoy the beaches here—the
sand is soft, there are no riptides, there's a great view of the Atlantic,
and parking is both inexpensive and plentiful. However, on weekends,
be prepared for a long hike from your car to the beach. There are bathrooms, outdoor showers, plenty of picnic tables, and concession stands.
The family-friendly park offers abundant options for those who find
it challenging simply to sit and build sand castles. Kite-board rentals
and lessons are offered from the north water-sports concessions, as are
kayak rentals. Eco-tours and nature trails showcase the myriad ecosystems of Key Biscayne including mangroves, coastal hammock, and
sea-grass beds. Bird-watching is great at the southern end of the park.
The **Crandon's Family Amusement Center** at Crandon Park was once
the site of a zoo. There are swans, waterfowl, peacocks, and dozens of
huge iguanas running loose. Nearby you'll find a restored carousel (it's
open weekends and major holidays), an old-fashioned outdoor roller
rink, a dolphin-shape spray fountain, and a playground. **Amenities:**
food and drink; lifeguards; parking (fee); showers; toilets; water sports.
Best for: swimming; walking. ⊠ *6747 Crandon Blvd., Key Biscayne*
☎ *305/361–5421* ⊕ *www.miamidade.gov/Parks/crandon.asp* ⋈ *$5 per
vehicle weekdays, $7 weekends.*

SOUTH BEACH

Fodor'sChoice   **South Beach.** A 10-block stretch of white sandy beach hugging the tur-
★   quoise waters along Ocean Drive—from 5th to 15th streets—is one of
the most popular in America, known for drawing unabashedly model-
like sunbathers and posers. With the influx of new luxe hotels and hot
spots from 1st to 5th and 16th to 25th streets, the South Beach stand-
and-pose scene is now bigger than ever and stretches yet another dozen-
plus blocks. The beaches crowd quickly on the weekends with a blend of
European tourists, young hipsters, and sun-drenched locals. Separating
the sand from the traffic of Ocean Drive is palm-fringed **Lummus Park,**
with its volleyball nets and chickee huts (huts made of palmetto thatch
over a cypress frame) for shade. The beach at **12th Street** is popular
with gays, in a section often marked with rainbow flags. Locals hang out
on 3rd Street beach, in an area called **SoFi** (South of Fifth) where they
watch fit Brazilians play foot volley, a variation of volleyball that uses
everything but the hands. Because much of South Beach leans toward
skimpy sunning—women are often in G-strings and casually topless—
many families prefer the tamer sections of Mid- and North Beach (save
Haulover nude beach). Metered parking spots next to the ocean are a
rare find. Instead, opt for a public garage a few blocks away and enjoy
the people-watching as you walk to find your perfect spot on the sand.
Amenities: food and drink; lifeguards; parking (fee); showers; toilets.
Best for: partiers; sunrise; swimming; walking. ⊠ *Ocean Dr., from 5th
to 15th Sts., then Collins Ave. to 25th St., South Beach.*

NORTH BEACH

MIAMI BEACH

Haulover Beach Park. This popular clothing-optional beach is embraced
by naturists of all ages, shapes, and sizes; there are even sections primarily frequented by families, singles, and gays. However, Haulover
has more claims to fame than its casual attitude toward swimwear—
it's also the best beach in the area for bodyboarding and surfing, as
it gets what passes for impressive swells in these parts. Plus the sand
here is fine-grain white, unusual for the Atlantic coast. Once you
park in the North Lot, you'll walk through a short tunnel covered
with trees and natural habitat until you emerge on the unpretentious
beach, where nudity is rarely met by gawkers. There are volleyball
nets, and plenty of beach chair and umbrella rentals to protect your
birthday suit from too much exposure—to the sun, that is. The sections of beach requiring swimwear are popular, too, given the park's
ample parking and relaxed atmosphere. Lifeguards stand watch. More
active types might want to check out the kite rentals, or charter-fishing
excursions. **Amenities:** food and drink; lifeguards; parking (fee); showers; toilets. **Best for:** nudists; surfing; swimming; walking. ⊠ *10800
Collins Ave., north of Bal Harbour, North Beach* ☎ *305/947–3525
⊕ www.miamidade.gov/parks/haulover.asp* ⬛ *Parking $5 per vehicle
weekdays, $7 weekends.*

NORTH MIAMI BEACH

FAMILY **Oleta River State Park.** Tucked away in North Miami Beach, this urban park is a ready-made family getaway. Nature lovers will find it easy to embrace the 1,128 acres of subtropical beauty along Biscayne Bay. Swim in the calm bay waters and bicycle, canoe, kayak, and bask among egrets, manatees, bald eagles, and fiddler crabs. Dozens of picnic tables, along with 10 covered pavilions, dot the stunning natural habitat, which was restored with red mangroves to revitalize the ecosystem and draw endangered birds, like the roseate spoonbill. There's a playground for tots, a mangrove island accessible only by boat, 15 miles of mountain-bike trails, a half-mile exercise track, concessions, and outdoor showers. **Amenities:** food and drink; parking (fee); showers; toilets; water sports. **Best for:** solitude; sunrise; sunset; walking. ⌂ *3400 N.E. 163rd St., North Miami Beach* ☎ *305/919–1844* ⊕ *www.floridastateparks.org/park/Oleta-River* ⌦ *$6 per vehicle; $2 per pedestrian.*

WHERE TO EAT

Miami's restaurant scene has exploded in the past few years, with new restaurants springing up left and right every month. The melting pot of residents and visitors has brought an array of sophisticated, tasty cuisine. Little Havana is still king for Cuban fare, and Miami Beach is swept up in a trend of fusion cuisine, which combines Asian, French, American, and Latin cooking with sumptuous—and pricey—results. Locals spend the most time in downtown Miami, Wynwood, Midtown, and the Design District, where the city's ongoing foodie and cocktail revolution is most pronounced. Since Miami dining is a part of the trendy nightlife scene, most dinners don't start until 8 or 9 pm, and may go well into the night. To avoid a long wait among the late-night partiers at hot spots, come before 7 pm or make reservations. Attire is usually casual-chic, but patrons like to dress to impress. Don't be surprised to see large tables of women in skimpy dresses—this is common in Miami. Prices tend to stay high in hot spots like Lincoln Road, but if you venture off the beaten path you can find delicious food for reasonable prices. When you get your bill, check whether a gratuity is already included; most restaurants add between 15% and 20% (ostensibly for the convenience of, and protection from, the many Latin American and European tourists who are used to this practice in their homelands), but supplement it depending on your opinion of the service.

Restaurant reviews have been shortened. For full information, visit Fodors.com. Use the coordinate (⊕ C2) at the end of each review to locate a property on the Where to Eat and Stay in the Miami Area map.

WHAT IT COSTS				
	$	**$$**	**$$$**	**$$$$**
Restaurants	under $15	$15–$20	$21–$30	over $30

Restaurant prices are the average cost of a main course at dinner or, if dinner is not served, at lunch.

DOWNTOWN

$$$$ SEAFOOD 🍴 **Area 31.** High atop the 16th floor of downtown Miami's Kimpton Epic Hotel, memorable and sustainable ocean-to-table cuisine is prepared in the bustling, beautiful open kitchen. Executive chef Wolfgang Birk infuses his seafood-centric menu with innovative flavors and a hefty portion of ethos—all fruits of the sea here are certified by the Monterey Bay Aquarium's Seafood Watch. **Known for:** sustainable seafood; excellent bay-side views; artisanal cocktails. [$] *Average main: $35* ✉ *Kimpton Epic Hotel, 270 Biscayne Blvd. Way, 16th fl., Downtown* ☎ *305/424–5234* 🌐 *www.area31restaurant.com* ✣ *D4.*

$$$$ ECLECTIC 🍴 **Azul.** A restaurant known for producing celebrity chefs and delivering dining fantasies of Food Network proportions, Azul is a Miami foodie institution. With its Forbes five-star, award-winning team, Azul offers a haute-cuisine experience on par with a two- or three-Michelin-star restaurant. **Known for:** special-occasion dining; gastronomic excellence; sublime bay-side views. [$] *Average main: $48* ✉ *Mandarin Oriental, Miami, 500 Brickell Key Dr., Downtown* ☎ *305/913–8358* 🌐 *www.mandarinoriental.com/miami* 🕒 *Closed Sun. and Mon. No lunch* ✣ *D5.*

$$$ FRENCH 🍴 **db Bistro Moderne Miami.** One of America's most celebrated French chefs, Daniel Boulud brings his renowned cooking to the Miami scene with a menu that pays homage to Mediterranean cuisines and the specialties of his homeland. There's a good-value prix-fixe lunch during the workweek for Miami's business crowd. **Known for:** power lunches; beautiful interiors; coq au vin. [$] *Average main: $30* ✉ *JW Marriott Marquis Miami, 255 Biscayne Blvd. Way, Downtown* ☎ *305/421–8800* 🌐 *www.dbbistro.com/miami/* ✣ *D4.*

$$$ STEAKHOUSE Fodor's Choice ★ 🍴 **Edge, Steak & Bar.** It's farm-to-table surf and turf at this elegantly understated restaurant in the Four Seasons Hotel Miami, where hefty portions of the finest cuts and freshest seafood headline the menu, prepared by renowned chef Aaron Brooks. The innovative tartares are a surefire way to start the night right—try the corvina with baby cucumber, green apple, and a young celery-leaf, yellow-pepper sauce, or the ahi tuna with pickled shallots, watermelon, and mint. **Known for:** crudos; Sunday brunch; outdoor terrace seating. [$] *Average main: $30* ✉ *Four Seasons Miami, 1435 Brickell Ave, Downtown* ☎ *305/381–3190* 🌐 *www.edgerestaurantmiami.com* ✣ *D5.*

$$$ ECLECTIC 🍴 **15th & Vine Kitchen and Bar.** The signature restaurant of the swanky W Miami wows with a trifecta of sleek decor, delicious food, and a breathtaking backdrop from the property's famed terrace and deck hovering 15 stories above Brickell Avenue and Biscayne Bay. Seasonal menus tout contemporary American cuisine under global influences, all presented tapas-style. **Known for:** coconut mojitos; ecelctic small plates; dining under the stars. [$] *Average main: $27* ✉ *W Miami, 485 Brickell Ave., Downtown* ☎ *305/307–5413* 🌐 *www.wmiamihotel.com/downtown-miami-restaurants* ✣ *D4.*

$$$$ PERUVIAN Fodor's Choice ★ 🍴 **La Mar by Gaston Acurio.** Don't have time to make a foodie pilgrimage to Lima, Peru? Not to worry; the next best thing beckons in downtown Miami, where Peruvian celebrity-chef Gaston Acurio dazzles with a sublime menu and an atmospheric, bay-side setting to match. **Known for:** authentic Peruvian food; alfresco dining; desserts served in dollhouses.

2

$ *Average main: $34* ✉ *Mandarin Oriental, Miami, 500 Brickell Key Dr., Downtown* ⊕ *www.mandarinoriental.com/miami* ✛ *D5.*

$$$$ ✕ **NAOE.** By virtue of its petite size (eight patrons max) and strict seating
JAPANESE   times (at 6 and 9:30 nightly), the Japanese gem will forever remain intimate and original. Chef Kevin Cory prepares a gastronomic adventure a few feet from his patrons, using only the best Japanese ingredients and showcasing family treasures, like the renowned products of his centuries-old family shoyu (soy sauce) and sake brewery. **Known for:** freshest of fresh fish; authentic Japanese taste; $240 per person price tag. $ *Average main: $240* ✉ *661 Brickell Key Dr., Downtown* ☎ *305/947–6263* ⊕ *www.naoemiami.com* ☺ *Closed Sun. No lunch* ✛ *D5.*

$$$ ✕ **Perricone's Marketplace and Café.** Brickell Avenue south of the Miami
ITALIAN   River is a haven for Italian restaurants, and this lunch place for local bigwigs is arguably the best and most popular. It's housed partially outdoors and partially indoors in an 1880s barn that was brought down from Vermont. **Known for:** rustic setting; tree-lined garden seating area; excellent Italian food. $ *Average main: $22* ✉ *Mary Brickell Village, 15 S.E. 10th St., Downtown* ☎ *305/374–9449* ⊕ *www.perricones.com* ✛ *D5.*

$$ ✕ **Verde at PAMM.** As if the high-design Pérez Art Museum Miami
ECLECTIC   (PAMM) weren't cool enough, its waterfront restaurant also makes
Fodor's Choice   major waves across Biscayne Bay. The slick, contemporary restaurant
★   offers seating both indoors and out, with chic decor and accessories true to its "green" name that blend seamlessly with the living walls and hanging gardens strewn across the museum's exterior. **Known for:** fabulous bay views; light lunching; artisanal pizzas. $ *Average main: $18* ✉ *Pérez Art Museum Miami, 1103 Biscayne Blvd., Downtown* ☎ *305/375–3000* ⊕ *www.pamm.org/dining* ☺ *Closed Wed. No dinner Fri.–Tues.* ✛ *D4.*

COCONUT GROVE

$$$$ ✕ **Glass & Vine.** With a design that fuses the indoors and outdoors, this
MODERN   charming restaurant by celebrity-chef Giorgio Rapicavoli (a champion
AMERICAN   on Food Network's *Chopped*) is as picturesque as it is unexpected.
FAMILY   It happens to be smack in the middle of Coconut Grove's residential Peacock Park, fronting a playground, a baseball park, and the bay. **Known for:** local fish aguachile; locally sourced ingredients; garden atmosphere. $ *Average main: $34* ✉ *2820 McFarlane Rd., Coconut Grove* ☎ *305/200–5268* ⊕ *www.glassandvine.com* ✛ *C5.*

$$ ✕ **GreenStreet Cafe.** A tried-and-true locals' hangout since it was founded
MEDITERRANEAN   in the early 1990s—with regulars including athletes, politicians, entrepreneurs, artists, and other prominent area names—this cozy café serves up simple French-Mediterranean delights. Despite the restaurant's see-and-be-seen reputation, diners are encouraged to sit back and simply enjoy the experience with relaxed decor, good food, and friendly service. **Known for:** fruity cocktails; great breakfast; late-night lounging and noshing. $ *Average main: $17* ✉ *3468 Main Hwy., Coconut Grove* ☎ *305/444–0244* ⊕ *www.greenstreetcafe.net* ✛ *C5.*

$$$ ✕ **Monty's.** Connected to Prime Marina Miami, Monty's has a Carib-
SEAFOOD   bean flair, thanks especially to live calypso and island music on the
FAMILY   outdoor terrace. Though it has lost the luster it had back in the 1990s,

it's still a fun, chill, kid-friendly place where Mom and Dad can kick back in the early evening and enjoy a beer and the raw bar while the kids dance to live music. **Known for:** conch fritters; tropical cocktails; waterfront dining. $ *Average main: $23* ✉ *Prime Marina Miami, 2550 S. Bayshore Dr., at Aviation Ave., Coconut Grove* ☎ *305/856–3992* ⊕ *www.montysrawbar.com* ✧ *C5.*

$$
AMERICAN
FAMILY
✕ **Peacock Garden Café.** Reinstating the artsy and exciting vibe of Coconut Grove circa once-upon-a-time, this lovely spot offers an indoor-outdoor, teatime setting for light bites. By day, it's one of Miami's most serene lunch spots as the lushly landscaped courtyard is lined with alfresco seating, drawing some of Miami's most fabulous ladies who lunch. **Known for:** old-school charm; idyllic setting for lunch; homemade soups. $ *Average main: $19* ✉ *2889 McFarlane Rd., Coconut Grove* ☎ *305/774–3332* ⊕ *www.jaguarhg.com* ✧ *C5.*

CORAL GABLES

$$$
ECLECTIC
Fodor's Choice
★
✕ **eating house.** Check your calorie counter at the door when you enter the hippest eatery in Coral Gables. The ever-changing small-plates menu teems with extreme culinary innovation and unexpected flavor combinations. **Known for:** "dirt cup" dessert; innovative cuisine; foodie crowd. $ *Average main: $25* ✉ *804 Ponce de León Blvd., Coral Gables* ☎ *305/448–6524* ⊕ *www.eatinghousemiami.com* ⊗ *No lunch weekends* ✧ *B5.*

$
CUBAN
FAMILY
✕ **El Palacio de los Jugos.** To the northwest of Coral Gables proper, this joint is one of the easiest and truest ways to see Miami's local Latin life in action. It's also one of the best fruit-shake shacks you'll ever come across (ask for a tropical juice of mamey or guanabana). **Known for:** exotic fruit shakes; no-frills feel; great market for getting produce to go. $ *Average main: $6* ✉ *5721 W. Flagler St., Flagami, Coral Gables* ☎ *305/264–8662* ⊕ *www.elpalaciodelosjugos.com/en* ▬ *No credit cards* ✧ *B4.*

$$$
CARIBBEAN
✕ **Ortanique on the Mile.** Cascading *ortaniques*, a Jamaican hybrid orange, are hand-painted on columns in this warm, welcoming, yellow dining room. Food is vibrant in taste and color, as delicious as it is beautiful. **Known for:** creative, tropical cocktails; colorful decor; excellent seafood. $ *Average main: $29* ✉ *278 Miracle Mile, Coral Gables* ☎ *305/446–7710* ⊕ *www.ortaniquerestaurants.com* ⊗ *No lunch weekends* ✧ *B5.*

$$$$
FRENCH
✕ **Pascal's on Ponce.** This French gem amid the Coral Gables restaurant district is always full, thanks to chef-proprietor Pascal Oudin's assured and consistent cuisine. Oudin forgoes the glitz and fussiness often associated with French cuisine, and instead opts for a simple, small, refined dining room that won't overwhelm patrons. **Known for:** tomato tartine; crispy duck confit; refined atmosphere. $ *Average main: $34* ✉ *2611 Ponce de León Blvd., Coral Gables* ☎ *305/444–2024* ⊕ *www.pascalmiami.com* ⊗ *Closed Sun. No lunch Sat.* ✧ *B5.*

KEY BISCAYNE

$$$
MEXICAN
✕ **Cantina Beach.** Leave it to Ritz-Carlton to bring a small, sumptuous piece of coastal Mexico to Florida's fabulous beaches. The pool- and ocean-side Cantina Beach showcases authentic and divine Mexican cuisine, including fresh guacamole made table-side. **Known for:** top-shelf

margaritas; table-side guacamole; dining on the sand. [$] *Average main: $21* ✉ *The Ritz-Carlton Key Biscayne, Miami, 455 Grand Bay Dr., Key Biscayne* ☎ *305/365–4500* 🌐 *www.ritzcarlton.com/keybiscayne* ✥ *D6.*

$$$ MODERN AMERICAN Fodor's Choice ★ 🍴 **Rusty Pelican.** Whether you're visiting Miami for the first or 15th time, a meal at the Rusty Pelican is a memorable experience. Vistas of the bay and Miami skyline are sensational—whether you admire them through the floor-to-ceiling windows or from the expansive outdoor seating area, lined with alluring fire pits. **Known for:** views of Miami skyline; great seafood; outdoor fire pits. [$] *Average main: $26* ✉ *3201 Rickenbacker Causeway, Key Biscayne* ☎ *305/361–3818* 🌐 *www.therustypelican.com* ✥ *D5.*

WYNWOOD

$$$$ ECLECTIC Fodor's Choice ★ 🍴 **Alter Restaurant.** Chef Bradley Kilgore has risen to local superstardom with his progressive, seasonally inspired new American hot spot. Kilgore is always changing up the menu based on ingredient availability and then taking on the awesome task of transforming food into edible art. **Known for:** tasting menus; locavore patrons; great wine pairings. [$] *Average main: $34* ✉ *223 N.W. 23rd St., Wynwood* ☎ 🌐 *www.altermiami.com* ✥ *D4.*

$$ ITALIAN 🍴 **Joey's.** This small, modern Italian café offers a full line of flatbread pizzas, including the legendary *dolce e piccante* with figs, Gorgonzola, honey, and hot pepper—it's sweet-and-spicy goodness through and through. Joey's also serves the full gamut of Italian favorites and was cited in 2016 as one of Beyoncé and Jay Z's favorite Miami haunts. Opened in 2008, it was one of the first nongallery tenants in the area and the first restaurant in the Wynwood Art District, and it remains a favorite in the neighborhood despite an onslaught of fancy newcomers. **Known for:** fig-and-Gorgonzola pizza; true local feel; affordable wine selection. [$] *Average main: $19* ✉ *2506 N.W. 2nd Ave., Wynwood* ☎ *305/438–0488* 🌐 *www.joeyswynwood.com* ⏲ *No dinner Mon.* ✥ *D4.*

$$$ ECLECTIC Fodor's Choice ★ 🍴 **KYU.** Foodies and locavores love this eclectic, eco-minded restaurant in the heart of Wynwood. The small-plates menu wows with dishes from the Japanese wood-fired grill such as the epic roasted cauliflower and goat cheese, divine roasted grouper over sake-braised white beans, and simple yet delicious whole-grilled corn with miso-lime butter. **Known for:** living walls; apex of Wynwood atmosphere; flavor-rich small plates. [$] *Average main: $28* ✉ *251 N.W. 25th St., Wynwood* ☎ *786/577–0150* 🌐 *www.kyumiami.com* ✥ *D4.*

$ CAFÉ Fodor's Choice ★ 🍴 **Panther Coffee.** The eclectic coffee shop has made a triumphant return to Miami, and it goes by the name of Panther Coffee. The original location of the Miami-based specialty coffee roaster is smack in the center of the Wynwood Arts District (it has now expanded into Miami Beach and other South Florida neighborhoods), attracting a who's who of hipsters, artists, and even suburbanites to indulge in small-batch cups of joe and supermoist muffins and fresh-baked pastries. **Known for:** hipster clientele; great coffee; fabulous people-watching. [$] *Average main: $5* ✉ *2390 N.W. 2nd Ave., Wynwood* ☎ *305/677–3952* 🌐 *www.panthercoffee.com* ✥ *D4.*

$$$
ECLECTIC
Fodor'sChoice
★

✕ **Wynwood Kitchen & Bar.** At the center of Miami's artsy gallery-driven neighborhood, Wynwood Kitchen & Bar offers an experience that includes both cultural and gastronomic excitement. While you enjoy Latin-inspired small plates, you can marvel at the powerful, hand-painted interior and exterior murals, which also spill out onto the captivating Wynwood Walls. **Known for:** ropa vieja empanadas; hamburguesitas; graffiti art displays. $ *Average main: $22* ✉ *2550 N.W. 2nd Ave., Wynwood* ☎ *305/722–8959* ⊕ *www.wynwoodkitchenandbar.com* ✛ *D4.*

MIDTOWN

$$$
MODERN ITALIAN

✕ **Bocce.** A splendid slice of the Italian countryside thrives in Miami's trendy Midtown area, and the impressive 3,200-square-foot enclave houses a beautifully appointed rustic Italian restaurant, Miami's first official bocce court, and a throwback-style Italian market. Mosaic-tiled floors, antique mirrors, and exposed wood beams set the scene indoors while towering cypress trees, a traditional bocce court, and alfresco seating aplenty define the front patio. **Known for:** lively bocce court; great happy hour; melanzane (eggplant) parmigiana. $ *Average main: $24* ✉ *3252 N.E. 1st Ave., No. 107, Midtown* ☎ *786/245–6211* ⊕ *www.bocceristorante.com* ✛ *D4.*

$$$$
JAPANESE
FUSION
Fodor'sChoice
★

✕ **Sugarcane Raw Bar Grill.** Midtown's most popular restaurant rages seven nights (and days) a week, and it's not hard to see why. The vibrant, supersexy, high-design restaurant perfectly captures Miami's Latin vibe while serving eclectic Latin American tapas and modern Japanese delights from three separate kitchens (*robata* grill, raw bar, and hot kitchen). **Known for:** "night crab" sushi roll; spicy local-catch crudo; high-design interiors. $ *Average main: $38* ✉ *3252 N.E. 1st Ave., Midtown* ☎ *786/369–0353* ⊕ *sugarcanerawbargrill.com* ✛ *D4.*

DESIGN DISTRICT

$$
PIZZA
FAMILY
Fodor'sChoice
★

✕ **Harry's Pizzeria.** Harry's is a neighborhood spot with some seriously good pizza, as one would expect as the second restaurant under Miami culinary darling Michael Schwartz and his team. The casual, friendly-yet-funky ambience is inviting for all diner matchups: old chums, new dates, family members young and old. **Known for:** seasonally inspired pizzas; lively atmopshere; homemade ricotta. $ *Average main: $16* ✉ *3918 N. Miami Ave., Design District* ☎ *786/275–4963* ⊕ *www.harryspizzeria.com* ✛ *D3.*

$$$
MODERN GREEK
Fodor'sChoice
★

✕ **Mandolin Aegean Bistro.** A step inside this 1940s house-turned-bistro transports you to *ya-ya*'s home along the Aegean Sea. The food is fresh and the service warm, matching its charming dining garden enlivened by an awning of trees, a rustic wooden canopy, and traditional village furnishings. **Known for:** signature Greek salad; bucolic courtyard; spectacular meze. $ *Average main: $26* ✉ *4312 N.E. 2nd Ave., Design District* ☎ *305/576–6066* ⊕ *www.mandolinmiami.com* ✛ *D3.*

$$$
AMERICAN
Fodor'sChoice
★

✕ **Michael's Genuine Food & Drink.** Michael's is often cited as Miami's top restaurant, and it's not hard to see why: this indoor-outdoor bistro in Miami's Design District is an evergreen oasis for Miami dining sophisticates. Owner and chef Michael Schwartz aims for sophisticated

American cuisine with an emphasis on local and organic ingredients, and he gets it right. **Known for:** being at the forefront of modern American cuisine; sceney alfresco dining area; innovative cocktails. $ *Average main: $27* ⊠ *130 N.E. 40th St., Design District* ☎ *305/573–5550* ⊕ *www.michaelsgenuine.com* ✛ *D3.*

LITTLE HAITI

$$

CARIBBEAN

✕ **Chez Le Bebe.** Chez Le Bebe offers a short menu of Haitian home cooking—it's been going strong for 30 years and has been featured on shows like the Travel Channel's *Bizarre Foods with Andrew Zimmern* and *The Layover with Anthony Bourdain.* If you want to try stewed goat, this is the place to do it! **Known for:** authentic Haitian eats; no-frills atmosphere; stewed goat. $ *Average main: $15* ⊠ *114 N.E. 54th St., Little Haiti* ☎ *305/751–7639* ▭ *No credit cards* ✛ *D3.*

LITTLE HAVANA

$

CAFÉ
FAMILY
Fodor's Choice
★

✕ **Azucar Ice Cream Company.** Balmy weather and sweet-tooth cravings are tempered at this ice-cream shop specializing in homemade Cuban-style scoops. More crafty than churning, flavors are inspired and derived from ingredients at nearby fruit stands, international grocery shops, and farmers' markets. **Known for:** Abuela Maria ice cream; flan ice cream; one-of-a-kind frozen indulgences. $ *Average main: $6* ⊠ *1503 S.W. 8th St., Little Havana* ☎ *305/381–0369* ⊕ *www.azucaricecream.com* ✛ *C5.*

$

LATIN AMERICAN

✕ **El Exquisito Restaurant.** For a true locals' spot and some substantial Cuban eats in the heart of Little Havana, pop into this local institution that's been popular since the 1970s. The unassuming Cuban café serves up delectable, authentic Cuban favorites, including a great cubano (a grilled Cuban sandwich layered with ham, garlic-and-citrus-marinated slow-roasted pork, Swiss cheese, and pickles) and succulent yuca with garlic sauce. **Known for:** chatty regulars; insanely cheap prices; Cuban sandwiches. $ *Average main: $14* ⊠ *1510 S.W. 8th St., Little Havana* ☎ *305/643–0227* ⊕ *www.elexquisitomiami.com* ▭ *No credit cards* ✛ *C5.*

$

CUBAN

✕ **Las Pinareños Fruteria y Floreria.** In the mood for something refreshing or a high-octane jolt? Try Las Pinareños, a *fruteria* (fruit stand) that serves *coco frio* (fresh, cold coconut juice served in a whole coconut), mango juice, and other *jugos* (juices), as well as Cuban coffees and Cuban finger foods. **Known for:** exotic juices; coco frio; friendly staff. $ *Average main: $7* ⊠ *1334 S.W. 8th St., Little Havana* ☎ *305/285–1135* ◁▷ *C5.*

$$

CUBAN
FAMILY
Fodor's Choice
★

✕ **Versailles.** To the area's Cuban population, Miami without Versailles is like rice without black beans. First-time Miami visitors looking for that "Cuban food on Calle Ocho" experience, look no further: the storied eatery, where old émigrés opine daily about all things Cuban, is a stop on every political candidate's campaign trail, and it should be a stop for you as well. **Known for:** lechon asado; Cuban coffee; take-out window. $ *Average main: $15* ⊠ *3555 S.W. 8th St., Little Havana* ☎ *305/444–0240* ⊕ *www.versaillesrestaurant.com* ✛ *C5.*

SOUTH BEACH

$$$ MODERN AMERICAN 🍴 **Beachcraft.** Tom Colicchio made his Miami debut in late 2015 with this fabulous, farm-meets-ocean-to-table concept. A vast open kitchen anchors the restaurant, where guests can see and smell the action from their seats. **Known for:** grilled specialities; local products; intimate vibe. [$] *Average main: $28* ✉ *1 Hotel South Beach, 2395 Collins Ave., South Beach* ☎ *305/604–6700* 🌐 *www.beachcraftsobe.com* ✥ *E4.*

$$$$ ITALIAN 🍴 **Bianca at Delano South Beach.** In a hotel where style reigns supreme, this high-profile restaurant provides both glamour and solid Italian cuisine. The main attraction of dining here is to see and be seen, but you may leave talking about the shaved baby-artichoke salad and truffle tagliatelle just as much as the outfits, hairdos, and celebrity appearances. **Known for:** truffle tagliatelle; Sunday brunch; stylish crowd. [$] *Average main: $37* ✉ *Delano Hotel, 1685 Collins Ave., South Beach* ☎ *305/674–5752* 🌐 *www.delano-hotel.com* ✥ *H2.*

$$$ MODERN ITALIAN Fodor's Choice ★ 🍴 **Dolce Italian.** Best known as a top contender on the Bravo TV show *Best New Restaurant,* Dolce Italian buzzes in the center of the South Beach action, doling out an irresistible menage à trois: great food, great ambience, and an easy-on-the-eyes crowd. Italian-born chef Paolo Dorigato's menu is packed with modern incarnations of Italian classics that would make nonna proud. **Known for:** house-made mozzarella and pastas; Neopolitan-style pizzas; hot crowd. [$] *Average main: $29* ✉ *Gale South Beach, 1690 Collins Ave., South Beach* ☎ *786/975–2550* 🌐 *www.dolceitalianrestaurant.com* ✥ *G2.*

$$$$ MODERN AMERICAN 🍴 **The Dutch Miami.** Loft meets cozy kitchen at the Miami outpost of chef Andrew Carmellini's NYC foodie hot spot in the swank W South Beach. There's a bit of everything on the "roots-inspired American menu," from local line-caught fish to homemade pastas and 28-day dry-aged steaks. **Known for:** local crowd; sweet corn mezzaluna; artisanal cocktails. [$] *Average main: $34* ✉ *W South Beach, 2201 Collins Ave., South Beach* ☎ *305/938–3111* 🌐 *www.thedutchmiami.com* ✥ *H1.*

$$$$ ITALIAN 🍴 **Gianni's at the Villa.** Set within the glitz and ostentation of Gianni Versace's former mansion, the Villa Casa Casuarina, this restaurant doles out excellent Italian eats across the mansion's most prized nooks. You can expect stellar service, bedazzling dishes, and a gold-and-diamond-encrusted atmosphere. **Known for:** haute dining; wow-factor surrounds; only-in-Miami experience. [$] *Average main: $48* ✉ *The Villa Casa Casuarina, 1116 Ocean Dr., South Beach* ☎ *786/485–2200* 🌐 *www.vmmiamibeach.com/restaurant* ⏲ *Closed Mon.* ✥ *G3.*

$$$$ ASIAN FUSION 🍴 **Jaya at The Setai.** As the flagship restaurant of one of Miami's most exclusive hotels, The Setai, Jaya exceeds all expectations yet remains remarkably approachable. Chef Mathias Gervais delivers a pan-Asian extravaganza, representing the countries of Thailand, Vietnam, Singapore, Korea, India, China, and Japan, through dishes that range from tandoori sea bass to Peking duck to lobster laksa. **Known for:** beautiful interiors; tandoori sea bass; black pepper shrimp. [$] *Average main: $36* ✉ *The Setai, 2001 Collins Ave., South Beach* ☎ *855/923–7899* 🌐 *www.thesetaihotel.com/jaya.php* ✥ *H1.*

$$$$
SEAFOOD
Fodor'sChoice
★

✕ **Joe's Stone Crab Restaurant.** In South Beach's decidedly new-money scene, the stately Joe's Stone Crab is an old-school testament to good food and good service. Stone crabs, served with legendary mustard sauce, crispy hash brown potatoes, and creamed spinach, remain the staple. **Known for:** the best of the best stone crab claws; long waits (up to three hours on weekends); decadent side dishes. $ *Average main: $49* ✉ *11 Washington Ave., South Beach* ☎ *305/673–0365, 305/673–4611 for takeout* ⊕ *www.joesstonecrab.com* ⊗ *No lunch Sun. and Mon. and mid-May–mid-Oct.* ✛ *G5.*

$$$$
JAPANESE
FUSION
Fodor'sChoice
★

✕ **Juvia.** High atop South Beach's design-driven 1111 Lincoln Road parking garage, Juvia commingles urban sophistication with South Beach seduction. Three renowned chefs unite to deliver an amazing eating experience that screams Japanese, Peruvian, and French all in the same breath, focusing largely on raw fish and seafood dishes. **Known for:** city and beach views; sunset cocktails on the terrace; tuna poke. $ *Average main: $35* ✉ *1111 Lincoln Rd., South Beach* ☎ *305/763–8272* ⊕ *www.juviamiami.com* ✛ *F2.*

$$$
JAPANESE
FUSION

✕ **Katsuya South Beach.** Design impresario Philippe Starck opted to fill the smoking-hot SLS Hotel South Beach with a number of see-and-be-seen eateries, including Katsuya South Beach. At this popular Japanese restaurant, executive chef Jose Icardi (under the tutelage of master sushi chef Katsuya Uechi) employs four separate kitchens to serve up awesome eats like his legendary miso-marinated black cod, succulent lobster dynamite (in a creamy mushroom sauce), baked crab hand rolls, and amazing sushi rolls. **Known for:** sceney dining; baked crab hand rolls; high-design interiors. $ *Average main: $28* ✉ *SLS Hotel South Beach, 1701 Collins Ave., South Beach* ⊕ *www.katsuyarestaurant.com/southbeach* ✛ *H1.*

$$$
ITALIAN

✕ **Macchialina.** Framed by exposed brick walls, decorated with daily specials chalkboards, and packed with gregarious patrons, this local foodie hangout feels like a cozy, neighborhoody, New England tavern. And with a gorgeous menu showcasing the prowess of chef Michael Pirolo, Macchialina Taverna Rustica nails the concept of modern Italian cuisine. **Known for:** Italian-imported salumi; house panna cotta; devoted local following. $ *Average main: $26* ✉ *820 Alton Rd., South Beach* ☎ *305/534–2124* ⊕ *www.macchialina.com* ✛ *F3.*

$$$
THAI

✕ **NaiYaRa.** Combine the pulse of Bangkok with the glitz of South Beach and undertones of Tokyo, and you get this hypercool, Thai-meets-Japanese restaurant with a sleek, retro-contemporary design in the heart of Miami's burgeoning Sunset Harbour area. The lovable and highly talented owner, Piyarat Potha Arreeratn (aka Chef Bee), guarantees a memorable night of fun, fruity and wild cocktails, and a diverse menu that spans classic Thai dishes perfected (pad thai and papaya salad) to more daring taste creations like the Naiyara roll (a sushi roll filled with salmon belly, cucumber, avocado, scallion, truffle oil, and topped with salmon belly "crème brûlée"). **Known for:** fried chicken dumplings; dynamic atmosphere; Bangkok-imbued environs. $ *Average main: $28* ✉ *1854 Bay Rd., South Beach* ☎ *786/275–6005* ⊕ *www.naiyara.com* ✛ *E4.*

Where to Eat and Stay in the Miami Area

A   **B**   **C**   **D**

2 mi

2 km

Palmetto Expwy.

Okeechobee Rd.

HIALEAH

Red Rd.

W. 49th St.

E. 49th St.

N.W. 135th St.

N.W. 27th Ave.

N. Miami Beach Blvd.

NORTH MIAMI BEACH

N.E. 6th Ave.

N.E. 135th St.

Gratigny Rd.

NORTH MIAMI

Biscayne Blvd.

N.W. 103rd St.

N.W. 95th St.

N.E. 95th St.

N.W. 79th St.

JFK Causeway

N.W. 62nd St.

N.W. 58th St.

N.W. 72nd Ave.

N.W. 87th Ave.

Hialeah Dr.

N.W. 54th St.

DESIGN DISTRICT

N.W. 40th St.

N.W. 39th St.

Airport Expwy.

Chez Le Bebe

Mandolin Aegean Bistro

Harry's Pizzeria

Michael's Genuine Food & Drink

N.W. 36th St.

Bocce

Miami River

Sugarcane Raw Bar Grill

Wynwood Kitchen & Bar

Julia Tuttle Causeway

MIDTOWN

Dairy Rd.

Miami International Airport

WYNWOOD

N.W. 20th St.

KYU

Joey's

Doubletree by Hilton Biscayne Bay

Alter

Panther Coffee

Grand Hotel

DOWNTOWN MIAMI

Venetian Causeway

Dolphin Expwy.

db Bistro Moderne Miami

MacArthur Causeway

Verde at PAMM

JW Marriott Marquis Miami

El Palacio de los Jugos

N.W. 7th St.

Area 31

Kimpton EPIC Hotel

Azucar Ice Cream Company

15th & Vine

W Miami

W. Flagler St.

Versailles

W. Flagler St.

Perricone's Marketplace and Café

AZUL

NAOE

S.W. 8th St.

W. Flagler St.

eating house

El Exquisito

S.W. 8th St.

La Mar by Gaston Acurio

Tamiami Trail

LITTLE HAVANA

Conrad Miami

Mandarin Oriental, Miami

Biltmore Hotel

Hyatt Regency Coral Gables

Las Pinareños

24th St.

Ortanique on the Mile

S.W. 22nd St.

Edge, Steak and Bar

Rusty Pelican

Coral Way

COCONUT GROVE

Four Seasons Hotel Miami

Pascal's on Ponce

Glass & Vine

40th St.

Biltmore Hotel

Bird Rd.

CORAL GABLES

GreenStreet Café

Monty's

The Ritz-Carlton, Coconut Grove, Miami

S.W. 87th Ave.

S.W. 57th Ave.

Mayfair Hotel & Spa

S.W. 72nd St.

Peacock Garden Café

Crandon Park

KEY BISCAYNE

Rickenbacker Causeway

Biscayne Bay

N. Kendall Dr.

Red Rd.

Old Cutler Rd.

S. Dixie Hwy.

Matheson Hammock Park

Cantina Beach

The Ritz-Carlton Key Biscayne, Miami

A   **B**   **C**   **D**

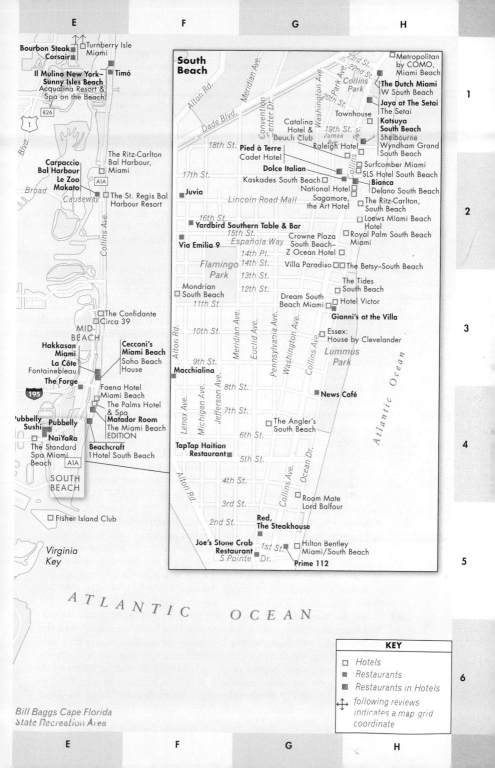

$$ AMERICAN 🍴 **News Café.** No first-time trip to Miami is complete without a stop at this Ocean Drive landmark, though the food is nothing special. The 24-hour café attracts a crowd with snacks, light meals, drinks, periodicals, and the people parade on the sidewalk out front. **Known for:** late-night and early-morning dining; people-watching; newspaper selection. [$] *Average main: $18* ✉ *800 Ocean Dr., South Beach* ☎ *305/538–6397* 🌐 *www.newscafe.com* ✢ *G4.*

$$$$ MODERN FRENCH 🍴 **Pied à Terre.** This cozy, 36-seat, French contemporary restaurant with Mediterranean influences resides in the heart of South Beach, but it's everything the beach is not. Quiet, classic, and elegant, this hidden gastro-sanctuary within the historic Cadet Hotel forgoes glitz and gimmicks for taste and sophistication. **Known for:** romantic dining; use of seasonal ingredients; visiting French chefs from top restaurants in France. [$] *Average main: $42* ✉ *Cadet Hotel, 1701 James Ave., South Beach* ☎ *305/531–4533* 🌐 *www.cadethotel.com* ⏲ *Closed Mon. No lunch* ✢ *G2.*

$$$$ STEAKHOUSE Fodor's Choice ★ 🍴 **Prime 112.** This wildly busy steak house is particularly prized for its highly marbleized prime beef, creamed corn, truffle macaroni and cheese, and buzzing scene. While you stand at the bar awaiting your table—everyone has to wait, at least a little bit—you'll clamor for a drink with all facets of Miami's high society, from the city's top real estate developers and philanthropists to striking models and celebrities. **Known for:** finest cuts of beef; decadent side dishes; stellar service. [$] *Average main: $45* ✉ *112 Ocean Dr., South Beach* ☎ *305/532–8112* 🌐 *www.mylesrestaurantgroup.com* ⏲ *No lunch weekends* ✢ *G5.*

$$$ ECLECTIC Fodor's Choice ★ 🍴 **Pubbelly.** This petite eatery, on a residential street in SoBe's western reaches, still attracts the who's who of beach socialites, hipsters, and the occasional tourist coming to chow down on inventive Asian-Latin small plates, dumplings, charcuterie, and seasonal large plates by executive chef–owner Jose Mendin. From bay scallops "à la escargot" to short-rib tartare, Pubbelly constantly pushes the envelope on inventive cuisine, and locals simply can't get enough. **Known for:** chef's tasting menu; hypercreative "pb culture" small plates; modern dim sum. [$] *Average main: $28* ✉ *1418 20th St., South Beach* ☎ *305/532–7555* 🌐 *www.pubbellyboys.com/miami/pubbelly* ✢ *E4.*

$$$$ JAPANESE 🍴 **Pubbelly Sushi.** The team behind South Beach's wildly popular Pubbelly gastropub teamed up with sushi chef Yuki Leto to create the original Pubbelly Sushi, a 40-seat canteen doling out contemporary, Japanese-inspired sharing plates. Now there are four spread between Miami and the Dominican Republic. **Known for:** happy hour; sake cocktails; flavorful sushi rolls. [$] *Average main: $35* ✉ *1424 20th St., South Beach* ☎ *305/531–9282* 🌐 *www.pubbellysushi.us* ✢ *E4.*

$$$$ STEAKHOUSE 🍴 **Red, the Steakhouse.** The carnivore glamour den seduces with its red-and-black dominatrix color scheme and overloads the senses with the divine smells and tastes of the extensive menu. Red boasts an equal number of seafood and more traditional meat offerings, each delicately prepared, meticulously presented, and gleefully consumed. **Known for:** sexy interiors; decadent, caloric side dishes; sublime steaks. [$] *Average main: $55* ✉ *119 Washington Ave., South Beach* ☎ *305/534–3688* 🌐 *www.redthesteakhouse.com* ✢ *G5.*

$$ CARIBBEAN 🍴 **Tap Tap Haitian Restaurant.** Tap Tap is anything but SoBe glitz and glam, but this Haitian restaurant will instantly immerse you in Haiti's cuisine and culture. An extensive collection of Haitian folk art is displayed throughout this house-turned-restaurant—so much so that every wall, table, and chair doubles as a piece of colorful art. **Known for:** unique dining experience; affordable pricing; vegetarian menu. [$] *Average main: $15 ✉ 819 5th St., South Beach ☎ 305/672–2898 🌐 www.taptapmiamibeach.com ✥ F4.*

$$ ITALIAN Fodor's Choice ★ 🍴 **Via Emilia 9.** If you're longing for a *true* taste of Italy and a respite from the overpriced SoBe dining scene, head to this adorable hole-in-the-wall restaurant off Alton Road. It is owned and operated by Italian chef Wendy Cacciatori and his lovely wife. **Known for:** authentic Italian fare; homemade flatbreads; variety of stuffed pastas. [$] *Average main: $17 ✉ 1120 15th St., South Beach ☎ 786/216–7150 🌐 www.viaemilia9.com ✥ F2.*

$$$ SOUTHERN 🍴 **Yardbird Southern Table & Bar.** There's a helluva lot of Southern lovin' from the Lowcountry at this lively and funky South Beach spot. Miami's A-list puts calorie-counting aside for decadent nights filled with comfort foods and innovative drinks. **Known for:** high-calorie delights; Mama's chicken biscuits; 27-hour marinated fried chicken. [$] *Average main: $30 ✉ 1600 Lenox Ave., South Beach ☎ 305/538–5220 🌐 www.runchickenrun.com ✥ F2.*

CHEAP EATS ON SOUTH BEACH

Miami Beach is notoriously overpriced, but locals know that you don't always have to spend $30 for lunch or $45 for a dinner entrée here to have a good meal. **Pizza Rustica** (✉ *8th St. and Washington Ave. and 667 Lincoln Rd.*) serves up humongous slices overflowing with mozzarella, steak, olives, and barbecue chicken until 4 am. **La Sandwicherie** (✉ *14th St. between Collins and Washington Aves.*) is a South Beach classic that's been here since 1988, serving gourmet French sandwiches, a delicious prosciutto salad, and healthful smoothies from a walk-up bar.

MID-BEACH

$$$ ITALIAN 🍴 **Cecconi's Miami Beach.** The wait for a table at this outpost of the iconic Italian restaurant is just as long as for its counterparts in West Hollywood and London, and the dining experience just as fabulous. The food is great, but atmosphere here is everything. **Known for:** light and succulent fish carpaccios; hearty pastas; sceney courtyard. [$] *Average main: $27 ✉ Soho Beach House Miami, 4385 Collins Ave., Mid-Beach ☎ 786/507–7902 🌐 www.cecconismiamibeach.com ✥ E3.*

$$$$ STEAKHOUSE 🍴 **The Forge.** Legendary for its opulence, this restaurant has been wowing patrons since 1968. After a face-lift in 2010, antiques, gilt-framed paintings, a chandelier from the Paris Opera House, and Tiffany stained-glass windows from New York's Trinity Church are the fitting background for some of Miami's best cuts. **Known for:** expansive enomatic wine system; dramatic interiors; prime cuts of beef. [$] *Average main: $44 ✉ 432 Arthur Godfrey Rd., Mid-Beach ☎ 305/538–8533 🌐 www.theforge.com ⏰ No lunch ✥ E4.*

$$$$ CANTONESE

🍴 **Hakkasan Miami.** This stateside sibling of the Michelin-star London restaurant brings the haute-Chinese-food movement to South Florida, adding pan-Asian flair to even quite simple and authentic Cantonese recipes, and producing an entire menu that can be classified as blow-your-mind delicious. Seafood and vegetarian dishes outnumber meat options. **Known for:** well-dressed patrons; superb Cantonese cuisine; dim sum perfected. [$] *Average main: $52* ✉ *Fontainebleau Miami Beach, 4441 Collins Ave., 4th fl., Mid-Beach* ☎ *786/276–1388 after 4 pm, 877/326–7412 before 4 pm* 🌐 *www.hakkasan.com/locations/hakkasan-miami/* ⏲ *No lunch weekdays* ✣ *E3.*

$$$$ FRENCH

🍴 **La Côte.** With clean white lines, colorful bursts of aqua-blue cushions, and elegant umbrellas, La Côte at the Fontainebleau whisks you away to the coast of southern France. The two-level, predominantly alfresco restaurant snuggled between the beach and the Fontainebleau's pools opens its arms in a generous embrace while flirting with your taste buds, and maybe your man: the female waitstaff wear bikinis and flip-flops. **Known for:** beach cuisine; stylish, alfresco surrounds; French Riviera ambience. [$] *Average main: $31* ✉ *Fontainebleau Hotel, 4441 Collins Ave., Mid-Beach* ☎ *305/674–4710* ⏲ *No dinner Sun.–Wed.* ✣ *E3.*

$$$ SPANISH
Fodor's Choice ★

🍴 **Matador Room.** In one of Miami's most captivating and seductive settings, the latest headline restaurant by celebrity-chef Jean-Georges Vongerichten fuses Spanish, Caribbean, and Latin American gastronomy, presenting the result in a diverse collection of small and large plates. Though the venue plays into a sexy matador theme, the name stems from the space's former incarnation—the eponymous, superglam supper club of yesteryear. **Known for:** tropically inspired bites; the epic pineapple elixir cocktail served in a massive copper pineapple; nice terrace for outdoor dining. [$] *Average main: $25* ✉ *The Miami Beach EDITION, 2901 Collins Ave., Mid-Beach* ☎ *786/257–4600* 🌐 *www.matadorroom.com* ✣ *E4.*

NORTH BEACH

BAL HARBOUR

$$$$ MODERN ITALIAN

🍴 **Carpaccio Bal Harbour.** As expected for its ritzy location, this upscale restaurant matches its high-fashion neighbors, albeit in a refreshing manner. There's no funky furniture nor slick decor, just simple white-clothed tables and charming Italian touches. **Known for:** myriad carpaccios; ladies who lunch; well-heeled crowd. [$] *Average main: $32* ✉ *Bal Harbour Shops, 9700 Collins Ave., Bal Harbour* ☎ *305/867–7777* 🌐 *www.carpaccioatbalharbour.com* ✣ *E2.*

$$$$ FRENCH

🍴 **Le Zoo.** Following success with Makoto in the swanky Bal Harbour shops, restaurateur Stephen Starr has shifted gears from Japan to France, bringing a bona fide Parisian brasserie—inclusive of vintage decorations, furnishings, and an entire bar, all of which were imported from France—to Miami's poshest region. Expect classics perfected such as onion soup gratiné, steak frites, and seafood plateaux (towers); a few delicious deviations like the escargots in hazelnut butter (rather than garlic butter); and plenty of excellent people-watching. **Known** for: Parisian flair; seafood towers; outdoor seating. ⓢ *Average main: $42* ✉ *Bal Harbour Shops, 9700 Collins Ave. No. 135, North Beach* ☎ *305/602–9663* ⊕ *www.lezoo.com* ✛ *E2.*

$$$$
JAPANESE
Fodor's Choice
★

✕ **Makoto.** Stephen Starr's Japanese headliner, executed by celebrity-chef Makoto Okuwa, is one of the most popular restaurants in all of South Florida (and in this swanky shopping center, too). There are two menus: one is devoted solely to sushi, sashimi, and maki, the other to Japanese cold and hot dishes. **Known for:** superfresh sushi; artistic presentation; well-dressed crowd. ⓢ *Average main: $31* ✉ *Bal Harbour Shops, 9700 Collins Ave., Bal Harbour* ☎ *305/864–8600* ⊕ *www. makoto-restaurant.com* ✛ *E2.*

SUNNY ISLES BEACH

$$$$
ITALIAN

✕ **Il Mulino New York – Sunny Isles Beach.** For more than two decades, Il Mulino New York has ranked among the top Italian restaurants in Gotham, so it's no surprise that the Miami outposts (one in Sunny Isles, one in South Beach) are similarly good. Everything that touches your palate will be perfectly executed, from simply prepared fried calamari and gnocchi pomodoro to the more complex scampi oreganata and ever-changing risottos. **Known for:** seasonal primavera risotto; fried zucchini and bruschetta; consistency. ⓢ *Average main: $45* ✉ *Acqualina Resort, 17875 Collins Ave., Sunny Isles Beach* ☎ *305/466–9191* ⊕ *www.ilmulino.com/miami* ✛ *E1.*

$$$
ITALIAN

✕ **Timó.** In a glorified strip mall, Timó (Italian for "thyme") is worth the trip from anywhere in South Florida. It's a kind of locals' secret. **Known for:** brick-oven pizza; seafood antipasto; vegetarian tasting menu. ⓢ *Average main: $28* ✉ *17624 Collins Ave., Sunny Isles Beach* ☎ *305/936–1008* ⊕ *www.timorestaurant.com* ☾ *No lunch weekends* ✛ *E1.*

AVENTURA

$$$$
STEAKHOUSE

✕ **Bourbon Steak.** Michael Mina's long-standing South Florida steak house has never gone out of style. The restaurant design is seductive, the clientele sophisticated, the wine list outstanding, the service phenomenal, and the food exceptional. **Known for:** duck-fat fries; Maine lobster potpie; apex of Aventura "scene". ⓢ *Average main: $60* ✉ *Turnberry Isle Miami, 19999 W. Country Club Dr., Aventura* ☎ *786/279–6600* ⊕ *www.michaelmina.net* ✛ *E1.*

$$$
MEDITERRANEAN
FAMILY

✕ **Corsair.** At Corsair, *Chopped* judge Scott Conant doles out experiential, seasonally inspired farm-to-table fare prepared in Mediterranean style. From start to finish, each course serves as testimony to his well-deserved win on *Chopped All-Stars,* where he competed against other celebrity chefs to prove himself best of the best. **Known for:** complex flavors; fresh ingredients; skillful preparation of dishes. ⓢ *Average main: $28* ✉ *Turnberry Isle Miami, 19999 W. Country Club Dr., Aventura* ☎ *786/279–6800* ⊕ *www.turnberryislemiami.com* ✛ *E1.*

WHERE TO STAY

Room rates in Miami tend to swing wildly. In high season, which is January through May, expect to pay at least $250 per night, even at value-oriented hotels. In fact, it's common nowadays for rates to begin around $500 at Miami's top hotels. In summer, however, prices can be as much as 50% lower than the dizzying winter rates. You can also find great deals between Easter and Memorial Day, which is actually a delightful time in Miami. Business travelers tend to stay in downtown Miami, and most vacationers stay on Miami Beach, as close as possible to the water. South Beach is no longer the only "in" place to stay. Mid-Beach and Downtown have taken the hotel scene by storm in the past few years and become home to some of the region's most avant-garde and luxurious properties to date. If money is no object, stay in one of the glamorous hotels lining Collins Avenue between 15th and 23rd streets or between 29th and 44th streets. Otherwise, stay on the quiet beaches farther north, or in one of the small boutique hotels on Ocean Drive, Collins, or Washington avenues between 10th and 15th streets. Two important considerations that affect price are balcony and view. If you're willing to have a room without an ocean view, you can sometimes get a much lower price than the standard rate, even at an oceanfront hotel.

Hotel reviews have been shortened. For full information, visit Fodors.com. Use the coordinate (⊕ C2) at the end of each review to locate a property on the Where to Eat and Stay in the Miami Area map.

WHAT IT COSTS

	$	$$	$$$	$$$$
Hotels	under $200	$200–$300	$301–$400	over $400

Hotel prices are the lowest cost of a standard double room in high season.

DOWNTOWN

Miami's skyline continues to grow by leaps and bounds. With Downtown experiencing a renaissance of sorts, the hotel scene here isn't just for business anymore. In fact, hotels that once relied solely on their Monday–Thursday traffic are now bustling on weekends, with a larger focus on cocktails around the rooftop pool and less on the business center. These hotels offer proximate access to Downtown's burgeoning food and cocktail scene, and historic sights, and are a short Uber ride away from Miami's beaches.

$$$ HOTEL **Conrad Miami.** Occupying floors 16 to 26 of a 36-story skyscraper in Miami's burgeoning city center, this hotel mixes business with pleasure, offering easy access to the best of Downtown. **Pros:** central Downtown location; excellent service; good spa. **Cons:** poor views from some rooms; expensive parking. $ *Rooms from: $319* ✉ *Espirito Santo Plaza, 1395 Brickell Ave., Downtown* ☎ *305/503–6500* 🌐 *www.conradmiami.com* *201 rooms* *No meals* ⊕ *D5.*

$$ 🖭 **DoubleTree by Hilton Grand Hotel Biscayne Bay.** Just 1 mile from Port-
HOTEL Miami at the north end of Downtown, this waterfront hotel offers
relatively basic, spacious rooms and convenient access to and from the
cruise ships, making it a good crash pad for budget-conscious cruise
passengers. **Pros:** marina; proximity to cruise port; spacious rooms.
Cons: still need a cab to get around; dark lobby and neighboring arcade
of shops; worn rooms. $ *Rooms from: $279* ✉ *1717 N. Bayshore Dr.,
Downtown* ☎ *305/372–0313* ⊕ *www.doubletree.com* ⤴ *202 rooms*
❑ *No meals* ✛ *D4.*

$$$$ 🖭 **Four Seasons Hotel Miami.** A favorite of business travelers visiting
HOTEL Downtown's busy, business-centric Brickell Avenue, this plush sanctu-
FodorsChoice ary offers a respite from the nine-to-five mayhem—a soothing water
★ wall greets you, the understated rooms impress you, and the seventh-
floor, 2-acre-pool terrace relaxes you. **Pros:** sensational service; window-
side daybeds; amazing gym and pool deck. **Cons:** no balconies; not
near the beach. $ *Rooms from: $519* ✉ *1435 Brickell Ave., Downtown*
☎ *305/358–3535* ⊕ *www.fourseasons.com/miami* ⤴ *221 rooms* ❑ *No
meals* ✛ *D5.*

$$$$ 🖭 **JW Marriott Marquis Miami.** The marriage of Marriott's JW and Mar-
HOTEL quis brands created a truly high-tech, contemporary, and stylish busi-
ness-minded hotel—you may never have seen another Marriott quite
like this one. **Pros:** entertainment center; amazing technology; pristine
rooms. **Cons:** swimming pool receives limited sunshine; lots of conven-
tioneers on weekdays; congestion at street entrance. $ *Rooms from:
$499* ✉ *255 Biscayne Blvd. Way, Downtown* ☎ *305/421–8600* ⊕ *www.
jwmarriottmarquismiami.com* ⤴ *313 rooms* ❑ *No meals* ✛ *D4.*

$$$ 🖭 **Kimpton EPIC Hotel.** In the heart of Downtown, Kimpton's pet-friendly,
HOTEL artful EPIC Hotel offers rooms with spacious balconies (many of them
overlook Biscayne Bay) and fabulous modern amenities—Frette linens,
iPod docks, spa-inspired luxury bath products—that match the modern
grandeur of the trendy common areas, which include a supersexy rooftop pool. **Pros:** sprawling rooftop pool deck; balcony in every room;
complimentary wine hour, coffee, and Wi-Fi. **Cons:** some rooms have
inferior views; congested valet area. $ *Rooms from: $319* ✉ *270 Biscayne Blvd. Way, Downtown* ☎ *305/424–5226* ⊕ *www.epichotel.com*
⤴ *411 rooms* ❑ *No meals* ✛ *D4.*

$$$$ 🖭 **Mandarin Oriental, Miami.** At the tip of prestigious Brickell Key in
HOTEL Biscayne Bay, the Mandarin Oriental feels as exclusive as it does glamor-
FodorsChoice ous, with luxurious rooms, exalted restaurants, and the city's top spa,
★ all of which marry the brand's signature Asian style with Miami's bold
tropical elegance. **Pros:** impressive lobby; intimate vibe; ultraluxuri-
ous. **Cons:** man-made beach; small infinity pool; few beach cabanas.
$ *Rooms from: $599* ✉ *500 Brickell Key Dr., Downtown* ☎ *305/913–
8288, 866/888–6780* ⊕ *www.mandarinoriental.com/miami* ⤴ *357
rooms* ❑ *No meals* ✛ *D5.*

$$$$ 🖭 **W Miami.** Formerly the Viceroy, Miami's second W hotel cultivates
HOTEL a brash, supersophisticated Miami attitude, likely stemming from its
guest rooms decked out with dramatic Kelly Wearstler, Asian-inspired
interiors and larger-than-life common areas designed by Philippe Starck.
Pros: amazing design elements; exceptional pool deck and spa; sleek

rooms. **Cons:** serious traffic getting in and out of hotel entrance; tiny lobby; some amenities shared with ICON Miami residents. $ *Rooms from: $528* ✉ *485 Brickell Ave., Downtown* ☎ *305/503–4400* ⊕ *www. wmiamihotel.com* ⇱ *168 rooms* ⦿ *No meals* ✛ *D4.*

COCONUT GROVE

Although this area certainly can't replace the draw of Miami Beach or the business convenience of Downtown, about 20 minutes away, it's an exciting bohemian-chic neighborhood with a gorgeous waterfront.

$$
HOTEL
▦ **Mayfair Hotel & Spa.** Some 30 years strong, the five-story Mayfair Hotel & Spa still reflects Coconut Grove's bohemian roots, best exemplified by its eclectic exteriors: handcrafted wooden doors, one-of-a-kind decorative moldings, mosaic tiles inspired by Spain's Alhambra, and Gaudi-like ornaments adorning the rooftop pool deck. **Pros:** in the heart of walkable Coconut Grove; details in exterior design; in-house spa. **Cons:** limited lighting within rooms; interiors not as exciting as exteriors; car needed to get to the beach. $ *Rooms from: $258* ✉ *3000 Florida Ave., Coconut Grove* ☎ *800/433–4555 reservations, 305/441–0000* ⊕ *www.mayfairhotelandspa.com* ⇱ *179 rooms* ⦿ *No meals* ✛ *C5.*

$$$$
HOTEL
▦ **The Ritz-Carlton Coconut Grove, Miami.** This business-centric Ritz-Carlton hotel in the heart of Coconut Grove has a lively lobby and lounge that complements its sophisticated guest rooms—all with marble baths and private balconies. **Pros:** elevated pool deck; near Coconut Grove and Coral Gables shopping; excellent service. **Cons:** near residential area; more business than leisure oriented. $ *Rooms from: $499* ✉ *3300 S. W. 27th Ave., Coconut Grove* ☎ *305/644–4680, 800/241–3333* ⊕ *www. ritzcarlton.com/coconutgrove* ⇱ *115 rooms* ⦿ *No meals* ✛ *C5.*

CORAL GABLES

Beautiful Coral Gables is set around its beacon, the national landmark Biltmore Hotel. It also has a couple of big business hotels and one smaller boutique property. The University of Miami is nearby.

$$$$
HOTEL
▦ **Biltmore Hotel.** Built in 1926, this landmark hotel has had several incarnations over the years—including a stint as a hospital during World War II—but through it all, this grande dame has remained an opulent reminder of yesteryear, with its palatial lobby and grounds, enormous pool (largest in the Lower 48), and distinctive 315-foot tower, which rises above the canopy of trees shading Coral Gables. **Pros:** historic property; gorgeous pool; great tennis and golf. **Cons:** in the suburbs; a car is necessary to get around. $ *Rooms from: $469* ✉ *1200 Anastasia Ave., Coral Gables* ☎ *855/311–6903* ⊕ *www.biltmorehotel.com* ⇱ *312 rooms* ⦿ *No meals* ✛ *B5.*

$$$
HOTEL
▦ **Hyatt Regency Coral Gables.** Within walking distance to the shops and businesses of Miami's most prestigious suburb and just 4 miles from Miami International Airport, the 250-room, Moorish-inspired Hyatt Regency Coral Gables mingles European charm with functionality. **Pros:** easy access to MIA; meets rigorous "green" standards; walking

distance to several local restaurants. **Cons:** small bathrooms; in suburbs; no spa. $ *Rooms from: $310* ✉ *50 Alhambra Plaza, Coral Gables* ☎ *305/441–1234* ⊕ *www.coralgables.regency.hyatt.com* ⤴ *253 rooms* †○† *No meals* ✛ *B5.*

KEY BISCAYNE

There's probably no other place in Miami where slowness is lifted to a fine art. On Key Biscayne there are no pressures, there's no nightlife outside of the Ritz-Carlton's great live Latin music weekends, and the dining choices are essentially limited to the hotel (which has four dining options, including the languorous, Havana-style RUMBAR).

$$$$
RESORT
FAMILY
Fodor'sChoice
★

⌨ **The Ritz-Carlton Key Biscayne, Miami.** In this ultra-laid-back setting, it's natural to appreciate the Ritz brand of pampering with luxurious rooms, attentive service, five on-property dining options, and ample recreational activities for the whole family. **Pros:** on the beach; quiet; luxurious family retreat. **Cons:** far from South Beach; beach sometimes seaweed strewn; rental car almost a necessity. $ *Rooms from: $499* ✉ *455 Grand Bay Dr., Key Biscayne* ☎ *305/365–4500, 800/241–3333* ⊕ *www.ritzcarlton.com/keybiscayne* ⤴ *402 rooms* †○† *No meals* ✛ *D6.*

SOUTH BEACH

If you are looking to experience the postcard image of Miami, look no further than South Beach. Most of the hotels along Ocean Drive, Collins Avenue, and Washington Avenue are housed in history-steeped art deco buildings, each one cooler than the next. From boutique hotels to high-rise structures, all South Beach hotels are in close proximity to the beach and never far from the action. Most hotels here cost a pretty penny, and for good reason. They are more of an experience than a place to crash (think designer lobbies, some of the world's best pool scenes, and unparalleled people-watching).

$$$
HOTEL

⌨ **The Angler's South Beach.** This boutique hotel, one of several in Miami under the Kimpton brand, has an air of serenity and privacy that pervades this discreet little oasis of personality-driven villas (built in 1930 by architect Henry Maloney) and modern tower units, together capturing the feel of a sophisticated private Mediterranean villa community. **Pros:** gardened private retreat; excellent service; daily complimentary wine hour. **Cons:** on busy Washington Avenue; not directly on beach. $ *Rooms from: $379* ✉ *660 Washington Ave., South Beach* ☎ *305/534–9600* ⊕ *www.anglershotelmiami.com* ⤴ *44 rooms* †○† *No meals* ✛ *G4.*

$$$
HOTEL
Fodor'sChoice
★

⌨ **The Betsy—South Beach.** After a two-year expansion, the original Betsy Ross Hotel (now christened the "Colonial" wing) has been joined with what was the neighboring, historic Carlton Hotel to create a retro-chic, art deco treasure that delivers the full-throttle South Beach experience with style, pizzazz, and cultural twist. **Pros:** unbeatable location; superfashionable; great beach club. **Cons:** some small rooms; service can be hit or miss. $ *Rooms from: $315* ✉ *1440 Ocean Dr., South Beach* ☎ *305/531–6100* ⊕ *www.thebetsyhotel.com* ⤴ *130 rooms* †○† *No meals* ✛ *G2.*

$ HOTEL Fodor's Choice ★ 🏨 **Cadet Hotel.** A former home to World War II air force cadets, this gem has been reimagined as an oasis in South Beach, offering the antithesis of the sometimes maddening jet-set scene, with 34 distinctive rooms exuding understated luxury. **Pros:** excellent service; lovely garden and spa pool; originality. **Cons:** tiny swimming pool; limited appeal for the party crowd. [$] *Rooms from: $189* ✉ *1701 James Ave., South Beach* ☎ *305/672–6688* 🌐 *www.cadethotel.com* 🛏 *34 rooms* 🍴 *No meals* ✣ *G2.*

$ HOTEL 🏨 **Catalina Hotel & Beach Club.** The Catalina is the budget party spot in the heart of South Beach's hottest block and attracts plenty of twentysomethings with its free nightly drink hour, airport shuttles, fitness classes, two fun pools, and beach chairs. **Pros:** free drinks; free airport shuttle; good people-watching. **Cons:** service not a high priority; loud; not all rooms well maintained. [$] *Rooms from: $183* ✉ *1720–1756 Collins Ave., South Beach* ☎ *305/674–1160* 🌐 *www.catalinahotel.com* 🛏 *190 rooms* 🍴 *No meals* ✣ *G2.*

$$ HOTEL 🏨 **Crowne Plaza South Beach – Z Ocean Hotel.** This is definitely not your grandmother's Crowne Plaza: the lauded firm of Arquitectonica designed this glossy and bold all-suites hideaway, including 27 rooftop suites endowed with terraces, each complete with Jacuzzi, plush chaise lounges, and a view of the South Beach skyline. **Pros:** incredible balconies; huge rooms; space-maximizing closets. **Cons:** gym is tiny and basic; not much privacy on rooftop suite decks. [$] *Rooms from: $263* ✉ *1437 Collins Ave., South Beach* ☎ *305/672–4554* 🌐 *www.ihg.com* 🛏 *79 suites* 🍴 *No meals* ✣ *G2.*

$$$$ HOTEL 🏨 **Delano South Beach.** The hotel that single-handedly made South Beach cool again in the 1990s is still making major waves across the beach as this Philippe Starck powerhouse continues to define the paradigm of South Beach decor and glamour. **Pros:** electrifying design; lounging among the beautiful and famous. **Cons:** crowded; scene-y; entry-level rooms are on small side. [$] *Rooms from: $409* ✉ *1685 Collins Ave., South Beach* ☎ *305/672–2000, 800/555–5001* 🌐 *www.morganshotelgroup.com/delano/delano-south-beach* 🛏 *208 rooms* 🍴 *No meals* ✣ *H2.*

$$$ HOTEL 🏨 **Dream South Beach Miami.** This trendy boutique hotel, which is right in the center of the South Beach action, merges two refurbished, archetypal, 1939 art deco buildings into a single project of eclectic modernism, with whimsically decorated interiors—and the result is at once trippy and cool. **Pros:** awesome interior design; easy-on-the-eyes crowd; amazing location. **Cons:** limited natural light in some rooms; lack of bathroom privacy; small pool. [$] *Rooms from: $309* ✉ *1111 Collins Ave., South Beach* ☎ *305/673–4747* 🌐 *www.dreamhotels.com/southbeach* 🛏 *108 rooms* 🍴 *No meals* ✣ *G3.*

$$ HOTEL 🏨 **Essex: House by Clevelander.** This restored art deco gem is a favorite with Europeans desiring good location and a relatively no-frills, practical base—expect average-size rooms with mid-century-style red furniture and marble tubs. **Pros:** a social, heated pool; access to amenities at neighboring Clevelander hotel; in-house sushi restaurant Zen Sai. **Cons:** small pool; not on the beach. [$] *Rooms from: $254* ✉ *1001 Collins Ave., South Beach* ☎ *877/532–4006* 🌐 *www.clevelander.com/essex-house.htm* 🛏 *70 rooms* 🍴 *No meals* ✣ *G3.*

Continued on page 83

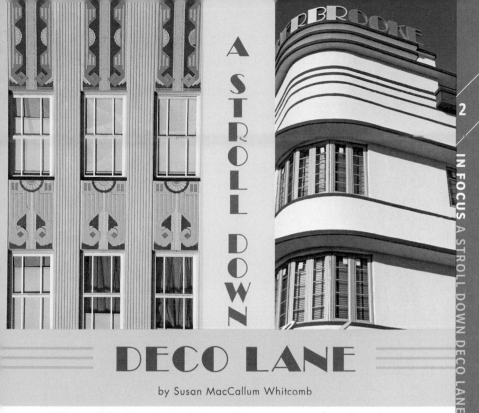

A STROLL DOWN

DECO LANE

by Susan MacCallum Whitcomb

"It was an age of miracles, it was an age of art,

it was an age of excess, and it was an age of satire."

—F. Scott Fitzgerald, *Echoes of the Jazz Age*

The 1920s and '30s brought us flappers and gangsters, plunging stock prices and soaring skyscrapers, and plenty of headline-worthy news from the arts scene, from talking pictures and the jazz craze to fashions where pearls piled on and sequins dazzled. These decades between the two world wars also gave us an art style reflective of the changing times: art deco.

Distinguished by geometrical shapes and the use of industrial motifs that fused the decorative arts with modern technology, art deco became the architectural style of choice for train stations and big buildings across the country (think New york's Radio City Music Hall and Empire State Building).

Using a steel-and-concrete box as the foundation, architects dipped into art deco's grab bag of accessories, initially decorating facades with spheres, cylinders, and cubes. They later borrowed increasingly from industrial design, stripping elements used in ocean liners and automobiles to their streamlined essentials.

The style was also used in jewelry, furniture, textiles, and advertising. The fact that it employed inexpensive materials, such as stucco or terrazzo, helped art deco thrive during the Great Depression.

MIAMI BEACH'S ART DECO DISTRICT

With its warm beaches and tropical surroundings, Miami Beach in the early 20th century was establishing itself as America's winter playground. During the roaring '20s luxurious hostelries resembling Venetian palaces, Spanish villages, and French châteaux sprouted up. In the 1930s, middle-class tourists started coming, and more hotels had to be built. Designers like Henry Hohauser chose art deco for its affordable yet distinctive design.

An antidote to the gloom of the Great Depression, the look was cheerful and tidy. And with the whimsical additions of portholes, colorful racing bands, and images of rolling ocean waves painted or etched on the walls, these South Beach properties created an oceanfront fantasy world for travelers.

Many of the candy-colored hotels have survived and been meticulously restored. They are among the more than 800 buildings of historical significance in South Beach's art deco district. Composing much of South Beach, the 1-square-mile district is bounded by Dade Boulevard on the north, the Atlantic Ocean on the east, 6th Street on the south, and Alton Road on the west.

Because the district as a whole was developed so rapidly and designed by like-minded architects—**Henry Hohauser, L. Murray Dixon, Albert Anis,** and their colleagues—it has amazing stylistic unity. Nevertheless, on this single street you can trace the evolution of period form from angular, vertically emphatic early deco to aerodynamically rounded Streamline Moderne. The relatively severe Cavalier and more curvaceous Cardozo are fine examples of the former and latter, respectively.

To explore the district, begin by loading up on literature in the **Art Deco Welcome Center** (✉ *1001 Ocean Dr.* ☎ *305/763-8026* ⊕ *www.mdpl.org*). If you want to view these historic properties on your own, just start walking. A four-block stroll north on Ocean Drive gets you up close to camera-ready classics: the **Clevelander** (1020), the **Tides** (1220), the **Leslie** (1244), the **Carlyle** (1250), the **Cardozo** (1300), the **Cavalier** (1320), and the **Winter Haven** (1400).

ARCHITECTURAL HIGHLIGHTS

FRIEZE DETAIL, CAVALIER HOTEL

The decorative stucco friezes outside the Cavalier Hotel at 1320 Ocean Drive are significant for more than aesthetic reasons. Roy France used them to add symmetry (adhering to the "Rule of Three") and accentuate the hotel's verticality by drawing the eye upward. The pattern he chose also reflected a fascination with ancient civilizations engendered by the recent rediscovery of King Tut's tomb and the Chichén Itzá temples.

Cavalier Hotel

LOBBY FLOOR, THE RALEIGH HOTEL

Terrazzo—a compound of cement and stone chips that could be poured, then polished—is a hallmark of deco design. Terrazzo floors typically had a geometric pattern, like this one in The Raleigh Hotel, a 1940 building by L. Murray Dixon at 1775 Collins Avenue.

The Raleigh Hotel

CORNER FACADE, ESSEX HOUSE HOTEL

Essex House Hotel, a 1938 gem that appears permanently anchored at 1001 Collins Avenue, is a stunning example of Maritime deco (also known as Nautical Moderne). Designed by Henry Hohauser to evoke an ocean liner, the hotel is rife with marine elements, from the rows of porthole-style windows and natty racing stripes to the towering smokestack-like sign. With a prow angled proudly into the street corner, it seems ready to steam out to sea.

Essex House Hotel

NEON SPIRE, THE HOTEL

The name spelled vertically in eye-popping neon on the venue's iconic aluminum spire—Tiffany—bears evidence of the hotel's earlier incarnation. When the L. Murray Dixon–designed Tiffany Hotel was erected at 801 Collins Avenue in 1939, neon was still a novelty. Its use, coupled with the spire's rocket-like shape, combined to create a futuristic look influenced by the sci-fi themes then pervasive in popular culture.

The Hotel

ENTRANCE, SEÑOR FROG'S

Inspired by everything from car fenders to airplane noses, proponents of art deco's Streamline Moderne look began to soften buildings' hitherto boxy edges. But when Henry Hohauser designed Hoffman's Cafeteria in 1940 he took moderne to the max. The landmark at 1450 Collins Avenue (now Señor Frog's) has a sleek, splendidly curved facade. The restored interior echoes it through semicircular booths and rounded chair backs.

Señor Frog's

ARCHITECTURAL TERMS

The Rule of Three: Early deco designers often used architectural elements in multiples of three, creating tripartite facades with triple sets of windows, eyebrows, or banding.

Eyebrows: Small shelf-like ledges that protruded over exterior windows were used to simultaneously provide much-needed shade and serve as a counterpoint to a building's strong vertical lines.

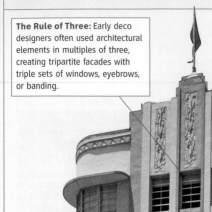

Tropical Motifs: In keeping with the setting, premises were plastered, painted, or etched with seaside images. Palm trees, sunbursts, waves, flamingoes, and the like were particularly common.

Banding: Enhancing the illusion that these immobile structures were rapidly speeding objects, colorful horizontal bands (also called "racing stripes") were painted on exteriors or applied with tile.

Stripped Classic: The most austere version of art deco (sometimes dubbed Depression Moderne) was used for buildings commissioned by the Public Works Administration.

(top) Hotel Marlin; (left) Sherbrooke Hotel; (right) U.S. Post Office in Miami Beach.

$$$$ ⌨ **Hilton Bentley Miami/South Beach.** Not to be confused with the budget-
HOTEL   oriented Bentley Hotel down the street, the Hilton Bentley Miami
FAMILY is a contemporary, design-driven, and artsy boutique hotel in the
emerging and trendy SoFi (South of Fifth) district, offering families
just the right mix of South Beach flavor and wholesome fun while
still providing couples a romantic base without any party madness.
Pros: quiet location; style and grace; family-friendly. **Cons:** small pool;
small lobby; daily resort charge. $ *Rooms from: $429* ⊠ *101 Ocean
Dr., South Beach* ☎ *305/938–4600* ⊕ *www.hilton.com* ⤳ *109 rooms*
⏻⃝ *No meals* ⊹ *G5.*

$$ ⌨ **Hotel Victor.** After a Yabu Pushelberg face-lift in late 2013, the sleek
HOTEL   Hotel Victor, originally influenced by Parisian designer Jacques Garcia,
has replaced the dated jellyfish motif with a newer incarnation of bold
modernism. **Pros:** views from pool deck; high hip factor; good service.
Cons: small rooms; street noise from some rooms. $ *Rooms from:
$269* ⊠ *1144 Ocean Dr., South Beach* ☎ *305/908–1462, 844/319–3854*
⊕ *www.hotelvictorsouthbeach.com* ⤳ *91 rooms* ⏻⃝ *No meals* ⊹ *G3.*

$$ ⌨ **Kaskades South Beach.** Though it's not directly on the beach—it's
HOTEL   across the street—this boutique hotel offers fabulous, style- and value-
conscious accommodations in the heart of South Beach. **Pros:** awesome
bathrooms; central location; complimentary wine hour. **Cons:** rooftop
deck often quiet; most amenities in sister hotel. $ *Rooms from: $240*
⊠ *300 17th St., South Beach* ☎ *305/673–0199* ⊕ *www.kaskadeshotel.
com* ⤳ *24 rooms* ⏻⃝ *Breakfast* ⊹ *G2.*

$$$$ ⌨ **Loews Miami Beach Hotel.** Loews Miami Beach, a two-tower mega-
HOTEL   hotel with top-tier amenities, a massive spa, a great pool, and direct
FAMILY beachfront access, is a good choice for families, businesspeople, groups,
and pet lovers. **Pros:** excellent on-site seafood restaurant; immense spa;
pets welcome. **Cons:** insanely large size; constantly crowded; pets des-
perate to go will need to wait several minutes to make it to the grass.
$ *Rooms from: $449* ⊠ *1601 Collins Ave., South Beach* ☎ *305/604–
1601, 800/235–6397* ⊕ *www.loewshotels.com/miami-beach* ⤳ *790
rooms* ⏻⃝ *No meals* ⊹ *H2.*

$$$ ⌨ **Metropolitan by COMO, Miami Beach.** The luxury COMO brand brings
RESORT its Zen-glam swagger to South Beach, reinventing the art deco Tray-
more hotel into a 74-room, Paola Navone–designed boutique hotel
that commingles brand signatures (excellent, health-driven cuisine,
and myriad spa elements) with Miami panache. **Pros:** easy access to
both South Beach and Mid-Beach; Como Shambhala toiletries; stylish
"P" and "C" door magnets signal "Clean" or "Privacy". **Cons:** two
people per room max; limited number of rooms with good views; small
bathrooms. $ *Rooms from: $383* ⊠ *2445 Collins Ave., South Beach*
☎ *305/695–3600* ⊕ *www.comohotels.com/metropolitanmiamibeach*
⤳ *74 rooms* ⏻⃝ *No meals* ⊹ *H1.*

$$ ⌨ **Mondrian South Beach.** The Mondrian South Beach infuses life into
HOTEL   the beach's lesser-known western perimeter and rises as a poster child of
SoBe design glam—head to toe, the hotel is a living and functioning work
of art, an ingenious vision of provocateur Marcel Wanders. **Pros:** great
pool scene; perfect sunsets; party vibe. **Cons:** could still use a bit more
refreshing; a short walk from most of the action; no direct beach access.

$ *Rooms from: $229* ⊠ *1100 West Ave., South Beach* ☎ *305/514–1500* ⊕ *www.meninhospitality.com* ⤳ *335 rooms* ⎮◎⎮ *No meals* ✛ *F3.*

$$ ⊞ **National Hotel.** Fully renovated in 2014, the National Hotel maintains
HOTEL   its distinct art deco heritage (the chocolate- and ebony-hued pieces in
the lobby date back to the 1930s, and the baby grand piano headlines
the throwback Blues Bar) while trying to keep up with SoBe's glossy
newcomers. **Pros:** stunning pool; perfect location; Blues Bar. **Cons:**
street noise on the weekends; smaller rooms in art deco tower; $19/
day resort fee. $ *Rooms from: $295* ⊠ *1677 Collins Ave., South Beach*
☎ *305/532–2311, 800/327–8370 reservations* ⊕ *www.nationalhotel.
com* ⤳ *152 rooms* ⎮◎⎮ *No meals* ✛ *H2.*

$$$$ ⊞ **1 Hotel South Beach.** This snazzy eco-minded hotel is one of Miami's
RESORT   all-around best. **Pros:** even basic level rooms are great; vibrant crowd;
Fodor's Choice sustainability mantra. **Cons:** many rooms face street; constantly busy.
★ $ *Rooms from: $416* ⊠ *2341 Collins Ave., South Beach* ☎ *305/604–
1000* ⊕ *www.1hotels.com/south-beach* ⤳ *426 rooms* ⎮◎⎮ *No meals* ✛ *E4.*

$$$ ⊞ **Raleigh Hotel.** This classy art deco gem, part of the sbe hotel group,
HOTEL   balances the perfect amount of style, comfort, and South Beach sultri-
ness, highlighted by the beach's sexiest pool, which was created for
champion swimmer Esther Williams. **Pros:** amazing historic swimming
pool; art deco design; beautiful courtyard. **Cons:** lobby is a bit dark;
not as social as other South Beach hotels; in need of soft renovation.
$ *Rooms from: $385* ⊠ *1775 Collins Ave., South Beach* ☎ *305/534–
6300, 800/848–1775 reservations* ⊕ *www.raleighhotel.com* ⤳ *105
rooms* ⎮◎⎮ *No meals* ✛ *H2.*

$$$ ⊞ **The Ritz-Carlton, South Beach.** The Ritz-Carlton is a surprisingly trendy
HOTEL   beachfront bombshell, with a dynamite staff, a snazzy Club Lounge,
FAMILY and a long pool deck that leads right out to the beach. **Pros:** great
service; pool with VIP cabanas; great location. **Cons:** larger property;
in-house restaurant Bistro ONE LR often quiet; $28/night resort fee.
$ *Rooms from: $391* ⊠ *1 Lincoln Rd., South Beach* ☎ *786/276–4000,
800/542–8680 reservations* ⊕ *www.ritzcarlton.com/southbeach* ⤳ *375
rooms* ⎮◎⎮ *No meals* ✛ *H2.*

$$ ⊞ **Room Mate Lord Balfour.** Quickly making a name for itself in South
HOTEL   Beach's emerging SoFi (South of Fifth) neighborhood, the luxurious, bou-
tique, and retro-chic Lord Balfour hotel—part of the Spain's RoomMate
brand—exudes style, sophistication, and the full-throttle, present-day
Miami Beach experience. **Pros:** great European crowd; whimsical interior
design; excellent service. **Cons:** rooms on smaller side; occasional street
noise from some rooms; small resort fee. $ *Rooms from: $219* ⊠ *350
Ocean Dr., South Beach* ☎ *855/471–2739, 305/673–0401* ⊕ *www.lord-
balfour.room-matehotels.com* ⤳ *64 rooms* ⎮◎⎮ *No meals* ✛ *G4.*

$$$ ⊞ **Royal Palm South Beach Miami.** The Royal Palm South Beach Miami,
RESORT   now part of Starwood's Tribute Portfolio, is a daily celebration of art
Fodor's Choice deco, Art Basel, modernity, and design detail. **Pros:** design blending
★   contemporary style with South Beach identity; impressive spa; multiple
pools; unbeatable location. **Cons:** small driveway for entering; older
elevators. $ *Rooms from: $338* ⊠ *1545 Collins Ave., South Beach*
☎ *305/604–5700, 866/716–8147 reservations* ⊕ *www.royalpalmsouth-
beach.com* ⤳ *393 rooms* ⎮◎⎮ *No meals* ✛ *G2.*

2

$$$$ HOTEL

Sagamore, the Art Hotel. This supersleek, all-white, all-suites hotel in the middle of the action looks and feels like an edgy art gallery, filled with brilliant contemporary works, the perfect complement to the posh, gargantuan, 500-square-foot crash pads. **Pros:** sensational pool; great location; good rate specials. **Cons:** can be quiet on weekdays; rooms could use some refreshing. [$] *Rooms from: $429* ✉ *1671 Collins Ave., South Beach* ☎ *305/535–8088* 🌐 *www.sagamorehotel.com* 🛏 *93 suites* 🍴 *No meals* ✥ *H2.*

$$$$ RESORT Fodor's Choice ★

The Setai Miami Beach. This opulent, all-suites hotel feels like an Asian museum: serene and beautiful, with heavy granite furniture lifted by orange accents, warm candlelight, and the soft bubble of seemingly endless ponds complemented by three oceanfront infinity pools (heated to different temperatures) that further spill onto the beach's velvety sands. **Pros:** quiet and classy; beautiful grounds; great celeb spotting. **Cons:** TVs are far from the beds; extremely high price point; many rooms lack ocean views. [$] *Rooms from: $875* ✉ *2001 Collins Ave., South Beach* ☎ *305/520–6111, 888/625–7500 reservations* 🌐 *www.thesetaihotel.com* 🛏 *130 suites* 🍴 *No meals* ✥ *H1.*

$$$ RESORT

Shelborne Wyndham Grand South Beach. After a major cash infusion from Wyndham hotels, the iconic Morris Lapidus–designed Shelborne hotel has reemerged as the retro-chic 200-room Shelborne Wyndham Grand South Beach, ushering in a new era of glory for both the brand and the hotel. **Pros:** location; prolific common spaces; Frette linens. **Cons:** entry-level rooms small; lack of balconies. [$] *Rooms from: $389* ✉ *1801 Collins Ave., South Beach* ☎ *305/531–1271* 🌐 *www.shelbornewyndhamgrand.com* 🛏 *200 rooms* 🍴 *No meals* ✥ *H1.*

$$$ RESORT Fodor's Choice ★

SLS Hotel South Beach. Smack in the center of South Beach, the SLS Hotel marks designer Philippe Starck's triumphant, large-scale return to South Beach; but this time he's teamed up with Sam Nazarian and chefs José Andrés and Katsuya Uech for the whimsical trip down the rabbit hole, creating the latest and greatest in the evolution of Miami's happening hotel-food-pool-beach scene. **Pros:** great in-house restaurants; masterful design; fun pool scene. **Cons:** some small rooms; no lobby per se; $30 per night resort fee. [$] *Rooms from: $395* ✉ *1701 Collins Ave., South Beach* ☎ *305/674–1701* 🌐 *www.slshotels.com/southbeach* 🛏 *140 rooms* 🍴 *No meals* ✥ *H2.*

$$ HOTEL

Surfcomber Miami, South Beach. As part of the hip Kimpton Hotel group, South Beach's legendary Surfcomber hotel reflects a vintage luxe aesthetic and an ocean-side freshness as well as a reasonable price point that packs the place with a young, sophisticated, yet unpretentious crowd. **Pros:** stylish but not pretentious; pet-friendly; on the beach. **Cons:** small bathrooms; front desk often busy. [$] *Rooms from: $279* ✉ *1717 Collins Ave., South Beach* ☎ *305/532–7715* 🌐 *www.surfcomber.com* 🛏 *186 rooms* 🍴 *No meals* ✥ *H2.*

$$$$ HOTEL

The Tides South Beach. The Tides South Beach, which celebrated its 80th anniversary in 2016, is an exclusive Ocean Drive art deco hotel of all ocean-facing suites adorned with soft pinks and corals, gilded accents, and marine-inspired decor. **Pros:** superior service; great beach location; ocean views from all suites plus the terrace restaurant (where we recommend cocktails only). **Cons:** tiny elevators; on touristy Ocean

Drive; taxidermy in rooms and common areas. $ *Rooms from: $445*
✉ *1220 Ocean Dr., South Beach* ☎ *305/604–5070* ⊕ *www.tidessouth-
beach.com* 🖅 *45 suites* ⦿ *No meals* ✛ *G3.*

$ ⛱ **Townhouse.** Though sandwiched between the glitzy high-rises of Col-
HOTEL   lins Avenue, Townhouse doesn't try to act all dolled up: it's comfortable being the shabby-chic, lighthearted, relaxed, fun hotel on South
Beach. **Pros:** a great budget buy for the style hungry; easy beach access;
hot rooftop lounge. **Cons:** no pool; small rooms not designed for long
stays; resort fee. $ *Rooms from: $195* ✉ *150 20th St., east of Collins
Ave., South Beach* ☎ *305/534–3800* ⊕ *www.townhousehotel.com* 🖅 *70
rooms* ⦿ *No meals* ✛ *H1.*

$ ⛱ **Villa Paradiso.** This hotel is one of South Beach's best deals for budget
B&B/INN   travelers (and for those who don't plan on lingering in their rooms all
day), with huge (but basic) rooms with kitchens and a charming tropical courtyard with benches for hanging out at all hours. **Pros:** great
hangout spot in courtyard; good value; great location. **Cons:** no pool;
no restaurant; not trendy. $ *Rooms from: $139* ✉ *1415 Collins Ave.,
South Beach* ☎ *305/532–0616* ⊕ *www.villaparadisohotel.com* 🖅 *17
rooms* ⦿ *No meals* ✛ *G2.*

$$$$ ⛱ **W South Beach.** Fun, fresh, and funky, the W South Beach represents
HOTEL   the brand's evolution towards young sophistication, which means less
Fodor'sChoice   club music in the lobby, more lighting, and more attention to the mul-
★   timillion-dollar art collection lining the lobby's expansive walls. **Pros:**
pool scene; masterful design; ocean-view balconies in each room. **Cons:**
not a classic art deco building; hit-or-miss service; room rates for top-
level suites can be $1,000 per night in high season. $ *Rooms from: $429*
✉ *2201 Collins Ave., South Beach* ☎ *305/938–3000* ⊕ *www.wsouth-
beach.com* 🖅 *248 rooms* ⦿ *No meals* ✛ *H1.*

MID-BEACH

The stretch of Miami Beach called Mid-Beach is undergoing a renaissance, as formerly run-down hotels are renovated and new hotels and
condos are built.

$ ⛱ **Circa 39 Hotel.** Located in the heart of Mid-Beach, this stylish yet
HOTEL   affordable boutique hotel pays attention to every detail and gets them
all right, with amenities that include a swimming pool and sundeck
complete with cabanas and umbrella-shaded chaises that invite all-day
lounging. **Pros:** affordable; beach chairs provided; art deco fireplace.
Cons: not on the beach side of Collins Avenue. $ *Rooms from: $170*
✉ *3900 Collins Ave., Mid-Beach* ☎ *305/538–4900* ⊕ *www.circa39.com*
🖅 *96 rooms* ⦿ *No meals* ✛ *E4.*

$$$ ⛱ **The Confidante.** Formerly the Thompson, this hotel in Miami's bur-
RESORT   geoning Mid-Beach district is a beachfront classic art deco building
reinvented by Martin Brudnizki to channel a colorful, modern incar-
nation of 1950s Florida glamour. **Pros:** valet only $15 for visitors din-
ing on-property; rooftop spa; USB ports built into wall. **Cons:** small
driveway; entry-level rooms are on the small side. $ *Rooms from: $379*
✉ *4041 Collins Ave., Mid-Beach* ☎ *786/605–4041* ⊕ *www.theconfi-
dante.unbound.hyatt.com* 🖅 *363 rooms* ⦿ *No meals* ✛ *E3.*

$$$$
RESORT
Fodor's Choice
★

⊞ **Faena Hotel Miami Beach.** Hotelier Alan Faena delivers on the high expectations of his Miami debut with the jaw-dropping, larger-than-life principal hotel within his in-progress, billion-dollar Faena Arts District in Miami Beach. **Pros:** incredible design; excellent service; spectacular beach club. **Cons:** pricey; construction in neighborhood. $ *Rooms from: $609* ⊠ *3201 Collins Ave., Mid-Beach* ☎ *305/535–4697* ⊕ *www. faena.com/miami-beach* ⌁ *169 rooms* |○| *No meals* ✛ *E4.*

$$$$
RESORT
FAMILY
Fodor's Choice
★

⊞ **Fontainebleau Miami Beach.** Vegas meets art deco at this colossal classic hotel, Miami's largest, which has undergone a $1 billion reinvention. **Pros:** excellent restaurants; historic design mixed with all-new facilities; fabulous pools. **Cons:** away from the South Beach pedestrian scene; massive size; wide mix of guests. $ *Rooms from: $449* ⊠ *4441 Collins Ave., Mid-Beach* ☎ *305/535–3283, 800/548–8886* ⊕ *www.fontainebleau.com* ⌁ *1504 rooms* |○| *No meals* ✛ *E3.*

$$$$
RESORT
Fodor's Choice
★

⊞ **The Miami Beach EDITION.** At this reinvention of the 1955 landmark Seville Hotel by unlikely hospitality duo Ian Schrager and Marriott, historic glamour parallels modern relaxation from the palm-fringed marble lobby to the beachy guest rooms. **Pros:** hotel's got incredible swagger; hanging gardens in the alfresco area; great beachfront service. **Cons:** a bit pretentious; open bathroom setup in select rooms offers little privacy; near a particularly rocky part of Miami Beach. $ *Rooms from: $459* ⊠ *2901 Collins Ave., Mid-Beach* ☎ *786/257–4500* ⊕ *www. editionhotels.com/miami-beach* ⌁ *294 rooms* |○| *No meals* ✛ *E4.*

$$
HOTEL

⊞ **The Palms Hotel & Spa.** If you're seeking an elegant, relaxed property away from the noise but close to both Mid-Beach and South Beach nightlife, you'll find an exceptional beach, an easy pace, and beautiful gardens with soaring palm trees and inviting hammocks here, with rooms as fabulous as the grounds. **Pros:** tropical garden; relaxed and quiet. **Cons:** standard rooms do not have balconies (but suites do); need a taxi or Uber to get most places. $ *Rooms from: $238* ⊠ *3025 Collins Ave., Mid-Beach* ☎ *305/534–0505, 800/550–0505* ⊕ *www.thepalmshotel.com* ⌁ *242 rooms* |○| *No meals* ✛ *E4.*

$$$$
HOTEL

⊞ **Soho Beach House.** The Soho Beach House is a throwback to swanky vibes of bygone decades, bedazzled in faded color palates, maritime ambience, and circa-1930s avant-garde furnishings, luring both somebodies and wannabes to indulge in the amenity-rich, retro-chic rooms as long as they follow stringent "house rules" (no photos, no mobile phones, no suits, and one guest only). **Pros:** two pools; fabulous restaurant; full spa. **Cons:** members have priority for rooms; lots of pretentious patrons; house rules are a bit much. $ *Rooms from: $545* ⊠ *4385 Collins Ave., Mid-Beach* ☎ *786/507–7900* ⊕ *www.sohobeachhouse. com* ⌁ *55 rooms* |○| *No meals* ✛ *E3.*

FISHER AND BELLE ISLANDS

$$$$
RESORT

⊞ **Fisher Island Club.** An exclusive private island, just south of Miami Beach but accessible only by ferry, Fisher Island houses an upscale residential community that includes a small inventory of overnight accommodations, including opulent cottages, villas, and junior suites, which surround the island's original 1920s-era Vanderbilt mansion. **Pros:** great private beaches; never crowded; varied on-island dining choices. **Cons:**

not the warmest fellow guests; ferry ride to get on and off island; limited cell service. $ *Rooms from: $1375* ⊠ *1 Fisher Island Dr., Fisher Island* ☎ *305/535–6000, 800/537–3708* ⊕ *www.fisherislandclub.com* ⤳ *60 rooms* ⏁ *No meals* ✛ *E5.*

$$ ⛝ **The Standard Spa Miami Beach.** An extension of André Balazs's trendy
RESORT   and hip—yet budget-conscious—brand, this shabby-chic boutique spa hotel is a mile from South Beach on an island just over the Venetian Causeway and boasts one of South Florida's most renowned spas, trendiest bars, and hottest pool scenes. **Pros:** free bike and kayak rentals; swank pool scene; great spa. **Cons:** slight trek to South Beach; small rooms with no views. $ *Rooms from: $263* ⊠ *40 Island Ave., Belle Isle* ☎ *305/673–1717* ⊕ *www.standardhotels.com* ⤳ *105 rooms* ⏁ *No meals* ✛ *E4.*

NORTH BEACH

BAL HARBOUR

$$$$ ⛝ **The Ritz-Carlton Bal Harbour, Miami.** In one of South Florida's poshest
RESORT   neighborhoods, the former ONE Bal Harbour exudes contemporary
FAMILY   beachfront luxury design with decadent mahogany-floor guest rooms featuring large terraces with panoramic views of the water and city, over-the-top bathrooms with 10-foot floor-to-ceiling windows, and LCD TVs built into the bathroom mirrors. **Pros:** proximity to Bal Harbour Shops; beachfront; great contemporary-art collection. **Cons:** narrow beach is a bit disappointing; far from nightlife; $25 daily resort fee. $ *Rooms from: $518* ⊠ *10295 Collins Ave., Bal Harbour* ☎ *305/455–5400* ⊕ *www.ritzcarlton.com/en/hotels/miami/bal-harbour* ⤳ *187 rooms* ⏁ *No meals* ✛ *E2.*

$$$$ ⛝ **The St. Regis Bal Harbour Resort.** When this $1 billion–plus resort
RESORT   opened in 2012, Miami's North Beach entered a new era of glamour
Fodor's Choice   and haute living, with A-list big spenders rushing to stay in this 27-story,
★   triple-glass-tower masterpiece. **Pros:** beachfront setting; beyond glamorous; large rooms. **Cons:** limited lounge space around main pool; limited privacy on balconies. $ *Rooms from: $929* ⊠ *9703 Collins Ave., Bal Harbour* ☎ *305/993–3300, 866/716–8116* ⊕ *www.stregisbalharbour. com* ⤳ *280 rooms* ⏁ *No meals* ✛ *E2.*

SUNNY ISLES BEACH

$$$$ ⛝ **Acqualina Resort & Spa on the Beach.** Following a complete room rede-
RESORT   sign in late 2014, Acqualina continues to raise the bar for Miami beach-
FAMILY   front luxury, delivering a fantasy of modern Mediterranean opulence,
Fodor's Choice   with sumptuously appointed, striking gray- and silver-accented interi-
★   ors, and expansive facilities. **Pros:** excellent beach; in-room check-in; huge spa. **Cons:** no nightlife near hotel; hotel's towering height shades the beach by early afternoon. $ *Rooms from: $846* ⊠ *17875 Collins Ave., Sunny Isles Beach* ☎ *305/918–8000* ⊕ *www.acqualinaresort.com* ⤳ *97 rooms* ⏁ *No meals* ✛ *E1.*

AVENTURA

$$$$ ⛝ **Turnberry Isle Miami.** Golfers and families favor this 300-acre tropical
RESORT   resort with jumbo-size rooms and world-class amenities, including a
FAMILY   majestic lagoon pool (winding waterslide and lazy river included), an

Cars whiz by the Avalon hotel and other art deco architecture on Ocean Drive, Miami South Beach.

acclaimed three-story spa and fitness center, and two celeb-chef restaurants—Michael Mina's Bourbon Steak and Scott Conant's Corsair restaurant. **Pros:** great golf, pools, and restaurants; free shuttle to Aventura Mall; situated between Miami and Fort Lauderdale. **Cons:** not on the beach; no nightlife. [$] *Rooms from: $548* ✉ *19999 W. Country Club Dr., Aventura* ☎ *305/932–6200, 866/612–7739* 🌐 *www.turnberryisle-miami.com* 🛏 *437 rooms* 🍴 *No meals* ✥ *E1.*

NIGHTLIFE

One of Greater Miami's most popular pursuits is barhopping. Bars range from intimate enclaves to showy see-and-be-seen lounges to loud, raucous frat parties. There's a New York–style flair to some of the newer lounges, which are increasingly catering to the Manhattan party crowd who escape to Miami and Miami Beach for long weekends. No doubt, Miami's pulse pounds with nonstop nightlife that reflects the area's potent cultural mix. On sultry, humid nights with the huge full moon rising out of the ocean and fragrant night-blooming jasmine intoxicating the senses, who can resist Cuban salsa with some disco and hip-hop thrown in for good measure? When this place throws a party, hips shake, fingers snap, bodies touch. It's no wonder many clubs are still rocking at 5 am. If you're looking for a relatively nonfrenetic evening, your best bet is one of the chic hotel bars on Collins Avenue, or a lounge away from Miami Beach in Wynwood, the Design District, or Downtown.

THE VELVET ROPES

How to get past the velvet ropes at the hottest South Beach night spots? First, if you're staying at a hotel, use the concierge. Decide which clubs you want to check out (consult *Ocean Drive* magazine celebrity pages if you want to be among the glitterati), and the concierge will email, fax, or call in your names to the clubs so you'll be on the guest list when you arrive. This means much easier access and usually no cover charge (which can be upward of $20) if you arrive before midnight. Guest list or no guest list, follow these pointers: Make sure there are more women than men in your group. Dress up: casual chic is the dress code. For men this means no sneakers, no shorts, no sleeveless vests, and no shirts unbuttoned past the top button. For women, provocative and seductive is fine; overly revealing is not. Black is always right. At the door: don't name-drop—no one takes it seriously. Don't be pushy while trying to get the doorman's attention. Wait until you make eye contact, then be cool and easygoing. If you decide to tip him (which most bouncers don't expect), be discreet and pleasant, not big-bucks obnoxious—a $10 or $20 bill quietly passed will be appreciated, however. With the right dress and the right attitude, you'll be on the dance floor rubbing shoulders with South Beach's finest clubbers in no time.

The *Miami Herald* (⊕ *www.miamiherald.com*) is a good source for information on what to do in town. The Weekend section of the newspaper, included in the Friday edition, has an annotated guide to everything from plays and galleries to concerts and nightclubs. The "Ticket" column details the week's entertainment highlights. Or you can pick up the *Miami New Times* (⊕ *www.miaminewtimes.com*), the city's largest free alternative newspaper, published each Thursday. It lists nightclubs, concerts, and special events; reviews plays and movies; and provides in-depth coverage of the local music scene. *MIAMI* (⊕ *www.modernluxury.com/miami*) and *Ocean Drive* (⊕ *www.oceandrive.com*), Miami's model-strewn, upscale fashion and lifestyle magazines, squeeze club, bar, restaurant, and events listings in with fashion spreads, reviews, and personality profiles. Paparazzi photos of local party people and celebrities give you a taste of Greater Miami nightlife before you even dress up to paint the town.

The Spanish-language *El Nuevo Herald* (⊕ *www.elnuevoherald.com*), published by the *Miami Herald*, has extensive information on Spanish-language arts and entertainment, including dining reviews, concert previews, and nightclub highlights.

DOWNTOWN

BARS AND LOUNGES

Bin No.18. Pop into this bistro and wine bar before or after a show at the nearby Adrienne Arsht Center, or simply while the evening away here. The setting masterfully fuses style with charm: wine barrels double as table bases, intimate and communal seating blend, a bar reveals an open kitchen, and chandeliers add a hint of luxe. The menu provides a good mix of seafood and meat, to share or not, but the real highlight is the wine list. Owner-chef Alfredo Patino handpicks from boutique wineries, finding gems from the most famed regions to remote locations around the globe. ■ TIP→ **The best time to explore new varietals is Tuesday, when all bottles under $50 are half price.** ⊠ *1800 Biscayne Blvd., Downtown* 🕾 *786/235–7575* ⊕ *www.bin18miami.com.*

Fodor'sChoice
★
Blackbird Ordinary. This local watering hole has been around since 2011, but it became supertrendy in 2015 and hasn't looked back since. With a vibe that's a bit speakeasy, a bit dive bar, a bit hipster hangout, and a bit Miami sophisticate, it's hands down one of the coolest places in the city and clearly appeals to a wide range of demographics. Mixology is a huge part of the Blackbird experience—be prepared for some awesome artisanal cocktails. There's something going on every night of the week, and the stylish outdoor space is great for cocktails under the stars, movie screenings, and live music. ⊠ *729 S.W. 1st Ave., Downtown* 🕾 *305/671–3307* ⊕ *www.blackbirdordinary.com.*

Fodor'sChoice
★
Sugar. This skyscraping rooftop bar is the essence of the new downtown Miami: futuristic, worldly, and beyond sleek. It crowns the 40th floor of East, Miami, the luxury hotel tucked inside one of Miami's most ambitious multiuse endeavors: the billion-dollar-plus Brickell City Centre complex. The sunsets here are spectacular, as are the Southeast Asian bites and the exotic cocktails. ⊠ *East, Miami, 788 Brickell Plaza, Downtown* 🕾 *305/712–7000* ⊕ *www.east-miami.com.*

DANCE CLUBS

Club Space. Want 24-hour partying? Here's the place, which revolutionized the Miami party scene back in 2000 and still gets accolades as one of the country's best dance clubs. But depending on the month, Space wavers between trendy and empty, depending on the DJ or the special event, so make sure you get the up-to-date scoop from your hotel concierge. Created from four Downtown warehouses, it has two levels, an outdoor patio, a New York–style industrial look, and a 24-hour liquor license. It's open on weekends only, and you'll need to look good to be allowed past the velvet ropes. Note that the crowd can sometimes be sketchy, and take caution walking around the surrounding neighborhood. ⊠ *34 N.E. 11th St., Downtown* 🕾 *305/375–0001* ⊕ *www.clubspace.com.*

Fodor'sChoice
★
E11EVEN Miami. The former Gold Rush building has been transformed into an ultraclub with LED video walls, intelligent lighting, and a powerful sound system that pulses sports by day and beats by night, providing partygoers the 24/7 action they crave. Hospitality and VIP experiences are ample throughout the private lounges and second-level Champagne room; however, the real action is in "The Pit," featuring burlesque performances and intermittent Cirque du Soleil–style shows from a hydraulic-elevating stage. The fusion of theatrics and technology attracts an A-list clientele, and it's not unusual to catch a celebrity or two sporadically jumping on the decks. On the roof, the intimate 50-seat Touché restaurant serves a tapas menu. Live music on the adjacent rooftop lounge warms you up for the long evening—or morning—ahead. ⊠ *29 N.E. 11th St., Downtown* 🕾 *305/829–2911* ⊕ *www.11miami.com.*

COCONUT GROVE

BARS AND LOUNGES

Vinos in the Grove. There's no swirling, sniffing, or pondering (unless you want to, of course); most are here to simply lean back and recoup from the day. Indeed this is a place to enjoy good wine without any airs. Socialization is easy via the staff, who are genuinely conversational with their wine knowledge; you can meet the locals in the casual outdoor seating area, which is front and center for the Grove activity. Inside, punched-out brick walls, chandeliers fastened from wineglasses, and chalkboard menus highlighting cheese plates add a quirky charm. ⊠ *3409 Main Hwy., Coconut Grove* ☎ *305/442–8840* ⊕ *www.vinosinthegrove.com.*

CORAL GABLES

BARS AND LOUNGES

The Bar. One of the oldest bars in South Florida (est. 1946), the old Hofbrau has been reincarnated a few times and now goes by the name "The Bar." The no-frills joint has become an institution in the South Florida bar scene, though it remains totally nontouristy. A massive American flag hangs on the wall of this locals' hangout, arguably the only "cool" nightlife in suburban Coral Gables. Owned by the same folks as Blackbird Ordinary in Downtown, The Bar delivers DJ-led tunes Wednesday through Saturday night and karaoke on Tuesday night. Oh, and they have pretty awesome, farm-fresh bar food, too, for both lunch and dinner. ⊠ *172 Giralda Ave., at Ponce de León Blvd., Coral Gables* ☎ *305/442–2730* ⊕ *www.thebargables.com.*

Fodor'sChoice
★ **El Carajo.** The back of a Mobil gas station is perhaps the most unexpected location for a wine bar, yet for nearly 25 years a passion for good food and drink has kept this family-run business among Miami's best-kept secrets. Tables are in the Old World–style wine cellar, stocked with bottles representing all parts of the globe (and at excellent prices). A waiter takes your order from the menu of exquisite cheeses and charcuterie, hot and cold tapas, paellas, and, of course, wine. Note that though this is an elusive spot, oenophiles are hardly deterred. Reservations are a must, as the place fills up quickly, especially since it closes by 10 pm weekdays, 11 pm weekends. ⊠ *2465 S.W. 17th Ave, Coral Gables* ☎ *305/856–2424* ⊕ *www.el-carajo.com.*

WYNWOOD

BARS AND LOUNGES

Cafeina Wynwood Lounge. This awesome Wynwood watering hole takes center stage during the highly social Gallery Night and Artwalk through the Wynwood Art District (⊕ *www.wynwoodartwalk.com*), the second Saturday of every month, which showcases the cool and hip art galleries between Northwest 20th and Northwest 36 streets west of North Miami Avenue. For those in the know, on any given Miami weekend, the evening either begins or ends this seductive, design-driven lounge with a gorgeous patio and plenty of art on display. It's simply a great place to hang out and get a true feel for Miami's cultural revolution. It's open only Thursday–Saturday (5 pm to midnight Thursday, 5 pm to 3 am Friday, 9 pm to 3 am Saturday). ⊠ *297 N.W. 23rd St., Wynwood* ☎ *305/438–0792* ⊕ *www.cafeinamiami.com.*

Wood Tavern. This is a neighborhood hangout where anything—and anyone—goes: suits mix with hoodies, fashionistas mingle with hipsters, but everyone in the crowd gives off a warm, welcoming vibe. The outdoor terrace is a block party scene with Latin bites served from grafitti-covered car countertops and bleacher-style stairs from which to people-watch or bob to the beats as the DJ jumps from Cypress Hill to Led Zepplin. The scene is a bit of a departure from the sultry nightlife typically associated with the Magic City (wine and cocktails are served in red plastic cups), but all in all it's an experience definitely worth checking out. ⊠ *2531 N.W. 2nd Ave., Wynwood* ☎ *305/748–2828* ⊕ *www.woodtavern.com.*

Wynwood Brewing Company. This family-owned craft brewery is hidden among the towering graffiti arts walls of Wynwood. Communal tables and ever-changing pop-up galleries by neighborhood artists make the taproom cozy; however, a peek through the window behind the bar reveals there is much more to the establishment: 15 pristine silver vats are constantly brewing variations of blond ale, IPA, barrel-aged strong ales, seasonal offerings, and national Gold Medalist the Robust Porter. All staff members are designated "Beer Servers" under the Cicerone Certification Program, ensuring knowledgeable descriptions and recommendations to your liking. ⊠ *565 N.W. 24 St., Wynwood* ☎ *305/982–8732* ⊕ *www.wynwoodbrewing.com.*

MIDTOWN

BARS AND LOUNGES

Fodor's Choice
★
Lagniappe. You may stumble upon this unassuming yet intriguing den across from the Midtown railroad tracks. Shelves house a selection of boutique-label wines with no corkage fee. Artisanal cheeses and meats are also available for the plucking and can be arranged into tapas-board displays. Once your selection is complete, take it back into the "living room" of worn sofas, antique lamps, and old-fashioned wall photos. Live musicians croon from the corner, with different bands each evening. Additional socializing can be found out in the "backyard" of mismatched seating and strung lighting, where as the evening wears on, you're apt to mingle and table-hop among the international crowd. ⊠ *3425 N.E. 2nd Ave., Midtown* ☎ *305/576–0108* ⊕ *www.lagniappehouse.com.*

LITTLE HAVANA

LIVE MUSIC

Fodor's Choice
★
Ball & Chain. Established in 1935 and steeped in legends of gambling, Prohibition protests, the rise of budding entertainers Billie Holiday, Count Basie, and Chet Baker, and the development of Cuban-centric Calle Ocho, this storied nightlife spot has now been renovated and

reestablished under its original name. The high-vaulted ceilings, floral wallpaper, black-and-white photos, and palm-fringed outdoor lounge nod to its torrid history and the glamour of Old Havana. Live music flows freely, as do the Latin-inspired libations and tapas of traditional Cuban favorites for an experience equally cultural as it is enjoyable. Reserved seating is available for a reasonable minimum. ⌧ *1513 S.W. 8th St., Little Havana* ☎ *305/643–7820* ⊕ *www.ballandchainmiami.com.*

SOUTH BEACH

BARS AND LOUNGES

Fodor'sChoice
★

Blues Bar. Dedicate at least one night of your Miami vacation to an art deco pub crawl, patronizing the hotel bars and lounges of South Beach's most iconic buildings, including the National Hotel. Though it's a low-key affair, the nifty wooden Blues Bar here is well worth a stop. The bar is one of many elements original to the 1939 building that give it such a sense of its era that you'd expect to see Ginger Rogers and Fred Astaire hoofing it along the polished terrazzo floor. Live music begins nightly at 8 pm. The adjoining Martini Room has a great collection of cigars, old airline stickers, and vintage Bacardi ads on the walls, but it's only available for private events (but if you ask for a peek, your request might be granted). ⌧ *National Hotel, 1677 Collins Ave., South Beach* ☎ *305/532–2311* ⊕ *www.nationalhotel.com/food/blues.*

FDR at Delano. Top DJs are on tap at this überexclusive subterranean lounge that caters to a stylish see-and-be-seen crowd. Seductive lighting illuminates the two-room, 200-person watering hole, decked out in dark and sexy decor. Bottle service is available for those with deep pockets. ⌧ *1685 Collins Ave., South Beach* ☎ *305/924–4071* ⊕ *www. morganshotelgroup.com/delano/delano-south-beach.*

Haven. This hipster-frequented gastrolounge may be cozy by South Beach standards, but it's just as flashy under the glow of backlit architecture, main bar, and lounge tables in ever-changing hues. Wall-to-wall TVs that double as light installations provide additional hypnotic entertainment. Clever mixology matches the innovative ambience with smoky craft cocktails fusing fresh-fruit flavors with herbs. Hungry? Your palate will be further appeased with the all-night menu of sushi and Asian-inspired bites, interspersed with fresh interpretations of American classics (including duck burgers and Maytag blue tater tots). ⌧ *1237 Lincoln Rd., South Beach* ☎ *305/987–8885.*

Lost Weekend. Slumming celebs and locals often patronize this pool hall–resto–dive bar on quaint Española Way. The hard-core locals are serious about their pastime, so it can be challenging to get a table on weekends. However, everyone can enjoy the pinball machines, the air hockey table, the bar grub, and the full bar, which has 150 kinds of beer (a dozen of which are on tap). Each night, Lost Weekend draws an eclectic crowd, from yuppies to drag queens to celebs on the down-low (and everyone gets equally bad service). So South Beach! ⌧ *218 Española Way, South Beach* ☎ *305/672–1707.*

Mac's Club Deuce Bar. Smoky, dark, and delightfully unpolished, this complete dive bar is anything but what you'd expect from glitzy South

Beach. The circa-1964 pool hall attracts a colorful crowd of clubbers, locals, celebs, and just about anyone else. Locals consider it a top spot for an inexpensive drink and cheap thrills. Visitors love it as a true locals' hangout. ⊠ *222 14th St., at Collins Ave., South Beach* ☎ *305/531–6200* ⊕ *www.macsclubdeuce.com.*

Onyx Bar. Fanny-packed tourists are sure to stop and pose outside the Villa Casa Casuarina, the 1930s-era oceanfront mansion that once belong to late fashion designer Gianni Versace. But travelers know the true way to explore Versace's eccentric and bold Mediterranean mansion: by grabbing a drink at this six-seat bar, a conversion of Versace's former kitchen. The drinks are as opulent as you'd expect from the locale, with gold-leafed accessories and over-the-top taste sensations (think: Berissace Collins—a vodka-and-blackberry-based libation, topped with gold flakes). ⊠ *1116 Ocean Dr., South Beach* ☎ *786/485–2200* ⊕ *www.vmmiamibeach.com.*

Palace Bar. South Beach's gay heyday continues at this fierce oceanfront bar where folks both gay and straight come to revel in good times, cheap cocktails, and great drag performances. Everyone's welcome, and there's no formal dress code. So for many, Speedos, tank tops, and two-pieces will do. The bar gets busiest in the afternoon and early evening; it's not really a late-night place. For out-of-towners, the Sunday Funday drag brunch is a must. It's a true showstopper—or car-stopper, shall we say: using Ocean Drive as a stage, drag queens direct oncoming traffic with street-side splits and acrobatic tricks in heels. ⊠ *1200 Ocean Dr., South Beach* ☎ *305/531–7234* ⊕ *www.palacesouthbeach.com.*

Fodor's Choice ★ **Radio Bar.** What began as a pop-up bar in South Beach's emerging SoFi district in 2013 has evolved into a permanent local favorite, offering a basement-style party where the cool kids love to party, drink, and play. Radio Bar draws a diverse crowd of dressed-down locals, stylish yuppies, and consignment-shop junkies. You'll quickly recognize the bar by the 600-foot radio tower that marks the back-door entrance. Inside, the bar serves awesome craft cocktails, local brews, and small bites. ⊠ *814 1st St., South Beach* ☎ *305/397–8382* ⊕ *www.radiosouthbeach.com.*

Fodor's Choice ★ **The Regent Cocktail Club.** This classic cocktail bar recalls an intimate gentleman's club (and not the stripper kind) with strong masculine cocktails, dark furnishings, bartenders dressed to the nines, and the sounds of jazz legends in the background. The intimate space exudes elegance and timelessness. It's a welcome respite from South Beach's predictable nightlife scene. Cocktails—each with bespoke ice cubes—change daily and are posted on the house blackboard. ⊠ *Gale South Beach, 1690 Collins Ave., South Beach* ☎ *786/975–2555* ⊕ *www.galehotel.com/nightlife.*

Rose Bar. Tucked away inside the chic Delano South Beach, Rose Bar is a Miami mainstay and an essential stop on any South Beach crawl, mixing classic art deco architecture with the best in mixology (and a bit of Vegas bling). Embodying Philippe Starck's original, iconic vision and design for the Delano South Beach, the bar features a rose quartz bar top, velvet wall curtains, and striking chandeliers. ⊠ *Delano Hotel, 1685 Collins Ave., South Beach* ☎ *305/674–5752* ⊕ *www.morganshotelgroup.com/delano/delano-south-beach.*

Sweet Liberty. Miami's bartender of-the-moment, John Lermayer, proves that he's in it for the long haul at this neighborhood hot spot, which took home the prize for Best New American Cocktail Bar 2016 in the Spirited Awards (the ultimate accolade in American bar scene). The bar is a tropical-chic, come-as-you-are joint with incredible spirit-forward cocktails. For something extra special, reserve the "Bartender's Table," which operates like a chef's table, but here you're in the thick of the bar action, tasting libations. ⊠ *237-B 20th St., South Beach* ☎ *305/763–8217* ⊕ *www.mysweetliberty.com.*

Tom on Collins. This lobby bar at the supersexy 1 Hotel South Beach is the brainchild of celebrity-chef Tom Colicchio. Don't expect a wild scene here. It has more of a sultry, laid-back vibe, a young-professional crowd, and plenty of conversation-worthy libations with cute names to match (like "Shiso-Pretty"). ⊠ *1 Hotel South Beach, 2341 Collins Ave., South Beach* ☎ *305/604–1000* ⊕ *www.beachcraftsobe.com/spaces/tom-on-collins/.*

DANCE CLUBS

Nikki Beach Miami Beach. Smack-dab on the beach, the full-service Nikki Beach Club was once upon a time a favorite of SoBe's pretty people and celebrities. Nowadays, it's filled with more suburbanites than the "in" crowd. Nikki's late-night parties are reserved for Sunday only. On Friday and Saturday, the Beach Club is open from noon to 11 pm, and closes at 6 pm on weekdays. Visitors can eat at the Nikki Beach Restaurant and get their food and drink on in the tepees, hammocks, and beach beds (expect rental fees). Sunday brunch at the club's restaurant is pretty spectacular. ⊠ *1 Ocean Dr., South Beach* ☎ *305/538–1111* ⊕ *www.nikkibeach.com.*

Fodor's Choice   **Rec Room.** Entering Rec Room is like stumbling upon an awesome base-
★   ment party that just happens to be packed with the hottest people ever. Amy Sacco's subterranean space at the Gale pays homage to everything 1977 (memorabilia included) and features a collection of more than 3,000 vinyl records at the disposal of resident DJs. The vibe is totally speakeasy meets modern day—the easy-on-the-eyes crowd lets loose, free of inhibitions, jamming out to old-school hip-hop and '80s and '90s throwbacks. ⊠ *Gale South Beach, 1690 Collins Ave., South Beach* ☎ *786/975–2555* ⊕ *www.recroomies.com.*

Score. Since the 1990s, Score has been the see-and-be-seen HQ of Miami's gay community, with plenty of global hotties coming from near and far to show off their designer threads and six-pack abs. After moving in 2013 to Washington Avenue from its longtime Lincoln Road location, this South Beach powerhouse shows no signs of slowing down. DJs spin five nights a week, but Planeta Macho Latin Tuesday is exceptionally popular, as are the weekend dance-offs, especially circuit-party-style "Bigger Saturdays." Dress to impress (and then be ready to go shirtless and show off your abs). ⊠ *1437 Washington Ave., South Beach* ☎ *305/535–1111* ⊕ *www.scorebar.net* ☉ *Closed Mon. and Wed.*

Twist. Twist is a gay institution in South Beach, having been the late-night go-to place for decades, filling to capacity around 2 am after the beach's fly-by-night bars and more established lounges begin to die down (though it's in fact open daily from 1 pm to 5 am). There's never a cover here—not even on holidays or during gay-pride events. The dark club has several rooms spread over two levels and patios, pumping out different tunes and attracting completely disparate groups. It's not uncommon to have college boys partying to Top 40 in one room and strippers showing off their stuff to the straight girls in another area, while an electronic dance throwdown is taking place upstairs. ⊠ *1057 Washington Ave., South Beach* ☎ *305/538–9478* ⊕ *www.twistsobe.com.*

MID-BEACH

BARS AND LOUNGES

Fodor's Choice ★ **The Broken Shakerbooks.** Popular with Miami's cool crowd, this indoor-outdoor craft cocktail joint lures in droves to the adult-chic Freehand hostel to revel in the art of mixology and people-watching. The vibe is Brooklyn meets Miami: everyone's Instagraming everything in faded filters, and there's lots of man buns, facial hair, and girls that look like Lana del Rey (though they may claim they don't like her music). The drinks are pretty daring and definitely awesome with ingredients like green bean juice and kale juice complementing the top-shelf liquors. It's no wonder the venue has been awarded national titles such as America's Best Bar. ⊠ *Freehand Miami, 2727 Indian Creek Dr., Mid-Beach* ☎ *786/476–7011* ⊕ *www.thefreehand.com.*

DANCE CLUBS

Fodor's Choice ★ **LIV.** Since its 2009 opening, this snazzy nightclub located at the Fontainebleau Miami Beach has garnered tons of global attention, and it shows no signs of stopping. It's not hard to see why LIV often makes lists of the world's best clubs—if you can get in, that is (LIV is notorious for lengthy lines, so don't arrive fashionably late). Past the velvet ropes, the dance palladium impresses with its lavish decor, well-dressed international crowd, sensational light-and-sound system, and seductive bi-level club experience. Sometimes the lobby bar, filled with LIV's overflow (and rejects), is just as fun as the club itself. ∎TIP➜ Men beware: groups of guys entering LIV are often coerced into insanely priced bottle service. ⊠ *Fontainebleau Miami Beach, 4441 Collins Ave., Mid-Beach* ☎ *305/674–4680 for table reservations* ⊕ *www.livnightclub.com.*

FISHER AND BELLE ISLANDS

BARS AND LOUNGES

Fodor's Choice ★ **The Lido Bayside Grill.** With all due respect to wonderful food by executive-chef Mark Zeitouni, many locals come to this eatery with drinking as their top priority. By day, the colorful and chic waterfront alfresco restaurant is idyllic for watching the bay-side boats and poolside hotties go by. In the evening, lights braided into the surrounding trees illuminate the terrace, sparking a seductive ambience. On weekdays from 4 to 7, the bar offers a SunDown'er Happy Hour menu. ∎TIP➜ The indoor, lobby-side Lido Bar and Lounge is great for a craft cocktail and a round of Ping-Pong, but the real scene is outdoors, on the opposite side of the hotel, at The Lido Bayside Grill. ⊠ *The Standard Spa, Miami Beach, 40 Island Ave., Belle Isle* ☎ *786/245–0880* ⊕ *www.standardhotels.com.*

SHOPPING

Beyond its fun-in-the-sun offerings, Miami has evolved into a world-class shopping destination. People fly to Miami from all over the world just to shop. The city teems with sophisticated malls—from multistory, indoor climate-controlled temples of consumerism to sun-kissed, open-air retail enclaves—and bustling avenues and streets, lined at once with affordable chain stores, haute couture boutiques, and one-off, "only in Miami"–type shops.

Following the incredible success of the Bal Harbour Shops in the highest of the high-end market (Chanel, Alexander McQueen, ETRO), the Design District has followed suit. Beyond fabulous designer furniture showrooms, the district's tenants now include Hermès, Dior Homme, Rolex, and Prada.

If you're from a region ripe with the climate-controlled slickness of shopping malls and food-court "meals," you'll love the choices in Miami. Head out into the sunshine and shop the city streets, where you'll find big-name retailers and local boutiques alike. Take a break at a sidewalk café to power up on some Cuban coffee or fresh-squeezed OJ and enjoy the tropical breezes.

Beyond clothiers and big-name retailers, Greater Miami has all manner of merchandise to tempt even the casual browser. For consumers on a mission to find certain items—art deco antiques or cigars, for instance—the city streets burst with a rewarding collection of specialty shops.

Stroll through Spanish-speaking neighborhoods where shops sell clothing, cigars, and other goods from all over Latin America or even head to Little Haiti for rare vinyl records.

COCONUT GROVE

CLOTHING

The Griffin. This small boutique packs a big punch with the most coveted shoe styles, from Aquazarra to Chloe to Valentino and Loeffler Randall. Walk around once, then do it again, and you're sure to find another style urging you to try it on. Need help pulling the trigger? The boutique's stocked bar eases the pain of pricey purchases. ⊠ *3112 Commodore Plaza, Coconut Grove* ☎ *786/631–3522.*

Maui Nix. Anchoring the corner of CocoWalk plaza, this Florida-based store sells anything and everything you might need for a trip to the beach. More beach storehouse than shack, the bleached blond-wood walls and racks display 100 surf and skate brands of apparel, shoes, accessories, and gear. Pair a Billabong sundress with a pooka bead necklace, Hurley hoodie with skateboard, Vans slip-ons with Oakely sunglasses or Beats headphones—the possibilities are endless for looking like a true "Grovite." ⊠ *CocoWalk, 3015 Grand Ave., No. 145, Coconut Grove* ☎ *305/444–6919* ⊕ *www.mauinix.com.*

Unika. A longtime fashion resident of Coconut Grove (circa 1989), Unika takes shoppers from day to night, and all affairs in between, with a wide range of inventory for men and women. The contemporary boutique has an it-girl vibe, but the cool, relaxed one you'd actually want to be friends with. High–low pricing appeases all budgets; expect to uncover up-and-coming designer gems tucked within the racks of well-known brands. Bonus: the staff is great with styling for a head-to-toe look. ⊠ *3444 Main Hwy., Suite 2, Coconut Grove* ☎ *305/445–4752.*

MALLS

CocoWalk. Though this three-story, indoor-outdoor mall anchors the Grove's shopping scene, but it's long passed its 1990s heydey. Some chain stores like Victoria's Secret and Gap remain alongside a few specialty shops like Maui Nix. Touristy kiosks with cigars, beads, incense, herbs, and other small items are scattered around the ground level, and commercial restaurants and nightlife (Cheesecake Factory, Fat Tuesday, and Cinépolis Coconut Grove—a multiscreen, state-of-the-art movie theater with a wine bar and lounge and in-seat food service) line the upstairs perimeter. Overall, the space mixes the bustle of a mall with the breathability of an open-air market. Note that hanging out and people-watching is something of a pastime here for Miami suburbanites. ⊠ *3015 Grand Ave., Coconut Grove* ☎ *305/444–0777* ⊕ *www. cocowalk.net.*

CORAL GABLES

BOOKS

FAMILY

Fodor'sChoice

★

Books & Books, Inc. Long live the classic bookstore! Greater Miami's only independent English-language bookshop, Books & Books, specializes in contemporary and classical literature as well as in books on the arts, architecture, Florida, and Cuba. The Coral Gables store is the largest of its four South Florida locations. Here, you can sip 'n' read in the courtyard lounge or dine at the old-fashioned in-store café while browsing the photography gallery. Multiple rooms are filled with myriad genres, making for a fabulous afternoon of book shopping; plus there's an entire area dedicated to kids. There are book signings, literary events, poetry, and other readings, too. Two smaller locations on Lincoln Road in South Beach and at the Bal Harbour Shops also carry great reads as does a petite outpost at the Miami International Airport. ⊠ *265 Aragon Ave., Coral Gables* ☎ *305/442–4408* ⊕ *www. booksandbooks.com.*

CLOTHING

Koko & Palenki. Shoe shopaholics come here for the well-edited selection of trendy footwear by Giuseppe Zanotti, Lola Cruz, Rachel Zoe, Rebecca Minkoff, and others. Handbags and belts add to the selection. Clothing hails from designers like Diane von Furstenberg, Misa, and J Brand. Koko & Palenki also has a store in Aventura Mall and a great online selection (they ship anywhere in the world). ⊠ *Village of Merrick Park, 342 San Lorenzo Ave., Suite 1090, Coral Gables* ☎ *305/444–0626* ⊕ *www.kokopalenki.com.*

FAMILY

Fodor'sChoice

★

Nic Del Mar. Attending one of Miami's famed pool parties practically requires a trip to this upscale swimwear boutique. From the teeny weeny to innovative one-pieces to sporty cuts, the varied suit selection includes Mara Hoffman, Tori Praver, Acacia, and Zimmerman, many of which include matching children's styles for mini beach babes. Flowy cover-ups by the same labels and more can easily double as dinner dresses, while hats, totes, lotions, and even metallic temporary tattoos add a sun-kissed touch. Men's styles are also available. ⊠ *475 Biltmore Way, Suite 105, Coral Gables* ☎ *305/442–8080* ⊕ *www.nicdelmar.com.*

Silvia Tcherassi. The famed, Miami-based Colombian designer's signature boutique in the Village of Merrick Park features ready-to-wear, feminine, and frilly dresses and separates accented with chiffon, toile, and sequins. You'll see plenty of Tcherassi's designs on Miami's Latin power players at events and A-list parties. A neighboring atelier at 270 San Lorenzo Avenue showcases the designer's bridal collection. ⊠ *Village of Merrick Park, 350 San Lorenzo Ave., No. 2140, Coral Gables* ☎ *305/461–0009* ⊕ *www.silviatcherassi.com.*

MALLS

Village of Merrick Park. At this open-air Mediterranean-style, tri-level, shopping-and-dining venue, Neiman Marcus and Nordstrom anchor 115 specialty shops. Outposts by Michael Kors, Jimmy Choo, Tiffany &Co., Burberry, CH Carolina Herrera, and Gucci fulfill most high-fashion needs, and haute-decor shopping options include Brazilian contemporary-furniture designer Artefacto. International food favorite C'est Bon offers further indulgences. ⊠ *358 San Lorenzo Ave., Coral Gables* ☎ *305/529–1215* ⊕ *www.villageofmerrickpark.com.*

ONLY IN MIAMI

Ramon Puig Guayaberas. This clothing shop sells custom-made Ramon Puig guayaberas, the natty four-pocket dress shirts favored by older Cuban men and hipsters alike. Ramon Puig is known as "the King of Guayaberas," and his shirts are top of the line as far as guayaberas go. Hundreds are available off the rack. There are styles for women, too. ⊠ *5840 S.W. 8th St., Coral Gables* ☎ *305/ 266–9680* ⊕ *www.ramon-puig.com.*

SHOPPING DISTRICTS

Miracle Mile. The centerpiece of the downtown Coral Gables shopping district, lined with trees and busy with strolling shoppers, is home to a host of exclusive couturiers and bridal shops as well as some men's and women's boutiques, jewelry, and home-furnishings stores. The half-mile "mile" runs from Douglas Road to LeJeune Road and Aragon Avenue to Andalusia Avenue, but many of the Gables' best non-bridal shops are found on side streets, off the actual mile. In addition, the street itself teems with first-rate restaurants—more than two dozen—facilitating a fabulous afternoon of shopping and eating. ■ TIP→ If debating Miracle Mile versus Bal Harbour or the Design District, check out the others first. ⊠ *Miracle Mile (Coral Way), Douglas Rd. to LeJeune Rd., and Aragon Ave. to Andalusia Ave., Coral Gables* ⊕ *www.shopcoralgables.com.*

WYNWOOD

ONLY IN MIAMI

FAMILY **Genius Jones.** This is a modern design store for kids and parents. It's the best—and one of the few—places to buy unique children's gifts in Miami. Pick up furniture, strollers, clothing, home accessories, and playthings, including classic wooden toys, vintage-rock T-shirts by Claude and Trunk, and toys designed by Takashi Murakami and Keith Haring. ⊠ 2800 N.E. 2nd Ave., Wynwood ☎ 305/571–2000 ⊕ www. geniusjones.com.

DESIGN DISTRICT

Fodor'sChoice ★ Miami is synonymous with good design, and this ever-expanding visitor-friendly shopping district—officially from Northeast 38th to Northeast 42nd streets, between North Miami Avenue and Northeast 2nd Avenue (though unofficially beyond)—is an unprecedented melding of public space and the exclusive world of design. High-design buildings don the creativity of architects like Aranda & Lasch, Sou Fujimoto, and the Leong Leong firm. Throughout the district, there are more than 100 showrooms and galleries, including Baltus, Animadomus, Kartell, Ann Sacks, Poliform USA, and Luminaire Lab. Upscale retail outlets also grace the district. Cartier, Dolce & Gabbana, Fendi, Marc Jacobs, Valentino, Giorgio Armani, Louis Vuitton, Prada, Rolex, and Scotch & Soda sit next to design showrooms. Meanwhile, restaurants like Michael's Genuine Food & Drink and Mandolin Aegean Bistro also make this trendy neighborhood a hip place to dine. Unlike most showrooms, which are typically the beat of decorators alone, the Miami Design District's showrooms are open to the public and occupy windowed, street-level spaces. The area also has its own website: ⊕ www. miamidesigndistrict.net.

CLOTHING

En Avance. This boutique offers a feminine compilation of on-the-cusp designers like Alexis, MSGM, Protagonist, Anjuna, and other young brands. Style and beauty enthusiasts will also enjoy the roving table displays of bespoke baubles, handbags, Assouline lifestyle books, and delicate lotions and potions. The owner's close connection with decorative artist Fornasetti brings to the store an extensive and exclusive selection of fashion-inspired furniture and accessories for the home. ⊠ 53 N.E. 40th St., Design District ☎ 305/576–0056 ⊕ www.enavance.com.

ONLY IN MIAMI

The Bazaar Project. Those looking for the rare and special need look no further than this boutique, curated by owner and Turkey-native Yeliz Titiz via her travels around the globe. Fashions, beauty, decor, and the wonderfully unusual exude the culture and craft akin to their respective regions. Highlights include whimsical housewares and candles by Seletti, linens and Turkish rugs by Haremlique, French wallpapers by Koziel, and intriguing jewelry by Titiz's own line, Sura. ⊠ 4308 N.E. 2nd Ave., Design District ☎ 786/703–6153 ⊕ www.thebazaarproject-shop.com.

V°73. Though high rents in Miami's Design District have translated to more big-name tenants like Fendi and Giorgio Armani, a number of more singular offerings still thrive. One case in point is the exquisite boutique by Italian handbag designer Elisabetta Armellin. It's the artist's only U.S. store and offers a wealth of colorful and understated leather totes and accessories at a number of different price points, catering to a broader demographic than the Design District's typical black-card holders. ⊠ *4218 N.E. 2nd Ave., Design District* ☎ *786/536–4140* ⊕ *www.v73.it/en.*

LITTLE HAITI

VINTAGE CLOTHING

Fly Boutique. After 13 years on South Beach, Fly Boutique found its new home in Miami's up-and-coming MIMO district, north of the Design District and bordering Little Haiti. This resale boutique is where Miami hipsters flock for the latest arrival of used clothing. 1980s glam designer pieces fly out at a premium price, but vintage camisoles and Levi's corduroys are still a resale deal. You'll find supercool art, furniture, luggage, and collectibles throughout the boutique. And be sure to look up—the eclectic lanterns are also for sale. ⊠ *7235 Biscayne Blvd., Little Haiti* ☎ *305/604–8508* ⊕ *www.flyboutiquevintage.com.*

Rebel. Rebel might be a little off the beaten path, though the trip here is well worth it. Half new, half vintage consignment, the goods offered here make you feel as if you are raiding your stylish friend's closet. Racks are packed with all different types of styles and designers—Flying Monkey, Ark & Co., Indah, Karina Grimaldi—requiring a little patience when sifting though. The store has a particularly strong collection of jeans, funky tees, and maxi dresses. ■TIP→ Be thorough, as cute finds are within every nook and corner. ⊠ *6621 Biscayne Blvd., Upper East Side, Little Haiti* ☎ *305/793–4104.*

LITTLE HAVANA

ONLY IN MIAMI

FAMILY **La Casa de los Trucos.** This popular costume store first opened in Cuba in the 1920s; the exiled owners reopened it here in the 1970s. You'll find cartoon costumes, rock star costumes, pet costumes, couples costumes, you name it. If you come any time near Halloween, expect to stand in line just to enter the tiny store. Wooden, life-sized costume cut-outs in the parking lot make for great photo ops. ⊠ *1343 S.W. 8th St., Little Havana* ☎ *305/858–5029* ⊕ *www.crazyforcostumes.com.*

SOUTH BEACH

ART GALLERIES

Fodor's Choice ★ **Romero Britto Gallery.** Though exhibited throughout galleries and museums in more than 100 countries, the vibrant, pop art creations by Brazilian artist Romero Britto have become most synonymous with Miami's playful spirit. His flagship gallery and store are now split between two locations on Lincoln Road. Together they carry the full range of his portfolio, but you'll find original paintings and limited-edition sculptures at the gallery location at 1102 Lincoln Road. Collectibles, fine art prints, and his signature interpretations in collaboration with some of America's most iconic characters and brands, including Disney and Coco-Cola, can be found at the Britto store at 532 Lincoln Road. Home-decor accessories and tech gadgets with Britto's artistic touch are also available. ⊠ *1102 Lincoln Rd., South Beach* ☎ *305/531–8821,* ⊕ *www.britto.com.*

CLOTHING

Fodor's Choice
★

Alchemist. Synonymous with the pinnacle of design and fashion in the Magic City, this boutique has so much personality that it requires not one but two cutting-edge spaces in the retail section of Lincoln Road's trendy Herzog and de Meuron–designed parking garage. There's an anchor store on street level as well as a glass-encased studio for men's clothing and jewelry on the fifth floor. The price tags skew high, yet represent brands known for innovation and edge. Selections span statement pieces and accessories by Alaia, Givenchy, Moschino; jewelry on an artistry level including Cristina Ortiz, Lydia Courteille, and Stephen Webster; and fashions for the home by Tom Dixon. In 2015, Alchemist opened a fine jewelry-focused outpost in the Design District at 140 Northeast 39th Street. ⊠ *1111 Lincoln Rd., Carpark Level 5, South Beach* ☎ *305/531–4643* ⊕ *www.alchemist.miami.*

Base Superstore. This is the quintessential South Beach fun-and-funky boutique experience. Stop here for men's eclectic clothing, shoes, jewelry, and accessories that mix Japanese design with Caribbean-inspired materials. Constantly evolving, this shop features an intriguing magazine section, a record section, groovy home accessories, and the latest in men's swimwear and sunglasses. The often-present house-label designer may help select your wardrobe's newest addition. ⊠ *927 Lincoln Rd., South Beach* ☎ *305/531–4982* ⊕ *www.baseworld.com.*

frankie. miami. Expect high style at moderate prices at this boutique. The studio-like ambience matches the highly edited collection of fashionista favorites Beck & Bridge, Sam & Lavi, Iro, For Love & Lemons, and Loeffers. Co-owner Cheryl Herger also designs her own private-label line especially for frankie. miami. Skirts and dresses with interesting silhouettes, uniquely cut tops, and swimwear almost too good for just the pool are interspersed with easy-chic basics and the boutique's renowned selection of denim shorts (it is a Miami Beach fashion staple, after all). Delicate jewelry and statement clutches provide that polished edge to your final look. ⊠ *1891 Purdy Ave., South Beach* ☎ *786/479–4898* ⊕ *www.frankiemiami.com.*

Intermix. This modern New York–based boutique has the variety of a department store. You'll find fancy dresses, stylish shoes, slinky accessories, and trendy looks by sassy and somewhat pricey designers like Chloé, Stella McCartney, Marc Jacobs, Moschino, and Diane von Furstenberg. Its popularity on Collins Avenue has translated into a second outpost down the beach at Lincoln Road Mall, which opened in late 2014. There is yet another branch at the Bal Harbour Shops at 9700 Collins Avenue. ⊠ *634 Collins Ave., South Beach* ☎ *305/531–5950* ⊕ *www.intermixonline.com.*

ONLY IN MIAMI

Dog Bar. Just north of Lincoln Road's main drag, this over-the-top pet boutique caters to enthusiastic animal owners with a variety of unique items for the superpampered pet. From luxurious, vegan "leather" designer dog purse/carriers to bling-bling-studded collars to chic poopy bag holders, Miami's "original pet boutique" carries pretty much every pet accessory imaginable. You'll also find plenty of gourmet food and treats as well as a wide variety of fancy toys for dogs, large and small. ⊠ *1684 Jefferson Ave., South Beach* ☏ *305/532–5654* ⊕ *www.dogbar.com.*

Fodor's Choice
★

The Webster Miami. Occupying an entire circa-1939 art deco building, The Webster is a tri-level, 20,000-square-foot, one-stop shop for fashionistas. This retail sanctuary carries ready-to-wear fashions by more than 100 top designers, plus in-store exclusive shirts, candles, books, and random trendy items you might need for your South Beach experience—a kind of haute Urban Outfitters for grown-ups. Too many choices? Sit down for a café au lait and pastry inside the store to mull over your future purchases. ⊠ *1220 Collins Ave., South Beach* ☏ *305/674–7899* ⊕ *www.thewebstermiami.com.*

SHOPPING DISTRICTS

Collins Avenue. Give your plastic a workout in South Beach shopping at the many high-profile tenants on this densely packed stretch of Collins between 5th and 10th streets, with stores like Steve Madden, Club Monaco, The Webster, MAC Cosmetics, Ralph Lauren, and Intermix. Sprinkled among the upscale vendors are hair salons, spas, cafés, and such familiar stores as the Gap and Sephora. Be sure to head over one street east to Ocean Drive or west to Washington Avenue for a drink or a light bite, or go for more retail therapy on Lincoln Road. ⊠ *Collins Ave. between 5th and 10th Sts., South Beach* ⊕ *www.lincolnroadmall. com/shopping/collins-avenue.*

Fodor's Choice
★

Lincoln Road Mall. The eight-block-long pedestrian mall between Alton Road and Washington Avenue is the trendiest place on Miami Beach. Home to more than 200 shops, art galleries, restaurants and cafés, and the renovated Colony Theatre, Lincoln Road is like the larger, more sophisticated cousin of Ocean Drive. The see-and-be-seen theme is furthered by outdoor seating at every restaurant, where tourists and locals lounge and discuss the people (and pet) parade passing by. An 18-screen movie theater anchors the west end of the street, which is where most of the worthwhile shops are; the far east end is mostly discount and electronics shops. Due to higher rents, you are more likely to see big corporate stores like Armani, H&M, and Victoria's Secret than original boutiques. However, a few emporiums and stores with unique personalities, like Alchemist, Base, and Books & Books, remain. ⊠ *Lincoln Rd. between Alton Rd. and Washington Ave., South Beach* ⊕ *www.lincolnroadmall.com.*

NORTH BEACH

BAL HARBOUR
CLOTHING

Le Beau Maroc. Shoppers can snag a piece of Moroccan exoticism and regality via pieces introduced to the United States for the very first time and available only within the boutique. Lavishly embellished couture kaftans by Souad Chraïbi and Siham Tazi, two of Morocco's most famed designers commissioned by a royal and celebrity clientele, can work for beach, day, and evening wear. Special orders created from the finest fabrics sourced from fashion houses Dior, Valentino, Hermès, Pucci, La Croix, Yves St. Laurent, Jakob Schlaepfer, and Ungaro are also available. Additional exclusive treasures are found at the "beauty bar," where you can adorn yourself with 18 carat-gold Moroccan jewelry and the "liquid gold" of Marokissime, an elixir of 100% pure Moroccan argan and prickly-pear oils coveted by Moroccan women for centuries for their beauty regimens. ⊠ *9507 Harding Ave., Bal Harbour* ☎ *305/763–8847* ⊕ *www.lebeaumaroc.com.*

100% Capri. This shop is one of only two stores by this Italian brand in the United States (the other is in Los Angeles). The collection is all pure linen (including the shopping bags). Designer Antonio Aiello sources and produces all pieces in Capri for an exciting interpretation that takes its wearers to exotic beach locales style-wise—and quite literally, given its clientele. You'll find clothing for women, men, and children, and even home goods with curated glass accessories brought over from Italy. Displays of gray, wood-slatted wall panels and pools of water build up the ambience, prompting you to linger longer. Now if only there was rosé. ⊠ *Bal Harbour Shops, 9700 Collins Ave., No. 236, Bal Harbour* ☎ *305/866–4117* ⊕ *www.100capri.com/en.*

Fodor'sChoice ★ **The Webster Bal Harbour.** Though smaller than its sister store in South Beach, The Webster Bal Harbour is still sizable with 2,600 square feet to house high-level fashions for both men and women. Nearly every great contemporary luxury designer is represented (Chanel, Céline, Alaia, Valentino, Givenchy, Proenza Schouler, Stella McCartney, etc.), as well as emerging runway darlings. Fashionably impatient? The store can snag ready-to-wear pieces from the latest shows. It also carries exclusive pieces, a real feat considering its influential mall neighbors, including a continuous flow of capsule collections in collaboration with the likes of Calvin Klein, Marc Jacobs, and Anthony Vaccarello, to name a few. ⊠ *Bal Habour Shops, 9700 Collins Ave., No. 204, Bal Harbour* ☎ *305/868–6544* ⊕ *www.thewebstermiami.com.*

SHOPPING CENTERS AND MALLS

Fodor'sChoice ★ **Bal Harbour Shops.** Beverly Hills meets the South Florida sun at this swank collection of 100 high-end shops, boutiques, and department stores, which currently holds the title as the country's greatest revenue-earner per square foot. Many European designers open their first North American signature store at this outdoor, pedestrian-friendly mall, and many American designers open their first boutique outside of New York here. The open-air enclave includes Florida's largest Saks Fifth Avenue; an 8,100-square-foot, two-story flagship Salvatore Ferragamo store; and stores by Alexander McQueen, Gucci, Valentino, and local juggernaut The Webster. Restaurants and cafés, in tropical garden settings, overflow with style-conscious diners; in fact, people-watching on the terrace of the Japanese restaurant Makoto and Italian restaurant Carpaccio might be the best in Miami (even trumping South Beach). ⊠ *9700 Collins Ave., Bal Harbour* ☎ *305/866–0311* ⊕ *www.balharbourshops.com.*

AVENTURA

JEWELRY

MIA Jewels. This jewelry and accessories boutique is known for its colorful gem- and bead-laden, gold and silver earrings, necklaces, bracelets, and brooches by lines such as Cousin Claudine, Amrita, and Alexis Bittar. This is a shoo-in store for everyone: you'll find things for trend lovers (gold-studded chunky Lucite bangles), classicists (long, colorful, wraparound beaded necklaces), and ice lovers (long Swarovski crystal cabin necklaces) alike. ⊠ *Aventura Mall, 19575 Biscayne Blvd., No. 1061, Aventura* ☎ *305/931–2000.*

SHOPPING CENTERS AND MALLS

Fodor's Choice ★ **Aventura Mall.** This three-story megamall offers the ultimate in South Florida retail therapy and welcomes more than 29 million visitors annually. Aventura houses many global top performers including the most lucrative outposts of several U.S. chain stores, a supersize Nordstrom and Bloomingdale's, and 300 other shops like a two-story flagship Louis Vuitton, Façonnable, Fendi, and MIA Jewels, which together create the third-largest mall in the United States. This is the one-stop, shop-'til-you-drop retail mecca for locals, out-of-towners, and—frequently—celebrities. ⊠ *19501 Biscayne Blvd., Aventura* ☎ *305/935–1110* ⊕ *www.aventuramall.com.*

SPORTS AND THE OUTDOORS

Sun, sand, and crystal-clear water mixed with an almost nonexistent winter and a cosmopolitan clientele make Miami and Miami Beach ideal for year-round sunbathing and outdoor activities. Whether the priority is showing off a toned body, jumping on a Jet Ski, or relaxing in a tranquil natural environment, there's a beach tailor-made to please. But tanning and water sports are only part of this sun-drenched picture. Greater Miami has championship golf courses and tennis courts, miles of bike trails along placid canals and through subtropical forests, and skater-friendly concrete paths amidst the urban jungle. For those who like their sports of the spectator variety, the city offers up a bonanza of pro teams for every season. There's even a crazy ball-flinging game called jai alai that's billed as the fastest sport on Earth.

BASEBALL

FAMILY **Marlins.** Miami's baseball team, formerly known as the Florida Marlins, then the Miami Marlins, and now simply the Marlins, plays at the state-of-the-art Marlins Park—a 37,442-seat retractable-roof, air-conditioned baseball stadium on the grounds of Miami's famous

Orange Bowl. Go see the team that came out of nowhere to beat the New York Yankees and win the 2003 World Series. Home games are April through early October. ⊠ *Marlins Park, 501 Marlins Way, Little Havana* ☎ *305/480–1300, 877/627–5467 for tickets* ⊕ *miami. marlins.mlb.com* ⊴ *$10–$395; parking from $20 and should be pre-purchased online.*

BIKING

Perfect weather and flat terrain make Miami–Dade County a popular place for cyclists; however, biking here can also be quite dangerous. Be very vigilant when biking on Miami Beach, or better yet, steer clear and bike the beautiful paths of Key Biscayne instead.

Key Cycling. On an island where biking is a way of life, this Key Biscayne bike shop carries a wide range of amazing bikes in its showroom, as well as any kind of bike accessory imaginable. Out-of-towners can rent mountain or hybrid bikes for $20 for two hours, $25 for the day, and $100 for the week. ⊠ *Galleria Shopping Center, 328 Crandon Blvd., Suite 121, Key Biscayne* ☎ *305/361–0061* ⊕ *www.keycycling.com.*

Miami Beach Bicycle Center. If you don't want to opt for the hassle of CitiBike or if you want wheels with some style, the easiest and most economical place for a bike rental on South Beach is this shop near Ocean Drive. Rent a bike starting at $5 per hour, $18 per day, or $80 for the week. All bike rentals include locks, helmets, and baskets. ⊠ *601 5th St., South Beach* ☎ *305/674–0150* ⊕ *www.bikemiamibeach.com.*

BOATING AND SAILING

Boating, whether on sailboats, powerboats, luxury yachts, WaveRunners, or windsurfers, is a passion in Greater Miami. The Intracoastal Waterway, wide and sheltered Biscayne Bay, and the Atlantic Ocean provide ample opportunities for fun aboard all types of watercraft.

The best windsurfing spots are on the north side of the Rickenbacker Causeway at Virginia Key Beach or to the south at, go figure, Windsurfer Beach.

GOLF

Greater Miami has more than 30 private and public courses. Costs at most courses are higher on weekends and in season, but you can save by playing on weekdays and after 1 or 3 pm, depending on the course. Call ahead to find out when afternoon-twilight rates go into effect. For information on most courses in Miami and throughout Florida, you can visit ⊕ *www.floridagolferguide.com.*

Biltmore Golf Course. On the grounds of the historic circa 1926 Biltmore hotel, the Biltmore Golf Course provides a golf experience primarily for in-house guests, local residents, and those visiting the Coral Gables area. The 6,800-yard, 18-hole, par-71, championship golf course was designed in 1925 by Scotsman Donald Ross, the "it" golf designer of the Roaring '20s. Today, the lush, well-maintained course is easily accessible thanks to its advanced online booking system, where you can easily reserve your tee time and decide between pricing, depending on the time of day and year (weekdays are cheaper; and the later, the cheaper it gets). There's a pro shop on-site, and golf instruction is available through the Biltmore Golf Academy or the more extensive on-site Golf Channel Academy. ⊠ *The Biltmore Hotel, 1210 Anastasia Ave., Coral Gables* ☎ *305/460–5364* ⊕ *www. biltmorehotel.com/golf* ⌨ *$122 for 9 holes, $200 for 18 holes* 🏌 *18 holes, 6800 yards, par 71.*

Fodor's Choice ★ **Crandon Golf at Key Biscayne.** On the serene island of Key Biscayne, overlooking Biscayne Bay, this top-rated, championship municipal golf course is considered one of the state's most challenging par-72 courses. Enveloped by tropical foliage, mangroves, saltwater lakes, and bay-side waters, the course also happens to be the only one in North America with a subtropical lagoon. The Devlin/Von Hagge–designed course has a USGA rating of 75.4 and a slope rating of 129 and has received national awards from both *Golfweek* and *Golf Digest*. The course is located on the south side of Crandon Park. Nonresidents should expect to pay $200 for a round during peak hours in peak season (mid-December–mid-April) and roughly half that off-season. Deeply discounted twilight rates of $65 apply after 2 pm. Tee times can be booked online. ⊠ *Crandon Park, 6700 Crandon Blvd., Key Biscayne* ☎ *305/361–9129, 855/465–3305 for tee times* ⊕ *www.golfcrandon. com* ⌨ *$200* 🏌 *18 holes, 7400 yards, par 72.*

The Senator Course at Shula's Golf Club. Deep in the suburbs of west Miami, the Senator Course at Shula's Golf Club boasts the longest championship course in the area (7,055 yards, par 72), a lighted par-3 course, and a golf school. The championship, classic-style Senator Course was originally designed in 1962 by Bill Watts, updated by Kipp Schulties in 1998, and completely refreshed in late 2013, with improvements that included sparkling new Champion Bermuda greens and new Celebration Bermuda tees. The club hosts dozens of tournaments yearly. Because of its remote location, greens fees tend to be on the lower side, varying by season and time. You'll pay in the lower range on weekdays, more on weekends, and a third of prime-time rates after 2 pm. Golf carts are included. For true golf enthusiasts, there's the on-site Don Shula hotel—a comfortable base to eat, live, and breathe golf. ⊠ *7601 Miami Lakes Dr., 154th St. exit off Rte. 826, Miami Lakes* ☎ *305/820–8088* ⊕ *www.shulasgolfclub.com* ⌨ *$130* 🏌 *18 holes, 7055 yards, par 70.*

GUIDED TOURS

BOAT TOURS

FAMILY **Island Queen Cruises.** Working with nine boats, experiences on the very touristy Island Queen Cruises run the gamut—sunset cruises, dance cruises, fishing cruises, speedboat rides, and their signature, tours of Millionaire's Row, Miami's waterfront homes of the rich and famous. The *Island Queen, Island Lady,* and *Miami Lady* are three double-decker, 140-passenger tour boats docked at Bayside Marketplace that set sail daily for 90-minute narrated tours of the Port of Miami and Millionaires' Row. ⊠ *401 Biscayne Blvd., Downtown* ☎ *800/910–5119* ⊕ *www.islandqueencruises.com* ✆ *From $19.*

WALKING TOURS

FAMILY **Art Deco District Walking Tour.** Operated by the Miami Design Preservation League, this is a 90-minute guided walking tour that departs from the league's welcome center at Ocean Drive and 10th Street. It starts at 10:30 am daily, with an extra tour at 6:30 pm Thursday. Alternatively, you can go at your own pace with the league's self-guided iPod audio tour, which also takes roughly an hour and a half. ⊠ *1001 Ocean Dr., South Beach* ☎ *305/763–8026* ⊕ *www.mdpl.org* ✆ *$25 guided tour, $20 self-guided audio tour.*

Little Havana Arts & Culture Walk. Cultural institution HistoryMiami (formerly the Historical Museum of Southern Florida) runs some fabulous art and cultural tours of Little Havana (spiked with plenty of Cuban coffees and cigars, of course). Enjoy the unique architecture of this ethnic enclave and community history by visiting art galleries, botanicas, cigar factories, and the Cuba Ocho Art and Research Center, featuring rare Cuban art from early 19th and 20th century. The two-hour tour is offered monthly and leaves from the juice stand and market Los Pinareños Fruteria at 6 pm. Tours aren't available every month, so check the HistoryMiami calendar on the website ahead of time to book. ⊠ *1334 S.W. 8 St., Little Havana* ☎ *305/375–1492* ⊕ *www.historymiami.org* ✆ *$30.*

SCUBA DIVING AND SNORKELING

Diving and snorkeling on the offshore coral wrecks and reefs on a calm day can be very rewarding. Chances are excellent that you'll come face-to-face with a flood of tropical fish. One option is to find Fowey, Triumph, Long, and Emerald reefs in 10- to 15-foot dives that are perfect for snorkelers and beginning divers. On the edge of the continental shelf a little more than 3 miles out, these reefs are just a quarter-mile away from depths greater than 100 feet. Another option is to paddle around the tangled prop roots of the mangrove trees that line the coast, peering at the fish, crabs, and other creatures hiding there.

Perhaps the area's most unusual diving options are its artificial reefs. Since 1981, Miami-Dade County's Department of Environmental Resources Management has sunk tons of limestone boulders and a water tower, army tanks, and almost 200 boats of all descriptions to create a "wreckreational" habitat where divers can swim with yellow tang, barracudas, nurse sharks, snapper, eels, and grouper. The website offers an interactive map of wreck locations. ⇨ *For the best snorkeling in Miami–Dade, head to Biscayne National Park. See the Everglades, Chapter 3, for more information.*

Divers Paradise of Key Biscayne. This complete dive shop and diving-charter service, next to the Crandon Park Marina, includes equipment rental and scuba instruction with PADI and NAUI affiliation. Four-hour dive trips are offered on weekends at 8:30 and 1:30. Night dives are offered Thursday at 5:30; the company is generally closed on Mondays. ⊠ *Crandon Park Marina, 4000 Crandon Blvd., Key Biscayne* ☎ *305/361–3483* ⊕ *www.keydivers.com* ⊠ *$60.*

Fodor'sChoice **South Beach Dive and Surf.** Dedicated to all things ocean, this PADI five-
★ star dive shop offers multiple diving and snorkeling trips weekly as well as surfboard, paddleboard, and skateboard sales, rentals, and lessons. The Discover Scuba course (for noncertified divers) trains newcomers every Monday, Tuesday, Thursday, and Saturday at 10 am, which includes two dives in Key Largo's John Pennekamp Marine Sanctuary that same day. In some months of the year, night dives take place on Wednesday at 5. Wreck and reef dives take place on weekend mornings. The center also runs dives in Key Largo's Spiegel Grove, the second-largest wreck ever to be sunk for the intention of recreational diving, and in the Neptune Memorial Reef, inspired by the city of Atlantis and created in part using the ashes of cremated bodies. The dive shop itself is located in the heart of South Beach, but boats depart from marinas in Miami Beach and Key Largo, in the Florida Keys. ⊠ *850 Washington Ave., South Beach* ☎ *305/531–6110* ⊕ *www.southbeachdivers.com.*

THE EVERGLADES

WELCOME TO THE EVERGLADES

TOP REASONS TO GO

★ **Fun fishing:** Cast for some of the world's fightingest game fish—600 species in all—in the Everglades' backwaters.

★ **Abundant birdlife:** Check hundreds of birds off your life list, including—if you're lucky—the rare Everglades snail kite.

★ **Cool kayaking:** Do a half-day trip in Big Cypress National Preserve or grab a paddle for the ultimate—the 99-mile Wilderness Trail.

★ **Swamp cuisine:** Want to chow down on alligator tail or frogs' legs? Or how about swamp cabbage, made from hearts of palm? Better yet, try stone-crab claws fresh from the traps.

★ **Gator-spotting:** This is ground zero for alligator viewing in the United States, and odds are you'll leave having spotted your quota.

1 Everglades National Park. Alligators, Florida panthers, black bears, manatees, dolphins, bald eagles, and roseate spoonbills call this vast habitat home.

2 Biscayne National Park. Mostly under water, here's where the string of coral reefs and islands that form the Florida Keys begins.

3 Big Cypress National Preserve. Neighbor to Everglades National Park, it's an outdoor-lover's paradise.

Miccosukee
Indian Village

Tamiami Trail

Everglades
Gator Park

Shark
Valley

Hialeah

95

Miami

836

Everglades
Safari Park

41

Coral
Gables

826

Kendall

Observation
Tower **1**

997

1

2

Biscayne
National Park

Homestead

9336

Florida City

Convoy
Point

Biscayne
Bay

Boca Chita
Key

Elliott Key

Adams Key

1

Barnes
Sound

ATLANTIC
OCEAN

Snake
Bight

Joe Kemp
Key

*Florida
Bay*

Florida
Keys

GETTING ORIENTED

3

The southern third of the Florida peninsula is largely taken up by protected government land that includes Everglades National Park, Big Cypress National Preserve, and Biscayne National Park. Miami lies to the northeast, with Naples and Marco Island to the northwest. Land access to Everglades National Park is primarily by two roads. The park's main road traverses the southern Everglades from the gateway towns of Homestead and Florida City to the outpost of Flamingo, on Florida Bay. To the north, Tamiami Trail (U.S. 41) cuts through the Everglades from Greater Miami on the east coast or from Naples on the west coast to the western park entrance near Everglades City at Route 29.

THE FLORIDA
EVERGLADES

by Lynne Helm

Alternately described as elixir of life or swampland muck, the Florida Everglades is one of a kind—a 50-mi-wide "river of grass" that spreads across hundreds of thousands of acres. It moves at varying speeds depending on rainfall and other variables, sloping south from the Kissimmee River and Lake Okeechobee to estuaries of Biscayne Bay, Florida Bay, and the Ten Thousand Islands.

Today, apart from sheltering some 70 species on America's endangered list, the Everglades also embraces more than 7 million residents, 50 million annual tourists, 400,000 acres of sugarcane, and the world's largest concentration of golf courses.

Demands on the land threaten the Everglades' finely balanced ecosystem. Irrigation canals for agriculture and roadways disrupt natural water flow. Drainage for development leaves wildlife scurrying for new territory. Water runoff, laced with fertilizers, promotes unnatural growth of swamp vegetation. What remains is a miracle of sorts, given decades of these destructive forces.

Creation of the Everglades required unique conditions. South Florida's geology, linked with its warm, wet subtropical climate, is the perfect mix for a marshland ecosystem. Layers of porous, permeable limestone create water-bearing rock, soil, and aquifers, which in turn affects climate, weather, and hydrology.

This rock beneath the Everglades reflects Florida's geologic history—its crust was once part of the African region. Some scientists theorize that continental shifting merged North America with Africa, and then continental rifting later pulled North America away from the African continent but took part of northwest Africa with it—the part that is today's Florida. The Earth's tectonic plates continued to migrate, eventually placing Florida at its current location as a land mass jutting out into the ocean, with the Everglades at its tip.

EXPERIENCING THE ECOSYSTEMS

Eight distinct habitats exist within Everglades National Park, Big Cypress National Preserve, and Biscayne National Park.

ECOSYSTEMS	EASY WAY	MORE ACTIVE WAY
COASTAL PRAIRIE: An arid region of salt-tolerant vegetation lies between the tidal mud flats of Florida Bay and dry land. **Best place to see it: The Coastal Prairie Trail**	Take a guided boat tour of Florida Bay, leaving from Flamingo Marina.	Hike the Coastal Prairie Trail from Eco Pond to Clubhouse Beach.
CYPRESS: Capable of surviving in standing water, cypress trees often form dense clusters called "cypress domes" in natural water-filled depressions. **Best place to see it: Big Cypress National Preserve**	Drive U.S. 41 (also known as Tamiami Trail—pronounced Tammy-Amee), which cuts across Southern Florida, from Naples to Miami.	Hike (or drive) the scenic Loop Road, which begins off Tamiami Trail, running from the Loop Road Education Center to Monroe Station.
FRESH WATER MARL PRAIRIE: Bordering deeper sloughs are large prairies with marl (clay and calcium carbonate) sediments on limestone. Gators like to use their toothy snouts to dig holes in prairie mud. **Best place to see it: Pahayokee Overlook**	Drive there from the Ernest F. Coe Visitor Center.	Take a guided tour, either through the park service or from permitted, licensed guides. You also can set up camp at Long Pine Key.
FRESH WATER SLOUGH AND HARDWOOD HAMMOCK: Shark River Slough and Taylor Slough are the Everglades' two sloughs, or marshy rivers. Due to slight elevation amid sloughs, dense stands of hardwood trees appear as teardrop-shaped islands. **Best place to see it: The Observation Tower**	Take a two-hour guided tram tour from the Shark Valley Visitor Center to the tower and back.	Walk or bike (rentals available) the route to the tower via the tram road and (walkers only) Bobcat Boardwalk trail and Otter Cave Hammock Trail.
MANGROVE: Spread over South Florida's coastal channels and waterways, mangrove thrives where Everglades fresh water mixes with salt water. **Best place to see it: The Wilderness Waterway**	Picnic at the area near Long Pine Key, which is surrounded by mangrove, or take a water tour at Biscayne National Park.	Boat your way along the 99-mi Wilderness Waterway. It's six hours by motorized boat, seven days by canoe.
MARINE AND ESTUARINE: Corals, sponges, mollusks, seagrass, and algae thrive in the Florida Bay, where the fresh waters of the Everglades meet the salty seas. **Best place to see it: Florida Bay**	Take a boat tour from the Flamingo Visitor Center marina.	Canoe or kayak on White Water Bay along the Wilderness Waterway Canoe Trail.
PINELAND: A dominant plant in dry, rugged terrain, the Everglades' diverse pinelands consist of slash pine forest, saw palmettos, and more than 200 tropical plant varieties. **Best place to see it: Long Pine Key trails**	Drive to Long Pine Key, about 6 mi off the main road from Ernest F. Coe Visitor Center.	Hike or bike the 28 mi of Long Pine Key trails.

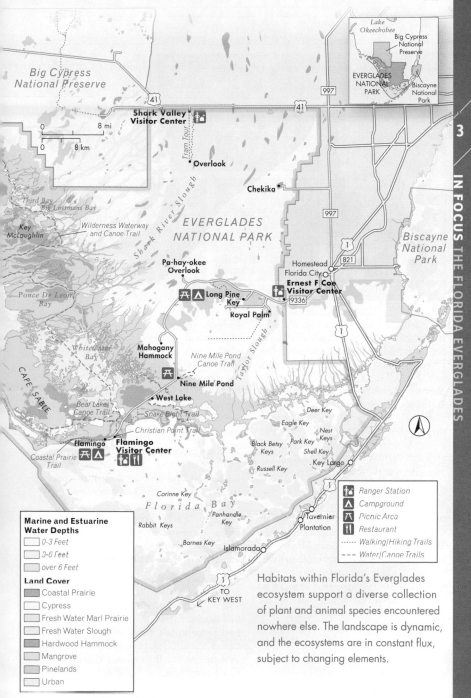

Lake
Okeechobee

Big Cypress
National
Preserve

EVERGLADES
NATIONAL
PARK

Biscayne
National
Park

Big Cypress
National Preserve

41

997

Shark Valley
Visitor Center

Tram Tour

0   8 mi
0   8 km

Overlook

Chekika

997

Third Bay

Big Lostmans Bay

Wilderness Waterway
and Canoe Trail

Key
McLaughlin

Shark River Slough

EVERGLADES
NATIONAL PARK

Biscayne
National
Park

Pa-hay-okee
Overlook

Homestead
Florida City

Ernest F Coe
Visitor Center

Ponce De Leon
Bay

Long Pine
Key

9336

Royal Palm

Whitewater
Bay

Mahogany
Hammock

Nine Mile Pond
Canoe Trail

Taylor Slough

821

CAPE SABLE

Nine Mile Pond

West Lake

Bear Lake
Canoe Trail

Snake Bight Trail

Christian Point Trail

Deer Key

Eagle Key

Nest
Keys

Flamingo

Flamingo
Visitor Center

Black Betsy
Keys

Park Key

Shell Key

Coastal Prairie
Trail

Russell Key

Key Largo

Corinne Key

Florida Bay

Panhandle
Key

Rabbit Keys

Tavernier
Plantation

Barnes Key

Islamorada

**Marine and Estuarine
Water Depths**
◻ 0-3 Feet
◻ 3-6 Feet
◻ over 6 Feet
Land Cover
◼ Coastal Prairie
◻ Cypress
◻ Fresh Water Marl Prairie
◻ Fresh Water Slough
◼ Hardwood Hammock
◻ Mangrove
◻ Pinelands
◻ Urban

1

TO
KEY WEST

🚹 Ranger Station
⛺ Campground
🌲 Picnic Area
🍴 Restaurant
······· Walking/Hiking Trails
- - - Water/Canoe Trails

Habitats within Florida's Everglades
ecosystem support a diverse collection
of plant and animal species encountered
nowhere else. The landscape is dynamic,
and the ecosystems are in constant flux,
subject to changing elements.

FLORA

❶ Cabbage Palm

It's virtually impossible to visit the Everglades and not see a cabbage palm, Florida's official state tree. The cabbage palm (or sabal palm), graces assorted ecosystems and grows well in swamps. **Best place to see them:** At Loxahatchee National Wildlife Refuge (embracing the northern part of the Everglades, along Alligator Alley), throughout Everglades National Park, and at Big Cypress National Preserve.

❷ Sawgrass

With spiny, serrated leaf blades resembling saws, sawgrass inspired the term "river of grass" for the Everglades. **Best place to see them:** Both Shark Valley and Pahayokee Overlook provide terrific vantage points for gazing over sawgrass prairie; you also can get an eyeful of sawgrass when crossing Alligator Alley, even when doing so at top speeds.

❸ Mahogany

Hardwood hammocks of the Everglades live in areas that rarely flood because of the slight elevation of the sloughs, where they're typically found. **Best place to see them:** Everglades National Park's Mahogany Hammock Trail (which has a boardwalk leading to the nation's largest living mahogany tree).

❹ Mangrove

Mangrove forest ecosystems provide both food and protected nursery areas for fish, shellfish, and crustaceans. **Best place to see them:** Along Biscayne National Park shoreline, at Big Cypress National Preserve, and within Everglades National Park, especially around the Caple Sable area.

❺ Gumbo Limbo

Sometimes called "tourist trees" because of peeling reddish bark (not unlike sunburns). **Best place to see them:** Everglades National Park's Gumbo Limbo Trail and assorted spots throughout the expansive Everglades.

FAUNA

❶ American Alligator

In all likelihood, on your visit to the Everglades you'll see at least a gator or two. These carnivorous creatures can be found throughout the Everglades swampy wetlands.

Best place to see them: Loxahatchee National Wildlife Refuge (also sheltering the endangered Everglades snail kite) and within Everglades National Park at Shark Valley or Anhinga Trail. Sometimes (logically enough) gators hang out along Alligator Alley, basking in early morning or late-afternoon sun along four-lane I–75.

❷ American Crocodile

Crocs gravitate to fresh or brackish water, subsisting on birds, fish, snails, frogs, and small mammals.

Best place to see them: Within Everglades National Park, Big Cypress National Preserve, and protected grounds in or around Billie Swamp Safari.

❸ Eastern Coral Snake

This venomous snake burrows in underbrush, preying on lizards, frogs, and smaller snakes.

Best place to see them: Snakes typically shy away from people, but try Snake Bight or Eco Pond near Flamingo, where birds are also prevalent.

❹ Florida Panther

Struggling for survival amid loss of habitat, these shy, tan-colored cats now number around 100, up from lows of near 30.

Best place to see them: Protected grounds of Billie Swamp Safari sometimes provide sightings during tours. Signage on roadway linking Tamiami Trail and Alligator Alley warns of panther crossings, but sightings are rare.

❺ Green Tree Frog

Typically bright green with white or yellow stripes, these nocturnal creatures thrive in swamps and brackish water.

Best place to see them: Within Everglades National Park, especially in or near water.

● =Extremely Common ● =Very Common ● =Somewhat Common ● =Rare

BIRDS

❶ Anhinga

The lack of oil glands for waterproofing feathers helps this bird to dive as well as chase and spear fish with its pointed beak. The Anhinga is also often called a "water turkey" because of its long tail, or a "snake bird" because of its long neck.

Best place to see them: The Anhinga Trail, which also is known for attracting other wildlife to drink during especially dry winters.

❷ Blue-Winged Teal

Although it's predominantly brown and gray, this bird's powder-blue wing patch becomes visible in flight. Next to the mallard, the blue-winged teal is North America's second most abundant duck, and thrives particularly well in the Everglades.

Best place to see them: Near ponds and marshy areas of Everglades National Park or Big Cypress National Preserve.

❸ Great Blue Heron

This bird has a varied palate and enjoys feasting on everything from frogs, snakes, and mice to shrimp, aquatic insects, and sometimes even other birds! The all-white version, which at one time was considered a separate species, is quite common to the Everglades.

Best place to see them: Loxahatchee National Wildlife Refuge or Shark Valley in Everglades National Park.

❹ Great Egret

Once decimated by plume hunters, these monogamous, long-legged white birds with S-shaped necks feed in wetlands, nest in trees, and hang out in colonies that often include heron or other egret species.

Best place to see them: Throughout Everglades National Park, along Alligator Alley, and sometimes even on the fringes of Greater Fort Lauderdale.

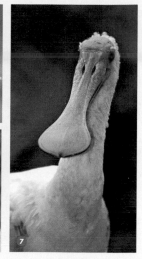

5 Greater Flamingo

Flocking together and using long legs and webbed feet to stir shallow waters and mud flats, color comes a couple of years after hatching from ingesting shrimplike crustaceans along with fish, fly larvae, and plankton.
Best place to see them: Try Snake Bight or Eco Pond, near Flamingo Marina.

6 Osprey

Making a big comeback from chemical pollutant endangerment, ospreys (sometimes confused with bald eagles) are distinguished by black eyestripes down their faces. Gripping pads on feet with curved claws help them pluck fish from water.
Best place to see them: Look near water, where they're fishing for lunch in the shallow areas. Try the coasts, bays, and ponds of Everglades National Park. They also gravitate to trees You can usually spot them from the Gulf Coast Visitor Center, or you can observe them via boating in the Ten Thousand Islands.

7 Roseate Spoonbill

These gregarious pink-and-white birds gravitate toward mangroves, feeding on fish, insects, amphibians, and some plants. They have long, spoon-like bills, and their feathers can have a touch of red and yellow. These birds appear in the Everglades year-round.
Best place to see them: Sandy Key, southwest of Flamingo, is a spoonbill nocturnal roosting spot, but at sunrise these colorful birds head out over Eco Pond to favored day hangouts throughout Everglades National Park.

8 Wood Stork

Recognizable by featherless heads and prominent bills, these birds submerge in water to scoop up hapless fish. They are most common in the early spring and often easiest to spot in the morning.
Best place to see them: Amid the Ten Thousand Island areas, Nine Mile Pond, Mrazek Pond, and in the mangroves at Paurotis Pond.

● =Extremely Common ● =Very Common ● =Somewhat Common ● =Rare

THE STORY OF THE EVERGLADES

Dreams of draining southern Florida took hold in the early 1800s, expanding in the early 1900s to convert large tracts from wetlands to agricultural acreage. By the 1920s, towns like Fort Lauderdale and Miami boomed, and the sugar industry—which came to be known as "Big Sugar"—established its first sugar mills. In 1947 Everglades National Park opened as a refuge for wildlife.

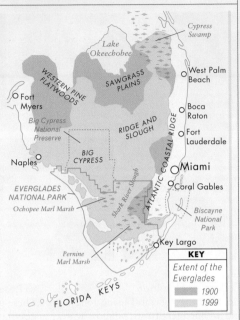

Cypress Swamp

Lake Okeechobee

WESTERN PINE FLATWOODS

SAWGRASS PLAINS

West Palm Beach

Fort Myers

Boca Raton

Big Cypress National Preserve

RIDGE AND SLOUGH

Fort Lauderdale

Naples

BIG CYPRESS

Miami

Coral Gables

EVERGLADES NATIONAL PARK

Ochopee Marl Marsh

ATLANTIC COASTAL RIDGE

Shark River Slough

Biscayne National Park

Key Largo

Pernine Marl Marsh

FLORIDA KEYS

KEY

Extent of the Everglades
- 1900
- 1999

Meanwhile, the sugar industry grew. In its infancy, about 175,000 tons of raw sugar per year was produced from fields totaling about 50,000 acres. But once the U.S. embargo stopped sugar imports from Cuba in 1960 and laws restricting acreage were lifted, Big Sugar took off. Less than five years later, the industry produced 572,000 tons of sugar and occupied nearly a quarter of a million acres.

Fast-forward to 2008, to what was hailed as the biggest conservation deal in U.S. history since the creation of the national parks. A trailblazing restoration strategy hinged on creating a water flow-way between Lake Okeechobee and the Everglades by buying up and flooding 187,000 acres of land. The country's largest producers of cane sugar agreed to sell the necessary 187,000 acres to the state of Florida for $1.75 billion. Environmentalists cheered.

But within months, news broke of a scaled-back land acquisition plan: $1.34 billion to buy 180,000 acres. By spring 2009, the restoration plan had shrunk to $536,000 to buy 73,000 acres. With the purchase still in limbo, critics claim the state might overpay for acreage appraised at pre-recession values and proponents fear dwindling revenues may derail the plan altogether.

The Big Sugar land deal is part of a larger effort to preserve the Everglades. In 2010, two separate lawsuits charged the state, along with the United States Environmental Protection Agency, with stalling Everglades cleanup that was supposed to begin in 2006. "Glacial delay" is how one judge put it. The state must reduce phosphorus levels in water that flows to the Everglades or face fines and sanctions for violating the federal Clean Water Act. The fate of the Everglades remains in the balance.

3

Updated by
Lynne Helm

More than 1.5 million acres of South Florida's 4.3 million acres of subtropical, watery wilderness were given national-park status and protection in 1947 with the creation of Everglades National Park. It's one of the country's largest national parks and is recognized by the world community as a Wetland of International Importance, an International Biosphere Reserve, and a World Heritage Site. Come here if you want to spend the day biking, hiking, or boating in deep, raw wilderness with lots of wildlife.

To the east of Everglades National Park, Biscayne National Park brings forth a pristine, magical, subtropical Florida. It's the nation's largest marine park and the largest national park within the continental United States boasting living coral reefs. A small portion of the park's 172,000 acres consists of mainland coast and outlying islands, but 95% remains submerged. Of particular interest are the mangroves and their tangled masses of stiltlike roots that thicken shorelines. These "walking trees," as some locals call them, have curved prop roots arching down from trunks, and aerial roots that drop from branches. The roots of these trees can filter salt from water and create a coastal nursery that sustains myriad types of marine life. You can see Miami's high-rise buildings from many of Biscayne's 44 islands, but the park is virtually undeveloped and large enough for escaping everything that Miami and the Upper Keys have become. To truly escape, grab scuba-diving or snorkeling gear and lose yourself in the wonders of the coral reefs.

On the northern edge of Everglades National Park lies Big Cypress National Preserve, one of South Florida's least developed watersheds. Established by Congress in 1974 to protect the Everglades, it comprises extensive tracts of prairie, marsh, pinelands, forested swamps, and sloughs. Hunting is allowed, as is off-road-vehicle use. Come here if you like alligators. Stop at the Oasis Visitor Center's boardwalk with alligators lounging underneath, and then drive Loop Road for a back-woods experience. If time and desire for watery adventure permits, kayak or canoe the Turner River.

Surrounding the parks and preserve are communities where you'll find useful outfitters: Everglades City, Florida City, and Homestead.

PLANNING

WHEN TO GO

Winter is the best, and busiest, time to visit the Everglades. Temperatures and mosquito activity are more tolerable, low water levels concentrate the resident wildlife, and migratory birds swell the avian population. In late spring the weather turns hot and rainy, and tours and facilities are less crowded. Migratory birds depart, and you must look harder to see wildlife. Summer brings intense sun and afternoon rainstorms. Water levels rise and mosquitoes descend, making outdoor activity virtually unbearable, unless you protect yourself with netting. Mosquito repellent is a necessity any time of year.

GETTING HERE AND AROUND

Miami International Airport (MIA) is 34 miles from Homestead and 47 miles from the eastern access to Everglades National Park. ⇨ *For MIA airline information, see the Travel Smart chapter.* Shuttles run between MIA and Homestead. Southwest Florida International Airport (RSW), in Fort Myers, a little over an hour's drive from Everglades City, is the closest major airport to the Everglades' western entrance. On-demand taxi transportation from the airport to Everglades City is available from MBA Airport Transportation and costs $150 for up to three passengers ($10 each for additional passengers).

Contacts MBA Airport Transportation. ☏ *239/225–0428* ⊕ *www.mbaairport.com.*

HOTELS

Accommodations near the parks range from inexpensive to moderate and offer off-season rates in summer, when rampant mosquito populations discourage spending time outdoors, especially at dusk. If you're devoting several days to exploring the east-coast Everglades, stay in park campgrounds; 11 miles away in Homestead–Florida City, where there are reasonably priced chain motels and RV parks; in the Florida Keys; or in the Greater Miami–Fort Lauderdale area. Lodgings and campgrounds are also plentiful on the Gulf Coast (in Everglades City, Marco Island, and Naples, the latter with the most upscale area accommodations).

RESTAURANTS

Dining in the Everglades area centers on mom-and-pop places serving hearty home-style food, and small eateries specializing in fresh local fare: alligator, fish, stone crab, frogs' legs, and Florida lobster from the Keys. American Indian restaurants serve local favorites as well as catfish, Indian fry bread (a flour-and-water flatbread), and pumpkin bread. A growing Hispanic population around Homestead means plenty of authentic, inexpensive Latin cuisine, with an emphasis on Cuban and

Mexican dishes. Restaurants in Everglades City, especially those along the river, specialize in fresh (often just hours out of the water) seafood including particularly succulent, sustainable stone crab. These mostly rustic places are ultracasual and often close in late summer or fall. For finer dining, head for Marco Island or Naples.

Hotel and restaurant reviews have been shortened. For full information, visit Fodors.com.

WHAT IT COSTS				
	$	**$$**	**$$$**	**$$$$**
Restaurants	under $15	$15–$20	$21–$30	over $30
Hotels	under $200	$200–$300	$301–$400	over $400

Restaurant prices are the average cost of a main course at dinner or, if dinner is not served, at lunch. Hotel prices are the lowest cost of a standard double room in high season.

ABOUT ACTIVITIES

While outfitters are listed with the parks and preserve, see our What's Nearby section later in this chapter for information about each town.

EVERGLADES NATIONAL PARK

45 miles southwest of Miami International Airport.

If you're heading across South Florida on U.S. 41 from Miami to Naples, you'll breeze right through the Everglades. Also known as Tamiami Trail, this mostly two-lane road skirts the edge of Everglades National Park and cuts across the Big Cypress National Preserve. You'll also be near the park if you're en route from Miami to the Florida Keys on U.S. 1, which cuts through Homestead and Florida City—communities east of the main park entrance. Basically, if you're in South Florida, you can't escape at least fringes of the Everglades. With tourist strongholds like Miami, Naples, and the Florida Keys so close, travelers from all over the world typically make day trips to the park.

Everglades National Park has three main entry points: the park headquarters at Ernest F. Coe Visitor Center, southwest of Homestead and Florida City; the Shark Valley area, accessed by Tamiami Trail (U.S. 41); and the Gulf Coast Visitor Center, south of Everglades City to the west and closest to Naples.

Explore on your own or participate in ranger-led hikes, bicycle or bird-watching tours, and canoe trips. The variety of these excursions is greatest from mid-December through Easter, and some adventures (canoe trips, for instance) typically aren't offered in sweltering summer. Among the more popular are the Anhinga Amble, a 50-minute walk around the Taylor Slough (departs from the Royal Palm Visitor Center), and the Early Bird Special, a 90-minute walk centered on birdlife (departs from Flamingo Visitor Center). Check with visitor centers for details.

CLOSE UP

War on Pythons

In 2013, Florida launched its first Python Challenge™ to put the kibosh on Burmese pythons, those deadly snakes literally squeezing the life out of Everglades wonders, from colorful birds to full-grown deer to gators.

The state-sponsored winter competition was a trailblazer, attracting amateurs and professionals alike from 38 states and Canada to help decimate this growing environmental threat. Sadly, only 68 pythons were captured of thousands estimated lurking in the Everglades.

Then the Challenge was scrapped, although the state continued its war with a python-removal program, issuing hunting permits to qualified applicants. In 2016, the Challenge made a comeback and now seems to be on again.

Even experienced Gladesmen with special permits to stalk these predators have trouble finding them—partly because tan, splotchy skin provides natural camouflage for slithering about and causing mayhem within the ecosystem. Unseasonably warm winter weather also leaves pythons, growing up to 26 feet long, without incentive to boldly expose themselves for sunning.

In 2012, the U.S. Department of the Interior—hailing a milestone in Everglades protection—announced a nationwide ban on the importation of Burmese pythons and other nonnative, large constrictor snakes, including African pythons and the yellow anaconda. The ban has stuck thus far and is helping with the problem.

No matter what the format for the state's effort to eradicate pythons, its war against invasive species and the efforts to protect Everglades wildlife continue unabated.

—Lynne Helm

PARK ESSENTIALS

Admission Fees The fee is $25 per vehicle; and $8 per pedestrian, bicycle, or motorcycle. Payable at gates, the admission is good for seven consecutive days at all park entrances. Annual passes are $40.

Admission Hours Open daily, year-round, both the main entrance near Florida City and Homestead, and the Gulf Coast entrance are open 24 hours a day. The Shark Valley entrance is open 8:30 am to 6 pm.

COE VISITOR CENTER TO FLAMINGO

About 30 miles southwest of Miami.

The most utilized access to Everglades National Park is via the park headquarters entrance southwest of Homestead and Florida City. If you're coming to the Everglades from Miami, take Route 836 West to Route 826/874 South to the Homestead Extension of Florida's Turnpike, U.S. 1, and Krome Avenue (Route 997/old U.S. 27). To reach the Ernest F. Coe Visitor Center from Homestead, go right (west) from U.S. 1 or Krome Avenue onto Route 9336 (Florida's only four-digit route) in Florida City and follow signage to the park entrance.

Route 9336 travels 38 miles from the Ernest F. Coe Visitor Center southwest to the Florida Bay at Flamingo. It crosses a section of the park's eight distinct ecosystems: hardwood hammock, freshwater prairie, pinelands, freshwater slough, cypress, coastal prairie, mangrove, and marine-estuarine. Route highlights include a dwarf cypress forest, the transition zone between saw grass and mangrove forest, and a wealth of wading birds at Mrazek and Coot Bay ponds—where in early morning or late afternoon you can observe them feeding. Be forewarned, however, that flamingo sightings are extremely rare. Boardwalks, looped trails, several short spurs, and observation platforms help you stay dry. You may want to stop along the way to walk several short trails (each takes about 30 minutes): the wheelchair-accessible Anhinga Trail, which cuts through saw-grass marsh and allows you to see lots of wildlife (be on the lookout for alligators and the trail's namesake waterbirds: anhingas); the junglelike—yet also wheelchair-accessible—Gumbo-Limbo Trail; the Pinelands Trail, where you can see the park's limestone bedrock; the Pahayokee Overlook Trail, ending at an observation tower; and the Mahogany Hammock Trail, with its dense growth. ■TIP→ Before heading out on the trails, inquire about insect and weather conditions to plan accordingly, stocking up on bug repellent, sunscreen, and water as necessary. Even on seemingly sunny days, it's smart to bring rain gear.

EXPLORING

To explore this section of the park, follow Route 9336 from the park entrance to Flamingo; you'll find plenty of opportunities to stop along the way, and assorted activities to pursue in the Flamingo area. Other than campgrounds, there are no lodging options within the national park at this writing.

FAMILY **Ernest F. Coe Visitor Center.** Get your park map here, 365 days a year, but don't just grab and go; this visitor center's numerous interactive exhibits and films are well worth your time. The 15-minute film *River of Life*, updated frequently, provides a succinct park overview. A movie on hurricanes and a 35-minute wildlife film for children are available upon request. Learn about the Great Water Debate, detailing how the last century's gung ho draining of swampland for residential and agricultural development also cut off water-supply routes for precious wetlands in the Everglades ecosystem. You'll also find a schedule of daily ranger-led activities, mainly walks and talks; information on the popular Nike missile site tour (harking back to the Cuban missile crisis era); and details about canoe rentals and boat tours at Flamingo. The Everglades Discovery Shop stocks books, kids' stuff, plus insect repellent, sunscreen, and water. Coe Visitor Center, which has restrooms, is outside park gates, so you can stop in without paying park admission. ⊠ *40001 State Rd. 9336, Homestead ✚ 11 miles southwest of Homestead* ☎ *305/242–7700* ⌫ *Free.*

FAMILY **Flamingo.** At the far end of the main road to the Flamingo community along Florida Bay, you'll find a marina (with beverages, snacks, and a gift shop), visitor center, and campground, with nearby hiking and nature trails. Despite the name, what you are unlikely to find here are flamingos. To improve your luck for glimpsing these flamboyant pink birds with toothpick legs, check out Snake Bight Trail, starting about 5 miles from the Flamingo outpost, but they are a rare sight indeed. Before

Hurricanes Katrina and Wilma hit in 2005, a lodge, cabins, and restaurant facilities in Flamingo provided Everglades National Park's only accommodations. Rebuilding of Flamingo Lodge, long projected, has yet to materialize. For now, you can still pitch tents or bring RVs to the campground, where improvements include solar-heated showers and electricity for RV sites. A houseboat rental concession offers a pair of 35-footers each sleeping six and equipped with shower, toilet, bedding, kitchenware, stereo, and depth finder. The houseboats (thankfully air-conditioned) have 60-horsepower outboards and rent for $350 per night, plus a $200 fuel deposit. ⌧ *Flamingo* ⊕ *www.nps.gov/ever/planyourvisit/flamdirections*.

> ### GOOD READS
>
> ■ *The Everglades: River of Grass.* This circa-1947 classic by pioneering conservationist Marjory Stoneman Douglas (1890–1998) is a must-read.
>
> ■ *Everglades Wildguide.* Jean Craighead George gives an informative account of the park's natural history in this official National Park Service handbook.
>
> ■ *Everglades: The Park Story.* Wildlife biologist William B. Robertson Jr. presents the park's flora, fauna, and history.

NEED A BREAK Worthwhile spots to pull over for a picnic are **Paurotis Pond**, about 10 miles north of Florida Bay, or **Nine Mile Pond**, less than 30 miles from the main visitor center. Another option is along **Bear Lake**, 2 miles north of the Flamingo Visitor Center.

FAMILY **Flamingo Visitor Center.** Check the schedule here for ranger-led activities, such as naturalist talks, trail hikes, and evening programs in the 100-seat campground amphitheater, replacing the old gathering spot destroyed by 2005 hurricanes. Mosquito repellent will be your favorite take-along here. If you're famished and haven't packed your own picnic, the center's Buttonwood Cafe (closed in summer) serves sandwiches, salads, and such. There's no other option for miles. You'll find natural history exhibits and pamphlets on canoe, hiking, and biking trails in the second-floor Florida Bay Flamingo Museum, accessible only by stairway and a steep ramp. You can get drinks and snacks at the marina store when the café is closed. ⌧ *1 Flamingo Lodge Hwy., Flamingo* ☎ *239/695–2945, 239/695–3101 marina* ⌦ *Free*.

FAMILY **Royal Palm Visitor Center.** Ideal for when there's limited time to experience the Everglades, this small center with a bookstore and vending machines permits access to the popular, paved **Anhinga Trail boardwalk,** where in winter spotting alligators congregating in watering holes is virtually guaranteed. Neighboring **Gumbo Limbo Trail** takes you through a hardwood hammock. Combining these short strolls (½ mile or so) allows you to experience two Everglades ecosystems. Rangers conduct Anhinga Ambles in season (call ahead for times). A Glades Glimpse program takes place afternoons in season, as do starlight walks and bike tours. As always, arm yourself with insect repellent. If you have a mind for history, ask about narrated Nike missile site tours, stemming from the '60s-era Cuban missile crisis. ⌧ *Rte. 9336, Everglades National Park* ✛ *4 miles west of Ernest F. Coe Visitor Center* ☎ *305/242–7700*.

SPORTS AND THE OUTDOORS

BIRD-WATCHING

Some of the park's best birding is in the Flamingo area.

BOATING

The 99-mile inland **Wilderness Trail** between Flamingo and Everglades City is open to motorboats as well as canoes, although, depending on water levels, powerboats may have trouble navigating above White-water Bay. Flat-water canoeing and kayaking are best in winter, when temperatures are moderate, rainfall diminishes, and mosquitoes back off—a little, anyway. You don't need a permit for day trips, although there's a seven-day, $5 launch fee for all motorized boats brought into the park. The Flamingo area has well-marked canoe trails, but be sure to tell someone where you're going and when you expect to return. Getting lost is easy, and spending the night without proper gear can be unpleasant, if not dangerous.

FAMILY **Flamingo Lodge, Marina, and Everglades National Park Tours.** Everglades National Park's official concessionaire operates a marina, runs tours, and rents canoes, kayaks, and skiffs, secured by credit cards. A one-hour, 45-minute backcountry cruise aboard the 50-passenger *Pelican* winds under a heavy canopy of mangroves, revealing abundant wildlife—from alligators, crocodiles, and turtles to herons, hawks, and egrets. You can rent a 17-foot, 40-hp skiff starting at 7 am for a full day (returning by 4 pm), a half day, or for as little as two hours; there is a $100 credit card deposit required. Canoes for up to three paddlers can be rented for two hours (minimum), four hours, eight hours, or overnight. Family canoes for up to four are available, and the concessionaire also rents bikes, binoculars, rods, reels, and other equipment for up to a full day. Feeling sticky after a day in the Glades? Hot showers are available ($). Flamingo Lodge, a victim of massive hurricane damage in 2005, remains closed pending a long-delayed fresh start. ■TIP➔ An experimental Eco Tent of canvas and wood, unveiled in winter 2012–13, was booked solid for the season. Built by University of Miami architecture students, Eco Tent sleeps four, has a table and chairs, and wins rave reviews from designers, park officials, and campers. It's a prototype for up to 40 more units, once funding is secured. ⊠ 1 *Flamingo Lodge Hwy., on Buttonwood Canal, Flamingo* ☏ *239/695–3101, 239/695–0124 Eco Tent reservations* ⊕ *www.evergladesnationalparkboattoursflamingo.com* ☏ *Pelican cruise from $37.63; skiff rentals from $80 (2 hrs); 3-person canoe rentals from $20.*

GULF COAST ENTRANCE

To reach the park's western gateway, take U.S. 41 west from Miami for 77 miles, turn left (south) onto Route 29, and travel another 3 miles through Everglades City to the Gulf Coast Ranger Station. From Naples on the Gulf Coast, take U.S. 41 east for 35 miles, and turn right onto Route 29.

FAMILY **Gulf Coast Visitor Center.** The best place to bone up on Everglades National Park's watery western side is at this center just south of Everglades City (5 miles south of Tamiami Trail) where rangers can give you the park lowdown and address your inquiries. In winter, backcountry campers purchase permits here and canoeists check in for trips to the Ten Thousand Islands and 99-mile Wilderness Waterway Trail. Nature lovers view interpretive exhibits on local flora and fauna while waiting for naturalist-led boat trips. In season (Christmas through Easter), rangers lead bike tours and canoe trips. A selection of about 30 nature presentations and orientation films are available by request for view on a TV screen. Admission is free only to this section, since no direct roads from here link to other parts of the park. ⊠ *815 Oyster Bar La., off Rte. 29, Everglades City* ☎ *239/695–3311.*

SPORTS AND THE OUTDOORS
BOATING AND KAYAKING
FAMILY **Everglades National Park Boat Tours.** In conjunction with boat tours at Flamingo, this operation runs 1½-hour trips through the Ten Thousand Islands National Wildlife Refuge. Adventure-seekers often see dolphins, manatees, bald eagles, and roseate spoonbills. In peak season (November–April), 49-passenger boats run on the hour and half hour daily. Mangrove wilderness tours on smaller boats are for up to six passengers. These one-hour, 45-minute trips are the best option to see alligators. The outfitter also rents canoes and kayaks. Ask about group discounts. ⊠ *Gulf Coast Visitor Center, 815 Oyster Bar La., Everglades City* ☎ *239/695–2591, 866/628–7275* ⊕ *www.evergladesnationalparkboattoursgulfcoast.com/index.php* ⌦ *Tours from $40.*

Fodor'sChoice **Everglades Rentals & Eco Adventures.** Ivey House Inn houses this estab-
★ lished, year-round source for guided Everglades paddling tours and rentals for canoes and kayaks. Shuttles can deliver you to major launching areas such as Turner River. Highlights include bird and gator sightings, mangrove forests, no-man's-land beaches, and spectacular sunsets. Longer adventures include equipment rental, guide, and meals. ⊠ *Ivey House, 107 Camellia St., Everglades City* ☎ *877/567–0679, 239/695–3299* ⊕ *www.evergladesadventures.com* ⌦ *Rentals from $35.*

SHARK VALLEY

23½ miles west of Florida's Turnpike, off Tamiami Trail. Approximately 45 mins west of Miami.

You won't see sharks at Shark Valley. The name comes from the Shark River, also called the River of Grass, flowing through the area. Several species of shark swim up this river from the coast (about 45 miles south of Shark Valley) to give birth, though not at this particular spot.

Much skill is required to navigate boats through the shallow, muddy waters of the Everglades.

Young sharks (called pups), vulnerable to being eaten by adult sharks and other predators, gain strength in waters of the slough before heading out to sea.

The Shark Valley entrance to the national park is on U.S. 41 (Tamiami Trail), 25 miles west of Florida's Turnpike (SR 821) or 39 miles east of SR 29. Some GPS units don't recognize it. If asked for a cross street, use U.S. 41.

EXPLORING

Although Shark Valley is the national park's north entrance, no roads here lead directly to other parts of the park. However, it's still worth stopping to take the two-hour narrated bio-diesel tram tour from Shark Valley Tram Tours. Stop at the halfway point and ascend the Shark Valley Observation Tower via the ramp.

Prefer to do the trail on foot? It takes nerve to walk the paved 15-mile loop in Shark Valley, because in the winter months alligators lie alongside the road, basking in the sun—most, however, do move out of the way.

You also can ride a bicycle (the folks who operate the tram tours also rent one-speed, well-used bikes daily from 8:30 to 4 for $9 per hour with helmets available). Near the bike-rental area a short boardwalk trail meanders through saw grass, and another passes through a tropical hardwood hammock.

FAMILY **Shark Valley Observation Tower.** At the Shark Valley trail's end (really, the halfway point of the 15-mile loop), you can pause to navigate this tower, first built in 1984, spiraling nearly 50 feet upward. Once on top, you'll find the River of Grass gloriously spreads out as far as you can see.

Observe waterbirds as well as alligators, and maybe even river otters crossing the road. The tower has a wheelchair-accessible ramp to the top. If you don't want to take the tram from the Shark Valley Visitor Center, you can either hike or bike in, but private cars are not allowed. ⊠ *Shark Valley Loop Rd., Miami* ⊕ *www.sharkvalleytramtours.com.*

FAMILY **Shark Valley Visitor Center.** The old ramshackle outpost has been razed altogether to make room for a nice picnic area, and a new, white, concrete-block building nearby is now in place with the bike-rental concession and a bookstore (run by the Everglades Association) with hats, sunscreen, insect repellent, postcards, and other souvenirs. Park rangers are still here, ready for your questions. ⊠ *36000 S.W. 8th St., Miami* ✛ *23½ miles west of Florida's Tpke., off Tamiami Trail* ☎ *305/221–8776.*

> ### THE EVERGLADES WITH KIDS
>
> Although kids of all ages can enjoy the park, those six and older typically get the most out of the experience. Predators including alligators abound. Consider how much you as a supervising adult will enjoy keeping tabs on tiny ones around so much water and so many teeth. Some children are frightened by sheer wilderness.

SPORTS AND THE OUTDOORS

BIKING

FAMILY **Shark Valley Bicycle Rentals.** You can gaze at gators while getting your exercise, too, by renting a bike at the Shark Valley Visitor Center from the same outfitter that operates the tram tours. Pedal along 15 miles of paved, level roadway (no hills or dales) to the observation tower and back while keeping an eye on plentiful roadside reptiles. Bikes are single gear, coaster-style two-wheelers with baskets and helmets available, along with some child seats for kids under 35 pounds. The well-used fleet also includes a few 20-inch junior models. You'll need a driver's license or other ID for a deposit. Arm yourself with water, insect repellent, and sunscreen. ⊠ *Shark Valley Visitor Center, Shark Valley Loop Rd., Shark Valley* ☎ *305/221–8776* ⊕ *www.sharkvalleytramtours.com/biking* 🖙 *Rentals from $9 per hr.*

BOATING

Many Everglades-area tours operate only in season, roughly November through April.

FAMILY **Buffalo Tiger's Airboat Tours.** A former chief of Florida's Miccosukee tribe—Buffalo Tiger, who died in January 2015 at the age of 94—founded this Shark Valley–area tour operation, and his spirit carries on. Savvy guides narrate the trip to an old Indian camp on the north side of Tamiami Trail from the Native American perspective. Don't worry about airboat noise, since engines are shut down during informative talks. The 45-minute tours go 10–5 Saturday through Thursday, with longer private tours available. Look online for discount coupons. Reservations are not required, and credit cards are now accepted at this outpost. ⊠ *29708 S.W. 8th St., 5 miles east of Shark Valley, 25 miles west of Florida's Tpke., Miami* ☎ *305/559–5250* ⊕ *www.buffalotigersairboattours.com* 🖙 *From $24.75.*

GUIDED TOURS

FAMILY **Shark Valley Tram Tours.** Starting at the Shark Valley Visitor Center, these popular two-hour, narrated tours ($24) on bio-diesel trams follow a 15-mile loop road—great for viewing gators—into the interior, stopping at a wheelchair-accessible observation tower. Bring your own water. Reservations are strongly recommended December through April. ⊠ *Shark Valley Visitor Center, Shark Valley Loop Rd., Miami* ☎ *305/221–8455* ⊕ *www.sharkvalleytramtours.com* ⌨ *$24.*

BIG CYPRESS NATIONAL PRESERVE

3

Through the early 1960s the world's largest cypress-logging industry prospered in Big Cypress Swamp until nearly all the trees were cut down. With the demise of the industry, government entities began buying parcels. Now more than 729,000 acres, or nearly half of the swamp, form this national preserve. "Big" refers not to the new-growth trees but to the swamp, jutting into the north edge of Everglades National Park like a jigsaw-puzzle piece. Size and strategic location make Big Cypress an important link in the region's hydrological system, where rainwater first flows through the preserve, then south into the park, and eventually into Florida Bay. Its variegated pattern of wet prairies, ponds, marshes, sloughs, and strands provides a wildlife sanctuary, and thanks to a policy of balanced land use—"use without abuse"—the watery wilderness is devoted to recreation as well as to research and preservation. Bald cypress trees that may look dead are actually dormant, with green needles springing to life in spring. The preserve allows—in limited areas—hiking, hunting, and off-road-vehicle use (airboat, swamp buggy, four-wheel drive) by permit. Compared with Everglades National Park, the preserve is less developed and hosts fewer visitors. That makes it ideal for naturalists, birders, and hikers preferring to see more wildlife than people.

Several scenic drives link from Tamiami Trail, some requiring four-wheel-drive vehicles, especially in wet summer months. A few lead to camping areas and roadside picnic spots. Apart from the Oasis Visitor Center, popular as a springboard for viewing alligators, the newer Big Cypress Swamp Welcome Center features a platform for watching manatees. Both centers, along Tamiami Trail between Miami and Naples, feature a top-notch 25-minute film on Big Cypress.

PARK ESSENTIALS

Admission Fees There's no admission fee to visit the preserve.

Admission Hours The park is open 24 hours daily, year-round. Accessible only by boat, Adams Key is for day use only.

Contacts Big Cypress National Preserve. ☎ *239/695–1201* ⊕ *www.nps.gov/bicy.*

EXPLORING

FAMILY **Big Cypress Swamp Welcome Center.** As a sister to the Oasis Visitor Center, the newer Big Cypress Swamp Welcome Center on the preserve's western side has abundant information, as well as restrooms, picnic facilities, and a 70-seat auditorium. An outdoor breezeway showcases an interactive Big Cypress watershed exhibit, illustrating Florida water flow. It's a convenient place to stop when crossing from either coast. ■TIP→ Love manatees? A platform allows for viewing these intriguing mammals, attracted to warm water. (They were possibly once mistaken for mermaids by thirsty or love-starved ancient sailors.) ✉ *33000 Tamiami Trail E, 5 miles east of SR29, Ochopee* ☎ *239/695–4758* ⊕ *www.nps.gov/bicy/planyourvisit/visitorcenters.htm* ✎ *Free.*

FAMILY **Clyde Butcher's Big Cypress Gallery.** For taking home swamp memories in stark black and white, you can't do better than picking up a postcard, calendar, or more serious pieces of artwork by photographer Clyde Butcher at his namesake trailside gallery. Butcher, a big guy with an even bigger beard, is an affable personality renowned for his knowledge of the Glades and his ability to capture its magnetism through a large-format lens. Even if you can't afford his big stuff, you're warmly invited to gaze. Out back, Butcher and his wife, Niki, also rent a bungalow ($225 per night, October–April) and a cottage ($350 per night, year-round). ■TIP→ Ask about Clyde's private photography Swamp Walk Tours, bookable in advance, September through March. You'll need a hat, long pants, old sneakers, and—because you *will* get wet—spare, dry clothing. ✉ *MM 54.5, 52388 Tamiami Trail, Ochopee* ☎ *239/695–2428* ⊕ *www.clydebutchersbigcypressgallery.com.*

FAMILY **Oasis Visitor Center.** The big attraction at Oasis Visitor Center, on the east side of Big Cypress Preserve, is the observation deck for viewing fish, birds, and other wildlife. A small butterfly garden's native plants seasonally attract winged wonders. Inside, you'll find an exhibit area, bookshop, and a theater showing an informative 25-minute film on Big Cypress Preserve swamplands. Get your gator watch on at the center's observation deck where big alligators congregate. Leashed pets are allowed, but not on the boardwalk deck. Here's where you also can get off-road-vehicle permits. ✉ *52105 Tamiami Trail, Ochopee* ✛ *24 miles east of Everglades City, 50 miles west of Miami, 20 miles west of Shark Valley* ☎ *239/695–1201* ⊕ *www.nps.gov/bicy/planyourvisit/ visitorcenters* ✎ *Free.*

FAMILY **Ochopee Post Office.** North America's smallest post office is a former irrigation pipe shed on the Tamiami Trail's south side. Blink and you'll risk missing it. To support this picturesque outpost during an era of postal service cutbacks, why not buy a postcard of this one-room shack with a U.S. flag outside for mailing to whomever would appreciate it? Mail packages or buy money orders here, too. ✉ *38000 E. Tamiami Trail, 4 miles east of Rte. 29, Ochopee* ☎ *239/695–2099.*

WHERE TO EAT

$ ✕ **Joanie's Blue Crab Cafe.** West of the nation's tiniest post office by a
SEAFOOD   quarter mile or so, you'll find this red barn of a place dishing out
catfish, frogs' legs, gator, grouper, burgers, salads, and (no surprise
here) an abundance of soft-shell crabs, crab cakes, and she-crab soup.
Entrées are reasonably priced, and peanut butter pie makes for a solid
finish. Known for: beer and wine only; indoor/outdoor seating; early
closing (5 pm). $ *Average main: $13* ✉ *39395 Tamiami Trail, Ochopee*
✛ *About 3½ miles east of Hwy. 29, less than a mile west of Ochopee
post office* ☎ *239/695–2682* ⊕ *www.joaniesbluecrabcafe.com* ☾ *Closed
Mon. (varies seasonally; call to confirm).*

SPORTS AND THE OUTDOORS

There are three types of trails—walking (including part of the extensive
Florida National Scenic Trail), canoeing, and bicycling. All three trail
types are easily accessed from the Tamiami Trail near the preserve visitor center, and one boardwalk trail departs from the center. Canoe and
bike equipment can be rented from outfitters in Everglades City, 24
miles west, and Naples, 40 miles west.

Hikers can tackle the Florida National Scenic Trail, which begins in
the preserve and is divided into segments of 6½ to 28 miles each. Two
5-mile trails, Concho Billy and Fire Prairie, can be accessed off Turner
River Road, a few miles east. Turner River Road and Birdon Road
form a 17-mile gravel loop drive that's excellent for birding. Bear Island
has about 32 miles of scenic, flat, looped trails that are ideal for bicycling. Most trails are hard-packed lime rock, but a few miles are gravel.
Cyclists share the road with off-road vehicles, most plentiful from mid-
November through December.

To see the best variety of wildlife from your vehicle, follow 26-mile
Loop Road, south of U.S. 41 and west of Shark Valley, where alligators,
raccoons, and soft-shell turtles crawl around beside the gravel road,
often swooped upon by swallowtail kites and brown-shouldered hawks.
Stop at H. P. Williams Roadside Park, west of the Oasis, and walk along
the boardwalk to spy gators, turtles, and garfish in the river waters.

RANGER PROGRAMS

From the Oasis Visitor Center you can get in on the seasonal ranger-
led or self-guided activities, such as campfire and wildlife talks, hikes,
slough slogs, and canoe excursions. The 8-mile Turner River Canoe
Trail begins nearby and crosses through Everglades National Park
before ending in Chokoloskee Bay, near Everglades City. Rangers lead
four-hour canoe trips and two-hour swamp walks in season; call for
days and times. Bring shoes and long pants for swamp walks and be
prepared to wade at least knee-deep in water. Ranger program reservations are accepted up to 14 days in advance.

BISCAYNE NATIONAL PARK

Occupying 172,000 acres along the southern portion of Biscayne Bay, south of Miami and north of the Florida Keys, Biscayne National Park is 95% submerged, its terrain ranging from 4 feet above sea level to 60 feet below. Contained within are four distinct zones: Biscayne Bay, undeveloped upper Florida Keys, coral reefs, and coastal mangrove forest. Mangroves line mainland shores much as they do elsewhere along South Florida's protected waters. Biscayne Bay serves as a lobster sanctuary and a nursery for fish, sponges, crabs, and other sea life. Manatees and sea turtles frequent its warm, shallow waters. The park hosts legions of boaters and landlubbers gazing in awe over the bay.

3

GETTING HERE

To reach Biscayne National Park from Homestead, take Krome Avenue to Route 9336 (Palm Drive) and turn east. Follow Palm Drive about 8 miles until it becomes Southwest 344th Street, and follow signs to park headquarters in Convoy Point. The entry is 9 miles east of Homestead and 9 miles south and east of Exit 6 (Speedway Boulevard/Southwest 137th Avenue) off Florida's Turnpike.

PARK ESSENTIALS

Admission Fees There's no fee to enter Biscayne National Park, and you don't pay a fee to access the islands, but there's a $25 overnight camping fee that includes a $5 dock charge to berth vessels at some island docks. The park concession charges for trips to the coral reefs and islands.

Admission Hours The park is open daily, year-round.

Contacts Biscayne National Park. ✉ *Dante Fascell Visitor Center, 9700 S.W. 328th St., Homestead* ☎ *305/230–7275* ⊕ *www.nps.gov/bisc.*

EXPLORING

Biscayne is a magnet for diving, snorkeling, canoeing, birding, and, to some extent (if you have a private boat), camping. Elliott Key is the best place to hike.

Biscayne's corals range from soft, flagellant fans, plumes, and whips found chiefly in shallow patch reefs to the hard brain corals, elkhorn, and staghorn forms that can withstand depths and heavier shoreline wave action.

To the east, about 8 miles off the coast, 44 tiny keys stretch 18 nautical miles north to south, and are reached only by boat. No mainland commercial transportation operates to the islands, and only a handful are accessible: Elliott, Boca Chita, Adams, and Sands Keys, lying between Elliott and Boca Chita. The rest are wildlife refuges or have rocky shores or waters too shallow for boats. December through April, when the mosquito population is less aggressive, is the best time to explore. Bring repellent, sunscreen, and water.

Adams Key. A stone's throw from the western tip of Elliott Key and 9 miles southeast of Convoy Point, the island is open for day use. It was the onetime site of the Cocolobo Club, a yachting retreat known for hosting Presidents Harding, Hoover, Johnson, and Nixon as well as

other famous and infamous lumi-
naries. Hurricane Andrew blew
away what remained of club facilities in 1992. Adams Key has picnic
areas with grills, restrooms, dockage, and a short trail running along
the shore and through a hardwood
hammock. Rangers live on-island.
Access is by private boat, with no
pets or overnight docking allowed.
⊠ *Biscayne National Park* ⊕ *www.
nps.gov/bisc.*

Boca Chita Key. Ten miles northeast
of Convoy Point and about 12
miles south of the Cape Florida
Lighthouse on Key Biscayne, this
key once was owned by the late
Mark C. Honeywell, former president of Honeywell Company, and is
on the National Register of Historic Places for its 10 historic structures.
A half-mile hiking trail curves around the island's south side. Climb the
65-foot-high ornamental lighthouse (by ranger tour only) for a panoramic view of Miami or check out the cannon from the HMS *Fowey.*
There's no freshwater, access is by private boat only, and no pets are
allowed. Only portable toilets are on-site, with no sinks or showers. A
$25 fee for overnight docking (6 pm to 6 am) covers a campsite; pay at
the harbor's automated kiosk. ⊠ *Biscayne National Park.*

> ### BISCAYNE IN ONE DAY
>
> Most visitors come to snorkel
> or dive. Divers should plan to
> spend the morning on the water
> and the afternoon exploring the
> visitor center. The opposite is true
> for snorkelers, as snorkel trips
> (and one-tank shallow-dive trips)
> depart in the afternoon. If you
> want to hike as well, turn to the
> trails at Elliott Key—just be sure
> to apply insect repellent (and
> sunscreen, too, no matter what
> time of year).

FAMILY
Fodor's Choice
★

Dante Fascell Visitor Center. Go outside on the wide veranda to soak up
views across mangroves and Biscayne Bay at this Convoy Point visitor
center, which opened in 2002. Inside the museum, artistic vignettes and
on-request videos including the 11-minute *Spectrum of Life* explore
the park's four ecosystems, while the Touch Table gives both kids and
adults a feel for bones, feathers, and coral. Facilities include the park's
canoe and tour concession, restrooms with showers, a ranger information area, gift shop with books, and vending machines. Various ranger
programs take place daily during busy fall and winter seasons. Rangers give informal tours on Boca Chita key, but these must be arranged
in advance. A short trail and boardwalk lead to a jetty, and there are
picnic tables and grills. This is the only area of the park accessible
without a boat. You can snorkel from shore, but the water is shallow,
with sea grass and a mud bottom. ⊠ *9700 S.W. 328th St., Homestead*
☏ *305/230–7275* ⊕ *www.nps.gov/bisc* ⊡ *Free.*

FAMILY
Elliott Key. The largest of the islands, 9 miles east of Convoy Point,
Elliott Key has a mile-long loop trail on the bay side at the north end
of the campground. Boaters may dock at any of 36 slips; the fee for
staying overnight includes use of a tent area for up to six people in two
tents. Head out on your own to hike the 6-mile trail along so-called
Spite Highway, a 225-foot-wide swath of green that developers mowed
down in hopes of linking this key to the mainland. Luckily the federal
government stepped in, and now it's a hiking trail through tropical
hardwood hammock. Facilities include restrooms, picnic tables, fresh

drinking water, cold (occasionally lukewarm) showers, grills, and a campground. Leashed pets are allowed in developed areas only, not on trails. A 30-foot-wide sandy shoreline about a mile north of the harbor on the west (bay) side of the key is the only one in the national park, and boaters like to anchor off here to swim. You can fish (check on license requirements) from the maintenance dock south of the harbor. The beach, fun for families, is for day use only; it has picnic areas and a short trail that cuts through the hammock. ⊠ *Biscayne National Park* ⌖ *$25 docking fee for campers.*

SPORTS AND THE OUTDOORS

BIRD-WATCHING

More than 170 species of birds have been identified in and around the park. Expect to see flocks of brown pelicans patrolling the bay—suddenly rising, then plunging beak first to capture prey in their baggy pouches. White ibis probe exposed mudflats for small fish and crustaceans. Although all the keys are excellent for birding, Jones Lagoon (south of Adams Key, between Old Rhodes Key and Totten Key) is outstanding. It's approachable only by nonmotorized craft.

DIVING AND SNORKELING

Diving is great year-around but best in summer, when calmer winds and smaller seas result in clearer waters. Ocean waters, 3 miles east of the Keys, showcase the park's main attraction—the northernmost section of Florida's living tropical coral reefs. Some are the size of an office desk, others as large as a football field. Glass-bottom-boat rides, when operating, showcase this underwater wonderland, but you really should snorkel or scuba dive to fully appreciate it.

A diverse population of colorful fish—angelfish, gobies, grunts, parrot fish, pork fish, wrasses, and many more—flits through the reefs. Shipwrecks from the 18th century are evidence of the area's international maritime heritage, and a Maritime Heritage Trail has been developed to link six of the major shipwreck and underwater cultural sites including the Fowey Rocks Lighthouse, built in 1878. Sites, including a 19th-century wooden sailing vessel, have been plotted with GPS coordinates and marked with mooring buoys.

WHAT'S NEARBY

EVERGLADES CITY

35 miles southeast of Naples and 83 miles west of Miami.

Aside from a chain gas station or two, Everglades City retains its Old Florida authenticity. No high-rises (other than an observation tower named for pioneer Ernest Hamilton) mar the landscape at this western gateway to Everglades National Park, just off the Tamiami Trail. Everglades City was developed in the late 19th century by Barron Collier, a wealthy advertising entrepreneur, who built it as a company town to house workers for his numerous projects, including construction of the

Tamiami Trail. It grew and prospered until the Depression and World War II. Today this ramshackle town draws adventure seekers heading to the park for canoeing, fishing, and bird-watching excursions. Airboat tours, though popular, are banned within the park because of the environmental damage they cause to the mangroves. The Everglades Seafood Festival, launched in 1970 and held the first full weekend of February, draws huge crowds for delights from the sea, music, and craft displays. At quieter times, dining choices center on a handful of rustic eateries big on seafood. The town is small, fishing-oriented, and unhurried, making it excellent for boating, bicycling, or just strolling around. You can pedal along the waterfront on a 2-mile strand out to Chokoloskee Island.

VISITOR INFORMATION
Everglades Area Chamber of Commerce Welcome Center. Pick up brochures, flyers and pamphlets for area lodging, restaurants, and attractions here, and ask for additional information from friendly staffers. Open daily 9 to 4. ⊠ *32016 E. Tamiami Trail, at Rte. 29* ☏ *239/695–3941* ⊕ *www. evergladeschamber.net.*

EXPLORING
Collier-Seminole State Park. Opportunity to try biking, hiking, camping, and canoeing in Everglades territory makes this 7,000-plus-acre park a prime introduction to this often forbidding mangrove swampland. Of historical interest, a Seminole War blockhouse has been re-created to hold the interpretive center, and one of the "walking dredges"—a towering black machine invented to carve the Tamiami Trail out of the muck—stands silent on grounds amid tropical hardwood forest. Kayaks and canoes can be launched into the Blackwater River here. Bring your own, or rent a canoe from the park by the hour or day. After a lengthy campground closure, upgraded campsites for tents to motor homes now include three restrooms and a laundry room. ⊠ *20200 E. Tamiami Trail, Naples* ☏ *239/394–3397* ⊕ *www.floridastateparks.org/ park/Collier-Seminole* 🅿 *$5 per car, $4 with lone driver, $2 for pedestrians or bikers; canoe rentals from $5 per hr.*

OFF THE BEATEN PATH

Fakahatchee Strand Preserve State Park. The half-mile Big Cypress Bend boardwalk through this linear swamp forest provides opportunity to see rare plants, nesting eagles, and Florida's largest stand of native royal palms coexisting—unique to Fakahatchee Strand—with bald cypress under the forest canopy. Fakahatchee Strand, about 20 miles long and 5 miles wide, is also the orchid and bromeliad capital of the continent with 44 native orchids and 14 native bromeliads, many blooming most extravagantly in hotter months. It's particularly famed for its ghost orchids (as featured in Susan Orlean's novel *The Orchid Thief*), visible on guided hikes. In your quest for ghost orchids, keep alert for white-tailed deer, black bears, bobcats, and the Florida panther. For park nature on parade, take the 12-mile-long (one-way) W. J. Janes Memorial Scenic Drive (deposit your admission fee at the honor box; have exact change). Hike its spur trails if you have time. Rangers lead swamp walks and canoe trips November through April. ⊠ *Boardwalk on north side of Tamiami Trail, 7 miles west of Rte. 29; W. J. Janes Scenic Dr., ¾ mile north of Tamiami Trail on Rte. 29; ranger station on W. J. Janes Scenic Dr., 137 Coastline Dr., Copeland* ☏ *239/695–4593*

OFF THE BEATEN PATH

Native plants hem paddlers in on both sides, and alligators lurk nearby.

🌐 www.floridastateparks.org/fakahatcheestrand 🎫 Free; W. J. Janes Memorial Scenic Drive $3 per car, $2 per motorcycle or pedestrian.

FAMILY **Museum of the Everglades.** Through artifacts and photographs you can meet American Indians, pioneers, entrepreneurs, and anglers playing pivotal roles in southwest Florida development. Exhibits and a short film chronicle the tremendous feat of building the Tamiami Trail across mosquito-ridden, gator-infested Everglades wetlands. Permanent displays and monthly exhibits rotate works of local artists. The small museum is housed in the Laundry Building, completed in 1927 and once used for washing linens from Everglades City's Rod and Gun Club and Everglades Inn. *✉ 105 W. Broadway ☎ 239/695–0008 🎫 Free.*

WHERE TO EAT

$$ SEAFOOD 🍴 **City Seafood.** Owner Richard Wahrenberger serves up gems from the sea delivered fresh from his own boats. Enjoy breakfast, lunch, or dinner inside this rustic haven, or sit outdoors to watch pelicans, gulls, tarpon, manatees, and the occasional gator play off the dock in the Barron River. **Known for:** serving sustainable stone crab in season; full bar open on weekends; wrapping and/or shipping fresh seafood. [$] *Average main: $15 ✉ 702 Begonia St. ☎ 239/695–4700 🌐 www.cityseafood1.com.*

$$ SEAFOOD 🍴 **Everglades Adventure Center and Taste of the Everglades Restaurant.** Formerly Everglades Seafood Depot, this restaurant still offers tasty, affordable meals in a scenic setting in a storied 1928 Spanish-style stucco structure fronting Lake Placid. Seafood, steaks, burgers, and dogs are the stars here. **Known for:** simple, affordable fare; views from tables on the back porch or by the windows; historic setting. [$] *Average main: $20 ✉ 102 Collier Ave. ☎ 239/695–0075.*

$$
CUBAN

×**Havana Cafe.** Cuban specialties are a welcome alternative from the typical seafood houses of Everglades City. This cheery eatery—3 miles south of Everglades City on Chokoloskee Island—has a dozen or so tables inside, and more seating on the porch amid plenty of greenery. **Known for:** good café con leche in the mornings; cash only when Internet is down; house-made hot sauce that you can take home in a bottle. $ *Average main: $15* ⊠ *191 Smallwood Dr., Chokoloskee* ☎ *239/695–2214* ⊕ *www.myhavanacafe.com* ⊗ *No dinner Apr.–Oct.; no dinner Sun.–Thurs. Nov.–Mar.*

$$
SEAFOOD
FAMILY

×**Oyster House Restaurant.** One of the town's oldest fish houses, Oyster House serves, along with the requisite oysters, all the local staples— shrimp, gator tail, frogs' legs, stone crab, and grouper—in a lodge- like setting with mounted wild game on walls and rafters. Deep-frying remains an art in these parts, so if you're going to indulge, do it here where you can create your own fried platter for under $30. **Known for:** fried everything; will do you-catch-we-cook; nice views at sunset. $ *Average main: $20* ⊠ *901 S. Copeland Ave.* ☎ *239/695–2073* ⊕ *www. oysterhouserestaurant.com.*

$$$
SEAFOOD

×**Rod and Gun Club.** Striking, polished pecky-cypress woodwork in this historic building dates from the 1920s, when wealthy hunters, anglers, and yachting parties arrived for the winter season. Fresh seafood domi- nates, from stone crab in season (October 15–May 15) to a surf-and- turf combo of steak and grouper or a swamp-and-turf duet of frogs' legs and steak, or pasta pairings. **Known for:** languorous service; will do you-catch-we cook; cash only. $ *Average main: $25* ⊠ *200 Riverside Dr.* ☎ *239/695–2101* ⊕ *www.everglades-rodandgun.com* ▬ *No credit cards* ⊗ *Sometimes shuts down in summer. Call ahead.*

$$
SEAFOOD
FAMILY

×**Triad Seafood.** Along the Barron River, seafood houses, fishing boats, and crab traps populate one shoreline; mangroves the other. Selling fresh off the boat, some seafood houses added picnic tables and eventually grew into restaurants, like this one. **Known for:** best grouper sandwich in the area; screened porch for dining; expensive all-you-can-eat stone crab in season. $ *Average main: $15* ⊠ *401 School Dr.* ☎ *239/695–0722* ⊕ *www.triadseafoodmarketcafe.com* ⊗ *Closed May 16–Oct. 15.*

WHERE TO STAY

$
HOTEL

🏨 **Glades Haven Cozy Cabins.** Bob Miller wanted to build a Holiday Inn next to his Oyster House Restaurant on marina-channel shores, but when that didn't fly, he sent for cabin kits and set up mobile-home-size units around a pool on his property as part of "Miller's World." Rent a cabin (no two are alike), and you get free boat docking. **Pros:** great nearby food options; convenient to ENP boating; free docking. **Cons:** trailer-park, crowded feel with a noisy bar nearby; no phones; no pets. $ *Rooms from: $99* ⊠ *801 Copeland Ave.* ☎ *239/695–2746, 888/956–6251* ⊕ *www. gladeshaven.com* ⇗ *24 cabins, 2 3-bedroom houses* ⦿*No meals.*

$
B&B/INN
Fodor's Choice
★

🏨 **Ivey House.** A remodeled 1928 boardinghouse built for crews working on the Tamiami Trail, Ivey House (originally operated by Mr. and Mrs. Ivey) now fits adventurers on assorted budgets. **Pros:** historic; pleasant; affordable. **Cons:** not on water; some small rooms. $ *Rooms from: $169* ⊠ *107 Camellia St.* ☎ *877/567–0679, 239/695–3299* ⊕ *www.iveyhouse. com* ⇗ *30 rooms, 18 with bath; 1 2-bedroom cottage* ⦿*Breakfast.*

SPORTS AND THE OUTDOORS

AIR TOURS

Wings Ten Thousand Islands Aero Tours. These 20-minute to nearly two-hour flightseeing tours of the Ten Thousand Islands National Wildlife Refuge, Big Cypress National Preserve, Everglades National Park, and Gulf of Mexico operate November through April. Aboard an Alaskan Bush plane, you can see saw-grass prairies, American Indian shell mounds, alligators, and wading birds. Flights also can be booked to the Keys, connecting to the Dry Tortugas. ⊠ *Everglades Airpark, 650 Everglades City Airpark Rd.* ☎ *239/695–3296* ☞ *From $50 per person (based on group of 3 or 4).*

BOATING AND CANOEING

On the Gulf Coast explore the nooks, crannies, and mangrove islands of Chokoloskee Bay and Ten Thousand Islands National Wildlife Refuge, as well as rivers near Everglades City. The Turner River Canoe Trail, popular and populated even on Christmas as a pleasant day trip with almost guaranteed bird and alligator sightings, passes through mangrove tunnels, dwarf cypress, coastal prairie, and freshwater slough ecosystems of Everglades National Park and Big Cypress National Preserve.

Glades Haven Marina. Access Ten Thousand Islands waters in a 19-foot Sundance or a 17-foot Flicker fishing boat. Basic rates are per day, but there are half-day and hourly options. The full-service marina outfitter also rents kayaks and canoes and has a 24-hour boat ramp and dockage for up to 24-foot vessels, where you can launch for a fee. ⊠ *801 Copeland Ave. S* ☎ *239/695–2628* ⊕ *www.gladeshaven.com* ☞ *Boat rentals from $200 per day.*

FLORIDA CITY

3 miles southwest of Homestead on U.S. 1.

Florida's Turnpike ends in Florida City, the southernmost town on the Miami Dade County mainland, spilling thousands of vehicles onto U.S. 1 and eventually west to Everglades National Park, east to Biscayne National Park, or south to the Florida Keys. Although Florida City begins immediately south of Homestead, the difference in towns couldn't be more noticeable. As the last outpost before 18 miles of mangroves and water, this stretch of U.S. 1 is lined with fast-food eateries, service stations, hotels, bars, dive shops, and restaurants. Hotel rates increase significantly during NASCAR races at the nearby Homestead-Miami Speedway. Like Homestead, Florida City is rooted in agriculture, with expanses of farmland west of Krome Avenue and a huge farmers' market that ships produce nationwide.

GETTING HERE AND AROUND

SuperShuttle. This 24-hour service runs air-conditioned vans between MIA and PortMiami or wherever else you'd like to go in the Miami-Dade County area; pickup is outside baggage claim. The shared van between MIA and PortMiami is $17 per person. ⊠ *Miami* ☎ *305/871–2000* ⊕ *www.supershuttle.com.*

EXPLORING

Tropical Everglades Visitor Center. Run by the nonprofit Tropical Everglades Visitor Association, this pastel-pink center with teal signage offers abundant printed material plus tips from volunteer experts on exploring South Florida, especially Homestead, Florida City, and the Florida Keys. ⊠ *160 U.S. 1* ☎ *305/245–9180, 800/388–9669* ⊕ *www. tropicaleverglades.com.*

WHERE TO EAT

$ | SEAFOOD ✕**Farmers' Market Restaurant.** Although this eatery is within the farmers' market on the edge of town and is big on serving fresh vegetables, seafood figures prominently on the menu. A family of anglers runs the place, so fish and shellfish are only hours from the sea, and there's a fish fry on Friday nights. **Known for:** early opening for breakfast; seafood-centric menu; using fresh produce from the market. $ *Average main: $13* ⊠ *300 N. Krome Ave.* ☎ *305/242–0008.*

$$ | SEAFOOD ✕**Mutineer Restaurant.** Families and older couples flock to this kitschy roadside outpost that is shaped like a ship. Florida lobster tails, stuffed grouper, shrimp, and snapper top the menu, along with another half dozen daily seafood specials. **Known for:** family-friendly atmosphere; kitschy decor; the Wharf Lounge, with live entertainment on weekends. $ *Average main: $20* ⊠ *11 S.E. 1st Ave. (U.S. 1), at Palm Dr.* ☎ *305/245–3377* ⊕ *www.mutineerrestaurant.com.*

WHERE TO STAY

$ | HOTEL **Best Western Gateway to the Keys.** For easy access to Everglades and Biscayne National Parks as well as the Keys, you'll be well situated at this sprawling, two-story motel two blocks off Florida's Turnpike. **Pros:** convenient to parks, outlet shopping, and dining; free Wi-Fi and breakfast; attractive pool area. **Cons:** traffic noise; fills up fast in high season. $ *Rooms from: $135* ⊠ *411 S. Krome Ave.* ☎ *305/246–5100, 888/981–5100* ⊕ *www.bestwestern.com/gatewaytothekeys* ⇴ *114 rooms* ¶⊙¶ *Breakfast.*

$ | HOTEL **Fairway Inn.** With a waterfall pool, this two-story motel with exterior room entry has some of the area's lowest chain rates, and it's next to the Chamber of Commerce visitor center so you'll have easy access to tourism brochures and other information. **Pros:** affordable; convenient to restaurants, parks, and raceway. **Cons:** plain, small rooms; no-pet policy. $ *Rooms from: $89* ⊠ *100 S.E. 1st Ave.* ☎ *305/248–4202, 888/340–4734* ⇴ *160 rooms* ¶⊙¶ *Breakfast.*

$ | HOTEL **Ramada Inn.** If you're seeking an uptick from other chains, this kid-friendly property offers more amenities and comfort, such as 32-inch flat-screen TVs, free Wi-Fi, duvet-covered beds, closed closets, and stylish furnishings. **Pros:** extra room amenities; convenient location; guest laundry facilities. **Cons:** chain anonymity. $ *Rooms from: $99* ⊠ *124 E. Palm Dr.* ☎ *305/247–8833* ⊕ *www.wyndhamhotels.com* ⇴ *118 rooms* ¶⊙¶ *Breakfast.*

$ | HOTEL **Travelodge.** This bargain motor lodge is close to Florida's Turnpike, Everglades and Biscayne National Parks, and Homestead-Miami Speedway. **Pros:** convenience to track and U.S. 1; nice pool; complimentary breakfast. **Cons:** busy location; some small rooms; no pets. $ *Rooms from: $89* ⊠ *409 S.E. 1st Ave.* ☎ *305/248–9777, 800/758–0618* ⊕ *www. tlflcity.com* ⇴ *88 rooms* ¶⊙¶ *Breakfast.*

SHOPPING

FAMILY **Robert Is Here.** Want take-home gifts? This historic fruit stand sells more than 100 types of jams, jellies, honeys, and salad dressings along with its vegetables, juices, fabulous fresh-fruit milk shakes (try the papaya key lime or guanabana, under $6), and some 30 kinds of tropical fruits, including (in season) carambola, lychee, egg fruit, monstera, sapodilla, dragonfruit, genipa, sugar apple, and tamarind. Back in 1960, the stand got started when pint-sized Robert sat at this spot hawking his father's bumper cucumber crop. Now with his own book (*Robert Is Here: Looking East for a Lifetime*), Robert remains on the scene daily with wife and kids, ships nationwide, and donates seconds to needy families. An assortment of animals out back—goats to iguanas and emus, along with a splash pool—adds to the fun. Picnic tables, benches, and a waterfall with a koi pond provide serenity. It's on the way to Everglades National Park, and Robert opens at 8 am, operating until at least 7, shutting down from Labor Day until November. ⊠ *19200 S.W. 344th St.* ☎ *305/246–1592.*

HOMESTEAD

30 miles southwest of Miami.

Since recovering from Hurricane Andrew in 1992, Homestead has redefined itself as a destination for tropical agro- and ecotourism. At a crossroads between Miami and the Keys as well as Everglades and Biscayne National Parks, the area has the added dimension of shopping centers, residential development, hotel chains, and the Homestead-Miami Speedway—when car races are scheduled, hotels hike rates and require minimum stays. The historic downtown has become a preservation-driven Main Street. Krome Avenue, where it cuts through the city's heart, is lined with restaurants, an arts complex, antiques shops, and low-budget, sometimes undesirable, accommodations. West of north–south Krome Avenue, miles of fields grow fresh fruits and vegetables. Some are harvested commercially, and others beckon with "U-pick" signs. Stands selling farm-fresh produce and nurseries that grow and sell orchids and tropical plants abound. In addition to its agricultural legacy, the town has an eclectic flavor, attributable to its population mix: descendants of pioneer Crackers, Hispanic growers and farm workers, professionals escaping the Miami hubbub, and latter-day northern retirees.

EXPLORING

FAMILY
Fodor's Choice
★

Fruit & Spice Park. Because it officially qualifies for tropical status, this 37-acre park in Homestead's Redland historic agricultural district is the only public botanical garden of its type in the United States. More than 500 varieties of fruit, nuts, and spices typically grow here, and there are 75 varieties of bananas alone, plus 160 of mango. Tram tours (included in admission) run three times daily, and you can sample fresh fruit at the gift shop, which also stocks canned and dried fruits plus cookbooks. The Mango Café, open daily from 11:30 am to 4:30 pm, serves mango salsa, smoothies, and shakes along with salads, wraps, sandwiches, and a yummy Mango Passion Cheesecake. Picnic in the garden at provided

Are baby alligators more to your liking than their daddies? You can pet one at Gator Park.

tables or on your own blankets. Annual park events include January's Redland Heritage Festival and June's Summer Fruit Festival. Kids age six and under are free. ✉ *24801 S.W. 187th Ave.* ☎ *305/247–5727* ⊕ *www.fruitandspicepark.com* ✉ *$8.*

Schnebly Redland's Winery. Homestead's fruity bounty comes in liquid form at this growing enterprise that began producing wines of lychee, mango, guava, and other fruits as a way to avoid waste from family groves each year—bounty not perfect enough for shipping. Over the years, this grape-free winery (now with a beer brewery, too) has expanded with a reception-tasting indoor area serving snacks and a lush plaza picnic area landscaped in coral rock, tropical plants, and waterfalls—topped with an Indian thatched chickee roof. Tours and tastings are offered daily. The Ultimate Tasting includes five wines and an etched Schnebly glass you can keep. Redlander Restaurant operates daily with an ever-changing menu. On Sunday, and on other occasions, there's yoga on the lawn. Count on a cover charge at the restaurant after 6 pm on Friday and Saturday nights. ✉ *30205 S.W. 217th Ave.* ☎ *305/242–1224, 888/717–9463 (WINE)* ⊕ *www.schneblywinery.com* ✉ *Winery tours (weekends only) $7; tastings $11.95.*

WHERE TO EAT

$ ⚹ **Royal Palm Grill.** You may have a déjà vu moment if you drive down
AMERICAN Krome Avenue, where two Royal Palm Grills are just a hop-skip away from each other. This popular "breakfast all day, every day" enterprise has two locations, only a few blocks apart, to accommodate a steady stream of customers for the aforementioned breakfast fare from omelets and pancakes to biscuits and gravy, plus salads, steaks, and seafood. **Known**

for: early open, early close; popular for breakfast; nostalgic setup at the original location. $ *Average main: $10* ✉ *Royal Palm Pharmacy, 806 N. Krome Ave.* ☎ *305/246–5701* ⊕ *royalpalmgrillfl.com* ☾ *No dinner.*

$$ ✕ **Shiver's BBQ.** Piggin' out since the 1960s, Shiver's ranks as a lip-smackin' must for lovers of hickory-smoked barbecued pork, beef, and chicken in assorted forms from baby back ribs to briskets. Longtime owners Martha and Perry Curtis are typically on hand attending to traditions with original recipes, although Martha does offer her new, alternative "secret recipe" sauce. **Known for:** corn-bread soufflé; picnic table seating; popular for takeout. $ *Average main: $15* ✉ *28001 S. Dixie Hwy.* ☎ *305/248–2272* ⊕ *www.shiversbbq.com.*

BARBECUE
FAMILY

$$ ✕ **White Lion Cafe.** Although the antique shop space within the bunga-low-style café is now history, this 45-seat comfort-food haven, with full bar, remains embellished with reminders of the past, from a 1950s-era wooden wall phone to a metal icebox and a Coca-Cola machine. A mounted jackalope oversees a wide menu of blue-plate specials (Home-stead crab cakes, burgers, fried chicken, meat loaf). **Known for:** comfort food galore; lots of potato options; kitschy decor. $ *Average main: $18* ✉ *146 N.W. 7th St.* ☎ *305/248–1076* ⊕ *www.whitelioncafe.com* ☾ *Closed. Sun. and Mon.*

ITALIAN

WHERE TO STAY

$ ⌂ **Hotel Redland.** Of downtown Homestead's smattering of mom-and-pop lodging options, this historic inn is by far the most desirable with its Victorian-style rooms done up in pastels and reproduction antique furniture. **Pros:** historic character; convenient to downtown and near antiques shops; free Wi-Fi. **Cons:** traffic noise; small rooms. $ *Rooms from: $120* ✉ *5 S. Flagler Ave.* ☎ *305/246–1904, 800/595–1904* ⊕ *www.hotelredland.com* ⌁ *13 rooms* ❋❋ *No meals.*

HOTEL

SPORTS AND THE OUTDOORS
AUTO RACING

Homestead-Miami Speedway. Buzzing more than 280 days each year, the 600-acre speedway hosts racing, manufacturer testing, car-club events, driving schools, and ride-along programs. The facility has 65,000 grandstand seats, club seating eight stories above racing action, and two tracks—a 2.21-mile continuous road course and a 1.5-mile oval. A packed schedule includes GRAND-AM and NASCAR events. Two tunnels on the grounds are below sea level. Parking includes space for 30,000 vehicles. ✉ *1 Speedway Blvd.* ☎ *866/409–7223* ⊕ *www.home-steadmiamispeedway.com.*

WATER SPORTS

Homestead Bayfront Park. Boaters, anglers, and beachgoers give high rat-ings to facilities at this recreational area adjacent to Biscayne National Park. The 174-slip Herbert Hoover Marina, accommodating up to 50-foot vessels, has a ramp, dock, bait-and-tackle shop, fuel station, ice, and dry storage. The park also has a snack bar, tidal swimming area, a beach with lifeguards, playground, ramps for people with disabilities, and a picnic pavilion with grills, showers, and restrooms. ✉ *9698 S.W. 328th St.* ☎ *305/230–3033* ⌁ *$7 per passenger vehicle on weekends; $12 per vehicle with boat Mon.–Thurs., $15 Fri.–Sun.; $15 per RV or bus.*

TAMIAMI TRAIL

U.S. 41, between Naples and Miami.

An 80-mile stretch of U.S. 41 (known as the Tamiami Trail) traverses the Everglades, Big Cypress National Preserve, and Fakahatchee Strand Preserve State Park. The road was conceived in 1915 to link Miami to Fort Myers and Tampa. When it finally became a reality in 1928, it cut through the Everglades and altered the natural flow of water as well as the lives of the Miccosukee Indians who were trying mightily to eke out a living fishing, hunting, farming, and frogging here. The landscape is surprisingly varied, changing from hardwood hammocks to pinelands, then abruptly to tall cypress trees dripping with Spanish moss and back to saw-grass marsh. Slow down to take in the scenery and you'll likely be rewarded with glimpses of alligators sunning themselves along the banks of roadside canals and hundreds of waterbirds, especially in the dry winter season. The man-made landscape includes Native American villages, chickee huts, and airboats parked at roadside enterprises. Between Miami and Naples the road goes by several names, including Tamiami Trail, U.S. 41, 9th Street in Naples, and, at the Miami end, Southwest 8th Street. ■TIP➜ Businesses along the trail give their addresses based on either their distance from Krome Avenue, Florida's Turnpike, or Miami on the east coast or Naples on the west coast.

EXPLORING

FAMILY **Everglades Safari Park.** A perennial favorite with tour-bus operators, this family-run park open 365 days has an arena, seating up to 300 for shows with alligator wrestling. Before and after, get a closer look at both alligators and crocodiles on Gator Island, follow a jungle trail, walk through a small wildlife museum, or board an airboat for a 35-minute ride on the River of Grass (included in admission). There's also a restaurant, gift shop, and an observation platform overlooking the Glades. Smaller, private airboats can be chartered for tours lasting 40 minutes to two hours. Check online for coupons and count on free parking. ✉ *26700 S.W. 8th St., Miami* ✛ *15 miles west of Florida's Tpke.* ☎ *305/226–6923, 305/223–3804* ⊕ *www.evergladessafaripark.com* ✎ *$25.*

FAMILY **Gator Park.** Here you can get face-to-face with and even touch an alligator—albeit a baby one—during the park's Wildlife Show. You also can squirm in a "reptilium" of some 30 different venomous and nonpoisonous native snakes or learn about American Indians of the Everglades through a reproduction of a Miccosukee village. The park, open rain or shine, also has 35-minute airboat tours as well as a gift shop and restaurant serving fare from burgers to gator tail and sausage. Admission includes the wildlife show and an airboat ride. ✉ *24050 Tamiami Trail, Miami* ✛ *12 miles west of Florida's Tpke.* ☎ *305/559–2255, 800/559–2205* ⊕ *www.gatorpark.com* ✎ *$19.99.*

FAMILY **Miccosukee Indian Village and Gift Shop.** Showcasing the skills and lifestyle of the Miccosukee Tribe of Florida, this cultural center offers craft demonstrations and insight into interaction with alligators. Narrated 30-minute airboat rides take you into the wilderness where natives hid after the Seminole Wars and Indian Removal Act of the mid-1800s. In modern times, many of the Miccosukee have relocated to this village along Tamiami Trail, but most still maintain their hammock farming and hunting camps. The museum shows two films on tribal culture and displays chickee structures and artifacts. Guided tours run throughout the day, and a gift shop stocks dolls, apparel, silver jewelry, beadwork, and other handcrafts. The Miccosukee Everglades Music and Craft Festival, going strong for four decades, falls on a July weekend, and the 10-day Miccosukee Indian Arts Festival is in late December. ✉ *U.S. 41, just west of Shark Valley entrance, 25 miles west of Florida's Tpke., Miami* ☎ *305/552–8365* 🌐 *www.miccosukee.com* 🎟 *Village $10, airboat rides $16.*

CROCS OR GATORS?

You can tell you're looking at a crocodile, not an alligator, if you can see its lower teeth protruding when those powerful jaws are shut. Gators are much darker in color—a grayish black—compared with the lighter tan shades of crocodiles. Alligator snouts—sort of U-shape—are also much broader than their long, thin A-shape crocodilian counterparts. South Florida is the world's only place where the two coexist in the wild. Alligators are primarily found in freshwater habitats, whereas crocodiles (better at expelling salt from water) are typically in coastal estuaries.

3

WHERE TO EAT

$$ SOUTHWESTERN FAMILY

🍴 **Miccosukee Restaurant.** For breakfast or lunch (or dinner until 9 pm, November–April), this roadside cafeteria a quarter mile from the Miccosukee Indian Village provides the best menu variety along Tamiami Trail in Everglades territory. Atmosphere comes from the view overlooking the River of Grass, friendly servers wearing traditional Miccosukee patchwork vests, and a mural depicting American Indian women cooking while men powwow. **Known for:** catfish and frogs' legs; Indian fry bread; basic diner staples. [$] *Average main: $15* ✉ *U.S. 41, 18 miles west of Miccosukee Resort & Gaming; 25 miles west of Florida's Tpke., Miami* ☎ *305/894–2374* ⏲ *No dinner May–Oct.*

$ BARBECUE FAMILY

🍴 **Pit Bar-B-Q.** This old-fashioned roadside eatery along Tamiami Trail near Krome Avenue was launched in 1965 by the late Tommy Little, who wanted to provide easy access to cold drinks and rib-sticking fare for folks heading into or out of the Everglades. Now spiffed up, this backwoods heritage vision remains a popular, affordable family option. **Known for:** double-decker barbecue sandwiches; a few Latin specialties; family-friendly atmosphere (with weekend pony rides). [$] *Average main: $12* ✉ *16400 S.W. 8th St., 5 miles west of Florida's Tpke., Miami* ☎ *305/226–2272* 🌐 *www.thepitbarbq.com.*

WHERE TO STAY

$ RESORT

🏨 **Miccosukee Resort & Gaming.** Like an oasis on the horizon of endless saw grass, this nine-story resort at the southeastern edge of the Everglades can't help but attract attention, even if you're not on the lookout for 24-hour gaming action. **Pros:** casino; most modern resort in these parts; golf. **Cons:** smoky lobby; hotel guests find parking lot fills with gamblers; feels incompatible with the Everglades. [$] *Rooms from: $149* ✉ *500 S.W. 177th Ave., Miami* ✣ *6 miles west of Florida's Tpke.* ☎ *305/925–2555, 877/242–6464* 🌐 *www.miccosukee.com* 🛏 *256 rooms, 46 suites* 🍽 *No meals.*

SPORTS AND THE OUTDOORS
BOAT TOURS

Many Everglades-area tours operate only in season, roughly November through April.

Coopertown Airboats. In business since 1945, the oldest airboat operator in the Everglades offers 35- to 40-minute tours that take you 9 miles to hammocks and alligator holes to see red-shouldered hawks or turtles. You also can book longer private charters. ⊠ *22700 S.W. 8th St., Miami* ✛ *11 miles west of Florida's Tpke.* ☎ *305/226–6048* ⊕ *www.coopertownairboats.com.* 🖻 *From $23.*

Everglades Alligator Farm. Open daily near the entrance to Everglades National Park, this working farm—home of the late 14-foot "Grandpa" gator (now mounted for display)—runs a 4-mile, 30-minute airboat tour with departures 25 minutes after the hour. The tour includes free hourly alligator, snake, and wildlife shows; or see only the gator farm and show. Alligator feedings are at noon and 3 pm. Look for online coupons. ⊠ *40351 S.W. 192nd Ave., Homestead* ☎ *305/247–2628* ⊕ *www. everglades.com.* 🖻 *From $19.50.*

FAMILY **Wooten's Everglades Airboat Tours.** This classic Florida roadside attraction, with a change of ownership a few seasons back, runs airboat tours through the Everglades for up to 22 people and swamp-buggy rides through the Big Cypress Swamp for up to 25. Each lasts approximately 30 minutes. (Swamp-buggies are giant tractorlike vehicles with huge rubber wheels.) More personalized airboat tours on smaller boats, seating six to eight, last about an hour. An on-site animal sanctuary with a live gator show shelters the typical Everglades array of alligators, snakes, and other creatures. Some packages include an airboat ride, swamp-buggy adventure, and sanctuary access. Rates change frequently, but check website for combo packages. ⊠ *32330 Tamiami Trail E, Ochopee* ✛ *1½ miles east of Rte. 29* ☎ *239/695–2781, 800/282–2781* ⊕ *www. wootenseverglades.com* 🖻 *Tours from $24; gator show $8.*

THE FLORIDA KEYS

WELCOME TO THE FLORIDA KEYS

TOP REASONS TO GO

★ **John Pennekamp Coral Reef State Park:** A perfect introduction to the Florida Keys, this nature reserve offers snorkeling, diving, camping, and kayaking. An underwater highlight is the massive *Christ of the Deep* statue.

★ **Viewing the Underwater World:** Whether you scuba dive, snorkel, or ride a glass-bottom boat, don't miss gazing at the coral reef and its colorful denizens.

★ **Sunset at Mallory Square:** Sure, it's touristy, but just once while you're here, you've got to witness the circuslike atmosphere of this nightly celebration.

★ **Duval crawl:** Shop, eat, drink, repeat. Key West's Duval Street and the nearby streets make a good day's worth of window-shopping and people-watching.

★ **Getting on the water:** From angling for trophy-size fish to zipping out to the Dry Tortugas, a boat trip is in your future. It's really the whole point of the Keys.

1 **The Upper Keys.** As the doorstep to the islands' coral reefs and blithe spirit, the Upper Keys introduce all that's sporting and sea-oriented about the Keys. They stretch from Key Largo to the Long Key Channel (MM 105–65).

2 **The Middle Keys.** Centered on the town of Marathon, the Middle Keys hold most of the chain's historic and natural attractions outside of Key West. They go from Conch (pronounced *konk*) Key through Marathon to the south side of the Seven Mile Bridge, including Pigeon Key (MM 65–40).

3 **The Lower Keys.** Pressure drops another notch in this laid-back part of the region, where key-deer viewing and fishing reign supreme. The Lower Keys go from Little Duck Key west through Big Coppitt Key (MM 40–9).

4 **Key West.** The ultimate in Florida Keys craziness, this party town isn't for the closed-minded or those seeking a quiet retreat. The Key West area encompasses MM 9–0.

4

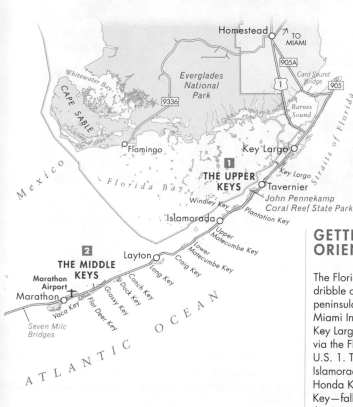

GETTING ORIENTED

The Florida Keys are the dribble of islands off the peninsula's southern tip. From Miami International Airport, Key Largo is a 56-mile drive via the Florida Turnpike and U.S. 1. The rest of the Keys— Islamorada, Marathon, Bahia Honda Key, and Big Pine Key—fall in succession for the 85 miles between Key Largo and Key West along the Overseas Highway. At their north end, the Florida Keys front Florida Bay, part of Everglades National Park. The Middle and Lower keys front the Gulf of Mexico; the Atlantic Ocean borders the length of the chain on its eastern shores.

SEAFOOD IN THE FLORIDA KEYS

Fish. It's what's for dinner in the Florida Keys. The Keys' runway between the Gulf of Mexico or Florida Bay and Atlantic warm waters means fish of many fin. Restaurants take full advantage by serving it fresh, whether you caught it or a local fisherman did.

Menus at a number of colorful waterfront shacks such as **Snapper's** (⊠ *139 Seaside Ave., Key Largo* ☎ *305/852–5956*) in Key Largo and **Half Shell Raw Bar** (⊠ *231 Margaret St., Key West* ☎ *305/294–7496*) range from basic raw, steamed, broiled, grilled, or blackened fish to some Bahamian and New Orleans–style interpretations. Other seafood houses dress up their fish in creative haute cuisine styles, such as **Pierre's** (⊠ *MM 81.5 BS, Islamorada* ☎ *305/664–3225* ⊕ *www.pierres-restaurant.com*) hogfish meunière, or yellowtail snapper with pear-ricotta pasta purses with caponata and red pepper coulis at **Café Marquesa** (⊠ *600 Fleming St., Key West* ☎ *305/292–1244* ⊕ *www.marquesa.com*). Try a Keys-style breakfast of "grits and grunts"—fried fish and grits—at the **Stuffed Pig** (⊠ *3520 Overseas Hwy., Marathon* ☎ *305/743–4059*).

BUILT-IN FISH

You know it's fresh when you see a fish market as soon as you open the door to the restaurant where you're dining. It happens frequently in the Keys. You can even peruse the seafood showcases and pick the fish fillet or lobster tail you want.

Many of the Keys' best restaurants are found in marina complexes, where the commercial fishermen bring their catches straight from the sea. Those in **Stock Island** (one island north of Key West) and at **Keys Fisheries Market & Marina** (⊠ *MM 49 BS, end of 35th St., Marathon* ☎ *305/743–4353, 866/743–4353*) take some finding.

CONCH

One of the tastiest legacies of the Keys' Bahamian heritage (and most mispronounced), conch (pronounced *konk*) shows up on nearly every menu in some shape or form. It's so prevalent in local diets that natives refer to themselves as Conchs. Conch fritters are the most popular culinary manifestations, followed by cracked (pounded, breaded, and fried) conch, and conch salad, a ceviche-style refresher. Since the harvesting of queen conch is now illegal, most of the islands' conch comes from the Bahamas.

FLORIDA LOBSTER

Where are the claws? Stop looking for them: Florida spiny lobsters don't have 'em, never did. The sweet tail meat, however, makes up for the loss. Commercial and sport divers harvest these glorious crustaceans from late July through March. Check with local dive shops on restrictions, and then get ready for a fresh feast. Restaurants serve them broiled with drawn butter or in creative dishes such as lobster Benedict, lobster spring rolls, lobster Reuben, and lobster tacos.

GROUPER

Once central to Florida's trademark seafood dish—fried grouper sandwich—its populations have been overfished in recent years, meaning that the state has exerted more control over bag regulations and occasionally closes grouper fishing on a temporary basis during the winter season. Some restaurants have gone antigrouper to try to bring back the abundance, but most grab it when they can. Black grouper is the most highly prized of the several varieties.

STONE CRAB

In season October 15 through May 15, it gets its name from its rock-hard shell. Fishermen take only one claw, which can regenerate in a sustainable manner. Connoisseurs prefer them chilled with tangy mustard sauce. Some restaurants give you a choice of hot claws and drawn butter, but this means the meat will be cooked twice, because it's usually boiled or steamed as soon as it's taken from its crab trap.

YELLOWTAIL SNAPPER

The preferred species of snappers, it's more plentiful in the Keys than in any other Florida waters. As pretty as it is tasty, it's a favorite of divers and snorkelers. Mild, sweet, and delicate, its meat lends itself to any number of preparations. It's available pretty much year-round, and many restaurants will give you a choice of broiled, baked, fried, or blackened. Chefs top it with everything from key lime beurre blanc to mango chutney. **Ballyhoo's** in Key Largo (⊠ *MM 97.8, in median* ☎ *305/852–0822*) serves it 10 different ways.

Updated by
Jill Martin

Your Keys experience begins on your 18-mile drive south on "The Stretch," a portion of U.S. 1 with a specially colored blue median that takes you from Florida City to Key Largo. The real magic begins at mile marker 113, where the Florida Keys Scenic Highway begins. As the only All-American Road in Florida, it is a destination unto itself, one that crosses 42 bridges over water, including the Seven Mile Bridge—with its stunning vistas—and ends in Key West. Look for crocodiles, alligators, and bald eagles along the way.

Key West has a Mardi Gras mood with Fantasy Festival, a Hemingway look-alike contest, and the occasional threat to secede from the Union. It's an island whose eclectic natives, known as "Conchs," mingle well with visitors (of the spring-break variety as well as those seeking to escape reality for a while) on this scenic, sometimes raucous 4x2-mile island paradise.

Although life elsewhere in the island chain isn't near as offbeat, it is as diverse. Overflowing bursts of bougainvillea, shimmering waters, and mangrove-lined islands can be admired throughout. The one thing most visitors don't admire much in the Keys are their beaches. They're not many, and they're not what you'd expect. The reason? The coral reef. It breaks up the waves and prevents sand from being dumped on the shores. That's why the beaches are mostly rough sand, as it's crushed coral. Think of it as a trade-off: the Keys have the only living coral reef in the United States, but that reef prevents miles of shimmering sands from ever arriving.

In season, a river of traffic gushes southwest on this highway. But that doesn't mean you can't enjoy the ride as you cruise along the islands. Gaze over the silvery blue-and-green Atlantic and its living coral reef, with Florida Bay, the Gulf of Mexico, and the backcountry on your right (the Keys extend southwest from the mainland). At a few points the ocean and gulf are as much as 10 miles apart; in most places, however, they're from 1 to 4 miles apart, and on the narrowest landfill islands they're separated only by the road.

While the views can be mesmerizing, to appreciate the Keys you need to get off the highway, especially in more developed regions like Key Largo, Islamorada, and Marathon. Once you do, rent a boat, anchor, and then fish, swim, or marvel at the sun, sea, and sky. Or visit one of the many sandbars, which are popular places to float the day away. Ocean side, dive or snorkel spectacular coral reefs or pursue grouper, blue marlin, mahimahi, and other deepwater game fish. Along Florida Bay's coastline, kayak to secluded islands through mangrove forests, or seek out the bonefish, snapper, snook, and tarpon that lurk in the shallow grass flats and mangrove roots of the backcountry.

PLANNING

WHEN TO GO
In high season, from mid-December through mid-April, traffic is inevitably heavy. From November to mid-December, crowds are thinner, the weather is superlative, and hotels and shops drastically reduce their prices. Summer is a second high season, especially among families, Europeans, bargain-seekers, and lobster divers.

Florida is rightly called the Sunshine State, but it could also be dubbed the "Humidity State." From June through September, 90% humidity levels are not uncommon. Thankfully, the weather in the Keys is more moderate than in mainland Florida. Temperatures can be 10°F cooler during the summer and up to 10°F warmer during the winter. The Keys also get substantially less rain than mainland Florida, mostly in quick downpours on summer afternoons. In hurricane season, June through November, the Keys get their fair share of warnings; pay heed, and evacuate earlier rather than later, when flights and automobile traffic get backed up.

GETTING HERE AND AROUND
AIR TRAVEL
About 450,000 passengers use Key West International Airport (EYW) each year; its most recent renovation includes a beach where travelers can catch their last blast of rays after clearing security. Because direct flights to Key West are few, many prefer flying into Miami International Airport (MIA) and driving the 110-mile Overseas Highway (aka U.S. 1).

BOAT AND FERRY TRAVEL
Key West Express operates air-conditioned ferries between the Key West Terminal (Caroline and Grinnell streets) and Marco Island and Fort Myers Beach. The trip takes at least four hours each way and costs $95 one way, from $125 round-trip (a $3 convenience fee is added to all online bookings). Ferries depart from Fort Myers Beach at 8:30 am and from Key West at 6 pm. The Marco Island ferry departs at 8:30 am (the return trip leaves Key West at 5 pm). A photo ID is required for each passenger. Advance reservations are recommended.

Boaters can travel to and through the Keys either along the Intracoastal Waterway (5-foot draft limitation) through Card, Barnes, and Blackwater sounds and into Florida Bay, or along the deeper Atlantic Ocean route through Hawk Channel, a buoyed passage. Refer to NOAA Nautical Charts Nos. 11451, 11445, and 11441. The Keys are full of marinas that welcome transient visitors, but they don't have enough slips for everyone. Make reservations in advance, and ask about channel and dockage depth—many marinas are quite shallow.

Contact Key West Express. ⊠ *100 Grinnell St., Key West* ☎ *239/463–5733 in Key West, 239/463–5733 in Fort Myers Beach, 239/463–5733 in Marco Island* ⊕ *www.seakeywestexpress.net.*

BUS TRAVEL

Keys Transportation provides private airport transfers to any destination in the Keys from either MIA or FLL. Prices start at $49 per person for transportation to Key Largo and get more expensive as you move south. Call or email for a price quote.

Greyhound Lines runs a special Keys shuttle twice a day (times depend on the day of the week) from Miami International Airport (departing from Concourse E, lower level) and stops throughout the Keys. Fares run from around $25 for Key Largo (⊠ *MM 99.6*) or Islamorada (⊠ *Burger King, MM 82*) to around $45 for Key West (⊠ *3535 S. Roosevelt, Key West International Airport*).

Keys Shuttle runs scheduled service six times a day in 15-passenger vans (9 passengers maximum) between Miami and Fort Lauderdale airports and Key West with stops throughout the Keys for $60 to $90 per person sharing rides.

SuperShuttle charges $191 for up to two passengers for trips to the Upper Keys; to go farther, you must book an entire 11-person van, which costs $402. For a trip to the airport, place your request 24 hours in advance.

Contacts Greyhound. ☎ *800/231–2222* ⊕ *www.greyhound.com.* **Keys Shuttle.** ⊠ *1333 Overseas Hwy., Marathon* ☎ *888/765–9997* ⊕ *www.keysshuttle.com.* **Keys Transportation.** ☎ *305/395–0299* ⊕ *www.keystransportation.com.* **SuperShuttle.** ☎ *800/258–3826* ⊕ *www.supershuttle.com.*

CAR TRAVEL

By car, from Miami International Airport, follow signs to Coral Gables and Key West, which puts you on LeJeune Road, then Route 836 west. Take the Homestead Extension of Florida's Turnpike south (toll road), which ends at Florida City and connects to the Overseas Highway (U.S. 1). Tolls from the airport run approximately $3. Payment is collected via SunPass, a prepaid toll program, or with Toll-By-Plate, a system that photographs each vehicle's license plate and mails a monthly bill for tolls, plus a $2.50 administrative fee, to the vehicle's registered owner.

Vacationers traveling in their own cars can obtain a mini-SunPass sticker via mail before their trip for $4.99 and receive the cost back in toll credits and discounts. The pass also is available at many major Florida retailers and turnpike service plazas. It works on all Florida toll roads and many bridges. For details on purchasing a mini-SunPass, call or visit the website.

For visitors renting cars in Florida, most major rental companies have programs allowing customers to use the Toll-By-Plate system. Tolls, plus varying service fees, are automatically charged to the credit card used to rent the vehicle (along with a hefty service charge in most cases). For details, including pricing options at participating rental-car agencies, check the program website. Under no circumstances should motorists attempt to stop in high-speed electronic tolling lanes. Travelers can contact Florida's Turnpike Enterprise for more information about the all-electronic tolling on Florida's Turnpike.

The alternative from Florida City is Card Sound Road (Route 905A), which has a (cash-only) bridge toll of $1. SunPass isn't accepted. Continue to the only stop sign and turn right on Route 905, which rejoins the Overseas Highway 31 miles south of Florida City.

Except in Key West, a car is essential for visiting the Keys.

Contacts Florida's Turnpike Enterprise. ☎ 800/749–7453 ⊕ www.floridas-turnpike.com. **SunPass.** ☎ 888/865–5352 ⊕ www.sunpass.com.

THE MILE MARKER SYSTEM

Getting lost in the Keys is almost impossible once you understand the unique address system. Many addresses are simply given as a mile marker (MM) number. The markers are small, green, rectangular signs along the side of the Overseas Highway (U.S. 1). They begin with MM 126, 1 mile south of Florida City, and end with MM 0, in Key West. Keys residents use the abbreviation BS for the bay side of Overseas Highway and OS for the ocean side. From Marathon to Key West, residents may refer to the bay side as the gulf side.

HOTELS

Throughout the Keys, the types of accommodations are remarkably varied, from 1950s-style motels to cozy inns to luxurious resorts. Most are on or near the ocean, so water sports are popular. Key West's lodging portfolio includes historic cottages, restored Conch houses, and large resorts. Some larger properties throughout the Keys charge a mandatory daily resort fee, which can cover equipment rental, fitness-center use, and other services. You can expect another 12.5% (or more) in state and county taxes. Some guesthouses and inns don't welcome children, and many don't permit smoking.

RESTAURANTS

Seafood rules in the Keys, which is full of chef-owned restaurants with not-too-fancy food. Many restaurants serve cuisine that reflects the proximity of the Bahamas and Caribbean (you'll see the term "Floribbean" on many menus). Tropical fruits figure prominently—especially on the beverage side of the menu. Florida spiny lobster should be local and fresh from August to March, and stone crabs from mid-October to mid-May. And don't dare leave the islands without sampling conch, be it in a fritter or in ceviche. Keep an eye out for authentic key lime pie—yellow custard in a graham-cracker crust. If it's green, just say "no." Note: Particularly in Key West and particularly during spring break, the more affordable and casual restaurants can get loud and downright rowdy, with young visitors often more interested in drinking than eating. Live music contributes to the decibel levels. If you're more of the quiet, intimate-dining type, avoid such overly exuberant scenes by eating early or choosing a restaurant where the bar isn't the main focus.

Hotel and restaurant reviews have been shortened. For full information, visit Fodors.com.

WHAT IT COSTS			
	$	$$	$$$	$$$$
Restaurants	under $15	$15–$20	$21–$30	over $30
Hotels	under $200	$200–$300	$301–$400	over $400

Restaurant prices are the average cost of a main course at dinner or, if dinner is not served, at lunch. Hotel prices are the lowest cost of a standard double room in high season.

VISITOR INFORMATION
There are several separate tourism offices in the Florida Keys, and you can use Visit Florida's website (⊕ *www.visitflorida.com*) for general information and referrals to local agencies. *See individual chapters for local visitor information centers.*

In addition to traditional tourist information, many divers will be interested in the Florida Keys National Marine Sanctuary, which has its headquarters in Key West and has another office in Key Largo.

Contact Florida Keys National Marine Sanctuary. ☎ *305/809–4700* ⊕ *floridakeys.noaa.gov.*

THE UPPER KEYS

Diving and snorkeling rule in the Upper Keys, thanks to North America's only living coral barrier reef that runs a few miles off the Atlantic coast. Divers of all skill levels benefit from accessible dive sites and an established tourism infrastructure. Fishing is another huge draw, especially around Islamorada, known for its sportfishing in both deep offshore waters and in the backcountry. Offshore islands accessible only by boat are popular destinations for kayakers. In short, if you don't like the water you might get bored here.

But true nature lovers won't feel shortchanged. Within 1½ miles of the bay coast lie the mangrove trees and sandy shores of Everglades National Park, where naturalists lead tours of one of the world's few saltwater forests. Here you'll see endangered manatees, curious dolphins, and other marine creatures. Although the number of birds has dwindled since John James Audubon captured their beauty on canvas, bird-watchers will find plenty to see, including the rare Everglades snail kite, bald eagles, ospreys, and a colorful array of egrets and herons. At sunset flocks take flight as they gather to find their night's roost, adding a swirl of activity to an otherwise quiet time of day.

GETTING HERE AND AROUND

Keys Transportation provides private airport transfers to any destination in the Keys from either MIA or FLL. Prices start at $49 per person for transportation to Key Largo and get more expensive as you move south. Call or email for a price quote. SuperShuttle charges $165 to $185 for two passengers for trips from Miami International Airport to Key Largo; reservations are required. For a trip to the airport, place your request 24 hours in advance. *For more information, see Getting Here and Around: Bus Travel.*

KEY LARGO

56 miles south of Miami International Airport.

4

The first of the Upper Keys reachable by car, 30-mile-long Key Largo is the largest island in the chain. Key Largo—named Cayo Largo ("Long Key") by the Spanish—makes a great introduction to the region. This is the gateway to the Keys, and an evening of fresh seafood and views of the sunset on the water will get you in the right state of mind.

The history of Largo reads much like that of the rest of the Keys: a succession of native people, pirates, wreckers, and developers. The first settlement on Key Largo was named Planter, back in the days of pineapple, and later, key lime plantations. For a time it was a convenient shipping port, but when the railroad arrived Planter died on the vine. Today three communities—North Key Largo and Key Largo as well as the separately incorporated city of Tavernier—make up the whole of Key Largo.

What's there to do on Key Largo besides gaze at the sunset? Not much if you're not into diving or snorkeling. Nobody comes to Key Largo without visiting John Pennekamp Coral Reef State Park, one of the jewels of the state park system. Water-sports enthusiasts head to the adjacent Key Largo National Marine Sanctuary, which encompasses about 190 square miles of coral reefs, sea-grass beds, and mangrove estuaries. If you've never tried diving, Key Largo is the perfect place to learn. Dozens of companies will be more than happy to show you the ropes.

Fishing is the other big draw, and world records are broken regularly in the waters around the Upper Keys. There are plenty of charter companies to help you find the big ones and teach you how to hook the elusive bonefish, sometimes known as the ghost fish.

On land, Key Largo provides all the conveniences of a major resort town, including restaurants that will cook your catch or prepare their own creations with inimitable style. You'll notice that some unusual specialties pop up on the menu, such as cracked conch, spiny lobster, and stone crab. Don't pass up a chance to try the local delicacies, especially the key lime pie.

Most businesses are lined up along U.S. 1, the four-lane highway that runs down the middle of the island. Cars whiz past at all hours—something to remember when you're booking a room. Most lodgings are on the highway, so you'll want to be as far back as possible. At MM 95, look for the mural painted in 2011 to commemorate the 100th anniversary of the railroad to the Keys.

GETTING HERE AND AROUND

Key Largo is 56 miles south of Miami International Airport, with its mile markers ranging from 106 to 91. The island runs northeast–southwest, with the Overseas Highway, divided by a median most of the way, running down the center. If the highway is your only glimpse of the island, you're likely to feel barraged by its tacky commercial side. Make a point of driving Route 905 in North Key Largo and down side streets to get a better feel for it.

VISITOR INFORMATION

In addition to traditional tourist information, many divers will be interested in the Florida Keys National Marine Sanctuary, which has an office in Key Largo.

Contacts Florida Keys National Marine Sanctuary. ☎ *305/809–4700* ⊕ *floridakeys.noaa.gov.* **Key Largo Chamber of Commerce.** ⊠ *MM 106 BS, 10600 Overseas Hwy.* ☎ *305/451–4747, 800/822–1088* ⊕ *www.keylargochamber.org.*

EXPLORING

TOP ATTRACTIONS

FAMILY **Dagny Johnson Key Largo Hammock Botanical State Park.** American crocodiles, mangrove cuckoos, white-crowned pigeons, Schaus swallowtail butterflies, mahogany mistletoe, wild cotton, and 100 other rare critters and plants inhabit these 2,400 acres, sandwiched between Crocodile Lake National Wildlife Refuge and the waters of Pennekamp Coral Reef State Park. The park is also a user-friendly place to explore the largest remaining stand of the vast West Indian tropical hardwood hammock and mangrove wetland that once covered most of the Keys. Interpretive signs describe many of the tropical tree species along a wide, 1-mile, paved road (2 miles round-trip) that invites walking and biking. A new, unpaved, extended loop trail can add 1–2 miles to your walk. There are also more than 6 additional miles of nature trails, most of which are accessible to both bikes and wheelchairs with a permit, easily obtainable from John Pennekamp State Park. Pets are welcome if on a leash no longer than 6 feet. You'll also find restrooms, information kiosks, and picnic tables. ■TIP➔ Rangers recommend not visiting when it's raining as the trees can drip poisonous sap. ⊠ *Rte. 905 OS, ½ mile north of Overseas Hwy., North Key Largo* ☎ *305/451–1202* ⊕ *www.floridastateparks.org/keylargohammock* ➱ *$2.50 (exact change needed).*

FAMILY **Dolphins Plus Bayside.** This educational program begins at the facility's bay-side lagoon with a get-acquainted session from a platform. After that, you slip into the water for some frolicking with your new dolphin pals. Options range from a shallow-water swim to a hands-on structured swim with a dolphin. You can also spend the day shadowing a trainer for a hefty $695 fee. ⊠ *MM 101.9 BS, 101900 Overseas Hwy.* ☎ *305/451–4060, 877/365–2683* ⊕ *www.dolphinsplus.com* ➱ *$10 admission only; interactive programs from $150.*

FAMILY **Dolphins Plus Oceanside.** A sister property to Dolphins Plus Bayside, this Dolphins Plus offers some of the same programs, and the age requirement is lower. The cheapest option, a shallow-water program, begins with a one-hour briefing, after which you enter the water up to your waist to interact with the dolphins. You only get to see them: part pants can snorkel but are not allowed to touch the dolphins. Prefer stay mostly dry? Opt to paint with a dolphin, or get a dolphin "kiss. For tactile interaction (fin tows, for example), sign up for the structured swim program, which is more expensive. ⊠ *MM 99, 31 Corrine Pl.* ☎ *305/451–1993, 866/860–7946* ⊕ *www.dolphinsplus.com* ✉ *Programs from $165.*

FAMILY **Florida Keys Wild Bird Center.** Have a nose-to-beak encounter with ospreys, hawks, herons, and other unreleasable birds at this bird rehabilitation center. The birds live in spacious screened enclosures along a boardwalk running through some of the best waterfront real estate in the Keys. Rehabilitated birds are set free, but about 30 have become permanent residents. Free birds—especially pelicans and egrets—come to visit every day for a free lunch from the center's staff. A short nature trail runs into the mangrove forest (bring bug spray May to October). A new addition is the interactive education center, now open about 1½ miles south. ⊠ *MM 93.6 BS, 93600 Overseas Hwy., Tavernier* ☎ *305/852–4486* ⊕ *www.keepthemflying.org* ✉ *Free, donations accepted.*

FAMILY **Jacobs Aquatic Center.** Take the plunge at one of three swimming pools: an eight-lane, 25-meter lap pool with two diving boards; a 3- to 4-foot-deep pool accessible to people with mobility challenges; and an interactive children's play pool with a waterslide, pirate ship, waterfall, and sloping zero entry instead of steps. Because so few of the motels in Key Largo have pools, it remains a popular destination for visiting families. ⊠ *Key Largo Community Park, 320 Laguna Ave., at St. Croix Pl.* ☎ *305/453–7946* ⊕ *www.jacobsaquaticcenter.org* ✉ *$12 ($2 discount weekdays).*

BEACHES

FAMILY **John Pennekamp Coral Reef State Park.** This state park is on everyone's
Fodor's Choice list for easy access to the best diving and snorkeling in Florida. The
★ underwater treasure encompasses 78 nautical square miles of coral reefs and sea-grass beds. It lies adjacent to the Florida Keys National Marine Sanctuary, which contains 40 of the 52 species of coral in the Atlantic Reef System and nearly 600 varieties of fish, from the colorful parrot fish to the demure cocoa damselfish. Whatever you do, get in the water. Snorkeling and diving trips ($30 and $75, respectively, equipment extra) and glass-bottom-boat rides to the reef ($24) are available, weather permitting. One of the most popular snorkel trips is to see *Christ of the Deep*, the 2-ton underwater statue of Jesus. The park also has nature trails, two man-made beaches, picnic shelters, a snack bar, and a campground. **Amenities:** food and drink; parking (fee); showers; toilets; water sports. **Best for:** snorkeling; swimming. ⊠ *MM 102.5 OS, 102601 Overseas Hwy.* ☎ *305/451–1202 for park, 305/451–6300 for excursions* ⊕ *www.pennekamppark.com, www. floridastateparks.org/pennekamp* ✉ *$4 for 1 person in vehicle, $8 for 2–8 people, $2 for pedestrians and cyclists or extra people (plus a 50¢ per-person county surcharge).*

WHERE TO EAT

$ ✕ **Alabama Jack's.** Calories be damned—the conch fritters here are
SEAFOOD heaven on a plate. Don't expect the traditional, golf-ball-size spheres
of dough; these are an unusual, mountainous, free-form creation of
fried, loaded-with-flavor perfection. **Known for:** heavenly conch fritters;
unique setting; weekend afternoon jam sessions. $ *Average main: $11*
✉ *58000 Card Sound Rd.* ☎ *305/248–8741.*

$$$ ✕ **Ballyhoo's.** Occupying a 1930s Conch house with outdoor seating
SEAFOOD right alongside U.S. 1 under the sea grape trees, this local favorite is all
about the fish (including the nautical decor). Yellowtail snapper, one
of the moistest, most flavorful local fish, is served 10 different ways on
the all-day menu, including blackened, stuffed with crab, and Parmesan
crusted. **Known for:** all-you-can-eat specials like Friday fish dinners
and in-season stone crab; Harvey's fish sandwich. $ *Average main: $21*
✉ *MM 97.8 median, 97800 Overseas Hwy.* ☎ *305/852–0822* ⊕ *www.
ballyhoosrestaurant.com.*

$$$ ✕ **Buzzard's Roost Grill and Pub.** The views are nice at this waterfront
SEAFOOD restaurant but the food is what gets your attention. Burgers, fish tacos,
Fodor's Choice and seafood baskets are lunch faves. **Known for:** marina views; daily
★ chef's specials. $ *Average main: $21* ✉ *Garden Cove Marina, 21 Garden Cove Dr.* ☎ *305/453–3746* ⊕ *www.buzzardsroostkeylargo.com.*

$ ✕ **Chad's Deli & Bakery.** It's a deli! It's a bakery! It's a pasta place! It's
AMERICAN also where the locals go. **Known for:** homemade soups and chowders;
eight varieties of supersized homemade cookies. $ *Average main: $10*
✉ *MM 92.3 BS, 92330 Overseas Hwy., Tavernier* ☎ *305/853–5566*
⊕ *www.chadsdeli.com.*

$$$ ✕ **The Fish House.** Restaurants not on the water have to produce the
SEAFOOD highest quality food to survive in the Keys. That's how the Fish House
has succeeded since the 1980s—so much so that it built the Fish House
Encore (a fancier version) next door to accommodate fans. **Known
for:** smoked fish appetizer; excellent key lime pie; fresh-as-can-be sea-
food. $ *Average main: $21* ✉ *MM 102.4 OS, 102341 Overseas Hwy.*
☎ *305/451–4665* ⊕ *www.fishhouse.com* ⊘ *Closed Sept.*

$$$ ✕ **The Fish House Encore.** To accommodate the crowds that gather at
SEAFOOD the Fish House, the owners opened this place with similar but more
refined cuisine ranging from sushi to steak. It's come into its own as a
more formal dining venue than its sister establishment. **Known for:** formal dining venue; off-season all-you-can-eat specials; live piano music
Thursday–Sunday. $ *Average main: $27* ✉ *MM 102.3 OS, 102341
Overseas Hwy.* ☎ *305/451–4665, 305/451–0650* ⊕ *www.fishhouse.
com* ⊘ *Closed Tues. and Oct. No lunch.*

$ ✕ **Harriette's Restaurant.** If you're looking for comfort food—like melt-
AMERICAN in-your-mouth biscuits the size of a salad plate—try this refreshing
throwback. Since the early 1980s, owner Harriette Mattson has been
here to personally greet guests who come for the to-die-for omelets and
old-fashioned hotcakes with sausage or bacon. **Known for:** breakfast
and lunch that's worth the wait; 13 muffin flavors. $ *Average main: $8*
✉ *MM 95.7 BS, 95710 Overseas Hwy.* ☎ *305/852–8689* ⊘ *No dinner*
⌗ *American Express not accepted.*

4

$$ ✕ **Jimmy Johnson's Big Chill.** Owned by former NFL coach Jimmy John-
SEAFOOD son, this waterfront establishment offers three entertaining experiences,
and all are big winners. You'll find the best sports bar in the Upper
Keys, complete with the coach's Super Bowl trophies; a main restaurant
with all-glass indoor seating and a waterfront deck; and an enormous
outdoor tiki bar with entertainment seven nights a week. **Known for:**
great sports bar; fantastic bay views; tuna nachos. $ *Average main:*
$19 ✉ *MM 104 BS, 104000 Overseas Hwy.* ☎ *305/453–9066* ⊕ *www.*
jjsbigchill.com.

$$ ✕ **Key Largo Conch House.** Tucked into the trees along the Overseas High-
AMERICAN way, this Victorian-style home (family owned since 2004) and its true-
to-the-Keys style of cooking is worth seeking out—at least the Food
Network and the Travel Channel have thought so in the past. The Old
South veranda and patio seating are ideal for winter dining, but indoors
the seating is tighter. **Known for:** serving lionfish; all-season outside
dining. $ *Average main: $16* ✉ *MM 100.2, 100211 Overseas Hwy.*
☎ *305/453–4844* ⊕ *www.keylargoconchhouse.com.*

$$ ✕ **Mrs. Mac's Kitchen.** Townies pack the counters and booths at this tiny
SEAFOOD eatery, where license plates are stuck on the walls and made into chande-
FAMILY liers, for everything from blackened prime rib to crab cakes. Every night
is themed including Meatloaf Monday, Italian Wednesday, and Sea-
food Sensation (offered Friday and Saturday). **Known for:** Champagne
breakfast; nightly themed dinners. $ *Average main: $17* ✉ *MM 99.4*
BS, 99336 Overseas Hwy. ☎ *305/451–3722, 305/451–6227* ⊕ *www.*
mrsmacskitchen.com ⊗ *Closed Sun.*

$$ ✕ **Snapper's.** In a lively, mangrove-ringed, waterfront setting, Snapper's
SEAFOOD has live music, Sunday brunch (including a build-your-own Bloody
Mary bar), killer rum drinks, and seating alongside the fishing dock.
"You hook 'em, we cook 'em" is the motto here but you have to clean
your own fish and dinner is $14 for a single diner, $15 per person
family-style meal with a mix of preparations when you provide the fish.
Known for: you hook, we cook; nightlife; fresh yellowtail. $ *Average*
main: $17 ✉ *MM 94.5 OS, 139 Seaside Ave.* ☎ *305/852–5956* ⊕ *www.*
snapperskeylargo.com.

$$$ ✕ **Sundowners.** If it's a clear night and you can snag a reservation, this
AMERICAN restaurant will treat you to a sherbet-hue sunset over Florida Bay. The
food is also excellent: try the key lime seafood, a happy combo of sau-
téed shrimp, lobster, and lump crabmeat swimming in a tangy sauce
spiked with Tabasco served over penne or rice. **Known for:** great sunset
viewing; Friday-night fish fry. $ *Average main: $22* ✉ *MM 104 BS,*
103900 Overseas Hwy. ☎ *305/451–4502* ⊕ *sundownerskeylargo.com.*

WHERE TO STAY

$ ⛺ **Amy Slate's Amoray Dive Resort.** You can read this hotel's name either
RESORT as "a moray" (referring to the moray eels you'll encounter on the reef)
or "amore" (Italian for love, which calls to mind the place's roman-
tic atmosphere), and you'll understand the place's dual charms. **Pros:**
top-notch dive operation; free use of snorkel equipment. **Cons:** noise
from highway; minimum stays during peak times. $ *Rooms from: $159*
✉ *MM 104.2 BS, 104250 Overseas Hwy.* ☎ *305/451–3595, 800/426–*
6729 ⊕ *www.amoray.com* ➫ *23 rooms, 8 apartments* ⦿ *No meals.*

$$
B&B/INN
🏨 **Azul del Mar.** The dock points the way to many beautiful sunsets at this no-smoking, adults-only boutique hotel, which Karol Marsden (an ad exec) and her husband Dominic (a travel photographer) have transformed from a run-down mom-and-pop place into a waterfront gem. **Pros:** great garden; good location; sophisticated design. **Cons:** small beach; high priced; minimum stays during holidays. $ *Rooms from: $299* ✉ *MM 104.3 BS, 104300 Overseas Hwy.* ☎ *305/451–0337, 888/253–2985* ⊕ *www.azulkeylargo.com* 🛏 *6 units* ⏹ *No meals.*

$
RESORT
🏨 **Coconut Bay Resort & Bay Harbor Lodge.** Some 200 feet of waterfront is the main attraction at these side-by-side sister properties that offer a choice between smaller rooms and larger separate cottages. **Pros:** bay front; neatly kept gardens; walking distance to restaurants; free use of kayaks, paddleboat, and paddleboards. **Cons:** a bit dated; small sea-walled sand beach. $ *Rooms from: $195* ✉ *MM 97.7 BS, 97702 Overseas Hwy.* ☎ *305/852–1625, 800/385–0986* ⊕ *www.coconut-baykeylargo.com* 🛏 *21 units* ⏹ *Breakfast.*

$$
B&B/INN
🏨 **Coconut Palm Inn.** You'd never find this waterfront haven unless someone told you it was there, as it's tucked into a residential neighborhood beneath towering palms and native gumbo limbos. **Pros:** secluded; quiet; sophisticated feel. **Cons:** front desk closes early each evening; no access to ice machine when staff leaves; breakfast is ho-hum. $ *Rooms from: $299* ✉ *MM 92 BS, 198 Harborview Dr., via Jo-Jean Way off Overseas Hwy., Tavernier* ☎ *305/852–3017* ⊕ *www.coconutpalminn.com* 🛏 *20 rooms* ⏹ *Breakfast.*

$$
B&B/INN
🏨 **Dove Creek Lodge.** With its sherbet-hued rooms and plantation-style furnishings, these tropical-style units (19 in all) range in size from simple lodge rooms to luxury two-bedroom suites. **Pros:** luxurious rooms; walk to Snapper's restaurant; complimentary kayaks and Wi-Fi. **Cons:** no beach; some find the music from next door bothersome. $ *Rooms from: $269* ✉ *MM 94.5 OS, 147 Seaside Ave.* ☎ *305/852–6200, 800/401–0057* ⊕ *www.dovecreeklodge.com* 🛏 *19 rooms* ⏹ *Breakfast.*

$$
RESORT
Fodor's Choice
★
🏨 **Hilton Key Largo Resort.** Nestled within a hardwood hammock (localese for uplands habitat where hardwood trees such as live oak grow) near the southern border of Everglades National Park, this sprawling, 13-acre resort underwent a $25 million renovation in 2017 without skipping a beat. **Pros:** nice nature trail on bay side; pretty pools with waterfalls; awesome trees; bicycles available for rent. **Cons:** some rooms overlook the parking lot; pools near the highway; expensive per-night resort fee. $ *Rooms from: $269* ✉ *MM 97 BS, 97000 Overseas Hwy.* ☎ *305/852–5553, 888/871–3437* ⊕ *www.keylargoresort.com* 🛏 *205 rooms* ⏹ *No meals.*

$$
RENTAL
🏨 **Island Bay Resort.** When Mike and Carol Shipley took over this off-the-beaten-path resort in 2000, they revamped the 10 bay-side cottages, improved the landscaping, and added touches such as hammocks and Adirondack chairs that make you feel like this is your own personal tropical playground. **Pros:** on the water; sunset views. **Cons:** most units are small; no pool; lacks on-site amenities. $ *Rooms from: $249* ✉ *92530 Overseas Hwy.* ☎ *305/852–4087* ⊕ *www.islandbayresort.com* 🛏 *10 units* ⏹ *No meals.*

$$ ⊞ **Kona Kai Resort, Gallery & Botanic Gardens.** Brilliantly colored bou-
RESORT   gainvillea, coconut palm, and guava trees—and a botanical garden of
Fodor'sChoice   other rare species—make this 2-acre adult hideaway one of the prettiest
★   places to stay in the Keys. **Pros:** free custom tours of botanical gardens
for guests; free use of sports equipment; knowledgeable staff. **Cons:**
expensive; some rooms are very close together. $ *Rooms from: $299*
⊠ *MM 97.8 BS, 97802 Overseas Hwy.* ☎ *305/852–7200, 800/365–*
7829 ⊕ *www.konakairesort.com* ⤳ *13 rooms* |○| *No meals.*

$$$ ⊞ **Marriott's Key Largo Bay Beach Resort.** This 17-acre bay-side resort has
RESORT   plenty of diversions, from diving to parasailing to a day spa. **Pros:** lots of
FAMILY   activities; free covered parking; dive shop on property; free Wi-Fi. **Cons:**
rooms facing highway can be noisy; thin walls. $ *Rooms from: $359*
⊠ *MM 103.8 BS, 103800 Overseas Hwy.* ☎ *305/453–0000, 866/849–*
3753 ⊕ *www.marriottkeylargo.com* ⤳ *153 rooms* |○| *No meals.*

$ ⊞ **The Pelican.** This 1950s throwback is reminiscent of the days when
HOTEL   parents packed the kids into the station wagon and headed to no-
frills seaside motels, complete with old-fashioned fishing off the dock.
Pros: free use of kayaks and a canoe; well-maintained dock; reasonable
rates. **Cons:** some small rooms; basic accommodations and amenities.
$ *Rooms from: $159* ⊠ *MM 99.3, 99340 Overseas Hwy.* ☎ *305/451–*
3576, 877/451–3576 ⊕ *www.hungrypelican.com* ⤳ *17 rooms, 4 effi-*
ciencies |○| *Breakfast.*

$$$ ⊞ **Playa Largo Resort and Spa, Autograph Collection.** This luxurious retreat,
RESORT   the first new hotel in Key Largo in over 21 years, is nestled on 14½ bay-
Fodor'sChoice   front acres. **Pros:** comfortable rooms, most with balconies; soft-sand
★   beach; excellent service; Playa Largo Kids Club. **Cons:** $25 a day resort
fee; pricey spa; $18 daily charge for valet parking. $ *Rooms from:*
$399 ⊠ *97450 Overseas Hwy.* ☎ *305/853–1001* ⊕ *playalargoresort.*
com ⤳ *178 units* |○| *No meals* ▭ *No credit cards.*

$ ⊞ **Popp's Motel.** Stylized metal herons mark the entrance to this 50-year-
HOTEL   old family-run motel. **Pros:** beach; intimate feel; discounts for multiple-
night stays. **Cons:** limited amenities; worn, outdated interiors. $ *Rooms*
from: $149 ⊠ *MM 95.5 BS, 95500 Overseas Hwy.* ☎ *305/852–5201,*
877/852–5201 ⊕ *www.poppsmotel.com* ⤳ *9 units* |○| *No meals.*

$ ⊞ **Seafarer Resort and Beach.** If you're looking for modern and updated,
HOTEL   this very basic, budget lodging isn't it. **Pros:** sandy beach; complimen-
tary kayak use; cheap rates. **Cons:** can hear road noise in some rooms;
some complaints about cleanliness. $ *Rooms from: $139* ⊠ *MM 97.6*
BS, 97684 Overseas Hwy. ☎ *305/852–5349* ⊕ *www.seafarerkeylargo.*
com ⤳ *15 units* |○| *No meals.*

NIGHTLIFE

The semiweekly *Keynoter* (Wednesday and Saturday), weekly *Reporter*
(Thursday), and Friday through Sunday editions of the *Miami Herald*
are the best sources of information on entertainment and nightlife.
Daiquiri bars, tiki huts, and seaside shacks pretty well summarize Key
Largo's bar scene.

Breezers Tiki Bar & Grille. Since its total makeover in 2016, you can now
mingle with locals over cocktails and catch amazing sunsets from the
comfort of an enclosed, air-conditioned bar. Floor-to-ceiling doors
can be opened on cool days and closed on hot days. It's located at

Marriott's Key Largo Bay Beach Resort. ⊠ *Marriott's Key Largo Bay Beach Resort, 103800 Overseas Hwy.* ☎ *305/453–0000.*

Caribbean Club. Walls plastered with Bogart memorabilia remind customers that the classic 1948 Bogart–Bacall flick *Key Largo* has a connection with this worn watering hole. Although no food is served and the floors are bare concrete, this landmark draws boaters, curious visitors, and local barflies to its humble bar stools and pool tables. But the real magic is around back, where you can grab a seat on the deck and catch a postcard-perfect sunset. Live music draws revelers Thursday through Sunday. ⊠ *MM 104 BS, 104080 Overseas Hwy.* ☎ *305/451–4466* ⊕ *caribbeanclubkl.com.*

SHOPPING

For the most part, shopping is sporadic in Key Largo, with a couple of shopping centers and fewer galleries than you find on the other big islands. If you're looking to buy scuba or snorkel equipment, you'll have plenty of choices.

Gallery at Kona Kai. Wander the gallery and get a peek of island life as you admire original works by local artists, as well as works from frequent guests who dabble in a variety of mediums. The exhibits are geared toward the environment and what you might experience while you're visiting—botanicals, wildlife, sunrises, and sunsets. ⊠ *MM 97.8 BS, 97802 Overseas Hwy.* ☎ *305/852–7200* ⊕ *www.g-k-k.com.*

FAMILY
Fodor'sChoice
★

Key Largo Chocolates. Specializing in key lime truffles made with quality Belgian chocolate, this is the only chocolate factory in the Florida Keys. But you'll find much more than just the finest white-, milk-, and dark-chocolate truffles; try the cupcakes, ice cream, and famous "chocodiles." The salted turtles, a fan favorite, are worth every calorie. Chocolate classes are also available for kids and adults, and a small gift area showcases local art, jewelry, hot sauces, and other goodies. Look for the bright-green-and-pink building. ⊠ *MM 100 BS, 100471 Overseas Hwy.* ☎ *305/453–6613* ⊕ *www.keylargochocolates.com.*

Key Lime Products. Go into olfactory overload—you'll find yourself sniffing every single bar of soap and scented candle inside this key lime treasure trove. Take home some key lime juice (supereasy pie-making directions are right on the bottle), marmalade, candies, sauces, even key lime shampoo. Outside, you'll find a huge selection of wood carvings, pottery, unique patio furniture, and artwork. The fresh fish sandwiches and conch fritters served here are alone worth the stop. ⊠ *MM 95.2 BS, 95231 Overseas Hwy.* ☎ *305/853–0378, 800/870–1780* ⊕ *www.keylimeproducts.com.*

Randy's Florida Keys Gift Co. Since 1989, Randy's has been *the* place for unique gifts. Owner Randy and his wife Lisa aren't only fantastic at stocking the store with a plethora of items, they're also well respected in the community for their generosity and dedication. Stop in and say hello, then browse the tight aisles and loaded shelves filled with key lime candles, books, wood carvings, jewelry, clothing, T-shirts, and eclectic, tropical decor items. This friendly shop prides itself on carrying wares from local craftsmen, and there's something for every budget. ⊠ *102421 Overseas Hwy.* ✛ *On U.S. 1, next to the Sandal Factory Outlet* ☎ *305/453–9229* ⊕ *www.keysmermaid.com.*

Shell World. You can find lots of shops in the Keys that sell cheesy souvenirs—snow globes, alligator hats, and shell-encrusted anything. This is the granddaddy of them all. But this sprawling building in the median of Overseas Highway contains much more than the usual tourist trinkets—you'll find high-end clothing, jewelry, housewares, artwork, and a wide selection of keepsakes, from delightfully tacky to tasteful. ⊠ *MM 97.5, 97600 Overseas Hwy.* ☏ *305/852–8245, 888/398–6233* ⊕ *www.shellworldflkeys.com.*

SPORTS AND THE OUTDOORS

BOATING

FAMILY **Everglades Eco-Tours.** For over 30 years, Captain Sterling has operated Everglades and Florida Bay ecology tours and more expensive sunset cruises. With his expert guidance, you can see dolphins, manatees, and birds from the casual comfort of his pontoon boat, equipped with PVC chairs. Bring your own food and drinks; each tour has a maximum of six people. ⊠ *Sundowners Restaurant, MM 104 BS, 103900 Overseas Hwy.* ☏ *305/853–5161, 888/224–6044* ⊕ *www.captainsterling.com* ▣ *From $59.*

FAMILY **M.V. Key Largo Princess.** Two-hour glass-bottom-boat trips and more expensive sunset cruises on a luxury 70-foot motor yacht with a 280-square-foot glass viewing area depart from the Holiday Inn docks three times a day. ■ **TIP→** Purchase tickets online to save big. ⊠ *Holiday Inn, MM 100 OS, 99701 Overseas Hwy.* ☏ *305/451–4655, 877/648–8129* ⊕ *www.keylargoprincess.com* ▣ *$35.*

CANOEING AND KAYAKING

Sea kayaking continues to gain popularity in the Keys. You can paddle for a few hours or the whole day, on your own or with a guide. Some outfitters even offer overnight trips. The **Florida Keys Overseas Paddling Trail,** part of a statewide system, runs from Key Largo to Key West. You can paddle the entire distance, 110 miles on the Atlantic side, which takes 9 to 10 days. The trail also runs the chain's length on the bay side, which is a longer route.

Coral Reef Park Co. At John Pennekamp Coral Reef State Park, this operator has a fleet of canoes and kayaks for gliding around the 2½-mile mangrove trail or along the coast. Powerboat rentals are also available. ⊠ *MM 102.5 OS, 102601 Overseas Hwy.* ☏ *305/451–6300* ⊕ *www. pennekamppark.com* ▣ *Rentals from $12 per hr.*

Florida Bay Outfitters. Rent canoes, sea kayaks, or Hobie Eclipses (the newest craze) from this company, which sets up self-guided trips on the Florida Keys Paddling Trail, helps with trip planning, and matches equipment to your skill level. It also runs myriad guided tours around Key Largo. Take a full-moon paddle or a one- to seven-day kayak tour to the Everglades, Lignumvitae Key, or Indian Key. ⊠ *MM 104 BS, 104050 Overseas Hwy.* ☏ *305/451–3018* ⊕ *www.paddlefloridakeys. com* ▣ *From $15.*

FISHING

Private charters and big "head" boats (so named because they charge "by the head") are great for anglers who don't have their own vessel.

Sailors Choice. Fishing excursions depart twice daily (half-day trips are cash only), but the company also does private charters. The 65-foot boat leaves from the Holiday Inn docks. Rods, bait, and license are included. ⊠ *Holiday Inn Resort & Marina, MM 100 OS, 99701 Overseas Hwy.* ☎ *305/451–1802, 305/451–0041* ⊕ *www.sailorschoicefishingboat.com* ✉ *From $40.*

SCUBA DIVING AND SNORKELING

Much of what makes the Upper Keys a singular dive destination is variety. Places like Molasses Reef, which begins 3 feet below the surface and descends to 55 feet, have something for everyone from novice snorkelers to experienced divers. The *Spiegel Grove*, a 510-foot vessel, lies in 130 feet of water, but its upper regions are only 60 feet below the surface. On rough days, Key Largo Undersea Park's Emerald Lagoon is a popular spot. Expect to pay about $80 to $85 for a two-tank, two-site dive trip with tanks and weights, or $35 to $40 for a two-site snorkel outing. Get big discounts by booking multiple trips.

Amy Slate's Amoray Dive Resort. This outfit makes diving easy. Stroll down to the full-service dive shop (PADI, TDI, and BSAC certified), then onto a 45-foot catamaran. Certification courses are also offered. ⊠ *MM 104.2 BS, 104250 Overseas Hwy.* ☎ *305/451–3595, 800/426–6729* ⊕ *www.amoray.com* ✉ *From $85.*

Conch Republic Divers. Book diving instruction as well as scuba and snorkeling tours of all the wrecks and reefs of the Upper Keys. Two-location dives are the standard, and you'll pay an extra $15 for tank and weights. ⊠ *MM 90.8 BS, 90800 Overseas Hwy.* ☎ *305/852–1655, 800/274–3483* ⊕ *www.conchrepublicdivers.com* ✉ *From $70.*

Coral Reef Park Co. At John Pennekamp Coral Reef State Park, this company gives 3½-hour scuba and 2½-hour snorkeling tours of the park. In addition to the great location and the dependability it's also suited for water adventurers of all levels. ⊠ *MM 102.5 OS, 102601 Overseas Hwy.* ☎ *305/451–6300* ⊕ *www.pennekamppark.com* ✉ *From $30.*

Horizon Divers. The company has customized diving and snorkeling trips that depart daily aboard a 45-foot catamaran. ⊠ *105800 Overseas Hwy* ☎ *305/453–3535, 800/984–3483* ⊕ *www.horizondivers.com* ✉ *From $50 for snorkeling, from $80 for diving.*

Island Ventures. If you like dry, British humor and no crowds, this is the operator for you. It specializes in small groups for snorkeling or dive trips, no more than 10 people per boat. Scuba trips are two tank, two locations, and include tanks and weights; ride-alongs pay just $35. Choose morning or afternoon. ⊠ *Jules Undersea Lodge, 51 Shoreland Dr.* ☎ *305/451–4957* ⊕ *www.islandventure.com* ✉ *Snorkel trips $50, diving $85.*

Ocean Divers. The PADI five-star facility has been around since 1975 and offers day and night dives, a range of courses, and dive-lodging packages. Two-tank reef dives include tank and weight rental. There are also organized snorkeling trips with equipment. ⊠ *MM 100 OS, 522 Caribbean Dr.* ☎ *305/451–1113, 800/451–1113* ⊕ *www.oceandivers.com* ✉ *Snorkel trips from $30, diving from $80.*

4

Fodor's Choice **Quiescence Diving Services.** This operator sets itself apart in two ways: it
★ limits groups to six to ensure personal attention and offers both two-
dive day and night dives, as well as twilight dives when sea creatures
are most active. There are also organized snorkeling excursions. ⊠ *MM
103.5 BS, 103680 Overseas Hwy.* ☎ *305/451–2440* ⊕ *www.quiescence.
com* 🖃 *Snorkel trips $49, diving from $69.*

ISLAMORADA

Islamorada is between MM 90.5 and 70.

Early settlers named this key after their schooner, *Island Home,* but to
make it sound more romantic they translated it into Spanish: *Isla Morada.*
The Chamber of Commerce prefers to use its literal translation, "Purple
Island," which refers either to a purple-shelled snail that once inhabited
these shores or to the brilliantly colored orchids and bougainvilleas.

Early maps show Islamorada as encompassing only Upper Matecumbe
Key. But the incorporated "Village of Islands" is made up of a string of
islands that the Overseas Highway crosses, including Plantation Key,
Windley Key, Upper Matecumbe Key, Lower Matecumbe Key, Craig
Key, and Fiesta Key. In addition, two state-park islands accessible only
by boat—Indian Key and Lignumvitae Key—belong to the group.

Islamorada (locals pronounce it *"eye-*la-mor-*ah-*da") is one of the
world's top fishing destinations. For nearly 100 years, seasoned anglers
have fished these clear, warm waters teeming with trophy-worthy fish.
There are numerous options for those in search of the big ones, including chartering a boat with its own crew or heading out on a vessel
rented from one of the plethora of marinas along this 20-mile stretch
of the Overseas Highway. More than 150 backcountry guides and 400
offshore captains are at your service.

GETTING HERE AND AROUND
Most visitors arrive in Islamorada by car. If you're flying in to Miami
International Airport or Key West International Airport, you can easily
rent a car (reserve in advance) to make the drive.

TOURS
Contact **Florida Keys Food Tours.** ☎ *305/393–9183*
⊕ *www.flkeysfoodtours.com.*

VISITOR INFORMATION
Contact **Islamorada Chamber of Commerce & Visitors Center.** ⊠ *MM 87.1
BS, 87100 Overseas Hwy.* ☎ *305/664–4503, 800/322–5397* ⊕ *www.islamorada-
chamber.com.*

EXPLORING
TOP ATTRACTIONS
Florida Keys Memorial / Hurricane Monument. On Monday, September 2,
1935, more than 400 people perished when the most intense hurricane
to make landfall in the United States swept through this area of the
Keys. Two years later, the Florida Keys Memorial was dedicated in
their honor. Native coral rock, known as keystone, covers the 18-foot
obelisk monument that marks the remains of more than 300 storm

Islamorada's warm waters attract large fish and the anglers and charter captains who want to catch them.

victims. A sculpted plaque of bending palms and waves graces the front (although many are bothered that the palms are bending in the wrong direction). In 1995, the memorial was placed on the National Register of Historic Places. ⊠ *MM 81.8, in front of the public library, 81831 Old State Hwy. 4A, Upper Matecumbe Key* ✛ *Just south of the Cheeca Lodge entrance* ⌦ *Free.*

History of Diving Museum. Adding to the region's reputation for world-class diving, this museum plunges into the history of man's thirst for undersea exploration. Among its 13 galleries of interactive and other interesting displays are a submarine and helmet re-created from the film *20,000 Leagues Under the Sea.* Vintage U.S. Navy equipment, diving helmets from around the world, and early scuba gear explore 4,000 years of diving history. For the grand finale, spend $3 for a mouth-piece and sing your favorite tune at the helium bar. There are extended hours (until 7 pm) on the third Wednesday of every month. ⊠ *MM 83 BS, 82990 Overseas Hwy., Upper Matecumbe Key* ☎ *305/664–9737* ⊕ *www.divingmuseum.org* ⌦ *$12.*

FAMILY **Robbie's Marina.** Huge, prehistoric-looking denizens of the not-so-deep, silver-sided tarpon congregate around the docks at this marina on Lower Matecumbe Key. Children—and lots of adults—pay $3 for a bucket of sardines to feed them and $1 each for dock admission. Spend some time hanging out at this authentic Keys community, where you can grab a bite to eat indoors or out, shop at a slew of artisans' booths, or charter a boat, kayak, or other watercraft. ⊠ *MM 77.5 BS, 77522 Overseas Hwy., Lower Matecumbe Key* ☎ *305/664–9814, 877/664–8498* ⊕ *www.robbies.com* ⌦ *Dock access $1.*

FAMILY **Theater of the Sea.** The second-oldest marine-mammal center in the world doesn't attempt to compete with more modern, more expensive parks. Even so, it's among the better attractions north of Key West, especially if you have kids in tow. In addition to marine-life exhibits and shows, you can make reservations for up-close-and-personal encounters like a swim with a dolphin or sea lion, or stingray and turtle feedings (which include general admission; reservations required). These are popular, so reserve in advance. Ride a "bottomless" boat to see what's below the waves and take a guided tour of the marine-life exhibits. Nonstop animal shows highlight conservation issues. You can stop for lunch at the grill, shop in the extensive gift shop, or sunbathe and swim at the private beach. This easily could be an all-day attraction. ✉ *MM 84.5 OS, 84721 Overseas Hwy., Windley Key* ☎ *305/664–2431* 🌐 *www.theaterofthesea.com* 🎟 *$31.95; interaction programs $45–$195.*

BEACHES

FAMILY **Anne's Beach Park.** On Lower Matecumbe Key this popular village park is named for a local environmental activist. Its "beach" (really a typical Keys-style sand flat with a gentle slope) is best enjoyed at low tide. The nicest feature here is an elevated, wooden half-mile boardwalk that meanders through a natural wetland hammock. Covered picnic areas along the way give you places to linger and enjoy the view. Restrooms are at the north end. Weekends are packed with Miami day-trippers as it's the only public beach until you reach Marathon. **Amenities:** parking (no fee); toilets. **Best for:** partiers; snorkeling; swimming; windsurfing. ✉ *MM 73.5 OS, Lower Matecumbe Key* ☎ *305/853–1685.*

WHERE TO EAT

$$$ SEAFOOD Fodor's Choice ★ 🍴 **Chef Michael's.** This local favorite whose motto is "Peace. Love. Hogfish." has been making big waves since its opening in 2011 with chef Michael Ledwith at the helm. Seafood is selected fresh daily, then elegantly prepared with a splash of tropical flair. **Known for:** fresh seafood daily; gluten-free and vegetarian options; melt-in-your-mouth steaks. [$] *Average main: $30* ✉ *MM 81.7, 81671 Overseas Hwy., Upper Matecumbe Key* ☎ *305/664–0640* 🌐 *www.foodtotalkabout.com* 🕒 *No lunch Mon.–Sat.*

$$$ SEAFOOD 🍴 **Green Turtle Inn.** This circa-1947 landmark inn and its vintage neon sign is a slice of Florida Keys history. Period photographs decorate the wood-paneled walls. **Known for:** turtle chowder; a piece of Florida Keys history. [$] *Average main: $24* ✉ *MM 81.2 OS, 81219 Overseas Hwy., Upper Matecumbe Key* ☎ *305/664–2006* 🌐 *www.greenturtlekeys.com* 🕒 *Closed Mon.*

$$ SEAFOOD 🍴 **Hungry Tarpon.** As part of the colorful, bustling Old Florida scene at Robbie's Marina, you know that the seafood here is fresh and top quality. The extensive menu seems as if it's bigger than the dining space, which consists of a few tables and counter seating indoors, plus tables out back under the mangrove trees, close to where tourists pay to feed the tarpon in the marina. **Known for:** extensive menu; heart-of-the-action location. [$] *Average main: $19* ✉ *MM 77.5 BS, 77522 Overseas Hwy., Lower Matecumbe Key* ☎ *305/664–0535* 🌐 *www.hungrytarpon.com.*

$$ SEAFOOD FAMILY 🍴 **Islamorada Fish Company.** When a restaurant is owned by Bass Pro Shops, you know the seafood should be as fresh as you can get it. The restaurant is housed in an open-air, oversized tiki hut right on Florida Bay, making this the quintessential Keys experience. **Known for:** tourist hot spot; great views; seafood baskets. [$] *Average main: $18* ✉ *MM 81.5 BS, 81532 Overseas Hwy., Windley Key* ☎ *305/664–9271* 🌐 *restaurants.basspro.com/fishcompany/Islamorada/.*

$ SEAFOOD 🍴 **Island Grill at Snake Creek.** Don't be fooled by appearances; this shack on the waterfront takes island breakfast, lunch, and dinner up a notch. The eclectic menu tempts you with such dishes as its famed "original tuna nachos," lobster rolls, and a nice selection of seafood and sandwiches. **Known for:** eclectic seafood options; slow service; nice views. [$] *Average main: $14* ✉ *MM 85.5 OS, 85501 Overseas Hwy., Windley Key* ☎ *305/664–8400* 🌐 *www.keysislandgrill.com.*

$$$ JAPANESE 🍴 **Kaiyo Grill & Sushi.** The decor—an inviting setting that includes colorful abstract mosaics, polished wood floors, and upholstered banquettes—almost steals the show at Kaiyo, but the food is equally interesting. The menu, a fusion of East and West, offers sushi rolls that combine local ingredients with traditional Japanese tastes. **Known for:** excellent wine and sake pairings; show-stopping decor; East-meets-West menu. [$] *Average main: $28* ✉ *MM 81.5 OS, 81701 Overseas Hwy., Upper Matecumbe Key* ☎ *305/664–5556* 🌐 *www.kaiyogrill.com* 🕒 *No lunch.*

$$ AMERICAN 🍴 **Lorelei Restaurant & Cabana Bar.** While local anglers gather here for breakfast, lunch and dinner bring a mix of islanders and visitors for straightforward food and front-row seats to the sunset. Live music seven nights a week ensures a lively nighttime scene, and the menu staves off inebriation with burgers, barbecued baby back ribs, and Parmesan-crusted snapper. **Known for:** amazing sunset views; nightly live music. [$] *Average main: $15* ✉ *MM 82 BS, 81924 Overseas Hwy., Upper Matecumbe Key* ☎ *305/664–2692* 🌐 *www.loreleicabanabar.com.*

$$$$ SEAFOOD 🍴 **Marker 88.** A few yards from Florida Bay, this popular seafood restaurant has large picture windows that offer great sunset views. The bay is lovely no matter what time of day you visit, though, and most diners opt to sit outdoors. **Known for:** great outdoor seating; key lime baked Alaska; extensive wine list. [$] *Average main: $34* ✉ *MM 88 BS, 88000 Overseas Hwy., Plantation Key* ☎ *305/852–9315* 🌐 *www.marker88.info.*

$$$ ECLECTIC FAMILY 🍴 **Morada Bay Beach Café.** This bay-front restaurant wins high marks for its surprisingly stellar cuisine, tables planted in the sand, and tiki torches that bathe the evening in romance. Entrées feature alluring combinations like fresh fish of the day sautéed with Meyer lemon butter and whole fried snapper with coconut rice. **Known for:** feet-in-the-sand dining; full-moon parties. [$] *Average main: $27* ✉ *MM 81 BS, 81600 Overseas Hwy., Upper Matecumbe Key* ☎ *305/664–0604* 🌐 *www.moradabay.com.*

$$$$ FRENCH Fodor's Choice ★ 🍴 **Pierre's.** One of the Keys' most elegant restaurants, Pierre's marries colonial style with modern food trends. Full of interesting architectural artifacts, the place oozes style, especially the wicker-chair-strewn veranda overlooking the bay. **Known for:** romantic spot for that special

night out; seasonally changing menu; full-moon parties. $ *Average main: $43* ⊠ *MM 81.5 BS, 81600 Overseas Hwy., Upper Matecumbe Key* ☎ *305/664–3225* ⊕ *www.moradabay.com* ⊗ *No lunch.*

WHERE TO STAY

$$
RESORT

⚏ Amara Cay Resort. Simple yet chic, Islamorada's newest resort is an oceanfront gem. **Pros:** free shuttle to local attractions; on-site dive shop; large heated pool. **Cons:** pricey $28 a day resort fee; expensive restaurant; living area of rooms lack seating. $ *Rooms from: $299* ⊠ *MM 80 OS, 80001 Overseas Hwy.* ☎ *305/664–0073* ⊕ *www.amaracayresort. com* ⌫ *110 rooms* ⦿⧵ *No meals.*

$$$
B&B/INN
Fodor's Choice
★

⚏ Casa Morada. This relic from the 1950s has been restyled into a suave, design-forward, all-suites property with outdoor showers and Jacuzzis in some of the suites. **Pros:** cool design; complimentary snacks and bottled water; complimentary use of bikes, kayaks, and snorkel gear. **Cons:** trailer park across the street; beach is small and inconsequential. $ *Rooms from: $309* ⊠ *MM 82 BS, 136 Madeira Rd., Upper Matecumbe Key* ☎ *305/664–0044, 888/881–3030* ⊕ *www.casamorada.com* ⌫ *16 suites* ⦿⧵ *Breakfast.*

$$$$
RESORT
Fodor's Choice
★

⚏ Cheeca Lodge & Spa. At 27 acres, this may be the largest resort in the Keys, and it's also big on included amenities. **Pros:** beautifully landscaped grounds; new designer rooms; water-sports center on property. **Cons:** expensive rates; expensive resort fee; very busy. $ *Rooms from: $499* ⊠ *MM 82 OS, 81801 Overseas Hwy., Upper Matecumbe Key* ☎ *305/664– 4651, 800/327–2888* ⊕ *www.cheeca.com* ⌫ *123 rooms* ⦿⧵ *No meals.*

$
HOTEL

⚏ Drop Anchor Resort and Marina. Immaculately maintained, this place has the feel of an old friend's beach house. **Pros:** bright and colorful; attention to detail; laid-back charm. **Cons:** noise from the highway; beach is better for fishing than swimming. $ *Rooms from: $159* ⊠ *MM 85 OS, 84959 Overseas Hwy., Windley Key* ☎ *305/664–4863, 888/664–4863* ⊕ *www.dropanchorresort.com* ⌫ *18 suites* ⦿⧵ *No meals.*

$$
RESORT

⚏ The Islander Resort, A Guy Harvey Outpost. Guests here get to choose between a self-sufficient townhome on the bay side or an oceanfront resort with on-site restaurants and oodles of amenities. **Pros:** spacious rooms; nice kitchens; eye-popping views. **Cons:** pricey for what you get; beach has rough sand. $ *Rooms from: $249* ⊠ *MM 82.1 OS, 82200 Overseas Hwy., Upper Matecumbe Key* ☎ *305/664–2031, 800/753– 6002* ⊕ *www.guyharveyoutpostislamorada.com* ⌫ *122 rooms, 24 townhomes* ⦿⧵ *Breakfast.*

$$$$
HOTEL
Fodor's Choice
★

⚏ The Moorings Village. This tropical retreat is everything you imagine when you envision the laid-back Keys—from hammocks swaying between towering trees to manicured sand lapped by aqua-green waves. **Pros:** romantic setting; good dining options with room-charging privileges; beautiful views. **Cons:** no room service; $25 daily resort fee for activities. $ *Rooms from: $529* ⊠ *MM 81.6 OS, 123 Beach Rd., Upper Matecumbe Key* ☎ *305/664–4708* ⊕ *www.themooringsvillage. com* ⌫ *18 cottages* ⦿⧵ *No meals.*

$$$
HOTEL
Fodor's Choice
★

⚏ Ocean House. This adults-only boutique hotel is situated right on the Atlantic, yet it's hidden from passersby amid lush gardens. **Pros:** complimentary use of kayaks, snorkel equipment, and bicycles; luxurious facilities and amenities. **Cons:** limited number of units means it's often booked solid; luxury comes at a price. $ *Rooms from: $319* ⊠ *MM 82 OS, 82885 Old Hwy., Windley Key* ☎ *866/540–5520* ⊕ *www.ocean-housefloridakeys.com* ↯ *8 suites* ¶◎¶ *Some meals.*

$$
RESORT

⊞ **Postcard Inn Beach Resort & Marina at Holiday Isle.** After an $11 million renovation that encompassed updating everything from the rooms to the public spaces, this iconic property (formerly known as the Holiday Isle Beach Resort) has found new life. **Pros:** large private beach; heated pools; on-site restaurants including Ciao Hound Italian Kitchen. **Cons:** rooms near tiki bar are noisy; minimum stay required during peak times; rooms without an oceanfront view overlook a parking lot. $ *Rooms from: $267* ⊠ *MM 84 OS, 84001 Overseas Hwy., Plantation Key* ☎ *305/664–2321* ⊕ *www.holidayisle.com* ↯ *143 rooms* ¶◎¶ *No meals.*

$
HOTEL
FAMILY

⊞ **Ragged Edge Resort.** Nicely tucked away in a residential area at the ocean's edge, this family-owned hotel draws returning guests who'd rather fish off the dock and grill up dinner than loll around in Egyptian cotton sheets. **Pros:** oceanfront; boat docks and ramp; cheap rates. **Cons:** dated decor; off the beaten path. $ *Rooms from: $169* ⊠ *MM 86.5 OS, 243 Treasure Harbor Rd., Plantation Key* ☎ *305/852–5389, 800/436–2023* ⊕ *www.ragged-edge.com* ↯ *10 units* ¶◎¶ *No meals.*

SHOPPING

Art galleries, upscale gift shops, and the mammoth World Wide Sportsman (if you want to look the part of a local fisherman, you must wear a shirt from here) make up the variety and superior style of Islamorada shopping.

Banyan Tree. Stroll and shop among the colorful orchids and lush plants at this outdoor garden and indoor boutique known for its tropical splendor, unique gifts, and free-spirited clothing. There is nothing quite like it in the area. ⊠ *MM 81.2 OS, 81197 Overseas Hwy., Upper Matecumbe Key* ☎ *305/664–3433* ⊕ *www.banyantreegarden.com* ☉ *Closed Sun.*

Casa Mar Village. Change is good, and in this case, it's fantastic. What was once a row of worn-down buildings is now a merry blend of gift shops and galleries with the added bonus of a place selling fresh-roasted coffee. By day, these colorful shops glisten at their canal-front location; by nightfall, they're lit up like a lovely Christmas town. The offerings include What The Fish Rolls & More restaurant; Casa Mar Seafood fish market; and Paddle The Florida Keys, where you can rent paddleboards and kayaks. ⊠ *MM 90 OS, 90775 Old Hwy., Upper Matecumbe Key* ⊕ *www.casamarvillage.com.*

Gallery Morada. This gallery is a go-to destination for one-of-a-kind gifts, beautifully displayed blown glass, original sculptures, paintings, and jewelry by 200 artists. Its location, front and center, makes it the gateway to the Morada Way Arts and Cultural District, an area with artist galleries, shops, potters, gardens, and culinary classes. ⊠ *MM 81.6 OS, 81611 Old Hwy., Upper Matecumbe Key* ☎ *305/664–3650* ⊕ *www.gallerymorada.com.*

Rain Barrel Artisan Village. This is a natural and unhurried shopping showplace. Set in a tropical garden of shady trees, native shrubs, and orchids, the crafts village has shops selling the work of local and national artists as well as resident artists who sell work from their own studios. Take a selfie with "Betsy," the giant Florida lobster, roadside. ⊠ *MM 86.7 BS, 86700 Overseas Hwy., Plantation Key* ☎ *305/852–3084* ⊕ *www. seefloridaonline.com/rainbarrel/index.html.*

Redbone Gallery. This gallery stocks hand-stitched clothing, giftware, and jewelry, in addition to works of art by watercolorists C.D. Clarke, Christine Black, and Julie Joyce; and painters David Hall, Steven Left, Tim Borski, and Jorge Martinez. Proceeds benefit cystic fibrosis research. Find them in the Morada Way Arts & Cultural District. ⊠ *MM 81.5 OS, 200 Morada Way, Upper Matecumbe Key* ☎ *305/664–2002* ⊕ *www.redbone.org.*

World Wide Sportsman. This two-level retail center sells upscale and everyday fishing equipment, resort clothing, sportfishing art, and other gifts. When you're tired of shopping, relax at the Zane Grey Long Key Lounge, located on the second level—but not before you step up and into *Pilar,* a replica of Hemingway's boat. ⊠ *MM 81.5 BS, 81576 Overseas Hwy., Upper Matecumbe Key* ☎ *305/664–4615, 800/327–2880.*

SPORTS AND THE OUTDOORS
BOATING

Bump & Jump. You can rent both fishing and deck boats here (from 15 to 29 feet) by the day or the week. Free local delivery with seven-day rentals from each of their locations is available. ⊠ *MM 85.9 BS and 99.7 OS, 85920 Overseas Hwy., Upper Matecumbe Key* ☎ *305/664–9404, 877/453–9463* ⊕ *www.keysboatrental.com* ☒ *Rentals from $185 per day.*

Early Bird Fishing Charters. Captain Ross knows these waters well and he'll hook you up with whatever is in season—mahimahi, sailfish, tuna, and wahoo, to name a few—while you cruise on a comfy and stylish 43-foot custom Willis charter boat. The salon is air-conditioned for those hot summer days, and everything but booze and food is included. ⊠ *Postcard Inn Marina, MM 84.5 OS, 84001 Overseas Hwy.* ☎ *305/942–3618* ⊕ *www.fishearlybird.com* ☒ *4 hrs $800; 6 hrs $1,000; 8 hrs $1,200.*

Nauti-Limo. Captain Joe Fox has converted the design of a 1983 pink Caddy stretch limo into a less-than-luxurious but certainly curious watercraft. The seaworthy hybrid—complete with wheels—can sail with the top down if you're in the mood. Only in the Keys! One-hour and longer tours are available. ⊠ *Lorelei Restaurant & Yacht Club, MM 82 BS, 96 Madeira Rd., Upper Matecumbe Key* ☎ *305/942–3793* ⊕ *www.nautilimo.com* ☒ *From $60.*

Robbie's Boat Rentals & Charters. This full-service company will even give you a crash course on how not to crash your boat. The rental fleet includes an 18-foot skiff with a 90-horsepower outboard to a 21-foot deck boat with a 130-horsepower engine. Robbie's also rents snorkeling gear (there's good snorkeling nearby) and sells bait, drinks, and snacks. Want to hire a guide who knows the local waters and where the fish lurk? Robbie's offers offshore-fishing trips, patch-reef trips, and party-boat fishing. Backcountry flats trips are a specialty. ⊠ *MM 77.5 BS, 77522 Overseas Hwy., Lower Matecumbe Key* ☎ *305/664–9814, 877/664–8498* ⊕ *www.robbies.com* ☒ *From $185 per day.*

Kayak ready to be used on the beach in the Florida Keys

FISHING

Here in the self-proclaimed "Sportfishing Capital of the World," sailfish is the prime catch in the winter and mahimahi in the summer. Buchanan Bank just south of Islamorada is a good spot to try for tarpon in the spring. Blackfin tuna and amberjack are generally plentiful in the area, too. ■TIP→ **The Hump at Islamorada ranks highest among anglers' favorite fishing spots in Florida (declared Florida Monthly magazine's best for seven years in a row) due to the incredible offshore marine life.**

Captain Ted Wilson. Go into the backcountry for bonefish, tarpon, redfish, snook, and shark aboard a 17-foot boat that accommodates up to three anglers. Choose half-day (four hours), three-quarter-day (six hours), or full-day (eight hours) trips, or evening tarpon fishing excursions. Rates are for one or two anglers. There's a $75 charge for an additional person. ⊠ *MM 79.9 OS, 79851 Overseas Hwy., Upper Matecumbe Key* ☎ *305/942–5224, 305/664–9463* ⊕ *www.captaintedwilson.com* ⌛ *Half-day and evening trips from $450.*

Florida Keys Fly Fish. Like other top fly-fishing and light-tackle guides, Captain Geoff Colmes helps his clients land trophy fish in the waters around the Keys, from Islamorada to Flamingo in the Everglades. ⊠ *105 Palm La., Upper Matecumbe Key* ☎ *305/853–0741* ⊕ *www.florida-keysflyfish.com* ⌛ *From $550.*

Florida Keys Outfitters. Long before fly-fishing became popular, Sandy Moret was fishing the Keys for bonefish, tarpon, and redfish. Now he attracts anglers from around the world on a quest for the big catch. His weekend fly-fishing classes include classroom instruction, equipment, and daily lunch. Guided fishing trips can be done for a half day or

DID YOU KNOW?

The coral making up the Barrier Reef is living and provides an ecosystem for small marine creatures. Bumping against or touching the coral can kill these creatures as well as damage the reef itself.

full day. Packages combining fishing and accommodations at Islander Resort are available. ⊠ *Green Turtle, MM 81.2, 81219 Overseas Hwy., Upper Matecumbe Key* ☎ *305/664–5423* ⊕ *www.floridakeysoutfitters. com* ✆ *Half day trips from $495.*

Hubba Hubba Charters. Captain Ken Knudsen has fished the Keys waters since the 1950s. A licensed backcountry guide, he's ranked among Florida's top 10 by national fishing magazines. He offers four-hour sunset trips for tarpon and two-hour sunset trips for bonefish, as well as half- and full-day outings. Prices are for one or two anglers, and tackle and bait are included. ⊠ *Bud n' Mary's Marina, MM 79.8 OS, Upper Matecumbe Key* ☎ *305/664–9281* ✆ *From $250.*

Miss Islamorada. This 65-foot party boat offers full-day trips. Bring your lunch or buy one from the dockside deli. ⊠ *Bud n' Mary's Marina, MM 79.8 OS, 79851 Overseas Hwy., Upper Matecumbe Key* ☎ *305/664– 2461, 800/742–7945* ⊕ *www.budnmarys.com* ✆ *$65.*

SCUBA DIVING AND SNORKELING

San Pedro Underwater Archaeological Preserve State Park. About 1¼ nautical miles south of Indian Key is the San Pedro Underwater Archaeological Preserve State Park, which includes the remains of a Spanish treasure-fleet ship that sank in 1733. The state of Florida protects the site for divers; no spearfishing or souvenir collecting is allowed. Seven replica cannons and a plaque enhance what basically amounts to a 90-foot-long pile of ballast stones. Resting in only 18 feet of water, its ruins are visible to snorkelers as well as divers and attract a colorful array of fish. ⊠ *MM 85.5 OS* ☎ *305/664–2540* ⊕ *www.floridastateparks.org/sanpedro.*

Florida Keys Dive Center. Dive from John Pennekamp Coral Reef State Park to Alligator Reef with this outfitter. The center has two 46-foot Coast Guard–approved dive boats, offers scuba training, and is one of the few Keys dive centers to offer Nitrox and Trimix (mixed gas) diving. ⊠ *MM 90.5 OS, 90451 Overseas Hwy., Plantation Key* ☎ *305/852– 4599, 800/433–8946* ⊕ *www.floridakeysdivectr.com* ✆ *Snorkeling from $38, diving from $65.*

Islamorada Dive Center. This one-stop dive shop has a resort, pool, restaurant, lessons, and twice-daily dive and snorkel trips and the newest fleet in the Keys. You can take a day trip with a two-tank dive or a one-tank night trip with their equipment or yours. Snorkel and spearfishing trips are also available. ⊠ *MM 84 OS, 84001 Overseas Hwy., Windley Key* ☎ *305/664–3483, 800/327–7070* ⊕ *www.islamoradadivecenter. com* ✆ *Snorkel trips from $45, diving from $85.*

WATER SPORTS

The Kayak Shack. You can rent kayaks for trips to Indian (about 20 minutes one way) and Lignumvitae (about 45 minutes one way) keys, two favorite destinations for paddlers. Kayaks can be rented for a half day (and you'll need plenty of time to explore those mangrove canopies). The company also offers guided two-hour tours, including a snorkel trip to Indian Key or backcountry ecotours. It also rents stand-up paddleboards, including instruction, and canoes. ⊠ *Robbie's Marina, MM 77.5 BS, 77522 Overseas Hwy., Lower Matecumbe Key* ☎ *305/664–4878* ⊕ *www.kayaktheflorida-keys.com* ✆ *From $40 for single, $55 for double; guided trips from $45.*

THE MIDDLE KEYS

Most of the activity in the Middle Keys revolves around the town of Marathon, the region's third-largest metropolitan area. On either end of it, smaller keys hold resorts, wildlife research and rehab facilities, a historic village, and a state park. The Middle Keys make a fitting transition from the Upper Keys to the Lower Keys not only geographically but also mentally. Crossing Seven Mile Bridge prepares you for the slow pace and don't-give-a-damn attitude you'll find a little farther down the highway. Fishing is one of the main attractions—in fact, the region's commercial fishing industry was founded here in the early 1800s. Diving is another popular pastime. There are also beaches and natural areas to enjoy in the Middle Keys, where mainland stress becomes an ever more distant memory.

DUCK KEY

MM 61.

Duck Key holds one of the region's nicest marina resorts, Hawks Cay, plus a boating-oriented residential community.

WHERE TO EAT

$$$
LATIN AMERICAN

✕ **Alma.** A refreshing escape from the Middle Keys' same-old menus, Alma serves expertly prepared Florida and Latin-Caribbean dishes in an elegant setting. Nightly changing menus might include a trio of dishes that could include ceviche, ahi tuna with a wonderful garbanzo bean tomato sauce, gnocchi and exotic mushroom ragout, or pan-seared Wagyu steak. **Known for:** seafood and steaks with a Latin influence; nightly changing menu; high prices. $ *Average main: $28* ⊠ *Hawks Cay Resort, 61 Hawks Cay Blvd.* ☎ *305/743–7000, 888/432–2242* ⊕ *www. hawkscay.com* ⊙ *No lunch.*

WHERE TO STAY

$$$
RESORT
FAMILY
Fodor'sChoice
★

⊡ **Hawks Cay Resort.** The 60-acre, Caribbean-style retreat with a full-service spa and restaurants has plenty to keep the kids occupied (and adults happy). **Pros:** huge rooms; restful spa; full-service marina and dive shop. **Cons:** no real beach; far from Marathon's attractions. $ *Rooms from: $315* ⊠ *MM 61 OS, 61 Hawks Cay Blvd.* ☎ *305/743–7000, 888/432–2242* ⊕ *www.hawkscay.com* ⇝ *161 rooms, 16 suites, 254 2- and 3-bedroom villas* ⊙*No meals.*

GRASSY KEY

MM 60–57.

Local lore has it that this sleepy little key was named not for its vegetation—mostly native trees and shrubs—but for an early settler by the name of Grassy. A few families operating small fishing camps and roadside motels primarily inhabit the key. There's no marked definition between it and Marathon, so it feels sort of like a suburb of its much larger neighbor to the south. Grassy Key's sights tend toward the natural, including a worthwhile dolphin attraction and a small state park.

DID YOU KNOW?

Dolphins in Florida are predominantly of the Atlantic bottlenose variety. These playful and smart creatures love to leap out of the water and synchronize their movements with others. By swimming next to boats, dolphins can conserve energy.

GETTING HERE AND AROUND

Most visitors arriving by air drive to this destination either from Miami International Airport or Key West International Airport. Rental cars are readily available at both, and in the long run, are the most convenient means of transportation for getting here and touring around the Keys.

EXPLORING

TOP ATTRACTIONS

Curry Hammock State Park. Looking for a slice of the Keys that's far removed from tiki bars? On the ocean and bay sides of Overseas Highway are 260 acres of upland hammock, wetlands, and mangroves. On the bay side, there's a trail through thick hardwoods to a rocky shoreline. The ocean side is more developed, with a sandy beach, a clean bathhouse, picnic tables, a playground, grills, and a 28-site campground, each with electric and water. Locals consider the paddling trails under canopies of arching mangroves one of the best kayaking spots in the Keys. Manatees frequent the area, and it's a great spot for bird-watching. Herons, egrets, ibis, plovers, and sanderlings are commonly spotted. Raptors are often seen in the park, especially during migration periods. ⊠ *MM 57 OS, 56200 Overseas Hwy., Little Crawl Key* ☎ *305/289–2690* ⊕ *www. floridastateparks.org/curryhammock* ⊠ *$4.50 for 1 person, $6 for 2, 50¢ per additional person* ⚲ *Campsites are $43 per night.*

FAMILY **Dolphin Research Center.** The 1963 movie *Flipper* popularized the notion of humans interacting with dolphins, and Milton Santini, the film's creator, also opened this center, which is home to a colony of dolphins and sea lions. The nonprofit center has educational sessions and programs that allow you to greet the dolphins from dry land or play with them in their watery habitat. You can even paint a T-shirt with a dolphin—you pick the paint, the dolphin "designs" your shirt. The center also offers five-day programs for children and adults with disabilities. ⊠ *MM 59 BS, 58901 Overseas Hwy.* ☎ *305/289–1121 information, 305/289–0002 reservations* ⊕ *www.dolphins.org* ⊠ *$28.*

WHERE TO EAT

$$$ ✕ **Hideaway Café.** The name says it all. Tucked between Grassy Key
AMERICAN and Marathon, it's easy to miss if you're mindlessly driving through the middle islands. **Known for:** seclusion and quiet; amazing escargot; hand-cut steaks and fresh fish. $ *Average main: $30* ⊠ *Rainbow Bend Resort, MM 58 OS, 57784 Overseas Hwy.* ☎ *305/289–1554* ⊕ *www. hideawaycafe.com* ⊗ *No lunch.*

MARATHON

MM 53–47.5.

New Englanders founded this former fishing village in the early 1800s. The community on Vaca Key subsequently served as a base for pirates, salvagers (also known as "wreckers"), spongers, and, later, Bahamian farmers who eked out a living growing cotton and other crops. More Bahamians arrived in the hope of finding work building the railroad. According to local lore, Marathon was renamed when a worker commented that it was a marathon task to position the tracks across the 6-mile-long island.

During the building of the railroad, Marathon developed a reputation for lawlessness that rivaled that of the Old West. It is said that to keep the rowdy workers from descending on Key West for their off-hours endeavors, residents would send boatloads of liquor up to Marathon. Needless to say, things have quieted down considerably since then.

Still, Marathon is a bustling town, at least compared to other communities in the Keys. As it leaves something to be desired in the charm department, Marathon may not be your first choice of places to stay, but water-sports types will find plenty to enjoy, and its historic and natural attractions merit a visit. Surprisingly good dining options abound, so you'll definitely want to stop for a bite even if you're just passing through on the way to Key West.

Throughout the year, Marathon hosts fishing tournaments (practically monthly), a huge seafood festival in March, and lighted boat parades around the holidays.

GETTING HERE AND AROUND

SuperShuttle charges $102 per passenger for trips from Miami International Airport to the Upper Keys. To go farther into the Keys, you must book an entire 11-person van, which costs about $280 to Marathon. For a trip to the airport, place your request 24 hours in advance. *See Getting Here and Around: Bus Travel.*

VISITOR INFORMATION

Contact Greater Marathon Chamber of Commerce and Visitor Center.
✉ *MM 53.5 BS, 12222 Overseas Hwy.* ☎ *305/743–5417, 800/262–7284* ⊕ *www.floridakeysmarathon.com.*

EXPLORING

TOP ATTRACTIONS

FAMILY **Crane Point Museum, Nature Center, and Historic Site.** Tucked away from the highway behind a stand of trees, Crane Point—part of a 63-acre tract that contains the last-known undisturbed thatch-palm hammock—is delightfully undeveloped. This multiuse facility includes the **Museum of Natural History of the Florida Keys,** which has displays about local wildlife, a seashell exhibit, and a marine-life display that makes you feel you're at the bottom of the sea. Kids love the replica 17th-century galleon and pirate dress-up room where they can play, and the re-created **Cracker House** filled with insects, sea-turtle exhibits, and children's activities. On the 1-mile indigenous loop trail, visit the **Laura Quinn Wild Bird Center** and the remnants of a Bahamian village, site of the restored **George Adderly House.** It is the oldest surviving example of Bahamian tabby (a concretelike material created from sand and seashells) construction outside of Key West. A boardwalk crosses wetlands, rivers, and mangroves before ending at Adderly Village. From November to Easter, docent-led tours are available; bring good walking shoes and bug repellent during warm weather. ✉ *MM 50.5 BS, 5550 Overseas Hwy.* ☎ *305/743–9100* ⊕ *www.cranepoint.net* ▨ *$14.95.*

FAMILY **Florida Keys Aquarium Encounters.** This isn't your typical large-city aquarium. It's more hands-on and personal, and it's all outdoors with several tiki huts to house the encounters and provide shade as you explore, rain or shine; plan to spend at least two to three hours here. You'll find a 200,000-gallon aquarium and plenty of marine encounters (extra cost), as well as guided tours, viewing areas, and a predator tank. The Coral Reef encounter ($95 snorkel, $130 scuba) lets you dive in a reef environment without hearing the theme from *Jaws* in your head (although you can see several sharks on the other side of the glass). Touch tanks are great for all ages and even have unique critters like slipper lobsters. Hungry? The on-site Eagle Ray Cafe serves up wings, fish tacos, salads, burgers, and more. Note that general admission is required, even if you're signed up for a marine encounter. ⊠ *MM 53 BS, 11710 Overseas Hwy.* ☎ *305/407–3262* ⊕ *www.floridakeysaquariumencounters.com* ✉ *$20.*

Pigeon Key. There's much to like about this 5-acre island under the Old Seven Mile Bridge. You might even recognize it from a season finale of the TV show *The Amazing Race.* You can reach it via a ferry that departs from behind the visitor center (look for the old red railroad car on Knight's Key, MM 47 OS). Once there, tour the island on your own or join a guided tour to explore the buildings that formed the early-20th-century work camp for the Overseas Railroad that linked the mainland to Key West in 1912. Later the island became a fish camp, a state park, and then government-administration headquarters. Exhibits in a small museum recall the history of the Keys, the railroad, and railroad baron Henry M. Flagler. The ferry ride with tour lasts two hours; visitors can self-tour and catch the ferry back in a half hour. ■ TIP→ Bring your own snorkel gear and dive flag and you can snorkel right from the shore. ⊠ *MM 45 OS, 1 Knights Key Blvd., Pigeon Key* ☎ *305/743–5999* ⊕ *pigeonkey.net* ✉ *$12.*

Seven Mile Bridge. This is one of the most photographed images in the Keys. Actually measuring slightly less than 7 miles, it connects the Middle and Lower keys and is believed to be the world's longest segmental bridge. It has 39 expansion joints separating its various concrete sections. Each April runners gather in Marathon for the annual Seven Mile Bridge Run. The expanse running parallel to Seven Mile Bridge is what remains of the **Old Seven Mile Bridge,** an engineering and architectural marvel in its day that's now on the National Register of Historic Places. Once proclaimed the Eighth Wonder of the World, it rested on a record 546 concrete piers. No cars are allowed on the old bridge today. ⊠ *Marathon.*

FAMILY **The Turtle Hospital.** More than 100 injured sea turtles check in here every year. The 90-minute guided tours take you into recovery and surgical areas at the world's only state-certified veterinary hospital for sea turtles. In the "hospital bed" tanks, you can see recovering patients and others that are permanent residents due to their injuries. After the tour, you can feed some of the "residents." Call ahead—space is limited and tours are sometimes canceled due to medical emergencies. The turtle ambulance out front makes for a memorable souvenir photo. ⊠ *MM 48.5 BS, 2396 Overseas Hwy.* ☎ *305/743–2552* ⊕ *www.turtlehospital.org* ✉ *$22.*

BEACHES

FAMILY **Sombrero Beach.** No doubt one of the best beaches in the Keys, here you'll find pleasant, shaded picnic areas that overlook a coconut palm–lined grassy stretch and the Atlantic Ocean. Roped-off areas allow swimmers, boaters, and windsurfers to share the narrow cove. Facilities include barbecue grills, a large playground, a pier, a volleyball court, and a paved, lighted bike path off Overseas Highway. Sunday afternoons draw lots of local families toting coolers. The park is accessible for those with disabilities and allows leashed pets. Turn east at the traffic light in Marathon and follow signs to the end. **Amenities:** showers; toilets. **Best for:** swimming; windsurfing. ⊠ *MM 50 OS, Sombrero Beach Rd.* ☎ *305/743–0033* 🎫 *Free.*

4

WHERE TO EAT

$ ✕ **Fish Tales Market and Eatery.** This no-frills, roadside eatery has a loyal
SEAFOOD local following, an unfussy ambience, a couple of outside picnic tables, and friendly service. Signature dishes include snapper on grilled rye with coleslaw and melted Muenster cheese, a fried fish burrito, and lobster bisque or tomato-based conch chowder. **Known for:** luscious lobster bisque; fresh and affordable seafood market; closing early. $ *Average main: $9* ⊠ *MM 52.5 OS, 11711 Overseas Hwy.* ☎ *305/743–9196, 888/662–4822* ⊕ *www.floridalobster.com* ⊙ *Closed Sun. No dinner Sat.*

$$ ✕ **Key Colony Inn.** The inviting aroma of an Italian kitchen pervades this
ITALIAN family-owned favorite known for its Sunday brunch, served November through April. For lunch there are fish and steak entrées served with fries, salad, and bread in addition to Italian specialties. **Known for:** friendly and attentive service; Italian specialties; Sunday brunch. $ *Average main: $20* ⊠ *MM 54 OS, 700 W. Ocean Dr., Key Colony Beach* ☎ *305/743–0100* ⊕ *www.kcinn.com.*

$$ ✕ **Keys Fisheries Market & Marina.** From the parking lot, you can't miss
SEAFOOD the enormous tiki bar on stilts, but the walk-up window on the ground
FAMILY floor is the heart of this warehouse-turned-restaurant. Order at the window, pick up your food, then dine at one of the waterfront tables outfitted with rolls of paper towels. **Known for:** huge lobster Reuben; walk-up takeout window; adults-only upstairs tiki bar. $ *Average main: $16* ⊠ *MM 49 BS, 3390 Gulfview Ave., at the end of 35th St.* ⊹ *Turn onto 35th St. from Overseas Hwy.* ☎ *305/743–4353, 866/743–4353* ⊕ *www.keysfisheries.com.*

$$$ ✕ **Lazy Days South.** Tucked into Marathon Marina a half mile north of the
SEAFOOD Seven Mile Bridge, this restaurant offers views just as spectacular as its
Fodor'sChoice highly lauded food. A spin-off of an Islamorada favorite, here you'll find
★ a wide range of daily offerings from fried or sautéed conch and a coconut-fried fish du jour sandwich to seafood pastas and beef tips over rice. **Known for:** water views; delicious seafood entrées. $ *Average main: $22* ⊠ *MM 47.3 OS, 725 11th St.* ☎ *305/289–0839* ⊕ *www.lazydayssouth.com.*

$ ✕ **The Stuffed Pig.** With only nine tables and a counter inside, this break-
DINER fast-and-lunch place is always hopping. When the weather's right, grab a table out back. **Known for:** famous "pig's" breakfast; daily lunch specials; large portions. $ *Average main: $9* ⊠ *MM 49 BS, 3520 Overseas Hwy.* ☎ *305/743–4059* ⊕ *www.thestuffedpig.com* ▭ *No credit cards* ⊙ *No dinner.*

$$$
SEAFOOD

✕ **Sunset Grille & Raw Bar.** After a walk or bike ride along the Old Seven Mile Bridge, treat yourself to a seafood lunch or dinner at this vaulted tiki hut by the bridge. For lunch, start with the conch chowder or fritters, and then move on to the Voodoo grouper sandwich topped with mango-guava mayo, and finish with a tasty key lime pie. **Known for:** weekend pool parties and barbecues; creative dinner specials. $ *Average main: $22* ✉ *MM 47 OS, 7 Knights Key Blvd.* ☎ *305/396-7235* ⊕ *www.sunsetgrille7milebridge.com.*

WHERE TO STAY

$$
RENTAL

🏨 **Glunz Ocean Beach Hotel & Resort.** The Glunz family got it right when they purchased this former time-share property and put a whole lot of love into renovating it to its full oceanfront potential. **Pros:** oceanfront; helpful service; excellent free Wi-Fi. **Cons:** neighbor noise; small elevator; no interior corridors; not cheap. $ *Rooms from: $280* ✉ *MM 53.5 OS, 351 E. Ocean Dr., Key Colony Beach* ☎ *305/289-0525* ⊕ *www. GlunzOceanBeachHotel.com* ⤴ *38 rooms, 8 villas* ⦿⏐ *No meals.*

$$$$
RESORT
FAMILY
Fodor's Choice
★

🏨 **Tranquility Bay.** Ralph Lauren could have designed the rooms at this stylish, luxurious resort on a nice beach. **Pros:** secluded setting; gorgeous design; lovely crescent beach. **Cons:** a bit sterile; no real Keys atmosphere; cramped building layout. $ *Rooms from: $425* ✉ *MM 48.5 BS, 2600 Overseas Hwy.* ☎ *305/289-0888, 866/643-5397* ⊕ *www.tranquilitybay.com* ⤴ *102 rooms* ⦿⏐ *No meals.*

SPORTS AND THE OUTDOORS

BIKING

Tooling around on two wheels is a good way to see Marathon. There's easy cycling on a 1-mile off-road path that connects to the 2 miles of the Old Seven Mile Bridge leading to Pigeon Key.

Bike Marathon Bike Rentals. "Have bikes, will deliver" could be the motto of this company, which gets beach cruisers to your hotel door, including a helmet and basket. They also rent kayaks. Note that there's no physical location, but services are available Monday through Saturday 9–4 and Sunday 9–2. ✉ *Marathon* ☎ *305/743-3204* ⊕ *www.bikemarathonbikerentals.com* ⌨ *$45 per wk.*

Overseas Outfitters. Aluminum cruisers and hybrid bikes are available for rent at this outfitter. It's open weekdays 9–5:30 and Saturday 9–3. All rentals include a helmet and lock. ✉ *MM 48 BS, 1700 Overseas Hwy.* ☎ *305/289-1670* ⊕ *www.overseasoutfitters.com* ⌨ *Rentals from $15 per day.*

BOATING

Sail, motor, or paddle: whatever your choice of modes, boating is what the Keys are all about. Brave the Atlantic waves and reefs or explore the backcountry islands on the gulf side. If you don't have a lot of boating and chart-reading experience, it's a good idea to tap into local knowledge on a charter.

Captain Pip's. This operator rents 18- to 24-foot outboards as well as tackle and snorkeling gear. Fishing charters are also available with a captain and a mate (full-day charters are also available). Ask about multiday deals, or try one of their accommodation packages and walk right from your bay-front room to your boat. ⊠ *MM 47.5 BS, 1410 Overseas Hwy.* ☎ *305/743–4403, 800/707–1692* ⊕ *www. captainpips.com* ⛴ *Rentals from $195 per day; half-day charters from $650.*

Fish 'n Fun. Get out on the water on 19- to 26-foot powerboats. Rentals can be for a half or full day. The company also offers free delivery in the Middle Keys. ⊠ *Duck Key Marina, MM 61 OS, 1149 Greenbriar Rd.* ☎ *305/743–2275, 800/471–3440* ⊕ *www.fishnfunrentals.com* ⛴ *From $175.*

FISHING

For recreational anglers, the deepwater fishing is superb in both bay and ocean. Marathon West Hump, one good spot, has depths ranging from 500 to more than 1,000 feet. Locals fish from a half dozen bridges, including Long Key Bridge, the Old Seven Mile Bridge, and both ends of Tom's Harbor. Barracuda, bonefish, and tarpon all frequent local waters. Party boats and private charters are available.

Marathon Lady. Morning, afternoon, and night, fish for mahimahi, grouper, and other tasty catch aboard this 73-footer, which departs on half-day excursions from the Vaca Cut Bridge (MM 53), north of Marathon. Join the crew for night fishing ($55) from 6:30 to midnight from Memorial Day to Labor Day; it's especially beautiful on a full-moon night. ⊠ *MM 53 OS, 11711 Overseas Hwy., at 117th St.* ☎ *305/743–5580* ⊕ *www.marathonlady.net* ⛴ *From $50.*

Sea Dog Charters. Captain Jim Purcell, a deep-sea specialist for ESPN's *The American Outdoorsman,* provides one of the best values in Keys fishing. Next to the Seven Mile Grill, his company offers half- and full-day offshore, reef and wreck, and backcountry fishing trips, as well as fishing and snorkeling trips aboard 30- to 37-foot boats. The per-person for a half-day trip is the same regardless of whether your group fills the boat, and includes bait, light tackle, ice, coolers, and fishing licenses. If you prefer an all-day private charter on a 37-foot boat, he offers those, too, for up to six people. A fuel surcharge may apply. ⊠ *MM 47.5 BS, 1248 Overseas Hwy.* ☎ *305/743–8255* ⊕ *www. seadogcharters.net* ⛴ *From $60.*

SCUBA DIVING AND SNORKELING

Local dive operations take you to Sombrero Reef and Lighthouse, the most popular down-under destination in these parts. For a shallow dive and some lobster nabbing, Coffins Patch, off Key Colony Beach, is a good choice. A number of wrecks such as *Thunderbolt* serve as artificial reefs. Many operations out of this area will also take you to Looe Key Reef.

Hall's Diving Center & Career Institute. The institute has been training divers for more than 40 years. Along with conventional twice-a-day snorkel and two-tank dive trips to the reefs at Sombrero Lighthouse and wrecks like the *Thunderbolt,* the company has more unusual offerings like rebreather, photography, and Nitrox courses. ⊠ *MM 48.5 BS, 1994 Overseas Hwy.* ☎ *305/743–5929, 800/331–4255* ⊕ *www.hallsdiving. com* ⛴ *From $45.*

Spirit Snorkeling. Join regularly scheduled snorkeling excursions to Sombrero Reef and Lighthouse Reef on this company's comfortable catamaran. They also offer sunset cruises and private charters. ⊠ *MM 47.5 BS, 1410 Overseas Hwy., Slip No. 1* ☎ *305/289–0614* ⊕ *www. captainpips.com* ☞ *From $30.*

Tildens Scuba Center. Since the mid-1980s, Tildens Scuba Center has been providing lessons, tours, gear rental, and daily snorkel, scuba, and Snuba adventures. Look for the huge, colorful angelfish sculpture outside the building. ⊠ *MM 49.5 BS, 4650 Overseas Hwy.* ☎ *305/743–7255, 888/728–2235* ☞ *From $60 for snorkel trips; from $70 for dive trips.*

THE LOWER KEYS

Beginning at Bahia Honda Key, the islands of the Florida Keys become smaller, more clustered, and more numerous, a result of ancient tidal water flowing between the Florida Straits and the gulf. Here you're likely to see more birds and mangroves than other tourists, and more refuges, beaches, and campgrounds than museums, restaurants, and hotels. The islands are made up of two types of limestone, both denser than the highly permeable Key Largo limestone of the Upper Keys. As a result, freshwater forms in pools rather than percolating through the rock, creating watering holes that support alligators, snakes, deer, rabbits, raccoons, and migratory ducks. (Many of these animals can be seen in the National Key Deer Refuge on Big Pine Key.) Nature was generous with her beauty in the Lower Keys, which have both Looe Key Reef, arguably the Keys' most beautiful tract of coral, and Bahia Honda State Park, considered one of the best beaches in the world for its fine sand dunes, clear warm waters, and panoramic vista of bridges, hammocks, and azure sky and sea. Big Pine Key is fishing headquarters for a laid-back community that swells with retirees in the winter. South of it, the dribble of islands can flash by in a blink of an eye if you don't take the time to stop at a roadside eatery or check out tours and charters at the little marinas. They include Little Torch Key, Middle Torch Key, Ramrod Key, Summerland Key, Cudjoe Key, Sugarloaf Keys, and Saddlebunch Key. Lying offshore of Little Torch Key, Little Palm Island once welcomed U.S. presidents and other notables to its secluded fishing camp. It was also the location for the movie *PT 109* about John F. Kennedy's celebrated World War II heroism. Today it still offers respite to the upper class in the form of an exclusive getaway resort accessible only by boat or seaplane.

GETTING HERE AND AROUND

To get to the Lower Keys, fly into either Miami International Airport or Key West International Airport. Key West is considerably closer, but there are far fewer flights coming in and going out. Rental cars are available at both airports. In addition, there is bus service from the Key West airport; $4 one way with Key West Transit. *See Getting Here and Around: Bus Travel in Key West, below.*

BAHIA HONDA KEY

MM 38.5–36.

All of Bahia Honda Key is devoted to its eponymous state park, which keeps it in a pristine state. Besides the park's outdoor activities, it offers an up-close view of the original railroad bridge.

EXPLORING

TOP ATTRACTIONS

FAMILY Fodor's Choice ★ **Bahia Honda State Park.** Most first-time visitors to the region are dismayed by the lack of beaches—but then they discover Bahia Honda Key. The 524-acre park sprawls across both sides of the highway, giving it 2½ miles of fabulous sandy coastline. The snorkeling isn't bad, either; there's underwater life (soft coral, queen conchs, random little fish) just a few hundred feet offshore. Although swimming, kayaking, fishing, and boating are the main reasons to visit, you shouldn't miss biking along the 2½ miles of flat roads or hiking the Silver Palm Trail, with rare West Indies plants and several species found nowhere else in the nation. Along the way you'll be treated to a variety of butterflies. Seasonal ranger-led nature programs take place at or depart from the Sand and Sea Nature Center. There are rental cabins, a campground, snack bar, gift shop, 19-slip marina, nature center, and facilities for renting kayaks and arranging snorkeling tours. Get a panoramic view of the island from what's left of the railroad—the Bahia Honda Bridge. ✉ *MM 37 OS, 36850 Overseas Hwy.* ☎ *305/872–2353* 🌐 *www.floridastateparks.org/park/Bahia-Honda* 🎫 *$4.50 for single occupant vehicle, $8 for vehicle with 2–8 people, plus $0.50 per person up to 8.*

BEACHES

Sandspur Beach. Bahia Honda Key State Beach contains three beaches in all—on both the Atlantic Ocean and the Gulf of Mexico. Sandspur Beach, the largest, is regularly declared the best beach in the Florida Keys, and you'll be hard-pressed to argue. The sand is baby-powder soft, and the aqua water is warm, clear, and shallow. With their mild currents, the beaches are great for swimming, even with small fry. **Amenities:** food and drink; showers; toilets; water sports. **Best for:** snorkeling; swimming. ✉ *MM 37 OS, 36850 Overseas Hwy.* ☎ *305/872–2353* 🌐 *www.floridastateparks.org/park/Bahia-Honda* 🎫 *$4.50 for single-occupant vehicle, $9 for vehicle with 2–8 people.*

WHERE TO STAY

$ RENTAL 🏨 **Bahia Honda State Park Cabins.** Elsewhere you'd pay big bucks for the wonderful water views available at these cabins on Florida Bay. Each of three cabins have two, two-bedroom units with a full kitchen and bath and air-conditioning (but no television, radio, or phone). **Pros:** great bay-front views; beachfront camping; affordable rates. **Cons:** books up fast; area can be buggy. [$] *Rooms from: $163* ✉ *MM 37 OS, 36850 Overseas Hwy.* ☎ *305/872–2353, 800/326–3521* 🌐 *www.reserveamerica.com* 🛏 *6 cabins* 🍴 *No meals.*

DID YOU KNOW?

An old railroad bridge connected Bahia Honda Key with Key West until a hurricane destroyed it in 1935. The bridge is no longer in operation, yet it's standing, barely. Falling debris prevents snorkeling below or exploring, but it makes for pretty photos, especially at sunrise and sunset.

SPORTS AND THE OUTDOORS
SCUBA DIVING AND SNORKELING

Bahia Honda Dive Shop. The concessionaire at Bahia Honda State Park manages a 19-slip marina; rents wet suits, snorkel equipment, and corrective masks; and operates twice-a-day offshore-reef snorkel trips. Park visitors looking for other fun can rent kayaks and beach chairs. ✉ *MM 37 OS, 36850 Overseas Hwy.* ☎ *305/872–3210* ⊕ *www.bahiahondapark. com* ⊘ *Kayak rentals from $10 per hr.; snorkel tours from $30.*

BIG PINE KEY

MM 32–30.

4

Welcome to the Keys' most natural holdout, where wildlife refuges protect rare and endangered animals. Here you have left behind the commercialism of the Upper Keys for an authentic backcountry atmosphere. How could things get more casual than Key Largo, you might wonder? Find out by exiting U.S. 1 to explore the habitat of the charmingly diminutive Key deer or cast a line from No Name Bridge. Tours explore the expansive waters of National Key Deer Refuge and Great White Heron National Wildlife Refuge, one of the first such refuges in the country. Along with Key West National Wildlife Refuge, it encompasses more than 200,000 acres of water and more than 8,000 acres of land on 49 small islands. Besides its namesake bird, the Great White Heron National Wildlife Refuge provides habitat for uncounted species of birds and three species of sea turtles. It is the only U.S. breeding site for the endangered hawksbill turtle.

GETTING HERE AND AROUND

Most people rent a car to get to Big Pine Key so they can also explore Key West and other parts of the chain.

VISITOR INFORMATION

Contact Big Pine and the Lower Keys Chamber of Commerce. ☎ *305/872–2411, 800/872–3722* ⊕ *www.lowerkeyschamber.com.*

EXPLORING
TOP ATTRACTIONS

National Key Deer Refuge. This 84,824-acre refuge was established in 1957 to protect the dwindling population of the Key deer, one of more than 22 animals and plants federally classified as endangered or threatened, including 5 that are found nowhere else on Earth. The Key deer, which stands about 30 inches at the shoulders and is a subspecies of the Virginia white-tailed deer, once roamed throughout the Lower and Middle keys, but hunting, destruction of their habitat, and a growing human population caused their numbers to decline to 27 by 1957. The deer have made a comeback, increasing their numbers to approximately 750. The best place to see Key deer in the refuge is at the end of Key Deer Boulevard and on No Name Key, a sparsely populated island just east of Big Pine Key. Mornings and evenings are the best time to spot them. Deer may turn up along the road at any time of day, so drive slowly. They wander into nearby yards to nibble tender grass and bougainvillea blossom, but locals do not appreciate tourists driving into their neighborhoods after them. Feeding them is against the law and puts them in danger.

A quarry left over from railroad days, the **Blue Hole** is the largest body of freshwater in the Keys. From the observation platform and nearby walking trail, you might see the resident alligator, turtles, and other wildlife. There are two well-marked trails, recently revamped: the Jack Watson Nature Trail (0.6 mile), named after an environmentalist and the refuge's first warden; and the Fred Mannillo Nature Trail (0.2 mile), one of the most wheelchair-accessible places to see an unspoiled pine-rockland forest and wetlands. The visitor center has exhibits on Keys biology and ecology. The refuge also provides information on the Key West National Wildlife Refuge and the Great White Heron National Wildlife Refuge. Accessible only by water, both are popular with kayak outfitters. ✉ *Visitor Center–Headquarters, Big Pine Shopping Center, MM 30.5 BS, 28950 Watson Blvd.* ☎ *305/872–2239* 🌐 *www.fws.gov/nationalkeydeer* 🎟 *Free.*

WHERE TO EAT

$ VEGETARIAN
🍴 **Good Food Conspiracy.** Like good wine, this small natural-foods eatery and market surrenders its pleasures a little at a time. Step inside to the aroma of brewing coffee, and then pick up the scent of fresh strawberries or carrots blending into a smoothie, the green aroma of wheatgrass juice, followed by the earthy odor of hummus. **Known for:** vegetarian and vegan dishes; sandwiches and smoothies; organic items. [$] *Average main: $10* ✉ *MM 30.2 OS, 30150 Overseas Hwy.* ☎ *305/872–3945* 🌐 *www.goodfoodconspiracy.com* 🕒 *No dinner Sun.*

$$ AMERICAN
🍴 **No Name Pub.** This no-frills honky-tonk has been around since 1936, delighting inveterate locals and intrepid vacationers who come for the excellent pizza, cold beer, and *interesting* companionship. The decor, such as it is, amounts to the autographed dollar bills that cover every inch of the place. **Known for:** shrimp pizza and fish sandwich; local and tourist favorite; decor of dollar bills. [$] *Average main: $15* ✉ *MM 30 BS, 30813 Watson Blvd.* ✥ *From U.S. 1, turn west on Wilder Rd., left on South St., right on Ave. B, right on Watson Blvd.* ☎ *305/872–9115* 🌐 *www.nonamepub.com.*

WHERE TO STAY

$ HOTEL
🏨 **Big Pine Key Fishing Lodge.** There's a congenial atmosphere at this lively, family-owned lodge-campground-marina—a happy mix of tent campers (who have the fabulous waterfront real estate), RVers (who look pretty permanent), and motel dwellers who like to mingle at the rooftop pool and challenge each other to a game of poker. **Pros:** local fishing crowd; nice pool; great price. **Cons:** RV park is too close to motel; deer will eat your food if you're camping. [$] *Rooms from: $134* ✉ *MM 33 OS, 33000 Overseas Hwy.* ☎ *305/872–2351* 🌐 *www.bpkfl.com* 🛏 *16 rooms* 🍽 *No meals* ☞ *To protect Key deer, no dogs allowed.*

$$$ B&B/INN
🏨 **Deer Run Bed & Breakfast.** Innkeepers Jen DeMaria and Harry Appel were way ahead of the green-lodging game when they opened in 2004, and guests love how Key deer wander the grounds of this beachfront B&B on a residential street lined with mangroves. **Pros:** quiet location; vegan, organic breakfasts; complimentary bikes, kayaks, and state park passes. **Cons:** price is a bit high; hard to find. [$] *Rooms from: $375* ✉ *MM 33 OS, 1997 Long Beach Dr.* ☎ *305/872–2015* 🌐 *www.deerrunfloridabb.com* 🛏 *4 rooms* 🍽 *Breakfast.*

SPORTS AND THE OUTDOORS

BIKING

A good 10 miles of paved roads run from MM 30.3 BS, along Wilder Road, across the bridge to No Name Key, and along Key Deer Boulevard into the National Key Deer Refuge. Along the way you might see some Key deer. Stay off the trails that lead into wetlands, where fat tires can damage the environment.

Big Pine Bicycle Center. Owner Marty Baird is an avid cyclist and enjoys sharing his knowledge of great places to ride. He's also skilled at selecting the right bike for the journey, and he knows his repairs, too. His old-fashioned single-speed, fat-tire cruisers rent by the half or full day. Helmets, baskets, and locks are included. ⊠ *MM 30.9 BS, 31 County Rd.* ☎ *305/872–0130* ⊛ *www.bigpinebikes.com* ⊠ *From $10.*

FISHING

Cast from No Name Key Bridge or hire a charter to take you into backcountry or deep waters for fishing year-round.

Strike Zone Charters. Glass-bottom-boat excursions venture into the backcountry and Atlantic Ocean. The five-hour Island Excursion emphasizes nature and Keys history; besides close encounters with birds, sea life, and vegetation, there's a fish cookout on an island. Snorkel and fishing equipment, food, and drinks are included. This is one of the few nature outings in the Keys with wheelchair access. Deep-sea charter rates for up to six people can be arranged for a half or full day. It also offers flats fishing in the Gulf of Mexico. Dive excursions head to the wreck of the 110-foot *Adolphus Busch*, and scuba and snorkel trips to Looe Key Reef, prime scuba and snorkeling territory, aboard glass-bottom boats. ⊠ *MM 29.6 BS, 29675 Overseas Hwy.* ☎ *305/872–9863, 800/654–9560* ⊛ *www.strikezonecharter.com* ⊠ *From $38.*

KAYAKING

There's nothing like the vast expanse of pristine waters and mangrove islands preserved by national refuges from here to Key West. The maze-like terrain can be confusing, so it's wise to hire a guide at least the first time out.

Big Pine Kayak Adventures. There's no excuse to skip a water adventure with this convenient kayak rental service, which delivers them to your lodging or anywhere between Seven Mile Bridge and Stock Island. The company, headed by *The Florida Keys Paddling Guide* author Bill Keogh, will rent you a kayak and then ferry you—called taxi-yakking—to remote islands with clear instructions on how to paddle back on your own. Rentals are by the half day or full day. Three-hour group kayak tours are the cheapest option and explore the mangrove forests of Great White Heron and Key Deer National Wildlife Refuges. More expensive four-hour custom tours transport you to exquisite backcountry areas teeming with wildlife. Kayak fishing charters are also popular. Paddleboard ecotours, rentals, and yoga are available. ⊠ *Old Wooden Bridge Fishing Camp, 1791 Bogie Dr.* ⊕ *From MM 30, turn right at traffic light, continue on Wilder Rd. toward No Name Key; the fishing camp is just before the bridge with a big yellow kayak on the sign out front* ☎ *305/872–7474* ⊛ *www.keyskayaktours.com* ⊠ *From $50.*

LITTLE TORCH KEY

MM 29–10.

Little Torch Key and its neighbor islands, Ramrod Key and Summerland Key, are good jumping-off points for divers headed for Looe Key Reef. The islands also serve as a refuge for those who want to make forays into Key West but not stay in the thick of things.

The undeveloped backcountry at your door makes Little Torch Key an ideal location for fishing and kayaking. Nearby **Ramrod Key,** which also caters to divers bound for Looe Key, derives its name from a ship that wrecked on nearby reefs in the early 1800s.

WHERE TO EAT

$ ✕ **Baby's Coffee.** The aroma of rich, roasting coffee beans arrests you at
AMERICAN the door of "the Southernmost Coffee Roaster in America." Buy beans by the pound or coffee by the cup, along with sandwiches and sweets. **Known for:** best coffee in the Keys; gluten-free, vegan, and vegetarian specialty foods. Ⓢ *Average main: $8* ⊠ *MM 15 OS, 3180 Overseas Hwy.* ☎ *305/744–9866, 800/523–2326* ⊕ *www.babyscoffee.com.*

$$ ✕ **Geiger Key Smokehouse Bar & Grill.** There's a strong hint of the Old
AMERICAN Keys at this ocean-side marina restaurant, where local fisherman stop for breakfast before heading out to catch the big one, and everyone shows up on Sunday for the barbecue from 4 to 9. "On the backside of paradise," as the sign says, its tiki structures overlook quiet mangroves at an RV park marina. **Known for:** Sunday barbecue. Ⓢ *Average main: $16* ⊠ *MM 10, 5 Geiger Key Rd., off Boca Chica Rd., Bay Point* ☎ *305/296–3553, 305/294–1230* ⊕ *www.geigerkeymarina.com.*

$$$$ ✕ **Little Palm Island Restaurant.** The restaurant at the exclusive Little Palm
ECLECTIC Island Resort—its dining room and adjacent outdoor terrace lit by candles and warmed by live music—is one of the most romantic spots in the Keys. However, it's only open to nonguests on a reservations-only basis and no one under 16 is allowed on the island. **Known for:** oceanfront tables in the sand; Key deer meandering by your table; Sunday brunch buffet. Ⓢ *Average main: $65* ⊠ *MM 28.5 OS, 28500 Overseas Hwy.* ☎ *305/872–2551* ⊕ *www.littlepalmisland.com.*

$$ ✕ **Mangrove Mama's Restaurant.** This could be the prototype for a Keys
SEAFOOD restaurant, given its shanty appearance, lattice trim, and roving sort of indoor-outdoor floor plan. Then there's the seafood, from the ubiquitous fish sandwich (fried, grilled, broiled, or blackened) to lobster Reubens, crab cakes, and coconut shrimp. **Known for:** pizza; award-winning conch chowder; all kinds of seafood dishes. Ⓢ *Average main: $20* ⊠ *MM 20 BS, Sugarloaf Key* ☎ *305/745–3030* ⊕ *www.mangrovemamasrestaurant.com.*

$$$ ✕ **Square Grouper.** In an unassuming warehouse-looking building right
SEAFOOD off U.S. 1, chef and owner Lynn Bell is creating seafood magic. Just ask
Fodor'sChoice the locals, who wait in line for a table along with visitors in the know.
★ But don't let the exterior fool you: the dining room is surprisingly suave, with butcher paper–lined tables, mandarin-colored walls, and textural components throughout. **Known for:** everything made fresh, in-house; long lines in season. Ⓢ *Average main: $25* ⊠ *MM 22.5 OS, Cudjoe Key* ☎ *305/745–8880* ⊕ *www.squaregrouperbarandgrill.com* ☉ *Closed Sun.; Mon. May–Dec.; and Sept.*

WHERE TO STAY

$$$$
RESORT
Fodor's Choice
★

⌇ **Little Palm Island Resort & Spa.** *Haute tropicale* best describes this luxury retreat, and "second mortgage" might explain how some can afford the extravagant prices. **Pros:** secluded setting; heavenly spa; easy wildlife viewing. **Cons:** expensive; might be too quiet for some; only accessible by boat or seaplane. $ *Rooms from: $1590* ⊠ *MM 28.5 OS, 28500 Overseas Hwy.* ☎ *305/872–2524, 800/343–8567* ⊕ *www. littlepalmisland.com* ⇋ *30 suites* ⏇ *Some meals* ⌒ *No one under 16 allowed on island.*

$
HOTEL

⌇ **Looe Key Reef Resort & Center.** If your Keys vacation is all about diving, you won't mind the no-frills, basic motel rooms with dated furniture at this scuba-obsessed operation because it's the closest place to stay to the stellar reef. **Pros:** guests get discounts on dive and snorkel trips; inexpensive rates. **Cons:** some reports of uncleanliness; unheated pool; close to the road. $ *Rooms from: $115* ⊠ *MM 27.5 OS, 27340 Overseas Hwy., Ramrod Key* ☎ *305/872–2215, 877/816–3483* ⊕ *www.diveflakeys.com* ⇋ *23 rooms, 1 suite* ⏇ *No meals.*

$
HOTEL

⌇ **Parmer's Resort.** Almost every room at this budget-friendly option has a view of South Pine Channel, with the lovely curl of Big Pine Key in the foreground. **Pros:** bright rooms; pretty setting; good value. **Cons:** a bit out of the way; housekeeping costs extra; little shade around the pool. $ *Rooms from: $159* ⊠ *MM 28.7 BS, 565 Barry Ave.* ☎ *305/872–2157* ⊕ *www.parmersresort.com* ⇋ *47 units* ⏇ *Breakfast.*

SPORTS AND THE OUTDOORS

BOATING

Dolphin Marina. Dolphin Marina rents 19- and 22-foot boats with 150 horsepower for up to eight people by the half day and full day. An onsite marina store has all the supplies you'll need for a day on the water. ⊠ *28530 Overseas Hwy.* ☎ *305/872–2685* ⊕ *www.dolphinmarina.net* ⌗ *From $200 half day; from $250 full day.*

SCUBA DIVING AND SNORKELING

This is the closest you can get on land to Looe Key Reef, and that's where local dive operators love to head.

In 1744 the HMS *Looe*, a British warship, ran aground and sank on one of the most beautiful coral reefs in the Keys. Today the key owes its name to the ill-fated ship. The 5.3-square-nautical-mile reef, part of the **Florida Keys National Marine Sanctuary,** has strands of elkhorn coral on its eastern margin, purple sea fans, and abundant sponges and sea urchins. On its seaward side, it drops almost vertically 50 to 90 feet. In its midst, **Shipwreck Trail** plots the location of nine historic wreck sites in 14 to 120 feet of water. Buoys mark the sites, and underwater signs tell the history of each site and what marine life to expect. Snorkelers and divers will find the sanctuary a quiet place to observe reef life—except in July, when the annual Underwater Music Festival pays homage to Looe Key's beauty and promotes reef awareness with six hours of music broadcast via underwater speakers. Dive shops, charters, and private boats transport about 500 divers and snorkelers to hear the spectacle, which includes classical, jazz, New Age, and Caribbean music, as well as a little Jimmy Buffett. There are even underwater Elvis impersonators.

Looe Key Reef Resort & Dive Center. This center, the closest dive shop to Looe Key Reef, offers two affordable trips daily, 7:30 am or 12:15 pm (for divers, snorkelers, or bubble watchers). The maximum depth is 30 feet, so snorkelers and divers go on the same boat. Call to check for availability for wreck and night dives. The dive boat, a 45-foot catamaran, is docked at the full-service Looe Key Reef Resort. ⊠ *Looe Key Reef Resort, MM 27.5 OS, 27340 Overseas Hwy., Ramrod Key* ☎ *305/872–2215, 877/816–3483* ⊕ *www.diveflakeys.com* ✎ *From $40.*

WATER SPORTS

Reelax Charters. For a guided kayak tour, join Captain Andrea Paulson of Reelax Charters, who takes you to remote locations. Charters carry up to three people and can include snorkeling and beaching on a secluded island in the Keys backcountry. ⊠ *Sugarloaf Marina, MM 17 BS, 17015 Overseas Hwy., Sugarloaf Key* ☎ *305/304–1392* ⊕ *www.keyskayaking.com* ✎ *From $240.*

Sugarloaf Marina. Rates for one-person kayaks are based on an hourly or daily rental. Two-person kayaks are also available. Delivery is free for rentals of three days or more. The folks at the marina can also hook you up with an outfitter for a day of offshore or backcountry fishing. There's also a well-stocked ship store. ⊠ *MM 17 BS, 17015 Overseas Hwy., Sugarloaf Key* ☎ *305/745–3135* ⊕ *www.sugarloafkeymarina.com* ✎ *From $15 per hr.*

KEY WEST

Situated 150 miles from Miami, 90 miles from Havana, and an immeasurable distance from sanity, this end-of-the-line community has never been like anywhere else. Even after it was connected to the rest of the country—by the railroad in 1912 and by the highway in 1938—it maintained a strong sense of detachment. The United States acquired Key West from Spain in 1821, along with the rest of Florida. The Spanish had named the island Cayo Hueso, or Bone Key, after the Native American skeletons they found on its shores. In 1823, President James Monroe sent Commodore David S. Porter to chase pirates away. For three decades, the primary industry in Key West was wrecking—rescuing people and salvaging cargo from ships that foundered on the nearby reefs. According to some reports, when pickings were lean the wreckers hung out lights to lure ships aground. Their business declined after 1849, when the federal government began building lighthouses.

In 1845, the army began construction on Ft. Taylor, which kept Key West on the Union side during the Civil War. After the fighting ended, an influx of Cubans unhappy with Spain's rule brought the cigar industry here. Fishing, shrimping, and sponge gathering became important industries, as did pineapple canning. Throughout much of the 19th century and into the 20th, Key West was Florida's wealthiest city in per-capita terms. But in 1929, the local economy began to unravel. Cigar making moved to Tampa, Hawaii dominated the pineapple industry, and the sponges succumbed to blight. Then the Depression hit, and within a few years half the population was on relief.

Tourism began to revive Key West, but that came to a halt when a hurricane knocked out the railroad bridge in 1935. To help the tourism industry recover from that crushing blow, the government offered incentives for islanders to turn their charming homes—many of them built by shipwrights—into guesthouses and inns. That wise foresight has left the town with more than 100 such lodgings, a hallmark of Key West vacationing today. In the 1950s, the discovery of "pink gold" in the Dry Tortugas boosted the economy of the entire region. Catching Key West shrimp required a fleet of up to 500 boats and flooded local restaurants with some of the sweetest shrimp alive. The town's artistic community found inspiration in the colorful fishing boats.

Key West reflects a diverse population: Conchs (natives, many of whom trace their ancestry to the Bahamas), freshwater Conchs (longtime residents who migrated from somewhere else years ago), Hispanics (primarily Cuban immigrants), recent refugees from the urban sprawl of mainland Florida, military personnel, and an assortment of vagabonds, drifters, and dropouts in search of refuge. The island was once a gay vacation hot spot, and it remains a decidedly gay-friendly destination. Some of the once-renowned gay guesthouses, however, no longer cater to an exclusively gay clientele. Key Westers pride themselves on their tolerance of all peoples, all sexual orientations, and even all animals. Most restaurants allow pets, and it's not surprising to see stray cats, dogs, and even chickens roaming freely through the dining rooms. The chicken issue is one that government officials periodically try to bring to an end, but the colorful fowl continue to strut and crow, particularly in the vicinity of Old Town's Bahamian Village.

As a tourist destination, Key West has a lot to sell—an average temperature of 79°F, 19th-century architecture, and a laid-back lifestyle. Yet much has been lost to those eager for a buck. Duval Street is starting to resemble a shopping mall with name-brand storefronts, garish T-shirt shops, and tattoo shops with sidewalk views of the inked action. Cruise ships dwarf the town's skyline and fill the streets with day-trippers gawking at the hippies with dogs in their bike baskets, gay couples walking down the street holding hands, and the oddball lot of locals, some of whom bark louder than the dogs.

GETTING HERE AND AROUND
AIR TRAVEL
You can fly directly to Key West on a limited number of flights, most of which connect at other Florida airports. But a lot of folks fly into Miami or Fort Lauderdale and drive down or take the bus.

BOAT TRAVEL
Key West Express operates air-conditioned ferries between the Key West Terminal (Caroline and Grinnell streets) and Marco Island, and Fort Myers Beach. The trip from Fort Myers Beach takes at least four hours each way and costs $95 one way, $155 round-trip. Ferries depart from Fort Myers Beach at 8:30 am and from Key West at 6 pm. The Miami and Marco Island ferry costs $95 one way and $155 round-trip, and departs at 8:30 am. A photo ID is required for each passenger. Advance reservations are recommended and can save money.

BUS AND SHUTTLE TRAVEL TO KEY WEST

Greyhound Lines runs a special Keys Shuttle up to twice a day (depending on the day of the week) from Miami International Airport (departing from Concourse E, lower level) that stops throughout the Keys. Fares run about $45 (Web fare) to $57 for Key West. Keys Shuttle runs scheduled service three times a day in 15-passenger vans between Miami Airport and Key West with stops throughout the Keys for $70 to $90 per person. SuperShuttle charges $102 per passenger for trips from Miami International Airport to the Upper Keys. To go farther into the Keys, you must book an entire 11-person van, which costs about $350 to Key West. You need to place your request for transportation back to the airport 24 hours in advance. Uber is also available throughout the Keys and from the airport, but you must download the company's smartphone app and register a credit card in order to use the service. *For detailed information on these services, see Getting Here and Around: Bus Travel*

BUS TRAVEL AROUND KEY WEST

Between mile markers 4 and 0, Key West is the one place in the Keys where you could conceivably do without a car, especially if you plan on staying around Old Town. If you've driven the 106 miles down the chain, you're probably ready to abandon your car in the hotel parking lot anyway. Trolleys, buses, bikes, scooters, and feet are more suitable alternatives. When your feet tire, catch a rickshaw-style pedicab ride, which will run you about $1.50 a minute. But to explore the beaches, New Town, and Stock Island, you'll need a car or taxi.

The City of Key West Department of Transportation has six color-coded bus routes traversing the island from 5:30 am to 11:30 pm. Stops have signs with the international bus symbol. Schedules are available on buses and at hotels, visitor centers, shops, and online. The fare is $2 one way. Its Lower Keys Shuttle bus runs between Marathon to Key West ($4 one way), with scheduled stops along the way.

VISITOR INFORMATION

Contacts Gay & Lesbian Community Center. ⊠ *513 Truman Ave.* ☎ *305/292–3223* ⊕ *www.lgbtcenter.com.* **Greater Key West Chamber of Commerce.** ☎ *305/294–2587, 800/527–8539* ⊕ *www.keywestchamber.org.*

TOURS

BIKE TOURS

Lloyd's Original Tropical Bike Tour. Explore the natural, noncommercial side of Key West at a leisurely pace, stopping on backstreets and in backyards of private homes to sample native fruits and view indigenous plants and trees with a 30-year Key West veteran. The behind-the-scenes tours run two hours and include a bike rental. ⊠ *Truman Ave. and Simonton St.* ☎ *305/304–4700* ⊕ *www.lloydstropicalbiketour.com* ☎ *$39.*

BUS TOURS

City View Trolley Tours. In 2010, City View Trolley Tours began service, offering a little competition to the Conch Train and Old Town Trolley, which are owned by the same company. Purchase your tickets online or with your smartphone, and save $5 per person. Tours depart every 30 minutes from 9:30 to 4:30. Passengers can board and disembark at any of nine stops, and can reboard at will. ⊠ *Key West* ☎ *305/294–0644* ⊕ *www.cityviewtrolleys.com* ✉ *From $19.*

Conch Tour Train. The Conch Tour Train is a 90-minute narrated tour of Key West, traveling 14 miles through Old Town and around the island. Board at Mallory Square or Angela Street and Duval Street depot every half hour (9–4:30 from Mallory Square). Discount tickets are available online. ⊠ *Key West* ☎ *305/294–5161, 888/916–8687* ⊕ *www.conchtourtrain.com* ✉ *$30.45.*

Gay & Lesbian Trolley Tour. Decorated with a rainbow, the Gay and Lesbian Trolley Tour rumbles around the town beginning at 11 am every Saturday morning. The 70-minute tour highlights Key West's influential gay history. ⊠ *513 Truman Ave.* ☎ *305/294–4603* ⊕ *www.keywestsites. com* ✉ *$20.*

Old Town Trolley. Old Town Trolley operates trolley-style buses, departing from Mallory Square every 30 minutes from 9 to 4:30, for 90-minute narrated tours of Key West. The smaller trolleys go places the larger Conch Tour Train won't fit and you can ride a second consecutive day for free. You may disembark at any of 13 stops and reboard a later trolley. You can save $3 by booking online. It also offers package deals with Old Town attractions. ⊠ *201 Front St.* ☎ *305/296–6688, 888/910–8687* ⊕ *www.trolleytours.com* ✉ *$30.45.*

WALKING TOURS

Historic Florida Keys Foundation. In addition to publishing several good guides on Key West, the foundation conducts tours of the City Cemetery on Tuesday and Thursday at 9:30 am. ⊠ *Old City Hall, 510 Greene St.* ☎ *305/292–6718* ⊕ *www.historicfloridakeys.org* ✉ *$15.*

Key West Promotions. If you're not entirely a do-it-yourselfer, Key West Promotions offers a variety of guided tours, including the famous pub crawl, a historic homes and gardens walking tour, a southernmost bike tour, a chilling ghost tour, and a palate-pleasing, Taste of Key West restaurant experience. ⊠ *218 Whitehead St.* ☎ *305/294–7170* ⊕ *www. keywestwalkingtours.com.*

EXPLORING

OLD TOWN

The heart of Key West, the historic Old Town area runs from White Street to the waterfront. Beginning in 1822, wharves, warehouses, chandleries, ship-repair facilities, and eventually, in 1891, the U.S. Custom House, sprang up around the deep harbor to accommodate the navy's large ships and other sailing vessels. Wreckers, merchants, and sea captains built lavish houses near the bustling waterfront. A remarkable number of these fine Victorian and pre-Victorian structures have been restored to their original grandeur and now serve as homes, guesthouses, shops, restaurants, and museums. These, along with the dwellings of famous writers, artists, and politicians who've come to Key West over the past 175 years, are among the area's approximately 3,000 historic structures. Old Town also has the city's finest restaurants and hotels, lively street life, and popular nightspots.

TOP ATTRACTIONS

Audubon House and Tropical Gardens. If you've ever seen an engraving by ornithologist John James Audubon, you'll understand why his name is synonymous with birds. See his works in this three-story house, which was built in the 1840s for Captain John Geiger and filled with period furniture. It now commemorates Audubon's 1832 stop in Key West while he was traveling through Florida to study birds. After an introduction by a docent, you can do a self-guided tour of the house and gardens. An art gallery sells lithographs of the artist's famed portraits. ⌂ *205 Whitehead St.* ☎ *305/294–2116, 877/294–2470* ⊕ *www.audubonhouse.com* ✉ *$12.*

Fodor's Choice
★

Custom House. When Key West was designated a U.S. port of entry in the early 1820s, a customhouse was established. Salvaged cargoes from ships wrecked on the reefs were brought here, setting the stage for Key West to become—for a time—the richest city in Florida. The imposing redbrick-and-terra-cotta Richardsonian Romanesque–style building reopened as a museum and art gallery in 1999. Smaller galleries have long-term and changing exhibits about the history of Key West, including a Hemingway room and a permanent Henry Flagler exhibit that commemorates the arrival of Flagler's railroad to Key West in 1912. ⌂ *281 Front St.* ☎ *305/295–6616* ⊕ *www.kwahs.com* ✉ *$10.*

Dry Tortugas National Park and Historic Key West Bight Museum. If you can't see Ft. Jefferson in the Dry Tortugas in person, this is the next best thing. Opened in 2013 by the national park's official ferry commissioner, this free attraction located in Key West's historic seaport has an impressive (1:87) scale model of the fort; life-size figures including the fort's most famous prisoner, Dr. Samuel Mudd; and even a junior ranger station for the little ones with hands-on educational fun. The exhibits are housed in a historic site as well, the old Thompson Fish House, where local fisherman would bring their daily catch for processing. History lingers on within these walls, but to get a whiff of the sea and days gone past, you'll have to walk the docks out front. ⌂ *240 Margaret St.* ☎ *305/294–7009* ⊕ *www.drytortugas.com* ✉ *Free.*

Fodor's Choice
★

The Ernest Hemingway Home and Museum. Amusing anecdotes spice up the guided tours of Ernest Hemingway's home, built in 1801 by the town's most successful wrecker. While living here between 1931 and 1942, Hemingway wrote about 70% of his life's work, including classics like *For Whom the Bell Tolls*. Few of his belongings remain aside from some books, and there's little about his actual work, but photographs help you visualize his day-to-day life. The famous six-toed descendants of Hemingway's cats—many named for actors, artists, authors, and even a hurricane—have free rein of the property. Tours begin every 10 minutes and take 30 minutes; then you're free to explore on your own. Be sure to find out why there is a urinal in the garden! ⌂ *907 Whitehead St.* ☎ *305/294–1136* ⊕ *www.hemingwayhome.com* ✉ *$13.*

Fort Zachary Taylor Historic State Park. Construction of the fort began in 1845 but was halted during the Civil War. Even though Florida seceded from the Union, Yankee forces used the fort as a base to block Confederate shipping. More than 1,500 Confederate vessels were detained in Key West's harbor. The fort, finally completed in 1866, was also used in the Spanish-American War. Take a 30-minute guided walking tour

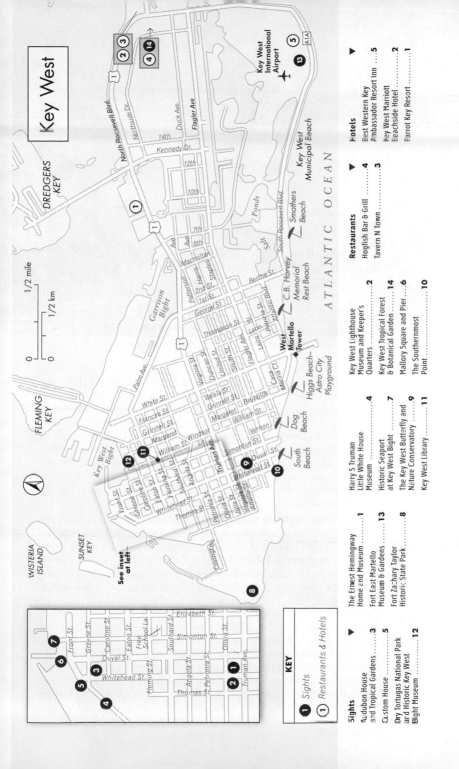

Key West

KEY

▶ Sights

① Restaurants & Hotels

Sights ▶

Audubon House
and Tropical Gardens **3**

Custom House **5**

Dry Tortugas National Park
and Historic Key West
Bight Museum **12**

The Ernest Hemingway
Home and Museum **1**

Fort East Martello
Museum & Gardens **13**

Fort Zachary Taylor
Historic State Park **8**

Harry S Truman
Little White House
Museum **4**

Historic Seaport
at Key West Bight **7**

The Key West Butterfly and
Nature Conservatory **6**

Key West Library **11**

Key West Lighthouse
Museum and Keeper's
Quarters **2**

Key West Tropical Forest
& Botanical Garden **14**

Mallory Square and Pier ... **6**

The Southernmost
Point **10**

Restaurants ▶

Hogfish Bar & Grill **4**

Tavern N Town **3**

Hotels ▶

Best Western Key
Ambassador Resort Inn ... **5**

Key West Marriott
Beachside Hotel **2**

Parrot Key Resort **1**

See the typewriter Hemingway used at his home office in Key West. He lived here from 1931 to 1942.

of the redbrick fort, a National Historic Landmark, at noon and 2, or self-guided tour anytime between 8 and 5. In February a celebration called Civil War Heritage Days includes costumed reenactments and demonstrations. From mid-January to mid-April the park serves as an open-air gallery for pieces created for Sculpture Key West. One of its most popular features is its man-made beach, a rest stop for migrating birds in the spring and fall; there are also picnic areas, hiking and biking trails, and a kayak launch. ⊠ *Southard St., at end of street, through Truman Annex* ☎ *305/292–6713* ⊕ *www.floridastateparks.org/park/ Fort-Taylor* ⊠ *$4 for single-occupant vehicles, $6 for 2–8 people in a vehicle, plus a 50¢ per person county surcharge.*

Harry S Truman Little White House Museum. Renovations to this circa-1890 landmark have restored the home and gardens to the Truman era, down to the wallpaper pattern. A free photographic review of visiting dignitaries and presidents—John F. Kennedy, Jimmy Carter, and Bill Clinton are among the chief executives who passed through here—is on display in the back of the gift shop. Engaging 45-minute tours begin every 20 minutes until 4:30. They start with an excellent 10-minute video on the history of the property and Truman's visits. On the grounds of **Truman Annex,** a 103-acre former military parade grounds and barracks, the home served as a winter White House for presidents Truman, Eisenhower, and Kennedy. Entry is cheaper when purchased in advance online; tickets bought on-site add sales tax. ■ **TIP→ The house tour does require climbing steps. Visitors can do a free self-guided botanical tour of the grounds with a brochure from the museum store.** ⊠ *111 Front St.* ☎ *305/294–9911* ⊕ *www.trumanlittlewhitehouse.com* ⊠ *$16.13.*

CLOSE UP

Hemingway Was Here

In a town where Pulitzer Prize–winning writers are almost as common as coconuts, Ernest Hemingway stands out. Many bars and restaurants around the island claim that he ate or drank there.

Hemingway came to Key West in 1928 at the urging of writer John Dos Passos and rented a house with his second wife, Pauline Pfeiffer. They spent winters in the Keys and summers in Europe and Wyoming, occasionally taking African safaris. Along the way, they had two sons, Patrick and Gregory. In 1931, Pauline's wealthy uncle Gus gave the couple the house at 907 Whitehead Street. Now known as the Ernest Hemingway Home & Museum, it's Key West's number one tourist attraction. Renovations included the addition of a pool and a tropical garden.

In 1935, when the visitor bureau included the house in a tourist brochure, Hemingway promptly built the brick wall that surrounds it today. He wrote of the visitor bureau's offense in a 1935 essay for *Esquire,* saying, "The house at present occupied by your correspondent is listed as number eighteen in a compilation of the forty-eight things for a tourist to see in Key West. So there will be no difficulty in a tourist finding it or any other of the sights

of the city, a map has been prepared by the local F.E.R.A. authorities to be presented to each arriving visitor. This is all very flattering to the easily bloated ego of your correspondent but very hard on production."

During his time in Key West, Hemingway penned some of his most important works, including *A Farewell to Arms, To Have and Have Not, Green Hills of Africa,* and *Death in the Afternoon.* His rigorous schedule consisted of writing almost every morning in his second-story studio above the pool, then promptly descending the stairs at midday. By afternoon and evening he was ready for drinking, fishing, swimming, boxing, and hanging around with the boys.

One close friend was Joe Russell, a craggy fisherman and owner of the rugged bar Sloppy Joe's, originally at 428 Greene Street but now at 201 Duval Street. Russell was the only one in town who would cash Hemingway's $1,000 royalty check. Russell and Charles Thompson introduced Hemingway to deep-sea fishing, which became fodder for his writing.

Hemingway stayed in Key West for 11 years before leaving Pauline for his third wife. Pauline and the boys stayed on in the house, which sold in 1951 for $80,000, 10 times its original cost.

4

Historic Seaport at Key West Bight. What was once a funky—in some places even seedy—part of town is now an 8½-acre historic restoration of 100 businesses, including waterfront restaurants, open-air bars, museums, clothing stores, bait shops, dive shops, docks, a marina, and water-sports concessions. It's all linked by the 2-mile waterfront **Harborwalk,** which runs between Front and Grinnell streets, passing big ships, schooners, sunset cruises, fishing charters, and glass-bottom boats. ⌂ *100 Grinnell St.* ⊕ *www.keywestseaport.com.*

NEED A
BREAK
Coffee Plantation. Get your morning (or afternoon) buzz, and hook up to the Internet in the comfort of a homelike setting in a circa-1890 Conch house. Munch on sandwiches, wraps, and pastries, and sip a hot or cold espresso beverage. ⊠ *713 Caroline St.* ☏ *305/295–9808* ⊕ *www.coffee-plantationkeywest.com.*

FAMILY **The Key West Butterfly and Nature Conservatory.** This air-conditioned refuge for butterflies, birds, and the human spirit gladdens the soul with hundreds of colorful wings—more than 45 species of butterflies alone—in a lovely glass-encased bubble. Waterfalls, artistic benches, paved pathways, birds, and lush, flowering vegetation elevate this above most butterfly attractions. The gift shop and gallery are worth a visit on their own. ⊠ *1316 Duval St.* ☏ *305/296–2988, 800/839–4647* ⊕ *www.keywestbutterfly.com* ✆ *$12.*

Key West Library. Check out the pretty palm garden next to the Key West Library at 700 Fleming Street, just off Duval. This leafy, outdoor reading area, with shaded benches, is the perfect place to escape the frenzy and crowds of downtown Key West. There's free Internet access in the library, too. ⊠ *700 Fleming St.* ☏ *305/292–3595* ⊕ *www.keyslibraries.org.*

Key West Lighthouse Museum and Keeper's Quarters. For the best view in town, climb the 88 steps to the top of this 1847 lighthouse. The 92-foot structure has a Fresnel lens, which was installed in the 1860s at a cost of $1 million. The keeper lived in the adjacent 1887 clapboard house, which now exhibits vintage photographs, ship models, nautical charts, and lighthouse artifacts from all along the Key reefs. A kids' room is stocked with books and toys. ⊠ *938 Whitehead St.* ☏ *305/295–6616* ⊕ *www.kwahs.com* ✆ *$10.*

Mallory Square and Pier. For cruise-ship passengers, this is the disembarkation point for an attack on Key West. For practically every visitor, it's the requisite venue for a nightly sunset celebration that includes street performers—human statues, sword swallowers, tightrope walkers, musicians, and more—plus craft vendors, conch fritter fryers, and other regulars who defy classification. With all the activity, don't forget to watch the main show: a dazzling tropical sunset. ⊠ *Mallory Sq.*

The Southernmost Point. Possibly the most photographed site in Key West (even though the actual geographic southernmost point in the continental United States lies across the bay on a naval base, where you see a satellite dish), this is a must-see. Who wouldn't want his picture taken next to the big striped buoy that marks the southernmost point in the continental United States? A plaque next to it honors Cubans who lost their lives trying to escape to America and other signs tell Key West history. ⊠ *Whitehead and South Sts.*

NEW TOWN

The Overseas Highway splits as it enters Key West, the two forks rejoining to encircle New Town, the area east of White Street to Cow Key Channel. The southern fork runs along the shore as South Roosevelt Boulevard (Route A1A) and skirts Key West International Airport, while the northern fork runs along the north shore as North Roosevelt

Divers examine the intentionally scuttled 327-foot former U.S. Coast Guard cutter *Duane* in 120 feet of water off Key Largo.

Boulevard and turns into Truman Avenue once it hits Old Town. Part of New Town was created with dredged fill. The island would have continued growing this way had the Army Corps of Engineers not determined in the early 1970s that it was detrimental to the nearby reef.

TOP ATTRACTIONS

Fort East Martello Museum & Gardens. This redbrick Civil War fort never saw a lick of action during the war. Today it serves as a museum, with historical exhibits about the 19th and 20th centuries. Among the latter are relics of the USS *Maine,* cigar factory and shipwrecking exhibits, and the citadel tower you can climb to the top. The museum, operated by the Key West Art and Historical Society, also has a collection of Stanley Papio's "junk art" sculptures inside and out, and a gallery of Cuban folk artist Mario Sanchez's chiseled and painted wooden carvings of historic Key West street scenes. ⊠ *3501 S. Roosevelt Blvd.* ☎ *305/296–3913* ⊕ *www.kwahs.com* ⊠ *$9.*

Key West Tropical Forest & Botanical Garden. Established in 1935, this unique habitat is the only frost-free botanical garden in the continental United States. You won't see fancy topiaries and exotic plants, but you'll see a unique ecosystem that naturally occurs in this area and the Caribbean. There are paved walkways that take you past butterfly gardens, mangroves, Cuban palms, lots of birds like herons and ibis, and ponds where you can spy turtles and fish. It's a nice respite from the sidewalks and shops, and offers a natural slice of Keys paradise. ⊠ *5210 College Rd.* ☎ *305/296–1504* ⊕ *www.kwbgs.org* ⊠ *$7.*

THE CONCH REPUBLIC

Beginning in the 1970s, pot smuggling became a source of income for islanders who knew how to dodge detection in the maze of waterways in the Keys. In 1982, the U.S. Border Patrol threw a roadblock across the Overseas Highway just south of Florida City to catch drug runners and undocumented aliens. Traffic backed up for miles as Border Patrol agents searched vehicles and demanded that the occupants prove U.S. citizenship. Officials in Key West, outraged at being treated like foreigners by the federal government, staged a protest and formed their own "nation," the so-called Conch Republic. They hoisted a flag and distributed mock border passes, visas, and Conch currency. The embarrassed Border Patrol dismantled its roadblock, and now an annual festival recalls the city's victory.

BEACHES

OLD TOWN

Dog Beach. Next to Louie's Backyard restaurant, this tiny beach—the only one in Key West where dogs are allowed unleashed—has a shore that's a mix of sand and rocks. **Amenities:** none. **Best for:** walking. ⊠ *Vernon and Waddell Sts.* ⊟ *Free.*

FAMILY **Fort Zachary Taylor Beach.** The park's beach is the best and safest place to swim in Key West. There's an adjoining picnic area with barbecue grills and shade trees, a snack bar, and rental equipment, including snorkeling gear. A café serves sandwiches and other munchies. Water shoes are recommended since the bottom is rocky here. **Amenities:** food and drink; showers; toilets; water sports. **Best for:** swimming; snorkeling. ⊠ *Southard St., at end of street, through Truman Annex* ☎ *305/292–6713* ⊕ *www.floridastateparks.org/forttaylor* ⊟ *$4 for 1-occupant vehicles, $6 for 2–8 people in a vehicle, plus 50¢ per person county surcharge.*

FAMILY **Higgs Beach–Astro City Playground.** This Monroe County park with its groomed pebbly sand is a popular sunbathing spot. A nearby grove of Australian pines provides shade, and the West Martello Tower provides shelter should a storm suddenly sweep in. Kayak and beach-chair rentals are available, as is a volleyball net. The beach also has the largest AIDS memorial in the country and a cultural exhibit commemorating the grave site of 295 enslaved Africans who died after being rescued from three South America–bound slave ships in 1860. An athletic trail with 10 fitness stations is a new addition. Hungry? Grab a bite to eat at the on-site restaurant, Salute. Across the street, **Astro City Playground** is popular with young children. **Amenities:** parking; toilets; water sports. **Best for:** swimming; snorkeling. ⊠ *Atlantic Blvd., between White and Reynolds Sts.* ⊟ *Free.*

NEW TOWN

C.B. Harvey Memorial Rest Beach. This beach and park were named after Cornelius Bradford Harvey, former Key West mayor and commissioner. Adjacent to Higgs Beach, it has half a dozen picnic areas

across the street, dunes, a pier, and a wheelchair and bike path. **Amenities:** none. **Best for:** walking. ✉ *Atlantic Blvd., east side of White St. Pier* 🎫 *Free.*

Smathers Beach. This wide beach has nearly 1 mile of nice white sand, plus beautiful coconut palms, picnic areas, and volleyball courts, all of which make it popular with the spring-break crowd. Trucks along the road rent rafts, Windsurfers, and other beach "toys." **Amenities:** food and drink; parking; toilets; water sports. **Best for:** partiers. ✉ *S. Roosevelt Blvd.* 🎫 *Free.*

WHERE TO EAT

Bring your appetite, a sense of daring, and a lack of preconceived notions about propriety. A meal in Key West can mean overlooking the crazies along Duval Street, watching roosters and pigeons battle for a scrap of food that may have escaped your fork, relishing the finest in what used to be the dining room of a 19th-century Victorian home, or gazing out at boats jockeying for position in the marina. And that's just the diversity of the setting. Seafood dominates local menus, but the treatment afforded that fish or crustacean can range from Cuban and New World to Asian and Continental.

OLD TOWN

$$ JAPANESE 🍴 **Ambrosia.** Ask any savvy local where to get the best sushi on the island and you'll undoubtedly be pointed to this bright and airy dining room with a modern indoor waterfall literally steps from the Atlantic. Grab a seat at the sleek bar, where the back wall glows from purple to blue, or sit at the sushi bar and watch owner and head sushi chef Masa (albeit not the famous chef from New York and Las Vegas) prepare an impressive array of superfresh sashimi delicacies. **Known for:** consistently good fish; great tempura and teriyaki bento lunch specials; the Ambrosia special, with a mix of sashimi, sushi, and rolls. [$] *Average main: $20* ✉ *Santa Maria Resort, 1401 Simonton St.* ☎ *305/293–0304* 🌐 *www.ambrosiasushi.com* ⏲ *Closed 2 wks after Labor Day. No lunch weekends.*

$$$ ECLECTIC 🍴 **Azur Restaurant.** Fuel up on the finest fare at this former gas station, now part of the Eden House complex. In a contemporary setting with indoor and outdoor seating, welcoming staff serves original, eclectic dishes for breakfast, lunch, and dinner that stand out from those at the hordes of Key West restaurants. **Known for:** four varieties of gnocchi; medium plates; Sunday brunch. [$] *Average main: $26* ✉ *425 Grinnell St.* ☎ *305/292–2987* 🌐 *www.azurkeywest.com.*

$$$ CARIBBEAN 🍴 **Blue Heaven.** The outdoor dining area here is often referred to as "the quintessential Keys experience," and it's hard to argue. There's much to like about this historic Caribbean-style restaurant where Hemingway refereed boxing matches and customers cheered for cockfights. **Known for:** house-made desserts and breads; lobster Benedict with key lime hollandaise; the wait for a table. [$] *Average main: $24* ✉ *729 Thomas St.* ☎ *305/296–8666* 🌐 *www.blueheavenkw.com* ⏲ *Closed after Labor Day for 6 wks.*

$$ ✕ **B.O.'s Fish Wagon.** What started out as a fish house on wheels appears
SEEAFOOD to have broken down on the corner of Caroline and William streets
Fodor's Choice and is today the cornerstone for one of Key West's junkyard-chic din-
★ ing institutions. Step up to the wood-plank counter window and order
the specialty: a grouper sandwich fried or grilled and topped with key
lime sauce. **Known for:** lots of Key West charm; self-service; all seating
on picnic tables in the yard $ *Average main: $18* ✉ *801 Caroline St.*
☎ *305/294-9272.*

$ ✕ **The Café.** You don't have to be a vegetarian to love this new-age café
VEGETARIAN decorated with bright artwork and a corrugated-tin-fronted counter.
Local favorites include homemade soup, veggie sandwiches and burg-
ers (order them with a side of sweet-potato fries), grilled portobello
mushroom salad, seafood, vegan specialties, stir-fry dinners, and grilled
Gorgonzola pizza with caramelized onions, walnuts, and spinach.
Known for: vegan options; wine and beer only; some seafood served.
$ *Average main: $11* ✉ *509 Southard St.* ☎ *305/296-5515* ⊕ *www.
thecafekw.com.*

$$$ ✕ **Café Marquesa.** Chef Susan Ferry presents seven or more inspired
EUROPEAN entrées on her changing menu each night. Delicious dishes can include
Fodor's Choice anything from yellowtail snapper to Australian rack of lamb. **Known**
★ **for:** relaxed but elegant setting; good wine and martini lists; desserts
worth ordering. $ *Average main: $29* ✉ *600 Fleming St.* ☎ *305/292–
1244* ⊕ *www.marquesa.com* ☾ *No lunch.*

$$$ ✕ **Café Solé.** This little corner of France hides behind a high wall in a
FRENCH residential neighborhood. Inside, French training intertwines with local
ingredients, creating delicious takes on classics, including a must-try
conch carpaccio, yellowtail snapper with mango salsa, and some of
the best bouillabaisse that you'll find outside of Marseilles. **Known
for:** hogfish in several different preparations; intimate, romantic atmo-
sphere; worthy desserts. $ *Average main: $27* ✉ *1029 Southard St.*
☎ *305/294-0230* ⊕ *www.cafesole.com.*

$$$ ✕ **Camille's Restaurant.** Break out the stretchy pants because everything
MODERN on the menu at this affordable hot spot not only sounds scrumptious,
AMERICAN it is. Locals have tried to keep this place a secret for over 20 years,
but the word is out for great breakfast, lunch, and dinner. **Known for:**
popularity with both locals and tourists; great grilled stone-crab cakes;
unique Barbie doll collection. $ *Average main: $21* ✉ *1202 Simonton
St., at Catherine St.* ☎ *305/296-4811* ⊕ *www.camilleskeywest.com.*

$$$ ✕ **Conch Republic Seafood Company.** Because of its location where the
SEAFOOD fast ferry docks, Conch Republic does a brisk business. It's huge, open-
air, and on the water, so the place is hard to miss. **Known for:** ambi-
tious menu of Caribbean-inspired seafood; no reservations; live music
most nights. $ *Average main: $25* ✉ *631 Greene St., at Elizabeth St.*
☎ *305/294-4403* ⊕ *www.conchrepublicseafood.com.*

$ ✕ **Croissants de France.** Pop into the bakery for something sinfully sweet
FRENCH or spend some time people-watching at the sidewalk café next door.
You can get breakfast or lunch at the café, and the bakery is open late.
Known for: gluten-free buckwheat crepes; popularity with both locals
and visitors; great coffee and croissants. $ *Average main: $14* ✉ *816
Duval St.* ☎ *305/294-2624* ⊕ *www.croissantsdefrance.com.*

4

$$
SEAFOOD
✕ **Dante's Key West Restaurant and Pool Bar.** With the motto "Come be an aquaholic," Dante's is as unique as Key West itself. Sun loungers, tiki bars, and tables with umbrellas and chairs surround a large free-form swimming pool. **Known for:** menu of typical bar food and snacks with a few entrées; popular happy hour; raucous weekend pool parties. $ *Average main: $18* ✉ *Conch Harbor Marina, 951 Caroline St.* ☎ *305/423–2001* ⊕ *www.danteskeywest.com.*

$$$
MODERN
AMERICAN
✕ **Deuce's Off the Hook Grill.** It's a tight fit with only six tables (and six counter seats), but if you don't mind sitting close to fellow diners, you will be rewarded with a made-from-scratch meal almost anytime of day. A specials board lists plenty of tempting options, but be sure to ask the price—seafood risotto might *sound* great, but when the reality hits your bill, your wallet won't be happy. **Known for:** excellent fresh seafood; small and can be busy; popular brunch spot. $ *Average main: $21* ✉ *728 Simonton St.* ☎ *305/414–8428* ⊕ *www.offthehookkeywest. com* ⊘ *Closed Tues.*

$$
CUBAN
✕ **El Meson de Pepe.** If you want to get a taste of the island's Cuban heritage, this is the place. After watching a Mallory Square sunset, you can dine alfresco or in the dining room on refined versions of Cuban classics. **Known for:** oversized mojitos; Latin band during the nightly sunset celebration; touristy atmosphere. $ *Average main: $19* ✉ *Mallory Sq., 410 Wall St.* ☎ *305/295–2620* ⊕ *www.elmesondepepe.com.*

$
CUBAN
✕ **El Siboney.** Dining at this family-style restaurant is like going to Mom's for Sunday dinner—if your mother is Cuban. The dining room is noisy, and the food is traditional *cubano*. To make a good thing even better, the prices are very reasonable and the homemade sangria is *muy bueno*. **Known for:** memorable paella and traditional dishes; wine and beer only; cheaper than more touristy options close to Duval. $ *Average main: $11* ✉ *900 Catherine St.* ☎ *305/296–4184* ⊕ *www. elsiboneyrestaurant.com.*

$$
SEAFOOD
FAMILY
✕ **Half Shell Raw Bar.** Smack-dab on the docks, this legendary institution gets its name from the oysters, clams, and peel-and-eat shrimp that are a departure point for its seafood-based diet. It's not clever recipes or fine dining (or even air-conditioning) that packs 'em in; it's fried fish, po'boy sandwiches, and seafood combos. **Known for:** cheap oysters for happy hour; few non-seafood options; good people-watching spot. $ *Average main: $16* ✉ *Lands End Village at Historic Seaport, 231 Margaret St.* ☎ *305/294–7496* ⊕ *www.halfshellrawbar.com.*

$$
AMERICAN
✕ **Jimmy Buffett's Margaritaville Cafe.** If you must have your cheeseburger in paradise, it may as well be here, where you can chew along with the songs playing on the sound system, TV monitors, and movie screen. The first of Buffett's line of chain eateries, it belongs here more than anywhere else, but quite frankly it's more about the name, music, and attitude (and margaritas) than the food. **Known for:** typical Caribbean bar food; live music at night; raucous party atmosphere almost all the time. $ *Average main: $16* ✉ *500 Duval St.* ☎ *305/292–1435* ⊕ *www. margaritaville.com.*

$$$
ECLECTIC
✕ **Latitudes.** For a special treat, take the short boat ride to lovely Sunset Key for lunch or dinner on the beach. Creativity and quality ingredients combine for dishes that are bound to impress as much as the setting.

Known for: seating both inside and outside on the patio; sophisticated atmosphere and expensive food; free 10-minute ferry ride (and reservations) required. [$] *Average main: $28* ✉ *Sunset Key Guest Cottages, 245 Front St.* ☎ *305/292–5300, 888/477–7786* 🌐 *www.sunsetkeycottages.com/latitudes-key-west.*

$$$$ ECLECTIC 🍴 **Louie's Backyard.** Feast your eyes on a steal-your-breath-away view and beautifully presented dishes prepared by executive chef Doug Shook. Once you get over sticker shock on the seasonally changing menu, settle in on the outside deck and enjoy dishes like cracked conch with mango chutney, lamb chops with sun-dried tomato relish, and tamarind-glazed duck breast. **Known for:** the more affordable Cafe at Louie's, upstairs for dinner only; cheaper versions of the same food at lunch; drinks at Afterdeck Bar, directly on the water. [$] *Average main: $36* ✉ *700 Waddell Ave.* ☎ *305/294–1061* 🌐 *www.louiesbackyard.com* 🕒 *Closed Labor Day–mid-Sept. Cafe closed Sun. and Mon.*

4

$$ ITALIAN 🍴 **Mangia Mangia.** This longtime favorite serves large portions of homemade pastas that can be matched with any of their homemade sauces. Tables are arranged in a brick garden hung with twinkling lights and in a cozy, casual dining room in an old house. **Known for:** extensive wine list with many old and rare vintages; wine and beer only; nice garden for outdoor seating. [$] *Average main: $16* ✉ *900 Southard St.* ☎ *305/294–2469* 🌐 *www.mangia-mangia.com* 🕒 *No lunch.*

$$$$ AMERICAN 🍴 **Michaels Restaurant.** White tablecloths, subdued lighting, and romantic music give Michaels the feel of an urban eatery, while garden seating reminds you that you are in the Keys. Chef-owner Michael Wilson flies in prime rib, cowboy steaks, and rib eyes from Allen Brothers in Chicago, which has supplied top-ranked steak houses for more than a century. **Known for:** elegant, romantic atmosphere; small plates available until 7:30 Sunday–Thursday; steak and seafood, which dominate the menu. [$] *Average main: $32* ✉ *532 Margaret St.* ☎ *305/295–1300* 🌐 *www.michaelskeywest.com* 🕒 *No lunch.*

$$$$ ECLECTIC 🍴 **Nine One Five.** Twinkling lights draped along the lower- and upper-level outdoor porches of a 100-year-old Victorian home set an unstuffy and comfortable stage here. If you like to sample and sip, you'll appreciate the variety of smaller-plate selections and wines by the glass. **Known for:** signature "tuna dome" with fresh crab wrapped in ahi-tuna sashimi; intimate and inviting atmosphere; outdoor dining overlooks upper Duval. [$] *Average main: $32* ✉ *915 Duval St.* ☎ *305/296–0669* 🌐 *www.915duval.com* 🕒 *No lunch.*

$$$$ EUROPEAN 🍴 **Pisces.** In a circa-1892 former store and home, chef William Arnel and staff create a contemporary setting with a stylish granite bar, Andy Warhol originals, and glass oil lamps. Favorites include "lobster tango mango," flambéed in cognac and served with saffron butter sauce and sliced mangoes. **Known for:** dressy, upscale setting; excellent wine list; gracious service. [$] *Average main: $35* ✉ *1007 Simonton St.* ☎ *305/294–7100* 🌐 *www.pisceskeywest.com* 🕒 *Closed summer. No lunch.*

$$$ ITALIAN 🍴 **Salute on the Beach.** Sister restaurant to Blue Heaven, this colorful establishment sits on Higgs Beach, giving it one of the island's best lunch views—and a bit of sand and salt spray on a windy day. The intriguing menu is Italian with a Caribbean flair and will not disappoint. **Known**

Where to Eat and Stay in Old Town

KEY

1 Restaurants
1 Hotels

ATLANTIC OCEAN

for: amazing water views; casual, inviting atmosphere; popular with locals as well as visitors. $ *Average main: $22* ✉ *Higgs Beach, 1000 Atlantic Blvd.* ☎ *305/292–1117* ⊕ *www.saluteonthebeach.com.*

$ ✗ **Santiago's Bodega.** If you've ever wondered where chefs go for a great TAPAS meal in the Lower Keys, this is their secret spot. Picky palates will be **Fodor's**Choice satisfied at this funky, dark, and sensuous corner house, which is well ★ off the main drag. **Known for:** only small plates served, so great for sharing; outdoor dining on the front porch; desserts as good as everything else. $ *Average main: $13* ✉ *Bahama Village, 207 Petronia St.* ☎ *305/296–7691* ⊕ *www.santiagosbodega.com.*

$$ ✗ **Sarabeth's.** Named for the award-winning jam-maker and pastry chef AMERICAN Sarabeth Levine, who runs the kitchen, it naturally is proclaimed for its all-morning, all-afternoon breakfast, best enjoyed in the picket-fenced front yard of this circa-1870 synagogue. Lemon ricotta pancakes, pumpkin waffles, omelets, and homemade jams make the meal. **Known for:** breakfast and brunch specialties, including famous lemon-ricotta pancakes; daily specials; good desserts. $ *Average main: $20* ✉ *530 Simonton St., at Souhard St.* ☎ *305/293–8181* ⊕ *www.sarabethskey-west.com* ⊘ *Closed Mon. Christmas through Easter, and Tues.*

$$$ ✗ **Seven Fish.** This local hot spot has relocated to a new, easy-to-find SEAFOOD location that exudes a casual Key West vibe, but you'll still find the same eclectic mix of dishes. Their specialty, however, will always be the local fish of the day (like snapper with creamy Thai curry). **Known for:** fresh seafood; busy spot requiring reservations; casual, inviting atmosphere. $ *Average main: $26* ✉ *921 Truman Ave.* ☎ *305/296–2777* ⊕ *www.7fish.com* ⊘ *Closed Tues. No lunch.*

$$ ✗ **Turtle Kraals.** Named for the kraals, or corrals, where sea turtles were SEAFOOD once kept until they went to the cannery, this place calls to mind the FAMILY island's history. The lunch–dinner menu offers an assortment of marine cuisine that includes seafood enchiladas, mesquite-grilled fish of the day, and mango crab cakes. **Known for:** wood-smoked entrées as good as the fish; happy-hour turtle races; location overlooking the Historic Seaport. $ *Average main: $16* ✉ *231 Margaret St.* ☎ *305/294–2640* ⊕ *www.turtlekraals.com.*

NEW TOWN

$ ✗ **Hogfish Bar & Grill.** It's worth a drive to Stock Island, one of Florida's SEAFOOD last surviving working waterfronts, just outside Key West, to indulge in the freshness you'll witness at this down-to-earth spot. Hogfish is the specialty, of course. **Known for:** "Killer Hogfish Sandwich" on Cuban bread; a spot to watch the shrimpers and fishermen unload their catch; ultracasual atmosphere with picnic tables outside. $ *Average main: $13* ✉ *6810 Front St., Stock Island* ☎ *305/293–4041* ⊕ *www.hogfishbar.com.*

$$$ ✗ **Tavern N Town.** This handsome and warm restaurant has an open ECLECTIC kitchen that adds lovely aromas from the wood-fired oven. The dinner menu offers a variety of options, including small plates and full entrées. **Known for:** upscale atmosphere (and prices); popular happy hour; winning the Master Chef's Classic at Key West Food & Wine Festival. $ *Average main: $26* ✉ *Key West Marriott Beachside Resort, 3841 N. Roosevelt Blvd.* ☎ *305/296–8100, 800/546–0885* ⊕ *www. beachsidekeywest.com* ⊘ *No lunch.*

WHERE TO STAY

Historic cottages, restored century-old Conch houses, and large resorts are among the offerings in Key West, the majority charging between $100 and $300 a night. In high season, Christmas through Easter, you'll be hard-pressed to find a decent room for less than $200, and most places raise prices considerably during holidays and festivals. Many guesthouses and inns do not welcome children under 16, and most do not permit smoking indoors. Most tariffs include an expanded Continental breakfast and, often, an afternoon glass of wine or snack.

LODGING ALTERNATIVES

The Key West Lodging Association is an umbrella organization for dozens of local properties. Vacation Rentals Key West lists historic cottages, homes, and condominiums for rent. Rent Key West Vacations specializes in renting vacation homes and condos for a week or longer. Vacation Key West lists all kinds of properties throughout Key West. In addition to these local agencies, 🌐 *airbnb.com* and 🌐 *vrbo.com* have many offerings in Key West.

Contacts Key West Lodging Association. ☎ *800/492–1911* 🌐 *www.keywestinns.com.* **Key West Vacations.** ☎ *888/775–3993* 🌐 *www.keywestvacations.com.* **Rent Key West Vacations.** ✉ *1075 Duval St., Suite C11* ☎ *305/294–0990, 800/833–7368* 🌐 *www.rentkeywest.com.* **Vacation Key West.** ✉ *100 Grinnell St., Key West Ferry Terminal* ☎ *305/295–9500, 800/595–5397* 🌐 *www.vacationkw.com.*

OLD TOWN

$$$ B&B/INN 🏨 **Ambrosia Key West.** If you desire personal attention, a casual atmosphere, and a dollop of style, stay at these twin inns spread out on nearly 2 acres. **Pros:** spacious rooms; poolside breakfast; friendly staff. **Cons:** on-street parking can be tough to come by; a little too spread out. [$] *Rooms from: $325* ✉ *615, 618, 622 Fleming St.* ☎ *305/296–9838, 800/535–9838* 🌐 *www.ambrosiakeywest.com* 🛏 *16 rooms, 3 town houses, 1 cottage* 🍴 *Breakfast.*

$ B&B/INN 🏨 **Angelina Guest House.** In the heart of Old Town, this home away from home offers simple, clean, attractively priced accommodations. **Pros:** good value; nice garden; friendly staff. **Cons:** thin walls; basic rooms; shared balcony. [$] *Rooms from: $134* ✉ *302 Angela St.* ☎ *305/294–4480, 888/303–4480* 🌐 *www.angelinaguesthouse.com* 🛏 *13 rooms* 🍴 *Breakfast.*

$$ B&B/INN 🏨 **Azul Key West.** The ultramodern—nearly minimalistic—redo of this classic circa-1903 Queen Anne mansion is a break from the sensory overload of Key West's other abundant Victorian guesthouses. **Pros:** lovely building; marble-floored baths; luxurious linens. **Cons:** on a busy street. [$] *Rooms from: $269* ✉ *907 Truman Ave.* ☎ *305/296–5152, 888/253–2985* 🌐 *www.azulhotels.us* 🛏 *11 rooms* 🍴 *Breakfast.*

$$$ RESORT FAMILY 🏨 **Casa Marina, A Waldorf-Astoria Resort.** At any moment, you expect the landed gentry to walk across the oceanfront lawn of this luxurious resort, just as they did when this 6½-acre resort opened on New Year's Eve in 1920. **Pros:** nice beach; historic setting; away from the crowds. **Cons:** long walk to central Old Town; expensive resort fee. [$] *Rooms from: $399* ✉ *1500 Reynolds St.* ☎ *305/296–3535, 866/203–6392* 🌐 *www.casamarinaresort.com* 🛏 *311 rooms* 🍴 *No meals.*

$$ ⬚ **Courtney's Place.** If you like kids, cats, and dogs, you'll feel right at
B&B/INN home in this collection of accommodations ranging from cigar-maker
cottages to shotgun houses. **Pros:** near Duval Street; fairly priced. **Cons:**
small parking lot; small pool; minimum-stay requirements. Ⓢ *Rooms
from: $249* ✉ *720 Whitmarsh La., off Petronia St.* ☎ *305/294–3480,
800/869–4639* ⊕ *www.courtneysplacekeywest.com* ⤳ *10 rooms, 8 cot-
tages* ⭘ *Breakfast.*

$$$ ⬚ **Crowne Plaza Key West–La Concha.** History and franchises can mix, as
HOTEL this 1920s-vintage hotel proves with its handsome atrium lobby and
sleep-conducive rooms. **Pros:** restaurant and Starbucks in-house; close
to downtown attractions; free Wi-Fi. **Cons:** high-traffic area; confusing layout; expensive valet-only parking. Ⓢ *Rooms from: $339* ✉ *430
Duval St.* ☎ *305/296–2991* ⊕ *www.laconchakeywest.com* ⤳ *178
rooms* ⭘ *No meals.*

$$ ⬚ **Eden House.** From the vintage metal rockers on the street-side porch
HOTEL to the old neon hotel sign in the lobby, this 1920s rambling Key West
mainstay hotel is high on character, low on gloss. **Pros:** free parking; hot
tub is actually hot; daily happy hour around the pool. **Cons:** pricey; a bit
of a musty smell in some rooms; no TV in some rooms. Ⓢ *Rooms from:
$200* ✉ *1015 Fleming St.* ☎ *305/296–6868, 800/533–5397* ⊕ *www.
edenhouse.com* ⤳ *44 rooms* ⭘ *No meals.*

$$$$ ⬚ **The Gardens Hotel.** Built in 1875, this gloriously shaded, well-loved
HOTEL property was a labor of love from the get-go, and it covers a third
Fodor'sChoice of a city block in Old Town. **Pros:** luxurious bathrooms; secluded
★ garden seating; free Wi-Fi. **Cons:** hard to get reservations; expensive;
nightly secure parking fee. Ⓢ *Rooms from: $415* ✉ *526 Angela St.*
☎ *305/294–2661, 800/526–2664* ⊕ *www.gardenshotel.com* ⤳ *23
rooms* ⭘ *Breakfast.*

$ ⬚ **Harborside Motel & Marina.** This little motel neatly packages three
HOTEL appealing characteristics—affordability, safety, and a pleasant location
between Old Town and New Town at Garrison Bight. **Pros:** grills for
cookouts; friendly fishing atmosphere; boat slips. **Cons:** more than a
mile from Duval Street; cash deposit for keys required. Ⓢ *Rooms from:
$189* ✉ *903 Eisenhower Dr.* ☎ *305/294–2780, 800/501–7823* ⊕ *www.
keywestharborside.com* ⤳ *12 rooms, 4 houseboats* ⭘ *No meals.*

$$ ⬚ **Heron House.** Conch-style architecture harks back to this property's
B&B/INN circa-1900 origins as a boardinghouse and cigar-maker cottages. **Pros:**
charming; fluffy bathrobes. **Cons:** faces noisy Eaton Street; owner's
suite smells musty. Ⓢ *Rooms from: $229* ✉ *412 Frances St.* ☎ *305/296–
4719, 888/265–2395* ⊕ *www.heronhousecourt.com* ⤳ *15 rooms*
⭘ *Breakfast.*

$$$$ ⬚ **Hyatt Centric Key West Resort and Spa.** With its own man-made beach,
RESORT the Hyatt Key West is one of few resorts where you can dig your toes
FAMILY in the sand, then walk a short distance away to the streets of Old
Town. **Pros:** a little bit away from the bustle of Old Town; plenty of
activities; Wi-Fi and bottled water included in resort fee. **Cons:** beach
is small; cramped-feeling property; $15 a night self-parking fee, $20
valet. Ⓢ *Rooms from: $419* ✉ *601 Front St.* ☎ *305/809–1234* ⊕ *www.
keywest.hyatt.com* ⤳ *118 rooms* ⭘ *No meals.*

$$$
B&B/INN
⛱ **Island City House Hotel.** A private garden with brick walkways, tropical plants, and a canopy of palms sets this convivial guesthouse apart from the pack. **Pros:** lush gardens; knowledgeable staff. **Cons:** spotty Wi-Fi service; no front-desk staff at night; some rooms are small. $ *Rooms from: $320* ✉ *411 William St.* ☎ *305/294–5702, 800/634–8230* ⊕ *www.islandcityhouse.com* ⇕ *24 suites* †○† *No meals.*

$$$$
HOTEL
⛱ **Island House.** Geared specifically toward gay men, this hotel features a health club, a video lounge, a café and bar, and rooms in historic digs. **Pros:** lots of privacy; just the place to get that all-over tan; free happy hour for guests. **Cons:** no women allowed; three rooms share a bath. $ *Rooms from: $459* ✉ *1129 Fleming St.* ☎ *305/294–6284, 800/890–6284* ⊕ *www.islandhousekeywest.com* ⇕ *34 rooms, 31 with bath* †○† *No meals.*

$$
B&B/INN
⛱ **Key Lime Inn.** This 1854 Grand Bahama–style house on the National Register of Historic Places succeeds by offering amiable service, a great location, and simple rooms with natural-wood furnishings. **Pros:** walking distance to clubs/bars; some rooms have private outdoor spaces; free Wi-Fi. **Cons:** standard rooms are pricey; pool faces a busy street; mulch-covered paths. $ *Rooms from: $259* ✉ *725 Truman Ave.* ☎ *305/294–5229, 800/549–4430* ⊕ *www.keylimeinn.com* ⇕ *37 rooms* †○† *Breakfast.*

$
B&B/INN
⛱ **Key West Bed and Breakfast/The Popular House.** There are accommodations for every budget here, but the owners reason that budget travelers deserve as pleasant an experience (and lavish a tropical Continental breakfast) as their well-heeled counterparts. **Pros:** lots of art; tiled outdoor shower; hot tub and sauna area is a welcome hangout. **Cons:** some rooms are small; four rooms have shared baths. $ *Rooms from: $135* ✉ *415 William St.* ☎ *305/296–7274, 800/438–6155* ⊕ *www.keywest-bandb.com* ⇕ *10 rooms, 6 with bath* †○† *Breakfast.*

$$
B&B/INN
⛱ **La Pensione.** Hospitality and period furnishings make this 1891 home, once owned by a cigar executive, a wonderful glimpse into Key West life in the late 19th century. **Pros:** pine-paneled walls; off-street parking; some rooms have wraparound porches. **Cons:** street-facing rooms are noisy; rooms do not have TVs; rooms can only accommodate two people. $ *Rooms from: $258* ✉ *809 Truman Ave.* ☎ *305/292–9923, 800/893–1193* ⊕ *www.lapensione.com* ⇕ *9 rooms* †○† *Breakfast.*

$$$$
RESORT
⛱ **Margaritaville Key West Resort & Marina.** This elegant waterfront resort's two three-story, Keys-style buildings huddle around its 37-slip marina in the middle of Old Town overlooking Mallory Square. **Pros:** rooms are large by Key West standards; access to Sunset Key; free Wi-Fi. **Cons:** feels too big for Key West; often crowded; heavy on conference clientele. $ *Rooms from: $409* ✉ *245 Front St.* ☎ *305/294–4000* ⊕ *www. margaritavillekeywest.com* ⇕ *210 rooms* †○† *No meals.*

$$$
RESORT
⛱ **The Marker.** As the first new hotel to open in Key West since the early 1990s, The Marker is a welcome and luxurious addition to the waterfront in Old Town, with Conch-style architecture and an authentic Keys aesthetic. **Pros:** convenient Old Town location; on-site restaurant Cero Bodega; three saltwater pools. **Cons:** $30 per night resort fee; underground parking $30 a night; lots of walking if your room isn't near the

amenities. $ *Rooms from: $400* ✉ *200 William St.* ☎ *305/501–5193* ⊕ *www.themarkerkeywest.com* ⌦ *96 rooms* ⦿ *No meals.*

$$$
HOTEL
Fodor's Choice
★

⬚ **Marquesa Hotel.** In a town that prides itself on its laid-back luxury, this complex of four restored 1884 houses stands out. **Pros:** room service; romantic atmosphere; turndown service. **Cons:** street-facing rooms can be noisy; expensive rates. $ *Rooms from: $395* ✉ *600 Fleming St.* ☎ *305/292–1919, 800/869–4631* ⊕ *www.marquesa.com* ⌦ *27 rooms* ⦿ *No meals.*

$$
B&B/INN

⬚ **Merlin Guesthouse.** Key West guesthouses don't usually welcome families, but this laid-back jumble of rooms and suites is an exception. **Pros:** good location near Duval Street; good rates. **Cons:** neighbor noise, especially in the front rooms; street parking or $10 nightly for their private lot. $ *Rooms from: $279* ✉ *811 Simonton St.* ☎ *305/296–3336, 800/642–4753* ⊕ *www.historickeywestinns.com* ⌦ *16 rooms, 4 cottages* ⦿ *Breakfast.*

$$
B&B/INN

⬚ **Mermaid & the Alligator.** An enchanting combination of flora and fauna makes this 1904 Victorian house a welcoming retreat. **Pros:** hot plunge pool; massage pavilion; island-getaway feel. **Cons:** minimum stay required (length depends on season); dark public areas; plastic lawn chairs. $ *Rooms from: $278* ✉ *729 Truman Ave.* ☎ *305/294–1894, 800/773–1894* ⊕ *www.kwmermaid.com* ⌦ *9 rooms* ⦿ *Breakfast.*

$$$
B&B/INN

⬚ **NYAH: Not Your Average Hotel.** From its charming white picket fence, it may look similar to other Victorian-style, Key West B&Bs, but that's where the similarities end. **Pros:** central location; expert staff; free daily happy hour. **Cons:** small rooms; even smaller closets; no toiletries provided. $ *Rooms from: $349* ✉ *420 Margaret St.* ☎ *305/296–2131* ⊕ *www.nyahotels.com* ⌦ *36 rooms* ⦿ *Breakfast* ⌐ *Age 18 and over only.*

$$$$
RESORT
Fodor's Choice
★

⬚ **Ocean Key Resort & Spa.** This full resort—relatively rare in Key West—has large, tropical-look rooms with private balconies and excellent amenities, including a pool and bar overlooking Sunset Pier and a Thai-inspired spa. **Pros:** well-trained staff; lively pool scene; best spa on the island. **Cons:** $20 per night valet parking; too bustling for some; pricey. $ *Rooms from: $495* ✉ *Zero Duval St.* ☎ *305/296–7701, 800/328–9815* ⊕ *www.oceankey.com* ⌦ *100 rooms* ⦿ *No meals.*

$$$$
RESORT

⬚ **Pier House Resort and Spa.** This upscale resort is near Mallory Square in the heart of Old Town, offering a wide range of amenities, including a beach, and comfortable, traditionally furnished rooms. **Pros:** beautiful beach; free Wi-Fi; nice spa. **Cons:** lots of conventions; poolside rooms are small; not really suitable for children under 16. $ *Rooms from: $470* ✉ *1 Duval St.* ☎ *305/296–4600, 800/327–8340* ⊕ *www.pierhouse.com* ⌦ *145 rooms* ⦿ *No meals.*

$$$
RESORT

⬚ **The Reach, A Waldorf Astoria Resort.** Embracing Key West's only natural beach, this full-service, luxury resort offers sleek rooms, all with balconies and modern amenities as well as reciprocal privileges to its sister Casa Marina resort nearby. **Pros:** removed from Duval hubbub; great sunrise views; pullout sofas in most rooms. **Cons:** expensive resort fee; high rates; some say it lacks the grandeur you'd expect of a Waldorf property. $ *Rooms from: $399* ✉ *1435 Simonton St.*

4

Sunset Key cottages are right on the water's edge, far away from the action of Old Town.

☎ 305/296–5000, 888/318–4316 🌐 www.reachresort.com 🛏 72 rooms, 78 suites 🍴 No meals.

$$$$ RENTAL Fodor's Choice ★ **Santa Maria Suites.** It's odd to call this a hidden gem when it sits on a prominent corner just one block off Duval, but you'd never know what luxury awaits behind its concrete facade, which creates total seclusion from the outside world. **Pros:** amenities galore; front desk concierge services; private parking lot. **Cons:** daily resort fee; beds low to the ground; only two-bedroom units available. *[$] Rooms from: $549 ✉ 1401 Simonton St. ☎ 866/726–8259, 305/296–5678 🌐 www.santamariasuites.com 🛏 35 suites 🍴 No meals.*

$$$ B&B/INN **Simonton Court.** A small world all its own, this adults-only B&B makes you feel deliciously sequestered from Key West's crasser side but keeps you close enough to get there on foot. **Pros:** lots of privacy; well-appointed accommodations; friendly staff. **Cons:** minimum stays required in high season; $25 a night off-street parking; some street noise in basic rooms. *[$] Rooms from: $310 ✉ 320 Simonton St. ☎ 305/294–6386, 800/944–2687 🌐 www.simontoncourt.com 🛏 23 rooms, 6 cottages 🍴 Breakfast.*

$$$ HOTEL **Southernmost Beach Resort.** Rooms at this hotel on the quiet end of Duval—a 20-minute walk from downtown—are modern and sophisticated, far enough from the hubub that you can relax but close enough that you can participate if you wish. **Pros:** pool attracts a lively crowd; access to nearby properties and beach; free parking and Wi-Fi. **Cons:** can get crowded around the pool and public areas; expensive nightly resort fee; beach is across the street. *[$] Rooms from: $359 ✉ 1319 Duval St. ☎ 305/296–6577, 800/354–4455 🌐 www.southernmost-beachresort.com 🛏 118 rooms 🍴 No meals.*

$$
B&B/INN
🏨 **Southwinds.** Operated by the same company as the ultra-high-end Santa Maria Suites, this motel-style property, though still pretty basic, has been modestly upgraded and is a good value-oriented option in pricey Key West. **Pros:** early (2 pm) check-in may be available; clean and spacious rooms; free parking and Wi-Fi. **Cons:** bland decor; small pools. $ *Rooms from: $200* ✉ *1321 Simonton St.* ☎ *305/296–2829, 877/879–2362* ⊕ *www.keywestsouthwinds.com* ⤳ *58 rooms* ⦿ *Breakfast.*

$
B&B/INN
🏨 **Speakeasy Inn.** During Prohibition, Raul Vasquez made this place popular by smuggling in rum from Cuba; today its reputation is for having reasonably priced rooms within walking distance of the beach. **Pros:** good location; all rooms have kitchenettes; free parking, first come first served. **Cons:** no pool; on busy Duval; rooms are fairly basic. $ *Rooms from: $189* ✉ *1117 Duval St.* ☎ *305/296–2680* ⊕ *www.speakeasyinn. com* ⤳ *7 suites* ⦿ *Breakfast.*

$$$$
RESORT
Fodor's Choice
★
🏨 **Sunset Key.** This luxurious private island retreat with its own sandy beach feels completely cut off from the world, yet you're just minutes away from the action: a 10-minute ride from Mallory Square on the 24-hour free ferry. **Pros:** all units have kitchens; roomy verandas; free Wi-Fi. **Cons:** luxury doesn't come cheap; beach shore is rocky; launch runs only every 30 minutes. $ *Rooms from: $780* ✉ *245 Front St.* ☎ *305/292–5300, 888/477–7786* ⊕ *www.westinsunsetkeycottages.com* ⤳ *40 cottages* ⦿ *Breakfast.*

NEW TOWN

$$
HOTEL
🏨 **Best Western Key Ambassador Resort Inn.** You know what to expect from this chain hotel: well-maintained rooms, predictable service, and competitive prices. **Pros:** big pool area; popular tiki bar; most rooms have screened-in balconies. **Cons:** airport noise; lacks personality. $ *Rooms from: $300* ✉ *3755 S. Roosevelt Blvd., New Town* ☎ *305/296–3500, 800/432–4315* ⊕ *www.keyambassador.com* ⤳ *100 rooms* ⦿ *Breakfast.*

$$$$
HOTEL
🏨 **Key West Marriott Beachside Hotel.** This hotel vies for convention business with the biggest ballroom in Key West, but it also appeals to families with its spacious condo units decorated with impeccable good taste. **Pros:** private beach; poolside cabanas; complimentary shuttle to Old Town and airport. **Cons:** small beach; lots of conventions and conferences; cookie-cutter facade. $ *Rooms from: $409* ✉ *3841 N. Roosevelt Blvd., New Town* ☎ *305/296–8100, 800/546–0885* ⊕ *www. keywestmarriottbeachside.com* ⤳ *93 rooms, 93 1-bedroom suites, 10 2-bedroom suites, 26 3-bedroom suites* ⦿ *No meals.*

$$$
HOTEL
🏨 **Parrot Key Resort.** This revamped destination resort feels like an old-fashioned beach community with picket fences and rocking-chair porches. **Pros:** four pools; finely appointed units; access to marina and other facilities at three sister properties in Marathon. **Cons:** outside of walking distance to Old Town; no transportation provided; hefty resort fee. $ *Rooms from: $329* ✉ *2801 N. Roosevelt Blvd., New Town* ☎ *305/809–2200* ⊕ *www.parrotkeyresort.com* ⤳ *74 rooms, 74 suites, 74 3-bedroom villas* ⦿ *No meals.*

4

NIGHTLIFE

Rest up: much of what happens in Key West occurs after dark. Open your mind and take a stroll. Scruffy street performers strum next to dogs in sunglasses. Characters wearing parrots or iguanas try to sell you your photo with their pet. Brawls tumble out the doors of Sloppy Joe's. Drag queens strut across stages in Joan Rivers garb. Tattooed men lick whipped cream off women's body parts. And margaritas flow like a Jimmy Buffett tune.

BARS AND LOUNGES

Capt. Tony's Saloon. When it was the original Sloppy Joe's in the mid-1930s, Hemingway was a regular. Later, a young Jimmy Buffett sang here and made this watering hole famous in his song "Last Mango in Paris." Captain Tony was even voted mayor of Key West. Yes, this place is a beloved landmark. Stop in and take a look at the "hanging tree" that grows through the roof, listen to live music seven nights a week, and play some pool. ⊠ *428 Greene St.* ☎ *305/294–1838* ⊕ *www. capttonyssaloon.com.*

Cowboy Bill's Honky Tonk Saloon. Ride the mechanical bucking bull, listen to live bands croon cry-in-your-beer tunes, and grab some pretty decent chow at the indoor-outdoor spread known as Cowboy Bill's Honky Tonk Saloon. There's live music from Tuesday through Saturday. Wednesday brings—we kid you not—sexy bull riding. ⊠ *610½ Duval St.* ☎ *305/295–8219* ⊕ *www.cowboybillskw.com.*

Durty Harry's. This megasize entertainment complex is home to eight different bars and clubs, both indoor and outdoor. Their motto is, "Eight Famous Bars, One Awesome Night," and they're right. You'll find pizza, dancing, live music, Rick's Key West, and the infamous Red Garter strip club. ⊠ *208 Duval St.* ☎ *305/296–5513* ⊕ *www. ricksbarkeywest.com.*

The Garden of Eden. Perhaps one of Duval's more unusual and intriguing watering holes, The Garden of Eden sits atop the Bull & Whistle saloon and has a clothing-optional policy. Most drinkers are looky-lous, but some actually bare it all, including the barmaids. ⊠ *Bull & Whistle Bar, 224 Duval St.* ☎ *305/396–4565.*

Green Parrot Bar. Pause for a libation in the open air and breathe in the spirit of Key West. Built in 1890 as a grocery store, this property has been many things to many people over the years. It's touted as the oldest bar in Key West and the sometimes-rowdy saloon has locals outnumbering out-of-towners, especially on nights when bands play. ⊠ *601 Whitehead St., at Southard St.* ☎ *305/294–6133* ⊕ *www. greenparrot.com.*

Hog's Breath Saloon. Belly up to the bar for a cold mug of the signature Hog's Breath Lager at this infamous joint, a must-stop on the Key West bar crawl. Live bands play daily 1 pm–2 am (except when the game's on TV). You never know who'll stop by and perhaps even jump on stage for an impromptu concert (can you say Kenny Chesney?). ⊠ *400 Front St.* ☎ *305/296–4222* ⊕ *www.hogsbreath.com.*

THE HOLIDAYS KEY WEST STYLE

On New Year's Eve, Key West celebrates the turning of the calendar page with three separate ceremonies that parody New York's dropping-of-the-ball drama. Here they let fall a 6-foot conch shell from Sloppy Joe's Bar, a pirate wench from the towering mast of a tall ship at the Historic Seaport, and a drag queen (elegantly decked out in a ball gown and riding an oversize red high-heel shoe) at Bourbon Street Pub. You wouldn't expect any less from America's most outrageous city.

Key West is one of the nation's biggest party towns, so the celebrations here take on a colorful hue.

In keeping with Key West's rich maritime heritage, its monthlong Bight Before Christmas begins Thanksgiving Eve at Key West Bight. The Lighted Boat Parade creates a quintessential Florida spectacle with live music and decorated vessels of all shapes and sizes.

Some years, Tennessee Williams Theatre hosts a Key West version of the *Nutcracker*. In this unorthodox retelling, the heroine sails to a coral reef and is submerged in a diving bell. (What? No sugar-plum fairies?) Between Christmas and New Year's Day, the Holiday House and Garden Tour is another yuletide tradition.

Margaritaville Café. A youngish, touristy crowd mixes with aging Parrot Heads. It's owned by former Key West resident and recording star Jimmy Buffett, who has been known to perform here. The drink of choice is, of course, a margarita, made with Jimmy's own brand of Margaritaville tequila. There's live music nightly, as well as lunch and dinner. ⊠ *500 Duval St.* ☎ *305/292–1435* ⊕ *www.margaritaville.com.*

Pier House. The party here begins at the Beach Bar with live entertainment daily to celebrate the sunset on the beach, then moves to the funky Chart Room. It's small and odd, but there are free hot dogs and peanuts, and its history is worth learning. ⊠ *1 Duval St.* ☎ *305/296–4600,* *800/327–8340* ⊕ *www.pierhouse.com.*

Schooner Wharf Bar. This open-air waterfront bar and grill in the historic seaport district retains its funky Key West charm and hosts live entertainment daily. Its margaritas rank among Key West's best, as does the bar itself, voted Best Local's Bar six years in a row. For great views, head up to the second floor and be sure to order up some fresh seafood and fritters and Dark and Stormy cocktails. ⊠ *202 William St.* ☎ *305/292–3302* ⊕ *www.schoonerwharf.com.*

Sloppy Joe's. There's history and good times at the successor to a famous 1937 speakeasy named for its founder, Captain Joe Russell. Decorated with Hemingway memorabilia and marine flags, the bar is popular with travelers and is full and noisy all the time. A Sloppy Joe's T-shirt is a de rigueur Key West souvenir, and the gift shop sells them like crazy. Grab a seat (if you can) and be entertained by the bands and by the parade of people in constant motion. ⊠ *201 Duval St.* ☎ *305/294–5717* ⊕ *www.sloppyjoes.com.*

Sloppy Joe's is one must-stop on most Key West visitors' bar-hop stroll, also known as the Duval Crawl.

Two Friends Patio Lounge. Love karaoke? Get it out of your system at Two Friends Patio Lounge, where your performance gets a live Internet feed via the bar's Karaoke Cam. The singing starts at 8:30 pm most nights. The Bloody Marys are famous. ⊠ *512 Front St.* ☎ *305/296–3124* ⊕ *www.twofriendskeywest.com.*

SHOPPING

On these streets, you'll find colorful local art of widely varying quality, key limes made into everything imaginable, and the raunchiest T-shirts in the civilized world. Browsing the boutiques—with frequent pub stops along the way—makes for an entertaining stroll down Duval Street. Cocktails certainly help the appreciation of some goods, such as the figurine of a naked man blowing bubbles out his backside or the swashbuckling pirate costumes that are no longer just for Halloween.

ARTS AND CRAFTS

Alan S. Maltz Gallery. The owner, declared the state's official wildlife photographer by the Wildlife Foundation of Florida, captures the state's nature and character in stunning portraits. Spend four figures for large-format images on canvas or save on small prints and closeouts. ⊠ *1210 Duval St.* ☎ *305/294–0005* ⊕ *www.alanmaltz.com.*

Art@830. This inviting gallery carries a little bit of everything, from pottery to paintings and jewelry to sculptures. Most outstanding is its selection of glass art, particularly the jellyfish lamps. Take time to admire all that is here. ⊠ *830 Caroline St., Historic Seaport* ☎ *305/295–9595* ⊕ *www.art830.com.*

Gallery on Greene. This is the largest gallery–exhibition space in Key West and it showcases 37 museum-quality artists. They pride themselves on being the leader in the field of representational fine art, painting, sculptures, and reproductions from the Florida Keys and Key West. You can see the love immediately from gallery curator Nancy Frank, who aims to please everyone, from the casual buyer to the established collector. ⊠ *606 Greene St.* ☎ *305/294–1669* ⊕ *www.galleryongreene.com.*

Gingerbread Square Gallery. The oldest private art gallery in Key West represents local and internationally acclaimed artists on an annually changing basis, in mediums ranging from paintings to art glass. ⊠ *1207 Duval St.* ☎ *305/296–8900* ⊕ *www.gingerbreadsquaregallery.com.*

Glass Reunions. Find a collection of wild and impressive fine-art glass here. It's worth a stop in just to see the imaginative and over-the-top glass chandeliers, jewelry, dishes, and platters. ⊠ *825 Duval St.* ☎ *305/294–1720* ⊕ *www.glassreunions.com.*

Key West Pottery. You won't find any painted coconuts here, but you will find a collection of contemporary tropical ceramics. Wife-and-husband owners Kelly Lever and Adam Russell take real pride in this working studio that, in addition to their own creations, features artists from around the country. This is one of the island's few specialty galleries. ⊠ *1203 Duval St.* ☎ *305/900–8303* ⊕ *www.keywestpottery.com.*

Lucky Street Gallery. High-end contemporary paintings are the focus at this gallery that has been in business for over 30 years. There are also a few pieces of jewelry by internationally recognized Key West–based artists. Changing exhibits, artist receptions, and special events make this a lively venue. Although the location has changed, the passionate staff remains the same. ⊠ *1204 White St.* ☎ *305/294–3973* ⊕ *www.luckystreetgallery.com.*

BOOKS

Key West Island Bookstore. This home away from home for the large Key West writers' community carries new, used, and rare titles. It specializes in Hemingway, Tennessee Williams, and South Florida mystery writers. ⊠ *513 Fleming St.* ☎ *305/294–2904* ⊕ *www.keywestislandbooks.com.*

CLOTHING AND FABRICS

Fairvilla Megastore. Don't leave town without a browse through the legendary shop. Although it's not really a clothing store, you'll find an astonishing array of fantasy wear, outlandish costumes (check out the pirate section), as well as other "adult" toys. (Some of the products may make you blush.) ⊠ *520 Front St.* ☎ *305/292–0448* ⊕ *www.fairvilla.com.*

Kino Sandals. A pair of Kino sandals was once a public declaration that you'd been to Key West. The attraction? You can watch these inexpensive items being made. The factory has been churning out several styles since 1966. Walk up to the counter, grab a pair, try them on, and lay down some cash. It's that simple. ⊠ *107 Fitzpatrick St.* ☎ *305/294–5044* ⊕ *www.kinosandalfactory.com.*

Seam Shoppe. Take home a shopping bag full of scarlet hibiscus, fuchsia heliconias, blue parrot fish, and even pink flamingo fabric, selected from the city's widest selection of tropical-print fabrics. ⌗ *1113 Truman Ave.* ☎ *305/296–9830* ⊕ *www.tropicalfabricsonline.com.*

FOOD AND DRINK

Fausto's Food Palace. Since 1926 Fausto's has been the spot to catch up on the week's gossip and to chill out in summer—it has groceries, organic foods, marvelous wines, a sushi chef on duty 8 am–3 pm, and box lunches to go. There are two locations you can shop at in Key West (the other is at 1105 White Street) plus a recently opened online store. ⌗ *522 Fleming St.* ☎ *305/296–5663* ⊕ *www.faustos.com.*

Fodor's Choice ★ **Kermit's Key West Lime Shoppe.** You'll see Kermit himself standing on the corner every time a trolley passes, pie in hand. Besides pie, his shop carries a multitude of key lime products from barbecue sauce to jelly beans. His prefrozen pies, topped with a special long-lasting whipped cream instead of meringue, travels well. This is a must-stop shop while in Key West. The key lime pie is the best on the island; once you try it frozen on a stick, dipped in chocolate, you may consider quitting your job and moving here. Savor every bite on the outdoor patio/garden area. Heaven. ⌗ *200 Elizabeth St., Historic Seaport* ☎ *305/296–0806, 800/376–0806* ⊕ *www.keylimeshop.com.*

Peppers of Key West. If you like it hot, you'll love this collection of hundreds of sauces, salsas, and sweets guaranteed to light your fire. Sampling encouraged. ⌗ *602 Greene St.* ☎ *305/295–9333, 800/597–2823* ⊕ *www.peppersofkeywest.com.*

GIFTS AND SOUVENIRS

Cayo Hueso y Habana. Part museum, part shopping center, this circa-1879 warehouse includes a hand-rolled-cigar shop, one-of-a-kind souvenirs, a Cuban restaurant, and exhibits that tell of the island's Cuban heritage. Outside, a memorial garden pays homage to the island's Cuban ancestors. ⌗ *410 Wall St., Mallory Sq.* ☎ *305/293–7260.*

Montage. For that unique (but slightly overpriced) souvenir of your trip to Key West head here, where you'll discover hundreds of handcrafted signs of popular Key West guesthouses, inns, hotels, restaurants, bars, and streets. If you can't find what you're looking for, they'll make it for you. ⌗ *291 Front St.* ✛ *Next to Margaritaville* ☎ *305/395–9101, 877/396–4278* ⊕ *www.montagekeywest.com.*

SHOPPING CENTERS

Bahama Village. Where to start your shopping adventure? This cluster of spruced-up shops, restaurants, and vendors is responsible for the restoration of the colorful historic district where Bahamians settled in the 19th century. The village lies roughly between Whitehead and Fort streets and Angela and Catherine streets. Hemingway frequented the bars, restaurants, and boxing rings in this part of town. ⌗ *Between Whitehead and Fort Sts. and Angela and Catherine Sts.*

SPORTS AND THE OUTDOORS

Unlike the rest of the region, Key West isn't known primarily for outdoor pursuits. But everyone should devote at least half a day to relaxing on a boat tour, heading out on a fishing expedition, or pursuing some other adventure at sea. The ultimate excursion is a boat or seaplane trip to Dry Tortugas National Park for snorkeling and exploring Ft. Jefferson. Other excursions cater to nature lovers, scuba divers, and snorkelers, and folks who just want to get out in the water and enjoy the scenery and sunset. For those who prefer land-based recreation, biking is the way to go. Hiking is limited, but walking the streets of Old Town provides plenty of exercise.

BIKING

Key West was practically made for bicycles, but don't let that lull you into a false sense of security. Narrow and one-way streets along with car traffic result in several bike accidents a year. Some hotels rent or lend bikes to guests; others will refer you to a nearby shop and reserve a bike for you. Rentals usually start at about $12 a day, but some places also rent by the half day. ■TIP→ Lock up; bikes—and porch chairs!—are favorite targets for local thieves.

A&M Rentals. Rent beach cruisers with large baskets, scooters, and electric mini-cars. Look for the huge American flag on the roof, or call for free airport, ferry, or cruise-ship pickup. ⊠ *523 Truman Ave.* ☎ *305/294–0399* ⊕ *www.amscooterskeywest.com* 📧 *Bicycles from $15, scooters from $35, electric cars from $99.*

Eaton Bikes. Tandem, three-wheel, and children's bikes are available in addition to the standard beach cruisers and hybrid bikes. Delivery is free for all Key West rentals. ⊠ *830 Eaton St.* ☎ *305/294–8188* ⊕ *www. eatonbikes.com* 📧 *From $18 per day.*

Moped Hospital. This outfit supplies balloon-tire bikes with yellow safety baskets for adults and kids, as well as scooters and even double-seater scooters. ⊠ *601 Truman Ave.* ☎ *305/296–3344, 866/296–1625* ⊕ *www.mopedhospital.com* 📧 *Bicycles from $12 per day, scooters from $35 per day.*

BOATING

Key West is surrounded by marinas, so it's easy to find what you're looking for, whether it's sailing with dolphins or paddling in the mangroves. In addition to its popular kayaking trips, Key West Eco-Tours offers sunset sails and private charters *(see Kayaking).*

Classic Harbor Line. The *Schooner America 2.0* is refined and elegant, and her comfortable seating makes her a favorite when she sails Key West each November–April. Two-hour sunset Champagne cruises are an island highlight. ⊠ *202-R Williams St.* ☎ *305/293–7245* ⊕ *www. sail-keywest.com* 📧 *From $55 day sail, from $85 sunset sail.*

Dancing Dolphin Spirit Charters. Victoria Impallomeni-Spencer, a wilderness guide and environmental marine science expert, invites up to six nature lovers—especially children—aboard the *Imp II,* a 25-foot Aquasport, for four- and seven-hour ecotours that frequently include encounters with wild dolphins. While island-hopping, you visit underwater gardens, natural shoreline, and mangrove habitats. For the "Dolphin Day for Humans" tour, you'll be pulled through the water, equipped with mask and snorkel, on a specially designed "dolphin water massage board" that simulates dolphin swimming motions. Sometimes dolphins follow the boat and swim among participants. All equipment is supplied. Captain Victoria is known around these parts as the dolphin whisperer as she's been guiding for over 40 years. ⊠ *MM 5 OS, Murray's Marina, 5710 Overseas Hwy.* ☎ *305/304–7562, 305/745–9901* ⊕ *www.dancingdolphinspirits.com* ▧ *From $500.*

FISHING

Any number of local fishing guides can take you to where the big ones are biting, either in the backcountry for snapper and snook or to the deep water for the marlins and shark that lured Hemingway here.

Key West Bait & Tackle. Prepare to catch a big one with the live bait, frozen bait, and fishing equipment provided here. They even offer rod and reel rentals (starting at $15 for one day, $5 each additional day). Stop by their on-site Live Bait Lounge where you can sip $3.25 ice-cold beer while telling fish tales. ⊠ *241 Margaret St.* ☎ *305/292–1961* ⊕ *www. keywestbaitandtackle.com.*

Key West Pro Guides. This outfitter offers private charters, and you can choose four-, five-, six-, or eight-hour trips. Choose from flats, backcountry, reef, offshore fishing, and even specialty trips to the Dry Tortugas. Whatever your fishing (even spearfishing) pleasure, their captains will hook you up. ⊠ *G–31 Miriam St.* ☎ *866/259–4205* ⊕ *www.keywestproguides.com* ▧ *From $450.*

GOLF

Key West Golf Club. Key West isn't a major golf destination, but there is one course on Stock Island designed by Rees Jones that will downright surprise you with its water challenges and tropical beauty. It's also the only "Caribbean" golf course in the United States, boasting 200 acres of unique Florida foliage and wildlife. Hole 8 is the famous "Mangrove Hole," which will give you stories to tell. It's a 143-yard, par 3 that is played completely over a mass of mangroves with their gnarly roots and branches completely intertwined. Bring extra balls and book your tee time early in season. Nike rental clubs available. ⊠ *6450 E. College Rd.* ☎ *305/294–5232* ⊕ *www.keywestgolf.com* ▧ *$55–$99* ⚑ *18 holes, 6500 yards, par 70.*

KAYAKING

Key West Eco-Tours. Key West is surrounded by marinas, so it's easy to find a water-based activity or tour, whether it's sailing with dolphins or paddling in the mangroves. These sail-kayak-snorkel excursions take you into backcountry flats and mangrove forests without the crowds. The 4½-hour trip includes a light lunch, equipment, and even dry camera bags. Private sunset sails, kayak, and paddleboard tours are available, too. ⊠ *Historic Seaport, 100 Grinnell St.* ☎ *305/294–7245* ⊕ *www.keywestecotours.com* ▧ *From $115.*

Lazy Dog. Take a two- or four-hour guided sea kayak–snorkel tour around the mangrove islands just east of Key West. Costs include transportation, bottled water, a snack, and supplies, including snorkeling gear. Paddleboard tours and PaddleYoga and PaddleFit classes are also available, as are rentals for self-touring. ⊠ *5114 Overseas Hwy.* ☎ *305/295–9898* ⊕ *www.lazydog.com* 🖭 *From $40.*

SCUBA DIVING AND SNORKELING

The Florida Keys National Marine Sanctuary extends along Key West and beyond to the Dry Tortugas. Key West National Wildlife Refuge further protects the pristine waters. Most divers don't make it this far out in the Keys, but if you're looking for a day of diving as a break from the nonstop party in Old Town, expect to pay about $65 and upward for a two-tank dive. Serious divers can book dive trips to the Dry Tortugas. The USS *Vandenberg* is another popular dive spot, known for its world's-first underwater transformative art exhibit on an artificial reef.

Captain's Corner. This PADI-certified dive shop has classes in several languages and twice-daily snorkel and dive trips to reefs and wrecks aboard the 60-foot dive boat *Sea Eagle.* Use of weights, belts, masks, and fins is included. ⊠ *125 Ann St.* ☎ *305/296–8865* ⊕ *www.captainscorner.com* 🖭 *From $45.*

Dive Key West. Operating over 40 years, Dive Key West is a full-service dive center that has charters, instruction, gear rental, sales, and repair. You can take either snorkel excursions or scuba trips with this outfit that is dedicated to coral reef education and preservation. ⊠ *3128 N. Roosevelt Blvd.* ☎ *305/296–3823* ⊕ *www.divekeywest.com* 🖭 *Snorkeling from $69, scuba from $95.*

FAMILY **Snuba of Key West.** If you've always wanted to dive but never found the time to get certified, Snuba is for you. You can dive safely using a regulator tethered to a floating air tank with a simple orientation. Ride out to the reef on a catamaran, then follow your guide underwater for a one-hour tour of the coral reefs. It's easy and fun. No prior diving or snorkeling experience is necessary, but you must know how to swim and be at least eight years old. The price includes beverages. ⊠ *Garrison Bight Marina, Palm Ave., between Eaton St. and N. Roosevelt Blvd.* ☎ *305/292–4616* ⊕ *www.snubakeywest.com* 🖭 *From $109.*

STAND-UP PADDLEBOARDING

SUP Key West. This ancient sport from Hawaii involves a surfboard and a paddle and has quickly become a favorite Florida water sport known as SUP (stand-up paddleboarding). SUP Key West gives lessons and morning, afternoon, or sunset tours of the estuaries. What's more, your tour guides are experts (one's even a PhD) in marine biology and ecology. Call ahead to make arrangements. ⊠ *110 Grinnell St.* ☎ *305/240–1426* ⊕ *www.supkeywest.com* 🖭 *From $45.*

EXCURSION TO DRY TORTUGAS NATIONAL PARK

70 miles southwest of Key West.

The Dry Tortugas lie in the central time zone. Key West Seaplane pilots like to tell their passengers that they land 15 minutes before they take off. If you can't do the time-consuming and (by air, at least, expensive) trip, the national park operates an interpretive center in the Historic Seaport at Old Key West Bight.

GETTING HERE AND AROUND

For now, the ferryboat *Yankee Freedom III* departs from a marina in Old Town and does day trips to Garden Key. Key West Seaplane Adventures has half- and full-day trips to the Dry Tortugas, where you can explore Ft. Jefferson, built in 1846, and snorkel on the beautiful protected reef. Departing from the Key West airport, the flights include soft drinks and snorkel equipment for $265 half day, $465 full day, plus there's a $10 park fee (cash only). If you want to explore the park's other keys, look into renting a boat or hiring a private charter. The Dry Tortugas National Park and Historic Key West Bight Museum at 240 Margaret Street is a way to experience it for free. *See Exploring in Key West.*

Key West Seaplane Adventures. The 35- to 40-minute trip to the Dry Tortugas skims above the trademark windowpane-clear waters of the Florida Keys. The seaplane perspective provides an awesome experience that could result in a stiff neck from craning to look out the window and down from 500 feet above. In the flats that edge Key West, you can spot stingrays, sea turtles, and sharks in the shallow water. In the area dubbed The Quicksands, water plunges to 30-foot depths and sand undulates in dunelike formations. Shipwrecks also festoon these waters; here's where Mel Fisher harvested treasure from the *Atocha* and *Margarita*. His 70-foot work ship, the *Arbutus,* deteriorated and eventually sank at the northern edge of the treasure sites. With its mast poking out above water, it's easy to spot and fun to photograph. From there, the water deepens from emerald hues to shades of deep blue as depths reach 70 feet. Seaplanes of Key West's most popular trip is the half-day option, where you spend about 2½ hours on Garden Key. The seaplanes leave during your stay, so be prepared to carry all of your possessions with you. The morning trip beats the ferries to the island, so you'll have it to yourself until the others arrive. Snorkeling equipment, soft drinks, and birding lists are supplied. ✉ *3471 S. Roosevelt Blvd., Key West* ☎ *305/293–9300* ⊕ *www.keywestseaplanecharters.com* ✉ *From $317.*

Yankee Freedom III. The fast, sleek, 110-foot catamaran *Yankee Freedom III* travels to the Dry Tortugas in 2¼ hours. The time passes quickly on the roomy vessel equipped with four restrooms, three warm freshwater showers, and two bars. Stretch out on two decks that are both air-conditioned, with cushioned seating. There is also an open sundeck with sunny and shaded seating. Continental breakfast and lunch are included. On arrival, a naturalist leads a 45-minute guided tour, which is followed by lunch and a free afternoon for swimming, snorkeling (gear included), and exploring. The vessel is

ADA certified for visitors using wheelchairs. The Dry Tortugas lies in the central time zone. ✉ *Lands End Marina, 240 Margaret St., Key West* ☎ *305/294–7009, 800/634–0939* ⊕ *www.yankeefreedom. com* ✆ *$175; parking $13 in city garage.*

EXPLORING

Dry Tortugas National Park. This park, 70 miles off the shores of Key West, consists of seven small islands. Tour the fort; then lay out your blanket on the sunny beach for a picnic before you head out to snorkel on the protected reef. Many people like to camp here ($15 per site for one of eight sites, plus a group site and overflow area; first come, first served), but note that there's no freshwater supply and you must carry off whatever you bring onto the island.

The typical visitor from Key West, however, makes it no farther than the waters of Garden Key. Home to 19th-century Ft. Jefferson, it is the destination for seaplane and fast ferry tours out of Key West. With 2½ to 6½ hours to spend on the island, visitors have time to tour the mammoth fort-prison and then cool off with mask and snorkel along the fort's moat wall.

History buffs might remember long-deactivated Ft. Jefferson, the largest brick building in the western hemisphere, as the prison that held Dr. Samuel Mudd, who unwittingly set John Wilkes Booth's leg after the assassination of Abraham Lincoln. Three other men were also held there for complicity in the assassination. Original construction on the fort began in 1846 and continued for 30 years, but was never completed because the invention of the rifled cannon made it obsolete. That's when it became a Civil War prison and later a wildlife refuge. In 1935 President Franklin Roosevelt declared it a national monument for its historic and natural value.

The brick fort acts as a gigantic, almost 16-acre reef. Around its moat walls, coral grows and schools of snapper, grouper, and wrasses hang out. To reach the offshore coral heads requires about 15 minutes of swimming over sea-grass beds. The reef formations blaze with the color and majesty of brain coral, swaying sea fans, and flitting tropical fish. It takes a bit of energy to swim the distance, but the water depth pretty much measures under 7 feet all the way, allowing for sandy spots to stop and rest. (Standing in sea-grass meadows and on coral is detrimental to marine life.)

Serious snorkelers and divers head out farther offshore to epic formations, including Palmata Patch, one of the few surviving concentrations of elkhorn coral in the Keys. Day-trippers congregate on the sandy beach to relax in the sun and enjoy picnics. Overnight tent campers have use of restroom facilities and achieve a total getaway from noise, lights, and civilization in general. Remember that no matter how you get here, the park's $10 admission fee must be paid in cash.

The park has set up with signage a self-guided tour that takes about 45 minutes. You should budget more time if you're into photography, because the scenic shots are hard to pass up. Ranger-guided tours are also available at certain times. Check in at the visitor center for a schedule. The small office also shows an orientation video, sells books and other educational materials, and, most importantly, provides a blast of air-conditioning on hot days.

Birders in the know bring binoculars to watch some 100,000 nesting sooty terns at their only U.S. nesting site, Bush Key, adjacent to Garden Key. Noddy terns also nest in the spring. During winter migrations, birds fill the airspace so thickly they literally fall from the sky to make their pit stops, birders say. Nearly 300 species have been spotted in the park's seven islands, including frigate birds, boobies, cormorants, and broad-winged hawks. Bush Key is closed to foot traffic during nesting season, January through September. ⊠ *Key West* ⊕ *www.nps.gov/drto* ✈ *$10.*

FORT LAUDERDALE

WELCOME TO FORT LAUDERDALE

TOP REASONS TO GO

★ **Blue waves:** The cerulean waters of the Atlantic Ocean hugging Broward County's entire coast form a 23-mile stretch of picturesque beaches between Miami-Dade and Palm Beach counties.

★ **Inland waterways:** More than 300 miles of inland waterways, including downtown Fort Lauderdale's historic New River and Intracoastal, create what's known as the "Venice of America."

★ **Everglades adventures:** The untamed landscape of the Everglades—home to alligators, crocodiles, colorful birds, and other elusive wildlife—is a short trip from beachfront luxury.

★ **Emerging arts scene:** Experience the local contemporary art scene as it grows into a major force in the region.

★ **Cruise gateway:** A dozen supermodern terminals serve about 4 million cruisers and ferry guests a year at Port Everglades, the busiest cruise port in the country.

1 Fort Lauderdale. Anchored by the New River and an eclectic downtown hub, Fort Lauderdale comprises high-rise condos along with single-family homes, museums, parks, and attractions. Las Olas Boulevard's boutiques, sidewalk cafés, and restaurants complement 23 miles of sparkling beaches.

2 Lauderdale-by-the-Sea. North of Fort Lauderdale on State Road A1A, old-school seaside charm draws families and cost-conscious travelers to a more low-rise, low-key beach alternative to Fort Lauderdale.

3 Hollywood. From the beachside Broadwalk to historic Young Circle (now ArtsPark), this South Broward destination provides grit and good times in a laid-back manner.

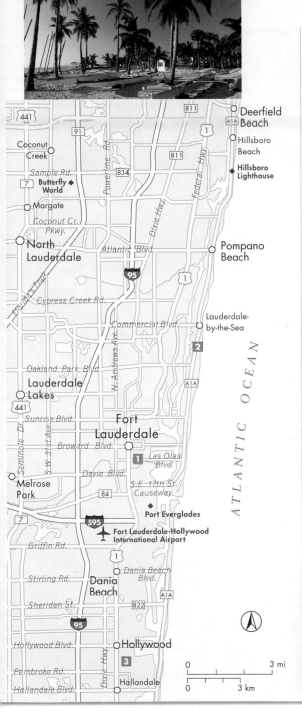

Deerfield Beach

Hillsboro Beach

Hillsboro Lighthouse

Pompano Beach

Lauderdale-by-the-Sea

Coconut Creek

Sample Rd.

Butterfly World

Margate

Coconut Cr. Pkwy.

North Lauderdale

Atlantic Blvd.

Cypress Creek Rd.

Commercial Blvd.

Oakland Park Blvd.

Lauderdale Lakes

Sunrise Blvd.

Fort Lauderdale

Broward Blvd.

Las Olas Blvd.

Davie Blvd.

Melrose Park

S.E. 17th St. Causeway

Port Everglades

Fort Lauderdale-Hollywood International Airport

Griffin Rd.

Stirling Rd.

Dania Beach

Dania Beach Blvd.

Sheridan St.

Hollywood Blvd.

Hollywood

Pembroke Rd.

Hallandale

Hallandale Blvd.

ATLANTIC OCEAN

0   3 mi

0   3 km

GETTING ORIENTED

Along Florida's Gold Coast, Fort Lauderdale and Broward County present a delightful middle ground between the posh Palm Beaches and the extravagance of Miami. From downtown Fort Lauderdale, it's about a four-hour drive to Orlando or Key West, but Broward's allure is undeniable. From ocean side to inland, the county's sprawling geography encompasses 31 communities with a resident population of nearly 1.8 million.

5

Updated
by Galena
Mosovich

It was only a matter of time before the sun-soaked streets of Fort Lauderdale faced an identity crisis. What was once a hotbed of dive bars, diners, and all-day beach parties is now a more upscale destination with a deeper focus on quality in the pursuit of leisure. The city's elevated personality has paved the way for creative organizations, notable eateries, and premium entertainment options to stake their claims and has attracted a menagerie of world-class hotel brands and condo developments. Fortunately, the upscaling is generally guided by an understated interpretation of luxury that doesn't follow Miami's over-the-top lead. Fort Lauderdale is still a place where flip-flops are acceptable, if not encouraged.

Along The Strip and west to the Intracoastal, many of the mid-century-modern boutique properties are trying to preserve the neighborhood's vintage design aesthetic. Somehow, Greater Fort Lauderdale gracefully melds disparate eras into nouveau nirvana, seasoned with a lot of sand. This could be the result of its massive territory: Broward County encompasses more than 1,100 square miles of land—ranging from dense residential enclaves to agricultural farms and subtropical wilds. But it's the county's beautiful beaches and some 3,000 hours of sunshine each year that make all this possible.

Fort Lauderdale was named for Major William Lauderdale, who built a fort in 1838 during the Second Seminole War. It was incorporated in 1911 with only 175 residents, but it grew quickly during the Florida boom of the 1920s, and it became a popular spring break destination in the 1960s. Today's population is more than 176,000, and the suburbs continue to grow. Of Broward County's 31 municipalities and unincorporated areas, Fort Lauderdale is the largest. And now, showstopping hotels, a hot food scene, and a burgeoning cultural platform accompany the classic beach lifestyle.

PLANNING

WHEN TO GO

Peak season is Thanksgiving through April, when cultural events (performing arts, visual art, concerts, and other outdoor entertainment) go full throttle. Expect extreme heat and humidity along with rain in the summer. Hurricanes come most notably in August and September. Tee times are harder to get on weekends year-round. Regardless of season, remember that Fort Lauderdale sunshine will burn even on a cloudy day.

GETTING HERE AND AROUND

AIR TRAVEL

Fort Lauderdale–Hollywood International Airport (FLL) serves more than 26 million passengers a year. FLL is 3 miles south of downtown Fort Lauderdale—just off U.S. 1 (South Federal Highway) between Fort Lauderdale and Hollywood, and near Port Everglades and Fort Lauderdale Beach. Other options include **Miami International Airport (MIA)**, which is about 32 miles southwest, and the far less chaotic **Palm Beach International Airport (PBI)**, which is about 50 miles north.

Airport Information Fort Lauderdale–Hollywood International Airport *(FLL).* ☎ *866/435–9355* ⊕ *www.broward.org/airport.* **Miami International Airport** *(MIA).* ☎ *800/825–5642* ⊕ *www.miami-airport.com.* **Palm Beach International Airport** *(PBI).* ☎ *561/471–7420* ⊕ *www.pbia.org.*

BUS TRAVEL

Broward County Transit (BCT) operates Bus Route 1 between the airport and its main terminal at Broward Boulevard and Northwest First Avenue in downtown Fort Lauderdale. Service from the airport is every 20 to 30 minutes and begins at 5:29 am on weekdays, 6:04 am Saturday, and 6:44 am Sunday; the last bus leaves the airport at 11:36 pm on weekdays, 11:44 pm Saturday, and 9:44 pm Sunday. The one-way cash fare is $2 (exact change). ■TIP➔ The Northwest First Avenue stop is in a sketchy part of town. Exercise caution there, day or night. Better yet, take an Uber, Lyft, or taxi to and from the airport. BCT also covers the county on fixed routes to four transfer terminals: Broward Central Terminal, West Regional Terminal, Lauderhill Mall Transfer Facility, and Northeast Transit Center. The fare for an all-day bus pass is $5 (exact change). Service starts around 4:30 am and continues to 12:40 am, except on Sunday.

Bus Contacts Broward County Transit. ☎ *954/357–8400* ⊕ *www.broward.org/BCT.*

CAR TRAVEL

Renting a car to get around Broward County is highly recommended. Traditional cabs are unreliable and expensive; ride-hailing apps such as Uber and Lyft are a cheaper, better option. Public transportation is not a realistic option for most travelers, but the Sun Trolley can be sufficient for some visitors who don't need or wish to explore beyond the downtown core and beaches.

By car, access to Broward County from north or south is via Florida's Turnpike, Interstate 95, U.S. 1, or U.S. 441. Interstate 75 (Alligator Alley, requiring a toll despite being part of the nation's interstate-highway system) connects Broward with Florida's west coast and runs parallel to State Road 84 within the county. East–west Interstate 595 runs from westernmost Broward County and connects Interstate 75 with Interstate 95 and U.S. 1, providing easy access to the airport and seaport. State Road A1A, designated a Florida Scenic Highway by the state's Department of Transportation, runs parallel to the beach.

TRAIN TRAVEL

Amtrak provides daily service to Fort Lauderdale and stops in Deerfield Beach and Hollywood.

All three of the region's airports link to Tri-Rail, a commuter train operating daily through Palm Beach, Broward, and Miami-Dade counties.

New, privately operated high-speed Brightline service began in summer 2017, connecting downtown Miami, Fort Lauderdale, and West Palm Beach. The trip from downtown Miami to Fort Lauderdale takes about 30 minutes; it's another 30 minutes to West Palm Beach.

Contacts Brightline. ⊕ *gobrightline.com.*

HOTELS

A collection of relatively young luxury beachfront hotels—the Atlantic Hotel & Spa, Hilton Fort Lauderdale Beach Resort, the Ritz-Carlton, the W, the Westin—that opened within the last decade are welcoming newcomers to the "Luxe Lauderdale" corridor. Seriously sophisticated places to stay include The Conrad, Four Seasons, and The Gale, while smaller retro spots are disappearing. You can also find hotel chains along the Intracoastal Waterway. If you want to be *on* the beach, be sure to ask when booking your room as many hotels on the inland waterways or on A1A advertise "waterfront" accommodations.

RESTAURANTS

Greater Fort Lauderdale offers one of the best and most diverse dining scenes of any U.S. city its size. There are more than 4,000 eateries in Broward offering everything from new American and South American to pan-Asian cuisines. Go beyond the basics, and you'll find an endless supply of hidden gems.

Hotel and restaurant reviews have been shortened. For full information, visit Fodors.com.

WHAT IT COSTS			
$	$$	$$$	$$$$
Restaurants	under $15	$15–$20	$21–$30	over $30
Hotels	under $200	$200–$300	$301–$400	over $400

Restaurant prices are the average cost of a main course at dinner or, if dinner is not served, at lunch. Hotel prices are the lowest cost of a standard double room in high season.

FORT LAUDERDALE

Like most of southeast Florida, Fort Lauderdale has long been revitalizing. Despite wariness of pretentious overdevelopment, city leaders have allowed a striking number of glittering high-rises and new hotels. Nostalgic locals and frequent visitors fret over the diminishing vision of sailboats bobbing in waters near downtown; however, Fort Lauderdale remains the yachting capital of the world, and the water toys don't seem to be going anywhere. Sharp demographic changes are also changing the face of Greater Fort Lauderdale with increasingly cosmopolitan communities, more minorities (including Hispanics and people of Caribbean descent), as well as gays and lesbians. Young professionals and families are settling into Fort Lauderdale proper, whereas longtime residents are heading north for more space. Downtown Fort Lauderdale's burgeoning arts district, cafés, and nightlife venues continue to the main drag of Las Olas Boulevard, where boutiques and restaurants dot the pedestrian-friendly street. Farther east is the sparkling shoreline. There are myriad neighborhoods to the north and south of Las Olas Boulevard that all offer their own brand of charm.

GETTING HERE AND AROUND

The Fort Lauderdale metro area is laid out in a grid system, and only a few waterways and bridges interrupt the relatively straight path of streets and roads. Nomenclature is important here: streets, roads, courts, and drives run east–west; avenues, terraces, and ways run north–south; boulevards can (and do) run any which way. For visitors, Las Olas Boulevard is one of the most important east–west passageways. It runs from the beach to downtown; whereas State Road A1A—dubbed Atlantic Boulevard, Ocean Boulevard, and Fort Lauderdale Beach—runs parallel to the north–south oceanfront. These names are confusing, and visitors can get mixed up with the streets called Atlantic and Ocean in both Hollywood and Pompano Beach, respectively.

The city's road system suffers from traffic overload. Interstate 595 connects the city and suburbs and provides a direct route to the Fort Lauderdale–Hollywood International Airport and Port Everglades, but lanes slow to a crawl during rush hours. The Intracoastal Waterway is the nautical equivalent of an interstate highway; it runs north–south through Fort Lauderdale and provides easy boating access to local hot spots as well as neighboring waterfront communities.

To bounce around Fort Lauderdale for free (with exceptions), catch a multicolored Sun Trolley. There are seven routes and each operates on its own schedule. Simply wave at the trolley driver: trolleys will stop for pickups anywhere along their route. Luggage is not allowed on the trolley, so this isn't a viable option for airport transportation. The most popular routes—Las Olas/Beaches—is $1 per ride or $3 for a day pass (cash only). It's best to review Sun Trolley's routes and schedules before trying this service.

Yellow Cab covers most of Broward County, but it's very expensive, and there's a $10 minimum for all trips originating from seaport or airport, and an additional $3 service charge when you start at the airport. You can book by phone, text, app, or website, and all Yellow Cab vehicles accept major credit cards. The Uber and Lyft apps are more concerned with the user experience and charge cheaper rates, hence their significant presence in the area.

Contacts Sun Trolley. ☎ 954/876–5539 ⊕ www.suntrolley.com. **Yellow Cab.** ☎ 954/777–7777 ⊕ yellowcabbroward.com.

TOURS

The labyrinthine waterways of Fort Lauderdale are home to thousands of privately owned vessels, but you don't need to be or know a boat owner to play on the water. To fully understand this city of canals (aka the "Venice of America"), you must see it from the water. Kick back on a boat tour or hop on a Water Taxi, Fort Lauderdale's floating trolley.

Carrie B Cruises. Board the *Carrie B*, a 112-foot paddle wheeler, for a 90-minute sightseeing tour of the New River, Intracoastal Waterway, and Port Everglades. Cruises depart at 11 am, 1 pm, and 3 pm daily from October through April; Thursday–Monday between May and September. The cost is $23.95 plus tax. Book ahead online for discounts. ⊠ *440 N. New River Dr. E, off Las Olas Blvd.* ☎ *888/238–9805* ⊕ *www.carriebcruises.com.*

FAMILY **Jungle Queen Riverboats.** The kitschy *Jungle Queen* and *River Queen* riverboats cruise through the heart of Fort Lauderdale on the New River. It's an old-school experience because this company launched its tours in 1935, and the touristy charm is just part of the fun. The daily morning sightseeing cruise at 11 am costs $23.50. The afternoon cruise and tour of Tropical Isle at 1:30 pm is $29.95. The daily afternoon and evening cruises at 4:30 and 7:30 pm are Thursday–Sunday and cost $23.50. The 6 pm all-you-can-eat barbecue dinner cruise runs Tuesday–Sunday and costs $52.95. ⊠ *Bahia Mar Yachting Center, 801 Seabreeze Blvd.* ☎ *954/462–5596* ⊕ *www.junglequeen.com.*

FAMILY **Water Taxi.** At once a sightseeing tour and a mode of transportation, Fodor's Choice the Water Taxi is a smart way to experience most of Fort Lauderdale ★ and Hollywood's waterways. The system has three connected routes: the Fort Lauderdale, the Margaritaville Express, and the Hollywood Local. The Fort Lauderdale route runs every 30 minutes from around 9:45 am to 11 pm; the other two routes have published schedules (check out the website). It's possible to cruise all day while taking in the sights. Captains and crew share fun facts and white lies about the city's history, as well as quirky tales about celebrity homes. A day pass is $26. ⊠ *Fort Lauderdale* ☎ *954/467–6677* ⊕ *www.watertaxi.com.*

VISITOR INFORMATION

Greater Fort Lauderdale Convention and Visitors Bureau. ⊠ *101 N.E. 3rd Ave., #100* ☎ *954/765–4466* ⊕ *www.sunny.org.*

EXPLORING

DOWNTOWN AND LAS OLAS

The jewel of downtown is the Arts and Entertainment District, where Broadway shows, ballet, and theater take place at the riverfront Broward Center for the Performing Arts. A cluster of cultural entities are within a five-minute walk: the Museum of Discovery and Science, the Fort Lauderdale Historical Society, and NSU's art museum. Restaurants, sidewalk cafés, bars, and dance clubs flourish along Las Olas's downtown extension, and its main presence brings a more upscale atmosphere. Riverwalk ties these two areas together with a 2-mile stretch along the New River's north and south banks, though the commercial success of this section has been tepid. Tropical gardens with benches and interpretive displays line the walk on the north, with boat landings on the south side.

TOP ATTRACTIONS

Fodor's Choice
★
Flagler Arts and Technology Village (FATVillage). Inspired by Miami's Wynwood Arts District, Flagler Arts & Technology Village (or FATVillage) encompasses several square blocks of a formerly blighted warehouse district in downtown Fort Lauderdale. It's now thriving with a slew of production studios, art studios, loft-style apartments, and a fabulous coffee shop. On the last Saturday of the month, FATVillage hosts an evening art walk, in which businesses display contemporary artworks by local talent, and where food trucks gather. There are libations, of course, and the village erupts into a giant, culture-infused street party. Many tourists come specifically for this monthly affair, but if you are visiting by day, check out one of Fort Lauderdale's coolest coffee shops, Next Door at C&I Studios. It's nestled inside a creative agency's lofty space, where the decor alone will keep you stimulated. Adorned with antique nods to the literary world, tufted couches, and an eerie 1972 Airstream trailer, Next Door serves the locally made Brew Urban Cafe. ⊠ *521 N.W. 1st Ave., Downtown* ☎ *954/760–5900* ⊕ *www.fatvillage.com.*

Historic Stranahan House Museum. The city's oldest surviving structure was once home to businessman Frank Stranahan, who arrived from Ohio in 1892. With his wife, Ivy, the city's first schoolteacher, he befriended and traded with Seminole Indians. In 1901 he built a store that would later become his home after serving as a post office, a general store, and a restaurant. The couple's tale is filled with ups and downs. Their home remains Fort Lauderdale's principal link to its brief history and has been on the National Register of Historic Places since 1973. Self-guided tours of the museum are not allowed. ⊠ *335 S.E. 6th Ave., Downtown* ✛ *Just off Las Olas Blvd. on the New River* ☎ *954/524–4736* ⊕ *www. stranahanhouse.org* ⊒ *$12.*

Fodor's Choice
★
Las Olas Boulevard. What Lincoln Road is to South Beach, Las Olas Boulevard is to Fort Lauderdale. Regarded as the heart and soul of Broward County, Las Olas is the premier street for restaurants, art galleries, museums, shopping, dining, and people-watching. Lined with high-rises in the downtown area and original boutiques and ethnic eateries along 10 blocks of the main stretch, it's also home to beautiful mansions and traditional Florida homes along the Intracoastal Waterway to the east, which typify the modern-day aesthetic of Fort Lauderdale. The ocean appears beyond the residential swath, and that's where you see that the name "Las Olas" (Spanish for "The Waves") begins to make more sense. It's a pedestrian-friendly thoroughfare, but it's not closed to vehicular traffic at any point. ⊠ *E. Las Olas Blvd., Downtown* ⊕ *www. lasolasboulevard.com.*

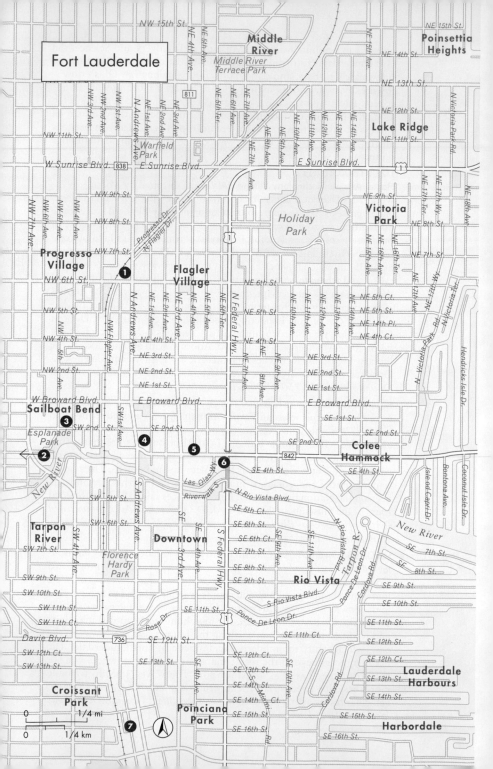

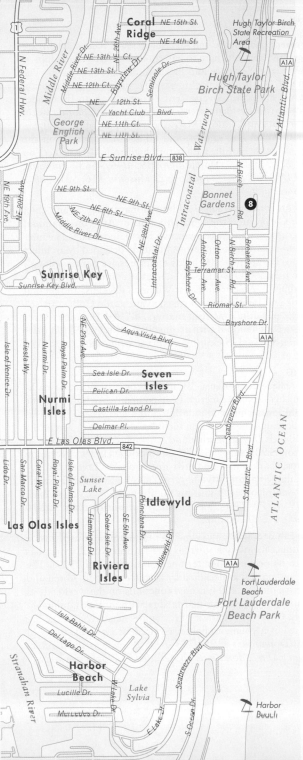

FAMILY **Museum of Discovery and Science and AutoNation IMAX Theater.** There are
Fodors Choice   dozens of interactive exhibits here to entertain children—*and* adults—
★   through the wonders of science and Florida's delicate ecosystem. The
state-of-the-art "7-D" theater takes guests on a virtual tour of aviation
technology, while the Ecodiscovery Center comes with an Everglades
Airboat Adventure ride, resident otters, and an interactive Florida storm
center. The 300-seat AutoNation IMAX theater is part of the complex
and shows mainstream and educational films, some in 3-D, on the
biggest screen in South Florida with a rare high-tech laser projection
system. ✉ *401 S.W. 2nd St., Downtown* ☎ *954/467–6637 museum,
954/463–4629 IMAX* ⊕ *www.mods.org* ✎ *Museum $16, $21 with 1
classic IMAX screening.*

Fodors Choice   **NSU Museum of Art Fort Lauderdale.** Led by visionary director and chief
★   curator Bonnie Clearwater, the NSU Museum of Art's international
exhibition programming ignites downtown Fort Lauderdale. The interior of the 83,000-square-foot modernist building, designed by architect
Edward Larrabee Barnes in 1986, holds an impressive permanent collection of more than 7,000 works, including the country's largest collection of paintings by American realist William Glackens, and pivotal
works by female and multicultural artists, avant-garde CoBrA artists,
and a wide array of Latin American masters. ■TIP➜ The lobby-level
Museum Café is a cool hangout with art-inspired gifts. ✉ *1 E. Las Olas
Blvd., Downtown* ☎ *954/525–5500* ⊕ *www.nsuartmuseum.org* ✎ *$12*
⊙ *Closed Mon.*

WORTH NOTING

FAMILY **Fort Lauderdale Antique Car Museum.** To preseve the history of the Packard, a long-vanished luxury American car company, Arthur O. Stone
and his wife, Shirley, set up a foundation and a showroom in downtown Fort Lauderdale. The collection includes about two dozen of the
buggy-style Packards (all in pristine and working condition) made in
the Midwest from 1909 to 1958. The collection includes everything
from grease caps, spark plugs, and gearshift knobs to Texaco Oil signage, plus an enlarged automotive library. There's also a gallery saluting Franklin Delano Roosevelt and his family. ✉ *1527 S.W. 1st Ave.,
Downtown* ☎ *954/779–7300* ⊕ *www.antiquecarmuseum.net* ✎ *$10
minimum donation* ⊙ *Closed Sun.*

FAMILY **Fort Lauderdale Fire and Safety Museum.** The museum is housed inside
the historic building formerly known as Fire Station No. 3, which has
been restored to its original Mediterranean beauty (circa 1927). The
Sailboat Bend landmark was designed by architect Francis Abreu and
retired from active duty in 2004; it now functions on the weekends as
a historical, cultural, and educational facility with vintage equipment
including a 1942 Chevrolet "Parade" fire engine. Legend has it the fire
station is haunted by a young firefighter. ✉ *1022 W. Las Olas Blvd., at
S.W. 11th Ave., Downtown* ☎ *954/763–1005* ⊕ *www.fortlauderdale-
firemuseum.com* ✎ *Free; donations appreciated* ⊙ *Closed weekdays.*

ALONG THE BEACH

If you want to stop for a bite to eat or a drink before or after visiting
Bonnet House, consider **Casablanca Café** (⊠ *3049 Alhambra St.*) or **Steak
954** (⊠ *W Fort Lauderdale, 401 N. Fort Lauderdale Beach Blvd.*)

FAMILY

Fodor's Choice

★

Bonnet House Museum and Gardens. This 35-acre subtropical estate
endures as a tribute to Old South Florida. Prior to its "modern" history, the grounds had already seen 4,000 years of activity when settler
Hugh Taylor Birch purchased the site in 1895. Birch gave it to his
daughter Helen as a wedding gift when she married Frederic Bartlett,
and the newlyweds built a charming home for a winter residence in
1920. Years after Helen died, Frederic married his second wife, Evelyn,
and the artistically gifted couple embarked on a mission to embellish
the property with personal touches and surprises that are still evident
today. This historic place is a must-see for its architecture, artwork, and
horticulture. While admiring the fabulous gardens, look out for playful monkeys swinging from the trees. ⊠ *900 N. Birch Rd., Beachfront*
☎ *954/563–5393* ⊕ *www.bonnethouse.org* ⊠ *$20 for house tours, $10
for gardens only; $2 for tram tour* ☺ *Closed Mon.*

WILTON MANORS AND OAKLAND PARK

North of Fort Lauderdale, Wilton Manors is the hub of gay life in the
greater Fort Lauderdale area and has several popular restaurants and
bars. Oakland Park, immediately to the north, also has several restaurants that are worth a visit.

WESTERN SUBURBS AND BEYOND

West of Fort Lauderdale is an ever-evolving suburbia, where most of
Broward's gated communities, golf courses, shopping outlets, casinos,
and chain restaurants exist. As you reach the county's western side, the
terrain takes on more characteristics of the Everglades, and you can see
alligators sunning on canal banks with other exotic reptiles and birds.
Tourists flock to the actual Everglades for airboat rides, but the best
way to experience the largest subtropical wilderness in the United States
is to visit the Everglades National Park itself.

TOP ATTRACTIONS

FAMILY

Fodor's Choice

★

Ah-Tah-Thi-Ki Museum. A couple of miles from Billie Swamp Safari is
Ah-Tah-Thi-Ki Museum, which means "a place to learn, a place to
remember" in the Seminole language. This Smithsonian Institution
Affiliate documents the living history and culture of the Seminole Tribe
of Florida through artifacts, exhibits, and experiential learning. There's
a mile-long boardwalk above the swamplands (wheelchair-accessible)
that leads you through the Big Cypress Reservation. At the midpoint
of the boardwalk, you can take a break at the re-created ceremonial
grounds. ⊠ *30290 Josie Billie Hwy., Clewiston* ✛ *At corner of W.
Boundary Rd.* ☎ *877/902–1113* ⊕ *www.ahtahthiki.com* ⊠ *$10.*

FAMILY

Billie Swamp Safari. Four different ecosystems in the "River of Grass"
are preserved by the Seminole Tribe of Florida, and these daily tours
by airboat or swamp buggy can introduce you to the elusive wildlife
that resides in each area. Sightings of deer, turtles, raccoons, wild hogs,
hawks, eagles, and alligators are likely but certainly not guaranteed.
Animal exhibits, a petting zoo, and snake/critter shows provide a solid

contingency plan. For the rugged adventurer, overnight camping in a native-style chickee (thatched-roof dwelling) is available. If a sleepover is too much, Twilight Expeditions offer a campfire with storytelling followed by a nighttime tour. Head to the Swamp Water Café to try Native American dishes like Indian fry bread with honey, Indian tacos, and bison burgers. Check the website for showtimes and tour schedules. ⊠ *Big Cypress Seminole Indian Reservation, 30000 Gator Tail Trail, Clewiston* ☎ *863/983–6101* ⊕ *www.billieswamp.com* ☒ *Swamp Safari Day Package $50; Twilight Swamp Expedition $43.*

FAMILY **Butterfly World.** More than 80 native and international butterfly species live inside the first and largest butterfly house in the United States. The 3-acre site inside Tradewinds Park in Coconut Creek has aviaries, observation decks, waterfalls, ponds, and tunnels. There are lots of birds, too: kids love the lorikeet aviary, where birds alight on every limb. ⊠ *Tradewinds Park, 3600 W. Sample Rd., Coconut Creek* ☎ *954/977–4400* ⊕ *www.butterflyworld.com* ☒ *$26.95.*

FAMILY **Everglades Holiday Park.** Many episodes of Animal Planet's *Gator Boys* are filmed here, making this wetland "park" an extremely popular tourist attraction. Take an hour-long airboat tour, snap a selfie with a python, and catch the alligator wrestling in the pit. ⚠ **The airboats tend to be supersized, and the overall experience can feel very commercialized.** ⊠ *21940 Griffin Rd.* ☎ *954/434–8111* ⊕ *www.evergladesholiday-park.com* ☒ *$29.99 (includes group photo).*

FAMILY **Flamingo Gardens.** Wander through the aviary, arboretum wildlife sanctuary, and Everglades museum in the historic Wray Home. A half-hour guided tram ride winds through tropical fruit groves and wetlands, where the largest collection of native wildlife lives (flamingos, alligators, bobcats, otters, panthers, and more). ⊠ *3750 S. Flamingo Rd., Davie* ☎ *954/473–2955* ⊕ *www.flamingogardens.org* ☒ *$19.95.*

FAMILY **Sawgrass Recreation Park.** Catch a good glimpse of plants and wildlife—from ospreys and alligators to turtles, snakes, and fish—on a half-hour airboat ride through the Everglades. The fee covers admission to all nature exhibits as well as a visit to a model Seminole village. ■ **TIP→ Nature truly comes alive at night. Sawgrass Recreation Park offers nighttime airboat rides on Wednesday and Saturday at 8 pm, reservatons required.** ⊠ *1006 N. U.S. 27, Weston* ✛ *GPS does not work with this address. Call for directions.* ☎ *888/424–7262, 954/389–0202 for directions* ⊕ *www.evergladestours.com* ☒ *$22.95; night tours $40.*

BEACHES

FAMILY

Fodor'sChoice

★

Fort Lauderdale Beach. The same stretch of sand that once welcomed America's wild spring breakers is now miles of beachside sophistication. It remains gloriously open and uncluttered when compared to other major beaches along the Florida coastline; walkways line both sides of the road, and traffic is trimmed to two gently curving northbound lanes. Fort Lauderdale Beach unofficially begins between the B Ocean Resort (formerly the Sheraton Yankee Clipper) and the DoubleTree by Hilton Bahia Mar Resort, starting with the quiet **Fort Lauderdale Beach Park,** where picnic tables and palm trees rule. Going north, a younger crowd

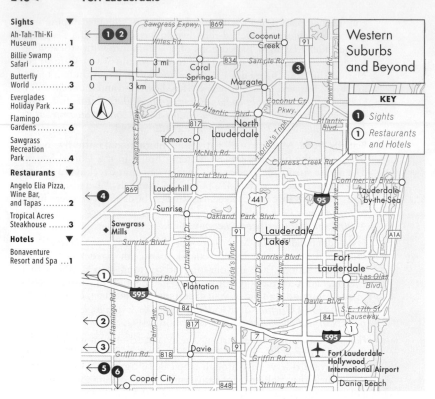

gravitates toward the section near Las Olas Boulevard. The beach is actually most crowded from here to **Beach Place,** home of Marriott's vacation rentals and touristy places like Hooters and Fat Tuesday (and a beach-themed CVS Pharmacy). An LGBT crew soaks up the sun along **Sebastian Street Beach,** just north of the Ritz-Carlton. Families with children enjoy hanging out between Seville Street and Vistamar Street, between the Westin Fort Lauderdale Beach and the Atlantic Resort and Spa. High-spirited dive bars dot The Strip and epitomize its "anything goes" attitude. **Amenities:** food and drink; lifeguards; parking (fee). **Best for:** sunrise; swimming; windsurfing; walking; partiers. ⊠ *S.R. A1A, from Holiday Dr. to Sunrise Blvd., Beachfront.*

FAMILY **Harbor Beach.** The posh Harbor Beach community includes Fort Lauderdale's most opulent residences on the Intracoastal Waterway. Due east of this community, a stunning beach has adopted the name of its neighborhood. The Harbor Beach section has some of the few private beaches in Fort Lauderdale, most of which belong to hotels like the Marriott Harbor Beach Resort and the Lago Mar Resort & Club. (Only hotel guests have access.) Such status allows the hotels to provide guests with full-service amenities and dining options on their own slices of heaven. **Amenities:** water sports. **Best for:** solitude; swimming; walking. ⊠ *S. Ocean La. and Holiday Dr., Beachfront.*

FAMILY **Hugh Taylor Birch State Park.** North of the bustling beachfront and Sunrise
Fodor's Choice Boulevard, quieter sands run parallel to Hugh Taylor Birch State Park,
★ an exquisite patch of Old Florida. The 180-acre subtropical oasis forms a barrier island between the Atlantic Ocean and the Intracoastal Waterway—surprisingly close to the urban core. Lush vegetation includes mangroves, and there are lovely nature trails through the hammock system. Visit the Birch House Museum, enjoy a picnic, play volleyball, or grab a canoe, kayak, or stand-up paddleboard. **Amenities:** toilets, water sports. **Best for:** solitude; walking. ✉ *3109 E. Sunrise Blvd., Intracoastal and Inland* ☎ *954/564–4521* 🌐 *www.floridastateparks.org/HughTaylorBirch* 🎫 *$4 for 1-person in vehicle; $6 for group in vehicle; $2 per pedestrian or bicyclist.*

WHERE TO EAT

DOWNTOWN AND LAS OLAS

$$ 🍴 **American Social.** In the sports bar desert of South Florida, it's nice
MODERN AMERICAN to know you can eat well while watching your team. American Social flaunts a seafood mac 'n' cheese skillet, shrimp-pesto flatbread, and a full spectrum of gourmet burgers with sides of Parmesan-truffle fries or sweet-potato fries. **Known for:** upscale bar food; live sports on TV; craft beers and good cocktails. [$] *Average main: $20* ✉ *721 E. Las Olas Blvd., Downtown* ☎ *954/764–7005* 🌐 *www.americansocialbar.com.*

$$$ 🍴 **Big City Tavern.** A must-visit Las Olas landmark, Big City Tavern
MODERN AMERICAN mingles Asian entrées like shrimp pad thai, Italian four-cheese ravioli, and an American grilled chicken Cobb salad. The crispy flatbread
FAMILY changes every day. ■ **TIP→ Big City is open late for drinks, with a special
Fodor's Choice late-night food menu.** **Known for:** eclectic menu; weekend brunch; fun
★ bar scene. [$] *Average main: $26* ✉ *609 E. Las Olas Blvd., Downtown* ☎ *954/727–0307* 🌐 *www.bigcitylasolas.com.*

$$ 🍴 **The Floridian.** This classic 24-hour diner serves up no-nonsense break-
DINER fast favorites (no matter the hour) like oversized omelets with biscuits,
FAMILY toast or English muffins, and a choice of grits or sliced tomatoes. Good hangover eats abound, but don't expect anything exceptional besides the location and the low prices. **Known for:** breakfast anytime; low prices; always open. [$] *Average main: $15* ✉ *1410 E. Las Olas Blvd., Downtown* ☎ *954/463–4041* 🌐 *www.thefloridiandiner.com.*

$ 🍴 **Gran Forno Bakery.** Most days, the Italian sandwiches, specialty
BAKERY breads, and pastries sell out before noon at this aptly named bakery
FAMILY ("large oven" in Italian). Customers line up in the morning to get Gran Forno's hot artisanal breads like ciabatta (800 loaves are made a day), returning later for the decadent desserts. **Known for:** great Italian-style breads; desserts; strong coffee. [$] *Average main: $14* ✉ *1235 E. Las Olas Blvd., Downtown* ☎ *954/467–2244* 🌐 *www.granforno.com.*

$$$$ 🍴 **Grille 401.** Grille 401's new American cuisine merges Osaka-style
MODERN AMERICAN pressed sushi, classic filet mignon, and crispy crab fritters with stuffed pork chops. The house-made desserts include a white-chocolate brioche bread pudding and a carrot cake made with shredded carrots and toasted pecans. **Known for:** power lunchers by day, sophisticated diners by night; outdoor deck; good cocktails. [$] *Average main: $33* ✉ *401 E. Las Olas Blvd., Downtown* ☎ *954/767–0222* 🌐 *www.grille401.com.*

5

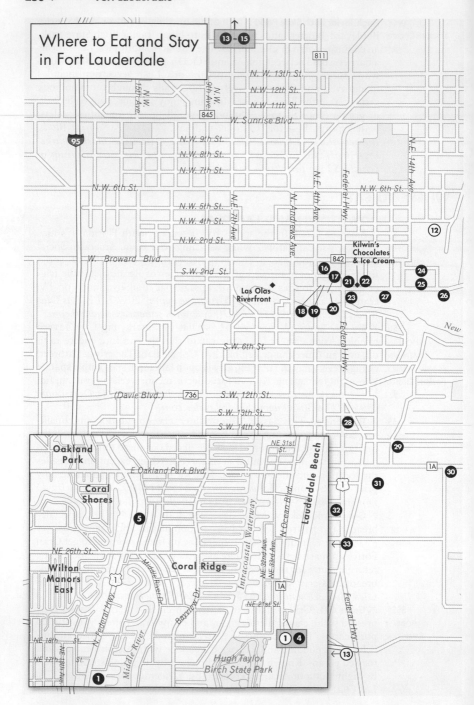

Where to Eat and Stay in Fort Lauderdale

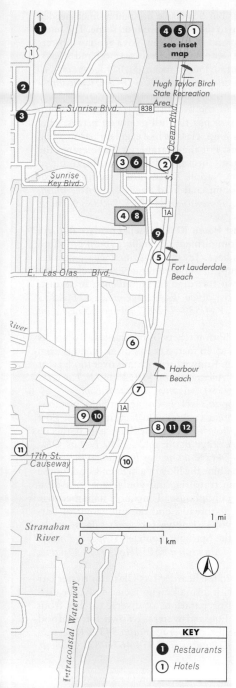

Restaurants ▼

American Social **22**

Anthony's Coal Fired Pizza **32**

Beauty and the Feast Bar | Kitchen **7**

Big City Tavern **21**

Canyon Southwest Cafe **3**

Casablanca Cafe **9**

Casa D'Angelo Ristorante **2**

Coco Asian Bistro and Bar **31**

Eduardo de San Angel **13**

The Floridian **26**

Gran Forno Bakery **27**

Grille 401 ....**19**

Kitchenetta **5**

Lips **14**

Lobster Bar Sea Grille **20**

Luigi's Coal Oven Pizza ...**24**

Mai-Kai Restaurant and Polynesian Show **15**

Market 17 ....**30**

Ocean 2000 Restaurant **4**

Old Fort Lauderdale Breakfast House (O-B House) **16**

Old Heidelberg Restaurant **33**

Pelican Landing **10**

Rocco's Tacos and Tequila Bar **25**

The Royal Pig Pub **18**

S3 .... **6**

Sea Level Restaurant and Ocean Bar **11**

Southport Raw Bar **29**

Steak 954 .... **8**

Sublime Restaurant and Bar **1**

3030 Ocean **12**

Timpano Italian Chophouse **17**

Tom Jenkins' Bar-B-Q **28**

Wild Sea Oyster Bar and Grille **23**

Hotels ▼

The Atlantic Resort and Spa **2**

B Ocean Resort **7**

Bahia Mar Fort Lauderdale Beach Hotel, a DoubleTree by Hilton **6**

Bonaventure Resort and Spa **13**

Fort Lauderdale Marriott Harbor Beach Resort and Spa **8**

Hilton Fort Lauderdale Beach Resort **3**

Hilton Fort Lauderdale Marina **11**

Hyatt Regency Pier Sixty-Six **9**

Lago Mar Resort and Club **10**

Pelican Grand Beach Resort **1**

Pineapple Point **12**

The Ritz-Carlton, Fort Lauderdale **5**

W Fort Lauderdale **4**

5

KEY

● Restaurants

① Hotels

$$$$
SEAFOOD
Fodor's Choice
★

✕ Lobster Bar Sea Grille. Lobster Bar Sea Grille brought a much-needed infusion of sophisticated dining to the downtown food scene. The selection of seafood and fish is solid and ranges from Nova Scotian lobsters to Atlantic char from Iceland. **Known for:** fresh seafood and steaks; sophisticated atmosphere; separate lounge menu. $ *Average main: $40* ⊠ *450 E. Las Olas Blvd., Downtown* ☎ *954/772–2675* ⊕ *www.buckheadrestaurants.com/lobster-bar-sea-grille.*

$$
PIZZA
FAMILY
Fodor's Choice
★

✕ Luigi's Coal Oven Pizza. One of the best little pizza joints in South Florida, Luigi's Coal Oven Pizza has the full gamut of pizzas, phenomenal salads with fresh dressings, classics like eggplant parmigiana, and oven-baked chicken wings. For the Margherita Napoletana, the quality and flavors of the crust, cheese, and sauce are the result of Luigi's century-old recipe from Napoli. **Known for:** traditional Neopolitan pizza; petite dining room; coal-fired oven. $ *Average main: $19* ⊠ *1415 E. Las Olas Blvd., Downtown* ☎ *954/522–9888* ⊕ *www.luigiscoalovenpizza.com.*

$$$
AMERICAN
Fodor's Choice
★

✕ Old Fort Lauderdale Breakfast House (O-B House). Locals can't get enough of the O-B House's commitment to quality; you'll only find fresh and organic ingredients here. Try cheesy grits, mega-pancakes with real Vermont maple syrup, or the free-range-egg omelets with wild-caught mahimahi. **Known for:** organic ingredients; breakfast; unique renovation of an old post office. $ *Average main: $21* ⊠ *333 Himmarshee St., Downtown* ☎ *954/530–7520* ⊕ *www.o-bhouse.com* ⌇ *No lunch Sun.*

$$
MODERN
MEXICAN
Fodor's Choice
★

✕ Rocco's Tacos and Tequila Bar. With pitchers of margaritas, Rocco's is more of a scene than a restaurant. In fact, Rocco's drink menu is even larger than its sizable food menu. **Known for:** cocktails over food; great guacamole; busy atmosphere. $ *Average main: $19* ⊠ *1313 E. Las Olas Blvd., Downtown* ☎ *954/524–9550* ⊕ *www.roccostacos.com.*

$$$
CAJUN

✕ The Royal Pig Pub. This gastropub revels in doling out hefty portions of Cajun comfort food and potent cocktails. In fact, it's one of Fort Lauderdale's busiest watering holes. **Known for:** busy bar; barbecue shrimp; weekend brunch. $ *Average main: $22* ⊠ *350 E. Las Olas Blvd., Downtown* ☎ *954/617–7447* ⊕ *www.royalpigpub.com.*

$$$
ITALIAN

✕ Timpano Italian Chophouse. Combine the likes of a high-end steak house with a typical Italian-American trattoria, and you've got yourself a successful recipe for an Italian chophouse. Timpano's Italian-centric offerings include fresh pastas, flatbreads, and the full gamut of Parmesans, marsalas, and fra diavolos. **Known for:** great salads; steakhouse favorites; live music in the Starlight Lounge. $ *Average main: $21* ⊠ *450 E. Las Olas Blvd., Downtown* ☎ *954/462–9119* ⊕ *www.timpanochophouse.net.*

$$$$
SEAFOOD

✕ Wild Sea Oyster Bar and Grille. In the heart of Las Olas, this oyster bar and grill keeps things simple with a small menu focused on a beautiful raw bar and ever-changing preparations of diverse catches from Florida, Hawaiian, and New England waters. **Known for:** seafood galore; raw bar; extensive wine list. $ *Average main: $43* ⊠ *Riverside Hotel, 620 E. Las Olas Blvd., Downtown* ☎ *954/467–0671* ⊕ *www.WildSeaLasOlas.com.*

ALONG THE BEACH

$$$
MODERN
AMERICAN
FAMILY
Fodor's Choice
★
✕ **Beauty and the Feast Bar | Kitchen.** Feast on a creative array of small plates with a Southern twist. The oceanfront restaurant is ideal for hungry and adventurous eaters who don't mind mixing and matching flavor profiles. **Known for:** small-plates menu; casual atmosphere; weekend brunch. $ *Average main: $26 ✉ The Atlantic Hotel and Spa, 601 N. Fort Lauderdale Beach Blvd., Beachfront ☎ 954/567–8070 ⊕ www. atlantichotelfl.com.*

$$$
ECLECTIC
FAMILY
✕ **Casablanca Cafe.** The menu at this piano bar and restaurant offers a global hodgepodge of American, Mediterranean, and Asian flavors, with a specific focus on eclectic preparations of Florida fish. The food isn't particularly good, but the ambience at this historic home is excellent. **Known for:** outdoor dining; historic setting in Jova House; popular piano bar. $ *Average main: $28 ✉ 3049 Alhambra St., Beachfront ☎ 954/764–3500 ⊕ www.casablancacafeonline.com.*

$$$$
SEAFOOD
FAMILY
Fodor's Choice
★
✕ **Ocean2000 Restaurant.** Locals know where to go for inspired regional cooking. At Ocean2000, the ethos is guided by freshness, and the seafood is unrivaled. **Known for:** fresh seafood; beachfront location; elegant, romantic atmosphere. $ *Average main: $32 ✉ Pelican Grand Beach Resort, 2000 N. Ocean Blvd., Beachfront ☎ 954/556–7667 ⊕ www.pelicanbeach.com/ocean2000.aspx.*

$$$
FUSION
✕ **S3.** S3 stands for the fabulous trio of sun, surf, and sand, paying homage to its prime beachfront location. The menu features a variety of Japanese-inspired raw dishes, sushi rolls, and small plates, and large plates with a new American focus. **Known for:** eclectic Asian and American flavors; solid selection of wine and cocktails; drawing both locals and visitors. $ *Average main: $29 ✉ Hilton Fort Lauderdale Beach Resort, 505 N. Fort Lauderdale Beach Blvd., Beachfront ⊕ www.s3restaurant.com.*

$$$
SEAFOOD
FAMILY
✕ **Sea Level Restaurant and Ocean Bar.** You have to take the road less traveled to find Sea Level, a haven for fresh seafood. The indoor-outdoor restaurant literally overlooks the ocean from sea level at Marriott's Harbor Beach Resort and Spa and its seasonal menu wows with daily specials and cocktails featuring ingredients from the chef's organic garden. **Known for:** the freshest seafood; outdoor dining; good cocktail menu. $ *Average main: $25 ✉ Fort Lauderdale Marriott Harbor Beach Resort and Spa, 3030 Holiday Dr., Beachfront ☎ 954/765–3041 ⊕ www.marriott.com/hotel-restaurants/fllsb-fort-lauderdale-marriott-harbor-beach-resort-and-spa/sea-level/5152470/about.mi.*

$$$$
MODERN
AMERICAN
Fodor's Choice
★
✕ **Steak 954.** It's not just the steaks that impress at Stephen Starr's superstar spot inside the chic W Fort Lauderdale, the seafood selections shine, too. Order as many dishes as possible, like the lobster and crab-coconut ceviche, the red snapper tiradito, and the Colorado lamb chops. **Known for:** high-quality (and expensive) steaks and seafood; outdoor dining; Sunday brunch. $ *Average main: $55 ✉ W Fort Lauderdale, 401 N. Fort Lauderdale Beach Blvd., Beachfront ☎ 954/414–8333 ⊕ www.steak954.com.*

$$$$
SEAFOOD
Fodor's Choice
★
✕ **3030 Ocean.** 3030 Ocean's unpredictable menus are guided by award-winning chef Adrienne Grenier's perfectionist flair. Her interpretation of modern American seafood focuses on balancing complex flavors to enhance her fresh ingredients—without subtracting from their integrity. **Known for:** ever-changing menu; fresh seafood; consistently

5

Sand can sometimes be forgiving if you fall, and bicyclists also appreciate the ocean views.

good food. $ *Average main: $39* ✉ *Fort Lauderdale Marriott Harbor Beach Resort and Spa, 3030 Holiday Dr., Beachfront* 🕾 *954/765–3030* ⊕ *www.3030ocean.com.*

INTRACOASTAL AND INLAND

$$
PIZZA
FAMILY

✕ **Anthony's Coal Fired Pizza.** Before this legendary South Florida pizzeria spread to more than 50 outposts across six states, Anthony's original coal-fired oven was heating up Fort Lauderdale in a big way. Its flagship location still packs the house nightly, serving a simple menu of pizza made with fresh ingredients in an 800°F oven, chicken wings, and salads. **Known for:** approachable menu with pizza and Italian favorites; casual, fun atmosphere; coal-fired oven. $ *Average main: $17* ✉ *2203 S. Federal Hwy., Intracoastal and Inland* 🕾 *954/462–5555* ⊕ *www.acfp.com.*

$$$$
SOUTHWESTERN-
INTERNATIONAL
Fodor's Choice
★

✕ **Canyon Southwest Cafe.** Inside this magical enclave, Southwestern fusion boasts Central and South American flavors and a twist of Asian influence. Pair the fresh seafood or wild game with a robust selection of tequilas, a few mezcals, and a decent wine list. **Known for:** local ingredients; long waits; large slection of tequilas. $ *Average main: $31* ✉ *1818 E. Sunrise Blvd., Intracoastal and Inland* ✛ *At N.E. 18th Ave.* 🕾 *954/765–1950* ⊕ *www.canyonfl.com* ☾ *No lunch.*

$$$$
ITALIAN
Fodor's Choice
★

✕ **Casa D'Angelo Ristorante.** Casa D'Angelo is always packed. The Tuscan-style fine-dining restaurant is beloved for its rustic and refined philosophy. **Known for:** everything made from scratch; grilled tiger prawns; extensive wine list. $ *Average main: $38* ✉ *1201 N. Federal Hwy., Intracoastal and Inland* 🕾 *954/564–1234* ⊕ *www.casa-d-angelo.com.*

$$$
ASIAN
Fodor's Choice
★

× **Coco Asian Bistro and Bar.** The best of Thailand and Japan unite in an unassuming Fort Lauderdale strip mall. Chef-owner Mike Ponluang's lobster pad thai and classic curries are the go-to for loyal locals, as are sushi rolls and more traditional Japanese selections. **Known for:** eclectic and extensive pan-Asian menu; soothing, elegant atmosphere; good desserts. $ *Average main: $27* ✉ *Harbor Shops, 1841 Cordova Rd., Intracoastal and Inland* ☎ 954/525–3541 ⊕ *www.cocoasianbistro. com* ⊗ *No lunch weekends.*

$$
ITALIAN
FAMILY
Fodor's Choice
★

× **Kitchenetta.** Kitchenetta is a modern trattoria serving gourmet Italian-American favorites in an industrial-chic setting. The best things to come out of this family-owned kitchen include the spaghetti with Neopolitan-style stuffed artichokes (seasonal), gnocchi Gorgonzola, and the wood-fired mushroom pizza. **Known for:** family-sized portions; good pastas; special Sunday supper. $ *Average main: $19* ✉ *2850 N. Federal Hwy., Intracoastal and Inland* ☎ 954/567–3333 ⊕ *www.kitchenetta. com* ⊗ *Closed Mon. No lunch.*

$$$$
AMERICAN
CONTEMPORARY

× **Market 17.** Market 17 sources ingredients exclusively from local farmers and fishermen and guests are able to see which farms and purveyors on the restaurant's website. As such, the menu changes daily. **Known for:** entirely locavore menu; constantly evolving offerings; house-made charcuterie. $ *Average main: $31* ✉ *1850 S.E. 17th St., Intracoastal and Inland* ⊹ *Next to the Convention Center* ☎ 954/835–5507 ⊕ *www. market17.net* ⊗ *Closed Mon. No lunch.*

$$$
GERMAN
FAMILY

× **Old Heidelberg Restaurant.** Old Heidelberg is like a Bavarian mirage on State Road 84 with a killer list of German specialties and beers on tap. Classics like bratwurst, knockwurst, kielbasa, and spaetzle dovetail nicely with four types of Wiener schnitzel. **Known for:** kitschy decor; large selection of German imports on tap; extensive menu of German favorites. $ *Average main: $25* ✉ *900 W. S.R. 84, Intracoastal and Inland* ☎ 954/463–6747 ⊕ *www.heidelbergfl.com* ⊗ *No lunch weekends.*

$$
SEAFOOD
FAMILY

× **Pelican Landing.** Somehow Pelican Landing has managed to stay under the radar in spite of its high-quality seafood, burgers, and Caribbean dishes. The fish is caught daily, served simply blackened or grilled, and presented with sides. **Known for:** fresh seafood; casual atmosphere; sunset views. $ *Average main: $19* ✉ *Hyatt Regency Pier Sixty Six, 2301 S.E. 17th St., Intracoastal and Inland* ⊹ *At end of main dock* ☎ 954/525–6666 ⊕ *www.pier66.hyatt.com.*

$$
SEAFOOD

× **Southport Raw Bar.** You can't go wrong at this unpretentious dive where seafood reigns. Feast on raw or steamed clams, raw oysters, and peel-and-eat shrimp. **Known for:** low prices; fresh seafood; ample choices for meat lovers. $ *Average main: $19* ✉ *1536 Cordova Rd., Intracoastal and Inland* ☎ 954/525–2526 ⊕ *www.southportrawbar.com.*

$$
VEGETARIAN
FAMILY

× **Sublime Restaurant and Bar.** Sublime's dishes are organic and free from any animal products. It's known for showing the world that veganism doesn't have to compromise flavor or creativity; innovative pizzas, pastas, and meat substitutes can satisfy any carnivore craving. **Known for:** strictly vegan cuisine; all-organic ingredients; elegant atmosphere. $ *Average main: $20* ✉ *1431 N. Federal Hwy., Intracoastal and Inland* ☎ 954/615–1431 ⊕ *www.sublimerestaurant.com* ⊗ *Closed Mon.*

5

$ BARBECUE FAMILY 🍴 **Tom Jenkins' Bar-B-Q.** Big portions of dripping barbecue are dispensed at this chill spot for eat-in or takeout. Dinners come with two sides like baked beans, collards, or mighty tasty mac 'n cheese. **Known for:** ample portions; very reasonable prices; good sides. [$] *Average main: $12* ✉ *1236 S. Federal Hwy., Intracoastal and Inland* ☎ *954/522–5046* 🌐 *www.tomjenkinsbbq.com* ⏲ *Closed Sun. and Mon.*

WESTERN SUBURBS AND BEYOND

$$ PIZZA FAMILY Fodor's Choice ★ 🍴 **Angelo Elia Pizza, Bar and Tapas.** This casual Weston outpost is one of chef Angelo Elia's popular Tuscan-inspired restaurants in Broward County. Affordable small plates, salads, ceviches, and pizzas are neighborhood favorites. **Known for:** moderate prices; family-friendly atmosphere; house-made gelato. [$] *Average main: $20* ✉ *Country Isles Shopping Center, 1370 Weston Rd., Weston* ☎ *954/306–0037* 🌐 *www.angeloeliapizza.com.*

$$$ STEAKHOUSE FAMILY 🍴 **Tropical Acres Steakhouse.** This old-school, family-owned steak house hasn't changed much since it opened in 1949. Sizzling steaks are served from a fiery grill, and there are dozens of other entrées to choose from (like frogs' legs, rack of lamb, boneless New York strip). **Known for:** nostalgia galore; family-friendly dining; popular happy hour. [$] *Average main: $24* ✉ *2500 Griffin Rd.* ☎ *954/989–2500* 🌐 *www.tropicalacres.com* ⏲ *Closed Sun. in July–Nov. No lunch.*

WILTON MANORS AND OAKLAND PARK

$$$ MEXICAN 🍴 **Eduardo de San Angel.** Authentic chilies, spices, and herbs enhance classic seafood, meat, and poultry dishes at this inviting Mexican enclave known for its hospitality. The restaurant has packed the house for over 20 years, a testament to its popularity and excellent cuisine. **Known for:** authentic upscale Mexican cuisine; sautéed beef tenderloin tips with mushrooms and onions; cilantro soup. [$] *Average main: $30* ✉ *2822 E. Commercial Blvd., Oakland Park* ☎ *954/772–4731* 🌐 *www.eduardodesanangel.com* ⏲ *Closed Sun.*

$$ AMERICAN 🍴 **Lips.** The 1990s are still alive and well at Lips. The hit restaurant and drag-show bar is a hot spot for groups celebrating birthdays, bachelorette parties, and other milestones requiring glitz and glamour. **Known for:** drag performances while you dine; Sunday brunch; raucous celebrations. [$] *Average main: $20* ✉ *1421 E. Oakland Park Blvd., Oakland Park* ☎ *954/567–0987* 🌐 *www.fladragshow.com* ⏲ *Closed Mon.*

$$$$ SOUTH PACIFIC FAMILY 🍴 **Mai-Kai Restaurant and Polynesian Show.** Touristy to some yet downright divine to others, Mai-Kai merges the South Pacific with South Florida. This torch-lit landmark is undeniably gimmicky, but it's the only place in town for tiki cocktails and Polynesian dance and fire shows. **Known for:** Peking duck; good wine list; long waits—reservations are essential. [$] *Average main: $39* ✉ *3599 N. Federal Hwy., Oakland Park* ☎ *954/563–3272* 🌐 *www.maikai.com.*

WHERE TO STAY

DOWNTOWN AND LAS OLAS

$$
B&B/INN

Pineapple Point. Tucked a few blocks behind Las Olas Boulevard in the residential neighborhood of Victoria Park, clothing-optional Pineapple Point is a magnificent maze of posh tropical cottages and dense foliage catering to the gay community and is nationally renowned for its stellar service. **Pros:** superior service; tropical setting. **Cons:** difficult to find at first; need a vehicle for beach jaunts. $ *Rooms from: $298 ⊠ 315 N.E. 16th Terr., Downtown* ☎ *954/527–0094, 888/844–7295* ⊕ *www. pineapplepoint.com* ⇨ *25 rooms* ⦿*Breakfast.*

ALONG THE BEACH

$$$
HOTEL
FAMILY

The Atlantic Resort and Spa. This towering oceanfront beauty has fantastic views of the ocean from its beds (unless, of course, you select a city view). **Pros:** oceanfront property; en suite kitchenettes; member of the Preferred Hotels & Resorts portfolio. **Cons:** dated decor in the rooms; expensive parking. $ *Rooms from: $350 ⊠ 601 N. Fort Lauderdale Beach Blvd., Beachfront* ☎ *954/567–8020* ⊕ *www.atlantichotelfl.com* ⇨ *124 rooms* ⦿*No meals.*

$$
HOTEL

B Ocean Resort. Formerly the Sheraton Yankee Clipper Hotel, this classic riverboat-shaped landmark is chic yet functional, but it's the views and beach access that truly set it apart. **Pros:** retro mermaid show in swimming pool; proximity to beach; excellent gym. **Cons:** small rooms; low ceilings in lobby; faded exteriors. $ *Rooms from: $250 ⊠ 1140 Seabreeze Blvd., Beachfront* ☎ *954/564–1000* ⊕ *www. boceanfortlauderdale.com* ⇨ *486 rooms* ⦿*No meals.*

$$
HOTEL
FAMILY

Bahia Mar Fort Lauderdale Beach Hotel, A DoubleTree by Hilton. This nicely situated resort has identical rooms in both its marina building and its tower building; however, the latter offers superior views. **Pros:** crosswalk from hotel to beach; on-site yacht center; Water Taxi stop. **Cons:** dated exteriors; small bathrooms; snug rooms. $ *Rooms from: $215 ⊠ 801 Seabreeze Blvd., Beachfront* ☎ *954/764–2233* ⊕ *www.bahiamar-hotel.com* ⇨ *296 rooms* ⦿*No meals.*

$$$$
RESORT
FAMILY
Fodor's Choice
★

Fort Lauderdale Marriott Harbor Beach Resort and Spa. Bill Marriott's personal choice for his annual four-week family vacation, the Marriott Harbor Beach sits on a quarter-mile of private beach; it bursts with the luxe personality of a top-notch island resort. **Pros:** private beachfront; all rooms have balconies; great eateries; no resort fees. **Cons:** Wi-Fi isn't free; expensive parking; large resort feel. $ *Rooms from: $450 ⊠ 3030 Holiday Dr., Beachfront* ☎ *954/525–4000* ⊕ *www.marriott.com* ⇨ *650 rooms* ⦿*No meals.*

$$$
HOTEL
FAMILY
Fodor's Choice
★

Hilton Fort Lauderdale Beach Resort. This oceanfront sparkler features tasteful guest rooms and a fabulous sixth-floor pool deck. **Pros:** fun poolscape and adults-only lounge; most rooms have balconies; great spa. **Cons:** charge for Wi-Fi; expensive valet parking. $ *Rooms from: $329 ⊠ 505 N. Fort Lauderdale Beach Blvd., Beachfront* ☎ *954/414–2222* ⊕ *www.hilton.com* ⇨ *374 rooms* ⦿*No meals.*

$$$
RESORT
FAMILY

Lago Mar Resort and Club. The sprawling family-friendly Lago Mar retains its sparkle and authentic Florida feel thanks to frequent renovations and committed owners. **Pros:** secluded setting; fun activities;

upscale spa. **Cons:** not easy to find; far from restaurants and beach action. $ *Rooms from: $400* ⊠ *1700 S. Ocean La., Beachfront* 🕾 *855/209–5677* ⊕ *www.lagomar.com* ⇥ *204 rooms* |◯| *No meals.*

$$
RESORT
FAMILY
Fodor's Choice
★

⛱ Pelican Grand Beach Resort. This bright yellow Key West–style Noble House property fuses a heritage seaside charm with understated luxury. **Pros:** incredible spa; directly on the beach; Ocean 2000 restaurant. **Cons:** small fitness center; slightly dated room decor; small property. $ *Rooms from: $270* ⊠ *2000 N. Atlantic Blvd., Beachfront* 🕾 *954/568–9431* ⊕ *www.pelicanbeach.com* ⇥ *159 rooms* |◯| *No meals.*

$$$$
HOTEL
Fodor's Choice
★

⛱ The Ritz-Carlton, Fort Lauderdale. Twenty-four dramatically tiered, glass-walled stories rise from the sea, forming a sumptuous resort that is helping to revive a golden age of luxury travel. **Pros:** prime beach location; ultramodern elegance; organic spa treatments. **Cons:** expensive valet parking; limited dining options. $ *Rooms from: $750* ⊠ *1 N. Fort Lauderdale Beach Blvd., Beachfront* 🕾 *954/465–2300* ⊕ *www.ritzcarlton.com/FortLauderdale* ⇥ *192 rooms* |◯| *No meals.*

$$$$
HOTEL

⛱ W Fort Lauderdale. Fort Lauderdale's trendiest hotel has a glamorous poolscape, übermodern rooms and suites, and dramatic views from every direction. **Pros:** amazing pool; very pet-friendly; complimentary Wi-Fi. **Cons:** party atmosphere not for everyone; hard to navigate the property; hectic valet. $ *Rooms from: $500* ⊠ *435 N. Fort Lauderdale Beach Blvd., Beachfront* 🕾 *954/462–1633* ⊕ *www.wfortlauderdale-hotel.com* ⇥ *465 rooms* |◯| *No meals.*

INTRACOASTAL AND INLAND

$
RESORT
FAMILY
Fodor's Choice
★

⛱ Hilton Fort Lauderdale Marina. Since its $72 million renovation in 2011, the mammoth, 589-room, 20-boat-slip Hilton Fort Lauderdale Marina has maintained its modern edge without compromising its charming, old-school Key West style. **Pros:** sexy fire pit; outdoor bar popular with locals; easy water-taxi access. **Cons:** no bathtubs in tower rooms; small fitness center. $ *Rooms from: $169* ⊠ *1881 S.E. 17th St., Intracoastal and Inland* 🕾 *954/463–4000* ⊕ *www.fortlauderdalemarinahotel.com* ⇥ *589 rooms* |◯| *No meals.*

$$$
RESORT

⛱ Hyatt Regency Pier Sixty-Six. Don't let the 1970s exterior of the iconic waterfront tower fool you; this 22-acre resort is more contemporary than it seems, with conveniences and activities galore. **Pros:** great views; free beach shuttle and easy Water Taxi access; complimentary Wi-Fi. **Cons:** rooms need a refresh; rotating rooftop venue is exclusively for private events; dated exterior. $ *Rooms from: $380* ⊠ *2301 S.E. 17th St. Causeway, Intracoastal and Inland* 🕾 *954/525–6666* ⊕ *www.pier66.hyatt.com* ⇥ *384 rooms* |◯| *No meals.*

WESTERN SUBURBS AND BEYOND

$$
RESORT
FAMILY

⛱ Bonaventure Resort and Spa. This suburban enclave targets conventions and business travelers as well as international vacationers who value golf, the Everglades, and shopping over beach proximity. **Pros:** lush landscaping; pampering spa. **Cons:** difficult to find; 30-minute drive from airport; poor views from some rooms; rental car necessary. $ *Rooms from: $284* ⊠ *250 Racquet Club Rd., Weston* 🕾 *954/389–3300* ⊕ *www.bonaventureresortandspa.com* ⇥ *501 rooms* |◯| *No meals.*

ROK: BRG. Downtown Fort Lauderdale loves this personality-driven burger bar and gastropub as it gives the grown-ups something to enjoy in the teenage-infested nightlife district. The long and narrow venue, adorned with exposed-brick walls and flat-screen TVs, is great for watching sports and for mingling on weekends. Locals come here for the great cocktails and beer selection. The burgers are also locally famous. ⊠ *208 S.W. 2nd St., Downtown* ☎ *954/525–7656* ⊕ *www.rokbrgr.com.*

Stache, 1920's Drinking Den. Inspired by the Roaring Twenties, this speak-easy-style drinking den and nightclub infuses party-hard downtown Fort Lauderdale with some class and pizzazz. Expect awesome craft cocktails, inclusive of bespoke ice cubes, especially for old-school drinks like manhattans and sidecars. Late night on Friday and Saturday anticipate great house music and a fun, easy-on-the-eyes, young, sophisticated crowd. ⊠ *109 S.W. 2nd Ave., Downtown* ☎ *954/449–1044* ⊕ *www.stacheftl.com.*

Fodor's Choice
★ **Tap 42 Bar and Kitchen.** With 42 rotating draft beers from around the United States, 50-plus bourbons, a few dozen original cocktails (including beer cocktails), and 66 bottled craft beers, good times await. The drafts adorn a stylish wall constructed of pennies, which creates an interesting trompe l'oeil. The venue attracts large crowds of young professionals for nights of heavy drinking and high-calorie bar eats. ⊠ *1411 S. Andrews Ave., Downtown* ☎ *954/463–4900* ⊕ *www.tap42.com.*

Tarpon Bend. This casual two-story restaurant transforms into a hopping bar scene in the early evening. It's consistently busy, especially late night, and is one of the only places that's survived all the ups and downs of downtown Fort Lauderdale. ⊠ *200 S.W. 2nd St., Downtown* ☎ *954/523–3233* ⊕ *www.tarponbend.com.*

ALONG THE BEACH

Given its roots as a beachside party town, it's hard to believe that Fort Lauderdale Beach offers very few options in terms of nightlife. A few dive bars are at opposite ends of the main strip, near Sunrise Boulevard and Route A1A, as well as Las Olas Boulevard and A1A. On the main thoroughfare between Las Olas and Sunrise, a few high-end bars at the beach's showstopping hotels have become popular, namely those at the W Fort Lauderdale.

Elbo Room. You can't go wrong wallowing in the past, lifting a drink, and exercising your elbow at the Elbo, a noisy, suds-drenched hot spot since 1938. It seems like nothing has changed here since Fort Lauderdale's spring break heyday. The watering hole phased out food (except for light nibbles) ages ago, but kept a hokey sense of humor: upstairs a sign proclaims "We don't serve women here. You have to bring your own." ⊠ *241 S. Fort Lauderdale Blvd., Beachfront* ☎ *954/463–4615* ⊕ *www.elboroom.com.*

McSorley's Beach Pub. This modern take on a classic Irish pub offers standard pub fun—from a jukebox to 35 beers on tap—but remains wildly popular thanks to its location right across from Fort Lauderdale beach. Indeed it's one of the few places on the beach to get an affordable drink and attracts its fair share of tourists and locals. Upstairs, the pub has a second lounge that's far more clubby as well as a rooftop terrace. ⊠ *837 N. Fort Lauderdale Beach Blvd., Beachfront* ☎ *954/565–4446* ⊕ *www.mcsorleysftl.com.*

Lago Mar Resort and Club in Fort Lauderdale has its own private beach on the Atlantic Ocean.

NIGHTLIFE AND PERFORMING ARTS

NIGHTLIFE

DOWNTOWN AND LAS OLAS

The majority of Fort Lauderdale nightlife takes place near downtown, beginning on Himmarshee Street (2nd Street) and continuing on to the Riverfront, and then to Las Olas Boulevard. The downtown Riverfront tends to draw a younger demographic somewhere between underage teens and late twenties. On Himmarshee Street, a dozen rowdy bars and clubs, ranging from the seedy to the sophisticated, entice a wide range of partygoers. Toward East Las Olas Boulevard, near the financial towers and boutique shops, bars cater to the yuppie crowd.

Fodor's Choice
★

Laser Wolf. Far from the main drag of Fort Lauderdale's nightlife district, Laser Wolf celebrates the urban grit on the other side of the tracks as an artsy, hipster, craft-beer bar. It's located on the railroad tracks in a cool indoor-outdoor space and might be the most popular bar for locals because of its great drinks, music, and overall vibe. Motto: "No jerks. Yes beer." ■TIP➔ Drive or Uber it here. It's best not to walk from other bars off Las Olas and Himmarshee due to distance and safety concerns. ✉ 901 Progresso Dr., No. 101, Downtown ☎ 954/667–9373 ⊕ www. laserwolf.bar/home.html.

Maguire's Hill 16. With the requisite lineup of libations and pub-style food, this classic Irish pub is good for no-frills fun, fried eats, and daily live music. It's famous locally as the oldest traditional Irish pub and restaurant in Fort Lauderdale. ✉ 535 N. Andrews Ave., Downtown ☎ 954/764–4453 ⊕ www.maguireshill16.com.

FAMILY **The World Famous Parrot Lounge.** A venerable Fort Lauderdale hangout, this dive bar–sports bar is particularly popular with Philadelphia Eagles fans and folks reminiscing about the big hair and spray tans of 1980s Fort Lauderdale (i.e., its heyday). This place is stuck in the past, but it's got great bartenders, wings, chicken fingers, poppers, and skins. 'Nuff said, ⊠ *911 Sunrise La., Beachfront* ☎ *954/563–1493* ⊕ *www. parrotlounge.com.*

The Wreck Bar. Travel back in time to the 1950s at this "under the sea" dive bar, where huge aquariums and a porthole show off live mermaids, who perform in the pool on Friday and Saturday. ⊠ *B Ocean Resort, 1140 Seabreeze Blvd., Beachfront* ☎ *954/564–1000* ⊕ *www.bocean-fortlauderdale.com.*

INTRACOASTAL AND INLAND

Bars and pubs along Fort Lauderdale's Intracoastal cater to the city's large, transient boating community. Heading inland along Sunrise Boulevard, the bars around Galleria Mall target thirty- and forty-something singles.

WILTON MANORS AND OAKLAND PARK

The hub of Fort Lauderdale's gay nightlife is in Wilton Manors. Wilton Drive, aka "The Drive," has numerous bars, clubs, and lounges that cater to the LGBT community.

Georgie's Alibi Monkey Bar Ptown / FTL. An anchor for the Wilton Manors gay community fills to capacity for cheap Long Island Iced Teas and stands out as a kind of gay Cheers—a chill neighborhood drinking hole with darts, pool, and friendly people. ⊠ *2266 Wilton Dr., Wilton Manors* ☎ *954/565–2526* ⊕ *www.alibiwiltonmanors.com.*

Rosie's Bar and Grill. Rosie's is very lively, pumping out pop tunes and award-winning burgers. It's the go-to gay-friendly place for affordable drinks and great times. Sunday brunch, with its cast of alternating DJs, is wildly popular. ⊠ *2449 Wilton Dr., Wilton Manors* ☎ *954/563–0123* ⊕ *www.rosiesbng.com.*

Village Pub and Pub Grub. Arguably the most consistently busy spot on "The Drive" in Wilton Manors, this gay pub delivers good times and cheap drinks nightly. Regardless of where you start or end your gay pub crawl in Wilton Manors, you'll invariably end up here at some point—and you'll be dancing. ⊠ *2283 Wilton Dr., Wilton Manors* ☎ *754/200–5244* ⊕ *www.villagepubwm.com.*

WESTERN SUBURBS AND BEYOND

Florida's cowboy country, Davie, offers country-western fun out in the 'burbs. In addition, South Florida's Native American tribes have long offered gambling on Indian Territory near Broward's western suburbs. With new laws, Broward's casinos offer Vegas-style slot machines and even blackjack. Hollywood's Seminole Hard Rock Hotel & Casino offers the most elegant of Broward's casino experiences. *See Nightlife in Hollywood.*

5

SHOPPING

FOOD

FAMILY **Living Green Fresh Market.** Living Green Fresh Market is a fabulous alternative to overpriced behemoths for the health-conscious in Oakland Park. This green shop and café is bursting with colorful, local, fresh produce, wild-caught fish, prepared foods, and other goods. The quality is top-notch yet the prices are affordable. You can grab breakfast or lunch and cross things off your grocery list, while knowing that each item has a ton of integrity. Plus, there's Puro fair-trade coffee. ⊠ *1305 E. Commercial Blvd., Oakland Park* ☎ *954/771–9770* ⊕ *www.livinggreenfreshmarket.com.*

MALLS

FAMILY **The Galleria at Fort Lauderdale.** Fort Lauderdale's most sophisticated mall is just west of the Intracoastal Waterway. The split-level emporium comprises Neiman Marcus, Apple, Cole Haan, Macy's, and 100 specialty shops. You can chow down at The Capital Grille, Truluck's, P.F. Chang's China Bistro, or Seasons 52. The mall itself is open Monday through Saturday 10–9, Sunday noon–6. The stand-alone restaurants and bars are open later. ⊠ *2414 E. Sunrise Blvd., Intracoastal and Inland* ☎ *954/564–1036* ⊕ *www.galleriamall-fl.com.*

FAMILY **Sawgrass Mills.** This alligator-shaped megamall draws millions of shoppers a year to its collection of 350 outlet stores. According to the mall, it's the second largest attraction in Florida—second only to Walt Disney World. While this may be an exaggeration, prepare for insane crowds. ⊠ *12801 W. Sunrise Blvd., at Flamingo Rd., Sunrise* ⊕ *www.simon. com/mall/sawgrass-mills.*

Fodor's Choice
★

SHOPPING DISTRICTS

FAMILY **The Gallery at Beach Place.** Just north of Las Olas Boulevard on Route A1A, this shopping gallery is attached to the mammoth Marriot Beach Place time-share. Spaces are occupied by touristy shops that sell everything from sarongs to alligator heads, chain restaurants like Hooter's, bars serving frozen drinks, and a supersize CVS pharmacy, which sells everything you need for the beach. ■TIP➔ Beach Place has covered parking, and usually has plenty of spaces, but you can pinch pennies by using a nearby municipal lot. ⊠ *17 S. Fort Lauderdale Beach Blvd., Beachfront* ⊕ *www.galleryatbeachplace.com.*

FAMILY **Las Olas Boulevard.** Las Olas Boulevard is the epicenter of Fort Lauderdale's lifestyle. Not only are 50 of the city's best boutiques, 30 top restaurants, and a dozen art galleries found along this landscaped street, but Las Olas links the growing downtown with its beautiful beaches. ⊠ *E. Las Olas Blvd., Downtown* ⊕ *www.lasolasboulevard.com.*

Fodor's Choice
★

SPORTS AND THE OUTDOORS

BIKING

Among the most popular routes are Route A1A and Bayview Drive, especially in early morning before traffic builds, and a 7-mile bike path that parallels State Road 84 and New River and leads to Markham Park, which has mountain-bike trails. ■TIP➔ Alligator alert: Do not dangle your legs from seawalls.

FAMILY **Broward BCycle.** The big-city trend of "pay and ride" bicycles is alive and well in Broward County. With 40 station locations over 20 scenic miles, from as far south as Hallandale to as far north as Pompano Beach and Coconut Creek, bikes can be rented for as little as 30 minutes or as long as a week, and can be picked up and dropped off at any and all stations in Broward County. Most stations are found downtown and along the beach. This is an excellent green and health-conscious way to explore Fort Lauderdale. Please note, however, that helmets are not provided at the kiosks. ⊕ *broward.bcycle.com.*

FISHING

FAMILY **Bahia Mar Yachting Center.** If you're interested in a saltwater charter, check out the offerings at the marina of the Bahia Mar Fort Lauderdale. Sportfishing and drift fishing bookings can be arranged. Snorkeling and diving outfitter Sea Experience also leaves from here, as does the famous *Jungle Queen* steamboat. In addition, the Water Taxi makes regular stops here. ⊠ *Bahia Mar Fort Lauderdale Beach – A DoubleTree by Hilton Hotel, 801 Seabreeze Blvd., Beachfront* ☎ *954/627–6309.*

RODEOS

FAMILY **Davie Pro Rodeo.** South Florida has a surprisingly large cowboy scene, concentrated in the western suburb of Davie. And for decades, the Bergeron Rodeo Grounds (also known as the Davie Pro Rodeo Arena) has hosted the area's best riders and ropers. Throughout the year, the rodeo hosts national tours and festivals as well as the annual Southeaster Circuit Finals. Check the website for the exact dates of these rodeos. ⊠ *Bergeron Rodeo Grounds, 4271 Davie Rd., Davie* ☎ *954/680–8005* ⊕ *www.davieprorodeo.com.*

SCUBA DIVING AND SNORKELING

FAMILY **Lauderdale Diver.** This dive center facilitates daily trips on a bevy of hard-core dive boats up and down Broward's shoreline (they don't have their own boats, but they work with a handful of preferred outfitters). A variety of snorkeling, reef-diving, and wreck-diving trips are offered as well as scuba-diving lessons. ⊠ *1334 S.E. 17th St., Intracoastal and Inland* ☎ *954/467–2822* ⊕ *www.lauderdalediver.com.*

FAMILY

Fodor's Choice

★

Sea Experience. The *Sea Experience I* leaves daily at 10:15 am and 2:15 pm for two-hour glass-bottom-boat-and-snorkeling combination trips through offshore reefs. Beginner and advanced scuba-diving experiences are available. ⊠ *Bahia Mar Fort Lauderdale Beach – A DoubleTree by Hilton Hotel, 801 Seabreeze Blvd., Beachfront* ☎ *954/770–3483* ⊕ *www.seaxp.com.*

TENNIS

FAMILY **Jimmy Evert Tennis Center.** This grande dame of Fort Lauderdale's public tennis facilities is where legendary champ Chris Evert learned her two-handed backhand under the watchful eye of her now-retired father, Jimmy, the center's tennis pro for 37 years. There are 22 courts (18 lighted clay courts, three hard courts, and a low-compression "beach" court). ⊠ *Holiday Park, 701 N.E. 12th Ave., Intracoastal and Inland* ☎ *954/828–5378* ⊕ *www.fortlauderdale.gov/departments/parks-recreation/tennis-centers/jimmy-evert-tennis-center* 🖭 *$18 per day for nonresidents.*

LAUDERDALE-BY-THE-SEA

Lauderdale-by-the-Sea is 5 miles north of Fort Lauderdale.

North of Fort Lauderdale's Birch Recreation Area, Route A1A edges away from the beach through a stretch known as Galt Ocean Mile, and a succession of ocean-side communities line up against the sea. Traffic can line up, too, as it passes through a changing pattern of beach-blocking high-rises and modest family vacation towns and back again. As far as tourism goes, these communities, which include Pompano Beach and Deerfield Beach, tend to cater to a different demographic than Fort Lauderdale.

Just north of Fort Lauderdale proper, the low-rise family resort town of Lauderdale-by-the-Sea boasts shoreline access that's rapidly disappearing in neighboring beach towns. The closest and most convenient of the A1A cities to Fort Lauderdale proper embraces its quaint personality by welcoming guests to a different world, drawing a mix of Europeans and cost-conscious families who are looking for fewer frills and longer stays.

GETTING HERE AND AROUND

Lauderdale-by-the-Sea is just north of Fort Lauderdale. From Interstate 95, exit at Commercial Boulevard and head east past the Intracoastal Waterway. From U.S. 1 (Federal Highway), go east at Commercial Boulevard. If driving north on State Road A1A, simply continue north from Fort Lauderdale Beach.

ESSENTIALS

Visitor Information Lauderdale-by-the-Sea Chamber of Commerce. ⊠ *4201 N. Ocean Dr., Lauderdale-by-the-Sea* ☎ *954/776–1000* ⊕ *www.lbts.com.*

BEACHES

FAMILY **Lauderdale-by-the-Sea Beach.** Preferred by divers and snorkelers, this laid-back beach is a gateway to magnificent coral reefs. When you're not underwater, look up and you'll likely see a pelican flying by. It's a super-relaxing retreat from the buzz of Fort Lauderdale's busy beaches. That said, the southern part of the beach is crowded near the restaurants at the intersection of A1A and Commercial Boulevard. The no-frills hotels and small inns for families and vacationers visiting for a longer stay are filled with Europeans. Look for metered parking around Commercial Boulevard and A1A. **Amenities:** food and drink; lifeguards; parking (fee). **Best for:** snorkeling; swimming. ⊠ *Commercial Blvd. at State Rd. A1A, Lauderdale-by-the-Sea.*

WHERE TO EAT

$$$ ✕ **Aruba Beach Café.** This casual beachfront eatery is arguably Lauder-
CARIBBEAN dale-by-the-Sea's most famous restaurant. Aruba Beach serves Carib-
FAMILY bean-American cuisine with standouts including Caribbean conch chowder and conch fritters. **Known for:** Bimini bread with Aruba glaze; live music; Sunday breakfast buffet. $ *Average main: $21* ⊠ *1 Commercial Blvd., Lauderdale-by-the-Sea* ☎ *954/776–0001* ⊕ *www. arubabeachcafe.com.*

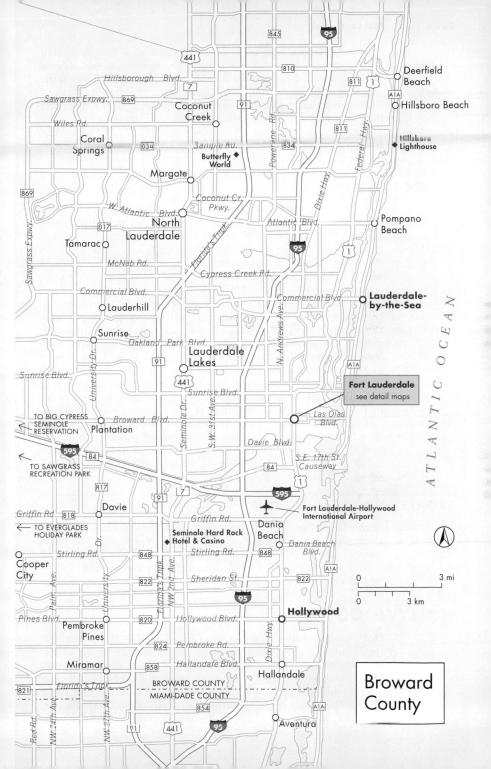

$ ✕ **LaSpada's Original Hoagies.** The crew at this seaside hole-in-the-wall
AMERICAN   puts on quite a show while assembling their sandwiches—locals rave
FAMILY   that this Broward County chain has the best around. Fill up on the
Fodor's Choice   foot-long "Monster" (ham, turkey, roast beef, and cheese), "Mama"
★   (turkey and Genoa salami), or hot meatballs marinara. **Known for:**
the "Monster," a foot-long with ham, turkey, roast beef, cheese; fresh
bread; freshly sliced meats. $ *Average main: $12* ✉ *233 Commercial
Blvd., Lauderdale-by-the-Sea* ☎ *954/776–7893* ⊕ *www.laspadashoa-
gies.com* ↝ *There are 4 additional locations in Broward County.*

WHERE TO STAY

$ ⌂ **Blue Seas Courtyard.** Husband-and-wife team Cristie and Marc Furth
B&B/INN   have run this whimsical Mexican-themed motel in Lauderdale-by-the-
FAMILY   Sea since 1971. **Pros:** south-of-the-border vibe; friendly owners; vintage
Fodor's Choice   stoves from 1972; across the street from the beach. **Cons:** no ocean
★   views; old bathtubs in some rooms. $ *Rooms from: $178* ✉ *4525 El
Mar Dr., Lauderdale-by-the-Sea* ☎ *954/772–3336* ⊕ *www.blueseas-
courtyard.com* ↝ *12 rooms* ⦿ *Breakfast.*

$$ ⌂ **High Noon Beach Resort.** This family-run hotel sits on 300 feet of beachy
B&B/INN   paradise with plenty of cozy spots, two heated pools, and an ambience
FAMILY   that keeps visitors coming back for more. **Pros:** directly on the beach;
friendly vibe; great staff. **Cons:** dated room decor; no maid service on
Sunday; no guarantee for room type. $ *Rooms from: $226* ✉ *4424
El Mar Dr., Lauderdale-by-the-Sea* ☎ *954/776–1121, 800/382–1265*
⊕ *www.highnoonresort.com* ↝ *40 rooms, 1 beach house* ⦿ *Breakfast.*

$ ⌂ **Sea Lord Hotel and Suites.** This gem is one of the nicest in Lauderdale-
B&B/INN   by-the-Sea. Many of the rooms have great ocean views, balconies,
Fodor's Choice   and full kitchens. **Pros:** gorgeous beach location; great staff; rooms
★   have balconies and full kitchens. **Cons:** limited parking; no restau-
rant. $ *Rooms from: $190* ✉ *4140 El Mar Dr., Lauderdale-by-the-
Sea* ☎ *954/776–1505, 800/344–4451* ⊕ *www.sealordhotel.com* ↝ *47
rooms* ⦿ *Breakfast.*

SPORTS AND THE OUTDOORS

FAMILY   **Anglins Fishing Pier.** A longtime favorite for 24-hour fishing, it's a spot
where you may catch snapper, snook, cobia, blue runner, and pom-
pano. The on-site bait-and-tackle shop can advise newbies to advanced
anglers. ✉ *2 Commercial Blvd., Lauderdale-by-the-Sea* ☎ *954/491–
9403* ⊕ *www.boatlessfishing.com/anglins.htm.*

HOLLYWOOD

Hollywood has had several face-lifts to shed its old-school image, but
there's still something delightfully retro about the city. Young Circle,
once down-at-heel, is now Broward's first ArtsPark. On Hollywood's
western outskirts, the flamboyant Seminole Hard Rock Hotel & Casino
has enlivened this previously downtrodden section of the State Road
7/U.S. 441 corridor, drawing local weekenders, architecture buffs, par-
tiers, and gamblers. But Hollywood's redevelopment efforts don't end

there: new shops, restaurants, and art galleries open at a persistent clip, and the city has continually spiffed up its boardwalk—a wide pedestrian walkway along the beach—where local joggers are as commonplace as sun-seeking snowbirds from the north. On the coast of Hallandale, the beach is backed by older, towering condominiums. Inland, Hallandale has been trying to get some business from neighboring Aventura and Sunny Isles in Dade County with the development of the high-end Village at Gulfstream Park, a luxury retail arcade anchored by a reinvented casino and racetrack.

GETTING HERE AND AROUND

From Interstate 95, exit east on Sheridan Street or Hollywood Boulevard for Hollywood, or Hallandale Beach Boulevard for either Hollywood or Hallandale.

ESSENTIALS

Visitor Information Hollywood Community Redevelopment Agency.
☎ 954/924–2980 ⊕ www.visithollywoodfl.org.

EXPLORING

FAMILY

Fodor'sChoice

★

Art and Culture Center/Hollywood. The Center, which is southeast of Young Circle, has a great reputation for presenting übercool contemporary art exhibitions and providing the community with educational programming for adults and children. Check online for the latest exhibition schedule. ⊠ 1650 Harrison St. ☎ 954/921–3274 ⊕ www.artandculturecenter.org ☑ $7.

FAMILY **ArtsPark at Young Circle.** In the center of downtown Hollywood, this 10-acre urban park has promenades and green spaces, public art, a huge playground for kids, a state-of-the-art amphitheater, and spaces for educational workshops like weekly glassblowing and jewelry making. ⊠ 1 N. Young Cir. ☎ 954/921–3500 ⊕ www.visithollywoodfl.org/artspark.aspx.

Design Center of the Americas (DCOTA). Though access is typically reserved strictly to those in the design biz, the Design Center of the Americas still permits visitors to browse the myriad showrooms, which parade the latest and greatest in home furnishings and interior design. Note, however, that this is purely for inspiration as direct consumer sales are not permitted. ⊠ 1855 Griffin Rd., Dania Beach ☎ 954/920–7997 Ext. 240 ⊕ www.dcota.com.

FAMILY **West Lake Park and Anne Kolb Nature Center.** Grab a canoe or kayak, or take a 40-minute guided boat tour at this lakeside park on the Intracoastal Waterway. At 1,500 acres, it's one of Florida's largest urban nature facilities. Extensive boardwalks traverse mangrove wetlands that shelter endangered and threatened species. A 65-foot observation tower showcases the entire park. At the **Anne Kolb Nature Center,** there's a 3,500-gallon aquarium. The center's exhibit hall has interactive displays explaining the park's delicate ecosystem. ⊠ 1200 Sheridan St. ☎ 954/357–5161 ⊕ www.broward.org/parks/WestLakePark ☑ Park: weekdays free, weekends and holidays $1.50. Exhibit hall: $2.

BEACHES

FAMILY

Fodor'sChoice

★

Dr. Von D. Mizell-Eula Johnson State Park. Formerly known as John U. Lloyd Beach State Park, this 310-acre park was renamed Dr. Von D. Mizell-Eula Johnson State Park in honor of the duo who led efforts to change the "colored beach" into a state park in 1973 and create appropriate access for residents. Native sea grapes, gumbo-limbo trees, and other native plants offer shade. Nature trails and a marina are large draws; canoeing on Whiskey Creek is also popular. The beaches are excellent, but beware of mosquitoes in summer **Amenities:** parking (fee); toilets. **Best for:** solitude; sunrise. ✉ *6503 N. Ocean Dr.* ☎ *954/923-2833* ⊕ *www.floridastateparks.org/park/Mizell-Johnson* 🗺 *$6 per vehicle for 2–8 passengers; $4 for lone driver.*

FAMILY

Fodor'sChoice

★

Hollywood Beach and Broadwalk. The name might be Hollywood, but there's nothing hip or chic about **Hollywood North Beach Park,** which sits at the north end of Hollywood (State Road A1A and Sheridan Street), before the 2½-mile pedestrian Broadwalk begins. And this is a good thing. It's an easygoing place to enjoy the sun, sand, and sea. The year-round **Dog Beach of Hollywood,** between Pershing and Custer streets, allows canine companions to join the fun a few days a week. Walk along the **Broadwalk** for a throwback to the 1950s, with mom-and-pop stores and ice-cream parlors, where elderly couples go for long strolls, and families build sand castles. The popular stretch has spiffy features like a pristine pedestrian walkway, a concrete bike path, a crushed-shell jogging path, an 18-inch decorative wall separating the Broadwalk from the sand, and places to shower off after a dip. Expect to hear French spoken throughout Hollywood since its beaches are a getaway for Quebecois. **Amenities:** food and drink; lifeguards; showers; parking (fee); toilets. **Best for:** sunrise; swimming; walking. ✉ *320 Johnson St.* ⊕ *www.visithollywoodfl.org* 🗺 *Parking in public lots $1.50 per hr weekdays, $2 per hr weekends.*

5

WHERE TO EAT

$$

AMERICAN

FAMILY

Fodor'sChoice

★

✕ Jaxson's Ice Cream Parlour and Restaurant. This mid-century landmark whips up malts, shakes, and jumbo sundaes from ice cream that is made on-site daily. Owner Monroe Udell's trademarked Kitchen Sink— a small sink full of ice cream, topped by sparklers—is a real hoot for parties. **Known for:** license-plate decor; house-made ice cream; salads and sandwiches for those without a sweet tooth. 💲 *Average main: $15* ✉ *128 S. Federal Hwy., Dania Beach* ☎ *954/923-4445* ⊕ *www.jaxsonsicecream.com.*

$$$

GREEK

FAMILY

✕ Taverna Opa. It's a Greek throwdown every night at this Hollywood institution. Expect a lively night of great eats (including amazing hot and cold meze, wood-fire-grilled meats and seafood), table-top dancing, and awkward moments (especially when suburban dads with two left feet decide to get in on the act), and lots of wine to make it all okay. **Known for:** location near Water Taxi stop; louder atmosphere as the night wears on; menu of Greek favorites. 💲 *Average main: $29* ✉ *410 N. Ocean Dr.* ☎ *954/929-4010* ⊕ *www.tavernaopa.com.*

WHERE TO STAY

$$$
RESORT
FAMILY
Fodor's Choice
★
Margaritaville Beach Resort. The funky boardwalk of Hollywood Beach has a tropical destination inspired by Jimmy Buffett's lifelong search for paradise. **Pros:** oceanfront location; fun water activities; daily live entertainment. **Cons:** the surrounding area isn't very upscale; touristy vibe; must be a Jimmy Buffett fan. $ *Rooms from: $349* ✉ *1111 N. Ocean Dr.* ☎ *954/874–4444* ⊕ *www.margaritavillehollywoodbeachresort.com* ↘ *349 rooms* ⦿ *No meals.*

$$$
HOTEL
Seminole Hard Rock Hotel & Casino. On the industrial flatlands of western Hollywood, the Seminole Hard Rock Hotel & Casino is a magnet for folks looking for Las Vegas–style entertainment casinos that never close, clubbing, and hedonism. **Pros:** limitless entertainment; solid bars and restaurants. **Cons:** in an unsavory neighborhood; no tourist sights in close proximity; rental car necessary. $ *Rooms from: $399* ✉ *1 Seminole Way* ☎ *866/502–7529* ⊕ *www.seminolehardrockhollywood.com* ↘ *469 rooms* ⦿ *No meals.*

NIGHTLIFE

Hollywood may have a sleepy, small-town feel on the east side, but the Seminole Hard Rock Hotel & Casino brings a twist of Vegas to the west.

Fodor's Choice
★
Seminole Hard Rock Hotel & Casino. Seminole Hard Rock Hotel & Casino is a Vegas-inspired gaming and entertainment complex in a fairly forlorn area of Hollywood. Once inside the Hard Rock fortress, you'll feel the excitement immediately. In addition to the AAA Four Diamond hotel, there's a monster casino, a 5,500-seat concert venue (Hard Rock Live), plus dozens of restaurants, bars, and nightclubs. ■TIP→ The Seminole Hard Rock Hotel & Casino is not to be confused with its neighbor, the Seminole Classic Casino. ✉ *1 Seminole Way* ☎ *866/502–7529* ⊕ *www. seminolehardrockhollywood.com.*

PALM BEACH AND THE TREASURE COAST

WELCOME TO PALM BEACH AND THE TREASURE COAST

TOP REASONS TO GO

★ **Exquisite resorts:** Two grandes dames, The Breakers and the Boca Raton Resort & Club, perpetually draw the rich, the famous, and anyone else who can afford the luxury. The Eau Palm Beach and Four Seasons sparkle with service fit for royalty.

★ **Beautiful beaches:** From Jupiter, where dogs run free, to Stuart's tubular waves, to the broad stretches of sand in Delray Beach and Boca Raton, swimmers, surfers, sunbathers—and sea turtles looking for a place to hatch their eggs—all find happiness.

★ **Top-notch golf:** The Champion Course and re-envisioned Fazio Course at PGA National Resort & Spa are world renowned; pros sharpen up at PGA Village.

★ **Horse around:** Wellington, with its popular polo season, is often called the winter equestrian capital of the world.

★ **Excellent fishing:** The Atlantic Ocean, teeming with kingfish, sailfish, and wahoo, is a treasure chest for anglers.

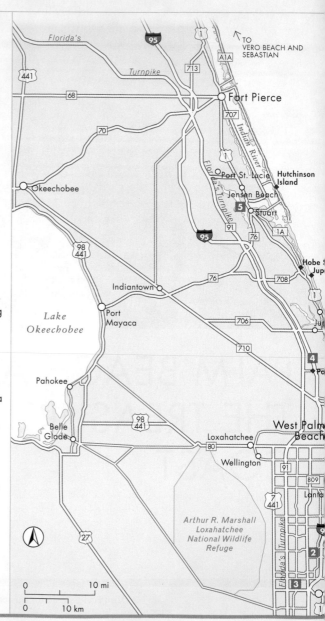

1 **Palm Beach.** With Gatsby-era architecture, stone-and-stucco estates, and extravagant dining, Palm Beach is a must-see for travelers to the area. Plan to spend time on Worth Avenue, a collection of more than 200 chic shops, and at Whitehall, the palatial retreat for Palm Beach's founder, Henry Flagler. West Palm Beach and its environs, including Lake Worth, are bustling with their own identities. Culture fans have plenty to cheer about with the Kravis Center and Norton Museum of Art; sports enthusiasts will have a ball golfing or boating or catching a spring-training game at the new stadium in West Palm Beach; and kids love Lion Country Safari.

2 **Delray Beach.** Its lively downtown, with galleries, independent boutiques, and trendy restaurants blocks from the ocean, is perfect for strolling. The Tennis Center draws the Love-Love crowds. To the west is the unique Morikami Museum and Japanese Gardens.

3 **Boca Raton.** An abundance of modern shopping plazas mix with historic buildings from the 1920s, masterpieces by renowned architect Addison Mizner. Parks line much of the oceanfront.

4 **North County.** Palm Beach Gardens, Jupiter, quaint Juno Beach, and Tequesta are more laid-back cousins to the areas south, with country clubs, newer malls, and family-oriented activities at the baseball stadium subbing for nightlife here. It's a golfer's paradise with PGA courses that make the pros.

GETTING ORIENTED

This diverse region extends 120 miles from laid-back Sebastian to tony Boca Raton. The area's glitzy epicenter, Palm Beach, attracts socialites, the well-heeled, and interested onlookers. The northernmost cities are only about 100 miles from Orlando, making that area an ideal choice for families wanting some beach time to go with their visit to Mickey Mouse. Delightfully funky Delray Beach is only an hour north of Miami. The Intracoastal Waterway runs parallel to the ocean and transforms from a canal to a tidal lagoon separating islands from the mainland, starting with Palm Beach and moving northward to Singer Island (Palm Beach Shores and Riviera Beach), Jupiter Island, Hutchinson Island (Stuart, Jensen Beach, and Fort Pierce), and Orchid Island (Vero Beach and Sebastian).

5 **Treasure Coast.** The area north of Palm Beach county—from Stuart and beyond—remains blissfully low-key, with fishing towns, spring-training stadiums, and ecotourism attractions until you hit the cosmopolitan—yet understated—Vero Beach.

6

Updated by
Jan Norris

A golden stretch of the Atlantic shore, the Palm Beach area resists categorization, and for good reason: the territory stretching south to Boca Raton, appropriately coined the Gold Coast, defines old-world glamour and new-age sophistication.

To the north you'll uncover the comparatively undeveloped Treasure Coast—liberally sprinkled with seaside gems and wide-open spaces along the road awaiting your discovery. Speaking of discovery, its moniker came from the 1715 sinking of a Spanish fleet that dumped gold, jewels, and silver in the waters; today the *Urca de Lima,* one of the original 11 ships and now an undersea "museum," can be explored by scuba divers.

Altogether, there's a delightful disparity between Palm Beach, pulsing with old-money wealth, and under-the-radar Hutchinson Island. Seductive as the gorgeous beaches, eclectic dining, and leisurely pursuits can be, you should also take advantage of flourishing commitments to historic preservation and the arts, as town after town yields intriguing museums, galleries, theaters, and gardens.

Palm Beach, proud of its status as America's first luxe resort destination and still glimmering with its trademark Mediterranean-revival mansions, manicured hedges, and highbrow shops, can rule supreme as the focal point for your sojourn any time of year. From there, head off in one of two directions: south toward Delray Beach and Boca Raton along an especially scenic estate-dotted route known as A1A, or back north to the beautiful barrier islands of the Treasure Coast. For rustic inland activities such as bass fishing and biking atop the dike around Lake Okeechobee, head west.

PLANNING

WHEN TO GO

The weather is optimal from November through May, but the trade-off is that roads, hotels, and restaurants are more crowded and prices higher. If the scene is what you're after, try the early weeks of December when the "season" isn't yet in full swing. However, be warned that after Easter, the crowd relocates to the Hamptons, and Palm Beach feels like another universe. For some, that's a blessing—and a great time to take advantage of lower summer lodging rates and dining deals—but you'll need to bring your tolerance for heat, humidity, and afternoon downpours.

GETTING HERE AND AROUND

AIR TRAVEL

Palm Beach International Airport is in West Palm, but it's possible (and sometimes cheaper) to fly to Fort Lauderdale, Miami, or Orlando. Do rent a car if you plan on exploring. Scenic Route A1A, also called Ocean Boulevard or Ocean Drive, depending on where you are, ventures out onto the barrier islands. Interstate 95 runs parallel to U.S. 1, a main north–south thoroughfare in the region (also known as Federal Highway), but a few miles inland.

Airport Palm Beach International Airport (*PBI*). ✉ *1000 Turnage Blvd., West Palm Beach* ✛ *From I–95, use the airport flyover exit; from Florida's Tpke., use the Southern Blvd. exit and drive east to the airport exit* ☎ *561/471-7420* ⊕ *www.pbia.org.*

Airport Transfers SuperShuttle. ☎ *800/258-3826* ⊕ *www.supershuttle.com.*

BUS TRAVEL

The county's bus service, Palm Tran, runs two routes (Nos. 44 and 40) that offer daily service connecting the airport, the Tri-Rail stop near it, and locations in central West Palm Beach. A network of 34 routes joins towns all across the area; it's $5 for a day pass. The free Downtown Trolley connects the West Palm Beach Amtrak station and the Tri-Rail stop in West Palm on its Green Line. Its Yellow Line makes continuous loops down Clematis Street, the city's main stretch of restaurants and watering holes interspersed with stores, and through CityPlace, a shopping-dining-theater district, and to the Kravis Center. Hop on and off at any of the stops. The trolley's Yellow Line runs Sunday to Wednesday 11–9 and Thursday to Saturday 11–11. The trolley's Green Line, which stretches farther east, west, and south, and connects to Tri-Rail and Amtrak, runs weekdays 7–7, Saturday 9–7, and Sunday 11–7. A seasonal Blue Line, operating from fall to spring, runs from downtown West Palm Beach to Northwood Village, and the Palm Beach Outlets mall. Times are Thursday–Saturday, 11–10.

Contacts Downtown Trolley. ☎ *561/833-8873* ⊕ *www.downtownwpb.com/trolley/.* **Palm Tran.** ☎ *561/841-4287* ⊕ *www.pbcgov.com/palmtran.*

6

TAXI TRAVEL

Several taxi companies serve the area, including the Southeastern Florida Transportation Group. Also available are limousine services to Palm Beach or out of county. The ride-sharing services Uber (⊕ *www.uber. com*) and Lyft (⊕ *www.lyft.com*) are accessible as apps from your phone.

Contacts AmeriCab. ☎ *561/337–7777* ⊕ *www.americabtaxi.com.* **Limos of Palm Beach.** ☎ *561/459–7128* ⊕ *www.limosofpb.com.* **Palm Beach Yellow Cab.** ☎ *561/721–2222* ⊕ *www.palmbeachyellowcab.com.* **Southeastern Florida Transportation Group.** ☎ *561/777–7777* ⊕ *www.yellowcabflorida.com.*

TRAIN TRAVEL

Amtrak stops daily in West Palm Beach. The station is at the same location as the Tri-Rail stop, so the same free shuttle, the Downtown Trolley, is available (via the trolley's Green Line).

Tri-Rail Commuter Service is a rail system with 18 stops altogether between West Palm Beach and Miami; tickets can be purchased at each stop, and a one-way trip from the first to the last point is $6.90 weekdays, $5 weekends. Three stations—West Palm Beach, Lake Worth, and Boca—have free shuttles to their downtowns, and taxis are on call at others.

A new high-speed train line, Brightline began running in late summer, 2017. It will connect downtown Miami to Fort Lauderdale and West Palm Beach in 30 and 60 minutes respectively.

Contacts Amtrak. ☎ *800/872–7245* ⊕ *www.amtrak.com.* **Brightline.** ⊕ *gobrightline.com.* **Tri-Rail.** ☎ *800/874–7245* ⊕ *www.tri-rail.com.*

HOTELS

Palm Beach has a number of smaller hotels in addition to the famous Breakers. Lower-priced hotels and bed-and-breakfasts can be found in West Palm Beach, Palm Beach Gardens, and Lake Worth. Heading south, the ocean-side town of Manalapan has the Eau Palm Beach Resort & Spa. The Seagate Hotel & Spa sparkles in Delray Beach, and the posh Boca Beach Club lines the superlative swath of shoreline in Boca Raton. In the opposite direction there's the PGA National Resort & Spa, and on the opposite side of town on the ocean is the Marriott on Singer Island, a well-kept secret for spacious, sleek suites. Even farther north, Vero Beach has a collection of luxury boutique hotels, as well as more modest options along the Treasure Coast. To the west, towns close to Lake Okeechobee offer country-inn accommodations geared to bass-fishing pros.

RESTAURANTS

Numerous elegant establishments offer upscale American, Continental, and international cuisine, but the area also is chock-full of casual waterfront spots serving affordable burgers and fresh seafood feasts. Snapper and grouper are especially popular here, along with the ubiquitous shrimp. Happy hours and early-bird menus, Florida hallmarks, typically entice the budget-minded with several dinner entrées at reduced prices offered during certain hours, usually before 5 or 6.

Hotel and restaurant reviews have been shortened. For full information, visit Fodors.com.

WHAT IT COSTS				
	$	$$	$$$	$$$$
Restaurants	under $15	$15–$20	$21–$30	over $30
Hotels	under $200	$200–$300	$301–$400	over $400

Restaurant prices are the average cost of a main course at dinner or, if dinner is not served, at lunch. Hotel prices are the lowest cost of a standard double room in high season.

VISITOR INFORMATION

Contacts Discover the Palm Beaches. ✉ *1555 Palm Beach Lakes Blvd., Suite 800, West Palm Beach* ☎ *561/233–3000* ⊕ *www.palmbeachfl.com.*

PALM BEACH

70 miles north of Miami, off I–95.

Long reigning as the place where the crème de la crème go to shake off winter's chill, Palm Beach, which is actually on a barrier island, continues to be a seasonal hotbed of platinum-grade consumption. The town celebrated its 100th birthday in 2011, and there's no competing with its historic social supremacy. It's been the winter address for heirs of the iconic Rockefeller, Vanderbilt, Colgate, Post, Kellogg, and Kennedy families. Even newer power brokers, with names like Kravis, Peltz, and Trump, are made to understand that strict laws govern everything from building to landscaping, and not so much as a pool awning gets added without a Town Council nod. Only three bridges allow entry, and huge tour buses are a no-no.

All this fabled ambience started with Henry Morrison Flagler, Florida's premier developer, and cofounder, along with John D. Rockefeller, of Standard Oil. No sooner did Flagler bring the railroad to Florida in the 1890s than he erected the famed Royal Poinciana and Breakers hotels. Rail access sent real-estate prices soaring, and ever since, princely sums have been forked over for personal stationery engraved with 33480, the zip code of Palm Beach (which didn't actually get its status as an independent municipality until 1911). Setting the tone in this town of unparalleled Florida opulence is the ornate architectural work of Addison Mizner, who began designing homes and public buildings here in the 1920s and whose Moorish-Gothic Mediterranean-revival style has influenced virtually all landmarks.

But the greater Palm Beach area is much larger and encompasses several communities on the mainland and to the north and south. To provide Palm Beach with servants and other workers, Flagler created an off-island community across the Intracoastal Waterway (also referred to as Lake Worth in these parts). West Palm Beach, now cosmopolitan and noteworthy in its own right, evolved into an economically vibrant business hub and a sprawling playground with some of the best nightlife and cultural attractions around, including the glittering Kravis Center for the Performing Arts, the region's principal entertainment venue. The mammoth Palm Beach County Judicial Center and Courthouse and the State Administrative Building underscore the breadth of the city's governmental and corporate activity.

The burgeoning equestrian development of Wellington, with its horse shows and polo matches, lies a little more than 10 miles west of downtown, and is the site of much of the county's growth.

Spreading southward from the Palm Beach/West Palm Beach nucleus set between the two bridges that flow from Royal Poinciana Way and Royal Palm Way into Flagler Drive on the mainland are small cities like Lake Worth, with its charming artsy center, Lantana, and Manalapan (home to the fabulous Eau Palm Beach resort, formerly the Ritz-Carlton Palm Beach). All three have turf that's technically on the same island as Palm Beach, and at its bottom edge across the inlet is Boynton Beach, a 20-minute drive from Worth Avenue.

GETTING HERE AND AROUND

Palm Beach is 70 miles north of Miami (a 90-minute trip with traffic). To access Palm Beach off Interstate 95, exit east at Southern Boulevard, Belvedere Road, or Okeechobee Boulevard. To drive from Palm Beach to Lake Worth, Lantana, Manalapan, and Boynton Beach, head south on Ocean Boulevard/Route A1A; Lake Worth is roughly 6 miles south, and Boynton is another 6. Similarly, to reach them from West Palm Beach, take U.S. 1 or Interstate 95. To travel between Palm Beach and Singer Island, you must cross over to West Palm before returning to the beach. Once there, go north on U.S. 1 and then cut over on Blue Heron Boulevard/Route 708. If coming straight from the airport or somewhere farther west, take Interstate 95 up to the same exit and proceed east. The main drag in Palm Beach Gardens is PGA Boulevard/Route 786, which is 4 miles north on U.S. 1 and Interstate 95; A1A merges with it as it exits the top part of Singer Island. Continue on A1A to reach Juno Beach and Jupiter.

TOURS

FAMILY **DivaDuck Amphibious Tours.** Running 75 minutes, these duck tours go in and out of the water on USCG-inspected amphibious vessels around West Palm Beach and Palm Beach. The tours depart two or three times most days for $29 per person (adults); there are discounts for seniors and kids. ⊠ *CityPlace, 600 S. Rosemary Ave., West Palm Beach* ✦ *Corner of Hibiscus St. and Rosemary Ave.* ☎ 877/844–4188 ⊕ *www. divaduck.com.*

Island Living Tours. Book a private mansion-viewing excursion around Palm Beach, and hear the storied past of the island's upper crust. Owner Leslie Diver also hosts an Antique Row Tour and a Worth Avenue Shopping Tour. Vehicle tours are 90 minutes for the "Best of Palm Beach" and 2½ hours for a more extensive architecture and history tour. Costs are from $60 to $150 per person, depending on the vehicle used. Leslie also runs 90-minute bicycle tours through Palm Beach ($45, not including bike rental). One bicycle tour explores the Estate Section and historic Worth Avenue; another explores the island's lesser known North End. Call in advance for location and to reserve. ☎ 561/868–7944 ⊕ *www.islandlivingpb.com.*

Draped in European elegance, The Breakers in Palm Beach sits on 140 acres along the oceanfront.

EXPLORING

PALM BEACH

Most streets around major attractions and commercial zones have free parking as well as metered spaces. If you can stake out a place between a Rolls-Royce and a Bentley, do so, but beware of the "Parking by Permit Only" signs, as a $50 ticket might take the shine off your spot. Better yet, if you plan to spend an entire afternoon strolling Worth Avenue, park in the Apollo lot behind Tiffany's midway off Worth on Hibiscus; some stores will validate your parking ticket.

TOP ATTRACTIONS

Fodor'sChoice
★ **The Breakers.** Built by Henry Flagler in 1896 and rebuilt by his descendants after a 1925 fire, this magnificent Italian Renaissance–style resort helped launch Florida tourism with its Gilded Age opulence, attracting influential wealthy Northerners to the state. The hotel, still owned by Flagler's heirs, is a must-see even if you aren't staying here. Walk through the 200-foot-long lobby, which has soaring arched ceilings painted by 72 Italian artisans and hung with crystal chandeliers. Meet for a drink at the HMF, one of the most beautiful bars in the state. ■TIP→ Book a pampering spa treatment or dine at the popular oceanfront Seafood Bar that was renovated in 2016. The $25 parking fee is waived if you spend at least $25 anywhere in the hotel (just have your ticket validated). ⊠ *1 S. County Rd.* ☎ *561/655–6611* ⊕ *www. thebreakers.com.*

Fodor'sChoice
★ **Henry Morrison Flagler Museum.** The worldly sophistication of Florida's Gilded Age lives on at Whitehall, the plush 55-room "marble palace" Henry Flagler commissioned in 1901 for his third wife, Mary Lily

Kenan. Architects John Carrère and Thomas Hastings were instructed to create the finest home imaginable—and they outdid themselves. Whitehall rivals the grandeur of European palaces and has an entrance hall with a baroque ceiling similar to Louis XIV's Versailles. Here you'll see original furnishings; a hidden staircase Flagler used to sneak from his bedroom to the billiards room; an art collection; a 1,200-pipe organ; and Florida East Coast Railway exhibits, along with Flagler's personal railcar, No. 91, showcased in an 8,000-square-foot beaux arts–style pavilion behind the mansion. Docent-led tours and audio tours are included with admission. The museum's Café des Beaux-Arts, open from Thanksgiving through mid-April, offers a Gilded Age–style early afternoon tea for $40 (11:30 am–2:30 pm); the price includes museum admission. ⊠ *1 Whitehall Way* ☎ *561/655–2833* ⊕ *www.flaglermuseum.us* ⌦ *$18.*

Fodor's Choice
★
Worth Avenue. Called "the Avenue" by Palm Beachers, this half-mile-long street is synonymous with exclusive shopping. Nostalgia lovers recall an era when faces or names served as charge cards, purchases were delivered home before customers returned from lunch, and bills were sent directly to private accountants. Times have changed, but a stroll amid the Spanish-accented buildings, many designed by Addison Mizner, offers a tantalizing taste of the island's ongoing commitment to elegant consumerism. Explore the labyrinth of nine pedestrian "vias" off of each side that wind past boutiques, tiny plazas, bubbling fountains, and bougainvillea-festooned balconies; this is where the smaller, unique shops are. The Worth Avenue Association holds historic walking tours on Wednesdays at 11 am during "season" (after Thanksgiving to late April). The $10 fee benefits local nonprofit organizations. ⊠ *Worth Ave., between Cocoanut Row and S. Ocean Blvd.* ☎ *561/659–6909* ⊕ *www.worth-avenue.com.*

WORTH NOTING

Bethesda-by-the-Sea. This Gothic-style Episcopal church had a claim to fame upon its creation in 1926: it was built by the first Protestant congregation in southeast Florida. Church lecture tours, covering Bethesda's history, architecture, and more, are offered at 12:15 on the second and fourth Sunday each month from September to mid-May (excluding December) and at 11:15 on the fourth Sunday each month from end of May to August. Also notable are the annual Boar's Head and Yule Log festivals in January. Adjacent is the formal, ornamental Cluett Memorial Garden. ⊠ *141 S. County Rd.* ☎ *561/655–4554* ⊕ *www.bbts.org* ⌦ *Free.*

El Solano. No Palm Beach mansion better represents the town's luminous legacy than the Spanish-style home built by Addison Mizner as his own residence in 1925. Mizner later sold El Solano to Harold Vanderbilt, and the property was long a favorite among socialites for parties and photo shoots. Vanderbilt held many a gala fund-raiser here. Beatle John Lennon and his wife, Yoko Ono, bought it less than a year before Lennon's death. It's still privately owned and not open to the public, but it's well worth a drive-by on any self-guided Palm Beach mansion tour. ⊠ *720 S. Ocean Blvd.*

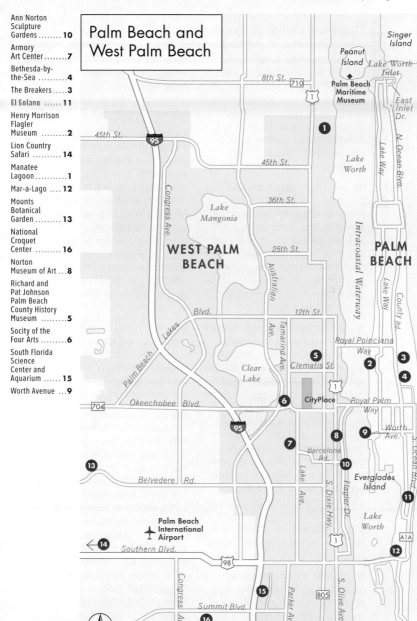

Palm Beach and West Palm Beach

6

CLOSE UP

The Mansions of Palm Beach

Whether you aspire to be a former president (Kennedy), a current one (Trump), or a rock legend (John Lennon, Rod Stewart, Jimmy Buffett—all onetime or current Palm Beach residents)—no trip to the island is complete without gawking at the megamansions lining its perfectly manicured streets.

No one is more associated with how the island took shape than Addison Mizner, architect extraordinaire and society darling of the 1920s. But what people may not know is that a "fab four" was really the force behind the residential streets as they appear today: Mizner, of course, plus Maurice Fatio, Marion Sims Wyeth, and John Volk.

The four architects dabbled in different genres, some more so than others, but the unmissable style is Mediterranean revival, a Palm Beach hallmark mix of stucco walls, Spanish red-tile roofs, Italianate towers, Moorish-Gothic carvings, and the uniquely Floridian use of coquina, a grayish porous limestone made of coral rock with fossil-like imprints of shells. As for Mizner himself, he had quite the repertoire of signature elements, including using differently sized and shaped windows on one facade, blue tile work inside and out, and tiered roof lines (instead of one straight-sloping panel across, having several sections overlap like scales on a fish).

The majority of preserved estates are clustered in three sections: along Worth Avenue; the few blocks of South County Road after crossing Worth and the streets shooting off it; and the 5-mile stretch of South Ocean Boulevard from Barton Avenue to near Phipps Ocean Park, where the condos begin cropping up.

If 10 miles of riding on a bike while cars zip around you isn't intimidating, the two-wheeled trip may be the best way to fully take in the beauty of the mansions and surrounding scenery. Many hotels have bicycles for guest use. Another option is the dependable Palm Beach Bicycle Trail Shop (☎ 561/659–4583 ⊕ www.palmbeach-bicycle.com). Otherwise, driving is a good alternative. Just be mindful that Ocean Boulevard is a one-lane road and the only route on the island to cities like Lake Worth and Manalapan, so you can't go too slowly, especially at peak travel times.

If gossip is more your speed, in-the-know concierges rely on Leslie Diver's "Island Living Tours" (☎ 561/868–7944 ⊕ www.islandlivingpb.com); she's one of the town's leading experts on architecture *and* dish, both past and present.

Top 10 Self-Guided Stops: (1) Casa de Leoni (✉ *450 Worth Ave.*, Addison Mizner); (2) Villa des Cygnes (✉ *456 Worth Ave.*, Addison Mizner and Marion Sims Wyeth); (3) 17 Golfview Road (Marion Sims Wyeth); (4) 220 and 252 El Bravo Way (John Volk); (5) 126 South Ocean Boulevard (Marion Sims Wyeth); (6) El Solano (✉ *720 S. Ocean Blvd.*, Addison Mizner); (7) Casa Nana (✉ *780 S. Ocean Blvd.*, Addison Mizner); (8) 920 and 930 South Ocean Boulevard (Maurice Fatio); (9) Mar-a-Lago (✉ *1100 S. Ocean Blvd.*, Joseph Urban); (10) Il Palmetto (✉ *1500 S. Ocean Blvd.*, Maurice Fatio).

—Dorothea Hunter Sönne

Mar-a-Lago. Breakfast-food heiress Marjorie Merriweather Post commissioned a Hollywood set designer to create Ocean Boulevard's famed Mar-a-Lago, a 114-room, 110,000-square-foot Mediterranean-revival palace. Its 75-foot Italianate tower is visible from many areas of Palm Beach and from across the Intracoastal Waterway in West Palm Beach. Its notable owner, President Donald Trump, has turned it into a private membership club and has realized Marjorie Post's dream of turning the estate into a presidential retreat. Tourists have to enjoy the view from the car window or bicycle seat, but even the gates are impressive. ⌂ *1100 S. Ocean Blvd.* ☎ *561/832–2600* ⊕ *www. maralagoclub.com.*

FAMILY **Society of the Four Arts.** Despite widespread misconceptions of its members-only exclusivity, this privately endowed institution—founded in 1936 to encourage appreciation of art, music, drama, and literature—is funded for public enjoyment. The Esther B. O'Keeffe gallery building artfully melds an exhibition hall that houses traveling exhibits with a 700-seat theater. A library designed by prominent Mizner-peer Maurice Fatio, a children's library, a botanical garden, and the Philip Hulitar Sculpture Garden round out the facilities and are open daily. A complete schedule of programming is available on the society's website. ⌂ *2 Four Arts Plaza* ☎ *561/655–7227* ⊕ *www.fourarts.org* ⌂ *$5 gallery; special program costs vary.*

WEST PALM BEACH

Long considered Palm Beach's less privileged stepsister, West Palm Beach has come into its own over the past 35 years, and just in this millennium the $30 million Centennial Square waterfront complex at the eastern end of Clematis Street, with piers, a pavilion, and an amphitheater, has transformed West Palm into an attractive, easy-to-walk downtown area—not to mention there's the Downtown Trolley that connects the shopping-and-entertainment mecca CityPlace with restaurant-and-lounge-lined Clematis Street. The recently opened Palm Beach Outlet Mall gives options to those looking for tony bargains. West Palm is especially well regarded for its arts scene, with unique museums and performance venues; a number of public art projects have appeared around the city. New attractions, such as the Manatee Lagoon, where the gentle sea creatures are visible up close in winter by the dozens, and a new stadium and sports complex for spring-training games, offer families many options while vacationing.

The city's outskirts, vast flat stretches with strip malls and car dealerships, may not inspire, but are worth driving through to reach attractions scattered around the southern and western reaches. Several sites are especially rewarding for children and other animal and nature lovers.

TOP ATTRACTIONS

Ann Norton Sculpture Gardens. This landmarked complex is a testament to the creative genius of the late American sculptor Ann Weaver Norton (1905–82), who was the second wife of Norton Museum founder, industrialist Ralph H. Norton. A set of art galleries in the studio and main house where she lived is surrounded by 2 acres of gardens with 300 species of rare palm trees, eight brick megaliths, a monumental

The Armory Art Center in West Palm Beach helps students of all ages create works of art in various mediums.

figure in Norwegian granite, and plantings designed to attract native birds. ✉ *253 Barcelona Rd., West Palm Beach* ☎ *561/832–5328* ⊕ *www.ansg.org* ✉ *$10* ⊙ *Closed Aug.*

FAMILY **Lion Country Safari.** Drive your own vehicle along 4 miles of paved roads through a cageless zoo with free-roaming animals (chances are you'll have a giraffe nudging at your window) and then let loose in a 55-acre fun-land with camel rides, bird feedings, and a pontoon-boat cruise past islands with monkeys. A CD included with admission narrates the winding trek past white rhinos, zebras, and ostriches grouped into exhibits like Gir Forest that's modeled after a sanctuary in India and has native twisted-horned blackbuck antelope and water buffalo. (For obvious reasons, lions are fenced off, and no convertibles or pets are allowed.) Aside from dozens more up-close critter encounters after debarking, including a petting zoo, kids can go paddleboating, do a round of mini-golf, climb aboard carnival rides, or have a splash in a 4,000-square-foot aquatic playground (some extra fees apply). ✉ *2003 Lion Country Safari Rd., at Southern Blvd. W, West Palm Beach* ☎ *561/793–1084* ⊕ *www.lioncountrysafari.com* ✉ *$35, $7 parking.*

FAMILY

Fodor's Choice

★

Manatee Lagoon. Once a casual spot next to the local electric plant's discharge waters, this center celebrating the manatee—South Florida's popular winter visitors—opened in 2016 at a spot where the peaceful creatures naturally congregate. The airy, two-story facility is surrounded by wraparound decks to accommodate sea-cow spotters from fall to spring. Educational, interactive displays tell the story of this once-endangered species. A long deck along the seawall leads to picnic pavilions from where you can watch the action at nearby Peanut Island

and the Port of Palm Beach. Free admission makes it group-friendly; a live "manatee cam" shows manatee counts before you go. ⊠ *6000 N. Flagler Dr., West Palm Beach* ✛ *Entrance is on Flagler Dr., via 58th St. east of U.S. 1 and south of the Port of Palm Beach flyover* ☎ *561/626–2833* ⊕ *www.visitmanateelagoon.com* ✉ *Free* ⊙ *Closed Mon.*

Mounts Botanical Garden. The oldest public green space in the county is, unbelievably, across the road from the West Palm Beach airport; but the planes are the last thing you notice while walking around and relaxing amid the nearly 14 acres of exotic trees, rain-forest flora, and butterfly and water gardens. The gift shop contains a selection of rare gardening books on tropical climes. Frequent plant sales are held here, and numerous plant societies with international ties hold meetings open to the public in the auditorium. Experts in tropical edible and ornamental plants are on staff. ⊠ *531 N. Military Trail, West Palm Beach* ☎ *561/233–1757* ⊕ *www.mounts.org* ✉ *$5 (suggested donation).*

Norton Museum of Art. Constructed in 1941 by steel magnate Ralph H. Norton and his wife, Elizabeth, the museum has grown to become one of the most impressive in South Florida with an extensive collection of 19th- and 20th-century American and European paintings—including works by Picasso, Monet, Matisse, Pollock, Cassatt, and O'Keeffe—plus Chinese art, earlier European art, and photography. To accommodate a growing collection, the museum is undergoing an extensive expansion to include 12,000 additional square feet of gallery space in a new west wing, event spaces, and a great hall. A garden will also be incorporated into the space. Until the opening of the expansion, which is expected in 2018, admission is free; until then, the museum is only open in the afternoon. ■TIP→ The popular Art After Dark, Thursday from 5 to 9 pm, is a gathering spot for art lovers, with wine and music in the galleries. ⊠ *1451 S. Olive Ave., West Palm Beach* ☎ *561/832–5196* ⊕ *www.norton.org* ✉ *Free* ⊙ *Closed Mon.*

WORTH NOTING

Armory Art Center. Built by the Works Progress Administration (WPA) in 1939, this art deco facility is now a nonprofit art school hosting rotating exhibitions and art classes throughout the year. The Armory Art Center became an institution for art instruction when the Norton Museum Gallery and School of Art dropped the latter part of its name in 1986 and discontinued art-instruction classes. ⊠ *1700 Parker Ave., West Palm Beach* ☎ *561/832–1776* ⊕ *www.armoryart.org* ✉ *Free.*

National Croquet Center. The world's largest croquet complex, the 10-acre center is also the headquarters for the U.S. Croquet Association. Vast expanses of orderly lawns are the stage for fierce competitions. There's also a clubhouse with a pro shop and the Croquet Grille, with verandas for dining and viewing (armchair enthusiasts can enjoy the games for no charge). You don't have to be a member to try your hand out on the lawns, and on Saturday morning at 10 am, there's a free group lesson with an introduction to the game, and open play; call in advance to reserve a spot. ⊠ *700 Florida Mango Rd., at Summit Blvd., West Palm Beach* ☎ *561/478–2300* ⊕ *www.croquetnational.com* ✉ *Center free; full day of croquet $30.*

Richard and Pat Johnson Palm Beach County History Museum. A beautifully restored 1916 courthouse in downtown opened its doors in 2008 as the permanent home of the Historical Society of Palm Beach County's collection of artifacts and records dating back before the town's start—a highlight is furniture and decorative objects from Mizner Industries (a real treat since many of his mansions are not open to the public). ⊠ *300 N. Dixie Hwy., West Palm Beach* ☎ *561/832–4164* ⊕ *www. historicalsocietypbc.org* ⧉ *Free* ☉ *Closed Sun.*

FAMILY **South Florida Science Center and Aquarium.** Both fresh- and saltwater aquariums greet the curious at this interactive, family-friendly science museum. Permanent exhibits of moon and Mars rocks and meteorites, a giant sphere with global animation projection for Earth sciences, and Everglades conservation exhibit teach while entertaining. A planetarium with daily themed shows and a conservation 9-hole mini-golf course designed by Gary Fazio and Jim Niklaus are popular with all ages and carry separate admission charges. ⊠ *4801 Dreher Trail N, West Palm Beach* ☎ *561/832–1988* ⊕ *www.sfsciencecenter.org* ⧉ *$16.95; planetarium $5; mini-golf $7.*

LAKE WORTH

For years, tourists looked here mainly for inexpensive lodging and easy access to Palm Beach, since a bridge leads from the mainland to a barrier island with Lake Worth's beach. Now Lake Worth has grown into an arts community, with several blocks of restaurants, nightclubs, shops, and galleries, making this a worthy destination on its own.

TOP ATTRACTIONS

Museum of Polo and Hall of Fame. The history of the sport of kings is displayed in a time line here, with other exhibits focusing on polo ponies, star players, trophies, and a look at how mallets are made. It provides a great introduction to the surprisingly exciting, hoof-pounding sport that is played live on Sundays from January to April in nearby Wellington. ⊠ *9011 Lake Worth Rd., Lake Worth* ☎ *561/969–3210* ⊕ *www. polomuseum.com* ⧉ *Free (donations accepted)* ☉ *Closed Sun. Closed Sat. May–Dec.*

LANTANA

Lantana—just a bit farther south from Palm Beach than Lake Worth—has inexpensive lodging and a bridge connecting the town to its own beach on a barrier island. Tucked between Lantana and Boynton Beach is **Manalapan,** a tiny but posh residential community.

BOYNTON BEACH

In 1884, when fewer than 50 settlers lived in the area, Nathan Boynton, a Civil War veteran from Michigan, paid $25 for 500 acres with a mile-long stretch of beachfront thrown in. How things have changed, with today's population at about 118,000 and property values still on an upswing. Far enough from Palm Beach to remain low-key, Boynton Beach has two parts, the mainland and the barrier island—the town of Ocean Ridge—connected by two bridges.

The posh Palm Beach area has its share of luxury villas on the water; many are Mediterranean in style.

TOP ATTRACTIONS

FAMILY **Arthur R. Marshall Loxahatchee National Wildlife Refuge.** The most robust part of the northern Everglades, this 221-square-mile refuge is one of two huge water-retention areas accounting for much of the "River of Grass" outside the national park near Miami. Start at the visitor center, which has fantastic interactive exhibits and videos like "Night Sounds of the Everglades" and an airboat simulator. From there, you can take a marsh trail to a 20-foot-high observation tower, or stroll a ½-mile boardwalk lined with educational signage through a dense cypress swamp. There are also guided nature walks (including some specifically for bird-watching), and there's great bass fishing (bring your own poles and bait) and a 5½-mile canoe and kayak trail loop (both can be rented from a kiosk by the fishing pier). ⊠ *10216 Lee Rd., off U.S. 441 between Rte. 804 and Rte. 806, Boynton Beach* ☎ *561/732–3684* ⊕ *www.fws.gov/refuge/arm_loxahatchee/* ⊠ *$5 per vehicle; $1 per pedestrian or bicyclist.*

BEACHES

PALM BEACH

Phipps Ocean Park. About 2 miles south of "Billionaire's Row" on Ocean Boulevard sits this public ocean-side park, with two metered parking lots separated by a fire station. There are four entry points to the beach, but the north side is better for beachgoers. At the southern entrance, there is a six-court tennis facility. The beach is narrow and has natural rock formations dotting the shoreline, making it ideal for snorkelers. There are picnic tables and grills on-site, as well as the Little Red

Schoolhouse, an 1886 landmark that hosts educational workshops for local kids. If a long walk floats your boat, venture north to see the mega-mansions, but don't go too far inland, because private property starts at the high-tide line. Parking is metered, and time limits strictly enforced. There's a two-hour time limit for free parking—but read the meter carefully: it's valid only during certain hours at some spots. **Amenities:** parking (no fee); toilets; showers; lifeguards. **Best for:** walking; solitude. ⊠ *2201 S. Ocean Blvd.* ☎ *561/838–5400 Ext. 8, 561/227–6450 tennis reservations* ☞ *Free.*

Town of Palm Beach Municipal Beach. You know you're here if you see Palm Beach's younger generation frolicking on the sands and locals setting up chairs as the sun reflects off their gleaming white veneers. The Worth Avenue clock tower is within sight, but the gateways to the sand are actually on Chilean Avenue, Brazilian Avenue, and Gulfstream Road. It's definitely the most central and longest lifeguarded strip open to everyone and a popular choice for hotel guests from the Colony, Chesterfield, and Brazilian Court. Lifeguards are present from Brazilian Avenue down to Chilean Avenue. It's also BYOC (bring your own chair). You'll find no water-sport or food vendors here; however, casual eateries are a quick walk away. Metered spots line A1A. **Amenities:** lifeguards; showers. **Best for:** swimming; sunset. ⊠ *S. Ocean Blvd. from Brazilian Ave. to Gulfstream Rd.* ☎ *561/838–5483 beach patrol.*

LAKE WORTH

FAMILY **Lake Worth Beach.** This public beach bustles with beachgoers of all ages thanks to the prolific family offerings. The waterfront retail promenade—the old-fashioned nongambling Lake Worth "casino"—has a Mulligan's Beach House Bar & Grill, a T-shirt store, a pizzeria, and a Kilwin's ice-cream shop. The beach also has a municipal Olympic-sized public swimming pool, a playground, a fishing pier—not to mention the pier's wildly popular daytime eatery, Benny's on the Beach (open for dinner weekends in season). Tideline Ocean Resort and Four Seasons guests are steps away from the action; Eau Palm Beach guests are a short bike ride away. **Amenities:** food and drink; lifeguards; parking (fee); showers; toilets; water sports. **Best for:** sunset; swimming. ⊠ *10 S. Ocean Blvd., at A1A and Lake Ave., Lake Worth* ⊕ *www.lakeworth. org* ☞ *$1 to enter pier, $3 to enter and fish, $2 per hr for parking.*

LANTANA

Town of Lantana Public Beach. Ideal for quiet ambles, this sandy stretch is also noteworthy for a casual restaurant, the no-frills breezy Dune Deck Café, which is perched above the waterline and offers great views for an oceanfront breakfast or lunch. The beach's huge parking lot is directly adjacent to the Eau Palm Beach (meters take credit cards), and diagonally across the street is a sizable strip mall with all sorts of conveniences, including boutiques and more eateries. Note: the beach is very narrow and large rocks loom in the water. However, these are some of the clearest waters along the Florida coastline, and they make an idyllic background for long walks and great photos. **Amenities:** food and drink; lifeguards; parking (fee); showers; toilets. **Best for:** walking. ⊠ *100 E. Ocean Ave., Lantana* ☞ *$1.50 per hr for parking.*

WHERE TO EAT

PALM BEACH

$$$$ ITALIAN 🍴 **Bice Ristorante.** The bougainvillea-laden trellises set the scene at the main entrance on Peruvian Way, off posh Worth Avenue. Even though it's a chain, this is a favorite of Palm Beach society, and both the restaurant and the bar become packed and noisy during high season. **Known for:** seafood risotto; homemade pizzaccia bread made with basil, chives, and oregano; outdoor dining where you can watch the scene on Worth Avenue. [$] *Average main: $35* ✉ *313½ Worth Ave.* ✣ *Entrance is on Peruvian Ave.* ☎ *561/835–1600* 🌐 *www.palmbeach.bicegroup.com.*

$$$$ FRENCH 🍴 **Bistro Chez Jean-Pierre.** With walls adorned by avant-garde contemporary art, this family-run bistro is where the Palm Beach old guard likes to let down its hair, all the while partaking of sumptuous northern French cuisine along with an impressive wine selection. Forget calorie or cholesterol concerns, and indulge in scrambled eggs with caviar or house-made foie gras, or the best-selling Dover sole. **Known for:** Dover sole; foie gras prepared in-house; dessert soufflés. [$] *Average main: $39* ✉ *132 N. County Rd.* ☎ *561/833–1171* 🌐 *www.chezjean-pierre.com* 🕒 *Closed mid-July–Aug. and Sun. No lunch.*

6

$$$$ ECLECTIC Fodor's Choice ★ 🍴 **bûccan.** Young blue bloods rocking D&G jeans slip into tightly packed copper-topped tables alongside groups of silver-haired oil scions with the kitchen in view. It's island casual in its trendiest, most boisterous, yet still refined incarnation, with a regional American menu to match. **Known for:** small sharing plates; hot dog panini; short rib empanadas. [$] *Average main: $32* ✉ *350 S. County Rd.* ☎ *561/833–3450* 🌐 *www.buccanpalmbeach.com* 🕒 *No lunch.*

$$$$ FRENCH Fodor's Choice ★ 🍴 **Café Boulud.** Palm Beach socialites just can't get enough of this prized restaurant by celebrated chef Daniel Boulud. This posh, French-American venue in the Brazilian Court hotel, which was renovated in 2016 and added a new contemporary bar with its own menu, is casual yet elegant. **Known for:** house-cured charcuterie; seared duck breast with cherry duck jus; an extensive wine list. [$] *Average main: $38* ✉ *The Brazilian Court Hotel & Beach Club, 301 Australian Ave.* ☎ *561/655–6060* 🌐 *www.cafeboulud.com.*

$$$$ INTERNATIONAL 🍴 **Café L'Europe.** Since 1980, the favorite spot of society's movers and shakers—and a few celebs—has remained a regular stop on foodie itineraries. Service and consistency are big reasons for its longevity. **Known for:** veal chops; romantic setting; Champagne and caviar bar with extensive selections. [$] *Average main: $47* ✉ *331 S. County Rd.* ☎ *561/655–4020* 🌐 *www.cafeleurope.com* 🕒 *Closed Mon. June–Nov.*

$$$ ASIAN 🍴 **Echo.** Palm Beach's window on Asia has a sleek sushi bar and floor-to-ceiling glass doors separating the interior from the popular terrace dining area. Chinese, Japanese, Thai, and Vietnamese selections are neatly categorized: Wind (small plates starting your journey), Water (seafood mains), Fire (open-flame wok creations), Earth (meat dishes), and Flavor (desserts, sweets). **Known for:** sushi and specialty rolls; fresh seafood; cocktails in the Dragonfly Lounge. [$] *Average main: $30* ✉ *230-A Sunrise Ave.* ☎ *561/802–4222* 🌐 *www.echopalmbeach.com* 🕒 *Closed Mon. No lunch.*

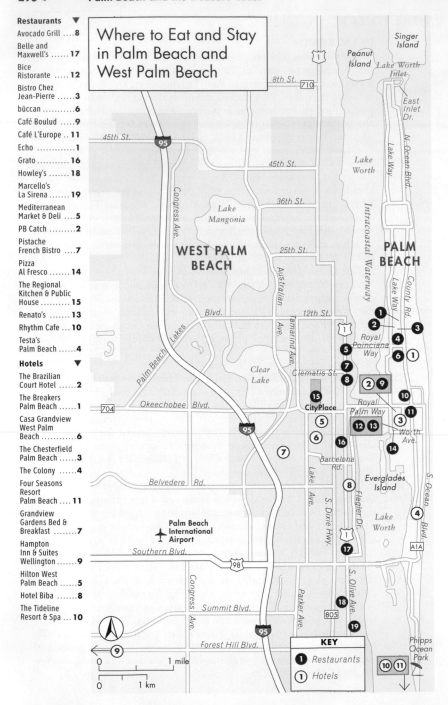

Restaurants ▼

Avocado Grill **8**

Belle and Maxwell's **17**

Bice Ristorante **12**

Bistro Chez Jean-Pierre **3**

bûccan **6**

Café Boulud **9**

Café L'Europe .. **11**

Echo **1**

Grato **16**

Howley's **18**

Marcello's La Sirena **19**

Mediterranean Market & Deli **5**

PB Catch **2**

Pistache French Bistro **7**

Pizza Al Fresco **14**

The Regional Kitchen & Public House **15**

Renato's **13**

Rhythm Cafe ... **10**

Testa's Palm Beach **4**

Hotels ▼

The Brazilian Court Hotel **2**

The Breakers Palm Beach **1**

Casa Grandview West Palm Beach **6**

The Chesterfield Palm Beach **3**

The Colony **4**

Four Seasons Resort Palm Beach **11**

Grandview Gardens Bed & Breakfast **7**

Hampton Inn & Suites Wellington **9**

Hilton West Palm Beach **5**

Hotel Biba **8**

The Tideline Resort & Spa ...**10**

Where to Eat and Stay in Palm Beach and West Palm Beach

$$$$ ✕ **PB Catch.** As the name implies, it's all about fins and shells here,
SEAFOOD including the live ones that entertain diners in their tanks in the modern dining room. The menu includes a raw bar with a good selection of raw (or grilled) oysters, clams, and the chef's "seacuterie" platter, a build-your-own sampler of such choices as salmon pastrami, citrus-cured fluke, cured sea bass, or octopus torchon. **Known for:** in-house cured fish; shellfish tower from the raw bar; craft cocktails. $ *Average main: $35* ✉ *251 Sunrise Blvd.* ☎ *561/655–5558* ⊕ *www.pbcatch.com* ⊙ *Closed Sun.*

$$ ✕ **Pizza Al Fresco.** The hidden-garden setting is the secret to the success of
PIZZA this European-style pizzeria, where you can dine under a canopy of century-old banyans in an intimate courtyard. Specialties are 12-inch hand-tossed brick-oven pizzas with such interesting toppings as prosciutto, arugula, and caviar. **Known for:** caviar-and-smoked-salmon pizza; fresh salads; garden setting. $ *Average main: $19* ✉ *14 Via Mizner, at Worth Ave.* ⊹ *Tucked in a courtyard off Worth Ave.* ☎ *561/832–0032* ⊕ *www.pizzaalfresco.com.*

$$$$ ✕ **Renato's.** Here, at one of the most romantic restaurants in Palm Beach,
ITALIAN guests can dine Italiano. Sit in the beautiful courtyard, with stars above and twinkling lights on the bougainvillea, or in the intimate, low-lighted dining room flickering with candles and enhanced with fresh flowers and quiet classical music. **Known for:** fresh pasta dishes; house-made soups; romantic setting. $ *Average main: $37* ✉ *87 Via Mizner* ☎ *561/655–9752* ⊕ *www.renatospalmbeach.com* ⊙ *No lunch Sun.*

$$$ ✕ **Testa's Palm Beach.** Attracting a loyal clientele since 1921 (Howdy
AMERICAN Doody is listed among its "celebs"), this restaurant is still owned by the
FAMILY Testa family. Dine inside in an intimate pine-paneled room with cozy bar, out back in a gazebo-style room for large groups, or outside—popular at breakfast—at sidewalk tables that are pet-friendly. **Known for:** shrimp-and-artichoke scampi; blueberry pancakes for breakfast; signature strawberry pie. $ *Average main: $27* ✉ *221 Royal Poinciana Way* ☎ *561/832–0992* ⊕ *www.testasrestaurants.com.*

WEST PALM BEACH

$$ ✕ **Avocado Grill.** In downtown West Palm Beach's waterfront district,
ECLECTIC this hot spot is an alternative to the bar food, tacos, and burgers more common in the area. "Green" cuisine seasonal salads, vegetarian dishes, and sustainably produced meats and seafood is making waves at the avocado-themed restaurant. **Known for:** everything avocado, including wonderful guacamole; mushroom fricassee with cheddar grits; kale and duck salad. $ *Average main: $19* ✉ *125 Datura St., West Palm Beach* ☎ *561/623–0822* ⊕ *www.avocadogrillwpb.com.*

$$ ✕ **Belle and Maxwell's.** Palm Beach ladies who lunch leave the island for
AMERICAN an afternoon at Belle and Maxwell's, while young professionals loosen up after work at the wine bar, part of the bistro's expanded dining area. Tucked along Antique Row, it looks like a storybook tea party at lunch, with eclectic furnishings and decor, and charming garden. **Known for:** classic chicken marsala; extensive list of lunch salads; house-made desserts. $ *Average main: $18* ✉ *3700 S. Dixie Hwy., West Palm Beach* ☎ *561/832–4449* ⊕ *www.belleandmaxwells.com* ⊙ *Closed Sun. No dinner Mon.*

6

$$$ TUSCAN 🍴 **Grato.** At this boisterous, trendy sibling to bûccan, pizzas and pastas are served up to neighborhood and Palm Beach island diners in a chic, open space. An open kitchen also hosts a small bar to accommodate viewing the chef in action. **Known for:** wood-fired-oven pizzas; fresh pastas; busy bar scene. [$] *Average main: $24* ✉ *1901 Dixie Hwy., West Palm Beach* ☎ *561/404–1334* 🌐 *www.gratowpb.com.*

$ AMERICAN 🍴 **Howley's.** Since 1950, this diner's eat-in counter and "cooked in sight, it must be right" motto have made it a congenial setting for meeting old friends and making new ones. Nowadays, Howley's prides itself on its kitsch factor and old-school eats like turkey potpie and a traditional Thanksgiving feast, as well as its retro-redux dishes like potato-and-brisket burrito. **Known for:** kitschy setting; retro diner specialties; late-night dining. [$] *Average main: $13* ✉ *4700 S. Dixie Hwy., West Palm Beach* ☎ *561/833–5691* 🌐 *www.sub-culture.org/howleys/.*

$$$$ ITALIAN 🍴 **Marcello's La Sirena.** A longtime favorite of locals, this sophisticated Italian restaurant is in an unexpected, nondescript location on Dixie Highway away from downtown and central hubs. But warm hospitality from a husband-and-wife team, along with smart service and delectable traditional dishes, await. **Known for:** fresh pasta dishes; award-winning wine list; great desserts. [$] *Average main: $31* ✉ *6316 S. Dixie Hwy., West Palm Beach* ☎ *561/585–3128* 🌐 *www.lasirenaonline.com* 🕒 *Closed Sun.*

$ MIDDLE EASTERN Fodor's Choice ★ 🍴 **Mediterranean Market & Deli.** This hole-in-the-wall Middle Eastern bakery, deli, and market is packed at lunchtime with regulars who are on a first-name basis with the gang behind the counter. From the nondescript parking lot the place doesn't look like much, but inside, delicious hot and cold Mediterranean treats await the take-out crowd. **Known for:** lamb salad; gyros; freshly baked pita bread. [$] *Average main: $10* ✉ *327 5th St., West Palm Beach* ☎ *561/659–7322* 🌐 *www.mediterraneanmarketanddeli.com* 🕒 *Closed Sun.*

$$$ FRENCH 🍴 **Pistache French Bistro.** Although "the island" is no doubt a bastion of French cuisine, this cozy bistro across the bridge on the Clematis Street waterfront entices a lively crowd looking for an unpretentious good meal. The outdoor terrace can't be beat, and the fabulous modern French menu with twists such as roasted sliced duck with truffled polenta is a delight. **Known for:** fresh seafood; cheese and charcuterie; great desserts. [$] *Average main: $27* ✉ *101 N. Clematis St., West Palm Beach* ☎ *561/833–5090* 🌐 *www.pistachewpb.com.*

$$$ SOUTHERN 🍴 **The Regional Kitchen & Public House.** *Top Chef* Lindsay Autry debuted her own Southern-inspired American cuisine in CityPlace to the acclaim of local critics. The menu of updated comfort food includes tea-brined fried chicken, creamy tomato pie, pimento cheese done table-side, and shrimp and grits. **Known for:** reinvented Southern classics; table-side pimento cheese; weekend brunch. [$] *Average main: $24* ✉ *CityPlace, 651 Okeechobee Blvd., West Palm Beach* ✥ *Directly across from the Convention Center* ☎ *561/557–6460* 🌐 *www.eatregional.com.*

$$$ MODERN AMERICAN 🍴 **Rhythm Cafe.** West Palm Beach's Rhythm Cafe is anything but Palm Beach formal (the decor includes a feathered pink flamingo perched on the terrazzo floor). Fun, funky, cheesy, campy, and cool all at once, the former 1950s-era drugstore-cum-restaurant on West Palm Beach's

Antique Row features an ever-changing creative menu of house-made items with Italian, Greek, American, and Creole influences. **Known for:** "tapas-tizer" small plates; fresh fish; graham-cracker-crusted key lime chicken. [$] *Average main: $24* ✉ *3800 S. Dixie Hwy., West Palm Beach* ☎ *561/833–3406* 🌐 *www.rhythmcafe.com* ⏲ *No lunch.*

LAKE WORTH

$ AMERICAN 🍴 **Benny's on the Beach.** Perched on the Lake Worth Pier, Benny's has a walk-up bar, a take-out window, and a full-service beach-themed restaurant serving casual fare at bargain prices. "Beach Bread" is a take on a waffle sandwich; the fresh seafood is from Florida waters. **Known for:** Florida seafood; beach brunch; afternoon drinks. [$] *Average main: $12* ✉ *Lake Worth Beach, 10 S. Ocean Blvd., Lake Worth* ✥ *On Lake Worth Pier* ☎ *561/582–9001* 🌐 *www.bennysonthebeach.com* ⏲ *No dinner May–early Dec.*

LANTANA

$$ SEAFOOD 🍴 **Old Key Lime House.** An informal seafood spot—serving crab cakes, fish sandwiches, and fillets—and a favorite of locals and tourists, is perched on the Intracoastal Waterway with spectacular views. Observation decks with separate bars wrap around the back where boats can dock; indoors is more family-oriented. **Known for:** unpretentious, casual atmosphere; fried and grilled fish; great key lime pie. [$] *Average main: $20* ✉ *300 E. Ocean Ave., Lantana* ☎ *561/582–1889* 🌐 *www.oldkeylimehouse.com.*

6

WHERE TO STAY

PALM BEACH

$$$$ HOTEL Fodor's Choice ★ 🏨 **The Brazilian Court Hotel.** This posh boutique hotel, stomping ground of Florida's well-heeled, is full of historic touches and creature comforts—from its yellow facade with dramatic white-draped entry, to modern draws like the renowned spa and Daniel Boulud restaurant. **Pros:** stylish and hip local crowd; charming courtyard; free beach shuttle. **Cons:** small fitness center; nondescript pool; 10-minute ride to ocean and suggested 24-hour advance reservation for shuttle. [$] *Rooms from: $609* ✉ *301 Australian Ave.* ☎ *561/655–7740* 🌐 *www.thebraziliancourt.com* 🛏 *80 rooms* 🍽 *No meals.*

$$$$ RESORT FAMILY Fodor's Choice ★ 🏨 **The Breakers Palm Beach.** More than an opulent hotel, The Breakers is a legendary 140-acre self-contained jewel of a resort built in a Mediterranean style and loaded with amenities, from a 20,000-square-foot luxury spa and grandiose beach club with four pools and a half-mile private beach, to 10 tennis courts, croquet courts, and two 18-hole golf courses. **Pros:** impeccable attention to detail; fantastic service; beautiful room views; extensive activities for families. **Cons:** big price tag; short drive to reach off-property attractions. [$] *Rooms from: $699* ✉ *1 S. County Rd.* ☎ *561/655–6611, 888/273–2537* 🌐 *www.thebreakers.com* 🛏 *540 rooms* 🍽 *No meals.*

$$$$ HOTEL 🏨 **The Chesterfield Palm Beach.** A distinctly upper-crust northern European feel pervades the peach stucco walls and elegant rooms here; the hotel sits just north of the western end of Worth Avenue, and high tea, a cigar parlor, and daily turndown service recall a bygone, more refined

era. **Pros:** gracious, attentive staff; Leopard Lounge entertainment; free valet parking. **Cons:** long walk to beach; only one elevator; to some, can come off as a bit stuffy. $ *Rooms from: $495* ⊠ *363 Cocoanut Row* ☎ *561/659–5800, 800/243–7871* ⊕ *www.chesterfieldpb.com* ⇴ *52 rooms* ⑩ *No meals.*

$$$$
HOTEL
🏨 **The Colony.** In 2014, nearly $10 million was spent to redecorate and refurbish every room at the island's legendary British-colonial-style hotel. **Pros:** unbeatable location; famous bar at Polo Steakhouse; pillow-top mattresses; full English breakfast included. **Cons:** lobby is small; elevators are tight. $ *Rooms from: $600* ⊠ *155 Hammon Ave.* ☎ *561/655–5430, 800/521–5525* ⊕ *www.thecolonypalmbeach.com* ⇴ *90 rooms* ⑩ *Breakfast.*

$$$$
RESORT
FAMILY
Fodor'sChoice
★
🏨 **Four Seasons Resort Palm Beach.** Couples and families seeking relaxed seaside elegance in a luxe yet understated setting will love this manicured 6-acre oceanfront escape at the south end of Palm Beach, with serene, bright, airy rooms in a cream-colored palette and spacious marble-lined baths. **Pros:** accommodating service; all rooms have balconies; outstanding complimentary kids' program. **Cons:** 10-minute drive to downtown Palm Beach (but can walk to Lake Worth); pricey. $ *Rooms from: $739* ⊠ *2800 S. Ocean Blvd.* ☎ *561/582–2800, 800/432–2335* ⊕ *www.fourseasons.com/palmbeach* ⇴ *210 rooms* ⑩ *No meals.*

$$$
RESORT
🏨 **The Tideline Resort & Spa.** This Zenlike boutique hotel, a member of the Kimpton group, has a loyal following of young, hip travelers, who appreciate the guest rooms that were updated in 2016 and the full-service spa. **Pros:** most rooms have beautiful views of the private beach; ultracontemporary vibe; luxury setting. **Cons:** a hike from shopping and nightlife; the infinity pool is across the driveway. $ *Rooms from: $340* ⊠ *2842 S. Ocean Blvd.* ☎ *561/540–6440, 888/344–4321* ⊕ *www. tidelineresort.com* ⇴ *144 rooms* ⑩ *No meals.*

WEST PALM BEACH

$$
B&B/INN
🏨 **Casa Grandview West Palm Beach.** In West Palm's charming Grandview Heights historic district—and just minutes away from both downtown and the beach—this warm and personalized B&B offers a wonderful respite from South Florida's big-hotel norm. **Pros:** daily dry cleaning of all linens; complimentary soft drinks, coffee, and snacks (and lots of them) in lobby; simple keyless entry (number code lock system). **Cons:** cottages and suites have seven-day minimum; free breakfast in B&B rooms only; art deco suites don't have air-conditioning. $ *Rooms from: $289* ⊠ *1410 Georgia Ave., West Palm Beach* ☎ *561/655–8932* ⊕ *www.casagrandview.com* ⇴ *17 rooms* ⑩ *Breakfast.*

$$
B&B/INN
🏨 **Grandview Gardens Bed & Breakfast.** Defining the Florida B&B experience, this 1925 Mediterranean-revival home overlooks a serene courtyard pool and oozes loads of charm and personality, while the fabulous owners provide heavy doses of bespoke service. **Pros:** multilingual owners; outside private entrances to rooms; free bicycle use; innkeepers offer historic city tours. **Cons:** not close to the beach; in a residential area; rental car needed. $ *Rooms from: $225* ⊠ *1608 Lake Ave., West Palm Beach* ☎ *561/833–9023* ⊕ *www.grandview-gardens.com* ⇴ *5 rooms, 2 cottages* ⑩ *Breakfast.*

$$ ⊞ **Hampton Inn & Suites Wellington.** The only hotel near the polo fields
HOTEL in the equestrian mecca of Wellington—10 miles west of downtown
Palm Beach—feels a bit like a tony clubhouse, with rich wood paneling,
hunt prints, and elegant chandeliers; but inside the rooms are standard
Hampton Inn fare. **Pros:** complimentary hot breakfast; free Wi-Fi; out-
door swimming pool; close to a large shopping center; near the county
fairgrounds. **Cons:** no restaurant; Intracoastal Waterway is a 30-minute
drive, and beach is farther. $ *Rooms from: $250* ⊠ *2155 Wellington
Green Dr., West Palm Beach* ☎ *561/472–9696* ⊕ *hamptoninn3.hilton.
com* ⇆ *122 rooms, 32 suites* ⏹ *Breakfast.*

$$ ⊞ **Hilton West Palm Beach.** In downtown, the contemporary business
HOTEL hotel situated next door to the county convention center has a pool with
FAMILY cabanas many resorts would envy. **Pros:** walking distance to convention
center, CityPlace, Kravis Center; resort-style pool; amenities geared toward
business travelers. **Cons:** long ride to the beach; noise from downtown
construction and trains. $ *Rooms from: $279* ⊠ *600 Okeechobee Blvd.,
West Palm Beach* ⊹ *Adjacent to the Palm Beach County Convention
Center* ☎ *561/231–6000* ⊕ *www3.hilton.com* ⇆ *400 rooms* ⏹ *No meals.*

$ ⊞ **Hotel Biba.** In the El Cid historic district, this 1940s-era motel has got-
HOTEL ten a fun, stylish revamp from designer Barbara Hulanicki: each room
has a vibrant mélange of colors, along with handcrafted mirrors, mosaic
bathroom floors, and custom mahogany furnishings. **Pros:** cool, punchy
design and luxe fixtures; popular wine bar; free Continental breakfast
with Cuban pastries. **Cons:** water pressure is weak; bathrooms are tiny;
noisy when the bar is open late and trains run nearby; not all rooms
have central air-conditioning. $ *Rooms from: $160* ⊠ *320 Belvedere
Rd., West Palm Beach* ☎ *561/832–0094* ⊕ *www.hotelbiba.com* ⇆ *43
rooms* ⏹ *Breakfast.*

LAKE WORTH

$ ⊞ **Sabal Palm House.** Built in 1936, this romantic, two-story B&B is
B&B/INN a short walk from Lake Worth's downtown shops, eateries, and the
Intracoastal Waterway, and each room is decorated with antiques and
inspired by a different artist, including Renoir, Dalí, Norman Rockwell,
and Chagall. **Pros:** on quiet street; hands-on owners; chairs and totes
with towels provided for use at nearby beach. **Cons:** no pool; peak times
require a two-night minimum stay; no parking lot. $ *Rooms from:
$159* ⊠ *109 N. Golfview Rd., Lake Worth* ☎ *561/582–1090, 888/722–
2572* ⊕ *www.sabalpalmhouse.com* ⇆ *5 rooms, 2 suites* ⏹ *Breakfast.*

SOUTH PALM BEACH AND MANALAPAN

$$$$ ⊞ **Eau Palm Beach.** In the coastal town of Manalapan (just south of
RESORT Palm Beach), this sublime, glamorous destination resort (formerly the
FAMILY Ritz-Carlton) showcases a newer, younger face of luxury, including a
Fodor'sChoice 3,000-square-foot oceanfront terrace, two sleek pools, a huge fitness
★ center, and a deluxe spa. **Pros:** magnificent aesthetic details throughout;
indulgent pampering services; excellent on-site dining; kids love the cool
cyber-lounge just for them. **Cons:** golf course is off property; 15-min-
ute drive to Palm Beach. $ *Rooms from: $560* ⊠ *100 S. Ocean Blvd.,
Manalapan* ☎ *561/533–6000, 800/241–3333* ⊕ *www.eaupalmbeach.
com* ⇆ *309 rooms* ⏹ *No meals.*

6

NIGHTLIFE AND PERFORMING ARTS

PALM BEACH

NIGHTLIFE

Palm Beach is teeming with restaurants that turn into late-night hot spots, plus hotel lobby bars perfect for tête-à-têtes.

Fodor's Choice **bûccan.** At this hip Hamptons-esque scene, society darlings crowd the
★ lounge, throwing back killer cocktails like the Basil Rathbone (gin, orange juice, mint, basil, strawberry) and Buccan T (vodka, black tea, cranberry, citrus, basil, and agave nectar). ⊠ *350 S. County Rd.* ☎ *561/833–3450* ⊕ *www.buccanpalmbeach.com.*

Café Boulud. A sleek, redesigned dining room bar with bar bites from a special menu plus an extended happy hour draws locals and visitors alike. ■TIP→ Dress to impress. ⊠ *301 Australian Ave.* ☎ *561/655–6060* ⊕ *www.cafeboulud.com/palmbeach.*

Cucina Dell' Arte. Though this spot is popular for lunch and dinner, it's even more popular later in the night. The younger, trendier set comes late to party, mingle, and dance into the wee hours. ⊠ *257 Royal Poinciana Way* ☎ *561/655–0770* ⊕ *www.cucinadellarte.com.*

The Leopard Lounge. In the Chesterfield hotel, this enclave feels like an exclusive club. The trademark ceiling and spotted floors of the renovated lounge are a nod to this hotel's historic roots, but the rest of the decor is new age Palm Beach glam. Though it starts each evening as a restaurant, as the night progresses the Leopard is transformed into an old-fashioned club with live music for Palm Beach's old guard. The bartenders know how to pour a cocktail here. ⊠ *The Chesterfield Palm Beach, 363 Cocoanut Row* ☎ *561/659–5800* ⊕ *www.chesterfieldpb.com.*

WEST PALM BEACH

NIGHTLIFE

West Palm is known for its exuberant nightlife—Clematis Street and CityPlace are the prime party destinations. In fact, downtown rocks every Thursday from 6 pm on with Clematis by Night (⊕ *www.wpb. org/clematis-by-night*), a celebration of music, dance, art, and food at Centennial Square.

Blue Martini. The CityPlace outpost of this South Florida hot spot for thirty-, forty-, and fiftysomething adults gone wild has a menu filled with tons of innovative martini creations (42 to be exact), tasty tapas, and lots of cougars on the prowl, searching for a first, second, or even third husband. And the guys aren't complaining! The drinks are great and the scene is fun for everyone, even those who aren't single and looking to mingle. Expect DJs some nights, live music others. ⊠ *CityPlace, 550 S. Rosemary Ave., #244, West Palm Beach* ☎ *561/835–8601* ⊕ *www.bluemartinilounge.com.*

ER Bradley's Saloon. People of all ages congregate to hang out and socialize at this kitschy open-air restaurant and bar to gaze at the Intracoastal Waterway; the mechanical bull is a hit on Saturdays. Live music's on tap five to seven nights a week. ⊠ *104 Clematis St., West Palm Beach* ☎ *561/833–3520* ⊕ *www.erbradleys.com.*

Fodor'sChoice
★ **Rocco's Tacos and Tequila Bar.** In the last few years, Rocco's has taken root in numerous South Florida downtowns and become synonymous with wild nights of chips 'n' guac, margaritas, and intoxicating fun. This is more of a scene than just a restaurant, and when Rocco's in the house and pouring shots, get ready to party hearty. With pitchers of margaritas continuously flowing, the middle-age crowd is boisterous and fun, recounting (and reliving) the days of spring break debauchery from their pre-professional years. Get your party started here with more than 220 choices of tequila. There's another branch at 5250 Town Center Circle in Boca Raton; at 110 Atlantic Avenue in Delray Beach; and in Palm Beach Gardens in PGA Commons at 5090 PGA Boulevard. ⊠ *224 Clematis St., West Palm Beach* ☎ *561/650–1001* ⊕ *www. roccostacos.com.*

PERFORMING ARTS
Palm Beach Dramaworks (pbd). Housed in an intimate venue with only 218 seats in downtown West Palm Beach, the modus operandi is "theater to think about," with plays by Pulitzer Prize winners on rotation. ⊠ *201 Clematis St., West Palm Beach* ☎ *561/514–4042* ⊕ *www.palmbeach-dramaworks.org.*

Palm Beach Opera. The organization celebrates its 55th anniversary with the 2017 season. Three main-stage productions are offered during the season from January through April at the Kravis Center with English-language supertitles. There's an annual Children's Performance where all tickets are $5, plus a free outdoor concert at the Meyer Amphitheatre in downtown West Palm Beach. Tickets start at $25. ⊠ *1800 S. Australian Ave., Suite 301, administrative office, West Palm Beach* ☎ *561/833–7888* ⊕ *www.pbopera.org.*

Fodor'sChoice
★ **Raymond F. Kravis Center for the Performing Arts.** This is the crown jewel amid a treasury of local arts attractions, and its marquee star is the 2,195-seat Dreyfoos Hall, a glass, copper, and marble showcase just steps from the restaurants and shops of CityPlace. The center also boasts the 289-seat Rinker Playhouse, 170-seat Persson Hall, and the Gosman Amphitheatre, which holds 1,400 total in seats and on the lawn. A packed year-round schedule features a blockbuster lineup of Broadway's biggest touring productions, concerts, dance, dramas, and musicals; the Miami City Ballet, Palm Beach Opera, and the Palm Beach Pops perform here. ⊠ *701 Okeechobee Blvd., West Palm Beach* ☎ *561/832–7469 box office* ⊕ *www.kravis.org.*

SHOPPING

As is the case throughout South Florida, many of the smaller boutiques in Palm Beach close in the summer, and most stores are closed on Sunday. Consignment stores in Palm Beach are definitely worth a look; you'll often find high-end designer clothing in impeccable condition.

PALM BEACH
SHOPPING AREAS
Royal Poinciana Way. Cute shops dot the north side of Royal Poinciana Way between Bradley Place and North County Road. Wind through the courtyards past upscale consignment stores to Sunset Avenue, then

Worth Avenue is the place in Palm Beach for high-end shopping, from international boutiques to independent jewelers.

stroll down Sunrise Avenue: this is the place for specialty items like out-of-town newspapers, health foods, and rare books. ✉ *Royal Poinciana Way, between Bradley Pl. and N. County Rd.*

Fodor's Choice
★
Worth Avenue. One of the world's premier showcases for high-quality shopping runs half a mile from east to west across Palm Beach, from the beach to Lake Worth. The street has more than 200 shops (more than 40 of them sell jewelry), and many upscale chain stores (Gucci, Hermès, Saks Fifth Avenue, Neiman Marcus, Louis Vuitton, Chanel, Cartier, Tiffany & Co., and Tourneau) are represented—their merchandise appealing to the discerning tastes of the Palm Beach clientele. Don't miss walking around the vias, little courtyards lined with smaller boutiques; historic tours are available each month during "season" from the Worth Avenue Association. ■TIP➔ For those looking to go a little lighter on the pocket book, just north of Worth Avenue, the six blocks of South County Road have interesting and somewhat less expensive stores. ✉ *Worth Ave., between Cocoanut Row and S. Ocean Blvd.* ⊕ *www.worth-avenue.com.*

WEST PALM BEACH
SHOPPING AREAS

Fodor's Choice
★
Antique Row. West Palm's U.S. 1, "South Dixie Highway," is the destination for those who are interested in interesting home decor. From thrift shops to the most exclusive stores, it is all here within 40 stores—museum-quality furniture, lighting, art, junk, fabric, frames, tile, and rugs. So if you're looking for an art deco, French-provincial, or Mizner pièce de résistance, big or small, schedule a few hours for an Antique Row stroll. You'll find bargains during the off-season (May to November).

Antique Row runs north–south from Belvedere Road to Forest Hill Boulevard, although most stores are bunched between Belvedere Road and Southern Boulevard. ⊠ *U.S. 1, between Belvedere Rd. and Forest Hill Blvd., West Palm Beach* ⊕ *www.westpalmbeachantiques.com.*

CityPlace. The 72-acre, four-block-by-four-block commercial and residential complex centered on Rosemary Avenue attracts people of all ages to with restaurants like Italian-inspired Il Bellagio, bars like Blue Martini, a 20-screen Muvico and IMAX theater, Revolutions—a bowling alley and sports bar, the Harriet Himmel Theater, and the Improv Comedy Club. In the courtyard, a 36,000-gallon water fountain and light show entertains, along with live bands on weekends. The dining, shopping, and entertainment are all family-friendly; at night, however, a lively crowd likes to hit the outdoor bars. Among CityPlace's stores are such popular national retailers as H&M, Tommy Bahama, and Restoration Hardware. Anushka Spa and Salon draws locals and visitors. ⊠ *700 S. Rosemary Ave., West Palm Beach* ☎ *561/366–1000* ⊕ *www.cityplace.com.*

FAMILY **Clematis Street.** If lunching is just as important as window-shopping, the renewed downtown West Palm around Clematis Street that runs west to east from South Rosemary Avenue to Flagler Drive is the spot for you. Centennial Park by the waterfront has an attractive design—and fountains where kids can cool off—which adds to the pleasure of browsing and resting at one of the many outdoor cafés. Hip national retailers such as Design Within Reach mix with local boutiques like third-generation Pioneer Linens, and both blend in with restaurants and bars. ⊠ *Clematis St., between S. Rosemary Ave. and Flagler Dr., West Palm Beach* ⊕ *www.westpalmbeach.com/clematis.*

Palm Beach Outlets. An outlet mall worthy of Palm Beach finally opened in 2014 in West Palm Beach. It features more than 130 retailers, with big names among the usual suspects. Off Fifth (Saks Fifth Avenue's store), Nordstrom Rack, White House | Black Market, Brooks Brothers, DKNY, and Calvin Klein are interspersed with stores selling shoes, discounted home decor, sports gear, kids fashions, and more. The mall has several restaurants as well as coffee shops and a food court. And it continues to expand, so check the website for an updated list of shops. ■TIP→ The wine bar in Whole Foods Market is the "see and be seen" scene at this outdoor mall. ⊠ *1751 Palm Beach Lakes Blvd., West Palm Beach* ☎ *561/515–4400* ⊕ *www.palmbeachoutlets.com.*

SPORTS AND THE OUTDOORS

PALM BEACH

Palm Beach Island has two good golf courses—The Breakers and the Palm Beach Par 3 Golf Course, but only the latter is open to the public. Not to worry, there are more on the mainland, as well as myriad other outdoor sports opportunities, including a new spring-training baseball stadium where two teams will play.

BIKING

Bicycling is a great way to get a closer look at Palm Beach. Only 14 miles long, half a mile wide, flat as the top of a billiard table, and just as green, it's a perfect biking place.

FAMILY **Lake Trail.** This palm-fringed trail, about 4 miles long, skirts the back-yards of mansions and the edge of Lake Worth. The start ("south trail" section) is just up from Royal Palm Way behind the Society of the Four Arts; follow the signs and you can't miss it. As you head north, the trail gets a little choppy around the Flagler Museum, so most people just enter where the "north trail" section begins at the very west end of Sunset Avenue. The path stops just short of the tip of the island, but people follow the quiet residential streets until they hit North Ocean Boulevard and the dock there with lovely views of Peanut Island and Singer Island, and then follow North Ocean Boulevard the 4 miles back for a change of scenery. ⊠ *Parallel to Lake Way ✛ Behind Society of the Four Arts.*

Fodor's Choice **Palm Beach Bicycle Trail Shop.** Open daily year-round, the shop rents bikes
★ by the hour or day, and it's about a block from the north Lake Trail entrance. The shop has maps to help you navigate your way around the island, or you can download the main map from the shop's website. They are experts on the nearby, palm-fringed, 4-mile Lake Trail. ⊠ *223 Sunrise Ave.* ☎ *561/659–4583* ⊕ *www.palmbeachbicycle.com.*

GOLF

Fodor's Choice **Palm Beach Par 3 Golf Course.** This course has been named the best par-3
★ golf course in the United States by *Golf Digest* magazine. The 18-hole course—originally designed by Dick Wilson and Joe Lee in 1961—was redesigned in 2009 by Hall of Famer Raymond Floyd. The par-3 course includes six holes directly on the Atlantic Ocean, with some holes over 200 yards. The grounds are exquisitely landscaped, as one would expect in Palm Beach. A lavish clubhouse houses Al Fresco, an Italian restaurant. A cart is an extra $15, but walking is encouraged. Summer rates are greatly discounted. ⊠ *2345 S. Ocean Blvd.* ☎ *561/547–0598* ⊕ *www.golfontheocean.com* ⌦ *$50 for 18 holes* ⚑ *18 holes, 2458 yards, par 58.*

WEST PALM BEACH
BASEBALL

FAMILY **Ballpark of the Palm Beaches.** There's a lot to root for at the new-in-2017 state-of-the-art baseball stadium. It plays host to spring training for the Houston Astros and the Washington Nationals, along with farm team play and numerous tournaments in the summer on its many fields. Seating includes lawn, bleacher, field boxes, and suites, with full food service in the latter two. A full bar overlooks left field. With free (and plenty) parking—as well as reasonably priced tickets—it's a value day out. Check the website to see the other teams coming to play in Florida's "Grapefruit League" against the home teams. The stadium complements Roger Dean Stadium in Jupiter, which hosts the spring games for the Miami Marlins and St. Louis Cardinals. Fields for lacrosse, football, and soccer are part of the massive complex and expected to draw those games; other community events are staged here. ⊠ *5444 Haverhill Rd., West Palm Beach ✛ Best exit off I–95 is 45th St.; off Florida's Tpke. is Okeechobee Blvd.* ☎ *844/676–2017* ⊕ *www.ballparkpalmbeaches.com* ⌦ *From $17.*

POLO

Fodor'sChoice **International Polo Club Palm Beach.** Attend matches and rub elbows with ★ celebrities who make the pilgrimage out to Palm Beach polo country (the western suburb of Wellington) during the January–April season. The competition is not just among polo players. High society dresses in their best polo couture week after week, each outfit more fabulous than the next; they tailgate out of their Bentleys and Rolices. An annual highlight at the polo club is the U.S. Open Polo Championship at the end of season. ■TIP➜ One of the best ways to experience the polo scene is by enjoying a gourmet brunch on the veranda of the International Polo Club Pavilion; it'll cost you from $100–$120 per person depending on the month, but it's well worth it. ⊠ *3667 120th Ave. S* ☎ *561/204–5687* ⊕ *www.internationalpoloclub.com.*

LAKE WORTH

GOLF

Palm Beach National Golf and Country Club. Despite the name, this classic 18-hole course resides in Lake Worth, not in Palm Beach. It is, however, in Palm Beach County and prides itself on being "the most fun and friendly golf course" in Palm Beach County. The championship layout was designed by Joe Lee in the 1970s and is famous for its 3rd and 18th holes. The 3rd: a par-3 island hole with a sand bunker. The 18th: a short par 4 of 358 yards sandwiched between a wildlife preserve and water. Due to the challenging nature of the course, it's more popular with seasoned golfers. The Steve Haggerty Golf Academy is also based here. Summer rates are significantly discounted. ⊠ *7500 St. Andrews Rd., Lake Worth* ☎ *561/965–0044* ⊕ *www.palmbeachnational.com* ⊠ *$94 for 18 holes* ⅃. *18 holes, 6734 yards, par 72.*

DELRAY BEACH

15 miles south of West Palm Beach.

A onetime artists' retreat with a small settlement of Japanese farmers, Delray has grown into a sophisticated beach town. Delray's current popularity is caused in large part by the fact that it has the feel of an organic city rather than a planned development or subdivision— and it's completely walkable. Atlantic Avenue, which fell from a tony downtown to a dilapidated main drag, has been reinvented into a mile-plus-long stretch of palm-dotted sidewalks lined with stores, art galleries, and restaurants. Running east–west and ending at the beach, it's a happening place for a stroll, day or night. Another active pedestrian area, the Pineapple Grove Arts District, begins at Atlantic and stretches northward on Northeast 2nd Avenue about half a mile, and yet another active pedestrian way begins at the eastern edge of Atlantic Avenue and runs along the big, broad swimming beach that extends north to George Bush Boulevard and south to Casuarina Road. Renovations and buildings in progress in adjoining areas both south and north of the avenue will offer more shops and restaurants, as well as condos.

Morikami Museum and Japanese Gardens gives a taste of the Orient through its exhibits and tea ceremonies.

GETTING HERE AND AROUND
To reach Delray Beach from Boynton Beach, drive 2 miles south on Interstate 95, U.S. 1, or Route A1A.

ESSENTIALS
VISITOR INFORMATION
Contacts Discover the Palm Beaches. ✉ *1555 Palm Beach Lakes Blvd., Suite 800, West Palm Beach* ☎ *561/233–3000* ⊕ *www.palmbeachfl.com.*

EXPLORING

Colony Hotel. The chief landmark along Atlantic Avenue since 1926 is this sunny Mediterranean-revival-style building, which is a member of the National Trust's Historic Hotels of America. Walk through the lobby to the parking lot where original garages still stand—relics of the days when hotel guests would arrive via chauffeured cars and stay there the whole season. The bar is a locals' gathering spot. ✉ *525 E. Atlantic Ave.* ☎ *561/276–4123* ⊕ *www.thecolonyhotel.com.*

FAMILY **Delray Beach Center for the Arts at Old School Square.** Instrumental in the revitalization of Delray Beach circa 1995, this cluster of galleries and event spaces were established in restored school buildings dating from 1913 and 1925. The **Cornell Museum of Art & American Culture** offers ever-changing exhibits on fine arts, crafts, and pop culture, plus a hands-on children's gallery. From November to April, the 323-seat **Crest Theatre** showcases national-touring Broadway musicals, cabaret concerts, dance performances, and lectures. ✉ *51 N. Swinton Ave.* ☎ *561/243–7922* ⊕ *www.oldschool.org* 🎫 *$10 for museum* ⊘ *Closed Mon.*

FAMILY
Fodor'sChoice ★
Morikami Museum and Japanese Gardens. The boonies west of Delray Beach seems an odd place to encounter one of the region's most important cultural centers, but this is exactly where you can find a 200-acre cultural and recreational facility heralding the Yamato Colony of Japanese farmers that settled here in the early 20th century. A permanent exhibit details their history, and all together the museum's collection has more than 7,000 artifacts and works of art on rotating display. Traditional tea ceremonies are conducted monthly from October to June, along with educational classes on topics like calligraphy and sushi making (these require advance registration and come with a fee). The six main gardens are inspired by famous historic periods in Japanese garden design and have South Florida accents (think tropical bonsai), and the on-site Cornell Café serves light Asian fare at affordable prices and was recognized by the Food Network as being one of the country's best museum eateries. ✉ *4000 Morikami Park Rd.* ☎ *561/495–0233* 🌐 *www.morikami.org* 🎟 *$15* 🕒 *Closed Mon.*

BEACHES

Fodor'sChoice ★
Delray Municipal Beach. If you're looking for a place to see and be seen, head for this wide expanse of sand, the heart of which is where Atlantic Avenue meets A1A, close to restaurants, bars, and quick-serve eateries. Singles, families, and water-sports enthusiasts alike love it here. Lounge chairs and umbrellas can be rented every day, and lifeguards man stations half a mile out in each direction. The most popular section of beach is south of Atlantic Avenue on A1A, where the street parking is found. There are also two metered lots with restrooms across from A1A at Sandoway Park and Anchor Park (bring quarters if parking here). On the beach by Anchor Park, north of Casuarina Road, are six volleyball nets and a kiosk that offers Hobie Wave rentals, surfing lessons, and snorkeling excursions to the 1903 SS *Inchulva* shipwreck half a mile offshore. The beach itself is open 24 hours, if you're at a nearby hotel and fancy a moonlight stroll. **Amenities:** water sports; food and drink; lifeguards; parking (fee); toilets; showers. **Best for:** windsurfing; partiers; swimming. ✉ *Rte. A1A and E. Atlantic Ave.* 🎟 *$1.50 per 1 hr parking.*

WHERE TO EAT

$$
BRITISH
🍴 **Blue Anchor.** Yes, this pub was actually shipped from England, where it had stood for 150 years in London's historic Chancery Lane. There it was a watering hole for famed Englishmen, including Winston Churchill; here you may hear stories of lingering ghosts told over some suds. **Known for:** fish-and-chips; beer selection; late-night food spot. [$] *Average main: $18* ✉ *804 E. Atlantic Ave.* ☎ *561/272–7272* 🌐 *www.theblueanchor.com.*

$$$
SEAFOOD
Fodor'sChoice ★
🍴 **City Oyster & Sushi Bar.** This trendy restaurant mingles the personalities and flavors of a New England oyster bar, a modern sushi eatery, an eclectic seafood grill, and an award-winning dessert bakery to create a can't-miss foodie haven in the heart of Delray's bustling Atlantic Avenue. Dishes like the oyster bisque, New Orleans–style shrimp and

crab gumbo, tuna crudo, and lobster fried rice are simply sublime. **Known for:** large selection of oysters; excellent desserts; loud and busy, especially in high season. *Average main: $26 213 E. Atlantic Ave. 561/272–0220 www.cityoysterdelray.com.*

$$$ MODERN AMERICAN Fodor's Choice ★ **Max's Harvest.** A few blocks off Atlantic Avenue in the artsy Pineapple Grove neighborhood, a tree-shaded, fenced-in courtyard welcomes foodies eager to dig into its "farm-to-fork" offerings. The menu encourages people to experiment with "to share," "start small," and "think big" plates. **Known for:** menu aimed at sharing; cocktails made from artisanal spirits; Sunday brunch. *Average main: $27 169 N.E. 2nd Ave. 561/381–9970 www.maxsharvest.com No lunch Mon.–Sat.*

$$$ AMERICAN Fodor's Choice ★ **The Office.** Scenesters line the massive indoor-outdoor bar from noon 'til the wee hours at this cooler-than-thou retro library restaurant, but it's worth your time to stop here for the best burger in town. There's a whole selection, but the Prime CEO steals the show: Maytag bleu cheese and Gruyère with tomato-onion confit, arugula, and bacon. **Known for:** upscale comfort food; weekend brunch; alcoholic shakes. *Average main: $24 201 E. Atlantic Ave. 561/276–3600 www.theofficedelray.com.*

$$$$ AMERICAN Fodor's Choice ★ **32 East.** Although restaurants come and go every year on Atlantic Avenue, 32 East remains one of the best—if not the best—in Delray Beach. An ever-changing daily menu defines modern American cuisine. **Known for:** local seafood; extensive wine list; busy bar. *Average main: $36 32 E. Atlantic Ave. 561/276–7868 www.32east.com No lunch.*

WHERE TO STAY

$ HOTEL **Colony Hotel & Cabaña Club.** Not to be confused with the luxurious Colony in Palm Beach, this charming hotel in the heart of downtown Delray dates back to 1926; and although it's landlocked, it does have a cabana club 2 miles away for hotel guests only. **Pros:** pet-friendly; full breakfast buffet included with rooms; free use of cabanas, umbrellas, and hammocks. **Cons:** no pool at main hotel building; must walk to public beach for water-sport rentals. *Rooms from: $195 525 E. Atlantic Ave. 561/276–4123, 800/552–2363 www.thecolonyhotel.com 70 rooms Breakfast.*

$$$ HOTEL **Crane's Beach House Boutique Hotel & Luxury Villas.** A tropical oasis, this boutique hotel is a hidden jungle of lush exotic and tropical plants, only a block from the beach. **Pros:** private location within the city setting; short walk to the beach; free parking; property is smoke-free. **Cons:** pricey; no restaurants on-site; no fitness or spa facilities. *Rooms from: $349 82 Gleason St. 866/372–7263, 561/278–1700 www.cranesbeachhouse.com 28 rooms, 4 villas No meals.*

$$$$ HOTEL FAMILY **Delray Beach Marriott.** By far the largest hotel in Delray Beach, the Marriott has two towers on a stellar plot of land at the east end of Atlantic Avenue—it's the only hotel that directly overlooks the water, yet it is still within walking distance of restaurants, shopping, and nightlife. **Pros:** fantastic ocean views; pampering spa; two pools. **Cons:** chain-hotel feel; charge for parking; must rent beach chairs. *Rooms from: $499 10 N. Ocean Blvd. 561/274–3200 www.delraybeachmarriott.com 269 rooms No meals.*

$$$$ | RESORT | FAMILY | Fodor's Choice ★

The Seagate Hotel & Spa. Those who crave 21st-century luxury in its full glory (ultraswank tile work and fixtures, marble vanities, seamless shower doors) will love this LEED-certified hotel that offers a subtle Zen-coastal motif throughout. **Pros:** two swimming pools; fabulous beach club; exceptionally knowledgeable concierge team. **Cons:** main building not directly on beach; daily resort fee; separate charge for parking. [$] *Rooms from: $489* ✉ *1000 E. Atlantic Ave.* ☎ *561/665–4800, 877/577–3242* 🌐 *www.theseagatehotel.com* 🛏 *154 rooms* 🍴 *No meals.*

$$ | B&B/INN | Fodor's Choice ★

Sundy House. Just about everything in this bungalow-style B&B is executed to perfection—especially its tropical, verdant grounds, which are actually a nonprofit botanical garden (something anyone can check out during free weekday tours) with a natural, freshwater swimming pool where your feet glide along limestone rocks and mingle with fish. **Pros:** charming eclectic decor; each room is unique; renowned restaurant with popular indoor-outdoor bar and free breakfast; in quiet area off Atlantic Avenue. **Cons:** need to walk through garden to reach rooms (i.e., no covered walkways); beach shuttle requires roughly half-hour advance notice; no private beach facilities. [$] *Rooms from: $299* ✉ *106 Swinton Ave.* ☎ *561/272–5678, 877/434–9601* 🌐 *www.sundyhouse.com* 🛏 *11 rooms* 🍴 *Breakfast.*

$$$ | HOTEL | FAMILY

Wright by the Sea. Here's a 1950s throwback to beachfront hotels in Florida—down to the venetian blinds and tropical-beachy decor in the rooms, which were last remodeled in fall 2014. **Pros:** directly on the beach; free laundry; free beach cabanas; free parking. **Cons:** dated decor in some rooms; no elevators; no restaurant. [$] *Rooms from: $314* ✉ *1901 S. Ocean Blvd.* ☎ *561/257–0885* 🌐 *www.wbtsea.com* 🛏 *29 rooms* 🍴 *No meals.*

6

NIGHTLIFE

Boston's on the Beach. You'll find beer flowing and the ocean breeze blowing at this beach bar and eatery, a local watering hole since 1983. The walls are laden with paraphernalia from the Boston Bruins, New England Patriots, and Boston Red Sox, including a shrine to Ted Williams. Boston's can get loud and rowdy (or lively, depending on your taste) later at night. Groove to reggae on Monday, live blues bands on Tuesday, and other live music from rock to country on Friday, Saturday, and Sunday. ✉ *40 S. Ocean Blvd.* ☎ *561/278–3364* 🌐 *www.bostonsonthebeach.com.*

Dada. Bands play in the living room of this historic house, though much of the action is outdoors on the lawn in fair weather, where huge trees and lanterns make it a fun stop for drinks or a group night out. It's a place where those who don't drink will also feel comfortable, however, and excellent gourmet nibbles are a huge bonus (a full dinner menu is available, too). A bohemian, younger crowd gathers later into the night. ✉ *52 N. Swinton Ave.* ☎ *561/330–3232* 🌐 *www.sub-culture.org/dada.*

Jellies Bar at the Atlantic Grille. Within the Seagate Hotel, the fun and fabulous bar at the Atlantic Grille is known locally as Jellies Bar. The over-thirty set consistently floats over to this stunning bar to shimmy to live music Tuesday to Saturday; the namesake jellyfish tank never fails to entertain as well. ✉ *The Seagate Hotel & Spa, 1000 E. Atlantic Ave.* ☎ *561/665–4900* 🌐 *www.theatlanticgrille.com.*

SHOPPING

Atlantic Avenue and Pineapple Grove, both charming neighborhoods for shoppers, have maintained Delray Beach's small-town integrity. Atlantic Avenue is the main street, with art galleries, boutiques, restaurants, and bars lining it from just west of Swinton Avenue all the way east to the ocean. The now established Pineapple Grove Arts District is centered on the half-mile strip of Northeast 2nd Avenue that goes north from Atlantic; these areas are broadening as the downtown area expands south and east.

Furst. This studio-shop gives you the chance to watch designer Flavie Furst or her pupils at work—and then purchase their fine, handcrafted gold, gold-filled, and silver jewelry. The other half of this space is the Ronald Furst bespoke handbag store, selling unique bags, purses, and sacks. ⊠ *123 N.E. 2nd Ave.* ☎ *561/272–6422* ⊕ *www.flaviefurst.com.*

Snappy Turtle. Jack Rogers sandals and Trina Turk dresses mingle with other fun resort fashions and beachy gifts for the home and family at this family-run store. ⊠ *1100 E. Atlantic Ave.* ☎ *888/762–7798* ⊕ *www. snappy-turtle.com.*

SPORTS AND THE OUTDOORS

BIKING

There's a bicycle path in Barwick Park, but the most popular place to ride is up and down the special oceanfront bike lane along Route A1A. The city also has an illustrated and annotated map on key downtown sights available through the Palm Beach Convention and Visitors Bureau.

Richwagen's Bike & Sport. Rent bikes by the hour, day, or week (they come with locks, baskets, and helmets); Richwagen's also has copies of city maps on hand. A seven-speed cruiser rents for $60 per week, or $30 a day. They also rent bike trailers, child seats, and electric carts. The shop is closed Sunday. ⊠ *298 N.E. 6th Ave.* ☎ *561/276–4234* ⊕ *www. delraybeachbicycles.com.*

TENNIS

Delray Beach Tennis Center. Each year this complex hosts simultaneous professional tournaments where current stars like Ivo Karlovic and Marin Cilic along with legends like Andy Roddick, Ivan Lendl, and Michael Chang duke it out. Florida's own Chris Evert hosts the Pro-Celebrity Tennis Classic charity event here. The rest of the time, you can practice or learn on 14 clay courts and seven hard courts; private lessons and clinics are available, and it's open from 7:30 am to 9 pm weekdays and until 6 pm weekends. Since most hotels in the area do not have courts, tennis players visiting Delray Beach often come here to play. ⊠ *201 W. Atlantic Ave.* ☎ *561/243–7360* ⊕ *www.delraytennis.com.*

BOCA RATON

6 miles south of Delray Beach.

Less than an hour south of Palm Beach and anchoring the county's south end, upscale Boca Raton has much in common with its fabled cousin. Both reflect the unmistakable architectural influence of Addison Mizner, their principal developer in the mid-1920s. The meaning of the name Boca Raton (pronounced boca rah-*tone*) often arouses curiosity, with many folks mistakenly assuming it means "rat's mouth." Historians say the probable origin is Boca Ratones, an ancient Spanish geographical term for an inlet filled with jagged rocks or coral. Miami's Biscayne Bay had such an inlet, and in 1823 a mapmaker copying Miami terrain confused the more northern inlet, thus mistakenly labeling this area Boca Ratones. No matter what, you'll know you've arrived in the heart of downtown when you spot the historic town hall's gold dome on the main street, Federal Highway. Much of the Boca landscape was heavily planned, and many of the bigger sights are clustered in the area around town hall and Lake Boca, a wide stretch of the Intracoastal Waterway between Palmetto Park Road and Camino Real (two main east–west streets at the southern end of town).

GETTING HERE AND AROUND

To get to Boca Raton from Delray Beach, drive south 6 miles on Interstate 95, Federal Highway (U.S. 1), or Route A1A.

ESSENTIALS

VISITOR INFORMATION

Contacts Discover the Palm Beaches. ⊠ *1555 Palm Beach Lakes Blvd., Suite 800, West Palm Beach* ☎ *561/233–3000* ⊕ *www.palmbeachfl.com.*

EXPLORING

FAMILY **Boca Raton Museum of Art.** Changing-exhibition galleries on the first floor showcase internationally known artists—both past and present—at this museum in a spectacular building that's part of the Mizner Park shopping center; the permanent collection upstairs includes works by Picasso, Degas, Matisse, Klee, Modigliani, and Warhol, as well as notable African and pre-Columbian art. Daily tours are included with admission. In addition to the treasure hunts and sketchbooks you can pick up from the front desk, there's a roster of special programs that cater to kids, including studio workshops and gallery walks. Another fun feature is the cell phone audio guide—certain pieces of art have a corresponding number you dial to hear a detailed narration. ⊠ *501 Plaza Real, Mizner Park* ☎ *561/392–2500* ⊕ *www.bocamuseum.org* ⊑ *$12* ⊘ *Closed Mon.*

FAMILY **Gumbo Limbo Nature Center.** A big draw for kids, this stellar spot has four huge saltwater tanks brimming with sea life, from coral to stingrays to spiny lobsters, touch tanks, plus a sea turtle rehabilitation center. Nocturnal walks in spring and early summer, when staffers lead a quest to find nesting female turtles coming ashore to lay eggs, are popular; so are the hatching releases in August and September. (Call to purchase tickets in advance as there are very limited spaces.) This is one of only a handful of centers that offer this. There is also a nature trail and butterfly garden, a ¼-mile boardwalk, and a 40-foot observation tower, where you're likely to see brown pelicans and osprey. ⊠ *1801 N. Ocean Blvd.* ☏ *561/544–8605* ⊕ *www.gumbolimbo.org* ✉ *Free ($5 suggested donation); turtle walks $15.*

Old Floresta. This residential area was developed by Addison Mizner starting in 1925 and is beautifully landscaped with palms and cycads. Its houses are mainly Mediterranean in style, many with balconies supported by exposed wood columns. Explore by driving northward on Paloma Avenue (Northwest 8th Avenue) from Palmetto Park Road, then weave in and out of the side streets. ⊠ *Paloma Ave., north of W. Palmetto Park Rd.*

BEACHES

Boca's three city beaches (South Beach, Red Reef Park, and Spanish River Park, south to north, respectively) are beautiful and hugely popular; but unless you're a resident or enter via bicycle, parking can be very expensive. Save your receipt if you care to go in and out, or park hop—most guards at the front gate will honor a same-day ticket from another location if you ask nicely. Another option is the county-run South Inlet Park that's walking distance from the Boca Raton Bridge Hotel at the southern end of Lake Boca; it has a metered lot for a fraction of the cost, but not quite the same charm as the others.

FAMILY   **Red Reef Park.** The ocean with its namesake reef that you can wade up to is just one draw: a fishing zone on the Intracoastal Waterway across the street, a 9-hole golf course next door, and the Gumbo Limbo Environmental Education Center at the northern end of the park can easily make a day at the beach into so much more. But if pure old-fashioned fun in the sun is your focus, there are tons of picnic tables and grills, and two separate playgrounds. Pack snorkels and explore the reef at high tide when fish are most abundant. Swimmers, be warned: once lifeguards leave at 5, anglers flock to the shores and stay well past dark. **Amenities:** lifeguards; parking (fee); showers; toilets. **Best for:** snorkeling; swimming; walking. ⊠ *1400 N. Rte. A1A* ☏ *561/393–7974, 561/393–7989 for beach conditions* ⊕ *www.ci.boca-raton.fl.us/rec/parks/redreef.shtm* ✉ *$16 parking (weekdays), $18 parking (weekends).*

South Beach Park. Perched high up on a dune, a large open-air pavilion at the east end of Palmetto Park Road offers a panoramic view of what's in store below on the sand that stretches up the coast. Serious beachgoers need to pull into the main lot ¼ mile north on the east side of A1A, but if a short-but-sweet visit is what you're after, the 15 or so one-hour spots with meters in the circle driveway will do (and not cost you the normal $15 parking fee). During the day, pretty young things blanket the shore, and windsurfers practice tricks in the waves. Quiet quarters are farther north. **Amenities:** lifeguards; parking (fee); toilets; showers. **Best for:** sunset; windsurfing; walking; swimming. ⊠ *400 N. Rte A1A* ⊕ *www.ci.boca-raton.fl.us/rec/parks/southbeach.shtm* ✉ *$15 parking (weekdays), $17 parking (weekends).*

Spanish River Park. At 76 acres and including extensive nature trails, this is by far one of the largest ocean parks in the southern half of Palm Beach County and a great pick for people who want more space and fewer crowds. Big groups, including family reunions, favor it because of the number of covered picnic areas for rent, but anyone can snag a free table (there are plenty) under the thick canopy of banyan trees. Even though the vast majority of the park is separated from the surf, you never actually have to cross A1A to reach the beach, because tunnels run under it at several locations. **Amenities:** lifeguards; parking (fee); showers; toilets. **Best for:** swimming; walking; solitude. ⊠ *3001 N. Rte. A1A* ☎ *561/393–7815* ⊕ *www.ci.boca-raton.fl.us/rec/parks/spanishriver.shtm* 🖅 *$16 parking (weekdays), $18 parking (weekends).*

WHERE TO EAT

$$$$
TUSCAN
Fodor's Choice
★
✕ **Casa D'Angelo Ristorante.** The lines are deservedly long at chef Angelo Elia's upscale Tuscan restaurant in tony Boca Raton. The outpost of his renowned Casa D'Angelo in Broward impresses with an outstanding selection of antipasti, carpaccios, pastas, and specialties from the wood-burning oven. **Known for:** wide range of antipasti; veal osso buco and scaloppine; extensive wine list. $ *Average main: $38* ⊠ *171 E. Palmetto Park Rd.* ☎ *561/996–1234* ⊕ *www.casa-d-angelo.com* ☺ *No lunch.*

$$$
MODERN
AMERICAN
✕ **Farmer's Table.** Taking up the local-food mantle, the menu here includes inventive dishes following the seasons using locally sourced meats, seafood, and vegetables. Whenever possible, the foods are organic or sustainable. **Known for:** Buddha bowl with stir-fried vegetables and udon; good wine, cocktails, and beer; some vegan options. $ *Average main: $22* ⊠ *Wyndham Boca Raton, 1901 N. Military Trail* ☎ *561/417–5836* ⊕ *www.farmerstableboca.com.*

$$$
AMERICAN
✕ **Racks Downtown Eatery & Tavern.** Whimsical indoor–outdoor decor and comfort food with a twist help define this popular eatery in tony Mizner Park. Instead of dinner rolls, pretzel bread and mustard get things started. **Known for:** menu made for sharing; raw bar; popular happy hour. $ *Average main: $23* ⊠ *402 Plaza Real, Mizner Park* ☎ *561/395–1662* ⊕ *www.racksboca.com.*

$$$$
SEAFOOD
Fodor's Choice
★
✕ **Truluck's.** This popular Florida and Texas seafood chain is so serious about its fruits of the sea that it supports its own fleet of 16 fishing boats. Stone crabs are the signature dish, and you can have all you can eat on Monday night from October to May. **Known for:** fresh seafood; large portions; gluten-free menu. $ *Average main: $35* ⊠ *351 Plaza Real, Mizner Park* ☎ *561/391–0755* ⊕ *www.trulucks.com.*

$$$
CHINESE
✕ **Uncle Tai's.** The draw at this longtime upscale eatery offers up some of the best Hunan cuisine on Florida's east coast. Specialties include sliced duck with snow peas and water chestnuts in a tangy plum sauce, and orange beef delight—flank steak stir-fried until crispy and then sautéed with pepper sauce, garlic, and orange peel. **Known for:** spicy cuisine that can be toned down on request; General Tso's chicken; sunset dinner specials. $ *Average main: $21* ⊠ *5250 Town Center Circle* ☎ *561/368–8806* ⊕ *www.uncletais.com.*

6

WHERE TO STAY

$$$$ RESORT FAMILY Fodor's Choice ★ **Boca Beach Club.** Dotted with turquoise lounge chairs, ruffled umbrellas, and white-sand beaches, this newly reconceived and rebranded hotel is now part of the Waldorf-Astoria collection and looks as if it was carefully replicated from a retro-chic postcard. **Pros:** great location on the beach; kids' activity center. **Cons:** pricey; shuttle ride away from the main building; resort fee. [$] *Rooms from: $542* ✉ *900 S. Ocean Blvd.* ☎ *888/564–1312* 🌐 *www.bocabeachclub.com* 🛏 *212 rooms* 🍴 *No meals.*

$$$ RESORT FAMILY Fodor's Choice ★ **Boca Raton Resort & Club.** Addison Mizner built this Mediterranean-style hotel in 1926, and additions over time have created a sprawling, sparkling resort, one of the most luxurious in all of South Florida and part of the Waldorf-Astoria collection. **Pros:** superexclusive—grounds are closed to the public; decor strikes the right balance between historic roots and modern comforts; plenty of activities. **Cons:** daily resort charge; conventions often crowd common areas. [$] *Rooms from: $309* ✉ *501 E. Camino Real* ☎ *561/447–3000, 888/543–1277* 🌐 *www.bocaresort.com* 🛏 *635 rooms* 🍴 *No meals.*

$$ HOTEL **Waterstone Resort & Marina.** The former Bridge Hotel was transformed into a sleek, modern resort with a $20 million restoration in 2014. **Pros:** short walk to beach; pet-friendly; waterfront views throughout. **Cons:** parking fee; no quiet common space; some rooms noisy from nearby bridge traffic. [$] *Rooms from: $289* ✉ *999 E. Camino Real* ☎ *561/368–9500* 🌐 *www.waterstoneboca.com* 🛏 *139 rooms* 🍴 *No meals.*

SHOPPING

Mizner Park. This distinctive 30-acre shopping center off Federal Highway, one block north of Palmetto Park Road, intersperses apartments and town houses among its gardenlike commercial areas. Some three dozen retailers—including Lord and Taylor, which moved in as the only national department store east of Interstate 95 in Boca—line the central axis. It's peppered with fountains and green space, restaurants, galleries, a jazz club, a movie theater, the Boca Raton Museum of Art, and an amphitheater that hosts major concerts as well as community events. ✉ *327 Plaza Real* ☎ *561/362–0606* 🌐 *www.miznerpark.com.*

Royal Palm Place. The retail enclave of Royal Palm is filled with independent boutiques selling fine jewelry and apparel. By day, stroll the walkable streets and have your pick of sidewalk cafés for a bite alongside Boca's ladies who lunch. Royal Palm Place assumes a different personality come nightfall, as its numerous restaurants and lounges attract throngs of patrons for great dining and fabulous libations. Parking here is free. ✉ *101 Plaza Real S* ☎ *561/392–8920* 🌐 *www.royalpalmplace.com.*

Town Center at Boca Raton. Over on the west side of the interstate in Boca, this indoor megamall has over 220 stores, with anchor stores including Saks and Neiman Marcus and just about every major high-end designer, including Kate Spade and Anne Fontaine. But not every shop here requires deep pockets. The Town Center at Boca Raton is also firmly rooted with a variety of more affordable national brands like Gap and Guess. ✉ *6000 Glades Rd.* ☎ *561/368–6000* 🌐 *www.simon.com/mall/town-center-at-boca-raton.*

SPORTS AND THE OUTDOORS

GOLF

Red Reef Park Executive Golf Course. This executive golf course offers 9 holes with varying views of the Intracoastal and the Atlantic Ocean. The Joe Palloka– and Charles Ankrom–designed course dates back to 1957. It was refreshed in 2001 through a multimillion-dollar renovation. The scenic holes are between 54 and 227 yards each—great for a quick round. Carts are available, but the short course begs to be walked. Park in the lot across the street from the main beach entrance, and put the greens fees receipt on the dash; that covers parking. ✉ *1221 N. Ocean Blvd.* ☎ *561/391–5014* ⊕ *www.bocacitygolf.com* ✍ *$17 to to walk; $27 to ride* ⚑ *9 holes, 1357 yards, par 32.*

SCUBA AND SNORKELING

Force-E. This company, in business since the late 1970s, rents, sells, and repairs scuba and snorkeling equipment—and organizes about 80 dive trips a week from the Palm Beach Inlet to Port Everglades in Broward County. The PADI–affiliated five-star center has instruction for all levels and offers private charters, too. They have two other outposts besides this Boca Raton location—one north in Riviera Beach and one south in Pompano Beach. ✉ *2181 N. Federal Hwy.* ☎ *561/368–0555, 561/368–0555* ⊕ *www.force-e.com.*

6

NORTH COUNTY

Just over the bridge at the Port of Palm Beach are the more laid-back towns of North County, where families and golf pros, not to mention the celebs on Jupiter Island, call home. On **Singer Island,** visible from Palm Beach across the Palm Beach Inlet, and a mere 20 minutes by land, are the towns of **Palm Beach Shores** and **Riviera Beach.** With good beach access and waterfront parks, surf- and sun-seekers have several options, including the nearby Peanut Island. On the mainland north and west, suburban **Palm Beach Gardens** is the golf capital of the county, with PGA courses and country club greens making for greenspace throughout, along with a shoppers' paradise (malls abound). The tiny seaside **Juno Beach,** with turtle-rich beaches, melds quickly into Jupiter, where the beach is the star—for both two- and four-legged sun worshippers—with parks and public pavilions providing gathering sites for groups.

PALM BEACH GARDENS

13½ miles north of West Palm Beach.

About 15 minutes northwest of Palm Beach is this relaxed, upscale residential community known for its high-profile golf complex, the **PGA National Resort & Spa.** Although not on the beach, the town is less than a 15-minute drive from the ocean. Malls and dining are centered on the main street, PGA Boulevard, running east from the resort to U.S. 1.

WHERE TO EAT

$$$$
AMERICAN

✕ **Café Chardonnay.** A longtime local favorite, Café Chardonnay is charming, romantic, and has some of the most refined food in the suburban town of Palm Beach Gardens. Soft lighting, warm woods, white tablecloths, and cozy banquettes set the scene for a quiet lunch or romantic dinner. **Known for:** outstanding wine list; innovative specials; many locally sourced ingredients. $ *Average main: $34* ⊠ *The Gardens Square Shoppes, 4533 PGA Blvd.* ☎ *561/627–2662* ⊕ *www. cafechardonnay.com* ⊘ *No lunch weekends.*

$$$
AMERICAN

✕ **Coolinary Cafe.** It's tucked away in a strip mall and has only 50 seats inside (counting the bar) and a handful out on the sidewalk, but everything down to the condiments is made in-house here. Rabbit sausage and noodles or lamb meatball risotto are examples on the seasonal one-page menus the chef puts together daily. **Known for:** small, focused regular menu; fresh fish specials; long waits for dinner in season. $ *Average main: $22* ⊠ *Donald Ross Village Plaza, 4650 Donald Ross Rd., Suite 110* ☎ *561/249–6760* ⊕ *www.coolinarycafe. com* ⊘ *Closed Sun.*

$$$
AMERICAN

✕ **The Cooper.** With a contemporary farm-to-table menu, and spacious dining rooms and bars, this spot in PGA Commons has plenty of local fans. Happy-hour crowds fill the patio bar-lounge area to sip the craft cocktails and nibble from a cheese or salumi board. **Known for:** wide-ranging American menu; extensive wine list; gluten-free options. $ *Average main: $23* ⊠ *PGA Commons, 4610 PGA Blvd.* ☎ *561/622–0032* ⊕ *www.thecooperrestaurant.com.*

$$$$
STEAKHOUSE

✕ **Ironwood Steak & Seafood.** Located in the PGA National Resort & Spa, this eatery draws guests, locals, and tourists alike eager for a taste of its fired-up Vulcan-cooked steaks (Vulcan to meat eaters is like Titleist to golfers—the best equipment around). Wagyu and Angus beef cuts are featured. **Known for:** wide range of steaks; raw bar; extensive wine list. $ *Average main: $38* ⊠ *PGA National Resort & Spa, 400 Ave. of the Champions* ☎ *561/627–4852* ⊕ *www.pgaresort.com/restaurants/ ironwood-grille.*

$$$
SEAFOOD

✕ **Spoto's Oyster Bar.** If you love oysters and other raw bar nibbles, head here, where black-and-white photographs of oyster fisherman adorn the walls. The polished tables give the eatery a clubby look. **Known for:** wide range of oysters and clams; fresh seafood; live music in the Blue Point Lounge. $ *Average main: $26* ⊠ *PGA Commons, 4560 PGA Blvd.* ☎ *561/776–9448* ⊕ *www.spotosoysterbar.com.*

WHERE TO STAY

$$
HOTEL

🏨 **Hilton Garden Inn Palm Beach Gardens.** A hidden find in Palm Beach Gardens, this hotel sits on a small lake next to a residential area, but near two shopping malls and close to PGA golf courses. **Pros:** 24-hour free business center; walk to two different malls with shops, restaurants, and movie theaters. **Cons:** outdoor self-parking; no bell service; pool closes at dusk; 15 minutes from the beach. $ *Rooms from: $209* ⊠ *3505 Kyoto Gardens Dr.* ☎ *561/694–5833, 561/694–5829* ⊕ *hilton-gardeninn3.hilton.com* ⇥ *180 rooms* ⦙⦙ *No meals.*

$$$

RESORT

Fodor's Choice

★

PGA National Resort & Spa. This golfer's paradise (five championship courses and the site of the yearly Honda Classic pro-tour tournament) is a sleek modern playground with a gorgeous zero-entry lagoon pool, seven different places to eat, and a full-service spa with unique mineral-salt therapy pools. **Pros:** dream golf facilities; affordable rates for top-notch amenities; close to shopping malls. **Cons:** no beach shuttle; difficult to get around if you don't have a car; long drive to Palm Beach proper. $ *Rooms from: $348* ⌧ *400 Ave. of the Champions* ☎ *561/627–2000, 800/633–9150* ⊕ *www.pgaresort.com* ⤢ *339 rooms* ⦿ *No meals.*

SHOPPING

FAMILY **Downtown at The Gardens.** This open-air pavilion down the street from The Gardens Mall has boutiques, chain stores, a grocery store, day spas, a 16-screen movie theater, and a lively restaurant and nighttime bar scene that includes the Dirty Martini and the Yard House, both of which stay open late. A carousel, children's barbershop, boutiques, and Cool Beans (an indoor playground), make this a family-friendly mall. ⌧ *11701 Lake Victoria Gardens Ave.* ☎ *561/340–1600* ⊕ *www. downtownatthegardens.com.*

Fodor's Choice

★

The Gardens Mall. One of the most refined big shopping malls in America, the 160-store Gardens Mall in northern Palm Beach County has stores like Chanel, Gucci, Louis Vuitton, and David Yurman, along with Saks Fifth Avenue and Nordstrom. There are also plenty of reasonably priced national retailers like H&M and Abercrombie & Fitch, Bloomingdale's, and Macy's. This beautiful mall has prolific seating pavilions, making it a great place to spend a humid summer afternoon. ⌧ *3101 PGA Blvd.* ☎ *561/775–7750* ⊕ *www.thegardensmall.com.*

SPORTS AND THE OUTDOORS

Spring-training fans travel to the area to see the Cardinals and Marlins tune up for their seasons at Roger Dean Stadium in Palm Beach Gardens, and to watch their AAA feeder teams in summer. Port St. Lucie and Vero Beach stadiums and more teams are only a short drive up Interstate 95.

GOLF

Fodor's Choice

★

PGA National Resort & Spa. If you're the kind of traveler who takes along a set of clubs, you'll achieve nirvana on the greens of PGA National Resort & Spa. The five championship courses are open only to hotel guests and club members, which means you'll have to stay to play, but packages that include a room and a round of golf are reasonably priced. The Champion Course, redesigned by Jack Nicklaus and famous for its Bear Trap holes, is the site of the yearly Honda Classic pro tournament. The four other challenging courses are also legends in the golfing world: the Palmer, named for its architect, the legendary Arnold Palmer; the Fazio (formerly the "Haig," the resort's first course reopened in November 2012 after a major renovation) and the Squire, both from Tom and George Fazio; and the Karl Litten–designed Estates, the sole course not on the property (it is located 5 miles west of the PGA resort). Lessons are available at the David Leadbetter Golf Academy, and they also run a summertime kids' golf camp. ⌧ *PGA National Resort & Spa, 1000*

6

Ave. of the Champions ☎ *561/627–1800* ⊕ *www.pgaresort.com/golf/
pga-national-golf* ⌨ *$409 for 18 holes for Champion Course, Fazio
Course, and Squire Course. $250 for 18 holes for Palmer Course and
Estates Course.* 🏌 *Champion Course: 18 holes, 7048 yards, par 72.
Palmer Course: 18 holes, 7079 yards, par 72. Fazio Course: 18 holes,
6806 yards, par 72. Squire Course: 18 holes, 6465 yards, par 72. Estates
Course: 18 holes, 6694 yards, par 72.*

SINGER ISLAND

6 miles north of West Palm Beach.

Across the inlet from the northern end of Palm Beach is Singer Island,
which is actually a peninsula that's big enough to pass for a barrier
island, rimmed with mom-and-pop motels and high-rises. Palm Beach
Shores occupies its southern tip (where tiny Peanut Island is a stone's
throw away); farther north are Riviera Beach and North Palm Beach,
which also straddle the inlet and continue on the mainland.

EXPLORING

Palm Beach Maritime Museum. Though the main building of the Palm
Beach Maritime Museum is found in Currie Park in West Palm Beach,
its main treasure—the restored "Kennedy Bunker," a bomb shelter
built for President John F. Kennedy, and a historic Coast Guard station—is located on Peanut Island. You can take a guided tour of the
bunker through the museum's Peanut Island outpost. The museum also
has a nice little gift shop, an outdoor deck on the water, and a lawn
where you can play games including horseshoes. To get there, catch a
water taxi from Riviera Beach Municipal Marina, but be aware that
the boats won't run in choppy waters. ⊠ *Peanut Island, Riviera Beach*
☎ *561/848–2960* ⊕ *www.pbmm.info* ⌨ *$17 (not including water trans-
portation)* ⊘ *Closed Mon.–Wed.*

BEACHES

FAMILY   **John D. MacArthur Beach State Park.** If getting far from rowdy crowds is
Fodor'sChoice   your goal, this spot on the north end of Singer Island is a good choice.
★   Encompassing 2 miles of beach and a lush subtropical coastal habitat, inside you'll find a great place for kayaking, snorkeling at natural
reefs, bird-watching, fishing, and hiking. You might even get to see a
few manatees. A 4,000-square-foot nature center has aquariums and
displays on local flora and fauna, and there's a long roster of monthly
activities, such as surfing clinics, art lessons, and live bluegrass music.
Guided sea turtle walks are available at night in season, and daily
nature walks depart at 10 am. Check the website for times and costs
of activities. **Amenities:** water sports; parking (fee); toilets; showers.
Best for: swimming; walking; solitude; surfing. ⊠ *10900 Jack Nicklaus
Dr., North Palm Beach* ☎ *561/624–6950* ⊕ *www.macarthurbeach.org*
⌨ *Parking $5, bicyclists and pedestrians $2.*

Peanut Island Park. Partiers, families, and overnight campers all have a
place to go on the 79 acres here. The island, in a wide section of the
Intracoastal between Palm Beach Island and Singer Island with an open
channel to the sea, is accessible only by private boat or water taxi, two

of which set sail regularly from the Riviera Beach Municipal Marina (🌐 *peanutislandferry.com*) and the Sailfish Marina (🌐 *www.sailfishmarina.com/water_taxi*). Fun-loving seafarers looking for an afternoon of Jimmy Buffett and picnics aboard pull up to the day docks or the huge sandbar on the north—float around in an inner tube, and it's spring break déjà vu. Walk along the 20-foot-wide paver-lined path encircling the island, and you'll hit a 170-foot fishing pier, a campground, the lifeguarded section to the south that is particularly popular with families because of its artificial reef, and last, but not least, the Palm Beach Maritime Museum's "Kennedy Bunker" (a bomb shelter prepared for President John F. Kennedy that was restored and opened to the public in 1999). There are picnic tables and grills, but no concessions. A new ordinance means alcohol possession and consumption is restricted to permit areas. **Amenities:** lifeguards (summer only); toilets; showers. **Best for:** partiers; walking; swimming; sunrise. ✉ *6500 Peanut Island Rd., Riviera Beach* ☎ *561/845–4445* 🌐 *www.pbcgov.com/parks/peanutisland* 🎫 *Beach free; water taxi $10; park stay $17.*

WHERE TO STAY

$$$$ RESORT FAMILY 🏨 **Palm Beach Marriott Singer Island Beach Resort & Spa.** Families with a yen for the cosmopolitan but requiring the square footage and comforts of home revel in these one- and two-bedroom suites with spacious, marble-tiled, granite-topped kitchens. **Pros:** wide beach; genuinely warm service; plenty of kids' activities; sleek spa. **Cons:** no upscale dining nearby; unspectacular room views for an ocean-side hotel. [$] *Rooms from: $509* ✉ *3800 N. Ocean Dr., Singer Island, Riviera Beach* ☎ *561/340–1700, 877/239–5610* 🌐 *www.marriott.com* 🛏 *202 suites* 🍴 *No meals.*

$ HOTEL 🏨 **Sailfish Marina Resort.** A marina with deepwater slips—and prime location at the mouth to the Atlantic Ocean on the Intracoastal Waterway across from Peanut Island—lures boaters and anglers here to these rather basic rooms, studios, and efficiencies. **Pros:** inexpensive rates; great waterfront restaurant; has a water taxi; pretty grounds. **Cons:** no real lobby; not directly on beach; area attracts a party crowd and can be noisy; dated decor. [$] *Rooms from: $150* ✉ *98 Lake Dr., Palm Beach Shores* ☎ *561/844–1724* 🌐 *www.sailfishmarina.com* 🛏 *30 units* 🍴 *No meals.*

SPORTS AND THE OUTDOORS

FISHING

Sailfish Marina. Book a full or half day of deep-sea fishing for up to six people with the seasoned captains and large fleet of 28- to 65-foot boats. A ship's store and restaurant are also on-site. ✉ *Sailfish Marina Resort, 98 Lake Dr., Palm Beach Shores* ☎ *561/844–1724* 🌐 *www.sailfishmarina.com.*

JUNO BEACH

12 miles north of West Palm Beach.

This small town east of Palm Beach Gardens has 2 miles of shoreline that becomes home to thousands of sea turtle hatchlings each year, making it one of the world's densest nesting sites. A 990-foot-long pier lures fishermen and beachgoers seeking a spectacular sunrise.

EXPLORING

FAMILY

Fodor's Choice

★

Loggerhead Park Marine Life Center of Juno Beach. Located in a certified green building in Loggerhead Park—and established by Eleanor N. Fletcher, the "turtle lady of Juno Beach"—the center focuses on the conservation of sea turtles, using education, research, and rehabilitation. The education center houses displays of coastal natural history, detailing Florida's marine ecosystems and the life and plight of the various species of sea turtles found on Florida's shores. You can visit recovering turtles in their outdoor hospital tanks; volunteers are happy to tell you the turtles' heroic tales of survival. The center has regularly scheduled activities, such as Kid's Story Time and Junior Vet Lab, and most are free of charge. During peak nesting season, the center hosts night walks to experience turtle nesting in action. Given that the adjacent beach is part of the second biggest nesting ground for loggerhead turtles in the world, your chances of seeing this natural phenomenon are pretty high (over 15,000 loggerheads nested here in 2016). ⊠ *14200 U.S. 1* ☎ *561/627–8280* ⊕ *www.marinelife.org* ⟹ *Free.*

BEACHES

FAMILY

Juno Beach Ocean Park. An angler's dream, this beach has a 990-foot pier that's open daily, like the beach, from sunrise to sunset—but from November through February, pier gates open at 6 am and don't close until 10 pm on weeknights and midnight on weekends, making it an awesome place to catch a full sunrise and sunset (that is, if you don't mind paying the small admission fee). A concession stand on the pier sells fish food as well as such human favorites as burgers, sandwiches, and ice cream. Rods and tackle are rented here. Families adore this shoreline because of the amenities and vibrant atmosphere. There are plenty of kids building castles but also plenty of teens having socials and hanging out along the beach. Pets are not allowed here, but they are allowed on Jupiter Beach. **Amenities:** lifeguards; food and drink; parking (no fee); showers; toilets. **Best for:** sunrise; sunset; swimming. ⊠ *14775 U.S. 1* ☎ *561/799–0185 for pier* ⊕ *www.pbcgov.com/parks/ locations/junobeach.htm* ⟹ *$4 to fish, $1 to enter pier; beach free.*

JUPITER AND VICINITY

12 miles north of West Palm Beach.

Jupiter is one of the few towns in the region not fronted by an island but still quite close to the fantastic hotels, shopping, and dining of the Palm Beach area. The beaches here are on the mainland, and Route A1A runs for almost 4 miles along the beachfront dunes and beautiful homes.

Northeast across the Jupiter Inlet from Jupiter is the southern tip of Jupiter Island, which stretches about 15 miles to the St. Lucie Inlet. Here expansive and expensive estates often retreat from the road behind screens of vegetation, and the population dwindles the farther north you go. At the very north end, which adjoins tiny Hobe Sound in Martin County on the mainland, sea turtles come to nest.

GETTING HERE AND AROUND

If you're coming from the airport in West Palm Beach, take Interstate 95 to Route 706. Otherwise, Federal Highway (U.S. 1) and Route A1A are usually more convenient.

Contacts Discover the Palm Beaches. ⊠ *1555 Palm Beach Lakes Blvd., Suite 800, West Palm Beach* ☎ *561/233–3000* ⊕ *www.palmbeachfl.com.*

EXPLORING

FAMILY

Fodor'sChoice

★

Blowing Rocks Preserve. Managed by the Nature Conservancy, this protected area on Jupiter Island is headlined by an almost otherworldly looking limestone shelf that fringes South Florida's most turquoise waters. Also protected within its 73 acres are plants native to beachfront dunes, coastal strand (the landward side of the dunes), mangrove swamps, and tropical hardwood forests. There are two short walking trails on the Intracoastal side of the preserve, as well as an education center and a butterfly garden. The best time to come and see the "blowing rocks" is when a storm is brewing: if high tides and strong offshore winds coincide, the sea blows spectacularly through the holes in the eroded outcropping. During a calm summer day, you can swim in crystal-clear waters on the mile-long beach and climb around the rock formations at low tide. Park in one of the two lots because police ticket cars on the road. ⊠ *574 S. Beach Rd., CR 707, Hobe Sound* ☎ *561/744–6668* ⊕ *www.nature.org/blowingrocks* ⊠ *$2.*

FAMILY

Fodor'sChoice

★

Hobe Sound Nature Center. Though located in the Hobe Sound National Wildlife Refuge, this nature center is an independent organization. The exhibit hall houses live baby alligators, crocodiles, a scary-looking tarantula, and more—and is a child's delight. Just off the center's entrance is a mile-long nature trail loop that snakes through three different kinds of habitats: coastal hammock, estuary beach, and sand pine scrub, which is one of Florida's most unusual and endangered plant communities and what composes much of the refuge's nearly 250 acres. ■TIP➔ Among the center's more popular events are the annual nighttime sea turtle walks, held between May and June; reservations are accepted as early as April 1. ⊠ *13640 S.E. U.S. 1, Hobe Sound* ☎ *772/546–2067* ⊕ *www.hobesoundnaturecenter.com* ⊠ *Free (donation requested)* ⊗ *Closed Sun.*

FAMILY

Fodor'sChoice

★

Jonathan Dickinson State Park. This serene state park provides a glimpse of predevelopment "real" Florida. A beautiful showcase of Florida inland habitat, the park teems with endangered gopher tortoises and manatees. From Hobe Mountain, an ancient dune topped with a tower, you are treated to a panoramic view of this park's more than 11,000 acres of varied terrain and the Intracoastal Waterway. The Loxahatchee River, named a National Wild and Scenic River, cuts through the park, and is home to plenty of charismatic manatees in winter and alligators year-round. Two-hour boat tours of the river depart daily. Kayak rentals are available, as is horseback riding (it was reintroduced after a 30-year absence). Among the amenities are a dozen newly redone cabins for rent, tent sites, bicycle and hiking trails, two established campgrounds and some primitive campgrounds, and a snack bar. Palmettos on the Loxahatchee is a new food-and-beverage garden with wine, beer, and

6

Away from developed shorelines, Blowing Rocks Preserve on Jupiter Island lets you wander the dunes.

local foods featured. Don't skip the Elsa Kimbell Environmental Education and Research Center, which has interactive displays, exhibits, and a short film on the natural history of the area. The park is also a fantastic birding location, with about 150 species to spot. ✉ *16450 S.E. U.S. 1, Hobe Sound* ☎ *772/546–2771* ⊕ *www.floridastateparks. org/jonathandickinson* ✉ *Vehicles $6, bicyclists and pedestrians $2.*

FAMILY

Fodor'sChoice

★

Jupiter Inlet Lighthouse & Museum. Designed by Civil War hero Lieutenant George Gordon Meade, this working brick lighthouse has been under the Coast Guard's purview since 1860. Tours of the 108-foot-tall landmark are held approximately every half hour and are included with admission. (Children must be at least 4 feet tall to go to the top.) The museum tells about efforts to restore this graceful spire to the way it looked from 1860 to 1918; its galleries and outdoor structures, including a pioneer home, also showcase local history dating back 5,000 years. ✉ *Lighthouse Park, 500 Capt. Armour's Way, Jupiter* ☎ *561/747–8380* ⊕ *www.jupiterlighthouse.org* ✉ *$12* ⊙ *Closed Mon. May–Dec.*

BEACHES

Carlin Park. About ½ mile south of the Jupiter Beach Resort and Indiantown Road, the quiet beach here is just one draw; otherwise, the manicured park, which straddles A1A, is chock-full of activities and amenities, and it has the most free parking of any beach park in the area. Several picnic pavilions, including a few beachside, two bocce ball courts, six lighted tennis courts, a baseball diamond, a wood-chip-lined running path, and an amphitheater that hosts free concerts and Shakespeare productions are just some of the highlights. Locals also swear by the Lazy Loggerhead Café that's right off the seaside parking lot for a great casual breakfast and lunch. **Amenities:** lifeguards; food and drink; parking (no fee); toilets; showers. **Best for:** swimming; walking. ✉ *400 S. Rte. A1A, Jupiter* 🌐 *www.pbcgov.com/parks/locations/carlin.htm.*

Hobe Sound National Wildlife Refuge. Nature lovers seeking to get as far as possible from the madding crowds will feel at peace at this refuge managed by the U.S. Fish & Wildlife service. It's a haven for people who want some quiet while they walk around and photograph the gorgeous coastal sand dunes, where turtles nest and shells often wash ashore. The beach has been severely eroded by high tides and strong winds (surprisingly, surfing is allowed and many do partake). You can't actually venture within most of the 735 protected acres, so if hiking piques your interest, head to the refuge's main entrance a few miles away on Hobe Sound (✉ *13640 S.E. U.S. 1 in Hobe Sound*) for a mile-long trek close to the nature center, or to nearby Jonathan Dickinson State Park (✉ *16450 S.E. U.S. 1 in Hobe Sound*). **Amenities:** parking (fee); toilets. **Best for:** solitude; surfing; walking. ✉ *198 N. Beach Rd., at end of N. Beach Rd., Jupiter Island* ☎ *772/546–6141* 🌐 *www.fws.gov/hobesound* 🎟 *$5.*

Fodor's Choice ★ **Jupiter Beach.** Famous throughout all of Florida for a unique pooch-loving stance, the town of Jupiter's beach welcomes Yorkies, Labs, pugs—you name it—along its 2½-mile oceanfront. Dogs can frolic unleashed (once they're on the beach) or join you for a dip. Free parking spots line A1A in front of the sandy stretch, and there are multiple access points and continuously refilled dog-bag boxes (29 to be exact). The dog beach starts on Marcinski Road (Beach Marker #25) and continues north until Beach Marker #59. Before going, read through the guidelines posted on the Friends of Jupiter Beach website; the biggest things to note are be sure to clean up after your dog and steer clear of lifeguarded areas to the north and south. **■ TIP→ Dogs fare best early morning and late afternoon, when the sand isn't too hot for their paws.** **Amenities:** toilets; showers. **Best for:** walking. ✉ *2188 Marcinski Rd., across the street from the parking lot, Jupiter* ☎ *561/748–8140* 🌐 *www.friendsofjupiterbeach.com.*

6

WHERE TO EAT

$$ SEAFOOD 🍴 **Guanabanas.** Expect a wait for dinner, which is not necessarily a bad thing at this island paradise of a waterfront restaurant and bar. Take the wait time to explore the bridges and trails of the open-air tropical oasis, or grab a chair by the river to watch the sunset, listen to the live band, or nibble on some conch fritters at the large tiki bar until your table is ready. **Known for:** water views from the outdoor dining area; live music; weekend breakfast. [$] *Average main: $18* ✉ *960 N. Rte. A1A, Jupiter* ☎ *561/747–8878* 🌐 *www.guanabanas.com.*

$$ SEAFOOD 🍴 **Little Moir's Food Shack.** This local favorite is not much to look at and a bit tricky to find, but well worth the search. The fried-food standards you might expect at such a casual, small place that uses plastic utensils are not found on the menu; instead there are fried tuna rolls with basil, and panko-crusted fried oysters with spicy fruit salad. **Known for:** fresh fish; good beer selection; long lines during the season. [$] *Average main: $17* ✉ *103 S. U.S. 1, Jupiter* ☎ *561/741–3626* 🌐 *www.littlemoirs.com/food-shack* ⏲ *Closed Sun.*

$$$$ ✕ **Sinclair's Ocean Grill.** This upscale restaurant at the Jupiter Beach Resort
SEAFOOD   & Spa has a slick, contemporary look and is a favorite of locals in the know. The menu has a daily selection of fresh fish, such as Atlantic black grouper over lemon crab salad, sesame-seared tuna, and mahimahi with fruit salsa. **Known for:** fresh fish; weekend brunch; drinks in Sinclair's Lounge. $ *Average main: $31* ✉ *Jupiter Beach Resort, 5 N. Rte. A1A, Jupiter* ☎ *561/746–2511* ⊕ *www.jupiterbeachresort.com.*

$$ ✕ **Taste Casual Dining.** Located in the center of historic Hobe Sound, this
AMERICAN   cozy dining spot with a pleasant, screened-in patio offers piano dinner music on Fridays. Locals like to hang out at the old, English-style wine bar; however, the food itself is the biggest draw here. **Known for:** fresh fish specials; slow-cooked prime rib; signature Gorgonzola salad. $ *Average main: $18* ✉ *11750 S.E. Dixie Hwy., Hobe Sound* ☎ *772/546–1129* ⊕ *www.tastehobesound.com* ☉ *May–Oct., closed Sun.*

WHERE TO STAY

$$$ 🛏 **Jupiter Beach Resort & Spa.** Families love this nine-story hotel filled
RESORT   with rich Caribbean-style rooms containing mahogany sleigh beds and
FAMILY   armoires; all rooms have balconies, and many have stunning views of
Fodor's Choice   the ocean and local landmarks like the Jupiter Lighthouse and Juno
★   Pier. **Pros:** fantastic beachside pool area with hammocks and a fire pit; marble showers; great restaurant. **Cons:** $25 nightly resort fee; no covered parking; bathtubs only in suites. $ *Rooms from: $360* ✉ *5 N. Rte. A1A, Jupiter* ☎ *561/746–2511, 800/228–8810* ⊕ *www.jupiterbeachresort.com* ⇆ *168 rooms* ⏋◯⏌ *No meals.*

$$$ 🛏 **Wyndham Grand Jupiter at Harbourside Place.** This luxury waterfront
HOTEL   hotel is in an upscale complex of business and retail development just minutes from the beach. **Pros:** convenient to plaza shops and restaurants; only minutes from the beach; boat docks and fitness center available. **Cons:** no covered walkway to restaurant; no green spaces; pricey. $ *Rooms from: $309* ✉ *Harbourside Place, 122 Soundings Ave., Jupiter* ☎ *561/273–6600* ⊕ *www.wyndhamgrandjupiter.com* ⇆ *179 rooms* ⏋◯⏌ *No meals.*

SPORTS AND THE OUTDOORS

BASEBALL

Roger Dean Stadium. It's a spring-training doubleheader: both the St. Louis Cardinals and the Miami Marlins call this 6,600-seat facility home base from February to April. The rest of the year two minor-league teams (Jupiter Hammerheads and Palm Beach Cardinals) share its turf. In the Abacoa area of Jupiter, the grounds are surrounded by a mix of restaurants and sports bars for pre- and postgame action. ✉ *4751 Main St., Jupiter* ☎ *561/775–1818* ⊕ *www.rogerdeanstadium.com* ⌸ *From $12.*

BOATING AND CANOEING

Fodor's Choice   **Canoe Outfitters of Florida.** See animals, from otters to eagles, along 8
★   miles of the Loxahatchee River in Riverbend County Park daily except Tuesday and Wednesday. Canoe and two-person kayaks are available for rent. Bike rentals are available, too. ✉ *Riverbend County Park, 9060 W. Indiantown Rd., Jupiter* ☎ *561/746–7053* ⊕ *www.canoeoutfittersofflorida.com* ⌸ *From $35 for 4 hrs for kayak rentals.*

FAMILY
Fodor's Choice
★

Jonathan Dickinson State Park River Tours. Boat tours of the Loxahatchee River and guided horseback rides, along with canoe, kayak, bicycle, and boat rentals, are offered daily. The popular Wilderness Guided Boat Tour leaves four times daily at 9 and 11 am and 1 and 3 pm (for best wildlife photos take the 11 or 1 tour). The pontoon cruises for 90 minutes up the Loxahatchee in search of manatees, herons, osprey, alligators, and more. The skipper details the region's natural and cultural history; and from Thursday to Monday the boat also stops at the Trapper Nelson Interpretive Site for a tour of the home of a local legend, the so-called Wildman of the Loxahatchee. ⊠ *Jonathan Dickinson State Park, 16450 S.E. U.S. 1, Hobe Sound* ☏ *561/746–1466* ⊕ *www.floridaparktours.com* ⊠ *$6 park admission; boat tours $20.*

GOLF

Abacoa Golf Club. Built in 1999, the tagline for this Joe Lee–designed 18-hole course in Jupiter is "public golf at its finest." Most of the courses in this golfing community are private, but the range at Abacoa is on par with them and membership (nor deep pockets) *isn't* required. Since 2013, $1 million has been spent to renovate the facilities throughout the course and clubhouse. One of the course's more interesting features includes the several elevation changes throughout, which is a rarity in flat Florida. The course caters to golfers at all skill levels. The greens fee ranges from $45 to $110 (including cart), depending on time of year, time of day, and weekday versus weekend. ⊠ *105 Barbados Dr., Jupiter* ☏ *561/622–0036* ⊕ *www.abacoagolfclub.com* ⊠ *$100 for 18 holes* ⏂ *18 holes, 7200 yards, par 72.*

Golf Club of Jupiter. Locally owned and operated since 1981, this Lamar Smith–designed golf club features a public, championship golf course— the "Jupiter" course—with 18 holes of varying difficulty. It has a course rating of 69.9 and a slope rating of 117 on Bermuda grass. There's a full-time golf pro on staff and an on-site bar and restaurant. ⊠ *1800 S. Central Blvd., Jupiter* ☏ *561/747–6262* ⊕ *www.golfclubofjupiter.com* ⊠ *$59 for 18 holes* ⏂ *18 holes, 6275 yards, par 70.*

OFF THE
BEATEN
PATH

Forty miles west of West Palm Beach, amid the farms and cattle pastures rimming the western edges of Palm Beach and Martin counties, is **Lake Okeechobee,** the second-largest freshwater lake completely within the United States. It's girdled by 120 miles of road yet remains shielded from sight for almost its entire circumference. (The best place to view it is in Port Mayaca on the north side—where you can get great sunset shots—and the Okeechobee docks on the northwest.) Lake Okeechobee—the Seminole's "Big Water" and the gateway of the great Everglades watershed—measures 730 square miles, at its longest roughly 33 miles north–south and 30 miles east–west, with an average natural depth of only 10 feet (flood control brings the figure up to 12 feet and deeper). Six major lock systems and 32 separate water-control structures manage the water and allow boaters to cross the state through its channels from the Atlantic Ocean to the Gulf of Mexico. Encircling the lake is a 34-foot-high grassy levee that locals call "the dike," and atop it, the Lake Okeechobee Scenic Trail, a segment of the Florida National Scenic Trail that's an easy, flat ride for

6

bikers. Anglers have a field day here as well, with great bass and perch catches. ■TIP➜ There's no shade, so wear a hat, sunscreen, and bug repellent (a must). Be sure to bring lots of bottled water, too, because restaurants and stores are few and far between.

TREASURE COAST

In contrast to the glitzy, überplanned Gold Coast that includes Greater Palm Beach and Boca Raton, the more bucolic Treasure Coast stretches from south Martin County into St. Lucie and Indian River counties. Along the east are barrier islands all the way to Sebastian and beyond, starting with Jupiter Island, then Hutchinson Island, and finally Orchid Island—and reefs, too. Those reefs are responsible for the region's nickname: they've caused ships carrying riches dating back as far as 1715 to fall asunder and cast their treasures ashore. The Intracoastal Waterway here is called the Indian River starting at the St. Lucie Inlet in Stuart and morphs into a broad tidal lagoon with tiny uninhabited islands and wildlife galore. Inland, there's cattle ranching and tracts of pine and palmetto scrub, along with sugar and citrus production.

Despite a growing number of malls and beachfront condominiums, much of the Treasure Coast remains untouched, something not lost on ecotourists, game fishers, and people who want a break from the over-saturated digital age. Consequently, there are fewer lodging options in this region of Florida, but if 30 minutes in the car sounds like a breeze, culture vultures can live in the lap of luxury in Vero Beach and detour south to Fort Pierce's galleries and botanical gardens. Likewise, families will revel in every amenity imaginable at the Hutchinson Island Marriott and be able to swing northwest to hit up the Mets spring-training stadium in Port St. Lucie or down to Jupiter for the Cardinals and the Marlins.

STUART AND JENSEN BEACH

10 miles north of Hobe Sound.

The compact town of Stuart lies on a peninsula that juts out into the St. Lucie River off the Indian River and has a remarkable amount of shoreline for its size. It scores huge points for its charming historic district and is the self-described "Sailfish Capital of the World." On the southern end, you'll find Port Salerno and its waterfront area, the Manatee Pocket, which are a skip away from the St. Lucie Inlet.

Immediately north of Stuart is down-to-earth Jensen Beach. Both Stuart and Jensen Beach straddle the Indian River and occupy Hutchinson Island, the barrier island that continues into the town of Fort Pierce. Between late April and August, hundreds, even thousands, of turtles come here to nest along the Atlantic beaches. Residents have taken pains to curb the runaway development that has created commercial crowding to the north and south, although some high-rises have popped up along the shore.

GETTING HERE AND AROUND

To get to Stuart and Jensen Beach from Jupiter and Hobe Sound, drive north on Federal Highway (U.S. 1). Route A1A crosses through downtown Stuart and is the sole main road throughout Hutchinson Island. Route 707 runs parallel on the mainland directly across the tidal lagoon.

EXPLORING

Strict architectural and zoning standards guide civic-renewal projects in the heart of Stuart. Antiques stores, restaurants, and more than 50 specialty shops are rooted within the two-block area of Flagler Avenue and Osceola Street north of where A1A cuts across the peninsula (visit ⊕ *www.stuartmainstreet.org* for more information). A self-guided walking-tour pamphlet is available at assorted locations to clue you in on this once-small fishing village's early days.

FAMILY **Elliott Museum.** Opened in March 2013, the museum's glittering, green-certified, 48,000-square-foot facility is double its previous size and houses a permanent collection along with traveling exhibits. The museum was founded in 1961 in honor of Sterling Elliott, an inventor of an early automated-addressing machine, the egg crate, and a four-wheel bicycle, and it celebrates history, art, and technology, much of it viewed through the lens of the automobile's effect on American society. There's an impressive array of antique cars, plus paintings, historic artifacts, and nostalgic goods like vintage baseball cards and toys. ⊠ *825 N.E. Ocean Blvd., Jensen Beach* ☎ *772/225–1961* ⊕ *elliottmuseum.org* ☞ *$14.*

FAMILY **Florida Oceanographic Coastal Center.** This hydroland is the place to go for an interactive marine experience and live the center's mission "to inspire environmental stewardship of Florida's coastal ecosystems through education and research." Petting and feeding stingrays can be done at various times; in the morning, a sea turtle program introduces you to three full-time residents. Make sure to catch the "feeding frenzy" when keepers toss food into the 750,000-gallon lagoon tank and sharks, tarpon, and snook swarm the surface. Join a 1-mile guided walk through the coastal hardwood hammock and mangrove swamp habitats, or explore the trails on your own—you may see a dolphin or manatee swim by. ⊠ *890 N.E. Ocean Blvd., Stuart* ☎ *772/225–0505* ⊕ *www.floridaocean.org* ☞ *$12.*

Gilbert's Bar House of Refuge Museum. Built in 1875 on Hutchinson Island, this is the only remaining example of 10 such structures that were erected by the U.S. Life-Saving Service (a predecessor of the Coast Guard) to aid stranded sailors. The displays here include antique lifesaving equipment, maps, artifacts from nearby wrecks, and boatbuilding tools. The museum is affiliated with the nearby Elliott Museum; package tickets are available. ⊠ *301 S.E. MacArthur Blvd., Jensen Beach* ☎ *772/225–1875* ⊕ *www.houseofrefugefl.org* ☞ *$8.*

6

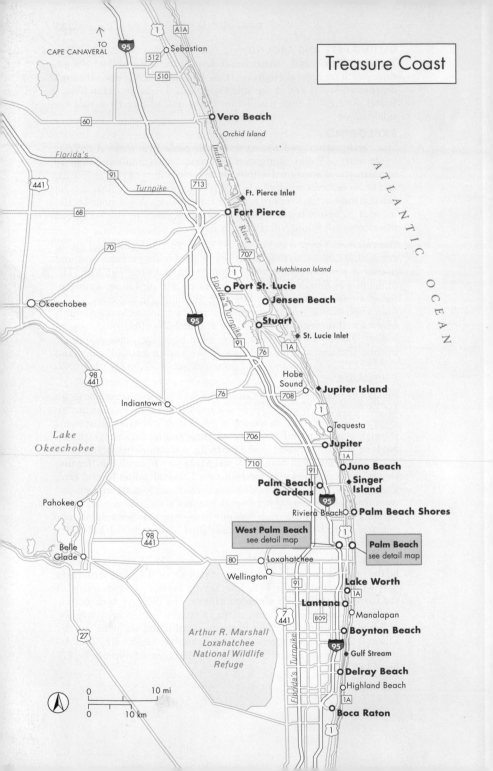

Treasure Coast

CLOSE UP

Florida's Sea Turtles: The Nesting Season

From May to October, turtles nest all along the Florida coast. Female loggerhead, Kemp's ridley, and other species living in the Atlantic Ocean or Gulf of Mexico swim as much as 2,000 miles to the Florida shore. By night they drag their 100- to 400-pound bodies onto the beach to the dune line. Then each digs a hole with her flippers, drops in 100 or so eggs, covers them up, and returns to sea.

The babies hatch about 60 days later. Once they burst out of the sand, the hatchlings must get to sea rapidly or risk becoming dehydrated from the sun or being caught by crabs, birds, or other predators.

Instinctively, baby turtles head toward bright light, probably because for millions of years starlight or moonlight reflected on the waves was the brightest light around, serving to guide hatchlings to water. Many coastal towns enforce light restrictions during nesting months. Florida homeowners are asked to dim their lights on behalf of baby sea turtles.

At night, volunteers walk the beaches, searching for signs of turtle nests. Upon finding telltale scratches in

the sand, they cordon off the sites, so beachgoers will leave the spots undisturbed. (It is illegal to disturb turtle nests.) Volunteers also keep watch over nests when babies are about to hatch, and assist disoriented hatchlings.

Several local organizations offer nightly turtle walks during nesting season. Most are in June and July, starting around 8 pm and sometimes lasting until midnight. Expect a $10 to $15 fee. Call in advance to confirm times and to reserve a spot—places usually take reservations as early as April. If you're in southern Palm Beach County, contact Boca Raton's **Gumbo Limbo Nature Center** (☎ 561/338–1473 ⊕ www.gumbolimbo.org). The **John D. MacArthur Beach State Park** (☎ 561/624–6952 ⊕ www. macarthurbeach.org) is convenient for Palm Beach–area visitors at the northern end of Singer Island. **Hobe Sound Nature Center** (☎ 772/546–2067 ⊕ www.hobesoundnaturecenter.com) is farther up. Treasure Coasters in or near Vero Beach can go to **Sebastian Inlet State Park** (☎ 321/984–4852 ⊕ www.floridastateparks.org/ sebastianinlet).

6

BEACHES

FAMILY **Bathtub Reef Beach.** Rough tides are often the norm in this stretch of the Atlantic Ocean, and frequently take away the beach, but a charming enclave at the southern end of Hutchinson Island—after the Marriott's beach and right by the Indian River Plantation luxury development—provides a perfect escape for families with young children and anyone who likes to snorkel. The waters are shallow and usually calm, and youngsters can walk up to the reef and see a dazzling assortment of fish. The parking lot is small, so get there early. Erosion is a problem, and sometimes lifeguards can't pull their hefty chairs out, leaving the beach unguarded (but it shouldn't deter you, because the sea isn't rough). **Amenities:** toilets; parking (no fee); lifeguards. **Best for:** swimming; snorkeling. ⊠ *1585 S.E. MacArthur Blvd., Stuart.*

FAMILY **Stuart Beach.** When the waves robustly roll in, the surfers are rolling in, too. Beginning surfers are especially keen on Stuart Beach because of its ever-vigilant lifeguards, and pros to the sport like the challenges that the choppy waters here bring. But the beach is equally popular with surf fishers. Families enjoy the snack bar known for its chicken fingers, the basketball courts, the large canopy-covered playground, and the three walkways interspersed throughout the area for easy ocean access. **Amenities:** lifeguards; food and drink; parking (no fee); showers; toilets. **Best for:** surfing; swimming. ✉ *889 N.E. Ocean Blvd., Stuart.*

WHERE TO EAT

$$$ SEAFOOD 🍴 **Conchy Joe's.** Like a hermit crab sliding into a new shell, Conchy Joe's moved up from West Palm Beach in 1983 to its current home, a 1920s rustic stilt house on the Indian River. It's full of antique fish mounts, gator hides, and snakeskins, and is a popular tourist spot—but the waterfront location, very casual vibe, and delicious seafood lures locals, too. **Known for:** conch chowder; grouper marsala; live reggae Thursday–Sunday. [$] *Average main: $27* ✉ *3945 N.E. Indian River Dr., Jensen Beach* ☎ *772/334–1130* 🌐 *www.conchyjoes.com.*

$$$ FRENCH 🍴 **Courtine's.** A husband-and-wife team oversees this quiet and hospitable restaurant under the Roosevelt Bridge. French and American influences are clear in the Swiss chef's dishes, from rack of lamb with Dijon mustard to grilled filet mignon stuffed with Roquefort and fresh spinach. **Known for:** refined Continental cuisine; elegant atmosphere; more casual bar menu. [$] *Average main: $25* ✉ *514 N. Dixie Hwy., Stuart* ☎ *772/692–3662* 🌐 *www.courtines.com* ⏲ *Closed Sun. and Mon. No lunch.*

$$$ SOUTHERN 🍴 **District Table and Bar.** Farm-fresh foods with a Southern accent are served up at this chef-owned restaurant with a theater kitchen, where comfort foods are taken to new levels. (Slow Foods, a group that celebrates local foods and artisans, has given the restaurant a "Snail of Approval.") **Known for:** farm-to-table menu; lively bar scene; everything house made, including condiments and jams. [$] *Average main: $23* ✉ *900 S.E. Indian St., Stuart* ☎ *772/324–8357* 🌐 *www.districttableandbar.com* ⏲ *Closed Mon.*

$$$$ ECLECTIC 🍴 **11 Maple Street.** This cozy spot is as good as it gets on the Treasure Coast. Soft music and a friendly staff set the mood in the antiques-filled dining room of this old house, which holds only 21 tables. **Known for:** nice selection of wines; good desserts; Old Florida setting in vintage house. [$] *Average main: $42* ✉ *3224 N.E. Maple Ave., Jensen Beach* ☎ *772/334–7714* 🌐 *www.elevenmaple.com* ⏲ *Closed Sun. and Mon. No lunch.*

$$$ SEAFOOD 🍴 **Ian's Tropical Grill.** Tucked inside a small plaza, the restaurant has a small, cozy dining room and covered alfresco patio. The menu changes often, depending on what's fresh in the markets and from local farms, which are named. **Known for:** fresh Florida seafood; primarily locally sourced ingredients; inventive cocktails. [$] *Average main: $25* ✉ *2875 S.E. Ocean Blvd., Stuart* ☎ *772/334–4563* ⏲ *Closed Sun.*

WHERE TO STAY

$$

RESORT

FAMILY

⌂ **Hutchinson Island Marriott Beach Resort & Marina.** With a 77-slip marina, a full water-sports program, a golf course, two pools, tons of tennis courts, and children's activities, this self-contained resort is excellent for families, most of whom prefer to stay in the tower directly on the ocean. **Pros:** attentive, warm staff; rooms are comfortable and casually chic; all rooms have balconies. **Cons:** only one sit-down indoor restaurant; common areas are a bit dated; no spa; daily resort fee. $ *Rooms from: $230* ✉ *555 N.E. Ocean Blvd., Stuart* ☎ *772/225–3700, 800/775–5936* ⊕ *www.marriott.com/pbiir* ⇘ *274 rooms* ⦿ *No meals.*

$

RESORT

⌂ **Pirate's Cove Resort & Marina.** This cozy enclave on the banks of the Manatee Pocket with ocean access at the southern end of Stuart is the perfect place to set forth on a day at sea or wind down after one—it's relaxing and casual, and has amenities like a swimming-pool courtyard, restaurant, and fitness center. **Pros:** spacious tropical-themed rooms; great for boaters, with a 50-slip, full-service, deepwater marina; each room has a balcony overlooking the water; free Wi-Fi and parking. **Cons:** lounge gets noisy at night; decor and furnishings are pretty but not luxurious; pool is on the small side. $ *Rooms from: $150* ✉ *4307 S.E. Bayview St., Port Salerno* ☎ *772/287–2500* ⊕ *www.piratescoveresort.com* ⇘ *50 rooms* ⦿ *No meals.*

SHOPPING

More than 60 restaurants and shops with antiques, art, and fashion draw visitors downtown along Osceola Street.

B&A Flea Market. A short drive from downtown and operating for more than two decades, the oldest and largest weekend-only flea market on the Treasure Coast has a street-bazaar feel, with shoppers happily scouting the 500 vendors for the practical and unusual. A produce market carries local tropical fruits and vegetables. If you have an open mind and love to shop garage sales, you'll do just fine here. ✉ *2885 S.E. U.S. 1, Stuart* ☎ *772/288–4915* ⊕ *www.bafleamarket.com* ▤ *Free.*

SPORTS AND THE OUTDOORS

BOAT TOURS

Island Princess **Cruises.** Cruise the Indian River and St. Lucie River as well as Jupiter Sound aboard the *Island Princess,* an 82-footer that docks at the Sailfish Marina in Stuart. In season, there are nature cruises and cruises that go through the St. Lucie River locks. Have lunch during their Jupiter Island cruise, embarking Tuesday and weekends year-round. The schedule, which changes often, is posted on the company's website. All ages are welcome, and advance reservations are required. ✉ *Sailfish Marina, 3585 S.E. St. Lucie Blvd., Stuart* ☎ *772/225–2100* ⊕ *www.islandprincesscruises.com* ▤ *Cruises from $25.*

FISHING

Sailfish Marina of Stuart. Nab a deep-sea charter here to land a sailfish, a popular sport fish that is prolific off the St. Lucie Inlet. This is the closest public marina to the St. Lucie Inlet. Recently expanded, it is home to *Island Princess* Cruises, which takes visitors to Vero Beach or Jupiter via the Intracoastal Waterway. ✉ *3565 S.E. St. Lucie Blvd., Stuart* ☎ *772/283–1122* ⊕ *www.sailfishmarinastuart.com*

FORT PIERCE AND PORT ST. LUCIE

11 miles north of Jensen Beach.

About an hour north of Palm Beach, Fort Pierce has a distinctive rural feel—but it has a surprising number of worthwhile attractions for a town of its size, including those easily seen while following Route 707 on the mainland (A1A on Hutchinson Island). The downtown is expanding, and sports new theater revivals, restaurants, and shops. A big draw is an inlet that offers fabulous fishing and excellent surfing. Nearby Port St. Lucie is largely landlocked southwest of Fort Pierce and is almost equidistant from there and Jensen Beach. It's not a big tourist area except for two sports facilities near Interstate 95: the St. Lucie Mets' training grounds, Tradition Field, and the PGA Village. If you want a hotel directly on the sand or crave more than simple, motel-like accommodations, stay elsewhere and drive up for the day.

GETTING HERE AND AROUND

You can reach Fort Pierce from Jensen Beach by driving 11 miles north on Federal Highway (U.S. 1), Route 707, or Route A1A. To get to Port St. Lucie, continue north on U.S. 1 and take Prima Vista Boulevard west. From Fort Pierce, Route 709 goes diagonally southwest to Port St. Lucie, and Interstate 95 is another choice.

ESSENTIALS

Visitor Information St. Lucie County Tourist Development Council. ⊠ *2300 Virginia Ave., Fort Pierce* ☎ *800/344–8443* ⊕ *www.visitstluciefla.com.*

EXPLORING

Heathcote Botanical Gardens. Stroll through this 3½-acre green space, which includes a palm walk, a Japanese garden, and a collection of 100 bonsai trees. There is also a gift shop with whimsical and botanical knickknacks. Guided tours are available by appointment for an extra fee. ⊠ *210 Savannah Rd., Fort Pierce* ☎ *772/464–0323* ⊕ *www. heathcotebotanicalgardens.org* ☜ *$6* ⊙ *Closed Mon.*

FAMILY **National Navy UDT-SEAL Museum.** Commemorating the more than 3,000 troops who trained on these shores during World War II when this elite military unit got its start, there are weapons, vehicles, and equipment on view. Exhibits honor all frogmen and underwater demolition teams and depict their history. The museum houses the lifeboat from which SEALs saved the *Maersk Alabama* captain from Somali pirates in 2009. Kids get a thrill out of the helicopters and aircraft on the grounds. ⊠ *3300 N. Rte. A1A, Fort Pierce* ☎ *772/595–5845* ⊕ *www.navysealmuseum. com* ☜ *$10* ⊙ *Closed Mon.*

FAMILY **Savannas Recreation Area.** Once a reservoir, the 550 acres have been returned to their natural wetlands state. Today the wilderness area has campgrounds, interpretive trails, and a boat ramp, and the recreation area is open year-round. Canoe and kayak rentals are available Thursday through Monday. A dog park (open daily) is also on-site. Amenities include showers, toilets, and free Wi-Fi for campers. ⊠ *1400 E. Midway Rd., Fort Pierce* ☎ *772/464–7855* ⊕ *www.stlucieco.gov/parks/savannas.htm* ☜ *Free; $25.25 for campers (full service).*

BEACHES

Fort Pierce Inlet State Park. Across the inlet at the northern side of Hutchinson Island, a fishing oasis lures beachgoers who can't wait to reel in snook, flounder, and bluefish, among others. The park is also known as a prime wave-riding locale, thanks to a reef that lies just outside the jetty. Summer is the busiest season by a long shot, but don't be fooled: it's a laid back place to sun and surf. There are covered picnic tables but no concessions; however, from where anglers perch, a bunch of casual restaurants can be spotted on the other side of the inlet that are a quick drive away. Note that the area of Jack Island Preserve has been closed indefinitely. **Amenities:** toilets; showers; parking (fee); lifeguards (summer only). **Best for:** surfing; walking; solitude. ✉ *905 Shorewinds Dr., Fort Pierce* ☎ *772/468–3985* 🌐 *www.floridastateparks.org/fortpierceinlet* 🎟 *Vehicle $6, bicyclists and pedestrians $2.*

WHERE TO STAY

$ HOTEL 🏨 **Dockside Inn.** This hotel is the best of the lodgings lining the scenic Fort Pierce Inlet on Seaway Drive (and that's not saying much); it's a practical base for fishing enthusiasts with nice touches like two pools and a waterfront restaurant. **Pros:** good value; overnight boat docking available; reasonable rates at marina; parking included. **Cons:** basic decor; some steps to climb; grounds are nothing too fancy but have great views. [$] *Rooms from: $125* ✉ *1160 Seaway Dr., Fort Pierce* ☎ *772/468–3555, 800/286–1745* 🌐 *www.docksideinn.com* 🛏 *36 rooms* 🍴 *No meals.*

SPORTS AND THE OUTDOORS

BASEBALL

Tradition Field. Out west by Interstate 95, this Port St. Lucie baseball stadium, formerly known as Digital Domain Park as well as Thomas J. White Stadium, is where the New York Mets train; it's also the home of the St. Lucie Mets minor-league team. ✉ *525 N.W. Peacock Blvd., Port St. Lucie* ☎ *772/871–2115* 🌐 *www.stluciemets.com.*

GOLF

PGA Village. Owned and operated by the PGA of America, the national association of teaching pros, PGA Village is the winter home to many Northern instructors, along with permanent staff. The facility is a little off the beaten path and the clubhouse is basic, but serious golfers will appreciate the three championship courses by Pete Dye and Tom Fazio and the chance to sharpen their skills at the 35-acre PGA Center for Golf Learning and Performance, which has nine practice bunkers mimicking sands and slopes from around the globe. Between the Fazio-designed Wanamaker Course, the Ryder Course, and the Dye-designed Dye Course, there are 54 holes of championship golf at PGA Village. Also affiliated is the nearby St. Lucie Trail Golf Club, another Fazio design. Beginners can start out on the lesser known (and easier) 6-hole PGA Short Course. Holes are 35 to 60 yards each, and course play is free. ✉ *1916 Perfect Dr., Port St. Lucie* ☎ *772/467–1300, 800/800–4653* 🌐 *www.pgavillage.com* 🎟 *Wanamaker Course $131; Ryder Course $131; Dye Course $131; St. Lucie Trail Golf Club $89*

Wanamaker Course: 18 holes, 7123 yards, par 72; Ryder Course: 18 holes, 7037 yards, par 72; Dye Course: 18 holes, 7279 yards, par 72; St. Lucie Golf Club Trail Course: 18 holes, 6901 yards, par 72.

SCUBA DIVING

The region's premier dive site is actually on the National Register of Historic Places. The *Urca de Lima* was part of the storied treasure fleet bound for Spain that was destroyed by a hurricane in 1715. It's now part of an underwater archaeological preserve about 200 yards from shore, just north of the National Navy UDT-SEAL Museum and under 10 to 15 feet of water. The remains contain a flat-bottom, round-bellied ship and cannons that can be visited on an organized dive trip.

Dive Odyssea. This full-service dive shop offers kayak rentals, tank rentals, and scuba lessons. The shop can arrange a scuba charter in Jupiter or Palm Beach (two-tank dive trips typically start at $65), but Dive Odyssea no longer offers dive trips of its own. ⊠ *Fort Pierce Inlet, 621 N. 2nd St., Fort Pierce* ☎ *772/460–1771* ⊕ *www.diveodyssea.com.*

VERO BEACH

12 miles north of Fort Pierce.

Tranquil and picturesque, this upscale Indian River County town has a strong commitment to the environment and culture, and it's also home to eclectic galleries and trendy restaurants. Downtown Vero is centered on the historic district on 14th Avenue, but much of the fun takes place across the Indian River (aka the Intracoastal Waterway) around Orchid Island's beaches. It was once home to the Dodgers Spring Training base, and there's still a strong affinity for baseball here, and it's kid-friendly, with the former Dodgertown Stadium hosting LIttle League tournaments, and plenty of parks around. Its western edges still are home to cattlemen and citrus growers, so there is a juxtaposition of country and gentry.

GETTING HERE AND AROUND

To get here, you have two basic options: Route A1A along the coast (not to be confused with Ocean Drive, an offshoot on Orchid Island), or either U.S. 1 or Route 605 (also called Old Dixie Highway) on the mainland. As you approach Vero on the latter, you pass through an ungussied-up landscape of small farms and residential areas. On the beach route, part of the drive bisects an unusually undeveloped section of the Florida coast. If flying in, consider Orlando International Airport, which is larger and a smidge closer than Palm Beach International Airport.

VISITOR INFORMATION

Contacts Indian River County Chamber of Commerce. ⊠ *1216 21st St.* ☎ *772/567–3491* ⊕ *www.indianriverchamber.com.*

EXPLORING

Environmental Learning Center. Off Wabasso Beach Road, the 64 acres here are almost completely surrounded by water. In addition to a 600-foot boardwalk through the mangrove shoreline and a 1-mile canoe trail, there are aquariums filled with Indian River creatures. Boat and kayak trips to see the historic Pelican Island rookery are on offer along with guided nature walks and touch-tank encounters. Call or check the center's website for times. ⊠ *255 Live Oak Dr.* ☎ *772/589–5050* ⊕ *www. discoverelc.org* ✉ *$5* ⊘ *Closed Mon.*

Fodor's Choice ★
McKee Botanical Garden. On the National Register of Historic Places, the 18-acre plot is a tropical jungle garden—one of the most lush and serene around. This is *the* place to see spectacular water lilies, and the property's original 1932 Hall of Giants, a rustic wooden structure that has stained-glass and bronze bells, contains what is claimed to be the world's largest single-plank mahogany table at 35 feet long. There's a Seminole bamboo pavilion, a gift shop, and café (open for lunch Tuesday through Saturday—and Sunday in season), which serves especially tasty snacks and sandwiches. ⊠ *350 U.S. 1* ☎ *772/794–0601* ⊕ *www. mckeegarden.org* ✉ *$12* ⊘ *Closed Mon.*

Pelican Island National Wildlife Refuge. Founded in 1903 by President Theodore Roosevelt as the country's first national wildlife refuge, the park encompasses the historic Pelican Island rookery itself—a small island in the Indian River lagoon and important nesting place for 16 species of birds such as endangered wood storks and, of course, brown pelicans—and the land surrounding it overlooking Sebastian. The rookery is a closed wilderness area, so there's no roaming alongside animal kingdom friends; however, there is an 18-foot observation tower across from it with direct views and more than 6 miles of nature trails in the refuge. Another way to explore is via guided kayak tours from the Florida Outdoor Center. Make sure to bring a camera—it's a photographer's dream. ⊠ *Rte. A1A, 1 mile north of Treasure Shores Park* ✛ *Take A1A and turn on Historic Jungle Trail* ☎ *772/581–5557* ⊕ *www.fws. gov/pelicanisland* ✉ *Free.*

BEACHES

Most of the hotels in the Vero Beach area are clustered around South Beach Park or line Ocean Drive around Beachland Boulevard just north of Humiston Park. Both parks have lifeguards daily. South Beach, at the end of East Causeway Boulevard, is one of the widest, quietest shores on the island, and has plenty of hammock shade before the dunes to picnic in, plus volleyball nets on the beach. Humiston Park is smack-dab in the main commercial zone with restaurants galore, including the lauded Citrus Grillhouse at its southern tip.

Humiston Park. Just south of the Driftwood Resort on Ocean Drive sits Humiston Park, one of the best beaches in town. Parking is free and plentiful, as there's a large lot on Easter Lily Lane and there are spots all over the surrounding business district. The shore is somewhat narrow and there isn't much shade, but the vibrant scene and other amenities make it a great choice for people who crave lots of activity. With lifeguards on call daily, there's a children's playground, plus a ton of hotels, restaurants, bars, and shops within walking distance. **Amenities:** lifeguards; food and drink; toilets; showers. **Best for:** swimming; partiers; sunsets; walking. ⊠ *3000 Ocean Dr., at Easter Lily La.* ☎ *772/231–5790.*

6

FAMILY
Fodor'sChoice
★

Sebastian Inlet State Park. The 1,000-acre park, which runs from the tip of Orchid Island across the passage to the barrier island just north, is one of the Florida park system's biggest draws, especially because of the inlet's highly productive fishing waters. Views from either side of the tall bridge are spectacular, and a unique hallmark is that the gates never close—an amazing feature for die-hard anglers who know snook bite better at night. Two jetties are usually packed with fishers and spectators alike. The park has two entrances, the entrance in Vero Beach and the main entrance in Melbourne (⊠ 9700 Rte. A1A). Within its grounds, you'll observe a wonderful two-story restaurant that overlooks the ocean, a fish and surfing shop (by the way, this place has some of the best waves in the state, but there are also calmer zones for relaxing swims), two museums, guided sea turtle walks in season, 51 campsites with water and electricity, and a marina with powerboat, kayak, and canoe rentals. **Amenities:** food and drink; parking (fee); showers; toilets; water sports. **Best for:** surfing; sunrise; sunset; walking. ⊠ 14251 N. Rte. A1A ☎ 321/984–4852 ⊕ www.floridastateparks. org/sebastianinlet ⊠ $8 vehicles with up to 8 people, $4 single drivers, $2 bicyclists and pedestrians.

FAMILY

Wabasso Beach Park. A favorite for local surfboarding teens and the families at the nearby Disney's Vero Beach Resort, the park is nestled in a residential area at the end of Wabasso Road, about 8 miles up from the action on Ocean Drive and 8 miles below the Sebastian Inlet. Aside from regular amenities like picnic tables, restrooms, and a dedicated parking lot (which really is the "park" here—there's not much green space—and it's quite small, so arrive early), the Disney crowd walks there for its lifeguards (the strip directly in front of the hotel is unguarded) and the local crowd appreciates its conveniences, like a pizzeria and a store that sells sundries, snacks, and beach supplies. **Amenities:** food and drink; lifeguards; parking (no fee); toilets; showers. **Best for:** swimming; surfing. ⊠ 1820 Wabasso Rd.

WHERE TO EAT

$$$
MODERN
AMERICAN
Fodor'sChoice
★

✕ **Citrus Grillhouse.** There are rooms with a view, and then there's this view: uninterrupted sea from a wraparound veranda at the southern end of Humiston Park. Even better, the food here is a straightforward, delicious celebration of fresh and fabulous. **Known for:** fresh Florida seafood, especially snapper; some gluten-free options; bargain prix fixe Monday–Wednesday 5–6. $ Average main: $24 ⊠ Humiston Park, 1050 Easter Lily La. ☎ 772/234–4114 ⊕ www.citrusgrillhouse.com ⊗ No lunch Sun.

$
DINER
FAMILY

✕ **The Lemon Tree.** If Italy had old-school luncheonettes, this is what they'd look like: a storefront of yellow walls, dark-green booths, white linoleum tables, and cascading sconces of faux ivy leaves and hand-painted Tuscan serving pieces for artwork. It's self-described by the husband-and-wife owners (who are always at the front) as an "upscale diner," and locals swear by it for breakfast (served all day) and lunch. **Known for:** shrimp scampi; treats on the house; waits during the high season. $ Average main: $11 ⊠ 3125 Ocean Dr. ⊕ www.lemontreevero. com ⊗ No lunch or dinner Sun. No dinner June–Sept.

6

$$$ ✕ **Ocean Grill.** Opened in 1941, this family-owned Old Florida–style
SEAFOOD restaurant combines its ocean view with Tiffany-style lamps, wrought-
iron chandeliers, and paintings of pirates. Count on at least three
kinds of seafood any day on the menu, along with steaks, pork chops,
soups, and salads. **Known for:** just OK food; great drinks; the Pusser's
Painkiller. $ *Average main: $28* ✉ *1050 Beachland Blvd.* ☎ *772/231–
5409* ⊕ *www.ocean-grill.com* ⊘ *Closed 2 wks around Labor Day. No
lunch Sun.*

$$$ ✕ **The Tides.** A charming cottage restaurant west of Ocean Drive pre-
ECLECTIC pares some of the best food around—not just in Vero Beach, but all
Fodor's Choice of South Florida. The chefs, classically trained, give a nod to interna-
★ tional fare with disparate dishes such as tuna tataki, Asian-inspired
carpaccio with satay, penne *quattro formaggi,* and classic lobster
bisque. **Known for:** fresh Florida fish; jumbo crab cakes with corn-
and-pepper sauce; chef's table with wine pairings. $ *Average main:
$29* ✉ *3103 Cardinal Dr.* ☎ *772/234–3966* ⊕ *www.tidesofvero.com*
⊘ *No lunch.*

WHERE TO STAY

$ 🏨 **Costa d'Este Beach Resort.** This stylish, contemporary boutique hotel
RESORT in the heart of Vero's bustling Ocean Drive area has a gorgeous infinity
Fodor's Choice pool overlooking the ocean and a distinctly Miami Beach vibe—just
★ like its famous owners, singer Gloria Estefan and producer Emilio
Estefan, who bought the property in 2004. **Pros:** all rooms have balconies or secluded patios; huge Italian marble showers; complimentary signature mojitos on arrival. **Cons:** spa is on small side; rooms
have only blackout shades; daily resort fee. $ *Rooms from: $139*
✉ *3244 Ocean Dr.* ☎ *772/562–9919* ⊕ *www.costadeste.com* ⇄ *94
rooms* ⦿ *No meals.*

$$$ 🏨 **Disney's Vero Beach Resort.** This oceanfront, family-oriented retreat
RESORT tucked away in a residential stretch of Orchid Island has a retro Old
FAMILY Florida design and not too much Mickey Mouse, which is a welcome
surprise for adults. **Pros:** a great pool with waterslide and kiddie splash
pool; campfire circle; several dining options on property. **Cons:** far from
shopping and dining options; minimal Disney-themed decor. $ *Rooms
from: $365* ✉ *9250 Island Grove Terr.* ☎ *772/234–2000, 407/939–
7540* ⊕ *www.disneybeachresorts.com/vero-beach-resort/* ⇄ *181 rooms*
⦿ *No meals.*

$ 🏨 **The Driftwood Resort.** On the National Register of Historic Places,
RESORT the two original buildings of this 1935 inn were built entirely from
FAMILY ocean-washed timbers with no blueprints; over time more buildings
were added, and all are now decorated with such artifacts as ship's
bells, Spanish tiles, a cannon from a 16th-century Spanish galleon,
and plenty of wrought iron, which create a quirky, utterly charming
landscape. **Pros:** central location and right on the beach; free Wi-Fi;
laundry facilities; weekly treasure hunt is a blast. **Cons:** older prop-
erty; rooms can be musty; no-frills furnishings. $ *Rooms from: $150*
✉ *3150 Ocean Dr.* ☎ *772/231–0550* ⊕ *www.verobeachdriftwood.com*
⇄ *100 rooms* ⦿ *No meals.*

$$
RESORT
FAMILY
Fodor's Choice
★

Vero Beach Hotel & Spa. With a sophisticated, relaxed British West Indies feel, this luxurious five-story beachfront hotel at the north end of Ocean Drive is an inviting getaway and, arguably, the best on the Treasure Coast. **Pros:** beautiful pool; complimentary daily wine hour with hors d'oeuvres. **Cons:** separate charge for valet parking; some rooms overlook parking lot. $ *Rooms from: $299* ⊠ *3500 Ocean Dr.* ☎ *772/231–5666* ⊕ *www.verobeachhotelandspa.com* ⏦ *102 rooms* ⦿*No meals.*

SHOPPING

The place to go when in Vero Beach is **Ocean Drive.** Crossing over to Orchid Island from the mainland, the Merrill P. Barber Bridge turns into Beachland Boulevard; its intersection with Ocean Drive is the heart of a commercial zone with a lively mix of upscale clothing stores, specialty shops, restaurants, and art galleries.

Just under 3 miles north of that roughly eight-block stretch on A1A is a charming outdoor plaza, the **Village Shops.** It's a delight to stroll between the brightly painted cottages that have more unique, high-end offerings.

Back on the mainland, take 21st Street westward and you'll come across a small, modern shopping plaza with some independent shops and national chains. Keep going west on 21st Street, and then park around 14th Avenue to explore a collection of art galleries and eateries in the historic downtown.

RECOMMENDED STORES

Maison Beach. Formerly called Christine, the owner changed the name of this cute shop and moved to Pelican Plaza. It still is *the* place to find gorgeous hostess and dining entertainment gifts like Mariposa napkin holders, Julia Knight bowls, and Michael Aram picture frames, along with trendy Mudpie household ware. ⊠ *Pelican Plaza, 4895 Hwy. A1A* ☎ *772/492–0383* ⊕ *www.christineshop.com.*

Sassy Boutique. One of the chicest spots in town sells bright, punchy, and pretty women's designer fashions such as Calypso St. Barth, Tory Burch, Kate Spade New York, Kenneth Jay Lane, Stacia, and Nanette Lepore. ⊠ *3375 Ocean Dr.* ☎ *772/234–3998* ⊕ *www.sassyboutique.com.*

Shells & Things. Stop here for lovely handcrafted goods inspired by the sea, many by local artisans. Choose from jewelry, candles, gifts for kids, home decor items, and artwork. ⊠ *3119 Ocean Dr.* ☎ *772/234–4790* ⊕ *www.shellsandthings.com.*

SHOPPING CENTERS AND MALLS

Vero Beach Outlets. Need some retail therapy? Just west of Interstate 95 off Route 60 is a discount shopping destination with 50 high-end brand-name stores, including Ann Taylor, Calvin Klein, Christopher & Banks, Dooney & Bourke, Polo Ralph Lauren, Restoration Hardware, and White House/Black Market. ⊠ *1824 94th Dr.* ✛ *On Rte. 60, west of I–95 at Exit 147* ☎ *772/770–6097* ⊕ *www.verobeachoutlets.com.*

6

SPORTS AND THE OUTDOORS
GOLF

Sandridge Golf Club. The Sandridge Golf Club features two public 18-hole courses designed by Ron Garl: the Dunes course, with 6 holes located on a sand ridge; and the Lakes course, named for—you guessed it—the ubiquitous lakes around the course. The Dunes course, opened in 1987, follows a history-steeped pathway once used during mining operations. The Lakes course, opened in 1992, is renowned for the very challenging, par-4 14th hole with an island green. There's a pro shop on-site offering lessons and clinics. Florida and Indian River County residents can get membership cards to book tee times eight days out—and get discounts for play. ⊠ *5300 73rd St.* ☎ *772/770–5000* ⊕ *www.sandridgegc.com* ⊠ *$50 for 18 holes with cart* ⅃. *Dunes course: 18 holes, 6817 yards, par 72; Lakes course: 18 holes, 6181 yards, par 72.*

THE TAMPA
BAY AREA

WELCOME TO
THE TAMPA BAY AREA

TOP REASONS
TO GO

★ **Art gone wild:** Whether you take the guided tour or chart your own course, experience the one-of-a-kind collection at the Salvador Dalí Museum, which has relocated to a gorgeous waterfront building in downtown St. Petersburg.

★ **Cuban roots:** You'll find great food and vibrant nightlife in historic Ybor City, just east of downtown Tampa.

★ **Beachcomber bonanza:** Caladesi Island State Park has some of the best shelling on the Gulf Coast, and its five-star sunsets are a great way to end the day.

★ **Culture fix:** If you love the arts, there's no finer offering in the Bay Area than at the Florida State University Ringling Center for the Cultural Arts in Sarasota.

1 Tampa. Situated on a large bay of the same name, Tampa is a growing waterfront metropolis that's packed with state-of-the-art zoos, plenty of museums, and inviting shopping districts. Among the main draws is Busch Gardens, which doubles as a theme park and a zoo.

2 St. Petersburg. Although downtown St. Petersburg can be rowdy, there are also pockets of culture. The mellow but pricey Pinellas County beach towns include St. Pete Beach and Treasure Island.

3 Clearwater and Vicinity. Quiet during the winter, the beach areas north of St. Petersburg buzz all spring and summer. In addition to Clearwater, the area includes Dunedin and Tarpon Springs.

4 Citrus County. North of the Tampa/St. Petersburg area, the area known as the "Nature Coast" is filled with protected natural areas inhabited by manatees.

5 Sarasota and Vicinity. Sarasota County's barrier islands lure travelers to a battery of white-sand beaches, but Sarasota's cultural treasures are the true draw for many of its visitors.

GETTING ORIENTED

On the east side of the bay, Tampa is a sprawling cosmopolitan city offering attractions like Busch Gardens and Ybor City. To the west, St. Petersburg and Clearwater boast lovely barrier island beaches. Moving to the south, Sarasota's arts scene is among the finest in Florida.

7

Updated by Kate Bradshaw

If you seek a destination that's no one-trick pony, the Tampa Bay region is a spot you can't miss. Encompassing an area from Tarpon Springs to Tampa proper and all the way south to Sarasota, it's one of those unsung places as dynamic as it is appealing—and word has definitely started to spread about its charms. With its long list of attractions—from pristine beaches to world-class museums—it's easy to see why.

First and foremost, Tampa Bay's beaches are some of the best in the country. Whether you want coarse or fine sand, and whether you seek a mellow day of shelling or a raucous romp on a crowded stretch of waterfront, this place has it all. Of course, you can choose from a range of water activities, including charter fishing, parasailing, sunset cruises, kayaking, and more.

The region has its share of boutique districts spotted with shops and sidewalk cafés. Tampa's Hyde Park Village and downtown St. Petersburg's Beach Drive are among the top picks if you're looking to check out some upscale shops and dine alfresco while getting the most of the area's pleasant climate. Vibrant nightlife tops off Tampa Bay's list of assets. Ybor City attracts the club set, and barrier islands like St. Pete Beach offer loads of live music and barefoot dancing into the wee hours.

Tampa Bay has lots of family-friendly attractions, too. You can check out Busch Gardens, Adventure Island, and the Clearwater Marine Aquarium, to name a few. And art fanatics will find an astonishing array of attractions, including Sarasota's Ringling Museum of Art, St. Petersburg's enrapturing Salvador Dalí and Dale Chihuly collections (both permanent and housed in exquisite new digs), and Tampa's Museum of Art. Come prepared to explore and see for yourself what a compelling, unforgettable place the Tampa Bay area really is.

PLANNING

WHEN TO GO

Winter and spring are high season, and the amount of activity during this time is double that of the off-season. Beaches do stay pretty packed throughout the sweltering summer, which is known for massive, almost-daily afternoon thunderstorms. Summer daytime temperatures hover around or above 90°F. Luckily the mercury drops to the mid-70s at night, and the beaches have a consistent onshore breeze that starts just before sundown, which enabled civilization to survive here before air-conditioning arrived.

GETTING HERE AND AROUND

AIR TRAVEL

Tampa International Airport, the area's largest and busiest airport, with 19 million passengers per year, is served by most major carriers and offers ground transportation to surrounding cities. Many of the large U.S. carriers also fly into and out of Sarasota–Bradenton International Airport. St. Petersburg–Clearwater International Airport, 9 miles west of downtown St. Petersburg, is much smaller than Tampa International and has limited service.

Airport Transfers: SuperShuttle is one of the easiest ways to get to and from the airport if you forgo a rental car. All you need to do is call or visit the SuperShuttle website to book travel—they'll pick you up and drop you off wherever you're staying at any hour. Basic service costs around $28.

Blue One Transportation provides service to and from Tampa International Airport for areas including Hillsborough (Tampa, Plant City), Pinellas (St. Petersburg, St. Pete Beach, Clearwater), and Polk (Lakeland) counties. Rates vary by pickup location, destination, and fuel costs.

Airport Sarasota–Bradenton International Airport. ☎ 941/359–2770 ⊕ www.srq-airport.com. **St. Petersburg–Clearwater International Airport.** ☎ 727/453–7800 ⊕ www.fly2pie.com. **Tampa International Airport.** ☎ 813/870–8700 ⊕ www.tampaairport.com.

Airport Transfers Blue One Transportation. ☎ 813/282–7351 ⊕ www.blueonetransportation.com. **SuperShuttle.** ☎ 800/258–3826 ⊕ www.supershuttle.com.

BUS TRAVEL

Several transit lines serve Hillsborough (Tampa), Pinellas (St. Petersburg and Clearwater), Sarasota, and Manatee (Bradenton) counties, and if you are staying in a resort, they may meet your needs, but none is as convenient as a car.

CAR TRAVEL

Interstates 75 and 275 span the Bay Area from north to south. Coming from Orlando, you're likely to drive west into Tampa on Interstate 4. Along with Interstate 75, U.S. 41 (the Tamiami Trail) stretches the length of the region and links the business districts of many communities; avoid this route during rush hours (7–9 am and 4–6 pm).

HOTELS

Many convention hotels in the Tampa Bay area double as family-friendly resorts—taking advantage of nearby beaches, marinas, spas, tennis courts, and golf links. However, unlike Orlando and some other parts of Florida, the area has been bustling for more than a century, and its accommodations often reflect a sense of its history.

You'll find a turn-of-the-20th-century beachfront resort where Zelda and F. Scott Fitzgerald stayed, a massive all-wood building from the 1920s, plenty of art deco, and Spanish-style villas. But one thing they all have in common is a certain Gulf Coast charm.

RESTAURANTS

Fresh Gulf seafood is plentiful—raw bars serving oysters, clams, and mussels are everywhere. Tampa's many Cuban and Spanish restaurants serve paella with seafood and chicken, *boliche criollo* (sausage-stuffed eye-round roast) with black beans and rice, *ropa vieja* (shredded flank steak in tomato sauce), and other treats. Tarpon Springs adds classic Greek specialties. In Sarasota the emphasis is on ritzier dining, though many restaurants offer extra-cheap early-bird menus.

Hotel and restaurant reviews have been shortened. For full information, visit Fodors.com.

WHAT IT COSTS				
	$	$$	$$$	$$$$
Restaurants	under $15	$15–$20	$21–$30	over $30
Hotels	under $200	$200–$300	$301–$400	over $400

Restaurant prices are the average cost of a main course at dinner or, if dinner is not served, at lunch. Hotel prices are the lowest cost of a standard double room in high season.

TAMPA

84 miles southwest of Orlando via I–4.

Tampa, the west coast's business-and-commercial hub, has a sprinkling of high-rises and heavy traffic. A concentration of restaurants, nightlife, stores, and cultural events is amid the bustle. The city has really come into its own in recent years. The downtown Tampa waterfront features stunning views and excellent museums. Animal lovers flock here for attractions like Lowry Park Zoo, Busch Gardens, Big Cat Rescue, and Giraffe Ranch. Revelers will enjoy the strip of bars and clubs that constitutes Ybor City, a historic area with a heavy Cuban influence. The city also abounds with art museums, shops, and a wide array of restaurants. Downtown and Ybor City are both excellent spots to look for live music. Not too far out of town are some great golf courses and nature trails. Tampa is also a short drive from a long stretch of gorgeous Gulf Coast beaches.

GETTING AROUND

Downtown Tampa's Riverwalk, on Ashley Drive at the Hillsborough River, connects waterside entities such as the Florida Aquarium, the Channelside shopping-and-entertainment complex, and Marriott Waterside. The landscaped park is 6 acres and extends along the Garrison cruise-ship channel and along the Hillsborough River downtown. The walkway is being expanded as waterside development continues.

Hillsborough Area Regional Transit and TECO Line Street Cars replicate Tampa's first electric streetcars, transporting cruise-ship passengers to Ybor City and downtown Tampa.

Although downtown Tampa, the Channelside District, and Ybor City are easy to navigate without a car, you'll want to rent one if you plan on hitting the beaches or heading to Busch Gardens, Hyde Park, International Plaza, or any of the zoos.

Bus and Trolley Contacts Hillsborough Area Regional Transit. ☎ *813/254–4278* ⊕ *www.gohart.org.* **TECO Line Street Cars.** ☎ *813/254–4278* ⊕ *www. tecolinestreetcar.org.*

VISITOR INFORMATION

Contacts Tampa Bay Beaches Chamber of Commerce. ✉ *6990 Gulf Blvd., St. Pete Beach* ☎ *727/360–6957* ⊕ *www.tampabaybeaches.com.* **Visit Tampa Bay.** ✉ *401 E. Jackson St., Suite 2100* ☎ *800/448–2672, 813/223–1111* ⊕ *www. visittampabay.com.* **Ybor City Chamber Visitor Information Center.** ✉ *1600 E. 8th Ave., Suite B104, Ybor City* ☎ *813/241–8838* ⊕ *www.ybor.org.*

EXPLORING

TOP ATTRACTIONS

Fodor'sChoice **Big Cat Rescue.** Suburban Citrus Park in North Tampa is probably
★ the last place you'd expect to be able to get face-to-face with an 800-pound tiger. Yet at the end of a shaded road just yards off the Veterans' Expressway, you can do just that. This nonprofit, accredited sanctuary rescues and provides a permanent home for lions, tigers, ocelots, bobcats, cougars, and members of any other large-cat species you can imagine. Each and every one of these marvelous creatures has a unique story. Some arrived here after narrowly avoiding becoming an expensive coat. Others were kept as pets until the owners realized how pricey 15 pounds of meat per day (what it takes to feed some of these creatures) can be. They're all kept in large enclosures. A volunteer guide will lead you around the property and tell you the story of every cat you see. You'll also get an earful of little-known facts about these big cats, from the true origin of the white tiger to why some cats have white spots on the backs of their ears. Tours (no unescorted visits are allowed) are every day but Thursday, and special tours for children under 10 accompanied by an adult are offered on weekends. Night tours, feeding tours, and appointment-only private tours are also available. ✉ *12802 Easy St., Citrus Park* ☎ *813/920–4130* ⊕ *bigcatrescue.org* ⊠ *$36.*

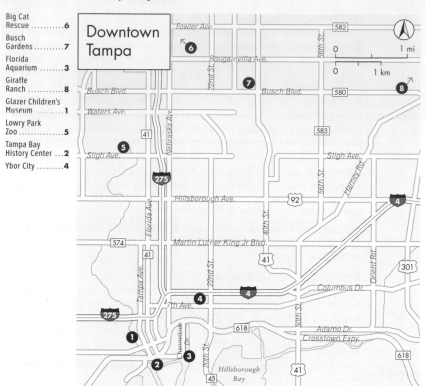

Downtown Tampa

FAMILY
Fodor's Choice
★

Busch Gardens. The Jungala exhibit at Busch Gardens brings Bengal tigers to center stage and puts them at eye level—allowing you to view them from underground caves and underwater windows. The big cats are just one of the reasons the theme park attracts some 4.5 million visitors each year. This is a world-class zoo, with more than 2,000 animals, and a live-entertainment venue that provides a full day (or more) of fun for the whole family. If you want to beat the crowds, start in the back of the park and work your way around clockwise.

The 335-acre adventure park's habitats offer views of some of the world's most endangered and exotic animals. For the best animal sightings, go to their habitats early, when it's cooler. You can experience up-close animal encounters on the Serengeti Plain, a 65-acre free-roaming habitat, home to reticulated giraffes, Grevy's zebras, white rhinos, bongos, impalas, and more. Myombe Reserve allows you to view lowland gorillas and chimpanzees in a lush, tropical-rain-forest environment. Down Under–themed Walkabout Way offers those ages five and up an opportunity to hand-feed kangaroos and wallabies (a cup of vittles is $5).

Interested in watching a tiger get a dental checkup? Then head over to the Animal Care and Nutrition Center, where you can observe veterinary care for many of the park's animals.

One of the park's newer thrill rides is Falcon's Fury, a 335-foot drop that is reportedly the tallest freestanding drop ride on the continent. It's the centerpiece of the park's Pantopia section, a colorful collection of rides, cafés, and retail space that replaced its Timbuktu section.

Many consider the seven roller coasters to be the biggest lure. On the wings of an African hawk, SheiKra—North America's first dive coaster—takes riders on a three-minute journey 200 feet up, then (gulp!) plunges 90 degrees straight down at 70 mph. The park's coaster lineup also includes steel giants Kumba, Scorpion, and Montu, and Sand Serpent, a five-story family coaster full of hairpin turns and breathtaking dips. When it's running, the Cheetah Hunt is an absolutely exhilarating 4,429-foot-high launch coaster. With three different launch points, this coaster takes you through the Serengeti and into a rocky gorge with a top speed of 60 mph.

Catering to the shorter set, the Sesame Street Safari of Fun is a 5-acre kids' playground with Sesame-themed rides, shows, and water adventures. The Air Grover Rollercoaster takes kids (and parents) on minidives and twisty turns over the Sahara, while Jungle Flyers gets them swinging and screeching. If you're looking to cool off, your best bets are Congo River Rapids, Stanleyville Falls (a flume ride), or Bert and Ernie's Water Hole—complete with bubblers, geysers, water jets, and dumping buckets. Character lunches are available (but you might want to wait until after your rides). ✉ *10165 N. Malcolm McKinley Dr., Central Tampa* ☎ *813/884–4386, 888/800–5447* ⊕ *www.buschgardens.com* ✉ *$102; parking $15.*

FAMILY **Florida Aquarium.** Although eels, sharks, and stingrays are the headliners, the Florida Aquarium is much more than a giant fishbowl. This architectural landmark features an 83-foot-high, multitier, glass dome; 250,000 square feet of air-conditioned exhibit space; and more than 20,000 aquatic plants and animals representing species native to Florida and the rest of the world—from black-tip sharks to leafy sea dragons.

Floor-to-ceiling interactive displays, behind-the-scenes tours, and in-water adventures allow kids to really get hands-on—and even get their feet wet. Adventurous types (certified divers age 15 and up) can dive with mild-mannered sharks and sea turtles or shallow-water swim with thousands of reef fish, eels and stingrays (for age six and up).

However, you don't have to get wet to have an interactive experience: the Ocean Commotion exhibit offers virtual dolphins and whales and multimedia displays and presentations. The Coral Reef Gallery, the aquarium's premier exhibit, is a 500,000-gallon tank with viewing windows, an awesome 43-foot-wide panoramic opening, and a walk-through tunnel that gives the illusion of venturing into underwater depths. There you see a thicket of elkhorn coral teeming with tropical fish, and a dark cave reveals sea life you would normally see only on night dives. The Journey to Madagascar exhibit features ring-tailed lemurs, hissing cockroaches, and an Indian Ocean coral reef to showcase the nation's vast diversity of creatures and ecosystems.

If you have an extra 90 minutes, try the Wild Dolphin Adventure Cruise, which takes up to 130 passengers onto Tampa Bay in a 72-foot catamaran for an up-close look at bottlenose dolphins and other wildlife. The

7

DID YOU KNOW?

One of seven roller coasters at Busch Gardens, SheiKra dives and twists without a floor beneath your feet. While other coasters take you for a gentler ride, this one spares no punches.

outdoor Explore a Shore exhibit, which gives younger kids a chance to release some energy, is an aquatic playground with a waterslide, water-jet sprays, and a climbable replica pirate ship. Last but not least, South African penguins make daily appearances in the Coral Reef Gallery. For an extra cost, you can get an up-close look at the daily lives of these penguins during the half-hour-long Penguins: Backstage Pass demonstration. ⊠ *701 Channelside Dr., Downtown* ☎ *813/273-4000* ⊕ *www.flaquarium.org* ✍ *Aquarium $24.95; Aquarium/Dolphin Cruise combo $49.90; Penguins Backstage Pass combo $54.95; Behind the Scenes Combo $36.95; Dive with the Sharks $150; Swim with the Fishes $75; parking $6.*

OFF THE BEATEN PATH

Giraffe Ranch. Rural Dade City is known mostly for its strawberries, but word is quickly spreading about something else that makes people flock here: giraffes. These graceful creatures are the headliners at this nearly 50-acre ranch. You can view them as part of a tour in a safari-style vehicle, on the back of a camel or flanked by a llama, or on a Segway; on any tour, you get to hand-feed them cabbage leaves. You'll also see tons of zebras, a pair of pygmy hippos, a giant porcupine, ostriches, and many other animal species roaming the grounds. Near the ranch's welcome center and gift shop is a corral of enclosures where you can watch guinea pigs chomp on sweet-potato chunks, hold a baby goat, (for a little extra cash) feed a flock of resident lemurs or bongo cattle, or watch a group of otters. You can also feed and help bathe a pair of rhinos. The ranch's proprietors have encyclopedic knowledge of the animal kingdom, and the overall experience is meant to impart a sense of connection to the animal world—and the environment—on those who visit. Tours take about two hours, and reservations are required. Credit cards are not accepted. ⊠ *38650 Mickler Rd., Dade City* ☎ *813/482–3400* ⊕ *www.girafferanch.com* ✍ *$90 for tour in safari van; $180 for tour by camelback; $180 by Segway; $180 for a llama trek.*

FAMILY **Glazer Children's Museum.** It's all about play here, and, with 53,000 square feet, more than a dozen themed areas, and 175 "interactives," there's plenty of opportunity for it. Areas designed to nurture imagination and strengthen confidence allow children and families to experience everything from flying an airplane to shopping for groceries. Kids can also create art, control the weather, navigate a mini–shipping channel, and "drive" a miniature (stationary) fire truck through Tampa. The Water's Journey Tree lets kids climb the tree to the second floor and mimics the water cycle. ⊠ *110 W. Gasparilla Plaza, Downtown* ☎ *813/443–3861* ⊕ *glazermuseum.org* ✍ *$15.*

FAMILY **Lowry Park Zoo.** Natural-habitat exhibits including Safari Africa, where a herd of African elephants is free to roam, make the 56-acre Lowry Park Zoo one of the best midsize zoos in the country. Asia gardens features two clouded leopards, and residents of Ituri Forest include a cheetah and lovably plump pygmy hippos. As you stroll through, keep an eye out for okapis, a rare forest giraffe from Central Africa. The stars at Primate World range from cat-size lemurs to a family of heavyweight Bornean orangutans that love to ham for the camera.

For hands-on experiences, Lowry has more options than most large parks, including chances to feed a giraffe, hold a colorful lorikeet, stroll with

7

wallabies, or touch a slippery stingray. Majestic red-tailed hawks and other raptors put on a show at the Birds of Prey Center, and a flock of majestic macaws soars through the zoo in a one-of-a-kind free-flight experience each day at 10:15 and 2. You can come face-to-face with Florida manatees at the Manatee Aquatic Center, the only nonprofit manatee hospital on the planet.

Dwindling native species like Florida panthers, black bears, and red wolves may be tough to find in the wild, but you can easily find them at the Florida Wildlife Center. Adorable koalas, wallabies, and emus populate the Wallaroo Station children's zoo. There are also water-play areas, rides (all of which are included with zoo admission), shows, and restaurants. ⊠ *1101 W. Sligh Ave., Central Tampa* ☎ *813/935–8552* ⊕ *www.lowryparkzoo.com* ⊠ *$32.95.*

FAMILY **Tampa Bay History Center.** From the early civilizations that once flourished on its shores to the 2000 presidential vote recount, the Tampa Bay region has long had an integral role in Florida history and that of the country as a whole. The interactive exhibits here let you peer back in time at the people and events that helped shape the area. You'll learn about the Tocobaga and other people who lived in coastal areas and the Spanish explorers who encountered them. A new 8,500 square-foot space explores Tampa Bay's pirate lore with help from a massive replica pirate ship. You'll find a wealth of information and artifacts from the Seminole Wars, Ybor City's once-thriving cigar industry, and Florida crackers who, believe it or not, once drove their cattle in areas now saturated with busy roads and shopping centers. Exhibits also cover the sports teams that have called Tampa Bay home, not to mention the war heroes and politicians of the 20th and 21st centuries. Museumgoers looking for a bite to eat are in for a treat: the café here is a branch of none other than the Columbia, Tampa's most famous and historic restaurant. ⊠ *801 Old Water St.* ☎ *813/228–0097* ⊕ *tampabayhistorycenter.org* ⊠ *$12.95.*

Ybor City. Tampa's Latin quarter is one of only a few National Historic Landmark districts in Florida. Bordered by Interstate 4 to the north, 22nd Street to the east, Adamo Drive to the south, and Nebraska Avenue to the West, it has antique-brick streets and wrought-iron balconies. Cubans brought their cigar-making industry to Ybor (pronounced *ee*-bore) City in 1886, and the smell of cigars—hand-rolled by Cuban immigrants—still wafts through the heart of this east Tampa area, along with the strong aroma of roasting coffee. These days the neighborhood makes for an interesting visit as empty cigar factories and historic social clubs have been transformed into boutiques, art galleries, restaurants, and nightclubs. However, it can also be seedy and rowdy at times. ⊠ *Ybor City.*

WHERE TO EAT

$$ ✕ **Bella's Italian Café.** While this popular SoHo (South Howard Avenue)
ITALIAN eatery earned its wings by offering crowd-pleasing Italian classics, much of this mainstay's popularity stems from the creative takes on them. Carnivores are not slighted here, but it is often more delicious to go meatless. **Known for:** hearty Italian classics; house-made pasta; intimate dining environment. $ *Average main: $20* ⊠ *1413 S. Howard Ave., Hyde Park* ☎ *813/254–3355* ⊕ *www.bellasitaliancafe.com.*

$$$$ STEAKHOUSE Fodor's Choice ★ 🍴 **Bern's Steak House.** With the air of an exclusive club, this is one of—if not *the*—finest Florida's steak houses. Rich mahogany paneling and ornate chandeliers define the legendary circa-1956 Bern's, where the chef ages his own beef, grows much of his own produce, and roasts his own coffee. **Known for:** colossal wine list; exclusive atmosphere; after dinner, a trip upstairs to the famous dessert room. [$] *Average main: $36* ✉ *1208 S. Howard Ave., Hyde Park* ☎ *813/251–2421* 🌐 *www.bernssteakhouse.com* 👔 *Jacket and tie.*

$$$ ASIAN FUSION 🍴 **BT.** Local restaurateur B. T. Nguyen has earned quite a following with her modern take on high-style Vietnamese cuisine featuring fresh herbs grown on-site and a drink list that includes organic sake martinis—some flavored with herbs from that same garden. She opened her first eatery in the early 1990s. **Known for:** fresh, local ingredients; creative dishes like Shaken beef with cognac and shallots; intimate atmosphere. [$] *Average main: $28* ✉ *2507 S. MacDill Ave., Suite B, SoHo* ☎ *813/258–1916* 🌐 *www.restaurantbt.com* 🕓 *Closed Sun. and Mon. No lunch.*

$$$ MODERN AMERICAN 🍴 **Café Dufrain.** Dogs can tag along if you dine on the front patio at pet-friendly Café Dufrain, an eatery right on the Hillsborough River across from the Amalie Arena. Creative menu items, which vary by season, include teriyaki-glazed salmon and house-made dim-sum. **Known for:** internationally influenced American cuisine, such as a bánh mì–style chicken sandwich; excellent water and downtown views; large selection of craft beers and cocktails. [$] *Average main: $24* ✉ *707 Harbour Post Dr., Downtown* ☎ *813/275–9701* 🌐 *cafedufrain.com.*

$ PIZZA 🍴 **Cappy's Pizza.** Chicago may be the first place you think of when you hear the words "deep-dish pizza," which is why the high-quality pies this local chain offers may surprise (and please) you. The menu at this family-friendly spot is pretty simple: choose either a Chicago- or New York–style crust, and select your toppings. **Known for:** rich, Chicago-style deep-dish pizza (or New York–style if that's your thing); bottled beer selection—grab one yourself from the cooler; real-deal vintage decor. [$] *Average main: $14* ✉ *4910 N. Florida Ave., Seminole Heights* ☎ *813/238–1516* 🌐 *cappyspizzaonline.com* 💳 *No credit cards* 🕓 *No lunch.*

$$$ SPANISH Fodor's Choice ★ 🍴 **The Columbia Restaurant.** Make a date for some of the best Latin cuisine in Tampa. A fixture since 1905, this magnificent structure with an Old World air and spacious dining rooms takes up an entire city block and seems to feed the entire city—locals as well as visitors—throughout the week, but especially on weekends. **Known for:** paella à la Valenciana with seafood, chicken, and pork; 1905 salad with ham, olives, cheese, and garlic; delicious sangria. [$] *Average main: $23* ✉ *2117 E. 7th Ave., Ybor City* ☎ *813/248–4961* 🌐 *www.columbiarestaurant.com.*

$$ ECLECTIC 🍴 **Datz Tampa.** Fans of a hearty meal will not be slighted here; the eclectic menu is mostly massive sandwiches and hefty plates (and printed on tabloid paper, an indication of how much it changes). The show-stealer here is the Cheesy Todd, a hamburger patty sandwiched between two deep-fried mounds of bacon-jalapeño mac-and-cheese. **Known for:** large portions; extensive beer and cocktail list; over-the-top sweets from Datz Dough. [$] *Average main: $17* ✉ *2616 S. MacDill Ave., SoHo* ☎ *813/831–7000* 🌐 *datztampa.com.*

$$$$ ECLECTIC 🍴 **Edison Food + Drink Lab.** In the relatively short time this gastropub has been around, it has handily earned a spot at the table of Tampa culinary musts. The internationally influenced, creative menu changes almost every day as chef/owner Jeannie Pierola experiments with a revolving list of intriguing ingredients. **Known for:** grilled octopus appetizer; interesting cocktails; extensive wine list. [$] *Average main: $32* ✉ *912 W. Kennedy Blvd., Downtown* ☎ *813/254–7111* 🌐 *edison-tampa.com* 🕒 *Closed Sun. No lunch Sat.*

$ HOT DOG 🍴 **Mel's Hot Dogs.** Look for the red wiener-mobile parked on the north side of the highway near the theme park, and you'll find this 1950s-style diner that specializes in dogs and fries. It's a must after a long day of riding roller coasters and scoping out zebras at Busch Gardens. **Known for:** long list of hot dogs; crispy, gold fries; decent beer selection. [$] *Average main: $8* ✉ *4136 E. Busch Blvd., Central Tampa* ☎ *813/985–8000* 🌐 *www.melshotdogs.com* 🕒 *Closed Sun.*

$$$ MODERN AMERICAN 🍴 **Mise en Place.** Known to locals as "Mise" (pronounced *meez*), this upscale, modern downtown space is a popular lunch spot for Tampa's political and social elite. At night, it transforms into an elegant, understated dining destination with an ever-changing, seasonal menu that offers adventurous yet meticulously crafted modern American cuisine. **Known for:** five-course "Get Blitzed" tasting menu of the week's highlights; lovingly assembled wine and cocktail list; staples like chicken liver pâté and rack of lamb. [$] *Average main: $29* ✉ *442 W. Kennedy Blvd., Suite 110, Downtown* ☎ *813/254–5373* 🌐 *www.miseonline.com* 🕒 *Closed Sun. and Mon. No lunch Sat.*

$ MEXICAN 🍴 **Taco Bus.** It's a Mexican joint with a simple name in a less-than-magnificent location, but that matters not to anyone who's ever eaten to this legendary late-night establishment. Its popularity has turned what was little more than a food truck into a small local chain. **Known for:** chicken burrito preñado; butternut squash tostadas; vegetarian protein options like tofu, tempeh, portabello mushrooms, vegan cheese. [$] *Average main: $11* ✉ *913 E. Hillsborough Ave., Central Tampa* ☎ *813/232–5889.*

$$$ ECLECTIC Fodor's Choice ★ 🍴 **Ulele.** Named after a 16th-century Tocobagan princess, this hot spot from the same family behind the historic Columbia restaurant in Ybor City has become the go-to spot for Tampa diners in the know. The diverse menu focuses on locally available ingredients but has an easy-to-detect Southern accent. **Known for:** Florida pompano and seafood potpie; spectacular views of the Hillsborough River; creative cocktail menu and house-brewed beer. [$] *Average main: $25* ✉ *1810 N. Highland Ave.* ☎ *813/999–4952* 🌐 *ulele.com.*

WHERE TO STAY

$$ HOTEL 🏨 **Aloft Tampa Downtown.** Right on the Hillsborough River, this high-rise used to be a bank but now offers sweeping downtown and water views close to some of Tampa's best restaurants and entertainment venues. **Pros:** right in the middle of everything; tech-friendly; excellent views. **Cons:** parking is valet only; no full-service restaurant; DJ on weekend nights can be loud for early birds on lower floors. [$] *Rooms from: $224* ✉ *100 W. Kennedy Blvd., Downtown* ☎ *813/898–8000* 🌐 *alofttampa-downtown.com* 🛏 *130 rooms* 🍽 *No meals.*

$$$ HOTEL Fodor's Choice ★ 🏨 **Epicurean.** Brought to you in part by the people at Bern's Steak House (which happens to be across the street), this vibrant, cuisine-centric installment of Marriott's Autograph Collection is an absolute must for foodies, but it doesn't make nonfoodies feel left out. **Pros:** excellent service; great location; tons of amenities. **Cons:** can get pricey; exclusive vibe; not the best option for families. [$] *Rooms from: $329* ✉ *1207 S. Howard Ave., SoHo* ☎ *813/999–8700, 855/829–2536* 🌐 *epicureanhotel.com* 🛏 *137 rooms* 🍴 *No meals.*

$$ RESORT 🏨 **Grand Hyatt Tampa Bay.** On the southwestern edge of Tampa, near the airport and overlooking the Courtney Campbell Causeway, the Grand Hyatt has a lot to offer—both in its guest rooms and on the property. **Pros:** extensive amenities; amazing views; world-class dining. **Cons:** far from beach; getting here can be tough due to traffic and awkward road layout; lots of business conventions and travelers. [$] *Rooms from: $299* ✉ *2900 Bayport Dr., West Tampa* ☎ *813/874–1234* 🌐 *www.grandtampabay.hyatt.com* 🛏 *442 rooms* 🍴 *No meals.*

$$ HOTEL 🏨 **Hilton Garden Inn Tampa Ybor Historic District.** Although its modern architecture and rooms (updated in 2016) make it seem out of place in this historic district, this chain hotel's location across from Centro Ybor is a plus. **Pros:** located in top cultural and nightlife district; free Wi-Fi; free parking. **Cons:** neighborhood can be rowdy on weekends; chain-hotel feel; limited amenities. [$] *Rooms from: $269* ✉ *1700 E. 9th Ave., Ybor City* ☎ *813/769–9267* 🌐 *www.hiltongardeninn.com* 🛏 *95 rooms* 🍴 *No meals.*

7

$$ HOTEL 🏨 **Le Méridien Tampa.** A meticulous renovation transformed this historic, marble-lined former federal courthouse into Tampa's most talked-about boutique hotel. **Pros:** close to downtown attractions; fascinating for history buffs; lots of amenities. **Cons:** traffic in surrounding area can be a nightmare; all that marble makes for loud echoes in the hallways. [$] *Rooms from: $269* ✉ *601 N. Florida Ave., Downtown* ☎ *813/221–9555, 877/782–0116 reservations* 🌐 *lemeridientampa.com* 🛏 *130 rooms* 🍴 *No meals.*

$$ RESORT 🏨 **Saddlebrook Resort Tampa.** If you can't get enough golf and tennis, here's your fix. **Pros:** away from urban sprawl; great choice for the fitness minded. **Cons:** a bit isolated; very far from attractions. [$] *Rooms from: $249* ✉ *5700 Saddlebrook Way, Wesley Chapel* ☎ *813/973–1111, 800/729–8383* 🌐 *www.saddlebrook.com* 🛏 *540 rooms* 🍴 *No meals.*

$ HOTEL 🏨 **Tampa Marriott Waterside Hotel & Marina.** Across from the Tampa Convention Center, this downtown hotel was built for conventioneers but is also convenient to tourist spots such as the Florida Aquarium and the Ybor City and Hyde Park shopping and nightlife districts. **Pros:** great downtown location; near sights, dining, nightlife. **Cons:** gridlock during rush hour; streets tough to maneuver. [$] *Rooms from: $199* ✉ *700 S. Florida Ave., Downtown* ☎ *888/268–1616 for reservations, 813/221–4900* 🌐 *www.marriott.com* 🛏 *719 rooms* 🍴 *No meals.*

$ HOTEL 🏨 **Westin Tampa Harbour Island.** Few folks think of the islands when visiting Tampa, but this 12-story hotel on a 177-acre man-made islet is a short drive from downtown Tampa and even closer to the cruise terminal. **Pros:** close to downtown; nice views; on the TECO streetcar line. **Cons:** lots of traffic in immediate area; chain-hotel feel; lots of business travelers. [$] *Rooms from: $199* ✉ *725 S. Harbour Island Blvd., Harbour Island* ☎ *813/229–5000* 🌐 *westintampaharbourisland.com* 🛏 *318 rooms* 🍴 *No meals.*

Where to Eat and Stay in Tampa

600 92

W. Hillsborough Ave.

WELLSWOOD

W South Ave.
N Lois Ave.
92
W Osborne Ave.
N Grady Ave.
Al Lopez Field
W Osborne Ave.
W Plaza
N Manhattan Ave.
N Habana Ave.
N Armenia Ave.
N Howard Ave.
N Rome Ave.
Hillsborough River

W Cayuga St.
DREW PARK
N Dale Mabry Hwy.
PLAZA TERRACE
W Alva St.

574

W Dr. Martin Luther King Jr. Blvd.
West Virginia Ave.
RIVERSIDE HEIGHTS
West Virginia Ave.
574

Hillsborough Community College
Raymond James Stadium
W Lake Ave.
W Indiana Ave.
RIVERSIDE HEIGHTS
W Woodlawn Ave.
W Woodlawn Ave.
N Perry Ave.
N Oakley Ave.
W Pribley St.
W Collins St.
North Blvd.

W Tampa Bay Blvd.
N Nixon St.
N Glen Ave.
N Matanzas Ave.
N Macdill Ave.
Braddock St.
W Dewey St.
W Ivy St.
W Aileen St.
N Perry Ave.
N Karger Ave.
Myrtle Ave.
Braddock St.

Tampa International Airport
W Columbus Dr.
W Spruce Blvd.
W Columbus Dr.

CARVER CITY / LINCOLN GARDENS
MacFARLANE PARK
W St. Louis St.
W St. Joseph St.
W St. Conrad St.
W Beach St.
OLD WEST TAMPA
W St. Conrad St.
W Francis
W Cherry St.
N Lois Ave.
N Grady Ave.
1
Laurel St.
W Spruce St.
MacFarlane Park
W Green St.
N Gomer Ave.
N Habana Ave.
N Tampania Ave.
W Union St.
W Green St.
W Spruce St.
W Main St.

275
W La Salle St.
NORTH HYDE PARK
W Arch St.
N Hubert Ave.
W Cypress St.
W Cass St.
Nassau St.
W Cypress St.
275
W Lemon St.
600
NORTH BON AIR
92
OAKFORD PARK
W Cass St.
N Gomez Ave.
N Habana Ave.
W Lemon St.
W Carmen St.
N Oregon St.
North Blvd.
W Fig St.
W North B St.
W North A St.
W Fig St.

W. Kennedy Blvd.
60
GRAY GABLES
685 60
W. Kennedy Blvd.
W Cleveland St.
5
SWANN ESTATES
BON AIR
S Hubert Ave.
S Glen Ave.
S Church Ave.
Dale Ave.
685
S Macdill Ave.
S Trask St.
W A'zeele St.
W De Leon St.
S Audubon Ave.
S Armenia Ave.
S Howard Ave.
S Albany Ave.
W Horatio
S Oregon St.
W Platt St.
W Swann Ave.
S Boulevard
S Edison Ave.
S Rome Ave.
HYDE PARK
W Swann Ave.
W Inman Ave.
S Lois Ave.
W Morrison Ave.
PARKLAND ESTATES
W Watrous Ave.
S Dakota Ave.
W Neptune St.
GOLFVIEW
W Watrous Ave.
W Prospect Rd.
4
Lee Roy Selmon Expwy (Toll)
S Willis Ave.
South Blvd.
Newport Ave.
PALMA CEIA WEST
685
Palma Ceia Golf and Country Club
1 2
2
3
Bayshore
South Dale Mabry Hwy.
Henderson Blvd.
S Sterling Ave.
S Himes Ave.
S Glen Ave.

1/2 mi
0   1/2 km

KEY
🌑 Restaurants
① Hotels

NIGHTLIFE

When it comes to entertainment, there's never a dull moment in Tampa. Colorful Ybor City, a heavily Cuban-influenced area minutes from downtown, is a case in point. It has by far the biggest concentration of nightclubs (too many to list here), all situated along 7th and 8th avenues. Ybor comes alive at night and on weekends, when a diverse array of bars and clubs open their doors to throngs of partygoers. Whether it's bumping house music or some live rock and roll you seek, you'll find it here. Downtown Tampa is also becoming a formidable nightlife destination. When it comes to the arts—visual, musical, performing, or otherwise—Tampa is one of the South's leading spots.

BARS

Centro Cantina. There are lots of draws here: a balcony overlooking the crowds on 7th Avenue, live music Thursday through Sunday nights, a large selection of margaritas, and more than 30 brands of tequila. Food is served until 2 am. ⊠ *1600 E. 8th Ave., Ybor City* ☎ *813/241–8588* ⊕ *www.centroybor.com.*

Cigar City Brewing Tasting Room. Offering the fruits of the adjacent Cigar City brewery, the large tasting room here puts Tampa on the map for craft beer enthusiasts. On tap, it offers mainstay brews like Jai Alai IPA and Maduro Brown Ale as well as an interesting rotation of seasonal beers. It's a spot with friendly staff and generally good music. But beware: happy hour can be packed. Brewery tours are available on the hour Wednesday through Sunday between 11 am and 3 pm during the week (a bit later on weekends) for a nominal fee. ⊠ *3924 W. Spruce St., Suite A, Central Tampa* ☎ *813/348–6363 Ext. 206* ⊕ *cigarcitybrewing.com.*

Fly Bar. A happy-hour mecca for hip young professionals, Fly Bar and Restaurant offers an intriguing selection of creative cocktails with ingredients like violets, walnut bitters, and salted celery-apple puree. The list goes on. If you're hungry, you'll find a food menu to match. There's live music on weekends and occasionally during the week. A huge draw—in fair weather, anyway—is the rooftop deck, which offers killer views of surrounding downtown Tampa. ⊠ *1202 N. Franklin St., Downtown* ☎ *813/275–5000* ⊕ *www.flybarandrestaurant.com.*

Gaspar's Grotto. Spanish pirate Jose Gaspar was known for swashbuckling up and down Florida's west coast in the late 18th and early 19th century. His legend has inspired a massive, raucous street festival each winter. This Ybor City drinkery has adopted his name, and rightly so. Decked out in tons of pirate memorabilia, it's the cornerstone to any night spent barhopping on the Ybor strip. The sangria is a good choice, but the aged rums may be a better fit here. You'll also find a food menu that goes well beyond standard bar fare. ⊠ *1805 E. 7th Ave., Ybor City* ☎ *813/248–5900* ⊕ *www.gasparsgrotto.com.*

The Hub Bar. Considered something of a dive—but a lovable one—by a loyal and young local following that ranges from esteemed jurists to nose-ring-wearing night owls. The Hub, which dates back to 1946, is known for strong drinks and a jukebox that goes well beyond the usual. ⊠ *719 N. Franklin St., Downtown* ☎ *813/229–1553* ⊕ *thehubbartampa.com.*

CASINO

Seminole Hard Rock Hotel & Casino. In addition to playing one of the hundreds of Vegas-style slot machines, gamers can get their kicks at the casino's poker tables and video-gaming machines. The lounge serves drinks 24 hours a day. Hard Rock Cafe, of course, has live music, dinner, and nightlife. There is a heavy smell of cigarette smoke here, as with most casinos. ⊠ 5223 N. Orient Rd., off I–4 at N. Orient Rd. exit, East Tampa ☎ 813/627–7625 ⊕ www.seminolehardrock.com.

MUSIC CLUB

Skippers Smokehouse. A junkyard-style restaurant and oyster bar, Skippers is known for hosting Uncle John's Band (a long-running Grateful Dead cover act) every Thursday, and for having great smoked fish every night. Check their calendar for exceptional musical lineups on the weekends; it's closed on Mondays. ⊠ 910 Skipper Rd., North Tampa ☎ 813/971–0666 ⊕ www.skipperssmokehouse.com.

SHOPPING

MALLS

Centro Ybor. Ybor City's destination within a destination is this dining-and-entertainment palace. It has shops, bars, and restaurants, a 20-screen movie theater, and even a gourmet Popsicle shop. ⊠ 1600 E. 8th Ave., Ybor City ⊕ www.centroybor.com.

Channelside Bay Plaza. Right next to Tampa's cruise-ship terminal, this outdoor mall offers a vast array of shopping and dining options, as well as live music in a large courtyard. Look out for Hablo Taco, a poplar Mexican food stop; daiquiri spot Wet Willie's; and Splitsville, a 21-and-up bowling alley and restaurant chain targeting a younger crowd. ⊠ 615 Channelside Dr., Downtown ⊕ www.channelsidebayplaza.com.

SPORTS AND THE OUTDOORS

BASEBALL

George M. Steinbrenner Field. Locals and tourists flock each March to see the New York Yankees play about 17 spring training games at this 11,000-seat facility. (Call or visit the website for tickets.) From April through September, the stadium belongs to a Yankee farm team, the Tampa Yankees, who play 70 games against the likes of the Daytona Cubs and the Sarasota Red Sox. ⊠ 1 Steinbrenner Dr., near the corner of Dale Mabry Hwy., off I–275 Exit 41B, Central Tampa ☎ 813/875–7753 ⊕ www.steinbrennerfield.com.

GOLF

The Claw at USF. Named for its many dog-legged fairways, this University of South Florida course is one of the most challenging public courses in the area. Live oaks as well as cypress and pine trees line the tight twists and turns of the fairways. This is one of the few places in Tampa Bay where you'll find deer grazing along the fairway (especially early in the morning) and gators sunning themselves next to the course's ponds. You'll also find a driving range and a golf shop. After you play, grab a beer at Rocky's Sports Grill, where you'll be able to catch the game on one of several flat- or plasma-screen TVs. ⊠ *13801 N. 46th St., North Tampa* ☎ *813/632–6893* ⊕ *www.theclawatusfgolf.com* ⊠ *$20–$45* ⚑ *18 holes, 6863 yards, par 71.*

Saddlebrook Golf Club. This expansive complex half an hour northeast of Tampa offers not one but two courses designed by Arnold Palmer. The Palmer Golf Course's hilly terrain contrasts with Tampa Bay's generally flat landscape, and it make you think you're playing on a course somewhere in New England. With its Spanish moss–draped cypress hammocks, the Saddlebrook Golf Course has more of an Old Florida feel to it. As you make your way past this course's green ponds, keep an eye out for turtles—and gators. There's also a golf shop, driving range, on-site pros, and, if you're aching from a grueling day on the course, a luxury spa on the resort property. ⊠ *Saddlebrook Resort, 5700 Saddlebrook Way, Wesley Chapel* ☎ *813/973–1111* ⊕ *www.saddlebrook. com* ⊠ *$50–$145 (varies seasonally)* ⚑ *Palmer Course: 18 holes, 6243 yards, par 71; Saddlebrook Course: 18 holes, 6480 yards, par 70.*

Tournament Players Club of Tampa Bay. A stop along the PGA Champion's Tour, this public course sits about 15 miles north of Tampa. It was designed by Bobby Weed with consultation from Chi Chi Rodriguez and is laid out along natural wetlands, which means you can spot plenty of local wildlife as you play. The course was designed to be challenging while still giving novices a fair shake. Practice ahead of time at the driving, chipping, or putting range. There's a golf shop on-site as well as the Cuatro, where you can grab a sandwich and a cold one after your game. ⊠ *5300 W. Lutz Fern Rd., Lutz* ☎ *813/949–0090* ⊕ *www. tpctampabay.com* ⊠ *$169* ⚑ *18 holes, 6898 yards, par 71.*

WALKING

Bayshore Boulevard Trail. Considered the world's longest continuous sidewalk, this 4½-mile trail is a good spot for just standing still and taking it all in, with its spectacular views of downtown Tampa and the Hillsborough Bay area. Of course, you can also walk, talk, jog, bike, and in-line skate with locals. The trail is open from dawn to dusk daily. ⊠ *Bayshore Blvd.* ☎ *813/274–8615.*

ST. PETERSBURG

21 miles west of Tampa.

Nicknamed the Sunshine City, St. Pete is much more than a mass of land between the airport and the beaches. In recent years it's seen a fierce arts and cultural revival, which you can plainly see as you stroll through the city's lively downtown area. The Salvador Dalí Museum building is a testament to the great pride residents of the 'Burg take in their waterfront city. But the city has other arts-oriented attractions, including the Dale Chihuly Collection, the Fine Arts Museum, and the burgeoning young artist hub known as the 600 Block, where eateries and bars attract crowds in the evening. Beach Drive offers some upscale options, whereas Central Avenue appeals more to night owls. The Grand Central District offers some unique vintage and antiques shopping. Gulfport is a stylishly low-key suburb southwest of St. Petersburg. The long strip of

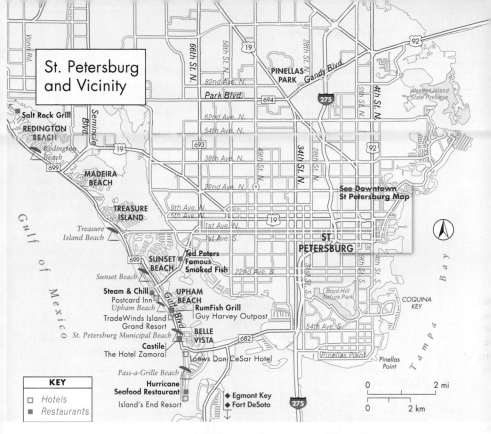

barrier islands lining St. Pete's west coast offer miles of gorgeous white beaches as well as dining, nightlife, and phenomenal sunsets. Nearby beach towns include St. Pete Beach, Treasure Island, Madeira Beach, and Redington Shores. No trip to this area is complete without a visit to the remote, pristine beaches of Fort De Soto.

GETTING HERE AND AROUND

Interstate 275 heads west from Tampa across Tampa Bay to St. Petersburg, swings south, and crosses the bay again on its way to Terra Ceia, near Bradenton. U.S. 19 is St. Petersburg's major north–south artery; traffic can be heavy, and there are many lights, so try to avoid it. Alternatives include 66th and 4th streets. One key thing to remember about St. Pete is that the roads form an easy-to-navigate grid: streets run north to south; avenues run east to west. Central Avenue connects downtown to the beaches.

Around St. Petersburg, Pinellas Suncoast Transit Authority serves Pinellas County. Look for buses that cover the beaches and downtown exclusively.

St. Petersburg Trolley will get you to key destinations throughout downtown St. Pete, and even offers free service between the Chamber of Commerce Visitor's Bureau and certain destinations.

Contacts Pinellas Suncoast Transit Authority. ☎ 727/540–1800 ⊕ www.psta. net. **St. Petersburg Trolley.** ☎ 727/821–5166 ⊕ www.stpetetrolley.com.

TOURS

All About Fun Tours. What sets this tour apart from others is you are not going by bus or boat—your self-guided chariot is a motorized Segway. Each tour starts with an easy 15- to 20-minute training session. Tours are 60 or 90 minutes and are offered up to three times daily. It's a carefree way to see downtown St. Petersburg, the park system, and the waterfront while learning about local history. Reservations are required. ✉ *335 N.E. 2nd Ave.* ☎ *727/896–3640* ⊕ *www.gyroglides.com* ⌦ *Tours $35–$50.*

Dolphin Landings Tours. This operation runs a four-hour shelling trip, a two-hour dolphin-sighting excursion powered mostly by sail, back-bay or party-boat fishing, and other outings to Egmont Key and Shell Key. It's not easy to spot from the road: the boats are docked behind a strip mall. ✉ *4737 Gulf Blvd., St. Pete Beach* ☎ *727/360–7411* ⊕ *www.dolphinlandings.com* ⌦ *From $35.*

FAMILY　**Island Boat Adventures.** Another popular option for getting out to Egmont Key, this company offers snorkeling adventures as well as dolphin-watching and snorkeling trips out of where the boats dock near Ft. De Soto. ✉ *224 Pinellas Bayway S, St. Petersburg* ☎ *727/871–2628* ⊕ *islandboatadventures.com* ⌦ *$39.95.*

VISITOR INFORMATION

Contacts Visit St. Petersburg-Clearwater. ✉ *8200 Bryan Dairy Rd., Suite 200, Largo* ☎ *727/464–7200, 877/352–3224* ⊕ *www.visitstpeteclearwater.com.*

EXPLORING

DOWNTOWN ST. PETERSBURG
TOP ATTRACTIONS

Fodor'sChoice　**Chihuly Collection.** In October 2016, the first permanent collection of
★　world-renowned glass sculptor Dale Chihuly's work received a new, 10,000-square-foot home in an electrifying Albert Alfonso–designed building. Now, such impossibly vibrant, larger-than-life pieces as "Float Boat" and "Ruby Red Icicle" sit next to some of the famed sculptor's smaller and more under-the-radar works. You can tour the museum independently or with one of its volunteer docents (no added cost; tours are given hourly on the half hour during the week). Each display is perfectly lit against a shade of gray paint on the walls Chihuly himself handpicked, which adds to the drama of the designs. Don't miss "Mille Fiore" ("Thousand Flowers"), a spectacular, whimsical glass montage mimicking a wildflower patch, critters and all. Check out the gift shop at the end if you'd like to take some of the magic home with you. Your admission includes access to Morean Arts Center's glassblowing studio, where you can watch resident artisans create a unique glass piece before your eyes. ✉ *720 Central Ave., Downtown* ☎ *727/856–4527* ⊕ *www. moreanartscenter.org/chihuly* ⌦ *$19.99.*

Fodor'sChoice　**The Dalí Museum.** Inside and out, the waterfront Dalí Museum, which
★　opened on 1/11/11 (Dalí is said to have been into numerology), is almost as remarkable as the Spanish surrealist's work. The state-of-the-art building has a surreal geodesic-like glass structure called the Dalí Enigma, as well as an outdoor labyrinth and a DNA-inspired spiral

staircase leading up to the collection. All this, before you've even seen the collection, which is one of the most comprehensive of its kind—courtesy of Ohio magnate A. Reynolds Morse, a friend of Dalí's.

Here, you can scope out his early impressionistic works and see how the painter evolved into the visionary he's now seen to be. The mind-expanding paintings in this downtown headliner include *Eggs on a Plate Without a Plate, The Hallucinogenic Toreador,* and more than 90 other oils. You'll also discover more than 2,000 additional works including watercolors, drawings, sculptures, photographs, and objets d'art. The museum also hosts temporary collections from the likes of Pablo Picasso and Andy Warhol. Free hour-long tours are led by well-informed docents. ⊠ *1 Dali Blvd.* ☎ *727/823–3767* ⊕ *www.thedali.org* 🎟 *$24.*

FAMILY **Sunken Gardens.** A cool oasis amid St. Pete's urban clutter, this lush 4-acre plot was created from a lake that was drained in 1903. Explore the cascading waterfalls and koi ponds, and walk through the butterfly house and exotic gardens where more than 50,000 tropical plants and flowers from across the globe thrive amid groves of some of the area's most spectacular palm trees. The flock of wading flamingoes is a favorite here. The on-site restaurant (Carrabba's), bakery/dessert spot (St. Pete Bakery), and hands-on kids' museum (Great Exploration) make this place a family favorite. ⊠ *1825 4th St. N* ☎ *727/551–3102* ⊕ *www.sunkengardens.org* 🎟 *$10.*

ST. PETE BEACH AND VICINITY
TOP ATTRACTIONS
Egmont Key. In the middle of the mouth of Tampa Bay lies the small (350 acres), largely unspoiled but critically eroding island Egmont Key, now a state park, national wildlife refuge, national historic site, and bird sanctuary. On the island are the ruins of Ft. De Soto's sister fortification, Ft. Dade, built during the Spanish-American War to protect Tampa Bay. The primary inhabitants of the less-than-2-mile-long island are the threatened gopher tortoise and box turtles. The only way to get here is by boat—you can catch a ferry from Ft. De Soto, among other places. Nature lovers will find the trip well worth it—the beach here is excellent for shelling, secluded beach bathing, wildlife viewing, and snorkeling. Multiple ferry operators run trips here, including Hubbard's Marina, Dolphin Landings, and Island Boat Adventures. ⊠ *Tierra Verde* ⊕ *www.floridastateparks.org/egmontkey.*

WORTH NOTING
FAMILY
Fodor'sChoice
★

Fort De Soto Park. Spread over five small islands, 1,136-acre Fort De Soto Park lies at the mouth of Tampa Bay. It has 7 miles of waterfront (much of it beach), two fishing piers, a 4-mile hiking, cycling, and skating trail, picnic-and-camping grounds, and a historic fort that kids of any age can explore. For those traveling with their canine family members, there is a long and popular dog beach just north of the main fishing pier. The fort for which it's named was built on the southern end of Mullet Key to protect sea lanes in the gulf during the Spanish-American War. Roam the fort or wander the beaches of any of the islands within the park. Kayaks and beach cruisers are available for rental, and mementos can be found at a souvenir shop/grille on the park's north side. ⊠ *3500 Pinellas Bayway St., Tierra Verde* ☎ *727/582–2267* ⊕ *www.pinellascounty.org/park/05_ft_desoto.htm* 🎟 *$5.*

7

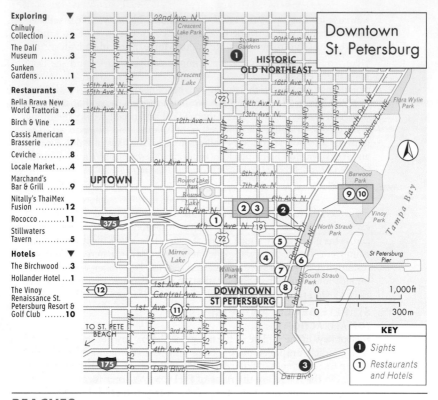

BEACHES

ST. PETE BEACH & VICINITY

Egmont Beach. An undeveloped island teeming with birds, shells, and native plants is a short ferry ride away. You'll find serene lengths of beach, abandoned former military buildings, a lighthouse and a herd of gopher tortoises patrolling nearby hiking paths. You can grab a ferry here from Dolphin Landings, John's Pass, or Ft. De Soto for as little as $15. **Amenities:** none. **Best for:** solitude; walking. ⊠ *Egmont Key National Wildlife Refuge, accessible by boat only, Tierra Verde* ☎ *727/867–6569* ⊕ *floridastateparks.org/egmontkey.*

Madeira Beach. Known to locals as "Mad Beach," this lively barrier island town occupies the southern tip of Shell Key. The beachfront consists of a long stretch of soft, shell-strewn sand, and it's often crowded with families as well as clusters of twentysomething beachgoers. You can get to the beach via numerous public access points, but your best bet is to park at the municipal beach parking lot and head to the sand from there. It's easily accessible from Treasure Island, northern St. Petersburg, and Clearwater Beach. **Amenities:** food and drink; parking; showers; toilets. **Best for:** partiers; swimming; walking. ⊠ *14400 Gulf Blvd., Madeira Beach.*

FAMILY
Fodor's Choice
★

Pass-a-Grille Beach. At the southern tip of St. Pete Beach (past the Don Cesar), this is the epitome of Old Florida. One of the most popular beaches in the area, it skirts the west end of charming, historic Pass-a-Grille, a neighborhood that draws tourists and locals alike with its stylish yet low-key mom-and-pop motels and restaurants. There's a sunset celebration each night at a pavilion/snack shop on the stretch of beach between the ends of 9th and 10th avenues. On weekends, check out the Art Mart, an open-air market showcasing the work of local artisans. **Amenities:** food and drink; parking; showers; toilets. **Best for:** sunset; windsurfing. ⊠ *1000 Pass-a-Grille Way, St. Pete Beach.*

Redington Beach. Sand Key, the landmass that is home to Madeira Beach at the south end and Belleaire Beach in the north, is spotted with public beach access points. This particular spot has a bigger parking area than the others, though it's not free. It's also within walking distance of the Redington Pier, one of the most popular areas for fishing. **Amenities:** food and drink; parking; toilets. **Best for:** solitude; swimming; walking. ⊠ *160th Ave. at Gulf Blvd., Redington Beach.*

FAMILY

St. Petersburg Municipal Beach. Though the beach is technically in the city of Treasure Island, the city of St. Petersburg owns and maintains this stretch. Due in part to a concession stand and playground, it's excellent for families. The beach here is very, very wide, near hotels, and great for beach volleyball. **Amenities:** food and drink; parking; showers; toilets. **Best for:** solitude; partiers; sunset; swimming. ⊠ *11260 Gulf Blvd., Treasure Island.*

7

Shell Key. If you want to find the most pristine beach possible without heading to some remote outpost, this is your best bet. Shuttles to this seemingly remote paradise run out of Pass-A-Grille and Dolphin Landings. You can catch them in the morning and early afternoon most days. If you do, expect some amazing snorkeling, shelling, and bird-watching. (You can also kayak or canoe here from a launch near Ft. De Soto.) Rustic overnight camping is allowed here in the part of the island not designated as a bird sanctuary. Watch for rip currents when swimming, as they can be pretty strong. **Amenities:** none. **Best for:** solitude; swimming; walking. ⊠ *Shell Key Shuttle, 801 Pass-A-Grille Way, St. Pete Beach* ☎ *727/360–1348* ⊕ *shellkeyshuttle.com* ⌂ *$25.*

FAMILY
Fodor's Choice
★

Sunset Beach. A peninsula that's technically part of Treasure Island, this 2-mile-long outcrop is one of Tampa Bay's best-kept secrets. The northern end has a mixed crowd—from bikers to spring breakers, the middle portion is good for families (there's a pavilion and playground at around 78th and West Gulf Boulevard), and the southern tip attracts the LGBT crowd. Surfers hit up Sunset Beach on the rare occasion that the Gulf has some swells to offer. Once you turn onto West Gulf, you can find multiple paid parking lots. There are several pay lots starting to your right just south of 82nd Avenue. But if you would rather take advantage of the abundant street parking on the neighborhood's side streets, make sure you park legally—it's all too easy to unwittingly get a parking ticket here. **Amenities:** parking; toilets. **Best for:** partiers; solitude; sunset. ⊠ *West Gulf Blvd., Treasure Island.*

A St. Petersburg pelican stares down passersby on the wharf.—photo by Seymour Levy, Fodors.com member.

FAMILY **Treasure Island.** Large, wide swaths of sand that are sans crowd abound, but you can also find some good crowds, especially on weekends. The Sunday-evening drum circle, which happens around sunset just southwest of the Bilmar, makes for some interesting people-watching, as do the many festivals occurring here each month. It's also the only beach that allows alcohol, as long as it's not contained in glass. Plus, getting here is super easy—just head west on St. Petersburg's Central Avenue, which dead-ends smack-dab in the middle of T.I. (that's what the locals call it), where the iconic Thunderbird Beach Resort sign towers over the boulevard. Hang a left at the light. There's a Publix right across the street if you're up for an impromptu picnic or don't want to pay beach-bar prices for a beer. **Amenities:** food and drink; parking; showers; toilets. **Best for:** partiers; solitude; sunsets. ⊠ *10400 Gulf Blvd., Treasure Island.*

FAMILY **Upham Beach.** One of the most notable things about this popular beach is the series of large objects that look like yellow school buses buried in the sand. These are actually designed to stabilize the shoreline (this beach is known for rapid erosion). The structures, called T-groins, may not please the eye, but that doesn't keep locals from flocking here. Upham is a wide beach with tons of natural landscaping, and it's near Postcard Inn and the TradeWinds. There's a snack bar that slings burgers and beer at its north end. **Amenities:** food and drink; showers; toilets. **Best for:** partiers; sunset; swimming; walking. ⊠ *900 Gulf Way, St. Pete Beach.*

WHERE TO EAT

DOWNTOWN ST. PETERSBURG

$$ ITALIAN 🍴 **Bella Brava New World Trattoria.** This trendy eatery is one of the more sought-after places on equally trendy Beach Drive. It offers a fresh, imaginative approach to Italian fare. **Known for:** ravioli Genovese (stuffed with pine nuts and goat cheese); pasta brava (with wood-grilled chicken, cotto ham, peas, and Aslago cream); lively happy hour and people-watching scene. [$] *Average main: $18* ✉ *204 Beach Dr. NE, Downtown* ☎ *727/895–5515* 🌐 *bellabrava.com.*

$$$ MODERN AMERICAN 🍴 **Birch & Vine.** Seasonal, locally sourced ingredients work equally well in both the surf and the turf columns at Birch & Vine, which has turned The Birchwood hotel lobby and patio into an evening dining destination for hungry diners in downtown St. Petersburg. Take particular note of the maple cream sous vide scallops, and the duck breast seared and topped with blackberry-5-spice sauce, contemporary preparations that complement the reimagined 1920s property. **Known for:** maple cream sous vide scallops; blackberry 5-spice duck; outdoor dining with views of downtown waterfront parks. [$] *Average main: $28* ✉ *The Birchwood, 340 Beach Dr. NE, Downtown* ☎ *727/896–1080* 🌐 *www.thebirchwood.com/birchandvine.*

$$$ BRASSERIE 🍴 **Cassis American Brasserie.** If you drop in for a drink at one of the best places in St. Petersburg for happy hour, it's worth sticking around for the French-inspired cuisine for dinner. More casual options include a croque monsieur, but there are also entrées like bouillabaisse and Atlantic salmon, which is served with smashed peas, baby-carrot confit, and an orange-coriander glaze. **Known for:** European-inspired fare such as bouillabaisse; happy-hour deals, especially on good wine; dog-friendly outdoor dining (including a "mutt menu"). [$] *Average main: $29* ✉ *170 Beach Dr. NE, Downtown* ☎ *727/827–2927* 🌐 *www.cassisab.com.*

$$$ TAPAS 🍴 **Ceviche.** A choice romantic destination as well as an excellent launchpad for a night out, this tapas bar offers an astonishing spate of pleasant sensations for those with savvy taste buds. You can't go wrong with a huge order of seafood or chicken and pork paella. **Known for:** wide range of small plates; delicious sangria; live jazz, salsa, and flamenco music. [$] *Average main: $25* ✉ *10 Beach Dr., Downtown* ☎ *727/209–2299* 🌐 *www.ceviche.com.*

$$ CONTEMPORARY 🍴 **Locale Market.** The brainchild of celebrity chefs Michael Mina and Don Pintabona, this unconventional farm-to-table food court in the new upscale Sundial St. Pete shopping and dining complex allows you to choose your own culinary adventure. Multiple stations are scattered throughout the two-story culinary fortress. **Known for:** robust turkey burger with avocado, pepperjack cheese, and aioli; brussels sprout halves roasted with apples and garlic; bakery/chocolate counter featuring a variety of cupcakes and pastries. [$] *Average main: $15* ✉ *179 2nd Ave. N, Downtown* ☎ *727/523–6300* 🌐 *localegourmetmarket.com.*

$$$$ ECLECTIC 🍴 **Marchand's Bar & Grill.** Opened in 1925, this wonderful restaurant in the posh Renaissance Vinoy Resort has frescoed ceilings and a spectacular view of Tampa Bay. Upscale and special-occasion diners are drawn to Marchand's dynamic menu, which changes often and embraces a

farm-to-table approach. **Known for:** Wednesday through Saturday sushi; 1925 early-bird menu; great happy hour. [$] *Average main: $34* ✉ *Renaissance Vinoy Resort, 501 5th Ave. NE* ☎ *727/824–8072* 🌐 *www.marchandsbarandgrill.com.*

$$ ECLECTIC

🍴 **Nitally's ThaiMex Fusion.** For those who take pride in their ability to handle the heat, this casual yet acclaimed fusion eatery is a must. It's run by a married couple, one of whom is from Thailand and the other from, as you may have guessed, Mexico. **Known for:** food that is rich in spice (so dial it down if you don't like your food too hot); large portions; inferno soup with ghost peppers if you dare. [$] *Average main: $18* ✉ *2462 Central Ave.* ☎ *727/321–8424* 🌐 *nitallys.com* ⏲ *Closed Sun. and Mon.*

$$$ STEAKHOUSE

🍴 **Rococo.** Yet another spot inspired by the St. Pete of yesteryear, this happening steak house sits in what was once a historic YWCA building. Possibly the only independent steak house in St. Petersburg, it gets its name from the late-baroque art movement (but displays the work of local artists on its walls). **Known for:** solid steak offerings; famous lobster bisque; variety of craft cocktails and beer. [$] *Average main: $30* ✉ *655 2nd Ave. S* ☎ *727/822–0999* 🌐 *rococosteak.com* ⏲ *No lunch.*

$$ MODERN AMERICAN

🍴 **Stillwaters Tavern.** Equal parts happy-hour spot and go-to dinner locale, this trendy Beach Drive trattoria—from the folks who brought us Bella Brava—has something for everyone. Their take on fish-and-chips gets cheers, as does the catch of the day (whatever that might be), the falafel (served on a bed of hummus), and most of the menu's other diverse, often locally sourced options. **Known for:** catch of the day; craft cocktails; outdoor seating. [$] *Average main: $19* ✉ *224 Beach Dr. NE, Downtown* ☎ *727/350–1019* 🌐 *stillwaterstavern.com.*

ST. PETE BEACH & VICINITY

$$$ SPANISH

🍴 **Castile.** Within the chic Hotel Zamora, this popular dining spot has been getting much praise from local and national press since it opened in 2014. As the name suggests, much of the menu's inspiration comes from Spain, but many items—all the creations of executive chef Ted Dorsey—have other influences. **Known for:** creative Spanish fusion offering a particularly deft touch with seafood; Caesar salad with Parmesan custard and white anchovies; lovely views. [$] *Average main: $28* ✉ *Hotel Zamora, 3701 Gulf Blvd., St. Pete Beach* ☎ *727/456–8660* 🌐 *www.castilerestaurant.com.*

$$ SEAFOOD Fodor's Choice ★

🍴 **Hurricane Seafood Restaurant.** Sunsets and Gulf views are the bait that hooks regulars as well as travelers who find their way to this somewhat hidden pit stop in historic Pass-A-Grille. Dating to 1977, it's mainly heralded as a watering hole where you can hoist a cold one while munching on one of the area's better grouper sandwiches. **Known for:** genuine grouper sandwiches and delicious crab cakes; spectacular views, especially at sunset; great tropical mixed drinks. [$] *Average main: $15* ✉ *809 Gulf Way, St. Pete Beach* ☎ *727/360–9558* 🌐 *www.thehurricane.com.*

$$$ SEAFOOD FAMILY

🍴 **RumFish Grill.** While the fish served at this upbeat restaurant at the Guy Harvey Outpost resort is deserving of much attention, the ones swimming in the 33,500-gallon aquarium lining the restaurant's back wall are the real draw. The menu consists primarily of local seafood prepared with a Carribbean touch. **Known for:** dishes featuring local seafood; adjacent sports bar with its own menu; alluring aquarium vistas. [$] *Average main: $28* ✉ *Guy Harvey Outpost, 6000 Gulf Blvd., St. Pete Beach* ☎ *727/329–1428* 🌐 *www.rumfishgrill.com.*

$$$ SEAFOOD 🍴 **Salt Rock Grill.** Tourists and locals converge to enjoy a fun and lively waterfront atmosphere, but the rock-solid (if slightly less than imaginative) menu is the best reason to come. Don't believe the Caribbean fire roasted lobster tails is "jumbo"—at 1¼ pounds it's on the small side, but it's twice cooked, including a finish on the grill, and quite tasty. **Known for:** consistently fresh, local seafood; great waterfront views; upscale atmosphere. [$] *Average main: $25* ✉ *19325 Gulf Blvd., Indian Shores* ☎ *727/593–7625* 🌐 *www.saltrockgrill.com* 🕒 *No lunch Mon.–Sat.*

$ CAFÉ 🍴 **Steam & Chill.** In addition to its long, creative lunch and dinner menus, this gem on St. Pete Beach offers creative breakfast options that tend to be a bit healthier—and more worldly—than their greasy-spoon counterparts (think: vegan hash and berry-and-Brie crepes). It's also pretty much the only neighborhood spot in St. Pete Beach where you'll find proper espresso drinks, not to mention formidable brunch and tapas menus. **Known for:** great omelets for breakfast and brunch; large selection of tapas for lunch and dinner; bloody Mary/mimosa bar. [$] *Average main: $12* ✉ *357 Corey Ave., St. Pete Beach* ☎ *727/367–2445* 🌐 *chillstpetebeach.com.*

$ SEAFOOD Fodor's Choice ★ 🍴 **Ted Peters Famous Smoked Fish.** Picture this: flip-flop-wearing anglers and beach-towel-clad bathers lolling on picnic benches, sipping a beer, and devouring oak-smoked salmon, mullet, mahimahi, and mackerel. Dinner comes to the table with heaped helpings of potato salad and coleslaw. **Known for:** red oak-smoked fish; region's best burger; smoked fish spread. [$] *Average main: $13* ✉ *1350 Pasadena Ave. S, South Pasadena* ☎ *727/381–7931* 🌐 *tedpetersfish.com* 💳 *No credit cards* 🕒 *Closed Tues.*

WHERE TO STAY

DOWNTOWN ST. PETERSBURG

$$ B&B/INN 🏨 **The Birchwood.** Few things are as emblematic of Beach Drive's renaissance as this boutique hotel, which like many of downtown St. Pete's best attractions, seamlessly blends old and new. **Pros:** highly sought-after location; exquisite furnishings; close to downtown attractions. **Cons:** service seems more like a B&B than a hotel and sometimes staff is MIA; not the best choice for families with kids; 20 minutes from the beach. [$] *Rooms from: $300* ✉ *340 Beach Dr. NE, Downtown* ☎ *727/896–1080* 🌐 *thebirchwood.com* 🛏 *18 rooms* 🍽 *No meals.*

$ HOTEL Fodor's Choice ★ 🏨 **Hollander Hotel.** This charming, chicly renovated 1933 hotel and restaurant on the edge of downtown has become a hub for visitors and locals alike and offers a less pricey alternative to the Vinoy. **Pros:** some rooms have refurbished vintage bathtubs; close to action; good for nightlife. **Cons:** smaller rooms; small bathrooms; some blight nearby. [$] *Rooms from: $145* ✉ *421 4th Ave. N, Downtown* ☎ *727/873–7900* 🌐 *hollanderhotel.com* 🛏 *100 rooms* 🍽 *No meals.*

7

$$$
RESORT
Fodor'sChoice
★

The Vinoy Renaissance St. Petersburg Resort & Golf Club. Built in 1925 (making it roughly the same vintage as the Don CeSar), the Vinoy is a luxury resort in St. Petersburg's gorgeous Old Northeast. **Pros:** charming property; friendly service; close to downtown museums. **Cons:** pricey; small rooms; drive to the beach. $ *Rooms from: $389* ⊠ *501 5th Ave. NE* 🕾 *727/894–1000* ⊕ *www.vinoyrenaissanceresort. com* ⇒ *361 rooms/suites* ¶◎¶ *No meals.*

ST. PETE BEACH & VICINITY

$$$
RESORT
FAMILY

Guy Harvey Outpost. The namesake artist's trademark vibrantly painted swordfish, mahimahi, and other sea creatures adorn the walls of this high-rise beachfront hotel that offers good options for both dining and exploring. **Pros:** large rooms with kitchenettes; lots of resort amenities; close to other beach attractions. **Cons:** layout can be confusing; $35 nightly resort fee; can be busy and noisy. $ *Rooms from: $315* ⊠ *6000 Gulf Blvd., St. Pete Beach* 🕾 *727/360–5551* ⊕ *www.tradewindsresorts. com* ⇒ *211 rooms* ¶◎¶ *No meals.*

$$$
HOTEL

The Hotel Zamora. An excellent choice for a romantic getaway, this new hotel offers modern rooms with a flamenco twist—you may think you've been swept away to a luxurious Spanish villa. **Pros:** stylish, flamenco-inspired decor and furnishings; great restaurant; beautiful views of Gulf and intracoastal. **Cons:** beach is across busy street; can get surprisingly pricey in high season; rooftop bar can close for private parties without much notice. $ *Rooms from: $339* ⊠ *3701 Gulf Blvd., St. Pete Beach* 🕾 *877/798–2434* ⊕ *thehotelzamora.com* ⇒ *36 rooms 36 suites* ¶◎¶ *No meals.*

$
HOTEL

Island's End Resort. This converted 1950s-vintage motel has some of the area's best sunrise and sunset views and, like the rest of historic Pass-A-Grille, is totally friendly and totally Old Florida. **Pros:** good value; nice views; near restaurants and shops. **Cons:** access via a traffic-clogged road; parking can be tricky; not directly on the beach. $ *Rooms from: $168* ⊠ *1 Pass-A-Grille Way, St. Pete Beach* 🕾 *727/360–5023* ⊕ *www. islandsend.com* ⇒ *6 cottages* ¶◎¶ *Breakfast.*

$$
RESORT
Fodor'sChoice
★

Loews Don CeSar Hotel. Today the "Pink Palace," as it's called thanks to its paint job, is a storied resort and Gulf-coast architectural landmark, with exterior and public areas oozing turn-of-the-20th-century elegance. **Pros:** romantic destination; great beach with cabanas and paddleboards available; tasty dining options, namely popular Maritana. **Cons:** small rooms; can be quite pricey; $25 daily resort fee adds to already-hefty tab. $ *Rooms from: $299* ⊠ *3400 Gulf Blvd., St. Pete Beach* 🕾 *727/367–6952, 800/282–1116* ⊕ *www.doncesar.com* ⇒ *317 rooms* ¶◎¶ *No meals.*

$$
HOTEL

Postcard Inn. Take a Waikiki surf shack from back in Duke's day, shake it up with a little mid-century Miami chic, and give it a clean modern twist—that's this ultrahip beachfront hotel to a T. This place was the toast of the beaches when it opened in 2010, and it's easy to see why. **Pros:** on the beach; walking distance to restaurants and nightlife; friendly staff. **Cons:** can be crowded; not for squares. $ *Rooms from: $239* ⊠ *6300 Gulf Blvd., St. Pete Beach* 🕾 *727/367–2611, 800/237–8918* ⊕ *www.postcardinn.com* ⇒ *196 rooms* ¶◎¶ *Breakfast.*

$$ RESORT FAMILY 🏨 **TradeWinds Island Grand Resort.** The only resort on the beach offering up its own fireworks display, the island-chic TradeWinds is very popular with foreign travelers and the go-to place for beach weddings. **Pros:** great beachfront location; close to restaurants; pet-friendly. **Cons:** large, sprawling complex; lots of conventions; pesky resort fee. [$] *Rooms from: $285* ✉ *5500 Gulf Blvd., St. Pete Beach* ☎ *727/363–2212* 🌐 *www.tradewindsresort.com* 🛏 *687 rooms* 🍴 *No meals.*

NIGHTLIFE

DOWNTOWN ST. PETERSBURG

BARS AND PUBS

Ale and the Witch. Situated in the courtyard of an office building just off trendy Beach Drive, this establishment is a live-music hub—mostly jam bands—as well as the cornerstone of St. Petersburg's exploding craft beer scene. Fans of IPAs, saisons, stouts, you name it, will find their beer of choice somewhere amid the lengthy list of brews on tap. There's some seating inside, but all the action happens outside in the courtyard, where there are plenty of tables and a makeshift band shell. Patrons are welcome to grab food from one of the complex's several restaurants to go along with their brews. Although it's a late-night draw, kids and dogs are welcome. ✉ *111 2nd Ave. NE, Downtown* ☎ *727/821–2533* 🌐 *thealeandthewitch.com.*

Green Bench Brewing Company. The name of this bar is a nod to the green benches that once lined Central Avenue, which retirees occupied in a bygone era. St. Pete has shaken its rap as a sleepy retirement town, and this brewery embodies the Sunshine City's recent emergence as a craft beer town. Barkeeps here serve up brews made on-site as well as a few guest kegs. The interior has a lodgelike feel (as much as a bar can in Florida), but the real ambience lies outside, where Adirondack chairs and badminton sets are scattered across the lawn. It's also conveniently located a couple of blocks from Tropicana Field, so the place can get packed before and after the Rays play. ✉ *1133 Baum Ave., Downtown* ☎ *727/800–9836* 🌐 *greenbenchbrewing.com.*

The Mandarin Hide. Perhaps the epitome of downtown St. Pete's bold transformation into a stylish nightlife destination, this place exudes a classy yet jubilant speakeasy vibe. Just as vintage as the decor is the drinks menu, which features numerous classic cocktails (made the old-fashioned way), tasty concoctions you'll find nowhere else, and craft beers. You'll find either live music or a DJ most nights. On weekends you can get a mean Bloody Mary when the bar opens early. ✉ *231 Central Ave., Downtown* ☎ *727/231–4007* 🌐 *www.mandarinhide.com* 🕒 *Closed Mon.*

St. Pete Brewing Company. A welcoming spot just off the main drag in downtown, this tasting room offers tons of craft beer options (the St. Pete Orange Wheat is a longtime local favorite). There's plenty of outdoor and indoor seating, and the clientele tends to be friendly. It's not far from St. Pete's dining and other nightlife. If you are looking to bring your dog, this is one of the best places to have a beer. ✉ *544 1st Ave. N, Downtown* ☎ *727/623–1837* 🌐 *stpetebrewingcompany.com.*

3 Daughters Brewing. This local craft brewery and tasting room is something of an oasis within the Warehouse Arts District, but it's close enough to Central Avenue to be within easy walking distance from Tropicana Field and the restaurants of the Grand Central District (or drive/trolley ride from downtown). On tap in this converted industrial space is a spate of excellent creations made in-house (their Bimini Twist IPA is a favorite). There's live music some nights as well as a few game options. ⊠ *222 22nd St. S, Warehouse Arts District* ☎ *727/495–6002* ⊕ *3dbrewing.com.*

ST. PETE BEACH & VICINITY
BARS AND PUBS

Daiquiri Shak. If frozen DayGlo concoctions spinning around in washing machine–like mechanisms are your thing, this place should certainly be on your list. If not, this is still a good go-to weekend watering hole on Madeira Beach (technically, it's across the street from the beach). In addition to selections like the Grape Ape and the Voodoo Loveshake, there's a respectable selection of beer on tap and a full bar. Entertainment includes some excellent funk and rock bands Thursday through Sunday. The food menu includes loads of seafood, of course (oysters are a winner), and the late-night menu is served until 1:30 am. ⊠ *14995 Gulf Blvd., Madeira Beach* ☎ *727/393–2706* ⊕ *www.daiquirishak.com.*

Jimmy B's Beach Bar. This is a default stop for tourists and locals alike. The newly renovated, open-air beach bar has seating for all as well as three full bars. It overlooks the vast dunes leading down to the beach. There's live music virtually every afternoon and each night on one of two stages. The beer selection isn't too exotic here, but they make a mean mai tai. The food menu is mostly bar food. Sports fans can catch the game at Player's, a bar located on the same property. ⊠ *6200 Gulf Blvd., behind the Beachcomber Resort, St. Pete Beach* ☎ *727/367–1902.*

Mad Beach Craft Brewing Company. Until very recently, Tampa Bay's beach towns were something of a craft beer dead zone, even as the rest of the region teemed with such establishments. This spot, located in John's Pass, is a shining example of how things are changing. Most of the beers on tap are brewed on-site, though there are a few guest taps. While there is plenty of space at the bar, the barroom is massive and styled after a German beer hall, large tables and all. There's foosball and indoor beanbag tossing if you're feeling competitive, live music many nights, and a menu featuring bar food. ⊠ *12945 Village Blvd., Madeira Beach* ☎ *727/362–0008* ⊕ *madbeachbrewing.com.*

SHOPPING

There's no need for a trip to the mall here. Few places in the Tampa Bay area offer so many eclectic shopping options as the St. Petersburg area. Downtown St. Petersburg's Beach Drive is sprinkled with tons of smart yet pricey boutiques. The Grand Central district has plenty of antiques and vintage clothing shops. Beach shopping hubs John's Pass Village and 8th Avenue offer souvenir shopping that goes well beyond the norm. Each of these is also packed with a range of enticing eateries, many with outdoor seating and live entertainment.

Epitomizing St. Petersburg's cultural rebirth, the block-long stretch of Central Avenue between 6th and 7th streets has loads of art galleries and indie shops, as well as dive bars frequented by tattooed hipsters. The central point is Crislip Arcade, where you'll find a vintage clothing shop (Ramblin' Rose), local art galleries (eve-N-odd and Olio, to name a couple), and a unique jewelry shop (Kathryn Cole). Local businesses line the street, including one that specializes in Moroccan imports (Treasures of Morocco), one that hawks a colorful array of vintage clothing and campy memorabilia (Star Booty), and a smoky bar specializing in craft beer and punk rock (Fubar). Local 662 and the State Theater are two music venues on this block that attract national indie music acts.

DOWNTOWN ST. PETERSBURG

ARTpool Gallery. This local gallery/boutique offers scores of works by local artists and so much more. With one of the flashier storefronts in St. Pete's bustling Grand Central District, this sprawling store is a must for lovers of real-deal vintage clothing and accessories, not to mention furnishings and handmade crafts. There's a courtyard connecting the two buildings that constitute this creative megaplex. In the second building, where you can score everything from record albums to antique ashtrays and typewriters, there's a café with a diverse menu as well as wine and craft beer. Occasionally, owner Marina Williams opens her doors up for after-hours art-centric special events. ⊠ *2030 Central Ave., Gulfport* ☏ *727/324–3878* ⊕ *www.artpoolrules.com* ☾ *Closed Sun.*

Charlie Parker Pottery. For those who like to look beyond the well-worn paths when they shop, this spot in St. Pete's growing Warehouse Arts District offers the pottery of Charlie Parker, a true master of his craft, as well as those of his apprentices. Some of what's created here belongs more rightly on a wall rather than on a table filled with fruit. But many of the works are useful, too; and there's even a $5 rack for those not looking to spend a fortune on a colorful platter. Parker himself offers pottery classes daily; they're worth it for his witty repartee. ⊠ *2724 6th Ave. S, Warehouse Arts District* ☏ *727/321–2071* ⊕ *www.charlieparkerpottery.com.*

Craftsman House Gallery. In a lovingly renovated historic Craftsman-style bungalow, this spot offers a variety of wares, mostly from both local national artists and craftspeople. The jewelry counter has some particularly intriguing finds. You'll also come across art made from glass, wood, and other media. Toward the back is a small café where you can order a wrap or bowl of soup and a craft beer or espresso drink, which you can take onto the large front porch as you watch the action along bustling Central Avenue. Occasionally, owner Jeff Schorr opens the gallery up for house concerts by touring musicians. ⊠ *2955 Central Ave., Gulfport* ☏ *727/323–2787* ⊕ *craftsmanhousegallery.com.*

Duncan McClellan Glass. One of the better-known artists to call St. Petersburg home, Duncan McClellan set up this studio and gallery in a former fish-processing plant, helping spur a renaissance in what was until recently known as a gritty industrial district. The main draw is an enormous gallery featuring diverse works from a rotating cast of artists from around the globe, as well as glassblowing demonstrations. If you happen to be in town for the second Saturday evening of the month,

7

this spot is the hub for a trendy monthly art walk through the area. There are regular hours from Tuesday through Saturday, but it's open by appointment only on Sunday and Monday. ✉ *2342 Emerson Ave. S* ☎ *855/436–4527* ⊕ *dmglass.com.*

Florida CraftArt. Downtown St. Pete's bursting art revival is epitomized at this nonprofit, formerly known as Florida Craftsmen Gallery, that gives 125 artisans from throughout the state a chance to exhibit glassware, jewelry, furniture, and more. (Imagine a vivid coral reef seascape made entirely out of yarn. Stuff like that.) You can also book a walking tour of downtown St. Pete's colorful murals. The gallery is open seven days from 10 to 5:30 but stays open late for the famed Second Saturday Art Walk. ✉ *501 Central Ave.* ☎ *727/821–7391* ⊕ *www.floridacraftart.org.*

Haslam's. One of the state's most notable bookstores, this family-owned emporium has been doing business in St. Petersburg's Grand Central District since the 1930s. Rumored to be haunted by the ghost of *On the Road* author Jack Kerouac (indeed, the renowned Beat Generation author used to frequent Haslam's before he died in St. Pete in 1969), the store carries some 300,000 volumes, from cutting-edge best sellers to ancient tomes. If you value a good book or simply like to browse, you could easily spend an afternoon here. ✉ *2025 Central Ave.* ☎ *727/822–8616* ⊕ *www.haslams.com.*

Sundial St. Pete. With a gigantic (and functional) sundial in the middle of the plaza, this open-air collection of upscale shops occupies the space of former shopping and dining hub Baywalk. The renovation of the space created a more open atmosphere that has attracted a Ruth's Chris Steakhouse, a St. Pete branch of the restaurant Sea Salt, and celebrity Chef Michael Mina's Locale. The shopping here is equally high-end, and retail here includes Diamonds Direct, Tracy Negoshian, as well as local retailers like Florida Jean Company. If that's not enough, there's the Shave Cave, something a masculine take on a salon, and its feminine counterpart Marilyn Monroe Glamour Room. At the back of the complex is a 19-screen Muvico theater with an IMAX theater. ✉ *153 2nd Ave. N, Downtown* ☎ *727/800–3201* ⊕ *sundialstpete.com.*

Zen Glass Studio. Glass art is pretty big in St. Pete, and this place showcases all the ways in which it can be done. There's a gallery here with some thoroughly intriguing pieces as well as a retail shop where you can find glassware, jewelry, decor items, and much more. Those not afraid of the flame can even take part in the glassblowing process themselves in the on-site hot shop. Classes offer amateur glassblowers the opportunity to make everything from beads to beer- and wineglasses. ✉ *600 27th St. S, Gulfport* ☎ *727/323–3141* ⊕ *www.zenglass.com* ☾ *Closed Sun.*

SPORTS AND THE OUTDOORS

BASEBALL

Tampa Bay Rays. Major League Baseball's Tampa Bay Rays completed an improbable worst-to-first turnaround when they topped the American League Eastern Division in 2008, and again in 2010. Then there was that dramatic end-of-season comeback in 2011, and the World Series near-miss in 2014. Tickets are available at the box office for most games, but you may have to rely on the classifieds sections of the *Tampa Bay Times* for popular games. Get here early; parking is often at a premium (pre-gaming at Ferg's or Green Bench is always a safe bet). ⊠ *Tropicana Field, 1 Tropicana Dr., off I–175* ☎ *727/825–3137* ⊕ *tampabay.rays.mlb.com.*

CLEARWATER AND VICINITY

12 miles north of St. Petersburg via U.S. 19.

In Clearwater itself, residential areas are a buffer between the commercial zone that centers on U.S. 19 and the beach, which is moderately quiet during winter but buzzing with life during spring break and in the busy summer season. There's a quaint downtown area on the mainland, just east of the beach, with a theater and a couple of small eateries.

On the beach itself, which is part of the city of Clearwater, you'll find a nightly sunset celebration at Pier 60 and tons of options for dining and entertainment, not to mention the beautiful sand. Among this area's celebrity residents is Winter, the dolphin who was fitted with a prosthetic tail and depicted in the 2011 film *Dolphin Tale,* along with her friend Hope, her costar in the 2014 sequel.

The smaller towns surrounding Clearwater are generally more low-key. To the southwest, Indian Rocks Beach and its neighboring towns are less crowded alternatives to their busy neighbor to the north. To the north on U.S. 19 is Dunedin, a Scottish settlement that's packed with cute shops, restaurants, and craft beer bars, as well as the Toronto Blue Jays' spring training facility. Farther north is Palm Harbor, a key destination for cyclists and craft beer enthusiasts. Charming Tarpon Springs has a highly Greek-influenced downtown; you'll find historic sponge docks, a Greek restaurant or two, and some great beaches for watching the sunset.

GETTING HERE AND AROUND

Clearwater is due west from Tampa International Airport via State Road 60, and it's about 45 minutes north of St. Petersburg. If you want to fly directly to Clearwater instead of Tampa, though, St. Pete/Clearwater International Airport is another option. From St. Pete you can get here via U.S. 19, which is notorious for its congestion, Alternate U.S. 19, or County Road 1. If you're up for a scenic yet slower drive, Gulf Boulevard takes you all the way to Clearwater from St. Pete Beach—as does a beach trolley that runs along that route.

VISITOR INFORMATION

Contacts Clearwater Regional Chamber of Commerce. ☎ *727/461–0011* ⊕ *clearwaterflorida.org.* **Greater Dunedin Chamber of Commerce.** ☎ *727/733–3197* ⊕ *www.dunedinfl.com.* **Tarpon Springs Chamber of Commerce.** ☎ *727/937–6109* ⊕ *tarponspringschamber.com.*

EXPLORING

CLEARWATER

Clearwater Marine Aquarium. This aquarium gives you the opportunity to participate in the work of saving and caring for endangered marine species. Many of the sea turtles, dolphins, and other animals living at the aquarium were brought here to be rehabilitated from an injury or saved from danger. The dolphin exhibit has an open-air arena giving the dolphins plenty of room to jump during their shows. This aquarium is also home to Winter, a dolphin fitted with a prosthetic tail that was the subject of the 2011 film *Dolphin Tale* (and its 2014 sequel), as well as her friend Hope. The aquarium conducts tours of the bays and islands around Clearwater, including a daily cruise on a pontoon boat (you might just see a wild dolphin or two), and kayak tours of Clearwater Harbor and St. Joseph Sound. ⊠ *249 Windward Passage* ☎ *727/441–1790* ⊕ *seewinter.com* ☒ *$21.95.*

FAMILY   **Pier 60.** This spot is the terminus of State Road 60 (hence the name), which runs under various names between Vero Beach on the east coast and Clearwater Beach on the west coast. Around 3:30 pm each day, weather permitting, the area surrounding the pier starts to liven up. Local artists and craftspeople populate their folding tables with beaded jewelry, handmade skin-care products, and beach landscape paintings. Jugglers, musicians, break-dancers, and fire breathers put on some lively shows for those in attendance. And the grand finale is the sun setting over the Gulf of Mexico. On weekends when the weather is mild, there are also free, family-friendly movie screenings. ⊠ *10 Pier 60 Dr., Clearwater Beach* ☎ *727/449–1036* ⊕ *www.sunsetsatpier60.com.*

TARPON SPRINGS

FAMILY   **Konger Tarpon Springs Aquarium.** Although it's not on par with larger facilities in Tampa and Clearwater, this is certainly an entertaining attraction. There are some good exhibits, including a 120,000-gallon shark tank complete with a coral reef. (Divers feed the sharks several times daily.) Also look for tropical fish exhibits and a tank where you can touch baby sharks and stingrays. ⊠ *850 Dodecanese Blvd., off U.S. 19, Tarpon Springs* ☎ *727/938–5378* ⊕ *www.tarponspringsaquarium. com* ☒ *$7.75.*

The Sponge Docks. Paralleled by a busy boulevard lined with sponge shops and Greek restaurants, this several-blocks-long waterfront spot showcase's Tarpon Spring's Greek roots as well as the industry that first made the town thrive over a century ago. Stroll along the docks and you'll find an aquarium, tons of small boutiques, bakeries specializing in baklava and the like, and several boat tours of the surrounding waters. Pop into the Sponge Docks Museum to see a film about the much-sought-after creatures from the phylum *porifera* and how they helped the town prosper in the early 1900s. You'll come away converted to (and loaded up with) natural sponges. ⊠ *Dodecanese Blvd., off Alt. U.S. 19, Tarpon Springs* ⊕ *www.spongedocks.net* ☒ *Free.*

Continued on page 378

SPRING TRAINING, FLORIDA-STYLE

by Jim Tunstall and Connie Sharpe

Sunshine, railroads, and land bargains were Florida's first tourist magnets, but baseball had a hand in things, too. The Chicago Cubs led the charge when they opened spring training in Tampa in 1913 — the same year the Cleveland Indians set up camp in Pensacola.

Over the next couple of decades, World War I and the Great Depression interrupted normal lives, but the Sunshine State became a great fit for the national pastime. Soon, big-league teams were flocking south to work off the winter rust.

At one point, the Florida "Grapefruit League" held a monopoly on spring training, but in 1947 Arizona's "Cactus League" started cutting into the action.

Today, roughly half of Major League Baseball's 30 teams arrive in Florida in February for six weeks of calisthenics, tryouts, and practice games. The clubs range from the Detroit Tigers, who have been in the same city (Lakeland) longer than any other team (since 1934), to the Tampa Bay Rays, who moved to a new spring home (Port Charlotte) in 2009.

Popular teams still draw large crowds for spring training games, which have gentler pricing than regular seasons.

HERE COME THE FANS

Fan appreciate the relative intimacy of Spring Training stadiums.

Florida's spring training teams play 25 or 30 home and away games, to the delight of 1.68 million annual ticker buyers. Diehards land as soon as the first troops—pitchers and catchers—come to practice around the third week of February. Intersquad games start in the fourth week, while the real training schedule begins by the end of February or first of March and lasts until the end of the month or early April. These games don't count in the regular season, but they give managers and fans a good idea of which players will be on the opening-day rosters, and who will be traded, sent to the teams' minor leagues, or told it's time to find a regular day job.

Spring training games provide a great excuse for local baseball fans to cut out of work early, while visitors from the North can leave ice, snow, and sleet behind. And who doesn't want a few chili dogs,

brats, burgers, and brews on a March day? Spring training's draw is more than just a change of venue with an early sample of concession-stand staples. There is also the ample choice of game sites. Teams are scattered around most of the major tourist areas of central and southern Florida, so those coming to watch the games can try a different destination each spring—or even make a road trip to several. Baseball fans also like that it's a melting pot—teams from more than a dozen cities are represented here.

Finally, you can't beat the price—tickets are usually cheaper than during the regular season—nor the access you have to baseball celebrities. In fact, the relaxed atmosphere of spring training makes most players more willing to sign your ball, glove, or whatever. You can get autographs during pregame workouts (practice sessions), which are free, as well as after the game.

4 TIPS

■ **Have a game plan.** Don't just show up. Most teams only have about 15 home games, and those involving popular teams often sell out weeks in advance. Consider buying tickets ahead of time, and if needed, make hotel room reservations at the same time.

■ **Beat the crowds.** The best chance to do this is to go to a weekday game. You'll still encounter lots of fans, but weekday games generally aren't as well attended as weekenders. Also, each team only has a few night games.

■ **Pack a picnic.** Some stadiums let you bring coolers through the turnstiles. Many game attendees also gather for a tailgate party, grilling burgers and sipping a lemonade or beer while jawing with fellow fans (have a chair in tow).

■ West coast games get a lot of sun. Seats in the shade are premium.

(above) Hammond Stadium in Ft. Myers is where the Minnesota Twins practice.
(right) Former St. Louis Cardinals player Chris Duncan is tagged out at Roger Dean Stadium in Jupiter.

Atlanta Braves	2	New York Yankees	4
Baltimore Orioles	7	Philadelphia Phillies	1
Boston Red Sox	14	Pittsburgh Pirates	10
Detroit Tigers	9	St. Louis Cardinals/ Florida Marlins	12
Houston Astros	11	Tampa Bay Rays	3
Minnesota Twins	8	Toronto Blue Jays	5
New York Mets	6	Washington Nationals	13

7

PLAY BALL!

Spring training schedules are determined around Thanksgiving. Ticket prices change each year. For all of these teams, you also can order spring training tickets through Ticketmaster (☎ 866/448–7849 ⊕ www.ticketmaster.com) or through the respective team's box office or team Web site. For more information about any of the teams, visit ⊕ www.florida-grapefruitleague.com.

SPRING TRAINING GUIDE
Order a free Guide to *Florida Spring Training* from the **Florida Sports Foundation** (⊠ 101 N. Monroe St., Suite 1000, Tallahassee, FL ☎ 850/410–5286 ⊕ www.flasports.com). Published in February each year, it's packed with information about teams, sites, tickets, and more.

Former New York Mets catcher Ramon Castro.

ATLANTA BRAVES
Home Field: Champion Stadium, ESPN Wide World of Sports, 700 S. Victory Way, Kissimmee. **Tickets:** $15–$59 ☎ 407/939–4263 ⊕ www.braves.mlb.com

BALTIMORE ORIOLES
Home Field: Ed Smith Stadium, 2700 12th St., Sarasota. **Tickets:** $24–$36
☎ 941/893–6300 ⊕ www.orioles.mlb.com

BOSTON RED SOX
Home Field: JetBlue Park, 11500 Fenway South Dr., Fort Myers. **Tickets:** $10–$49
☎ 239/334–4700, 888/733–7696 ⊕ www.redsox.mlb.com

DETROIT TIGERS
Home Field: Joker Marchant Stadium, 2301 Lakeland Hills Blvd., Lakeland. **Tickets:** $10–$32
☎ 863/686–8075 ⊕ www.tigers.mlb.com

HOUSTON ASTROS
Home Field: The Ballpark of the Palm Beaches, 5444 Haverhill Rd., West Palm Beach. **Tickets:** $15–$42
☎ 844/676–2017 ⊕ www.astros.mlb.com

MIAMI MARLINS
Home Field: Roger Dean Stadium (shared with St. Louis Cardinals), 4751 Main St., Jupiter. **Tickets:** $15–$42
☎ 561/630–1828 ⊕ www.marlins.mlb.com

MINNESOTA TWINS
Home Field: Hammond Stadium, CenturyLink Sports Complex, 14100 Six Mile Cypress Parkway, Fort Myers. **Tickets:** $5–$15
☎ 800/338-9467 ⊕ www.twins.mlb.com

NEW YORK METS
Home Field: First Data Field, 525 NW Peacock Blvd., Port St. Lucie. **Tickets:** $8–$25
☎ 772/871-2115 ⊕ www.mets.mlb.com

NEW YORK YANKEES
Home Field: George M. Steinbrenner Field, 1 Steinbrenner Dr., Tampa. **Tickets:** $17–$33
☎ 813/879-2244 ⊕ www.yankees.mlb.com

PHILADELPHIA PHILLIES
Home Field: Bright House Networks Field, 601 N. Old Coachman Rd., Clearwater. **Tickets:** $17–$39
☎ 727/467-4457 ⊕ www.phillies.mlb.com

PITTSBURGH PIRATES
Home Field: McKechnie Field, 1611 9th St. W, Bradenton. **Tickets:** $12–$22
☎ 941/747-3031 ⊕ www.pirates.mlb.com

ST. LOUIS CARDINALS
Home Field: Roger Dean Stadium (shared with Miami Marlins), 4751 Main St., Jupiter. **Tickets:** $10–$29
☎ 561/630-1828 ⊕ www.cardinals.mlb.com

TAMPA BAY RAYS
Home Field: Charlotte County Sports Park, 2300 El Jobean Rd., Port Charlotte. **Tickets:** $10–$27
☎ 888/326-7297 ⊕ www.rays.mlb.com

TORONTO BLUE JAYS
Home Field: Florida Auto Exchange Park, 373 Douglas Ave., Dunedin. **Tickets:** $15–$30
☎ 727/733-0429 ⊕ www.bluejays.mlb.com

WASHINGTON NATIONALS
Home Field: The Ballpark of the Palm Beaches, 5444 Haverhill Rd., West Palm Beach. **Tickets:** $15–$42
☎ 844/676-2017 ⊕ www.nationals.mlb.com

BEACHES

CLEARWATER

Fodor's Choice
★
Clearwater Beach. On a narrow island between Clearwater Harbor and the Gulf is a stretch of sand with a widespread reputation for beach volleyball. Pier 60, which extends from shore here, is the site of a nightly sunset celebration, complete with musicians and artisans. It's one of the area's nicest and busiest beaches, especially on weekends and during spring break, but it's also one of the costliest in terms of parking fees, which can reach $2 per hour. ■ TIP→ Traffic can get pretty gnarly here and parking spots scarce, especially approaching sunset, so get here early or opt for public or on-foot transportation as much as possible. Amenities: food and drink; showers; toilets. Best for: partiers; sunset; walking. ⊠ *Western end of Rte. 60, 2 miles west of downtown Clearwater.*

Sand Key Park. This is a mellow counterpart to often-crowded Clearwater Beach to the north. It has a lovely beach, plenty of green space, a playground, and a picnic area in an otherwise congested area. Parking is a flat $5. Amenities: food and drink; lifeguards; showers; toilets. Best for: solitude; sunset; swimming. ⊠ *1060 Gulf Blvd.* ☎ *727/588–4852* 🖅 *$5.*

DUNEDIN

Caladesi Island State Park. Quiet, secluded, and still wild, this 3½-mile-long barrier island is one of the best shelling beaches on the Gulf Coast, second only to Sanibel. The park also has plenty of sights for birders—from common sandpipers to majestic blue herons to rare black skimmers—and miles of trails through scrub oaks, saw palmettos, and cacti (with tenants such as armadillos, rabbits, and raccoons). The landscape also features mangroves and dunes, and the gradual slope of the sea bottom makes this a good spot for novice swimmers and kids. You have to get to Caladesi Island by private boat (there's a 108-slip marina) or through its sister park, Honeymoon Island State Recreation Area, where you take the hourly ferry ride across to Caladesi; ferry rides cost $14 per person. You can also paddle yourself over in a kayak. Amenities: food and drink; showers; toilets. Best for: solitude; swimming. ⊠ *Dunedin Causeway, Dunedin* ☎ *727/469–5918* ⊕ *floridastateparks.org/caladesiisland* 🖅 *$6 per boat; $2 per kayaker.*

Honeymoon Island State Park. If you're seeking an almost completely undeveloped beach that's still easily accessible by car, this is one of your best bets. Northwest of Clearwater, this large state park offers some of the best shell hunting you'll find, as well as thousands of feet of serene beachfront. If you head north along the park road, you find extensive hiking trails, along which you'll see an astonishing array of birds. You can also catch a ferry to Caladesi Island from here. Amenities: food and drink; showers; toilets. Best for: solitude; swimming; walking. ⊠ *1 Causeway Blvd., Dunedin* ⊕ *floridastateparks.org/honeymoonisland* 🖅 *$8 per vehicle; $4 per single-occupant vehicle.*

Clearwater's Bait House lures in those heading to the pier to fish. —photo by watland, Fodors.com member.

INDIAN ROCKS BEACH

Indian Rocks Beach. This beach community is a mellow alternative to the oft-crowded shorelines of Clearwater and St. Pete Beach along the Gulf Coast. This is a town in which the road narrows to two lanes and is lined with upscale residential condos instead of busy hotels. There are quite a few beach access points, though your best bet is a landscaped facility offering ample parking, nearby food and drink, and an occasional event. **Amenities:** food and drink; parking; showers; toilets. **Best for:** solitude; swimming; walking. ✉ *Indian Rocks Beach Nature Preserve, 1700 Gulf Blvd., Indian Rocks Beach* ⊕ *indian-rocks-beach.com.*

TARPON SPRINGS

Fred Howard Park Beach. It comes in two parts: a shady mainland picnic area with barbecues and a white-sand beach island. The causeway is a popular hangout for windsurfers, and the entire area is great for birding. The beach itself is very relaxed and family-friendly, and you can find kayak rentals on the island's eastern side. **Amenities:** showers; toilets. **Best for:** sunset; swimming; windsurfing. ✉ *1700 Sunset Dr., Tarpon Springs* 🚗 *$5 flat fee to park.*

Sunset Beach. As the name suggests, this beach park is known as one of the best places in North Pinellas County to watch the sunset. It's a small beach but a great place to barbecue. From April through November there's a weekly concert. **Amenities:** toilets. **Best for:** sunset; swimming. ✉ *1715 Gulf Rd., Tarpon Springs.*

WHERE TO EAT

CLEARWATER

$$$ AMERICAN
🍴 **Bob Heilman's Beachcomber.** The Heilman family has fed hungry diners since 1920. Although it's very popular with tourists, you'll also rub shoulders with devoted locals. **Known for:** classic sautéed chicken with mashed potatoes, vegetables, and fresh bread; Gulf shrimp prepared several ways; good wine selection. [$] *Average main: $25* ✉ *447 Mandalay Ave., Clearwater Beach* ☎ *727/442–4144* 🌐 *www.bobheilmans.com.*

$$ SEAFOOD
🍴 **Frenchy's Rockaway Grill.** Quebec native Mike "Frenchy" Preston runs four eateries in the area, including the fabulous Rockaway Grill. Visitors and locals alike keep coming back for the grouper sandwiches that are moist and not battered into submission. **Known for:** she-crab soup, grouper sandwiches, and egg rolls; beachfront sunset vistas. [$] *Average main: $15* ✉ *7 Rockaway St.* ☎ *727/446–4844* 🌐 *www.frenchysonline.com.*

$$ SEAFOOD
🍴 **Palm Pavilion Beachside Grill & Bar.** Long heralded as one of the best spots for watching sunsets, this place also gets high marks for its fresh seafood offerings. The grouper cheeks and wasabi scallops in particular are among more intriguing menu items. **Known for:** surprisingly good bar fare; sunset festivities with live music; a bit less casual than some other beachside spots. [$] *Average main: $17* ✉ *10 Bay Esplande, Clearwater Beach* ☎ *727/446–2642* 🌐 *www.palmpavilion.com.*

DUNEDIN

$$$ EUROPEAN
🍴 **Bon Appétit.** Known for its creative fare, this waterfront restaurant has a menu that changes frequently, offering such entrées as broiled rack of lamb in herbed pecan crust, and red snapper on a bed of lobster hash. The creative grouper options, including grouper medallions, get well-deserved plaudits from many patrons. **Known for:** real Gulf grouper on the menu; live music Thursday through Sunday; gorgeous water views. [$] *Average main: $25* ✉ *148 Marina Plaza, Dunedin* ☎ *727/733–2151* 🌐 *www.bonappetitrestaurant.com.*

$$ MEXICAN
Fodor's Choice ★
🍴 **Casa Tina.** At this colorful Dunedin institution, vegetarians can veg out on roasted chiles rellenos (cheese-stuffed peppers), enchiladas with vegetables, and a cactus salad that won't prick your tongue but will tickle your taste buds with the tantalizing flavors of tender pieces of cactus, cilantro, tomatoes, onions, lime, and queso fresco. The chayote squash relleno also makes the grade. **Known for:** chayote squash relleno; duck sopas with cotija cheese and guava sauce; good margaritas and sangria. [$] *Average main: $15* ✉ *365 Main St., Dunedin* ☎ *727/734–9226* 🌐 *casatinas.com.*

$ MEDITERRANEAN
🍴 **The Living Room on Main.** Hand-picked antique furnishings add charm to this downtown Dunedin spot, which specializes in Mediterranean-inspired small plates and spectacular cocktails. For a little more sustenance, check out the sandwich menu—the seared tuna club with avocado and caper aioli, and the deconstructed egg salad sandwich make for some good options. **Known for:** creative small plates; excellent craft cocktails; vintage-inspired ambience. [$] *Average main: $13* ✉ *487 Main St., Dunedin* ☎ *727/736–5202* 🌐 *thelivingroomonmain.com.*

WHERE TO STAY

CLEARWATER

$$$$ RESORT **Hyatt Regency Clearwater Beach.** One of the more recent additions to the Clearwater Beach skyline, this upscale resort towers above almost everything else in the immediate area, both in terms of height and luxury. **Pros:** gorgeous hotel; plenty of amenities, including a full-service spa; near the action. **Cons:** beach is across busy street; renovation underway throughout 2017. [$] *Rooms from: $450 ✉ 301 S. Gulfview Blvd. ☎ 727/373–1234 🌐 www.clearwaterbeach.hyatt.com 🛏 250 suites 🍴 No meals.*

$$$ RESORT **Sandpearl Resort.** Two things set this expansive, luxurious Clearwater Beach resort apart from other upscale accommodations in the vicinity: it's not part of a major chain, and the property has deep local ties. **Pros:** on the beach; tons of amenities and dining options. **Cons:** resort fee; lots of conventions. [$] *Rooms from: $344 ✉ 500 Mandalay Ave. ☎ 727/441–2425 🌐 sandpearl.com 🛏 253 rooms 🍴 No meals.*

$$ RESORT **Sheraton Sand Key Resort.** Expect something special when you stay here, including a modern property and one of the few uncluttered beaches in the area. **Pros:** secluded beach; great views; no resort fee and parking is also free. **Cons:** near Clearwater Beach traffic; views come with a high price tag. [$] *Rooms from: $290 ✉ 1160 Gulf Blvd., Clearwater Beach ☎ 727/595–1611 🌐 sheratonsandkey.com 🛏 389 rooms/suites 🍴 No meals.*

$$ RESORT FAMILY **Wyndham Grand Clearwater Beach.** The new resort, which opened in January 2017 near Pier 60, guarantees sweeping water views (of either the Gulf or the Intracoastal Waterway) from your balcony regardless of where your room is located. **Pros:** excellent views; good accommodations for families; brand-new resort. **Cons:** residential building on property; lots of beach traffic; busy with events and meetings. [$] *Rooms from: $299 ✉ 100 Coronado Dr., Clearwater Beach ☎ 727/281–9000 🌐 wyndhamgrandclearwater.com 🛏 343 rooms 🍴 No meals.*

PALM HARBOR

$ RESORT **Innisbrook Resort & Golf Club.** A massive pool complex with a 15-foot waterfall, two winding waterslides, and a sandy waterfront are part of the allure of this sprawling resort, but it may be the 72 holes of golf, including the challenging Copperhead course, that are the real draw. **Pros:** good seasonal golf packages; varied dining options, namely Packard's Steakhouse; lots of family-friendly activities and amenities. **Cons:** far from attractions; surrounding environment is unattractive, traffic-strangled U.S. 19; $20 resort fee can add up. [$] *Rooms from: $185 ✉ 36750 U.S. 19 N, Palm Harbor ☎ 727/942–2000, 888/794–8627 🌐 www.innisbrookgolfresort.com 🛏 600 rooms 🍴 No meals.*

SAFETY HARBOR

$$ RESORT **Safety Harbor Resort & Spa.** Built over natural mineral springs, this resort, which has been consistently expanded and renovated, has been drawing visitors since 1927. **Pros:** charm to spare; good choice for pampering; large spa with natural springs. **Cons:** far from beach; not ideal for families with children. [$] *Rooms from: $209 ✉ 105 N. Bayshore Dr., Safety Harbor ☎ 727/726–1161, 877/237–8772 🌐 www.safetyharborspa.com 🛏 191 rooms 🍴 No meals.*

7

NIGHTLIFE

PALM HARBOR

Stilt House Brewery. If you happen to be riding on the Pinellas Trail between Clearwater and Tarpon Springs, this place is right on the trail. It's also right on Alternate U.S. 19, though it can be hard to spot from the road since it's in a small strip mall. Beers are brewed on-site (like the Norbert's Valkyrie Belgian Tripel or the Soul Candy Milk Stout), though there are also some guest taps. There's always a friendly crowd. Off to the side you'll notice a small room packed with vintage video games. ⊠ *625 Alt. U.S. 19, Palm Harbor* ☏ *727/270–7373* ⊕ *www.stilthousebrewery.com.*

DUNEDIN

Dunedin Brewery. Tampa Bay is seen by many as a flourishing craft beer hub. If it weren't for Dunedin Brewery, that might not be the case. It was the first of its kind in the area and continues to offer delicious brews to throngs of patrons. It doesn't hurt that it offers live music many nights of the week, either. ⊠ *937 Douglas Ave., Dunedin* ☏ *727/736–0606* ⊕ *dunedinbrewery.com.*

7venth Sun Brewery. Northern Pinellas County is a hotbed for craft brewing. This small tasting room features this brewery's offerings, largely Belgian-style, spirit barrel-aged sour beer as well as IPAs, and a handful of others. It's near downtown Dunedin's shopping, dining, and nightlife and isn't too far from the Pinellas Trail. ⊠ *1012 Broadway, Dunedin* ☏ *727/733–3013* ⊕ *www.7venthsun.com.*

SPORTS AND THE OUTDOORS

BASEBALL

Philadelphia Phillies. The Phillies get ready for the season with spring training here (late February to early April). The stadium also hosts the Phillies' farm team. Check out their minor-league team, the Clearwater Threshers, at Spectrum Field during the summer months. ⊠ *Spectrum Field, 601 N. Old Coachman Rd.* ☏ *727/712–4300* ⊕ *philadelphia.phillies.mlb.com.*

Toronto Blue Jays. The Jays play around 15 to 20 spring training games here, starting in February, which is why Dunedin is packed with Canadians this time of year. The team has trained here since its 1977 inception—and this consistency is not common for a major-league team. A farm team plays here in the summer. The training fields are located several miles away, at 1700 Solon Avenue. ⊠ *Florida Auto Exchange Stadium, 373 Douglas Ave., north of Hwy. 580, Dunedin* ☏ *727/733–0429* ⊕ *toronto.bluejays.mlb.com.*

BIKING

Pinellas Trail. This 42-mile paved route spans Pinellas County, from near the southernmost point all the way north to Tarpon Springs. Along a former railway line, the trail runs adjacent to major thoroughfares, no more than 10 feet from the roadway, so you can access it from almost any point. The trail, also popular with in-line skaters, has spawned trailside businesses such as repair shops, breweries, and cafés. There are also many lovely rural areas to bike through and plenty of places to rent bikes. Be wary of traffic in downtown Clearwater and on the

7

congested areas of the Pinellas Trail, which still needs more bridges for crossing over busy streets, and avoid the trail at night. To start riding from the route's south end in downtown St. Petersburg (1st Street South at Shore Boulevard) in St. Petersburg. To ride south from the north end, park your car in downtown Tarpon Springs (East Tarpon Avenue at North Stafford Avenue). ☎ *727/582–2100 Pinellas County Parks & Conservation Department* ⊕ *www.pinellascounty.org/trailgd.*

GOLF

Dunedin Golf Club. Dunedin is Tampa Bay's little Scotland, the birthplace of golf, so it's only natural that one of the area's better courses is here. Designed by influential golf-course architect Donald Ross, this semi-private, recently restored facility also has a driving range, a pro shop, and a clubhouse. The course itself offers numerous challenging holes with names like "Isn't Easy," "Calamity Jane," and "Devil's Kick," with the twists and turns to match. Water hazards aren't too overwhelming here, except on the 14th hole, known as "Round the Lake." ✉ *1050 Palm Blvd., Dunedin* ☎ *727/733–2134* ⊕ *www.dunedingolfclub.com* 🎫 *$47.99* ⚑ *18 holes, 6625 yards, par 72.*

Innisbrook. Considered one of the top 100 golf destinations in Florida, this resort is home to Larry Packard–designed Copperhead Course, which hosts the annual PGA Tour Valspar Championship. Open to resort guests as well as the public, the four courses here take full advantage of the fact that they're on the coast, with plenty of ponds and sand traps adding to the scenery as well as the challenge. Fairways here on the Copperhead Course consist of rolling hills lined with trees, which are prime for spotting blue herons, squirrels, and even an alligator or two. The Island Course offers narrow fairways, some of which are lined by Lake Innisbrook, others by tall stands of pine and cypress trees. The North Course features tight fairways, numerous bunkers, and 11 water hazards, while the South Course has more of a links course–like layout. The Fox Squirrel Course is a quick 9-hole course available to guests only. ✉ *36750 U.S. Hwy. 19 N, Palm Harbor* ☎ *888/794–8627, 727/942–2000* ⊕ *innisbrookgolfresort. com* 🎫 *Copperhead Course, $280; Island Course, $240; North and South Courses, $190* ⚑ *Copperhead Course: 18 holes, 7209 yards, par 71; Island Course: 18 holes, 7194 yards, par 72; North Course: 18 holes, 6085 yards, par 70; South Course, 18 holes, 6642 yards, par 71; Fox Squirrel Course: 9 holes, 1236 yards, par 36 (resort guests only, closed during high season).*

Saddlebrook. The courses of this golf-centric resort 30 minutes northeast of Tampa are open to the public, and offer a remoteness that's hard to find in such a densely populated metro area. The star here is the Palmer Course, which, as one might expect, is named for Arnold Palmer, who designed it. It's characterized by a hilly terrain uncharacteristic of Florida as well as island-dotted ponds and plenty of troublesome bunkers. The Saddlebrook Course is more scenic than it is challenging (but is very much both), with long fairways lined with rows of pine trees. There's a pro on-site Tuesday, Thursday, and Saturday to help you perfect your game, not to mention a full-fledged golf academy. ✉ *5700 Saddlebrook Way, Wesley Chapel* ☎ *813/907–4401* ⊕ *saddlebrook.com* 🎫 *$96 for 9 holes, $145 for 18 holes* ⚑ *Palmer Course: 18 holes, 6243 yards, par 71; Saddlebrook Course: 18 holes, 6480 yards, par 70.*

SURFING

FlowRider at Surf Style. Surf Style, in the towering Hyatt, is a chain store that sells beach essentials like sarongs, sunblock, and souvenirs. But what sets this particularly enormous store apart is the FlowRider, an indoor pool that generates artificial waves suitable for surfing; for $20 per half hour, you and the kids can surf or learn to surf, something you can't usually do out in the Gulf. An instructor is on hand to show you the ropes. ⊠ *Hyatt Regency Clearwater Beach, 311 S. Gulfview Blvd.* ☎ *888/787–3789 Ext. 175* ⊕ *flowrider.surfstyle.com* ✆ *$30 for 30 mins.*

CITRUS COUNTY

The coastal and western inland areas of Citrus County north of Tampa and St. Petersburg are sometimes called the Nature Coast, and aptly so. Flora and fauna have been well preserved in this area, and West Indian manatees are showstoppers. These gentle vegetarian marine mammals, distantly related to elephants, remain an endangered species, though their numbers have grown to 3,500 or more today. Many manatees have massive scars on their backs from run-ins with boat propellers. Extensive nature preserves and parks have been created to protect them and other wildlife indigenous to the area, and these are among the best spots to view manatees in the wild. Although they're far from mythical beauties, it's believed that manatees inspired ancient mariners' tales of mermaids. This is one of the few spots in the world where you can legally swim with—and even touch—these gentle creatures.

GETTING HERE AND AROUND

U.S. 19 and the Suncoast Parkway, a toll road, are the prime north–south routes through this rural region, and traffic flows freely once you've left the congestion of St. Petersburg, Clearwater, and Port Richey. In most cases, the Suncoast Parkway is a far quicker drive than U.S. 19, though you'll have to pay several dollars in tolls. If you're planning a day trip from the Bay Area, pack a picnic lunch before leaving, since most of the sights are outdoors.

WEEKI WACHEE

Weeki Wachee Springs. At Weeki Wachee Springs, the spring flows at the remarkable rate of 170 million gallons a day with a constant temperature of 74°F. The spring has long been famous for its live "mermaids," clearly not the work of Mother Nature, as they wear bright costumes and put on an Esther Williams–like underwater choreography show that's been virtually unchanged since the park opened in 1947. The park is considered a classic piece of Florida history and culture. It also features snorkel tours and canoe trips on the river, and a wilderness boat ride gives an up-close look at raccoons, otters, egrets, and other semi-tropical Florida wetlands wildlife. In summer, Buccaneer Bay water park opens for swimming, beaching, and riding its thrilling slides and flumes. ⊠ *6131 Commercial Way, at U.S. 19 and Rte. 50* ☎ *352/592–5656* ⊕ *weekiwachee.com* ✆ *$13.*

HOMOSASSA SPRINGS

65 miles north of St. Petersburg on U.S. 19.

A little more than an hour north of Clearwater, you'll come upon this small and friendly hub for water lovers. Along with a phenomenal manatee-centric state park, you'll find more than a handful of charming restaurants, some featuring live music in the evening. This and Crystal River provide you with the once-in-a-lifetime chance to swim with manatees, something best done in winter. Summer's scallop season is also a massive draw.

EXPLORING

FAMILY **Ellie Schiller Homosassa Springs Wildlife State Park.** Here you can see many manatees and several species of fish through a floating glass observatory known as the Fish Bowl—except in this case the fish are outside the bowl and you are inside it. The park's wildlife walk trails lead you to excellent manatee, alligator, and other animal programs. Among the species are bobcats, a western cougar, white-tailed deer, a black bear, pelicans, herons, snowy egrets, river otters, whooping cranes, and even a hippopotamus named Lu, a keepsake from the park's days as an exotic-animal attraction. Boat cruises on Pepper Creek lead you to the Homosassa wildlife park (which takes its name from a Creek Indian word meaning "place where wild peppers grow"). ⊠ *4150 S. Suncoast Blvd., U.S. 19* ☎ *352/628–5343* ⊕ *floridastateparks.org/ homosassasprings* ➾ *$13.*

Yulee Sugar Mill Ruins Historic State Park. This state park has the remains of a circa-1851 sugar mill and other remnants of a 5,100-acre sugar plantation owned by Florida's first U.S. Senator, David Levy Yulee. Interpretive panels spaced throughout the mill ruins describe early methods of the sugar-making process. ⊠ *Rte. 490 (Yulee Dr.), 3 miles off U.S. 19/98* ☎ *352/795–3817* ⊕ *floridastateparks.org/yuleesugarmill* ➾ *Free.*

WHERE TO EAT

$ ✕ **Dan's Clam Stand.** Four reasons to go: the fried grouper sandwich,
SEAFOOD the clam "chowda," anything else seafood, and the beef burgers. The original location is about 2 miles east of Homosassa Springs State Wildlife Park. **Known for:** local favorite; clams and lobster; reasonable prices. $ *Average main: $10* ⊠ *7364 Grover Cleveland Blvd.* ☎ *352/628–9588* ⊙ *Closed Sun.*

$ ✕ **Museum Cafe.** A short trip west of Homosassa Springs State Wildlife
CUBAN Refuge, this tiny eatery is housed in the Olde Mill House Printing Museum. It's only open for lunch, but it's well worth making room for a visit here in your itinerary. **Known for:** Cuban sandwiches; occasional live blues shows; takeout for picnics. $ *Average main: $7* ⊠ *10466 W. Yulee Dr.* ☎ *352/628–1081* ⊙ *No dinner.*

CRYSTAL RIVER

6 miles north of Homosassa Springs on U.S. 19.

Situated along the peaceful Nature Coast, this area is *the* low-key getaway spot in one of the most pristine and beautiful areas in the state. It's also one of the few places on the planet where you can legally swim with manatees. The river's fed by a spring that's a constant 72°F, which is why manatees enjoy spending their winters here. Boating and snorkeling are popular, as is scalloping in the summer. This is a true paradise for nature lovers, and absolutely worth making room for in your vacation itinerary.

EXPLORING

Crystal River National Wildlife Refuge. This is a U.S. Fish and Wildlife Service sanctuary for the endangered manatee. Kings Bay, around which manatees congregate in winter (generally from November to March), feeds crystal-clear water into the river at 72°F year-round. This is one of the sure-bet places to see manatees in winter since hundreds congregate near this 90-acre refuge. The small visitor center has displays about the manatee and other refuge inhabitants. If you want to get an even closer look at these gentle giants, several dive companies provide opportunities for you to swim among them—if you don't mind shelling out some extra cash, donning a wet suit, and adhering to some strict interaction guidelines. In warmer months, when most manatees scatter, the main spring is fun for a swim or scuba diving. ⊠ *1502 S.E. Kings Bay Dr.* ☎ *352/563–2088* ⊕ *www.fws.gov/crystalriver* ⌗ *Free.*

BEACHES

Fort Island Gulf Beach. This is one of the most remote beaches you will find north of Ft. De Soto, the isolated beach south of St. Petersburg. One of the best parts of coming here is the drive. The beach sits as the terminus of Fort Island Trail, the same road where you'll find the Plantation Inn & Golf Resort. A 9-mile drive through the wetlands gets you here, offering sweeping views along the way (though the Crystal River nuclear plant looms to the north). The beach itself is raw and subdued, though there are picnic shelters, barbecues, and a fishing pier. Don't expect many frills, but if you need to relax after a long day of playing in the water, this is your place. **Amenities:** showers; toilets. **Best for:** solitude; sunset. ⊠ *16000 W. Fort Island Trail* ⊕ *www.citrusbocc.com/commserv/parksrec/parks/ft-isl-beach/fib-park.jsp?parkid=18.*

SPORTS AND THE OUTDOORS

MANATEE DIVES

American Pro Diving Center. This is one of several local operators in the area conducting manatee tours of Crystal River National Wildlife Refuge or Homosassa River, something you can't legally do pretty much anywhere else in the country. ⊠ *821 S.E. U.S. 19* ☎ *352/563–0041* ⊕ *www.americanprodiving.com* ⌗ *From $58.*

Crystal Lodge Dive Center. This dive center is one of the more popular operators offering dives, swims, and snorkel trips to see manatees. ⊠ *525 N.W. 7th Ave.* ☎ *352/795–6798* ⊕ *www.manatee-central.com* ⌗ *From $35.*

Plantation Adventure Center. An obvious choice if you're staying at the Plantation on Crystal River, this dive tour company stands on its own as a manatee tour operator. The guides bring you out to various spots along the river to interact with manatees, and tend to be longtime residents who know their subject well. Day trips to nearby Rainbow River, scenic cruises, and sunset/sunrise kayak tours are also available. If the weather is warm, that means no manatees, so plan accordingly. ✉ *Plantation on Crystal River, 9301 Fort Island Trail* ☎ *352/795–4211* ⊕ *www.crystalriverdivers.com* ✎ *$65.*

SARASOTA AND VICINITY

Widely thought of as one of the best places in Florida to live, Sarasota County anchors the southern end of Tampa Bay. A string of barrier islands borders it with 35 miles of Gulf and bay beaches. Sarasota County has something for everyone, from the athletic to the artistic. Thirteen public beaches, two state parks, 22 municipal parks, plus more than 60 public and private golf courses will help keep the active in motion. Spring training was an original destination attraction that now shares the stage with international rowing, swimming, and sailing events. Add to that a plentiful cultural scene dating to the era of circus magnate John Ringling, who chose this area for the winter home of his circus and his family.

BRADENTON

49 miles south of Tampa.

In 1539 Hernando de Soto landed near this Manatee River city, which has some 20 miles of beaches. Bradenton is well situated for access to fishing, both fresh- and saltwater, and it also has its share of golf courses and historic sites dating to the mid-1800s. Orange groves and cattle ranches mix with farmlands between Bradenton's beaches and Interstate 75. Anna Maria Island, a nearby barrier island connected to Bradenton by a causeway, contains the towns of Anna Maria, Holmes Beach, and Bradenton Beach.

GETTING HERE AND AROUND

You can get to Bradenton via Interstate 75, Interstate 275, and U.S. 41/301. West Manatee Avenue gets you out to the beaches. Manatee County Area Transit (MCAT) has buses throughout Bradenton and the nearby towns of Palmetto and Ellenton, as well as connections to Sarasota attractions. Fares for local bus service range from $1.25 to $3 (for an all-day pass); exact change is required. A $30 monthly "M-Card" is available for unlimited rides on all MCAT routes. However, if you want to get around efficiently—and want access to more places—you're best off renting a car.

Contacts Manatee County Area Transit. ☎ 941/749–7116 ⊕ ridemcat.org.

VISITOR INFORMATION

Contacts Bradenton Area Convention and Visitors Bureau. ☎ 941/729–9177 ⊕ www.bradentongulfislands.com.

EXPLORING

De Soto National Memorial. One of the first Spanish explorers to land in North America, Hernando de Soto came ashore with his men and 200 horses near what is now Bradenton in 1539; this federal park commemorates De Soto's expedition and the Native Americans he and his crew encountered. During the height of tourist season, from mid-December to late April, park staff and volunteers dress in period costumes at Camp Uzita, demonstrate the use of 16th-century weapons, and show how European explorers prepared and preserved food for their overland journeys. The season ends with a reenactment of the explorer's landing. The site also offers a film and short nature trail through the mangroves. ⊠ *8300 De Soto Memorial Hwy.* ☎ *941/792–0458* ⊕ *www.nps.gov/deso* ☞ *Free (donations accepted).*

Gamble Plantation Historic State Park. Built in the 1840s, this antebellum mansion 5 miles northeast of Bradenton was home to Major Robert Gamble and is the headquarters of an extensive sugar plantation. It is the only surviving plantation house in South Florida. The Confederate secretary of state took refuge here when the Confederacy fell to Union forces. Picnic tables are available. Guided tours of the house are available six times a day. ⊠ *3708 Patten Ave., Ellenton* ☎ *941/723–4536* ⊕ *floridastateparks.org/gambleplantation* ☞ *Free, tours $6* ☉ *Museum/visitor center closed Tues. and Wed.*

Pine Avenue. Anna Maria Island's newly restored "Main Street" features numerous upscale mom-and-pop boutiques, including beach-appropriate clothiers, beach-inspired home decor stores, and antique furniture shops. You can also find shops offering items such as quality jewelry and infused olive oil. The Anna Maria City Pier, which overlooks the southern end of Tampa Bay, sits at the end of the street. If you're here in the morning, check out Anna Maria Donuts, which offers made-to-order custom donuts, some having sriracha sauce among their ingredients. ⊠ *Pine Ave., Anna Maria* ☎ *941/592–6642* ⊕ *www.pineavenueinfo.com.*

Robinson Preserve. With miles of trails that wind through wetlands and mangroves to lookout towers and peaceful waterfront spots, this Manatee County park is a must for anyone who likes a quiet walk (or run) and sweeping views of the landscape and the wildlife that inhabit it. There's also a kayak launch here, which links into a network of trails for small watercraft. Toward the front of the property the historic Valentine House, which was moved from its original site in Palmetto and restored, now serves as a visitor center and offers a few wonders of its own, including reptiles and shells the kids will dig. ⊠ *1704 99th St. NW* ☎ *941/745–3723* ⊕ *robinsonpreserve.com.*

OFF THE BEATEN PATH

Solomon's Castle. For a visit to the wild and weird side, particularly fun for children, head to this "castle" about 45 minutes east of Bradenton through orange groves and cattle farms. Artist and Renaissance man Howard Solomon began building the 12,000-square-foot always-in-progress work out of thousands of aluminum offset printing plates. Inside, you'll find tons of intrigues—everything from a knight assembled with Volkswagen parts to a chair fashioned out of 86 beer cans to an elephant made from seven oil drums. A restaurant serves sit-down lunches in a full-scale model of a Spanish galleon. ⊠ *4533 Solomon Rd., Ona* ☎ *863/494–6077* ⊕ *www.solomonscastle. org* ⊟ *$12.50* ☉ *Closed Aug. and Sept.*

FAMILY **South Florida Museum and Parker Manatee Aquarium.** Snooty, the oldest manatee in captivity, is the headliner here. Programs about the endangered marine mammals run four times daily, and the first-floor gallery features fossils that tell the story of prehistoric Florida. View changing exhibits in the East Gallery; glass cases and roll-out drawers on the second floor allow you to look at exhibits normally out of public view. At the Bishop Planetarium (with a domed theater screen), programs presented range from black holes to the origin of life itself. ⊠ *201 10th St. W* ☎ *941/746–4131* ⊕ *www.southfloridamuseum.org* ⊟ *$19* ☉ *Closed Mon.*

Fodor's Choice ★ **TreeUmph! Adventure Course** Daredevils of all ages will love this collection of aerial ropes courses and zip lines. Those who partake will traverse swinging bridges, Tarzan ropes, treacherous hanging nets, and other obstacles suspended high in the air between the tall trees here, not to mention the many zip lines at the end of each set of obstacles. Adrenaline will flow more than once during this half-day adventure, but cautious parents need not worry; everyone is secured in a harness, and staff require everyone to demonstrate that they understand the park's many rules by watching a safety video and traversing a small demo course. There's a course that's just for small kids aged 7–12, but most can test their bravery on the five main courses, which get progressively more difficult (culminating in the ultratough Summit Course; most people don't get that far). At the end, everyone, regardless of whether they finished, can partake in a 650 foot-long zip line that starts at 60 feet high and offers spectacular views (the only way to get there is to climb a series of ladders). ■TIP→ Check the weather before you go. If there's lightning within a small radius, staff has to ground you for at least half an hour, and the clock gets set back every time there's a nearby strike. ⊠ *21805 E. State Rd. 70* ☎ *941/322–2130, 855/322–2130* ⊕ *treeumph.com* ⊟ *$54.95.*

BEACHES

Anna Maria Island, Bradenton's 7-mile barrier island to the west, has a number of worthwhile beaches, as does Longboat Key. Manatee Avenue connects the mainland to the island via the Palma Sola Causeway, adjacent to which is a long, sandy beach fronting Palma Sola Bay. There are boat ramps, a dock, and picnic tables.

Coquina Beach. Singles and families flock to Coquina Beach, a wider swath of sand at the southern end of Anna Maria Island. Beach walkers love this stretch since it's Anna Maria's longest beach, and it also attracts crowds of young revelers. **Amenities:** food and drink; showers; toilets. **Best for:** solitude; swimming; walking. ⊠ *2650 Gulf Dr. S, Anna Maria.*

DID YOU KNOW?

Sometimes called "sea cows," manatees are aquatic relatives of elephants. They can weigh more than 1,500 pounds and live 50-plus years. There are more than 3,000 in Florida's coastal waters.

Cortez Beach. Towering Australian pines greet you at the entrance of this popular beach park, a favorite among locals and visitors alike. **Amenities:** showers; toilets. **Best for:** solitude; swimming; walking. ✉ *Gulf Dr., between 5th and 13th Aves., Bradenton Beach.*

Greer Island Beach. Just across the inlet on the northern tip of Longboat Key, Greer Island Beach is accessible by boat or by car via North Shore Boulevard (you can walk here at low tide, but be sure to leave before the tide comes in). You'll also hear this place referred to as Beer Can Island. The secluded peninsula has a wide beach and excellent shelling, but no facilities. **Amenities:** none. **Best for:** solitude; walking. ✉ *7500 Gulf of Mexico Dr., Longboat Key.*

Manatee Beach Park. In the middle of Anna Maria Island, Manatee County Beach is popular with beachgoers of all ages. Paid parking is in the gravel lot next to the beach. **Amenities:** food and drink; parking (fee); showers; toilets. **Best for:** solitude; swimming; walking. ✉ *4000 S.R. 64, at Gulf Dr., Holmes Beach.*

WHERE TO EAT

$$$$ CONTEMPORARY

🍴 **Beach Bistro.** The menu at this cozy beachfront spot offers such standards as a melt-in-your-mouth, herb-rubbed rack of lamb; seafood bouillabaisse; and duckling confit with peppercorn-and-cognac demi-glace. But the menu also includes a variety of specials and small plates. **Known for:** "One Helluva Soup" with plum tomatoes, cream, and blue cheese; beachfront dining with amazing sunset views; prix-fixe tasting menu. [$] *Average main: $49* ✉ *6600 Gulf Dr., Holmes Beach* ☎ *941/778–6444* 🌐 *www.beachbistro.com* 🕒 *No lunch.*

$$$$ STEAKHOUSE
Fodor's Choice ★

🍴 **Euphemia Haye.** A lush tropical setting on the barrier island of Longboat Key, this is one of the most romantic restaurants around. Signature dishes include crisp roast duckling with bread stuffing, and flambéed prime peppered steak; the popular dessert display is a sweet ending. **Known for:** crispy roast duckling with bread stuffing and tangy, fruit-based sauce; upstairs dessert bar offers delicious, heaping portions; quaint, intimate atmosphere. [$] *Average main: $40* ✉ *5540 Gulf of Mexico Dr., Longboat Key* ☎ *941/383–3633* 🌐 *www.euphemiahaye.com* 🕒 *No lunch.*

$ AMERICAN

🍴 **Gulf Drive Café & Tiki.** Especially popular for breakfast (served all day), this unassuming landmark squats on the beach and serves cheap sit-down eats: mostly sandwiches, but also a wide array of entrées after 4 pm. The dinner menu at this beachfront spot, which is great for watching sunsets, features all the seafood options, from lobster mac-and-cheese to grilled or blackened mahimahi. **Known for:** Greek-inspired foods like lemon chicken topped with feta; baked Gulf grouper stuffed with crab cake; beachfront sunset vistas. [$] *Average main: $14* ✉ *900 Gulf Dr. N, Bradenton Beach* ☎ *941/778–1919* 🌐 *gulfdrivetiki.com.*

$$$ AMERICAN

🍴 **Sandbar Restaurant.** While their ever-evolving menu features cutting-edge fare for the most sophisticated of palates, the margarita-and-coconut-shrimp crowd will thoroughly enjoy it here as well. Much of what you'll find on the menu at this beachfront spot is harvested nearby, whether it's herbs and vegetables from one of the gardens along Pine Avenue or fresh fish from nearby Cortez. **Known for:**

unconventional, locally sourced ingredients like grouper cheeks and crab bellies; private-label wines; cocktails on the beach at sunset. [$] *Average main: $22* ✉ *100 Spring Ave., Anna Maria* ☎ *941/778–0444* 🌐 *sandbar.groupersandwich.com*.

WHERE TO STAY

$$ RENTAL 🏨 **BridgeWalk.** This circa-1947 Caribbean colonial-style property is across from the beach and a community within itself. **Pros:** great location; units are roomy; spa and restaurant on property. **Cons:** can be pricey; minimum stays required February–April; not all units have full kitchens. [$] *Rooms from: $229* ✉ *100 Bridge St., Bradenton Beach* ☎ *941/779–2545, 866/779–2545* 🌐 *www.silverresorts.com* 🛏 *28 units* 🍴 *Breakfast.*

$$$$ RENTAL 🏨 **Mainsail Beach Inn.** If you're looking for upscale digs on low-key Anna Maria Island, you'll find them at this small, amenity-laden complex on the beach. **Pros:** on beach; upscale apartments; full of amenities. **Cons:** not for the thrifty; early (10 am) checkout. [$] *Rooms from: $589* ✉ *101 66th St., Holmes Beach* ☎ *888/849–2642* 🌐 *mainsailbeachinn.com* 🛏 *6 2-bedroom condos, 6 3-bedroom condos* 🍴 *No meals.*

$$$$ RESORT 🏨 **The Resort at Longboat Key Club.** This spectacularly landscaped property is one of the best places to play golf in the state, and among the top tennis resorts in the country. **Pros:** resort offers an impressive number of amenities; lovely grounds; all rooms have private balcony. **Cons:** facilities are for guests and members only; few off-site dining options nearby; daily $24 resort fee can add up. [$] *Rooms from: $569* ✉ *220 Sands Point Rd., Longboat Key* ☎ *941/383–8821, 855/314–2619* 🌐 *www.longboatkeyclub.com* 🛏 *223 rooms* 🍴 *No meals.*

$$ RESORT 🏨 **Silver Surf Gulf Beach Resort.** A sister to BridgeWalk, the Silver Surf has the air of a well-maintained 1960s motel with a modern twist, thanks to recent renovations to all of the studios and full apartments. **Pros:** location; freshly renovated rooms and exterior; good value for your money. **Cons:** while nice, the rooms are still pretty basic (this is not luxury). [$] *Rooms from: $219* ✉ *Anna Maria Island, 1301 Gulf Dr. N, Bradenton Beach* ☎ *941/778–6626, 800/441–7873* 🌐 *www.silverresorts.com* 🛏 *26 rooms* 🍴 *No meals.*

SPORTS AND THE OUTDOORS

GOLF

Buffalo Creek Golf Course. The excellent county-owned course was designed by Ron Garl to resemble a Scottish links course, making it among the more challenging courses in the area. Still, novice golfers have a shot here. There are water hazards on several holes (not to mention a gator or two), and the terrain varies throughout. Some consider it to be the best public golf course in the Tampa Bay area. All greens were renovated in 2014. Players can choose to play the whole course or just a quick 9-hole game. The clubhouse offers cold beer at the end of the course. ✉ *8100 Erie Rd., Palmetto* ☎ *941/7792–6773* 🌐 *www.golfmanatee.com* 🎟 *$20 for 9 holes, $39 for 18 holes* 🏌 *18 holes, 7005 yards, par 72.*

7

SARASOTA

30 miles south of Tampa and St. Petersburg.

Sarasota is a year-round destination and home to some of Florida's most affluent residents. Circus magnate John Ringling and his wife, Mable, started the city on the road to becoming one of the state's hotbeds for the arts. Today sporting and cultural events can be enjoyed anytime of the year, and there's a higher concentration of upscale shops, restaurants, and hotels here than in other parts of the Tampa Bay area. Across the water from Sarasota lie the barrier islands of Siesta Key and Lido Key, with myriad beaches, shops, hotels, condominiums, and houses.

GETTING HERE AND AROUND

Sarasota is accessible from Interstate 75, Interstate 275, and U.S. 41. The town's public transit company is Sarasota County Area Transit (SCAT). Fares for local bus service range from $0.75 to $3 (for an all-day pass); exact change is required. A $60 monthly "R-Card" is available for unlimited rides on all SCAT and Manatee County Area Transit (MCAT) routes. If you want to make it to the farther reaches of the area, though, renting a car is probably your best bet.

Contacts **Sarasota County Area Transit (SCAT).** ☎ *941/861–5000* ⊕ *www.scgov.net/scat.*

VISITOR INFORMATION

Contacts **Sarasota Convention and Visitors Bureau.** ✉ *1710 Main St.* ☎ *941/957–1877* ⊕ *www.sarasotafl.org.*

EXPLORING

TOP ATTRACTIONS

FAMILY

Fodor's Choice

★

John and Mable Ringling Museum of Art. Administered by Florida State University, the museum encompasses the entire Ringling estate, far more than just the art museum; there's also the Tibbals Learning Center and Circus Museums as well as Ca' d'Zan Mansion, the original Ringling home, and its expansive gardens. The entire compound covers 20 waterfront acres and also has the Historic Asolo Theater, restaurants, and a research library.

The **Art Museum** was a dream long in the making for John Ringling (of Ringling Brothers fame). Finally finished in 1931 after setbacks including a land bust and the death of his wife Mable, this enormous museum was originally built to house Ringling's mind-blowingly expansive art collection. You'll find works ranging from Indian doorways elaborately carved with Jain deities to opalescent baroque paintings from the likes of Rubens. There seems to be an endless number of rooms, themselves decorated in an appropriately gorgeous manner, housing these masterpieces. Contemporary art—both visiting and permanent exhibits—has dedicated space here, as do rotating exhibits from the museum's permanent photography collection. A newer wing, with its facade of jade-tinged terra-cotta, houses ancient and contemporary works of Asian art. The museum's exit opens out into an enormous courtyard, over which a towering replica statue of *David* presides, flanked by royal palms.

Ringling Mansion Sarasota

Circus magnate John Ringling's grand home, **Ca' d'Zan,** which was built along Sarasota Bay, was patterned after the Doge's Palace in Venice. This exquisite mansion of 32 rooms, 15 bathrooms, and a 61-foot Belvedere Tower was completed in 1925, and today is the crowning jewel at the site of the Ringling Estate. Its 8,000-square-foot terrace overlooks the dock where Ringling's wife, Mable, moored her gondola. Mansion tours occur on the hour, and last half an hour. If you don't want a guided tour, show up on the half hour for a self-guided tour.

Allot some extra time to wander around in the Mable Ringling's **Rose Garden,** a lush labyrinth surrounded by towering banyans and full of rare roses and haunting statues.

Don't let the name **Tibbals Learning Center** fool you. This Ringling estate attraction offers a colorful glimpse into a most wondrous element of a bygone era: the traveling circus. The center focuses on the history of the American circus and the collection of Howard Tibbals, master model builder, who spent 40 years building the world's largest miniature circus. Perhaps the center's main attraction, this impressive to-scale replica of the circa 1920s and '30s Ringling Bros. and Barnum & Bailey Circus is an astonishingly accurate portrayal of a circus coming through town—the number of pancakes the circus cooks are flipping, the exact likenesses and costumes of the performers, the correct names of the animals marked on the miniature mess buckets—you name it. Tibbals's passion to re-create every exact detail continues in his on-site workshop, where kids can ask him questions and watch him carving animals and intricate wagons.

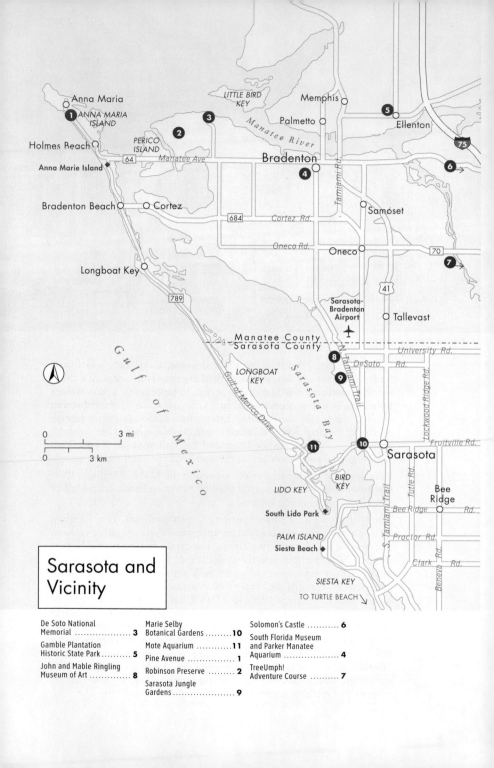

Sarasota and Vicinity

If you're looking for clown noses, ringmaster hats, and circus-themed T-shirts, don't leave before checking out the **Ringling Museum of Art Store.**

The **Historic Asolo Theater** is also on the estate grounds and is home to the Asolo Repertory Company. ✉ *5401 Bay Shore Rd. ✛ ½ mile west of Sarasota-Bradenton Airport* ☎ *941/359–5700* ⊕ *www.ringling. org* 🎫 *$25 (art museum only free Mon.); $20 Ca d'Zan docent tours.*

Marie Selby Botanical Gardens. Orchids make up nearly a third of the 20,000 species of flowers and plants here. You can stroll through the Tropical Display House, home of orchids and colorful bromeliads gathered from rain forests, and wander the garden pathway past plantings of bamboo, ancient banyans, and mangrove forests along Little Sarasota Bay. Although spring sees the best blooms, the greenhouses make this an attraction for all seasons. The added bonus is a spectacular view of downtown. There are rotating exhibits of botanical art and photography in a 1934 restored Southern Colonial mansion. Enjoy lunch at the Local Coffee + Tea, a café in the historic Selby House. ✉ *811 S. Palm Ave.* ☎ *941/366–5731* ⊕ *www.selby.org* 🎫 *$20.*

WORTH NOTING

FAMILY **Mote Aquarium.** A renowned research facility, the Mote is also a popular tourist attraction that draws families and others interested in its international array of ocean creatures. Its newest draw is a large outdoor habitat featuring a family of frolicking river otters. In the main building, 135,000-gallon shark tank lets you view various types of sharks from above and below the surface. Other tanks show off eels, rays, and other marine creatures native to the area. Touch tanks abound here for the little ones, and the not-so faint of heart can scope out a preserved giant squid; a rare find out in the wild. The expanded Seahorse Conservation Lab offers a glimpse into the unusual creatures' lives and how the aquarium is working to help them survive and thrive. Hugh and Buffett are the resident manatees and, though not as venerable as Snooty at the Parker Manatee Aquarium, they have lived here since 1996 as part of a research program. There's also a permanent sea-turtle exhibit. For an extra fee, **Sarasota Bay Explorers** offers boat tours from the museum's dock (reservations required), guided kayak tours through the mangroves, private tours, and a "Nature Safari." ✉ *City Island, 1600 Ken Thompson Pkwy.* ☎ *941/388–4441* ⊕ *www.mote.org* 🎫 *$19.75.*

FAMILY **Sarasota Jungle Gardens.** One of Old Florida's charming, family-owned and -operated attractions, Sarasota Jungle Gardens fills 10 acres with native and exotic animals as well as tropical plants. The lush gardens date to 1939, and still have the small-world feel of yesterday's Florida. You'll find red-tailed hawks and great horned owls in the Wildlife Wonder show, American alligators and a variety of snakes in the reptile encounter, and an exotic bird show. Among more cuddly residents here are lemurs, monkeys, and prairie dogs. You can talk to trainers and get to know such plants as the rare Australian nut tree and the Peruvian apple cactus in the gardens. Also on-site are flocks of flamingos that guests can hand-feed, plus reptiles and a butterfly garden. ✉ *3701 Bay Shore Rd.* ☎ *941/355–5305* ⊕ *www.sarasotajunglegardens.com* 🎫 *$17.99.*

BEACHES

Fodor's Choice ★ **Siesta Beach.** With 40 acres of nature trails, this park is popular; you'll find tons of amenities. This beach has fine, powdery quartz sand that squeaks under your feet, very much like the sand along the state's northwestern coast. Don't forget to bring a volleyball—or a tennis racket. **Amenities:** food and drink; lifeguards; toilets. **Best for:** partiers; sunset; swimming; walking. ✉ *948 Beach Rd., Siesta Key.*

South Lido County Park. At the southern tip of the island, South Lido County Park has one of the best beaches in the region, but there are no lifeguards. The 100-acre park interacts with four significant bodies of water: the Gulf of Mexico, Big Pass, Sarasota Bay, and Brushy Bayou. The sugar-sand beach has plenty of early morning sand dollars and is a popular place to fish. Picnic as the sun sets through the Australian pines into the water. Facilities include nature trails, canoe and kayak trails, restrooms, and picnic grounds. This park was purchased by John Ringling in 1920 as part of his ambitious plan to develop island properties. His plan collapsed with the great Florida Land bust of 1926. Because of swift rip currents, swimming here is not recommended. **Amenities:** showers; toilets. **Best for:** solitude; walking. ✉ *2201 Ben Franklin Dr., Lido Key.*

Turtle Beach. A 14-acre beach-park that's popular with families, Turtle has 2,600 linear feet of beach frontage and is more secluded than most Gulf beaches. Though narrower than most of the region's beaches, it's also much less crowded, so it doesn't feel so narrow. It's known for abundant sea turtles. It has covered picnic shelters, grills, and a volleyball court. Locals like the 40-site campground that is also open to visitors with advance reservations. Fittingly enough, this beach is near the übermellow Turtle Beach Resort. **Amenities:** toilets. **Best for:** solitude; sunset; swimming; walking. ✉ *8918 Midnight Pass Rd., Siesta Key* ☎ *941/349–3839.*

WHERE TO EAT

$$$ FRENCH Fodor's Choice ★ 🍴 **Bijou Café.** This 1920s-era gas station–turned–restaurant has been expanded over the years so that it is now a 140-seat restaurant. The enchanting decor is what you might expect in a quaint, modern European café—think French windows and doors, sparkling glassware, bouquets of freshly picked flowers, and the soft glow of candlelight. **Known for:** contemporary takes on traditional dishes, heavy on the seafood; cheaper bar menu; pre- or post-show dining. [$] *Average main: $30* ✉ *1287 1st St.* ☎ *941/366–8111* 🌐 *www.bijoucafe.net* ⏲ *Closed Sun. No lunch weekends.*

$$$ MODERN AMERICAN 🍴 **Boca.** One of four locations, this regional chain fits right into downtown Sarasota's hopping dining and shopping scene. The menu is as locally inspired as it gets—from the catch of the day courtesy of local fishing boats, to the fresh herbs that literally grow on the walls here. **Known for:** locally sourced seafood; craft cocktails; prime downtown location. [$] *Average main: $23* ✉ *19 S. Lemon Ave.* ☎ *941/256–3565* 🌐 *bocasarasota.com.*

$$$$ EUROPEAN 🍴 **Café L'Europe.** Located in St. Armand's Circle, this sidewalk and indoor café has a spectacular menu featuring table-side specialties such as chateaubriand for two. Other popular entrées range from potato-crusted

grouper and brandied duckling to rack of lamb. **Known for:** rich, classic French fare; great wine list; Parisian-sidewalk-café feel. $ *Average main: $33* ⊠ *431 St. Armands Circle, Lido Key* 🕾 *941/388–4415* ⊕ *www.cafeeurope.net.*

$$$
AMERICAN
✕ **Michael's on East.** Not only do the lounge and piano bar, with their extensive wines and vintage cocktails, lure the after-theater set, but inspired cuisine and superior service also entice. Dinner fare ranges from pompano sautéed with Gulf shrimp, tomatoes, and fresh herbs to pan-roasted chicken breast with anise-scented sweet potato puree. **Known for:** large menu of seafood and meat dishes; extensive wine list; supper club atmosphere with piano bar. $ *Average main: $26* ⊠ *1212 East Ave. S* 🕾 *941/366–0007* ⊕ *www.michaelsoneast.com* ☉ *Closed Sun. No lunch Sat.*

$$
AMERICAN
✕ **The Old Salty Dog.** A menu of steamer and raw-bar options has been added to the much-enjoyed old favorites, including quarter-pound hot dogs, fish-and-chips, wings, and burgers—and early birds can catch breakfast here now, too. With views of New Pass between Longboat and Lido Keys, this is a popular stop for locals and visitors en route from Mote Aquarium and the adjoining bay-front park. **Known for:** oysters and raw bar; hot dogs, burgers, and sandwiches; outdoor dining and sunset views. $ *Average main: $15* ⊠ *1601 Ken Thompson Pkwy., City Island* 🕾 *941/388–4311* ⊕ *www.theoldsaltydog.com.*

$$$$
AMERICAN
✕ **Ophelia's on the Bay.** Enjoy the flowering gardens while dining alfresco on the outdoor patio on the dock at Market #48 or in one of two casually elegant dining rooms. An ever-evolving menu highlights Florida seafood, such as Gulf mangrove snapper served with a side of tropical fruit jam and habañero potatoes. **Known for:** creative, internationally influenced seafood dishes; intimate, romantic atmosphere; lovely water vistas. $ *Average main: $32* ⊠ *9105 Midnight Pass Rd., Siesta Key* 🕾 *941/349–2212* ⊕ *www.opheliasonthebay.net* ☉ *No lunch Mon.–Sat.*

$$
SOUTHERN
✕ **Owen's Fish Camp.** Nestled in a banyan-shaded corner of the hip Burns Court district of downtown Sarasota, this spot dishes out quintessentially Southern fare (though the menu is not geographically limited) that is particularly heavy on the seafood options. You'll find everything from the shrimp and oyster po'boy with bacon to chicken-fried lobster tail, a popular appetizer. **Known for:** fresh oysters and locally caught seafood; casual, low-key setting; no reservations and occasionally long waits. $ *Average main: $16* ⊠ *516 Burns Ct.* 🕾 *941/951–6936* ⊕ *owensfishcamp.com* ☉ *No lunch.*

$$
MODERN
AMERICAN
✕ **Shore.** If you're a sucker for mid-century modern flair, the aesthetic alone at this partially open-air St. Armand's Circle spot is a draw. But the menu here, whether you're in the mood for the St. Louis "Jenga" ribs or roasted cauliflower quinoa, is the real draw, especially when paired with the right local brew served on tap. **Known for:** Maine lobster sliders; spareribs with a Mongolian glaze; chic atmosphere. $ *Average main: $20* ⊠ *465 John Ringling Blvd., Suite 200* 🕾 *941/296–0301* ☉ *dineshore.com.*

$ AMERICAN 🍴 **Yoder's.** Lines for meals stretch well beyond the hostess podium here. Pies—key lime, egg custard, banana cream, peanut butter, strawberry rhubarb, and others—are the main event at this family restaurant in the heart of Sarasota's Amish community. **Known for:** fresh-baked pies; comfort food; good breakfast. [$] *Average main: $10* ✉ *3434 Bahia Vista* ☎ *941/955–7771* 🌐 *www.yodersrestaurant.com* 🕒 *Closed Sun.*

WHERE TO STAY

$$ RENTAL 🏨 **Gulf Beach Resort.** Lido Key's first motel, this beachfront condo complex has been designated a historic property. **Pros:** near shopping; most units have kitchens or kitchenettes; free Wi-Fi. **Cons:** decor is fairly basic; motel feel; limited amenities. [$] *Rooms from: $205* ✉ *930 Ben Franklin Dr., Lido Key* ☎ *941/388–2127, 800/232–2489* 🌐 *www.gulfbeachsarasota.com* 🛏 *49 rooms* 🍽 *No meals.*

$$$ HOTEL 🏨 **Hyatt Regency Sarasota.** Popular among business travelers, the Hyatt Regency is contemporary in design and sits in the heart of the city across from the Van Wezel Performing Arts Hall. **Pros:** great location; stellar views. **Cons:** chain-hotel feel; not on the beach. [$] *Rooms from: $379* ✉ *1000 Blvd. of the Arts* ☎ *941/953–1234, 941/953–1234* 🌐 *www.sarasota.hyatt.com* 🛏 *294 rooms* 🍽 *Breakfast; No meals.*

$$$ RENTAL 🏨 **Lido Beach Resort.** Superb Gulf views can be found at this stylish beachfront resort. **Pros:** beachfront location; many rooms have kitchens. **Cons:** bland, somewhat dated furnishings; high per-night fee for pets. [$] *Rooms from: $369* ✉ *700 Ben Franklin Dr., Lido Key* ☎ *941/388–2161, 866/306–5457* 🌐 *www.lidobeachresort.com* 🛏 *222 rooms* 🍽 *No meals.*

$$$$ HOTEL 🏨 **Ritz-Carlton, Sarasota.** With a style that developers like to say is circus magnate John Ringling's realized dream, The Ritz is appointed with fine artwork and fresh-cut flowers. **Pros:** Ritz-style glitz; lots of amenities; attentive staff. **Cons:** long distance to golf course; not on the beach. [$] *Rooms from: $649* ✉ *1111 Ritz-Carlton Dr.* ☎ *941/309–2000,* 🌐 *www.ritzcarlton.com/sarasota* 🛏 *296 rooms* 🍽 *No meals.*

$$$ HOTEL Fodor's Choice ★ 🏨 **Turtle Beach Resort & Inn.** Reminiscent of a quieter time, many of the cottages at this friendly, affordable, family- and pet-friendly resort date to the 1940s, a romantic plus for yesteryear lovers. **Pros:** nice location; romantic setting; self-serve laundry and Wi-Fi included. **Cons:** far from the area's cultural attractions; amenities are lacking; not family-friendly. [$] *Rooms from: $350* ✉ *9049 Midnight Pass Rd., Siesta Key* ☎ *941/349–4554* 🌐 *www.turtlebeachresort.com* 🛏 *7 rooms, 3 suites, 10 cottages* 🍽 *No meals.*

NIGHTLIFE AND PERFORMING ARTS

NIGHTLIFE

JDub's Brewing Company. Sarasota is no exception to the Tampa Bay area's thriving craft beer scene. Though JDub's may be best known for the popular milk chocolate porter, the ever-rotating cast of options on tap include the Left on Lido Mosaic Pale Ale and the warm-weather appropriate Poolside Kolsch. The brewery/tasting room is well off the beaten path—it's situated in an industrial area a solid 15 minutes from the beach—but the atmosphere here is excellent. Out back, there's a dog-friendly area with yard games like bean bag toss. There are also food trucks most days out front. Brewery tours are available every day at 1 and 6 for $5 (which includes a free "flagship" beer). ⊠ *1215 Mango Ave.* ☎ *941/955–2739* ⊕ *jdubsbrewing.com.*

PERFORMING ARTS

Asolo Repertory Theatre. One of the best theaters in Sarasota stages productions year round in varying venues, which include the Historic Asolo Theater in the Ringling Estate. ⊠ *5555 Tamiami Trail* ☎ *941/351–8000* ⊕ *www.asolorep.org.*

The Players Theatre. A long-established community theater, having launched such actors as Montgomery Clift and Paul Reubens, this troupe performs comedies, special events, live concerts, and musicals. ⊠ *838 N. Tamiami Trail, U.S. 41 at 9th St.* ☎ *941/365–2494* ⊕ *www. theplayers.org.*

Sarasota Opera. Performing in a historic 1,122-seat downtown theater, the Sarasota Opera features internationally known artists singing the principal roles, supported by a professional chorus of young apprentices. The season typically lasts from February through March, though a few special events take place at the venue throughout the year. ⊠ *61 N. Pineapple Ave.* ☎ *941/328–1300* ⊕ *sarasotaopera.org.*

SPORTS AND THE OUTDOORS

BOAT TOURS

Sarasota Bay Explorers. Many visitors to the Mote Aquarium take the 105-minute boat trip onto Sarasota Bay. Conducted by Sarasota Bay Explorers, all boat trips are done in conjunction with the aquarium and leave from the aquarium's dock. The crew brings marine life on board, explains what it is, and throws it back to swim away. You are almost guaranteed to see bottlenose dolphins. Reservations are recommended. You can also charter the *Miss Explorer,* a 24-foot Sea Ray Sundeck, or take a guided kayak or nature tour. ⊠ *Mote Aquarium, 1600 Ken Thompson Pkwy.* ☎ *941/388–4200* ⊕ *www.sarasotabayexplorers.com* ▤ *Boat tour $27, kayak tour $55, nature tour $45, charters $295–$445.*

FISHING

Flying Fish Fleet. Several boats can be chartered for deep-sea fishing by the day or half day, and there are daily group trips on a "party" fishing boat. ⊠ *2 Marina Plaza, on the bay front at Marina Jack* ☎ *941/366–3373* ⊕ *www.flyingfishfleet.com* ▤ *Group trips from $60 per person, charters from $650.*

GOLF

Bobby Jones Golf Course. This public 45-hole course is over a century old and caters to a range of golfers. The setting is lush and green, with plenty of live oak trees and water. The grounds here are so pleasant that many choose to walk their chosen course, of which there are three. The American Course is best for less experienced golfers or those who want to practice their short shot, and features a range of lakes and varied terrain. The British Course is slightly more challenging, offering longer fairways dotted with water hazards and sand bunkers. The Gillespie Executive Course is recommended for beginners or those lacking the time needed for a full 18 holes. A large ravine divides much of the course from several of its greens approaches. ✉ *1000 Circus Blvd.* ☎ *941/365–4653* ⊕ *bjgc365.com* ✉ *$20 for 9 holes, $28 for 18 holes* 🏌 *American Course: 18 holes, 6028 yards, par 71; British Course: 18 holes, 6700 yards, par 72; Gillespie Executive Course: 9 holes, 1716 yards, par 30.*

KAYAKING

Sarasota Bay Explorers, which operates from the Mote Aquarium, also offers guided kayaking trips *(see Boat Tours).*

Siesta Sports Rentals. Up for rent here are kayaks, stand-up paddleboards, bikes, beach chairs, scooters, and beach wheelchairs and strollers. Guided kayaking trips are also available. ✉ *6551 Midnight Pass Rd., Siesta Key* ☎ *941/346–1797* ⊕ *www.siestasportsrentals.com.*

THE LOWER GULF COAST

WELCOME TO
THE LOWER GULF COAST

TOP REASONS
TO GO

★ **Heavenly beaches:**
Whether you go to the
beach to sun, swim,
gather shells, or watch
the sunset, the region's
Gulf of Mexico beaches
rank among the best.

★ **Edison & Ford Winter
Estates:** A rare complex
of two famous inventors'
winter homes comes
complete with botanical-
research gardens, Edison's
lab, and a museum.

★ **Island hopping:** Rent a
boat or jump aboard a
charter for lunch, picnicking, beaching, or shelling
on a subtropical island
adrift from the mainland.

★ **Naples shopping:**
Flex your buying power
in downtown Naples's
charming shopping dis-
tricts or in lush outdoor
centers around town.

★ **Watch for wildlife:**
On the edge of Everglades
National Park, the region
protects vast tracts of
fragile land and water
where you can see alliga-
tors, manatees, dolphins,
roseate spoonbills, and
hundreds of other birds.

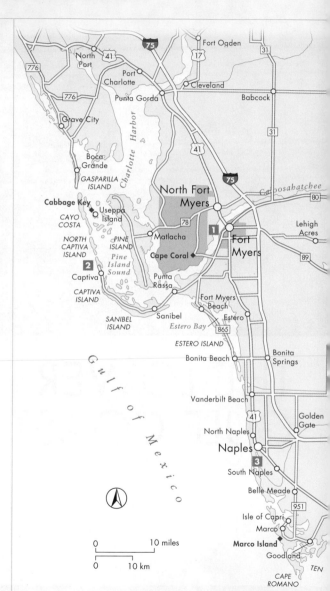

1 Fort Myers and Vicinity.
Don't miss the Edison & Ford
Winter Estates along royal
palm–lined McGregor Boulevard. For museums, theater,
and art, the up-and-coming
downtown River District
rules.

2 The Coastal Islands.
Shells and wildlife refuges
bring nature lovers to
Sanibel and Captiva islands.
Fort Myers Beach is known
for its lively clubs and shrimp
fleet. For true seclusion,
head to the area's unbridged
island beaches.

3 Naples and Vicinity.
Some of the region's best
shopping and dining take up
residence in historic buildings trimmed with blossoms
and street sculptures in Old
Naples. Hit Marco Island
for the boating lifestyle
and funky fishing-village
character.

GETTING ORIENTED

The Lower Gulf Coast of
Florida, as its name suggests,
occupies a stretch of coastline along southernmost west
Florida, bordered by the Gulf
of Mexico. It lies south of
Tampa and Sarasota, directly
on the other side of the state
from West Palm Beach and
Fort Lauderdale. In between
the two coasts stretch heart-
land agricultural areas and
Everglades wilderness. The
region encompasses the
major resort towns of Fort
Myers, Fort Myers Beach,
Sanibel Island, Naples, and
Marco Island, along with a
medley of suburban commu-
nities and smaller islands.

8

Updated by Jill
Martin

With its subtropical climate and beckoning family-friendly beaches known for their powdery sand, calm surf, and nary a freighter in sight, the Lower Gulf Coast, also referred to as the state's southwestern region, is a favorite vacation spot of Florida residents as well as visitors. Vacationers tend to spend most of their time outdoors— swimming, sunning, shelling, fishing, boating, and playing tennis or golf.

The region has several distinct travel destinations. Small and historic downtown Fort Myers rises inland along the Caloosahatchee River, and the rest of the town sprawls in all directions. It got its nickname, the City of Palms, from the hundreds of towering royal palms that inventor Thomas Edison planted between 1900 and 1917 along McGregor Boulevard, a historic residential street and site of his winter estate. Edison's idea caught on, and more than 2,000 royal palms now line 14-mile-long McGregor Boulevard. Museums and educational attractions are the draw here. Across the river, Cape Coral has evolved from a mostly residential community to a resort destination for water-sports enthusiasts.

Off the coast west of Fort Myers are more than 100 coastal islands in all shapes and sizes. Connected to the mainland by a 3-mile causeway, Sanibel is known for its superb shelling, fine fishing, beachfront resorts, and wildlife refuge. Here and on Captiva, to which it is connected by a short bridge, multimillion-dollar homes line both waterfronts. Just southwest of Fort Myers is Estero Island, home of busy Fort Myers Beach, and farther south, Lovers Key State Park and Bonita Beach.

Farther down the coast lies Naples, once a small fishing village and now a thriving and sophisticated enclave. It's like a smaller, more understated version of Palm Beach, with fine restaurants, chichi shopping areas, luxury resorts, and—locals will tell you—more golf holes per capita than anywhere else in the world. A half hour south basks Marco Island, best known for its beaches and fishing. See a maze of pristine miniature mangrove islands when you take a boat tour from the island's marinas into Ten Thousand Islands National Wildlife Refuge. Although high-rises line much of Marco's waterfront, the tiny fishing village of Goodland, an outpost of Old Florida, tries valiantly to stave off new development.

PLANNING

WHEN TO GO

In winter this is one of the warmest areas of the United States. Occasionally temperatures drop in December or January, but rarely below freezing. From February through April you may find it next to impossible to find a hotel room.

Numbers drop the rest of the year, but visitors within driving range, European tourists, and convention clientele still keep things busy. Temperatures and humidity spike, but discounted room rates make summer attractive. Summer is also rainy season, but most storms occur in the afternoon and last for a flash. Hurricane season runs from June through November.

GETTING HERE AND AROUND

AIR TRAVEL

The area's primary airport is Southwest Florida International in Fort Myers, where many airlines offer flights; private pilots land at both RSW and Page Field, also in Fort Myers. Gulf Coast Airways to Key West and a couple of private charter services also land at Naples Municipal Airport, and North Captiva Island has a private airstrip.

Airport Transfer Contacts Aaron Airport Transportation. ☎ 239/768–1898 ⊕ www.aarontaxi.com. **Sanibel Taxi.** ☎ 239/472–4160, 888/527–7806 ⊕ www.sanibeltaxi.com.

Airport Contacts Naples Municipal Airport. ✉ 160 Aviation Dr. N, Naples ☎ 239/643–0733 ⊕ www.flynaples.com. **Southwest Florida International Airport (RSW).** ✉ 11000 Terminal Access Rd., Fort Myers ☎ 239/590–4800 ⊕ www.flylcpa.com.

CAR TRAVEL

If you're driving, U.S. 41 (the Tamiami Trail) runs the length of the region. Sanibel Island is accessible from the mainland via the Sanibel Causeway (toll $6 round-trip). Captiva Island lies across a small pass from Sanibel's north end, accessible by bridge.

Be aware that the destination's popularity, especially during winter, means traffic congestion at peak times of day. Avoid driving when the locals are getting to and from work and visitors to and from the beach.

HOTELS

Lodging in Fort Myers, the islands, and Naples can be pricey, but there are affordable options even during the busy winter season. If these destinations are too rich for your pocket, consider visiting in the off-season, when rates drop drastically, or look to Fort Myers Beach and Cape Coral for better rates. Beachfront properties tend to be more expensive; to spend less, look for properties away from the water. In high season—Christmastime and Presidents' Day through Easter—always reserve ahead for the top properties. Fall is the slowest season: rates are low and availability is high, but this is also hurricane season (June–November).

RESTAURANTS

In this part of Florida, fresh seafood reigns supreme. Succulent native stone-crab claws, a particularly tasty treat, in season from mid-October through mid-May, are usually served hot with drawn butter or chilled with tangy mustard sauce. Supplies are typically steady, since claws regenerate in time for the next season. Other seafood specialties include fried grouper sandwiches and Sanibel pink shrimp. In Naples's highly hailed restaurants and sidewalk cafés, mingle with locals, winter visitors, and other travelers, and catch up on the latest culinary trends.

Hotel and restaurant reviews have been shortened. For full information, visit Fodors.com.

WHAT IT COSTS			
$	$$	$$$	$$$$
Restaurants	under $15	$15–$20	$21–$30	over $30
Hotels	under $200	$200–$300	$301–$400	over $400

Restaurant prices are the average cost of a main course at dinner or, if dinner is not served, at lunch. Hotel prices are the lowest cost of a standard double room in high season.

TOURS

Captiva Cruises. Shelling, dolphin, luncheon, beach, sunset, and history cruises run to and around the out islands of Cabbage Key, Useppa Island, Cayo Costa, and Gasparilla Island. Night sky cruises and excursions also go to historic Tarpon Lodge and Calusa Indian Mound Trail on Pine Island. Excursions are from $27.50, and there may be a charge for parking. ✉ *McCarthy's Marina, 11401 Andy Rosse La., Captiva* ☎ *239/472–5300* ⊕ *www.captivacruises.com* 🎫 *Tours from $27.50.*

FAMILY **Manatee Sightseeing Adventure.** You are guaranteed to see manatees or you don't pay. Tours depart at Port of the Islands. Discount tickets are available online. ✉ *525 Newport Dr., Naples* ☎ *239/642–8818* ⊕ *www. see-manatees.com* 🎫 *Admission $58.*

Tarpon Bay Explorers. One of the best ways to see the J.N. "Ding" Darling National Wildlife Refuge is by taking one of these guided or self-guided nature tours. There are many options to choose depending on your activity level and desire—including a sea life cruise, open-air tram tours, and nature cruises, to name a few. Rentals of kayaks, canoes, stand-up paddleboards, bikes, and pontoon boats are right on-site. Charter boats are also available. ✉ *900 Tarpon Bay Rd., Sanibel* ☎ *239/472–8900* ⊕ *www.tarponbayexplorers.com* 🎫 *Tours from $13.*

FORT MYERS AND VICINITY

In parts of Fort Myers, old Southern mansions and their modern-day counterparts peek out from behind stately palms and blossomy foliage. Views over the broad Caloosahatchee River, which borders the city's small but businesslike cluster of office buildings downtown, soften the look of the area. These days it's showing the effects of age and urban sprawl, but planners work at reviving what has been termed the River District at the heart of downtown. North of Fort Myers are small fishing communities and new retirement towns, including Boca Grande on Gasparilla Island; Englewood Beach on Manasota Key; and Port Charlotte, north of the Peace River.

FORT MYERS

80 miles southeast of Sarasota, 125 miles west of Palm Beach.

The city core lies inland along the banks of the Caloosahatchee River, a half hour from the nearest beach. The town is best known as the winter home of inventors Thomas A. Edison and Henry Ford.

GETTING HERE AND AROUND

The closest airport to Fort Myers is Southwest Florida International Airport (RSW), about 15 miles southeast of town. A taxi for up to three passengers costs about $25–$40; extra people are charged $10 each. LeeTran bus service serves most of the Fort Myers area.

If you're driving here from Florida's East Coast, consider Alligator Alley, a toll section of Interstate 75 that runs from Fort Lauderdale to Naples. Interstate 75 then runs north–south the length of the region. U.S. 41 (the Tamiami Trail, also called South Cleveland Avenue in Fort Myers) runs parallel to the interstate to the west and goes through downtown Naples and Fort Myers. McGregor Boulevard (Route 867) and Summerlin Road (Route 869), Fort Myers's main north–south city streets, head toward Sanibel and Captiva islands. San Carlos Boulevard (Route 865) runs southwest from Summerlin Road to Fort Myers Beach, and Pine Island–Bayshore Road (Route 78) leads from North Fort Myers through northern Cape Coral onto Pine Island.

Bus Contacts LeeTran. ☎ *239/275–8726, 239/533–8726* ⊕ *www.rideleetran.com.*

VISITOR INFORMATION

Contacts Lee County Visitor & Convention Bureau. ✉ *2201 2nd St., Suite 600* ☎ *239/338–3500, 800/237–6444* ⊕ *www.fortmyers-sanibel.com.*

EXPLORING

TOP ATTRACTIONS

Fodor's Choice **Edison & Ford Winter Estates.** Fort Myers's premier attraction pays homage
★ to two of America's most ingenious inventors: Thomas A. Edison, who gave the world the stock ticker, the incandescent lamp, and the phonograph, among other inventions; and his friend and neighbor, automaker Henry Ford. Donated to the city by Edison's widow, his once 12-acre estate has been expanded into a remarkable 25 acres, with three homes, two caretaker cottages, a laboratory, botanical gardens, and a museum.

8

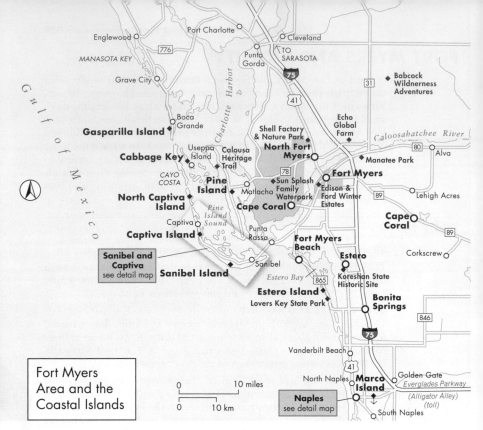

Fort Myers
Area and the
Coastal Islands

0   10 miles

0   10 km

The laboratory contains the same gadgets and gizmos as when Edison last stepped foot into it. Visitors can see many of his inventions, along with historic photographs and memorabilia, in the museum. Edison traveled south from New Jersey and devoted much of his time here to inventing things (there are 1,093 patents to his name), experimenting with rubber for friend and frequent visitor Harvey Firestone, and planting hundreds of plant species collected around the world. Next door to Edison's two identical homes is Ford's "Mangoes," the more modest seasonal home of Edison's fellow inventor. The property's oldest building, the Edison Caretaker's House, dates to 1860. Tours are guided or audio self-guided. One admission covers homes of both men; museum and laboratory-only tickets and botanical-garden tour tickets are also available. ✉ 2350 McGregor Blvd. ☎ 239/334–7419 ⊕ www.edisonfordwinterestates.org 🎫 Complete Estate Tour $20; other tours available.

FAMILY   **Imaginarium Science Center.** Kids can't wait to get their hands on the won-
Fodor's Choice   derful interactive exhibits at this lively museum–aquarium combo that
★   explores technology, physics, weather, and other science topics. Check out the stingrays and other marine life in the aquariums, touch tanks, and the USS *Mohawk* artificial reef tank featured on Animal Planet's "Tanked!" Feed the fish, turtles, and swans in the outdoor lagoon; visit a tarantula, python, hissing cockroach, juvenile alligator, and other live

critters in the Animal Lab; dig for dinosaur bones; watch a 3-D movie in the theater; take part in a hands-on Animal Encounter demonstration, and touch a cloud. Other highlights include the Mini Museum early childhood area, Backyard Nature, aquaponics area, Nano Lab, and Idea Lab engineering design center, as well as Build-Your-Own-Coaster and Science of Motion. Look for history exhibits to be integrated in 2017, with underwater plane wrecks, a Columbian mammoth, and giant ground sloth, as well as a replica Cracker House. ✉ *2000 Cranford Ave.* ☎ *239/321–7420* 🌐 *www.imaginariumfortmyers.com* 🎟 *$12* 🕒 *Closed Mon.*

FAMILY **Manatee Park.** Here you may glimpse Florida's most famous, yet often hard to spot, marine mammal. When Gulf waters drop to 68°F or below—usually from November to March—the sea cows congregate in these waters, which are warmed by the outflow of a towering nearby power plant. Pause at any of the three observation decks (the first nearest the outflow and last at the lagoon usually yield the most sightings, as does the fishing pier) and watch for bubbles. Hydrophones on the last deck allow you to eavesdrop on their songs. Periodically, one of these gentle giants—mature adults weigh an average of 1,000 pounds—will surface. Calusa Blueway Outfitters run the visitor center/gift shop and offer kayak and canoe rentals, as well as clinics and tours to paddle the canals and get a closer look. ✉ *10901 Palm Beach Blvd., 1¼ miles east of I–75 Exit 141* ☎ *239/690–5030* 🌐 *www.leeparks.org* 🎟 *Free. Parking (cash only) May–Nov. $1 per hr, $5 daily; Dec.–Apr. $2 per hr, $5 daily* 🕒 *Concessions closed Apr.–Nov.*

WHERE TO EAT

$$$ AMERICAN 🍴 **Bistro 41.** Amid brightly painted, textured walls and a display kitchen, shoppers and businesspeople meet here for some of the town's most dependable and inventive cuisine. To experience the kitchen at its imaginative best, check the night's specials, which often include daringly done seafood. **Known for:** 41 Prime Dip sandwich; nightly specials; creative seafood dishes. [$] *Average main: $23* ✉ *13499 S. Cleveland Ave.* ☎ *239/466–4141* 🌐 *www.bistro41.com.*

$$$ ITALIAN 🍴 **Cibo.** Its flavor-bursting Italian food and its propensity for fresh, quality ingredients keep Cibo (pronounced *chee-bo*) at the head of the class for local Italian restaurants. In contrast to the sophisticated black-and-white setting, the menu comes in colors from the classic Caesar salad with shaved Grana Padano and spaghetti and meatballs to salmon piccata and veal porterhouse with porcini risotto. **Known for:** classic Italian dishes; excellent service; great wine list. [$] *Average main: $24* ✉ *12901 McGregor Blvd.* ☎ *239/454–3700* 🌐 *www.cibofortmyers.com* 🕒 *No lunch.*

$$ ITALIAN 🍴 **Il Pomodoro Cucina Italiana.** We may say *tomato* or *tomahtoe,* but in Italy, they say *pomodoro.* But there's much more than the use of fresh tomatoes to recommend this place to the locals who find their way off the beaten culinary path. **Known for:** rigatoni Bolognese; good pizza; chicken Sinatra. [$] *Average main: $15* ✉ *9681 Gladiolus Dr.* ☎ *239/985–0080* 🌐 *www.ilpomodororestaurant.com* 🕒 *No lunch Sat. May–Dec., closed Sun.*

View 200 phonographs, an invention Thomas Edison patented in 1878, at his Fort Myers winter estate.

$$$ VIETNAMESE 🍴 **Saigon Paris Bistro.** Irish omelets, Belgian waffles, crepes, steak au poivre, Vietnamese sea bass, Waldorf chicken salad: this eatery's extensive menu clearly travels farther abroad than its name implies. And it does so with utmost taste and flavor, as its faithful local clientele will attest. **Known for:** pho soup; two-for-one breakfast deals; international cuisine. [$] *Average main: $21* ✉ *12995 S. Cleveland. Ave., Suite 118* ☎ *239/936–2233* 🌐 *www.saigonparisbistro.com* ⏲ *Closed Mon. June–Sept.*

$ SEAFOOD FAMILY 🍴 **Shrimp Shack.** Seafood lovers, families, and retired snowbirds flock to this venue with its vivacious staff, bustle, and colorful, cartoonish wall murals. Southern-style deep frying prevails—whole-belly clams, grouper, shrimp, onion rings, hush puppies, and fried pork loins—though you can get certain selections broiled or blackened, and there's some New England flavor with seafood rolls at lunch. **Known for:** fried seafood; great burgers; online coupons for free kids meals. [$] *Average main: $13* ✉ *13361 Metro Pkwy.* ☎ *239/561–6817* 🌐 *www.shrimpshackusa.com.*

$$$$ SOUTHERN 🍴 **The Veranda.** Restaurants come and go quickly as downtown reinvents itself, but this one has endured since 1978. A favorite of business and government bigwigs at lunch (the fried-green-tomato salad is signature), it serves imaginative Continental fare with a trace of a Southern accent for dinner. **Known for:** Caesar salad made tableside; prime rib; fresh seafood. [$] *Average main: $34* ✉ *2122 2nd St.* ☎ *239/332–2065* 🌐 *www.verandarestaurant.com* ⏲ *Closed Sun. No lunch Sat.*

WHERE TO STAY

$ HOTEL **Baymont Inn & Suites Fort Myers Airport Hotel.** A top option for its value and facilities, this spot is close to the airport and interstate, with complete business services, a basic gym, and a warm, cozy lobby. **Pros:** near airport; many dining options nearby. **Cons:** no frills; high-traffic area. $ *Rooms from: $160* ✉ *9401 Marketplace Rd.* ☎ *239/454–0040* 🌐 *www.baymontinns.com* 🛏 *85 rooms* 🍴 *Breakfast.*

$$ HOTEL **Crowne Plaza Hotel Fort Myers at the Bell Tower Shops.** Baseball fans often make this hotel home base since spring training and other sports parks are just a few miles away. **Pros:** free airport shuttle; complimentary transportation within a 3-mile radius; laundry facilities. **Cons:** showing signs of age; rooms a bit tight; meeting traffic crowds the lobby. $ *Rooms from: $210* ✉ *13051 Bell Tower Dr.* ☎ *239/482–2900* 🌐 *www.ihg.com* 🛏 *225 rooms* 🍴 *No meals.*

$$ HOTEL **Hilton Garden Inn Fort Myers.** This compact, prettily landscaped low-rise is near Fort Myers's cultural and commercial areas, and a business clientele favors it for its convenience. **Pros:** near lots of shops and restaurants; enjoyable on-site restaurant; large rooms. **Cons:** chain feel; small pool; at busy intersection. $ *Rooms from: $210* ✉ *12600 University Dr.* ☎ *239/790–3500* 🌐 *www.fortmyers.stayhgi.com* 🛏 *126 rooms* 🍴 *Breakfast.*

$ HOTEL **Hotel Indigo, Ft. Myers Downtown River District.** The only modern boutique hotel downtown, it attracts a cosmopolitan set that wants to be in the center of the River District's art, dining, and shopping scene—and just minutes from other attractions. **Pros:** sleek design; walking distance to restaurants and nightlife; tower built in 2009 and lobby part of historic arcade; rooftop bar. **Cons:** must drive to beach; no suites have full kitchens. $ *Rooms from: $199* ✉ *1520 Broadway* ☎ *239/337–3446* 🌐 *www.hotelindigo.com* 🛏 *67 rooms* 🍴 *No meals.*

$$$ RESORT FAMILY Fodor's Choice ★ **Sanibel Harbour Marriott Resort & Spa.** Vacationing families and businesspeople who want luxury pick this sprawling resort complex that towers over the island-studded San Carlos Bay at the last mainland exit before the Sanibel Causeway. **Pros:** top-notch accommodations; full amenities; updated spa. **Cons:** daily parking fee as well as resort fee added to rate; unspectacular beach. $ *Rooms from: $369* ✉ *17260 Harbour Pointe Dr.* ☎ *239/466–4000, 800/767–7777* 🌐 *www.marriott.com* 🛏 *347 rooms* 🍴 *No meals.*

NIGHTLIFE

Buddha Rock Club. A giant gold statue of his Zen-ness out front greets fans—a fun mix of frat boys, retirees, and young professionals—who crowd the casual, smoky bar and groove to hits from live bands and DJs. This is a local favorite. It's closed on Monday nights. ✉ *12701 McGregor Blvd.* ☎ *239/482–8565* 🌐 *buddharockclub.com.*

Crü. Trendsters in the mood for a drink and excellent global tapas crowd the lounge area of this cutting-edge restaurant. The lounge serves food until midnight on weekends. ✉ *13499 S. Cleveland Ave., Suite 241* ☎ *239/466–3663* 🌐 *www.eatcru.com.*

8

Florida Rep. In the restored circa-1915 Arcade Theatre downtown, this top professional company stages Tony- and Pulitzer-winning plays and musicals. There's also an adjacent, more intimate space for edgier works and a Lunchbox Theatre Series for children. ⊠ *2267 1st St.* ☎ *239/332–4488* ⊕ *www.floridarep.org.*

Laugh-In Comedy Cafe. For more than 20 years, this is the place to watch top comedians perform every Friday and Saturday, in a no-smoking atmosphere. ⊠ *College Plaza, 8595 College Pkwy., Suite 300* ☎ *239/479–5233* ⊕ *www.laughincomedycafe.com.*

Stevie Tomato's Sports Page. Five miles up on Interstate 75 from the buzzing Gulf Coast Town Center bars, this is a low-key spot to catch a game and feast on good food; earlier in the evening it's very family-friendly. Best bets are their baby back ribs, Chicago-style pizza, and Italian beef. ⊠ *9510 Market Place Rd.* ☎ *239/939–7211* ⊕ *stevietomato.com.*

SHOPPING

Fleamasters Fleamarket. Just east of downtown, more than 900 vendors sell new and used goods Friday through Sunday 9–5. Its music hall hosts live entertainment. ⊠ *4135 Dr. Martin Luther King Jr. Blvd., 1.7 miles west of I–75 Exit 138* ☎ *239/334–7001* ⊕ *www.fleamall.com.*

Sanibel Outlets. Its boardwalks are lined with outlets for Nike, Van Heusen, Maidenform, Coach, Under Armour, Calvin Klein, and Samsonite, among others. ⊠ *20350 Summerlin Rd.* ☎ *888/471–3939* ⊕ *www.sanibeloutlets.com.*

SPORTS AND THE OUTDOORS

BASEBALL

The region is a popular outpost for spring training teams, with two in Fort Myers.

Boston Red Sox. The Sox settled into new digs in 2012 at JetBlue Park at Fenway South, a 10,823-capacity stadium and 106-acre training facility. The field itself is an exact duplicate of their famous home turf, with a Green Monster wall and manual scoreboard. ⊠ *JetBlue Park, 11581 Daniels Pkwy.* ☎ *239/334–4700, 888/733–7696* ⊕ *boston.redsox.mlb.com.*

Minnesota Twins. The team plays exhibition games in town during March and early April. From April through September, the Miracle (⊕ *www.miraclebaseball.com*), a Twins single-A affiliate, plays home games at Hammond Stadium. ⊠ *Lee County Sports Complex, 14100 6 Mile Cypress Pkwy.* ☎ *800/338–9467* ⊕ *minnesota.twins.mlb.com.*

BIKING

One of the longest bike paths in Fort Myers is along Summerlin Road. It passes commercial areas and gets close to Sanibel through dwindling wide-open spaces. Linear Park, which runs parallel to Six Mile Cypress Parkway, offers more natural, less congested views. Trailhead Park is linked to the new John Yarbrough Linear Park to create a 30-mile pathway, the longest in Lee County.

Bike Route. Since 1974, this is the place to come for a good selection of rentals. ⊠ *8595 College Pkwy., Suite 200* ☎ *239/481–3376* ⊕ *www.thebikeroute.com* ☉ *Closed Sun.*

BOATING AND SAILING

Southwest Florida Yachts. Charter a sailboat or powerboat, or take lessons. With 30 years in the business, they can help you explore southwest Florida like a native. ⊠ *6095 Silver King Blvd., Cape Coral* ☎ *239/656–1339, 800/257–2788* ⊕ *www.swfyachts.com.*

GOLF

Eastwood Golf Course. Golfers love how this Robert von Hagge– and Bruce Devlin–designed course is in an area where there is little development, meaning no homes around the course, just plenty of water, trees, and wildlife (aka gators). The driving range and course are affordable, too, especially if you don't mind playing at unfavorable times (midday in summer, for example). Test your skills on the short par 4 on hole 7, where your second shot is over water. The 10th hole will have you shooting over water, too. ⊠ *4600 Bruce Herd La.* ☎ *239/321–7487* ⊕ *www.cityftmyers.com/eastwood* ⚑ *From $45; rental clubs $15* ⚐ *18 holes, 6772 yards, par 72.*

Fort Myers Country Club. Walk in the footsteps of Thomas Edison and Henry Ford when you play this course known as "The Fort" to its huge fan base. Located less than a mile from the winter estates of these famous inventors, this course is one of the oldest on Florida's west coast. In fact, it was designed in 1916 by Donald Ross and opened in 1917. Number 10 is a par 3 where you can hit anything from a 7 iron to a hybrid as the hole stretches out 203 yards. The Coors Light Open is held here early each year. Next door is a lively restaurant and bar, The Edison. ⊠ *3591 McGregor Blvd.* ☎ *239/321–7488* ⊕ *www.cityftmyers.com/countryclub* ⚑ *$45–$70* ⚐ *18 holes, 6400 yards, par 72.*

Shell Point Golf Club. Newbies to heavy hitters enjoy the layout of this Gordon Lewis–designed course with its challenging fairways and share of water hazards—eight tees on every hole. The front nine play like a symphony, but the back nine can be rough and slow with the wind and their somewhat compacted layouts. If you're looking for a 19th hole where you can toast your one-under-par score, you won't find it here as no alcohol is served. One nice feature at "The Shell" is that they offer Laser Link for accurate yardage to the pin. ⊠ *17401 On Par Blvd.* ☎ *239/433–9790* ⊕ *www.shellpointgolf.com* ⚑ *$85* ⚐ *18 holes, 6880 yards, par 71.*

KAYAKING

Calusa Blueway Outfitters. Paddling enthusiasts can rent kayaks to explore the Manatee Park environs daily from Thanksgiving to Easter and on weekends in the summer; clinics and guided tours are also available, but go in winter if spotting sea cows is your aim. ⊠ *Manatee Park, 10901 Palm Beach Blvd., 1¼ miles east of I-75 Exit 141* ☎ *239/481–4600* ⊕ *www.calusabluewayoutfitters.com.*

8

CAPE CORAL, PINE ISLAND, AND NORTH FORT MYERS

13 miles from downtown Fort Myers.

Cape Coral is determinedly trying to move from its pigeonhole as a residential community by attracting tourism with its downtown reconfiguration, the Resort at Marina Village, and destination restaurants at the Cape Harbour residential marina development.

GETTING HERE AND AROUND

Four bridges cross from Fort Myers to Cape Coral and North Fort Myers. Pine Island–Bayshore Road (Route 78) leads from North Fort Myers through northern Cape Coral onto off-the-beaten path Pine Island, known for its art galleries, fishing, and exotic fruit farms.

EXPLORING

Calusa Heritage Trail. Affiliated with the University of Florida's natural history museum in Gainesville, this 0.7-mile interpretive walkway explores the site of an ancient Calusa village—more than 1,500 years old—with excellent signage, two intact shell mounds you can climb, the remains of a complex canal system, and ongoing archaeological research. Guided tours are given three times a week from January to April. Check the website for special tours and lecture events. ⌂ *Randell Research Center, 13810 Waterfront Dr., Bokeelia, Pineland* ☎ *239/283–2157* ⊕ *www.flmnh.ufl.edu/rrc* ✍ *$7 (suggested donation).*

OFF THE
BEATEN
PATH

ECHO Global Farm Tours & Nursery. ECHO is an international Christian nonprofit striving to end world hunger via creative farming. A 90-minute tour of its working farm is honestly fascinating; it takes you through seven simulated tropic-zone gardens and has you tasting leaves, walking through rain-forest habitat, visiting farm animals, stopping at a simulated Haitian school, witnessing urban gardens grown inside tires on rooftops, and learning about ECHO's mission. Although the group is religiously based, the tour guides are far from preachy, plus the organization's scope is all-inclusive, equipping and training people who deserve it no matter what their beliefs are. If you have time, spring for the Appropriate Technology Tour. It's held in a covered facility and runs slightly shorter than the basic Global Farm Tour, and you'll see simple contraptions that give ingenious solutions to everyday challenges in the developing world, like pressing seeds and making rope (spoiler alert—one involves a bicycle-powered saw). The ECHO Global Nursery and Gift Shop sells fruit trees and the same seeds ECHO distributes to impoverished farmers in 180 countries. ⌂ *17391 Durrance Rd., North Fort Myers* ☎ *239/543–3246* ⊕ *www.echonet.org* ✍ *$12.50.*

FAMILY

Shell Factory & Nature Park. This entertainment complex, once just a quirky shopping destination and a survivor from Florida's roadside-attraction era, now contains eateries, an arcade, bumper boats, miniature golf, and a mining sluice where kids can pan for shells, fossils, and gemstones. Strolling the grounds is free, including seeing over $6 million worth of exhibits and displays, but some activities carry individual fees, and a separate admission is required to enter the Nature Park, which has the feel of a small zoo. There you can find llamas; a

PUNTA GORDA DAY TRIP

A half hour (23 miles) north of Fort Myers, the small, old town of Punta Gorda merits a day trip for its restaurants and historic sites. If you're driving to Boca Grande via U.S. 41, it also makes a nice stop along the way. On the mouth of the Peace River, where it empties into Charlotte Harbor, a new riverfront park, water views, and murals enliven the compact downtown historic district. Away from the downtown area, a classic-car museum, wildlife rehabilitation center, and waterfront shopping complex built into an old fish-packing plant fills out a day of sightseeing. Fishing and nature-watching tours also depart from the Fishermen's Village complex.

petting farm with sheep, pigs, and goats; a walk-through aviary; an EcoLab; a touch center; and a gator slough. The Shell Factory hosts family-friendly events throughout the year, such as the Gumbo Fest in January. It's newest addition is the Soaring Eagle Zipline. ✉ *2787 N. Tamiami Trail, North Fort Myers* ☎ *239/995–2141* 🌐 *www.shellfactory.com* 🎟 *Shell Factory free; attractions starting at $2 each; Nature Park $12* 🕒 *Shell Factory daily 9–7; Nature Park daily 10–5.*

FAMILY Fodor's Choice ★ **Sun Splash Family Waterpark.** Head here to cool off when summer swelters. Nearly two dozen wet and dry attractions include 10 thrill waterslides; the Sand Dollar Walk, where you step from one floating "sand dollar" to another; pint-sized Pro Racer flumes; a professional sand volleyball court; a family pool and Tot Spot; and a river-tube ride. Rates go down after 2 pm, plus the park offers Family Fun Night specials. ✉ *400 Santa Barbara Blvd., Cape Coral* ☎ *239/574–0558* 🌐 *www.sunsplashwaterpark.com* 🎟 *$17.95.*

8

OFF THE BEATEN PATH

Babcock Wilderness Adventures. To see what Florida looked like centuries ago, visit Babcock's Crescent B Ranch, northeast of Fort Myers. During the 90-minute swamp-buggy-style excursion you ride in a converted school bus through several ecosystems, including the unusual and fascinating Telegraph Cypress Swamp. Along the way an informative and typically amusing guide describes the area's social and natural history while you keep an eye peeled for alligators, wild pigs, all sorts of birds, Florida panthers, and other denizens of the wild. The tour also takes in the ranch's resident cattle and cougar in captivity. Reservations are needed for tours. An on-site restaurant serves "Cracker" chow in season. ✉ *8000 Rte. 31, Punta Gorda* ☎ *800/500–5583* 🌐 *www.babcockranch.com* 🎟 *Ecotour $24; cost for other specialty tours varies* ✍ *Reservations essential.*

WHERE TO EAT

$ AMERICAN 🍴 **Bert's Bar & Grill.** Looking to hang out with the locals of Pine Island? Here you'll find cheap eats, live entertainment, a pool table, and a water view to boot. **Known for:** great views; grouper Reuben sandwiches; homemade key lime pie. [$] *Average main: $9* ✉ *4271 Pine Island Rd., Matlacha* ☎ *239/282–3232* 🌐 *www.bertsbar.com.*

$ ✕ **Rumrunners.** Cape Coral's best casual cuisine is surprisingly afford-
AMERICAN able, considering the luxury condo development that rises around it and the size of the yachts that pull up to the docks. Caribbean in spirit, with lots of indoor and outdoor views of a mangrove-fringed waterway, it serves bistro specialties such as conch fritters, seafood potpie, bronzed salmon, and a warm chocolate bread pudding that is addictive. **Known for:** coconut fried shrimp; seafood potpie; Rumrun-ner cocktails. $ *Average main: $13* ✉ *Cape Harbour Marina, 5848 Cape Harbour Dr., off Chiquita Blvd., Cape Coral* ☎ *239/542–0200* ⊕ *www.rumrunnersrestaurant.com.*

$ ✕ **Siam Hut.** Lunch and dinner menus at this Cape Coral fixture let
THAI you design your own stir-fry, noodle, or fried-rice dish. Dinner spe-cialties include fried crispy frogs' legs with garlic and black pepper, a sizzling shrimp platter, fried whole tilapia with curry sauce, salads, and pad Thai (rice noodles, egg, ground peanuts, vegetables, and choice of protein). **Known for:** duck royal with pineapple, tomato, and red curry; stir-fry dishes; special fried rice with meat and sea-food. $ *Average main: $14* ✉ *4521 Del Prado Blvd., Cape Coral* ☎ *239/945–4247* ⊕ *www.siamhutcapecoral.com* ☾ *Closed Sun. No lunch Sat.*

WHERE TO STAY

$ ⛆ **Casa Loma Motel.** Stay at this pretty little motel, 15 minutes from
HOTEL Fort Myers at the end of the Croton Canal, to be close to Cape Coral's attractions and escape the sticker shock of beachfront lodgings. **Pros:** kitchen facilities in rooms; free Wi-Fi; large sundeck with canal access. **Cons:** must drive to beach; on a busy street; decor a bit dated; no res-taurant. $ *Rooms from: $119* ✉ *3608 Del Prado Blvd., Cape Coral* ☎ *239/549–6000, 877/227–2566* ⊕ *www.casalomamotel.com* ⇗ *49 rooms* ⦿ *No meals.*

$ ⛆ **Tarpon Lodge.** A no-frills escape, this lodge, named for a local game
B&B/INN fish, was built in 1926 on a sweep of green lawn with magnificent views out to sea. **Pros:** waterfront view; historic property; great res-taurant; can dock boats overnight. **Cons:** some rooms are basic; far from other restaurants; quite far from beach by land. $ *Rooms from: $185* ✉ *13771 Waterfront Dr., Pineland* ☎ *239/283–3999* ⊕ *www. tarponlodge.com* ⇗ *20 rooms, 2 cottages* ⦿ *Breakfast.*

$$$ ⛆ **The Westin Cape Coral Resort at Marina Village.** Cape Coral's only luxury
RESORT resort, this modern 19-story tower sits alongside a marina fringed with mangroves and caters to families and water-sports enthusiasts. **Pros:** designer touches; kids club; great kayaking. **Cons:** 45-minute ferry to beach; high-rise. $ *Rooms from: $309* ✉ *5951 Silver King Blvd., Cape Coral* ☎ *239/541–5000, 888/372–9256* ⊕ *www.westincapecoral.com* ⇗ *264 units* ⦿ *No meals.*

THE COASTAL ISLANDS

A maze of islands in various stages of habitation fronts Fort Myers mainland, separated by the Intracoastal Waterway. Some are accessible via a causeway; to reach others, you need a boat. If you cut through bay waters, you have a good chance of being escorted by bottlenose dolphins. Mostly birds and other wild creatures inhabit some islands, which are given over to state parks. Traveler-pampering hotels on Sanibel, Captiva, and Fort Myers Beach give way to rustic cottages, old inns, and cabins on quiet Cabbage Key and Pine Island, which have no beaches because they lie between the barrier islands and mainland. Others are devoted to resorts. When exploring barrier island beaches, keep one eye on the sand: collecting seashells is a major pursuit in these parts.

GASPARILLA ISLAND (BOCA GRANDE)

43 miles northwest of Fort Myers.

Before roads to the Lower Gulf Coast were even talked about, wealthy Northerners came by train to spend the winter at the Gasparilla Inn. The inn was completed in 1913 in Boca Grande on Gasparilla Island, named, legend has it, for a Spanish pirate who set up headquarters in these waters. Although condominiums and modern mansions occupy the rest of Gasparilla, much of the town of Boca Grande evokes another era. The mood is set by the Old Florida homes and tree-framed roadways. The island's calm is disrupted in the spring when anglers descend with a vengeance on Boca Grande Pass, considered among the best tarpon-fishing spots in the world.

8

GETTING HERE AND AROUND

Boca Grande is more than an hour's drive northwest of Fort Myers. Day-trippers can catch a charter boat or rent a boat, dock at a marina, and rent a bike or golf cart for a day of exploring and lunching. North of it stretches a long island, home to Don Pedro Island State Park and Palm Island Resort, both accessible only by boat. Also nearby is the off-the-beaten-path but car-accessible island of Manasota Key and its fishing resort community of Englewood Beach.

EXPLORING

Gasparilla Island State Park and Port Boca Grande Lighthouse Museum. The island's beaches are its greatest prize and lie within the state park at the south end. The long, narrow beach ends at Boca Grande Pass, famous for its deep waters and tarpon fishing. The pretty, two-story, circa-1890 lighthouse once marked the pass for mariners. In recent years it has been restored as a museum that explores the island's fishing and railroad heritage. The lighthouse is closed in August. ⊠ *880 Belcher Rd., Boca Grande* ☎ *941/964–0060* ⊕ *www.floridastateparks. org/gasparillaisland* ☜ *$3 per vehicle; $3 suggested donation to lighthouse (exact change only).*

WHERE TO EAT

$$$ AMERICAN 🍴 **The Loose Caboose.** Revered by many—including Katharine Hepburn in her time—for its homemade ice cream, this is also a good spot for solid, affordable fare. Housed in the town's historic depot, it offers indoor and patio seating in an all-American setting. **Known for:** extremely rich (16% butterfat) ice cream; green tomatoes and crab cake appetizer; Caboose Thai shrimp. [$] *Average main: $24* ✉ *433 W. 4th St., Boca Grande* ☎ *941/964–0440* 🌐 *www.loosecaboose.biz* ⏰ *No dinner Wed. or Apr.–Dec.*

WHERE TO STAY

$$$ HOTEL 🏨 **Gasparilla Inn & Club.** Once the playground of social-register members such as the Vanderbilts and DuPonts, the gracious pale-yellow wooden hotel was built by shipping industrialists in the early 1900s. **Pros:** historic property; nicely renovated. **Cons:** expensive rates; the quirks of a very old building. [$] *Rooms from: $385* ✉ *500 Palm Ave., Boca Grande* ☎ *941/964–2201, 800/996–1913* 🌐 *www.gasparillainn.com* 🛏 *137 rooms, 23 cottages* 🍽 *Some meals.*

CABBAGE KEY

5 miles south of Boca Grande.

Cabbage Key is the ultimate island-hopping escape in these parts. Some say Jimmy Buffett was inspired to write "Cheeseburger in Paradise" after a visit to its popular restaurant.

GETTING HERE AND AROUND

You'll need to take a boat—from Bokeelia or Pineland, on Pine Island, or from Captiva Island—to get to this island, which sits at mile marker 60 on the Intracoastal Waterway. Local operators offer day trips and luncheon cruises.

8

WHERE TO STAY

$ HOTEL 🏨 **Cabbage Key Inn.** Atop an ancient Calusa Indian shell mound and accessible only by boat, the friendly, somewhat quirky inn built by novelist and playwright Mary Roberts Rinehart in 1938 welcomes guests seeking quiet and isolation. **Pros:** plenty of solitude; Old Florida character. **Cons:** two-night minimum stay; accessible only by boat or seaplane; limited amenities, some rooms have no TV; in season the restaurant is busy. [$] *Rooms from: $175* ✉ *Cabbage Key* ☎ *239/283–2278* 🌐 *www.cabbagekey.com* 🛏 *6 rooms, 8 cottages* 🍽 *No meals.*

SANIBEL AND CAPTIVA ISLANDS

23 miles southwest of downtown Fort Myers.

Sanibel Island is famous as one of the world's best shelling grounds, a function of the unusual east–west orientation of the island's south end. Just as the tide is going out and after storms, the pickings can be superb, and shell seekers performing the telltale "Sanibel stoop" patrol every beach carrying bags of conchs, whelks, cockles, and other bivalves and gastropods. (Remember, it's unlawful to pick up live shells.) Away from the beach, flowery vegetation decorates small shopping complexes, pleasant resorts and condo complexes, mom-and-pop motels, and casual restaurants. But much of the two-lane road down the spine of the island is bordered by nature reserves that have made Sanibel as well known among bird-watchers as it is among seashell collectors.

Captiva Island, connected to the northern end of Sanibel by a bridge, is quirky and engaging. At the end of a twisty road lined with million-dollar mansions lies a delightful village of shops, eateries, and beaches.

GETTING HERE AND AROUND

Sanibel Island is approximately 23 miles southwest of downtown Fort Myers, and Captiva lies north of 12-mile-long Sanibel. If you're flying into Southwest Florida International Airport, an on-demand taxi for up to three passengers to Sanibel or Captiva costs about $60 to $68; additional passengers are charged $10 each. Sanibel Island is accessible from the mainland via the Sanibel Causeway (toll $6 round-trip). Captiva Island lies across a small pass from Sanibel's north end, accessible by bridge.

ESSENTIALS

Visitor Information Sanibel and Captiva Islands Chamber of Commerce. ✉ *1159 Causeway Rd., Sanibel* ☎ *239/472–1080* ⊕ *www.sanibel-captiva.org.*

EXPLORING

FAMILY

Fodor'sChoice

★

Bailey-Matthews National Shell Museum. There have been big changes here at the museum and it all starts before you even enter, with giant shell photos on the exterior of the building by nature photographer Henry Domke. Once inside, there are more than 30 permanent and short-term exhibits. See a life-size display of native Calusa and how they used shells. From tiny to enormous, view local specimens and a variety from around the world. Play in the colorful kids' lab. Watch movies about how shells are formed and where to find them. Get a close-up look at mollusks in the 8-foot-long, live-viewing tank. The museum has also added two full-time marine biologists who lead daily tank talks (at 11:30 and 3), host daily guided beach walks, and lead a weekly marine naturalist cruise (Thursday). From colossal squids to Shelling 101, make this your first stop and you'll be giving your own talks on the beach. Don't miss the museum store, filled with upscale nautical gifts. ✉ *3075 Sanibel–Captiva Rd., Sanibel* ☎ *239/395–2233, 888/679–6450* ⊕ *www. shellmuseum.org* 🎟 *$15.*

Clinic for the Rehabilitation of Wildlife (C.R.O.W.). In existence for more than 40 years, the clinic currently cares for more than 4,000 wildlife patients each year. The center offers a look inside the world of wildlife medicine through exhibits, videos, interactive displays, touch screens, and critter cams that feed live footage from four different animal spaces. Wildlife walks give a behind-the-scenes look and can be reserved for $20 per person. This is an excellent facility, but the displays may be too graphic for young visitors. ✉ *3883 Sanibel–Captiva Rd., Sanibel* ☎ *239/472–3644* ⊕ *www.crowclinic.org* 🎟 *$7.*

Continued on page 426

SHELL-BENT ON SANIBEL ISLAND

by Chelle Koster Walton

Sanibel Island beachgoers are an unusual breed: they pray for storms; they muck around tidal pools rather than play in the waves; and instead of lifting their faces to the sun, they have their heads in the sand—almost literally—as they engage in the so-called "Sanibel Stoop."

Odd? Not when you consider that this is Florida's prime shelling location, thanks to the island's east-west bend (rather than the usual north-south orientation of most beaches along the coastline). The lay of the land means a treasure trove of shells—more than 400 species—wash up from the Caribbean.

These gifts from the sea draw collectors of all levels. Come winter, when the cold and storms kill the shellfish and push them ashore, a parade of stoopers forms on Sanibel's shores.

The reasons people shell are as varied as the shellers themselves. The hardcore compete and sell, whereas others collect simply for the fun of discovery, for displaying, for use in gardens, or for crafts. The typical Sanibel tourist who comes seeking shells is usually looking for souvenirs and gifts to take home.

WHERE TO SHELL

Shelling is good anywhere along Sanibel's gulf-front. Remote **Bowman's Beach** (*off Sanibel-Captiva Road at Bowman's Beach Rd.*) offers the least competition. Other public accesses include **Lighthouse Beach** (Periwinkle Way), **Tarpon Bay Beach** (Tarpon Bay Rd.), and **Turner Beach** (Sanibel-Captiva Rd.). If you want to ditch your car (and crowds), walk or bike using **resident access beaches** (along the Gulf drives). If you want to search with others and get a little guidance, you can join shelling cruises from Sanibel and Captiva islands to the unbridged island of Cayo Costa. Cruises leave from both islands and usually include pickup from your hotel or condo. Most are done on a covered catamaran.

Captiva
Island

Captiva

Turner
Beach

Bowman's
Beach

SANIBEL ISLAND

Sanibel

Lighthouse
Beach

Tarpon Bay
Beach

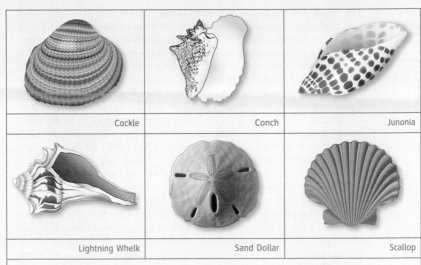

Cockle	Conch	Junonia
Lightning Whelk	Sand Dollar	Scallop

TYPES OF SHELLS

Cockles: The common Sanibel bivalve (hinged two-shelled mollusk), the heart cockle (named for its Valentine shape) is larger and more bowl-like than the scallop, which makes it a popular, colorful find for soap dishes, ashtrays, and catch-alls.

Conchs: Of the large family of conchs, fighting conchs are most commonly found on Sanibel. Contrary to its macho name, the fighting conch is one of the few vegetarian gastropods. While alive, the shell flames brilliant orange; it fades under tropical sunshine.

Junonias: These olive-shaped, spotted gastropods (single-shell mollusks) are Sanibel's signature, though somewhat rare, finds. People who hit upon one get their picture in the local paper. Resorts have been accused of planting them on their beaches for publicity.

Lightning Whelks: The lightning variety of whelk is "left-handed"—opening on the opposite side from most gastropods. Early islanders used them for tools. The animals lay their miniature shell eggs in papery egg-case chains on the beach.

Sand Dollars: Classified as an echinoderm not a mollusk, the thin sand dollar is brown and fuzzy while alive, studded with tiny tubes for breathing and moving. Unoccupied shells bleach to a beautiful white textured pattern, ideal for hanging on Christmas trees.

Scallops: No surprise that these pretty little bivalves have "scalloped" edges. They invented the word. Plentiful on Sanibel beaches, they come in a variety of colors and sizes.

SHELLING LIKE A PRO

Veteran shell-seekers go out before the sun rises so they can be the first on the beach after a storm or night of high tides. (Storms and cold fronts bring in the best catches.)

Most shellers use a bag to collect their finds. But once you're ready to pack shells for transit, wash them thoroughly to remove sand and debris. Then wrap fragile species such as sand dollars and sea urchins in tissue paper or cotton, then newspaper. Last, place your shells in a cardboard or plastic box. To display them, restore the shell's luster by brushing it with baby oil.

Sanibel shops sell books and supplies for identifying your finds and turning them into craft projects.

FAMILY
Fodor's Choice
★

J.N. "Ding" Darling National Wildlife Refuge. More than half of Sanibel is occupied by the subtly beautiful 6,300 acres of wetlands and jungly mangrove forests named after a conservation-minded Pulitzer prize–winning political cartoonist. The masses of roseate spoonbills and ibis and the winter flock of white pelicans here make for a good show even if you're not a die-hard bird-watcher. Birders have counted some 230 species, including herons, ospreys, and the timid mangrove cuckoo. Raccoons, otters, alligators, and a lone American crocodile also may be spotted. The 4-mile Wildlife Drive is the main way to explore the preserve; drive, walk, or bicycle along it, or ride a specially designed open-air tram with an onboard naturalist. QR-coded signs link to interactive YouTube videos and a new "Discover Ding" app combines social media, GPS, and trivia to make learning on-site fun. There are also a couple of short walking trails, including one to a Calusa shell mound. Or explore from the water via canoe or kayak (guided tours are available). The best time for bird-watching is in the early morning and about an hour before or after low tide; the observation tower along the road offers prime viewing. Interactive exhibits in the free visitor center, at the entrance to the refuge, demonstrate the refuge's various ecosystems and explain its status as a rest stop along a major bird-migration route. A new hands-on manatee exhibit was recently unveiled, too. Wildlife Drive is closed to vehicular traffic on Friday, but you can still kayak and do tours from the Tarpon Bay Recreation Area. ⊠ *1 Wildlife Dr., off Sanibel–Captiva Rd. at MM 2, Sanibel* ☎ *239/472–1100 for refuge, 239/472–8900 kayaking and tours* ⊕ *www.fws.gov/dingdarling* ⊒ *$5 per car, $1 for pedestrians and bicyclists, tram $13.*

FAMILY
Sanibel–Captiva Conservation Foundation. For a quiet walk to watch for inhabitants of Sanibel's interior wetlands, follow some or all of the 4½ miles of interlocking walking trails here and climb the observation tower. View information about wildlife research projects, a butterfly house, live turtles, snakes, and a marine touch tank at the nature center. In winter, guided walks and programs are available on and off property. ⊠ *3333 Sanibel–Captiva Rd., Sanibel* ☎ *239/472–2329* ⊕ *www.sccf.org* ⊒ *$5; 17 and under are free.*

Sanibel Historical Museum & Village. Charming buildings from the island's past include a general store, a one-room schoolhouse, a 1927 post office, a tearoom, a 1925 winter-vacation cottage, a 1898 fishing cottage, and the 1913 Rutland House Museum, containing old documents and photographs, artifacts, and period furnishings. All buildings are authentic and have been moved from their original locations to the museum grounds. ⊠ *950 Dunlop Rd., Sanibel* ☎ *239/472–4648* ⊕ *www.sanibelmuseum.org* ⊒ *$10.*

BEACHES

Red tide, an occasional natural beach occurrence that kills fish, also has negative effects on the human respiratory system. It causes scratchy throats, runny eyes and noses, and coughing. Although the effects aren't long-term, it's a good idea to avoid the beach when red tide is in the vicinity (look for posted signs).

SANIBEL

FAMILY **Bowman's Beach.** This long, wide beach on Sanibel's northwest end is the island's most secluded strand, but it also has the most amenities. Park facilities include a playground, picnic tables, grills, bathrooms, and bike racks. It is famed for its shell collecting and spectacular sunsets at the north end—try to spot the green flash, said to occur just as the sun sinks below the horizon. For utmost seclusion, walk north from the two main access points where bridges cross an estuary to reach the beach. It's a long walk from the parking lot over the estuary to the beach, so pack accordingly and plan on a long stay. Tall Australian pines provide shade behind the white sands. Typically gentle waves are conducive to swimming and wading with kids. **Amenities:** parking (fee); showers; toilets. **Best for:** sunsets; swimming; walking. ⊠ *Bowman Beach Rd., at Blind Pass, Sanibel* ☎ *239/472–3700* 🅿 *Parking $4 per hr.*

FAMILY **Gulfside Park Preserve.** The beach is quiet, safe from strong currents, and good for solitude, bird-watching, and shell-finding. There are restrooms, and long stretches to stroll. The white sand is slightly coarse and borders a park with shade, picnic tables, and a loop nature trail. Low-rise resorts and homes lie to the east and west of the parking lot accesses. **Amenities:** parking (fee); toilets. **Best for:** swimming; walking. ⊠ *Algiers La., off Casa Ybel Rd., Sanibel* ☎ *239/472–3700* 🅿 *Parking $4 per hr.*

Lighthouse Beach. At Sanibel's eastern tip, the beach is guarded by the frequently photographed Sanibel Lighthouse, built in 1884, before the island was settled. The lighthouse is not currently open to the public, but there's talk of refurbishing the tower so visitors can climb to the top. The park rounds the island's east end for waterfront on both the Gulf and bay, where a fishing pier draws avid anglers. Shaded nature trails connect the two shores; the park is listed on the Great Florida Birding Trail because of its fall and spring migration fallouts. A pair of ospreys frequently perch on the lighthouse railing; look and listen for these local residents while you're there. **Amenities:** parking (fee); toilets. **Best for:** sunrise; walking; windsurfing. ⊠ *East end of Periwinkle Way, Sanibel* ☎ *239/472–3700* 🅿 *Parking $4 per hr.*

Tarpon Bay Beach. This centrally located beach is safer for swimming than beaches at the passes, where waters move swiftly. It is, however, one of the more populated beaches, lined with low-rise condos and resorts set back behind vegetation. Casa Ybel Resort lies east of the public access; other smaller resorts can be found along the stretch to the west. The parking lot is a five-minute walk from the beach, so drop off your gang and gear before you park (the lot is open daily from 7 am to 7 pm). At the beach, you can walk for miles in either direction on soft white sand studded with shells. **Amenities:** parking (fee); toilets. **Best for:** swimming; walking. ⊠ *Off Sanibel–Captiva Rd., Tarpon Bay Rd. at Gulf Dr., Sanibel* ✚ *Drive to the end of W. Gulf Dr. and east to Casa Ybel Rd.* ☎ *239/472–3700* 🅿 *Parking $4 per hr.*

CAPTIVA

FAMILY **Alison Hagerup Beach Park.** This park, once called Captiva Beach, is acclaimed as one of the nation's most romantic beaches for its fabulous sunsets—the best view on Sanibel and Captiva. Shells stud the white, wide sands. The parking lot is filled with potholes and is small, so arrive early, watch where you're driving, and bring an umbrella if you need shade. The beach can get crowded, especially in the busy winter and spring seasons. Facilities are limited to portable restrooms and a volleyball net, but stores and restaurants are nearby. South Seas Island Resort lines the north end of the beach. **Amenities:** parking (fee); toilets. **Best for:** sunsets; swimming; walking. ✉ *Captiva Dr., at the north end, Captiva* 🎫 *Parking 2 hrs $5, 5 hrs $10.*

Turner Beach. Looking for some romance? This is a prime sunset-watching spot on the southern point of Captiva. Strong currents through Blind Pass make swimming tricky but shelling amazing, and parking is limited. Surfers head here when winds whip up the waves. The beach is narrower than in other parts of the island. No buildings sit on the beach, but 'Tween Waters Resort is across the road to the north of the public access, and Castaways Beach & Bay Cottages is beachfront across the bridge on the Sanibel side of Blind Pass. Restaurants are nearby. **Amenities:** parking (fee); toilets. **Best for:** sunsets; surfing; walking. ✉ *Captiva Dr., at Blind Pass, Captiva* 🎫 *Parking $4 per hr.*

WHERE TO EAT

SANIBEL

$ AMERICAN FAMILY

🍴 **Lazy Flamingo.** At two Sanibel locations, plus two more in neighboring Fort Myers and Pine Island Sound, this is a friendly neighborhood hangout enjoyed by locals and visitors alike. All of these restaurants have a funky nautical look à la Key West and a popular following for their Dead Parrot Wings (buffalo wings coated with tongue-scorching hot sauce), mesquite-grilled grouper sandwiches, burgers, and steamer pots. **Known for:** mesquite-grilled grouper; family-friendly atmosphere; fiery Dead Parrot Wings. [$] *Average main: $12* ✉ *6520C Pine Ave., Sanibel* ☎ *239/472–5353* 🌐 *www.lazyflamingo.com.*

$$ AMERICAN

🍴 **Over Easy Café.** Locals head to this chicken-theme eatery mainly for breakfast and lunch, although it also serves dinner in season. Kickstart the day with the egg Reuben sandwich, veggie Benedict, pancakes, or omelets such as crab and asparagus or "meat-lovers." **Known for:** smoked salmon Benedict; all-day breakfast; egg Reuben sandwich. [$] *Average main: $16* ✉ *630-1 Tarpon Bay Rd., Sanibel* ☎ *239/472–2625* 🌐 *www.overeasycafesanibel.com* 🕒 *No dinner.*

$$$ MODERN AMERICAN Fodor's Choice ★

🍴 **Sweet Melissa's Cafe.** You've seen them before, those people who take photos of their food: you'll become one of them when you eat here. Choose from full portions or small plates, but the latter are recommended so that you can savor more outstanding dishes in one sitting. **Known for:** imaginative cuisine; fish stew; impeccable service. [$] *Average main: $25* ✉ *1625 Periwinkle Way, Sanibel* ☎ *239/472–1956* 🌐 *www.sweetmelissascafe.com* 🕒 *No lunch weekends.*

$$$$ CONTEMPORARY Fodor's Choice ★

🍴 **Thistle Lodge Restaurant.** Now this is romance: the lodge was built as a wedding gift from a husband to his wife and is now a gift to those lucky enough to dine here. Lush green grounds are right outside the window, then just beyond is the Gulf of Mexico and Sanibel's seashell-laden shores. **Known for:** romantic atmosphere; fresh seafood; Gulf views. [$] *Average main: $35* ✉ *Casa Ybel Resort, 2255 W. Gulf Dr., Sanibel* ☎ *239/472–9200* 🌐 *www.thistlelodge.com.*

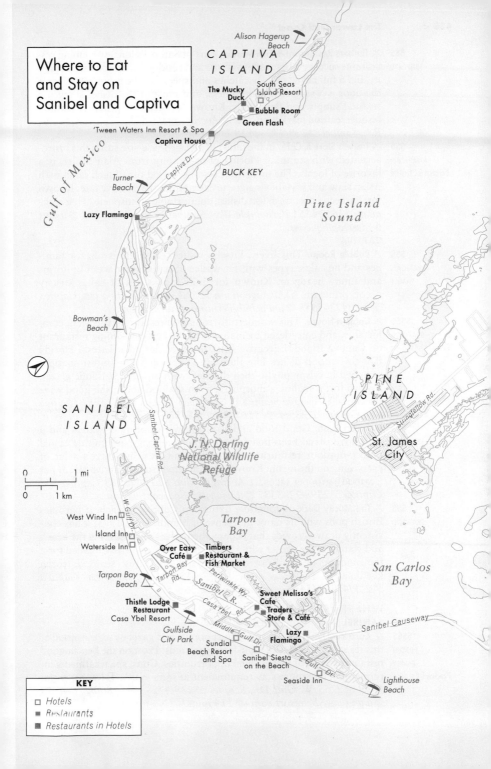

Where to Eat and Stay on Sanibel and Captiva

Alison Hagerup Beach

CAPTIVA ISLAND

The Mucky Duck

South Seas Island Resort

Bubble Room

Green Flash

'Tween Waters Inn Resort & Spa

Captiva House

Captiva Dr.

BUCK KEY

Gulf of Mexico

Turner Beach

Pine Island Sound

Lazy Flamingo

Bowman's Beach

SANIBEL ISLAND

Sanibel-Captiva Rd.

J. N. Darling National Wildlife Refuge

PINE ISLAND

Stringfellow Rd.

St. James City

0   1 mi
0   1 km

Tarpon Bay

West Wind Inn

W. Gulf Dr.

Island Inn

Waterside Inn

Over Easy Café

Timbers Restaurant & Fish Market

Tarpon Bay Rd.

Tarpon Bay Beach

Periwinkle Wy.

Sanibel E. R.

Sweet Melissa's Cafe

San Carlos Bay

Thistle Lodge Restaurant

Casa Ybel Rd.

Traders Store & Café

Casa Ybel Resort

Gulfside City Park

Middle Gulf Dr.

Sundial Beach Resort and Spa

Lazy Flamingo

Sanibel Siesta on the Beach

Sanibel Causeway

E. Gulf Dr.

Seaside Inn

Lighthouse Beach

KEY

□ *Hotels*
■ *Restaurants*
■ *Restaurants in Hotels*

$$$ SEAFOOD

🍴 **Timbers Restaurant & Fish Market.** One of Sanibel's longest-running restaurants successfully satisfies visitors and residents with consistent quality and a full net of nightly catches and specials. The fish market inside the door is a sure sign of freshness, and most of the dishes showcase seafood simply and flavorfully. **Known for:** crunchy grouper; seafood bisque; seafood market on-site. [$] *Average main: $21* ✉ *703 Tarpon Bay Rd., Sanibel* ☎ *239/472–3128* 🌐 *www.prawnbroker.com.*

$$$ AMERICAN Fodor's Choice ★

🍴 **Traders Store & Café.** In the midst of a warehouse-size store, this bistro, accented with stunning Florida photography from Alan Maltz, is a favorite of locals. The marvelous sesame-seared tuna lunch salad with Asian slaw and wasabi vinaigrette exemplifies the creative fare. **Known for:** barbecue ribs; fresh fish dishes; comfortable atmosphere. [$] *Average main: $26* ✉ *1551 Periwinkle Way, Sanibel* ☎ *239/472–7242* 🌐 *www.traderssanibel.com.*

CAPTIVA

$$$ AMERICAN FAMILY

🍴 **Bubble Room.** This lively, kitschy visitors' favorite is fun for families and nostalgic types with fat wallets. Servers wear scout uniforms and funny headgear. **Known for:** mile-high slices of cake; kitschy decor; prime rib. [$] *Average main: $25* ✉ *15001 Captiva Dr., Captiva* ☎ *239/472–5558* 🌐 *www.bubbleroomrestaurant.com.*

$$$$ SEAFOOD Fodor's Choice ★

🍴 **Captiva House.** This wonderfully romantic restaurant is casual, comfortable, and considered by many to be the best fine-dining restaurant on Captiva Island. Executive Chef Jason Miller adds a fresh, Florida flair to seafood dishes like the island snapper wrap (moist snapper wrapped in crispy phyllo then drizzled with an aged balsamic glaze). **Known for:** romantic atmosphere; fresh seafood and sushi; good wine selection. [$] *Average main: $32* ✉ *'Tween Waters Inn, 15951 Captiva Dr., Captiva* ☎ *239/472–5161* 🌐 *captiva-house.com.*

$$$ SEAFOOD

🍴 **Green Flash.** Good food and sweeping views of quiet waters and a mangrove island keep boaters and others coming back to this casual indoor-outdoor restaurant. Seafood dominates, but there's a bit of everything on the menu. **Known for:** shrimp bisque; Captiva steam pot (seafood); grouper tacos. [$] *Average main: $23* ✉ *15183 Captiva Dr., Captiva* ☎ *239/472–3337* 🌐 *www.greenflashcaptiva.com.*

$$$ SEAFOOD

🍴 **The Mucky Duck.** A longtime fixture on Captiva's beach, it parodies British pubs with its name and sense of humor. Since 1975, it has consistently drawn crowds that occupy themselves with walking the beach and watching the sunset while waiting for their name to be called for a table indoors or out. **Known for:** fish-and-chips; fresh seafood; frozen key lime pie. [$] *Average main: $24* ✉ *11546 Andy Rosse La., Captiva* ☎ *239/472–3434* 🌐 *www.muckyduck.com.*

WHERE TO STAY

SANIBEL

$$$$ RESORT FAMILY Fodor's Choice ★

🏨 **Casa Ybel Resort.** Palm trees, quiet ponds, and gazebos set the mood at this resort on 23 acres of Gulf-facing grounds. **Pros:** on the beach; good restaurants; lots of recreational opportunities. **Cons:** spa treatments in-room only; minimum-stay requirement in some units. [$] *Rooms from: $599* ✉ *2255 W. Gulf Dr., Sanibel* ☎ *239/472–3145, 800/276–4753* 🌐 *www.casaybelresort.com* 🛏 *114 units* 🍴 *No meals.*

$$$ RESORT

Island Inn. Choose from your own cottage on the beach, or take your pick from six different styles of modernized hotel rooms at the most established inn on Sanibel. **Pros:** right on the beach; free breakfast; laundry facilities. **Cons:** minimum stays in season; furniture and bathrooms are dated in some units. [$] *Rooms from: $360* ✉ *3111 W. Gulf Dr., Sanibel* ☎ *239/472–1561* 🌐 *www.islandinn.com* 🛏 *42 rooms, 7 cottages* 🍴 *Breakfast.*

$$$ RENTAL FAMILY Fodor's Choice ★

Sanibel Siesta on the Beach. You might want to move right in and never leave once you discover these luxurious two-bedroom/two-bath condos right on the sand. **Pros:** on the beach; swimming pool; free Wi-Fi. **Cons:** minimum stays; office closes early. [$] *Rooms from: $330* ✉ *1246 Fulgur St., Sanibel* ☎ *239/472–4117* 🌐 *www.sanibelsiesta.com* 🛏 *67 units* 🍴 *No meals.*

$$ HOTEL

Seaside Inn. Tucked among the tropical greenery, this beachfront inn is a pleasant alternative to the area's larger resorts. **Pros:** intimate feel; lots of character; beautiful beachfront. **Cons:** no on-site restaurant; cramped parking lot. [$] *Rooms from: $289* ✉ *541 E. Gulf Dr., Sanibel* ☎ *239/472–1400, 866/565–5092* 🌐 *www.seasideinn.com* 🛏 *36 rooms, 6 cottages* 🍴 *Breakfast.*

$$ RESORT FAMILY

Sundial Beach Resort and Spa. With multimillion-dollar renovations completed in 2015, Sanibel's largest resort encompasses 400 privately owned studio, one-, two-, and three-bedroom low-rise condo units, about half of which are in its rental program. **Pros:** great beach; plenty of amenities; no charge for beach chairs. **Cons:** conference crowds; packed pool area; $30 per night resort fee. [$] *Rooms from: $279* ✉ *1451 Middle Gulf Dr., Sanibel* ☎ *239/472–4151, 866/565–5093* 🌐 *www.sundialresort.com* 🛏 *184 units* 🍴 *No meals.*

8

$$ HOTEL

Waterside Inn. Palm trees, sea-grape trees, pastel cottages, and a tiki on the Gulf set the scene at this quiet beachside vacation spot. **Pros:** beachfront location; intimate feel; small pets allowed in most cottages. **Cons:** office closes at night; cottage interiors are worn; parking for only one car per unit. [$] *Rooms from: $293* ✉ *3033 W. Gulf Dr., Sanibel* ☎ *239/472–1345, 800/741–6166* 🌐 *www.watersideinn.net* 🛏 *14 rooms, 13 cottages* 🍴 *No meals.*

$$$ HOTEL

West Wind Inn. Families and couples flock to this resort for its upscale, West Gulf Drive location on the residential side of the island. **Pros:** on the beach; quiet side of the island; laundry facilities on-site. **Cons:** Wi-Fi can be sporadic; pool towels are small and wafer thin. [$] *Rooms from: $340* ✉ *3345 W. Gulf Dr., Sanibel* ☎ *239/472–1541* 🌐 *www.westwindinn.com* 🛏 *103 rooms* 🍴 *No meals.*

CAPTIVA

$$$ RESORT FAMILY Fodor's Choice ★

South Seas Island Resort. This full-service 330-acre resort feels as lush as its name suggests. **Pros:** full range of amenities; exclusive feel; car-free transportation. **Cons:** high rates in season; a bit isolated; spread out. [$] *Rooms from: $339* ✉ *5400 Plantation Rd., Captiva* ☎ *239/472–5111, 888/222–7848* 🌐 *www.southseas.com* 🛏 *471 rooms* 🍴 *No meals.*

$$ B&B/INN

'Tween Waters Inn Resort & Spa. Besides its great beach-to-bay location, this inn has historic value and in 2011 was listed in the National Register of Historic Places. **Pros:** great views; lots of water-sports options; free Wi-Fi. **Cons:** beach is across the road. [$] *Rooms from: $280* ✉ *Captiva Dr., Captiva* ☎ *239/472–5161, 800/223–5865* 🌐 *www.tween-waters.com* 🛏 *119 units, 19 cottages* 🍴 *Breakfast.*

SHOPPING

Sanibel is known for its art galleries, shell shops, and one-of-a-kind boutiques; the several small open-air shopping complexes are inviting, with their tropical flowers and shady ficus trees.

SANIBEL

Seashells.com. Among the island's cache of shell shops, this one is favored by serious collectors and crafters because of its reasonable prices and the knowledgeable family that runs it. For shell gifts, the family operates another little shop right behind the warehouse-sized one. It's super easy to find, located right on the main drag. ✉ *905 Fitzhugh St., Sanibel* ☎ *239/472–1603* 🌐 *www.seashells.com.*

She Sells Sea Shells. At She Sells Sea Shells, everything imaginable is made from shells, from mirrors to lamps to Christmas ornaments. The owner wrote the book on shell art, and you can buy it here. You can also purchase local shells, like the prized junonia and pick up a T-shirt at a fair price. A second location is on the same road at 2422 Periwinkle Way. ✉ *1157 Periwinkle Way, Sanibel* ☎ *239/472–6991* 🌐 *www.sanibelshellcrafts.com.*

CAPTIVA

Fodor's Choice ★ **Jungle Drums.** Expect the unexpected in wildlife art, where fish, sea turtles, and other creatures are depicted with utmost creativity and touches of whimsy. If you're looking for souvenirs above and beyond the usual, or unique jewelry, paintings, sculptures, and pottery—this is the place. ✉ *11532 Andy Rosse La., Captiva* ☎ *239/395–2266* 🌐 *www.jungledrumsgallery.com* ⏲ *Closed Sun.*

SPORTS AND THE OUTDOORS

BIKING

Everyone bikes around flat-as-a-pancake Sanibel and Captiva—on bikeways that edge the main highway in places, on the road through the wildlife refuge, and along side streets. Free maps are available at bicycle liveries.

Billy's Bikes. Rent by the hour or the day from this Sanibel outfitter, which also rents motorized scooters and leads Segway tours. They even have beach gear like chairs, umbrellas, and boogie boards. ✉ *1470 Periwinkle Way, Sanibel* ☎ *239/472–5248* 🌐 *www.billysrentals.com.*

Yolo Watersports. Bikes and water-sports recreation rentals of all kinds (sailboats, WaveRunners, paddleboards) are available at this Captiva operator. Gear is also for sale. ✉ *11534 Andy Rosse La., Captiva* ☎ *239/472–1296* 🌐 *www.yolowatersports.com.*

CANOEING AND KAYAKING

Tarpon Bay Explorers. One of the best ways to scout out the wildlife refuge is by paddle. Rent a canoe or kayak from the refuge's official concessionaire and explore at your leisure. The kayak water trail is easy to follow, simply paddle your way along 17 markers and see a bevy of birds and other wildlife. Guided tours by kayak or pontoon boat are also offered and worthwhile for visitors unfamiliar with the ecosystem. Their on-site touch tank gives a hands-on learning experience about local sea life. ⊠ *900 Tarpon Bay Rd., Sanibel* ☎ *239/472–8900* ⊕ *www. tarponbayexplorers.com.*

FISHING

Local anglers head out to catch mackerel, pompano, grouper, snook, snapper, tarpon, and shark.

Sanibel Marina. To find a charter captain on Sanibel, visit their on-site Ship Store or give them a call. ⊠ *634 N. Yachtsman Dr., Sanibel* ☎ *239/472–2723* ⊕ *www.sanibelmarina.com.*

'Tween Waters Marina. On Captiva, this is the place to look for guides. You can also rent kayaks, canoes, stand-up paddleboards, and other recreational watercrafts. ⊠ *'Tween Waters Inn, 15951 Captiva Dr., Captiva* ☎ *239/472–5161* ⊕ *www.tween-waters.com/marina.*

GOLF

Dunes Golf & Tennis Club. When your back nine are sanctioned as a wildlife preserve by the Audubon Cooperative Society—even if you play poorly—you're rewarded with lusher than lush fairways and more wildlife than you can shake a stick at. Bring your camera if you golf here, as it's not every day that bald eagles watch you play. Water hazards at every hole will have you losing more balls than usual, so bring plenty. Hole 10 is the toughest, which explains why most wish it were a par 5 instead of a par 4. Go for a long, straight tee shot and watch out for the water (and the gators). ⊠ *949 Sandcastle Rd., Sanibel* ☎ *239/472–2535* ⊕ *www.dunesgolfsanibel.com* ⌦ *$115* ⛳ *18 holes, 5583 yards, par 70.*

FORT MYERS BEACH (ESTERO ISLAND)

18 miles southwest of Fort Myers.

Crammed with motels, hotels, and restaurants, Estero Island is one of Fort Myers's more frenetic Gulf playgrounds. Dolphins frequently frolic in Estero Bay, part of the Intracoastal Waterway, and marinas provide a starting point for boating adventures, including sunset cruises, sightseeing cruises, and deep-sea fishing. At the southern tip, a bridge leads to Lovers Key State Park.

GETTING HERE AND AROUND

San Carlos Boulevard in Fort Myers leads to Fort Myers Beach's high bridge, Times Square, and Estero Boulevard, the island's main drag. Estero Island is 18 miles southwest of Fort Myers.

BEACHES

Lovers Key State Park. Once a little-known secret, this out-of-the-way park encompassing 1,616 acres on four barrier islands and several uninhabited islets is popular among beachgoers and birders. Bike, hike, walk, or paddle the park's trails (rentals available); go shelling on its 2½ miles of white-sand beach; take a boat tour; or have a beach picnic under the trees. Trams run regularly from 9 to 4:30 to deliver you and your gear to South Beach. The ride is short but often dusty. North Beach is a five-minute walk from the concession area and parking lot. Watch for osprey, bald eagles, herons, ibis, pelicans, and roseate spoonbills, or sign up for a free excursion to learn fishing and nature photography. On the park's bay side, across the road from the beach entrance, playgrounds and a picnic area cater to families, plus there are boat ramps, kayak rentals, and a bait shop. **Amenities:** food and drink; parking (fee); showers; toilets; water sports. **Best for:** swimming; walking. ⊠ *8700 Estero Blvd., Fort Myers Beach* ☎ *239/463–4588* ⊕ *www.floridastateparks.org/loverskey* ▨ *$4–$8 per vehicle, $2 for pedestrians and bicyclists.*

FAMILY **Lynn Hall Memorial Park.** At the 17-acre park in the commercial northern part of Estero Island, the wide, sandy shore slopes gradually into the usually tranquil and warm Gulf waters, providing safe swimming for children. And since houses, restaurants, condominiums, and hotels (including the Best Western Beach Resort and Pink Shell Resort north of the parking lot) line most of the beach, you're never far from civilization. There are picnic pavilions and barbecue grills, as well as playground equipment and a free fishing pier. The park is part of a pedestrian mall with a number of beach shops and restaurants steps away. The parking lot fills early on sunny days. **Amenities:** food and drink; parking (fee); showers; toilets; water sports. **Best for:** partiers; sunsets; walking. ⊠ *Estero Blvd. at San Carlos Blvd., to Bowditch Point Park, Fort Myers Beach* ☎ *239/463–1116* ⊕ *www.leeparks.org* ▨ *Parking $2 per hr.*

WHERE TO EAT

$$ ✕ **Doc Ford's Rum Bar & Grille.** For dependably well-prepared food with
MODERN a water view, Doc Ford's is the top choice in Fort Myers Beach. A
AMERICAN spin-off of a Sanibel Island original, its name and theme come from a murder-mystery series by local celebrity author Randy Wayne White. **Known for:** Yucatan shrimp, steamed with spicy key lime butter; fish tacos; lively atmosphere. Ⓢ *Average main: $20* ⊠ *708 Fisherman's Wharf, Fort Myers Beach* ☎ *239/765–9660* ⊕ *www.docfordsfortmyersbeach.com.*

$$ ✕ **Matanzas Inn.** Watch boats coming and going whether you sit inside or
SEAFOOD out at this rustic Old Florida–style restaurant right on the docks alongside the Intracoastal Waterway. When the weather cooperates, enjoy the view from the shaded outdoor tables. **Known for:** pizza at Petey's Upper Deck; fresh seafood; slow, sometimes grumpy servers. Ⓢ *Average main: $18* ⊠ *416 Crescent St., Fort Myers Beach* ☎ *239/463–3838* ⊕ *www.matanzas.com.*

$$ ✕ **Parrot Key Caribbean Grill.** For something more contemporary than
SEAFOOD Fort Myers Beach's traditional shrimp and seafood houses, head to San Carlos Island on the east side of the high bridge where the shrimp boats dock. Parrot Key sits marina-side near the shrimp docks, offering a casual vibe that exudes merriment with its Floribbean cuisine and island music. **Known for:** Caribbean-inspired cuisine; seafood nachos; live music most nights. Ⓢ *Average main: $20* ⊠ *2500 Main St., Fort Myers Beach* ☎ *239/463–3257* ⊕ *www.myparrotkey.com.*

$ ✕ **The Plaka.** A casual long-timer and a favorite for a quick break-
GREEK fast, filling lunch, and sunset dinner, Plaka—named after the historic neighborhood in Athens—has typical Greek fare. Expect standards

like moussaka, pastitsio, gyros, and roast lamb, as well as burgers, sandwiches, fried seafood, and strip steak. **Known for:** gyro platters; pastitsio (Greek lasagna); sunset views. $ *Average main: $13* ⊠ *1001 Estero Blvd., Fort Myers Beach* ☎ *239/463–4707.*

WHERE TO STAY

$$$$
RESORT
FAMILY
🏨 **DiamondHead.** This 12-story resort sits on the beach, and many of the suites, especially those on higher floors, have stunning views. **Pros:** on the beach; well-organized childlen's programs; kitchens in all units. **Cons:** heavy foot and car traffic; tiny fitness center; not the best value on the beach. $ *Rooms from: $429* ⊠ *2000 Estero Blvd., Fort Myers Beach* ☎ *239/765–7654, 888/765–5002* ⊕ *www.diamondheadfl.com* ↘ *121 suites* ❍| *No meals.*

$$
RENTAL
🏨 **Harbour House.** This condo-hotel adds a degree of beach luxury with brightly painted and sea-motif studios and one- and two-bedroom condos, all privately owned. **Pros:** close to lots of restaurants; roomy units; all have private balconies or lanais; free covered parking. **Cons:** a walk to the beach; not great views from most rooms. $ *Rooms from: $245* ⊠ *450 Old San Carlos Blvd., Fort Myers Beach* ☎ *239/463–0700, 866/998–9250* ⊕ *www.harbourhouseattheinn.com* ↘ *34 units* ❍| *No meals.*

$
HOTEL
🏨 **Lighthouse Resort Inn & Suites.** These pastel-painted buildings hold fairly basic but spacious rooms, standing tall and welcoming at the foot of the Fort Myers bridge, an ideal location for exploring. **Pros:** convenient location; on-site laundry; views of the area from balconies. **Cons:** can be noisy; may have to park across the street if under-building parking is full. $ *Rooms from: $175* ⊠ *1051 5th Ave., Fort Myers Beach* ☎ *239/463–9392* ⊕ *www.lighthouseislandresort.com* ↘ *79 units* ❍| *No meals.*

$$
RENTAL
🏨 **Lovers Key Resort.** Views can be stupendous from upper floors in this 14-story tower just north of Lovers Key State Park. **Pros:** excellent views; off the beaten path; spacious accommodations. **Cons:** not a true beach; far from shopping and restaurants; limited amenities. $ *Rooms from: $280* ⊠ *8771 Estero Blvd., Fort Myers Beach* ☎ *239/765–1040, 877/798–4879* ⊕ *www.loverskey.com* ↘ *100 units* ❍| *No meals.*

$
RESORT
FAMILY
🏨 **Outrigger Beach Resort.** On a wide Gulf beach, this casual resort has rooms and efficiencies with configurations to suit different guests' needs, including some kitchenettes. **Pros:** beautiful beach; water-sports rentals; family-friendly vibe. **Cons:** can be noisy; crowded pool area; old-school feel. $ *Rooms from: $199* ⊠ *6200 Estero Blvd., Fort Myers Beach* ☎ *239/463–3131, 800/657–5659* ⊕ *www.outriggerfmb.com* ↘ *144 rooms* ❍| *No meals.*

SPORTS AND THE OUTDOORS

BIKING

Fort Myers Beach has no designated trails, so most cyclists ride along the road.

Fun Rentals. Bike rentals are available from anywhere between two hours and a week. Not your speed? Rent a Harley or a scooter instead. ⊠ *1901 Estero Blvd., Fort Myers Beach* ☎ *239/463–8844* ⊕ *www.funrentals.org.*

8

Lover's Key Adventures and Events. This company rents one-speed bikes, kayaks, canoes, paddleboards, and concessions in Lovers Key State Park. ⊠ 8700 Estero Blvd., Fort Myers Beach 🕾 239/765–7788 ⊕ www. loverskeyadventures.com 🖅 $20 for half day, $25 for full day.

CANOEING

Lover's Key Adventures and Events. Lovers Key State Park offers kayak, canoe, and paddleboard rentals and guided kayaking tours of its bird-filled estuary. Call ahead for a guided tour schedule. ⊠ 8700 Estero Blvd., Fort Myers Beach 🕾 239/765–7788 ⊕ www.loverskeyadventures. com 🖅 Guided tours $60; rentals from $38 for 2 hrs.

FISHING

Getaway Deep Sea Fishing. Arrange anything from half-day party-boat charters to full-day excursions, fishing equipment included. ⊠ 18400 San Carlos Blvd., Fort Myers Beach 🕾 800/641–3088, 239/466–3600 ⊕ www.getawaymarina.com 🖅 From $65.

NAPLES AND VICINITY

As you head south from Fort Myers on U.S. 41, you soon come to Estero and Bonita Springs, followed by the Naples and Marco Island areas, which are sandwiched between Big Cypress Swamp and the Gulf of Mexico. East of Naples the land is largely undeveloped and mostly wetlands, all the way to Fort Lauderdale. Naples itself is a major vacation destination that has sprouted pricey high-rise condominiums and golfing developments, plus a spate of restaurants and shops to match. A similar but not as thorough evolution has occurred on Marco Island, the largest of the Ten Thousand Islands.

ESTERO/BONITA SPRINGS

10 miles south of Fort Myers via U.S. 41.

Towns below Fort Myers have started to flow seamlessly into one another since the opening of Florida Gulf Coast University in San Carlos Park and as a result of the growth of Estero and Bonita Springs, which were agricultural communities until the 1990s. In recent years the area has become a shopping mecca of mega–outdoor malls mixing big-box stores, smaller chains, and restaurants. Bonita Beach, the closest beach to Interstate 75, has evolved from a fishing community into a strip of upscale homes and beach clubs built to provide access for residents of inland golf developments.

GETTING HERE AND AROUND

U.S. 41 (Tamiami Trail) runs right through the heart of these two adjacent communities. You can also reach them by exits 123 and 116 off Interstate 75.

EXPLORING

FAMILY **Everglades Wonder Gardens.** Opened in 1936 by two retired moonshiners from Detroit, the Everglades Wonder Gardens was one of the first roadside attractions in the state and remained little changed until 2013, when the family decided to close its doors—and thus a rich chapter of

Florida tourism history—forever. In stepped Florida landscape photographer John Brady, who negotiated a lease with the founding family and transformed the old-style cramped zoological gardens (that once featured Florida panthers, black bears, crocodiles, alligators, and tame Florida deer) into a botanical garden by conserving the flora and fauna following contemporary standards. Now in focus are diverse gardens that include old-growth trees like kapok, banyan, candle nut, egg fruit, plumeria, jaboticaba, mahogany, cashew, avocado, and mango, as well as integrated animal exhibits with tortoises, turtles, smaller alligators, flamingos, and a butterfly garden. The original buildings have been preserved and made into a modern gallery that showcases Brady's photography. ✉ *27180 Old 41 Rd., Bonita Springs* ☎ *239/992–2591* ⊕ *www. evergladeswondergardens.com* 🖭 *$12.*

Koreshan State Historic Site. Tour one of Florida's quirkier chapters from the past. Named for a religious cult that was active at the turn of the 20th century, Koreshan preserves a dozen structures where the group practiced arts, worshipped a male-female divinity, and created its own branch of science called cosmogony, which claimed the universe existed within a giant hollow sphere. The cult floundered when leader Cyrus Reed Teed died in 1908, and in 1961 the four remaining members deeded the property to the state. Rangers and volunteers lead tours and demonstrations, and the grounds are lovely for picnicking and camping. Canoeists paddle the Estero River, fringed by a forest of exotic vegetation the Koreshans planted. ✉ *3800 Corkscrew Rd., at U.S. 41 (Tamiami Trail), Estero* ☎ *239/992–0311* ⊕ *www.floridastateparks.org/ park/koreshan* 🖭 *$5 per vehicle with up to 8 passengers; $4 for single motorist; $2 per bicyclist, pedestrian, or extra passenger.*

BEACHES

Barefoot Beach Preserve. This one isn't exactly easy to find since it's accessible only by a quiet neighborhood road around the corner from buzzing Bonita Beach Park, but it's well worth the effort if you appreciate natural coastal habitats with fun interpretive programs. Shells here are bountiful, as are gopher tortoises that may park in shade of your car. Stop by the nature center to join a ranger-led walk through the trails and gardens, or take up a paddle and go kayaking. There's no towel-jockeying here along the wide-open space (the preserve as a whole is 342 acres), and refreshments and beach rentals provide ample comfort while you unwind in the pristine sands. **Amenities:** food and drink; parking (fee); showers; toilets; water sports. **Best for:** solitude; walking. ✉ *5901 Bonita Beach Rd., at Barefoot Beach Rd., Bonita Springs* ☎ *239/591–8596* ⊕ *www.collierparks.com* 🖭 *Parking $8.*

Bonita Beach Park. The joint is always jumping on this rowdy stretch of coast, the easiest by far to reach from the inland areas south of Fort Myers. Local favorite hangout Doc's Beach House, open from breakfast until the wee hours of the night, keeps bellies full and libations flowing. Other food and sports vendors camp out here, too, making it nearly impossible to resist an ice cream or a ride on a Jet Ski. Shaded pavilions between the parking lot and dunes are a great way to cool off from the sweltering heat—just don't sit too close to the picnickers barbecuing. **Amenities:** food and drink; parking (fee); showers; toilets water sports. **Best for:** partiers; windsurfing. ✉ *27954 Hickory Blvd., at Bonita Beach Rd., Bonita Springs* ☎ *239/949–4615* 🌐 *www.leeparks.org* 🅿 *Parking $2 per hr.*

WHERE TO EAT

$$$$ ITALIAN Fodor's Choice ★ 🍴 **Angelina's Ristorante.** Here it's all about the experience—one of the most indulgent, pampered meals you'll ever eat. Formally trained waitstaff attend to your every need in this temple of traditional Italian cuisine. **Known for:** phenomenal service; homemade pastas; the freshest seafood. [$] *Average main: $36* ✉ *24041 U.S. 41, Bonita Springs* ☎ *239/390–3187* 🌐 *www.angelinasofbonitasprings.com* 🕘 *No lunch.*

$$$ SEAFOOD 🍴 **Blue Water Bistro.** For the convenience of shoppers at Coconut Point, several excellent restaurants cluster in the midst of the shopping center. This one, although part of a Naples–Bonita Springs dining dynasty, has a personality all its own, with a suave indoor-outdoor bar scene and seafood that's anything but timid. **Known for:** international fish dishes; creative sushi; inventive cocktails. [$] *Average main: $24* ✉ *Coconut Point Mall, 23151 Village Shops Way, Suite 109, Estero* ☎ *239/949–2583* 🌐 *www.bluewaterbistro.net* 🕘 *No lunch.*

$ AMERICAN FAMILY 🍴 **Doc's Beach House.** Right next door to the public access point for Barefoot Beach, Doc's has fed hungry beachgoers for decades. Come barefoot and grab a quick libation or meal downstairs, outside on the beach, or in the courtyard. **Known for:** spicy conch chowder; juicy burgers; unfancy seafood; dining right on the water. [$] *Average main: $10* ✉ *27908 Hickory Blvd., Bonita Springs* ☎ *239/992–6444* 🌐 *www.docsbeachhouse.com* 💳 *No credit cards.*

$ AMERICAN 🍴 **Old 41 Restaurant.** A mostly local clientele populates the cheery dining room with its Philadelphia allegiances, offering a great Philly cheesesteak. For breakfast, don't miss the incredible Texas French toast with homemade caramel and pecans, Carbon's malted Belgian waffles, or eggs and homemade hash with Boar's Head meat. **Known for:** slow-cooked turkey and roast beef; chipped beef for breakfast; no reservations (but a call-ahead wait list on weekends). [$] *Average main: $7* ✉ *25091 Bernwood Dr., Bonita Springs* ☎ *239/948–4123* 🌐 *www.old41.com* 🕘 *No dinner.*

WHERE TO STAY

$$$$ RESORT FAMILY Fodor's Choice ★ 🏨 **Hyatt Regency Coconut Point Resort & Spa.** This secluded luxury resort, with its marble-and-mahogany lobby and championship golf course, makes a lovely sanctuary for families who want a refined atmosphere. **Pros:** pampering spa; insane water park with lazy river and high-speed slides; private island beach. **Cons:** need water shuttle to reach the beach; expensive restaurants. [$] *Rooms from: $649* ✉ *5001 Coconut Rd., Bonita Springs* ☎ *239/444–1234, 800/554–9288* 🌐 *www.coconutpoint.hyatt.com* 🛏 *454 rooms* 🍴 *No meals.*

$$ HOTEL 🏨 **Trianon Bonita Bay.** Convenient to Bonita Springs's best shopping and dining, this branch of a refined downtown Naples favorite has a peaceful, sophisticated feel and a poolside–lakeside alfresco bar and grill. **Pros:** spacious rooms; intimate atmosphere. **Cons:** sometimes less-than-friendly staff; far from beach; slightly stuffy. [$] *Rooms from: $239* ✉ *3401 Bay Commons Dr., Bonita Springs* ☎ *239/948–4400, 800/859–3939* 🌐 *www.trianonbonitabay.com* 🛏 *100 rooms* 🍴 *No meals.*

SHOPPING

Miromar Outlets. The complex includes Adidas, Guess, Michael Kors, Nike, Nautica, and more than 140 other stores and eateries, plus a free Playland for kids. ⊠ *10801 Corkscrew Rd., at I–75 Exit 123, near Germain Arena, Estero* ☎ *239/948–3766* ⊕ *www.miromaroutlets.com.*

SPORTS AND THE OUTDOORS

BIRDING

The last leg of the Great Florida Birding Trail has more than 20 stops in the Lower Gulf Coast. Go to ⊕ *www.floridabirdingtrail.com* for a complete list.

CANOEING

The meandering Estero River is pleasant for canoeing as it passes through Koreshan State Historic Site to the bay.

Estero River Outfitters. Since 1977, this is the place to rent canoes, kayaks, paddleboards, and equipment. They're also a full-service tackle shop. ⊠ *20991 Tamiami Trail S, Estero* ☎ *239/992–4050* ⊕ *www.esteroriveroutfitters.com.*

NAPLES

21 miles south of Bonita Springs, on U.S. 41.

Poised between the Gulf of Mexico and the Everglades, Naples belies its wild setting and Indian past with the trappings of wealth—neo-Mediterranean-style mansions, neatly manicured golfing developments, revitalized downtown streets lined with galleries and one-of-a-kind shops, and a reputation for lively and eclectic dining. Visitors come for its luxury hotels—including two Ritz-Carltons—its fabulous white-sand beaches, fishing, shopping, theater and arts, and a lofty reputation for golf. Yet with all the highfalutin living, Naples still appeals to families, especially with its water park and the Golisano Children's Museum of Naples that opened in 2012.

Old Naples, the historic downtown section, has two main commercial areas, 5th Avenue South and 3rd Street South, and there's also a small cluster of restaurants right by City Dock on Naples Bay. Farther north on U.S. 41 (the Tamiami Trail, or 9th Street here), hotels, shopping centers, and developments have fast been filling in the area around and south of Vanderbilt Beach, including the dining and shopping meccas Waterside Shops, and the Village on Venetian Bay.

GETTING HERE AND AROUND

The Naples Municipal Airport is a small facility east of downtown principally serving private planes, commuter flights, and charters. A taxi for up to three passengers is about $60 to $90 from Southwest Florida International Airport (RSW) in Fort Myers to Naples; each additional person is charged $10. You don't need to reserve in advance; simply go to the ground-transportation booth. If you prefer to book a car or limo pickup in advance, three major companies are Aaron Airport Transportation, Naples Taxi & Limo Services, and Naples Airport Shuttle.

8

Downtown Naples is 15 miles south of Bonita Springs, on U.S. 41. If you're driving here from Florida's east coast, consider Alligator Alley, a toll section of Interstate 75 that's a straight shot from Fort Lauderdale to Naples. In Naples, east–west county highways exiting off Interstate 75 include, from north to south, Immokalee Road (Route 846), Pine Ridge Road (Route 896), and Collier Boulevard (Route 951), which actually goes north–south and takes you also to Marco Island.

Contacts Aaron Airport Transportation. ☎ *239/768–1898* ⊕ *www.aarontaxi.com.* **Naples Airport Shuttle.** ☎ *239/430–4747, 888/569–2227* ⊕ *www.naplesairportshuttle.com.* **Naples Taxi & Limo Services.** ☎ *239/435–0000, 800/472–1371* ⊕ *www.naplestaxiflorida.com.*

TOURS

Naples Trolley Tours. If you want someone to be your guide as you go about town, Naples Trolley Tours offers eight narrated tours daily, covering more than 100 points of interest in town. The tour lasts about two hours, but you can get off and on at no extra cost. ⊠ *1010 6th Ave. S* ☎ *239/262–7300, 800/592–0848* ⊕ *www.naplestrolleytours.com.*

VISITOR INFORMATION

Contacts Naples, Marco Island, Everglades Convention and Visitors Bureau. ☎ *800/688–3600, 239/225–1013* ⊕ *www.paradisecoast.com.*

EXPLORING
TOP ATTRACTIONS

Fodor's Choice ★ **The Baker Museum.** This cool, contemporary museum at Artis–Naples displays provocative, innovative pieces, including renowned miniatures, antique walking sticks, modern and contemporary American and Mexican masters, and traveling exhibits. Dazzling installations by glass artist Dale Chihuly include a fiery cascade of a chandelier and an illuminated ceiling layered with many-hued glass bubbles, glass corkscrews, and other shapes that suggest the sea; alone, this warrants a visit, but with three floors and 15 galleries, your cultural curiosity is sure to pique, perhaps in the glass-domed conservatory. Reward your visual arts adventure with lunch at the on-site Cafe Intermezzo. ⊠ *5833 Pelican Bay Blvd.* ☎ *239/597–1900, 800/597–1900* ⊕ *www.artisnaples. org* ⊠ *$10* ⊘ *Closed Mon.*

FAMILY **Collier County Museum.** To get a feel for local history, stroll the nicely presented indoor vignettes and traveling exhibits and outdoor parklike displays at this museum. A Seminole *chickee* village, native plant garden, swamp buggy, reconstructed 19th-century fort, steam logging locomotive, and more capture important Naples-area developments from prehistoric times to the World War II era. ⊠ *3331 Tamiami Trail E* ☎ *239/252–8476* ⊕ *www.colliermuseums.com* ⊠ *Free.*

FAMILY **Conservancy of Southwest Florida Nature Center.** If you're looking to connect with nature, this is the place, regardless of age. Take a 45-minute electric boat tour (ages 2+) along the Gordon River, rent a kayak, or go on a guided nature walk. The Dalton Discovery Center features interactive exhibits on six Florida ecosystems, including a touch tank where you can learn about many of the same animals you find on the local beaches, and meet the area's only loggerhead sea turtle living in

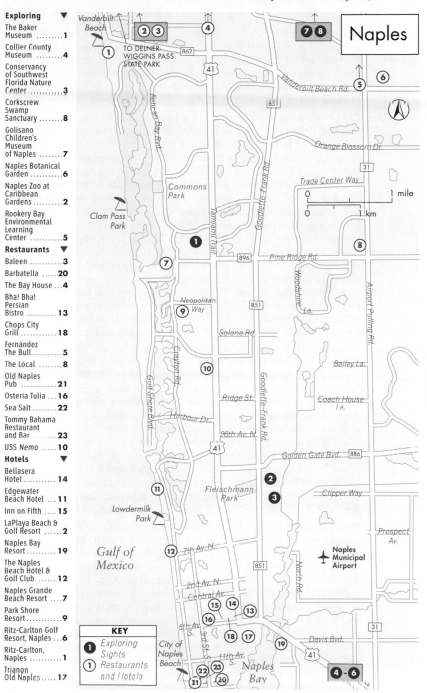

a spectacular aquarium. Preschoolers can have hands-on fun at the Little Explorer Play Zone. The on-site wildlife hospital's viewing area gives you a peek at staff working on any number of animals. Check out Cinema Sunday and other events in their Nature Center. ■TIP→ The electric boat tours are free, and you don't have to pay the admission fee for the center to ride. ⊠ 1495 Smith Preserve Way ☎ 239/262–0304 ⊕ www.conservancy.org ☜ $12.95.

Fodor'sChoice ★ **Corkscrew Swamp Sanctuary.** To get a feel for what this part of Florida was like before civil engineers began draining the swamps, drive 17 miles east of North Naples to these 13,000 acres of pine flatwood and cypress, grass-and-sedge "wet prairie," saw-grass marshland, and lakes and sloughs filled with water lettuce. Managed by the National Audubon Society, the sanctuary protects North America's largest remaining stand of ancient bald cypress, 600-year-old trees as tall as 130 feet, as well as endangered birds, such as wood storks, which often nest here. This is a favorite destination for serious birders and is the gateway to the Great Florida Birding and Wildlife Trail. If you spend a couple of hours to take the 2¼-mile self-guided tour along the boardwalk, you'll spot ferns, orchids, and air plants, as well as wading birds and possibly alligators and river otters. A nature center educates you about this precious, unusual habitat with a dramatic re-creation of the preserve and its creatures in the Swamp Theater. ■TIP→ The boardwalks are completely wheelchair-accessible. ⊠ 375 Sanctuary Rd. W, 17 miles east of I–75 on Rte. 846 ☎ 239/348–9151 ⊕ corkscrew.audubon.org ☜ $14.

FAMILY **Golisano Children's Museum of Naples.** This bright, cheery 30,000-square-foot ode to playful learning burst onto Naples's cultural scene in 2012 after a decade of much-anticipated planning, and its 12 state-of-the-art permanent galleries do not disappoint. Kids of many ages and abilities (exhibits were designed to be accessible for children with special needs, too) will love the gigantic Banyan Tree, a focal point at 45 feet tall and a climbing obstacle of sorts; the Farm & Market, a cooperative playground where roles are assigned (a harvester or cashier, for example) to subtly enforce team building and math skills; and the Green Construction zone, where hard hats and eco-friendly building materials will inspire future architects. ■TIP→ It's in the same park as Sun-n-Fun Lagoon, and it's possible to do both in one day. ⊠ North Collier Regional Park, 15080 Livingston Rd. ☎ 239/514–0084 ⊕ www.cmon.org ☜ $10 ☉ Closed Wed.

Naples Botanical Garden. An expansion and renovation of the botanical gardens that finished in 2010 elevated this attraction to one of Naples's most culturally and botanically exciting. Its "gardens with latitude" flourish with plants and architectural and decorative elements from Florida and other subtropical locales including Asia, Brazil, and the Caribbean. Highlights of the 170 acres include a Children's Garden with a butterfly house, tree house, waterfall, cave, Florida Cracker house, and hidden garden; an infinity water lily pool; an aromatic Enabling Garden with a how-to theme; and a dramatic waterfall feature. A visitor center offers a café, restaurant, and three gardens, including an orchid garden with more than 1,000 species and cultivars. ⊠ 4820 Bayshore Dr. ☎ 239/643–7275 ⊕ www.naplesgarden.org ☜ $14.95 ☞ Complimentary wheelchairs; fee for scooters.

FAMILY **Naples Zoo at Caribbean Gardens.** The lush 44-acre zoo got its start as a botanical garden in 1919 and has since drawn visitors curious to see lions, tigers, bears, leopards, gazelles—and a wildly popular giraffe herd added in 2011. For an extra fee you can feed the gentle, eyelash-batting giants or, in the winter season only, ride aboard dromedary camels. Other exhibits include the rare Malayan Tigers (approximately 60 in the nation), an endangered Florida panther (as few as 180 cats left in the wild), and a "Reptile Rendezvous" show; a giant anteater and critically endangered cotton-top tamarins in the South American exhibits; and the "Primate Expedition Cruise" that sails past islands populated with monkeys, apes, and lemurs. Youngsters can amuse themselves in two play zones, and there are daily meet-the-keeper times, alligator feedings, and a live educational Safari educational animal presentation. Newer exhibits include critically endangered red-ruffed lemurs, rare juvenile clouded leopards, and francois langur primates. ■**TIP→ Purchase tickets online for a $3 discount per ticket.** ⊠ *1590 Goodlette-Frank Rd.* ☏ *239/262–5409* ⊕ *www.napleszoo.org* ⊠ *$22.95; giraffe feeding and camel rides (seasonal) $5 each.*

FAMILY **Rookery Bay Environmental Learning Center.** In the midst of 110,000-acre Rookery Bay National Marine Estuary, the center dramatically interprets the Everglades environment and local history with interactive models, aquariums, an art gallery, a film, tours, and "coastal connections" programs (45 minutes, at 11 and 2 daily). It's on the edge of the estuary, about five minutes east of Marco's north bridge on Collier Boulevard. Take a walk along Observation Bridge, a 440-foot pedestrian bridge that spans the reserve's creek from the center's second floor, and connects with 1½ miles of nature trails and leads to a creekside viewing platform. Guided and self-guided walks are available. Kayak and boat tours are also available through advance registration. Exhibits include an interactive research boat, a display on the importance of the Gulf of Mexico to coastal communities, and another on global climate change. Geocaches can be found on the trail and parking area. ■**TIP→ Kids go free on Friday in June and July. Also, visit the website for a printable coupon for admission.** ⊠ *300 Tower Rd.* ☏ *239/530–5940* ⊕ *www. rookerybay.org* ⊠ *$5.*

BEACHES

FAMILY **City of Naples Beach.** There's something here for everyone just west of the 3rd Street South shopping area, but what gets the most attention by far is the historic pier that extends deep into the Gulf and has the best free dolphin-viewing seats around. Sunsets are a nightly ritual, and dodging anglers' poles is par for the course. The concession stand sells food for humans as well as for fishy friends, and on the sand below, teenagers hold court at the volleyball nets and families picnic on blankets, while a handful of people can always be seen swooping up cockles, fighting conchs, and coquinas. For a charming landscape away from the commotion, head south on Gulf Shore Boulevard and take your pick of the public access points. They may not have the amenities of the pier—or amenities, period—but the solitude can't be beat. **Amenities:** food and drink; parking (fee); showers; toilets. **Best for:** sunsets; swimming. ⊠ *12th Ave. S at Gulf Shore Blvd.* ☏ *239/213–3062* ⊠ *Parking 25¢ per 6 mins.*

8

Clam Pass Beach Park. A quiet day at the beach gets an adventurous start when you board a tram and career down a ¾-mile boardwalk through shaded mangroves and a network of canals. At the end is a pretty, secluded patch of sand that still has notable activities because of the family-vacation-magnet Naples Grande Beach Resort just a few steps from the public parking lot. The surf is calm, perfect for swimming, and aside from the usual lying out, shelling, and sand-castle building, you can spring for a kayak and meander around the marsh for a different kind of water experience. **Amenities:** food and drink; parking (fee); showers; toilets; water sports. **Best for:** solitude; swimming. ⊠ *465 Seagate Dr.* ☎ *239/252–4000* ⊕ *www.collierparks. com* 🚗 *Parking $8.*

Fodor's Choice
★

Delnor-Wiggins Pass State Park. This wide, virtually untouched expanse—about 166 acres—of open beach makes visitors feel transported from the bustling high-rises and resorts just a few blocks south. A full roster of eco-inclined features, like a designated fishing zone, hard-bottom reef (one of the few in the region and close enough to swim up to), boat dock, and observation tower hooks anglers, nature lovers, and water-sports enthusiasts drawn to the peaceful, laid-back vibe. Moms and dads love the educational displays on the local environment and the ranger-led sea turtle and birding programs, not to mention the picnic tables, grills, and plenty of shade offshore. A concession stand offers food, drinks, and beach gear easily accessible to those less inclined to self-catering. **Amenities:** food and drink; parking (fee); showers; toilets; water sports. **Best for:** solitude; snorkeling; walking. ⊠ *11135 Gulf Shore Dr. N* ☎ *239/597–6196* ⊕ *www.floridastateparks.org/park/ delnor-wiggins* 🚗 *$6 per vehicle with up to 8 people, $4 for single drivers, $2 for pedestrians and bicyclists.*

FAMILY

Lowdermilk Park. Do you prefer your beach loud and active with a big dose of good old-fashioned fun? Kids running around in the surf, volleyballers hitting the sand, and tykes getting up close and personal with the park's most colorful residents, the red-throated Muscovy ducks, are all part of the Lowdermilk experience. Shallow waters and little-to-no wave action beg for a dip from even the most hesitant swimmer, and thatched umbrellas dotting the shoreline complete the happy tiki vibe and are yours for the taking—assuming you can snag one (they are strictly first come, first served). Even more, a food stand, two playgrounds, and some casual eateries down the strand at the Naples Beach Hotel make digging your feet into the sand a no-brainer. **Amenities:** food and drink; parking (fee); showers; toilets. **Best for:** swimming; walking. ⊠ *1301 Gulf Shore Blvd. N* ☎ *239/213–3029* ⊕ *www.naples-gov.com* 🚗 *Parking 25¢ per 6 mins.*

Vanderbilt Beach. If a day at the shore just doesn't seem quite complete without a piña colada and serious people-watching, this place is for you. The white powdery sand often looks like a kaleidoscope, with multihued towels and umbrellas dotting the landscape in front of the nearly 3 miles of tony north Naples condos and luxe resorts, including the Ritz-Carlton and LaPlaya. If you walk far enough—which many people do—you come across eye candy of a different kind: the architecturally stunning megamansions of Bay Colony perched up on the dunes.

A covered public parking garage gives easy access, and the beach really comes alive at sunset with onlookers. **Amenities:** food and drink; parking (fee); showers; toilets; water sports. **Best for:** partiers; sunsets; walking. **■ TIP→ Stroll up to Gumbo Limbo at the Ritz for the best Floribbean, yet surprisingly not wallet-busting, lunches and panoramic views from a shaded deck.** ✉ *100 Vanderbilt Beach Rd.* ☎ *239/252–4000* 🌐 *www.collierparks.com* 🎫 *Parking $8.*

WHERE TO EAT

$$$$ SEAFOOD 🍴 **Baleen.** The mood cast in this well-appointed dining room and the romantic Gulf-view patio that spills onto the sand feels like the perfect Florida restaurant experience. There's only one small problem: lighting is so low at dinner that you can't read the menu, even with its built-in flashlight. **Known for:** lobster frittata breakfast; signature blackened grouper; water views. [$] *Average main: $37* ✉ *La Playa Beach & Golf Resort, 9891 Gulf Shore Dr.* ☎ *239/598–5707, 800/237–6883* 🌐 *www.laplayaresort.com.*

$$ ITALIAN 🍴 **Barbatella.** This trattoria with an edge is still just as popular as it was when it opened in 2012. The restaurant has three dining spaces to suit any whim: the wine bar, with sleek eclectic decor, has a communal table, green ceiling medallions, crystal chandeliers wrapped in birdcages, and a wine dispenser that allows guests to sip their way through 32 bottles (Italian, of course) by the 1-, 3-, or 6-ounce glass. **Known for:** pizzettes (small pizzas); Venetian-style meatballs; amazing gelato. [$] *Average main: $20* ✉ *1290 3rd St. S* ☎ *239/263–1955* 🌐 *www.barbatellanaples.com.*

$$$$ SEAFOOD 🍴 **The Bay House.** Nestled in a hidden expanse of twisted mangrove trees and flowing canals is one of the area's best restaurants for casual fine dining—and beautifully natural scenery. Restored wooden rowboats and modern chandeliers hang from the ceiling of the main dining room, which is packed almost every night in season. **Known for:** crab bisque; coastal pan roast with fresh Gulf fish; live music. [$] *Average main: $32* ✉ *799 Walkerbilt Rd.* ☎ *239/591–3837* 🌐 *www.bayhousenaples.com* 🕑 *No lunch May–Nov.*

$$$ MIDDLE EASTERN 🍴 **Bha! Bha! Persian Bistro** Long considered one of Naples's best ethnic restaurants, loyal fans of Bha! Bha! have flocked to a tiny north Naples strip mall year in and year out to indulge in the restaurant's chic Persian atmosphere and cuisine. On the eve of its 15th birthday came a well-deserved present: a brand-new location on bustling Fifth Avenue South. **Known for:** authentic Persian cuisine; signature plum lamb; slow-braised duck. [$] *Average main: $25* ✉ *865 5th Ave. S* ☎ *239/594–5557* 🌐 *www.bhabhapersianbistro.com.*

$$$$ ECLECTIC 🍴 **Chops City Grill.** Count on high-quality cuisine that fuses Asian cuisine and steak-house mainstays. It's sophisticated and popular, yet resort-wear casual, drawing everyone from young businesspeople to local retirees. **Known for:** succulent dry-aged steaks; region's best clam chowder; delicious side dishes. [$] *Average main: $32* ✉ *837 5th Ave. S* ☎ *239/262–4677* 🌐 *www.chopscitygrill.com* 🕑 *No lunch.*

$$ CUBAN 🍴 **Fernández The Bull.** Intrepid palates venture several miles inland to get a taste of the "Best Cuban Food in Naples," as voted by readers of *Gulfshore Life* magazine. You'll get authentic, home-cooked specialties, without pretension, at this simple storefront café. **Known**

for: slow-roasted pork; old-school black beans and rice; Palomilla steak with onions. [$] *Average main: $17* ✉ *1201 Piper Blvd., Suite 10* ☎ *239/254–9855* 🌐 *www.fernandezthebull.com.*

$$ CONTEMPORARY Fodor's Choice ★ 🍴 **The Local.** You'll find an epicurean take on healthy eating at this farm-and-sea-to-table bistro that, as the name declares, looks almost exclusively to local suppliers to stock its kitchen. Though in a strip mall a few blocks inland, the setting is hip and polished with an interior that evokes both the beach and the farm, no doubt a reflection of the young and stylish owners' passion for nourishment. **Known for:** pot roast with grandma's veggies; flatbreads and pizzas; fresh ingredients. [$] *Average main: $18* ✉ *5323 Airport Pulling Rd. N* ☎ *239/596–3276* 🌐 *www.thelocalnaples.com.*

$$ AMERICAN 🍴 **Old Naples Pub.** Local blue- and white-collar workers gather with shoppers for affordable sandwiches and seafood in the vaulted, vine-twisted courtyard of this traditional pub, which has been tucked away from shopping traffic off upscale 3rd Street since 1990. It strikes one as an everybody-knows-your-name kind of place, with jars of pickles on the tables and friendly bartenders. **Known for:** casual, fun vibe; wide selection of beers; fresh fish platters. [$] *Average main: $15* ✉ *255 13th Ave. S* ☎ *239/649–8200* 🌐 *www.naplespubs.com.*

$$$ ITALIAN Fodor's Choice ★ 🍴 **Osteria Tulia.** An ancestral air pervades at this intimate yet lively restaurant on 5th Avenue, where the Sicilian-born chef (and part owner) drives an authentic celebration of the Italian table. Opened in 2013, the concept is a refreshing departure from long, ornate menus and focuses on simple, finely produced, house-made Italian cuisine in a rustic, refined setting. **Known for:** homemade sausage and cheeses; freshly made pastas; rustic, family setting. [$] *Average main: $25* ✉ *466 5th Ave. S* ☎ *239/213–2073* 🌐 *www.tulianaples.com.*

$$$$ MEDITERRANEAN Fodor's Choice ★ 🍴 **Sea Salt.** The city's hottest upscale restaurant draws a crowd of connoisseurs to a modern, coral stone dining room that spills out onto the sidewalk. Venetian-born Chef Fabrizio Aielli puts a New World spin on traditional Italian favorites on his nightly changing menu, utilizing 130 different types of salt from around the globe. **Known for:** charred octopus appetizer; daily prix-fixe sunset menu from 5 to 6; house-made pappardelle with Wagyu beef. [$] *Average main: $40* ✉ *1186 3rd St. S* ☎ *239/434–7258* 🌐 *www.seasaltnaples.com.*

$$$ CARIBBEAN 🍴 **Tommy Bahama Restaurant and Bar.** Here Naples takes a youthful curve. Island music sounds on the umbrella-shaded courtyard at this eatery, the original prototype for a small national chain inspired by the clothing line. **Known for:** coconut fried shrimp; fantastic crab bisque; island-style ambience. [$] *Average main: $30* ✉ *1220 3rd St. S* ☎ *239/643–6889* 🌐 *www.tommybahama.com.*

$$$ SEAFOOD Fodor's Choice ★ 🍴 **USS Nemo.** Don't be fooled by the tacky glowing sign from the highway: most Neapolitans swear this is *the* place for seafood in town, which is why you should still make a reservation even in the heat of summer. The food is in the vein of fine dining but served in a whimsical setting with portholes, antique bronze diving gear, and colorful sculptures of fish. **Known for:** miso-broiled sea bass; swordfish cioppino; fresh tuna with your choice of savory sauce. [$] *Average main: $26* ✉ *3745 Tamiami Trail N* ☎ *239/261–6366* 🌐 *www.ussnemorestaurant.com* 🕒 *No lunch weekends.*

WHERE TO STAY

$$$$
HOTEL
Bellasera Hotel. This downtown hotel is just far enough "off 5th" to be away from the dining-and-shopping foot traffic but close enough for convenience, and it feels like a lovely Italian villa with its red tile roofs and burnt-ocher stucco. **Pros:** spacious, full apartment units; free bikes for guests; first-come, first-served private cabanas at pool. **Cons:** must take shuttle to beach; on a busy highway (though surprisingly quiet). $ *Rooms from: $489 ⊠ 221 9th St. S ☎ 239/649–7333, 888/612–1115 ⊕ www.bellaseranaples.com ➭ 95 units �ⓄⅠ No meals.*

$$$$
HOTEL
Edgewater Beach Hotel. At this all-suite, beachfront property at the north end of scenic Gulf Shore Boulevard, the rooms are large and refreshing, exuding a relaxed, contemporary vibe. **Pros:** beautiful beach; quiet; exquisite views. **Cons:** far from shopping; surrounded closely by high-rises; pool area must be vacated at 10 pm. $ *Rooms from: $479 ⊠ 1901 Gulf Shore Blvd. N ☎ 239/403–2000, 888/564–1308 ⊕ www. edgewaternaples.com ➭ 125 suites ⓄⅠ No meals.*

$$$$
HOTEL
Inn on Fifth. You can't top this luxe hotel if you want to plant yourself in the heart of Naples nightlife and shopping. **Pros:** central location; metro vibe; spa has free sauna for guests. **Cons:** pool is eye-level with power lines; beach is a long stroll or shuttle ride away. $ *Rooms from: $425 ⊠ 699 5th Ave. S ☎ 239/403–8777, 888/403–8778 ⊕ www.innon-fifth.com ➭ 119 rooms ⓄⅠ No meals.*

$$$$
RESORT
Fodor's Choice
★
LaPlaya Beach & Golf Resort. LaPlaya bespeaks posh and panache down to the smallest detail—note the Balinese-style spa, marble bathrooms, and a stuffed sea turtle toy to cuddle during your stay. **Pros:** right on the beach; high-end amenities; beautiful rooms, which were renovated in 2012. **Cons:** golf course is off property; no locker rooms in spa. $ *Rooms from: $619 ⊠ 9891 Gulf Shore Dr. ☎ 239/597–3123, 800/237–6883 ⊕ www.laplayaresort.com ➭ 189 rooms ⓄⅠ No meals.*

$$$
RESORT
FAMILY
Naples Bay Resort. Dual personalities are at work in this sprawling resort, and both are upscale and polished at every turn: at one end, a 97-slip marina with a luxury hotel (a boater's dream), and at the other a cottage resort with a busy, water-oriented recreation park. **Pros:** walk to downtown; $5 water taxi to other bay-side hot spots. **Cons:** no beach; some highway noise. $ *Rooms from: $369 ⊠ 1500 5th Ave. S ☎ 239/530–1199, 866/605–1199 ⊕ www.naplesbayresort. com ➭ 85 rooms, 108 cottages ⓄⅠ No meals ☞ 6-night minimum stay in cottages.*

$$$$
RESORT
FAMILY
The Naples Beach Hotel & Golf Club. Family-owned and -managed since 1946, this art-deco resort is a piece of Naples history—and its stretch of powdery sand has lots of action at all times. **Pros:** terrific beach scene; golf course and driving range on property; complimentary kids' program. **Cons:** expensive nightly rates; have to cross street to reach spa and breakfast dining; though interiors are freshly renovated, signature old-school exterior may not appeal to sleek tastes. $ *Rooms from: $459 ⊠ 851 Gulf Shore Blvd. N ☎ 239/261–2222, 800/237–7600 ⊕ www.naplesbeachhotel.com ➭ 319 rooms ⓄⅠ No meals.*

$$$$ RESORT FAMILY Fodor's Choice ★ **Naples Grande Beach Resort.** Beach access, a golf club, and top-shelf luxury are all yours at this ultramodern high-rise formerly known as the Waldorf Astoria Naples. **Pros:** indulgent spa; beach service with cabanas; attentive service. **Cons:** not directly on the beach; golf course is 6 miles away with no shuttle. [$] *Rooms from: $729* ✉ *475 Seagate Dr.* ☎ *239/597–3232, 888/722–1267* 🌐 *www.naplesgrande.com* 🛏 *553 rooms* 🍴 *No meals.*

$$$ RENTAL **Park Shore Resort.** Well situated near the beaches and shopping off Gulf Shore Boulevard, this hidden retreat is practical and comfortable. **Pros:** good value; tropical pool and shaded grounds; quiet. **Cons:** no restaurant; long walk to beach; no shuttle service. [$] *Rooms from: $349* ✉ *600 Neapolitan Way* ☎ *800/548–2077* 🌐 *www.parkshorefl.com* 🛏 *156 rooms* 🍴 *No meals.*

$$$$ RESORT Fodor's Choice ★ **Ritz-Carlton Golf Resort, Naples.** Ardent golfers with a yen for luxury will find their dream vacation at Naples's most elegant golf resort where Ritz style prevails and service exceeds your wildest expectations. **Pros:** best golf academy in area; two championship courses at the front door; plush setting; access to Ritz spa and beach via shuttle; service par excellence. **Cons:** 10-minute drive to beaches; expensive rates; farther inland than most properties. [$] *Rooms from: $649* ✉ *2600 Tiburón Dr.* ☎ *239/593–2000* 🌐 *www.ritzcarlton.com* 🛏 *295 rooms* 🍴 *No meals.*

$$$$ RESORT FAMILY Fodor's Choice ★ **Ritz-Carlton, Naples.** This is a regal Ritz-Carlton, with marble statues and antique furnishings blended with artistic modernity in the rooms and public spaces. **Pros:** flawless service; fun tiki bar and water-sports options; near north Naples shopping and restaurants; ultraindulgent spa. **Cons:** high price tag; hike to downtown; valet parking only; extra charge for beach umbrellas annoying at this nice a place. [$] *Rooms from: $999* ✉ *280 Vanderbilt Beach Rd.* ☎ *239/598–3300* 🌐 *www.ritzcarlton.com* 🛏 *450 rooms* 🍴 *No meals.*

$$$ HOTEL **Trianon Old Naples.** Refined ladies and gents will feel at home in this classy boutique hotel that's right smack in the central historic district, yet enrobed in an aura of privacy two quiet residential blocks south of 5th Avenue's bustle. **Pros:** can't-beat location for urbanites; large rooms. **Cons:** limited facilities; long walk (or short drive) to beach. [$] *Rooms from: $319* ✉ *955 7th Ave. S* ☎ *239/435–9600, 877/482–5228* 🌐 *www.trianonoldnaples.com* 🛏 *58 rooms* 🍴 *No meals.*

NIGHTLIFE AND PERFORMING ARTS

NIGHTLIFE

The heart of Old Naples, 5th Avenue South, already known for its scene of lively bars and sidewalk cafés, has undergone a renaissance of sorts.

Burn by Rocky Patel. At this part cigar bar, part dance club, you can expect pretty young things grooving to a house DJ. ✉ *9110 Strada Pl.* ☎ *239/653–9013* 🌐 *www.burnbyrockypatel.com.*

Naples Beach Brewery. With the opening of Naples Beach Brewery in 2013, the Naples scene isn't only about fine wine anymore. This microbrewery's concoctions can be found in almost 50 local bars and restaurants including some of Naples's finest dining establishments. Twenty-plus house brews range from the straw-colored Weizen to the Naples Beach Stout. Look for a palm tree logo on bottles and taps signifying the local craft beers, or head directly to the brewery on Friday and Saturday afternoons for guided tours, tastings, and pizza made with their spent grain. But don't expect to be wowed by a big gleaming factory, as this brewery is small and authentic, located in an industrial neighborhood sandwiched between hardware manufacturers—the real deal. ⊠ *4110 Enterprise Ave., Suite 217* ☎ *239/304–8795* ⊕ *www.naplesbeachbrewery.com* ▨ *$15.*

The Pub. Long lists of brews, flat-screens, and fun British decor attract a lively crowd to this popular outpost of a small, family-run chain. Brunch is served on weekends from 10 to 2. ⊠ *9118 Strada Pl.* ☎ *239/594–2748* ⊕ *www.experiencethepub.com.*

Silverspot Cinema. More than a plush movie theater, Silverspot offers a full evening's entertainment, including a lounge where you can sip specialty cocktails before showtime. You can even have dinner right in your comfy movie seat; just order, and it will be delivered to you while you're enjoying the show. ⊠ *9118 Strada Pl., 2nd fl.* ☎ *239/592–0300* ⊕ *www.silverspot.net.*

Vergina. The mature crowd hits the dance floor for Gloria Gaynor and the Bee Gees. Upscale professionals gather here for daily happy-hour specials and the lighter bar menu. ⊠ *700 5th Ave. S* ☎ *239/659–7008* ⊕ *www.verginarestaurant.com.*

PERFORMING ARTS

Naples is the cultural capital of this stretch of coast.

Naples Philharmonic. See the 85-piece Naples Philharmonic Orchestra perform more than 140 plays, ballets, orchestral, and chamber concerts each year at the Hayes Hall at Artis–Naples from September to June. The Miami City Ballet performs here during its winter season. ⊠ *Artis–Naples, 5833 Pelican Bay Blvd.* ☎ *239/597–1900, 800/597–1900* ⊕ *www.artisnaples.org.*

Naples Players. Musicals and dramas are performed year-round; winter shows often sell out well in advance. ⊠ *Sugden Community Theatre, 701 5th Ave. S* ☎ *239/263–7990* ⊕ *www.naplesplayers.org.*

SHOPPING

Old Naples encompasses two distinct shopping areas marked by historic buildings and flowery landscaping: 5th Avenue South and 3rd Street South. Both are known for their abundance of fine-art galleries and monthly musical entertainment. Elsewhere, malls, outdoor plazas, and independent boutiques pepper the landscape, mostly on and around U.S. 41.

SPECIALTY SHOPS

Gattle's. Started in 1904, this downtown shop stocks pricey-but-pretty linens. ⊠ *1250 3rd St. S* ☎ *239/262–4791, 800/344–4552* ⊕ *www.gattles.com.*

It's New to You. The most upscale clothes sometimes go to this consignment shop, furniture too. ⊠ *933 Creech Rd.* ☎ *239/263–8400.*

Marissa Collections. *The* destination in Naples for ultra-high-end designer women's wear. ⊠ *1167 3rd St. S* ☎ *239/263–4333* ⊕ *www.marissacollections.com.*

Regatta. Among 5th Avenue South's selection with a decidedly local flair, this shop sells personal and home accessories with a sense of humor and style. ✉ *760 5th Ave. S* ☎ *239/262–3929* ⊕ *www.fifthavenuesouth.com/regatta.*

The Shelter Options Shoppe. Naples's ladies who lunch often donate their year-old Armani cast-offs and fine collectibles to this terrific thrift shop whose proceeds benefit the Shelter for Abused Women & Children. ✉ *968 2nd Ave. N* ☎ *239/434–7115* ⊕ *www.optionsnaples.org.*

SPORTS AND THE OUTDOORS
BIKING
Naples Cyclery. Daily or hourly rentals of two- and four-passenger surreys, tandems, and more are available at this convenient store in the Pavilion Shopping Center; weekly rentals are also available. ■TIP→ If you need a little boost, have breakfast, lunch, or an espresso at the store's Fit & Fuel Café, where there's a serious fitting room if you're in the market for a custom-fit bike. ✉ *Pavilion Shopping Center, 813 Vanderbilt Beach Rd.* ☎ *239/566–0600* ⊕ *www.naplescyclery.com* 🎫 *From $14.*

BOATING AND FISHING
Mangrove Outfitters. Take a guided boat and learn to cast and tie flies. ✉ *4111 Tamiami Trail E* ☎ *239/793–3370, 888/319–9848* ⊕ *www.mangroveoutfitters.com.*

Port Of Naples Marina. All new boats makes this the youngest fleet to rent. Choose pontoon or deck boats. ✉ *550 Port-O-Call Way* ☎ *239/774–0479* ⊕ *www.portofnaplesmarina.com* 🎫 *From $169.*

FAMILY **Pure Naples.** Half-day deep-sea and backwater fishing trips depart twice daily. Sightseeing cruises and thrilling jet tours are also available, along with Jet Ski and boat rentals and private charters. ✉ *Tin City, 1200 5th Ave. S* ☎ *239/263–4949* ⊕ *www.purenaples.com.*

GOLF
Lely Resort Golf and Country Club. Flamingo Island (designed by Robert Trent Jones) and The Mustang (designed by Lee Trevino) are the two championship courses open to the public at Lely Resort. Flamingo Island features white-sand bunkers, hourglass fairways, and large greens, along with its signature 3200-yard hole 5 with a water-rimmed rolling fairway, bunkers, and two bridges providing the only access to the mainland. The Mustang features 12 lakes and rolling fairways. If you do more shanking than swinging, schedule time with their PGA teaching professional Charles Lostracco. ✉ *8004 Grand Lely Blvd.* ☎ *239/793–2600* ⊕ *www.lelyresortgolfandcountryclub.com* 🎫 *$169* ⛳ *Flamingo Island: 18 holes, 7171 yards, par 72; The Mustang: 18 holes, 7217 yards, par 72.*

The Naples Beach Hotel & Golf Club. This historic club has weekly clinics, a driving range, and a putting green and is replete with nostalgia as the region's oldest course, built in 1929. But lately, it's all about the "dramatic" $9-million renovations by acclaimed designer Jack Nicklaus, and architect John Stanford. You'll find an all new, par-71 consisting of five tees, ranging from 4800 yards to over 6900 yards. ■TIP→ It has been voted "Top 50 Women Friendly Golf Courses in the U.S." by the magazine *Golf for Women.* ✉ *851 Gulf Shore Blvd. N* ☎ *239/435–2475*

8

⊕ *www.naplesbeachhotel.com* ⌸ *$55 for 9 holes, $99 for 18 holes* ⚑ *18 holes, 6488 yards, par 72.*

Tiburón Golf Club. There are two 18-hole Greg Norman–designed courses, the Gold and the Black—an especially difficult course carved right out of a cypress preserve. Challenging and environmentally pristine, the links include narrow fairways, stacked sod wall bunkers, coquina sand, and no roughs. New this year is the Impact Zone Golf Academy. ■TIP→ You cannot book months in advance unless you're staying at one of the Ritz-Carlton hotels. Nonguests can book 10 days out. ⌸ *Ritz-Carlton Golf Resort, 2620 Tiburón Dr.* ☎ *239/593–2201* ⊕ *www.tiburongcnaples.com* ⌸ *$250* ⚑ *Tiburón Gold: 18 holes, 7271 yards, par 74.9; Tiburón Black: 18 holes, 6949 yards, par 75.01.*

MARCO ISLAND

20 miles south of Naples via Rte. 951.

High-rises dominate part of the shores of Marco Island, which is connected to the mainland by two bridges. Yet because of its distance from downtown Naples, it retains an isolated feeling much appreciated by those who love this corner of the world. Some natural areas have been preserved, and the down-home fishing village of Goodland, a 20-minute drive from historic Old Marco, resists change. Fishing, boating, sunning, swimming, and tennis are the primary activities here.

GETTING HERE AND AROUND

From Naples, Collier Boulevard (Route 951) takes you to Marco Island. If you're not renting a car, taxi rides cost about $100 from the regional airport in Fort Myers. Key West Express operates a ferry from Marco Island (from Christmas through Easter) and Fort Myers Beach (year-round) to Key West. The cost for the round-trip (less than four hours each way) is $147 from either Fort Myers Beach or Marco Island.

Contacts Key West Express. ✉ *951 Bald Eagle Dr.* ☎ *239/394–9700, 888/539–2628* ⊕ *www.keywestexpress.us.*

VISITOR INFORMATION

Contacts Naples, Marco Island, Everglades Convention and Visitors Bureau. ☎ *800/688–3600, 239/225–1013* ⊕ *www.paradisecoast.com.*

EXPLORING

Marco Island Historical Museum. Marco Island was once part of the ancient Calusa kingdom. The Key Marco Cat, a statue found in 1896 excavations, has become symbolic of the island's prehistoric significance. The original is part of the Smithsonian Institution's collection, but a replica of the Key Marco Cat is among displays illuminating the ancient past at this museum, which opened in 2011. Three rooms examine the island's history with dioramas, artifacts, and signage: the Calusa Room, Pioneer Room, and Modern Marco Room. A fourth hosts traveling exhibits focusing on the settlement history of the island. Outside, the yard was built to look like a Calusa village atop a shell mound with a water feature and *chickee* structure. ✉ *180 S. Heathwood Dr.* ☎ *239/642–1440* ⊕ *www.colliermuseums.com* ⌸ *Free.*

BEACHES

FAMILY **Tigertail Beach.** On the northwest side of the island is 2,500 feet of both developed and undeveloped areas. Once Gulf-front, in recent years a sand spit known as Sand Dollar Island has formed, which means the stretch especially at the north end has become mud flats—great for birding. There's plenty of powdery sand farther south and across the lagoon that draws a broad base of fans flocking there for its playgrounds, butterfly garden, volleyball nets, and kayak and umbrella rentals. Beach wheelchairs are also available for free use. ■TIP➔ **The Conservancy of Southwest Florida conducts free educational beach walks at Tigertail Beach every weekday from 8:30 to 9:30 from January to mid-April.** **Amenities:** food and drink; parking (fee); showers; toilets; water sports. **Best for:** sunset; swimming; walking. ⊠ *490 Hernando Dr.* ☎ *239/252–4000* ⊕ *www.collierparks.com* 🅿 *Parking $8.*

WHERE TO EAT

$$$ ✕ **Arturo's.** This place is huge, with expansive Romanesque dining rooms
ITALIAN and more seating on the patio. Still, it fills up year-round with a strong
Fodor's Choice well-dressed following that appreciates a fun attitude and serious Italian
★ cuisine done comprehensively and traditionally. **Known for:** signature stuffed pork chop; homemade pastas; rich and thick NY-style cheesecake. Ⓢ *Average main: $24* ⊠ *844 Bald Eagle Dr.* ☎ *239/642–0550* ⊕ *www.arturosmarcoisland.com* ⊘ *No lunch.*

$$$ ✕ **Café de Marco.** This cozy little bistro with cheery pastel walls and
ECLECTIC stained-glass windows has served expertly prepared local fish since 1983. The jumbo prawns—an entire pound butterflied and broiled in their shell—are the signature dish, but grilled filet mignon on phyllo pastry proves the kitchen also knows how to do meat. **Known for:** jumbo prawns in the shell; shrimp Lenny with crab and bacon; oysters Rockefeller. Ⓢ *Average main: $30* ⊠ *244 Palm St.* ☎ *239/394–6262* ⊕ *www.cafedemarco.com* ⊘ *Closed Sun. May–Dec. No lunch.*

$ ✕ **Crazy Flamingo.** Burgers, conch fritters, and chicken wings draw
AMERICAN mostly locals to this neighborhood bar. Order at the counter, and take a seat indoors or outdoors on the sidewalk. **Known for:** fresh steamed and fried seafood; Uncle Vinny's steak sandwich; ultracasual atmosphere. Ⓢ *Average main: $11* ⊠ *Marco Island Town Center, 1035 N. Collier Blvd.* ☎ *239/642–9600* ⊕ *www.thecrazyflamingo.com.*

$$$ ✕ **Old Marco Lodge Crab House.** Built in 1869, this waterfront restau-
SEAFOOD rant is Goodland's oldest landmark. Boaters often cruise in and tie up dockside to sit on the veranda and dine on local seafood and pasta entrées. **Known for:** simple seafood platters; homemade key lime pie; lively atmosphere. Ⓢ *Average main: $25* ⊠ *401 Papaya St., Goodland* ☎ *239/642–7227* ⊕ *www.oldmarcolodge.com* 🚫 *No credit cards* ⊘ *Closed Aug. and Sept.*

$$$$ ✕ **Sale e Pepe.** Marco's best dining view comes also with some of its fin-
ITALIAN est cuisine. The name means "salt and pepper," an indication that this palatial restaurant with terrace seating overlooking the beach adheres to the basics of southern Italian cuisine. **Known for:** beautiful Gulf views; house-made fresh pasta dishes; award-winning Italian cuisine. Ⓢ *Average main: $38* ⊠ *Marco Beach Ocean Resort, 480 S. Collier Blvd.* ☎ *239/393–1400* ⊕ *www.sale-e-pepe.com.*

$$$ ✗ **Snook Inn.** Situated on the water with live entertainment in the tiki
SEAFOOD   bar and a loaded salad bar, it's no wonder this place has been a casual
favorite for locals and visitors for decades. This is *the* place for good
food, good music, and a fun crowd every day of the week on Marco.
Known for: smoked fish dip appetizer; lively atmosphere and good
drinks under the chickee hut; expansive water views. Ⓢ *Average main:
$21* ✉ *1215 Bald Eagle Dr.* ☎ *239/394–3313* ⊕ *www.snookinn.com.*

$$ ✗ **Sunset Grille.** Head to this popular spot for casual dining with a view
AMERICAN   of the beach and a menu of munchies, sandwiches, burgers, seafood,
and steak. The lively sports-bar scene adds to the fun indoors; a porch
accommodates alfresco diners—just beware if you leave your table
that the porch has no screens, and the local gulls are thieves. **Known
for:** seasonally inspired small plates; chef's loaded nachos; famous
crab cake sandwich. Ⓢ *Average main: $16* ✉ *Apollo Condominiums,
900 S. Collier Blvd.* ☎ *239/389–0509* ⊕ *www.sunsetgrilleonmarcois-
land.com.*

$$$ ✗ **Verdi's American Bistro.** There's a Zen feel to this intimate bistro built
ECLECTIC   on creative American-Italian-Asian fusion cuisine. You'll feel like you're
dining in a home, and that's exactly how the owners want it to be:
inviting, warm, and welcoming. **Known for:** incredible crispy duck;
New Zealand rack of lamb; excellent service. Ⓢ *Average main: $28*
✉ *Sand Dollar Plaza, 241 N. Collier Blvd.* ☎ *239/394–5533* ⊕ *www.
verdisbistro.com* �) *Closed Sept. No lunch.*

WHERE TO STAY

$$ ☷ **The Boat House Motel.** For a great location at a good price, check into
HOTEL   this modest, but appealing, two-story motel at the north end of the
island on the Marco River, close to the Gulf. **Pros:** away from busy
beach traffic; affordable; boating docks and access. **Cons:** no beach;
hard to find; tight parking area. Ⓢ *Rooms from: $250* ✉ *1180 Edington
Pl.* ☎ *239/642–2400, 800/528–6345* ⊕ *www.theboathousemotel.com*
⇥ *20 rooms* ⦿ *No meals.*

$$$$ ☷ **Hilton Marco Island Beach Resort and Spa.** This 11-story hotel is smaller
RESORT   and more conservative than the Marriott—but it seems less busy and
crowded. **Pros:** gorgeous, wide beach; complete business services; exclusive feel. **Cons:** a little stuffy; charges for self-parking; business focus.
Ⓢ *Rooms from: $419* ✉ *560 S. Collier Blvd.* ☎ *239/394–5000, 800/445–
8667* ⊕ *www.hiltonmarcoisland.com* ⇥ *297 rooms* ⦿ *No meals.*

$$$$ ☷ **JW Marriott Marco Island Beach Resort.** A grandiose circular drive with
RESORT   rock waterfalls front this hilltop, beachfront resort that has nearly com-
FAMILY   pleted a $320-million makeover and rebranding journey to becoming
the first-ever JW Marriott on the beach in the continental U.S. Made
up of twin 11-story towers and villa-like suites, three on-site pools,
and the widest stretch of sand on the island (over 3 miles), it's an
island seekers dream. **Pros:** great spa; 10 on-site restaurants; appeals
to children and adults; two private golf courses. **Cons:** huge size; lots
of convention business; paid parking across the street in an uncovered
lot; $30 daily resort fee. Ⓢ *Rooms from: $579* ✉ *400 S. Collier Blvd.*
☎ *239/394–2511, 800/438–4373* ⊕ *www.jwmarco.com* ⇥ *810 rooms*
⦿ *No meals.*

8

$$$$ RESORT Fodor's Choice ★ 🏨 **Marco Beach Ocean Resort.** One of the island's first condo hotels, this 12-story beachfront class act has luxurious one- and two-bedroom suites decorated in elegant neutral tones with the finest fixtures. **Pros:** gourmet dining on-site; intimate atmosphere; sophisticated crowd. **Cons:** steep prices; squeezed between high-rises; near another busy resort. [$] *Rooms from: $609* ✉ *480 S. Collier Blvd.* ☎ *239/393–1400, 800/715–8517* 🌐 *www.marcoresort.com* 🛏 *98 rooms* 🍴 *No meals.*

$$$$ RENTAL 🏨 **Olde Marco Island Inn & Suites.** This Victorian with tin roofs and royal-blue shutters and awnings in the heart of quieter Old Marco used to be the only place to stay on the island, and if you are looking for a property with some historic flair, it's still a good choice. **Pros:** full kitchen in every unit; free Wi-Fi; laundry facilities; free covered parking. **Cons:** must drive to beach; annexed to a shopping center; office closes at night. [$] *Rooms from: $420* ✉ *100 Palm St.* ☎ *239/394–3131, 877/475–3466* 🌐 *www.oldemarcoinn.com* 🛏 *51 units* 🍴 *No meals.*

SPORTS AND THE OUTDOORS

BIKING

Scootertown Island Bike Shop. Rentals are available at Scootertown Island Bike Shop for use on the island's bike path along beachfront condos, resorts, and residential areas. You can rent by the day or week. ✉ *1095 Bald Eagle Dr.* ☎ *239/394–8400* 🌐 *www.islandbikeshops.com* 🎟 *From $12.*

FISHING

Sunshine Tours. Try a half-day deep-sea or three-hour backcountry fishing charter with this outfitter. ✉ *Rose Marina, 951 Bald Eagle Dr.* ☎ *239/642–5415* 🌐 *www.sunshinetoursmarcoisland.com* 🎟 *From $65.*

9

ORLANDO AND
ENVIRONS

WELCOME TO ORLANDO AND ENVIRONS

TOP REASONS TO GO

★ **Magic and fantasy:**
Unleash your inner child, in the glow of Cinderella Castle, at WDW's Magic Kingdom. Fireworks transform the night skies—and you—at this park and at Epcot. And, over at Universal Orlando we have just, two words: Harry Potter.

★ **Around the world:**
Visit Epcot's 11 countries, complete with perfect replicas of foreign monuments, unique crafts, and traditional cuisine.

★ **Amazing animals:**
Safari through Africa in Disney's Animal Kingdom, get splashed by Shamu at SeaWorld, kiss a dolphin at Discovery Cove, and watch gators wrestle at Gatorland.

★ **Shopping ops:**
Hit the national chains at Orlando's upscale malls, or browse Winter Park's unique Park Avenue boutiques. Don't forget the mouse ears: Main Street U.S.A. and Downtown Disney are filled with the best classic souvenirs and some quirkier items as well.

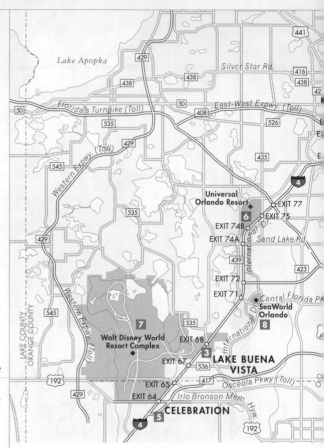

1 Orlando. Orlando offers more than theme parks, including museums, parks, and gardens. Beyond Central Orlando, the I-Drive area has a concentration of attractions, restaurants, and lodging. Other options are in South Orlando and the Sand Lake Road area, Winter Park, Kissimmee, and Downtown Orlando proper. Thanks to Disney World, Orlando is the gateway for many visitors to Central Florida.

2 Winter Park. Looking for more laid-back local flavor? You'll find it just 20 miles northeast of Orlando in the charming Winter Park suburb.

CENTRAL FLORIDA

TO MAITLAND
AND ALTAMONT SPRINGS

WINTER PARK **2**

SEMINOLE COUNTY
ORANGE COUNTY

Colonial Dr.

EXIT 83A
EXIT 83
EXIT 82B
EXIT 82A

1 ORLANDO

Orlando Executive Airport

EXIT 80

Central Florida Greenway (Toll)

Hafner Av.

Beachline Expwy. (Toll)

Florida's Turnpike (Toll)

da Pkwy

Orlando International Airport

Central Florida Greenway (Toll)

ORANGE COUNTY
OSCEOLA COUNTY

KISSIMMEE 4

East Lake
Tohopekaliga

0   4 mi

0   4 km

GETTING ORIENTED

Orlando is more or less equidistant from Tampa/ St. Petersburg on the Gulf of Mexico and the coastal attractions of Daytona Beach and Cape Canaveral on the Atlantic coast. Walt Disney World is about 25 miles southwest of the city.

9

culture, especially Harry Potter. The new Volcano Bay water park adds to the fun, and Universal has pledged to open a new attraction every year.

7 Walt Disney World.
Walt Disney's original decree was that his parks be ever-changing; the newest addition is Pandora–The World ot Avatar.

8 SeaWorld. Less glitzy than Walt Disney World or Universal, SeaWorld and its sister park Discovery Cove are worth a visit for a low-key, relaxing, ocean-theme experience.

3 Lake Buena Vista.
Adjacent to Walt Disney World, Lake Buena Vista offers a wide array of dining and lodging options adjacent to the area's biggest theme parks.

4 Kissimmee. Edging Orlando to the south is Kissimmee, with homegrown attractions like Gatorland.

5 Celebration. Walt Disney World's planned residential community also has hotels and dining.

6 Universal Orlando Resort. While Disney creates a fantasy world for those who love fairy tales, Universal Orlando is geared to older kids, adults, and anyone who enjoys pop

Updated by
Joseph Hayes
and Jennifer
Greenhill-Taylor

Most Orlando locals look at the theme parks as they would an unruly neighbor: it's big and loud, but it keeps a nice lawn (and they secretly love them). Central Florida's many theme parks can become overpowering for even the most enthusiastic visitor, and that's when an excursion into the "other" Orlando—the one the locals know and love—is in order.

There are ample opportunities for day trips. If the outdoors is your thing, you can swim or canoe at Wekiwa Springs State Park or one of the area's many other sparkling springs, where the water remains a refreshing 72°F no matter how hot the day. Alternatively, you can hike, horseback ride, canoe, and camp in the Ocala National Forest.

If museums are your thing, charming Winter Park has the Charles Hosmer Morse Museum of American Art with its huge collection of Tiffany glass. While in Winter Park, you can indulge in some high-end shopping and dining on Park Avenue or take a leisurely boat tour of the lakefront homes.

Got kids to educate and entertain? Check out WonderWorks or the Orlando Science Center, where you can view live gators and turtles. Even more live gators (some as long as 14 feet) can be viewed or fed (or even eaten) at Gatorland, just south of Orlando.

Do the kids prefer rockets and astronauts? Don't miss a day trip to Kennedy Space Center, where you can tour a rocket forest, sit in a space capsule, or see a space shuttle up close.

Kissimmee is a 19th-century cattle town south of Orlando that proudly hangs on to its roots with a twice-yearly rodeo where real cowboys ride bulls and rope cattle. The town sits on Lake Tohopekaliga, a favorite spot for airboat rides or fishing trips.

GETTING HERE AND AROUND

Orlando is spread out. During rush hour, car traffic crawls along the often-crowded Interstate 4 (particularly now that the multibillion-dollar upgrade, expected to end in 2021, has begun, relocating and closing key exits and entrances), which runs to both coasts. If you're heading east, you can also take Route 528 (aka the Beachline), a toll road that heads directly for Cape Canaveral and points along the Space Coast; no such option leads west.

If you avoid rush-hour traffic, traveling to points of interest shouldn't take too much time out of your vacation. Winter Park is no more than 20 minutes from Downtown; International Drive and the theme parks are about 30 minutes away in heavier traffic. Orlando International Airport is only 9 miles south of Downtown, but it will take about 30 minutes via a circuitous network of highways (Interstate 4 west to Florida's Turnpike south to Route 528 east).

VISITOR INFORMATION

Contacts Orlando Visitors Bureau. ⊠ *8723 International Dr., Suite 101* ☎ *407/363-5872, 800/972-3304* ⊕ *www.visitorlando.com.*

EXPLORING

Orlando is a diverse town. The Downtown area, though small, is dynamic, thanks to an ever-changing skyline of high-rises, sports venues, museums, restaurants, nightspots, a history museum, and several annual cultural events—including film festivals and a world-renowned theater fest. Downtown also has a central green, Lake Eola Park, which offers a respite from otherwise frantic touring.

Neighborhoods such as Thornton Park (great for dining) and College Park (an outpost of quirky shopping) are fun to wander. Not too far to the north, you can come in contact with natural Florida—its manatees, gators, and crystal-clear waters in spring-fed lakes.

Closer to the theme-park action, International Drive, the hub of resort and conference hotels, offers big restaurants and even bigger outlet-mall bargains. Sand Lake Road, between the two, is Orlando's Restaurant Row, with plenty of exciting dining prospects.

9

ORLANDO

There's more to Orlando than theme parks: a thriving Downtown with ample opportunity to stay, eat, and play. Internationally recognized cultural events, theater, and the evolving music scene make Downtown more than just a stopping point.

CENTRAL ORLANDO

FAMILY **Crayola Experience.** One of the company's three "experiences" in the country, Crayola offers a 70,000-square-foot haven of color at the Florida Mall. An overwhelming 25 interactive stations extend throughout the two-floor center, including painting and modeling stations, where tykes can create animals out of clay and melted crayons. Don't miss the younger set's favorite: You Design, a virtual studio for coloring and digitally accessorizing a car or fashion wardrobe before watching the personal design make its debut on a large projected screen. Also be sure to make it a priority to check out the Crayon Factory, where live demonstrations show the crayon creation process from wax to wrapper. ⊠ *The Florida Mall, 8001 Orange Blossom Trail, Central Orlando* ☎ *407/825-9234* ⊕ *www.crayolaexperience.com* ⊠ *$22.99.*

Fodor's Choice ★ **Harry P. Leu Gardens.** A few miles outside of Downtown—on the former lakefront estate of a citrus entrepreneur—is this 50-acre garden. Among the highlights are a collection of historical blooms (many varieties of which were established before 1900), ancient oaks, a 50-foot floral clock, and one of the largest camellia collections in eastern North America (in bloom November–March). Mary Jane's Rose Garden, named after Leu's wife, is filled with more than 1,000 bushes; it's the largest formal rose garden south of Atlanta. The simple 19th-century Leu House Museum, once the Leu family home, preserves the furnishings and appointments of a well-to-do, turn-of-the-20th-century Florida family. Admission is free on the first Monday of the month from January through September. ⊠ *1920 N. Forest Ave., Audubon Park* 🕾 *407/246–2620* ⊕ *www. leugardens.org* 🖅 *$10* ⊘ *Leu House Museum closed in July.*

FAMILY   **Lake Eola Park.** This beautifully landscaped 43-acre park is the verdant heart of Downtown Orlando, its mile-long walking path a gathering place for families, health enthusiasts out for a run, and culture mavens exploring area offerings. The well-lighted playground is alive with children, and ducks, swans, and native Florida birds call the lake home. A popular and expanded farmers' market takes up residence on Sunday afternoon.

The lakeside Walt Disney Amphitheater is a dramatic site for concerts, ethnic festivals, and spectacular Fourth of July fireworks. Don't resist the park's biggest draw: a ride in a swan-shaped pedal boat. Up to five adults can fit comfortably in each. (Children under 16 must be accompanied by an adult.)

The Relax Grill, by the swan-boat launch, is a great place for a snack. The park is surrounded by great Downtown and Thornton Park restaurants and lounges. The ever-expanding skyline rings the lake with modern high-rises, making the peace of the park even more welcome. The landmark fountain features an LED-light-and-music show on summer evenings at 9:30. ⊠ *195 N. Rosalind Ave., Downtown Orlando* ✛ *Center of Downtown Orlando* 🕾 *407/246–4485 park, 407/246–4485 swan boats* 🖅 *Swan boat rental $15 per ½ hr.*

Mennello Museum of American Folk Art. One of the few museums in the United States devoted to folk art has intimate galleries, some with lovely lakefront views. Look for the nation's most extensive permanent collection of Earl Cunningham paintings as well as works by many other self-taught artists. There's a wonderful video about Cunningham and his "curio shop" in St. Augustine, Florida. Temporary exhibitions have included the works of Wyeth, Cassatt, and Michael Eastman. At the museum shop you can purchase folk-art books, toys, and unusual gifts. The Mennello is the site of the annual Orlando Folk Festival, held the second weekend of February. ⊠ *900 E. Princeton St., Lake Ivanhoe* 🕾 *407/246–4278* ⊕ *www.mennellomuseum.org* 🖅 *$5* ⊘ *Closed Mon.*

FAMILY   **Orange County Regional History Center.** Exhibits here take you on a journey back in time to discover how Florida's Paleo-Indians hunted and fished the land, what the Sunshine State was like when the Spaniards first arrived, and how life in Florida was different when citrus was king. Exhibitions cover the history of citrus-growing in Central Florida, samples of the work of the famed Highwaymen painters, and the

Central Orlando

0   1/2 mi
0   1/2 km

TO
WINTER
PARK

To Winter Park

Orlando
Executive
Airport

TO
ORLANDO
INT'L AIRPORT
via Route 436
(Semoran Blvd.)

The Social / AERO

Wally's

Amway
Center

Florida Mall

advancement of the theme parks. Traveling exhibits bring modern technology and art to the museum. Free audio tours are available. ✉ *65 E. Central Blvd., Downtown Orlando* ☎ *407/836–8500, 800/965–2030* ⊕ *www.thehistorycenter.org* ✍ *$8.*

FAMILY

Fodor's Choice

★

Orlando Science Center. A new and very popular Kids Town and a new gift shop were opened in 2016, part of an ongoing $30-million renovation of the museum, which opened in 1997. With exhibits about the human body, mechanics, computers, math, nature, the solar system, and optics, the science center has something for every child's inner geek. Traveling shows include an astronaut experience, the science of human anatomy, and the annual interactive technology expo called Otricon.

The four-story internal atrium is home to live gators and turtles and is a great spot for simply gazing at what Old Florida once looked like. The 300-seat Dr. Phillips CineDome, a movie theater with a giant eight-story screen, offers large-format iWERKS films and planetarium programs. The Crosby Observatory and Florida's largest publicly accessible refractor telescope are here, as are several smaller telescopes.

Adults like the science center, too, thanks to events like the annual Science of Wine and Cosmic Golf Challenge; evenings of stargazing in the Crosby Observatory; and the very popular First Wednesdays wine and music gatherings. ✉ *777 E. Princeton St., Lake Ivanhoe* ☎ *407/514–2000* ⊕ *www.osc.org* ✍ *$19.95; parking $5* ⊙ *Closed Wed. (except for 1st Wed. evenings).*

INTERNATIONAL DRIVE

The Coca-Cola Orlando Eye. The 400-foot-tall Orlando Eye offers an almost unobstructed view of theme parks, lush green landscape, and the soaring buildings of the City Beautiful from the tallest observation wheel on the east coast. Only 15 minutes from Walt Disney World and Universal Studios Orlando, the 400-foot Ferris wheel anchors I-Drive 360 and the area's massive redevelopment projects. The wheel's 30 high-tech capsules complete a rotation every 30 minutes. Apple iPad Air tablets on board help to locate points of interest throughout the trip, including the nearby theme parks, scenic landscapes, and even the Atlantic coast. Visibility on clear days can be more than 50 miles, reaching all the way east to Cape Canaveral. ✉ *I-Drive 360, 8401 International Dr., International Drive* ☎ *407/270–8644* ⊕ *www.officialorlandoeye.com* ✍ *$25.*

FAMILY

Fun Spot America. Virtual reality met real excitement when Fun Spot added a VR system to its Freedom Flyer coaster last year, adding a high-tech element to a park known for wooden roller coasters, go-karts, and twirling teacups. Four go-kart tracks offer a variety of driving experiences. Though drivers must be at least 10 years old and meet height requirements, parents can drive younger children in two-seater cars on several of the tracks, including the Conquest Track. Nineteen rides range from the dizzying Paratrooper to an old-fashioned Revolver Ferris Wheel to the twirling toddler Teacups. Fun Spot features Central Florida's only wooden roller coaster as well as the Freedom Flyer steel suspension family coaster, a kiddie coaster, and SkyCoaster—part skydive, part hang-glide. There's also an arcade. ✉ *5700 Fun Spot Way, International Drive* ✛ *From Exit 75A, turn left onto International Dr.,*

The 300-seat Dr. Phillips CineDome, a movie theater with an eight-story screen at the Orlando Science Center, offers large-format iWERKS films.

then left on Fun Spot Way ☎ *407/363–3867* ⊕ *www.funspotattractions. com* ✉ *$39.95 for all rides (online discounts available) or pay per ride; admission for nonriders free; arcade extra.*

Ripley's Believe It or Not! Odditorium A 10-foot-square section of the Berlin Wall. A pain and torture chamber. Two African fertility statues that women swear have helped them conceive. These and almost 200 other oddities (shrunken heads included) speak for themselves in this museum-cum-attraction in the heart of tourist territory on International Drive. The building itself is designed to appear as if it's sliding into one of Florida's notorious sinkholes. Give yourself an hour or two to soak up the weirdness, but remember: this is a looking, not touching, experience; it might drive antsy youngsters—and their parents—crazy. ■ TIP→ Buy tickets online ahead of time, and you can get discounts. ✉ *I-Drive 360, 8201 International Dr., International Drive* ☎ *407/351–5803* ⊕ *www.ripleysorlando.com* ✉ *$19.99; parking free.*

9

FAMILY **SEA LIFE Orlando Aquarium.** In the shadow of the Orlando Eye within the I-Drive 360 entertainment complex stands a kaleidoscope of underwater colors, where you can see some 5,000 sea creatures and explore various habitats. Plan to spend the better part of an afternoon exploring the attraction, as all ages delight at the close encounters with the aquarium's sharks, green sea turtles, and jellyfish. With an emphasis on education and conservation, exhibits are playful and informative, with fun features that include a 360-degree ocean tunnel and a children's soft play area. Combo tickets are available for SEA LIFE, the Orlando Eye, and Madame Tussauds. ✉ *I-Drive 360, 8449 International Dr., International Drive* ☎ *866/622–0607* ⊕ *www2.visitsealife.com/orlando* ✉ *$25.*

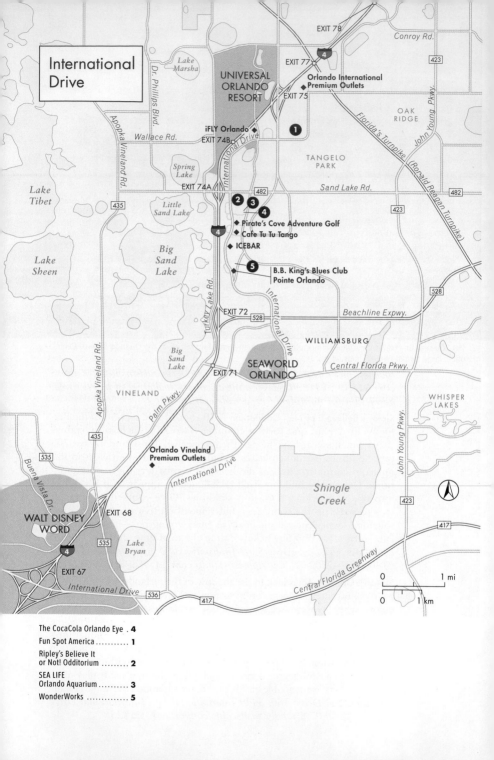

International Drive

EXIT 78

Conroy Rd.

EXIT 77

Lake Marsha

Dr. Phillips Blvd.

UNIVERSAL ORLANDO RESORT

Orlando International Premium Outlets

EXIT 75

Florida's Turnpike (Ronald Reagan Turnpike)

OAK RIDGE

iFLY Orlando
EXIT 74B

International Drive

Wallace Rd.

Apopka Vineland Rd.

TANGELO PARK

1

Spring Lake

EXIT 74A

Little Sand Lake

435

482

Sand Lake Rd.

482

423

Lake Tibet

2 **3** **4**

◆ **Pirate's Cove Adventure Golf**

Big Sand Lake

◆ **Cafe Tu Tu Tango**

Lake Sheen

◆ **ICEBAR**

5 ◆ **B.B. King's Blues Club Pointe Orlando**

528

Turkey Lake Rd.

International Drive

EXIT 72

528

Beachline Expwy.

WILLIAMSBURG

Big Sand Lake

EXIT 71

SEAWORLD ORLANDO

Central Florida Pkwy.

VINELAND

Palm Pkwy.

WHISPER LAKES

John Young Pkwy.

Apopka Vineland Rd.

435

◆ **Orlando Vineland Premium Outlets**

International Drive

Shingle Creek

423

535

Buena Vista Dr.

417

WALT DISNEY WORD

EXIT 68

Lake Bryan

Central Florida Greenway

417

EXIT 67

International Drive

536

417

0 ——— 1 mi

0 ——— 1 km

FAMILY **WonderWorks.** The building seems to be sinking into the ground—at a precarious angle and upside down. Many people stop to take pictures in front of the topsy-turvy facade, complete with upended palm trees and broken skyward-facing sidewalks. Inside, the upside-down theme continues only as far as the lobby. After that, it's a playground of 100 interactive experiences—some incorporating virtual reality, others educational (similar to those at a science museum), and still others pure entertainment. You can experience an earthquake or a hurricane, land a space shuttle using simulator controls, make giant bubbles in the Bubble Lab, play laser tag in the enormous laser-tag arena and arcade, design and ride your own roller coaster, lie on a bed of real nails, and play baseball with a virtual Major League batter. An "Outta Control Magic Comedy Dinner Show" is held here nightly. ⊠ *9067 International Dr., International Drive* ☎ *407/351–8800* ⊕ *www.wonderworksonline. com/orlando* ⊠ *$29.99; Outta Control Magic Comedy Dinner Show extra (online discounts available); parking $4–$10.*

WINTER PARK

6 miles northeast of Orlando, 20 miles northeast of WDW.

This peaceful, upscale community may be just outside the hustle and bustle of Orlando, but it feels like a different country. The town's name reflects its early role as a warm-weather haven for those escaping the frigid blasts of Northeast winters. From the late 1880s until the early 1930s, wealthy industrialists and their families would travel to Florida by rail on vacation, and many stayed, establishing grand homes and cultural institutions. The lovely, 8-square-mile village retains its charm with brick-paved streets, historic buildings, and well-maintained lakes and parkland. Even the town's bucolic 9-hole golf course (open to the public) is on the National Register of Historic Places.

On Park Avenue you can spend a few hours sightseeing, shopping, or both. The street is lined with small boutiques and fine restaurants and bookended by world-class museums: the Charles Hosmer Morse Museum of American Art, with the world's largest collection of artwork by Louis Comfort Tiffany. The campus of Rollins College (the oldest college in Florida) is also in Winter Park.

9

TOURS

FAMILY **Scenic Boat Tour.** Head east from Park Avenue and, at the end of Morse Boulevard, you'll find the launching point for this tour, a Winter Park tradition since 1938. The one-hour cruise takes in 12 miles of waterways, including three lakes and narrow, oak- and cypress-shaded canals built in the 1800s as a transportation system for the logging industry. A well-schooled skipper shares stories about the moguls who built their mansions along the shore and points out wildlife and remnants of natural Florida still surrounding the expensive houses. Cash or check only is accepted. ⊠ *312 E. Morse Blvd., Winter Park* ☎ *407/644–4056* ⊕ *www. scenicboattours.com* ⊠ *$14.*

EXPLORING

Fodor's Choice ★ **Charles Hosmer Morse Museum of American Art.** The world's most comprehensive collection of work by Louis Comfort Tiffany—including immense stained-glass windows, lamps, watercolors, and desk sets—is in this museum, which also contains American decorative art and paintings from the mid-19th to the early 20th century.

Among the draws is the 1,082-square-foot Tiffany Chapel, originally built for the 1893 World's Fair in Chicago. It took craftsmen 2½ years to painstakingly reassemble the chapel here. Many of the works were rescued from Tiffany's Long Island estate, Laurelton Hall, after a 1957 fire destroyed much of the property. The 12,000-square-foot Laurelton Hall wing allows for much more of the estate's collection to be displayed at one time. Exhibits in the wing include architectural and decorative elements from Laurelton's dining room, living room, and Fountain Court reception hall. There's also a re-creation of the striking Daffodil Terrace, so named for the glass daffodils that serve as the capitals for the terrace's marble columns. ⊠ *445 N. Park Ave., Winter Park* ☎ *407/645–5311* ⊕ *www. morsemuseum.org* ⊠ *$6; free Nov.–Apr., Fri. 4–8* ⊙ *Closed Mon.*

FAMILY **WinterClub Indoor Ski & Snowboard.** Snow enthusiasts can opt for the truly unique experience of skiing and snowboarding in shorts and a T-shirt at Orlando's WinterClub Indoor Ski & Snowboard, proving that heading south doesn't necessarily cancel out winter sports. The region's first indoor ski center welcomes participants at all levels to come practice and play on these high-tech "endless slopes." WinterClub's interactive Ski Simulator fuses high-definition large video wall ski runs with a unique chassis that allows skiers to experience the same G-force effects as they would skiing in real life. ⊠ *2950 Aloma Ave, Winter Park* ☎ *407/618–1123* ⊕ *www.winterclubski.com* ⊠ *From $49.*

KISSIMMEE

18 miles south of Orlando, 10 miles southeast of Walt Disney World (WDW).

Although Kissimmee is primarily known as the gateway to Disney (technically, the vast Disney property of theme parks and resorts lies in both Osceola and Orange counties), its non-WDW attractions just might tickle your fancy. They range from throwbacks to old-time Florida to dinner shows for you and 2,000 of your closest friends. Orlando used to be prime cattle country, and the best sampling of what life was like is here during the Silver Springs Rodeo in February and June.

With at least 100,000 acres of freshwater lakes, the Kissimmee area brings anglers and boaters to national fishing tournaments and speedboat races. A 50-mile-long series of lakes, the Kissimmee Waterway, connects Lake Tohopekaliga—a Native American name that means "Sleeping Tiger"—with huge Lake Okeechobee in South Florida, and from there, to both the Atlantic Ocean and the Gulf of Mexico.

FAMILY **Gatorland.** This campy attraction near the Orlando–Kissimmee border on U.S. 441 has endured since 1949 without much change, despite competition from the major parks. Over the years, the theme park and registered conservancy has gone through some changes while retaining its gator-rasslin' spirit. Kids get a kick out of this unmanufactured, old-timey thrill ride.

The Gator Gulley Splash Park is complete with giant "egrets" spilling water from their beaks, dueling water guns mounted atop giant gators, and other water-park splash areas. There's also a small petting zoo and an aviary. A free train ride is a high point, taking you through an alligator breeding marsh and a natural swamp setting where you can spot gators, birds, and turtles. A three-story observation tower overlooks the breeding marsh, swamped with gator grunts, especially come sundown during mating season.

For a glimpse of 37 giant, rare, and deadly crocodiles, check out the Jungle Crocs of the World exhibit. To see eager gators leaping out of the water to catch their food, come on cool days for the Gator Jumparoo Show (summer heat just puts them to sleep). The most thrilling is the first one in the morning, when the gators are hungriest. There's also a Gator Wrestlin' Show, and although there's no doubt who's going to win the match, it's still fun to see the handlers take on those tough guys with the beady eyes. In the educational Upclose Encounters show, the show's host handles a variety of snakes. Recent park additions include Panther Springs, featuring brother-and-sister endangered panthers, and the wheelchair-accessible Screamin' Gator Zip Line (additional cost). This is a real Florida experience, and you leave knowing the difference between a gator and a croc. ■ TIP→ Discount coupons are available online. ✉ *14501 S. Orange Blossom Trail, between Orlando and Kissimmee, Kissimmee* ☎ *407/855–5496, 800/393–5297* ⊕ *www.gatorland.com* ✉ *$23.99.*

WHERE TO EAT

Dining in Orlando ranges from fast food and national chains to celebrity chefs—both international and local—serving locally sourced foods, creative preparations, and clever international influences. The theme parks now have some of the best restaurants in town, although you may opt for a rental car to seek out the local treasures.

The signs of Orlando's dining progress are most evident in the last place one would look: Disney's fast-food outlets. Every eatery on Disney property offers a tempting vegetarian option, and kiddie meals come with healthful sides and drinks unless you specifically request otherwise. Chefs at Disney's table-service restaurants consult face-to-face with guests about food allergies. And big-name chefs are now well represented in Disney Springs, though less so at Universal's CityWalk.

Around town, locals flock to the Ravenous Pig, the Rusty Spoon, and other gastropubs where the menu changes regularly; Luma on Park, a suave home of thoughtfully created cutting-edge meals; and any number of dining establishments competing to serve the very finest steaks. Orlando's culinary blossoming began in 1995, when Disney's signature California Grill debuted, featuring farm-to-table cuisine and wonderful wines by the glass. Soon after, celebrity chefs started opening up shop. Disney has since completely revamped California Grill so it's a trendsetter once again.

9

Orlando's destination restaurants can be found in the theme parks, as well as in the outlying towns. Sand Lake Road is now known as Restaurant Row for its eclectic collection of worthwhile tables. Here you'll find fashionable outlets for sushi and seafood, Italian and chops, Hawaiian fusion, and upscale Lebanese. Heading into the residential areas, the neighborhoods of Winter Park (actually its own city), Thornton Park, and College Park are prime locales for chow. Scattered throughout Central Florida, low-key ethnic restaurants specialize in the fare of Turkey, India, Peru, Thailand, Vietnam—you name it. Prices in these family owned finds are usually delightfully low.

MAPS

Throughout the chapter, you'll see mapping symbols and coordinates (⊕ 1:F2) after property names or reviews. Maps are within the chapter. The first number after the symbol indicates the map number. After that is the property's coordinate on the map grid.

MEAL PLANS

Disney Magic Your Way Plus Dining Plan allows you one table-service meal, one counter-service meal, and one snack per day of your trip at more than 100 theme-park and resort restaurants, provided you stay in a Disney hotel. You'll also receive a refillable drink mug for use at your hotel's fast fooderies. For more money, you can upgrade the plan to include more; to save, you can downgrade to a counter-service-only plan. Used wisely, a Disney dining plan is a steal, but be careful to buy only the number of meals you'll want to eat. Moderate eaters can end up turning away appetizers and desserts to which they're entitled. Plan ahead, and use "extra" meals to your advantage by swapping two table-service meals for a Disney dinner show, say, or an evening at a high-end restaurant like California Grill.

Universal Dining Plan offers one sit-down and one quick-service meal at participating walk-up eateries inside Universal Studios and Islands of Adventure, plus a snack and soft drink. Meal plans can only be purchased with a resort stay. A quick-service-only arrangement, with one meal a day, can be purchased by anyone, as can all-you-can-drink soft drinks.

WHAT IT COSTS			
	$	$$	$$$	$$$$
At Dinner	under $15	$15–$20	$21–$30	over $30

Prices are per person for a median main course, at dinner, excluding tip and tax of 6.5%.

RESERVATIONS

Reservations are strongly recommended throughout the theme parks. Indeed, make reservations for Disney restaurants and character meals at both Universal and Disney at least 90 (and up to 180) days out. And be sure to ask about the cancellation policy—at a handful of Disney restaurants, for instance, you may be charged penalties if you don't give 24 to 48 hours' notice.

Kissimmee's Lake Tohopekaliga (affectionately known as Lake Toho) is famous with fishers the world over. It's also great for wildlife spotting—an especially exhilarating experience when done from an airboat.

For restaurant reservations within Walt Disney World, call ☎ *407/939–3463 (WDW–DINE)* or book online at 🌐 *www.disneyworld.com/dining*. You can also get plenty of information on the website, including the meal periods served, price range, and specialties of all Disney eateries. Menus for all restaurants are posted online and tend to be up to date. For Universal Orlando reservations, call ☎ *407/224–9255 (theme parks and CityWalk)* or ☎ *407/503–3463* (hotels). Learn about the complex's 50-plus restaurants at 🌐 *www.universalorlando.com/dining*.

Unless otherwise noted, the restaurants listed are open daily for lunch and dinner. Restaurant reviews have been shortened. For full information, visit Fodors.com.

9

ORLANDO

CENTRAL ORLANDO

$$ ASIAN FUSION Fodor's Choice ★

🍴 **Hawkers.** Hipsters, families, and business groups dine side by side at this popular restaurant, a laid-back spot that specializes in serving Asian street food. Travel the continent with scratch-made specialties from all around Southeast Asia. **Known for:** typical dishes like roti canai, sesame noodles, and stir-fried udon; hip and casual atmosphere; extensive and exotic beer selections. [$] *Average main: $16* ✉ *1103 Mills Ave., Mills 50 District* ☎ *407/237–0606* 🌐 *eathawkers.com* ✣ *1:F1.*

$$$$ AMERICAN Fodor's Choice ★

🍴 **K Restaurant & Wine Bar.** At the forefront of Orlando's local and sustainable dining scene, K is a hot spot for locals, serving upscale, eclectic American and Italian cuisine in an intimate setting. Besides happy-hour specials and dinner, K hosts wine tastings in the garden or on the patio

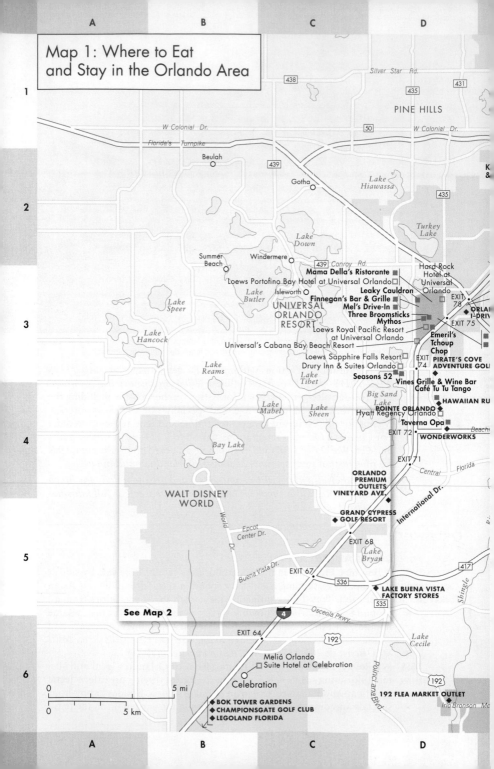

Map 1: Where to Eat and Stay in the Orlando Area

PINE HILLS

Silver Star Rd.

438
435
431

W Colonial Dr.
50
W Colonial Dr.

Florida's Turnpike

Beulah

439

Gotha

Lake Hiawassa

435

Lake Down

Turkey Lake

Summer Beach

Windermere

439 Conroy Rd.

Mama Della's Ristorante
Loews Portofino Bay Hotel at Universal Orlando

Hard Rock Hotel at Universal Orlando

Lake Speer

Lake Butler

Isleworth

Leaky Cauldron

EXIT 78

ORLA I-DRIV

Finnegan's Bar & Grille
Mel's Drive-In
Three Broomsticks
Mythos

EXIT 75

Lake Hancock

UNIVERSAL ORLANDO RESORT

Loews Royal Pacific Resort at Universal Orlando
Universal's Cabana Bay Beach Resort

Emeril's Tchoup Chop
PIRATE'S COVE ADVENTURE GOLF

Lake Reams

Loews Sapphire Falls Resort
Drury Inn & Suites Orlando
Seasons 52

EXIT 74

Lake Tibet

Vines Grille & Wine Bar
Café Tu Tu Tango

Lake Mabel

Lake Sheen

Big Sand Lake

HAWAIIAN RU

POINTE ORLANDO
Hyatt Regency Orlando
Taverna Opa

Beach

EXIT 72

WONDERWORKS

Bay Lake

EXIT 71

Central Florida

WALT DISNEY WORLD

World Dr.

Epcot Center Dr.

ORLANDO PREMIUM OUTLETS VINEYARD AVE.

International Dr.

GRAND CYPRESS GOLF RESORT

EXIT 68

Lake Bryan

Buena Vista Dr.

EXIT 67

536

417

LAKE BUENA VISTA FACTORY STORES

535

Shingle

See Map 2

4

Osceola Pkwy.

EXIT 64

192

Lake Cecile

Meliá Orlando Suite Hotel at Celebration

Celebration

Poinciana Blvd.

192

0   5 mi
0   5 km

BOK TOWER GARDENS
CHAMPIONSGATE GOLF CLUB
LEGOLAND FLORIDA

192 FLEA MARKET OUTLET

Irlo Bronson Me

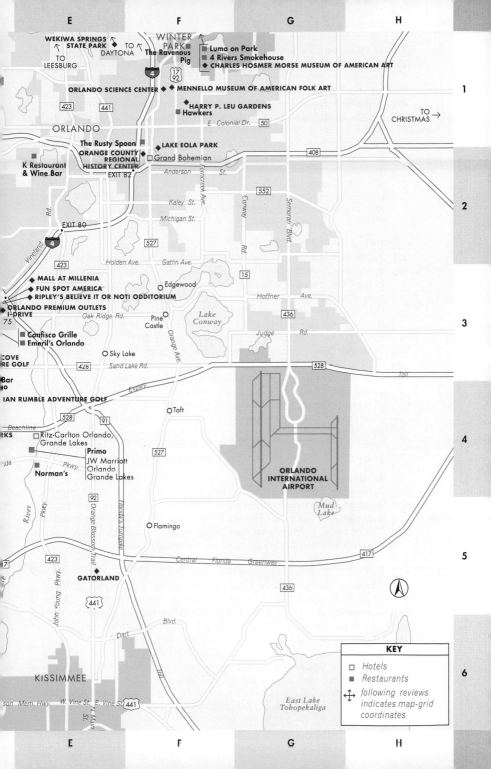

E

WEKIWA SPRINGS
↑ STATE PARK ↖ TO ↖
TO DAYTONA
↑ LEESBURG

F

WINTER
PARK
The Ravenous
Pig

■ Luma on Park
■ 4 Rivers Smokehouse
◆ CHARLES HOSMER MORSE MUSEUM OF AMERICAN ART

G   **H**

ORLANDO SCIENCE CENTER ◆ ◆ MENNELLO MUSEUM OF AMERICAN FOLK ART   1

[423] [441]   ◆ HARRY P. LEU GARDENS
                               ■ Hawkers
ORLANDO   E. Colonial Dr. [50]   TO →
                                                            CHRISTMAS

The Rusty Spoon ■ ◆ LAKE EOLA PARK   [408]
ORANGE COUNTY
REGIONAL   □ Grand Bohemian
K Restaurant   HISTORY CENTER
& Wine Bar   EXIT 82   Anderson   St.
                                                [552]   2
                Kaley St.
Vineland   Michigan St.   Conway
Rd. EXIT 80
   4   [527]   Semoran Blvd.
[423]   Holden Ave.   Gatlin Ave.   [15]

◆ MALL AT MILLENIA
◆ FUN SPOT AMERICA   ○ Edgewood   Hoffner   Ave.
◆ RIPLEY'S BELIEVE IT OR NOT! ODDITORIUM
ORLANDO PREMIUM OUTLETS   [436]   3
I-DRIVE   Oak Ridge Rd.   Pine   Lake
75   Castle   Conway
■ Confisco Grille   Judge   Rd.
■ Emeril's Orlando   Orange Ave.
                ○ Sky Lake   [528]
COVE   Sand Lake Rd.   Toll
RE GOLF   [428]
Bar   Expwy.
IO
IAN RUMBLE ADVENTURE GOLF
Beachline   ○ Taft   ORLANDO
[528] [91]   [527]   INTERNATIONAL   4
RKS □ Ritz-Carlton Orlando,   AIRPORT
   Grande Lakes
ida   Primo
   ■ JW Marriott
Norman's ■ Orlando
       Grande Lakes
   [92]   Mud
7   ○ Flamingo   Lake
River Pkwy.
[423]   Central Florida Greenway   [417]   5
7
       ◆ GATORLAND
[441]
                Blvd.
                Dart

KISSIMMEE   6

son Mem. Hwy. W. Vine St. E. Vine St. [441]   East Lake
                                                     Tohopekaliga

E   **F**   **G**   **H**

┌─────────────────────────────┐
│   KEY   │
│ □ Hotels   │
│ ■ Restaurants   │
│ ⬍ following reviews   │
│   indicates map-grid   │
│   coordinates   │
└─────────────────────────────┘

and popular prix-fixe wine dinners. **Known for:** ever-changing seasonal menu; great local meeting spot away from Downtown Orlando; mac-and-cheese specials. $ *Average main: $34 ⊠ 1710 Edgewater Dr., College Park* ☎ 407/872–2332 ⊙ *No dinner Sun.* ✛ *1:E2.*

$$$ ✕ **The Rusty Spoon.** Lovingly raised animals and locally grown produce
AMERICAN   are the menu foundation at this Downtown gastropub owned by chef
Fodor'sChoice   Kathleen Blake. An ideal spot for a business lunch or dinner before a
★   basketball game, theater, or concert, the wood-and-brick dining room is a comfortable backdrop to hearty, seasonal American meals with Italian and Southern elements. **Known for:** locally sourced and Florida-specific ingredients; "Lake Meadow" salad, with local greens and sautéed chicken livers; impressive service. $ *Average main: $22 ⊠ 55 W. Church St., Downtown Orlando* ☎ 407/401–8811 ⊕ *www.therustyspoon.com* ⊙ *No lunch weekends* ✛ *1:F1.*

INTERNATIONAL DRIVE

$$$ ✕ **Café Tu Tu Tango.** The food here is served tapas-style—everything is
ECLECTIC   appetizer size but plentiful, and relatively inexpensive. The restaurant is designed to resemble an artist's loft; artists paint at easels while diners take a culinary trip around the world. **Known for:** small plates ideal for sharing; live entertainment; "Wine Down Wednesday" drink specials. $ *Average main: $23 ⊠ 8625 International Dr., International Drive* ☎ 407/248–2222 ⊕ *www.cafetututango.com* ✛ *1:D4.*

$$$ ✕ **Taverna Opa.** This high-energy Greek restaurant offers a fun evening
GREEK   in lively environment to supplement excellent Greek staples and a nice
FAMILY   selection of meze (small plate) appetizers. Here the ouzo flows like a mountain stream, the Greek (and global) music almost reaches the level of a rock concert, and the roaming belly dancers actively encourage diners to join in. **Known for:** traditional Greek taverna food; live entertainment; large selection of meze, both vegetarian and not. $ *Average main: $27 ⊠ Pointe Orlando, 9101 International Dr., International Drive* ☎ 407/351–8660 ⊕ *www.opaorlando.com* ✛ *1:D4.*

SOUTH ORLANDO

$$$$ ✕ **Norman's.** Legendary Florida chef Norman Van Aken brings impres-
ECLECTIC   sive credentials to the restaurant that bears his name. Van Aken's culi-
Fodor'sChoice   nary roots go back to the Florida Keys, where he's credited with creating
★   "Floribbean" cuisine, part Key West and part Caribbean—although he now weaves in flavors from all continents. **Known for:** James Beard Award–winning chef; creative preparations with wide-ranging international influences; extensive wine list. $ *Average main: $49 ⊠ Ritz-Carlton Orlando Grande Lakes, 4000 Central Florida Pkwy., South Orlando* ☎ 407/393–4333 ⊕ *www.normans.com* ⊙ *No lunch* ✛ *1:E4.*

$$$$ ✕ **Primo.** Chef Melissa Kelly cloned her Italian-organic Maine restau-
ITALIAN   rant in an upscale Orlando hotel and brought her farm-to-table sen-
Fodor'sChoice   sibilities with her. Here the daily dinner menu pays tribute to Italian
★   cuisine utilizing produce grown in the hotel's organic garden. **Known for:** constantly changing menu using locally sourced ingredients; interesting pizzas; house-made pastas. $ *Average main: $43 ⊠ JW Marriott Orlando Grande Lakes, 4040 Central Florida Pkwy., South Orlando* ☎ 407/393–4444 ⊕ *www.primorestaurant.com* ⊙ *No lunch* ✛ *1:E4.*

SAND LAKE ROAD

$$$ AMERICAN

🍴 **Seasons 52.** Parts of the menu change every week at this innovative restaurant that serves different foods at different times of year, depending on what's in season. It's hard to believe that a chain restaurant can continue to serve healthful yet hearty and very flavorful food for more than a decade, yet it does. **Known for:** waits for tables, even when you have a reservation; $5 plates and wines during the daily happy hour; flatbread starters that are big enough to share. [$] *Average main: $21* ✉ *Plaza Venezia, 7700 Sand Lake Rd., I–4 Exit 75A, Sand Lake Rd. Area* ☎ *407/354–5212* 🌐 *www.seasons52.com* ✣ *1:D3.*

$$$$ STEAKHOUSE

🍴 **Vines Grille & Wine Bar.** Live jazz and blues music fills the night at the bar section of this dramatically designed restaurant, but the food and drink in the snazzy main dining room are headliners in their own right. The kitchen bills itself as a steak house, but it really is far more than that. **Known for:** extensive wine selection and cocktails; prime steaks cooked on a wood-fired grill; live jazz performances. [$] *Average main: $62* ✉ *The Fountains, 7533 W. Sand Lake Rd., Sand Lake Rd. Area* ☎ *407/351–1227* 🌐 *www.seasons52.com* 🕒 *No lunch* ✣ *1:D3.*

WINTER PARK

$ BARBECUE Fodor's Choice ★

🍴 **4 Rivers Smokehouse.** What started as a tiny business in a former tire repair shop has turned into a multistate dynasty. The popular 4 Rivers, now with 14 locations and more on the way, turns out slow-cooked barbecue standards like pulled pork and Texas-style brisket. **Known for:** giant portions; sweet shop bakeries; bacon-wrapped smoked jalapeños. [$] *Average main: $13* ✉ *1600 W. Fairbanks Ave., Winter Park* ☎ *855/368–7748* 🌐 *4rsmokehouse.com* 🕒 *Closed Sun.* ✣ *1:F1.*

$$$ MODERN AMERICAN Fodor's Choice ★

🍴 **Luma on Park.** One of the Orlando area's best restaurants, Luma on Park is a popular spot for progressive American cuisine served in a fashionable setting, run by chef Brandon McGlammery. Every ingredient is carefully sourced from local producers when possible, and scratch preparation—from pastas to sausages to pickled rhubarb—is the mantra. **Known for:** North Carolina flounder and Snake River flank steak; extensive wine list; attention to detail. [$] *Average main: $30* ✉ *290 S. Park Ave., Winter Park* ☎ *407/599–4111* 🌐 *www.lumaonpark.com* ✣ *1:F1.*

$$$$ MODERN AMERICAN Fodor's Choice ★

🍴 **The Ravenous Pig.** The first local restaurant to break into the "gastropub" category, the Pig is arguably Orlando's most popular foodie destination and has spawned several offshoots. Run by husband-and-wife chefs James and Julie Petrakis, the restaurant dispenses delicacies, from a pork porterhouse to a pub burger. **Known for:** merged with Cask & Larder brewery; open until midnight Thursday–Saturday; house-made charcuterie. [$] *Average main: $31* ✉ *565 W. Fairbanks Ave, Winter Park* ☎ *407/628–2333* 🌐 *www.theravenouspig.com* ✣ *1:F1.*

9

KISSIMMEE

$$$$ STEAKHOUSE 🍴 **Old Hickory Steakhouse.** This upscale steak house is designed to look like rustic cabins in the Everglades. Beyond the playful facade is a polished restaurant with a classic steak-house menu of steaks and chops. **Known for:** particularly good steaks; free valet parking; consistently good service. [$] *Average main: $47* ✉ *Gaylord Palms Resort, 6000 W. Osceola Pkwy., I–4 Exit 65, Kissimmee* ☎ *407/586–1600* 🌐 *www.gaylordpalms.com* 🕒 *No lunch* ✣ *2:F6.*

LAKE BUENA VISTA

$$$ ITALIAN 🍴 **La Luce by Donna Scala.** Originated by the late California restaurateur and chef Donna Scala, La Luce brings Italian cuisine with a Napa Valley farm-fresh flair to this upscale Hilton at the edge of Walt Disney World. Pastas are made fresh, steaks are handled with Italian care, and the cocktail bar is second to none. **Known for:** upscale and authentic Italian cuisine; extensive wine list; artwork created specially for the restaurant. [$] *Average main: $30* ✉ *Hilton Orlando Bonnet Creek, 14100 Bonnet Creek Resort La., Bonnet Creek* ☎ *407/597–3600* 🌐 *www.laluceorlando.com* 🕒 *No lunch* ✣ *2:E5.*

WALT DISNEY WORLD

MAGIC KINGDOM

$$$ FRENCH Fodor's Choice ★ 🍴 **Be Our Guest.** This massive restaurant offers a *Beauty and the Beast* theme, French flair, and the Magic Kingdom's first wine and beer served at dinner; breakfast and lunch remain a fast-casual affair. The breakfast, lunch, and dinner restaurant has three rooms: a gilded ballroom, whose ceiling sports cherubs with the faces of Imagineers' children; the tattered West Wing, with a slashed painting that changes from prince to beast during faux storms; and the Rose Gallery. **Known for:** sautéed shrimp and scallops with lobster; dessert cart treats; artwork that changes by the hour. [$] *Average main: $26* ✉ *Fantasyland, Magic Kingdom* ✣ *North end of Fantasyland* ☎ *407/939–3463* 🌐 *disneyworld.disney.go.com/dining* ✣ *2:B1.*

$$$$ AMERICAN 🍴 **Cinderella's Royal Table.** Cinderella and other Disney princesses appear at this eatery in the castle's old mead hall, offering prix-fixe Fairyland dining as only Disney can supply. The Fairytale Breakfast offers all-you-can-eat options such as lobster-crab crepes and caramel apple–stuffed French toast. **Known for:** food that may seem rich for little princesses; character appearances and autograph signings; distinctive medieval castle decor. [$] *Average main: $59* ✉ *Cinderella Castle, Magic Kingdom* ☎ *407/939–3463* 🌐 *disneyworld.disney.go.com/dining* ✣ *2:B1.*

$$$$ AMERICAN 🍴 **Liberty Tree Tavern.** Now serving beer and wine, this formerly "dry" tavern holds a prime spot on the parade route, so you can catch a good meal while you wait. Each of the six dining rooms commemorates a historical U.S. figure, like Betsy Ross or Benjamin Franklin. **Known for:** Patriot's Platter of roast turkey, sliced prime rib, and carved pork roast; authentic-looking Colonial decor; Samuel Adams Boston Lager. [$] *Average main: $39* ✉ *Liberty Square, Magic Kingdom* ☎ *407/939–3463* 🌐 *disneyworld.disney.go.com/dining* ✣ *2:B1.*

EPCOT

$$$$
SCANDINAVIAN

✕ **Akershus Royal Banquet Hall.** This restaurant has character buffets at all three meals, with an array of Disney princesses, including Ariel, Belle, Jasmine, Snow White, Aurora, Mary Poppins, and even an occasional cameo appearance by Cinderella. The breakfast menu is American, but lunch and dinner find an ever-changing assortment of Norwegian specialties, which may be foreign to children. **Known for:** an expansive buffet of Nordic specialties; Scandinavian appeal; scallops, mussels, and shrimp casserole. $ *Average main: $48* ✉ *Norway Pavilion, World Showcase, Epcot* ☎ *407/939–3463* ⊕ *disneyworld.disney.go.com/dining* ✛ *2:E4.*

$$$$
GERMAN

✕ **Biergarten Restaurant.** Oktoberfest runs 365 days a year here, where cheerful, sometimes raucous, crowds and an oompah band set the stage for a buffet of German specialties. The menu and level of frivolity are the same at lunch and dinner. **Known for:** bratwurst and other sausages; lively oompa band music; buffet-style servings. $ *Average main: $47* ✉ *Germany Pavilion, World Showcase, Epcot* ☎ *407/939–3463* ⊕ *disneyworld.disney.go.com/dining* ✛ *2:E4.*

$$$$
CANADIAN

✕ **Le Cellier Steakhouse.** This popular, charming eatery with stone arches and dark woods transports diners to a chic setting under the Canadian Parliament, offering a menu heavy on meat and a good selection of wines and Canadian beer. The à la carte menu includes the signature cheddar cheese soup and filet mignon with wild-mushroom risotto and truffle–butter sauce. **Known for:** Le Cellier signature coffee-rubbed black Angus rib eye; venison osso bucco; smoked soy-lacquered striped bass. $ *Average main: $45* ✉ *Canada Pavilion, World Showcase, Epcot* ☎ *407/939–3463* ⊕ *disneyworld.disney.go.com/dining* ✛ *2:D4.*

$$$$
FRENCH
Fodor's Choice
★

✕ **Monsieur Paul.** A mere staircase away from Epcot's busy World Showcase, Monsieur Paul is a subdued and sophisticated fine French restaurant. Make a reservation here if you are looking for an expensive, sophisticated, and delightful diversion from the theme park's bustle that is not particularly kid-friendly. **Known for:** knowledgeable service; magret de canard (roasted duck breast); an extensive wine list. $ *Average main: $42* ✉ *France Pavilion, World Showcase, Epcot* ☎ *407/939–3463* ⊕ *disneyworld.disney.go.com/dining* ✛ *2:D4.*

$$$
BRITISH
FAMILY

✕ **Rose & Crown Pub & Dining Room.** If you're an Anglophile and you love a beer so thick you could stand a spoon up in your mug, this is the place to soak up both the suds and British street culture and get the best fish-and-chips in town. Try the traditional English fare—cottage or shepherd's pie, and, at times, the ever-popular bangers-and-mash (sausage over mashed potatoes). **Known for:** beer-battered fish-and-chips; Angus beef burger with Welsh rarebit sauce; wide selection of beers and ciders from the pub. $ *Average main: $24* ✉ *United Kingdom Pavilion, World Showcase, Epcot* ☎ *107/939 3463* ⊕ *disneyworld.disney.go.com/dining* ✛ *2:D4.*

$$$
PIZZA

✕ **Via Napoli Ristorante e Pizzeria.** A menu of authentic, thin-crust Neapolitan-style pizzas from massive ovens named after Italian volcanoes is supplemented by a large menu of southern Italian favorites at this casual, family-friendly restaurant in the Italy Pavilion. Pizzas come topped with pepperoni, mushrooms, or eggplant, artichokes, cotto ham, cheese, and even prosciutto and melon. **Known for:** pizzas from wood-fired ovens; spaghetti with veal meatballs; generous kid portions. $ *Average main:*

9

$30 ✉ Italy Pavilion, World Showcase, Epcot ☎ 407/939–3463 🌐 disneyworld.disney.go.com/dining ✥ 2:E4.

DISNEY'S HOLLYWOOD STUDIOS

$$ AMERICAN FAMILY 🍴 **50's Prime Time Café.** If you grew up in middle America in the 1950s—or if you're just a fan of classic TV shows like *I Love Lucy* and *The Donna Reed Show*—you'll appreciate the vintage atmosphere and all-American classic menu at this diner-style restaurant. Clips of old TV shows will welcome you as you feast on meat loaf, pot roast, or fried chicken, all served on a Formica tabletop. **Known for:** showing clips of classic TV shows during dinner; "Mom" wandering around tables telling kids to eat their veggies; golden-fried chicken, pot roast, and meat loaf sampler. [$] *Average main: $18 ✉ Echo Lake, Disney's Hollywood Studios ☎ 407/939–3463 🌐 disneyworld.disney.go.com/dining ✥ 2:D5.*

$$$$ AMERICAN 🍴 **Hollywood Brown Derby.** At this reproduction of the famous 1940s Hollywood favorite, the walls are lined with movie-star caricatures, and the specialty is a Cobb salad, which was invented by Brown Derby founder Robert Cobb and still tossed table-side. While waiting for a table (it might take a while), or as an alternative, try the outdoor lounge, where appetizers and drinks may be ordered. **Known for:** old Hollywood atmosphere; mini dessert trio; famous crispy duck. [$] *Average main: $40 ✉ Hollywood Blvd., Disney's Hollywood Studios ☎ 407/939–3463 🌐 disneyworld.disney.go.com/dining ✥ 2:D5.*

$$$ AMERICAN 🍴 **Sci-Fi Dine-In Theater Restaurant.** If you don't mind zombies leering at you while you eat, then head to this enclosed faux drive-in, where you can eat in a table that looks like a candy-color 1950s convertible while watching trailers from classics like *Attack of the Fifty-Foot Woman* and *Teenagers from Outer Space*. The menu includes choices like steak and garlic-mashed potatoes, an Angus or veggie burger, shrimp with whole-grain pasta, and a huge Reuben sandwich with fries or cucumber salad. End with a hot-fudge sundae. **Known for:** menu of American classics like steak and Reuben sandwich; build-your-own Angus burger; wine, sangria, and fun cocktails. [$] *Average main: $25 ✉ Commissary La., Disney's Hollywood Studios ☎ 407/939–3463 🌐 disneyworld.disney.go.com/dining ✥ 2:D5.*

DISNEY'S ANIMAL KINGDOM

$ FAST FOOD 🍴 **Flame Tree Barbecue.** This counter-service eatery is one of the relatively undiscovered gems of Disney's culinary offerings; there's nothing fancy here, but you can dig into ribs and pulled-pork sandwiches. For something with a lower calorie count, try the smoked turkey sandwich served with cranberry mayo or a great barbecued chicken served with baked beans and coleslaw. **Known for:** reasonably priced barbecue in an Animal Kingdom setting; ribs, chicken, and pulled-pork sampler; variety of beer and wine. [$] *Average main: $12 ✉ Discovery Island, Animal Kingdom 🌐 disneyworld.disney.go.com/dining ✥ 2:B5.*

$$$$ INTERNATIONAL Fodor's Choice ★ 🍴 **Tiffins.** Inspired by the worldwide journeys of Disney Imagineers, Tiffins is the theme parks' newest upscale sit-down restaurant and possibly the best eatery on Disney property, serving a wide-ranging international menu that changes constantly. Superb cross-cultural food is served in an inventive space with enough unique decor to fill a museum. **Known for:** superbly cooked, changing menu with Asian, Latin, and African

flavors; elaborate decor; kids meals that aren't dumbed down. $ *Average main: $41* ⊠ *Discovery Island, Animal Kingdom* ☎ *407/939–1947* ⊕ *disneyworld.disney.go.com/dining* ✛ *2:B5.*

$$$ ✗ **Yak & Yeti.** This large, pan-Asian restaurant offers sit-down service in
ASIAN a two-story, 250-seat venue in the Asia section, offering everything from a variety of noodles to curries to Korean barbecued ribs. The decor is pleasantly faux-Asian, with cracked plaster walls, wood carvings, and tile mosaic tabletops. **Known for:** large menu with Indian, Japanese, Chinese, and Korean influences; welcoming lounge for escaping the weather; shareable dim sum and appetizer baskets. $ *Average main: $22* ⊠ *Asia, Animal Kingdom* ☎ *407/939–3463* ⊕ *disneyworld.disney.go.com/dining* ✛ *2:B5.*

DISNEY SPRINGS

$$$$ ✗ **The BOATHOUSE.** Contemporary and upscale, The BOATHOUSE sits
SEAFOOD directly on the Disney Springs waterfront, offering a menu of primarily fresh seafood and views of the restaurant's main attraction, so-called Amphicar tours. Boats that look like vintage, retrofitted vehicles offer the chance for a one-of-a-kind tour of Disney Springs as each vessel's four wheels submerge underwater, and a propeller jet glides riders throughout the lake. **Known for:** fresh seafood; lobster bake for two with whole Maine lobster and clams; "Amphicars" for rent. $ *Average main: $35* ⊠ *Disney Springs, The Landing, Disney Springs* ☎ *407/939–2628* ⊕ *disneyworld.disney.go.com/dining* ▤ *No credit cards* ✛ *2:F4.*

$$$$ ✗ **Morimoto Asia.** Created by the Iron Chef himself, Masaharu Morim-
ASIAN FUSION oto, this is Morimoto's first restaurant that moves outside the sushi realm. The pan-Asian menu includes interesting variations on Chinese duck, Korean noodles, Singaporean laksa, and more. **Known for:** high-end sushi and pan-Asian cuisine; late-night hours until 1 am on weekends; best views of the Disney Springs lagoon from the upstairs patio. $ *Average main: $35* ⊠ *Disney Springs, The Landing, Lake Buena Vista* ☎ *407/939–6686* ⊕ *www.patinagroup.com/morimoto-asia* ✛ *2:F4.*

$$$ ✗ **Raglan Road Irish Pub.** If an authentic Irish pub—actually transported
IRISH from the Old Country plank by plank—is your thing, Raglan Road is
FAMILY the place to go, for both superb traditional dishes and inventive twists.
Fodor's Choice International chef Kevin Dundon spends a lot of time here when he's
★ not in residence at his hotel in County Wexford, and the attention shows in the quality. **Known for:** first-rate dining and special chef-driven events; extensive beer and ale selections, including exclusive brews; nightly, sometimes hourly, entertainment. $ *Average main: $25* ⊠ *Disney Springs, The Landing, Disney Springs* ☎ *407/938–0300* ⊕ *www.raglanroadirishpub.com* ✛ *2:F4.*

$$$$ ✗ **Wolfgang Puck Grand Cafe.** With four restaurants in one building, there
AMERICAN are lots of choices here, from Puck's trademark wood-oven pizza at the informal Puck Express to fine-dining meals in the upstairs formal dining room. There's also a sushi bar and an informal café, which is quite literally a happy medium—and may be the best bet for families hoping for a bit of elegance without the pressure of a formal dinner. **Known for:** name-brand dining in familiar surroundings; casual meals, sushi, and fine dining in one location; world-famous pizza. $ *Average main: $32* ⊠ *Disney Springs, The Marketplace, Disney Springs* ☎ *407/938–9653* ⊕ *www.wolfgangpuckcafeorlando.com* ✛ *2:F4.*

9

WDW RESORTS

$$$$ ✕ **Boma—Flavors of Africa.** Boma takes Western-style ingredients and pre-
AFRICAN pares them with an African twist—then invites guests to walk through
FAMILY an African marketplace–style dining room to help themselves at coun-
Fodor'sChoice ters piled high with flavor from an upscale buffet like no other. The
★ dozen or so serving stations have entrées such as roasted pork, Durban-
style chicken, spice-crusted beef, and fish served with tamarind and
other robust sauces; intriguing salads; and some of the best hummus this
side of the Atlantic. **Known for:** superb food that appeals to the timid
and adventurous alike; African flavors and dishes; endless buffet with
wonderful service. $ *Average main: $43* ⊠ *Animal Kingdom Lodge,
2901 Osceola Pkwy., Animal Kingdom Resort Area* ☎ *407/939–3463*
⊕ *disneyworld.disney.go.com/dining* ⊗ *No lunch* ✛ *2:A5.*

$$$$ ✕ **California Grill.** The view from the surrounding Disney parks from this
AMERICAN 15th-floor restaurant—the World's signature dining establishment since
Fodor'sChoice 1995—is as stunning as the food, especially after dark, when you can
★ watch the nightly Magic Kingdom fireworks from an outdoor viewing
area. The space has stylish mid-century modern furnishings and chandeliers, while the exhibition kitchen is so well equipped that it has a cast-
iron flat grill designed specifically for cooking fish. **Known for:** stunning
views of the parks and fireworks; wild game charcuterie and fresh sushi;
Sunday brunch. $ *Average main: $42* ⊠ *Contemporary Resort, 4600
N. World Dr., Magic Kingdom Resort Area* ☎ *407/939–3463* ⊕ *disney-
world.disney.go.com/dining* ⊗ *No lunch* ✛ *2:C1.*

$$$$ ✕ **Chef Mickey's.** The fact that the Disney monorail zooms overhead right
AMERICAN through the Contemporary hotel, and that Mickey, Minnie, or Goofy
FAMILY hang around for breakfast and dinner, would be enough to make it
popular, but the food at Chef Mickey's is surprisingly good. The breakfast buffet includes "pixie-dusted" challah French toast, mountains of
pancakes, and even a breakfast pizza. **Known for:** character meals and
"Storybook Moments"; family fare buffet and lots of it; specialty cocktails for the grown-ups. $ *Average main: $47* ⊠ *Contemporary Resort,
4600 N. World Dr., Magic Kingdom Resort Area* ☎ *407/939–3463*
⊕ *disneyworld.disney.go.com/dining* ⊗ *No lunch* ✛ *2:C1.*

$$ ✕ **ESPN Club.** Not only can you watch sports on a big-screen TV here
AMERICAN (the restaurant has about 100 monitors), but you can also periodically
see ESPN programs being taped in the club itself while enjoying typi-
cal sports-bar food and beer. Food ranges from a variety of half-pound
burgers, made with Angus chuck (and one topped with peanut butter
and jelly), to Philly cheesesteaks and *char siu* sliders. **Known for:** gigan-
tic space that still fills up on game days; pub food: nachos, chicken and
waffles, big burgers; wine and regional beers. $ *Average main: $17*
⊠ *Disney's Boardwalk, 2101 Epcot Resorts Blvd., Epcot Resort Area*
☎ *407/939–3463* ⊕ *disneyworld.disney.go.com/dining* ✛ *2:D4.*

$$$$ ✕ **Flying Fish.** Completely renovated in 2016, Flying Fish maintains its
SEAFOOD place as one of Disney World's finest restaurants, with a menu heavy on
Fodor'sChoice the freshest seafood as well as steaks. The menu includes such options
★ as wild Alaskan King salmon, Wagyu beef, and even exotic fare like
bison. **Known for:** sophisticated dining on the Disney Boardwalk;
Chef's Counter personalized dining; AbracadaBAR cocktail lounge

next door. $ *Average main: $48* ⊠ *Disney's Boardwalk, 2101 Epcot Resorts Blvd., Epcot Resort Area* ☎ *407/939–2359* ⊕ *disneyworld.disney.go.com/dining* ☾ *No lunch* ✦ *2:D4.*

$$$$
AFRICAN
Fodor'sChoice
★

✕ **Jiko.** The name of this restaurant means "the cooking place" in Swahili, and it is certainly that, offering a menu that is more African-inspired than purely African as well as a strong selection of South African wines. The dining area surrounds two big, wood-burning ovens and a grill area where you can watch cooks in North African–style caps working on your meal. **Known for:** African cuisine with an American flair; sophisticated surroundings and decor; a remarkably popular macaroni and cheese. $ *Average main: $41* ⊠ *Animal Kingdom Lodge, 2901 Osceola Pkwy., Animal Kingdom Resort Area* ☎ *407/939–3463* ⊕ *disneyworld.disney.go.com/dining* ☾ *No lunch* ✦ *2:A5.*

$$$$
SEAFOOD
Fodor'sChoice
★

✕ **Todd English's bluezoo.** Celebrity chef Todd English designed the menu for this upscale seafood eatery. The sleek, modern restaurant resembles an underwater dining hall, with blue walls and carpeting, aluminum fish along the wall behind the bar, and bubblelike lighting fixtures. **Known for:** variety of seafood; celebrity chef dining; two hours of complimentary child care while dining. $ *Average main: $44* ⊠ *Walt Disney World Dolphin Hotel, 1500 Epcot Resorts Blvd., Epcot Resort Area* ☎ *407/934–1111* ⊕ *www.thebluezoo.com* ☾ *No lunch* ✦ *2:C4.*

$$$$
MODERN
AMERICAN
Fodor'sChoice
★

✕ **Victoria & Albert's.** At this ultraposh Disney restaurant, a well-polished service team will anticipate your every need, providing one of the plushest fine-dining experiences in Florida, with an ambience so sophisticated that children under 10 aren't on the guest list. The seven-course, prix-fixe menu changes daily, and you'd do well to supplement the pricey tab with an optional wine pairing. **Known for:** highest-priced restaurant at WDW; enormous and expensive wine list; exclusive additions like Osetra caviar and Miyazaki beef. $ *Average main: $200* ⊠ *Grand Floridian, 4401 Floridian Way, Magic Kingdom Resort Area* ☎ *407/939–3862* ⊕ *www.victoria-alberts.com* ☾ *No lunch* 🎩 *Jacket required* ✦ *2:B1.*

9

UNIVERSAL ORLANDO RESORT

UNIVERSAL STUDIOS

$$
IRISH

✕ **Finnegan's Bar & Grill.** This Irish pub would look just right in downtown Manhattan during the Ellis Island era. The menu offers classic Irish comfort food like shepherd's pie, corned beef and cabbage, bangers and mash, and fish-and-chips, plus Guinness on tap and a five-beer sampler. **Known for:** live music; typical pub menu; interesting atmosphere. $ *Average main: $16* ⊠ *New York, Universal Studios* ☎ *407/363–8757* ⊕ *www.universalorlando.com* ✦ *1:D3.*

$
BRITISH
FAMILY

✕ **Leaky Cauldron.** British pub staples are fitting fare for Diagon Alley's restaurant. The drinks menu complements those hearty meals with kooky-sounding beverages from the Harry Potter books like Tongue-Tying Lemon Squash, Otter's Fizzy Orange Juice, and Fishy Green Ale (it's minty, with blueberry-flavored boba). **Known for:** quick-service Potter-inspired meals; plowman's lunch of meats, cheeses, and salad; Butterbeer, of course. $ *Average main: $14* ⊠ *The Wizarding World of Harry Potter: Diagon Alley, Universal Studios* ☎ *407/224–9716* ⊕ *www.universalorlando.com* ✦ *1:D3.*

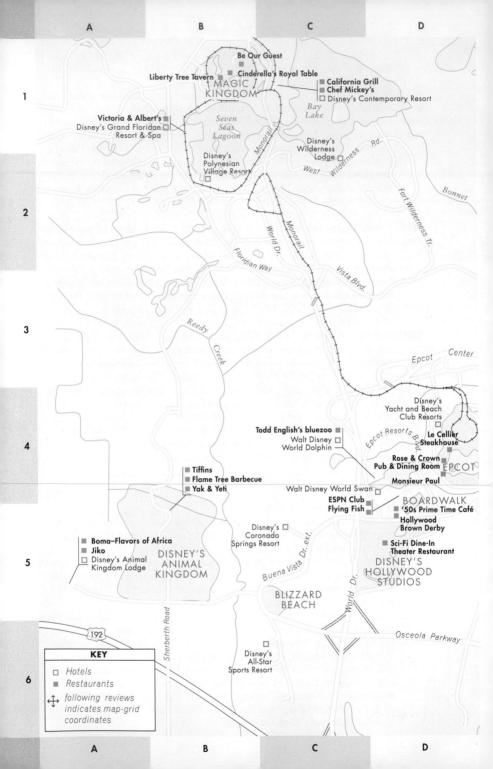

Be Our Guest

Cinderella's Royal Table

Liberty Tree Tavern

MAGIC KINGDOM

California Grill
Chef Mickey's
Disney's Contemporary Resort

Bay Lake

Victoria & Albert's
Disney's Grand Floridan
Resort & Spa

Seven Seas Lagoon

Disney's
Wilderness
Lodge

Monorail

Fort Wilderness Tr.

Bonnet

Disney's
Polynesian
Village Resort

West   Wilderness   Rd.

Floridian Way

World Dr.

Monorail

Vista Blvd.

Reedy   Creek

Epcot   Center

Disney's
Yacht and Beach
Club Resorts

Todd English's bluezoo
Walt Disney
World Dolphin

Epcot Resorts Blvd.

**Le Cellier
Steakhouse**

**Rose & Crown
Pub & Dining Room**
Monsieur Paul

EPCOT

Tiffins
Flame Tree Barbecue
Yak & Yeti

Walt Disney World Swan

ESPN Club
Flying Fish

BOARDWALK

'50s Prime Time Café

**Hollywood
Brown Derby**

Disney's
Coronado
Springs Resort

Buena Vista Dr. ext.

Boma–Flavors of Africa
Jiko
Disney's Animal
Kingdom Lodge

DISNEY'S
ANIMAL
KINGDOM

**Sci-Fi Dine-In
Theater Restaurant**

DISNEY'S
HOLLYWOOD
STUDIOS

World Dr.

BLIZZARD
BEACH

Osceola   Parkway

Sherberth Road

192

Disney's
All-Star
Sports Resort

KEY

□ *Hotels*
■ *Restaurants*
⬦ *following reviews
indicates map-grid
coordinates*

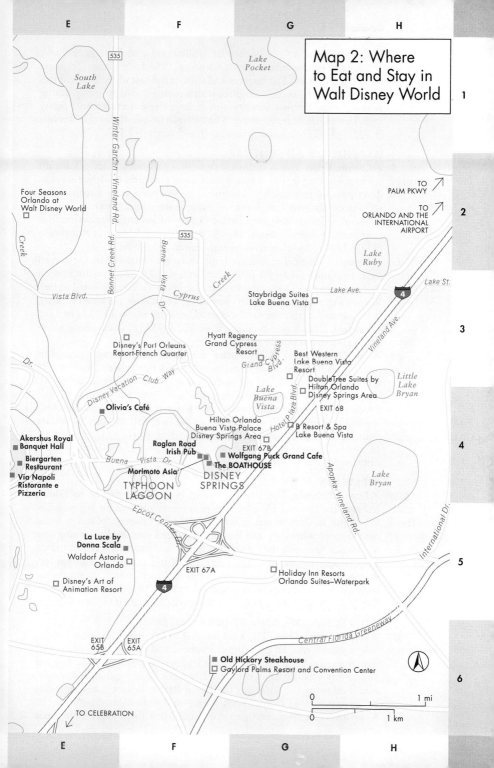

E   F   G   H

535

Lake
Pocket

South
Lake

**Map 2: Where
to Eat and Stay in
Walt Disney World**   1

TO
PALM PKWY

Four Seasons
Orlando at
Walt Disney World

TO
ORLANDO AND THE
INTERNATIONAL
AIRPORT   2

Creek

Winter Garden – Vineland Rd.

535

Lake
Ruby

Buena Vista Dr.

Vista Blvd.

Bonnet Creek Rd.

Cyprus   Creek

Lake Ave.

Lake St.

4

Vineland Ave.

3

Staybridge Suites
Lake Buena Vista

Hyatt Regency
Grand Cypress
Resort

Grand Cypress Blvd.

Best Western
Lake Buena Vista
Resort

Little
Lake
Bryan

Disney's Port Orleans
Resort-French Quarter

Disney Vacation Club Way

DoubleTree Suites by
Hilton Orlando
Disney Springs Area

Dr.

Olivia's Café

Lake
Buena
Vista

Hotel Plaza Blvd.

EXIT 68

4

**Akershus Royal
Banquet Hall**

Hilton Orlando
Buena Vista Palace
Disney Springs Area

B Resort & Spa
Lake Buena Vista

Lake
Bryan

**Biergarten
Restaurant**

**Raglan Road
Irish Pub**

EXIT 67B

**Via Napoli
Ristorante e
Pizzeria**

Buena   Vista   Dr.

The BOATHOUSE

Wolfgang Puck Grand Cafe

Apopka – Vineland Rd.

Morimoto Asia

**TYPHOON
LAGOON**

DISNEY
SPRINGS

International Dr.

Epcot Center Dr.

**La Luce by
Donna Scala**

4

EXIT 67A

Holiday Inn Resorts
Orlando Suites–Waterpark

5

Waldorf Astoria
Orlando

Disney's Art of
Animation Resort

Central Florida Greeneway

EXIT
65B

EXIT
65A

Old Hickory Steakhouse
Gaylord Palms Resort and Convention Center

6

0   1 mi

0   1 km

TO CELEBRATION

E   F   G   H

$ ✕ **Mel's Drive-In.** At the corner of Hollywood and Vine is a flashy
AMERICAN   1950s-style eatery with a pink-and-white 1956 Ford Crown Victoria
FAMILY   parked out in front. For burgers and fries, this is one of the best choices
in the park, and it comes complete with a roving doo-wop group during
peak seasons. **Known for:** drive-in styling; live entertainment; frosty
milk shakes. $ *Average main: $11* ✉ *Hollywood, Universal Studios*
📞 *407/363–8766* ⊕ *www.universalorlando.com* ✛ *1:D3.*

ISLANDS OF ADVENTURE

$ ✕ **Confisco Grille.** You could walk right past this full-service restaurant
AMERICAN   without noticing it, but if you want a good meal and sit-down service,
don't pass by too quickly. The menu is American with international
influences. **Known for:** Italian, Greek, Asian, and Mexican dishes;
overlooked location means better chance of seating; Backwater Bar
next door. $ *Average main: $13* ✉ *Port of Entry, Islands of Adventure*
📞 *407/224–4404* ⊕ *www.universalorlando.com* ✛ *1:D3.*

$$ ✕ **Mythos.** A magical restaurant built into a rock cliff, the inside is even
ECLECTIC   more enchanting than the foreboding exterior. The menu includes such
Fodor'sChoice   mainstays as pad Thai and pan-seared salmon with lemon-basil butter.
★   **Known for:** spectacular decor; one of the best theme park restaurants;
lamb burgers, crab cake sandwiches. $ *Average main: $17* ✉ *The Lost
Continent, Islands of Adventure* 📞 *407/224–4533* ⊕ *www.universalor-
lando.com* ⊘ *No dinner* ✛ *1:D3.*

$ ✕ **Three Broomsticks.** Harry Potter fans flock here to taste pumpkin
BRITISH   juice (with hints of honey and vanilla) and Butterbeer (sort of like
bubbly butterscotch cream soda, or maybe shortbread cookies).
They're on the menu along with barbecue and traditional British
foods at this Hogsmeade restaurant. **Known for:** quirky Harry Pot-
ter atmosphere; quick and courteous service; full English breakfast
daily. $ *Average main: $12* ✉ *The Wizarding World of Harry Potter:
Hogsmeade, Islands of Adventure* 📞 *407/224–4233* ⊕ *www.univer-
salorlando.com* ✛ *1:D3.*

CITYWALK

$$$$ ✕ **Emeril's Orlando.** The popular eatery is a culinary shrine to Emeril
CAJUN   Lagasse, the famous TV chef who occasionally makes an appearance.
Fodor'sChoice   While the modern interior, with its 30-foot ceilings, blond woods,
★   second-story wine loft, and lots of galvanized steel looks nothing like
the French Quarter, the hardwood floors and linen tablecloths create
an environment befitting the stellar nature of the cuisine. **Known for:**
inventive and creative Louisiana cooking; Emeril name; free parking
with lunch reservation. $ *Average main: $33* ✉ *6000 Universal Blvd.,
CityWalk* 📞 *407/224–2424* ⊕ *www.emerils.com* ✛ *1:D3.*

UNIVERSAL ORLAND RESORT HOTELS

$$$ ✕ **Emeril's Tchoup Chop.** The bold interior decor—with lots of bamboo,
SOUTH PACIFIC   bright glazed tile, an exposition kitchen, and a long zero-edge pool
with porcelain lily pads running the length of the dining room—is just
as ambitious as the food at Emeril Lagasse's Pacific-influenced restaurant. Following the theme of the Royal Pacific Resort, Lagasse melds
his signature bold flavors with Asian- and Polynesian-fusion tastes.
Known for: sophisticated pan-Asian cuisine; robata grill; sushi from

sustainable fish. $Average main: $29 ⊠ *Loews Royal Pacific Resort, 6300 Hollywood Way, Universal Orlando Resort* ☎ *407/503–2467* ⊕ *www.emerils.com* ✛ *1:D3.*

$$$

ITALIAN

✕ **Mama Della's Ristorante.** This playfully themed Italian restaurant happens to have excellent food. The premise is that you're eating at a home-turned-restaurant owned by Mama Della. **Known for:** intimate New York/Neapolitan environment; better-than-usual Italian cuisine; house-made gnocchi. $ *Average main: $30* ⊠ *Loews Portofino Bay Hotel, 5601 Universal Blvd., Universal Orlando Resort* ☎ *407/503–3463* ⊕ *www.loewshotels.com* ⊗ *No lunch* ✛ *1:D3.*

WHERE TO STAY

Updated by Jennifer Greenhill-Taylor

With tens of thousands of lodging choices available in the Orlando area, from tents to deluxe villas, there is no lack of variety in price or amenities. In fact, narrowing down the possibilities is part of the fun.

More than 60 million visitors come to the Orlando area each year, making it the most popular tourism destination on the planet. More upscale hotels are opening as visitors demand more luxurious surroundings, such as luxe linens, tasteful and refined decor, organic toiletries, or ergonomic chairs and work desks. But no matter what your budget or desires, lodging comes in such a wide range of prices, themes, color schemes, brands, meal plans, and guest-room amenities, you will have no problem finding something that fits.

Resorts on and off Disney property combine function with fantasy, as befits visitor expectations. Characters in costume perform for the kids, pools are pirates' caves with waterfalls, and some, like the Gaylord Palms, go so far as to re-create Florida landmarks under a gargantuan glass roof, giving visitors the illusion of having visited more of the state than they expected.

International Drive's expanding attractions, including the Orlando Eye, Madame Tussauds, and a widening array of eateries, are drawing more savvy conventioneers who bring their families along for the fun.

Many hotels have joined the trend toward green lodging, bringing recycling, water conservation, and other environmentally conscious practices to the table. Best of all, the sheer number and variety of hotel rooms means you can still find relative bargains throughout the Orlando area, even on Disney property, by researching your trip well, calling the lodgings directly, negotiating packages and prices, and shopping wisely.

RESERVATIONS

Always book your lodging months in advance in Orlando, regardless of where you stay.

Walt Disney Travel Co. Packages can be arranged through the Walt Disney Travel Co. Guests can find planning tools on the website that allow them to customize vacation itineraries based on interests as well as age, height restrictions, and medical needs. ☎ *407/939–5277* ⊕ *www. disneyworld.com.*

9

WDW Central Reservations Office. You can book many accommodations—Disney-owned hotels and some non-Disney-owned hotels—through the WDW Central Reservations Office. The website allows you to compare prices at the various on-site resorts

People with disabilities can also use this number, as the representatives are all knowledgeable about services available at resorts and parks for guests with disabilities. All representatives have TTY ability. The website is also a valuable source for specific needs. Go to Guest Services and search the word "Disabilities."☎ *407/939–7838* 🌐 *www.disneyworld.com.*

WHAT IT COSTS				
	$	$$	$$$	$$$$
For Two People	under $200	$200–$300	$301–$400	over $400

ABOUT OUR REVIEWS

Prices: Prices in the hotel reviews are the lowest cost of a standard double room in high season, excluding taxes, service charges, resort fees, and meal plans (except at all-inclusives). Prices for rentals are the lowest per-night cost for a one-bedroom unit in high season. Note that taxes in Central Florida can be as high as 12.5%.

Maps: *Throughout the chapter, you'll see mapping symbols and coordinates (⊕ 1:F2) after property names or reviews. Maps are within the chapter. The first number after the symbol indicates the map number. After that is the property's coordinate on the map grid.*

Hotel reviews have been shortened. For full information, visit Fodors.com.

ORLANDO

INTERNATIONAL DRIVE

$$ RESORT 🏨 **Hyatt Regency Orlando.** This deluxe high-rise conference hotel offers anything a full-service resort customer could want, with richly appointed rooms, two pools with cabanas, a full-service spa and fitness center the size of your local Y, two large restaurants, and a 360-seat, glass-walled lounge overlooking the pool. **Pros:** good spa; close to shops and more restaurants; on the I-Drive Trolley route. **Cons:** check-in can take a while if a convention is arriving; long walk from end to end; daily resort and parking fees. [$] *Rooms from: $259* ✉ *9801 International Dr., International Drive* ☎ *407/284–1234* 🌐 *www.orlando.regency.hyatt.com* 🛏 *1,639 rooms* 🍴 *No meals* ⊕ *1:D4.*

SOUTH ORLANDO

$$$ RESORT FAMILY 🏨 **JW Marriott Orlando Grande Lakes.** This lush resort, set in 500 acres of natural beauty, certainly caters to a convention clientele, but leisure-seekers and families are given equal attention. **Pros:** pool is great for kids and adults; shares amenities with the Ritz, including huge spa; free shuttle to SeaWorld and Universal. **Cons:** daily resort fees for parking and in-room Wi-Fi; the resort is huge and spread out; need a car to reach Disney or shopping. [$] *Rooms from: $319* ✉ *4040 Central Florida*

WHERE SHOULD WE STAY?

	VIBE	PROS	CONS
Disney	Thousands of rooms at every price; convenient to Disney parks; free transportation all over WDW complex.	Perks like early park entry, MagicBands or cards, and Magical Express, which lets you circumvent airport bag checks. Free Wi-Fi.	Without a rental car, you likely won't leave Disney. On-site buses, although free, can take a big bite of time out of your entertainment day; convenience comes at a price.
Universal	On-site hotels offer luxury, convenience, and value. There are less expensive options just outside the gates.	Central to Disney, Universal, SeaWorld, malls, and I–4; free water taxis to parks from on-site hotels.	Most on-site hotels are pricey; the Cabana Bay Beach Resort, however, is reasonable; expect heavy rush-hour traffic during drives to and from other parks.
I-Drive	A hotel, convention center, and activities bonanza. A trolley runs from one end to the other.	Outlet malls provide bargains; world-class restaurants; the Orlando Eye lifts visitors up for a bird's-eye view; many hotels offer free park shuttles.	Transportation can be pricey, in cash and in time, as traffic is often heavy. Crime is up, especially after dark, although area hotels and businesses have increased security.
Kissimmee	It offers mom-and-pop motels and upscale choices, restaurants, and places to buy saltwater taffy.	It's just outside Disney, very close to Magic Kingdom. Lots of Old Florida charm and low prices.	Some of the older motels here are a little seedy. Petty crime in which tourists are victims is rare—but not unheard of.
Lake Buena Vista	Many hotel and restaurant chains here. Adjacent to WDW, which is where almost every guest in your hotel is headed.	Really close to WDW; plenty of dining and shopping options; easy access to I–4.	Heavy peak-hour traffic. As in all neighborhoods near Disney, a gallon of gas will cost 10%–15% more than elsewhere.
Central Orlando	Parts of town have the modern high-rises you'd expect. Other areas have oak tree–lined brick streets winding among small, cypress-ringed lakes.	Locally owned restaurants, trendy hotels, vibrant nightlife, and some quaint B&Bs. City buses serve the parks. There's good access to I–4.	You'll need to rent a car. And you will be part of the traffic headed to WDW. Expect the 25-mile drive to take at least 45 minutes.
Orlando International Airport	Mostly business and flight-crew hotels and car-rental outlets.	Great if you have an early flight or just want to shop in a mall. There's even a Hyatt on-site.	Watching planes, buses, taxis, and cars arrive and depart is all the entertainment you'll get.

9

Pkwy., South Orlando ☎ *407/206–2300, 800/576–5750* 🌐 *www.grandelakes.com* 🛏 *1,000 rooms* 🍴 *Breakfast; Some meals* ✥ *1:E4.*

$$$$ RESORT FAMILY Fodor's Choice ★ 🏨 **Ritz-Carlton Orlando, Grande Lakes.** Orlando's only Ritz-Carlton is a particularly extravagant link in the luxury chain, which shares a lush 500-acre campus with the JW Marriott. **Pros:** truly luxurious; impeccable service; transportation to theme parks. **Cons:** remote from theme parks, attractions; lots of convention and meeting traffic; resort fee. [$] *Rooms from: $579* ✉ *4012 Central Florida Pkwy., South Orlando* ☎ *407/206–2400, 800/576–5760* 🌐 *www.ritzcarlton.com* 🛏 *582 rooms* 🍴 *Breakfast; Some meals* ✥ *1:E4.*

KISSIMMEE

$$ RESORT 🏨 **Gaylord Palms Resort and Convention Center.** Built in the style of a grand turn-of-the-20th-century Florida resort, this huge building is meant to inspire awe. **Pros:** you could have a great vacation without ever leaving the grounds; free shuttle to Disney; excellent on-site dining. **Cons:** daily resort and parking fee; rooms can be pricey; hotel is so big that you can take quite a hike inside the building. [$] *Rooms from: $299* ✉ *6000 W. Osceola Pkwy., I–4 Exit 65, Kissimmee* ☎ *407/586–0000* 🌐 *www.gaylordpalms.com* 🛏 *1,406 rooms* 🍴 *No meals* ✥ *2:F6.*

LAKE BUENA VISTA

$ RESORT FAMILY 🏨 **Holiday Inn Resorts Orlando Suites - Waterpark.** This 24-acre resort has undergone a $30-million renovation since Holiday Inn took it over from Nickelodeon in 2016. **Pros:** extremely kid-friendly; Disney shuttles included in resort fee; mini-golf course. **Cons:** daily resort fee of $30; way too frenetic for folks without kids; poolside rooms can be noisy. [$] *Rooms from: $199* ✉ *14500 Continental Gateway, Lake Buena Vista* ☎ *407/387–5437, 866/462–6425* 🌐 *www.nickhotel.com* 🛏 *777 rooms* 🍴 *No meals* ✥ *2:G5.*

$$ RESORT FAMILY Fodor's Choice ★ 🏨 **Hyatt Regency Grand Cypress Resort.** Sitting amid 1,500 palm-filled acres just outside Disney's gate, this huge luxury resort hotel has a private lake with watercraft, three golf courses, and miles of trails for strolling, bicycling, jogging, and horseback riding. **Pros:** elaborate spa; lots of recreation options, including huge pool and equestrian center; free Wi-Fi. **Cons:** need a car or taxi to get to Downtown Orlando or Universal; expensive daily resort fee; lots of conventioneers. [$] *Rooms from: $259* ✉ *1 Grand Cypress Blvd., Lake Buena Vista* ☎ *407/239–1234, 800/233–1234* 🌐 *www.hyattgrandcypress.com* 🛏 *815 rooms* 🍴 *No meals* ✥ *2:G3.*

$ HOTEL FAMILY 🏨 **Staybridge Suites Lake Buena Vista.** Just minutes from Disney Springs, this pleasant all-suites (one- and two-bedroom, two-bath) hotel is perfect for a big family on a small budget who wants a home away from home. **Pros:** free scheduled shuttle service to WDW; free hot breakfast; free Wi-Fi and parking. **Cons:** no restaurant; no shuttles to other parks; pool and dining areas can be crowded. [$] *Rooms from: $155* ✉ *8751 Suiteside Dr., Lake Buena Vista* ☎ *407/238–0777* 🌐 *www.staybridge.com* 🛏 *150 rooms* 🍴 *Breakfast; Some meals* ✥ *2:G3.*

DISNEY AND UNIVERSAL RESORT PERKS

DISNEY PERKS

Extra Magic Hours. You get special early and late-night admission to certain Disney parks on specified days. Call ahead for details so you can plan your early- and late-visit strategies.

Free Parking. Parking is free for Disney hotel guests at Disney hotel and theme-park lots.

Magical Express. If you're staying at a select Disney hotel, this free airport service means you don't need to rent a car or think about finding a shuttle or taxi or worry about baggage handling. You check your bags with special Disney tags, and they will be picked up and delivered to your room (though this can take a while). If your flight arrives before 5 am or after 10 pm, you will have to pick up your luggage and deliver it to the coach.

On departure, the process works in reverse (though only on some participating airlines, so check in advance). You get your boarding pass and check your bags at the hotel. At the airport you go directly to your gate, skipping check-in. You won't see your bags until you're in your hometown airport. Participating airlines include Alaska, American, Delta, JetBlue, Southwest, and United.

Charging Privileges. You can charge most meals and purchases throughout Disney to your hotel room, using your MagicBands or cards.

Package Delivery. Anything you purchase at Disney—at a park, a hotel, or in Downtown Disney—can be delivered to your Disney hotel for free.

Priority Reservations. Disney hotel guests get priority reservations at Disney restaurants and choice tee times at Disney golf courses up to 30 days in advance, using your MagicBand or card.

Guaranteed Entry. Disney theme parks sometimes reach capacity, but on-site guests can enter even when others would be turned away.

UNIVERSAL PERKS

Head-of-the-Line Access. Your hotel key (except Cabana Bay) lets you go directly to the head of the line for most Universal Orlando attractions. Unlike Disney's FastPass+ program, you don't need to use this at a specific time; it's always good. Hotel guests also get early admission to the often-crowded Harry Potter attractions.

Priority Seating. Many of Universal's restaurants offer priority seating to those staying at on-site hotels.

Charging Privileges. You can charge most meals and purchases throughout Universal to your hotel room.

Delivery Services. If you buy something in the theme parks, you can have it sent directly to your room, so you don't have to carry it around.

Free Loaners. Some on-site hotels have a "Did You Forget?" closet that offers everything from kids' strollers to dog leashes to computer accessories. There's no fee for using this service.

9

$$$$ RESORT Fodor's Choice ★ 🏨 **Waldorf Astoria Orlando.** While it can't duplicate the famed original in New York City, this Waldorf echoes it with imagination and flair, from the iconic clock in the center of the circular lobby to tiny, black-and-white accent tiles on guest room floors. **Pros:** lavish and luxurious hotel; free transportation to Disney parks; great spa and golf course. **Cons:** pricey, but you knew that; if you can bear to leave your cabana, you'll need a car to see anything else in the area; steep daily resort fee. [$] *Rooms from: $559* ✉ *14200 Bonnet Creek Resort La., Bonnet Creek* ☎ *407/597–5500* 🌐 *www.waldorfastoriaorlando.com* 🛏 *328 rooms* 🍴 *Breakfast* ✥ *2:F5.*

CELEBRATION

$ HOTEL FAMILY 🏨 **Meliá Orlando Suite Hotel at Celebration.** Much like a European boutique hotel in style, the Meliá Orlando is very human in scale, minimalist in decor, and is only minutes from Disney. **Pros:** shuttle to Celebration, Disney parks, Universal, and SeaWorld; golf privileges at Celebration Golf; spa privileges at Celebration Day Spa. **Cons:** busy U.S. 192 is close by; daily resort fee; need a car to go anywhere besides Celebration and the parks. [$] *Rooms from: $143* ✉ *225 Celebration Pl., Celebration* ☎ *866/404–6662, 407/964–7000* 🌐 *www.solmelia.com* 🛏 *240 rooms* 🍴 *Breakfast* ✥ *1:C6.*

WALT DISNEY WORLD

Disney-operated hotels are fantasies unto themselves. Each is designed according to a theme (quaint New England, the relaxed culture of the Polynesian Islands, an African safari village, and so on), and each offers the same perks: free transportation from the airport and to the parks, the option to charge all of your purchases to your room, special guest-only park-visiting times, and much more. If you stay on-site, you'll have better access to the parks and be more immersed in the Disney experience.

ON-SITE NON-DISNEY HOTELS

Although not operated by the Disney organization, the Swan and the Dolphin, just outside Epcot; Shades of Green, near the Magic Kingdom; and the hotels along Hotel Plaza Boulevard near Disney Springs call themselves "official" Walt Disney World hotels. Whereas the Swan, Dolphin, and Shades of Green have the special privileges of on-site Disney hotels, such as free transportation to and from the parks and early park entry, the Disney Springs resorts may use Disney transportation, but don't have all the same perks.

MAGIC KINGDOM RESORT AREA

$$$$ RESORT 🏨 **Disney's Contemporary Resort.** You're paying for location at this sleek, modern, luxury resort next to the Magic Kingdom. **Pros:** monorail access; Chef Mickey's, the epicenter of character-meal world; health and wellness suites. **Cons:** a mix of conventioneers and vacationers means it can be too frenzied for the former and too staid for the latter. [$] *Rooms from: $588* ✉ *4600 N. World Dr., Magic Kingdom Resort Area* ☎ *407/824–1000* 🌐 *www.disneyworld.com* 🛏 *950 rooms* 🍴 *No meals* ✥ *2:C1.*

$$$$
RESORT
Fodor'sChoice
★

Disney's Grand Floridian Resort & Spa. On the shores of the Seven Seas Lagoon, so close to the Magic Kingdom that you can see the colors change on the Cinderella Castle, this red-roofed Victorian-style resort emulates the look of the great railroad resorts of the past with beautifully appointed rooms, rambling verandas, delicate, white-painted woodwork, and brick chimneys. **Pros:** on the monorail route; Victoria & Albert's offers an evening-long experience in dining; if you're a couple with no kids, this is definitely the most romantic on-property hotel. **Cons:** pricey; draws a large convention clientele; vacationing couples may be more comfortable than families with young children. $ *Rooms from: $715* ✉ *4401 Floridian Way, Magic Kingdom Resort Area* ☎ *407/824–3000* ⊕ *www.disneyworld.com* ⚲ *867 rooms* ○| *No meals* ✦ *2:B1.*

$$$$
RESORT
FAMILY

Disney's Polynesian Village Resort. This South Pacific–themed resort with its tropical backdrop of orchids, ferns, and palms, lies directly across the lagoon from the Magic Kingdom, on the monorail and water taxi routes, and has lots of kids activities, making it a good family choice. **Pros:** on the monorail line; great atmosphere; free Wi-Fi. **Cons:** pricey; lots of loud children; Magic Kingdom ferry noise affects some bungalows. $ *Rooms from: $667* ✉ *1600 Seven Seas Dr., Magic Kingdom Resort Area* ☎ *407/824–2000* ⊕ *www.disneyworld.disney.go.com/resorts* ⚲ *864 rooms* ○| *No meals* ✦ *2:B2.*

$$$$
RESORT
FAMILY

Disney's Wilderness Lodge. The architects outdid themselves in designing this seven-story hotel modeled after majestic turn-of-the-20th-century lodges in the American West, with a cavernous lobby, supported by towering tree trunks, an 82-foot-high fireplace made of rocks from the Grand Canyon, two 55-foot-tall hand-carved totem poles that pay homage to the region's Native American culture, all lighted by enormous tepee-shaped chandeliers. **Pros:** boarding point for romantic cruises or free water taxi to Magic Kingdom; elegant dining options; children's activity center. **Cons:** no direct bus to Magic Kingdom; no monorail access; room safes are small and still use metal keys. $ *Rooms from: $508* ✉ *901 Timberline Dr., Magic Kingdom Resort Area* ☎ *407/824–3200* ⊕ *www.disneyworld.com* ⚲ *841 rooms* ○| *No meals* ✦ *2:C2.*

EPCOT RESORT AREA

$$
RESORT
FAMILY

Disney's Art of Animation Resort. This brightly colored, three-story resort is a kid's version of paradise: each of its four wings features images from *Finding Nemo, Cars, The Lion King,* or *The Little Mermaid,* and in-room linens and carpeting match the wing's theme. **Pros:** direct transportation to airport; free parking; images that kids adore. **Cons:** can be crowded; standard rooms fill up fast; the only on-site dining options are quick-service. $ *Rooms from: $217* ✉ *1850 Animation Way, Epcot Resort Area* ☎ *407/938–7000* ⊕ *www.disneyworld.disney.go.com/resorts* ⚲ *1,984 rooms* ○| *No meals* ✦ *2:E5.*

$$$$
RESORT

Disney's Yacht Club and Beach Club Resorts. These big Crescent Lake inns next door to Epcot seem straight out of a Cape Cod summer, with their nautical decor, waterfront locale, airy, light-filled rooms, rocking-chair porches, and family-friendly water-based activities. **Pros:** it's easy to walk or hop a ferry to Epcot or Hollywood Studios; gracious atmosphere; adjacent to Boardwalk entertainment and dining. **Cons:** distances within the hotel can seem vast; remote from other

9

parks; primarily corporate travelers. $ *Rooms from: $607* ✉ *1700 Epcot Resorts Blvd., Epcot Resort Area* ☎ *407/934–8000 Beach Club, 407/934–7000 Yacht Club* ⊕ *www.disneyworld.disney.go.com/resorts* ⌇ *1,773 rooms* †○† *No meals* ✚ *2:D4.*

$$$$ ⛬ **Four Seasons Orlando at Walt Disney World Resort.** The award-winning
RESORT   Four Seasons presides majestically over Disney's exclusive Golden Oak community, and its amenities and dedication to service are clear from the moment you step into the marble, flower-bedecked lobby and head for your room. **Pros:** free transportation to Disney parks; lots of on-site kids' entertainment; no resort fee. **Cons:** pricey, but then, it is the Four Seasons; long way from Universal or SeaWorld; remote from Disney parks. $ *Rooms from: $779* ✉ *10100 Dream Tree Blvd., Epcot Resort Area* ☎ *407/313–7777* ⊕ *www.fourseasons.com/orlando* ⌇ *444 rooms* †○† *No meals* ✚ *2:E2.*

$$$$ ⛬ **Walt Disney World Dolphin.** A pair of 56-foot-tall sea creatures book-
RESORT   ends this 25-story glass pyramid, a luxe resort designed, like the adjoining Swan, by world-renowned architect Michael Graves, and close enough to the parks that you can escape the midday heat for a dip in the pool. **Pros:** character meals available; access to all facilities at the Swan; free boat to BoardWalk, Epcot, and Hollywood Studios, buses to other parks. **Cons:** daily self-parking fee; a daily resort fee; no charging to room key at parks. $ *Rooms from: $645* ✉ *1500 Epcot Resorts Blvd., Epcot Resort Area* ☎ *407/934–4000, 800/227–1500* ⊕ *www. swandolphin.com* ⌇ *1,509 rooms* †○† *No meals* ✚ *2:C4.*

$$$ ⛬ **Walt Disney World Swan.** With Epcot and Hollywood Studios close by,
RESORT   guests here can hit the parks in the morning, return for a swim or nap on a hot afternoon, and go back to the parks refreshed and ready to play until the fireworks. **Pros:** free boats to BoardWalk, Epcot, and Hollywood Studios; good on-site restaurants; MagicBand and card service available. **Cons:** long bus ride to Magic Kingdom; daily resort fee; daily charge for self-parking. $ *Rooms from: $335* ✉ *1200 Epcot Resorts Blvd., Epcot Resort Area* ☎ *407/934–3000, 800/325–3535* ⊕ *www. swandolphin.com* ⌇ *756 rooms* †○† *No meals* ✚ *2:D4.*

ANIMAL KINGDOM RESORT AREA

$ ⛬ **Disney's All-Star Sports Resort.** Stay here if you want the All-American,
RESORT   sports-mad, quintessential Disney-with-your-kids experience, or if
FAMILY   you're a couple to whom all that pitter-pattering of little feet is a rea-
Fodor'sChoice   sonable trade-off for a good deal on a room, albeit a small one. **Pros:**
★   unbeatable price for a Disney property; kids love sports themes; heated pool. **Cons:** no kids clubs or programs; distances between rooms and on-site amenities can seem vast; farthest resort from Magic Kingdom means you'll spend time on the bus. $ *Rooms from: $105* ✉ *1701 W. Buena Vista Dr., Animal Kingdom Resort Area* ☎ *407/939–5000* ⊕ *www.disneyworld.disney.go.com/resorts* ⌇ *1,920 rooms* †○† *No meals* ✚ *2:C6.*

$$$$ ⛬ **Disney's Animal Kingdom Lodge.** Giraffes, zebras, and other wildlife
RESORT   roam three 11-acre savannas separated by the encircling arms of this
FAMILY   grand hotel, designed to resemble a *kraal,* or animal enclosure, in
Fodor'sChoice   Africa. **Pros:** extraordinary wildlife and cultural experiences; excel-
★   lent on-site restaurants; breakfast buffet in Boma is a bargain. **Cons:**

shuttle to parks other than Animal Kingdom can take more than an hour; concierge-level rooms have $100-plus surcharge; thin walls. [$] *Rooms from: $467* ✉ *2901 Osceola Pkwy., Animal Kingdom Resort Area* ☎ *407/938–3000* 🌐 *www.disneyworld.disney.go.com/resorts* 🛏 *1,421 rooms* 🍴 *No meals* ✥ *2:A5.*

$$ RESORT FAMILY Fodor's Choice ★ 🏨 **Disney's Coronado Springs Resort.** Popular with convention-goers who need huge meeting spaces, and with families who appreciate its casual Southwestern architecture; lively, Mexican-style food court; and elaborate swimming pool, colorful Coronado Springs Resort also offers a moderate price. **Pros:** great pool with a play-area arcade for kids and a bar for adults; lots of outdoor activities; wide range of dining choices. **Cons:** some accommodations are a long trek from the restaurants; standard rooms are on the small side; the lake is not for swimming. [$] *Rooms from: $261* ✉ *1000 W. Buena Vista Dr., Animal Kingdom Resort Area* ☎ *407/939–1000* 🌐 *www.disneyworld.disney.go.com/resorts* 🛏 *1,917 rooms* 🍴 *No meals* ✥ *2:C5.*

DISNEY SPRINGS RESORT AREA

$ RESORT FAMILY 🏨 **B Resort & Spa Lake Buena Vista.** The white-and-blue tower of the B Resort on Hotel Plaza Boulevard is the most recent addition to the cluster of hotels just outside Disney Springs, and a stay there combines an excellent location with a reasonable price. **Pros:** walk to Disney Springs; kids' activities; park shuttles. **Cons:** resort fee; parking fee; need a car to get to Universal or Downtown Orlando. [$] *Rooms from: $199* ✉ *1905 Hotel Plaza Blvd., Disney Springs Resort Area* ☎ *407/828–2828* 🌐 *www.bhotelsandresorts.com/b-walt-disney-world* 🛏 *394 rooms* 🍴 *No meals* ✥ *2:G4.*

$ RESORT FAMILY Fodor's Choice ★ 🏨 **Best Western Lake Buena Vista Resort.** Only a few minutes' walk from Disney Springs' growing number of shops and restaurants, this towering resort with its airy lobby offers luxury linens, flat-screen TVs, and, in many rooms, a bird's-eye view of the fireworks, all for a bargain price. **Pros:** a quick walk to shopping and restaurants; free transportation to parks, discount shops; kids eat free. **Cons:** inconvenient to Universal and Downtown Orlando; transportation to the parks can be slow and crowded; resort and parking fees. [$] *Rooms from: $174* ✉ *2000 Hotel Plaza Blvd., Disney Springs Resort Area* ☎ *407/828–2424, 800/780–7234* 🌐 *www.lakebuenavistaresorthotel.com* 🛏 *325 rooms* 🍴 *No meals* ✥ *2:G3.*

$$ HOTEL 🏨 **Disney's Port Orleans Resort–French Quarter.** Ornate, Big Easy–style row houses with wrought-iron balconies cluster around magnolia- and oak-shaded squares in this relatively quiet resort, which appeals to couples more than families. **Pros:** authentic—or as authentic as Disney can make it—fun, New Orleans–style; moderate price; lots of water recreation options, including boat rentals. **Cons:** even though there are fewer kids here, public areas can still be quite noisy; shuttle service is slow; food court is the only on-site dining option. [$] *Rooms from: $246* ✉ *2201 Orleans Dr., Disney Springs Resort Area* ☎ *407/934–5000* 🌐 *www.disneyworld.disney.go.com/resorts* 🛏 *1,008 rooms* 🍴 *No meals* ✥ *2:F3.*

$ HOTEL FAMILY **DoubleTree Suites by Hilton Orlando Disney Springs Area.** Price and location make this all-suites, Hilton-owned hotel a good choice for families and business travelers, as there are amenities for both, and it's a quick, free bus ride to any of the Disney parks. **Pros:** restaurants on-site; adult pool and splash pad for kids, adults; free shuttle to Disney attractions. **Cons:** of the properties on Hotel Plaza Boulevard, this is the farthest away from Disney Springs; inconvenient to Universal and Downtown Orlando; daily fee for parking, Wi-Fi. [$] *Rooms from: $185* ✉ *2305 Hotel Plaza Blvd., Disney Springs Resort Area* ☎ *407/934–1000, 800/222–8733* 🌐 *www.doubletreeguestsuites.com* 🛏 *229 units* 🍴 *No meals* ✣ *2:G4.*

$$ RESORT **Hilton Orlando Buena Vista Palace Disney Springs Area.** This towering hotel, just yards from Disney Springs, caters to business and leisure guests and gets kudos as much for its on-site amenities as for its location. **Pros:** good restaurants and bars on-site; kids' activities; spa is large and luxurious. **Cons:** inconvenient to Universal and Downtown Orlando; daily resort fee for Wi-Fi and fitness center; big convention clientele. [$] *Rooms from: $229* ✉ *1900 E. Buena Vista Dr., Disney Springs Resort Area* ☎ *407/827–2727* 🌐 *www.buenavistapalace.com* 🛏 *1,014 rooms* 🍴 *No meals* ✣ *2:G4.*

UNIVERSAL ORLANDO AREA

Universal Orlando's on-site hotels were built in a little luxury enclave that has everything you need, so you never have to leave Universal property. In minutes, you can walk from any hotel to CityWalk, Universal's dining and entertainment district, or take a water taxi that carries guests along a pleasant river ride to the parks.

The newest Universal Orlando Resort hotel, Sapphire Falls, with 1,000 guest rooms and family suites, joins the more affordable Cabana Bay Beach Resort and three other on-site hotels to offer free transportation to the Universal parks, as well as to SeaWorld and Aquatica.

A burgeoning hotel district across Kirkman Road and down to Sand Lake Road offers convenient accommodations and some even less expensive rates. Although these off-property hotels don't have the perks of the on-site places, you'll probably be smiling when you see your hotel bill.

$ HOTEL Fodor's Choice ★ **Drury Inn & Suites Orlando.** This reasonably priced, centrally located hotel offers free Wi-Fi, free parking, free shuttle to Universal, free hot breakfast, free long-distance and local phone calls, and free hot food and cold beverages in the late afternoon. **Pros:** free everything; central location; reasonable price. **Cons:** if Disney is your destination, this might be a little far afield; next to two busy roadways; pool and gym are small. [$] *Rooms from: $170* ✉ *7301 W. Sand Lake Rd., at I–4, Universal Studios* ☎ *407/354–1101* 🌐 *www.druryhotels.com* 🛏 *238 rooms* 🍴 *Some meals* ✣ *1:D3.*

$$$$ HOTEL **Hard Rock Hotel at Universal Orlando.** Music rules in this mission-style building, from the darkly amusing *Hotel California* quote above the entrance, "You can check out any time you like...But you can never leave," to public areas decorated with rock memorabilia, including an

Elvis jumpsuit, Madonna's "Like a Prayer" costume, and Elton John's boots. **Pros:** shuttle, water taxi, or short walk to Universal Parks and CityWalk; Universal Express Unlimited pass included; charge privileges extend to the other on-property Universal hotels. **Cons:** rooms and meals are pricey; fee for parking; loud rock music in public areas, even the pool. $ *Rooms from: $479* ⊠ *5800 Universal Blvd., CityWalk* ☎ *407/503–7625, 800/232–7827* ⊕ *www.hardrockhotelorlando.com* ⌇ *650 rooms* ⦿ *No meals* ✛ *1:D3.*

$$$$
HOTEL
Fodor'sChoice
★

⛨ **Loews Portofino Bay Hotel at Universal Orlando.** The charm and romance of Portofino, Italy—destination of Europe's rich and famous—are conjured up at this lovely luxury resort, where part of the fun is exploring the waterfront Italian "village" from end to end and not knowing what you'll find around a corner or down some steps. **Pros:** large spa; short walk or ferry ride to CityWalk, Universal; Universal Express Unlimited pass included. **Cons:** rooms and meals are pricey; daily fee for parking; not convenient to Disney parks. $ *Rooms from: $469* ⊠ *5601 Universal Blvd., Universal Orlando Resort* ☎ *407/503–1000, 800/232–7827* ⊕ *www.loewshotels.com/portofino-bay-hotel* ⌇ *750 rooms* ⦿ *Breakfast* ✛ *1:D3.*

$$$
RESORT
FAMILY

⛨ **Loews Royal Pacific Resort at Universal Orlando.** The entrance—a broad, covered footbridge high above a tropical stream—sets the tone for the Pacific Rim theme of this hotel. **Pros:** Universal Express Unlimited pass included; character dining; shuttle to CityWalk and parks. **Cons:** rooms can feel smallish; steep parking fee; can be busy with conventioneers. $ *Rooms from: $394* ⊠ *6300 Hollywood Way, Universal Orlando Resort* ☎ *407/503–3000, 800/232–7827* ⊕ *www.universalorlando.com* ⌇ *1,000 rooms* ⦿ *No meals* ✛ *1:D3.*

$$
RESORT
FAMILY
Fodor'sChoice
★

⛨ **Loews Sapphire Falls Resort.** Waterfalls cascade into aqua pools, and lush gardens fill the grounds at this latest Universal on-property hotel, which opened in 2016. **Pros:** newest Universal on-site hotel; biggest pool of any Universal resort; excellent restaurant. **Cons:** pricey parking; early entry to Universal but no Express pass; thin walls. $ *Rooms from: $225* ⊠ *6601 Adventure Way* ☎ *888/430–4999, 888/430–4999* ⊕ *www.loewshotels.com/sapphire-falls-resort* ⌇ *1,000 rooms* ⦿ *No meals* ✛ *1:D3.*

$$
RESORT
FAMILY
Fodor'sChoice
★

⛨ **Universal's Cabana Bay Beach Resort.** Universal's Cabana Bay Beach Resort takes guests back in time to a 1950s Florida beach town with a modern twist, and offers families a less expensive option to staying on-site at Universal. **Pros:** early access to Universal but no Express pass; food court on property; two swimming pools. **Cons:** parking fee; WDW isn't close; some rooms open onto outdoor passageways. $ *Rooms from: $229* ⊠ *6550 Adventure Way, Universal Orlando Resort* ☎ *407/503–4000* ⊕ *www.loewshotels.com/cabanabay* ⌇ *1,800 rooms* ⦿ *No meals* ✛ *1:D3.*

9

NIGHTLIFE

Updated by
Joseph Hayes

Outside of Downtown Disney and Universal's CityWalk, the focal point of adult Orlando nightlife is Downtown. If you stand on the corner of Orange Avenue and Church Street long enough, you can watch all types of gussied-up revelers walk by. The bars and music clubs here hop even after the 2 am last call.

ORLANDO

CENTRAL ORLANDO

BARS

AERO. You have to head up to the roof using the side staircase of The Social nightclub to reach the former Sky60 rooftop bar. Revamped and updated, it offers a hip and social view of Downtown Orlando, house and EDM parties on Saturdays, and Ladies Nights on Thursdays. ✉ *60 N. Orange Ave., Downtown Orlando* ☎ *407/274–8452* ⊕ *www.aeroorlando.com.*

Wally's. One of Orlando's oldest bars (circa 1954), this longtime local favorite is a hangout for a cross section of cultures and ages. Some would say it's a dive (which it is), but that doesn't matter to the students, bikers, lawyers, and barflies who land here to drink surrounded by the go-go-dancer wallpaper and '60s-era interior. Just grab a stool at the bar to take in the scene and down a cold one. ✉ *1001 N. Mills Ave., Downtown Orlando* ☎ *407/896–6975* ⊕ *www.wallysonmills. com* ☞ *Closed Sun.*

MUSIC CLUBS

Fodor's Choice
★

The Social. Beloved by locals, The Social is the premier Downtown music spot for indie artists. Up to seven nights a week you can sip trademark martinis while listening to anything from indie rock to rockabilly to undiluted jazz. Several now-national acts got their start here, including Matchbox Twenty, Seven Mary Three, and other groups that don't have numbers in their names. Hours vary, and there is usually a cover. ✉ *54 N. Orange Ave., Downtown Orlando* ☎ *407/246–1419* ⊕ *www.thesocial.org.*

Venue 578. Originally an old automotive repair shop, this multilevel, high-energy club, the former Firestone Live, went through several very costly renovations (and owners) to attract international music acts. Something's always going on to make the crowd hop: DJ mixes, big band, jazz, hip-hop, rock. Often the dance floor is more like semicontrolled chaos than a place to just listen, so be prepared. Hours and prices vary by event; check the website. ✉ *578 N. Orange Ave., Downtown Orlando* ☎ *407/872–0066* ⊕ *www.venue578.com.*

INTERNATIONAL DRIVE AREA

MUSIC CLUBS

B.B. King's Blues Club. The blues great was doing quite well as a musician before becoming a successful entrepreneur, with blues clubs in Memphis, Nashville, Las Vegas, and West Palm Beach as well as Orlando. Like the others, this club has music at its heart. There's a dance floor and stage for live performances by the B.B. King All-Star Band or visiting musicians seven nights a week. You can't really experience Delta blues without Delta dining, so the club doubles as a restaurant with fried dill pickles, catfish bites, po' boys, ribs, and other comfort foods. Oh yeah, and there's a full bar. ✉ *Pointe Orlando, 9101 International Dr., International Drive* ☎ *407/370–4550* ⊕ *www.bbking-clubs.com/orlando.*

NIGHTCLUBS

ICEBAR. Thanks to the miracle of refrigeration, this is Orlando's coolest bar—literally and figuratively. Fifty tons of pure ice is kept at a constant 27°F and has been cut and sculpted by world-class carvers into a cozy (or as cozy as ice can be) sanctuary of tables, sofas, chairs, and a bar. The staff loans you a thermal cape and gloves (upgrade to a fur coat for extra $), and when you enter the frozen hall your drink is served in a glass made of crystal-clear ice. There's no cover charge if you just want to hang out in the Fire Lounge or outdoor Polar Patio, but you will pay a cover to spend as much time as you can handle in the subfreezing ICEBAR. There's no beer or wine inside; it's simply too cold. ✉ *Pointe Orlando, 8967 International Dr., International Drive* ☎ *407/426–7555* ⊕ *www.icebarorlando.com.*

SHOPPING

Visitors from as far away as Britain and Brazil often arrive in Orlando with empty suitcases for their purchases. Although shopping has all but disappeared from Downtown, the metro area is filled with options. There really is something for everyone—from high-end fashion to outlet-mall chic, from a mall filled with handmade crafts to a boutique-filled town, from an antique treasure to a hand-hewn Florida find.

The College Park area, once an antiques-hunter's dream, still has some treasures to be found along North Orange Avenue and Edgewater Drive, including the largest vinyl-record shop in Florida.

The simultaneously glitzy and kitschy International Drive has almost 500 designer outlet stores and odd, off-brand electronics shops. The factory outlets on the north end of I-Drive once consisted of shops with merchandise piled on tables; today the shops here are equal to their higher-priced first-run cousins. The strip also has plenty of massive restaurants and, for those in your group who don't feel like shopping, movie theaters.

9

ORLANDO

CENTRAL ORLANDO

MALLS

Florida Mall. With 270-plus stores and 1.8 million square feet of shopping, it's big enough for you to vacation here—in fact, there's even an attached 511-room hotel. Only 7 miles from the airport, the mall attracts crowds of international visitors eager for American bargains. Exclusive shops include American Girl, Crayola Experience, and M&M World. Anchor stores include Sears, JCPenney, Dillard's, and Macy's. A revamped dining pavilion offers quick service as well as an American

Girl Bistro, Shake Shack, FAT ONE'S by singer Joey Fatone, and a Cake Boss–themed Carlo's Bakery. Stroller and wheelchair rentals are available; there are even concierge services and a currency exchange. The mall is 4½ miles east of Interstate 4 and International Drive at the corner of Sand Lake Road and South Orange Blossom Trail. ⊠ *8001 S. Orange Blossom Trail, South Orlando* ☎ *407/851–7234* ⊕ *www.simon. com/mall/the-florida-mall.*

INTERNATIONAL DRIVE AREA
FACTORY OUTLETS

Orlando International Premium Outlets. This is a prime destination for international shoppers, who can find shoes, clothing, cosmetics, electronics, and household goods at a fraction of their home-country prices. The massive complex at the north tip of International Drive includes hot brands such as 7 for All Mankind, Bebe, Janie and Jack, and Skagen, along with Saks OFF 5th, Coach, and Disney. Searching for bargains works up an appetite, and there are plenty of places to eat here, too, either in the well-lit food court or in one of several sit-down and highly regarded restaurants. ⊠ *4951 International Dr., International Drive* ☎ *407/352–9611* ⊕ *www.premiumoutlets.com/ outlet/orlando-international.*

Orlando Vineland Premium Outlets. This outlet capitalizes on its proximity to Disney (it's at the confluence of Interstate 4, State Road 535, and International Drive). It's easier to see from the highway than to enter, and parking is tedious and scarce, but smart shoppers have lunch on International Drive and take the I-Ride Trolley right to the front entrance (it runs every 15 minutes). The center's design makes this almost an open-air market, so walking can be pleasant on a nice day. You'll find Prada, Gap, Nike, Adidas, Tory Burch, Salvatore Ferragamo, and about 150 other stores. ⊠ *8200 Vineland Ave., International Drive* ☎ *407/238–7787* ⊕ *www.premiumoutlets.com/ outlet/orlando-vineland.*

MALLS

Pointe Orlando. What was once an enclosed shopping center is now a dining, shopping, and entertainment hot spot—one that's within walking distance of five top hotels and the Orange County Convention Center. It's a bit of a ramble and the parking garage is terribly confusing, so plan a day of it when you get there. In addition to WonderWorks and the enormous Regal IMAX theater, the complex has specialty shops such as Armani Exchange, Tommy Bahama, Chico's, Hollister, Charming Charlie, and Victoria's Secret. Restaurants have become a reason to visit, with the very high-end Capital Grille, the Oceanaire Seafood Room, Cuba Libre Restaurant and Rum Bar, The Pub, Marlow's Tavern, the popular Funky Monkey Bistro & Bar, B.B. King's Blues Club, and Taverna Opa. Blue Martini and Lafayette's provide after-hours entertainment and adult beverages. Check the website for a list of happy-hour specials. Winter hours tend to be longer than summer hours. ⊠ *9101 International Dr., International Drive* ☎ *407/248–2838* ⊕ *www.pointeorlando.com.*

SPORTS AND THE OUTDOORS

There are many ways to enjoy the outdoors here, but a few activities stand out. You can keep your feet planted firmly on the ground and play golf (or miniature golf), or you can take to the "skies."

BALLOONING

FAMILY

Fodor's Choice

★

Bob's Balloons. Bob's offers one-hour rides over protected marshland and even flies over the Disney area if wind and weather conditions are right. You meet at Champions Gate, near Disney World, at dawn, where Bob and his assistant take you by van to the launch site. It takes about 15 minutes to get the balloon in the air, and then you're off on an adventure that definitely surpasses Peter Pan's Flight in the Magic Kingdom.

You'll see farm and forest land for miles, along with horses, deer, wild boar, cattle, and birds flying *below* you. Bob may take you as high as 1,000 feet, and you may be able to see such landmarks as the Animal Kingdom's Expedition Everest mountain and Epcot's Spaceship Earth sphere. Several other balloons are likely to go up near you—there's a tight-knit community of ballooners in the Orlando area—so you'll view these colorful sky ornaments from an unparalleled sight line. There are seats in the basket, but you'll probably be too thrilled to sit down. Check the website for specials and call Bob to reserve. ✉ *Orlando* ☎ *407/466–6380, 877/824–4606* ⊕ *www.bobsballoons.com* ⛅ *$175.*

GOLF

If golf is your passion, you already know that Gary Player, Annika Sorenstam, Nick Faldo, and the late Arnold Palmer—in fact, almost half of the PGA tour—called Orlando their off-road home. It's not by accident that the Golf Channel originates from here. The Bay Hill Invitational and several LPGA tourneys (the headquarters is in Daytona) come to Orlando every year. And with more than 170 public and private courses, more than 20 golf academies, and dozens of mini golf putts, there's ample opportunity for you to play on world-class courses such as Grand Cypress or Champions Gate.

MINIATURE GOLF

FAMILY

Fodor's Choice

★

Hollywood Drive-In Golf at Universal CityWalk. The newest course in Orlando—and possibly the best—is two courses in one. With a science-fiction alien invasion course, and a 1950s horror movie monster course, there's something for kids and fun-loving adults alike. Spectacular lighting and sound effects mean that the play is different day and night. A 36-hole "Double Feature" package is available, and the course is open until 2 am. ✉ *6000 Universal Blvd., CityWalk* ☎ *407/802–4848* ⊕ *hollywooddriveingolf.com* ⛅ *From $15.99.*

FAMILY

Pirate's Cove Adventure Golf. Two 18-hole miniature golf courses wind around artificial mountains, through caves, beside waterfalls, and into lush foliage. The beginner's course is called Captain Kidd's Adventure;

9

the more advanced course is Blackbeard's Challenge. There's another Pirate's Cove on International Drive. ⊠ *Crossroads Shopping Center, 12545 State Rd. 535, Lake Buena Vista* ☎ *407/827–1242* ⊕ *www.piratescove.net* ⊟ *From $11.45.*

SKYDIVING

Fodor's Choice
★

iFLY Orlando. OK, so technically you aren't really skydiving, but you come pretty close in this 12-foot-high, 1,000-horsepower wind tunnel that lets you experience everything skydivers do, but closer to the ground.

The experience starts with instruction, after which you suit up and hit the wind tunnel, where you soar like a bird (or try to) under your instructor's watchful eye. It's all so realistic that skydiving clubs come to hone their skills. It's also pretty surreal as you look through the window and see people floating in midair. The attraction is safe for anyone under 250 pounds and older than three. The 90-minute introductory experience includes two flights. You can purchase a video of your "jump" at the end. ⊠ *6805 Visitors Circle, International Drive* ☎ *407/903–1150* ⊕ *iflyworld.com* ⊟ *From $59.95.*

DAY-TRIPS FROM ORLANDO

WEKIWA SPRINGS STATE PARK

13 miles northwest of Orlando, 28 miles north of WDW.

FAMILY
Fodor's Choice
★

Wekiwa Springs State Park. *Wekiva* is a Creek Indian word meaning "flowing water"; *wekiwa* means "spring of water." The river, springs, and surrounding 6,400-acre Wekiwa Springs State Park are well suited to camping, hiking, picnicking, swimming, canoeing, and fishing. The area is also full of Florida wildlife: otters, raccoons, alligators, bobcats, deer, turtles, and birds.

Canoe trips can range from a simple hour-long paddle around the lagoon to observe a colony of water turtles to a full-day excursion through the less congested parts of the river, which haven't changed much since the area was inhabited by the Timacuan Indians. You can rent canoes in the town of Apopka, near the park's southern entrance.

The park has 60 campsites: some are "canoe sites" that you can reach only via the river, and others are "trail sites," meaning you must hike a good bit of the park's 13½-mile trail to reach them. Most, however, are for the less hardy—you can drive right up to them. Sites have electric and water hookups.

To get here, take Interstate 4 Exit 94 (Longwood) and turn left on Route 434. Go 1¼ miles to Wekiwa Springs Road; turn right and go 4½ miles to the entrance, on the right. ⊠ *1800 Wekiva Circle, Apopka* ☎ *407/884–2008, 800/326–3521 campsites, 407/884–4311 canoe rentals* ⊕ *www.floridastateparks.org/park/wekiwa-springs* ⊟ *$2 per pedestrian or bicycle; $6 per vehicle.*

LEGOLAND

50 miles southwest of Orlando.

FAMILY **LEGOLAND Florida.** From 1936 to 2009, the sleepy town of Winter Haven was home to the Sunshine State's first theme park, Cypress Gardens. Today the spot holds the world's largest LEGOLAND, 150 acres of buildings built using nearly 56 million LEGOs. In addition to its 1:20-scale Lego miniature reproductions of U.S. cities, the park features more than 50 rides, shows, and attractions throughout 10 different zones, as well as the marvelous botanical gardens from the original park. The World of Chima presented by Cartoon Network invites guests into a fantastical world of animal tribal habitats anchored by an interactive water ride, the Quest for CHI. In Chima's Speedorz Arena, participants compete to win a supply of the mystical CHI energy source. A 4-D movie and Chima-character meet-and-greets round out the experience.

The Danish toy company's philosophy is to help children "play well." And play they do, as LEGOLAND attractions are very hands-on. Kids can hoist themselves to the top of a tower, power a fire truck, or navigate a LEGO robot. Sights include huge LEGO dragons, wizards, knights, pirates, castles, roller coasters, racetracks, villages, and cities.

The cityscapes in Miniland USA fascinate children and adults, who delight in discovering what's possible when you have enough bricks. Miniland opens with Kennedy Space Center, where a 6-foot shuttle waits on the launch pad. Miami Beach features bikini-clad bathers and art deco hotels; St. Augustine and its ancient fort play into LEGO's pirate theme; Key West's Mallory Square is accurate right down to the trained cats leaping through rings of fire. The rest of the United States is not ignored: New York City, Las Vegas, San Francisco, and Washington, D.C., appear in intricate detail. Visitors spend hours looking for amusing details hidden in each city, like New York's purse snatcher.

Among other highlights are Ninjago, where kids battle computer-generated bad guys; LEGO Kingdoms, whose castle towers over a jousting area and a roller coaster where knights, damsels, dragons, and ogres are found; Land of Adventure, where you can explore hidden tombs and hunt for treasure; and the Imagination Zone, showcasing LEGO Mindstorms robots, where a giant head of Albert Einstein invites kids to explore and invent. Things get wild in LEGO Technic, the most active of the park's zones, where Test Track, Aquazone Wave Racers, and Technicycle let the family expend some energy. And the live Pirates' Cove show, where seafaring sailors wearing LEGO suits defend a huge ship from attacking pirates on water skis.

LEGOLAND Water Park features a wave pool; Build-a-Raft, where families construct a LEGO vessel and float down a lazy river; a 375-foot pair of intertwined waterslides that plunge riders into a pool; and a DUPLO toddler water play area. Not to be forgotten, Cypress Gardens, at the heart of the park, preserves one of Florida's treasures.

Families can wander the lush, tropical foliage and gasp at one of the world's largest banyan trees. Two on-site hotels offer LEGO-themed accommodations and park packages.

For day-trippers, round-trip transportation from Orlando Premium Outlets, on Vineland Avenue, leaves at 9 and costs $5. ⊠ *1 Legoland Way, Winter Haven* ☎ *877/350–5346* ⊕ *www.legoland.com* ⊒ *$93; parking $15; water park $20 additional* ⊙ *Closed Tues. and Wed. during Jan. and Feb.*

BOK TOWER GARDENS

57 miles southwest of Orlando, 42 miles southwest of WDW.

Fodor's Choice ★ **Bok Tower Gardens.** You'll see citrus groves as you ride south along U.S. 27 to the small town of Lake Wales and the Bok Tower Gardens. This appealing sanctuary of plants, flowers, trees, and wildlife has been something of a local secret for years. Shady paths meander through pine forests with silvery moats, mockingbirds and swans, blooming thickets, and hidden sundials. The majestic, 200-foot Bok Tower is constructed of coquina—from seashells—and pink, white, and gray marble. The tower houses a carillon with 60 bronze bells that ring out each day at 1 and 3 pm during 30-minute recitals that might include early-American folk songs, Appalachian tunes, Irish ballads, or Latin hymns. The bells are also featured in recordings every half hour after 10 am, and sometimes even moonlight recitals.

The landscape was designed in 1928 by Frederick Law Olmsted Jr., son of the planner of New York's Central Park. The grounds include the 20-room, Mediterranean-style Pinewood Estate, built in 1930 and open for self-guided touring. From January through April, guides lead you on a 60-minute tour of the gardens (included in the admission price); tours of the inside of the tower are a benefit of membership.

Take Interstate 4 to Exit 55 and head south on U.S. 27 for about 23 miles. Proceed past Eagle Ridge Mall, then turn left after two traffic lights onto Mountain Lake Cut Off Road, and follow the signs. ⊠ *1151 Tower Blvd., Lake Wales* ☎ *863/676–1408* ⊕ *www. boktower.org* ⊒ *From $14* ⊙ *Hrs and access to Pinewood Estate vary seasonally.*

WALT DISNEY WORLD

WELCOME TO WALT DISNEY WORLD

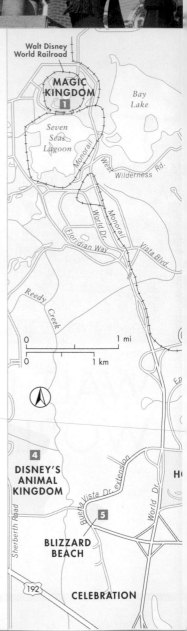

TOP REASONS TO GO

★ **Nostalgia:** Face it—Mickey and Company are old friends. And you probably have childhood pictures of yourself in front of Cinderella Castle. Even if you don't, nobody does yesteryear better: head to Main Street, U.S.A or Hollywood Boulevard and see.

★ **Memories in the making:** Who doesn't want to snap selfies on the Dumbo ride or of Junior after his Splash Mountain experience? The urge to pass that Disney nostalgia on to the next generation is strong.

★ **The thrills:** For some this means roller coasting to an Aerosmith sound track or simulating space flight; for others it's about cascading down a waterslide or going on safari.

★ **The chills:** If the Pirates of the Caribbean cave doesn't give you goose bumps, try the Haunted Mansion or Twilight Zone Tower of Terror.

★ **The spectacle:** The list is long—fireworks, laser-light displays, arcade games, parades....

1 Magic Kingdom. Disney's emblematic park is home to Space Mountain, Pirates of the Caribbean, and an expanded Fantasyland full of experiences.

2 Epcot. Future World's focus is science, technology, and hands-on experiences. In the World Showcase, you can tour 11 countries without getting jet-lagged and ride Frozen Ever After in Norway.

3 Disney's Hollywood Studios. Attractions at this re-creation of old-time Hollywood include Rock 'n' Roller Coaster Starring Aerosmith, Twilight Zone Tower of Terror, and a host of *Star Wars*–related rides and shows.

4 Disney's Animal Kingdom. Amid a 403-acre wildlife preserve are an Asian-themed water ride, an African safari ride, a runaway-train coaster, and the new Avatar-inspired land, Pandora.

5 Blizzard Beach. Water thrills range from steep flume rides to tubing expeditions in the midst of a park that you'd swear is a slowly melting ski resort. There's plenty for little ones, too.

6 Typhoon Lagoon. Sandy beaches, oceanlike waves, and a themed water coaster invite castaways to enjoy a

Orlando ⊙

CENTRAL FLORIDA

GETTING ORIENTED

Walt Disney World straddles Orange and Osceola counties to the west of Interstate 4. Four exits will get you to the parks and resort areas: 64B, 65, 67, and 68. To reach hotels along I-Drive, use Exit 72, 74A, or 75A.

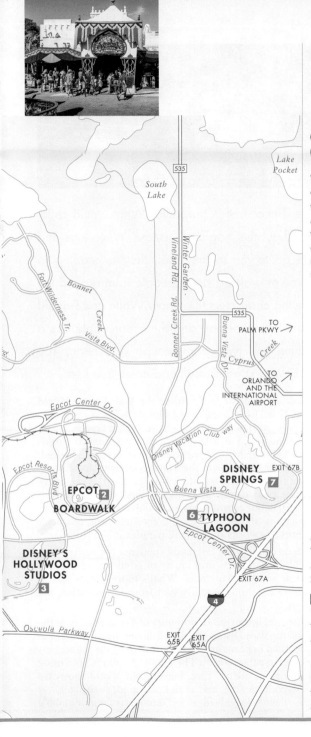

10

day of fun and relaxation. Take the kids on Bay Slides and don snorkels to explore Shark Reef.

7 Disney's Other Worlds. Disney Springs is the place to go for shopping, dining, and great entertainment. Disney's BoardWalk is a nostalgia trip, with bicycles built for two, surreys with fringe on top, pizza, bars, and a dance hall.

Updated by Jennifer Greenhill-Taylor and Joseph Hayes

Mickey Mouse. Tinker Bell. Cinderella. What would childhood be like without the magic of Disney? When kids and adults want to go to *the* theme park, they're heading to Disney. Here you're walking amid people from around the world and meeting characters like Snow White and Donald Duck while rides whirl nonstop and the irrepressible "it's a small world" tune and lyrics run through your head. You can't help but believe dreams really do come true here.

The **Magic Kingdom** is the heart and soul of the Walt Disney World empire. It was the first Disney outpost in Florida when it opened in 1971, and it's the park that launched Disney's presence in France, Japan, Hong Kong, and Shanghai. For a landmark that wields such worldwide influence, the 142-acre Magic Kingdom may seem small—indeed, Epcot is more than double the size of the Magic Kingdom, and Animal Kingdom is almost triple the size when including the park's expansive animal habitats. But looks can be deceiving. Packed into six different "lands" are nearly 50 major crowd-pleasers, and that's not counting all the ancillary attractions: shops, eateries, live entertainment, character meet-and-greet spots, fireworks shows, and parades.

Nowhere but at **Epcot** can you explore and experience the native food, entertainment, culture, and arts and crafts of countries in Europe, Asia, North Africa, and the Americas. What's more, employees at the World Showcase pavilions actually hail from the countries the pavilions represent.

Epcot, or "Experimental Prototype Community of Tomorrow," was the original inspiration for Walt Disney World. Walt envisioned a future in which nations coexisted in peace and harmony, reaping the miraculous harvest of technological achievement. The Epcot of today is both more and less than his original dream. Less, because the World Showcase presents views of its countries that are, as an Epcot guide once put it, "as Americans perceive them"—highly idealized. But this is a minor quibble in the face of the major achievement: Epcot is that rare paradox—a successful educational theme park that excels at entertainment, too.

Disney's Hollywood Studios was initially designed to be a trip back to Tinseltown's golden age, but the park is undergoing changes as it morphs into a future populated by characters and experiences from the *Star Wars* juggernaut and *Toy Story*.

The result is a theme park that blends movie-themed shows and attractions and high-tech wonders with breathtaking rides but that still retains a bit of Hollywood nostalgia. The park's old-time Hollywood atmosphere includes a rosy-hued view of the moviemaking business from the 1930s and '40s, amid sleek art-moderne buildings in pastel colors, funky diners, kitschy decorations, and sculptured gardens. But the future will include a 14-acre Star Wars land and an 11-acre Toy Story area.

Thanks to a rich library of film scores, the park is permeated with music—all familiar, all evoking the magic of the movies, and all constantly streaming from the camouflaged loudspeakers at a volume just right for humming along. Breaking through this musical background on a disconcertingly regular basis are the screams of fear from riders of the dropping elevator on the iconic Tower of Terror.

Disney's Animal Kingdom explores the stories of all animals—real, imaginary, and extinct. Enter through the Oasis, where you hear exotic background music and find yourself surrounded by gentle waterfalls and gardens alive with exotic birds, reptiles, and mammals. And the park now transforms as it opens at night.

At 403 acres and several times the size of the Magic Kingdom, Animal Kingdom is the largest in area of all Disney theme parks. Animal habitats take up much of that acreage. Creatures here thrive in careful re-creations of landscapes from Asia and Africa. Throughout the park, you'll also learn about conservation in a low-key way.

Amid all the nature are thrill rides, a 3-D show (housed in the "root system" of the iconic Tree of Life), two first-rate musicals, and character meet-and-greets. Cast members are as likely to hail from Kenya or South Africa as they are from Kentucky or South Carolina. It's all part of the charm. New park areas based on the movie *Avatar* opened in 2017, a fitting addition since the film's theme of living in harmony with nature reflects the park's eco-philosophy.

10

Typhoon Lagoon and **Blizzard Beach** are two of the world's best water parks. What sets them apart? It's the same thing that differentiates all Disney parks—the detailed themes. Whether you're cast away on a balmy island at Typhoon Lagoon or washed up on a ski-resort-turned-seaside-playground at Blizzard Beach, the landscaping and clever architecture will add to the fun of flume and raft rides, wave pools, and splash areas. Another plus: the vegetation has matured enough to create shade. The Disney water parks give you that lost-in-paradise feeling on top of all those high-speed, wedgie-inducing waterslides. They're so popular that crowds often reach overflow capacity in summer. If you're going to Disney for four days or more between April and October, add the Water Park Fun & More option to your Magic Your Way ticket.

PLANNING

ADMISSION

At the gate, the per-person, per-day price for Magic Kingdom guests varies depending on date and park. In high season the price is $124 for adults (ages 10 and older) and $118 for children (ages 3–9). At Disney's other three parks, Epcot, Hollywood Studios, and Animal Kingdom, the per-person, per-day price is $119 for adults (ages 10 and older) and $113 for children (ages 3–9). You can buy tickets at the Ticket and Transportation Center (TTC) in the Magic Kingdom, from booths at other park entrances, in all on-site resorts if you're a guest, at the Disney store in the airport, and at various other sites around Orlando. You can also buy them in advance online—the best way to save time and money.

If you opt for a multiday ticket, you'll be issued a nontransferable pass that uses your fingerprint for ID. Hold your pass up to the reader, just like people with single-day tickets, and also slip your finger into the V-shaped reader. If you're staying at a Walt Disney World resort (or if you choose to buy one), a MagicBand wristband serves as park ticket, attraction FastPass+ ticket, and even hotel room key.

OPERATING HOURS

Walt Disney World operates 365 days a year. Opening and closing times vary by park and by season, with the longest hours during prime summer months and year-end holidays. The parking lots open at least an hour before the parks do.

In general, openings hover around 9 am, though certain attractions might not start up till 10 or 11. Closings range between 5 and 8 pm in the off-season and between 8 and 10, 11, or even midnight in high season. Downtown Disney/Disney Springs and BoardWalk shops stay open as late as 11 pm.

EXTRA MAGIC HOURS

The Extra Magic Hours program gives Disney resort guests free early and late-night admission to certain parks on specified days—check ahead (⊕ *www.disneyworld.disney.go.com/calendars*) for information about each park's "magic hours" days to plan your early- and late-visit strategies.

PARKING AND IN-PARK TRANSPORT

Parking at Disney parks is free to resort guests; all others pay $20 for cars and $22 for RVs and campers. Parking is free for everyone at Typhoon Lagoon, Blizzard Beach, Disney Springs, and the Board-Walk. Trams take you between the theme-park lots (*note your parking location!*) and turnstiles. Disney's buses, boats, and monorails whisk you from resort to park and park to park. If you're staying on Disney property, you can use this system exclusively. Either take a Disney bus or drive to Typhoon Lagoon and Blizzard Beach. Once inside the water parks, you can walk, swim, slide, or chill out. Allow up to an hour for travel between parks and hotels on Disney transportation.

FASTPASS+

FastPass+ helps you avoid lines, and it's included in regular park admission. Using the new My Disney Experience app or FastPass+ kiosks in each park, you can select up to three attractions at one time; each appointment will give you a one-hour window within which you can experience each attraction. The FastPass+ appointments are loaded directly to your MagicBand or card. It's best to make appointments only for the most popular attractions and to stick with the standby queue for attractions that aren't in such demand. Strategy is everything.

Guests can get FastPass+ reservations for some designated character greetings, parades, and shows. These "experience" FastPass+ reservations count just the same as those for the rides. You get three to start with (in a single park) and can add as many more as you have time for (and these can be in a different park if you have the Park Hopper option). Best FastPass+ practices are explained by the program. It will direct you to the attractions where FastPass+ is most helpful. If these attractions don't meet your family's specific needs—your kids are too young to ride coasters, for example—the program will also help you customize your FastPass+ selections.

DISNEY STRATEGIES

Keep in mind these essential strategies, tried and tested by generations of Disney fans.

Buy tickets before leaving home. It saves money and gives you time to look into all the ticket options. It also offers an opportunity for you to consider vacation packages and meal plans and to register with the My Disney Experience program and mobile app for vacation planning.

Make dining reservations before leaving home. If you don't, you might find yourself eating fast food (again) or leaving Disney for dinner. On-site restaurants, especially those featuring character appearances, book up months ahead, and you can reserve 180 days before you arrive.

Arrive at least 30 minutes before the parks open. We know, it's your vacation and you want to sleep in. But you probably want to make the most of your time and money, too. Plan to be up by 7:30 am each day to get the most out of your park visits. After transit time, it'll take you 15–20 minutes to park, get to the gates, and pick up your park guide maps and *Times Guide*.

See top attractions in the morning. And we mean *first thing*. Decide in advance on your can't-miss attractions, find their locations, and hotfoot it to them before 10 am.

Use FastPass+. The system is free, easy, more streamlined than ever with the new FastPass+ online prebooking system, and it's your ticket to the top attractions with little or no waiting in line. Even if you wait to book once you're in the park, you can now schedule up to three FastPasses at one time; paper FastPass tickets are obsolete. Instead, your attraction appointments are loaded onto your MagicBand or plastic ticket, whichever you choose to use.

10

Use Baby Swap. Disney has a theme-park "rider switch" policy that works like this: one parent waits with the baby or toddler while the other parent rides the attraction. When the ride ends, they switch places with minimal wait.

Build in rest time. Start early and then leave the parks around 1 or 2 pm, thus avoiding the hottest and often most crowded period. After a couple of hours' rest at your hotel, head back for an evening spectacle or to ride a big-ticket ride (lines often are shorter around closing time).

Create an itinerary, but leave room for spontaneity. Don't try to plot your trip hour by hour. If you're staying at a Disney resort, find out which parks have Extra Magic Hours on which days.

Eat at off-hours. To avoid the mealtime rush hours, have a quick, light breakfast at 7 or 8 am, lunch at 11, and dinner at 5 or 6.

OTHER DISNEY SERVICES

If you can shell out $300–$500 an hour (with a six-hour minimum), you can take a customized **VIP Tour** with guides who help you park hop and get good seats at parades and shows. These tours include expedited entry to attractions, and they make navigating easy. Groups can have up to 10 people; book up to three months ahead.

FAMILY **WDW Tours.** Reserve with WDW Tours up to 180 days in advance for behind-the-scenes tours. Participant age requirements vary, so be sure to check before you book. ⊠ *Walt Disney World* ☎ *407/939–8687* ⊕ *www.disneyworld.com.*

DISNEY CONTACTS

Cruise Line: ☎ *800/370–0097* ⊕ *www.disneycruise.com*

Dining Reservations: ☎ *407/939–3463*

Extra Magic Hours: ⊕ *www.disneyworld.disney.go.com/calendars*

Fairy-Tale Weddings: ☎ *321/939–4610* ⊕ *www.disneyweddings.disney. go.com*

Golf Reservations: ☎ *407/939–4653*

Guest Info: ☎ *407/824–4321*

VIP Tours: ☎ *407/560–4033*

WDW Travel Company: ☎ *407/828–8101*

Web: ⊕ *www.disneyworld.disney.go.com*

THE MAGIC KINGDOM

Whether you arrive at the Magic Kingdom via monorail, boat, or bus, it's hard to escape that surge of excitement or suppress that smile upon sighting the towers of Cinderella Castle or the spires of Space Mountain. So what if it's a cliché by now? There's magic beyond the turnstiles, and you aren't going to miss one memorable moment.

Most visitors have some idea of what they'd like to see and do during their day in the Magic Kingdom. Popular attractions like Space Mountain and Splash Mountain are on the lists of any thrill seeker, and Fantasyland is Destination One for parents of small children and

TOP ATTRACTIONS

FOR AGES 7 AND UP	FOR AGES 6 AND UNDER
Big Thunder Mountain Railroad	Dumbo the Flying Elephant
Buzz Lightyear's Space Ranger Spin	Enchanted Tales with Belle
	The Magic Carpets of Aladdin
Haunted Mansion	The Many Adventures of Winnie the Pooh
Pirates of the Caribbean	
Seven Dwarfs Mine Train	Under the Sea: Journey of the Little Mermaid
Space Mountain	

seekers of moderate thrills like the Seven Dwarfs Mine Train. Visitors who steer away from wilder rides are first in line at the Jungle Cruise or Pirates of the Caribbean in Adventureland.

It's great to have a strategy for seeing the park's attractions, grabbing a bite to eat, or scouring the shops for souvenir gold. But don't forget that Disney Imagineers—the creative pros behind every themed land and attraction—are famous for their attention to detail. Your experience will be richer if you take time to notice the extra touches—from the architecture to the music and the costumes. The same genius is evident even in the landscape, from the tropical setting of Adventureland to the red-stone slopes of Frontierland's Big Thunder Mountain Railroad.

Wherever you go, watch for hidden Mickeys—silhouettes and abstract images of Mickey Mouse—tucked by Imagineers into every corner of the Kingdom. For instance, at the Haunted Mansion, look for him in the place settings in the banquet scene.

Much of the Magic Kingdom's pixie dust is spread by the people who work here, the costumed cast members who do their part to create fond memories for each guest who crosses their path. Maybe the grim ghoul who greets you solemnly at the Haunted Mansion will cause you to break down and giggle. Or the sunny shop assistant will help your daughter find the perfect sparkly shoes to match her princess dress. You get the feeling that everyone's in on the fun.

GETTING ORIENTED

The park is laid out on a north–south axis, with Cinderella Castle at the center and the various lands surrounding it in a broad circle.

As you pass underneath the railroad tracks, symbolically leaving behind the world of reality and entering a world of fantasy, you'll immediately notice the charming buildings lining Town Square and Main Street, U.S.A, which runs due north and ends at the Hub (also called Central Plaza), in front of Cinderella Castle. If you're lost or have questions, cast members are available at almost every turn to help you.

10

Parades are a part of the Walt Disney World experience. Most are held daily.

PARK AMENITIES

Guest Relations. To the left in Town Square as you face Main Street, **City Hall** houses Guest Relations (aka Guest Services), the Magic Kingdom's principal information center (☎ *407/824–4521*). Here you can search for misplaced belongings or companions, ask questions of staffers, and pick up a guide map and a *Times Guide* with schedules of events and character-greeting information. ■TIP→ If you're trying for a last-minute lunch or dinner reservation, you may be able to book it at City Hall.

Lockers: Lockers ($8 or $10 plus $5 deposit) are in an arcade under the Main Street railroad station. If you're park hopping, use your locker receipt to get a free locker at the next park.

Lost People and Things: Make plans for a place to meet in case of emergency or a lost member before you go any further. Instruct your kids to talk to anyone with a Disney name tag if they lose you. **City Hall** also has a lost-and-found and a computerized message center, where you can leave notes for your companions in the Magic Kingdom and other parks.

Stroller Rentals: You can rent strollers near the main entrance. Singles are $15 daily, $13 for multiday rental; doubles cost $31 daily, $27 for multiple days.

VISITING TIPS

Try to go toward the end of the week, because most families hit the Magic Kingdom early in a visit.

Ride a star attraction during a parade; lines ease considerably. (But be careful not to get stuck on the wrong side of the parade route when it starts, or you may never get across.)

At City Hall, near the park's Town Square entrance, pick up a map and a *Times Guide*, which lists showtimes, character-greeting times, and hours for attractions and restaurants.

Book character meals early. Main Street, U.S.A.'s The Crystal Palace, A Buffet with Character has breakfast, lunch, and dinner with Winnie the Pooh, Tigger, and friends. All three meals at Cinderella's Royal Table in Cinderella Castle are extremely popular—so much so that you should reserve your spot six months out. The same advice goes for booking the full-service dinner at the Be Our Guest Restaurant in the Beast's Castle in Fantasyland.

EXPLORING THE MAGIC KINGDOM

MAIN STREET, U.S.A.

With its pastel Victorian-style buildings, antique automobiles ahoohga-oohga-ing, sparkling sidewalks, and an atmosphere of what one writer has called "almost hysterical joy," Main Street is more than a mere conduit to the other enchantments of the Magic Kingdom. It's where the spell is first cast.

You emerge from beneath the Walt Disney World Railroad Station into a realization of one of the most tenacious American dreams. The perfect street in the perfect small town in a perfect moment of time is burnished to jewel-like quality, thanks to a four-fifths-scale reduction, nightly cleanings with high pressure hoses, and constant repainting. And it's a very sunny world, thanks to an outpouring of welcoming entertainment: live bands, barbershop quartets, and background music from Disney films and American musicals played over loudspeakers. Horse-drawn trolleys and omnibuses with their horns tooting chug along the street. Vendors in Victorian costumes sell balloons and popcorn. And Cinderella's famous castle floats whimsically in the distance where Main Street disappears.

Although attractions with a capital A are minimal on Main Street, there are plenty of inducements—namely, shops and eateries—to while away your time and part you from your money. The largest of these, the Emporium, is often the last stop for souvenir hunters at day's end. At the Main Street Bakery, you can find your favorite latte and a sandwich or baked treats like cupcakes and brownies. If you can't resist an interactive challenge while making your way through the park, head first to the Firehouse, next to City Hall, to join the legendary wizard Merlin in the Sorcerers of the Magic Kingdom role-playing game. For no extra charge, you can take ownership of special cards with "magic spells" that help you search for symbols and bring down Disney villains like Yzma, Cruella, Scar, Jafar, and Maleficent. Don't worry—you'll have time between fireball battles and cyclone spells to ride Space Mountain.

The Harmony Barber Shop lets you step back in time for a haircut ($18 for children 12 and under, $19 for anyone older). Babies or tots get Mickey Ears, a souvenir lock of hair, and a certificate if it's their first haircut ever, but you pay $25 for the experience. At the Town Square Theater, presented by Kodak, Mickey Mouse meets you for photos and autographs. And you can pick up a FastPass+ appointment for such meet-and-greets. While you're here, stock up on batteries and memory cards or disposable cameras.

10

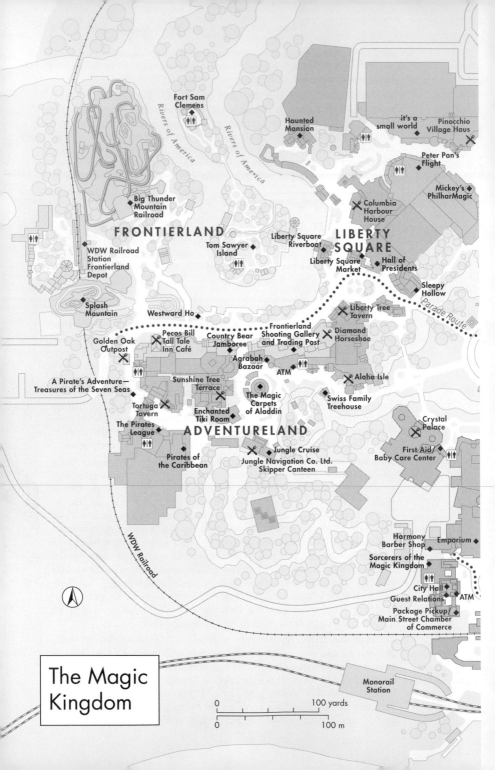

Fort Sam
Clemens

Haunted
Mansion

it's a
small world

Pinocchio
Village Haus

Peter Pan's
Flight

Mickey's
PhilharMagic

Big Thunder
Mountain
Railroad

FRONTIERLAND

Tom Sawyer
Island

Liberty Square
Riverboat

LIBERTY
SQUARE

Rivers of America

Rivers of America

Columbia
Harbour
House

WDW Railroad
Station
Frontierland
Depot

Liberty Square
Market

Hall of
Presidents

Sleepy
Hollow

Splash
Mountain

Westward Ho

Liberty Tree
Tavern

Parade Route

Golden Oak
Outpost

Pecos Bill
Tall Tale
Inn Café

Country Bear
Jamboree

Frontierland
Shooting Gallery
and Trading Post

Diamond
Horseshoe

A Pirate's Adventure—
Treasures of the Seven Seas

Sunshine Tree
Terrace

Agrabah
Bazaar

ATM

Aloha Isle

Tortuga
Tavern

Enchanted
Tiki Room

The Magic
Carpets
of Aladdin

Swiss Family
Treehouse

The Pirates
League

ADVENTURELAND

Crystal
Palace

Pirates of
the Caribbean

Jungle Cruise

First Aid/
Baby Care Center

Jungle Navigation Co. Ltd.
Skipper Canteen

WDW Railroad

Harmony
Barber Shop

Emporium

Sorcerers of the
Magic Kingdom

City Hall

ATM

Guest Relations

Package Pickup/
Main Street Chamber
of Commerce

Monorail
Station

The Magic
Kingdom

0   100 yards

0   100 m

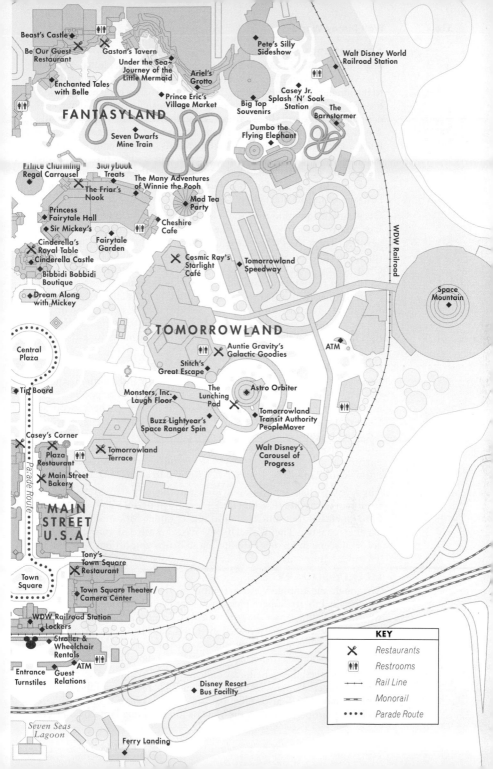

FANTASYLAND

Beast's Castle
Be Our Guest Restaurant
Gaston's Tavern
Under the Sea Journey of the Little Mermaid
Ariel's Grotto
Pete's Silly Sideshow
Walt Disney World Railroad Station
Enchanted Tales with Belle
Prince Eric's Village Market
Big Top Souvenirs
Casey Jr. Splash 'N' Soak Station
The Barnstormer
Seven Dwarfs Mine Train
Dumbo the Flying Elephant

Prince Charming Regal Carrousel
Storybook Treats
The Friar's Nook
The Many Adventures of Winnie the Pooh
Mad Tea Party
Princess Fairytale Hall
Sir Mickey's
Cheshire Cafe
Cinderella's Royal Table
Fairytale Garden
Cosmic Ray's Starlight Café
Tomorrowland Speedway
Cinderella Castle
Bibbidi Bobbidi Boutique
Dream Along with Mickey

TOMORROWLAND

Space Mountain

Auntie Gravity's Galactic Goodies
ATM
Stitch's Great Escape
Astro Orbiter
Monsters, Inc. Laugh Floor
The Lunching Pad
Tomorrowland Transit Authority PeopleMover
Buzz Lightyear's Space Ranger Spin
Central Plaza
Tip Board
Casey's Corner
Plaza Restaurant
Tomorrowland Terrace
Walt Disney's Carousel of Progress
Main Street Bakery

MAIN STREET U.S.A.

Tony's Town Square Restaurant
Town Square
Town Square Theater/Camera Center
WDW Railroad Station
Lockers
Stroller & Wheelchair Rentals
Entrance Turnstiles
Guest Relations
ATM
Disney Resort Bus Facility

Seven Seas Lagoon
Ferry Landing

WDW Railroad

Parade Route

KEY	
✕	Restaurants
▮▮	Restrooms
—•—	Rail Line
⊟	Monorail
••••	Parade Route

ADVENTURELAND

From the scrubbed brick, manicured lawns, and meticulously pruned trees of the Central Plaza, an artfully dilapidated wooden bridge leads to the jungles of Adventureland. Here, South African cape honeysuckle droops, Brazilian bougainvillea drapes, Mexican flame vines cling, spider plants clone, and three varieties of palm trees sway. The bright, all-American sing-along tunes that fill the air along Main Street and Central Plaza are replaced by the recorded repetitions of trumpeting elephants, pounding drums, and squawking parrots. The architecture is a mishmash of the best of Thailand, the Middle East, the Caribbean, Africa, and Polynesia, arranged in an inspired disorder that recalls comic-book fantasies of far-off places.

Once contained within the Pirates of the Caribbean attraction, Captain Jack Sparrow and the crew of the Black Pearl are brazenly recruiting new hearties at the Pirates League, adjacent to the ride entrance. You can get pirate and mermaid makeovers (for lots of doubloons) here. On a nearby stage furnished with pirate booty, the captain instructs scurvy dog recruits on brandishing a sword at Captain Jack Sparrow's Pirate Tutorial (several shows a day). And that's not all! At "A Pirate's Adventure: Treasures of the Seven Seas" park guests embark on an interactive quest with a pirate map and talisman to complete "raids" through Adventureland as they fight off pirate enemies along the way. Shiver me timbers—it's a pirate's life for ye!

FRONTIERLAND

Frontierland evokes the American frontier and is planted with mesquite, twisted Peruvian pepper trees, slash pines, and cacti. The period seems to be the latter half of the 19th century, and the West is being won by Disney cast members dressed in checked shirts, leather vests, cowboy hats, and brightly colored neckerchiefs. Banjo and fiddle music twangs from tree to tree, and every once in a while a flash-mob country-dance party breaks out. (Beware of hovering seagulls that migrate to the parks during cooler months—they've been known to snatch snacks.)

The screams that sometimes intrude into the jolly string music come from two of the Magic Kingdom's more thrilling rides: Splash Mountain, an elaborate flume ride, and Big Thunder Mountain Railroad, a roller coaster. The Walt Disney World Railroad tunnels past a colorful scene in Splash Mountain and drops you off between it and Thunder Mountain.

LIBERTY SQUARE

The rough-and-tumble Western frontier gently transforms into Colonial America as Liberty Square picks up where Frontierland leaves off. The weathered siding gives way to solid brick and neat clapboard. The mesquite and cactus are replaced by stately oaks and masses of azaleas. The theme is Colonial history, and the buildings, topped with weather vanes and exuding prosperity, are pure New England.

A replica of the Liberty Bell, crack and all, seems an appropriate prop to separate Liberty Square from Frontierland. There's even a Liberty Tree, a more-than-150-year-old live oak, transported here from elsewhere on Disney property. Just as the Sons of Liberty hung lanterns on trees

Coasting down Splash Mountain in Frontierland will put some zip in your doo-dah and some water on your clothes.

as a signal of solidarity after the Boston Tea Party, the Liberty Tree's branches are decorated with 13 lanterns representing the 13 original colonies. Around the square are tree-shaded tables for an alfresco lunch and plenty of carts and fast-food eateries to supply the goods.

FANTASYLAND

Walt Disney called this "a timeless land of enchantment," and Fantasyland does conjure pixie dust. Perhaps that's because the fanciful gingerbread houses, gleaming gold turrets, and, of course, the rides, are based on Disney-animated movies.

Many of these rides, which could ostensibly be classified as rides for children, are packed with enough delightful detail to engage the adults who accompany them. Fantasyland has always been the most heavily trafficked area in the park, and its rides and shows are almost always crowded.

A major expansion of Fantasyland was finished in 2014, including new rides and even a new castle. The Dumbo the Flying Elephant ride now is double the original size, flying above circus-themed grounds that also include the Great Goofini coaster, starring Goofy as stuntman. There's also a Walt Disney World Railroad station in Fantasyland. And a circus-themed Casey Jr. Splash 'N' Soak Station provides water-play respite for kids. Ariel of *The Little Mermaid* invites you to her own state-of-the-art attraction, Under the Sea: Journey of the Little Mermaid. Disney princesses welcome you for a photo op in the glittering Princess Fairytale Hall. You can be part of the show when you join Belle, Lumière, and Madame Wardrobe of *Beauty and the Beast* at the Enchanted Tales with Belle attraction for a story performance. Meanwhile, Beast may

10

be brooding in his castle, where the Be Our Guest dining room beckons to lunch and dinner guests. And the musical Seven Dwarfs Mine Train family coaster hurtles guests into the bejeweled depths of the earth to the tune of, what else, *Heigh Ho*.

You can enter Fantasyland on foot from Liberty Square, Tomorrowland, or via the Walt Disney World Railroad, but the classic introduction is through Cinderella Castle. As you exit the castle's archway, look left to discover a charming and often overlooked touch: Cinderella Fountain, with its lovely bronze casting of the castle's namesake, who's dressed in her peasant togs and surrounded by her beloved mice and bird friends.

From the southern end of Liberty Square, head toward the park hub and stop at the Disney PhotoPass picture spot for one of the park's best, unobstructed ground-level views of Cinderella Castle. It's a great spot for that family photo.

TOMORROWLAND

The "future that never was" spins boldly into view as you enter Tomorrowland, where Disney Imagineers paint the landscape with whirling spaceships, flashy neon lights, and gleaming robots. This is the future as envisioned by early-20th-century sci-fi writers and moviemakers, when space flight, laser beams, and home computers were fiction, not fact. Retro Jetsonesque styling lends the area lasting chic.

Gamers who want a break from the crowds can find their favorite video challenges in the arcade attached to Space Mountain. SEGA race car, NASCAR, and Fast and Furious Super Bikes games draw tweens and teens; Lil' Hoops give young kids a manageable basketball challenge. Though Tomorrowland Transit Authority (TTA) PeopleMover isn't a big-ticket ride, it's a great way to check out the landscape from above as it zooms in and out of Space Mountain and curves around the entire land.

EPCOT

Walt Disney said that Epcot would "take its cue from the new ideas and new technologies that are now emerging from the creative centers of American industry." He wrote that Epcot—never completed, always improving—"will never cease to be a living blueprint of the future, a showcase to the world for the ingenuity of American free enterprise."

But the permanent settlement that Disney envisioned wasn't to be. Epcot opened in 1982—16 years after his death—as a showcase, ostensibly, for the concepts that would be incorporated into the real-life Epcots of the future. (Disney's vision *has* taken an altered shape in the self-contained city of Celebration, an urban-planner's dream opened in 1996 on Disney property near Kissimmee.)

Epcot, the theme park, has two key areas: Future World, where most pavilions are collaborations between Walt Disney Imagineering and U.S. corporations and are designed to demonstrate technological advances through innovative shows and attractions; and the World Showcase, where shops, restaurants, attractions, and live entertainment create microcosms of 11 countries from four continents.

For years, Epcot was considered the more staid park, a place geared toward adults. But after its 10th anniversary, Epcot began to evolve into a livelier, more child-friendly park, with such "wow" attractions as Future World's Test Track, Mission: SPACE, and Soarin'.

There's something for everyone here. The World Showcase appeals to younger children with the Kidcot

TOP ATTRACTIONS

Frozen Ever After

IllumiNations

Mission: SPACE

Soarin'

Test Track

Fun Stop craft stations and the Norway pavilion's Frozen Ever After ride. Soarin', in the Land Pavilion, is a family favorite. The Seas with Nemo & Friends—with one of the world's largest saltwater aquariums and a Nemo-themed ride—is a must-see for all. Adrenaline junkie? Don't miss Test Track presented by Chevrolet, where you can design your own custom concept car, then put it through its high-speed paces.

Wear comfortable shoes—there's *a lot* of territory to cover here. Arrive early, and try to stay all day, squeezing in extras like high-tech games at Innoventions and a relaxing meal. If you enter through International Gateway before 11 am, cast members will direct you to Future World, which usually opens two hours before World Showcase, or you can indulge in a latte and éclair at the France bakery, the sole quick-service eatery open early in World Showcase.

GETTING ORIENTED

Epcot is composed of two areas: Future World and the World Showcase. The inner core of Future World's pavilions has the Spaceship Earth geosphere and a plaza anchored by the computer-animated Fountain of Nations.

Six pavilions compose Future World's outer ring. Each of the three east pavilions has a ride and the occasional post-ride showcase; a visit rarely takes more than 30 minutes. The blockbuster exhibits on the west side contain rides and interactive displays; each exhibit can take up to 90 minutes for the complete experience.

World Showcase pavilions are on the promenade that circles the World Showcase Lagoon. Each houses shops, restaurants, and friendly international staffers; some have films or displays. Mexico offers a tame ride. Live entertainment is scheduled at every pavilion except Norway. Disney's monorail and buses drop you off at the main entrance in front of Future World. But if you're staying at one of the Epcot resorts (the BoardWalk, Yacht Club, Beach Club, Dolphin, or Swan), you can use the International Gateway entrance between World Showcase's France and U.K. pavilions.

PARK AMENITIES

Guest Relations: To the right of the ticket windows at the park entrance and to the left of Spaceship Earth inside the park, this is the place to pick up schedules and maps. You also can get maps at the park's International Gateway entrance and most shops. Guest Relations will also assist with dining reservations, ticket upgrades, and services for guests with disabilities.

10

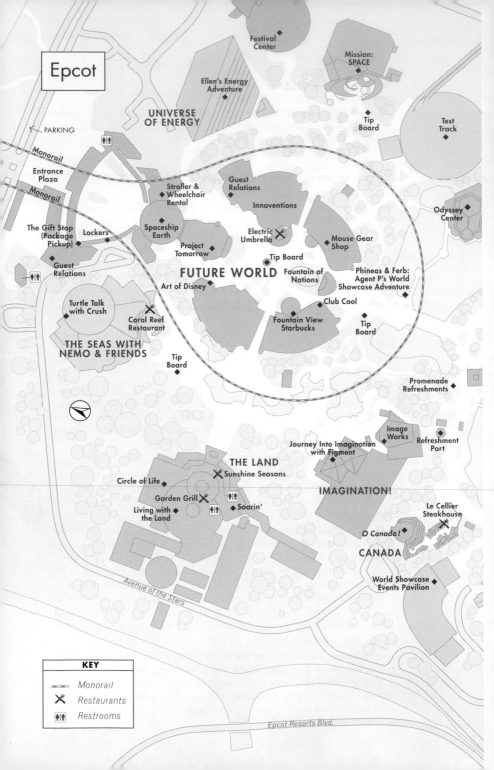

Epcot

PARKING

Monorail

Entrance Plaza

Monorail

UNIVERSE OF ENERGY

Festival Center

Ellen's Energy Adventure

Mission: SPACE

Tip Board

Test Track

The Gift Stop (Package Pickup)

Lockers

Stroller & Wheelchair Rental

Spaceship Earth

Guest Relations

Project Tomorrow

Innoventions

Electric Umbrella

Odyssey Center

Guest Relations

Tip Board

Mouse Gear Shop

FUTURE WORLD

Art of Disney

Fountain of Nations

Phineas & Ferb: Agent P's World Showcase Adventure

Turtle Talk with Crush

Coral Reef Restaurant

Club Cool

THE SEAS WITH NEMO & FRIENDS

Fountain View Starbucks

Tip Board

Tip Board

Promenade Refreshments

Journey Into Imagination with Figment

Image Works

Refreshment Port

THE LAND

Circle of Life

Sunshine Seasons

Garden Grill

Living with the Land

Soarin'

IMAGINATION!

Le Cellier Steakhouse

O Canada!

CANADA

Avenue of the Stars

World Showcase Events Pavilion

Epcot Resorts Blvd.

KEY

▨▨▨	*Monorail*
✕	*Restaurants*
⋔	*Restrooms*

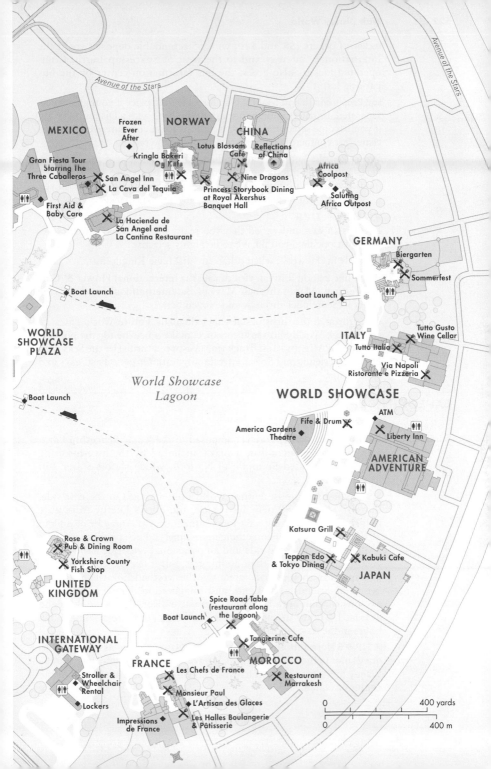

Avenue of the Stars

Avenue of the Stars

MEXICO

Frozen Ever After

NORWAY

CHINA

Gran Fiesta Tour Starring The Three Caballeros

Kringla Bakeri Og Kafe

Lotus Blossom Café

Reflections of China

San Angel Inn
La Cava del Tequila

Nine Dragons

Africa Coolpost

First Aid & Baby Care

Princess Storybook Dining at Royal Akershus Banquet Hall

Saluting Africa Outpost

La Hacienda de San Angel and La Cantina Restaurant

GERMANY

Biergarten

Sommerfest

Boat Launch

Boat Launch

WORLD SHOWCASE PLAZA

ITALY

Tutto Gusto Wine Cellar

Tutto Italia

Via Napoli Ristorante e Pizzeria

World Showcase Lagoon

WORLD SHOWCASE

Boat Launch

ATM

Fife & Drum

America Gardens Theatre

Liberty Inn

AMERICAN ADVENTURE

Katsura Grill

Rose & Crown Pub & Dining Room

Teppan Edo & Tokyo Dining

Kabuki Cafe

Yorkshire County Fish Shop

JAPAN

UNITED KINGDOM

Spice Road Table (restaurant along the lagoon)

INTERNATIONAL GATEWAY

Boat Launch

Tangierine Cafe

Stroller & Wheelchair Rental

FRANCE

Les Chefs de France

MOROCCO

Restaurant Marrakesh

Lockers

Monsieur Paul

L'Artisan des Glaces

Impressions de France

Les Halles Boulangerie & Pâtisserie

| 0 | | | 400 yards |
| 0 | | | 400 m |

Lockers: Lockers ($8 and $10, with $5 refundable deposit) are at the International Gateway and to the west of Spaceship Earth. Coin-operated lockers also are at the bus information center by the bus parking lot.

Lost People and Things: Make a plan for a meeting place if your group gets separated. Instruct children to speak to someone with a Disney name tag if you become separated. Guest Relations has a computerized message center for contacting companions in any of the parks.

Stroller Rentals: You can rent strollers on the east side of the Entrance Plaza and at the International Gateway. Singles are $15 daily, $13 for multiday rental; doubles cost $31 daily, $27 for multiple days. Even preschoolers will be glad for a stroller in this large park.

VISITING TIPS

Epcot is so vast and varied that you really need two days to explore. With just one day, you'll have to be highly selective.

Go early in the week, when others are at Magic Kingdom.

If you like a good festival, visit during the **International Flower & Garden Festival** (March through May) or the **International Food & Wine Festival** (September through mid-November).

Once through the turnstiles at either the main Future World entrance or the back World Showcase entrance, make a beeline for the popular Mission: SPACE and Test Track (for fast-paced thrills) or the Seas with Nemo & Friends and Soarin' (for family fun). Or get a FastPass+ and return later.

EXPLORING EPCOT

FUTURE WORLD

Future World's inner core is composed of the iconic Spaceship Earth geosphere and, beyond it, a plaza anchored by the awe-inspiring computer-animated Fountain of Nations, which shoots water 150 feet skyward.

Six pavilions compose Future World's outer ring. On the east side, they are Mission: SPACE, Test Track, and Ellen's Energy Adventure (which at 30+ is getting a bit long in the tooth, and may be closing in 2017 to make way for something more timely). Each pavilion presents a single, self-contained ride and an occasional post-ride showcase; a visit rarely takes more than 30 minutes, but it depends on how long you spend in the post-ride area. On the west side are the Seas with Nemo & Friends, The Land, and Imagination! These blockbuster exhibits contain both rides and interactive displays; you could spend at least 1½ hours at each of these pavilions, but there aren't enough hours in the day, so prioritize.

■TIP➜ Before setting out, look into the Disney PhotoPass at the Camera Center in the Entrance Plaza. It tracks photos of your group shot by Disney photographers, which you can view and purchase later at the center or online.

One of Epcot's most popular rides is Mission: Space, which simulates a shuttle launch.

WORLD SHOWCASE

Nowhere but at Epcot can you explore a little corner of nearly a dozen countries in one day. As you stroll the 1.3 miles around the 40-acre World Showcase Lagoon, you circumnavigate the globe-according-to-Disney by experiencing the architecture, native food, entertainment, culture, and arts and crafts at pavilions representing countries in Europe, Asia, North Africa, and the Americas. Pavilion employees are from the countries they represent—Disney hires them as part of its international college program.

Solid film attractions are featured at the Canada, China, and France pavilions; Norway houses the Frozen Ever After ride, a kid magnet if there ever was one; several art exhibitions; and the chance to try your foreign language skills with the staff. Each pavilion also has a designated Kidcot Fun Stop, open daily from 11 or noon until about 8 or 9, where youngsters can try a cultural crafts project. Live entertainment is an integral part of the experience, and you'll enjoy watching the incredibly talented Jeweled Dragon Acrobats in China and the Matsuriza Taiko drummers in Japan or laughing along with the mime and juggler in the Italy courtyard.

Dining is another favorite pastime at Epcot, and the World Showcase offers tempting tastes of the authentic cuisines of the countries here.

TOP ATTRACTIONS

FOR AGES 8 AND UP	Twilight Zone Tower of Terror
Indiana Jones Epic Stunt Spectacular!	Walt Disney: One Man's Dream
Rock 'n' Roller Coaster Starring Aerosmith	**FOR AGES 7 AND UNDER** Beauty and the Beast—Live on Stage
Star Tours—The Adventures Continue	Disney Junior—Live on Stage!
Toy Story Mania!	A Frozen Sing-along Celebration
	Muppet*Vision 3-D

DISNEY'S HOLLYWOOD STUDIOS

The first thing you notice when you pass through the Hollywood Studios turnstiles is the laid-back California attitude. Palm-lined Hollywood Boulevard oozes glamour—but in a casual way that makes you feel as if you belong. The second thing you notice is the growing presence of *Star Wars*.

When the park opened in May 1989 its name was Disney-MGM Studios. Disney changed the name to Disney Hollywood Studios in 2008 and combined Disney detail with a broader motion-picture legacy and Walt Disney's own animated classics. Imagineers built the park with real film and television production in mind, and during its first decade, the Studios welcomed films like *Ernest Saves Christmas* and TV shows like *Wheel of Fortune* to its soundstages.

Though production has mostly halted at the park, you can enjoy plenty of attractions that showcase how filmmakers practice their craft. If you're wowed by action-film stunts, you can learn the tricks of the trade at the Indiana Jones Epic Stunt Spectacular! The Great Movie Ride celebrates some of Hollywood's most famous products.

10

In a savvy effort to grab a bigger piece of the pop-culture pie, Disney is turning away from the past and moving toward the future, as the *Star Wars* attractions take over more space at the park. Add in the expanding *Toy Story* attractions and the park is sure to keep the whole family happy.

GETTING ORIENTED

The park is divided into sightseeing clusters. **Hollywood Boulevard** is the main artery to the heart of the park, and is where you find the glistening replica of Graumann's Chinese Theater.

Encircling it are **Sunset Boulevard**, the **Animation Courtyard, Mickey Avenue, Pixar Place, Commissary Lane, the Streets of America area**, and **Echo Lake**.

The entire park is 135 acres, and has fewer than 20 attractions (compared with Magic Kingdom's 40-plus). It's small enough to cover in a day and even repeat a favorite ride or two.

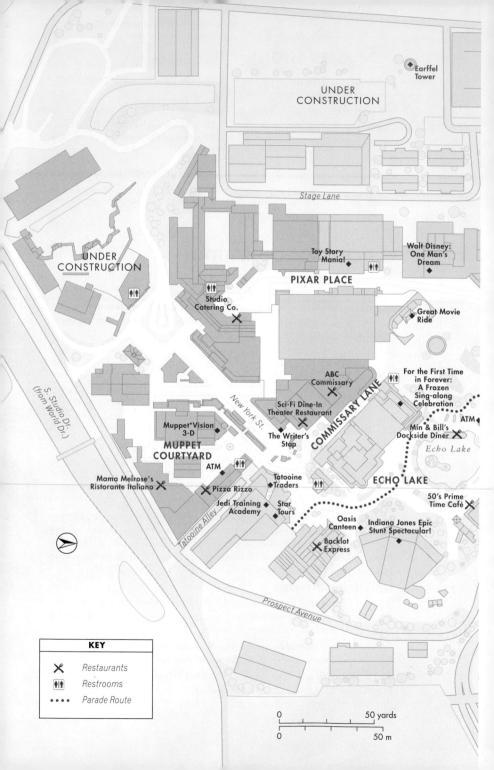

Earffel
Tower

UNDER
CONSTRUCTION

Stage Lane

UNDER
CONSTRUCTION

Toy Story
Mania!

Walt Disney:
One Man's
Dream

PIXAR PLACE

Studio
Catering Co.

Great Movie
Ride

ABC
Commissary

For the First Time
in Forever:
A Frozen
Sing-along
Celebration

ATM

Sci-Fi Dine-In
Theater Restaurant

New York St.

Min & Bill's
Dockside Diner

Muppet*Vision
3-D

The Writer's
Stop

COMMISSARY LANE

Echo Lake

MUPPET
COURTYARD

ATM

ECHO LAKE

Mama Melrose's
Ristorante Italiano

Pizza Rizzo

Tatooine
Traders

50's Prime
Time Café

S. Studio Dr.
(from World Dr.)

Jedi Training
Academy

Star
Tours

Oasis
Canteen

Indiana Jones Epic
Stunt Spectacular!

Tatooine Alley

Backlot
Express

Prospect Avenue

KEY

✗   Restaurants

🚻   Restrooms

••••   Parade Route

| 0 | | 50 yards |
| 0 | | 50 m |

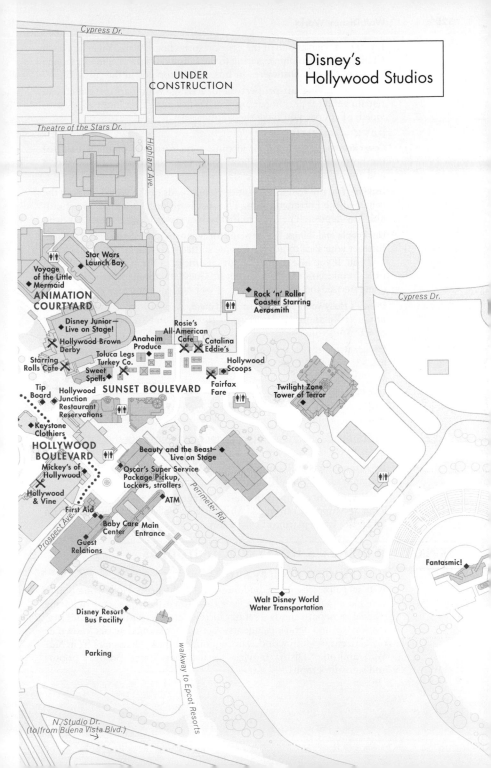

Disney's Hollywood Studios

Cypress Dr.

UNDER CONSTRUCTION

Theatre of the Stars Dr.

Highland Ave.

Cypress Dr.

Star Wars Launch Bay

Voyage of the Little Mermaid

ANIMATION COURTYARD

Rock 'n' Roller Coaster Starring Aerosmith

Disney Junior— Live on Stage!

Hollywood Brown Derby

Rosie's All-American Cafe

Anaheim Produce

Catalina Eddie's

Starring Rolls Cafe

Toluca Legs Turkey Co.

Hollywood Scoops

Sweet Spells

SUNSET BOULEVARD

Fairfax Fare

Twilight Zone Tower of Terror

Tip Board

Hollywood Junction Restaurant Reservations

Keystone Clothiers

HOLLYWOOD BOULEVARD

Beauty and the Beast— Live on Stage

Mickey's of Hollywood

Oscar's Super Service Package Pickup, Lockers, strollers

Hollywood & Vine

Perimeter Rd.

ATM

First Aid

Baby Care Center

Main Entrance

Guest Relations

Fantasmic!

Prospect Ave.

Walt Disney World Water Transportation

Disney Resort Bus Facility

Parking

walkway to Epcot Resorts

N. Studio Dr. (to/from Buena Vista Blvd.)

If you're staying at one of the Epcot resorts (BoardWalk, Yacht or Beach Club, Swan, or Dolphin), getting to the Entrance Plaza on a motor launch is part of the fun. Disney resort buses also drop you at the entrance.

If you're staying off-property and driving, your parking ticket will remain valid for parking at another Disney park later in the day—provided, of course, you have the stamina.

PARK AMENITIES

Guest Relations: You'll find it just inside the turnstiles on the left side of the Entrance Plaza. A **FastPass+ kiosk** is at the corner of Hollywood and Sunset boulevards.

Lockers: You can rent lockers at the Crossroads of the World kiosk in the center of the Entrance Plaza. The cost is $8 or $10 with a $5 refundable key deposit. The lockers themselves are at Oscar's Super Service.

Lost People and Things: Make plans for where to meet if you get separated. Instruct your kids to go to a Disney staffer with a name tag if they can't find you. If you lose them, ask any cast member for assistance; logbooks of lost children's names are kept at Guest Relations, which also has a computerized message center where you can leave notes for companions.

Disney's Hollywood Studios Lost and Found. Report lost or found articles at Guest Relations. ⊠ *Hollywood Blvd., Disney's Hollywood Studios* ☎ *407/560–4666.*

Stroller Rentals: Oscar's Super Service rents strollers. Single strollers are $15 daily, $13 for more than one day; doubles are $31 daily, $27 multiday.

VISITING TIPS

Visit early in the week, when most people are at Magic Kingdom and Animal Kingdom.

Check the Tip Board periodically for attractions with short wait times to visit between FastPass+ appointments.

Be at the Fantasmic! amphitheater at least an hour before showtime if you didn't book the VIP dinner package.

Need a burst of energy? On-the-run hunger pangs? Grab a slice at **Pizza Rizzo** at Muppet Courtyard. Alternatively, **Hollywood Scoops** ice cream on Sunset is the place to be on a hot day.

EXPLORING DISNEY'S HOLLYWOOD STUDIOS

HOLLYWOOD BOULEVARD

With its palm trees, pastel buildings, and flashy neon, Hollywood Boulevard paints a rosy picture of 1930s Tinseltown. There's a sense of having walked right onto a movie set of old, with art-deco storefronts and roving starlets and nefarious agents—actually costumed actors known as the Citizens of Hollywood. Throughout the park, characters from *Star Wars* and other Disney movies—such as *Toy Story*—pose for photos and sign autographs.

SUNSET BOULEVARD

This avenue honors Hollywood with facades derived from City of Angels landmarks, and leads straight to the Beauty and the Beast Live on Stage show.

ANIMATION COURTYARD

As you exit Sunset Boulevard, veer right through the high-arched gateway to the Animation Courtyard. Straight ahead are *Disney Junior— Live on Stage!*, *Voyage of the Little Mermaid,* and the Star Wars Launch Bay, where fans can meet Chewbacca and Kylo Ren.

PIXAR PLACE

Pixar Place is home to one of the park's biggest attractions, Toy Story Midway Mania! Where TV- and film-production soundstages once stood, warm brick facades welcome you to the land of Woody and Buzz. Open-air kiosks invite you to browse for themed toys and souvenirs. The brick building featuring Toy Story Friends is the place to mix and mingle with characters from the blockbuster movie *Toy Story.* Check schedules on your *Times Guide.*

STAR WARS LAND

Much of the southwest corner of the park has been behind walls and fences for the past two years, but 2017—to celebrate the 40th anniversary of the original film—is the year that *Star Wars* really begins to take over Hollywood Studios. Even though the land itself is not expected to be complete until 2019, the franchise, including characters and scenes from *Rogue One,* have already affected much of the entertainment and direction in the larger park. At 14 acres, Star Wars Land will be the largest single-themed expansion ever added to a Disney theme park. Visitors will be transported to a galaxy far, far away, to a planet on the outer rim of civilization, one of the last stops before wild space, and right into a battle between the dark and light sides of the Force. One of the signature attractions will put you behind the controls of the Millennium Falcon; and Star Tours—the Adventures Continue will include a new mission based on elements from the upcoming *Star Wars Episode VIII.* The food, entertainment, and attractions are all part of the story, including the Cantina and a supper club with alien entertainment.

ECHO LAKE

In the center of the park is a cool, blue lake—an oasis fringed with trees, benches, and things like pink-and-aqua, chrome-trimmed restaurants with sassy waitresses and black-and-white TVs at the tables; the shipshape Min & Bill's Dockside Diner; and Tatooine Traders, where kids can build their own lightsabers and browse a trove of *Star Wars*–inspired goods. You'll also find two of the park's longest-running attractions, the Indiana Jones Epic Stunt Spectacular! and Star Tours— The Adventures Continue, where guests can interact with scenes and characters from 2016's *Rogue One.*

10

ANIMAL KINGDOM

If you're thinking, "Oh, it's just another zoo, let's skip it," think again. Walt Disney World's fourth theme park, opened in 1998, takes its inspiration from humankind's enduring love for animals and pulls out all the stops. Your day will be packed with unusual animal encounters, enchanting entertainment, themed rides that will leave you breathless, and a brand-new land, Pandora—The World of Avatar, which takes visitors inside the culture and sights of James Cameron's film.

A large chunk of the park is devoted to animal habitats, especially the forest and savanna of Africa's Kilimanjaro Safaris. Towering acacia trees and tall grasses sweep across the land where antelopes, giraffes, and wildebeests roam. A lion kopje, warthog burrows, a zebra habitat, and an elephant watering hole provide ample space for inhabitants.

About 94 acres contain foliage like hibiscus and mulberry, perfect for antelope and many other species. The largest groups of Nile hippos and African elephants in North America live along the winding waterway that leads to the savanna. The generously landscaped Pangani Forest Exploration Trail provides roaming grounds for troops of gorillas, and authentic habitats for meerkats, birds, fish, and other creatures.

Beyond the park's Africa territory, similar large spaces are set aside for the homes of Asian animals like tigers and giant fruit bats, as well as for creatures such as Galápagos tortoises and a giant anteater.

Disney Imagineers didn't forget to include their trademark thrills, from the Kali River Rapids ride in Asia to the fast-paced DINOSAUR journey in DinoLand U.S.A. Expedition Everest, the park's current big thrill attraction, is a "runaway" train ride on a faux rugged mountain complete with icy ledges, dark caves, and a yeti legend. Next up: The glow-in-the-dark plants, flying banshees, floating mountains, and Na'vi culture of *Avatar* and its coming sequels.

Every evening, the Tree of Life Awakenings bathes the central icon with color, and several live entertainment ensembles perform, including the Discovery Island Carnivale and the popular Tam Tam Drummers of Harambe. A new evening show "Rivers of Light" also began after a long delay in 2017.

The only downside to the Animal Kingdom layout is that walking paths and spaces can get very crowded and hot in the warmest months. Your best bet is to arrive very early and see the animals first before the heat makes them (and you) woozy.

Just before the park opens, Minnie Mouse, Pluto, and other characters arrive at Trader's Outpost to welcome early guests into the park.

GETTING ORIENTED

Animal Kingdom's hub is the Tree of Life, in the middle of Discovery Island. The park's lands, each with a distinct personality, radiate from Discovery Island. To the southwest lies the new land of Pandora, based on the *Avatar* film and upcoming sequels. The land opened in May 2017. North of the hub is Africa, where Kilimanjaro Safaris travel across extensive savanna. In the northeast corner is Rafiki's Planet Watch with conservation activities.

Asia, with thrills like Expedition Everest and Kali River Rapids, is east of the hub, and DinoLand U.S.A. brings *T. rex* and other prehistoric creatures to life in the park's southeast corner.

If you're staying on-site, you can take a Disney bus to the Entrance Plaza. If you drive, the $20 parking fee allows you to park at other Disney lots throughout the day.

Although this is technically Disney's largest theme park, most of the land is reserved for the animals. Pedestrian areas are actually quite compact, with relatively narrow passageways. The only way to get around is on foot or in a wheelchair or electronic convenience vehicle (ECV).

TOP ATTRACTIONS

Africa
Festival of the Lion King
Kilimanjaro Safaris

Asia
Expedition Everest

DinoLand U S A
DINOSAUR
Finding Nemo: The Musical

Discovery Island
Tree of Life: It's Tough to Be a Bug!

Pandora—The World of Avatar
Avatar Flight of Passage

PARK AMENITIES

Guest Relations: This office will help with tickets at a window to the left just before you pass through the turnstile. Once you've entered, Guest Relations staffers in the Oasis can provide park maps, schedules, and answers to questions. They can also assist with dining reservations, ticket upgrades, and services for guests with disabilities.

Lockers: Lockers are in Guest Relations in the Oasis. Rental fees are $8 to $10 (depending on size) for a day plus a $5 key deposit.

Lost People and Things: Instruct your kids to speak to someone with a Disney name tag if you become separated. Lost children are taken to the baby-care center, where they can watch Disney movies, or to Guest Relations, whichever is closer. If you do lose your child, contact any cast member immediately and Disney security personnel will be notified.

Animal Kingdom Lost and Found. To retrieve lost articles on the same day, visit or call Lost and Found, which is in the lobby of Guest Relations, just inside the park. ⊠ *Oasis, Animal Kingdom* ☎ *407/938–2785.*

Stroller Rentals: Garden Gate Gifts in the Oasis rents strollers. Singles are $15 daily, $13 multiday; doubles run $31 daily, $27 multiday.

VISITING TIPS

Try to visit during the week. Pedestrian areas are compact, and the park can feel uncomfortably packed on weekends.

The new land of Pandora will likely draw particularly large crowds for at least a year after its opening in May 2017.

Plan on a full day here. That way, while exploring Africa's Pangani Forest Exploration Trail, say, you can spend 10 minutes (rather than just 2) watching vigilant meerkats stand sentry or tracking a mama gorilla as she cares for her youngster.

10

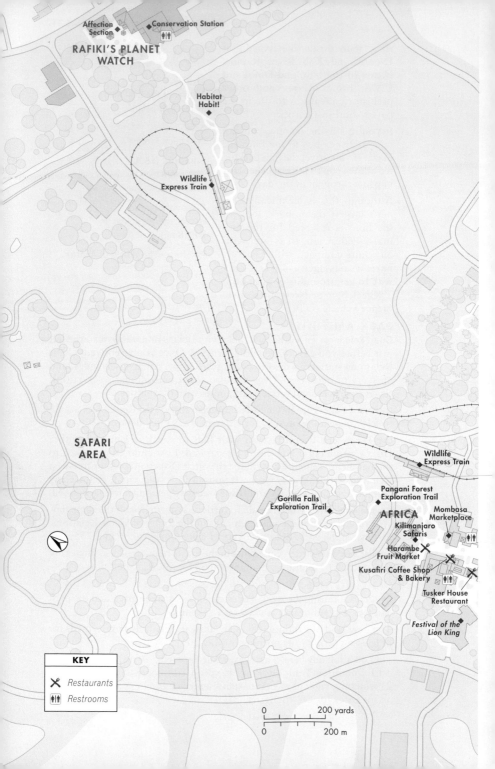

Affection
Section
Conservation Station

**RAFIKI'S PLANET
WATCH**

Habitat
Habit!

Wildlife
Express Train

Wildlife
Express Train

**SAFARI
AREA**

Pangani Forest
Exploration Trail

Gorilla Falls
Exploration Trail

Mombasa
Marketplace

AFRICA

Kilimanjaro
Safaris

Harambe
Fruit Market

Kusafiri Coffee Shop
& Bakery

Tusker House
Restaurant

Festival of the
Lion King

KEY

✗ *Restaurants*

🚻 *Restrooms*

0   200 yards

0   200 m

Disney's Animal Kingdom

ASIA

Expedition Everest

Kali River Rapids

Anandapur Ice Cream Truck

Serka Zong Bazaar

Rivers of Light

Maharajah Jungle Trek

Finding Nemo— The Musical

Rivers of Light

Discovery River

Yak & Yeti Restaurant

Dino Diner

Primeval Whirl

Fossil Fun Games

Flights of Wonder

Boneyard

TriceraTop Spin

Chester Hester's Dinosaur Treasures

ATM

Warung

Adventure Outpost

Flame Tree Barbecue

Trilo-Bites

DINOLAND U.S.A.

The Dino Institute Shop

Caravan Road

Mr Kamal's

Gardens Kiosk

Dino-Bite Snacks

DinoSue

Tree of Life, It's Tough to Be a Bug!

Discovery Trading Company

Restaurantosaurus

DINOSAUR

Harambe Market

Awakenings

Tamu Tamu Refreshments

DISCOVERY ISLAND

Isle of Java

Tips and Showtimes

Terra Treats

Discovery Island Trails

Island Mercantile

Garden Gate Gifts

Dawa Bar

Strollers & Wheelchairs

ATM

First Aid/ Baby Care Center

Creature Comforts

Pizzafari

OASIS

Entrance

Tiffins

Lockers

Guest Relations

PANDORA— THE WORLD OF AVATAR

Rainforest Café

Valley of Mo'ara

Guest Relations

Avatar Flight of Passage

Na'vi River Journey

Arrive a half hour before the park opens as much to see the wild animals at their friskiest (morning is a good time to do the safari ride) as to get a jump on the crowds.

For updates on line lengths, check the Tip Board, just after crossing the bridge into Discovery Island.

Good places to rendezvous include the outdoor Dawa Bar or Tamu Tamu Refreshments areas in Africa, in front of DinoLand U.S.A.'s Boneyard, or on one of the benches outside Expedition Everest in Asia.

EXPLORING ANIMAL KINGDOM

THE OASIS

This entrance makes you feel as if you've been plunked down in the middle of a rain forest. Cool mist, the aroma of flowers, playful animals, and colorful birds enliven a miniature landscape of streams and grottoes, waterfalls, and glades fringed with banana leaves and jacaranda. It's also where you can take care of essentials before entering. Here you'll find guide maps, stroller and wheelchair rentals, Guest Relations, and an ATM.

DISCOVERY ISLAND

The park hub and site of the Tree of Life, this island is encircled by Discovery River, which isn't an actual attraction but makes for attractive views from the bridge to Harambe and another between Asia and DinoLand U.S.A. The island's whimsical architecture, with wood carvings from Bali, lends charm and a touch of fantasy. The Discovery Island Trails that lead to the Tree of Life provide habitats for African crested porcupines, lemurs, Galápagos tortoises, and other creatures you won't want to miss.

You'll discover some great shops and good counter-service eateries here. Visitor services that aren't in the Oasis are here, on the border with Harambe, including the baby-care center and the first-aid center.

DINOLAND U.S.A.

Just as it sounds, this is the place to come in contact with re-created prehistoric creatures, including the fear-inspiring carnotaurus and the gentle iguanodon. The landscaping includes live plants that have evolved over the last 65 million years. In collaboration with Chicago's Field Museum, Disney displays a complete, full-scale skeleton cast of Dino-Sue—also known as "Sue"—the 65-million-year-old *Tyrannosaurus rex* discovered near the Black Hills of South Dakota.

After admiring Sue, you can go on the thrilling DINOSAUR ride, play in the Boneyard, or take in the Finding Nemo: The Musical show at the Theater in the Wild. Kids will want to try the TriceraTop Spin and the Primeval Whirl family coaster, which has spinning "time machines." There's no need to dig for souvenirs at Chester and Hester's Dinosaur Treasures gift shop—all you need is your wallet.

On Asia's Expedition Everest, you'll chug, twist, turn, and plunge up, through, and down Mt. Everest on nearly a mile of track. Oh, yeah, and beware of the yeti!

ASIA

Meant to resemble an Asian village, this land is full of remarkable rainforest scenery and ruins. Groupings of trees grow from a crumbling tiger shrine, and massive towers—representing Thailand and Nepal—are the habitat for gibbons, whose hooting fills the air.

AFRICA

The largest of the lands is an area of forests and grasslands, predominantly an enclave for wildlife from the continent. Harambe, on the northern bank of Discovery River, is Africa's starting point. Inspired by several East African villages, this Disney town has so much detail that it's mind-boggling to try to soak it all up. Signs on the apparently peeling stucco walls are faded, as if bleached by the sun, and everything has a hot, dusty look. For souvenirs with Disney and African themes, browse through the Mombasa Marketplace and Ziwani Traders.

RAFIKI'S PLANET WATCH

While in the Harambe, Africa, section, board the 250-passenger rustic Wildlife Express steam train for a ride to a unique center of eco-awareness named for the wise baboon from *The Lion King*. Young children especially enjoy the chance to explore these three animal-friendly areas.

PANDORA—THE WORLD OF AVATAR

The latest land at Animal Kingdom opened in May 2017. Inspired by the film *Avatar* the land has floating mountains, bioluminescent plants, and flying inhabitants, and it brims with dazzling high-tech effects that are particularly resonant by night. Visitors are greeted by members of Alpha Centauri Expeditions, an ecotour group preparing Pandora for explorers and adventure seekers. The land contains two major attractions: the family-friendly Na'vi River Journey travels along a river through a rain forest with glow-in-the-dark flowers to a meeting with a shaman. The more thrilling Avatar Flight of Passage allows guests to ride a Banshee over the world of Pandora, past the astonishing sight of giant, vine-covered mountains that seem to float in the air.

WALT DISNEY WORLD WATER PARKS

The beauty of Disney's water parks is that you can make either experience fit your mood. Like crowds? Head for the lounge chairs along the Surf Pool at Typhoon Lagoon or Melt-Away Bay at Blizzard Beach. Prefer peace? Walk past lush foliage along each park's circular path until you spot a secluded lean-to or tree-shaded patch of sand.

TYPHOON LAGOON

According to Disney legend, Typhoon Lagoon was created when the lush Placid Palms Resort was struck by a cataclysmic storm. It left a different world in its wake: surfboard-sundered trees, once-upright palms imitated the Leaning Tower of Pisa, and part of the original lagoon was cut off, trapping thousands of tropical fish—and a few sharks. Nothing, however, topped the fate of *Miss Tilly,* a shrimp boat from "Safen Sound, Florida," which was hurled high in the air and became impaled on Mt. Mayday, a magical volcano that periodically tries to dislodge *Miss Tilly* with huge geysers.

Ordinary folks, the legend continues, would have been crushed by such devastation. But the resourceful residents of Placid Palms were made of hardier stuff—and from the wreckage they created 56-acre Typhoon Lagoon, the self-proclaimed "world's ultimate water park."

GETTING ORIENTED

The layout is so simple. The wave and swimming lagoon is at the park's center. Note that the waves are born in the Mt. Mayday side and break on the beaches closest to the entrance. Any attraction requiring a gravitational plunge starts around the summit of Mt. Mayday. Shark Reef and Ketchakiddee Creek flank the head of the lagoon, to Mt. Mayday's right and left, respectively, as you enter. The Crush 'n' Gusher water coaster is due right of Singapore Sal's.

You can take WDW bus transportation or drive to Typhoon Lagoon. There's no parking charge. Once inside, your options are to walk, swim, or slide.

WDW Information. Call WDW Information or check ⊕ *www.disney-world.com*'s park calendars for days of operation. ⊠ *1534 Blizzard Beach Dr., Blizzard Beach* ☎ *407/824–4321.*

WHAT TO EXPECT

You can speed down waterslides with names like Crush 'n' Gusher and Humunga Kowabunga or bump through rapids and falls at Mt. Mayday. You can also bob along in 5-foot waves in a surf pool the size of two football fields or, for a mellow break, float in inner tubes along the 2,100-foot Castaway Creek. Go snorkeling in Shark Reef, rubberneck as fellow human cannonballs are ejected

from the Storm Slides, or hunker down in a hammock or lounge chair and read a book. Ketchakiddee Creek, for young children, replicates adult rides on a smaller scale. It's Disney's version of a day at the beach—complete with friendly Disney lifeguards. Most people agree that kids under seven and older adults prefer Typhoon Lagoon. Bigger kids and teens like Blizzard Beach.

During the off-season between October and April, Typhoon Lagoon closes for several weeks for routine maintenance and refurbishment.

PARK AMENITIES

Dressing Rooms and Lockers: There are thatched-roof dressing rooms and keyless lockers to the right on your way into the park. It costs $10 a day to rent a small locker and $15 for a large one. There are restrooms in every nook and cranny. Most have showers and are much less crowded than the dressing rooms. If you forgot your towel, rent ($2) or buy one at Singapore Sal's.

BLIZZARD BEACH

With its oxymoronic name, Blizzard Beach promises the seemingly impossible—a seaside playground with an alpine theme. As with its older cousin, Typhoon Lagoon, Disney Imagineers have created a legend to explain the park's origin.

10

The story goes that after a freak winter storm dropped snow over the western side of Walt Disney World, entrepreneurs created Florida's first downhill ski resort. Saunalike temperatures soon returned. But as the 66-acre resort's operators were ready to close up shop, they spotted a playful alligator sliding down the 120-foot-tall "liquid ice" slopes. The realization that the melting snow had created the world's tallest, fastest, and most exhilarating water-filled ski and toboggan runs gave birth to the ski resort–water park.

From its imposing ski-jump tower to its 1,200-foot series of rushing waterfalls, Blizzard Beach delivers cool fun even in the hot summertime. Where else can you wear your swimsuit on the slopes?

GETTING ORIENTED

The park layout makes it fairly simple to navigate. Once you enter and rent a locker, you'll cross a small bridge over Cross Country Creek before choosing a spot to park your towels and cooler. To the left is the

From the wreckage—like that shown here—in the wake of a storm, Placid Palms Resort residents created 56-acre Typhoon Lagoon. Or so the story goes....

Melt-Away Bay wave pool. Dead ahead you can see Mt. Gushmore, a chairlift to the top, and the park's many slopes and slides.

If thrills are your game, come early and line up for Summit Plummet, Slush Gusher, and Downhill Double Dipper before wait times go from light to moderate (or heavy). Anytime is a good time for a dip in Melt-Away Bay or a tube trip around Cross Country Creek. Parents with young children should claim their spot early at Tike's Peak, to the park's right even before you cross the bridge.

You can take WDW bus transportation or drive to Blizzard Beach. There's no charge for parking. Once inside, your options are to walk, swim, or slide.

WHAT TO EXPECT

Disney Imagineers have gone all out here to create the paradox of a ski resort in the midst of a tropical lagoon. Lots of verbal puns and sight gags play with the snow-in-Florida motif. The centerpiece is Mt. Gushmore, with its 120-foot-high Summit Plummet. Attractions have names like Teamboat Springs, a white-water raft ride. Themed speed slides include Toboggan Racers, Slush Gusher, and Snow Stormers. Between Mt. Gushmore's base and its summit, swim-skiers can also ride a chairlift converted from ski-resort to beach-resort use—with multihued umbrellas and snow skis on their undersides. Older kids and devoted waterslide enthusiasts generally prefer Blizzard Beach to other water parks.

PARK AMENITIES

Dressing Rooms and Lockers: Dressing rooms, showers, and restrooms are in the village area, just inside the main entrance. There are other restrooms in Lottawatta Lodge, at the Ski Patrol Training Camp, and just past the Melt-Away Bay beach area. Lockers are near the entrance, next to Snowless Joe's Rentals, and near Tike's Peak (the children's area and the most convenient if you have little swim-skiers in tow). It costs $10 to rent a small locker and $15 for a large one. Lockers are keyless, and require you to select a four-digit pin number. Note that there are only small lockers at Tike's Peak. The towels for rent ($2) at Snowless Joe's are tiny. If you forgot yours, you're better off buying a proper one at the Beach Haus.

DISNEY'S OTHER WORLDS

Budget a few hours to explore Disney's "other" places. Several are no-admission-required charmers; one is a high-tech, high-cover-charge gaming wonderland.

DISNEY SPRINGS

EXPLORING

This sprawling shopping, dining, and entertainment complex has four areas: the Marketplace, West Side, The Landing, and Town Center. A large number of new shops, high-end, celebrity-chef run restaurants, and promenades opened in 2016, along with two huge parking garages. You can rent lockers, strollers, or wheelchairs, and there are two Guest Relations centers.

FAMILY **DisneyQuest.** In a five-story virtual-reality mini-theme park at Disney Springs West Side, DisneyQuest offers an array of high-tech virtual adventures and video games. The entry fee lets you play all day, and there are cutting-edge games and interactive adventures that make the admission worthwhile. It's also a great place for teens and older tweens (children under 14 must be accompanied by a guest age 14 or older).

All attractions are wheelchair accessible, but most require transfer from wheelchair to the attraction itself. You can, however, wheel right onto Pirates of the Caribbean: Battle for Buccaneer Gold, Aladdin's Magic Carpet Ride, and Mighty Ducks Pinball Slam. Rent wheelchairs at the DisneyQuest Emporium or at Disney Springs Marketplace Guest Relations ($12 per day for hand operated, plus $100 refundable credit-card deposit); powered chairs are $50 plus deposit at the Marketplace location only. Guide dogs are permitted in all areas but aren't allowed to ride several attractions. Strollers are *not* permitted.

Four attractions have height requirements: Cyberspace Mountain (51 inches), Buzz Lightyear's AstroBlaster (51 inches), Mighty Ducks Pinball Slam (48 inches), and Pirates of the Caribbean (35 inches). Little ones ages two through seven can enjoy a Kids' Area on the fourth floor, where they can play smaller versions of video and other games like air hockey, basketball, and bowling.

Lost and Found is at the Guest Relations window and cash is available at ATMs inside the House of Blues merchandise shop not far from the DisneyQuest entrance. ⊠ *West Side, Disney Springs* ☎ *407/828–4600* 💲*$45 adults, $39 children 3–9, excluding sales tax.*

10

FAMILY **The Landing.** A family-oriented dining and entertainment district, this part of Disney Springs has nearly a dozen eateries, some run by celebrity chefs such as Morimoto, Art Smith, and Irish chef Kevin Dundon. The restaurants all offer indoor and patio dining, and some, such as Dundon's Raglan Road, also have offer entertainment, in this case music and traditional Irish step-dance performances every night and during weekend brunch. Paradiso 37 also welcomes diners indoors and alfresco. The BOATHOUSE features attractive water-front dining, with views of the water taxis delivering folks across the lake, and the tiny, colorful boat-cars tootling up and down the ramp. ⊠ *Disney Springs.*

Marketplace. In the Marketplace, the easternmost Disney Springs area, you can meander along winding sidewalks and explore hidden alcoves. Children love to splash in fountains that spring from the pavement and ride the miniature train and old-time carousel ($2). Toy stores entice with creation-stations and too many treasures to comprehend. There are plenty of spots to grab a bite, sip a cappuccino, or enjoy an ice cream along the lakefront, while watching the volcano atop the Rainforest Cafe erupt. Most Marketplace shops, boutiques, and eateries begin opening at 9:30 am and stay open through 11 pm to midnight. ⊠ *Disney Springs.*

Town Center. Once a parking lot, this newest area of Disney Springs is home to upscale shopping and dining, along meandering pathways, and through squares and plazas surrounded with architecturally interesting buildings. There's something for all tastes (and most budgets): from Lily Pulitzer to Ugg Boots, from Uniqlo's trendy Japanese-designs to Zara's Spanish-influenced clothing and accessories. Even if you are just looking, Town Center offers a rich window-shopping experience. Celebrity chef Rick Bayless has a waterfront eatery where he serves his take on Mexican, and the independently owned, local-chef-driven Polite Pig dishes up Southern charm and lots of pork-based dishes. ⊠ *1486 Buena Vista Dr., Orlando* ☎ *407/939–6244* ⊕ *www. disneysprings.com.*

West Side. The main attractions in the hip West Side are the House of Blues music hall, Cirque du Soleil, Splitsville Luxury Lanes, Disney-Quest virtual indoor theme park and arcade, and a new Starbucks with covered patio overlooking the waterfront. You can also take a ride in the Characters in Flight helium balloon tethered here ($18 ages 10 and up, $12 ages 3–9), shop in boutiques, or dine in such restaurants as the Wolfgang Puck Café and Planet Hollywood. Shops open at 9:30 or 10:30 am, and closing time is between 11 pm and 2 am. The Splitsville entertainment center offers plenty of fresh fun with 30 bowling lanes on two floors, weekend DJs, and upscale eats like fillet sliders and sushi at indoor and outdoor tables. ⊠ *Disney Springs.*

NIGHTLIFE
Bongos Cuban Café. Latin rhythms provide the beat at this restaurant and bar with a Havana theme owned by pop singer Gloria Estefan. Four bars are especially busy on weekends, when a Latin band kicks it up a notch

with *muy caliente* music. Samba, tango, salsa, and merengue rhythms roll throughout the week. ⊠ *West Side, Disney Springs* ☎ *407/828–0999.*

House of Blues. The restaurant serves up live blues performances and rib-sticking Mississippi Delta cooking all week long. The attached concert hall has showcased such artists as Aretha Franklin, David Byrne, Steve Miller, Willie Nelson, and Journey. Many swear by the "World Famous Gospel Brunch" each Sunday. There's often a cover charge, which varies. ⊠ *West Side, Disney Springs* ☎ *407/934–2583.*

La Nouba. If you've seen rave media reviews of this production, believe them. The surreal show by the world-famous Cirque du Soleil company starts at 100 mph and accelerates through 90 mesmerizing minutes of acrobatics, avant-garde costumes and staging, and captivating choreography. So much happens that even those who've seen the show once return to see what they missed last time.

The story of La Nouba—derived from the French phrase *faire la nouba* (live it up)—is alternately mysterious, dreamlike, comical, and sensual. A cast of 67 international performers—including two vocalists and six musicians who play 22 instruments from tower platforms—takes the stage in a 1,671-seat showroom of a big-top-style theater.

World-renowned jugglers manipulate balls, hoops, and clubs with breathtaking precision and speed. Another fresh act—Skipping Ropes—combines dance and acrobatics to elevate child's play to a seemingly impossible level. Acrobatic cyclists present tricks you don't see on the street.

The interplay is charming as the Cleaning Lady sweeps her way into a dreamworld of Technicolor characters who dance, tumble, and fly through the air on ribbons of red silk. Two silly clowns provide comic relief at intervals, and a troupe of adorable Chinese girls steal applause with their astonishing diabolo (Chinese yo-yo) performance. The jaw-dropping last act is a masterpiece of acrobatics and gymnastics synched to uplifting music.

Call ahead for good seats (there are three categories of seating), and hire a babysitter if necessary—you wouldn't want to miss one minute of this class act. ⊠ *West Side, Disney Springs* ☎ *407/939–7600 reservations* ⊕ *www.cirquedusoleil.com* ✉ *From $62.*

10

DISNEY'S BOARDWALK

In the good ol' days, Americans escaped their city routines for breezy seaside boardwalks. Disney's BoardWalk is within walking distance of Epcot, across Crescent Lake from Disney's Yacht and Beach Club Resorts, and fronting a hotel of the same name. You may be drawn to its good restaurants, bars, shops, surreys, and performers. After sunset, the mood is festive. ■TIP→ If you're here when Epcot is ready to close, you can watch the park fireworks from the bridge that connects BoardWalk to the Yacht and Beach Club resorts.

NIGHTLIFE

Atlantic Dance Hall. This high-energy dance club plays music from the '80s onward, with a huge screen showing videos requested by the crowd. The parquet dance floor is set off by furnishings of deep blue, maroon, and gold, and the ceiling glows with gold stars and twinkling lights. Signature cocktails are in demand, and you can sip a cognac or choose from a selection of popular beers to inspire your dance floor moves. ⊠ *BoardWalk, Epcot Resort Area* ☎ *407/939–2444* 🎬 *No cover.*

Big River Grille & Brewing Works. Disney World's only brewpub has intimate tables where brewmasters tend to their potions. You can order an $8 sampler with five to seven 3-ounce pours of whatever's on tap that day, usually including Red Rocket, Southern Flyer Light Lager, Gadzooks Pilsner, and Steamboat Pale Ale. Upscale pub grub and sandwiches pair well. There's also a sidewalk café. ⊠ *BoardWalk, Epcot Resort Area* ☎ *407/560–0253.*

Jellyrolls. In this rockin', boisterous piano bar, comedians act as emcees and play dueling grand pianos nonstop. The steady stream of conventions at Disney makes this the place to catch CEOs doing the conga to Barry Manilow's "Copacabana"—if that's your idea of a good time. There's generally a $12 cover. ⊠ *BoardWalk, Epcot Resort Area* ☎ *407/560–8770.*

UNIVERSAL ORLANDO RESORT

WELCOME TO UNIVERSAL ORLANDO RESORT

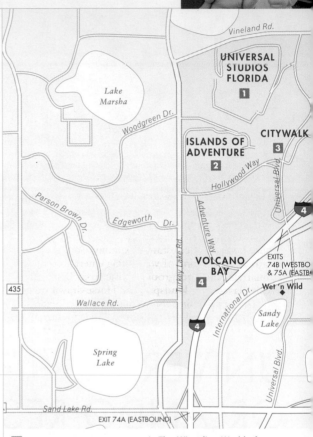

TOP REASONS TO GO

★ **Harry Potter:** For die-hard fans, there's no other place to head in Florida than The Wizarding World of Harry Potter.

★ **The variety:** Universal Orlando Resort consists of two complete theme parks, the CityWalk entertainment complex; and five on-site resorts. Universal's Volcano Bay Water Theme Park, which opened in 2017, is the region's newest and most exciting water park.

★ **Theme-park power-house:** No other Orlando theme park can match the collective energy at Universal Studios, Islands of Adventure, and Volcano Bay. Wild rides, clever shows, constantly updated attractions, and an edgy attitude all push the envelope here.

★ **Party central:** Throughout the year, Universal hosts festive park-wide events such as Mardi Gras, Halloween Horror Nights, Grinchmas, the Summer Concert Series, and the Rock the Universe Christian-music cel-ebration. And CityWalk is busy year-round.

1 Universal Studios Florida. The centerpiece of Universal Orlando is a creative and quirky tribute to Hollywood past, present, and future. Overall, the collection of wild rides, quiet retreats, live shows, street characters, and clever movies (both 3-D and 4-D) are as entertain-ing as the motion pictures they celebrate. Another plus is The Wizarding World of Harry Potter: Diagon Alley.

2 Islands of Adventure. While The Wizarding World of Harry Potter: Hogsmeade may top visitors' to-do lists, the park also is home to Spider-Man, the Hulk, velociraptors, the Cat in the Hat, and dozens of other characters that give guests every reason to head to the islands.

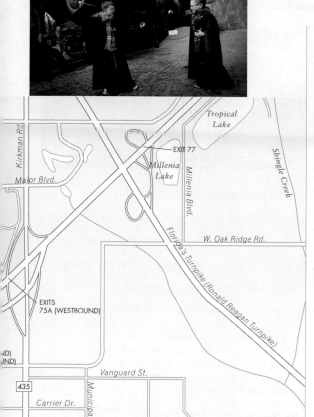

Orlando

CENTRAL FLORIDA

GETTING ORIENTED

Universal Orlando Resort is tucked into a corner created by the intersection of Interstate 4 and Kirkman Road (Highway 435), midway between Downtown Orlando and the Walt Disney World Resort. Here you'll be about 15 minutes from each and just 10 minutes from SeaWorld.

Tropical Lake

EXIT 77

Millenia Lake

Kirkman Rd.

Major Blvd.

Millenia Blvd.

Shingle Creek

Florida's Turnpike (Ronald Reagan Turnpike)

W. Oak Ridge Rd.

EXITS 75A (WESTBOUND)

ND) JND)

Vanguard St.

435

Carrier Dr.

Municipal Dr.

Mandarin Dr.

Pomelo Dr.

Sand Lake Rd.

3 CityWalk. Even when the parks are closed (*especially* when the parks are closed), locals and visitors come to this sprawling entertainment and retail complex to watch movies; dine at theme restaurants; shop for everything from cigars to surf wear; and stay up late at nightclubs celebrating the French Quarter, Jamaica, and the coolest clubs of NYC.

4 Volcano Bay. A sparkling new water park built around an "erupting" volcano, this park's wild rides and wave pool offer a very cool way to chill out during the blistering hot summers, and it will be open year-round, thanks to Orlando's mild temperatures.

Updated
by Jennifer
Greenhill-Tay-
lor and Joseph
Hayes

Universal Orlando's personality is revealed the moment you arrive on property. Mood music, cartoonish architecture, abundant eye candy, subtle and overt sound effects, whirling and whizzing rides, plus a throng of fellow travelers will follow you to nearly every corner of the park. For peace and quiet, seek out a sanctuary at one of the resort hotels.

If you can keep up a breathless pace, there's a chance you could visit both big Universal theme parks in a single day, but to do that you'll have to invest in an Express Pass. Without it, you'll spend a good portion of that day waiting in line at the premium attractions. So allow two days, three if you also want to visit Volcano Bay or to return to your favorite rides at a more leisurely pace. Which attractions are the main attractions? At both Islands and Universal Studios, it's definitely The Wizarding World of Harry Potter. But the thrilling coasters and theme rides like Revenge of The Mummy and The Simpsons attractions are always popular.

Universal Studios appeals primarily to those who like loud, fast, high-energy attractions—generally teens and adults. Covering 444 acres, it's a rambling montage of sets, shops, and soundstages housing themed attractions, reproductions of New York and San Francisco and London, and some genuine moviemaking paraphernalia.

When Islands of Adventure first opened in 1999, it took attractions to a new level. Most—from Marvel Super Hero Island and Toon Lagoon to Seuss Landing and the Lost Continent—are impressive; some even out-Disney Disney. In 2010, Islands received well-deserved worldwide attention when it opened the first section of the 20-acre Wizarding World of Harry Potter. And in 2014 Universal Studios made another huge leap forward when it opened a full-scale version of Diagon Alley, complete with Gringotts Bank and a magical train that departs for Islands from Platform 9¾.

PLANNING

GETTING HERE AND AROUND

East on Interstate 4 (from WDW and Tampa), exit at Universal Boulevard (75A); take a left into Universal Orlando Resort, and follow the signs. Heading west on Interstate 4 (from Downtown or Daytona), exit at Universal Boulevard (74B), turn right, and follow Hollywood Way.

Both Universal Studios and Islands require a lot of walking—a whole lot of walking. Start off by using the parking area's moving walkways as much as possible. Arrive early at either park, and you may be able to complete a single lap that will get you to the main attractions.

OPERATING HOURS

The parks are open 365 days a year, from 9 am to 7 pm, with hours as late as 10 pm in summer and at holidays. Universal's Volcano Bay will be open year-round, weather permitting, but with varying hours. Always call for exact hours since those at all three parks change seasonally.

PARKING

Universal's two main garages total 3.4 million square feet, so *note your parking space*. The cost is $20 for cars and motorcycles, $22 for RVs and buses, and $30 for preferred parking. Although moving walkways get you partway, you could walk up to a half mile to reach the gates. Valet parking ($20 for up to two hours, $40 for more than two hours) is much closer. Volcano Bay, which is next to Cabana Bay Beach Resort, has a separate entrance and a separate parking garage.

ADMISSION

The at-the-gate, per-person, per-day rate for either Universal Studios Florida or Islands of Adventure is $119 (ages 10 and up) and $114 for children (ages 3–9), but that number can vary by season. Tip: To ride the Hogwart's Express and enjoy both Harry Potter experiences on the same day, you *must* have a park-to-park ticket, which starts at $169 (ages 10 and up) and $164 for children (ages 3–9). Multiday passes that include the two main parks offer a far less expensive per-day price. Also available is a three-park ticket, which includes Volcano Bay. Volcano Bay also has a single-day admission price of $67

EXPRESS PASSES

The Express Pass ranges in price from about $50 off-season to around $84 for both parks in peak season. This pass gets you to the front of most lines and saves a tremendous amount of time. Keep in mind, the pass is for one use only at each attraction—a more expensive "unlimited" pass takes you to the head of the line again and again and again. If you're a guest at a Universal hotel, this perk is free; your room key serves as the pass.

UNIVERSAL DINING PLAN

If you prefer to pay in advance, Quick Service meals include one meal, two snacks, and a nonalcoholic beverage ($28). The kids' version covers a kids meal, one snack, and a beverage ($20). Universal Studios locations include Mel's Drive-In, Louie's Italian, Beverly Hills Boulangerie, and the Classic Monsters Café. At Islands of Adventure, your choices are the Comic Strip Café, Croissant Moon, the Burger Digs, and Café 4.

UNIVERSAL STRATEGIES

Arrive early. Come as early as 8 am if the parks open at 9. Seriously. Better to share them with hundreds of people than with thousands.

Visit on a weekday. Crowds are lighter, especially fall through spring, when kids are in school.

Don't forget anything in your car. Universal's parking areas are at least a half mile from park entrances, and a round-trip hike will eat up valuable time. Consider valet parking. It costs $40 for longer than two hours before 6 pm (twice as much as regular parking), but it puts you much closer to Universal's park entrances and just steps from CityWalk.

Know the restrictions. A few things aren't allowed in the parks: alcohol and glass containers; hard-sided coolers; soft-sided coolers larger than 8½ inches wide by 6 inches high by 6 inches deep; and coolers, suitcases, and other bags with wheels. But if your flight's leaving later, you can check your luggage at the parks (unless you just leave them in your car).

Look into the Express Pass. Jumping to the front of the line with this pass really is worth the extra cost on busy days—unless you stay at a resort hotel, in which case front-of-line access is one of the perks.

Ride solo. At Universal some rides have a single-rider line that moves much faster than regular lines.

Get expert advice. The folks at Guest Services (aka Guest Relations) have great insight. The reps can even create a custom itinerary free of charge.

Check out Child Swap. At certain Universal attractions, one parent can enter the attraction, take a spin, and then return to take care of the baby while the other parent rides without having to wait in line again.

TOURS

VIP Tours. Universal has several VIP tours that are worthwhile if you're in a hurry, if crowds are heavy, if you're with a large group—and if you have the money to burn. The tours include extras like front-of-the-line access (that is, the right to jump to the head of the line). You can also arrange for extras like priority restaurant seating, bilingual guides, gift bags, refreshments at check-in, wheelchairs and strollers, and valet parking. Prices cited here do not include sales tax or park admission, and may edge up in peak seasons (or may not be available in peak season, so call ahead).

Here's what you'll pay in off-peak/peak seasons: Nonexclusive one-day tours (i.e., you'll tour with other park guests) cost $89/$129 per person for one park (five hours) and $219/$329 for two parks (seven hours). Then there are exclusive tours for your group only. If you're traveling with up to 10 people, consider splitting the cost of an eight-hour tour customized to your interests, which includes a sit-down breakfast, lunch, and dinner at the park of your choice. The eight-hour two-park exclusive price is $4,605/$5,084; to see one park in eight hours will cost you only $20 less. ⊠ *Universal Orlando Resort* ☎ *866/346–9350* ⊕ *www.universalorlando.com.*

CONTACTS
Universal Orland Resort ☎ *407/363–8000* ⊕ *www.universalorlando.com*
Universal Dining and Tickets ☎ *407/224–7840*
Universal (Loews Resorts) Room Reservations ☎ *877/819–7884*
Universal Vacation Packages ☎ *800/407–4275*

11

UNIVERSAL STUDIOS

Inspired by the California original, Universal Studios celebrates the movies. The park is a jumble of areas and attractions. But the same is true of back-lot sets at a film studio. Suspend any disbelief you might have, and just enjoy the motion-picture magic.

At Production Central large soundstages house attractions based on TV programs and films like *Shrek, Despicable Me,* and *Twister.* Because it's right near the entrance it can be the park's most crowded area.

Here you see firsthand that not every film or program based in New York is actually shot in New York. Cleverly constructed sets mean that nearly every film studio can own its own Big Apple. Universal is no exception. As you explore Production Central, a collection of sparkling public buildings, well-worn neighborhoods, and back alleys are the next-best thing to Manhattan itself.

As you enter the area known as San Francisco, you're roughly one-third of the way through the park. The crowds spread out, and the pace seems to slow. You can stop to take in the view across the lake and have a snack, or dine at the waterfront Lombard's Seafood Grille.

After passing scenes from San Francisco, you'll reach the land everyone is talking about: the Wizarding World of Harry Potter: Diagon Alley. What the books suggest and what filmmakers created, Universal has replicated—putting you in the middle of a fantastic fantasyland. Just ahead, World Expo features two large attractions—MEN IN BLACK: Alien Attack and The Simpsons Ride. The colorful spectacle surrounding the Simpsons' hometown of Springfield gives you access to Moe's Tavern and Krusty Burger, along with the abundant attractions at Woody Woodpecker's KidZone. The latter matches the energy of toddlers and the under-10 crowd with diversions that include a junior-size roller coaster, a mini–water park, and a chance to meet E.T. and Barney the dinosaur. In Hollywood, quiet parks and flashy Rodeo Drive really do make you think you've stepped into vintage Tinseltown.

All in all, Universal Studios fulfills its promise: to put you in the movies.

GETTING ORIENTED

On a map, the park appears neatly divided into seven areas positioned around a huge lagoon. There's Production Central, which covers the entire left side of the Plaza of the Stars; New York, with street performances at 70 Delancey; San Francisco; the Wizarding World of Harry Potter: Diagon Alley; the futuristic World Expo; Woody Woodpecker's KidZone; and Hollywood.

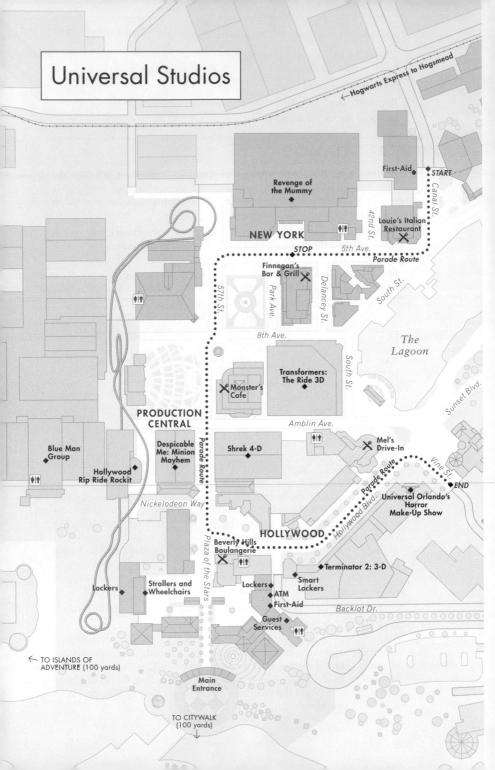

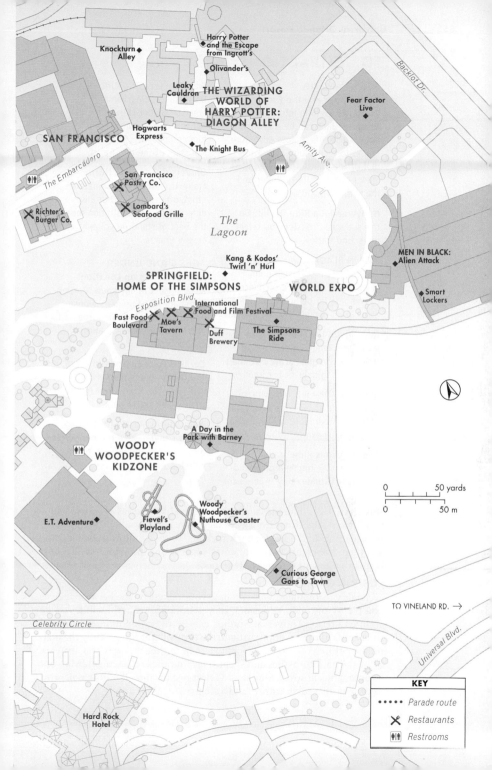

Knockturn Alley

Harry Potter and the Escape from Ingrott's

Olivander's

Leaky Cauldron

THE WIZARDING WORLD OF HARRY POTTER: DIAGON ALLEY

Backlot Dr.

Fear Factor Live

SAN FRANCISCO

Hogwarts Express

The Knight Bus

The Embarcadero

Amity Ave.

San Francisco Pastry Co.

Richter's Burger Co.

Lombard's Seafood Grille

The Lagoon

Kang & Kodos' Twirl 'n' Hurl

MEN IN BLACK: Alien Attack

SPRINGFIELD: HOME OF THE SIMPSONS

WORLD EXPO

Smart Lockers

Exposition Blvd.

Fast Food Boulevard

International Food and Film Festival

Moe's Tavern

Duff Brewery

The Simpsons Ride

A Day in the Park with Barney

WOODY WOODPECKER'S KIDZONE

E.T. Adventure

Fievel's Playland

Woody Woodpecker's Nuthouse Coaster

Curious George Goes to Town

TO VINELAND RD. →

| 0 | | | 50 yards |
| 0 | | | 50 m |

Celebrity Circle

Universal Blvd.

Hard Rock Hotel

KEY	
••••	*Parade route*
✗	*Restaurants*
🚻	*Restrooms*

TOP ATTRACTIONS

AGES 7 AND UP

Harry Potter and the Escape from Gringotts. Getting into the vault at Gringotts Bank can be a challenge, but it's also a first-class adventure thanks to technology similar to that of The Transformers and IOA's Spider-Man and Harry Potter and the Forbidden Journey.

Hollywood Rip Ride Rockit. On this superwild coaster, you select the sound track.

MEN IN BLACK: Alien Attack. The "world's first ride-through video game" gives you a chance to compete for points by plugging away at an endless swarm of aliens.

Revenge of the Mummy. It's a jarring, rocketing indoor coaster that takes you past scary mummies and billowing balls of fire (really).

Shrek 4-D. The 3-D film with sensory effects picks up where the original film left off—and adds some creepy extras in the process.

The Simpsons Ride. It puts you in the heart of Springfield on a wild-and-crazy virtual-reality experience.

Transformers: The Ride 3-D. Universal Studios' version of IOA's fantastic Spider-Man experience, but this one features a rough-and-tumble encounter with the mechanical stars of the film franchise.

Universal Orlando's Horror Make-Up Show. This sometimes gross, often raunchy, but always entertaining demonstration merges the best of stand-up comedy with creepy effects.

AGES 6 AND UNDER

Animal Actors on Location! It's a perfect family show starring a menagerie of animals whose unusually high IQs are surpassed only by their cuteness and cuddle-ability.

Curious George Goes to Town. The celebrated simian visits the Man with the Yellow Hat in a small-scale water park.

A Day in the Park with Barney. Young children love the big purple dinosaur and the chance to sing along.

What's tricky is that—because it's designed like a series of movie sets—there's no straightforward way to tackle the park. You'll probably make some detours and do some backtracking. To save time and shoe leather, ask theme park hosts for itinerary suggestions and time-saving tips. Here are a few of our own suggestions.

TOURING TIPS

We highly recommend you purchase your tickets online because it gives you plenty of time to consider your many options and includes a discount. Entering Universal Studios can be overwhelming as you and thousands of others flood through the turnstiles at once. Study the map online before you go, then pick up a map in the entryway to CityWalk or by the park turnstiles and spend a few minutes reviewing it. Map out a route, find show schedules, and select restaurants. If a host is nearby, ask for insider advice on what to see first.

The "right" way. Upon entering, avoid the temptation to go left toward the towering soundstages, looping the park clockwise. Instead, head right—bypassing shops, restaurants, and some crowds to primary attractions like The Simpsons Ride and MEN IN BLACK: Alien Attack.

Photo ops. Universal Studios posts signs that indicate photo spots and show how best to frame your shot.

Rendezvous. Good meeting spots include the Hello Kitty shop, near the entrance; Mel's Drive-In, midway through the park on the right; and the purple Knight Bus, just outside Diagon Alley, at the far end of the park.

PARK AMENITIES

Guest Services: Get strategy advice *before* visiting by calling Guest Services (☎ 407/224–4233).

Lockers: Daily rates for lockers near the park entrance are $10 for a small unit and $12 for a larger one. There are free lockers near the entrances of some high-speed attractions (such as MEN IN BLACK: Alien Attack, Harry Potter: Escape from Gringotts, and Revenge of the Mummy), where you can stash your stuff before your ride; they're available to you for up to 90 minutes total.

Lost People and Things: If you plan to split up, be sure everyone knows where and when to reconnect. Staffers take lost children to Guest Services near the main entrance. This is also where you might find lost personal items.

Stroller Rentals: Just inside the main entrance, there are strollers for $15 (single) and $25 (double) a day. You can also rent small kiddie cars ($18) or large ones ($28) by the day.

EXPLORING

PRODUCTION CENTRAL

Expect plenty of loud, flashy, rollicking rides that appeal to tweens, teens, and adults. Clear the turnstiles and go straight. You can use Express Pass at all attractions.

NEW YORK

Universal has gone all out to re-create New York's skyscrapers, commercial districts, ethnic neighborhoods, and back alleys—right down to the cracked concrete. Hidden within these structures are restaurants, arcades, gift shops, and key attractions. And, although they're from Chicago, the Blues Brothers drive from the Second City to New York City in their Bluesmobile for free performances at 70 Delancey. Here you can use Express Pass at Revenge of the Mummy and Twister.

SAN FRANCISCO

This area celebrates the West Coast with the wharves and warehouses of San Francisco's Embarcadero and Fisherman's Wharf districts.

WORLD EXPO

At the far end of the park is a futuristic set of buildings containing a few of Universal Studios' most popular attractions, MEN IN BLACK: Alien Attack, The Simpsons Ride, and Kang & Kodos' Twirl 'n' Hurl, which offer fast admission with Express Pass.

WOODY WOODPECKER'S KIDZONE

With its colorful compilation of rides, shows, and play areas, this entire section caters to preschoolers. It's a pint-size Promised Land, where kids can try out a roller coaster and get sprayed, splashed, and soaked in a water-park area. It's also a great place for parents, since it gives them a needed break after nearly circling the park. All shows and attractions except Curious George and Fievel accept Universal Express Pass.

HOLLYWOOD

The quintessential tribute to the golden age of the silver screen, this area to the right of the park entrance celebrates icons like the Brown Derby, Schwab's Pharmacy, and art deco Hollywood. There are only a few attractions here, and all accept Universal Express Pass.

THE WIZARDING WORLD OF HARRY POTTER: DIAGON ALLEY

Fronted by the purple Knight Bus, and hidden by a facade of London row homes, you may not think there's much to see. But when you spy an opening through a broken brick wall and step into Diagon Alley, you'll realize what an incredible blueprint J.K. Rowling created through her words. You can spend hours in this one district looking at the complete range of Potter-centric places: Ollivander's wand shop (where you can purchase interactive wands); Weasleys' Wizard Wheezes (magical jokes and novelty items); the Magical Menagerie (all creatures furry, feathered, or scaly); Madam Malkin's Robes for All Occasions (wizard wear); Wiseacre's Wizarding Equipment; and Quality Quidditch Supplies. Practitioners of the Dark Arts may venture down Knockturn Alley and step inside Borgin and Burkes. For an appetizing break, stop at the Leaky Cauldron, the land's signature restaurant, or cool off at Florean Fortescue's Ice-Cream Parlour.

And when you're ready to head to Hogsmeade (conveniently located at the neighboring Islands of Adventure), make sure you have a park-to-park pass before stepping aboard the wonderful, magical Hogwarts Express—now departing to Islands of Adventure from Platform 9¾. Be sure to get a photo of friends and family disappearing through the brick wall.

ISLANDS OF ADVENTURE

More so than just about any other theme park, Islands of Adventure has gone all out to create settings and attractions that transport you from reality into the surreal. What's more, no one island here has much in common with any other, so in a way, a visit here is almost like a visit to half a dozen different parks.

The park's unique nature is first revealed when you arrive at the Port of Entry and are greeted by a kaleidoscope of sights and a cacophony of sounds. It's all designed to put you in the frame of mind for adventure.

When you reach the central lagoon, your clockwise journey commences with Marvel Super Hero Island and its tightly packed concentration of roller coasters and thrill rides. Of special note is the amazingly high-tech and dazzling Amazing Adventures of Spider-Man. In just minutes you'll have experienced a day's worth of sensations—and you've only just begun.

Stepping into Toon Lagoon is like stepping into the pages of a comic book, just as entering the upcoming island, Jurassic Park, is like entering a research center where reconstituted dinosaur DNA is being used to create a new breed of *brontosaurus*.

You move from the world of science into the world of magic when you segue into the Wizarding World of Harry Potter. You can wander through the magnificently fictional—yet very realistic—realm of the young wizard and his Hogwarts classmates and tutors, including the village of Hogsmeade, with its snow-topped roofs, and the halls of Hogwarts Castle itself.

TOP ATTRACTIONS

Ages 7 and Up

Amazing Adventures of Spider-Man

Dudley Do-Right's Ripsaw Falls

Harry Potter and the Forbidden Journey

Incredible Hulk Coaster

Ages 6 and Under

The Cat in the Hat

Flight of the Hippogriff

Popeye & Bluto's Bilge-Rat Barges

But that's not the end of it. In the Lost Continent the mood is that of a Renaissance fair, where crafters work inside colorful tents. It's as pronounced an atmosphere as that of the final island, Seuss Landing, which presents the incredible, topsy-turvy world of Dr. Seuss. It's a riot of colors and shapes and fantastic wildlife that pay tribute to the good doctor's vivid imagination.

GETTING ORIENTED

Getting your bearings at Islands is far easier than at its sister park, Universal Studios. Brochures in a multitude of languages are in a rack a few steps beyond the turnstiles. The brochures include a foldout map that will acquaint you with the park's simple layout (it's a circle). And, ahead by the lagoon, boards are posted with up-to-the-minute ride and show information—including the length of lines at the major attractions.

You pass through the turnstiles and into the Port of Entry plaza, a bazaar that brings together bits and pieces of architecture, landscaping, music, and wares from many lands—Dutch windmills, Indonesian pedicabs, African masks, restrooms marked "Loo's Landing," and Egyptian figurines that adorn a massive archway inscribed with the notice "The Adventure Begins." From here, themed islands—arranged around a large lagoon—are connected by walkways that make navigation easy. When you've done the full circuit, you'll recall the fantastic range of sights, sounds, and experiences and realize there can be truth in advertising. This park really *is* an adventure.

TOURING TIPS

Hosts. Just about any employee is a host, whether they're at a kiosk or attraction or turnstile. Ask them about their favorite experiences—and for suggestions for saving time.

Photo ops. Islands of Adventure posts signs that indicate picture spots and show how best to frame your shot.

You never know who might be waiting around the next corner in Jurassic Park.

Retreat. Explore little-used sidewalks and quiet alcoves to counter the park's manic energy.

Split the difference. If the park's open late, split the day in half. See part of it in the morning, head off-site to a restaurant for lunch (your parking ticket is good all day) then head to your hotel for a swim or a nap (or both). Return in the cooler, less crowded evening.

ISLANDS OF ADVENTURES PLANNER
PARK AMENITIES

Guest Services: Guest Services (☎ 407/224–6350) is right near the turnstiles, both before and after you enter Islands of Adventure.

Lockers: There are $10-a-day lockers across from Guest Services at the entrance; for $12 a day you can rent a family-size model. You have unlimited access to both types throughout the day—although it's a hike back to retrieve things. Scattered strategically throughout the park— notably at the Incredible Hulk Coaster, Jurassic Park River Adventure, and Forbidden Journey—are so-called Smart Lockers. These are free for the first 45 to 75 minutes, $2 per hour afterward, and max out at $14 per day. Stash backpacks and cameras here while you're being drenched on a watery ride or going through the spin cycle on a twisty one.

Lost People and Things: If you've misplaced something, head to Guest Services in the Port of Entry. This is also where park staffers take lost children.

Stroller Rentals: You can rent strollers ($15 per day for singles, $25 for doubles) at the Port of Entry to your left after the turnstiles. You can also rent kiddie cars—small ones for $18, and large ones for $28.

EXPLORING

MARVEL SUPER HERO ISLAND

The facades on Stanley Boulevard (named for Marvel's famed editor and co-creator Stan Lee) put you smack in the middle of an alternatively pleasant and apocalyptic comic-book world—complete with heroes, villains, and cartoony colors and flourishes. Although the spiky, horrific towers of Doctor Doom's Fearfall and the vivid green of the Hulk's coaster are focal points, the Amazing Adventures of Spider-Man is the must-see attraction. At various times Doctor Doom, Spider-Man, and the Incredible Hulk are available for photos, and sidewalk artists are on hand to paint your face like your favorite hero (or villain). All rides here accept Universal Express Pass.

TOON LAGOON

The main street, Comic Strip Lane, makes use of cartoon characters that are recognizable to anyone—anyone born before 1940, that is. Pert little Betty Boop, gangly Olive Oyl, muscle-bound Popeye, Krazy Kat, Mark Trail, Flash Gordon, Pogo, and Alley Oop are all here, as are the relatively more contemporary Dudley Do-Right, Rocky, Bullwinkle, Beetle Bailey, Cathy, and Hagar the Horrible. With its colorful backdrops, chirpy music, hidden alcoves, squirting fountains, and highly animated scenery, Toon Town is a natural for younger kids (even if they don't know who these characters are). All attractions here accept Universal Express Pass except Me Ship, The Olive.

JURASSIC PARK

Pass through the towering gates of Jurassic Park and the music becomes slightly ominous, the vegetation tropical and junglelike. All of this, plus the high-tension wires and warning signs, does a great job of re-creating the Jurassic Park of Steven Spielberg's blockbuster movie (and its sequels). The half-fun, half-frightening Jurassic Park River Adventure (the only attraction here that uses Universal Express Pass) is the standout, bringing to life key segments of the movie's climax.

THE WIZARDING WORLD OF HARRY POTTER: HOGSMEADE

In 2010, Islands of Adventure fulfilled the fantasy of Harry Potter devotees when it unveiled the biggest theme-park addition since the arrival of Disney's Animal Kingdom in 1998. At the highly publicized premiere, even the actors from the Potter film franchise were amazed. Having performed their roles largely before a green screen, they had never seen anything like this. Neither have you. The movie-magic-perfect re-creations of mythical locales such as Hogwarts and Hogsmeade Village are here, while playing supporting roles are a handful of candy shops, souvenir stores, and restaurants expertly and exquisitely themed to make you believe you've actually arrived in the incredible fantasy world of J.K. Rowling. Wands, Bertie Bott's Every-Flavour Beans™, Chocolate Frogs™, and best of all, Butterbeer, are available for you to try. Expect to be impressed—and to wait in line. Even if you owned a wand and were a real wizard, the only attractions that accept the Universal Express Pass are Flight of the Hippogriff and Dragon Challenge.

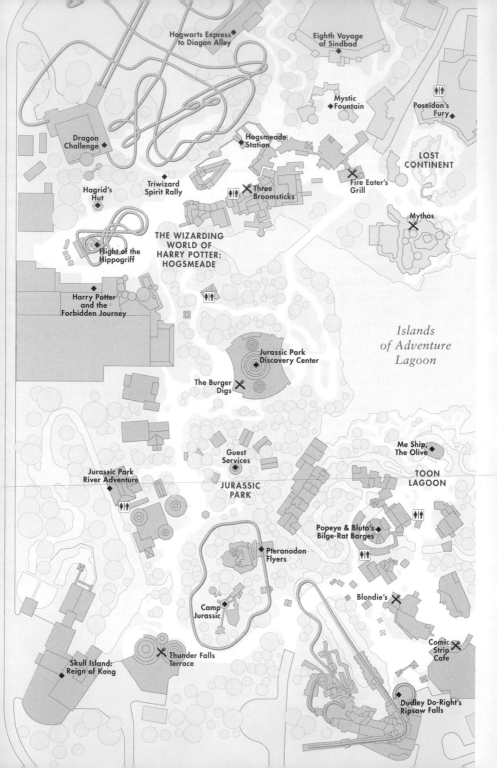

Hogwarts Express
to Diagon Alley

Eighth Voyage
of Sindbad

Mystic
Fountain

Poseidon's
Fury

Dragon
Challenge

Hogsmeade
Station

LOST
CONTINENT

Hagrid's
Hut

Triwizard
Spirit Rally

Three
Broomsticks

Fire Eater's
Grill

Mythos

Flight of the
Hippogriff

THE WIZARDING
WORLD OF
HARRY POTTER:
HOGSMEADE

Harry Potter
and the
Forbidden Journey

Islands
of Adventure
Lagoon

Jurassic Park
Discovery Center

The Burger
Digs

Me Ship,
The Olive

Guest
Services

TOON
LAGOON

Jurassic Park
River Adventure

JURASSIC
PARK

Popeye & Bluto's
Bilge-Rat Barges

Pteranodon
Flyers

Blondie's

Camp
Jurassic

Comic
Strip
Cafe

Skull Island:
Reign of Kong

Thunder Falls
Terrace

Dudley Do-Right's
Ripsaw Falls

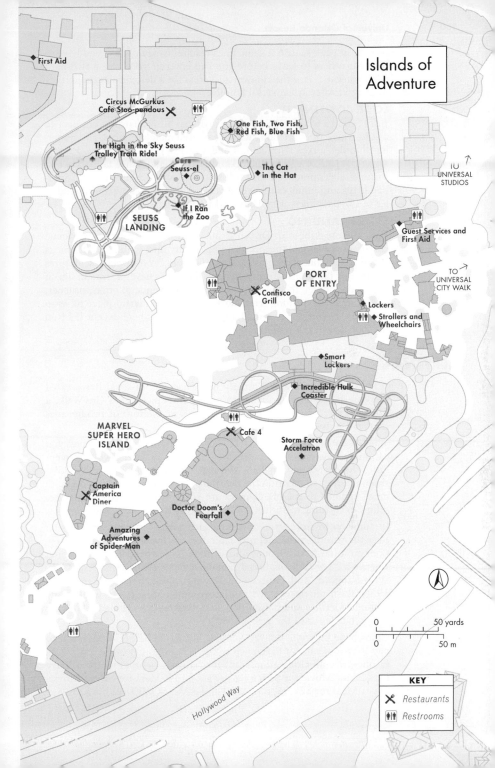

Islands of Adventure

First Aid

Circus McGurkus
Cafe Stoo-pendous ✕ ⚹

One Fish, Two Fish,
Red Fish, Blue Fish

The High in the Sky Seuss
Trolley Train Ride!

Caro
Seuss-el

The Cat
in the Hat

TO
UNIVERSAL
STUDIOS

If I Ran
the Zoo

SEUSS
LANDING

Guest Services and
First Aid

TO
UNIVERSAL
CITY WALK

PORT
OF ENTRY

Confisco ✕
Grill

Lockers

Strollers and
Wheelchairs

Smart
Lockers

Incredible Hulk
Coaster

MARVEL
SUPER HERO
ISLAND

✕ Cafe 4

Storm Force
Accelatron

Captain
America ✕
Diner

Doctor Doom's
Fearfall

Amazing
Adventures
of Spider-Man

Hollywood Way

0   50 yards

0   50 m

KEY

✕   *Restaurants*

⚹   *Restrooms*

In fact, in peak season it sometimes reaches capacity, and you have to wait for others to leave before you can enter. If you have a two-park pass, you can board the Hogwarts Express for a delightful train journey to Diagon Alley at Universal Studios.

LOST CONTINENT

Just beyond a wooden bridge, huge mythical birds guard the entrance to a land where trees are hung with weathered metal lanterns, and booming thunder mixes with chimes and vaguely Celtic melodies. Farther along the path, the scene looks similar to a Renaissance fair. Seers and fortune-tellers practice their trade in tents, and in a huge theater, Sindbad leaps and bounces all over Arabia. This stunt show and Poseidon let you bypass lines using Universal Express Pass.

SEUSS LANDING

This 10-acre tribute to Dr. Seuss puts you in the midst of his classic children's books. This means spending quality time with the Cat, Things 1 and 2, Horton, the Lorax, and the Grinch. From topiary sculptures to lurching lampposts to curvy fences (there was never a straight line in any of the books) to buildings that glow in lavenders, pinks, peaches, and oranges, everything seems surreal. It's a wonderful place to wrap up a day. Even the Cat would approve. All rides here except If I Ran the Zoo accept Express Pass.

CITYWALK

With an attitude that's distinctly non-Disney, Universal has created nightlife for adults who want to party. The epicenter is CityWalk, a 30-acre entertainment and retail complex at the hub of promenades that lead to two Universal parks.

When it comes to retail, much of the merchandise includes things you can find elsewhere—and most likely for less. But when you're swept up in the energy of CityWalk and dazzled by the degree of window-shopping (not to mention the fact that you're on vacation and you're more inclined to spend), chances are you'll want to drop into stores selling everything from surf wear and cigars to tattoos and timepieces.

In addition to stores, the open and airy gathering place includes an over-the-top discotheque, a theater for the fabulous and extremely popular Blue Man Group, and a huge hall where karaoke's king. There's a New Orleans bar, a Jamaican reggae lounge, a casual Key West hangout, and Hollywood Drive-In Golf, a pair of fun-filled 1950s sci-fi movie–themed miniature golf courses. On weeknights you find families and conventioneers; weekends a decidedly younger crowd parties until the wee hours.

Clubs have individual cover charges, but it's far more economical to pay for the whole kit and much of the caboodle. Choose a Party Pass (a one-price-all-clubs admission) for $11.99, or upgrade to a Party Pass-and-a-Movie for $15; a Party Pass-and-a-Meal for $21; a Movie-and-a-Meal for $21.95; or a Meal and a Mini-Golf Deal for $23.95.

At AMC Universal Cineplex, with its 20 screens (including IMAX), there's certain to be something you like—including nightly midnight movies. Meals (tax and gratuity included) are served at Jimmy Buffett's Margaritaville, the Hard Rock Cafe, and others. Nevertheless, it's a long haul from the garage to CityWalk—if you prefer, simply call a cab. They run at all hours. ☎ 407/354–3374, 407/363–8000 *Universal main line* ⊕ *www.citywalkorlando.com.*

NIGHTLIFE

With the wide range of nightlife you'll find at Universal, you may get the feeling that you're vacationing not in Orlando but in New York City. CityWalk's stores open by mid-morning, and its restaurants come to life between lunchtime and late afternoon. Eateries that double as nightclubs (such as Pat O'Brien's, Bob Marley's, and the Red Coconut Club) start charging a cover sometime in the evening and apply age restrictions (usually 21) around 9. For details on a particular establishment, check with Guest Services.

BARS AND CLUBS

Bob Marley—A Tribute to Freedom. Modeled after the King of Reggae's home in Kingston, Jamaica (even down to the air-conditioning window units), in a way this nightclub is also part museum, with more than 100 photographs and paintings showing pivotal moments in Marley's life. Though the place does serve Jamaican-influenced meals, most patrons are at the cozy bar or by the patio, where they can be jammin' to a (loud) live band that plays nightly. For a nice souvenir, pose by the wonderful Marley statue outside the club. Sunday is ladies' night from 9 pm until closing. ■TIP→ Often on Mondays and Tuesdays, CityWalk's pace is slow enough that some clubs will offer free admission. Ask before you pay. ⊠ *CityWalk* ☎ *407/224–2692* ⊕ *www.universalorlando.com.*

CityWalk's Rising Star. Here you and other hopeful (and hopeless) singers can really let loose. Instead of singing to recorded music, you're accompanied by a band complete with backup singers—in front of a live audience. Backup singers are on hand every night, while the live band plugs in Tuesday through Saturday, and a full bar is always on tap. ⊠ *6000 Universal Blvd., Suite 717, CityWalk* ☎ *407/224–2961* ⊕ *www.universalorlando.com.*

the groove. In this cavernous hall images flicker rapidly on several screens, and the lights, music, and mayhem appeal to a mostly under-30 crowd. Prepare for lots of fog, swirling lights, and sweaty bodies. The '70s-style Green Room is filled with beanbag chairs and everything you threw out when Duran Duran hit the charts. The Blue Room is sci-fi Jetson-y, and the Red Room is hot and romantic in a bordello sort of way. The music is equally diverse: Top 40, hip-hop, R&B, techno, and the occasional live band. ⊠ *6000 Universal Blvd., CityWalk* ☎ *407/224–2692* ⊕ *www. universalorlando.com.*

Jimmy Buffett's Margaritaville. Buffett tunes fill the air at the restaurant here and at the Volcano, Land Shark, and 12 Volt bars. Inside there's a miniature Pan Am Clipper suspended from the ceiling, music videos projected onto sails, limbo and hula-hoop contests, a huge

The Cat and his Hat, McGurkus and the Circus, and fish both red and blue are among the attractions geared to the under-7 set at Seuss Landing.

margarita blender that erupts "when the volcano blows," and live music nightly—everything that Parrotheads need to roost. Across the promenade, another full-size seaplane (emblazoned with "Jimmy Buffett, Captain") is the setting for the Lone Palm Airport, a pleasing and surprisingly popular outdoor waterfront bar. ✉ *6000 Universal Studios Plaza, Suite 704, CityWalk* ☎ *407/224–2155* ⊕ *www.margaritavilleorlando.com.*

Pat O'Brien's. An exact reproduction of the legendary New Orleans original, this comes complete with flaming fountain and dueling pianists who are playing for highly entertained regulars and visitors—even on weekday afternoons. Outside, the cozy and welcoming Patio Bar has a wealth of tables and chairs, allowing you to do nothing but enjoy the outdoors and your potent, rum-based Hurricanes in Orlando's version of the Big Easy. ✉ *6000 Universal Blvd., CityWalk* ☎ *407/224–2692* ⊕ *www.patobriens.com.*

Red Coconut Club. Paying tribute to kitsch design of the 1950s, the interior here is part Vegas lounge, part Cuban club, and part Polynesian tiki bar. It's "where tropical meets trendy." There are three full bars on two levels, signature martinis, an extensive wine list, and VIP bottle service. Hang out in the lounge, on the balcony, or at the bar. On a budget? Take advantage of the daily happy hours and gourmet appetizer menu. A DJ (Sunday–Wednesday) or live music (Thursday–Saturday) pushes the energy with tunes ranging from Sinatra to rock. Thursday is ladies' night. ✉ *6000 Universal Blvd., CityWalk* ☎ *407/224–2425* ⊕ *www.universalorlando.com.*

SHOWS

Blue Man Group. At their own venue, the ever-innovative Blue Man Group continues to pound out new music, sketches, and audience interaction that is nothing like you've ever seen. Attempting to understand the apps on a GiPad (a gigantic iPad), they may appear clueless and perplexed about cutting-edge technology (which for them can be as basic as a can of paint), but they're always excited when they can drum out rhythms on lengths of PVC pipes and throw a rave party finale for all in attendance. The show is a surreal comic masterpiece, so if you have the time and a little extra in your vacation budget, this is a must. Three levels of admission (Poncho, Tier 1, and Tier 2) hint at how messy things can get when the Blue Men cut loose. ⊠ *CityWalk* 📞 *407/258–3626* ⊕ *www.universalorlando.com* 🎟 *From $60.*

VOLCANO BAY

When you were a kid, chances are that the only thing you needed for cool summer fun was an inflatable pool and a garden hose. Well, you've grown up, and so have water parks. The choices for cool summer fun get no cooler than Universal's Volcano Bay, which opened in May 2017 and is a theme park all on its own.

Built around a central, fire-spewing volcano, the park offers numerous high-energy slides and drops for adults; lots of slides and fountains where the little ones can frolic; an area for older kids with bubbling geysers, water guns, slides, and dump cups. There's also a white-water rapids ride, a lazy-river ride, a surf pool, and some quiet, sandy beaches on which you can stretch out and get a tan.

Speaking of high energy, this is a park that requires a lot of it. A day here is often a marathon of climbing steps, sliding, swimming, and splashing, though you may not notice just how much your stamina is being drained as you scamper from slide to slide. Plan to take breaks: laze in a beach chair and eat high-protein meals and snacks to maintain your strength.

If you're not a strong swimmer, don't worry. There are plenty of low-key attractions, and all of the ride entrances are marked with warnings to let you know which ones are safe for you. Plus, during peak season, there are always lifeguards on duty daily. Also note that all the pools (if not the rides) are ADA-compliant and are heated in cooler weather. This, combined with Orlando's temperate climate, means that Volcano Bay is one of the few water parks in the country to stay open year-round.

SEAWORLD

WELCOME TO SEAWORLD

TOP REASONS TO GO

★ **Animal magnetism:**
If you love animals—slick, shiny, feathery, or furry—SeaWorld, Discovery Cove, and Aquatica are where you want to be. No robotic wildlife here; just dolphins, whales, seals, otters, penguins, cats, dogs....

★ **A slower pace:**
The shows and natural settings of SeaWorld and Discovery Cove let you enjoy a theme-park vacation without racing from one attraction to the next. Living in the moment is the lesson here.

★ **Getting smarter:** No one leaves these parks without learning a little something about nature through shows, backstage tours, instructional signage, and well-versed educators and naturalists who are always ready to answer questions.

★ **Memories in the making:**
Chances are SeaWorld and Discovery Cove will afford you the chance to pet a penguin, feed a dolphin, or watch a 5-ton whale leap out of the water. You can't forget things like that.

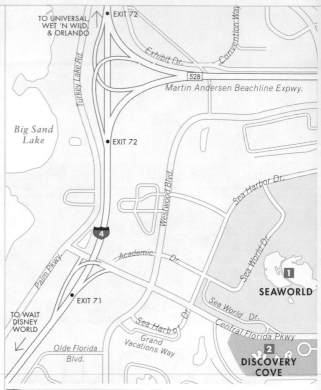

1 SeaWorld. With the exception of a handful of thrill rides, the original park (which opened in 1973 to reroute visitors heading to the then recently opened Walt Disney World) maintains a slow and easy pace. Here it's all about clever shows, shaded sidewalks, and plenty of opportunities to enjoy the natural grace and intriguing personalities of marine life and other animals.

Orlando

12

GETTING ORIENTED

SeaWorld is just off the intersection of Interstate 4 and the Beachline Expressway, equidistant from Universal Orlando and the Walt Disney World Resort, which are only about five minutes away. SeaWorld is also a mere 10 minutes from Downtown Orlando and 15 minutes from the airport. Discovery Cove is its own oasis across the street from SeaWorld. Aquatica, a little ways down the road from both, is the first of the three that you'll see after exiting the expressway.

TO WET 'N WILD & UNIVERSAL STUDIOS ↑

Universal Blvd.

EXIT 2
528
EXIT 1
EXIT 3A AND EXIT 3B

Gateway Ave.

3
AQUATICA

International Dr.

Orangewood Blvd.

D

423

0 ——— 1/4 mi
0 ——— 1/4 km

2 Discovery Cove. SeaWorld spun off this park to give you the chance to enjoy a lot more time (and to spend a little more cash) with the animals. A trip to this aquatic oasis feels like a trip to the islands; a daylong, all-inclusive experience that includes breakfast and lunch, drinks, a private beach, snorkeling equipment, and—for approximately an extra $100—the chance to swim with dolphins. Paradise.

3 Aquatica. SeaWorld's water park offers the chance to slip and slide at adrenaline-rush speeds, relax in the current of two wave pools, laze on a wide beach, and take the wee ones to pint-size play areas of their very own. All in all, there's something for everyone, showcased in a tropical, tiki-themed setting.

Updated
by Jennifer
Greenhill-Taylor

Just as Walt Disney World and Universal Orlando are much more than just a single park, the same is true of SeaWorld. The original park—which includes the Shamu shows as well as presentations featuring dolphins and seals—has expanded to include Discovery Cove (an immersive tropical retreat), and Aquatica (a water park loaded with aquatic excitement). So, as you plan your vacation, consider that SeaWorld can easily fill a single day or, if you're really eager to take to the waters, perhaps a day or two more.

There's a whole lot more to SeaWorld and Discovery Cove than being splashed by Shamu. You can see manatees face-to-snout, learn to love a shark, swim with dolphins, and be spat at by a walrus. These two parks celebrate all the mammals, birds, fish, and reptiles that live in and near the ocean.

Then there's Aquatica, a wild water park that takes its cues from Sea-World and Discovery Cove in design and mood—marine-life motifs are everywhere. It also gives competitor water parks a run for their money with thrilling slides, broad beaches, calming rivers, and an area for small kids.

The park also takes some tips from the tropics. Right after you clear the parking lot, you see a tropical pastiche of buildings. Yup. That's definitely an island vibe you're detecting. Upon entering Aquatica, you feel as if you've left Central Florida for the Caribbean or Polynesia, even.

You might be drawn to the series of superfast waterslides (some of which conclude by sending you into serene streams), or you might feel the pull of the white-sand beaches beside the twin wave pools, where you can laze in the sun, venturing out every so often to try a ride or climb into an inner tube and float down a river. Whether you're spending the day at SeaWorld, Discovery Cove, or Aquatica, just go with it. Get into a groove, relax, and enjoy yourself at some of the most pleasant theme parks in Orlando.

PLANNING

GETTING HERE AND AROUND

Heading west on Interstate 4 (toward Disney) take Exit 72; heading east, take Exit 71. After that you'll be going east on the Beachline Expressway (aka Route 528), and the first right-hand exit leads you to International Drive. Turn left, and you'll soon see the entrance to Aquatica on your left. Sea Harbor Drive—leading to SeaWorld's entrance—will be on your right. To reach Discovery Cove, follow International Drive past Aquatica a half mile to the Central Florida Parkway and turn right. The park's entrance will be on your left.

OPERATING HOURS

SeaWorld opens daily at 9 am and usually closes at 7 pm, with extended hours during the summer and holidays. Hours at Discovery Cove also vary seasonally, although it's generally open daily from 8 to 5:30, with check-in beginning 30 minutes earlier—which is not a bad idea considering Discovery Cove serves a complimentary breakfast until 10 am. Aquatica is open at 9 am, with closing times varying between 5 and 9 pm, depending on the season. Allow a full day to see each attraction.

ADMISSION

SeaWorld, Discovery Cove, Aquatica, and Busch Gardens Tampa Bay fall under the SeaWorld Parks & Entertainment umbrella, and you can save by buying combo tickets. Regular one-day tickets to **SeaWorld** cost $99 (adults and children three and older), excluding tax, but if you order in advance over the phone or online you'll save as much as $20 per ticket—which just may be the best money-saving option you'll find. Combo-park admission prices, which include 14 days at each park, are as follows:

SeaWorld/Aquatica Online $109

SeaWorld/Busch Gardens Tampa Online $109

SeaWorld/Aquatica/Busch Gardens Tampa Online $119

Flex Ticket (14 days at SeaWorld/Aquatica/Busch Gardens Tampa) $149

Aquatica Online $39 (at the gate $59)

Reserve **Discovery Cove** visits well in advance—attendance is limited to about 1,000 a day. Tickets (with a dolphin swim) start at about $229 (off-season, in January and February) but are generally around $289. Forgo the dolphin swim and save approximately $80. This park has what's called dynamic pricing (meaning prices change by season, and also at other times without notice). Admission is less expensive the earlier you book (so call well in advance) and includes access to all beach and snorkeling areas and the free-flight aviary; meals and snacks; use of a mask, snorkel, swim vest, towel, locker, and sunscreen; parking; and a pass for 14 days of unlimited admission to SeaWorld Orlando and Aquatica. Upgrade to an "ultimate" pass (about $20), which includes admission (and free parking) to Busch Gardens Tampa.

Quick Queue Unlimited Passes. SeaWorld's Quick Queue passes ($19–$35 per person, depending on season) get you to the front of the line at major attractions and shows for one admission each. The higher-priced unlimited pass is good for unlimited admissions. Neither Discovery Cove nor Aquatica has such a pass.

All-Day Dining Deal. Available at select SeaWorld restaurants (Voyager's Smokehouse, Seaport Pizza, Terrace Garden Buffet, The Spice Mill, Seafire Inn, and Mango Joe's), adults will pay about $30 and kids from $15 to chow down on an entrée, side dish, drink, and dessert for each meal. Skip it if you plan on having just one meal in the park.

CONTACTS

Aquatica ☎ 888/800–5447 ⊕ *aquaticabyseaworld.com*

Busch Gardens Tampa ☎ 888/800–5447 ⊕ *www.buschgardens.com/bgt*

Discovery Cove ☎ 877/557–7404 ⊕ *www.discoverycove.com*

SeaWorld ☎ 888/800–5447 ⊕ *www.seaworld.com*

Parking. Parking is $19 for a car or motorcycle; for $24 you can pull into one of the six Preferred Parking rows closest to the front gate. At Aquatica, cars and motorcycles are charged $12, RVs $16—although if you already have your parking slip from that day at SeaWorld, it's free. Parking is free at Discovery Cove.

SEAWORLD

Just as you wouldn't expect to arrive at Disney and see nothing but Mickey Mouse, don't expect to arrive at SeaWorld and see only Shamu. Only a few steps into the park you'll find baby dolphins and their mothers, a pool filled with stingrays, colorful flamingos, rescued sea turtles, rescued pelicans, and even rescued manatees. SeaWorld's objective is to educate as well as entertain.

You'll see how lumbering manatees live and what they look like up close; watch otters and seals perform slapstick routines based on their natural behaviors; learn about the lives of giant tortoises and sea turtles; and be absolutely amazed at the scope of marine life celebrated throughout the park.

Then there are the attractions, each and every one designed not only to showcase the marine world but also to demonstrate ways in which humans can protect the Earth's waters and wildlife. And, because there are more exhibits and shows than rides, the difference between SeaWorld and other theme parks is that you can go at your own pace, without that hurry-up-and-wait feeling. It's also worth noting that because shows, attractions, and exhibits are based primarily on nature and animals, designers have created a natural layout as well, with winding lanes and plenty of places to relax by the waterfront or beside bouquets of flowers. There's never a nagging urge to race through anything; indeed, the entire park encourages you to slow down and move at a casual pace. That said, theme parks like SeaWorld have been criticized by animal welfare groups. They argue that the conditions and treatment of marine life kept in captivity are harmful for the animals, and that human interaction further exacerbates this.

GETTING ORIENTED

SeaWorld's performance venues, attractions, and activities surround a 17-acre lagoon, and the artful landscaping, curving paths, and concealing greenery sometimes lead to wrong turns. But armed with a map that lists showtimes, it's easy to plan an approach that lets you move fluidly from one show and attraction to the next and still have time for rest stops and meal breaks.

TOP SEAWORLD ATTRACTIONS

Antarctica: Empire of the Penguin

Clyde and Seamor's Sea Lion High

Kraken

Manta

One Ocean

Pets Ahoy

TOURING TIPS

Before investing in front-of-the-line Quick Queue passes ($19–$35), remember that there are only a handful of big-deal rides, and space is seldom a problem at shows.

If you bring your own food, remove all straws and lids before you arrive—they can harm fish and birds.

Arrive at least 30 minutes early for the Shamu show, which generally fills to capacity. Prepare to get wet in the "splash zone" down front.

PARK AMENITIES

Guest Services: Ticket booths have become the new Guest Services (aka Guest Relations) center. If you ordered your tickets online, have questions about dining or attractions, or just need tickets to begin with, you can find it all here.

Information and Reservation Center: Right inside the entrance you can pick up the park map (which also has info on showtimes, services, and amenities); make dinner reservations; and buy tickets for Discovery Cove, Aquatica, and park tours.

Lockers: One-time-use, coin-op lockers ($1) are near flip-over coasters like Kraken and Manta, Journey to Atlantis, and Shamu's Happy Harbor as well as inside SeaWorld's main entrance. Also near the entrance, next to Shamu's Emporium, are day lockers ($8 small, $11 large per day). At Discovery Cove free lockers await you near the cabanas.

Lost People and Things: SeaWorld's Main Information Center operates as the park's Lost and Found. Lost children are brought here, and it's the place to report lost children. A park-wide paging system also helps reunite parents with kids. At Discovery Cove lost kids and items eventually find their way to the Check-In Lobby.

ANIMAL ENCOUNTERS AND TOURS

You can book tours up to three months in advance. For a list, check the SeaWorld website (⊕ *seaworldparks.com*) or call the park (☎ *407/351–3600*).

Behind the Scenes Tour. On this 90-minute program, you'll have a chance to see how SeaWorld's animal experts care for rescued manatees and sea turtles. Where else can you touch a shark, step inside a hidden polar bear den, and play with a penguin? ✉ *SeaWorld, 7007 SeaWorld Dr* ⊕ *seaworldparks.com* ☎ *From $29.*

DISCOVERY COVE

If you were pleasantly surprised by the pace at SeaWorld, believe it or not, you'll find it's even slower at Discovery Cove. Here your mission is to spend an entire day doing nothing but savoring a 32-acre tropical oasis. It's a task made easier by an all-inclusive admission that covers all meals, towels, a wet suit, masks, sunscreen, and the option of springing for the highlight of the day: a unique swimming experience with a bottlenose dolphin.

Even without a dolphin encounter, you can have a great time splashing around coral reefs, swimming into a spacious aviary, floating down a quiet river, and lazing on a sandy beach beneath lovely palms. Freshwater Oasis is a tropical rain-forest environment of sparkling clear springs offering face-to-face encounters with playful otters and curious marmoset monkeys, while, thanks to a special diving helmet, SeaVenture lets you walk underwater through a reef filled with tropical fish and rays that you can literally reach out and touch.

GETTING ORIENTED

Thanks to Discovery Cove's daily cap on crowds, it may seem as if you have the park to yourself. Navigating the grounds is simple; signs point to swimming areas, cabanas, or the free-flight aviary—aflutter with exotic birds and accessible via walkway or (even better) by swimming to it beneath a waterfall.

TOURING TIP

In Discovery Cove make the aviary one of your first stops, since the 250-plus birds within will be more active in the morning. Remember that check-in starts at 7:30 am, and the waterways open around 9.

PARK AMENITIES

Guest Services: You can get information on meals, cabanas, lockers, dolphin swims, merchandise, souvenir photos, and other aspects of the park at the **Discovery Cove Check-In Lobby** when you arrive, or at **Guest Services** (aka Guest Relations) just after you enter.

Lost People and Things: Lost kids and items are usually turned over to Discovery Cove attendants, who bring them to the attendants at the Check-In Lobby.

ANIMAL ENCOUNTERS

Fodor's Choice ★ **Trainer for a Day.** General admission to Discovery Cove includes meals, wet suit, and diving gear; this tour adds a gift bag, waterproof camera, trainer T-shirt, 30-minute dolphin swim, a private photo session with two dolphins, feeding fish in the Grand Reef, a meet-and-greet with tropical birds and small animals, and an almost exclusive (only eight guests in the entire lagoon) interaction that includes a "double-foot push" (two dolphins propel you across the lagoon by the soles of your feet). Ready for more? Shadow a trainer all day: head to the dolphin back area for a private tour and talk to trainers about how they teach and care for these amazing animals. Like other Discovery Cove admissions, this includes unlimited access to SeaWorld and Aquatica for 14 days. Call ahead to arrange a tour. ⊠ *Discovery Cove, 6000 Discovery Cove Way, Discovery Cove* ☎ *407/351–3600, 877/557–7404* ⊕ *www. discoverycove.com* ✉ *From $488.*

SeaWorld Orlando

← TO AQUATICA

Mako

Shark Encounter

Shark's Underwater Grill

Kraken

Pacific Point Preserve

Clyde and Seamore's Sea Lion High (Sea Lion & Otter Theater)

Lockers

Antarctica: Empire of the Penguins

ATM

Lockers

Journey to Atlantis

Antarctic Market

Voyager Smokehouse

Seaport Pizza

Guest Services, Information

Reservations and Show Schedules

Seaport Theater/ Pets Ahoy

Blue Horizons (Dolphin Theater)

Manta

Turtle Trek

Seafire Inn

Lockers

Dolphin Nursery

Pelican Preserve

ATM

Dolphin Cove

ATM

Lockers

Starbucks

Stingray Lagoon

First Aid

Information and Reservations

SeaWorld Rescue

Parking

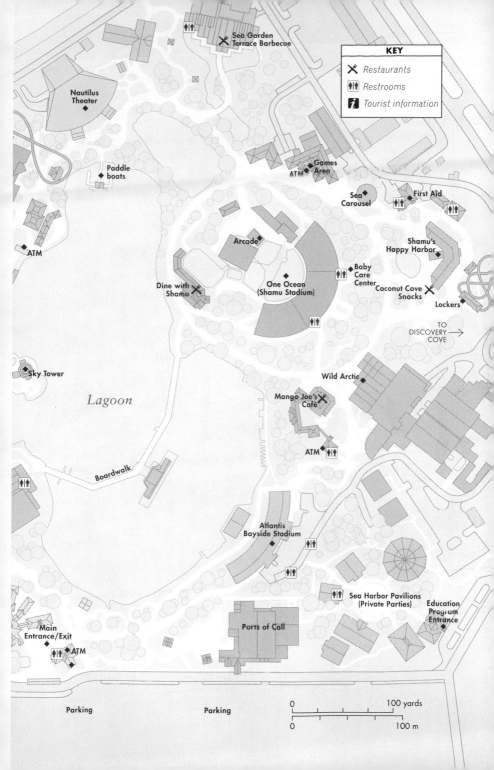

KEY

✕ *Restaurants*

🚻 *Restrooms*

ℹ *Tourist information*

Sea Garden Terrace Barbecue

Nautilus Theater

Paddle boats

ATM

Games Arena

Sea Carousel

First Aid

Arcade

Shamu's Happy Harbor

Dine with Shamu

One Ocean (Shamu Stadium)

Baby Care Center

Coconut Cove Snacks

Lockers

TO DISCOVERY COVE →

Sky Tower

Lagoon

Wild Arctic

Mango Joe's Café

ATM

Boardwalk

Atlantis Bayside Stadium

Sea Harbor Pavilions (Private Parties)

Education Program Entrance

Main Entrance/Exit

ATM

Ports of Call

Parking

Parking

0   100 yards

0   100 m

AQUATICA

Just across International Drive from SeaWorld, Aquatica is the 60-acre water park that does a wonderful job angling water-park lovers away from Disney's Typhoon Lagoon and Blizzard Beach and Universal's Wet 'n Wild. And, sure, Aquatica has all the slides you'd expect, but it also has plenty of whimsical SeaWorld touches.

Aquatica takes cues from SeaWorld and Discovery Cove in design and mood. The park also takes its cues from the tropics. Right after you clear the parking lot, you see a tropical pastiche of buildings that may convince you your ship just sailed into the Caribbean. So go with it. Get into a groove, relax, and enjoy yourself. In addition to superslippery waterslides, there are quiet coves, phenomenally creative kids' play areas, lazy streams, and an atmosphere that is guaranteed to relieve your pre-vacation stress.

Ideally you'll have arrived with some snacks and drinks to combat the fatigue you'll feel after scaling to the tops of all those watery thrill rides. If not, fear not—there are plenty of places to find food and drink.

You should also be toting beach towels, sunscreen, and water shoes. Again, if not, fear not—there are a number of shops and kiosks where you can buy (or rent) all of this stuff and more.

Many of the rides have height restrictions, so if you're traveling with kids, have their heights checked at the Information Center, which you'll see right when you enter the park. Each child will be issued a colored wristband that alerts attendants to which rides are appropriate for him or her (or just look for the height requirement signposted at the entrance to each attraction). If anyone in your group isn't comfortable in the water, this is also a good place to inquire about the swimming lessons that are offered.

After stashing excess supplies in a locker and generally settling in, it's time to explore. Unless it's peak season, several hours should be enough to visit each ride and attraction once or twice, and will also allow for some downtime, lazing on the beach, or enjoying a leisurely meal.

GETTING ORIENTED

Initially, you might find it hard to get your bearings amid the towering slides, Caribbean palms, winding sidewalks, and the seemingly random layout of restaurants, rides, slides, and facilities. And there are no paper maps, only posted diagrams throughout the park. But in reality, the park is fairly easy to navigate—its layout forms a simple circle. The services (restaurants, changing rooms, shops) form a core around which the attractions are situated.

At the entrance, turn right and you'll be at the premier attraction, Dolphin Plunge; but after that you may want to do an about-face and head straight to the shores of the beach at Cutback Cove. This way, you can set up a base and then work your way to other attractions around the circle while remaining conveniently close to meals at Waterstone Grill and the Banana Beach Cookout.

TOURING TIPS

Be aware of the sun. Avoid sunburn by reapplying sunscreen (they suggest SPF 30) often—even waterproof sunblock washes off. For even more sun protection, rent a standard cabana (about $60) or go all out and splurge on the "ultimate cabana" for eight, which includes an all-day locker, bottled water, towels, and discount coupons for merchandise.

Be aware of your feet. Wear sandals or water shoes (or even socks) to protect your feet from hot sand, sidewalks, and rough pool surfaces. At the major thrill rides, a "sneaker keeper" offers a place to stash your footwear while you experience the ride.

Buy tickets in advance. Prepurchased tickets get you early entrance, and this head start will enable you to hit the major flume and tube rides more than once.

Commune with nature. You can catch Commerson's dolphins at feeding times; spot macaws on tree limbs; or see small mammals in the Conservation Cabanas, where docents answer questions. A variety of animals are on display around the park.

PARK AMENITIES

Information: The Main Information Center is at the park entrance, just past the ticket kiosks. Also at the entrance are an ATM, telephones, and restrooms. This is where you check out the posted park map and plan your approach. On the walkways outside the information center and leading into the park, attendants are stationed to help you get your bearings and point out where to find strollers and wheelchairs, help you with lost-and-found inquiries, and describe combination-ticket packages.

Lockers: There are three areas with unlimited-access lockers to rent for a day. One is near the splashdown area at Walhalla Wave and HooRoo Run; two others are at the center and far end of the park, where there are also nursing facilities. You pay $7 for a small locker (enough for one backpack) and $11 for a large one (for about two backpacks); there's also a $10 deposit, which is refunded when you leave. The central locker area also rents towels for $4 ($1 of which is refunded upon return).

Lost People and Things: Lost items and people are taken to a small tent called the Concierge Cabana, which is right by the entrance to the beach area.

NORTHEAST
FLORIDA

WELCOME TO NORTHEAST FLORIDA

TOP REASONS TO GO

★ **Get out and play:** Beautiful beaches and a wealth of state and national parks mean swimming, sunbathing, kayaking, fishing, hiking, bird-watching, and camping opportunities are all nearby.

★ **Golfer's paradise:** "Above par" describes the golf scene, from award-winning courses to THE PLAYERS Championship to the World Golf Hall of Fame.

★ **Start your engines:** Few things get racing fans as revved up as tours of Daytona International Speedway, home of the Daytona 500, Coke Zero 400, and Rolex 24 at Daytona.

★ **Be in the now:** Whether you want a yoga retreat or the ultimate in sybaritic pampering, the oceanfront spas at Amelia Island and Ponte Vedra Beach make this region the place to be.

★ **The rest is history:** The nation's oldest city, St. Augustine, is a must-see for anyone interested in history.

1 **Jacksonville.** With a metro-area population of 1.3 million, Jacksonville has the social and cultural appeal of a big city but the down-to-earth charm of a small town.

2 **Jacksonville Beaches.** The laid-back beach towns on the barrier islands east of Jacksonville are popular family destinations.

3 **Amelia Island/Fernandina Beach.** At the northeast edge of Florida you'll find a historic downtown, beautiful beaches, and two superlative resorts.

4 **St. Augustine.** You don't have to be a history buff to enjoy America's oldest city, founded in 1565.

5 **Daytona Beach and Inland Towns.** The Daytona 500, Bike Week, and spring break put it on the map, but the region is popular with vacationing families, too. Gainesville is home to the University of Florida and its Gators.

6 **The Space Coast.** This area includes Canaveral National Seashore; the Kennedy Space Center; Port Canaveral and its cruise ships; Cocoa, offering quiet appeal; and Cocoa Beach, the ultimate surf and bodyboard destination.

GETTING ORIENTED

13

Northeast Florida has historic port cities such as Fernandina Beach on Amelia Island and St. Augustine and inland towns such as Micanopy and Gainesville, as well as the urban hub of Jacksonville. About two hours south of Jacksonville, on Interstate 95, Titusville is the entry point for the Kennedy Space Center. It marks the northern perimeter of the Space Coast, which includes Cocoa and Melbourne. If you take U.S. 1, it lengthens the trip, but the scenery makes up for the inconvenience. Route A1A/Atlantic Avenue is the main road on all the barrier islands. In many places on A1A, you can see the area's beautiful beaches from your car window.

THE SPACE SHUTTLE ATLANTIS

Even if you have never had the inclination to strap into a rocket or live in zero gravity, no trip to Florida would be complete without a visit to the Kennedy Space Center's *Atlantis* Exhibit. A full day can be spent experiencing the educational and emotional life and history of the American space shuttle program.

More than a mere "exhibit," the Space Shuttle *Atlantis* defies stereotypes with a hands-on approach that enables you to not only see and hear, but also touch and feel, so that you *experience* rather than observe. There are no fingerprint-covered glass cases separating you from getting up close and personal with the symbolic passageways, 60-plus interactive displays, games, simulators, and even a slide to get you back to the ground level (adults are allowed). The *Atlantis* shuttle, complete with tile damage from the heat of reentry, never fails to amaze visitors who see it as only astronauts have before. The

walk-through replicas of the shuttle's living quarters give visitors the ability to more accurately understand life on the shuttle. The *Atlantis* exhibit has an open atmosphere with a friendly, enthusiastic, and knowledgeable staff that has a way of stoking curiosity and bringing out the inner-astronaut in everyone.

THE EXPERIENCE

The Shuttle *Atlantis* exhibit is easily located from the moment you enter the Kennedy Space Center Visitor Complex; the 184-foot life-size replica of the twin rocket boosters and massive orange fuel tank used to transport the shuttle into orbit are displayed just outside the main entry. The *Atlantis* Experience begins with a dual-theater screening that showcases the history of the shuttle development. The motion-picturesque films provide a background and understanding of the necessity and evolution of the shuttle program. Passing through the theater and onto the upper level reveals *Atlantis*, with cargo doors open and robotic Canada arm extended.

Even for the space novice, it is easy to see the amount of thought, planning, and insight that went into the design and construction of the *Atlantis* facility, not to mention the engineering and transportation challenges overcome in order to display a real-life shuttle. Rotated 43.21 degrees and almost close enough to touch, this experience is the closest that many non-astronauts will ever come to something that has actually been into space—other than physically touching an astronaut (not recommended). The staff gladly answers any questions and provides an array of information regarding the facility, design, and interactive displays available for use. Touring *Atlantis* is an exploration in and of itself.

ACTIVITIES

The interactive games and displays are fun for children and parents alike, sometimes sparking fierce competition.

Try your hand on the shuttle crane simulator and experience the complex task of attaching the Shuttle *Atlantis* to the 58,500-pound fuel tank. Features like this are not only enjoyable, but also shed light on the often unheard engineering and physical obstacles encountered and conquered in order to prepare a shuttle for safe transport to the launch pad.

If you've ever wondered what it would be like to experience a shuttle liftoff, look no further. The Shuttle Launch Experience is the only place on Earth (and perhaps the galaxy) allowing non-astronauts to partake in a thrill only a select few Americans have known. After a series of informative videos, future astronauts are guided into the mock shuttle.

Once your safety belts have been fastened, the motion-based platform comes alive with specialized, interactive seating and high-fidelity video and audio to amaze the visitors with what astronauts call the most realistic simulation of a launch. After pushing through the high G-forces and separating from the rocket boosters and fuel tank, the simulation climaxes with a sense of weightlessness, along with a breathtaking view of the distant planet Earth. Be sure to secure belongings in the provided lockers to prevent inadvertent meteor showers of pocket debris during the launch.

Updated by
Steve Master
and Jennifer
Greenhill-Taylor

For many travelers, Florida is about fantasy, thanks in no small part to Central Florida's make-believe kingdoms. But the northeastern part of the state—you could call it "authentic Florida"—has its own allure, with unspoiled beaches and rivers, historic small towns, and urban arts and culture.

Northeastern Florida's beaches have wide, shell-strewn expanses of sand, in some places firm enough to ride bikes on, and breakers just the right height for kids to jump. Thanks to the temperate climate and waters warmed by the Gulf Stream, these beaches are a year-round playground—when it's too cold to swim, you can still enjoy surf-fishing or just riding on the beach, or strolling the shoreline looking for shells and sharks' teeth.

Sun and surf aren't the only reasons to explore northeastern Florida, though. There's historic St. Augustine and its horse-drawn carriages, Daytona and its classic spring-break flavor, and the Space Coast and its sense of discovery. Along the way is an array of little towns—from Fernandina and its shrimp fleets to Micanopy and its antiques stores— that invite quiet exploration.

There's city life in the northeast, too. In the last decade or so, Jacksonville has revitalized its institutions and infrastructure. And with the revitalization has come an arts renaissance—from virtuoso productions in the theaters of the Times-Union Center for the Performing Arts and the Florida Theatre, to world-class exhibitions in the Museum of Contemporary Art.

So, even if the ultimate reason for your Florida sojourn is Mickey and his friends, there's no reason to miss the northeast. Indeed, you'll find some authentic benefits—among them, a dearth of crowds and lines and an abundance of Southern hospitality, plus good value for the money.

PLANNING

WHEN TO GO

It's not 90°F and sunny here every day. In winter the weather is fair, averaging in the low 50s in Jacksonville and low 60s in Cocoa Beach, but the temperature sometimes dips below freezing for a day or two. Summer temperatures hover around 90°F, but the humidity makes it seem hotter, and late-afternoon thunderstorms are frequent. April and May are good months to visit, because the ocean is beginning to warm up and the beaches aren't yet packed. Fall is usually pleasant, too, but September is still hurricane season.

GETTING HERE AND AROUND

AIR TRAVEL

Jacksonville International Airport (JAX) is the region's air hub. A welcome center with information on local attractions, including St. Augustine and Amelia Island, is on the ground floor at the foot of the escalator near baggage claim. It's open daily 9 am–10 pm.

Daytona Beach International (DAB) and Gainesville Regional (GNV) are smaller operations with fewer flights; that said, they may be more convenient in certain travel situations.

Although Orlando isn't part of the area, visitors to northeastern Florida often choose to arrive at Orlando International Airport (MCO), because cheaper flights are usually available. Driving east from Orlando on toll road 528 (aka the Beachline Expressway) brings you to Cocoa Beach in about an hour. To reach Daytona from Orlando, take Interstate 4 or the Beachline Expressway to Interstate 95 and drive north for an hour or so.

CAR TRAVEL

East–west traffic travels the northern part of the state on Interstate 10, a cross-country highway stretching from Jacksonville, Florida, to Santa Monica, California. Farther south, Interstate 4 connects Florida's west and east coasts. Signs on Interstate 4 designate it an east–west route, but actually the road rambles northeast from Tampa to Orlando, then heads north–northeast to Daytona. Two interstates head north–south on Florida's peninsula: Interstate 95 on the east coast and Interstate 75 on the west.

If you want to drive as close to the Atlantic as possible, choose Route A1A, but accept the fact that it will add considerably to your drive time. It runs along the barrier islands, changing its name several times along the way.

The Buccaneer Trail, which overlaps part of Route A1A, goes from St. Augustine north to Mayport, through marshlands and beaches, crosses the St. Johns via Ferry, and then proceeds north into Fort Clinch State Park. The extremely scenic Route 13, also known as the William Bartram Trail, runs from Jacksonville to East Palatka along the east side of St. Johns River through tiny hamlets. U.S. 17 travels the west side of the river, passing through Green Cove Springs and Palatka. Route 40 runs east–west through the Ocala National Forest, giving a nonstop view of stately pines and bold wildlife.

13

HOTELS

For the busy seasons—during summer in and around Jacksonville and during spring, summer, winter, and holiday weekends all over Florida—reserve well ahead for top properties. Jacksonville's beach hotels fill up quickly for PGA's The Players Championship in mid-May. Daytona Beach presents similar problems during the Daytona 500 (late February), Bike Week (late February–early March), spring break (March), and the Coke Zero 400 (early July).

St. Augustine stays busy all year. In late summer and fall rates are low and availability is high, but it's also hurricane season. Although northeast Florida hasn't been hit directly since 1964, it's possible for threatening storms to disrupt plans.

RESTAURANTS

The ocean, St. Johns River, and numerous lakes and smaller rivers teem with fish, and so, naturally, seafood dominates local menus. Northeast Florida also has fine-dining restaurants, and its ethnic eateries include some excellent Middle Eastern places. And then there are the barbecue joints—more of them than you can shake a hickory chip at.

Hotel and restaurant reviews have been shortened. For full information, visit Fodors.com.

WHAT IT COSTS				
	$	$$	$$$	$$$$
Restaurants	under $15	$15–$20	$21–$30	over $30
Hotels	under $200	$200–$300	$301–$400	over $400

Restaurant prices are the average cost of a main course at dinner or, if dinner is not served, at lunch. Hotel prices are the lowest cost of a standard double room in high season.

TOURS

TourTime, Inc. This company offers custom group and individual motor-coach tours of Jacksonville, Amelia Island, Jekyll Island, and St. Augustine, as well as river cruises and trips to Silver Springs, Kennedy Space Center, Orlando, Okefenokee Swamp, and Savannah. Advance reservations are required. ☎ *904/282–8500* ⊕ *www.tourtimeinc.com.*

JACKSONVILLE

Updated by Jennifer Greenhill-Taylor

399 miles north of Miami, on I-95.

Jacksonville is an underrated vacation spot. It offers appealing downtown riverside areas, handsome residential neighborhoods, a thriving arts scene, spectacular beaches, and, for football fans, the NFL's Jaguars and the NCAA Gator Bowl.

Although the city has become the largest in area of the continental United States (841 square miles), its Old South flavor remains, especially in the Riverside/Avondale historic district. Here moss-draped oak trees frame prairie-style bungalows and Tudor Revival mansions, and palm trees, Spanish bayonet, and azaleas populate the landscape.

GETTING HERE AND AROUND

The main airport for the region is Jacksonville International Airport. Free shuttles run from the terminal to all parking lots (except the garage) around the clock, and transportation service into the city is available from numerous companies in vehicles that range from taxis to vans to elegant limousines. Check beforehand on prices, which vary widely, and on which credit cards are accepted. The average cost per person from airport to downtown is $35 to $45; it's $45 to $55 for trips to the beaches. The larger companies usually operate 24/7, but the smaller (and often less expensive ones) may be by appointment only.

Connecting the north and south banks of the St. Johns River, the St. Johns River Taxi runs between several locations, including Southbank Riverwalk at Friendship Park, the Doubletree Hotel, Lexington Hotel, Everbank Field/Metro Park, and the Jacksonville Landing. The one-way trip takes about five minutes. The water taxis run Sunday through Thursday, 11 to 9, and Friday and Saturday from 11 to 11 (except during rain or other bad weather), with special hours on game days and for special events. The fare is $10 for one day. Special ticketed tours are available to the Zoo, the Arts Fair, and other spots.

Jacksonville Transportation Authority buses and shuttles serve the city and its beaches. The city also operates a small monorail system that links the convention center and a few downtown areas to several other stations across the river on the Southbank and San Marco. It is free and runs weekdays from 6 am to 9 pm and Saturday and Sunday during special events only. JTA also operates the Mayport Ferry, which transports cars and pedestrians across the mouth of the St. Johns River.

Airport Jacksonville International Airport (*JAX*). ⊠ *14201 Pecan Park Rd.* ☎ *904/741–4902* ⊕ *www.flyjacksonville.com.*

Airport Transfers Dana's Limousine & Transportation. ☎ *904/744–3333* ⊕ *www.danaslimo.com.*

Ferries St. Johns River Taxi. ⊠ *Friendship Park, 1015 Museum Cir., Downtown* ☎ *904/860–8294* ⊕ *www.jaxrivertaxi.com.*

Public Transportation Jacksonville Transportation Authority (*JTA*). ☎ *904/630–3100* ⊕ *www.jtafla.com.*

Taxis Checker Cab–Jacksonville. ☎ *904/999–9999.* **Coastal Cab.** ☎ *904/246–9999* ⊕ *www.coastalcab-jax.com.*

VISITOR INFORMATION

Contacts Visit Jacksonville. ☎ *800/733–2668* ⊕ *www.visitjacksonville.com.*

EXPLORING

Jacksonville was settled along both sides of the twisting St. Johns River, and a number of attractions are on or near its banks. Both sides of the river, which is spanned by myriad bridges and crossed by water taxis and ferries, have downtown areas and waterfront complexes of shops, restaurants, parks, and museums.

You can reach some attractions by water taxi or Skyway Express monorail system—scenic alternatives to driving back and forth across the bridges. That said, a car is generally necessary.

In addition to the visitor information center at the airport, there are two downtown (one at the Jacksonville Landing marketplace and one at Hemming Plaza), and another in Jacksonville Beach at the Beaches Historical Museum (⊠ *425 Beach Blvd.*) that is open Tuesday through Saturday 10–4 and Sunday noon–4.

TOP ATTRACTIONS

Cummer Museum of Art & Gardens. The Wark Collection of early-18th-century Meissen porcelain is just one reason to visit this former estate on the St. Johns River, which includes 13 permanent galleries with more than 5,500 items spanning more than 4,000 years, and 3 acres of riverfront gardens, including a sculpture garden and outdoor plaza, that form a showcase for northeast Florida's blooming seasons and indigenous fauna. Art Connections allows kids of all ages to experience art through hands-on, interactive exhibits. The Thomas H. Jacobsen Gallery of American Art focuses on works by American artists, including Max Weber, N.C. Wyeth, and Paul Manship. Complimentary tour guide brochures at the front desk help visitors navigate the galleries, as do podcasts. ⊠ *829 Riverside Ave., Riverside* ☎ *904/356–6857* ⊕ *www.cummermuseum.org* 🖭 *$10, free Tues. 4–9* ☉ *Closed Mon.*

Jacksonville Landing. During the week, this riverfront market caters to locals (who sometimes arrive by boat) and tourists alike, with specialty shops, full-service restaurants—including a sushi bar, Italian bistro, Irish pub, steak house, and an indoor food court—all of which look out over the boat traffic on the St. Johns River. Water taxis shuttle across the river between the Landing and the Southbank. The Landing hosts more than 250 weekend events each year, ranging from the good clean fun of the Lighted Boat Parade and Christmas Tree Lighting to the just plain obnoxious Florida/Georgia game after-party, as well as live music (usually of the local cover-band variety) in the courtyard. ⊠ *2 W. Independent Dr., Downtown* ☎ *904/353–1188* ⊕ *www.jacksonvillelanding.com* 🖭 *Free.*

FAMILY
Fodor's Choice
★
Jacksonville Zoo and Gardens. The highly regarded zoo offers visitors the chance to hop on a train and explore different countries through the animals that live there, from the Land of the Tiger, a 2½-acre Asian attraction featuring Sumatran and Malayan tigers, to the Tuxedo Coast, a controlled Antarctic-like environment for a group of Magellanic penguins, and the African Plains area, which houses elephants, white rhinos, and two highly endangered leopards, in addition to other species of African birds and mammals. The Range of the Jaguar takes visitors

A rainbow lorikeet might pop by and say hello while you're touring the Jacksonville Zoo.

to a 4-acre Central and South American exhibit, with exotic big cats as well as 20 other species native to the region. Among the other highlights are rare waterfowl and the Reptile House in Wild Florida, which showcases some of the world's most venomous snakes. Wild Florida is a 2½-acre area with black bears, bald eagles, white-tailed deer, and other animals native to Florida, while RiverQuest reveals the ecology of the adjacent Trout River. Play Park contains a Splash Ground, a forest play area, two mazes, and a discovery building; Stingray Bay has a 17,000-gallon pool where visitors can pet and feed the mysterious creatures; and DinoTrek's life-size dinosaurs offer a glimpse into the past. The zoo opened a Manatee Critical Care Center in 2016. Parking is free. ⊠ *370 Zoo Pkwy., off Heckscher Dr. E* ☎ *904/757–4463* ⊕ *www.jacksonvillezoo.org* ✉ *$17.95.*

Fodor's Choice ★ **MOCA Jacksonville.** In this loftlike, five-story downtown building, the former headquarters of the Western Union Telegraph Company, a permanent collection of 20th-century art shares space with traveling exhibitions and a theater space. The museum, owned and managed by the University of North Florida, encompasses five galleries and ArtExplorium, a highly interactive educational exhibit for kids, as well as a funky gift shop and Nola MOCA, open for lunch on weekdays and for dinner on Thursdays. MOCA Jacksonville also hosts film series, theater performances, and workshops throughout the year, and packs a big art-wallop into a relatively small 14,000 square feet. A once-a-month Art Walk is free to all. ⊠ *Hemming Plaza, 333 N. Laura St., Downtown* ☎ *904/366–6911* ⊕ *www.mocajacksonville.unf.edu* ✉ *$8* ☺ *Closed Mon.*

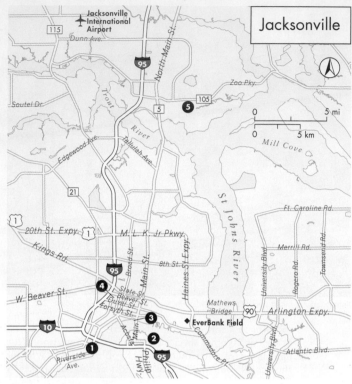

FAMILY   **Museum of Science & History.** Known locally as MOSH, this museum is home to the Bryan-Gooding Planetarium. As a next-generation planetarium, it can project 3-D laser shows that accompany the ever-popular weekend Cosmic Concerts. For those taking in the plane-tarium shows, the resolution is significantly sharper than that of the biggest HDTV on the market. Whether you're a kid taking in Sesame Street's *One World, One Sky,* or an adult star-gazing in the *Skies over Jacksonville* tour of the night sky, the experience is awesome. MOSH also has a wide variety of interactive exhibits and programs that include Health in Motion: Discover What Moves You; JEA Pow-erPlay: Understanding our Energy Choices, where you can energize the future city of MOSHtopia as you learn about alternative energy resources and the science of energy; the Florida Naturalist's Center, where you can interact with northeast Florida wildlife; and the Cur-rents of Time, where you'll navigate 12,000 years of northeast Florida history, from the region's earliest Native American settlers to modern-day events. Nationally acclaimed traveling exhibits are featured along with signature exhibits on regional history. ✉ *1025 Museum Circle* ☎ *904/396–6674* ⊕ *www.themosh.org* 🎟 *$12.50.*

WHERE TO EAT

$$$
AMERICAN

✕ **bb's.** Sleek yet cozy, this hip bistro is as popular with corporate types looking to close a deal as it is with young lovebirds seemingly on the verge of popping the question. The concrete floors and a stainless-steel wine bar provide an interesting backdrop for comfort-food-inspired entrées, but they also create a dining room that is uncommonly loud, especially on weekends. **Known for:** signature grilled pizzas; extensive selection of desserts from b the bakery; nightly entrée specials. $ *Average main: $21* ✉ *1019 Hendricks Ave., San Marco* ☎ *904/306–0100* ⊕ *www.bbsrestaurant.com* ☾ *Closed Sun.*

$$$
AMERICAN
Fodor's Choice
★

✕ **Biscottis.** The local artwork on the redbrick walls is a mild distraction from the crowds jockeying for tables here for brunch, lunch, and dinner. Elbows almost touch in the 100-seat restaurant, but no one seems to mind, as the constantly changing dinner specials offer so many unexpected delights. **Known for:** weekend brunch that is served until 3; decadent desserts from b the bakery; ever-changing nightly entrée specials. $ *Average main: $21* ✉ *3556 St. Johns Ave.* ☎ *904/387–2060* ⊕ *www.biscottis.net.*

$$$
FRENCH

✕ **Bistro Aix.** Named after the French city (and pronounced simply "X"), this sophisticated bistro-bar's leather booths, 1940s brickwork, olive drapes, and intricate marbled globes, provide a perfect home for well-prepared French food. Regulars can't get enough of the classic bistro entrées or delectable desserts. **Known for:** French onion soup and steak frites; smaller options for most menu items; attentive service. $ *Average main: $28* ✉ *1440 San Marco Blvd., San Marco* ☎ *904/398–1949* ⊕ *www.bistrox.com.*

$$
SEAFOOD

✕ **Clark's Fish Camp.** It's out of the way, but every mile will be forgotten once you step inside this former bait shop overlooking Julington Creek. Clark's has more than 160 appetizers and entrées, including the usual—shrimp, catfish, and oysters—and the unusual—ostrich, rattlesnake, and kangaroo. **Known for:** exotic meats; waterfront location; extensive taxidermy collection. $ *Average main: $20* ✉ *12903 Hood Landing Rd., Mandarin* ☎ *904/268–3474* ⊕ *www.clarksfishcamp.com.*

$
EUROPEAN

✕ **European Street Café.** Wicker baskets and lofty shelves brimming with European confections and groceries like Toblerone and Nutella fill practically every inch of space not occupied by café tables. The menu is similarly overloaded, with nearly 100 deli sandwiches and salads. **Known for:** raspberry-almond chicken salad; wide selection of beers on tap and in bottles; outdoor seating. $ *Average main: $9* ✉ *2753 Park St.* ☎ *904/384–9999* ⊕ *www.europeanstreet.com.*

$
ASIAN FUSION
Fodor's Choice
★

✕ **Hawkers Asian Street Fare.** Fans of Asian street food hit the jackpot here, as Hawkers replicates the small, varied, often spicy, dishes sold by street vendors in Asia, using recipes passed down for generations. Sharing bowls of noodles, steamed buns, small plates, soups, and more makes for a convivial atmosphere. **Known for:** roti canai with curry sauce; small plates; hip vibe. $ *Average main: $8* ✉ *1001 Park St.* ☎ *904/508–0342* ⊕ *www.eathawkers.com.*

$$$
ECLECTIC
Fodor's Choice
★

✕ **Matthew's.** No one can accuse chef Matthew Medure of resting on his laurels, of which there are many. Widely praised for culinary creativity and dazzling presentation at his signature San Marco restaurant, Medure's French- and Italian-inspired cuisine offers a wide range of

13

choices, from caviar to sweets. **Known for:** create-your-own charcuterie platters; huge wine list; six-course Chef's Adventure Menu. [$] *Average main: $25* ✉ *2107 Hendricks Ave., San Marco* ☎ *904/396–9922* 🌐 *www.matthewsrestaurant.com* 🕓 *Closed Sun. No lunch.*

$ THAI 🍴 **Taste of Thai.** Ravenous regulars dominate the tightly packed tables at this warm family-owned restaurant in a nondescript strip mall. Since 1997, chef/owner Aurathai Sellas, who might just be the most cheerful person in the entire restaurant business, has prepared the exotic dishes of her homeland, including *pla lad prig* (hot and spicy fish), *goog thod* (crispy shrimp), and chicken in peanut sauce, as well as pad thai. **Known for:** pla lad prig (whole hot and spicy fried fish); always a friendly welcome; great service. [$] *Average main: $14* ✉ *4317 University Blvd. S, San Jose* ☎ *904/737–9009* 🌐 *www.tasteofthaijax.com* 🕓 *Closed Sun.*

WHERE TO STAY

$$ HOTEL 🏨 **Hotel Indigo Jacksonville-Deerwood Park.** Bright, bold, and visually different from any other Jacksonville property, this contemporary boutique hotel—albeit a chain—makes you feel more like you're staying in a hip apartment rather than a by-the-night lodging. **Pros:** free Wi-Fi throughout; all rooms have kitchenettes; loaner PC. **Cons:** wood floors can be noisy; convenient to business parks but not downtown and its sights; lots of traffic at rush hour. [$] *Rooms from: $225* ✉ *9840 Tapestry Park Cir., Southside* ☎ *904/996–7199, 877/270–1392* 🌐 *www.hotelindigo.com* 🛏 *96 rooms* 🍽 *No meals.*

$ HOTEL 🏨 **Hyatt Regency Jacksonville Riverfront.** It doesn't get much more convenient than this 19-story, downtown, waterfront hotel within walking distance of Jacksonville Landing, EverBank Field, Florida Theatre, Times-Union Center, MOCA, and all things downtown. **Pros:** rooftop pool and hot tub; free Wi-Fi; 24-hour gym and business center. **Cons:** not all rooms are riverfront; packed with meetings; huge, with a chain hotel feel. [$] *Rooms from: $189* ✉ *225 E. Coastline Dr., Downtown* ☎ *904/588–1234* 🌐 *www.jacksonville.regency.hyatt.com* 🛏 *963 rooms* 🍽 *No meals.*

$ HOTEL FAMILY 🏨 **Omni Jacksonville Hotel.** Jacksonville's most luxurious and glamorous downtown hotel offers across-the-street convenience to the big theatrical or musical shows at the Times-Union Center. **Pros:** excellent on-site restaurant; rooftop pool; kids receive special backpack, milk, and cookies. **Cons:** fee for Wi-Fi and parking; restaurant pricey; can be chaotic when there's a show across the street. [$] *Rooms from: $199* ✉ *245 Water St.* ☎ *904/355–6664, 800/843–6664* 🌐 *www.omnijacksonville.com* 🛏 *354 rooms* 🍽 *No meals.*

$ B&B/INN 🏨 **Riverdale Inn.** In the early 1900s, Jacksonville's wealthiest residents built mansions along Riverside Avenue—dubbed the Row—and the three-story Riverdale Inn is one of only two such homes remaining. **Pros:** close to area restaurants and shops; private baths; charming, walkable neighborhood. **Cons:** small rooms; limited parking; strict cancellation policy. [$] *Rooms from: $175* ✉ *1521 Riverside Ave., Riverside* ☎ *904/354–5080* 🌐 *www.riverdaleinn.com* 🛏 *10 rooms* 🍽 *Breakfast.*

$ B&B/INN **St. Johns House.** You can enjoy the grace and elegance of the past and all the modern amenities at this surprisingly inexpensive B&B. **Pros:** historic home; beautiful Riverside location near parks, restaurants, and river; elegant antique furnishings. **Cons:** only open six months a year. [$] *Rooms from: $125* ✉ *1718 Osceola St., Riverside* ☎ *904/384–3724* 🌐 *www.stjohnshouse.com* 🕒 *Closed Mar. and June–Oct.* 🛏 *3 rooms* 🍴 *Breakfast.*

NIGHTLIFE

BARS

Mark's. This self-proclaimed "neighborhood lounge with a dash of dance club style" attracts beautiful people to a fairly classy bar with a small dance floor and a popular happy hour. ✉ *315 E. Bay St., Downtown* ☎ *904/355–5099* 🌐 *www.marksjax.com.*

Metro. It's more than just a gay bar: it's like eight gay bars rolled into one, including a piano bar, dance club, lounge, and drag-show cabaret. ✉ *859 Willow Branch Ave., Riverside* ☎ *904/388–8719* 🌐 *www.metrojax.com.*

COMEDY CLUBS

Comedy Zone. The area's premier comedy club is inside the Ramada Inn Mandarin, offering full food and bar service, in addition to laughs. It's closed Mondays and has a varying cover charge based on the night's headliner. ✉ *Ramada Inn Mandarin, 3130 Hartley Rd.* ☎ *904/292–4242* 🌐 *www.comedyzone.com.*

LIVE MUSIC CLUBS

Jack Rabbits. It's the place to catch the latest and greatest indie bands and budding rock stars, with a cover that varies by the headliner. ✉ *1528 Hendricks Ave.* ☎ *904/398–7496.*

Murray Hill Theatre. Fans of Christian music flock to this no-smoking, no-alcohol club. ✉ *932 Edgewood Ave. S, Westside* ☎ *904/388–3179* 🌐 *www.murrayhilltheatre.com.*

SHOPPING

SHOPPING AREAS

Five Points. This small but funky shopping district less than a mile southwest of downtown has new and vintage-clothing boutiques, shoe stores, and antiques shops. It also has a growing collection of inventive and offbeat eateries and bars, not to mention some of the city's most colorful characters. ✉ *Intersection of Park, Margaret, and Lomax Sts., Riverside* 🌐 *www.5pointsjax.com.*

MALLS

St. Johns Town Center. Some of the shops at this huge outdoor "lifestyle center" aren't found anywhere else in northeast Florida, including Anthropologie, Apple, Lucky Brand Jeans, Lululemon, and Sephora, as well as the Cheesecake Factory, P.F. Chang's China Bistro, and Maggiano's Little Italy. ✉ *4663 River City Dr., Southside* ☎ *904/998–7156* 🌐 *www.simon.com/mall/st-johns-town-center.*

San Marco Square. More than a dozen interesting apparel, home, and jewelry stores and upscale restaurants surround the open square in 1920s Mediterranean revival–style buildings. ⊠ *San Marco Blvd. at Atlantic Blvd., San Marco* ⊕ *mysanmarco.com.*

The Shoppes of Avondale. The highlights here include upscale clothing and accessories boutiques, art galleries, home-furnishings shops, a chocolatier, and trendy restaurants. ⊠ *St. Johns Ave., between Talbot Ave. and Dancy St., Avondale* ⊕ *www.shoppesofavondale.com.*

MARKETS

Riverside Arts Market. The unique location—under the Fuller-Warren Bridge, a block from the Cummer Museum of Art & Gardens and a healthy walk along the RiverWalk from downtown—might be as much of a draw as the merchandise for this Saturday-only market. RAM attracts larger and larger crowds of singles, couples, families, and their dogs. They all come to shop for locally created art and crafts, sample food from vendors that include some excellent area restaurants, and check out street performers or the live music shows on the riverfront stage. Quality is high in every aspect—artists and vendors all go through a fairly rigorous application/audition process—and what there is to see or hear or eat varies from week to week. Sometimes there's also a farmers' market, with licensed farmers and growers selling everything from just-laid eggs and local honey to salad greens that were still in the earth the day before. Inside the Children's Activity Center tent, several organizations offer free educational arts activities to kids. Because it's sheltered by the bridge, RAM goes on rain or shine. Free parking is available at EverBank and other adjacent businesses, and a "bike valet" service encourages people to travel on two wheels. ⊠ *715 Riverside Ave., Riverside* ☎ *904/389–2449* ⊕ *www. riversideartsmarket.com* 🎫 *Free.*

SPORTS AND THE OUTDOORS

BASEBALL

FAMILY **Jacksonville Jumbo Shrimp.** Formerly known as the Jacksonville Suns, this renamed AA minor-league affiliate of the Miami Marlins plays at the $34-million Baseball Grounds of Jacksonville. The Suns were Southern League champions in 2009, 2010, and 2014. ⊠ *Baseball Grounds of Jacksonville, 301 A. Philip Randolph Blvd., Downtown* ☎ *904/358– 2846* ⊕ *www.jaxshrimp.com.*

JACKSONVILLE BEACHES

Updated
by Jennifer
Greenhill-Taylor

The beach is 20 miles east of Jacksonville, on U.S. 90 (Beach Blvd.) or Atlantic Blvd.

Perhaps because the Intracoastal Waterway isn't all that wide where it separates the mainland from the beaches, people here aren't likely to think of themselves as "islanders." But they are, indeed, living on a barrier island, functioning with its own rhythms and led by its own elected officials. And, although there's only one island, there are four beach communities, each with its own mayor and city officials, tax base,

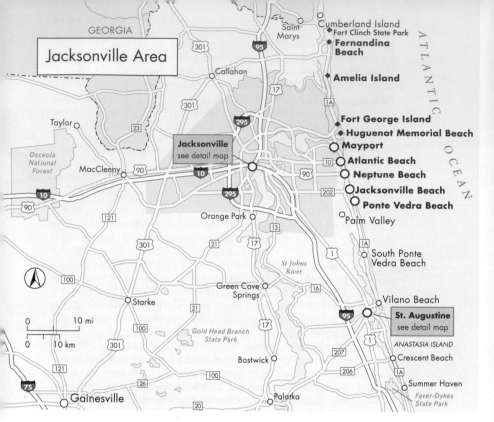

and local legislation. They are, from north to south, Atlantic Beach, Neptune Beach, Jacksonville Beach, and Ponte Vedra Beach. Technically, Ponte Vedra, which is home to the PGA Tour, crosses the border between Duval County and St. Johns County, but the four communities are all considered "Jacksonville's beaches." Farther north are two other popular coastal destinations, Mayport and Fort George Island. Some of the communities maintain height restrictions on beachfront buildings, adding to the old-fashioned beach vibe.

Oceanfront properties here can be worth millions, but a few blocks from the beach, things become more affordable. That means kids grow up and go to school together, and then stick around to live in and govern the towns together. Instead of pouring money into attractions designed to rake in tourism dollars, locals are likely to concentrate on subjects such as good schools and parks. Because of this, some visitors might find area beaches to be a little calmer and quieter than they expected.

But there's a real sense of community—and a laid-back pace. You might want to embrace it all. In fact, many vacationers like the easy pace so much that they decide to make the area their permanent home.

ATLANTIC BEACH

20 miles east of Jacksonville, on U.S. 90 (Beach Blvd.).

Beautiful sand and plentiful activities keep tourists coming back to this relatively tranquil, mostly residential, beach community. You can even rejuvenate with some prime pampering at the One Ocean resort's spa. Hotel guests and those wandering in from the beach can both use this luxurious oceanfront hotel's beach rental services, which offer umbrellas, lounge chairs, boogie boards, kayaks, and surfboards for a fee.

13

BEACHES

Atlantic Beach. If you're looking for sun-soaked relaxation, head for Atlantic Beach, where you can sink your feet into its white, sugary sands or catch some waves in the warm surf. Beachgoers with canine companions are welcome at Atlantic Beach during the day and evening as long as the dog is leashed. Atlantic Beach and next-door Neptune Beach share the trendy Town Center, which has lots of tempting dining and shopping within a block of the beach. **Amenities:** food and drink; lifeguards (seasonal); showers; water sports. **Best for:** sunrise; surfing; swimming; walking. ⊠ *Beach Ave., between 18th and 20th Sts.; Dewees Ave., between 1st and 16th Sts.; Ahern St. at Atlantic Blvd.* ☎ *904/247–5828* ⊕ *www.coab.us.*

WHERE TO EAT

$
ITALIAN

✕ Al's Pizza. The beach locations of this popular restaurant defy all expectations of a neighborhood pizza joint. The menu is fairly predictable; there's pizza by the slice and by the pie, plus standbys like lasagna and ravioli. **Known for:** pizza by the slice; beachy vibe; quick service. $ *Average main: $10* ⊠ *303 Atlantic Blvd.* ☎ *904/249–0002* ⊕ *www.alspizza.com.*

$$
SEAFOOD

✕ The Fish Company Restaurant and Oyster Bar. If you want fresh fish, this is the place, and the owners, Bill and Ann Pinner, have lots of local street cred. And there are plenty of offerings for meat lovers in the family, too. **Known for:** oyster happy hour on Tuesday and Wednesday; fresh, local seafood; shrimp and grits. $ *Average main: $20* ⊠ *725-12 Atlantic Blvd.* ☎ *904/246–0123* ⊕ *www.thefishcojax.com.*

$$$
ECLECTIC
Fodor'sChoice
★

✕ Ocean 60. Only a block from the Atlantic Ocean, this lively restaurant, wine bar, and martini room mixes fine dining and a laid-back, beachy atmosphere. The eclectic seasonal menu (which changes according to the fish available from the nearby Mayport docks) is quite sophisticated, including whole fried fish, pan-seared wild salmon, and locally caught shrimp. **Known for:** local, fresh-caught seafood; popular happy hour; live music on weekends. $ *Average main: $22* ⊠ *60 Ocean Blvd.* ☎ *904/247–0060* ⊕ *www.ocean60.com* ⊗ *Closed Sun. No lunch.*

$$
CAJUN

✕ Ragtime Tavern Seafood & Grill. A New Orleans theme prevails at this lively venue, a longtime favorite with locals and visitors alike. The crowd ranges in age from 21 to midlife-crisis, and they come both to sample the craft beer and eat the seafood-based fare. **Known for:** shrimp po'boys; large craft beer selection; popular Sunday brunch. $ *Average main: $20* ⊠ *207 Atlantic Blvd.* ☎ *904/241–7877* ⊕ *www. ragtimetavern.com.*

Beaches make great places to drop a line and see if the fish are biting.

WHERE TO STAY

$ RESORT FAMILY [H] **One Ocean.** Atlantic Beach's only high-rise oceanfront hotel captures the serenity of the sea through a color palette of translucent green, sand, and sky blue, and reflective materials such as glass and marble. **Pros:** exceptional service; walking distance to restaurants, shops, and the beach; all rooms have ocean view; 24-hour room service. **Cons:** tiny bathrooms; no self-parking on property; steep resort fee and separate parking fee. [$] *Rooms from: $199* ✉ *1 Ocean Blvd.* ☎ *904/249–7402* 🌐 *www.oneoceanresort.com* 🛏 *190 rooms* 🍴 *No meals.*

NEPTUNE BEACH

1.7 miles south of Atlantic Beach.

One of the quieter and less crowded beach towns in the area is a great destination if you want to escape for the day from the more crowded sands to the north and south. Slider's Bar and Grill is a local favorite, or make a pit stop at the oldest bar at the beaches, Pete's Bar, just to say you were there.

BEACHES

Neptune Beach. Between Atlantic and Jacksonville beaches, this is a great family spot. It's an excellent destination for those wishing to combine a day at the beach with other activities. Because Neptune and Atlantic beaches share Atlantic Avenue's Town Center, with its assortment of restaurants, galleries, stores, and boutiques, beachgoers can escape the sun when they're ready for great food, shopping, and live entertainment. **Amenities:** food and drink; lifeguards (seasonal); showers. **Best**

for: sunrise; swimming; walking. ✉ *Strand St., between Atlantic Blvd. and Gaillardia Pl.; Oak St. at Rose Pl.; North St. at 20th Ave.* 🌐 *ci.neptune-beach.fl.us.*

WHERE TO EAT

$ AMERICAN FAMILY

🍴 **Ellen's Kitchen.** Ellen's kitchen has been an institution in the area for years, and probably will be for generations, despite several moves, the most recent of which was from Jacksonville Beach to Neptune Beach. It's still a great place to salve your hangover on a Sunday morning, but it also welcomes families thanks to the kid-friendly menu, very reasonable prices, and relaxed atmosphere. **Known for:** early-bird specials; friendly staff; grilled biscuits. [$] *Average main: $9* ✉ *241 3rd St.* ☎ *904/372–4099* 🕒 *No dinner.*

WHERE TO STAY

$ HOTEL FAMILY Fodor'sChoice ★

🏨 **Sea Horse Oceanfront Inn.** This bright-pink-and-aqua 1950s-era throwback caters to budget-minded guests seeking an ultracasual, laid-back oceanfront experience. **Pros:** beach access with private walk-over; popular bar on-site; free breakfast baskets at the front desk. **Cons:** no-frills decor; no room service; no elevator. [$] *Rooms from: $139* ✉ *120 Atlantic Blvd.* ☎ *904/246–2175, 800/881–2330* 🌐 *www.seahorseoceanfrontinn.com* 🛏 *38 rooms* 🍽 *Breakfast.*

NIGHTLIFE

Pete's Bar. The oldest bar in the Jacksonville area is also notable for the cheapest drinks, cheapest pool tables, and most colorful clientele. It's also one of the only bars in the country where you can still smoke, so be warned. Serving locals and tourists for more than seven decades, Pete's has been written about by authors like John Grisham and James W. Hall, probably because it's across from The BookMark, a great independent bookstore where writers love to give readings. ✉ *117 1st St.* ☎ *904/249–9158.*

SHOPPING

BookMark. It may be small in size, but this book shop is big in prestige. Thanks to its knowledgeable owners, many famous authors love this place and always include it on their publicity tours. Once you've bought books here a time or two, the staff will be able to recommend ones you'll like with amazing accuracy. ✉ *220 1st St.* ☎ *904/241–9026* 🌐 *www.bookmarkbeach.com.*

JACKSONVILLE BEACH

2.2 miles south of Neptune Beach.

This family-friendly beach community has blossomed in recent years and remains busy during the spring and summer. The municipal Seawalk Pavilion hosts outdoor movies, concerts, and festivals, and the 2-acre Oceanfront Park (1st Street South, between 5th Avenue South and 6th Avenue South) has a small playground, volleyball court, and picnic areas. The popular fishing pier was seriously damaged in Hurricane Matthew in 2016, and is closed indefinitely. The historic Casa Marina Hotel, which opened its doors here in 1925, has a popular Sunday brunch.

EXPLORING

FAMILY **Adventure Landing and Shipwreck Island Water Park.** With go-karts, two miniature-golf courses, laser tag, batting cages, kiddie rides, and an arcade, Adventure Landing is more like an old-time boardwalk than a high-tech amusement park. But when the closest theme park is more than two hours away, you make do. The largest indoor/outdoor family-entertainment center in northeast Florida also encompasses Shipwreck Island Water Park, which features a lazy river for tubing, a 500,000-gallon wave pool, and four extreme slides—the Rage, HydroHalfpipe, Eye of the Storm, and Undertow. ✉ *1944 Beach Blvd.* ☎ *904/246–4386* 🌐 *www.adventurelanding.com* 🎟 *Adventure Landing free (fees for rides and games), Shipwreck Island $27.99.*

Beaches Museum & History Park. This charming museum has exhibitions on the history of the beaches communities, the St. Johns River, the fishing and shrimping industry, and the area's early settlers. Its gift shop is a good place to find Florida souvenirs of every variety, from tasteful histories of the local area to pure kitsch. Admission includes a guided tour of the adjacent Historical Park with its 1911 steam locomotive, railroad foreman's house, and the Mayport Depot. ✉ *381 Beach Blvd.* ☎ *904/241–5657* 🌐 *www.beachesmuseum.org* 🎟 *Free (donations accepted)* 🕒 *Closed Mon.*

BEACHES

Jacksonville Beach. Enjoy the waves at one of Jacksonville's busier beaches, which stretches along the coast for 4.1 miles. A boardwalk and a bevy of beachfront restaurants and shops are also draws, so expect moderate crowds during spring and summer school breaks. **Amenities:** food and drink; lifeguards (seasonal); parking (no fee); showers; toilets. **Best for:** partiers; sunrise; surfing; swimming. ✉ *1st St., between Seagate and S. 16th Aves.* ☎ *904/247–6100* 🌐 *www.jacksonvillebeach.org.*

WHERE TO EAT

$ AMERICAN 🍴 **European Street Café.** This colorful, quirky, beer-hall inspired, family-owned eatery is part of a local chain and has a menu with an ambitious list of sandwiches, salads, and soups. There's also an overflowing gourmet-food section; a mind-boggling beer list; cookies big enough to knock someone unconscious; and a range of other generous desserts. **Known for:** generous sandwiches; extensive beer list; giant cookies. [$] *Average main: $9* ✉ *992 Beach Blvd.* ☎ *904/249–3001* 🌐 *www.europeanstreet.com.*

$ BARBECUE 🍴 **Mojo Kitchen BBQ Pit & Blues Bar.** True barbecue aficionados know that the country's really divided into four territories: North Carolina, Memphis, Kansas City, and Texas, each renowned for its own barbecue style. Owner Todd Lineberry did some serious research into each region before deciding his restaurants would honor all four traditions—along with some original flavor. **Known for:** The Whole Hawg sampler with a bit of everything; house-made sides; burnt ends. [$] *Average main: $14* ✉ *1500 Beach Blvd.* ☎ *904/247–6636* 🌐 *www.mojobbq.com.*

WHERE TO STAY

$ HOTEL **Casa Marina Hotel.** Compared with nearby oceanfront inns, it's small, but Casa Marina's creature comforts and rich history—it opened in 1925 and hosted Franklin Delano Roosevelt and Al Capone in its early days—make it a hit with those looking for a characterful retreat. **Pros:** oceanfront location; comfortable beds; Continental breakfast. **Cons:** no pool; noise from lounge. [$] *Rooms from: $159* ✉ *691 1st St. N* ☎ *904/270–0025* 🌐 *www.casamarina-hotel.com* 🛏 *23 rooms* 🍴 *Breakfast.*

NIGHTLIFE

Lynch's Irish Pub. Hoist a pint o' Guinness and enjoy live local music. This popular Irish eatery also offers traditional fare, along with pub grub. ✉ *514 N. 1st St.* ☎ *904/249–5181* 🌐 *www.lynchsirishpub.com.*

Penthouse Lounge. This oceanfront spot, perched atop the historic Casa Marina Hotel, offers beautiful views of the night sky or the moonrise over the ocean in addition to a wide range of martinis and other cocktails. A full dinner is offered until 10 pm. ✉ *Casa Marina Hotel, 691 N. 1st St.* ☎ *904/270–0025* 🌐 *www.casamarinahotel.com.*

SPORTS AND THE OUTDOORS

BIKING

Champion Cycling. You can rent beach cruisers by the hour or the day—or get your high-end racing bike repaired—at this full-service bike shop. ✉ *1303 N. 3rd St.* ☎ *904/241–0900* 🌐 *www.championcycling.net* 🎟 *From $10.*

PONTE VEDRA BEACH

3.9 miles south of Jacksonville Beach.

Although this upscale coastal community 18 miles southeast of downtown Jacksonville is primarily known for its golf courses and swanky homes, it also has beautiful beaches as well as a number of resorts: the Ponte Vedra Inn & Club, The Lodge & Club, and the Sawgrass Marriott.

BEACHES

Ponte Vedra Beach. Public beach access for nonresort guests is minimal in most areas because of heavily restricted parking. However, thanks to its free public parking, Mickler's Landing, south of most residences, is the most popular beach access point. It's also famous as a great place to find fossilized sharks' teeth. **Amenities:** lifeguards (seasonal); parking (no fee); showers; toilets. **Best for:** solitude; sunrise; walking. ✉ *East of intersection of A1A S and Ponte Vedra Blvd.*

WHERE TO EAT

$$$ ECLECTIC 🍴 **Aqua Grill.** Come hungry. That might be the best advice for visitors to this Sawgrass Village restaurant, whose menu covers all the bases—steaks, pasta, pork chops, burgers, and lobster. **Known for:** local snapper and Mayport shrimp; lively bar scene that draws locals; lakefront dining. [$] *Average main: $25* ✉ *950 Sawgrass Village* ☎ *904/285–3017* 🌐 *www.aquagrill.net.*

WHERE TO STAY

$$$ RESORT FAMILY Fodor's Choice ★ **The Lodge & Club.** This Mediterranean-revival oceanfront resort is luxury lodging at its best, having been renovated in 2015. **Pros:** access to facilities at Ponte Vedra Inn & Club; accommodating service; private beach. **Cons:** most recreation facilities off-site; auto gratuity charge added to bill nightly; remote location. [$] *Rooms from: $319* ✉ *607 Ponte Vedra Blvd.* ☎ *904/273–9500, 866/330–9775* 🌐 *www.pontevedra.com* 🛏 *66 rooms* 🍴 *No meals.*

$$ RESORT FAMILY Fodor's Choice ★ **Ponte Vedra Inn & Club.** Considered northeast Florida's premier resort for decades, this award-winning 1928 landmark continues to wow guests with its stellar service and large guest rooms housed in white-brick, red-tile-roof buildings lining the beach. **Pros:** accommodating, friendly staff; private beach; adults-only pool. **Cons:** charge for umbrellas and chaises on the beach; crowded pools at some times of year; remote location. [$] *Rooms from: $289* ✉ *200 Ponte Vedra Blvd.* ☎ *904/285–1111, 800/234–7842* 🌐 *www.pontevedra.com* 🛏 *250 rooms, 33 suites* 🍴 *No meals.*

$$ RESORT FAMILY **Sawgrass Marriott Golf Resort & Spa.** Golf is at the heart of this luxurious resort, which underwent an extensive renovation in 2015, but there's no lack of opportunity for other recreation or for sheer indulgent relaxation, if that's what you're after. **Pros:** beautiful surroundings; readily available shuttle; efficient staff. **Cons:** beach requires a shuttle; steep resort fee covers Wi-Fi and parking; some rooms are noisy. [$] *Rooms from: $229* ✉ *1000 PGA Tour Blvd.* ☎ *904/285–7777, 800/457–4653* 🌐 *www.sawgrassmarriott.com* 🛏 *510 rooms* 🍴 *No meals.*

SPORTS AND THE OUTDOORS

BIKING

Ponte Vedra Bicycles. This outfitter includes free bike maps with your rental. ✉ *250 Solana Rd.* ☎ *904/273–0199.*

GOLF

Every May millions of golf fans watch golf's most elite competitors vie for the prestige of winning THE PLAYERS Championship. The event—considered by many to be the sport's "unofficial fifth major"—takes place each year at the Tournament Players Club (TPC) Sawgrass in Ponte Vedra Beach, 20 miles southeast of Jacksonville. Designed and built for major tournament golf, TPC has elevated seating areas that give more than 40,000 fans a great view of the action. And while you're in the area, be sure to visit the World Golf Hall of Fame a few miles down the road in St. Augustine.

Tournament Players Club Sawgrass. There are two golf courses here: the Stadium Course (with its world-renowned Island Green), which hosts The Players Championship each year, and the Pete Dye–designed Valley Course. In conjunction with the Sawgrass Marriott, TPC offers a wide variety of golf experiences. The Stadium Course underwent an extensive renovation in 2016, including resurfaced greens and some restructured holes. Though not as lauded as the Stadium Course, the Valley Course has hosted its share of major golf events, such as the Senior Players Championship and the NFL Golf Classic. Though challenging, it has wider fairways and more expansive greens than the Stadium Course, which was designed to test the world's best players. ⊠ *110 Championship Way* ☎ *904/273–3235, 800/457–4653* ⊕ *www.tpc.com/sawgrass* ▨ *Stadium Course $400; Dye's Valley Course $195* ⚑*. Stadium Course: 18 holes, 7215 yards, par 72; Dye's Valley Course: 18 holes, 6864 yards, par 72.*

MAYPORT

20 miles northeast of downtown Jacksonville, on Rte. A1A/105.

Dating back more than 300 years, this fishing village has several excellent and very casual seafood restaurants and markets, and a commercial shrimping fleet. It's also home to one of the largest naval facilities in the country, Naval Station Mayport.

GETTING HERE AND AROUND

St. Johns River Ferry. The arrival of the *Jean Ribault* ferry in 1948 made everyday life here more convenient, as it connects the north and south ends of Florida State Road A1A, allowing easy access to and from the islands to the north of Jacksonville. Since then, the ferry, known locally as the Mayport Ferry, continues to delight passengers young and old as they embark on the 10-minute cruise across the river between Mayport and Fort George Island. The cost is $5 per motorcycle, $6 per car. Pedestrians enjoy the ride for just $1 each way. Check the Web or call for departure times. ⊠ *Ferry Landing, Hwy. A1A* ☎ *904/241–9969* ⊕ *stjohnsriverferry.com.*

EXPLORING

Fodor'sChoice **Kathryn Abbey Hanna Park.** This 450-acre oceanfront city park and camp-
★ ground just north of Atlantic Beach is beloved by surfers, swimmers, campers, hikers, and especially bikers, who regularly hit the many off-road bike trails from novice right up to those named Grunt and Misery. You can rent canoes, kayaks, or paddleboats to go out on the 60-acre freshwater lake. Younger kids delight in the lakefront playground and a water park with fountains and squirting hoses. There are restrooms, picnic areas, and grills throughout, and from Memorial Day to Labor Day lifeguards supervise all water activities. ⊠ *500 Wonderwood Dr.* ☎ *904/249–4700* ▨ *$5 per vehicle (cash only).*

FORT GEORGE ISLAND

25 miles northeast of Jacksonville, on Rte. A1A/105.

One of the oldest inhabited areas of Florida, Fort George Island is lush with foliage, natural vegetation, and wildlife. A 4-mile nature and bike trail meanders across the island, revealing shell mounds dating as far back as 5,000 years.

EXPLORING

Kingsley Plantation. Built in 1792 by Zephaniah Kingsley, a landowner who produced Sea Island cotton, citrus, sugarcane, and corn with the aid of about 60 slaves, this is the oldest remaining cotton plantation in the state. The ruins of 23 tabby (a concretelike mixture of sand and crushed shells) slave houses, a barn, and the modest Kingsley home are open to the public via self-guided tours and reachable by bridge. ⊠ *11676 Palmetto Ave.* ☎ *904/251–3537* ⊕ *www.nps.gov/timu* ▨ *Free* ☺ *Plantation house closed weekdays.*

Talbot Island State Parks. These parks, including Big and Little Talbot islands, have 17 miles of gorgeous beaches, sand dunes, and golden marshes that hum with birds and native waterfowl. Come to picnic, fish, swim, snorkel, or camp. Little Talbot Island, one of the few undeveloped barrier islands in Florida, has river otters, marsh rabbits, raccoons, alligators, and gopher tortoises. Canoe and kayak rentals are available, and the north area is considered the best surfing spot in northeast Florida. A 4-mile nature trail winds across Little Talbot, and there are several smaller trails on Big Talbot. ⊠ *12157 Heckscher Dr.* ☎ *904/251-2320* ⊕ *www.floridastateparks.org/ park/big-talbot-island* ⊠ *$5 per vehicle, up to 8 people; $4 single occupant.*

BEACHES

Huguenot Memorial Park. Though it's officially a Jacksonville city park, this popular spot on the northern side of the St. Johns River is often grouped with Amelia's beaches. The park was closed after Hurricane Matthew caused severe damage in 2016, and officials have not announced an exact date for reopening. Call before you go to ensure access. Among a handful of places where driving on the beach is permitted, it's unusual in that no special permit is required. Families with lots of beach equipment like the option of parking close to the water, but it takes vigilance to avoid soft sand and incoming tides. The ocean side offers good surfing, boogie boarding, and surf fishing. On the western side is a shallow, sheltered lagoon that's a favorite with windsurfers, paddleboarders, and parents of small children. The eastern side offers views of the aircraft carriers and destroyers at Mayport Naval Station. The park is also an important stop for migrating birds, so at certain times of the year, some areas are closed to vehicles. **Amenities:** lifeguards (seasonal); parking (no fee); showers; toilets. **Best for:** surfing; swimming; windsurfing. ⊠ *10980 Heckscher Dr.* ☎ *904/251–3335* ⊠ *$3 per person 8–10 am, $4 per car after 10.*

AMELIA ISLAND AND FERNANDINA BEACH

Updated
by Jennifer
Greenhill-Taylor

35 miles northeast of Jacksonville.

At the northeasternmost reach of Florida, Amelia Island has beautiful beaches with enormous sand dunes along its eastern flank, a state park with a Civil War fort, sophisticated restaurants, interesting shops, and accommodations that range from bed-and-breakfasts to luxury resorts. The town of Fernandina Beach is on the island's northern end; a century ago casinos and brothels thrived here, but those are gone. Today there's little reminder of the town's wild days, though one event comes close: the Isle of Eight Flags Shrimp Festival, held during the first weekend of May.

TOURS

Amelia River Cruises and Charters. Narrated tours in shaded pontoon boats that glide near the area's marshes, rivers, and wilderness beaches, from American Beach and Fernandina on Amelia Island, to Cumberland Island in Georgia. ⊠ *1 N. Front St., Fernandina Beach* ☎ *904/261–9972, 877/264–9972* ⊕ *www.ameliarivercruises.com* ⊠ *From $22.*

VISITOR INFORMATION

Contact Amelia Island Convention and Visitors Bureau. ☎ *904/277–0717* ⊕ *www.ameliaisland.com.*

EXPLORING

Fernandina Historic District. This district in Fernandina Beach, which is home to Florida's oldest existing lighthouse, oldest bar, and oldest hotel, has more than 50 blocks of buildings listed on the National Register of Historic Places; 450 ornate structures built before 1927 offer some of the nation's finest examples of Queen Anne, Victorian, and Italianate homes. Many date from the haven's mid-19th-century glory days. Pick up a self-guided-tour map at the chamber of commerce, in the old train depot—once a stopping point on the first cross-state railroad—and take your time exploring the quaint shops, restaurants, and boutiques that populate the district, especially along Centre Street. ⊠ *Fernandina Beach.*

13

FAMILY
Fodor's Choice
★

Fort Clinch State Park. One of the country's best-preserved and most complete 19th-century brick forts, Ft. Clinch was built to discourage further British intrusion after the War of 1812 and was occupied in 1863 by the Confederacy; a year later it was retaken by the Union. During the Spanish-American War it was reactivated for a brief time, but no battles were ever fought on its grounds (which explains why it's so well preserved). Wander through restored buildings, including furnished barracks, a kitchen, and a repair shop. Living-history reenactments of Civil War garrison life are scheduled throughout the year. The 1,086-acre park surrounding the fort has full-facility camping, nature trails, carriage rides, a swimming beach, and surf and pier fishing. Nature buffs enjoy the variety of flora and fauna, especially since Fort Clinch is the only state park in northeast Florida designated by the Florida Fish and Wildlife Conservation Commission as a viewing destination for the eastern brown pelican, green sea turtle, and loggerhead sea turtle. ⊠ *2601 Atlantic Ave., Fernandina Beach* ☎ *904/277-7274* ⊕ *www. floridastateparks.org/fortclinch* ⊠ *$6 per vehicle, up to 8 people; $4 motorcycles; $2 per person entry to fort.*

BEACHES

There are a number of places on Amelia Island where driving on the beach is allowed in designated areas, including Seaside Park, Peters Point, Burney Park, and Amelia Island State Park. If you have a four-wheel-drive vehicle (and a lot of beach equipment to haul), you may want to try this. Be warned, though: it's easier to get stuck than you might think, and towing is expensive. You also need to watch the tides carefully if you don't want your car floating out to sea. And unless you're a county resident or disabled, you must buy a permit, which is available at the **Nassau County Historic Courthouse** (☎ *416 Centre St., Fernandina Beach* ☎ *904/491-6430*), **Flash Foods** (☎ *5518 S. Fletcher Ave., Fernandina Beach* ☎ *904/261-3113*), and several other locations. All city beaches have free admission.

Main Beach Park. Of all Fernandina Beach beach access points, this is likely to be the most crowded—but also the most fun for kids and teens. Not only are there sand volleyball courts, a beachfront playground, picnic tables, and a multipurpose court at the park itself, but there's old-school fun to be had at the adjacent skate park and vintage

WORD OF MOUTH

"On this particular day, the beach was strewn with starfish. They were everywhere. And they were still alive. I took a quick picture and then proceeded to run up and down the beach trying to save every one of them. I hope that I succeeded." —photo by funin-thetub, Fodors.com member

13

miniature-golf course, whose concession stand sells cold drinks, ice cream, and snow cones. A casual restaurant and bar are right on the beach. **Amenities:** food and drink; lifeguards (seasonal); parking (no fee); showers; toilets. **Best for:** swimming. ⊠ *32 N. Fletcher Ave., Fernandina Beach.*

Peters Point Beach. At the south end of the island, this beach allows you free access to the same gorgeous sands used by vacationers at the Ritz-Carlton. It has a large parking area, a picnic area, barbecue grills, and three lifeguard towers. **Amenities:** lifeguards (seasonal); parking (no fee); showers; toilets. **Best for:** sunrise; surfing; swimming; walking. ⊠ *1974 S. Fletcher Ave., Fernandina Beach.*

> **A BANNER BEACH**
>
> Fernandina Beach is also known as the "Isle of Eight Flags," derived from the fact that it's the only American site to have been under eight different flags (French, Spanish, British, Patriots, Green Cross of Florida, Mexican Revolutionary, National Flag of the Confederacy, and United States). Every May the Isle of Eight Flags Shrimp Festival celebrates another of Fernandina's claims to fame: birthplace of the modern shrimping industry.

Seaside Park Beach. Like Main Beach to the north and Peters Point to the south, Seaside Park allows limited beach driving if you have a permit, but beware—vehicles here frequently get stuck and have to be towed. There are several pavilions with picnic tables and dune walkovers to the beach. It's a great place to fish or to ride bikes at low tide. Bikes and other beach equipment can be rented at Beach Rentals and More, right across from the park (*2021 S. Fletcher Ave.*). Also nearby, Sliders Seaside Grill is a venerable oceanfront restaurant where you can enjoy food and drinks inside or at the tiki bar overlooking the beach, often with live music. **Amenities:** food and drink; lifeguards (seasonal); parking (no fee); showers; toilets. **Best for:** surfing; swimming; walking. ⊠ *Sadler Rd. at S. Fletcher Ave., Fernandina Beach* ⊕ *www.fbfl.us.*

Fodor'sChoice
★ **Talbot Islands State Parks Beaches.** A few miles south of Fernandina Beach, the Talbot Islands State Parks system consists of seven parks, three of which have beach settings. All of the oceanfront parks have picnic areas and a small admission charge but free parking. **Little Talbot** is popular for swimming and beachcombing. Sand dollars are often found at the far north end. **Big Talbot,** with its Boneyard Beach of wind-twisted trees, is not recommended for swimming but is a photographer's paradise. **Amelia Island State Park** is best known for letting you horseback ride on the beach as well as for the adjacent George Crady fishing pier. Kayak and canoe tours can be booked through the parks system's vendor, Kayak Amelia. **Amenities:** lifeguards (seasonal); parking (no fee); showers; toilets. **Best for:** solitude; sunrise; swimming; walking. ⊠ *Rte. A1A, south of Fernandina Beach, Fernandina Beach* ⊕ *www.floridastateparks.org* ▨ *Little Talbot, $5 per vehicle; Big Talbot, $3 per vehicle for The Bluffs picnic area; Amelia Island, $2 per person.*

WHERE TO EAT

$$ BARBECUE 🍴 **Gilbert's Underground Kitchen.** Celebrity Chef Kenny Gilbert opened this eclectic Fernandina Beach eatery after a stint on "Top Chef" brought him national fame. The menu is laden with authentic Old South recipes prepared with skill and flair and often with an individual twist. **Known for:** a wide variety of smoked meats; gator ribs; Brunswick stew. [$] *Average main: $16 ✉ 510 S. 8th St., Fernandina Beach ☎ 904/310–6374 🌐 www.undergroundkitchen.co ⏲ Closed Sun.*

$$$$ ECLECTIC Fodor's Choice ★ 🍴 **Salt.** The Ritz-Carlton's oceanfront restaurant serves inventive cuisine that utilizes seasonal ingredients. The signature dish is beef tenderloin served on a block of Himalayan salt. **Known for:** elegant oceanfront dining; beautifully prepared food; cooking classes. [$] *Average main: $56 ✉ The Ritz-Carlton, Amelia Island, 4750 Amelia Island Pkwy., Amelia Island ☎ 904/277–1000 🌐 www.ritzcarlton.com.*

$$ SEAFOOD FAMILY 🍴 **Sliders Seaside Grill.** After the condo-building boom of the last decade or so, not many oceanfront restaurants remain in the area, but thankfully this is one of them. Indeed there aren't many places where you can enjoy an ocean view like this—a surf break offshore makes it a good place to watch surfers do their thing. **Known for:** moderately priced and family-friendly; fresh Florida seafood; live music in the summer. [$] *Average main: $18 ✉ 1998 S. Fletcher Ave., Fernandina Beach ☎ 904/277–6652 🌐 www.slidersseaside.com.*

$$$$ SEAFOOD 🍴 **Verandah Restaurant.** Although it's at the Omni Amelia Island Plantation Resort, this family-friendly restaurant is open to nonresort guests, many of whom drive in from Jacksonville. The dining room has a casual vibe, with plush, roomy booths and tables overlooking the tennis courts, but the menu is all business, with a focus on Southern and local food. **Known for:** she-crab soup in season; Mayport shrimp and clams; excellent service. [$] *Average main: $39 ✉ Omni Amelia Island Plantation, 142 Raquet Park Dr., Amelia Island ☎ 904/277–5958 🌐 www.omnihotels.com ⏲ No lunch.*

WHERE TO STAY

$ HOTEL FAMILY 🏨 **Amelia Hotel at the Beach.** Across the street from the beach, this midsize inn is not only convenient but an economical and family-friendly alternative to the area's luxury resorts and romantic and kid-unfriendly B&Bs. **Pros:** complimentary breakfast; free Wi-Fi; walk to the beach. **Cons:** small pool; not all rooms have balconies; older motel. [$] *Rooms from: $139 ✉ 1997 S. Fletcher Ave., Fernandina Beach ☎ 904/206–5200, 877/263–5428 🌐 www.ameliahotel.com 🛏 86 rooms 🍽 Breakfast.*

$$ B&B/INN 🏨 **Elizabeth Pointe Lodge.** Guests at this beachfront inn, which resembles a Victorian-era beach cottage, can't say enough about the impeccable personal service, legendary breakfasts, and enjoyable evening social hour. **Pros:** hospitable staff; 24-hour desk attendant; free Wi-Fi. **Cons:** pricey for a B&B; not all rooms are oceanfront; must reserve well in advance in high season. [$] *Rooms from: $295 ✉ 98 S. Fletcher Ave., Fernandina Beach ☎ 904/277–4851, 800/772–3359 🌐 www.elizabethpointelodge.com 🛏 24 rooms, 1 cottage 🍽 Breakfast.*

$ B&B/INN **Florida House Inn.** This charming inn, which dates to the late 19th century, was once used by guests of the Vanderbilt, DuPont, and Carnegie families, whose "cottages" sat nearby on Cumberland and Jekyll islands. **Pros:** outstanding service; walk to restaurants and shops; free Wi-Fi. **Cons:** Mermaid Bar can be noisy; rooms are small; not on the beach and no pool. [$] *Rooms from: $172* ✉ *22 S. 3rd St., Fernandina Beach* ☎ *904/491–3322, 800/258–3301* 🌐 *www.floridahouseinn.com* 🛏 *16 rooms* 🍴 *Breakfast.*

$$$ RESORT FAMILY Fodor's Choice ★ **Omni Amelia Island Plantation Resort and the Villas of Amelia Island Plantation.** This huge resort (1,350 acres) was folded into the Omni hotel chain and transformed by an $85-million renovation and expansion in 2013, including 155 additional oceanfront rooms and stunning oceanfront Beach Club pools. **Pros:** all rooms oceanfront with private outdoor space; extensive kids' programs; largest poolscape in northern Florida. **Cons:** some facilities require a golf cart or shuttle ride; $25 a day resort fee for Wi-Fi, parking; remote from town. [$] *Rooms from: $349* ✉ *39 Beach Lagoon Rd., Amelia Island* ☎ *904/261–6161, 800/843–6664* 🌐 *www.omnihotels.com* 🛏 *404 rooms, more than 300 villas* 🍴 *No meals.*

$ HOTEL **Residence Inn Amelia Island.** Discerning, value-driven travelers love this newer all-suites property for its great location, modern design features, and family-friendly amenities. **Pros:** free Wi-Fi; bike rental on property; pet friendly (hefty fee, restrictions). **Cons:** no on-site restaurant or room service; historic district not within walking distance; not directly on the beach. [$] *Rooms from: $199* ✉ *2301 Sadler Rd., Fernandina Beach* ☎ *904/277–2440* 🌐 *www.residenceinnameliaisland.com* 🛏 *133 suites* 🍴 *Breakfast.*

$$$$ RESORT FAMILY Fodor's Choice ★ **The Ritz-Carlton, Amelia Island.** Guests know what to expect from the Ritz—elegance, superb comfort, excellent service—and the Amelia Island location is no exception. **Pros:** world-class spa; private beach access; great programs, activities, and amenities for kids, teens, and families. **Cons:** resort fee; no self-parking ($20 per day valet); a drive to sites and other restaurants. [$] *Rooms from: $519* ✉ *4750 Amelia Island Pkwy., Fernandina Beach* ☎ *904/277–1100* 🌐 *www.ritzcarlton.com/ameliaisland* 🛏 *496 rooms* 🍴 *No meals.*

SHOPPING

Within the Fernandina Beach Historic District, a 50-block area on the National Register of Historic Places, are numerous shops, art galleries, and boutiques, many clustered along Centre Street, including the Palace Saloon, the oldest continuously operating drinking establishment (since 1903) in the state. An entirely separate "Old Town," which had its 200th birthday in 2011, is considered the last town established under the 16th-century "Laws of the Indies" by the Spanish in the Americas. Old Town is located off North 14th Street.

Amelia SanJon Gallery. One of a cluster of "Ash and Third" galleries, the Amelia SanJon offers watercolors, acrylic paintings, fused-glass art, and custom jewelry. ✉ *218-A Ash St., Fernandina Beach* ☎ *904/491–8040* 🌐 *www.ameliasanjongallery.com.*

Book Loft. Popular for its readings and book signings, this old-fashioned bookstore fits perfectly in an old-fashioned town. In keeping with Fernandina's emphasis on its pirate heritage, the store includes kid-friendly pirate volumes like *The Pirate of Kindergarten* and *Do Pirates Change Diapers?* ⊠ *214 Centre St., Fernandina Beach* ☎ *904/261–8991.*

Celtic Charm. In addition to the obvious coffee cup with shamrocks and Irish-blessing plaque, this shop carries wonderful clothing—such as colorful and artistic Bill Baber Scottish sweaters—as well as Galway Irish crystal and Donegal Town Hana Hats. ⊠ *310 Centre St., Fernandina Beach* ☎ *904/277–8009* ⊕ *www.ameliaisland.com/shopping/celtic-charm.*

Fantastic Fudge. Right there in the window, resting in splendor on several marble-topped tables, are huge blocks of fudge just calling your name—enough fudge to put every citizen of the town into a coma—not to mention ice cream (with house-made waffle cones), hand-dipped chocolates, caramel corn, and so on. Indeed, if you hang out at one of the tables in front of this confectionery/ice cream shop, you'll see just about every kind of person imaginable pause by the door, sigh, and give in to temptation. The service is fast and friendly, and the ice cream is excellent, too. ⊠ *218 Centre St., Fernandina Beach* ☎ *904/277–4801* ⊕ *www.fantasticfudge.com.*

Gallery C. Up a wildly painted staircase, this gallery owned by artist Carol Winner (the "C" in the gallery's name) displays and sells one-of-a-kind semiprecious jewelry and mixed-media creations, as well as paintings of local nature scenes. ⊠ *218-B Ash St., Fernandina Beach* ☎ *904/583–4676* ⊕ *www.carolwinnerart.com.*

Lindy's Jewelry. For tasteful jewelry that reflects beach life, Lindy's is a good place to shop. Those who wish to commemorate their vacations in jewelry may be charmed by the Fernandina Beach and Cumberland Island map charms or fossilized shark teeth set into earrings and necklaces. ⊠ *110 Centre St., Fernandina Beach* ☎ *904/277–4880* ⊕ *www.lindysjewelry.com.*

Sea Jade. Inside, it's funny T-shirts and cheap souvenirs; outside, it's fishnet floats and seashells in all their natural beauty, heaped up in old-fashioned wooden baskets. Whether you want to buy sand dollars or saltwater taffy, if it's beach related, there's a good chance you'll find it here. ⊠ *208 Centre St., Fernandina Beach* ☎ *904/277–2977.*

Slightly Off Centre Gallery & Gifts. Just a block off the main drag, this store sells artistic ceramics as well as vivid photographs, paintings, pottery, and metalwork. It's closed on Tuesday. ⊠ *218-C Ash St., Fernandina Beach* ☎ *904/277–1147.*

SPORTS AND THE OUTDOORS

HORSEBACK RIDING

Kelly Seahorse Ranch. At this concession within the Amelia Island State Park, you can arrange horseback rides on the beach. It's closed on Monday. ⊠ *Amelia Island State Park, 9500 1st Coast Hwy., Amelia Island* ☎ *904/491–5166* ⊕ *www.kellyranchinc.net* 🖙 *$75 per person per hour for horse rental.*

KAYAKING

Kayak Amelia. This outfitter takes adventurous types on guided kayak tours of salt marshes and the Fort George River and also rents equipment for those looking to create their own adventures, whether on land or water. Reservations are required. There is also a Kayak Amelia shop on Centre Street, across from the Palace Saloon, in downtown Fernandina, but to rent a kayak or Segway, you must contact the Talbot Island location. ⊠ *13030 Heckscher Dr., Jacksonville* ☎ *904/251–0016* ⊕ *www.kayakamelia.com.*

13

ST. AUGUSTINE

Updated by
Steve Master

35 miles south of Jacksonville, on U.S. 1.

Along the banks of the shining Matanzas River lies St. Augustine, the nation's oldest city. It shows its age with charm, its history revealed in the narrow cobblestone streets, the horse-drawn carriages festooned with flowers, and the coquina bastions of the Spanish fort that guard the bay like sentinels. Founded in 1565 by Spanish explorers, St. Augustine is the site of the fabled Fountain of Youth, but travelers find additional treasures in the Historic District, which was built in the Spanish Renaissance Revival style. Terra-cotta roofs and narrow balconies overhang a wonderful hodgepodge of shops and eateries that can be happily explored for weeks.

St. Augustine also has miles of beaches on Anastasia Island to the east. From the idyllic, unspoiled beaches of Anastasia State Park to the more boisterous St. Augustine Beach, travelers have a full range of options when it comes to enjoying an ocean outing.

VISITOR INFORMATION

Centrally located between the south and north ends of St. Augustine's Historic District, the St. Augustine & St. Johns County Visitor Information Center is a smart place to start your day. You can park in the multistoried garage here ($1.25 per hour, $7.50 per day), as well as pick up maps, get information on and advice about attractions and restaurants, and hop aboard the sightseeing trolley.

Contacts St. Augustine, Ponte Vedra & the Beaches Visitors and Convention Bureau. ☎ *904/829–1711, 800/418–7529* ⊕ *www.floridashistoriccoast. com.* **St. Augustine & St. Johns County Visitor Information Center.** ⊠ *10 W. Castillo Dr.* ☎ *904/825–1000.*

TOURS

Old Town Trolley Tour. These fully narrated tours cover more than 100 points of interest and are, perhaps, the best way to take in the Historic District. Your pass is good for three days and, with parking at a premium and meters closely watched, it's nice to be able to park at one of the main stations (free) and get on and off at any of 23 stops throughout town. There are even shuttles to the beach. In the evening a macabre slant is added on the Ghosts and Graveyards Tour, which includes visits to the Old Jail and Lighthouse. ⊠ *167 San Marco Ave.* ☎ *904/829–3800, 888/910–8687* ⊕ *www.trolleytours.com/staugustine* 🚋 *From $25.*

Built to protect Spain's St. Augustine, the Castillo de San Marcos still stands along the shore.

EXPLORING

St. Augustine's neighborhoods are fairly compact. Most include a stretch of waterfront—whether ocean, river, or creek—which, along with Mediterranean architectural details like curves, archways, and red-tile roofs, gives the city its relaxed semitropical aura. Neighborhoods range from centuries old to mere decades, but all have sights worthy of attention.

It can be confusing to see references to the "Old City," "Old Town," and "Historic District." The Old City, like the Big Apple, refers not to a neighborhood but to the entire city of St. Augustine. Old Town is a small neighborhood, with the Plaza de la Constitución at its northern border, a row of shops and restaurants along King Street, many award-winning B&Bs, and the Oldest House museum toward the south. Old Town is actually within a larger neighborhood, the Historic District, a 144-block area filled with many of the city's most popular attractions, including museums, parks, restaurants, nightspots, shops, and historic buildings.

St. Augustine's Uptown is filled with the shops, restaurants, and galleries along San Marco Boulevard, as well as museums, parks, and historic structures, all of which attract crowds. The narrow streets and hustle and bustle make for a vibrant atmosphere.

Heading east across the Bridge of Lions, you enter Anastasia Island, much of which is within city limits. In the 1920s, real estate developer D. P. Davis had big plans for a Mediterranean-style development here, but the Florida land boom went bust. Today Davis Shores has a mélange of styles and a casual beach vibe.

TOP ATTRACTIONS

FAMILY
Fodor's Choice
★

Castillo de San Marcos National Monument. The focal point of St. Augustine, this massive and commanding structure was completed by the Spaniards in 1695 (English pirates were handy with a torch back then), and it looks every day of its three centuries. The fort was constructed of coquina, a soft limestone made of broken shells and coral that, unexpectedly, could absorb the impact of British cannonballs. (Unlike solid stone, the softer coquina wouldn't shatter when hit by large munitions.) The fort was also used as a prison during the Revolutionary and Civil wars.

Park rangers provide an introductory narration, after which you're on your own to explore the moat, turrets, and 16-foot-thick walls. Garrison rooms depict the life of the era, and special cannon-firing demonstrations are held several times a day Friday through Sunday year-round. Children 15 and under are admitted free and must be accompanied by an adult. Save the receipt, since admission is valid for seven days. ⊠ *1 S. Castillo Dr.* ☎ *904/829–6506* ⊕ *www.nps.gov/casa* ⊠ *$10.*

Cathedral Basilica of St. Augustine. This cathedral has the country's oldest written parish records, dating from 1594. The circa-1797 structure underwent changes after a fire in 1887 as well as restoration work in the mid-1960s. If you're around for the holidays, stop in for Christmas Eve's gorgeous midnight mass, conducted amid banks of flickering candles that reflect off gilded walls. Regular Sunday masses are held throughout the year at 7, 9, 11, and 5. ⊠ *38 Cathedral Pl.* ☎ *904/824– 2806* ⊕ *www.thefirstparish.org* ⊠ *Donations welcome.*

FAMILY
Colonial Quarter. This 2-acre living-history museum gives visitors a vivid sense of life in 16th-, 17th-, and 18th-century St. Augustine. The De Mesa–Sanchez House dates from the 1740s and the other buildings—including a soldier's home, print shop, blacksmith's shop, and gunsmith—are replicas, mostly built on the original foundations. Costumed reenactors help make the history come alive. New additions to the complex include a 35-foot watchtower from which you have a panoramic view of the city. You can also dig for replica artifacts, create a leather medallion, take part in a musket drill, watch a 16th-century ship being built, and more. Tours start 10:30, noon, 1:30, and 3. The complex also includes two restaurants: the Taberna del Caballo and the Bull and Crown Publick House. ⊠ *33 St. George St.* ☎ *904/342–2857* ⊕ *colonialquarter.com* ⊠ *$12.99.*

NEED A
BREAK

St. George Tavern. Although they serve food (sandwiches, mostly), the appeal of this joint is that, in a city of historic re-creations, this is the real deal: a noisy, packed, active bar where smokers smoke, drinkers drink, locals gather, and strangers blend right in. ⊠ *116-A St. George St.* ☎ *904/824–4204* ⊕ *www.stgeorgetavern.com.*

Lightner Museum. In his quest to turn Florida into an American Riviera, Henry Flagler built two fancy hotels in 1888: the Ponce de León, which became Flagler College, and the Alcazar, which closed during the Great Depression, was purchased by publisher Otto Lightner in 1946, and was donated to the city in 1948. It's now a museum with three floors of furnishings, costumes, Victorian art glass, not-to-be-missed ornate antique music boxes, and even an early 20th-century-era shrunken head from the Jivaro Indians of Ecuador. The Lightner Antiques Mall is on three levels of what was once the hotel's indoor pool. ⊠ *75 King St.* ☎ *904/824–2874* ⊕ *www.lightnermuseum.org* ▧ *$10.*

Old Jail Museum. At this 19th-century prison, felons were detained and released or detained and hanged from the gallows in back. A knowledgeable "inmate" will guide you through the men's, women's, and maximum- security cells, relaying tales of executions and the less-than-appealing sanitary conditions of the jail in its heyday. After learning the history of local crime and punishment and seeing displays of weapons and other artifacts, you can browse the surfeit of souvenirs in Cracker Bob's Trading Post and the adjacent Old Store Museum. Note that the museum is at the starting point for the Old Town Trolley Tour. ⊠ *167 San Marco Ave.* ☎ *904/829–3800* ▧ *$9.*

Ponce de León Hall, Flagler College. Originally one of two posh hotels Henry Flagler built in the 1880s, this building—which is now part of a small liberal-arts college—is a riveting Spanish Renaissance–revival structure with towers, turrets, and stained glass by Louis Comfort Tiffany. The former Hotel Ponce de León is a National Historic Landmark, having hosted U.S. presidents Grover Cleveland, Theodore Roosevelt, and Warren Harding. Visitors can view the building free or take a guided tour offered daily through Flagler's Legacy Tours. ⊠ *74 King St.* ☎ *904/829–6481, 904/823–3378 tour information* ⊕ *legacy.flagler.edu* ▧ *Tours $10.*

FAMILY **St. Augustine Alligator Farm Zoological Park.** Founded in 1893, the Alligator Farm is one of Florida's oldest (and, at times, smelliest) zoological attractions and is credited with popularizing the alligator in the national consciousness and helping to fashion an image for the state. In addition to oddities like Maximo, a 15-foot, 1,250-pound saltwater crocodile, and a collection of rare albino alligators, the park is also home to Land of Crocodiles, the only place in the world to see all 23 species of living crocodilians. Traversing the treetops in Crocodile Crossing is an inventive, ambitious, and expensive zip-line/rope course with more than 50 challenges and nine zip lines. In many places, a thin cable is all that keeps you from becoming croc cuisine. The shorter Sepik River course (three zip lines) is cheaper. Reptiles are the main attraction, but there's also a wading-bird rookery, an exotic-birds and mammals exhibit, and nature trails. Educational presentations are held throughout the day, and kids love the wild-animal shows. ⊠ *999 Anastasia Blvd.* ☎ *904/824–3337* ⊕ *www.alligatorfarm.com* ▧ *$24.99; zip lines $37–$67.*

St. Augustine Distillery. The first commercial block ice in Florida was made in this building over 100 years ago. Today, the historic structure has been restored into a small-batch, craft distillery that makes whiskey, rum, gin, and vodka using ingredients sourced from local farms. A free tour orients visitors to the building's rich history, partnerships with local farms, and the spirit-making process. Visitors are asked to punch a time card to enter the working distillery; they are "paid" at the end with samples of cocktails such as the Florida Mule and New World gin and tonic. A gift shop sells an assortment of bar gadgets and accessories, along with the bottles of the spirits. ⊠ *112 Riberia St.* ☎ *904/825–4962* ⊕ *www.staugustinedistillery.com* ▧ *Free.*

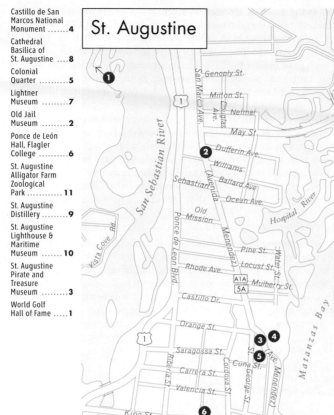

13

St. Augustine Lighthouse & Maritime Museum. It's unusual to find a lighthouse tucked into a residential neighborhood. This 1874 version replaced an earlier one built when the city was founded in 1565. Although its beacon no longer guides ships, it does draw thousands of visitors each year, in part because it has a reputation for being haunted. The visitor center has a museum featuring an exhibit called "Wrecked," which displays artifacts from an 1872 British loyalist shipwreck discovered off the shores of St. Augustine. You can also see exhibits on the U.S. Coast Guard, historic boatbuilding, maritime archaeology, and the life of a lighthouse keeper—whose work involved far more than light housekeeping. You have to climb 219 steps to reach the peak, 140 feet up, but the wonderful view and fresh ocean breeze are well worth it. Children must be at least 44 inches tall to make the ascent. The museum also conducts evening "Dark of the Moon Paranormal" tours ($25) and "Sunset-Moonrise" tours ($30) that include a Champagne toast and light hors d'oeuvres. ✉ *81 Lighthouse Ave.* ☎ *904/829–0745* ⊕ *www. staugustinelighthouse.org* ✆ *$12.95.*

FAMILY **St. Augustine Pirate and Treasure Museum.** Inside this small museum established by entrepreneur and motivational speaker Pat Croce is a collection of more than 800 pirate artifacts, including one of only two Jolly Rogers (skull-and-crossbone flags) known to have actually flown above a ship. Exhibits include a mock-up of a tavern, a captain's quarters, and a ship's deck. You'll learn about the lives of everyday and famous pirates, their navigation techniques, their weaponry, and the concoctions they drank (including something called Kill Devil, which is rum mixed with gunpowder). You'll get to touch an actual treasure chest; see piles of gold, jade, emeralds, and pearls; and leave knowing full well that there were pirates before Captain Jack Sparrow. ✉ *12 S. Castillo Dr.* ☎ *877/467–5863, 904/819–1444* ⊕ *www. thepiratemuseum.com* ✆ *$13.99.*

World Golf Hall of Fame. This stunning tribute to the game of golf is the centerpiece of World Golf Village, an extraordinary complex that includes 36 holes of golf, a golf academy, several accommodations options, a convention center, spa, and a variety of restaurants, including Murray Bros. Caddyshack. The Hall of Fame features an adjacent IMAX theater and houses a variety of exhibits combining historical artifacts and personal memorabilia with the latest in interactive technology. Stand up to the pressures of the TV camera and crowd noise as you try to sink a final putt, take a swing on the museum's simulator, or snap a photo as you walk across a replica of St. Andrews's Swilcan Burn Bridge. The "Major Moments" exhibit on golf's four major men's championships allows you to place your name atop a star-studded leaderboard. Once you're sufficiently inspired, see how you fare on the 18-hole natural-grass putting course. Admission includes a chance to score a hole-in-one on a 132-yard hole. If you do, you win a prize, such as admission to The Players Championship. ✉ *1 World Golf Pl.* ☎ *904/940–4123* ⊕ *www.worldgolfhalloffame.org* ✆ *$20.95 (includes museum, round on 18-hole putting course, and shot at hole-in-one challenge); IMAX $8.50–$13.*

BEACHES

Anastasia State Park Beach. If you don't mind paying a bit for beach access, this park offers some outstanding choices. At one end of the beach, there's a playground and snack bar, where you can order sandwiches and cold drinks or rent a beach chair, umbrella, surfboard, or other beach paraphernalia. If you walk north along the beach, however, all traces of civilization seem to vanish. An offshore break makes the park a good surfing spot, there's a boat launch, and canoes and kayaks can be rented. The campgrounds are very popular, too. **Amenities:** food and drink; lifeguards (seasonal); parking (no fee); showers; toilets; water sports. **Best for:** solitude; surfing; swimming; walking. ⊠ *1340-A Rte. A1A S* ☏ *904/461–2033* ⊕ *www.floridastateparks.org/park/anastasia* ⊠ *$8 per vehicle; $2 pedestrians.*

Butler Park Beach. In the days of racial segregation, Butler Beach, located south of St. Augustine and north of Crescent Beach, was an African-American beach. Today it is a county park that still provides access to the beachfront. **Amenities:** lifeguards (seasonal); parking (no fee); showers; toilets. **Best for:** swimming; walking. ⊠ *Rte. A1A, south of St. Augustine Beach, 5860 A1A S.*

Crescent Beach. A 15 minute-drive beyond the area's big tourist destinations, this quieter, less crowded spot offers wide, white-sand beaches with good shelling, making it particularly popular with beachcombers. Adding to the laid-back atmosphere are some good restaurants, where visitors can enjoy the beach from a distance, glass in one hand and plate of fresh seafood in the other. **Amenities:** lifeguards (seasonal); parking (no fee); showers; toilets. **Best for:** solitude; swimming; walking. ⊠ *South of Rtes. A1A and 206, Crescent Beach.*

North Beach. Just five minutes from St. Augustine, this site (aka Usina Beach) includes boat ramps, two campsites, and a picnic area with grills. If you'd rather opt for a restaurant than a picnic, you're in the right spot—a variety of eateries overlook the ocean or the Intracoastal Waterway. **Amenities:** lifeguards (seasonal); parking (no fee); showers; toilets. **Best for:** solitude; walking. ⊠ *Rte. A1A, north of Vilano Beach.*

St. Augustine Beach. Just south of Anastasia State Park, this beach has a livelier setting, thanks to the restaurants, bars, and shops along Beach-front Avenue and the 4-acre St. Johns County Ocean Pier Park. The park includes a playground, small splash park, sand volleyball courts, and a covered pavilion, where from May to September a series of Music by the Sea concerts are offered free. Speaking of free, the beach doesn't charge a fee, but the popular fishing pier does ($3). In addition, there are some areas designated for driving on the beach. **Amenities:** lifeguards (seasonal); parking (no fee); showers; toilets. **Best for:** swimming. ⊠ *Old A1A/Beach Blvd., south of Rte. 312.*

Vilano Beach. This beach, just 2 miles north of St. Augustine, is sandwiched between the Tolomato River and the Atlantic. In the 1920s it was home to the Grand Vilano Casino, but that was destroyed by a hurricane in 1937. Until recently, Vilano Beach had deteriorated into a small, somewhat run-down area, though with a nice, laid-back '60s surf vibe. That's changed rapidly, however. Now it's home to new stores and restaurants, the Vilano Beach Fishing Pier, and other community improvements. A Hampton Inn & Suites is within a few minutes' walk. The beach has some nice breakers for surfing—skimboarding is also popular—but strong currents sometimes make it dangerous for swimming. It's also one of the few beaches on which you can still drive a car. **Amenities:** lifeguards (seasonal); showers; toilets. **Best for:** solitude; surfing; walking. ✉ *3400 Coastal Hwy., Vilano Beach.*

WHERE TO EAT

$ CAFÉ

🍴 **The Bunnery Bakery & Café.** Hidden among the art galleries and trinket shops of St. George Street is this cozy little restaurant, which is very popular at breakfast and nearly as popular during lunch. There's nothing fancy—just high-back booths and a menu of pancakes, bacon, eggs, cinnamon buns, salads, and hot and cold sandwiches. **Known for:** all breads and buns made in-house; large selection of panini and grilled sandwiches; good omelets for breakfast. [$] *Average main: $7* ✉ *121 St. George St.* ☎ *904/829–6166* 🌐 *www.bunnerybakeryandcafe.com.*

$$ CAFÉ

🍴 **Café Alcazar.** Housed in the magnificent Lightner Museum—formerly the luxurious Hotel Alcazar in its 1890s incarnation—this lovely little lunch spot sits where wealthy winter tourists once frolicked in the nation's largest indoor pool. Curried chicken salad, panini, and artichokes "Giovanni"—an addictive dish of baked artichokes with cheese and mushrooms on linguine—are among the many favorites here. **Known for:** curried chicken salad; artichokes Giovanni; first-Friday-night dinner. [$] *Average main: $15* ✉ *25 Granada St.* ☎ *904/825–9948* 🌐 *thealcazarcafe.com.*

$$ LATIN AMERICAN

🍴 **Casa Maya.** Latin-inspired cuisine abounds in the nation's oldest city, but Casa Maya has created a niche—and passionate following—with fresh, eclectic cuisine from Mexico's Yucatán Peninsula. Everything is made from scratch here, from the sauces and marinades to the mixers for unique cocktails such as the cucumber jalapeño margarita. **Known for:** fresh seafood; Mayan soup with avocado and crispy tortillas; weekend breakfast. [$] *Average main: $15* ✉ *22 Hypolita St.* ☎ *904/823–0787.*

$$$$ ECLECTIC
Fodor's Choice ★

🍴 **Collage.** Tucked away on Hypolita Street in the Historic District, the 48-seat restaurant highlights local seafood, which, depending on the success of the fishermen, will include several fish entrées each day. The ever-changing menu also often has steak, lamb, or veal selections, all served in an intimate setting that is a tad more upscale than most area restaurants. **Known for:** locally caught seafood and lobster ravioli; beef tenderloin with a variety of sauces; large, reasonably priced wine list. [$] *Average main: $36* ✉ *60 Hypolita St.* ☎ *904/829–0055* 🌐 *www.collagestaug.com* 🕒 *No lunch.*

$$$ SPANISH

🍴 **Columbia.** With a long menu of time-honored Cuban and Spanish dishes, this branch of the Columbia is as popular as the original in Tampa, which was founded in 1905. Befitting its cuisine, the restaurant is decorated like an airy Spanish villa. **Known for:** paella Valenciana with seafood, chicken, and pork; long wine and cocktail list, including house-made sangria; 1905 salad with ham, cheese, tomatoes, and olives. [$] *Average main: $28* ✉ *98 St. George St.* ☎ *904/824–3341* 🌐 *www.columbiarestaurant.com.*

$$ MODERN AMERICAN FAMILY Fodor's Choice ★

🍴 **The Floridian.** Although vegetarians flock to this artsy and inspired eatery for the veggie-centric menu, there's plenty to tantalize omnivores as well. Delicious Southern food with flair ranges from fried-green-tomato bruschetta to a choice of shrimp, fish, or tofu with polenta cakes (here called "grits"). **Known for:** farm-to-table approach; vegetarian-friendly menu; entrée salads. [$] *Average main: $19* ✉ *72 Spanish St.* ☎ *904/829–0655* 🌐 *www.thefloridianstaug.com* ⏲ *Closed Tues.*

$$$ MEDITERRANEAN

🍴 **Michael's Tasting Room.** Mediterranean-style tapas are the specialty here, highlighted by dishes such as Spanish octopus and goat cheese terrine layered with sun-dried tomatoes, olives, and pesto. Large plates include adobo-braised short ribs and duck leg confit. **Known for:** tapas-style menu; fresh seafood; large selection of Spanish wines. [$] *Average main: $26* ✉ *25 Cuna St.* ☎ *904/810–2400* 🌐 *www.tastetapas.com.*

$$$ SEAFOOD

🍴 **O.C. White's Seafood & Spirits.** In the circa-1791 General Worth house across from the marina, this bustling little spot has a homey feel with a balanced clientele of locals, students, and visitors. Favorites include coconut shrimp, blue-crab cakes, and fresh local grouper. **Known for:** steamed shrimp; blue-crab cakes; preferred seating (but no real reservations). [$] *Average main: $21* ✉ *118 Ave. Menendez* ☎ *904/824–0808* 🌐 *www.ocwhitesrestaurant.com.*

$$ SEAFOOD

🍴 **O'Steen's.** Across the Bridge of Lions from downtown, this hole-in-the-wall restaurant is recognizable for the line of customers who wait patiently for fried shrimp (the specialty), seafood, and fried chicken. Needless to say it's been a popular local eatery for generations. **Known for:** fried shrimp with hush puppies; pies (particularly banana cream); cash only. [$] *Average main: $16* ✉ *205 Anastasia Blvd.* ☎ *904/829–6974* 🌐 *www.osteensrestaurant.com* 💳 *No credit cards* ⏲ *Closed Sun. and Mon.*

$$ SEAFOOD

🍴 **Sunset Grille.** They take their chowders seriously in St. Augustine, and many will tell you Sunset Grille's is the best—so good that it's poured over french fries as an appetizer. If you prefer a lighter version, a cup of the award-winning chowder works as a perfect prelude to the fresh fish dinners featuring Caribbean snapper and macadamia-crusted grouper. **Known for:** clam chowder (either creamy New England or tomato-based Minorcan); seared or blacked fresh fish; no-reservations policy. [$] *Average main: $18* ✉ *421 A1A Beach Blvd., St. Augustine Beach* ☎ *904/471–5555* 🌐 *www.sunsetgrillea1a.com.*

$$ ITALIAN

🍴 **Terra & Acqua.** Homemade pasta, fresh seafood, and brick-oven pizzas are just some of the delights attracting locals and tourists alike to this casual Italian gem a few blocks from the beach. Giant chalkboards signal the fresh fish creations of the day, but it's tough to resist the pasta dishes such as papardelle *cinghiale* (handmade papardelle with wild boar, plum tomatoes, and fresh herbs). **Known for:** handmade pasta; freshly caught seafood; brick-oven pizza. [$] *Average main: $19* ✉ *134 Sea Grove Main St., St. Augustine Beach* ☎ *904/429–9647* 🌐 *www.terraacquarestaurant.com* ⏲ *Closed Sun.*

WHERE TO STAY

$$ | B&B/INN | FAMILY

🏨 **Bayfront Marin House Historic Inn.** Children are rarely permitted at B&Bs, but this is a charming exception, thanks to separate entrances, several units large enough to accommodate families, and the warm welcome of the inn's owners, Mike and Sandy Wieber. **Pros:** personal service; child- and pet-friendly; riverfront location. **Cons:** parking a block away; dining area small if weather forces breakfast indoors. [$] *Rooms from: $219* ✉ *142 Ave. Menendez* ☎ *904/824–4301* 🌐 *www.bayfrontmarinhouse.com* 🛏 *15 rooms* 🍴 *Breakfast.*

$ | B&B/INN

🏨 **Bayfront Westcott House.** A bit more elegant and formal than the average B&B, this inn wows guests with a combination of English and American antiques and a wealth of complimentary food, from extravagant breakfasts to wine and canapés in the early evening. **Pros:** great views, most from private balconies; romantic rooms; free Wi-Fi. **Cons:** parking a short distance away; carriage house rooms not as elegant as main house. [$] *Rooms from: $189* ✉ *146 Ave. Menendez* ☎ *904/825–4602, 800/513–9814* 🌐 *www.westcotthouse.com* 🛏 *16 rooms* 🍴 *Breakfast.*

$ | B&B/INN

🏨 **Carriage Way Bed and Breakfast.** When it comes to location, the Victorian-era Carriage Way has the best of both worlds; it's far enough from the Historic District to avoid tourist noise but close enough to have easy access to excellent restaurants (try the nearby Floridian) and shops. **Pros:** great location; free on-site parking; personal attention; excellent breakfasts. **Cons:** some small rooms; street can get loud with traffic. [$] *Rooms from: $179* ✉ *70 Cuna St.* ☎ *904/829–2467, 800/908–9832* 🌐 *www.carriageway.com* 🛏 *13 rooms, 1 cottage* 🍴 *Breakfast.*

$ | B&B/INN

🏨 **Casa de Solana.** There's a reason you feel like you're stepping back in time when you enter this 1820s-era inn made of coquina and handmade bricks: It's on the oldest street in the oldest European-settled city in the country. **Pros:** excellent service; delicious breakfast; convenient location. **Cons:** some small rooms; free parking is three blocks away; "forced" socialization. [$] *Rooms from: $169* ✉ *21 Aviles St.* ☎ *904/824–3555* 🌐 *www.casadesolana.com* 🛏 *10 rooms* 🍴 *Breakfast.*

$$ | HOTEL | Fodor's Choice ★

🏨 **Casa Monica Hotel.** Hand-stenciled Moorish columns and arches, handcrafted chandeliers, and gilded iron tables decorate the lobby of this late-1800s Flagler-era masterpiece. **Pros:** downtown location near attractions; new spa in 2015; flat-screen TVs in all rooms. **Cons:** busy lobby; expensive ($24) parking; small rooms. [$] *Rooms from: $242* ✉ *95 Cordova St.* ☎ *904/827–1888, 800/648–1888* 🌐 *www.casamonica.com* 🛏 *127 rooms, 11 suites* 🍴 *No meals.*

$ | HOTEL

🏨 **DoubleTree by Hilton Historic District.** Despite being one of the newer additions to the St. Augustine lodging scene, the DoubleTree blends seamlessly into the city's Old World Spanish ethos. **Pros:** complimentary on-site parking; charming outdoor space with pool; comfortable beds. **Cons:** several-block walk to central tourist area; small lobby. [$] *Rooms from: $169* ✉ *116 San Marco Ave.* ☎ *904/825–1923* 🌐 *www.staugustinehistoricdistrict.doubletree.com* 🛏 *97 rooms* 🍴 *No meals.*

$ HOTEL FAMILY

Hilton St. Augustine Historic Bayfront. In the heart of historic St. Augustine, this Spanish-colonial-inspired hotel overlooking Matanzas Bay has 19 separate buildings in a village setting. **Pros:** good location for tourist sights; comfortable beds; great for families. **Cons:** expensive valet parking only ($21); late-night noise at street level. [$] *Rooms from: $199* ✉ *32 Ave. Menendez* ☎ *904/829–2277, 800/445–8667* 🌐 *www.hilton.com* 🛏 *72 rooms* 🍴 *No meals.*

$ B&B/INN

Inn on Charlotte Bed & Breakfast. Innkeeper Rodney Holeman says guests comment that staying at his inn reminds them of visiting a friend or family member's home, assuming that person offers an elegant two-course breakfast and cozy rooms with whirlpool tubs. **Pros:** location; excellent service; free parking. **Cons:** strict cancellation policy; tight parking in compact lot; weekend street noise. [$] *Rooms from: $149* ✉ *52 Charlotte St.* ☎ *904/829–3819, 800/355–5508* 🌐 *www.innoncharlotte.com* 🛏 *8 rooms* 🍴 *Breakfast.*

$ HOTEL

La Fiesta Ocean Inn & Suites. Chains have since taken over St. Augustine Beach, but this longtime favorite—the only remaining "Mom and Pop" on the beach—is still doing business (lots of it) and remains as beloved as ever. **Pros:** on the beach; breakfast delivered to rooms; refrigerators and microwaves in rooms. **Cons:** tiny lobby; resort fee; strict cancellation policy. [$] *Rooms from: $140* ✉ *810 A1A Beach Blvd., St. Augustine Beach* ☎ *904/471–2220* 🌐 *www.lafiestainn.com* 🛏 *46 rooms* 🍴 *Breakfast.*

$ RESORT Fodor's Choice ★

Renaissance Resort at World Golf Village. If you want to be within walking distance of all World Golf Village has to offer, this AAA Four Diamond resort is an excellent choice. **Pros:** breakfast buffet; large bathrooms; free shuttle to golf courses, spa, and downtown St. Augustine. **Cons:** small pool; daily fee for Internet/phone. [$] *Rooms from: $159* ✉ *500 S. Legacy Trail* ☎ *904/940–8000, 888/740–7020* 🌐 *www.worldgolfrenaissance.com* 🛏 *271 rooms, 30 suites* 🍴 *Breakfast; No meals.*

$ B&B/INN

St. Francis Inn Bed & Breakfast. This late-18th-century inn in the Historic District, a guesthouse since 1845, offers main-house rooms and suites, a room in the former carriage house, and a five-room cottage, all with a serene vibe and a delicious Southern breakfast buffet included. **Pros:** warm hospitality; lots of extras; short walk to Historic District attractions. **Cons:** small rooms; small pool. [$] *Rooms from: $169* ✉ *279 St. George St.* ☎ *904/824–6068, 800/824–6062* 🌐 *www.stfrancisinn.com* 🛏 *16 rooms, 1 cottage* 🍴 *Breakfast.*

$$ B&B/INN

St. George Inn. You can't be any closer to the St. George Street bustle than this 25-room inn nestled in the City Gate Plaza. **Pros:** convenient downtown location; balconies have views; comfortable beds. **Cons:** some street noise; parking two blocks away. [$] *Rooms from: $219* ✉ *4 St. George St.* ☎ *904/827–5740, 888/827–5740* 🌐 *www.stgeorge-inn.com* 🛏 *25 rooms* 🍴 *Breakfast.*

$ HOTEL

Wyndham Garden Sebastian St. Augustine. It's easy to mistake this colorful hotel, about a mile from the Historic District, for an upscale condominium complex. **Pros:** large rooms; on-site café and bar; inviting public areas. **Cons:** outside of the Historic District; few rooms have balconies. [$] *Rooms from: $161* ✉ *333 S. Ponce de Leon Blvd.* ☎ *904/209–5580* 🌐 *www.wyndhamhotels.com* 🛏 *95 rooms* 🍴 *No meals.*

NIGHTLIFE

A1A Aleworks. The Aleworks always seems to be filled with students and visitors taste-driving the microbrews and other selections from the full bar. Seats on the second-story balcony provide a great view of the marina and bay across the street. It's a little like being on Bourbon Street—but clean. ⊠ *1 King St.* ☎ *904/829–2977* ⊕ *www.a1aaleworks.com.*

Odd Birds Bar. You can catch live music under the stars here, or chill on a couch with a craft cocktail at the cozy upstairs bar. If you're lucky, you'll visit on a "Bartender Diplomacy Night" featuring a guest bartender from another city. For a late-night bite, the Venezuelan arepas hit the spot. ⊠ *33 Charlotte St.* ☎ *904/679–4933* ⊕ *www.oddbirdsbar.com.*

The Original Cafe Eleven. This live-music haven sets the stage for local groups, and tries to book national acts at least once a month. They also serve breakfast, lunch, and dinner seven days a week. ⊠ *501 Rte. A1A Beach Blvd.* ☎ *904/460–9311* ⊕ *www.originalcafe11.com.*

Scarlett O'Hara's. It's a popular and convenient spot to stop for lunch or dinner (preferably enjoyed on the front porch); later in the evening it turns up the volume with blues, jazz, disco, Top 40, or karaoke. Whatever's playing, it's always packed. ⊠ *70 Hypolita St.* ☎ *904/824–6535* ⊕ *www.scarlettoharas.net.*

Tini Martini Bar. The veranda overlooking Matanzas Bay at this Casablanca Inn bar is the perfect place to enjoy a cocktail, people-watch, and listen to live music. ⊠ *Casablanca Inn, 24 Ave. Menendez* ☎ *904/829–0928* ⊕ *www.tini-martini-bar.com.*

Tradewinds. It's been showcasing bands—from country to rock and roll—since 1964. Thanks to the music, beer, and margaritas, you may feel as if you're in Key West. ⊠ *124 Charlotte St.* ☎ *904/826–1590* ⊕ *www.tradewindslounge.com.*

The World Famous Oasis Deck and Restaurant. If you're staying on Anastasia Island, this is your best nightlife bet. It has a more than 20 draft beer selections, beach access, and what many locals consider the best burgers in town. ⊠ *4000 Rte. A1A S, at Ocean Trace Rd.* ☎ *904/471–3424* ⊕ *www.worldfamousoasis.com.*

SHOPPING

One of the most pleasing pastimes in St. Augustine is a stroll along St. George Street, a pedestrian mall with shoulder-to-shoulder art galleries and one-of-a-kind shops selling candles, home accents, handmade jewelry, aromatherapy products, pottery, books, and clothing. There are also restaurants, clubs, and a veritable orchestra of street musicians.

Several blocks north of the Castillo and the popular St. George Street, a string of shops—galleries, antiques, a bookstore—line both sides of San Marco Avenue. Although this strip isn't as eclectic as it used to be, you'll still find some interesting independent stores.

MALLS

St. Augustine Outlets. Several miles outside the city, Prime Outlets has almost 60 name-brand stores including Old Navy, Saks 5th Avenue's OFF 5TH, Kate Spade New York, and Michael Kors. ⊠ *500 Belz Outlet Blvd.* ☎ *904/826–1311* ⊕ *www.staugoutlets.com.*

St. Augustine Premium Outlets. Just north of St. Augustine, off Interstate 95, is this collection of 85 designer and brand-name outlet stores. ⊠ *2700 State Rd. 16* ☎ *904/825–1555* ⊕ *www.premiumoutlets.com.*

13

SPORTS AND THE OUTDOORS

BIKING

Solano Cycle. Here you can rent bicycles, scooters, and "scoot coups," which look like the offspring of a scooter and a bumper car and are $49 for the first hour (one-hour minimum) and $69 for two. ⊠ *32 San Marco Ave.* ☎ *904/825–6766* ⊕ *www.solanocycle.com.*

St. Augustine Bike Rentals. In addition to renting bicycles, scooters, and "scoot coups," you can catch a guided bicycle or Segway tour here. ⊠ *125A King St.* ☎ *904/547–2074* ⊕ *www.staugustinebikerentals.com* 🖅 *Rentals from $7; tours from $30.*

BOAT TOURS

EcoTours. Amid America's most enduring human history, EcoTours investigates St. Augustine's natural history. Scenic cruises, kayak tours, and catamaran excursions on Matanzas Bay offer a chance to see bottlenose dolphins, bird habitats, lakes, creeks, and saltwater marshes. Along the way are incredible photo ops of the city and the Castillo from the water. ⊠ *111 Ave. Menendez* ☎ *904/377–7245* ⊕ *www.staugustineecotours.com.*

FAMILY **The Pirate Ship** *Black Raven.* Whether you prefer Captain Hook or Captain Jack Sparrow, it's a pirate's life for everyone aboard the *Black Raven*, even if you're only sailing on the Mantanzas River. This "floating performance theater" hosts live pirate shows that include sea chanties, black-powder cannon firings, sword-fighting lessons for kids (with harmless foam blades), and treasure hunts on weekends. This is just entertainment, not historical education, so expect the jokes to be cheap and cheesy. However, the atmosphere's lively and the river's lovely. Kids can trade their "letters of marque" to get a share of the booty—if, that is, the crew and the kids can manage to get their treasure back from Blackbeard. There are also adults-only evening cruises—the ship includes a fully licensed bar, so grown-ups can live out the fantasy of "yo-ho-ho and a bottle of rum." Cruises can be cancelled for inclement weather, so call to check before making final travel plans. ⊠ *St. Augustine Municipal Marina, 111 Av. Menendez* ☎ *904/826–0000, 877/578–5050* ⊕ *www.blackravenadventures.com* 🖅 *$34.95.*

Ripple Effect Ecotours. Rent a kayak or take a boat or kayak tour at this outfitter south of St. Augustine. ⊠ *Town of Marineland Marina, 101 Tolstoy La.* ☎ *904/347–1565* ⊕ *www.rippleeffectecotours.com.*

Schooner *Freedom.* Cutting a sharp profile, this 72-foot replica of a 19th-century blockade-runner sails from the marina for excursions across Matanzas Bay. You can relax and savor the breeze, or you can help the crew prepare to set sail. There are two-hour day and sunset sails as well as a 75-minute moonlight tour. Precise times vary by season. Reservations are advised. ⊠ *St. Augustine Municipal Marina, 111 Ave. Menendez, Slip 86* ☎ *904/810–1010* ⊕ *www.schoonerfreedom.com* ⌦ *From $35.*

FISHING

Sea Love Charters. Tackle and bait are included on this outfit's half- or full-day deep-sea fishing trips. ⊠ *Cat's Paw Marina, 220 Nix Boat Yard Rd.* ☎ *904/824–3328* ⊕ *www.sealovefishing.com.*

GOLF

World Golf Village. The World Golf Hall of Fame complex has two 18-hole layouts named for and partially designed by golf legends Sam Snead, Gene Sarazen, Arnold Palmer, and Jack Nicklaus. The King & Bear course, a collaboration of Palmer and Nicklaus, features a design that symbolizes the styles of both golfing legends, including holes that especially reward outstanding power of the tees. Palmer chose the par-4 15th as one of his "Dream 18" in a *Sports Illustrated* report. It's the most picturesque hole on the course, with a dramatic rock wall surrounding the green. Snead and Sarazen consulted with designer Bobby Weed in creating The Slammer & Squire course, which features generous fairways and lots of water hazards. Amenities for both courses include complimentary range balls and fresh chilled apples on the 1st and 10th tees. ⊠ *1 World Golf Pl.* ☎ *904/940–6100 Slammer & Squire, 904/940–6200 King & Bear* ⊕ *www.worldgolfhalloffame. com* ⌦ *King & Bear, $179; Slammer & Squire, $139* ⌦ *King & Bear Course: 18 holes, 7279 yards, par 72; Slammer & Squite Course: 18 holes, 6939 yards, par 72.*

WATER SPORTS

Surf Station. Here you can rent surfboards, skimboards, and bodyboards. ⊠ *1020 Anastasia Blvd.* ☎ *904/471–9463, 800/460–6394* ⊕ *www.surf-station.com.*

DAYTONA BEACH AND INLAND TOWNS

Updated by
Steve Master

The section of the coast around Daytona Beach offers considerable variety, from the unassuming bedroom community of Ormond Beach to the auto-racing capital of Daytona Beach. (Go 75 miles to the south, and you've got speeding rockets instead of speeding cars.)

Peaceful little inland towns are separated by miles of two-lane roads, running through dense forest and flat pastureland and skirting one lake after another. There's not much to see but cattle and the state's few hills. Gentle and rolling, they're hardly worth noting to people from true hill country, but they're significant enough in Florida for much of this area to be called the "hill and lake region."

DAYTONA BEACH

65 miles south of St. Augustine.

Best known for the Daytona 500, Daytona has been the center of automobile racing since cars were first raced along the beach here in 1902. February is the biggest month for race enthusiasts, and there are weekly events at the International Speedway, which completed a $400-million renovation in 2016. During race weeks, bike weeks, spring-break periods, and summer holidays, expect extremely heavy traffic. On the mainland, near the inland waterway, several blocks of Beach Street have been "streetscaped," and shops and restaurants open onto an inviting, broad, brick sidewalk.

13

GETTING HERE AND AROUND

Several airlines have regular service to Daytona Beach International Airport, which is next to Daytona International Speedway on International Speedway Boulevard, an east–west artery that stretches from Interstate 95 to the beaches. The average drive time from the airport to beachside hotels is 20 minutes; Yellow Cab–Daytona Beach makes the trip for $15–$36.

DOTS Transit Service has scheduled service ($36 one-way, $67 round-trip) connecting Daytona Beach, DeLand, Deltona, and the Orlando International Airport, which serves more airlines and has more direct flights but is about a 70-mile commute via Interstate 4 and State Road 417 (allow at least 90 minutes).

Daytona Beach has an excellent bus network, Votran, which serves the beach area, airport, shopping malls, and major arteries, including service to DeLand and New Smyrna Beach and the DeBary SunRail station, where passengers can connect to various Orlando area locales. Exact fare is required for Votran ($1.75) if using cash.

Contacts Daytona Beach International Airport (*DAB*). ⊠ *700 Catalina Dr.* ☎ *386/248–8069* ⊕ *www.flydaytonafirst.com.* **DOTS Transit Service.** ☎ *386/257–5411, 800/231–1965* ⊕ *www.dots-daytonabeach.com.* **Votran.** ☎ *386/761–7700* ⊕ *www.votran.org.* **Yellow Cab–Daytona Beach.** ☎ *386/255–5555, 888/333–3356* ⊕ *www.daytonataxi.com.*

VISITOR INFORMATION

Contacts Daytona Beach Area Convention and Visitors Bureau. ☎ *800/544–0415* ⊕ *www.daytonabeach.com.*

EXPLORING

The Casements. Built in 1912 for Reverend Harwood Huntington and named for its handcrafted casement windows, the home was purchased by John D. Rockefeller Sr. in 1918 as a winter retreat. Once considered the richest man in the world, Rockefeller entertained famous friends such as Henry Ford, Will Rogers, and Henry Flagler at the home while remaining an active member of the Ormond Beach community. After Rockefeller's death in 1937, the property was bought and sold numerous times and is now a cultural center and museum. The waterfront estate and its formal gardens host daily tours and an annual lineup of events and exhibits; there's also a permanent exhibit of Hungarian folk art and Boy Scout memorabilia. ⊠ *25 Riverside Dr., Ormond Beach* ☎ *386/676–3216* ⊕ *www.thecasements.net* ☟ *Donations accepted* ☉ *Closed Sun.*

Halifax Historical Museum. Memorabilia from the early days of beach automobile racing are on display here, as are historic photographs, Native American and Civil War artifacts, a postcard exhibit, and a video that details city history. There's a shop for gifts and antiques, too. Admission is by donation on Thursday and on Saturday, kids 12 and under are free. ⊠ *252 S. Beach St.* ☎ *386/255–6976* ⊕ *www.hali-faxhistorical.org* ▨ *$7* ⊗ *Closed Sun. and Mon.*

FAMILY **Museum of Arts & Sciences.** This behemoth museum has displays of Chinese art and an eye-popping complete skeleton of a giant ground sloth that's 130,000 years old. The museum also boasts a new Visible Storage Building, one of the most significant collections of Cuban art outside of Cuba, a large Coca-Cola and Americana collection, a rare Napoleonic exhibit, and one of the more expansive collections of American art in the southeast. Kids love the Charles and Linda Williams Children's Museum, which features interactive science, engineering, and physics exhibits; a nature preserve with half a mile of boardwalks and nature trails; and a state-of-the-art planetarium with daily shows. Florida art dating back to the 18th century is featured in the recently opened Cici and Hyatt Brown Museum of Art, a free-standing, 26,000-square-foot Florida Cracker–style addition opened in 2015. Artists represented include John James Audubon, Thomas Hart Benton, and N.C. Wyeth. ⊠ *352 S. Nova Rd.* ☎ *386/255–0285* ⊕ *www.moas.org* ▨ *$12.95 for science museum; $10.95 for art museum; $18.95 combo ticket for both museums.*

OFF THE BEATEN PATH

Ponce de León Inlet Light Station. At the southern tip of the barrier island that includes Daytona Beach is the sleepy town of Ponce Inlet, with a small marina, a few bars, and casual seafood restaurants. Boardwalks traverse delicate dunes and provide easy access to the beach, although storms have caused serious erosion. Marking this prime spot is the bright-red, century-old Ponce de León Inlet Light Station, a National Historic Monument and museum, the tallest lighthouse in the state and the third tallest in the country. Climb to the top of the 175-foot-tall lighthouse tower for a bird's-eye view of Ponce Inlet. ⊠ *4931 S. Peninsula Dr., Ponce Inlet* ☎ *386/761–1821* ⊕ *www.ponceinlet.org* ▨ *$6.95.*

BEACHES

Fodor's Choice
★

Daytona Beach. At the World's Most Famous Beach you can drive right onto the sand (at least from one hour after sunrise to one hour before sunset), spread out a blanket, and have all your belongings at hand (with the exception of alcohol, which is prohibited). All that said, heavy traffic during summer and holidays makes it dangerous for children, and families should be extra careful or stay in the designated car-free zones. The speed limit is 10 mph, and there's a $10 fee, collected at the beach ramps.

The wide, 23-mile-long beach can get crowded in the "strip" area (between International Speedway Boulevard and Seabreeze Boulevard) with its food vendors, beachfront bars, volleyball matches, and motorized-water-sports enthusiasts. Those seeking a quieter experience can head north or south in either direction toward car-free zones in more residential areas. The hard-packed sand that makes the beach suitable for driving is also perfect for running and cycling. There's also excellent surf fishing directly from the beach. **Amenities:** food and drink; lifeguards; parking (some with fee); showers; toilets; water sports. **Best for:** sunrise; surfing; swimming; walking. **■ TIP→ Signs on Route A1A indicate car access via beach ramps. Sand traps aren't limited to the golf course, though—cars can get stuck.** ✉ *Rte. A1A* 🌐 *www.daytonabeach.com.*

WHERE TO EAT

$$$ SEAFOOD FAMILY

🍴 **Aunt Catfish's on the River.** Don't be surprised if your server introduces herself as your cousin, though you've never seen her before in your life. The silly Southern hospitality is only one of the draws at this wildly popular restaurant specializing in mouthwatering plates of fresh seafood and other Southern favorites. **Known for:** Southern-style seafood; Sunday brunch; hot cinnamon rolls. [$] *Average main: $24* ✉ *4009 Halifax Dr., Port Orange* ☎ *386/767–4768* 🌐 *www.auntcatfishontheriver.com.*

$$ AMERICAN

🍴 **Daytona Brickyard.** It's not just the locals who swear that the Brickyard's charbroiled sirloin burgers are the best they've ever tasted—devotees have been known to drive from Georgia just for lunch. Given its name and location in the heart of NASCAR country, the popular bar and grill is covered in racing memorabilia. **Known for:** giant sirloin burgers; wings with various sauces; racing memorabilia decor. [$] *Average main: $15* ✉ *747 International Speedway Blvd.* ☎ *386/253–2270* 🌐 *www.brickyardlounge.com.*

$$$$ STEAKHOUSE

🍴 **Hyde Park Prime Steakhouse.** This chophouse provides an upscale alternative to Daytona's more prevalent shorts-and-flip-flop joints. Steaks, especially the cuts named after race-car drivers, and mouthwatering sides (don't miss the potatoes Gruyère gratin) are the main attractions. **Known for:** wide selection of steaks; Gruyère gratin potatoes; happy hour on weekdays. [$] *Average main: $40* ✉ *Hilton Daytona Beach Resort/Ocean Walk Village, 100 N. Atlantic Ave.* ☎ *386/226–9844* 🌐 *www.hydeparkrestaurants.com* 🕒 *No lunch.*

$$$ CONTEMPORARY Fodor's Choice ★

🍴 **Martini's Chophouse.** The local beautiful people seem to flock to this trendy south Daytona eatery and lounge as much for the scene as for the food. The rotating menu emphasizes organic, locally sourced, seasonal ingredients, which owner/chef Clay Butters uses to create beef, seafood, and poultry dishes as appealing to the eye as the taste buds. **Known for:** fresh, organic ingredients; Bahamian lobster sauté; chic ambience. [$] *Average main: $24* ✉ *1815 S. Ridgewood Ave.* ☎ *386/763–1090* 🌐 *www.martinischophouse.com.*

$ MEXICAN

🍴 **Tia Cori's Tacos.** Mexican street food is the specialty at this tiny, counter-service eatery in the downtown riverfront shopping district. The namesake tacos come Mexican style (with onion, cilantro, and lime), but for 50¢ more you can get an Americanized version with cheese. **Known for:** authentic Mexican-style tacos; $5 margaritas; long lines. [$] *Average main: $7* ✉ *214 N. Beach St.* ☎ *386/947–4333* 🌐 *www.tiacoristacos.com* 🕒 *Closed Sun.*

WHERE TO STAY

$ HOTEL **Courtyard Daytona Beach Speedway/Airport.** For those visiting Daytona Beach for something other than surf and sand (a certain iconic racing facility comes to mind), this smartly located Marriott is the perfect base. **Pros:** proximity to speedway; welcoming indoor and outdoor public areas; dining on property. **Cons:** some noise from nearby airport; 15-minute drive to the beach. [$] *Rooms from: $134* ✉ *1605 Richard Petty Blvd.* ☎ *386/255–3388* 🌐 *www.marriott.com* 🛏 *122 rooms* 🍴 *No meals.*

$ RESORT **Hilton Daytona Beach Resort/Ocean Walk Village.** Perched on one of the few traffic-free strips of beach in Daytona, this high-rise is as popular with families as it is with couples. **Pros:** direct beach access; proximity to shops and restaurants. **Cons:** inconvenient self-parking; resort fee; not all rooms have balconies. [$] *Rooms from: $142* ✉ *100 N. Atlantic Ave.* ☎ *386/254–8200, 866/536–8477* 🌐 *www.daytonahilton.com* 🛏 *744 rooms* 🍴 *No meals.*

$ RESORT FAMILY **Perry's Ocean Edge Resort.** Perhaps more than any other property in Daytona, Perry's has a die-hard fan base, many of whom started coming to the oceanfront resort as children, then returned with their children and their children's children. **Pros:** spacious rooms; helpful staff; nice pools; family-friendly. **Cons:** small bathrooms; decor is dated. [$] *Rooms from: $179* ✉ *2209 S. Atlantic Ave.* ☎ *386/255–0581, 800/447–0002* 🌐 *www.perrysoceanedge.com* 🛏 *183 rooms* 🍴 *Breakfast.*

$ RESORT Fodor's Choice ★ **The Shores Resort & Spa.** Rustic furniture and beds swathed in mosquito netting are a nod to Old Florida at this 11-story beachfront resort, but there's nothing rustic about the amenities, including a luxury four-poster bed, doorless Italian marble showers and a 42-inch plasma TV in every room. **Pros:** beachfront; spa; friendly staff; 24-hour room service. **Cons:** expensive restaurant; overcrowding during special events. [$] *Rooms from: $189* ✉ *2637 S. Atlantic Ave., Daytona Beach Shores* ☎ *386/767–7350, 866/934–7467* 🌐 *www.shoresresort.com* 🛏 *212 rooms* 🍴 *No meals.*

NIGHTLIFE

BARS

Boot Hill Saloon. Despite its reputation as a biker bar, this place welcomes nonbikers and even nonbiker tourists! ✉ *310 Main St.* ☎ *386/258–9506* 🌐 *www.boothillsaloon.com.*

Ocean Walk Village. Lively and always hopping, Ocean Walk is a cluster of shops, restaurants, and bars (the Mai Tai Bar is a good bet) stretching along Atlantic Avenue and the ocean. ✉ *250 N. Atlantic Ave.* ☎ *386/258–9544* 🌐 *www.oceanwalkvillage.com.*

The Oyster Pub. Sports fans and oyster lovers congregate by the thousands here. ✉ *555 Seabreeze Blvd.* ☎ *386/255–6348* 🌐 *www.oysterpub.com.*

DANCE CLUBS

Razzle's Nightclub. DJs play high-energy dance music 9 pm–3 am. ✉ *611 Seabreeze Blvd.* ☎ *386/257–6236* 🌐 *www.razzlesnightclub.com.*

SHOPPING

Daytona Flea and Farmers' Market. One of the largest flea markets in the South draws residents from all over the state as well as visitors to the state. It's open weekends, including Friday, from 9 to 5. ⊠ *2987 Bellevue Ave.* ☎ *386/253–3330* ⊕ *www.daytonafleamarket.com.*

Destination Daytona. This 100-acre biker enclave is complete with an expansive Harley-Davidson dealership; retail shops; a restaurant; bars; a tattoo parlor; a hotel; and a pavilion used for concerts, conventions—even biker-inspired weddings. ⊠ *1635 N. U.S. 1, Ormond Beach* ⊕ *www.brucerossmeyer.com.*

One Daytona. A massive shopping, dining, and entertainment complex across the street from Daytona International Speedway, One Daytona will be anchored by luxury Cobb Theaters mulitplex and Bass Pro Shops Outpost. Scheduled for completion by the end of 2017, the complex will also include Oklahoma Joe's BBQ, Kilwin's Confections, and two hotels, including one from Marriott's Autograph Collection. ⊠ *1 Daytona Blvd.* ⊕ *www.onedaytona.com.*

TangerOutlets. Newly opened in November 2016, the 70-plus outlets here include Nike, Michael Kors, Polo Ralph Lauren, and Under Armor. ⊠ *1100 Cornerstone Blvd.* ☎ *386/843–7459* ⊕ *www.tangeroutlet.com/daytona.*

SPORTS AND THE OUTDOORS

AUTO RACING

Daytona International Speedway. If the beach is the main attraction in town, this iconic sports venue—home to the Daytona 500—is a close second. The massive speedway, which opened in 1959, completed a $400-million renovation in 2015 that transformed the aging structure into a bona fide "motorsports stadium." Now it's part racetrack, part sports stadium, and it seats more than 100,000 fans. Major racing events include the IMSA Rolex 24 at Daytona in January, Daytona 500 in February, Daytona 200 motorcycle race in March, and Coke Zero 400 in July. The venue hosts a multitude of other events throughout the year, including a country music festival, but racing is the focus. Those visiting on non-race days can enjoy one of the various tours. The three-hour VIP Tour (the most expensive option) includes having your photo taken in Victory Lane, a visit to the speedway's Archives and Research Center (home to Sir Malcolm Campbell's Bluebird III), and a close-up look at the most recent Daytona 500 winning car. ⊠ *1801 W. International Speedway Blvd.* ☎ *800/748–7467* ⊕ *www.daytonainternationalspeedway.com* 🎫 *Guided tours $18–$52.*

BIRD-WATCHING

Tomoka State Park. With more than 160 species to see, this scenic park is perfect for bird-watching. It also has wooded campsites, bicycle and walking paths, and kayak and canoe rentals on the Tomoka and Halifax rivers. It's on the site of a Timucuan Indian settlement discovered in 1605 by Spanish explorer Alvaro Mexia. ⊠ *2099 N. Beach St., Ormond Beach* ✛ *3 miles north of Ormond Beach* ☎ *386/676–4050* ⊕ *www.floridastateparks.org/tomoka* 🎫 *$5 per vehicle, up to 8 people; $2 pedestrians.*

BOATING

Cracker Creek. At this eco-adventure park you can rent kayaks, canoes, and hydrobikes, or take ecotours on scenic Spruce Creek. There are also on-site picnic facilities. ⊠ *1795 Taylor Rd., Port Orange* ☎ *386/304–0778* ⊕ *www.crackercreek.com.*

FISHING

Sea Spirit Fishing. Five- to nine-hour private and group charters are options with this operator. ⊠ *SeaLove Marina, 4884 Front St., Ponce Inlet* ☎ *386/763–4388* ⊕ *www.seaspiritfishing.com.*

GOLF

Club at Pelican Bay South Course. Golfers rave about the great value of Pelican Bay South, but one word of caution: what you save in greens fees you might give back in lost balls. No, this isn't the most difficult track. But the abundance of water—and challenging ocean breezes—can result in a lot of splashes for novices or overaggressive advanced players. Designed by Lloyd Clifton in 1984, the course is open to the public and features an island green on the par-4 15th. ⊠ *350 Pelican Bay Dr.* ☎ *386/756–0034* ⊕ *www.pelicanbaycc.com* ☞ *$29.95* ⚑ *18 holes, 6385 yards, par 72.*

LPGA International. This is where aspiring women professionals compete to earn a place on the LPGA Tour. The qualifying tournament—Q-school—is held every January, but the meticulously maintained courses are open to the public year-round. The Jones Course, designed by Rees Jones, is a links-style course with large, fast, undulating greens. Fairways are tighter on the Hills Course, designed by Arthur Hills, with long, difficult par-5s due to long carries and well-guarded greens. Wildlife is abundant, with bald eagles, owls, and deer as well as rattlesnakes and gators (some quite large). The course has driving, putting, and short-game practice areas, and an excellent restaurant, Malcolm's. ⊠ *1000 Champions Dr.* ☎ *386/523–2001* ⊕ *www.lpgainternational.com* ☞ *$65* ⚑ *Jones Course: 18 holes, 7088 yards, par 72; Hills Course: 18 holes, 6984 yards, par 72.*

Spruce Creek Golf & Country Club. Golfers distracted by loud noise might want to avoid this course, which is part of a fly-in community whose residents have included John Travolta and NASCAR star Mark Martin. Most, however, find the air traffic a unique amenity to this semiprivate course, considered one of the best golf values in the Daytona Beach area. The front 9 is challenging off the tees, with some tight, tree-lined fairways. Wind is more of a challenge on the more open back 9, where water lines 8 of the holes. A virtual tour on the club website gives golfers shot-by-shot advice in managing the course, which boasts a driving range as well as putting and short-game practice areas. ⊠ *1900 Country Club Dr., Port Orange* ☎ *386/756–6114* ⊕ *www.sprucecreekgolf.com* ☞ *$19 for 9 holes, $35 for 18 holes* ⚑ *18 holes, 6894 yards, par 72.*

MANATEE SPOTTING

Fodor's Choice ★ **Blue Spring State Park.** January and February are the top months for sighting sea cows at this designated manatee refuge, but they begin to head here in November, as soon as the water gets cold enough (below 68°F). Your best bet for spotting a manatee is to walk along the boardwalk.

The park, which is 30 miles southwest of Daytona Beach on Interstate 4, was once a river port where paddle wheelers stopped to take on cargoes of oranges. Home to the largest spring on the St. Johns River, the park offers hiking, camping, picnicking facilities, and two-bedroom cabins (two-night minimum weekends and holidays). It also contains a historic homestead that's open to the public. ⊠ *2100 W. French Ave., Orange City* 🏢 *386/775–3663* ⊕ *www.floridastateparks.org/bluespring* 🖻 *$6 per vehicle, up to 8 people; $2 pedestrians, bicyclists.*

FAMILY **Manatee Scenic Boat Tours.** This Ponce Inlet operator takes you on narrated cruises of the Intracoastal Waterway. Kids will love looking for the creatures also known as "sea cows," and your guide might tell you how (sun-delirious?) sailors may have mistaken them for mermaids. ⊠ *4884 Front St., Ponce Inlet* 🏢 *386/761–2027, 800/881–2628* ⊕ *www. manateecruise.com* 🖻 *$25.*

WATER SPORTS

Maui Nix. This is one of several outfitters that rent surf and boogie boards. ⊠ *635 N. Atlantic Ave.* 🏢 *386/253–1234* ⊕ *www.mauinix.com/store.*

Salty Dog Surf Shop. You can rent surfboards or paddleboards here. ⊠ *201 E. Granada Blvd., Ormond Beach* 🏢 *386/673–5277* ⊕ *www. saltydogsurfshop.com.*

NEW SMYRNA BEACH

19 miles south of Daytona Beach, 56 miles northeast of Orlando.

The long, dune-lined beach of this small town abuts the Canaveral National Seashore. Behind the dunes sit beach houses, small motels, and an occasional high-rise (except at the extreme northern tip, where none is higher than seven stories). Canal Street, on the mainland, and Flagler Avenue, with many beachside shops and restaurants, have both been "streetscaped" with wide brick sidewalks and stately palm trees. The town is also known for its internationally recognized artists' workshop and some of the best surfing on the East Coast.

EXPLORING

Arts on Douglas. In a warehouse that has been converted into a stunning 5,000-square-foot, high-ceiling art gallery, Arts on Douglas has a new exhibit of works by a Florida artist every month. Representing more than 50 Florida artists, the gallery has hosted exhibits on the handmade jewelry of Mary Schimpff Webb and landscape and still-life oils by Barbara Tiffany. The gallery also holds an opening reception every first Saturday of the month from 4 to 7 pm. ⊠ *123 Douglas St.* 🏢 *386/428–1133* ⊕ *www.artsondouglas.net* 🖻 *Free* ⊗ *Closed Sun. and Mon.*

Atlantic Center for the Arts. With exhibits that change every two months, the Atlantic Center for the Arts has works of internationally known artists. Mediums include sculpture, mixed materials, video, drawings, prints, and paintings. Intensive three-week residencies are periodically run by visual-, literary-, and performing-master artists. ⊠ *1414 Art Center Ave.* 🏢 *386/427–6975* ⊕ *www.atlanticcenterforthearts.org* 🖻 *Free* ⊗ *Closed Sun. and Mon.*

13

Canaveral National Seashore. Miles of grassy windswept dunes and a virtually empty beach await you at this remarkable 57,000-acre park on a barrier island with 24 miles of undeveloped coastline spanning from New Smyrna to Titusville. The unspoiled area of hilly sand dunes, grassy marshes, and seashell-sprinkled beaches is a large part of NASA's buffer zone and is home to more than 1,000 species of plants and 300 species of birds and other animals. Surf and lagoon fishing are available, and a hiking trail leads to the top of an American Indian shell midden at Turtle Mound. For an additional charge, visitors can take a pontoon-boat tour ($20) or participate in the turtle-watch interpretive program ($14). Reservations are required. A visitor center is on Route A1A at Apollo Beach. Weekends are busy, and parts of the park are closed when mandated by launch operations at the Kennedy Space Center, so call ahead. ⊠ *Visitor Information Center, 7611 S. Atlantic Ave.* ☎ *386/428–3384* ⊕ *www.nps.gov/cana* ⌨ *$10 cars; $1 pedestrians, bicycles.*

Smyrna Dunes Park. In this park, on a barrier island at the northernmost tip of New Smyrna Beach peninsula, 1½ miles of boardwalks crisscross sand dunes and delicate dune vegetation to lead to beaches and a fishing jetty. Botanical signs identify the flora, and there are picnic tables and an information center. It's also one of the few county parks where pets are allowed (on leashes, that is). ⊠ *2995 N. Peninsula Ave.* ☎ *386/424–2935* ⊕ *www.volusia.org/services/public-works/coastal-division/coastal-parks/smyrna-dunes-park.stml* ⌨ *$10 per vehicle, up to 8 people.*

BEACHES

Apollo Beach. In addition to typical beach activities, visitors to this beach on the northern end of Canaveral National Seashore can also ride horses here (with a permit), hike self-guided trails, and tour the historic Eldora Statehouse. From Interstate 95, take Exit 220 and head east. **Amenities:** lifeguards (seasonal); parking (fee); toilets. **Best for:** solitude; swimming; walking. ⊠ *Rte. A1A, at the southern end of New Smyrna Beach* ☎ *386/428–3384* ⌨ *$10 per vehicle for national seashore.*

New Smyrna Beach. This public beach extends 7 miles from the northernmost part of New Smyrna's barrier island south to the Canaveral National Seashore. It's mostly hard-packed white sand, and at low tide can be stunningly wide in some areas. The beach is lined with heaps of sandy dunes, but because they're endangered, it's against the law to walk on or play in them or to pick the sea grass, which helps to stabilize the dunes. From sunrise to sunset cars are allowed on certain sections of the beach (speed limit: 10 mph). In season there's a $10 beach-access fee for cars. **Amenities:** food and drink; lifeguards; parking (some with fee); showers; toilets; water sports. **Best for:** sunrise; surfing; swimming; walking. ⊠ *Rte. A1A.*

WHERE TO EAT

$$
SEAFOOD

✕ **J.B.'s Fish Camp and Restaurant.** Better known simply as J.B.'s, this local landmark is on the eastern shore of the Indian River (i.e., the middle of nowhere). Crowds gather around the picnic-style tables inside and out, or belly up to the bar to dine on mounds of spicy seafood, Cajun alligator, J.B.'s famous crab cakes, and rock shrimp by the dozen. **Known for:** spicy steamed shrimp and crabs; blackened alligator; delicious hush puppies. $ *Average main: $17* ✉ *859 Pompano Ave.* ☎ *386/427–5747* ⊕ *www.jbsfishcamp.com.*

$$$
SEAFOOD

✕ **Norwood's Restaurant & Wine Shop.** Fresh local fish and shrimp are the specialties at this bustling New Smyrna Beach landmark, open since 1946. Built as a gas station, the building later served as a general store and piggy-bank factory, but the remodeled interior belies this backstory; the place is replete with wood, from the chairs and booths to the walls and rafters. **Known for:** she-crab soup; vast wine selection; unique tree-house bar. $ *Average main: $22* ✉ *400 2nd Ave.* ☎ *386/428–4621* ⊕ *www.norwoods.com.*

$$$
CUBAN
Fodor's Choice
★

✕ **Spanish River Grill.** Michele and Henry Salgado own this modern Cuban and Spanish eatery, which many locals think is the best restaurant in New Smyrna Beach. Henry combines his Cuban grandmother's recipes with local ingredients for knockout results. **Known for:** yuca-crusted fish; churrasco steak; nice tapas selection. $ *Average main: $21* ✉ *737 E. 3rd Ave.* ☎ *386/424–6991* ⊕ *www.thespanishrivergrill.com* ☾ *Closed Mon.*

WHERE TO STAY

$
B&B/INN
Fodor's Choice
★

▤ **Black Dolphin Inn.** On a quaint residential street, this Spanish-style, three-story inn combines the charm and hospitality of a B&B with modern sensibilities and a chic, coastal-casual vibe. **Pros:** hospitable staff; river views; comfy beds. **Cons:** no pool; must drive to the beach. $ *Rooms from: $189* ✉ *916 S. Riverside Dr.* ☎ *386/410–4868, 855/410–4868* ⊕ *www.blackdolphininn.com* ⤳ *14 rooms* ⦿*| Breakfast.*

$$
B&B/INN

▤ **Riverview Hotel and Spa.** A landmark since 1885, this former bridge tender's home is set back from the Intracoastal Waterway at the edge of the north causeway, which still has an operating drawbridge. **Pros:** on-site spa and dining; hospitable staff; homey feel. **Cons:** small rooms in main house; strict cancellation policy; blocks from the beach. $ *Rooms from: $219* ✉ *103 Flagler Ave.* ☎ *386/428–5858, 800/945–7416* ⊕ *www.riverviewhotel.com* ⤳ *17 rooms, 1 suite* ⦿*| Breakfast.*

OCALA NATIONAL FOREST

Eastern entrance 40 miles west of Daytona Beach, northern entrance 52 miles south of Jacksonville.

This breathtaking 383,000-acre national forest off Route 40 has lakes, springs, rivers, hiking trails, campgrounds, and historic sites. It also has the largest off-highway vehicle trail system in the southeast and three major recreational areas: Alexander Springs, Salt Springs, and Juniper Springs. To get here, take Interstate 4 east to Exit 92, and head west on Route 436 to U.S. 441, which you take north to Route 19 north.

Alexander Springs Recreation Area. In this recreation area you'll find a stream for swimming, canoeing, and kayaking and a campground. ✉ *49525 Rte. 445 S, off Rte. 40, Altoona* ⊕ *www.fs.usda.gov/recarea/ ocala* ⌦ *$5.50.*

Juniper Springs Recreation Area. Here you'll find a stone waterwheel house, a campground, a natural-spring swimming pool, and hiking trails. The 7-mile Juniper Springs run is a narrow, twisting, and winding canoe ride, which, although exhilarating, isn't for the novice. ⊠ *14100 Rte. 40 N, Silver Springs* ⊕ *www.fs.usda.gov/recarea/ocala* ⊑ *$5.*

Salt Springs Recreation Area. The draw here is a natural saltwater spring where Atlantic blue crabs come to spawn each summer. ⊠ *Visitor Center, 14100 Rte. 19, Fort McCoy* ☎ *352/685–3070* ⊑ *$6.*

SPORTS AND THE OUTDOORS

CANOEING

Juniper Springs Canoe Rentals. This operator inside the national forest offers canoe rentals. ⊠ *Juniper Springs Recreation Area, 26701 Florida 40, Silver Springs* ☎ *877/444–6777* ⊑ *$33 (includes shuttle transports at end of run).*

FISHING

Captain Tom's Custom Charters. Charter fishing trips offered by this company range from two hours to a full day. You can arrange sightseeing cruises as well. Trips are by reservation only and are operated in a variety of areas within the national forest. ☎ *352/236–0872* ⊕ *www. captaintomscustomcharters.net.*

HORSEBACK RIDING

Adopt a Horse Club. Located within the Ocala National Forest, this outfitter offers trail riding and lessons (walk, gait, and canter) and guided rides for all ages. ⊠ *22651 S.E. Rte. 42, Umatilla* ☎ *352/821–4756, 800/731–4756* ⊕ *www.adoptahorseclub.com.*

GAINESVILLE

98 miles northwest of Daytona Beach.

The University of Florida (UF) anchors this sprawling town. Visitors are mostly Gator-football fans and parents of students, so the styles and costs of accommodations are aimed at budget-minded travelers rather than luxury-seeking vacationers. The surrounding area encompasses several state parks and interesting gardens and geological sites.

GETTING HERE AND AROUND

Gainesville Regional Airport is served by American and Delta. From the airport, taxi fare to the center of Gainesville is about $20; some hotels provide free airport pickup.

Contact Gainesville Regional Airport (*GNV*). ⊠ *3880 N.E. 39th Ave.* ☎ *352/373–0249* ⊕ *www.gra-gnv.com.*

VISITOR INFORMATION

Contact Gainesville/Alachua County Visitors and Convention Bureau. ☎ *352/374–5260, 866/778–5002* ⊕ *www.visitgainesville.com.*

EXPLORING

Devil's Millhopper Geological State Park. Scientists surmise that thousands of years ago an underground cavern collapsed and created this geological wonder that is designated as a National Natural Landmark. You pass a dozen small waterfalls as you head down 236 steps to the bottom of this botanical wonderland: exotic subtropical ferns and trees growing in a 500-foot-wide, 120-foot-deep sinkhole. You can pack a lunch to enjoy in one of the park's picnic areas. And bring Spot, too; just keep him on a leash. Guided walks with a park ranger are offered Saturday mornings at 10. ⊠ *4732 Millhopper Rd., off U.S. 441* ☎ *352/955–2008* ⊕ *www.floridastateparks.org/devilsmillhopper* ⌗ *$4 per vehicle, up to 8 people; $2 pedestrians and bicyclists* ⊙ *Closed Mon. and Tues.*

> ### LATER, GATORS
>
> Depending on what time of year you visit, Gainesville's population could be plus or minus 50,000. Home to one of the largest colleges in the country, the University of Florida, Gainesville takes on a different personality during the summer, when most students return home. During the fall and spring terms, the downtown streets are teeming with students on bikes, scooters, and foot, but in summer it's much more laid-back.

FAMILY **Florida Museum of Natural History.** On the campus of the University of Florida, the state's official museum of natural history and the largest natural history museum in the southeast has holdings of more than 40 million specimens of amphibians, birds, butterflies, fish, mammals, mollusks, reptiles, vertebrate and invertebrate fossils, recent and fossil plants, and archaeology and anthropology artifacts. It also holds one of the world's largest collections of butterflies and moths. Permanent exhibits include information on Florida's geological and fossil history, its early native peoples, and biodiversity of flora and fauna. Visitors can enjoy live butterflies, witness a Calusa Indian welcoming ceremony, experience a life-size limestone cave, and see fossil skeletons of a mammoth and mastodon from the last ice age. The museum features changing temporary exhibits, and kids eight and under will love the interactive Discovery Room. Butterfly releases take place weekdays at 2, and weekends at 2, 3, and 4, weather permitting. ⊠ *University of Florida Cultural Plaza, S.W. 34th St. at Hull Rd.* ☎ *352/846–2000* ⊕ *www.flmnh.ufl.edu* ⌗ *Free; Butterfly Rainforest $13; parking $4.*

FAMILY **Marjorie Kinnan Rawlings Historic State Park.** One of America's most cherished authors found inspiration in this out-of-the-way hamlet about 20 miles outside of Gainesville. The 90-acre park, set amid aromatic citrus groves, has a playground for kids and short hiking trails, where you might see owls, deer, or Rawlings' beloved "red birds." But the main attraction is the restored Florida Cracker–style home, where Rawlings wrote classics such as *The Yearling* and *Cross Creek* and entertained the likes of poet Robert Frost, author Thornton Wilder, and actor Gregory Peck. Although the house is guarded closely by spirited roosters, guided tours are offered seasonally. ⊠ *18700 S. County Rd. 325, Hawthorne* ☎ *352/466–3672* ⊕ *www.floridastateparks.org/marjoriekinnanrawlings* ⌗ *$3 per car; house tour is an additional $3* ⊙ *No house tours Aug. and Sept.*

Samuel P. Harn Museum of Art. This 112,800-square-foot museum has five main collections: Asian, with works dating back to the Neolithic era; African, encompassing costumes, domestic wares, and personal adornments; Modern, featuring the works of Georgia O'Keeffe, William Morris Hunt, Claude Monet, and George Bellows; Contemporary, with original pieces by Yayoi Kusama and El Anatsui; and Photography, including the work of Jerry N. Uelsmann, a retired University of Florida professor. ✉ *3259 Hull Rd.* ☎ *352/392–9826* 🌐 *www.harn.ufl.edu* 🎟 *Free* 🕒 *Closed Mon.*

WHERE TO EAT

$$ ECLECTIC 🍴 **Civilization.** "Eclectic" only begins to describe this wildly popular restaurant with the funny name, throwback policies (cash only), and inventive dishes representing all regions of the globe. The menu contains nods to any cuisine you might imagine—from Ethiopia to Greece to Thailand, and points in between. **Known for:** very vegetarian- and vegan-friendly; sheba plate (Ethiopian sampler); weekend brunch. [$] *Average main: $15* ✉ *1511 N.W. 2nd St.* ☎ *352/380–0544* 🌐 *welcometocivilization.com* 💳 *No credit cards.*

$$ LATIN AMERICAN 🍴 **Emiliano's Café.** Linen tablecloths and art deco–style artwork create a casual, elegant feel at this Gainesville institution that has been serving Pan-Latin cuisine since 1984. Start with the Spanish stew (a family recipe) and then move on to one of the chef's signature dishes such as mofongo or paella (Spanish saffron rice with shrimp, clams, mussels, fresh fish, chicken, artichoke hearts, peas, asparagus, and pimientos). **Known for:** seafood and chicken paella; mofongo; weekend brunch. [$] *Average main: $18* ✉ *7 S.E. 1st Ave.* ☎ *352/375–7381* 🌐 *www.emilianoscafe.com.*

$$$ EUROPEAN Fodor's Choice ★ 🍴 **Paramount Grill.** This tiny, fine-dining restaurant may have single-handedly changed the perception of Gainesville from a college town fueled by pizza, chicken wings, and pitchers of beer to an up-and-coming culinary destination with imaginative menus driven by fresh Florida produce. The ever-changing menu might include such items as an organic beet salad, grilled salmon over sweet potato and cotija cheese enchiladas, or pan-roasted angus fillet over chive mashed Yukon Golds. **Known for:** filet mignon; grilled duck breast; Sunday brunch. [$] *Average main: $29* ✉ *12 S.W. 1st Ave.* ☎ *352/378–3398* 🌐 *www.paramountgrill.com.*

WHERE TO STAY

$ HOTEL 🏨 **Hilton University of Florida Conference Center Gainesville.** With 25,000 square feet of meeting space, the University of Florida's flagship hotel caters most obviously to business travelers, but its location on the southwest corner of campus also makes it a good choice for UF visitors. **Pros:** proximity to college; spacious rooms; free use of business center. **Cons:** spotty service; overrated restaurant; charge for Wi-Fi. [$] *Rooms from: $199* ✉ *1714 S.W. 34th St.* ☎ *352/371–3600* 🌐 *www.hilton.com* 🛏 *248 rooms* 🍽 *No meals.*

$ B&B/INN 🏨 **Laurel Oak Inn.** Guests at this 1885 Queen Anne–style dwelling say they're so comfortable and at ease they feel like they're in a home, not an inn. **Pros:** three-course breakfast; location; hospitable staff. **Cons:** processing fee for cancellations; no pool. [$] *Rooms from: $135* ✉ *221 S.E. 7th St.* ☎ *352/373–4535* 🌐 *www.laureloakinn.com* 🛏 *5 rooms, 1 cottage* 🍽 *Breakfast.*

$ B&B/INN Fodor's Choice ★ 🏨 **The Magnolia Plantation.** Among only a handful of French Second Empire buildings in the southeastern United States, this inn consists of a main house, built in 1885, and six adorable cottages. **Pros:** friendly service; breakfast; nightly social hour. **Cons:** some small rooms; seven-day cancellation policy. [$] *Rooms from: $161* ✉ *309 S.E. 7th*

St. ☎ *352/375–6653, 800/201–2379* 🌐 *www.magnoliabnb.com* 🛏 *5 rooms, 9 cottages* 🍴 *Breakfast.*

$ B&B/INN 🏨 **Sweetwater Branch Inn Bed & Breakfast.** Modern conveniences such as hair dryers, complimentary Wi-Fi, a new pool, and business services mix with Southern charm and hospitality, all wrapped up in two grand Victorian homes surrounded by lush tropical gardens. **Pros:** Southern-style breakfast; Jacuzzi suites. **Cons:** occasional noise issues; frequent on-site weddings. [$] *Rooms from: $141* ✉ *625 E. University Ave.* ☎ *352/373–6760, 800/595–7760* 🌐 *www.sweetwaterinn.com* 🛏 *12 rooms, 8 cottages* 🍴 *Breakfast.*

13

SPORTS AND THE OUTDOORS

AUTO RACING

Gainesville Raceway. The site of professional and amateur auto and motorcycle races, including Gatornationals in March, is also home to Frank Hawley's Drag Racing School (🌐 *frankhawley.com*). ✉ *11211 N. County Rd. 225* ☎ *352/377–0046 Raceway, 866/480–7223 Drag Racing School* 🌐 *www.autoplusraceway.com.*

FOOTBALL

Ben Hill Griffin Stadium. The University of Florida Gators play their home games in the largest stadium in the state, also referred to as "The Swamp." ✉ *Lemerand Dr. at Stadium Rd.* ☎ *352/375–4683.*

THE SPACE COAST

Updated by Jennifer Greenhill-Taylor

South of the Daytona Beach area and Canaveral National Seashore are Merritt Island National Wildlife Refuge, the John F. Kennedy Space Center, and Cape Canaveral—hence the name "Space Coast." This area is also home to a popular cruise-ship port, Port Canaveral, and the laid-back town of Cocoa Beach, which attracts visitors on weekends year-round because of its proximity to Orlando, 50 miles to the west.

VISITOR INFORMATION

Contact Space Coast Office of Tourism. ☎ *877/572–3224, 321/433–4470* 🌐 *www.visitspacecoast.com.*

TITUSVILLE

34 miles south of New Smyrna Beach, 67 miles east of Orlando.

It's unusual that such a small, easily overlooked community could accommodate what it does, namely the magnificent Merritt Island National Wildlife Refuge and the entrance to the Kennedy Space Center, the nerve center of the U.S. space program.

EXPLORING

American Police Hall of Fame & Museum. Police officers deserve our respect, and you'll be reminded why at this intriguing attraction. In addition to memorabilia like the *Robocop* costume and *Blade Runner* car from the films, informative displays offer insight into the dangers officers face every day: drugs, homicides, and criminals who can create knives from dental putty and guns from a bicycle spoke. Other exhibits spotlight the gory history of capital punishment (from hangings to the guillotine to the electric chair) and crime scene investigation, terrorism, and a rotunda where more than 9,000 names are etched in marble to honor police officers who have died in the line of duty. A 24-stall shooting range provides rental guns. ⊠ *6350 Horizon Dr.* ☎ *321/264–0911* ⊕ *www.aphf.org* ✍ *$13.*

FAMILY

Fodor'sChoice

★

Kennedy Space Center Visitor Complex. America's space program—past, present, and future—is the star at this must-see attraction, just 45 minutes east of Orlando, where visitors are treated to a multitude of interactive experiences. Located on a 140,000-acre barrier island, Kennedy Space Center was NASA's launch headquarters from the beginning of the space program in the 1960s until the final shuttle launch in 2012. Thanks to an invigorated NASA program and to high-tech entrepreneurs who have turned their interests to space, visitors to the complex can once again view live rocket launches from the Cape. In fact, there were 15 launches in 2016—even more in 2017 (check the website for launch schedule).

In November 2016, the center opened its much-anticipated Heroes & Legends attraction, which celebrates the men and women who've journeyed to space, and features the relocated U.S. Astronaut Hall of Fame. The original *Mercury 7* team and the later *Gemini, Apollo, Skylab,* and shuttle astronauts have contributed artifacts and memorabilia to make it the world's premium archive of astronauts' personal stories. You can watch videos of historic moments in the space program and see one-of-a-kind items such as Wally Schirra's *Sigma 7* Mercury space capsule, Gus Grissom's space suit (colored silver only because NASA thought silver looked more "spacey"), and a flag that made it to the moon. The exhibit First on the Moon focuses on crew selection for *Apollo 11* and the Soviet Union's role in the space race. Don't miss Simulation Station, a hands-on discovery center with interactive exhibits that help you learn about space travel. One of the more challenging activities is a space-shuttle simulator that lets you try your hand at landing the craft—and afterward replays a side view of your rolling and pitching descent.

The IMAX film, *Journey To Space,* narrated by *Star Trek* legend Sir Patrick Stewart, fills a five-story movie screen with dramatic footage shot by NASA astronauts during missions, accentuating the bravery of all space travelers while capturing the spirit of the human desire to explore and expand. The film honors the milestones of the Space Shuttle Program—deploying and repairing the Hubble Space Telescope, assembling the International Space Station—and then looks forward to the deep-space exploration missions to come, offering a glimpse of the Space Launch System rocket that will send the *Orion* crew capsule toward Mars.

The drama of the IMAX films gives you great background for the many interactive programs available at the complex. The bus tour included with admission (buses depart every 15 minutes) takes you past iconic spots, including the 525-foot-tall Vehicle Assembly Building and launch pads, which are getting ready for future missions. Stops include the Apollo/Saturn V Center, where you can look up in awe at one of three remaining Saturn V moon rockets, the largest rocket ever built. Other exhibits include the Early Space Exploration display, which highlights the rudimentary yet influential Mercury and Gemini space programs; and the Lunar Theater, which shows the first moon landing. Visitors can dine next to a genuine moon rock at the cleverly named Moon Rock Café.

Several Up-Close tours offer more intimate views of the VAB, the Shuttle Landing Facility, the runway where the shuttles landed (now slated for use by the Sierra Nevada *Dream Chaser*, one of the commercial spacecraft under development), and the Cape Canaveral launch pads, where NASA, SpaceX, and the United Launch Alliance rockets await takeoff. Other iconic images include the countdown clock at NASA's Press Site, a giant crawler transporter that carried Apollo moon rockets and space shuttles to the launch pad, and the Launch Control Center. The Then and Now Guided Tour (extra charge), visits America's first launch sites from the 1960s and the 21st century's active unmanned-rocket program.

The space shuttle *Atlantis* attraction offers views of this historic spacecraft as only astronauts have seen it—rotated 43.21 degrees with payload bay doors open and its robotic arm extended, as if it has just undocked from the International Space Station. The attraction includes a variety of interactive highlights, including opportunities to perform an Extravehicular Activity (EVA), train like an astronaut, and create sonic booms while piloting *Atlantis* to a safe landing.

Don't miss the outdoor Rocket Garden, with walkways winding beside a group of historic vintage rockets, from early Atlas spacecraft to a *Saturn IB*. The Children's Playdome enables kids to play among the next generation of spacecraft, climb a moon-rock wall, and crawl through rocket tunnels. Astronaut Encounter Theater has two daily programs where retired NASA astronauts share their adventures in space travel and show a short film.

More befitting a theme park (complete with the health warnings), the Shuttle Launch Experience is the center's most spectacular attraction. Designed by a team of astronauts, NASA experts, and renowned attraction engineers, the 44,000-square-foot structure uses a sophisticated motion-based platform, special-effects seats, and high-fidelity visual and audio components to simulate the sensations experienced in an actual space-shuttle launch, including MaxQ, Solid Rocket Booster separation, main engine cutoff, and External Tank separation. The journey culminates with a breathtaking view of Earth from space.

A fitting way to end the day is a stop at the black-granite Astronaut Memorial, which honors those who lost their lives in the name of space exploration.

Other add-ons include Lunch with an Astronaut, where astronauts talk about their experiences and engage in a good-natured Q&A; the typical line of questioning from kids: "How do you eat/sleep/relieve yourself in space?" ⊠ *Kennedy Space Center, Rte. 405* ☎ *877/313–2610* ⊕ *www.*

kennedyspacecenter.com 🖼 *$50 (includes bus tour, IMAX movies, visitor complex shows and exhibits, and Astronaut Hall of Fame); specialty tours $21–$25; Lunch with an Astronaut $29.99.*

Valiant Air Command Warbird Museum & Tico Airshow. Don't judge a book by its cover: what's inside this very ordinary looking building is extraordinary. Operated mostly through the efforts of an enthusiastic team of volunteers, the museum is a treasure trove of aviation history, with memorabilia from World Wars I and II, Korea, and Vietnam, as well as extensive displays of vintage military flying gear and uniforms. There are posters that were used to help identify Japanese planes, plus a Huey helicopter and the cockpit of an F-106 that you can sit in. In the north hangar a group of dedicated aviation volunteers busily restores old planes. It's an inspiring sight, and a good place to hear some war stories. In the spring the museum puts on the Tico Warbird Airshow, featuring fighter and bomber aircraft that formerly flew in combat around the world. The lobby gift shop sells real flight suits, old flight magazines, bomber jackets, books, models, and T-shirts. ⊠ *6600 Tico Rd.* ☎ *321/268–1941* ⊕ *www.vacwarbirds.org* 🖼 *$20.*

BEACHES

Playalinda Beach. The southern access for the Canaveral National Seashore, remote Playalinda Beach has pristine sands and is the longest stretch of undeveloped coast on Florida's Atlantic seaboard. You can, however, see the shuttle launch pad at Cape Kennedy from the beach. Hundreds of giant sea turtles come ashore here from May through August to lay their eggs. Fourteen parking lots anchor the beach at 1-mile intervals. From Interstate 95, take Exit 249 and head east. Bring bug repellent in case of horseflies, and note that you may see some unauthorized clothing-optional activity. **Amenities:** lifeguards (seasonal); parking (fee); toilets. **Best for:** solitude; swimming; walking. ⊠ *Rte. 402, at northern end of Beach Rd.* ☎ *321/267–1110* ⊕ *www.nps.gov/cana* 🖼 *$5 per vehicle for national seashore.*

WHERE TO EAT

$$$ ✕ **Dixie Crossroads.** This sprawling restaurant is always crowded and
SEAFOOD   festive, but it's not just the rustic setting that draws the throngs—it's the seafood. The specialty is rock shrimp, which are served fried, broiled, or steamed. **Known for:** locally caught rock shrimp; corn fritters dusted with powdered sugar; long waits for tables at peak hours. Ⓢ *Average main: $23* ⊠ *1475 Garden St., 2 miles east of I–95 Exit 220* ☎ *321/268–5000* ⊕ *www.dixiecrossroads.com.*

WHERE TO STAY

$ ⛺ **Hampton Inn Titusville.** Proximity to the Kennedy Space Center and
HOTEL   reasonable rates make this four-story hotel a top pick for an overnight near the center. **Pros:** free Wi-Fi; extra-comfy beds; convenient to Interstate 95. **Cons:** thin walls; no restaurant on-site; no room service. Ⓢ *Rooms from: $139* ⊠ *4760 Helen Hauser Blvd.* ☎ *321/383–9191* ⊕ *www.hamptoninn.com* ↝ *90 rooms* ⧾⧾ *Breakfast.*

SPORTS AND THE OUTDOORS

Fodor's Choice **Merritt Island National Wildlife Refuge.** Owned by NASA, but part of
★ the National Wildlife Refuge System, this 140,000-acre refuge, which
adjoins the Canaveral National Seashore, acts as a buffer around
Kennedy Space Center while protecting 1,000 species of plants and
500 species of wildlife, including 15 federally considered threatened
or endangered. It's an immense area dotted by brackish estuaries and
marshes, coastal dunes, hardwood hammocks, and pine forests. You
can borrow field guides and binoculars at the visitor center (5 miles
east of U.S. 1 in Titusville on State Road 402) to track down falcons,
ospreys, eagles, turkeys, doves, cuckoos, owls, and woodpeckers, as
well as loggerhead turtles, alligators, wild boar, and otters. A 20-minute
video about refuge wildlife and accessibility—only 10,000 acres are
developed—can help orient you.

You might take a self-guided driving tour along the 7-mile Black Point
Wildlife Drive. Several roads and trails, including the Oak Hammock
Foot Trail, are closed indefinitely because of damage from 2016's Hurricane Matthew. Check with the website for updates on openings. If
you exit the north end of the refuge, look for the Manatee Observation
Area just north of the Haulover Canal (maps are at the visitor center).
They usually show up in spring and fall. There are also fishing camps,
fishing boat ramps, and six hiking trails scattered throughout the area.
If you do want to fish, a free, downloadable permit is required. The
refuge does not close when there is a launch. ⊠ *Visitor Center, Rte. 402,
5 miles east of U.S. 1 across Titusville Causeway* ☎ *321/861–0667,
321/861–0669 visitor center* ⊕ *www.fws.gov/refuge/merritt_island*
🖅 *Free; $5 per vehicle on Black Point Wildlife Dr. only.*

COCOA

17 miles south of Titusville.

Not to be confused with the seaside community of Cocoa Beach, the
small town of Cocoa sits smack-dab on mainland Florida and faces
the Intracoastal Waterway, known locally as Indian River. There's a
planetarium and a museum, as well as a rustic fish camp along the St.
Johns River, a few miles inland.

Folks in a rush to get to the beach tend to overlook Cocoa's Victorian-
style village, but it's worth a stop and is perhaps Cocoa's most interesting feature. Within the cluster of restored turn-of-the-20th-century
buildings and cobblestone walkways you can enjoy several restaurants,
indoor and outdoor cafés, snack and ice-cream shops, and more than
50 specialty shops and art galleries. The area hosts music performances
in the gazebo, arts-and-crafts shows, and other family-friendly events
throughout the year. To get to Cocoa Village, head east on Route 520—
named King Street in Cocoa—and when the streets get narrow and the
road curves, make a right onto Brevard Avenue; follow the signs for
the free municipal parking lot.

13

EXPLORING

FAMILY **Brevard Museum of History & Natural Science.** This is the place to come to see what the lay of the local land looked like in other eras. Hands-on activities draw children, who especially migrate toward the Imagination Center, where they can act out history or reenact a space shuttle flight. Not to be missed are Ice Age–era creatures such as a fully articulated mastodon, giant ground sloth, and saber-tooth cat. The Windover Archaeological Exhibit features 7,000-year-old artifacts indigenous to the region. In 1984, a shallow pond revealed the burial ground of more than 200 American Indians who lived in the area about 7,000 years ago. Preserved in the muck were bones and, to the archeologists' surprise, the brains of these ancient people. Nature lovers appreciate the museum's butterfly garden and the nature center with 22 acres of trails encompassing three distinct ecosystems—sand pine hills, lake lands, and marshlands. ✉ *2201 Michigan Ave.* ☎ *321/632–1830* 🌐 *www.myfloridahistory.org* 🎟 *$9* ⏲ *Closed Sun.–Tues.*

WHERE TO EAT

$$$ ECLECTIC Fodor's Choice ★ 🍴 **Café Margaux.** Eclectic, creative, and international is the best way to describe the cuisine and decor at this charming Cocoa Village spot, featured in 2015 on the Food Network. The menu blends French, Italian, and Asian influences with dishes such as lollipop pork chop over English pea-and-orzo risotto, sweet onion–crusted fresh red snapper, and braised veal scaloppine. **Known for:** great steaks; outdoor seating under umbrellas; vast wine list. [$] *Average main: $26* ✉ *220 Brevard Ave.* ☎ *321/639–8343* 🌐 *www.margaux.com* ⏲ *Closed Sun.*

$ ECLECTIC 🍴 **Lone Cabbage Fish Camp.** The word "rustic" doesn't even begin to describe this down-home, no-nonsense fish camp restaurant (translation: you eat off paper plates with plastic forks) housed in a weathered, old, clapboard shack along with a bait shop and airboat-tour company. Set your calorie counter on stun, as you peruse the plates of fried fish, frogs' legs, turtle, and alligator (as well as burgers and hot dogs). **Known for:** fried fish; frogs' legs and gator; airboat rides. [$] *Average main: $10* ✉ *8199 Rte. 520, at St. Johns River* ☎ *321/632–4199.*

SHOPPING

Cocoa Village. You could spend hours browsing in the more than 50 boutiques here, along Brevard Avenue and Harrison Street (the latter has the densest concentration of shops). Although most stores are of the gift and clothing variety, the village is also home to antiques shops, art galleries, restaurants, a tattoo parlor, and a spa. ✉ *Rte. 520 at Brevard Ave.* ☎ *321/631–9075* 🌐 *www.visitcocoavillage.com.*

Renninger's Super Flea & Farmers' Market. You're sure to find a bargain at one of the 800+ booths at this market, which is held every Friday, Saturday, and Sunday from 9 to 4. ✉ *4835 W. Eau Gallie Blvd., Melbourne* ☎ *321/242–9124* 🌐 *renningers.net/index.php/melbourne-home.*

SPORTS AND THE OUTDOORS

BOATING

FAMILY **Twister Airboat Rides.** If you haven't seen the swampy, alligator-ridden waters of Florida, then you haven't really seen Florida. This thrilling wildlife tour goes where eagles and wading birds coexist with water moccasins and gators. The Coast Guard–certified deluxe airboats hit speeds of up to 45 mph and offer unparalleled opportunities to photograph native species. The basic tour lasts 30 minutes, but 60- and 90-minute ecotours are also available at an additional cost by reservation only. Twister Airboat Rides is inside the Lone Cabbage Fish Camp, about 9 miles west of Cocoa's city limits, 4 miles west of Interstate 95. ✉ *8199 Rte. 520, at St. Johns River* ☎ *321/632–4199* 🌐 *www.twisterairboatrides.com* 🎫 *$24.*

CAPE CANAVERAL

5 miles east of Cocoa via Rte. A1A.

The once-bustling commercial fishing area of Cape Canaveral is still home to a small shrimping fleet, charter boats, and party fishing boats, but its main business these days is as a cruise-ship port. The north end of the port, where the Carnival, Disney, and Royal Caribbean cruise lines set sail, has some good waterfront restaurants, with big viewing decks. Port Canaveral is now Florida's second-busiest cruise port for multiday cruises, which makes this a great place to catch a glimpse of these giant ships. It's also a great place to catch sight of an unmanned rocket being launched from Cape Canaveral Air Force Base.

EXPLORING

FAMILY **Exploration Tower.** The best view at Port Canaveral is no longer from the top of your cruise ship. In fact, the view from atop this towering seven-story structure, which opened in late 2013, makes the cruise ships look—well, not so massive after all. The tower, a short walk from the cruise port, is equal parts museum and scenic overlook. The seventh-floor observation deck offers impressive views of the cruise port, the Atlantic Ocean, the Banana River, and even the Vehicle Assembly Building at Kennedy Space Center. Other floors house exhibits highlighting the cultural history of the area, from space flight to surfing, bird and sea life to the rich maritime history. Kids will enjoy interactive exhibits, including a virtual ship's bridge that allows you to pilot a boat through the Canaveral Channel and into the Atlantic. A theater shows a 20-minute film dedicated to the history of Brevard County, and a small café sells refreshments and baked goods. The ground floor houses a visitor information center. ✉ *670 Dave Nisbet Dr.* ☎ *321/394–3408* 🌐 *www.explorationtower.com* 🎫 *$6.50.*

WHERE TO EAT

$$ SEAFOOD 🍴 **Seafood Atlantic.** Locals think of this casual waterfront seafood market/eatery as a well-kept secret, but more and more cruise patrons are making their way here for a pre- or post-cruise treat. The market is connected to the restaurant, guaranteeing not only freshness but an array of choices. **Known for:** variety of shrimp; crab cakes; views of departing and arriving cruise ships. [$] *Average main: $19* ✉ *520 Glen Cheek Dr.* ☎ *321/784–1963* 🌐 *www.seafoodatlantic.org* 🕓 *Closed Mon. and Tues.*

$$ THAI 🍴 **Thai Thai III.** The mouthwatering photos on the menu aren't just a marketing ploy. The pictures don't do the real stuff justice. **Known for:** pad thai and curries; Beauty and the Beast roll with tuna, eel, avocado, and asparagus; great takeout. [$] *Average main: $20* ✉ *8660 Astronaut Blvd.* ☎ *321/784–1561.*

WHERE TO STAY

$ **Radisson Resort at the Port.** For cruise-ship passengers who can't wait to
HOTEL   get underway, this splashy resort, done up in pink and turquoise, already
feels like the Caribbean. **Pros:** nice pool area; free shuttle to beach and Port
Canaveral; free Wi-Fi. **Cons:** rooms around the pool can be noisy; loud
air-conditioning in some rooms; no complimentary breakfast. $ *Rooms
from: $124* ⊠ *8701 Astronaut Blvd.* ☎ *321/784–0000, 888/201–1718*
⊕ *www.radisson.com/capecanaveralfl* ➔ *356 rooms* ⦿ *No meals.*

$$ **Residence Inn Cape Canaveral Cocoa Beach.** Billing itself as the closest
HOTEL   all-suites hotel to the Kennedy Space Center is this four-story Residence
Inn, painted cheery yellow. **Pros:** helpful staff; free breakfast buffet; free
Wi-Fi. **Cons:** less than picturesque views; street noise in some rooms.
$ *Rooms from: $219* ⊠ *8959 Astronaut Blvd.* ☎ *321/323–1100,
800/331–3131* ⊕ *www.marriott.com* ➔ *150 suites* ⦿ *Breakfast.*

SHOPPING

Cove Marketplace. Whether you're at Port Canaveral for a cruise or are
just passing through, this area on the south side of the harbor has shops,
restaurants, and entertainment venues, including the seven-story Explora-
tion Tower. Since most of the bars and eateries are located on the public
waterfront area, you'll have a great view of the cruise ships. ⊠ *Glen Cheek
Dr., at Scallop Dr., Port Canaveral* ⊕ *www.visitspacecoast.com* ▧ *Free.*

COCOA BEACH

5 miles south of Cape Canaveral, 58 miles southeast of Orlando.

After crossing a long and high bridge just east of Cocoa Village, you
drop down upon a barrier island. A few miles farther and you'll reach
the Atlantic Ocean and picture-perfect Cocoa Beach at Route A1A.

In the early 1960s Cocoa Beach was a sleepy, little-known town. But
in 1965 the sitcom *I Dream of Jeannie* premiered. The endearing show
centered on an astronaut, played by Larry Hagman, and his "Jeannie"
in a bottle, Barbara Eden, and was set in Cocoa Beach. Though the
series was never shot in Florida, creator Sidney Sheldon paid homage
to the town with local references to Cape Kennedy (now known as the
Kennedy Space Center) and Bernard's Surf restaurant. Today the town
and its lovely beach are a mecca to Florida's surfing community.

VISITOR INFORMATION

Contacts Cocoa Beach Convention and Visitors Bureau. ☎ *321/454–2022,
877/321–8474* ⊕ *www.visitcocoabeach.com.*

EXPLORING

Cocoa Beach Pier. By day, it's a good place to stroll—if you don't mind
weatherworn wood and sandy, watery paths. Although most of the
pier is free to walk on, there's a small charge to enter the fishing area
at the end of the 800-foot-long boardwalk (even to look around), and
a separate fishing fee. You can rent rods and reels here for an additional
$20. Surf competitions can be viewed from the pier, as it's a popular
surf spot. By night, visitors and locals—beach bums and surfers among
them—head here to party. Weekends see live music. ■TIP➔ The pier is
a great place to watch launches from Kennedy Space Center or Cape

13

Canaveral. ⊠ *401 Meade Ave.* ☎ *321/783–7549* ⊕ *www.cocoabeach-pier.com* 🔖 *$7 to fish; $15 parking.*

BEACHES

Cocoa Beach. This is one of the Space Coast's nicest beaches—and the place where the great professional surfer Kelly Slater got his start. The beach boasts one of the steadiest surf breaks on the East Coast and has wide stretches of hard sand that are excellent for biking, jogging, power walking, and strolling. In some places there are dressing rooms, showers, playgrounds, picnic areas with grills, snack shops, and surfside parking lots. Beach vendors offer necessities, and lifeguards are on duty in the summer.

A popular entry road, Route 520 crosses the Banana River into Cocoa Beach. At its east end, 5-acre **Alan Shepard Park,** named for the famous astronaut, aptly provides excellent views of launches from Kennedy Space Center and Cape Canaveral. Facilities here include 10 picnic pavilions, shower and restroom facilities, and more than 300 parking spaces. Beach vendors carry necessities for sunning and swimming. Parking is $15. Shops and restaurants are within walking distance. Another enticing Cocoa Beach entry point is 10-acre **Sidney Fischer Park,** in the 2100 block of Route A1A in the central beach area. It has showers, playgrounds, changing areas, picnic areas with grills, snack shops, and plenty of well-maintained, inexpensive parking lots ($5 for cars). **Amenities:** food and drink; lifeguards (seasonal); parking (fee); showers; toilets; water sports. **Best for:** sunrise; surfing; swimming; walking. ⊠ *Rte. A1A from Cape Canaveral to Patrick Air Force Base, 401 Meade Ave.*

WHERE TO EAT

$$$
GERMAN
✕ **Heidelberg.** As the name suggests, the cuisine here is definitely German, from the sauerbraten served with potato dumplings and red cabbage to the beef Stroganoff and spaetzle to the classically prepared Wiener schnitzel. All the soups and desserts are homemade; try the Viennese-style apple strudel and the rum-zapped almond-cream tortes. **Known for:** classic Wiener schnitzel; delicious apple strudel; live music Wednesday through Saturday. $ *Average main: $29* ⊠ *7 N. Orlando Ave., opposite City Hall* ☎ *321/783–6806* ⊕ *www.heidelbergcocoa-beach.com* ⊘ *Closed Mon. and Tues. No lunch Sun.*

$
SEAFOOD
✕ **Keith's Oyster Bar.** At the only open-air seafood bar on the beach, at the entrance of the Cocoa Beach Pier, the main item is oysters, served on the half shell. You can also grab a fish sandwich or burger here, crab legs by the pound, or one of the popular buckets of steamed shrimp or coconut shrimp. **Known for:** fresh oysters on the half shell; pretty good cocktails; oceanfront dining. $ *Average main: $14* ⊠ *Cocoa Beach Pier, 401 Meade Ave.* ☎ *321/783–7549* ⊕ *www.cocoabeachpier.com.*

WHERE TO STAY

$
HOTEL
🏨 **Best Western Oceanfront Hotel & Suites.** Families love this Best Western for its affordable suites. **Pros:** free Wi-Fi and HBO; free parking; cruise terminal shuttle. **Cons:** not all rooms have an ocean view; small bathrooms; noise from the pier. $ *Rooms from: $150* ⊠ *5600 N. Atlantic Ave.* ☎ *321/783–7621, 800/962–0028* ⊕ *www.bestwesterncocoabeach.com* 🛏 *292 rooms* 🍽 *Breakfast.*

The Cocoa Beach Pier is a magnet for nightlife in Cocoa Beach.

$ HOTEL FAMILY **DoubleTree by Hilton Cocoa Beach Oceanfront.** Proximity to the beach and comforts like in-room microwaves and refrigerators—and DoubleTree's famous chocolate-chip walnut cookies—make this six-story hotel a favorite of vacationing families, particularly Orlandoans on weekend getaways. **Pros:** private beach access; free Wi-Fi; complimentary parking. **Cons:** extra charge for beach-chair rental; thin walls; slow elevators. [$] *Rooms from: $170* ✉ *2080 N. Atlantic Ave.* ☎ *321/783–9222* 🌐 *www.cocoabeachdoubletree.com* 🛏 *148 rooms, 12 suites* 🍴 *No meals.*

$ HOTEL FAMILY **Hilton Cocoa Beach Oceanfront.** You can't get any closer to the beach than this seven-story oceanfront hotel. **Pros:** beachfront; friendly staff. **Cons:** fees for Wi-Fi and parking; small pool and bathrooms; no balconies; room windows don't open. [$] *Rooms from: $189* ✉ *1550 N. Atlantic Ave.* ☎ *321/799–0003* 🌐 *www.hiltoncocoabeach.com* 🛏 *296 rooms* 🍴 *No meals.*

$ B&B/INN **Inn at Cocoa Beach.** This charming oceanfront inn has spacious, individually decorated rooms with four-poster beds, upholstered chairs, and balconies or patios; most have ocean views. **Pros:** quiet; romantic; honor bar. **Cons:** no on-site restaurant; "forced" socializing. [$] *Rooms from: $165* ✉ *4300 Ocean Beach Blvd.* ☎ *321/799–3460, 800/343–5307 outside Florida* 🌐 *www.theinnatcocoabeach.com* 🛏 *50 rooms* 🍴 *Breakfast.*

$$ RESORT FAMILY Fodor's Choice ★ **The Resort on Cocoa Beach.** Even if the beach weren't in its backyard, this family-friendly, oceanfront property offers enough activities and amenities—from tennis and basketball courts to a game room, pool, and 50-seat movie theater—to keep everyone entertained. **Pros:** kids' activities; full kitchens; in-room washers and dryers; large balconies; free Wi-Fi. **Cons:** check-in not until 4 and checkout at 10; not all rooms are

oceanfront; slow elevators. $ *Rooms from: $200* ⊠ *1600 N. Atlantic Ave.* ☎ *321/783–4000, 866/469–8222* ⊕ *www.theresortoncocoabeach. com* ⇆ *124 suites* ⦿ *No meals.*

SHOPPING

Merritt Square Mall. The area's only major shopping mall is about a 20-minute ride from the beach. Stores include Macy's, Dillard's, JCPenney, Sears, Foot Locker, Island Surf and Skate, and roughly 100 others. It's an indoor mall, a rapidly diminishing fixture in the Florida landscape, making for comfortable shopping in the heat of summer. There's a 16-screen multiplex, along with a food court and several restaurant chains. ⊠ *777 E. Merritt Island Causeway, Merritt Island* ☎ *321/452–3270* ⊕ *www.merrittsquaremall.com.*

SPORTS AND THE OUTDOORS

KAYAKING

Adventure Kayak of Cocoa Beach. Specializing in manatee encounters, this outfitter organizes one- and two-person kayak tours of mangroves, channels, and islands. Tours launch from various locations in the Cocoa Beach area. ⊠ *599 Ramp Rd.* ☎ *321/480–8632* ⊕ *www.kayakcocoabeach.com* ⌨ *From $30.*

SURFING

Cocoa Beach Surf Company. The world's largest surf complex sits inside the Four Points by Sheraton resort, and has three floors of boards, apparel, sunglasses, and anything else a surfer, wannabe-surfer, or souvenir-seeker could need. Also on-site are a 5,600-gallon fish and shark tank and the Shark Pit Bar and Grill. You can rent surfboards, bodyboards, and wet suits, as well as umbrellas, chairs, and bikes. And staffers teach wannabes—from kids to seniors—how to surf. There are group, semiprivate, and private lessons available in one-, two-, and three-hour sessions. All gear is provided. ⊠ *Four Points by Sheraton, 4001 N. Atlantic Ave.* ☎ *321/799–9930* ⊕ *www.cocoabeachsurf.com* ⌨ *From $40.*

Fodor's Choice ★ **Ron Jon Surf Shop.** It's impossible to miss the flagship and original Ron Jon: it takes up nearly two blocks along Route A1A and has a giant surfboard and an art-deco facade painted orange, blue, yellow, and turquoise. What started in 1963 as a small T-shirt and bathing-suit shop has evolved into a 52,000-square-foot superstore that's open every day 'round the clock. The shop rents water-sports gear as well as chairs and umbrellas, and it sells every kind of beachwear, surf wax, plus the requisite T-shirts and flip-flops. ⊠ *4151 N. Atlantic Ave., Rte. A1A* ☎ *321/799–8888* ⊕ *www.ronjonsurfshop.com.*

MELBOURNE

20 miles south of Cocoa Beach.

Despite its dependence on the high-tech space industry, this town is decidedly laid-back. Most of the city is on the mainland, but a small portion trickles onto a barrier island, separated by the Indian River Lagoon and accessible by several inlets, including the Sebastian.

EXPLORING

FAMILY

Fodor's Choice

★

Brevard Zoo. At the only Association of Zoo and Aquariums–accredited zoo built by a community, you can stroll along the shaded boardwalks and get a close-up look at rhinos, giraffes, cheetahs, alligators, crocodiles, giant anteaters, marmosets, jaguars, eagles, river otters, kangaroos, exotic birds, and kookaburras. Alligator, crocodile, and river-otter feedings are held on alternate afternoons—and no, the alligators don't dine on the otters. Stop by Paws-On, an interactive learning playground with a petting zone, wildlife detective training academy, and the Indian River Play Lagoon. Hand-feed a giraffe in Expedition Africa or a lorikeet in the Australian Free Flight Aviary; and step up to the Wetlands Outpost, an elevated pavilion that's a gateway to 22 acres of wetlands through which you can paddle kayaks and keep an eye open for the 4,000 species of wildlife that live in these waters and woods. Adventurers seeking a chimp's-eye view can zip-line through the zoo on Treetop Trek. ⊠ *8225 N. Wickham Rd.* ☎ *321/254–9453* ⊕ *www.brevardzoo. org* ⊠ *$17.95; $20.95 with train and giraffe and lorikeet food.*

BEACHES

Paradise Beach. Small and scenic, this 1,600-foot stretch of sand is part of a 10-acre park north of Indialantic, about 20 miles south of Cocoa Beach on Route A1A. It has a refreshment stand, volleyball courts, outdoor showers, a beachfront park with pavilions, grills, picnic tables, and lifeguards in summer. **Amenities:** food and drink; lifeguards (seasonal); parking; showers; toilets. **Best for:** sunrise; surfing; swimming; walking. ⊠ *2301 N. Rte. A1A* ⊕ *www.brevardcounty. us/parksrecreation/south/howardfutch.*

Satellite Beach. This sleepy little community just south of Patrick Air Force Base, about 15 miles south of Cocoa Beach on Route A1A, sits on a narrow barrier island with the Atlantic Ocean on one side and the Indian River lagoon on the other. Its beach is protected by dunes, and sea turtles flock there to lay their eggs. A popular spot for family vacations because of its slow pace and lack of crowds, Satellite Beach has several beachfront parks with playgrounds, pavilions, and picnic facilities. One park, which teaches visitors about the importance of the dune system, has boardwalks that meander over the dunes to the beach. **Amenities:** food and drink; lifeguards; parking; showers; toilets; water sports. **Best for:** sunrise; surfing; swimming; walking. ⊠ *Rte. A1A, Satellite Beach* ⊕ *www.satellitebeachfl.org.*

SPORTS AND THE OUTDOORS
BASEBALL

Space Coast Stadium. Even though they play in our nation's capital during the regular season, the Washington Nationals use this 8,000-seat stadium for their spring training site. For the rest of the season, the facility is home to the Brevard County Manatees, one of the Milwaukee Brewers' minor-league teams. ⊠ *5800 Stadium Pkwy., Viera* ☎ *321/633–4487 Stadium, 321/633–9200 Brevard County Manatees* ⊕ *www.viera.com/vieraoutdoors/spacecoaststadium.aspx.*

13

GOLF

Baytree National Golf Links. "Challenging but fair" is how golfers describe this award-winning, links-style course, designed by PGA legend Gary Player (aka "The Black Knight."). This semiprivate course, built in 1992, is known for its unique red shale coquina waste areas. A round can be something of a roller coaster ride, with an easy hole or two followed by a perplexingly challenging one. The 454-yard, par-4 18th, for instance, is rated among the toughest in Brevard County. It plays into the wind and requires an imposing carry over wetlands, followed by an approach into a green guarded by water on all sides. The club has a restaurant and full practice facility. ⊠ *8207 National Dr.* ☎ *321/259–9060* ⊕ *www.baytreenational.com* ✉ *$30 for 9 holes, $59–$70 for 18 holes* ✕ *18 holes, 7043 yards, par 72.*

Viera East Golf Club. Rated among the best public courses—and values— on the Space Coast, Viera East reflects course architect Joe Lee's credo that "golf should be enjoyable, not a chore." Novices appreciate the forgiving, open layout with generous landing areas; more advanced players embrace the challenge of Lee's strategically placed bunkers (there are 66), water hazards, and expansive, undulating greens. The coastal breezes can make club selection tricky at times. Opened in 1994, the course is framed by marshlands, lakes, ponds, and pine and cypress trees. The par-5 14th is among the more picturesque and challenging holes, with a green surrounded by water. ⊠ *2300 Clubhouse Dr., Viera* ☎ *321/639–6500* ⊕ *www.vieragolf.com* ✉ *$60* ✕ *18 holes, 6720 yards, par 72.*

THE PANHANDLE

WELCOME TO THE PANHANDLE

TOP REASONS TO GO

★ **Snowy white beaches:** Most of the Panhandle's Gulf Coast shoreline is relatively unobstructed by high-rise condos and hotels, and the white-powder sand is alluring.

★ **Lots of history:** Spanish, Native American, and, later, French and English influences shaped the direction of this region and are well represented in its architecture, historic sites, and museums.

★ **Slower pace:** The Panhandle is sometimes referred to as "L.A.," or Lower Alabama. Southern through and through, the pace here is as slow as molasses—a fact Tallahassee plays up by claiming to be "Florida with a Southern accent."

★ **Capital sites:** As the state capital (chosen because it was midway between the two earlier Spanish headquarters of St. Augustine and Pensacola), Tallahassee remains intriguing thanks to its history, historical museums, universities, and quiet country charm.

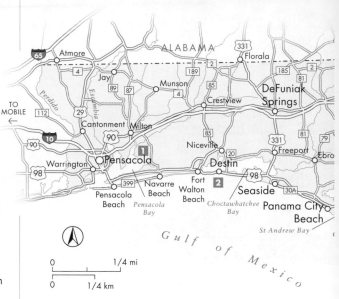

1 Around Pensacola Bay.

By preserving architecture from early Spanish settlements, Pensacola earns points for retaining the influence of these early explorers. The downtown district is compact, plus there's the city's Naval Air Museum and beaches nearby. Inland are some small towns with Old Florida appeal.

2 The Emerald Coast.

While the shoreline immediately east of Pensacola is nearly void of development, the tourist scene picks up along the so-called Emerald Coast between Fort Walton Beach and Panama City Beach, an area known for its blue-green waters and sugarlike sand beaches made of Appalachian quartz crystals. Farther east, Apalachicola and St. George Island are on what is known as the "Forgotten Coast."

GETTING ORIENTED

The Panhandle is a large area, and there are a number of airports to access the largest cities. Two major east–west routes offer alternatives to Interstate 10. Roughly parallel to its modern cousin, U.S. 90 is an early byway that goes from Tallahassee through small Old Florida towns like Marianna and DeFuniak Springs on its way to Pensacola. From Pensacola, U.S. 98 generally skirts along the Gulf of Mexico through seaside towns and communities like Fort Walton Beach, Destin, Panama City Beach, and Apalachicola, providing some breathtaking waterfront drives.

14

3 **Tallahassee.** In the state capital you can see the old and new capitols, visit the state's historical museum, attend an FSU football game, and go for a country ride down canopied roads.

Updated by
Ashley Wright

The sugar-white sands of the Panhandle's beaches stretch 227 miles from Pensacola east to Apalachicola. Sprinkle in clear emerald waters, towering dunes, and laid-back small towns where the fish are always biting and the folks are friendly, and you have a region with local color that's beloved by Floridians and visitors alike.

There are sights in the Panhandle, but sightseeing isn't the principal activity. The region is better known for its rich history, ample fishing and diving, and its opportunities for relaxation. Here it's about Southern drawls, a gentle pace, fresh seafood, and more grits and old-fashioned hospitality than anywhere else in the state. Sleepy (and not so sleepy) beach towns offer world-class golf, deep-sea fishing, relaxing spa treatments, and unbeatable shopping.

There's glamour here, too. Look for it in winning resorts throughout the region and in the abundance of nightlife, arts, and culture—from local symphonies to boutique art galleries—particularly in the more metropolitan areas. And then there's the food: from fresh catches of the day to some of the nation's finest oysters to mom-and-pop favorites offering fried seafood goodness.

Jump in a car, rent a bike, or buy a spot on a charter boat—you're never too far from outdoor adventure, with more miles of preserved coastline than anywhere else in the state. Destin is, after all, dubbed "The World's Luckiest Fishing Village," and the sport of YOLO Boarding (this region's term for the popular paddleboarding craze) has invaded the area in full force, offering a unique waterborne view of the entire region's unspoiled, natural beauty.

Don't forget to veer off the beach roads and venture into some of the area's picturesque historic districts. Pensacola is known as America's first settlement, and the rest of the region follows suit with rich history dating from the first settlers. The state's capital, Tallahassee, has its own unique history woven of politics, varying cultures, and innovation. Between the local charm, natural splendor, outdoor adventures, and miles of coastline, it's no wonder that the Panhandle is so beloved.

PLANNING

WHEN TO GO

Peak season is Memorial Day to Labor Day, with another spike during spring break. Inland, especially in Tallahassee, high season is during the fall (football) and March to April. Vendors, attractions, and other activities are in full swing in the summer. There's a "secret season" that falls around October and November: things quiet down as students go back to school, but restaurants and attractions keep normal hours and the weather is moderate.

GETTING HERE AND AROUND

AIR TRAVEL

The region is home to two primary airports—Northwest Florida Beaches International Airport (ECP) and Pensacola International Airport (VPS)—which offer flights from a number of major airlines. In addition, there are airports with regularly scheduled passenger service in Tallahassee, as well as a public airport—Northwest Florida Regional Airport—in Fort Walton Beach on the Eglin Air Force Base.

Contacts Northwest Florida Beaches International Airport (*ECP*). ✉ *6300 W. Bay Pkwy., Panama City* ☎ *850/763–6751* ⊕ *www.iflybeaches.com.* **Northwest Florida Regional Airport** (*VPS*). ☎ *850/651–7160* ⊕ *www.flyvps. com.* **Pensacola International Airport** (*PNS*). ✉ *2430 Airport Blvd., Pensacola* ☎ *850/436–5000* ⊕ *www.flypensacola.com.* **Tallahassee Regional Airport** (*TLH*). ✉ *3300 Capital Circle SW, Tallahassee* ☎ *850/891–7800* ⊕ *www.talgov. com/airport.*

CAR TRAVEL

The main east–west arteries across the top of the state are Interstate 10 and U.S. 90. Interstate 10 can be faster but monotonous, while U.S. 90 routes you along the main streets of several county seats. U.S. 98 snakes eastward along the coast, splitting into 98 and 98A at Inlet Beach before rejoining at Panama City and continuing on to Port St. Joe and Apalachicola. The view of the Gulf from U.S. 98 can be breathtaking, especially at sunset.

If you need to get from one end of the Panhandle to the other in a timely manner, drive inland to Interstate 10, where the speed limit runs as high as 70 mph in places. Major north–south highways that weave through the Panhandle are (from east to west) U.S. 231, U.S. 331, Route 85, and U.S. 29. From U.S. 331, which runs over a causeway at the east end of Choctawhatchee Bay between Route 20 and U.S. 98, the panorama of barge traffic and cabin cruisers on the twinkling waters of the Intracoastal Waterway will get your attention.

HOTELS

Many of the lodging selections here revolve around extended-stay options: resorts, condos, and time-shares that allow for a week or more in simple efficiencies, as well as fully furnished homes. There are also cabins, such as the ones that rest between the dunes at Grayton Beach. In any case, these are great for families and get-togethers, allowing you to do your own housekeeping and cooking, and explore the area without tour guides.

14

Local visitors' bureaus often act as clearinghouses for these types of properties, and you can also search online for vacation rentals. On the coast, but especially inland, the choices seem geared more toward mom-and-pop motels in addition to the usual line of chain hotels. ■TIP➔ During the summer and over holiday weekends, always reserve ahead for top properties.

RESTAURANTS

An abundance of seafood is served at coastal restaurants: oysters, crab, shrimp, scallops, and a variety of fish. Of course, that's not all there is on the menu. This part of Florida still impresses diners with old-fashioned comfort foods such as meat loaf, fried chicken, beans and corn bread, okra, and fried green tomatoes. You'll also find small-town seafood shacks where you can dine on local favorites such as deep-fried mullet, cheese grits, coleslaw, and hush puppies. Restaurants, like resorts, vary their operating tactics off-season, so call first if visiting during winter months.

Hotel and restaurant reviews have been shortened. For full information, visit Fodors.com.

WHAT IT COSTS			
$	$$	$$$	$$$$
Restaurants	under $15	$15–$20	$21–$30	over $30
Hotels	under $200	$200–$300	$301–$400	over $400

Restaurant prices are the average cost of a main course at dinner or, if dinner is not served, at lunch. Hotel prices are the lowest cost of a standard double room in high season.

PENSACOLA BAY

Nestled on the Gulf of Mexico at Florida's northwest tip, this region takes visitors back in time thanks to its rich cultural heritage. In 1559, Don Tristan de Luna first "discovered" the area, which today is divided into four distinct parts: North Pensacola, the walkable downtown historic district, Pensacola Beach, and Perdido Key. The historic district is the heart of the area. Just across the bay, Pensacola Beach is on Santa Rosa Island, while Perdido Key is farther west, hugging the Alabama state line.

PENSACOLA

59 miles east of Mobile, Alabama, via I–10.

Pensacola consists of four distinct districts—Seville, Palafox, East Hill, and North Hill—though they're easy to explore as a unit. Stroll down streets mapped out by the British and renamed by the Spanish, such as Cervantes, Palafox, Intendencia, and Tarragona.

An influx of restaurants and bars has brought new nightlife to the historic districts, especially Palafox Street, which is now home to a thriving entertainment scene. Taste buds water over fresh coastal cuisine from a number of award-winning, locally owned and operated restaurants, and the downtown entertainment district offers fun for any age throughout the year—festivals, events at bars and concert venues, and a growing Mardi Gras celebration.

At the southern terminus of Palafox Street is Plaza DeLuna, a 2-acre park with open grounds, interactive water fountains, and concessions. It's a quiet place to sit and watch the bay, fish, or enjoy an evening sunset.

GETTING HERE AND AROUND

Pensacola International Airport has dozens of daily flights and is served by American Airlines (American Eagle), Delta, Southwest, Silver Airways, United, and US Airways. From Pensacola International Airport via Yellow Cab, it costs about $14 to get downtown or about $32 to reach Pensacola Beach.

In Pensacola and Pensacola Beach, Escambia County Area Transit provides regular citywide bus service ($1.75), downtown trolley routes, tours through the historic districts, and free trolley service to the beach from mid-May to Labor Day on Friday, Saturday, and Sunday evenings as well as Saturday afternoon.

Contacts Escambia County Area Transit (*ECAT*). ☎ *850/595–3228* ⊕ *www.goecat.com.* **Yellow Cab.** ☎ *850/433–3333.*

VISITOR INFORMATION

Contacts Pensacola Visitor Information Center. ✉ *1401 E. Gregory St.* ☎ *850/434–1234, 800/874–1234* ⊕ *www.visitpensacola.com.*

EXPLORING

TOP ATTRACTIONS

Historic Pensacola Village. Within the Seville Square Historic District is this complex of several museums and historic homes whose indoor and outdoor exhibits trace the area's history back 450 years. The Museum of Industry (✉ *200 E. Zaragoza St.*), in a late-19th-century warehouse, is home to permanent exhibits dedicated to the lumber, maritime, and shipping industries—once mainstays of Pensacola's economy. A reproduction of a 19th-century streetscape is displayed in the Museum of Commerce (✉ *201 E. Zaragoza St.*). Also in the village are the Julee Cottage (✉ *210 E. Zaragoza St.*), the "first home owned by a free woman of color"; the 1871 Dorr House (✉ *311 S. Adams St.*); and the 1805 French-Creole Lavalle House (✉ *205 E. Church St.*).

Strolling through the area gives you a good (and free) look at many architectural styles, but to enter some of the buildings you must purchase an all-inclusive ticket at the Village gift shop in the Tivoli High House—which was once in the city's red-light district but now is merely a calm reflection of a restored home. Guided tours (at 11, 1, and 2:30, lasting 60–90 minutes) allow you to experience the history of Pensacola as you visit the Lavalle House, Dorr House, Old Christ Church, and the 1890s Lear Rocheblave House. ✉ *Tivoli High House, 205 E. Zaragoza St.* ⊕ *www.historicpensacola.org* 🎟 *$8* ⊗ *Closed Mon.*

Fodor'sChoice   **National Museum of Naval Aviation.** Within the Pensacola Naval Air Sta-
★   tion (widely considered to be the must-see attraction in Pensacola),
this 300,000-square-foot museum has more than 140 historic aircraft.
Among them are the NC-4, which in 1919 became the first plane to
cross the Atlantic; the famous World War II fighter the F-6 *Hellcat;* and
the Skylab Command Module.

Other attractions include an atomic bomb (it's defused, we promise),
and the restored Cubi Bar Café—a very cool former airmen's club trans-
planted here from the Philippines. Relive the morning's maneuvers in
the 14-seat motion-based simulator as well as an IMAX theater playing
Fighter Pilot, The Magic of Flight, and other educational films. Pensacola, also known as the "Cradle of Naval Aviation," celebrated the
100th Anniversary of Naval Aviation in 2011.

The museum also offers two MaxFlight Simulators that takes users
on a high-definition adventure in air-to-air combat and stunt flying in
an interactive 360-degree pitch-and-roll technology experience. The
$20 experience is for one or two. There's also two HD Motion-Based
Simulators that offer a larger group of up to 15 people a five-minute,
multisensory experience combining a high-definition projection screen
and surround-sound, with the motion of the ride compartment. Riders
can choose their own adventure, either a ride with the Blue Angels or
take off from an aircraft carrier and do battle in the Iraqi desert in the
Desert Storm Simulation." The ride costs $6

While at the museum you may hear the Navy's Blue Angels aerobatic
squadron buzzing overhead. This is their home base, and they practice
maneuvers here on most Tuesday and Wednesday mornings at 11:30
from March to November. The pilots usually stick around after the
show to shake hands and sign autographs. During the show, cover your
ears as the six F/A 18s blast off in unison for 45 minutes of thrills and
skill. Watching the Blue Angels practice their aerobatics is one of the
best "free" shows in all of Florida (well, your tax dollars are already
paying for these jets and their pilots).

The Pensacola Naval Air Station is also home to the National Flight
Academy, which teaches the principles of Science, Technology, Engineering, and Math (STEM) during an immersive experience for students aged 11–17. ⊠ *Pensacola Naval Air Station, 1750 Radford Blvd.*
☎ *800/327–5002* ⊕ *www.navalaviationmuseum.org* ⌦ *Museum free;*
IMAX film $9; flight simulators $6 or $20.

Pensacola Children's Museum. The Pensacola Children's Museum is the
newest museum in the West Florida Historic Preservation, Inc. complex. The museum offers a variety of programs for children of all
ages, including story time, art projects, and a plethora of interactive
historical exhibits from maritime to multicultural themes. ⊠ *115 E.*
Zaragoza St. ☎ *850/595–5985* ⊕ *www.historicpensacola.org* ⌦ *$8*
⊘ *Closed Mon.*

Seville Square Historic District. Established in 1559, this is the site of Pensacola's first permanent Spanish settlement (it beat St. Augustine's by
six years). Its center is Seville Square, a live oak–shaded park bounded
by Alcaniz, Adams, Zaragoza, and Government streets. Roam these

brick streets past honeymoon cottages and homes set in a parklike setting. Many buildings have been converted into restaurants, bars, offices, and shops that overlook broad Pensacola Bay and coastal road U.S. 98, which provides access to the Gulf Coast and beaches. ⊠ *Pensacola* ☎ *850/595–5985.*

FAMILY **T.T Wentworth, Jr. Florida State Museum.** Even if you don't like museums, this one is worth a look. Housed in the elaborate, Renaissance revival–style former city hall, it has an interesting mix of exhibits illustrating life in the Florida Panhandle over the centuries. One of these, the City of Five Flags, provides a good introduction to Pensacola's history. Mr. Wentworth was quite a collector (as well as a politician and salesman), and his eccentric collection includes a mummified cat (creepy) and the size 37 left shoe of Robert Wadlow, the world's tallest man (not creepy, but a really big shoe). A wide range of both permanent and traveling exhibits include a rare collection of dollhouses, Black Ink (a look at African-Americans' role in printing), Hoops to Hips (a review of fashion history), Civil War exhibits, and a kid-size interactive area with a ship and fort where kids can play and pretend to be colonial Pensacolans. ⊠ *330 S. Jefferson St.* ☎ *850/595–5985* ⊕ *www. historicpensacola.org* ⊑ *Free* ⊗ *Closed Mon.*

WORTH NOTING

Palafox Historic District. Palafox Street is the main stem of historic downtown Pensacola and the center of the Palafox Historic District. The commercial and government hub of Old Pensacola is now an active cultural and entertainment district, where locally owned and operated bars and restaurants attract flocks of locals and visitors. The opulent, renovated Spanish Renaissance–style Saenger Theater, Pensacola's 1925 movie palace, hosts performances by the local symphony and opera, as well as national acts.

On Palafox between Government and Zaragoza streets is a statue of Andrew Jackson, which commemorates the formal transfer of Florida from Spain to the United States in 1821. While in the area, stop by Veterans Memorial Park, just off Bayfront Parkway near 9th Avenue. The ¾-scale replica of the Vietnam Memorial in Washington, D.C., honors the more than 58,000 Americans who lost their lives in the Vietnam War. ⊠ *Palafox St.*

Pensacola Museum of Art. Pensacola's city jail once occupied the 1906 Spanish revival–style building that is now the secure home for the museum's permanent collection of paintings, sculptures, and works on paper by 20th- and 21st-century artists—and we do mean secure: you can still see the actual cells with their huge iron doors. Traveling exhibits have focused on photography (Wegman, Leibovitz, Ansel Adams), Dutch masters, regional artists, and the occasional art-world icon, such as Andy Warhol or Salvador Dalí. ⊠ *407 S. Jefferson St.* ☎ *850/432–6247* ⊕ *www.pensacolamuseum.org* ⊑ *$7* ⊗ *Closed Sun. and Mon.*

BEACHES

Perdido Key State Park. Part of Gulf Islands National Seashore, this state park is on Perdido Key, a 247-acre barrier island. Its beach, now referred to as Johnson Beach, was one of the few beaches open to African-Americans during segregation. Today the park offers primitive camping year-round. It is within walking distance of dining and nightlife on the key and is a short drive from Alabama. **Amenities:** showers; toilets. **Best for:** sunsets; swimming; walking. ✉ *5 miles southwest of Pensacola off Rte. 292, Perdido Key* 🌐 *www.floridastateparks.org/perdidokey* 🎟 *$3 per vehicle.*

WHERE TO EAT

$$$ SEAFOOD

🍴 **Fish House.** Come one, come all, come hungry, and come at 11 am to witness the calm before the lunch storm. The wide-ranging menu of fish dishes is the bait, and each can be served in a variety of ways: ginger-crusted, grilled, blackened, pecan-crusted, or Pacific-grilled, which puts any dish over the top. **Known for:** "Grits a Ya-Ya" (shrimp and cheese grits); large wine list; great water views. [$] *Average main: $28* ✉ *600 S. Barracks St.* ☎ *850/470–0003* 🌐 *fishhousepensacola.com.*

$$ IRISH Fodor's Choice ★

🍴 **McGuire's Irish Pub.** Since 1977 this authentic Irish pub has promised its patrons "feasting, imbibery, and debauchery" seven nights a week. A sense of humor pervades the place, evidenced by the range of prices on hamburgers—$10–$100 depending on whether you want it topped with cheddar or served with caviar and Champagne. **Known for:** large menu, including both meat and seafood; extensive wine cellar and cocktail list; house-brewed beer. [$] *Average main: $20* ✉ *600 E. Gregory St.* ☎ *850/433–6789* 🌐 *www.mcguiresirishpub.com.*

$$$$ SOUTHERN

🍴 **Restaurant IRON.** Contemporary Southern treats—in both the food and cocktail varieties—abound at this hip, sleek gem on Pensacola's hottest downtown strip. The modern menu takes its cue from Southern and seafood favorites prepared with modern methods and artistic plating (chicken and dumplings is a cheese-stuffed organic chicken served with gnocchi). **Known for:** modern twists on Southern favorites; extensive, ambitious cocktail menu; elegant ambience. [$] *Average main: $36* ✉ *22 N. Palafox St.* ☎ *850/476–7776* 🌐 *www.restaurantiron.com.*

WHERE TO STAY

$ HOTEL

🏨 **Crowne Plaza–Pensacola Grand Hotel.** On the site of the restored historic Louisville & Nashville (L&N) railroad passenger depot, the Crowne Plaza has a 15-story glass tower, attached to the train depot by a glass atrium, and incredible views of historic Pensacola. **Pros:** great location near downtown; amenities perfect for business travelers. **Cons:** standard chain hotel ambience; there are more intimate choices closer to downtown. [$] *Rooms from: $188* ✉ *200 E. Gregory St.* ☎ *850/433–3336, 800/348–3336* 🌐 *www.pensacolagrandhotel.com* 🛏 *200 rooms, 10 suites* 🍴 *No meals.*

$ B&B/INN

🏨 **New World Inn.** If you like your inns small, warm, and cozy, with the bay on one side and a short two-block walk to the downtown historic area on the other, then this is the one for you. **Pros:** steps away from downtown hot spots and attractions; historically inspired property; new local favorite restaurant on-site. **Cons:** not family-friendly; decor could use a refresh. [$] *Rooms from: $109* ✉ *600 S. Palafox St.* ☎ *850/432–4111* 🌐 *skopelosatnewworld.com* 🛏 *16 rooms* 🍴 *Breakfast.*

Like an Old West town with a Victorian twist, historic Pensacola is eye candy for architecture buffs.

$ HOTEL [icon] **Solé Inn and Suites.** If you want to stay in the middle of downtown action but within reasonable distance of Pensacola's beaches, this hotel offers a bit of style in a central location for a great price. **Pros:** upscale, fully renovated 1950s motel; complimentary happy hour; free Wi-Fi. **Cons:** small bathrooms; location can be loud in peak season; rooms open directly to the outdoors. [$] *Rooms from: $109* ✉ *200 N. Palafox St.* ☎ *850/470–9298, 888/470–9298* 🌐 *www.soleinnandsuites.com* 🛏 *45 rooms* 🍴 *Breakfast.*

NIGHTLIFE

Pensacola offers a wide variety of lively places to enjoy once the sun goes down, from Irish pubs to local watering holes that were once the haunts of old naval heroes. You can sample homegrown concoctions at upscale martini bars and the tunes of local and national music acts at numerous live-music venues.

Hopjacks Pizza Kitchen and Taproom. This restaurant and bar has one of the Panhandle's most extensive selections of specialty beers—more than 150, including 36 on tap. ✉ *10 S. Palafox St.* ☎ *850/497–6073* 🌐 *www.hopjacks.com.*

McGuire's Irish Pub. Those of Irish descent and anyone else who enjoys cold home-brewed ales, beers, or lagers will feel at home in this restaurant and microbrewery. Its 8,500-bottle wine cellar includes vintages ranging from $14 to $20,000. If you want a quiet drink, steer clear on Friday and Saturday nights—when crowds abound and live entertainment enlivens the masses. ✉ *600 E. Gregory St.* ☎ *850/433–6789* 🌐 *www.mcguiresirishpub.com.*

Seville Quarter. In the heart of the Historic District is Pensacola's equivalent of New Orleans's French Quarter. In fact, you may think you've traveled to Louisiana when you enter any of its seven bars and two courtyards offering an eclectic mix of live music. College students pack the place on Thursday, tourists come on the weekend, and military men and women from six nearby bases are stationed here nearly all the time. This is a classic Pensacola nightspot, and on most nights there's a small cover after 8 pm. ⊠ *130 E. Government St.* ☎ *850/434–6211* ⊕ *www.sevillequarter.com.*

Vinyl Music Hall. Music now fills the space of this 112-year-old former Masonic lodge. An impressive variety of bands and acts have floated through the intimate music venue, which offers mostly standing room. It's also home to 5½ bar, where mixologists create unique, handcrafted drinks from the classic to the contemporary in a swanky, downtown loft atmosphere. The box office is open weekdays between noon and 5 as well as before all events (one hour before start time). ⊠ *2 S. Palafox Pl.* ☎ *877/435–9849* ⊕ *www.vinylmusichall.com.*

SHOPPING

The Pensacola area is home to a variety of shopping options. The Palafox and Seville historic districts are enjoyable areas for browsing or buying; here boutiques sell trendy clothing and imported and eclectic home furnishings. Meanwhile, the area's main shopping staple, Cordova Mall, contains national chain stores.

Cordova Mall. Ten miles north of the historic districts, this mall is anchored by large stores such as Dillard's, Dick's Sporting Goods, Best Buy, and World Market. There are also more than 125 specialty shops and a food court. ⊠ *5100 N. 9th Ave.* ☎ *850/477–5355.*

SPORTS AND THE OUTDOORS
BASEBALL
Pensacola Blue Wahoos. The latest gem of the city sits on Pensacola's waterfront and offers a multi-use, public-private park development that is home to a 5,038-seat multipurpose stadium and Randall K. and Marth A. Hunter Amphitheater that overlooks beautiful Pensacola Bay. The stadium is home ot the Double A Pensacola Blue Wahoos. Keep an eye out for tickets—they sell out fast—as well as a variety of other events that fill the stadium and surrounding park year-round. ⊠ *Vince J. Whibbs Sr. Community Maritime Park, 301 W. Main St.* ☎ *850/436–5670* ⊕ *bluewahoos.com* ▨ *Tickets $7–$9.*

CANOEING AND KAYAKING
The Pensacola Bay area is known as the "Canoe Capital of Florida," and the pure sand-bottom Blackwater River is a particularly nice place to paddle. You can rent canoes and kayaks from a number of local companies as well as from outfits on nearby Perdido Key, home to the picturesque Perdido Watershed.

Adventures Unlimited. This outfitter on Coldwater Creek rents light watercraft as well as campsites and cabins along the Coldwater and Blackwater rivers in the Blackwater State Forest. Though prime canoe season lasts roughly from March through mid-November, Adventures Unlimited rents year-round. ⊠ *8974 Tomahawk Landing Rd., Milton* ☎ *850/623–6197, 800/239–6864* ⊕ *www.adventuresunlimited.com.*

Blackwater Canoe Rental. Canoe and kayak rentals for exploring the Blackwater River are available from this outfitter northeast of Pensacola off Interstate 10 Exit 31. ✉ *6974 Deaton Bridge Rd., Milton* ☎ *850/623–0235* ⊕ *www.blackwatercanoe.com.*

FISHING

With 52 miles of coastline and a number of inland waterways, the Pensacola area is a great place to drop a line. Bottom fishing is best for amberjack and grouper; offshore trolling trips search for tuna, wahoo, and sailfish; and inshore charters are out to hook redfish, cobia, and pompano. For a complete list of local fishing charters, visit ⊕ *www.pensacolafishing.com.*

Beach Marina. For a full- or half-day deep-sea charter, try the Beach Marina, which represents several charter outfits. ✉ *655 Pensacola Beach Blvd., Pensacola Beach* ☎ *850/932–0304* ⊕ *www.pensacola-beachmarina.com.*

GOLF

The bay area has a number of award-winning and picturesque golf courses. Some offer beach views, and others are local haunts.

Club at Hidden Creek. Hidden Creek is known for its lush landscape, rolling terrain, and scenic layout. The public course, designed by Ron Garl, offers challenging play for all levels of golfers with water throughout and well-guarded greens. It's rated one of the "Top 201 Courses to Play in North America" by *Golf Digest.* A natural grass practice facility with driving, putting, and chipping areas offers another unique feature. ✉ *3070 PGA Blvd., Navarre* ☎ *850/939–4604* ⊕ *theclubathiddencreek. com* 🖭 *$25–$47* ⛳ *18 holes, 6805 yards, par 72.*

Lost Key Golf Club. Framed by the natural beauty of Perdido Key, Lost Key is located a short drive from downtown Pensacola and features the new Sea Dwarf Paspalum grass from the tee through the green. The public Arnold Palmer Signature Design Course was the first golf course in the world to be certified as an Audubon International Silver Signature Sanctuary. The clubhouse has a full-service golf shop, men's and ladies' locker-room facilities with lounge areas, and a restaurant and bar with indoor and outdoor seating and panoramic views of the golf course. ✉ *625 Lost Key Dr.* ☎ *850/549–2160, 888/256–7853* ⊕ *www.lostkey. com* 🖭 *$39–$79* ⛳ *18 holes, 6801 yards, par 71.*

PENSACOLA BEACH

5 miles south of Pensacola via U.S. 98 to Rte. 399 (Bob Sikes) Bridge.

One of the longest barrier islands in the world, Pensacola Beach offers a low-key, family-friendly feel with many local hangouts, fishing galore, and historic Ft. Pickens. Connected to Pensacola by two long bridges, the island offers both a Gulf-front and "sound" side for those seeking a calmer seaside experience. Public beaches abound in the area, including Casino Beach at the tip of Pensacola Beach Road, which offers live entertainment at its pavilion in the summer, as well as showers and bathrooms. Quietwater Beach Boardwalk, across the street from Casino Beach, also offers boutique shopping, eateries, and nightlife.

Long home to chain hotels as well as locally owned motels, the beach has opened a number of condominiums and resorts in recent years. Don't miss renting a bike or taking a drive to explore both Fort Pickens Road and J. Earle Bowden Way (connecting Pensacola Beach to the Navarre Beach area), which have reopened after many years of being closed to vehicular traffic. They offer breathtaking, unobstructed views of the Gulf.

GETTING HERE

Pensacola Beach is a short drive (just 5 miles) from Pensacola across the Bob Sikes Bridge (Route 399).

EXPLORING

Ft. Pickens. Constructed of more than 21 million locally made bricks, this fort, dating back to 1834, once served as a prison for Apache chief Geronimo. A National Park Service plaque describes the complex as a "confusing jumble of fortifications," but the real attractions here are the beach, nature exhibits, a large campground, an excellent gift shop, and breathtaking views of Pensacola Bay and the lighthouse across the inlet. It's the perfect place for a picnic lunch and a bit of history, too. ✉ *Fort Pickens Rd., at western tip of island* ☎ *850/934–2600* 🎟 *$7 per person.*

BEACHES

Casino Beach. Named for the Casino Resort, the island's first tourist spot when it opened in 1931 (the same day as the first Pensacola Beach Bridge), this beach offers everything from seasonal live entertainment to public restrooms and showers. You can also lounge in the shade of the Pensacola Beach Gulf Pier. Casino Beach has the most parking for beach access on the island and is just a short stroll from dining, entertainment, and major hotels such as the Margaritaville Beach Hotel and Holiday Inn Resort Beachfront Hotel. **Amenities:** food and drink; lifeguards (seasonal); parking (free); showers; toilets. **Best for:** swimming; walking. ✉ *735 Pensacola Beach Blvd.*

Langdon Beach. The Panhandle is home to the Florida District of the Gulf Islands National Seashore, the longest tract of protected seashore in the United States. At the Ft. Pickens area of the park on the Gulf-side tip of Santa Rosa Island, this beach is one of the top spots to experience the unspoiled beauty and snow-white beaches this area is known for. Keep an eye out for wildlife of the flying variety; the Ft. Pickens area is known for its nesting shorebirds. A large covered pavilion is great for picnicking and a few minutes of shade. **Amenities:** lifeguards; parking (no fee); showers; toilets; water sports. **Best for:** snorkeling; solitude; sunrise; sunset; walking. ✉ *Fort Pickens Rd.* ✣ *3 miles west of Pensacola Beach on west end of Santa Rosa Island* 🌐 *www.nps.gov/guis/index.htm.*

WHERE TO EAT

$$ SEAFOOD

🍴 **Flounder's Chowder and Ale House.** The wide and peaceful Gulf spreads out before you at this casual restaurant where, armed with a fruity libation, you're all set for a night of "floundering" at its best. Funkiness comes courtesy of an eclectic collection of objets d'art; tastiness is served in specialties such as seafood nachos and the shrimp-boat platter. **Known for:** flounder chowder; live entertainment nightly in season; Gulf-inspired cocktails. [$] *Average main: $16* ✉ *800 Quietwater Beach Blvd.* ☎ *850/932–2003* 🌐 *www.flounderschowderhouse.com.*

$$$
SEAFOOD

✕ **Grand Marlin Restaurant and Oyster Bar.** This restaurant offers unforgettable views of Santa Rosa Sound and Pensacola Bay along with mouthwatering fresh local cuisine. Top-notch seafood shares the menu—printed daily—with specials. **Known for:** fresh seafood and Apalachicola oysters; breathtaking views; sophisticated atmosphere. $ *Average main: $21* ✉ *400 Pensacola Beach Blvd.* ☎ *850/677–9153* ⊕ *www.thegrandmarlin.com.*

WHERE TO STAY

$
HOTEL

⛱ **Hilton Pensacola Beach Gulf Front.** The name is fitting; right on the Gulf, this hotel offers incredible views at one of the beach's most affordable prices. **Pros:** impeccably well kept; great on-site dining; affordable rates. **Cons:** chain hotel feel; high price during season; renovation underway. $ *Rooms from: $179* ✉ *12 Via De Luna* ☎ *850/916–2999, 866/916–2999* ⊕ *www.pensacolabeachgulffront.hilton.com* ⤴ *272 rooms* ⦿ *No meals.*

$$
RESORT

⛱ **Holiday Inn Resort Pensacola Beach.** Known for its 250-foot lazy river and cascading waterfall, this Gulf-front hotel is one of the most family-friendly on the beach. **Pros:** indoor pool and large outdoor pool; beach-view fitness center; seasonal kids programs. **Cons:** some rooms have parking-lot views; pool area very crowded during peak season. $ *Rooms from: $200* ✉ *14 Via de Luna* ☎ *850/932–5331* ⊕ *holidayinnresortpensacolabeach.com* ⤴ *206 rooms* ⦿ *No meals.*

$$
HOTEL

⛱ **Margaritaville Beach Hotel.** This tropical getaway, inspired by the lyrics of Jimmy Buffett, gives you the relaxed, fun Margaritaville experience with the amenities of a top-notch hotel that oozes barefoot elegance. **Pros:** clean, inviting atmosphere; lots of dining options; local spa services available. **Cons:** somewhat off the beaten path. $ *Rooms from: $299* ✉ *165 Fort Pickens Rd.* ☎ *850/916–9755* ⊕ *www.margaritavillehotel.com* ⤴ *162 rooms* ⦿ *No meals.*

SPORTS AND THE OUTDOORS

DOLPHIN-SPOTTING CRUISES

FAMILY

Chase-N-Fins. Climb aboard this 50-foot navy utility launch, which cruises Pensacola Bay along Ft. Pickens, Pensacola Pass, and the Lighthouse at Pensacola Naval Air Station in search of friendly dolphins. ✉ *655 Pensacola Beach Blvd.* ☎ *850/492–6337* ⊕ *www.chase-n-fins.com* ✆ *From $25.*

FISHING

Pensacola Beach Gulf Pier. The 1,471-foot-long pier touts itself as "the most friendly pier around." It hosts serious anglers who find everything they'll need here—from pole rentals to bait—to land that big one, but those looking to catch only a beautiful sunset are welcome, too. Check the pier's website for the latest reports on what's biting. ✉ *41 Fort Pickens Rd.* ☎ *850/934–7200* ⊕ *www.fishpensacolabeachpier.com* ✆ *$7.50 fishers, $1.25 observers.*

STAND-UP PADDLEBOARDING

Coastal Paddle Company. Coastal Paddle Company offers a one-stop-shop for SUP experiences on Pensacola Beach with everything from all-day rentals to private lessons to on-board yoga classes. They also rent bikes, all from the bay-side dock across the street from Margaritaville Beach Resort. ✉ *136 Pensacola Beach Trail, across from Margaritaville Beach Hotel* ☎ *850/916–1600* ⊕ *coastalpaddlecompany.com* ✆ *From $35.*

14

DAY TRIPS FROM PENSACOLA

Inland, where the northern reaches of the Panhandle butt up against the back porches of Alabama and Georgia, you'll find a part of Florida that goes a long way toward explaining why the state song is "Swanee River" (and why its parenthetical title is "Old Folks at Home"). Stephen Foster's musical genius notwithstanding, the inland Panhandle area is definitely more Dixie than Sunshine State, with few lodging options other than the chain motels that flank the Interstate 10 exits and a decidedly slower pace of life than you'll find on the tourist-heavy Gulf Coast.

But the area's natural attractions—hills and farmland, untouched small towns, pristine state parks—make for great day trips from the coast should the sky turn gray or the skin red. Explore underground caverns where aeons-old rock formations create bizarre scenes, visit one of Florida's up-and-coming wineries, or poke around small-town America in DeFuniak Springs. Altogether, the inland area of the Panhandle is one of the state's most satisfyingly soothing regions.

DEFUNIAK SPRINGS

77 miles northeast of Pensacola on U.S. 90 off I–10.

This scenic spot has a rather unusual claim to fame: at its center lies a nearly perfectly symmetrical spring-fed lake, one of only two such naturally circular bodies of water in the world (the other is in Switzerland). A sidewalk encircles Lake DeFuniak (also called Circle Lake), which is dotted by pine and shade trees, creating a very pleasing atmosphere for a long-distance mosey. In 1848 the Knox Hill Academy was founded here, and for more than half a century it was the only institution of higher learning in northwestern Florida.

In 1885 the town was chosen as the location for the New York Chautauqua educational society's winter assembly. The Chautauqua programs were discontinued in 1922, but DeFuniak Springs attempts to revive them, in spirit at least, by sponsoring a countywide Chautauqua Festival in April. Christmas is a particularly festive time, when the sprawling Victorian houses surrounding the lake are decorated to the nines.

There's not a tremendous amount to see here, but if you have the good sense to travel U.S. 90 to discover Old Florida, at least take the time to travel Circle Drive to see its beautiful Victorian homes. Also take a little time to walk around the small downtown area and drop in its bookstores, cafés, and small shops.

EXPLORING

Chautauqua Winery. Open since 1989, this winery and its vintages have slowly won respect from oenophiles wary of what was once considered to be an oxymoron at best: "Florida wine." The winery has won honors in national and international competitions, with wines that vary from dry, barrel-fermented wines to Southern favorites like sweet muscadine and blueberry wines. Fourteen vats ranging in size from 1,500 to 6,000 gallons generate a total of 70,000 gallons of wine. Take a free tour to see how ancient art blends with modern technology;

then retreat to the tastefully decorated tasting room and gift shop. ⊠ *364 Hugh Adams Rd., DeFuniak Springs* ☎ *850/892–5887* ⊕ *www. chautauquawinery.com* ⊠ *Free.*

TAKE A TOUR

Circle Drive. Some of the finest examples of Victorian architecture in the state can be seen while you are walking or motoring around Circle Drive, the road that wraps around Circle Lake. The circumference is marked with beautiful Victorian specimens like the Walton-DeFuniak Public Library, the Dream Cottage, and the Pansy Cottage. Most of the other notable structures are private residences, but you can still admire them from the street. ⊠ *DeFuniak Springs.*

14

FALLING WATERS STATE PARK

35 miles east of DeFuniak Springs via U.S. 90 and Rte. 77.

Falling Waters State Park. This site of a Civil War–era whiskey distillery and, later, an exotic plant nursery (some species still thrive in the wild) is best known for also being the site of the Falling Waters Sink. The 100-foot-deep cylindrical pit provides the background for a waterfall, and there's an observation deck for viewing this natural phenomenon. The water free-falls 67 feet to the bottom of the sink, but where it goes after that is a mystery. ⊠ *1130 State Park Rd., Chipley* ☎ *850/638–6130* ⊕ *www.floridastateparks.org/fallingwaters* ⊠ *$5 per vehicle, up to 8 people.*

FLORIDA CAVERNS STATE PARK

13 miles northeast of Falling Waters off U.S. 90 on Rte. 166.

Florida Caverns State Park. A short drive from the center of Marianna, a cute and pristine community, you can see what's behind or—more accurately—what's beneath it all. Ranger-led cave tours reveal stalactites, stalagmites, soda straws, columns, rim stones, flowstones, and "waterfalls" of solid rock at these underground caverns, where the temperature hovers at an oh-so-pleasant 68°F year-round. Some of the caverns are off-limits to the public or open for scientific study by permit only, but you can still see enough to fill a half-day or more—and be amazed that caverns of this magnitude exist in the Sunshine State. Don't forsake the quiet, preserved, and peaceful woodlands, which encompass 10 distinct communities including upland glade, hardwood forests, floodplains, forests, and swamps. There are also hiking trails, campsites, and areas for swimming, horseback riding, and canoeing on the Chipola River. ⊠ *3345 Caverns Rd., off U.S. 90 on Rte. 166, Marianna* ☎ *850/482–9598, 800/326–3521 camping reservations* ⊕ *www.floridastateparks.org/floridacaverns* ⊠ *Park $5 per vehicle, up to 8 people; caverns $8.*

THE EMERALD COAST

On U.S. 98, several towns, each with its own personality, are strung along the shoreline from Pensacola southeast to St. George Island. The side-by-side cities of Destin and Fort Walton Beach seemingly merge into one sprawling destination and continue to spread as more con-dominiums, resort developments, shopping centers, and restaurants crowd the skyline each year. The view changes drastically—and for the better—farther along the coast as you veer off 98 and enter Route 30A, the main coastal road that leads to a quiet stretch known as South Walton. Here building restrictions prohibit high-rise developments, and the majority of dwellings are privately owned homes, most of which are available to vacationers.

Continuing southeast on U.S. 98, you come to Panama City Beach, whose Miracle Strip, once crammed with carnival-like amusement parks, junk-food vendors, T-shirt shops, and go-kart tracks, has been nearly replaced by up-to-date shopping and entertainment complexes and new condos that have given the area a much-needed face-lift. Far-ther east, past the up-and-coming sleeper cities of Port St. Joe and Mexico Beach, is the quiet blue-collar town of Apalachicola, Florida's main oyster fishery. Watch oystermen ply their trade, using long-han-dled tongs to bring in their catch. Cross the Apalachicola Bay via the Bryant Patton Bridge to St. George Island. This unspoiled 28-mile-long barrier island offers some of America's most scenic beaches, including St. George Island State Park, which has the longest beachfront of any state park in Florida.

GETTING HERE AND AROUND

Northwest Florida Regional Airport (VPS), on Highway 85 in North Eglin, is served by American Airlines (American Eagle), Delta (Delta Connection), United Airlines (Express Jet), and US Airways. From here you can take a number of car and cab services, including Checker Cab, to destinations such as Fort Walton Beach ($18) or Destin ($24).

Contacts Checker Cab. ☎ 850/650–8294.

VISITOR INFORMATION

Contacts Emerald Coast Convention and Visitors Bureau. ☎ 850/651–7131, 800/322–3319 ⊕ www.emeraldcoastfl.com.

FORT WALTON BEACH

46 miles east of Pensacola via U.S. 98.

This coastal town dates from the Civil War but had to wait more than 75 years to come into its own. Patriots loyal to the Confederate cause organized Walton's Guard (named in honor of Colonel George Walton, onetime acting territorial governor of West Florida) and camped at a site on Santa Rosa Sound, later known as Camp Walton. In 1940 fewer than 90 people lived in Fort Walton Beach, but within a decade the city became a boomtown, thanks to New Deal money for roads and bridges and the development of Eglin Field during World War II.

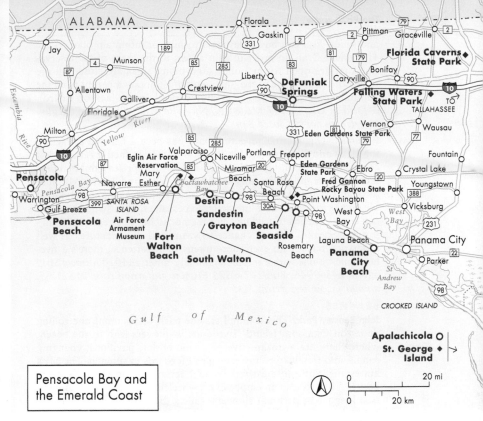

ALABAMA

Florala
Gaskin
Pittman
Graceville
Jay
Munson
Florida Caverns
State Park
Bonifay
Allentown
Liberty
Crestview
DeFuniak
Springs
Caryville
Falling Waters
State Park
Galliver
Floridale
TO
TALLAHASSEE
Milton
Vernon
Wausau
Eden Gardens State Park
Valparaiso
Fountain
Eglin Air Force
Reservation
Niceville
Portland
Freeport
Mary
Miramar
Eden Gardens
State Park
Ebro
Crystal Lake
Pensacola
Esther
Beach
Santa Rosa
Beach
Fred Gannon
Rocky Bayou State Park
Youngstown
Navarre
Chottawhatchee
Bay
Point Washington
Warrington
SANTA ROSA
ISLAND
Destin
West
Bay
Vicksburg
Gulf Breeze
Sandestin
Laguna Beach
Panama City
Pensacola
Beach
Air Force
Armament
Museum
Grayton Beach
Seaside
Panama
City
Beach
Parker
Fort
Walton
Beach
Rosemary
Beach
St
Andrew
Bay
South Walton
CROOKED ISLAND

Gulf of Mexico

Apalachicola
St. George
Island

Pensacola Bay and
the Emerald Coast

0   20 mi
0   20 km

Although off-limits to civilians, Eglin Air Force Base, which encompasses 724 square miles of land with 10 auxiliary fields and 21 runways, is Fort Walton Beach's main source of income. Tourism runs a close second. Despite inland sprawl, the town has a cute little shopping district with independent merchants along U.S. 98.

EXPLORING

Air Force Armament Museum. The collection at this museum just outside the Eglin Air Force Base's main gate contains more than 5,000 armaments (e.g., missiles, bombs, and aircraft) from World Wars I and II and the Korean and Vietnam wars. Included are uniforms, engines, weapons, aircraft, and flight simulators. You can't miss the museum—there's a squadron of aircraft including a B-17 Flying Fortress, an SR-71 Blackbird, a B-52, a B-25, and helicopters parked on the grounds in front. A continuously playing 32-minute movie, *Arming the Future*, features current weapons and Eglin's history and its role in their development. ⊠ *Eglin Air Force Base, 100 Museum Dr. (Rte. 85)* ☎ *850/882–4062* ⊕ *www.afarmamentmuseum.com* ☒ *Free* ⊗ *Closed Sun.*

Eglin Air Force Base Reservation. The 250,000 acres of the Eglin reservation conditionally open to the public include 21 ponds and plenty of challenging, twisting wooded trails that are all open to exploration. The area appeals to outdoors enthusiasts who want to hunt, fish, canoe, and swim. You can buy a day pass to hike or mountain bike on the Timberlake Trail. In order to gain access to the areas of the reservation that are open to the public (and many areas are closed all the time, others just some of the time), you must obtain a permit from the Natural Resource Division (also known locally as the Jackson Guard). ✉ *Jackson Guard, 107 Rte. 85 N, Niceville* ☎ *850/882–4165* 🌐 *eglin.isportsman.net* ⏲ *Closed Sun.*

FAMILY **Gulfarium.** This marine adventure park has been a beloved attraction for locals and visitors alike for almost 60 years. In fact, it is the oldest continuously operating marine park in Florida. Species exhibited here include otters, penguins, alligators, harbor seals, and sharks. Meander through a range of exhibits and get up close and personal with marine life thanks to several new interactive experiences, from swimming with our watery friends to feedings. For the not so faint of heart, the Stingray Bay Snorkel offers a chance to swim with the creatures as well as sharks, but for an even more intensive experience, there's a five-hour one-on-one with a marine-mammal trainer. ✉ *1010 Miracle Strip* ☎ *850/243–9046, 800/247–8575* 🌐 *www.gulfarium.com* 🎟 *$21.95, animal encounters extra.*

BEACHES

John Beasley Park. This tranquil seaside park rests among the rolling dunes on Okaloosa Island. Two dune walkovers lead to the beach, where there are a dozen covered picnic tables, pavilions, changing rooms, and freshwater showers—plus lifeguards in summer. The city's hottest nightlife is just down the road, but families can enjoy the scenic beauty. There is also an emphasis on wheelchair beach access. **Amenities:** lifeguards; parking; showers; toilets. **Best for:** sunset; walking. ✉ *Okaloosa Island.*

WHERE TO EAT

$$ AMERICAN 🍴 **Angler's Beachside Grill and Sports Bar.** Unless you sit in the water, you can't dine any closer to the Gulf than at this casual beachside bar and grill next to the Gulfarium. The waterfront setting is the image of a picturesque Gulf Coast eatery. **Known for:** typical sports bar fare plus fresh fish; warm smoked tuna dip; excellent Gulf views. [$] *Average main: $19* ✉ *1030 Miracle Strip Pkwy.* ☎ *850/796–0260* 🌐 *www.anglersgrill.com.*

WHERE TO STAY

$$ HOTEL 🏨 **Holiday Inn Resort Fort Walton Beach Hotel.** Located directly on the beach facing the Gulf of Mexico, this family-friendly resort has enough activities to keep all ages entertained—from one of the best pools in the area to an interactive mermaid to a secret tie to the rich military history of the Emerald Coast. **Pros:** steps from the beach; supervised kids programs; number of rooms with Gulf views. **Cons:** pay extra for beach services; loud music in lobby and pool areas. [$] *Rooms from: $276* ✉ *1299 Miracle Strip Pkwy. SE* ☎ *850/301–9000* 🌐 *holidayinnresortfortwaltonbeach.com* 🛏 *152 rooms* 🍽 *No meals.*

$ RESORT 🏨 **Ramada Plaza Beach Resort.** If your family loves the water, splash down at this beachside extravaganza, where activity revolves around a 194,000-gallon pool (allegedly the area's largest) with a spectacular swim-through waterfall that tumbles down from an island oasis. **Pros:**

very family-friendly; extravagant pool area; private beach. **Cons:** can be loud; chain hotel feel in rooms; draws spring breakers. $ *Rooms from: $199* ⊠ *1500 Miracle Strip Pkwy. SE* ☎ *850/243–9161, 800/874–8962* ⊕ *www.ramadafwb.com* ⤺ *335 rooms, 18 suites* ¶⊙¶ *No meals.*

NIGHTLIFE

The Boardwalk. This massive dining-and-entertainment complex at the entrance to the Okaloosa Island Pier includes several restaurants (Rockin Tacos, The Crab Trap, The Black Pearl, Floyd's Shrimp House, Al's Beach Club and Burger Bar, and Pino Gelato) as well as an assortment of night-clubs. ⊠ *1450 Miracle Strip Pkwy.* ⊕ *www.theboardwalkoi.com.*

SPORTS AND THE OUTDOORS

FISHING

FAMILY **Okaloosa Island Pier.** Don't miss a chance to go out to the end of this quar-ter-mile-long pier. There's an admission fee (and a fee to fish), and you can buy bait and tackle, and rent poles as well. ⊠ *1030 Miracle Strip Pkwy. E* ☎ *850/244–1023* ⊕ *www.okaloosaislandpier.net* ⤺ *$2; $8 to fish.*

SCUBA DIVING

Discovery Dive World. Run by military veterans, this full-service snor-keling and dive shop offers a variety of gear and lessons, though they specialize in spear fishing. ⊠ *92 S. John Sims Pkwy., Valparaiso* ☎ *850/678–5001* ⊕ *www.discoverydiveworld.com.*

DESTIN

8 miles east of Fort Walton Beach via U.S. 98.

Fort Walton Beach's "neighbor" lies on the other side of the strait that connects Choctawhatchee Bay with the Gulf of Mexico. Destin takes its name from its founder, Leonard A. Destin, a Connecticut sea captain who settled his family here sometime in the 1830s. For the next 100 years, Destin remained a sleepy little fishing village until the strait, or East Pass, was bridged in 1935. Then recreational anglers discovered its white sands, blue-green waters, and abundance of some of the most sought-after sport fish in the world. More billfish are hauled in around Destin each year than from all other Gulf ports combined, giving cre-dence to its nickname, the World's Luckiest Fishing Village.

But you don't have to be the rod-and-reel type to love Destin. There's plenty to entertain the sand-pail set as well as senior citizens, and there are many nice restaurants, which you'll have an easier time finding if you remember that the main drag through town is referred to as both U.S. 98 and Emerald Coast Parkway. The name makes sense, but part of what makes the Gulf look so emerald in these parts is the contrasting whiteness of the sand on the beach. Actually, it's not sand—it's pure, powder-soft Appalachian quartz that was dropped off by a glacier a few thousand years back. Since quartz doesn't compress (and crews clean and rake the beach each evening), your tootsies get the sole-satisfying benefit of soft, sugary "sand." Sand so pure it squeaks.

VISITOR INFORMATION

Contacts Destin Chamber of Commerce. ☎ *850/837–6241* ⊕ *www.destinchamber.com.*

Live oaks draped with Spanish moss are most common in the Panhandle.

EXPLORING

FAMILY **Big Kahuna's Lost Paradise.** The water park is the big draw here, with the Honolulu Half Pipe (a perpetual surfing wave), flume rides, steep and slippery slides, and assorted other methods of expending hydro-energy appealing to travelers who prefer freshwater thrills over the Gulf, which is just across the street. This complex also has dry family-friendly attractions: 54 holes of miniature golf, two go-kart tracks, an arcade, thrill rides, and an amphitheater. ✉ *1007 U.S. 98 E* ☎ *850/837–8319* 🌐 *www.bigkahunas.com* 🎟 *Grounds free, water park $37.99, miniature golf $6.99, go-karts $6.99, Sky Coaster or Cyclone $16.99* 🕓 *Water Park closed Labor Day–Apr. Adventure Park closed Labor Day–late Mar.*

BEACHES

Crab Island. All of the sugary, white-sand beaches of Destin and the surrounding Emerald Coast garner worldwide attention, but this is the locals' favorite. Actually a sandbar in East Pass rather than an island, Crab Island draws water-lovers and boaters, who wade the sandbar or drop anchor in droves on fair-weather days, especially weekends. People are friendly, so it's a great place to make new friends, and the shallow waters are good for families. A food barge comes around the "island" seasonally. **Amenities:** food and drink; water sports. **Best for:** partiers; snorkeling; swimming. ✉ *North side of East Pass and Marler Bridge.*

WHERE TO EAT

$$$ SEAFOOD ✕ **Marina Café.** A harbor view, impeccable service, and sophisticated fare create one of the finest dining experiences on the Emerald Coast. An ocean motif is expressed in shades of aqua, green, and sand accented with marine tapestries and sea sculptures. **Known for:** pan-seared

grouper with blue crab crust; extensive wine list; attentive service. Ⓢ *Average main: $24* ⊠ *404 U.S. 98 E* ☎ *850/837–7960* ⊕ *www.marinacafe. com* ☉ *No lunch.*

WHERE TO STAY

$$$$
RESORT
🖭 **Emerald Grande at HarborWalk Village.** Even locals seek out the views at this harbor-front destination within a destination, with luxurious hotel accommodations and a full menu of amenities, including a full-service spa, marina, health club, and indoor/outdoor pools. **Pros:** great for larger families and groups; many top-rated amenities are part of the complex. **Cons:** very family-oriented, so it's not ideal for a romantic couple's getaway; must water-taxi to the beach. Ⓢ *Rooms from: $487* ⊠ *10 Harbor Blvd.* ☎ *800/676–0091* ⊕ *www.emeraldgrande.com* ⤳ *269 rooms* ⑩ *No meals.*

SHOPPING

Destin Commons. Don't call it a mall. Call it an "open-air lifestyle center." More than 70 high-end specialty shops are here, as well as a 14-screen theater, Hard Rock Cafe, miniature train, and nautical theme park for kids. ⊠ *4300 Legendary Dr.* ☎ *850/337–8700* ⊕ *www.destincommons.com.*

Silver Sands Factory Stores. One of the southeast's largest retail designer outlets has more than 100 shops selling top-name merchandise. ⊠ *10562 Emerald Coast Pkwy. W* ☎ *850/654–9771* ⊕ *www.premiumoutlets.com/outlet/silver-sands.*

SPORTS AND THE OUTDOORS

FISHING

Destin has the largest charter-boat fishing fleet in the state. You can also pier-fish from the 3,000-foot-long Destin Catwalk and along East Pass Bridge.

Destin Charter Service. This company represents more than 90 charter services that offer deep-sea, bay-bottom, and light-tackle fishing excursions. ⊠ *East Pass Marina, 288 U.S. 98 E* ☎ *850/654–4070* ⊕ *www. destinfishingservice.com* ⌐ *From $120 per hr.*

Destin Dockside. It's a great place to pick up bait, tackle, and most anything else you'd need for a day of fishing. ⊠ *390 Harbor Blvd.* ☎ *850/428–3313* ⊕ *www.boatrentalsindestin.com.*

HarborWalk Marina. At this rustic-looking waterfront complex you can get bait, gas, tackle, and food. Regularly scheduled party-fishing-boat excursions are offered and are a much cheaper alternative to chartering or renting your own boat. ⊠ *66 Harbor Blvd. (U.S. 98 E)* ☎ *850/650–2400* ⊕ *www.harborwalk-destin.com* ⌐ *From $55.*

GOLF

Indian Bayou Golf Club. Indian Bayou offers three 9-hole courses with wide, forgiving fairways accented by well-manicured, lush greens, tall pines, and numerous lakes and water features. With challenging options for all skill levels, it is one of the more affordable options in the area. ⊠ *1 Country Club Dr. E, off Airport Rd., off U.S. 98* ☎ *850/837–6191* ⊕ *www.indianbayougolf.com* ⌐ *$45–$85 for nonmembers* ⚲ *Choctaw Course: 9 holes, 3464 yards, par 36; Creek Course: 9 holes, 3433 yards, par 36; Seminole Course: 9 holes, 3614 yards, par 36.*

14

Kelly Plantation Golf Club. Designed by Fred Couples and Gene Bates, this semiprivate course meanders along the Choctawhatchee Bay. The overall layout is encouraging for novice golfers from the forward tees, with hardly any forced carries; however, from the back tees, it's an entirely different game. Stretching 7,099 yards, the course offers a serious driving test for long hitters. Greens are unique on almost every hole. Keep an eye out for hole 4's spectacular, panoramic view of Choctawhatchee Bay, and take in the scents and sights of the surrounding magnolias and palmettos, native to the northwest Florida region. ⊠ *307 Kelly Plantation Dr.* ☎ *850/650–7600* ⊕ *www.kellyplantationgolf.com* ⊠ *$69–$145* ⚑ *18 holes, 7099 yards, par 72.*

Regatta Bay Golf and Country Club. Here you'll find a semiprivate course nestled among nature preserves along Choctawhatchee Bay. You'll also enjoy the golf club's amenities, including a state-of-the-art Parview GPS system on golf carts, and small touches that make the course and club unique, like chilled apples on the 1st and 10th tees and mango-scented iced towels. It's a favorite course for players in northwest Florida. ⊠ *465 Regatta Bay Blvd.* ☎ *850/337–8080* ⊕ *www.regattabay.com* ⊠ *$69– $95* ⚑ *18 holes, 6894 yards, par 72.*

SCUBA DIVING

Although visibility here (about 50 feet) isn't on par with the reefs of the Atlantic Coast, divers can explore artificial reefs, wrecks, and a limestone shelf at depths of up to 90 feet.

Emerald Coast Scuba. You can take diving lessons, arrange excursions, and rent all the necessary equipment through this operation. ⊠ *503 Harbor Blvd.* ☎ *850/837–0955* ⊕ *www.divedestin.com* ⊠ *Dive trips from $65, snorkel cruises from $30.*

STAND-UP PADDLEBOARDING

GUSU Paddleboards. The biggest craze in the region is YOLO ("You Only Live Once") boarding, or stand-up paddling (SUP), on what looks like a surfboard. It can be found at many resorts in the region and also through businesses such as GUSU Paddleboards. The company's website offers a map of paddle trails throughout the region and state, as well as rates for lessons and tours. Try one out on a one-hour rental or a SUP-lates class. They're located inside "TheXperience," a store that sells paddleboards and other wares in Destin. ⊠ *TheXperience, 111 Harbor Blvd.* ☎ *850/460–7300* ⊕ *www.thexperiencedestin.com* ⊠ *Rentals from $25.*

SOUTH WALTON

The 16 communities spread out along 26-mile stretch of coastline between Destin and Panama City Beach are referred to collectively as South Walton. Along this stretch of the Panhandle are monolithic condos of Destin and Panama City Beach in either direction, like massive bookends in the distance, flanking the area's low-slung, less imposing structures. A decidedly laid-back, refined mood prevails in these parts, where vacation homes go for millions and selecting a dinner spot is usually the day's most challenging decision. The South Walton neighborhood of Seaside is the birthplace of new urbanism and has been mimicked by several surrounding communities.

Accommodations consist primarily of private-home rentals, the majority of which are managed by local real-estate firms. Also scattered along Route 30A are a growing number of boutiques selling everything from fine art and unique hand-painted furniture to jewelry, gifts, and clothes.

VISITOR INFORMATION

Contacts Visit South Walton Information Center. ☎ *850/267–1216, 800/822–6877* 🌐 *www.visitsouthwalton.com.*

SANDESTIN

The resort community of Sandestin offers a one-stop shop for a family or quiet getaway offering everything from stunning golf courses to exceptional spa services. The Village of Baytowne Wharf offers a plethora of restaurants and nightlife options for those seeking entertainment. This is one of the areas in South Walton where you can also enjoy views of both the Gulf of Mexico and Choctawhatchee Bay a mere minutes from each other. Year-round events also make the area a draw for guests all four seasons.

WHERE TO STAY

$ RESORT 🏨 **Bayside at Sandestin.** Tucked into the Sandestin Beach Resort, this boutique hotel offers a different kind of experience on a quieter side of the resort, where breathtaking views of Choctawhatchee Bay steal the show. **Pros:** great amenities for the price and location; amazing bay views. **Cons:** check-in/check-out inconvenience during off-season; decor not up to par for boutique name. [$] *Rooms from: $169* ✉ *Sandestin Resort, 160 Sandestin Blvd. N, Sandestin* ☎ *877/953–2435* 🌐 *www.sandestin.com* 🛏 *109 rooms* 🍴 *No meals.*

$$$ HOTEL 🏨 **Hilton Sandestin Beach Golf Resort & Spa.** Constant refreshes—from incorporating beautiful seafoam and blue shades into the decor to new pool decking—make this chain property stand out as a Gulf-front gem as it blends in with the other vacation and condo rentals located on the Sandestin Golf and Beach resort property. **Pros:** plethora of dinning options; unbeatable Gulf views; affordable option for the region. **Cons:** chain hotel feel; can get busy during conference events. [$] *Rooms from: $369* ✉ *4000 Sandestin Blvd. S, Destin* ☎ *850/267–9500* 🌐 *www.hiltonsandestinbeach.com* 🛏 *602 rooms* 🍴 *No meals.*

$$ RENTAL Fodor'sChoice ★ 🏨 **Sandestin Golf and Beach Resort.** This place is its own little world—with shopping, charter fishing, spas, salons, tennis, water sports, golf, and special events—so it's no wonder newlyweds, conventioneers, and families all find something for them at this 2,400-acre resort. **Pros:** everything you'd ever need in a resort—and more; multiple and varied condo options throughout the property; varied price points and property types throughout. **Cons:** lacks the personal touches of a modest retreat; everything spread out far and wide; check in areas change during off season. [$] *Rooms from: $211* ✉ *9300 Emerald Coast Pkwy. W, Sandestin* ☎ *850/267–8000, 800/277–0800* 🌐 *www.sandestin.com* 🛏 *1,250 units* 🍴 *No meals.*

NIGHTLIFE

Sandestin Village of Baytowne Wharf. You can find funky blues, great sushi, and a set of dueling pianos here any night of the week. Music guests have included Graffiti & the Funky Blues Shack and John Wehner's Village Door Nightclub. ✉ *Sandestin Resort, 9300 Emerald Coast Pkwy. W, Sandestin* ☎ *800/622–1038.*

SHOPPING

The Market Shops. The two dozen or so upscale shops in this elegant Sandestin complex peddle everything from expensive chocolates to designer clothes. ✉ *Sandestin Resort, 9300 Emerald Coast Pkwy. W, Sandestin* ☎ *850/837–3077* ⊕ *www.themarketshops.com.*

Shops at Grand Boulevard at Sandestin Town Center. This town center–style shopping and dining complex is on the area's main thoroughfare, just a hop, skip, and jump from the Sandestin Resort. For the high-end shopper, the center offers everything from Fusion Art Glass Gallery to Brooks Brothers Country Club. A number of boutiques, such as Magnolia House, carry fare you can't find anywhere else. Dining options include Mitchell's Fish Market, P. F. Chang's China Bistro, and The Craft Bar, a Florida Gastropub. ✉ *600 Grand Blvd., Miramar Beach* ☎ *850/654–5929* ⊕ *www.grandboulevard.com.*

SPORTS AND THE OUTDOORS

For sheer number of holes, Sandestin tops the list with 72 (four courses): Baytowne Golf Club at Sandestin, the Burnt Pines Course, the Links Course, and the Raven Golf Club. For more information, see ⊕ *www.sandestin.com/golfers.*

Raven Golf Club. This picturesque course is a two-time home to the Boeing Championship—a stop on the PGA Champions Tour—and is carved through the marshes and pine trees of Sandestin Resort. Robert Trent Jones Jr. crafted the course as what he calls "a true modern traditional." The Raven Golf Club requires strategy on every tee as golfers are presented with a variety of shot options accompanied by changes in color and texture throughout the course. It will require almost every club and trick in your bag. ✉ *9300 Emerald Coast Pkwy. W, Sandestin* ☎ *850/267–8155* ⊕ *www.sandestin.com/golfers* ⌦ *$88–$135* ⌘ *18 holes, 6931 yards, par 71.*

GRAYTON BEACH

18 miles east of Destin via U.S. 98 on Rte. 30A (Exit 85).

Inland, pine forests and hardwoods surround the area's 14 dune lakes, giving anglers ample spots to drop a line and kayakers a peaceful refuge. Grayton Beach, the oldest community in this area, was founded in 1890. You can still see some of the old weathered-cypress homes scattered along narrow, crushed-gravel streets. The secluded off-the-beaten-path town has been noticed with the addition of adjacent WaterColor, a high-end development of vacation homes with a stylish boutique hotel as its centerpiece. The architecture is tasteful, development is carefully regulated—no buildings taller than four stories are allowed—and bicycles and kayaks are the preferred methods of transportation. Stringent building restrictions, designed to protect the pristine beaches and dunes, ensure that Grayton maintains its small-town feel and look.

EXPLORING

Eden Gardens State Park. Scarlett O'Hara could be at home here on the lawn of an antebellum mansion amid an arcade of moss-draped live oaks in nearby Point Washington. Tours of the mansion are given every hour on the hour, and furnishings inside the spacious rooms date as far back as the 17th century. The surrounding grounds—the perfect setting for a picnic lunch—are beautiful year-round, but they're nothing short of spectacular in mid-March, when the azaleas and dogwoods are in full bloom. ✉ *Rte. 395, Point Washington* ☎ *850/267–8320* 🎟 *Gardens $4, mansion tours $4* ⏲ *No mansion tours Tues. and Wed.*

BEACHES

Fodor's Choice ★ **Grayton Beach State Park.** This is the place to see what Florida looked like when only Native Americans lived here. One of the most scenic spots along the Gulf Coast, this 2,220-acre park is composed primarily of untouched Florida woodlands within the Coastal Lowlands region. It also has salt marshes, rolling dunes covered with sea oats, crystal-white sand, and contrasting blue-green waters. The park has facilities for swimming, fishing, and snorkeling, and there's an elevated boardwalk that winds over the dunes to the beach, as well as walking trails around the marsh and into the piney woods. Notice that the "bushes" you see are actually the tops of full-size slash pines and Southern magnolias, an effect created by the frequent shifting of the dunes. Even if you're just passing by, the beach here is worth a stop. Thirty fully equipped cabins and a campground provide overnight options. **Amenities:** fishing; parking (fee); showers; toilets; water sports. **Best for:** snorkeling; sunrise; swimming; walking. ✉ *357 Main Park Rd., off Rte. 30A, Grayton Beach* ☎ *850/267–8300* 🌐 *www.floridastateparks.org/graytonbeach* 🎟 *$5 per vehicle, up to 8 people; $2 pedestrians/cyclists.*

WHERE TO EAT

$$$ ECLECTIC Fodor's Choice ★ 🍴 **Fish Out of Water.** Time your appetite to arrive at sunset and you'll witness the best of both worlds: sea oats lumbering on gold-dusted dunes outside and a stylish interior that sets new standards of sophistication for the entire Panhandle. Colorful, handblown-glass accent lighting that "grows" out of the hardwood floors, plush taupe banquettes, oversize handmade lamp shades, and a sleek bar area create an atmosphere worthy of the inventive cuisine. **Known for:** small seasonal menus utilizing mostly local produce, meat, and fish; intimate, elegant atmosphere; extensive wine list. [$] *Average main: $26* ✉ *WaterColor Inn, 34 Goldenrod Circle, 2nd fl., Santa Rosa Beach* ☎ *850/534–5050* 🌐 *www.watercolorresort.com* ⏲ *No lunch.*

$$ SEAFOOD 🍴 **The Red Bar.** You could spend weeks here just taking in all the funky-junky, eclectic toy-chest memorabilia—from Marilyn Monroe posters to flags to dolls—dangling from the ceiling and tacked to every available square inch of wall. The contemporary menu is small, although it includes what you'd expect to find in the Panhandle: crab cakes, shrimp, and crawfish, to name a few. **Known for:** funky, kitschy decor; small, fish-heavy menu; live music nightly. [$] *Average main: $20* ✉ *70 Hotz Ave., Santa Rosa Beach* ☎ *850/231–1008* 🌐 *www.theredbar.com* 💳 *No credit cards.*

WHERE TO STAY

$ RENTAL 🏨 **Cabins at Grayton Beach State Park.** Back-to-nature enthusiasts and families love to visit these stylish accommodations set among the sand pines and scrub oaks of this pristine state park. **Pros:** rare and welcome preservation of Old Florida; pure peace and quiet; what a Gulf vacation is meant to be. **Cons:** few amenities; no daily maid service; no room TVs or phones. [$] *Rooms from: $130* ✉ *357 Main Park Rd., Santa Rosa Beach* ☎ *800/267–8300* 🛏 *30 cabins* 🍽 *No meals.*

14

If you saw *The Truman Show,* you may recognize several places in Seaside, where the movie was filmed.

$$$
HOTEL
Fodor's Choice ★

🏨 **WaterColor Inn and Resort.** Nature meets seaside chic at this boutique property, the crown jewel of the area's latest—and largest—planned communities. **Pros:** upscale and fancy; free Wi-Fi included; canoe use and tennis included in rates. **Cons:** clientele can be standoffish; you have to pay extra for beach gear. [$] *Rooms from: $333* ✉ *34 Goldenrod Circle, Santa Rosa Beach* ☎ *850/534–5000* 🌐 *www.watercolorresort.com* 🛏 *60 rooms* 🍴 *Breakfast.*

NIGHTLIFE

The Red Bar. The local watering hole presents red-hot blues or jazz acts every night. On Friday and Saturday nights it's elbow-to-elbow at the truly funky and colorful bar, which would be right at home on Miami's South Beach or in New York City's Greenwich Village. But credit cards aren't accepted. ✉ *70 Hotz Ave., Santa Rosa Beach* ☎ *850/231–1008* 🌐 *www.theredbar.com.*

SHOPPING

Shops of Grayton. This quaint shopping area offers eight cottages in a colorful complex where you can buy gifts, artwork, and antiques. ✉ *Rte. 283, 2 miles south of U.S. 98, Grayton Beach.*

SEASIDE

2 miles east of Grayton Beach on Rte. 30A.

This thriving planned community with old-fashioned Victorian architecture, brick streets, restaurants, retail stores, and a surfeit of art galleries was the brainchild of Robert Davis. Dubbed "new urbanism," the development style was designed to promote a neighborly, old-fashioned lifestyle. There's much to be said for an attractive, billboard-free village where you can park your car and walk everywhere you need to go.

Pastel-colored homes with white-picket fences, front-porch rockers, and captain's walks are set along redbrick streets, and all are within walking distance of the town center and its unusual cafés and shops. The community is so reminiscent of a storybook town that producers chose it for the set of the 1998 film *The Truman Show,* starring Jim Carrey.

The community has come into its own in the last few years, achieving a comfortable, lived-in look and feel that had escaped it since its founding in the late 1970s. Some of the once-shiny tin roofs are starting to rust around the edges and the foliage has matured, creating pockets of privacy and shade. There are also more signs of a real neighborhood with bars and bookstores added to the mix. Still, although Seaside's popularity continues to soar, it retains a suspicious sense of *Twilight Zone* perfection that can weird out some visitors.

Other planned neighborhoods, variations on the theme pioneered by Seaside's founders, have carved out niches along the dozen miles of Route 30A east to Rosemary Beach. The focus in the 107-acre planned community is on preserving the local environment (the landscape is completely made up of indigenous plants) and maintaining its small-town appeal. A nascent sense of community is sprouting at the Town Green, a perfect patch of manicured lawn fronting the beach, where locals gather with their wineglasses to toast the sunset. In total, South Walton touts 16 of these new urbanism–style beach communities and resorts.

WHERE TO EAT

$$$ EUROPEAN 🍴 **Bud & Alley's.** This down-to-earth beachside bistro (named for a pet cat and dog) has been a local favorite since 1986. Tucked in the dunes by the Gulf, the rooftop Tarpon Club bar makes a great perch for a sunset toast (guess the exact moment the sun will disappear and win a drink). **Known for:** Southern classics like gumbo and barbecue pork shank; fresh, seasonal fish and vegetables; sunset views. [$] *Average main: $30* ✉ *2236 E. Rte. 30A, Seaside* ☎ *850/231–5900* 🌐 *www.budandalleys.com.*

$$$$ EUROPEAN 🍴 **Café Thirty-A.** About a mile and half east of Seaside in a beautiful Florida-style home with high ceilings and a wide veranda, this restaurant has an elegant look—bolstered by white linen tablecloths—and impeccable service. The menu changes nightly and might include such entrées as wood-oven-roasted wild king salmon, sesame-crusted rare yellowfin tuna, and grilled filet mignon. **Known for:** excellent personal service; grilled quail with creamy grits appetizer; large martini and cocktail menu. [$] *Average main: $32* ✉ *3899 E. Rte. 30A, Seagrove Beach* ☎ *850/231–2166* 🌐 *www.cafethirtya.com* 🕓 *No lunch.*

$$$ SEAFOOD 🍴 **Great Southern Cafe.** Jim Shirley, founder of Pensacola's very popular Fish House, has brought his Grits a Ya-Ya to this restaurant on Seaside's town square. Breakfast is served from 8 to 11, when the menu segues to regional fare, including Gulf shrimp, Apalachicola oysters, and fresh sides such as collards, okra, black-eyed peas, fried green tomatoes, and sweet potatoes. **Known for:** Grits a Ya-Ya (blackened shrimp on cheese grits); shrimp po'boys; breakfast. [$] *Average main: $24* ✉ *83 Central Sq., Seaside* ☎ *850/231–7327* 🌐 *www.thegreatsoutherncafe.com.*

WHERE TO STAY

RENTAL AGENCIES

Seaside Cottage Rental Agency. When residents aren't using their pricey one- to six-bedroom, porticoed, faux-Victorian cottages, they rent them out. Homes have fully equipped kitchens, TV/VCR/DVDs, and vacuum cleaners and are a perfect option for a family vacation or a large group. And the rental agency helps by throwing in a bottle of wine, golf discounts, bicycles, and other perks. With Gulf breezes blowing off the water and proximity to unspoiled, sugar-white beaches, Seaside is an attractive vacation destination. And there are more than 200 different properties to choose from, sleeping from 2 to 14 people. What you won't find are the services and amenities of a full-service hotel. ✉ *2311 E. Rte. 30A, Santa Rosa Beach* ☎ *850/231–2222, 866/966–2565 reservations* 🌐 *www.cottagerentalagency.com* 🛏 *275 units* 🍴 *No meals.*

$$ B&B/INN

🏨 **The Rosemary Beach Inn.** European style meets understated chic beauty with Gulf-front views in this intimate inn in the small community of Rosemary Beach. **Pros:** caring owners; near activities and dining; beach chairs and umbrella included. **Cons:** most rooms fairly small; very limited parking (most is on-street); two-night minimum stay Thursday–Saturday. [$] *Rooms from: $300* ✉ *78 Main St., Rosemary Beach* ☎ *866/348–8952* 🌐 *www.therosemarybeachinn.com* 🛏 *11 rooms* 🍴 *Breakfast.*

SHOPPING

Seaside's central square and open-air market, along Route 30A, offer a number of unusual and whimsical boutiques carrying clothing, jewelry, and arts and crafts. In the heart of Seaside in an area called Ruskin Place, there's a collection of small shops and artists' galleries that has everything from toys and pottery to fine works of art.

Perspicacity. This shop sells simply designed women's clothing and accessories perfect for easy, carefree, beach-town casualness. ✉ *178 Market St., Seaside* ☎ *850/231–5829.*

SPORTS AND THE OUTDOORS

Butterfly Bike & Kayak. A few miles from Seaside in Seagrove Beach, this outfitter rents bikes, kayaks, scooters, and golf carts and has free delivery and pickup. ✉ *3657 E. Rte. 30A, Seagrove Beach* ☎ *850/231–2826* 🌐 *www.mybikerental.net* 🎫 *From $20 per day, from $45 per wk.*

SeaOats Beach Service. Whether it's a beach fire or surf lessons, this local couple's love for the beach shows through in a wide variety of luxury beach services. They don't have a brick-and-mortar store, but will meet you on the beach in Rosemary Beach instead. ☎ *850/951–3632* 🌐 *www.seaoatsbeachservice.com.*

PANAMA CITY BEACH

21 miles southeast of Seaside off U.S. 98.

Although Front Beach Road, the so-called Miracle Strip, is lined by high-rises (about two dozen in total) built mostly during the early 2000s, Panama City Beach's ample 27-mile coastline still gives you opportunities to avoid the crowds and congestion. Spring-break season in March and early April can bring extra congestion and noise, but the sprawling beach is long enough to accommodate everyone. The one constant in this ever-changing cityscape is the area's natural beauty, which, in many areas, helps you forget the commercialization in others.

The busiest section of Front Beach Road is book-ended by two undeveloped and fully protected state parks and their equally beautiful beaches. Stand on the pier and look in front of and behind you to see the abrupt end of the high-rises and the return of nature as far as the eye can see. The shoreline is so long that even when a mile is packed with partying students, there are 26 more where you can toss a beach blanket and find the old motels that have managed to survive. Or you travel inland, toward West Bay and find even quieter quarters, including expanses of undeveloped pinelands and a city park with ample biking trails. What's more, the beaches along the Miracle Strip, with their powder-soft sand and translucent emerald waters, are some of the finest in the state, so it's easy to understand why developers wanted to build here.

The busiest season stretches from spring (when college students descend en masse from neighboring states for spring break and a lot of raucous partying) to summer (when families and others come for the warm Gulf waters and beautiful beaches). Come before mid-March, when the temperatures can still be chilly and definitely not conducive to water activities, or after Labor Day until mid-October, when the water is still warm and inviting, and you will find a much quieter vacation destination.

Cabanas, umbrellas, sailboats, WaveRunners, and floats are available from any of dozens of vendors along the beach. To get an aerial view, for about $30 you can strap yourself beneath a parachute and go parasailing as you're towed aloft behind a speedboat a few hundred yards offshore. St. Andrews State Park, on the southeast end of the beaches, is treasured by locals and visitors alike. Camp Helen State Park, on the northwest end of the beaches, is a popular wedding venue with an incredible beach. The beautiful white sands, navigable waterways, and plentiful marine life that once attracted Spanish conquistadors today draw invaders of the vacationing kind—namely families, the vast majority of whom hail from nearby Georgia and Alabama. ■TIP→ When coming here, be sure to set your sights for Panama City Beach. Panama City is its beachless inland cousin.

GETTING HERE AND AROUND

The Northwest Florida Beaches International Airport on the east shore of Panama City's West Bay has only been open since 2010, with routes operated by Delta and Southwest, but it's the best of the region's airports. From the airport to the beach area, depending on the location of your hotel, it's about $15 to $27 by taxi. Try Yellow Cab or Checker Cab.

When navigating Panama City Beach by car, don't limit yourself to Front Beach Road—the stop-and-go traffic will drive you nuts. You can avoid the congestion by following parallel roads like Back Beach Road and U.S. 98. Also, anywhere along this long stretch of beachfront,

14

If you're lucky, you may see a great blue heron foraging on Shell Island in St. Andrews State Park.

look for "sunrise" signs, which indicate an access point to the beach. They're a treasure to find, especially when you happen across one in the midst of a quiet residential neighborhood and know that a private, quiet beach experience is just a few feet away. The Baytown Trolley serves Bay County, including downtown Panama City and the beaches ($1.50, $4 for an all-day pass); Panama City Beach is served by Route 7

Contacts Baytown Trolley. ☎ *850/769–0557* ⊕ *www.baytowntrolley.org.* **Checker Cab.** ☎ *850/236–6666.* **Yellow Cab.** ☎ *850/763–4691.*

VISITOR INFORMATION

Contacts Panama City Beach Convention and Visitors Bureau. ☎ *850/233–5070, 800/722–3224* ⊕ *www.visitpanamacitybeach.com.*

EXPLORING

FAMILY **Gulf World Marine Park.** It's certainly no SeaWorld, but with a tropical garden, tropical-bird theater, plus alligator and otter exhibits, the park is still a winner with kids. The stingray-petting pool and the shark-feeding and scuba demonstrations are big crowd pleasers, and the old favorites—performing sea lions, otters, and bottlenose dolphins—still hold their own. If you're particularly interested, consider a specialty program, such as Trainer for a Day, which takes you behind the scenes to assist in food preparation and training sessions and lets you make an on-stage appearance in the Dolphin Show. The $250, six-hour program includes a souvenir photo, lunch, and trainer T-shirt. ✉ *15412 Front Beach Rd.* ☎ *850/234–5271* ⊕ *www. gulfworldmarinepark.com* 🖃 *$29.*

FAMILY Fodor's Choice ★ **St. Andrews State Park.** At the southeastern tip of Panama City Beach, the hotels and condos and traffic stop, and there suddenly appears a pristine 1,260-acre park that offers a peek at what the entire beach area looked like before developers sank their claws into it. Here are beaches, pinewoods, and marshes with places to swim, pier-fish, and hike on clearly marked nature trails. A rock jetty creates a calm, shallow play area that is perfect for young children. There are also camping facilities and a snack bar. Board a ferry to Shell Island—a 700-acre barrier island in the Gulf of Mexico with some of the best shelling between here and southwest Florida's Sanibel Island. ✉ *4607 State Park La.* ☎ *850/233–5140* 🌐 *www.floridastateparks.org* 🎫 *$8 per vehicle, up to 8 people.*

FAMILY **Shipwreck Island Waterpark.** Once part of the Miracle Strip Amusement Park operation, this 6-acre water park has everything from speedy slides and tubes to the slow-moving Lazy River. Oddly enough, admission is based on height (whether you are over or under 50 inches), with under 35 inches free. Wear water shoes or flip-flops to protect your feet on the hot pavement. ✉ *12201 Middle Beach Dr.* ☎ *850/234–3333* 🌐 *www.shipwreckisland.com* 🎫 *$35.98* 🕒 *Closed Oct.–Mar.*

BEACHES

Mexico Beach. Just over 30 miles east of Panama City along scenic U.S. 98, this jewel of a beach is refreshingly free of the high-rises that populate many parts of Panama City Beach itself. Home to colorful, gracefully aging beach houses, the beach offers seclusion and a slower pace than its neighbor to the west. **Amenities:** food and drink; parking. **Best for:** solitude. ✉ *U.S. 98, 35 miles east of Panama City Beach, Mexico Beach* ☎ *888/723–2546* 🌐 *mexicobeach.com.*

Panama City Beach. With 27 miles of shoreline, the beaches of Panama City offer the same pure white sand and emerald-green waters as its neighbors. Here, however, the coastline is dotted with high-rises rather than unspoiled nature. On the plus side, there are plenty of places to play, swim, splash, and feast, and there's no excuse for getting bored or hungry. Although it was once known as party central, Panama City Beach is becoming more family-friendly. **Amenities:** lifeguards; parking; showers; toilets; water sports. **Best for:** partiers; swimming; walking. ✉ *Front Beach Rd., between U.S. 98 and St. Andrews State Park* ☎ *800/722–3224.*

WHERE TO EAT

While you'll find an almost endless array of chain restaurants in Panama City Beach, the city does have some extremely good locally owned restaurants as well if you are willing to look beyond Pier Park and the Miracle Strip.

$$ SEAFOOD 🍴 **Billy's Steamed Seafood Restaurant, Oyster Bar, and Crab House.** Join the throng of locals who really know their seafood. Then roll up your sleeves and dig into some of the Gulf's finest blue crabs and shrimp seasoned to perfection with Billy's special recipe. **Known for:** no-frills local hangout; fresh Gulf seafood; Billy's special spice blend. [$] *Average main: $16* ✉ *3000 Thomas Dr.* ☎ *850/235–2349* 🌐 *www.billysoysterbar.com.*

$$$ SEAFOOD 🍴 **Capt. Anderson's.** Come early to watch the boats unload the catch of the day on the docks and to beat the long line that forms each afternoon at this noted restaurant with a real family feel. Here since

1953, it doesn't seem to have changed much and that's a good thing. **Known for:** views of fishing boats; large selection of fresh seafood and steaks; Greek specialties. [$] *Average main: $30* ✉ *5551 N. Lagoon Dr.* ☎ *850/234–2225* 🌐 *www.captainandersons.com.*

$$$$ AMERICAN 🍴 **Firefly.** This local gem offers a fine-dining experience wrapped in a casual style. When you walk into Firefly and see the white-light adorned grand oak in the center, you automatically get a warm, wistful, and romantic feeling. **Known for:** upscale preparations of standards like bone-in pork chops and pan-roasted red snapper; romantic atmosphere; excellent service. [$] *Average main: $34* ✉ *535 N. Richard Jackson Blvd.* ☎ *850/249–3359* 🌐 *fireflypcb.com.*

$ AMERICAN 🍴 **Liza's Kitchen.** This local lunch favorite is popular with both locals and visitors for salads and delicious sandwiches on homemade focaccia bread; even many condiments, salad dressings, and all soups are made in-house. It's a casual spot, with seating both inside and out. **Known for:** gourmet sandwiches; weekend brunch; occasional live music. [$] *Average main: $8* ✉ *7328 Thomas Dr., Suite L* ☎ *580/233–9000* 🌐 *www.lovelizas.com* ⏲ *No dinner.*

$$ SEAFOOD 🍴 **Schooners.** This beachfront spot which is really tucked away down a small avenue bills itself as the "last local beach club," and more boldly, "the best place on Earth." Drawing a mix of locals and tourists, it's actually a perfect spot for a casual family lunch or early dinner: kids can have burgers and play on the beach while Mom and Dad enjoy grown-up drinks and simple fare such as homemade gumbo, steak, a burger, or seafood like crab-stuffed shrimp, fresh grouper, and grilled tuna steaks. **Known for:** basic burgers and seafood menu; lively, especially at sunset; family-friendly atmosphere. [$] *Average main: $17* ✉ *5121 Gulf Dr.* ☎ *850/235–3555* 🌐 *www.schooners.com.*

WHERE TO STAY

If you want a quieter experience, look for lodging on the bay side of Panama City Beach. You'll have a bit more traveling to get to the Miracle Strip and the beaches, but the quieter surroundings can be very pleasant, especially during the high season.

$ RENTAL FAMILY 🏨 **Carillon Beach Resort Inn.** Old-world charm and lovely architecture marry with a perfect location near the Gulf and Pier Park to make Carillion Beach Resort Inn one of the most unique properties in the area. **Pros:** showcases local wildlife and beauty; amenities abound; all rooms have kitchenettes. **Cons:** some decor could use updating; several miles away from Panana City Beach proper; it's a long walk to the beach. [$] *Rooms from: $199* ✉ *114 Carillon Market St.* ☎ *850/334–9100* 🌐 *www.carillonbeachresortinn.com* 🛏 *46 units* 🍽 *No meals.*

$$ RENTAL 🏨 **Edgewater Beach Resort.** You can sleep at least four and as many as eight in the luxurious one-, two-, and three-bedroom apartments in beachside towers and golf course villas. **Pros:** variety of lodging options; 110 acres of beautiful beachfront property. **Cons:** can get busy and noisy in season. [$] *Rooms from: $219* ✉ *11212 Front Beach Rd.* ☎ *855/874–8686 information, 877/278–0544 reservations* 🌐 *www.edgewaterbeachresort.com* 🛏 *520 units* 🍽 *No meals.*

$ HOTEL FAMILY 🏨 **Legacy by the Sea.** Nearly every room at this family-friendly, 14-story, pastel-peach hotel has a private balcony with commanding Gulf views. **Pros:** everything is within walking distance; plenty of resort amenities;

all units have full kitchens. **Cons:** crowded and congested area; lots of traffic in the area during peak season. [$] *Rooms from: $179* ✉ *15325 Front Beach Rd.* ☎ *850/249–8601, 888/886–8917* 🌐 *www.legacybythesea.com* 🛏 *139 rooms* 🍴 *Breakfast.*

$ RESORT 🏨 **Sheraton Bay Point Resort.** Across the Grand Lagoon from St. Andrews State Park, this expansive property offers quiet away from the madness of Panama City Beach as well as proximity to excellent golf. **Pros:** removed from the crush of tourists; excellent spa; private barrier island beach. **Cons:** large and sprawling; generic resort feel; draws a lot of meetings and conferences. [$] *Rooms from: $159* ✉ *4114 Jan Cooley Dr.* ☎ *850/236–6000, 866/912–1042 reservations* 🌐 *www.sheratonbaypoint.com* 🛏 *320 rooms* 🍴 *No meals.*

14

NIGHTLIFE

Club La Vela. Among the offerings that guarantee a full-tilt party here are a slate of concerts (acts have included Aerosmith, Creed, and Ludacris); international DJs; 48 bar stations; swimming pools; a tropical waterfall; and dance halls with names like Thunderdome, Underground, Night Gallery, Rock Arena, and the Pussykat Lounge. At spring-break time this club is transformed into a whirlpool of libido. ✉ *8813 Thomas Dr.* ☎ *850/234–1061, 850/234–3866* 🌐 *www.clublavela.com.*

Pineapple Willy's. This eatery and bar is geared to families and tourists—as well as sports fans. The signature rum drink, the Pineapple Willy, was the inspiration for its full slate of tropical drinks and the hangout's tiki attitude. ✉ *9875 S. Thomas Dr.* ☎ *850/235–0928* 🌐 *www.pwillys.com.*

Tootsie's Orchid House. A taste of Southern charm hits the beach at Tootsie's, which features country musical acts from Nashville on a regular basis. It's a lively atmosphere with cocktails and bar bites that tantalize a variety of palates. ✉ *600 Pier Park Dr.* ☎ *850/236–3459* 🌐 *www.tootsies.net.*

SHOPPING

Pier Park. Occupying a huge swath of land that was once an amusement park, this diverse 900,000-square-foot entertainment/shopping/dining complex creates the downtown feel that Panama City Beach otherwise lacks. Anchor stores including Dillard's, JCPenney, and Target keep things active during the day, along with a number of specialty shops, and clubs like Jimmy Buffett's Margaritaville and the 16-screen Grand Theatre keep things hopping after dark. Other stores, such as Ron Jon Surf Shop and Fresh Market, offer even more reason to see this vibrant and enjoyable complex. ✉ *600 Pier Park Dr.* ☎ *850/236–9974* 🌐 *www.simon.com/mall/pier-park.*

SPORTS AND THE OUTDOORS

CANOEING

Econfina Creek Canoe Livery. Rentals for a trip down Econfina Creek—known as Florida's most beautiful canoe trail—are supplied by this outfitter, and they will pick you up from the end of the trail and bring you back to your vehicle (even if you bring your own canoe, albeit for a price). You can rent single or double kayaks or canoes. No checks or credit cards. It's open by appointment only in the off-season (October–April). ✉ *5641 Porter Pond Rd., north of Rte. 20, Youngstown* ☎ *850/722–9032* 🌐 *www.canoeeconfinacreek.net* 🎟 *From $40.*

GOLF

Bay Point Resort Golf Club. Two golf courses—the Nicklaus Course and the Meadows Course—are nestled on a 1,100-acre wildlife sanctuary and are open to the public. The Nicklaus Course is the only Nicklaus Design golf course in northwest Florida and features generous plateaus and uncharacteristic elevation changes unique to the Florida Panhandle region. A few holes offer panoramic views of the Grand Lagoon and St. Andrews Bay.

The Meadows Course is also picturesque, and its occasionally tight fairways, numerous lakes, and bunkers provide an ever-changing set of challenges. ⊠ *4701 Bay Point Rd.* ☎ *850/235–6950, 877/235–6950* ⊕ *www.baypointgolf.com* ⊟ *Nicklaus Course, $34–$109; Meadows Course, $26–69* ⚑ *Nicklaus Course: 18 holes, 7000 yards, par 72; Meadows Course: 18 holes, 6913 yards, par 72.*

Hombre Golf Club. The Hombre opened in 1989 with 18 holes and hosted its first PGA Tour event (The Panama City Beach Classic) in 1990. It now has a total of 27 holes; the 9-hole groupings are known as "Good," "Bad," and "Ugly," and they can be played in varying combinations that give golfers three different 18-hole options as well as four sets of tees for different levels of difficulty to best fit their game and handicap. The original 18 holes plays from 5,400 yards (senior tees) to 6,836 yards (championship tees) for the men, while the ladies' layout is 4,901 yards. Each fall, Hombre hosts the PGA Tour Qualifying School, with the likes of Gary Nicklaus, Mike Weir, and Michael Campbell having come in the past. ⊠ *120 Coyote Pass* ☎ *850/234–3673* ⊕ *www.hombregolfclub.com* ⊟ *"Good" course, $39; "Bad" and "Ugly" courses, $55* ⚑ *"Good" course: 9 holes, 3170 yards, par 35; "Bad" course: 9 holes, 3393 yards, par 36; "Ugly" course: 9 holes, 3427 yards, par 36.*

STAND-UP PADDLEBOARDING

Fodor's Choice   **Walkin' on Water Paddleboards.** One of the most popular activities in the
★   Gulf area is stand-up paddleboarding, and the folks at WOW Paddleboards have a full-service operation, including guided paddling tours, equipment, instruction, and even equipment if you are in the business of buying. You can sign up for everything from cheaper group paddling trips to individual lessons. The instructors are competent and caring and can get almost anyone up onto a board, but you may find that you use muscles you never knew you had. ⊠ *108 Carillon Market St.* ☎ *850/588–6230* ⊕ *www.wowpaddleboards.com* ⊟ *From $45.*

SCUBA DIVING

Snorkeling and scuba diving are extremely popular in the clear waters here. If you have the proper certification, you can dive among dozens of ships sunk by the city to create artificial reefs.

Panama City Dive Center. Here you can arrange for instruction, gear rental, and charters. Two-day "Wreck Daze," for those interested in wreck diving, include boat accommodations and guides. ⊠ *4823 Thomas Dr.* ☎ *850/235–3390* ⊕ *www.pcdivecenter.com* ⊟ *From $34.*

WILDLIFE-WATCHING CRUISES

Fodor's Choice ★ **Dolphin and Snorkel Tours.** Captain Lorraine will take you on a cruise around the bay to see dolphins with stops for snorkeling and (on longer tours) lunch. Tours can be as short as two hours or as long as a full day. She knows all the best spots to find the most interesting sealife in the bay and, especially, around Andrews State Park and Shell Beach. She tries to make the trips educational and eco-friendly without causing undue disturbances for the wildlife. While she specializes in small private groups, Lorraine will work to put smaller groups together to avoid making trips unaffordable. ⊠ *Bay Point Marina, 3824 Hatteras La.* ☎ *850/866–8815* ⊕ *www.dolphinandsnorkeltours. com* ⌦ *From $65.*

Paradise Adventures. Known for an array of dolphin tours, sunset sails, and half-day sightseeing cruises, Paradise Adventures has showcased the natural beauty of the area for visitors and locals alike. They also offer a Shell Island Adventure Tour. ⊠ *3901 Thomas Dr.* ☎ *850/769–3866* ⊕ *paradiseadventurespcb.com* ⌦ *From $45.*

APALACHICOLA

65 miles southeast of Panama City Beach off U.S. 98.

It feels like a long haul between Panama City Beach and here. Add an odd name and a town's below-the-radar reputation to that long drive and you may be tempted to skip Apalachicola. But you shouldn't. It's a weirdly fascinating town that, for some reason, has a growing cosmopolitan veneer. And that makes it worth a visit.

Meaning "land of the friendly people" in the language of its original Native American inhabitants, Apalachicola—known in these parts as simply Apalach—lies on the Panhandle's southernmost bulge. European settlers began arriving in 1821, and by 1847 the southern terminus of the Apalachicola River steamboat route was a bustling port town. Although the town is now known as the Oyster Capital of the World, oystering became king only after the local cotton industry flagged—the city's extra-wide streets, built to accommodate bales of cotton awaiting transport, are a remnant of that trade—and the sponge industry moved down the coast after depleting local sponge colonies.

But the newest industry here is tourism, and visitors have begun discovering the Forgotten Coast, as the area is known, flocking to its intimate hotels and bed-and-breakfasts, dining at excellent restaurants, and browsing in unique shops selling anything from handmade furniture to brass fixtures recovered from nearby shipwrecks. If you like oysters or want to go back in time to the Old South of Gothic churches and spooky graveyards, Apalachicola is a good place to start.

VISITOR INFORMATION

Contacts Apalachicola Bay Chamber of Commerce. ☎ *850/653–9419* ⊕ *www.apalachicolabay.org.*

WHERE TO EAT

$$ SEAFOOD 🍴 **Apalachicola Seafood Grill & Steakhouse.** Where will you find the world's largest fish sandwich? Right here in downtown Apalachicola. **Known for:** "world's largest" fish sandwich; blue-crab cakes; diner atmosphere and gentle prices. [$] *Average main: $15* ✉ *100 Market St.* ☎ *850/653–9510* 🕒 *No dinner Sun.*

$$ SEAFOOD 🍴 **Boss Oyster.** "Shut up and shuck." That's the advice from this rustic Old Florida restaurant and it should know, since many consider this the top oyster restaurant in Florida's oyster capital. **Known for:** fresh oysters cooked and raw; fresh grouper; outdoor dining area on the riverfront. [$] *Average main: $20* ✉ *Apalachicola River Inn, 125 Water St.* ☎ *850/653–9364* 🌐 *www.bossoyster.com.*

$$$ AMERICAN 🍴 **Owl Café.** Located in a behemoth clapboard building on a prime corner in downtown Apalachicola, this old-fashioned, charming lunch-and-dinner spot pleases modern palates, both in the white-linen elegance of the dining room and in the colorful garden terrace. The food is an artful blend of old and new as well: the chicken wrap seems as much at home on the lunch menu as the crab quesadillas. **Known for:** varied menu, heavy on seafood selections; large wine selection; weekend brunch. [$] *Average main: $21* ✉ *15 Ave. D* ☎ *850/653–9888* 🌐 *www.owlcafeflorida.com.*

$$$ LATIN AMERICAN 🍴 **Tamara's Café.** Mixing Florida flavors with South American flair, Tamara, a native Venezuelan, opened this colorful bistro in a 1920s-era building in the 1990s and has been a local staple ever since. Now owned by her daughter and son-in-law, it continues to serve a menu reliable, Latin-accented Florida cuisine, especially seafood. **Known for:** Latin-influenced cuisine, especially seafood; tapas menu; small but excellent dessert menu. [$] *Average main: $23* ✉ *71 Market St.* ☎ *850/653–4111* 🌐 *www.tamarascafe.com.*

WHERE TO STAY

$ RENTAL 🏨 **The Consulate.** These four elegant suites, on the second story of the former offices of the French consul, range in size from 650 to 1,650 square feet and combine a 19th-century feel with 21st-century luxury. **Pros:** large rooms; more character than you'd find in a chain hotel; all units have kitchens and laundry facilities. **Cons:** a bit pricey for Apalachicola; balcony for front units is shared space. [$] *Rooms from: $155* ✉ *76 Water St.* ☎ *850/408–0556* 🌐 *www.consulatesuites.com* 🛏 *4 suites* 🍽 *No meals.*

$ B&B/INN 🏨 **Coombs Inn.** A combination of neighboring homes and a carriage house, this entire complex was created with Victorian flair. **Pros:** clean and comfortable; on-site, friendly owner who's happy to assist with travel tips and suggestions. **Cons:** be prepared to meet and greet other guests at the inn; if you favor complete privacy, a hotel may suit you better. [$] *Rooms from: $119* ✉ *80 6th St.* ☎ *850/653–9199* 🌐 *www.coombshouseinn.com* 🛏 *23 rooms* 🍽 *Breakfast.*

$ B&B/INN 🏨 **Gibson Inn.** One of a few inns on the National Register of Historic Places still operating as a full-service facility, this turn-of-the-20th-century hostelry in the heart of downtown is easily identified by its wraparound porches, intricate fretwork, and widow's walk. **Pros:** smack-dab in the center of town; peaceful veranda. **Cons:** may get a little busy when weddings are taking place in the main lobby; could use a refresh in some areas of the decor and building. $ *Rooms from: $120* ✉ *51 Ave. C* ☎ *850/653–2191* ⊕ *www.gibsoninn.com* ⤳ *30 rooms* ⦿ *Breakfast.*

SHOPPING

The best way to shop in Apalachicola is just to stroll around the tiny downtown area. There are always new stores joining old favorites, and somewhere along the way you'll find something that'll pique your interest.

Grady Market On the first floor of The Consulate inn is a collection of more than a dozen boutiques, including several antiques dealers and the gallery of Richard Bickel, known for his stunning black-and-white photographs of local residents. ✉ *The Consulate, 76 Water St.* ☎ *850/653–4099* ⊕ *www.downtownapalachicola.com/business/grady-market.*

14

ST. GEORGE ISLAND

8 miles southeast of Apalachicola via Bryant Patton Bridge off U.S. 98.

Cross the long, long bridge leading east out of Apalachicola and then look to your right for another lengthy span that takes you south to pristine St. George Island. Sitting 5 miles out in the Gulf of Mexico, the island is bordered by both Apalachicola Bay and the Gulf, offering the best of both to create a nostalgic seaside retreat.

The rich bay is an angler's dream, whereas the snowy-white beaches and clear Gulf waters satisfy even the most finicky beachgoer. Indulge in bicycling, hiking, canoeing, and snorkeling, or find a secluded spot for reading, gathering shells, or bird-watching. Accommodations mostly take the form of privately owned, fully furnished condos and single-family homes.

EXPLORING

Fodor'sChoice **St. George Island State Park.** This is Old Florida at its undisturbed best.
★ On the east end of the island are 9 miles of undeveloped beaches and dunes—the longest beachfront of any state park in Florida. Sandy coves, salt marshes, oak forests, and pines provide shelter for many birds, including bald eagles and ospreys. Spotless restrooms and plentiful parking make a day at this park a joy. Campers and boaters also welcome. **Amenities:** parking; showers; toilets. **Best for:** swimming; walking. ✉ *1900 E. Gulf Beach Dr.* ☎ *850/927–2111* ⊕ *www.floridastateparks.org/stgeorgeisland* 🎫 *$6 per vehicle, up to 8 people.*

WHERE TO EAT

$ ✕**BJs Pizza and Subs.** In any other locale you might think twice before
PIZZA dining at a restaurant that advertises "kegs-to-go" on the menu, but this is an island, so establishments tend to wear several hats (some even sell live bait). Fear not: this simple beach shack serves solid, if predictable, fare. **Known for:** good casual fare, but really good pizza; beer and wine served; game room for families. $ *Average main: $7* ✉ *105 W. Gulf Beach Dr.* ☎ *850/927–2805* ⊕ *www.sgipizza.com.*

$$ ✕**Blue Parrot.** You'll feel like you're sneaking in the back door as you
SEAFOOD climb the side stairs leading to an outdoor deck overlooking the Gulf (this is Apalach's only restaurant on the beach). Or if you can, grab a table indoors. **Known for:** good basic fried and grilled seafood; good frozen drinks; busy on the weekends. $ *Average main: $20* ✉ *68 W. Gorrie Dr.* ☎ *850/927–2987* ⊕ *www.blueparrotsgi.com.*

TALLAHASSEE

103 miles east of Panama City, 78 miles northeast of Apalachicola.

Tallahassee is Florida with a Southern accent. It maintains a tranquillity quite different from the sun-and-surf coastal towns. The only Southern capital spared in the Civil War, Tallahassee has preserved its history. Vestiges of the city's colorful past are found throughout. For example, in the capitol complex, the turn-of-the-20th-century Old Capitol building is strikingly paired with the New Capitol skyscraper.

The canopies of ancient oaks and spring bowers of azaleas line many streets; among the best "canopy roads" are St. Augustine, Miccosukee, Meridian, Old Bainbridge, and Centerville, all dotted with country stores and antebellum plantation houses. Between March and April, flowers bloom, the legislature is in session, and the Springtime Tallahassee festival is in full swing.

GETTING HERE AND AROUND

Just 14 miles south of the Georgia border and nearer to Atlanta than Miami, Tallahassee is midway between Jacksonville and Pensacola. Tallahassee Regional Airport is served by American, Delta, United Express, and US Airways. From the airport to downtown is around $20 via City Taxi or Yellow Cab.

Contacts City Taxi. ☎ *850/575–7575.* **Yellow Cab.** ☎ *850/999–9999* ⊕ *www.tallahasseeyellowcab.com.*

VISITOR INFORMATION

Contacts Tallahassee Area Convention and Visitors Bureau. ☎ *850/606– 2305, 800/628–2866* ⊕ *www.visittallahassee.com.*

EXPLORING

DOWNTOWN

TOP ATTRACTIONS

FAMILY **Challenger Learning Center.** Visitors of all ages can't help but get excited about math and science exploration at this museum that features a space mission simulator, an IMAX 3D theater, and the Downtown Digital Dome Theatre and Planetarium. Every kid, and kid at heart, can reenact a space mission with The Challenger Learning Center Space Mission Simulator. The next best thing to actual space flight, the simulator features a Mission Control room designed after NASA Johnson Space Center and an orbiting space station modeled after the laboratory on the International Space Station. Hands-on or demonstrational science techniques and equipment can be found throughout the museum. ⊠ *200 S. Duval St.* ☎ *850/645–7796, 850/644–4629 IMAX* ⊕ *www.challeng-ertlh.com* ⊟ *Planetarium $5, IMAX $8–$10.*

Museum of Florida History. If you thought Florida was founded by Walt Disney, stop in here. The displays explain the state's past by highlighting the unique geological and historical events that have shaped the state. Exhibits include a mammoth armadillo grazing in a savanna, the remains of a giant mastodon found in nearby Wakulla Springs, and a dugout canoe that once carried American Indians into Florida's backwaters.

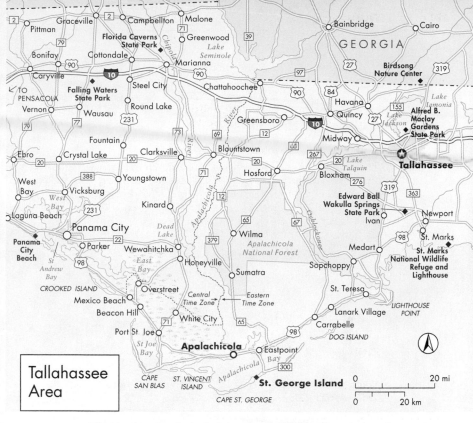

Tallahassee
Area

Florida's history also includes settlements by the Spanish, British, French, and Confederates who fought for possession of the state.

Gold bars, weapons, flags, maps, furniture, steamboats, and other artifacts underscore the fact that although most Americans date the nation to 1776, Florida's residents were building settlements hundreds of years earlier. If this intrigues you, one floor up is the Florida State Archives and Library, where there's a treasure trove of government records, manuscripts, photographs, genealogical records, and other materials. ■TIP➔ It was in these archives that researchers found footage of a young Jim Morrison appearing in a promotional film for Florida's universities. ⊠ *500 S. Bronough St.* ☎ *850/245–6400, 850/245–6600 library, 850/245–6700 archives* ⊕ *www.museumoffloridahistory.com* ✉ *Free.*

New Capitol. In the 1960s, when there was talk of relocating the capital to a more central location like Orlando, Panhandle legislators got to work and approved the construction of a 22-story skyscraper that would anchor the capital right where it was. It's perfectly placed at the crest of a hill, sitting prominently behind the low-rise Old Capitol. The governor's office is on the first floor, along with the Florida Artists Hall of Fame, a series of plaques that pay tribute to Floridians such as Ray Charles, Burt Reynolds, Tennessee Williams, Ernest Hemingway, and Marjorie Kinnan Rawlings.

The House and Senate chambers on the fifth floor provide viewer galleries for when the legislative sessions take place (March to May). Catch a panoramic view of Tallahassee and the surrounding countryside all the way into Georgia from the fabulous 22nd-floor observation deck. Although budget cuts have stopped scheduled guided tours, a free brochure can get you around; if you're traveling in a group you can call ahead to have a guide usher you. To pick up information about the area, stop at the Florida Visitors Center on the plaza level, and check out the plaque on the north wall facing the elevators. It's dedicated to Senator Lee Wissenborn "... whose valiant effort to move the Capitol to Orlando was the prime motivation for the construction of this building." ⊠ *400 S. Monroe St.* ☎ *850/488–6167* ⊕ *www.florida-capitol.myflorida.com* ▨ *Free* ⊗ *Closed weekends.*

TALLAHASSEE HISTORIC TRAIL

A route mapped and documented by an eager Eagle Scout is now a Tallahassee sightseeing staple. Start at the New Capitol, where you can pick up maps and descriptive brochures at the visitor center. You'll walk through the Park Avenue and Calhoun Street historic districts, which will take you back to territorial days and the era of postwar reconstruction. Along the way are landmark churches and cemeteries and outstanding examples of Greek Revival, Italianate, and prairie-style architecture. Some houses are open to the public.

Old Capitol. The centerpiece of the capitol complex, this 1842 structure has been added to and subtracted from several times. Having been restored, the jaunty red-and-white-striped awnings and combination gas-electric lights make it look much as it did in 1902. Inside, it houses a must-see museum of Florida's political history as well as the old Supreme Court chambers and Senate Gallery—a very interesting peek into the past. ⊠ *S. Monroe St., at Apalachee Pkwy.* ☎ *850/487–1902* ⊕ *www.flhistoriccapitol.gov* ▨ *Free.*

WORTH NOTING
Meginnis-Monroe House. This house served as a field hospital during the Civil War and is now the home of the LeMoyne Center for the Visual Arts. ⊠ *125 N. Gadsden St.* ⊕ *www.lemoyne.org* ▨ *Free* ⊗ *Closed Sun. and Mon.*

AWAY FROM DOWNTOWN
TOP ATTRACTIONS
Alfred B. Maclay Gardens State Park. Starting in December, the grounds at this 1,200-acre estate are afire with azaleas, dogwood, Oriental magnolias, spring bulbs of tulips and irises, banana shrubs, honeysuckle, silverbell trees, pansies, and camellias. Allow half a day to wander past the reflecting pool into the tiny walled garden and around the lakes and woodlands. The Maclay residence (open January through April) is furnished as it was in the 1920s; picnic areas, gardens, and swimming and boating facilities are open to the public. ⊠ *3540 Thomasville Rd.* ☎ *850/487–4556* ⊕ *www.floridastateparks.org/maclaygardens* ▨ *$6 per vehicle, up to 8 people; garden extra $6 per person Jan.–Apr. (blooming season), free rest of year.*

Guided tours are given daily at Florida's Old Capitol in Tallahassee. It sits in front of the 22-story New Capitol.

Fodor's Choice ★ **Edward Ball Wakulla Springs State Park.** Known for having one of the deepest springs in the world, this very picturesque and highly recommended park remains relatively untouched, retaining the wild and exotic look it had in the 1930s, when the films *Tarzan* and *Creature from the Black Lagoon* were shot here. Even if they weren't, you'd want to come here and see what Florida really looks like. Beyond the lodge is the spring where glass-bottom boats set off deep into the lush, jungle-lined waterways to catch glimpses of alligators, snakes, nesting limpkins, and other waterfowl. It costs $50 to rent a pontoon boat and go it alone—it may be worth it since an underground river flows into a pool so clear you can see the bottom more than 100 feet below. The park is 15 miles south of Tallahassee on Route 61. If you can't pull yourself away from this idyllic spot, spend the night in the 1930s Spanish Mediterranean–style lodge. ⊠ *465 Wakulla Park Dr., Wakulla Springs* ☎ *850/561-7276* ⊕ *www.floridastateparks.org/wakullasprings* ⊠ *$6 per vehicle, up to 8 people; boat tour $8.*

Mission San Luis Archaeological and Historic Site. Long before New England's residents began gaining a foothold in North America, the native Apalachee Indians as well as Spanish missionaries settled here. On the site of a 17th-century Spanish mission and Apalachee Indian town, this museum focuses on the archaeology of the late 1600s, when the Apalachee village here had a population of at least 1,400. By 1704, however, threatened by Creek Indians and British forces, the locals burned the village and fled. About once a year, researchers conduct digs, and then they spend the rest of the year analyzing their findings. If you're here when they are, you can watch them dig. Otherwise, you'll have to be content with roaming around the re-creation of a 17th-century Spanish village and speaking with the living-history guides, who offer tours by advance arrangement. Even without seeing researchers digging for clues, this is still a cool experience and a great way to learn about Florida's impressive history. A 24,000-square-foot, state-of-the-art visitor center offers an expanded exhibit hall and gift shop. ✉ *2100 W. Tennessee St.* ☎ *850/245–6406* 🌐 *www.missionsanluis.org* 🎟 *$5* 🕒 *Closed Mon.*

St. Marks National Wildlife Refuge and Lighthouse. As its name suggests, this attraction is of both natural and historical interest. Natural salt marshes, tidal flats, and freshwater pools used by early natives set the stage for the once-powerful Ft. San Marcos de Apalache, which was built nearby in 1639. Stones salvaged from the fort were used in the lighthouse, which is still in operation. In winter the 100,000-acre-plus refuge on the shores of Apalachee Bay is the resting place for thousands of migratory birds of more than 300 species, but the alligators seem to like it year-round (keep your camera ready). The visitor center has information on more than 75 miles of marked trails. Hardwood swamps and pine woodlands also provide habitat for wood ducks, black bears, otters, raccoons, deer, armadillos, coyotes, feral hogs, fox squirrels, gopher tortoises, and woodpeckers. Twenty-five miles south of Tallahassee, the refuge can be reached via Route 363. ✉ *1255 Lighthouse Rd., St. Marks* ☎ *850/925–6121* 🌐 *saintmarks.fws.gov* 🎟 *$5 per vehicle.*

WORTH NOTING

FAMILY **Tallahassee Museum.** Not exactly a museum, this is really an expansive, bucolic park that showcases a peaceful and intriguing look at Old Florida, located about 20 minutes from downtown. The theme and presentation here is of a working 1880s pioneer farm that offers daily hands-on activities for children, such as soap making and blacksmithing. A boardwalk meanders through the 52 acres of natural habitat that make up the zoo, which has such varied animals as panthers, bobcats, white-tailed deer, bald eagles, red wolves, hawks, owls, otters, and black bears—many of which were brought here injured or orphaned. Also on-site are nature trails, a one-room schoolhouse dating from 1897, and an 1840s Southern plantation manor, where you can usually find someone cooking on weekends. It's peaceful, pleasing, and educational. ✉ *3945 Museum Dr.* ☎ *850/575–8684* 🌐 *www.tallahasseemuseum.org* 🎟 *$11.50.*

WHERE TO EAT

$$$ ITALIAN 🍴 **Andrew's 228.** Part of a smart complex in the heart of the political district, this two-story "urban Tuscan villa" (contradiction noted) is the latest of owner Andy Reiss's restaurant incarnations to occupy the same space (the last was Andrew's Second Act). Leaning toward upscale, the food has Italian influences. **Known for:** menu of small plates; owned by a longtime local fixture; popular weekend brunch. [$] *Average main: $26* ✉ *228 S. Adams St.* ☎ *850/222–3444* 🌐 *www.andrewsdowntown.com* 🕒 *No dinner Sun.*

$$$ ✕**Avenue Eat and Drink.** Elegant yet unpretentious, this cozy restau-
SOUTHERN rant offers an eclectic mix of Southern fusion food that delights taste
buds in small bites and larger plates. You can't go wrong with tuna
two ways or the melt-in-your-mouth boneless short ribs served with
mashed parsnip and potatoes with a rosemary-Cabernet reduction.
Known for: upscale Southern-influenced menu; popular Sunday
brunch; large selection of wines by the glass and martinis. $ *Average
main: $28* ✉ *115 E. Park Ave.* ☎ *850/224–0115* ⊕ *www.avenuee-
atanddrink.com.*

$ ✕**Hopkins' Eatery.** Locals in the know flock here for superb salads, home-
AMERICAN made soups, and sandwiches—expect a short wait at lunchtime—via
simple counter service. Kids like the traditional peanut butter–and-jelly
sandwich (with bananas and sprouts, if they dare); adults might opt
for a chunky chicken melt, smothered beef, or garden vegetarian sub.
Known for: good salads and sandwiches; spearmint iced tea; cakes and
pies. $ *Average main: $6* ✉ *1415 Market St.* ☎ *850/668–0311* ⊕ *www.
hopkinseatery.com* ☾ *Closed Sun. No dinner Sat.*

$$ ✕**Kool Beanz Café.** The cuisine is as eclectic and cozy as the atmosphere
CARIBBEAN at this Tallahassee staple, loved by locals and visitors alike. The decor is
part of the charm, with a vibrant setting of dark pastels and modern art.
Known for: eclectic decor and menu; creative and colorful dishes; long
lines, especially on weekends. $ *Average main: $20* ✉ *921 Thomasville
Rd.* ☎ *850/224–2466* ⊕ *www.kool-beanz.com.*

WHERE TO STAY

$ ⌂**Aloft Tallahassee Downtown.** This urban-chic hotel provides the tree-
HOTEL lined downtown district with a bit of trendy fun courtesy of loft-style
rooms with bright, minimalist decor. **Pros:** convenient to downtown,
universities, and nightlife/restaurants; free Wi-Fi. **Cons:** small, utilitar-
ian rooms; lobby can get packed from the bar on weekend nights.
$ *Rooms from: $139* ✉ *200 N. Monroe St.* ☎ *850/513–0313, 866/513–
0313* ⇒ *162 rooms* ⚑ *No meals.*

$ ⌂**Governors Inn.** Only a block from the capitol, this plushly restored
B&B/INN historic warehouse is abuzz during the week with politicians, press, and
lobbyists. **Pros:** good service; the rooms and lobby are warm and inviting; near museums, restaurants, and the capitol. **Cons:** in a very busy
area; hotel can be busy with events and meetings; parking is valet-only.
$ *Rooms from: $169* ✉ *209 S. Adams St.* ☎ *850/681–6855* ⊕ *thegov-
inn.org* ⇒ *49 rooms* ⚑ *Breakfast.*

$ ⌂**Hotel Duval.** This boutique hotel, a renovated version of the land-
HOTEL mark build in 1951, sets a high standard for small luxury hotels
Fodor'sChoice in the capital. **Pros:** top-level amenities; good restaurants. **Cons:**
★ not suited to families; small rooms. $ *Rooms from: $109* ✉ *415 N.
Monroe St.* ☎ *850/224–6000* ⊕ *www.hotelduval.com* ⇒ *117 rooms*
⚑ *No meals.*

14

SHOPPING

Market District. Hop off Interstate 10 at Exit 203 to head to this shopping and dining district filled with locally owned specialty shops, salons, cafés, and restaurants. My Favorite Things and Cotton Colors are popular, as are many other stores scattered around the area in smaller enclaves. Not to worry, though—most are within walking distance of one another. The Market District is the place for a taste of true local culture. It's slightly west of Thomasville Road at the intersection of Timberline Road and Market Street. ⊠ *Timberline Rd. at Market St.* ⊕ *www.themarketdistrict.net.*

Midtown District. This area mixes a little bit of Southern charm with city chic, offering everything from the stylish and cutting-edge fashions of Cole Couture and Divas and Devils to luxury beauty and spa services at Kanvas. Shops adorn the sides of North Monroe Street heading toward downtown, as well as some of the side streets. If you get hungry picking up purchases, try the delicious treats at Lucy & Leo's Cupcakery, featured on *Cupcake Wars.* ⊠ *Between North Moore St. and Thomasville Rd., between W. 7th Ave. and W. 4th Ave.*

TRAVEL SMART
FLORIDA

GETTING HERE AND AROUND

■ AIR TRAVEL

Average flying time to Florida's international airports is 3 hours from New York, 4 hours from Chicago, 2¾ hours from Dallas, 4½–5½ hours from Los Angeles, and 8–8½ hours from London.

AIRPORTS

Florida has 21 commercial airports; the busiest are Orlando International Airport (MCO), Miami International Airport (MIA), Tampa (TPA), and Fort Lauderdale–Hollywood International Airport (FLL). Flying to alternative airports can save you both time and money. Fort Lauderdale is close to Miami, Palm Beach International (PBI) is close to Fort Lauderdale, and Sarasota Bradenton International (SRQ) is close to Tampa. FLL is a 30-minute drive from MIA. And what you might lose in driving time between Sarasota and downtown Tampa you'll make up for in spades with shorter security lines and fewer in-terminal navigation woes at SRQ.

■TIP→ Flying to secondary airports can save you money, so price things out before booking. Sometimes one-way car rentals in Florida can be more cost-effective than shared van shuttles.

Airport Information Daytona Beach International Airport (DAB). ✉ 700 Catalina Dr., Daytona Beach ☎ 386/248–8030 ⊕ www. flydaytonafirst.com. **Fort Lauderdale–Hollywood International Airport (FLL).** ✉ 100 Terminal Dr., Fort Lauderdale ☎ 866/435–9355 ⊕ www.broward.org/airport. **Jacksonville International Airport (JAX).** ✉ 2400 Yankee Clipper Dr., Jacksonville ☎ 904/741–4902 ⊕ www.flyjax.com. **Key West International Airport (EYW).** ✉ 3491 S. Roosevelt Blvd., Key West ☎ 305/809–5200, 305/296–5439 ⊕ www.eywairport.com. **Miami International Airport (MIA).** ✉ N.E. 20th St. and LeJeune Rd., Miami ☎ 305/876–7000 ⊕ www.miami-airport.com. **Northwest Florida Beaches International Airport (ECP).** ✉ 6300 W. Bay Pkwy., Panama City ☎ 850/763–6751 ⊕ www. iflybeaches.com. **Orlando International Airport (MCO).** ✉ 1 Jeff Fuqua Blvd., Orlando ☎ 407/825–2001 ⊕ www.orlandoairports. net. **Palm Beach International Airport (PBI).** ✉ 1000 Palm Beach International Airport, West Palm Beach ☎ 561/471–7420 ⊕ www. pbia.org. **Sarasota Bradenton International Airport (SRQ).** ✉ 6000 Airport Circle, Bradenton ☎ 941/359–5200 ⊕ www.srq-airport.com. **Southwest Florida International Airport (RSW).** ✉ 11000 Terminal Access Rd., Fort Myers ☎ 239/590–4800 ⊕ www.flylcpa.com. **St. Petersburg–Clearwater International Airport (PIE).** ✉ 14700 Terminal Blvd., Clearwater ☎ 727/453–7800 ⊕ www.fly2pie.com. **Tampa International Airport (TPA).** ✉ 4100 George J. Bean Pkwy., Tampa ☎ 813/870–8700 ⊕ www.tampaairport.com.

GROUND TRANSPORTATION

SuperShuttle service operates from several Florida airports: Fort Lauderdale, Miami, Orlando, Sarasota Bradenton, St. Petersburg–Clearwater, Tampa, and the Palm Beaches. That said, most airports offer some type of shuttle or bus service.

If you book a shuttle from your hotel to the airport, allow at least 24 hours, and expect to be picked up at least 2½ hours before your scheduled departure.

Cab fares from Florida's larger airports into town can be high, and there can be a departure fee from an airport. (In Fort Lauderdale, that airport departure fee is $3.) Note that in some cities airport cab fares are a single flat rate; in others, flat-rate fares vary by zone; and in others still, the fare is determined by the meter. Private car service fares are usually higher than taxi fares.

Shuttle Service SuperShuttle. ☎ 800/258–3826 ⊕ www.supershuttle.com.

FLIGHTS

American Airlines. Flies to Daytona Beach, Fort Lauderdale, Fort Myers, Fort Walton Beach, Gainesville, Jacksonville, Key West, Melbourne, Miami, Orlando,

Pensacola, Sarasota, Tallahassee, Tampa, and the Palm Beaches ☎ *800/433–7300* ⊕ *www.aa.com.*

Delta. Flies to Daytona Beach, Fort Lauderdale, Fort Myers, Fort Walton Beach, Gainesville, Jacksonville, Key West, Melbourne, Miami, Orlando, Panama City, Pensacola, Sarasota, Tallahassee, Tampa, and the Palm Beaches. ☎ *800/221–1212 for U.S. reservations, 800/241–4141 for international reservations* ⊕ *www.delta.com.*

Frontier. Flies to Fort Lauderdale, Fort Myers, Jacksonville, Orlando, and Tampa. ☎ *800/432–1359* ⊕ *www.frontierairlines.com.*

JetBlue. Flies to Fort Lauderdale, Fort Myers, Jacksonville, Key West, Sarasota, Tampa, and the Palm Beaches. ☎ *800/538–2583* ⊕ *www.jetblue.com.*

Southwest. Flies to Fort Lauderdale, Fort Myers, Jacksonville, Key West, Orlando, Panama City, Pensacola, Tampa, and the Palm Beaches. ☎ *800/435–9792* ⊕ *www.southwest.com.*

Spirit Airlines. Flies to Fort Lauderdale, Fort Myers, Orlando, Tampa, and the Palm Beaches. ☎ *801/401–2200* ⊕ *www.spirit.com.*

United. Flies to Daytona, Fort Lauderdale, Fort Myers, Fort Walton Beach, Gainesville, Jacksonville, Key West, Miami, Orlando, Panama City, Pensacola, Sarasota Bradenton, Tallahassee, Tampa, and the Palm Beaches. ☎ *800/864–8331 for U.S. reservations, 800/538–2929 for international reservations* ⊕ *www.united.com.*

▮ CAR TRAVEL

Three major interstates lead to Florida. Interstate 95 begins in Maine, runs south through the Mid-Atlantic states, and enters Florida just north of Jacksonville. It continues south past Daytona Beach, the Space Coast, Vero Beach, Palm Beach, and Fort Lauderdale, ending just south of Miami.

Interstate 75 begins in Michigan at the Canadian border and runs south through Ohio, Kentucky, Tennessee, and Georgia,

FROM–TO	MILES	HOURS +/-
Pensacola–Panama City	100	2
Tallahassee–Panama City	100	2
Tallahassee–Jacksonville	165	3
Jacksonville–St. Augustine	40	0:45
Cape/Port Canaveral–Orlando	60	1
Orlando–Tampa	85	1:30
Fort Lauderdale–Miami	30	0:45
Miami–Naples	125	2:15
Miami–Key Largo	65	1
Miami–Palm Beach	70	1:45
Key Largo–Key West	100	2

then moves south through the center of the state before veering west into Tampa. It follows the west coast south to Naples, then crosses the state through the northern section of the Everglades, and ends in Miami. Despite its interstate status, the Interstate 75 stretch between Naples and just west of Fort Lauderdale levies a toll each way per car, with higher tolls for motor homes, boat carriers, and such.

California and most southern and southwestern states are connected to Florida by Interstate 10, which moves east from Los Angeles through Arizona, New Mexico, Texas, Louisiana, Mississippi, and Alabama. It enters Florida at Pensacola and runs straight across the northern part of the state, ending in Jacksonville.

SUNPASS

To save time and money while on the road, you may want to purchase a SunPass for your personal or rental vehicle. It provides

CAR RENTAL RESOURCES

Local Agencies

Continental (Fort Lauderdale and Orlando)	800/221–4085 or 954/332–1125	www.continentalcar.com
Sunshine Rent A Car (Fort Lauderdale)	888/786–7446 or 954/467–8100	www.sunshinerentacar.com

Major Agencies

Alamo	877/222–9075	www.alamo.com
Avis	800/331–1212	www.avis.com
Budget	800/218–7992	www.budget.com
Hertz	800/654–3131	www.hertz.com
National Car Rental	800/227–7368	www.nationalcar.com

a discount on most tolls, and you'll be able to sail past collection booths without stopping. You also can use SunPass to pay for parking at Orlando, Tampa, Palm Beach, Miami, and Fort Lauderdale airports. (SunPass now interfaces with North Carolina's Quick Pass and Georgia's Peach Pass.) With SunPass—transponders can be purchased for $4.99 to $25, at drugstores, supermarkets, or tourism welcome centers—you can charge up with a credit card and reload as needed. For more info, check out ⊕ *www.sunpass.com.*

RENTAL CARS

Unless you're going to plant yourself at a beach or theme-park resort, you really need a vehicle to get around in Florida. Rental rates, which are loaded with taxes, fees, and other costs, sometimes can start around $35 a day/$160 a week, plus the aforementioned add-ons. In Florida you must be 21 to rent a car, must have a credit card, and need to know rates are higher if you're under 25.

ROAD CONDITIONS

Downtown areas of major cities can be extremely congested during rush hours, usually 7–9 am and 3:30–6:30 pm or later on weekdays. ■TIP→ Florida has a website (www.fl511.com) with real-time traffic information for six regional zones.

RULES OF THE ROAD

Speed limits are generally 60 mph on state highways, 30 mph within city limits and residential areas, and 70 mph on interstates, some Orlando-area toll roads, and Florida's Turnpike. Supervising adults must ensure that children under age seven are positioned in federally approved child car seats. Infants up to 20 pounds must be secured in rear-facing carriers in the backseat. Children younger than four years old must be strapped into a separate carrier or child seat; children four through five can be secured in a separate carrier, an integrated child seat, or by a seat belt. The driver will be held responsible for passengers under the age of 18 who aren't wearing seat belts, and all front-seat passengers are required to wear seat belts.

Florida's Alcohol/Controlled Substance DUI Law is one of the toughest in the United States. A blood-alcohol level of 0.08 or higher can have serious repercussions even for a first-time offender.

▮ FERRY TRAVEL

If you would like to avoid road traffic to the Keys and make the trip a watery adventure, Key West Express ferries people from Fort Myers Beach on a daily basis (and Marco Island in season) to Key West's historic seaport. The trip, just under four hours, is cheaper than airfare, and doesn't require months-in-advance booking.

Contact Key West Express. ⊠ *1200 Main St., Fort Myers* ☎ *888/539–2628* ⊕ *www.keywest-express.us.*

▮ TRAIN TRAVEL

A new high-speed train line, Brightline, began service in late summer 2017. It connects Downtown Miami to Fort Lauderdale and West Palm Beach in 30 and 60 minutes respectively.

Contacts Brightline. ⊕ *gobrightline.com.*

ESSENTIALS

■ ACCOMMODATIONS

In general, peak seasons are during Christmas/New Year's holidays and late January through Easter in the state's southern half, during the summer along the Panhandle and around Jacksonville and St. Augustine, and both time frames in Orlando and Central Florida. Holiday weekends at any point during the year are packed; if you're considering home or condo rentals, minimum-stay requirements are longer during these periods, too. Fall is the slowest season, with only a few exceptions (Key West is jam-packed for the 10-day Fantasy Fest at Halloween). Rates are low and availability is high, but this is also prime time for hurricanes.

Children are generally welcome throughout Florida, except for some Key West B&Bs and inns; however, the buck stops at spring-breakers. While many hotels allow them—and some even cater to them—most rental agencies won't lease units to anyone under 25 without a guardian present.

Pets, although allowed at many hotels (one upscale chain, Kimpton, with properties in Miami, Palm Beach, and Vero Beach, celebrates its pet friendliness with treats in the lobby and doggie beds for rooms), often carry an extra flat-rate fee for cleaning and de-allergen treatments, and are not a sure thing. Inquire ahead if Fido is coming with you.

APARTMENT AND HOUSE RENTALS

The state's allure for visiting snowbirds (Northerners "flocking" to Florida in winter) has caused private home and condo rentals to boom in popularity, at times affording better options for vacationers, particularly families who want to have some extra space and cooking facilities. In some destinations, home and condo rentals are more readily available than hotels. Fort Myers, for example, doesn't have many luxury hotel properties downtown. Everything aside from beach towels is provided during a stay, but some things to consider are that sizable down payments must be made at booking (15% to 50%), and the full balance is often due before arrival. Check for any cleaning fees (usually not more than $150). If being on the beach is of utmost importance, carefully screen properties that tout "water views," because they might actually be of bays, canals, or lakes rather than of the Gulf of Mexico or the Atlantic.

Finding a great rental agency can help you weed out the junk. Target offices that specialize in the area you want to visit, and have a personal conversation with a representative as soon as possible. Be honest about your budget and expectations. For example, let the rental agent know if having the living room couch pull double-duty as a bed is not OK. Although websites listing rentals directly from homeowners are growing in popularity, there's a higher chance of coming across Pinocchios advertising "gourmet" kitchens that have one or two nice gadgets but fixtures or appliances from 1982. To protect yourself, talk extensively with owners in advance, see if there's a system in place for accountability should something go wrong, and make sure there's a 24-hour phone number for emergencies.

Contacts American Realty of Captiva. ✉ 11526 Andy Rose La., Captiva ☎ 800/547–0127 ⊕ www.captiva-island.com. **Endless Vacation Rentals.** ☎ 877/782–9387 ⊕ www.evrentals.com. **Florida Keys Rental Store.** ✉ MM 82, 81800 Overseas Hwy., Upper Matecumbe Key ☎ 800/585–0584, 305/451–3879 ⊕ www.floridakeysrentalstore.com. **Freewheeler Vacations.** ✉ MM 98.5, 85992 Overseas Hwy., Key Largo ☎ 866/664–2075, 305/664–2075 ⊕ www.freewheeler-realty.com.

com. **Interhome.** ☎ 954/791–8282, 800/882–6864 ⊕ www.interhomeusa.com. **ResortQuest.** ✉ 14 Sylvan Way, Parsippany ☎ 800/275–5060 ⊕ www.resortquest. com. **Sand Key Realty.** ✉ 790 S. Gulfview Blvd., Clearwater Beach ☎ 800/257–7332, 727/443–0032 ⊕ www.sandkey.com. **Suncoast Vacation Rentals.** ✉ 224 Franklin Blvd., St. George Island ☎ 800/341–2021 ⊕ www.uncommonflorida.com. **Villas International.** ☎ 415/499–9490, 800/221–2260 ⊕ www.villasintl.com.

BED-AND-BREAKFASTS

Small inns and guesthouses in Florida range from modest, cozy places with home-style breakfasts and owners who treat you like family, to elegantly furnished Victorian houses with four-course breakfasts and rates to match. Since most B&Bs are small, they rely on various agencies and organizations to get the word out and coordinate reservations.

Reservation Services Bed & Breakfast Inns Online. ☎ 800/215–7365 ⊕ www.bbonline. com. **BedandBreakfast.com.** ☎ 512/322–2710, 800/462–2632 ⊕ www.bedandbreakfast.com. **Florida Bed & Breakfast Inns.** ☎ 561/223–9550 ⊕ www.florida-inns.com.

HOTELS AND RESORTS

Wherever you look in Florida you'll find lots of plain, inexpensive motels and luxurious resorts, independents alongside national chains, and an ever-growing number of modern properties as well as quite a few classics. All hotels listed have a private bath unless otherwise noted.

Hotel reviews have been shortened. For full reviews, visit Fodors.com.

▌EATING OUT

Smoking is banned statewide in most enclosed indoor workplaces, including restaurants. Exemptions are permitted for stand-alone bars where food takes a backseat to libations.

FLORIDA'S SCENIC TRAILS

Florida has some 8,000 miles of land-based routes (plus another 4,000 miles for paddling!). About 1,400 miles of these connect to create the Florida Trail, one of only 11 National Scenic Trails in the United States. Info on top segments is available at ⊕ www.floridatrail.org, and you can find a searchable list of all trails at ⊕ www.visitflorida.com/trails.

One caution: raw oysters pose a potential danger for people with chronic illness of the liver, stomach, or blood, or who have immune disorders. All Florida restaurants that serve raw oysters must post a notice in plain view warning of the risks associated with their consumption.

Restaurant reviews have been shortened. For full reviews, visit Fodors.com.

MEALS AND MEALTIMES

Unless otherwise noted, you can assume that the restaurants we recommend are open daily for lunch and dinner.

RESERVATIONS AND DRESS

We discuss reservations only when they're essential (there's no other way you'll ever get a table) or when they're not accepted. It's always smart to make reservations when you can, particularly if your party is large or if it's high season. It's critical to do so at popular restaurants (book as far ahead as possible, often 30 days, and reconfirm on arrival).

We mention dress only when men are required to wear a jacket or a jacket and tie. Expect places with dress codes to truly adhere to them.

Contacts OpenTable. ⊕ www.opentable.com.

▌HEALTH

Sunburn and heat prostration are concerns, even in winter. So hit the beach or play tennis, golf, or another outdoor sport before 10 am or after 3 pm. If you must be out at midday, limit exercise, drink plenty of nonalcoholic liquids, and wear both sunscreen and a hat. If you feel faint, get out of the sun and sip water slowly.

Even on overcast days, ultraviolet rays shine through the haze, so use a sunscreen with an SPF of at least 15, and have children wear a waterproof SPF 30 or higher.

While you're frolicking on the beach, steer clear of what look like blue bubbles on the sand. These are Portuguese men-of-war, and their tentacles can cause an allergic reaction. Also be careful of other large jellyfish, some of which can sting.

If you walk across a grassy area on the way to the beach, you'll probably encounter the tiny, light-brown, incredibly prickly sand spurs. If you get stuck with one, just pull it out.

▮ HOURS OF OPERATION

Many museums are closed Monday but have late hours on another weekday and are usually open on weekends. Some museums have days when admission is free. Popular attractions are usually open every day but Thanksgiving and Christmas Day. Watch out for seasonal closures at smaller venues; we list opening hours for all sights we recommend, but these can change on short notice. If you're visiting during a transitional month (for example, May in the southern part of the state), it's always best to call before showing up.

▮ MONEY

Prices here are given for adults. Substantially reduced fees are almost always available for children, students, and senior citizens.

CREDIT CARDS

We cite information about credit cards only if they aren't accepted at a restaurant or a hotel. Otherwise, assume that most major credit cards are acceptable.

> ### WORD OF MOUTH
>
> Did the food give you shivers of delight or leave you cold? Did the resort look as good in real life as it did in the photos? Did you sleep like a baby, or were the walls paper-thin? Was the service stellar or not up to snuff? Rate and review hotels and restaurants or start a discussion about your favorite (or not so favorite) places on ⊕ www.fodors.com. Your comments might even appear in our books. Yes, you, too, can be a correspondent!

Reporting Lost Cards American Express. ☏ 800/528–4800 ⊕ www.americanexpress. com. **Diners Club.** ☏ 800/234–6377 ⊕ www. dinersclub.com. **Discover.** ☏ 800/347–2683 ⊕ www.discovercard.com. **MasterCard.** ☏ 800/622–7747 ⊕ www.mastercard.com. **Visa.** ☏ 800/847–2911 ⊕ www.visa.com.

▮ PACKING

Northern Florida is much cooler in winter than southern Florida, so pack a heavy sweater or more. Even in summer, ocean breezes can be cool, so it's good to have a lightweight sweater or jacket.

Aside from an occasional winter cold spell (when the mercury drops to, say, 50), Miami and the Naples–Fort Myers areas are usually warm year-round and extremely humid in summer. Be prepared for sudden storms all over in summer, and note that plastic raincoats are uncomfortable in the high humidity. Often, storms are quick, often in the afternoons, and the sun comes back in no time. (This also means that it's best to get in your beach time earlier in the day; if it's nice in the morning in August, go to the beach. Don't wait.)

Dress is casual throughout the state—sundresses, sandals, or walking shorts are appropriate. Palm Beach is more polos and pearls, Miami is designer jeans, and elsewhere the Tommy Bahama–esque look dominates. Even beach gear is OK at a lot of places, but just make sure you've got a proper outfit on (shirt, shorts, and shoes). A very small number of restaurants request that men wear jackets and ties, but most don't. Where there are dress codes, they tend to be fully adhered to. Take note that the strictest places are golf and tennis clubs. Many ask that you wear whites or at least special sport shoes and attire. Be prepared for air-conditioning working in overdrive anywhere you go.

You can generally swim year-round in peninsular Florida from about New Smyrna Beach south on the Atlantic coast and from Tarpon Springs south on the Gulf Coast. Bring a sun hat and sunscreen.

▌SAFETY

Stepped-up policing against thieves preying on tourists in rental cars has helped address what was a serious issue in the mid-1990s. Still, visitors should be wary when driving in unfamiliar neighborhoods and leaving the airport, especially near Miami. Don't leave valuables unattended—and that can include food and drink—while you walk the beach or go for a dip. And never leave handbags, cameras, etc., in your vehicle. Visitors have reported theft of belongings while stopped for meals as they travel to or from the airport. Don't blatantly stow valuables in your car trunk just before walking away, either, since thieves can be adept at popping lids. And don't assume that valuables are safe in your hotel room; use in-room safes or the hotel's safety-deposit boxes. Try to use ATMs only during the day or in brightly lighted, well-traveled locales.

If you're visiting Florida during the June through November hurricane season and a hurricane is imminent, be sure to follow safety orders and evacuation instructions from local authorities.

▌TAXES

Florida has no state personal income tax, instead heavily relying on tourism revenues. The state sales tax in Florida is 6% (with the exception of most groceries and medicine); when combined with local taxes, the total sales tax rate is between 6% and 7.5%. Hotel taxes, often called "bed taxes," "resort taxes," or "transient rental taxes," vary. In Central Florida, including Orlando, for example, taxes on purchases range from 6.5% to 7%. A 6% resort tax is imposed on all hotel rooms in addition to the sales tax.

Palm Beach County has raised its bed tax to 6%, for a combined total of 12% with state sales tax. In Greater Fort Lauderdale, the bed tax is 5%, for a combined total of 11%.

▌TIME

The western portion of the Panhandle is in the Central time zone, and the rest of Florida is in the Eastern time zone.

▌TIPPING

Tip airport valets or hotel bellhops $1 to $3 per bag (there typically is also a charge to check bags outside the terminal, but this isn't a tip). Maids often get $1 to $2 per night per guest, more at high-end resorts or if you require special services, ideally left each morning since the person servicing your room or suite could change from day to day during your stay. Room-service waiters still hope to receive a 15% tip despite hefty room-service charges and service fees, which often don't go to the waiters. A door attendant or parking valet hopes to get $1 to $3. Waiters generally count on 15% to 20% (on the before-tax amount) or more, depending on your demands for special service. Bartenders get $1 or $2 per round of drinks. Golf caddies get 15% of the greens fee.

■ VISITOR INFORMATION

Florida welcome centers, with maps and citrus juice, are on Interstate 10 (near Pensacola), Interstate 75 (near Jennings), Interstate 95 (near Yulee, north of Jacksonville), and U.S. 231 (near Campbellton), and in the lobby of the New Capitol in Tallahassee.

Contact Visit Florida. ✉ *Visit Florida, 2540 W. Executive Center Circle, Tallahassee* ☎ *850/488–5607, 877/435–2872* ⊕ *www.visitflorida.com.*

INDEX

PHOTO CREDITS

ABOUT OUR WRITERS

Tampa Bay updater and beach lover **Kate Bradshaw** lives in St. Petersburg, where she edits the news and politics section of *Creative Loafing*, the alternative weekly in the Tampa Bay area. Born in the Chicago area, Kate is in love with her adopted home.

Jacksonville and Space Coast updater **Jennifer Greenhill-Taylor** has worked at both the *Florida Times Union* in Jacksonville and the *Orlando Sentinel*. Now an independent travel writer and editor, she lives in Orlando.

Orlando and Environs writer **Joseph Hayes** has informed the world about travel, food, and the arts in Central Florida for print and online publications for 20 years. He was the restaurant critic for *Orlando Magazine*. Born in Manhattan, he now lives full-time in Orlando. *jrhayes.net*

Fort Lauderdale–based freelance travel writer and editor **Lynne Helm** arrived from the Midwest anticipating a few years of palm-fringed fun. More than a quarter century later, she's still enamored of Florida's sun-drenched charms. Lynne updated the Everglades chapter and Travel Smart.

Miami native **Jill Martin** has written for the state's tourism website, Visit Florida, and also for various travel sites and print magazines. She is the creator of Sunshine Brain Games, a trivia card game all about Florida. She resides full time in the Redland and part time on Sanibel.

Northeast Florida updater **Steve Master** lives in Daytona Beach, 10 miles west of famed Daytona International Speedway. Originally a sports writer, he is now an associate professor of communication at Embry-Riddle Aeronautical University in Daytona Beach.

Galena Mosovich is known for covering cutting-edge developments and personalities in cocktail culture, gastronomy, travel, and visual art for top publications. She's considered an international expert on cocktails. Galena was raised in Coral Springs, in the northwest corner of Broward County, and she now lives in Miramar with her two dogs.

Jan Norris, contributing editor of *Florida Food & Farm,* is a career food journalist and publishes the website ⊕ *JanNorris. com.* She writes about the South Florida food and dining scene as well as travel in the Sunshine State after a 26-year career as food editor at *The Palm Beach Post.*

Paul Rubio's travels have taken him to 107 countries and counting. He graduated from Harvard in 2002, and in 2008 he gave into his passion and became a full-time travel writer. An award-winning writer, he is the travel editor of *Palm Beach Illustrated, Naples Illustrated,* and *Weddings Illustrated* and regularly contributes to several other publications.

Panhandle updater **Ashley Wright** is a northwest Florida native and a master-of-all-trades in the publishing world. She contributes to a number of local and regional publications, and loves sharing the hidden treasures of her native coast with travelers both near and far.